DERIVATIVES

DERIVATIVES

DERIVATIVES

WILEY

Published by John Wiley & Sons, Inc., Hoboken, New Jersey.
Published simultaneously in Canada.

For general information on our other products and services or for technical support, please contact our Customer Care Department within the United States at (800) 762-2974, outside the United States at (317) 572-3993 or fax (317) 572-4002.

Wiley publishes in a variety of print and electronic formats and by print-on-demand. Some material included with standard print versions of this book may not be included in e-books or in print-on-demand. If this book refers to media such as a CD or DVD that is not included in the version you purchased, you may download this material at http://booksupport.wiley.com. For more information about Wiley products, visit www.wiley.com.

Library of Congress Cataloging-in-Publication Data

Names: Pinto, Jerald E., author. | Pirie, Wendy L., author.
Title: Derivatives / Jerald E. Pinto, CFA, Wendy L. Pirie, CFA.
Description: Hoboken, New Jersey : John Wiley & Sons, Inc., [2017] | Series:
    CFA Institute investment series | Includes index. |
Identifiers: ISBN 9781119850588 (pdf) | ISBN 9781119850595 (epub) | ISBN 9781119850571
    (cloth)
Subjects: LCSH: Derivative securities.
Classification: LCC HG6024.A3 (ebook) | LCC HG6024.A3 P535 2017 (print) | DDC
    332.64/57—dc23

Printed in the United States of America

SKYF7199B01-664E-4C6B-8C66-CA271AC019BA_102921

CONTENTS

CHAPTER 7
Currency Management: An Introduction   **339**

CHAPTER 8
Options Strategies   421

CHAPTER 9
Swaps, Forwards, and Futures Strategies 493

FOREWORD

Since the breakthrough introduction of the Black–Scholes–Merton options pricing model in 1973, the field of financial derivatives has evolved into an extensive and highly scientific body of theoretical knowledge alongside a vast and vibrant market where economic producers, investors, finance professionals, and government regulators all interact to seek financial gains, manage risk, or promote price discovery. It is hard to imagine how even the most thoughtful and diligent practitioners can come to terms with such a broad and complex topic—until they read this book.

CFA Institute has compiled into a single book those parts of its curriculum that address this critically important topic. And it is apparent from reading this book that CFA Institute attracted preeminent scholars to develop its derivatives curriculum.

This book has several important virtues:

1. It is detailed, comprehensive, and exceptionally accessible.
2. It is efficiently organized in its coverage of topics.
3. It makes effective use of visualization with diagrams of transactions and strategy payoffs.
4. It includes numerous practice problems along with well-explained solutions.
5. And finally, unlike many academic textbooks, its focus is more practical than theoretical, although it does provide more-than-adequate treatment of the relevant theory.

The book begins by addressing the basics of derivatives, including definitions of the various types of derivatives and descriptions of the markets in which they trade.

It goes on to address the purpose of derivatives and the benefits they impart to society, including risk transfer, price discovery, and operational efficiency. It also discusses how derivatives can be misused to enable excessive speculation and how derivatives could contribute to the destabilization of financial markets.

The book provides comprehensive treatment of pricing and valuation with discussions of the law of one price, risk neutrality, the Black–Scholes–Merton options pricing model, and the binomial model. It also covers the pricing of futures and forward contracts as well as swaps.

The book then shifts to applications of derivatives. It discusses how derivatives can be used to create synthetic cash and equity positions along with several other positions. It relies heavily on numerical examples to illustrate these equivalencies.

It offers a comprehensive treatment of risk management with discussions of market risk, credit risk, liquidity risk, operational risk, and model risk, among others. It describes how to measure risk and, more importantly, how to manage it with the application of forward and futures contracts, swaps, and options.

This summary of topics is intended to provide a flavor of the book's contents. The contents of this book are far broader and deeper than I describe in this foreword.

Those who practice finance, as well as those who teach it, in my view, owe a huge debt of gratitude to CFA Institute—first, for assembling this extraordinary body of knowledge in its curriculum and, second, for organizing this knowledge with such cohesion and clarity. Anyone who wishes to acquire a solid knowledge of derivatives or to refresh and expand what they have learned about derivatives previously should certainly read this book.

Mark Kritzman

PREFACE

We are pleased to bring you *Derivatives, 1st Edition*, which focuses on key tools that are needed for today's professional investor. The book sets out the key features of derivatives, their purpose, benefits and risks for individuals, firms and society. The text teaches critical skills in the treatment of pricing and valuation of derivatives that challenge many professionals. It also provides a comprehensive treatment of risk management and shows how these techniques can be applied to manage risk with the application of forward and futures contracts, swaps, and options.

The content was developed in partnership by a team of distinguished academics and practitioners, chosen for their acknowledged expertise in the field, and guided by CFA Institute. It is written specifically with the investment practitioner in mind and is replete with examples and practice problems that reinforce the learning outcomes and demonstrate real-world applicability.

The CFA Program Curriculum, from which the content of this book was drawn, is subjected to a rigorous review process to assure that it is:

- Faithful to the findings of our ongoing industry practice analysis
- Valuable to members, employers, and investors
- Globally relevant
- Generalist (as opposed to specialist) in nature
- Replete with sufficient examples and practice opportunities
- Pedagogically sound

The accompanying workbook is a useful reference that provides Learning Outcome Statements, which describe exactly what readers will learn and be able to demonstrate after mastering the accompanying material. Additionally, the workbook has summary overviews and practice problems for each chapter.

We are confident that you will find this and other books in the CFA Institute Investment Series helpful in your efforts to grow your investment knowledge, whether you are a relatively new entrant or an experienced veteran striving to keep up to date in the ever-changing market environment. CFA Institute, as a long-term committed participant in the investment profession and a not-for-profit global membership association, is pleased to provide you with this opportunity.

THE CFA® PROGRAM

If the subject matter of this book interests you and you are not already a CFA charterholder, we hope you will consider registering for the CFA Program and starting progress toward earning the Chartered Financial Analyst designation. The CFA designation is a globally recognized standard of excellence for measuring the competence and integrity of investment professionals. To earn the CFA charter, candidates must successfully complete the CFA Program, a global graduate-level self-study program that combines a broad curriculum with professional conduct requirements as preparation for a career as an investment professional.

Anchored in a practice-based curriculum, the CFA Program Body of Knowledge reflects the knowledge, skills, and abilities identified by professionals as essential to the investment decision-making process. This body of knowledge maintains its relevance through a regular, extensive survey of practicing CFA charterholders across the globe. The curriculum covers 10 general topic areas, ranging from equity and fixed-income analysis to portfolio management to corporate finance—all with a heavy emphasis on the application of ethics in professional practice. Known for its rigor and breadth, the CFA Program curriculum highlights principles common to every market so that professionals who earn the CFA designation have a thoroughly global investment perspective and a profound understanding of the global marketplace.

CFA INSTITUTE

CFA Institute is the premier association for investment professionals around the world, with over 170,000 members from more than 160 countries. Since 1963 the organization has developed and administered the renowned Chartered Financial Analyst® Program. With a rich history of leading the investment profession, CFA Institute has set the highest standards in ethics, education, and professional excellence within the global investment community, and is the foremost authority on investment profession conduct and practice.

Each book in the CFA Institute Investment Series is geared toward industry practitioners along with graduate-level finance students and covers the most important topics in the industry. The authors of these cutting-edge books are themselves industry professionals and academics and bring their wealth of knowledge and expertise to this series.

ACKNOWLEDGMENTS

Special thanks to all the reviewers, advisors, and question writers who helped to ensure high practical relevance, technical correctness, and understandability of the material presented here.

We would like to thank the many others who played a role in the conception and production of this book: the Curriculum and Learning Experience team at CFA Institute with special thanks to the curriculum directors, past and present, who worked with the authors and reviewers to produce the chapters in this book, the Practice Analysis team at CFA Institute, and the Publishing and Technology team for bringing this book to production.

ABOUT THE CFA INSTITUTE INVESTMENT SERIES

CFA Institute is pleased to provide you with the CFA Institute Investment Series, which covers major areas in the field of investments. We provide this best-in-class series for the same reason we have been chartering investment professionals for more than 50 years: to lead the investment profession globally by setting the highest standards of ethics, education, and professional excellence.

The books in the CFA Institute Investment Series contain practical, globally relevant material. They are intended both for those contemplating entry into the extremely competitive field of investment management as well as for those seeking a means of keeping their knowledge fresh and up to date. This series was designed to be user friendly and highly relevant.

We hope you find this series helpful in your efforts to grow your investment knowledge, whether you are a relatively new entrant or an experienced veteran ethically bound to keep up to date in the ever-changing market environment. As a long-term, committed participant in the investment profession and a not-for-profit global membership association, CFA Institute is pleased to provide you with this opportunity.

THE TEXTS

Corporate Finance: A Practical Approach is a solid foundation for those looking to achieve lasting business growth. In today's competitive business environment, companies must find innovative ways to enable rapid and sustainable growth. This text equips readers with the foundational knowledge and tools for making smart business decisions and formulating strategies to maximize company value. It covers everything from managing relationships between stakeholders to evaluating merger and acquisition bids, as well as the companies behind them. Through extensive use of real-world examples, readers will gain critical perspective into interpreting corporate financial data, evaluating projects, and allocating funds in ways that increase corporate value. Readers will gain insights into the tools and strategies used in modern corporate financial management.

Fixed Income Analysis has been at the forefront of new concepts in recent years, and this particular text offers some of the most recent material for the seasoned professional who is not a fixed-income specialist. The application of option and derivative technology to the once staid province of fixed income has helped contribute to an explosion of thought in this area. Professionals have been challenged to stay up to speed with credit derivatives, swaptions, collateralized mortgage securities, mortgage-backed securities, and other vehicles, and this explosion of products has strained the world's financial markets and tested central banks to provide sufficient oversight. Armed with a thorough grasp of the new exposures, the professional investor is much better able to anticipate and understand the challenges our central bankers and markets face.

International Financial Statement Analysis is designed to address the ever-increasing need for investment professionals and students to think about financial statement analysis from a global perspective. The text is a practically oriented introduction to financial statement analysis that is distinguished by its combination of a true international orientation, a structured presentation style, and abundant illustrations and tools covering concepts as they are introduced in the text. The authors cover this discipline comprehensively and with an eye to ensuring the reader's success at all levels in the complex world of financial statement analysis.

Investments: Principles of Portfolio and Equity Analysis provides an accessible yet rigorous introduction to portfolio and equity analysis. Portfolio planning and portfolio management are presented within a context of up-to-date, global coverage of security markets, trading, and market-related concepts and products. The essentials of equity analysis and valuation are explained in detail and profusely illustrated. The book includes coverage of practitioner-important but often neglected topics, such as industry analysis. Throughout, the focus is on the practical application of key concepts with examples drawn from both emerging and developed markets. Each chapter affords the reader many opportunities to self-check his or her understanding of topics.

One of the most prominent texts over the years in the investment management industry has been Maginn and Tuttle's *Managing Investment Portfolios: A Dynamic Process*. The third edition updates key concepts from the 1990 second edition. Some of the more experienced members of our community own the prior two editions and will add the third edition to their libraries. Not only does this seminal work take the concepts from the other readings and put them in a portfolio context, but it also updates the concepts of alternative investments, performance presentation standards, portfolio execution, and, very importantly, individual investor portfolio management. Focusing attention away from institutional portfolios and toward the individual investor makes this edition an important and timely work.

Quantitative Investment Analysis focuses on some key tools that are needed by today's professional investor. In addition to classic time value of money, discounted cash flow applications, and probability material, there are two aspects that can be of value over traditional thinking. The first involves the chapters dealing with correlation and regression that ultimately figure into the formation of hypotheses for purposes of testing. This gets to a critical skill that challenges many professionals: the ability to distinguish useful information from the overwhelming quantity of available data. Second, the final chapter of *Quantitative Investment Analysis* covers portfolio concepts and takes the reader beyond the traditional capital asset pricing model (CAPM) type of tools and into the more practical world of multifactor models and arbitrage pricing theory.

The New Wealth Management: The Financial Advisor's Guide to Managing and Investing Client Assets is an updated version of Harold Evensky's mainstay reference guide for wealth managers. Harold Evensky, Stephen Horan, and Thomas Robinson have updated the core text of the 1997 first edition and added an abundance of new material to fully reflect today's investment challenges. The text provides authoritative coverage across the full spectrum of wealth management and serves as a comprehensive guide for financial advisors. The book expertly blends investment theory and real-world applications and is written in the same thorough but highly accessible style as the first edition. The first involves the chapters dealing with correlation and regression that ultimately figure into the formation of hypotheses for purposes of testing. This gets to a critical skill that challenges many professionals: the ability to distinguish useful information from the overwhelming quantity of available data. Second, the final chapter of *Quantitative Investment Analysis* covers portfolio concepts and takes the reader beyond the traditional capital asset pricing model (CAPM) type of tools and into the more practical world of multifactor models and arbitrage pricing theory.

All books in the CFA Institute Investment Series are available through all major booksellers. And, all titles are available on the Wiley Custom Select platform at http://customselect .wiley.com/ where individual chapters for all the books may be mixed and matched to create custom textbooks for the classroom.

DERIVATIVES

DERIVATIVES

CHAPTER 1

DERIVATIVE MARKETS AND INSTRUMENTS

Don M. Chance, PhD, CFA

LEARNING OUTCOMES

The candidate should be able to:

- define a derivative and distinguish between exchange-traded and over-the-counter derivatives;
- contrast forward commitments with contingent claims;
- define forward contracts, futures contracts, options (calls and puts), swaps, and credit derivatives and compare their basic characteristics;
- determine the value at expiration and profit from a long or a short position in a call or put option;
- describe purposes of, and controversies related to, derivative markets;
- explain arbitrage and the role it plays in determining prices and promoting market efficiency.

1. DERIVATIVES: INTRODUCTION, DEFINITIONS, AND USES

Equity, fixed-income, currency, and commodity markets are facilities for trading the basic assets of an economy. Equity and fixed-income securities are claims on the assets of a company. Currencies are the monetary units issued by a government or central bank. Commodities are natural resources, such as oil or gold. These underlying assets are said to trade in **cash markets** or **spot markets** and their prices are sometimes referred to as **cash prices** or **spot prices**, though we usually just refer to them as stock prices, bond prices, exchange rates, and commodity prices. These markets exist around the world and receive much attention in the financial and mainstream media. Hence, they are relatively familiar not only to financial experts but also to the general population.

Somewhat less familiar are the markets for **derivatives**, which are financial instruments that derive their values from the performance of these basic assets. This reading is an overview of derivatives. Subsequent readings will explore many aspects of derivatives and their uses in depth. Among the questions that this first reading will address are the following:

- What are the defining characteristics of derivatives?
- What purposes do derivatives serve for financial market participants?
- What is the distinction between a forward commitment and a contingent claim?
- What are forward and futures contracts? In what ways are they alike and in what ways are they different?
- What are swaps?
- What are call and put options and how do they differ from forwards, futures, and swaps?
- What are credit derivatives and what are the various types of credit derivatives?
- What are the benefits of derivatives?
- What are some criticisms of derivatives and to what extent are they well founded?
- What is arbitrage and what role does it play in a well-functioning financial market?

This reading is organized as follows. Section 1 explores the definition and uses of derivatives and establishes some basic terminology. Section 2 describes derivatives markets. Sections 3–9 categorize and explain types of derivatives. Sections 10 and 11 discuss the benefits and criticisms of derivatives, respectively. Section 12 introduces the basic principles of derivative pricing and the concept of arbitrage.

Derivatives: Definitions and Uses

The most common definition of a derivative reads approximately as follows:

> *A derivative is a financial instrument that derives its performance from the performance of an underlying asset.*

This definition, despite being so widely quoted, can nonetheless be a bit troublesome. For example, it can also describe mutual funds and exchange-traded funds, which would never be viewed as derivatives even though they derive their values from the values of the underlying securities they hold. Perhaps the distinction that best characterizes derivatives is that they usually *transform* the performance of the underlying asset before paying it out in the derivatives transaction. In contrast, with the exception of expense deductions, mutual funds and exchange-traded funds simply pass through the returns of their underlying securities. This transformation of performance is typically understood or implicit in references to derivatives but rarely makes its way into the formal definition. In keeping with customary industry practice, this characteristic will be retained as an implied, albeit critical, factor distinguishing derivatives from mutual funds and exchange-traded funds and some other straight pass-through instruments. Also, note that the idea that derivatives take their *performance* from an underlying asset encompasses the fact that derivatives take their value and certain other characteristics from the underlying asset. Derivatives strategies perform in ways that are derived from the underlying and the specific features of derivatives.

Derivatives are similar to insurance in that both allow for the transfer of risk from one party to another. As everyone knows, insurance is a financial contract that provides protection against loss. The party bearing the risk purchases an insurance policy, which transfers the risk to the other party, the insurer, for a specified period of time. The risk itself does not change, but the party bearing it does. Derivatives allow for this same type of transfer of risk. One type of derivative in particular, the put option, when combined with a position exposed to the risk, functions almost exactly like insurance, but all derivatives can be used to protect against loss. Of course, an insurance contract must specify the underlying risk, such as property, health, or life. Likewise, so do derivatives. As noted earlier, derivatives are associated with an underlying asset. As such, the so-called "underlying asset" is often simply referred to as the **underlying**, whose value is the source of risk. In fact, the underlying need not even be an asset itself. Although common derivatives underlyings are equities, fixed-income securities, currencies, and commodities, other derivatives underlyings include interest rates, credit, energy, weather, and even other derivatives, all of which are not generally thought of as assets. Thus, like insurance, derivatives pay off on the basis of a source of risk, which is often, but not always, the value of an underlying asset. And like insurance, derivatives have a definite life span and expire on a specified date.

Derivatives are created in the form of legal contracts. They involve two parties—the buyer and the seller (sometimes known as the writer)—each of whom agrees to do something for the other, either now or later. The buyer, who purchases the derivative, is referred to as the **long** or the holder because he owns (holds) the derivative and holds a long position. The seller is referred to as the **short** because he holds a short position.[1]

A derivative contract always defines the rights and obligations of each party. These contracts are intended to be, and almost always are, recognized by the legal system as commercial contracts that each party expects to be upheld and supported in the legal system. Nonetheless, disputes sometimes arise, and lawyers, judges, and juries may be required to step in and resolve the matter.

There are two general classes of derivatives. Some provide the ability to lock in a price at which one might buy or sell the underlying. Because they force the two parties to transact in the future at a previously agreed-on price, these instruments are called **forward commitments**. The various types of forward commitments are called forward contracts, futures contracts, and swaps. Another class of derivatives provides *the right but not the obligation* to buy or sell the underlying at a pre-determined price. Because the choice of buying or selling versus doing nothing depends on a particular random outcome, these derivatives are called **contingent claims**. The primary contingent claim is called an **option**. The types of derivatives will be covered in more detail later in this reading and in considerably more depth later in the curriculum.

The existence of derivatives begs the obvious question of what purpose they serve. If one can participate in the success of a company by holding its equity, what reason can possibly explain why another instrument is required that takes its value from the performance of the equity? Although equity and other fundamental markets exist and usually perform reasonably well without derivative markets, it is possible that derivative markets can *improve* the performance of the markets for the underlyings. As you will see later in this reading, that is indeed true in practice.

Derivative markets create beneficial opportunities that do not exist in their absence. Derivatives can be used to create strategies that cannot be implemented with the underlyings

---

[1]In the financial world, the *long* always benefits from an increase in the value of the instrument he owns, and the *short* always benefits from a decrease in the value of the instrument he has sold. Think of the long as having possession of something and the short as having incurred an obligation to deliver that something.

alone. For example, derivatives make it easier to go short, thereby benefiting from a decline in the value of the underlying. In addition, derivatives, in and of themselves, are characterized by a relatively high degree of leverage, meaning that participants in derivatives transactions usually have to invest only a small amount of their own capital relative to the value of the underlying. As such, small movements in the underlying can lead to fairly large movements in the amount of money made or lost on the derivative. Derivatives generally trade at lower transaction costs than comparable spot market transactions, are often more liquid than their underlyings, and offer a simple, effective, and low-cost way to transfer risk. For example, a shareholder of a company can reduce or even completely eliminate the market exposure by trading a derivative on the equity. Holders of fixed-income securities can use derivatives to reduce or completely eliminate interest rate risk, allowing them to focus on the credit risk. Alternatively, holders of fixed-income securities can reduce or eliminate the credit risk, focusing more on the interest rate risk. Derivatives permit such adjustments easily and quickly. These features of derivatives are covered in more detail later in this reading.

The types of performance transformations facilitated by derivatives allow market participants to practice more effective risk management. Indeed, the entire field of derivatives, which at one time was focused mostly on the instruments themselves, is now more concerned with the *uses* of the instruments. Just as a carpenter uses a hammer, nails, screws, a screwdriver, and a saw to build something useful or beautiful, a financial expert uses derivatives to manage risk. And just as it is critically important that a carpenter understand how to use these tools, an investment practitioner must understand how to properly use derivatives. In the case of the carpenter, the result is building something useful; in the case of the financial expert, the result is managing financial risk. Thus, like tools, derivatives serve a valuable purpose but like tools, they must be used carefully.

The practice of risk management has taken a prominent role in financial markets. Indeed, whenever companies announce large losses from trading, lending, or operations, stories abound about how poorly these companies managed risk. Such stories are great attention grabbers and a real boon for the media, but they often miss the point that risk management does not guarantee that large losses will not occur. Rather, **risk management** *is the process by which an organization or individual defines the level of risk it wishes to take, measures the level of risk it is taking, and adjusts the latter to equal the former.* Risk management never offers a guarantee that large losses will not occur, and it does not eliminate the possibility of total failure. To do so would typically require that the amount of risk taken be so small that the organization would be effectively constrained from pursuing its primary objectives. Risk taking is inherent in all forms of economic activity and life in general. The possibility of failure is never eliminated.

EXAMPLE 1   Characteristics of Derivatives

1. Which of the following is the best example of a derivative?
   A. A global equity mutual fund
   B. A non-callable government bond
   C. A contract to purchase Apple Computer at a fixed price
2. Which of the following is **not** a characteristic of a derivative?
   A. An underlying
   B. A low degree of leverage
   C. Two parties—a buyer and a seller

3. Which of the following statements about derivatives is **not** true?
   A. They are created in the spot market.
   B. They are used in the practice of risk management.
   C. They take their values from the value of something else.

Solution to 1: C is correct. Mutual funds and government bonds are not derivatives. A government bond is a fundamental asset on which derivatives might be created, but it is not a derivative itself. A mutual fund can technically meet the definition of a derivative, but as noted in the reading, derivatives transform the value of a payoff of an underlying asset. Mutual funds merely pass those payoffs through to their holders.

Solution to 2: B is correct. All derivatives have an underlying and must have a buyer and a seller. More importantly, derivatives have high degrees of leverage, not low degrees of leverage.

Solution to 3: A is correct. Derivatives are used to practice risk management and they take (derive) their values from the value of something else, the underlying. They are not created in the spot market, which is where the underlying trades.

Note also that risk management is a dynamic and ongoing process, reflecting the fact that the risk assumed can be difficult to measure and is constantly changing. As noted, derivatives are tools, indeed *the* tools that make it easier to manage risk. Although one can trade stocks and bonds (the underlyings) to adjust the level of risk, it is almost always more effective to trade derivatives.

Risk management is addressed more directly elsewhere in the CFA curriculum, but the study of derivatives necessarily entails the concept of risk management. In an explanation of derivatives, the focus is usually on the instruments and it is easy to forget the overriding objective of managing risk. Unfortunately, that would be like a carpenter obsessed with his hammer and nails, forgetting that he is building a piece of furniture. It is important to always try to keep an eye on the objective of managing risk.

2. THE STRUCTURE OF DERIVATIVE MARKETS

Having an understanding of equity, fixed-income, and currency markets is extremely beneficial—indeed, quite necessary—in understanding derivatives. One could hardly consider the wisdom of using derivatives on a share of stock if one did not understand the equity markets reasonably well. As you likely know, equities trade on organized exchanges as well as in over-the-counter (OTC) markets. These exchange-traded equity markets—such as the Deutsche Börse, the Tokyo Stock Exchange, and the New York Stock Exchange and its Eurex affiliate—are formal organizational structures that bring buyers and sellers together through market makers, or dealers, to facilitate transactions. Exchanges have formal rule structures and are required to comply with all securities laws.

OTC securities markets operate in much the same manner, with similar rules, regulations, and organizational structures. At one time, the major difference between OTC and exchange markets for securities was that the latter brought buyers and sellers together in a physical location, whereas the former facilitated trading strictly in an electronic manner. Today, these distinctions are blurred because many organized securities exchanges have gone completely to electronic systems. Moreover, OTC securities markets can be formally organized structures, such as NASDAQ, or can merely refer to informal networks of parties who buy and sell with each other, such as the corporate and government bond markets in the United States.

The derivatives world also comprises organized exchanges and OTC markets. Although the derivatives world is also moving toward less distinction between these markets, there are clear differences that are important to understand.

2.1. Exchange-Traded Derivatives Markets

Derivative instruments are created and traded either on an exchange or on the OTC market. Exchange-traded derivatives are standardized, whereas OTC derivatives are customized. To standardize a derivative contract means that its terms and conditions are precisely specified by the exchange and there is very limited ability to alter those terms. For example, an exchange might offer trading in certain types of derivatives that expire only on the third Friday of March, June, September, and December. If a party wanted the derivative to expire on any other day, it would not be able to trade such a derivative on that exchange, nor would it be able to persuade the exchange to create it, at least not in the short run. If a party wanted a derivative on a particular entity, such as a specific stock, that party could trade it on that exchange only if the exchange had specified that such a derivative could trade. Even the magnitudes of the contracts are specified. If a party wanted a derivative to cover €150,000 and the exchange specified that contracts could trade only in increments of €100,000, the party could do nothing about it if it wanted to trade that derivative on that exchange.

This standardization of contract terms facilitates the creation of a more liquid market for derivatives. If all market participants know that derivatives on the euro trade in 100,000-unit lots and that they all expire only on certain days, the market functions more effectively than it would if there were derivatives with many different unit sizes and expiration days competing in the same market at the same time. This standardization makes it easier to provide liquidity. Through designated market makers, derivatives exchanges guarantee that derivatives can be bought and sold.[2]

The cornerstones of the exchange-traded derivatives market are the market makers (or dealers) and the speculators, both of whom typically own memberships on the exchange.[3] The market makers stand ready to buy at one price and sell at a higher price. With

---

[2]It is important to understand that merely being able to buy and sell a derivative, or even a security, does not mean that liquidity is high and that the cost of liquidity is low. Derivatives exchanges guarantee that a derivative can be bought and sold, but they do not guarantee the price. The ask price (the price at which the market maker will sell) and the bid price (the price at which the market maker will buy) can be far apart, which they will be in a market with low liquidity. Hence, such a market can have liquidity, loosely defined, but the cost of liquidity can be quite high. The factors that can lead to low liquidity for derivatives are similar to those for securities: little trading interest and a high level of uncertainty.

[3]Exchanges are owned by their *members*, whose memberships convey the right to trade. In addition, some exchanges are themselves publicly traded corporations whose members are shareholders, and there are also non-member shareholders.

standardization of terms and an active market, market makers are often able to buy and sell almost simultaneously at different prices, locking in small, short-term profits—a process commonly known as scalping. In some cases, however, they are unable to do so, thereby forcing them to either hold exposed positions or find other parties with whom they can trade and thus lay off (get rid of) the risk. This is when speculators come in. Although speculators are market participants who are willing to take risks, it is important to understand that being a speculator does not mean the reckless assumption of risk. Although speculators will take large losses at times, good speculators manage those risks by watching their exposures, absorbing market information, and observing the flow of orders in such a manner that they are able to survive and profit. Often, speculators will hedge their risks when they become uncomfortable.

Standardization also facilitates the creation of a clearing and settlement operation. **Clearing** refers to the process by which the exchange verifies the execution of a transaction and records the participants' identities. **Settlement** refers to the related process in which the exchange transfers money from one participant to the other or from a participant to the exchange or vice versa. This flow of money is a critical element of derivatives trading. Clearly, there would be no confidence in markets in which money is not efficiently collected and disbursed. Derivatives exchanges have done an excellent job of clearing and settlement, especially in comparison to securities exchanges. Derivatives exchanges clear and settle all contracts overnight, whereas most securities exchanges require two business days.

The clearing and settlement process of derivative transactions also provides a credit guarantee. If two parties engage in a derivative contract on an exchange, one party will ultimately make money and the other will lose money. Derivatives exchanges use their clearinghouses to provide a guarantee to the winning party that if the loser does not pay, the clearinghouse will pay the winning party. The clearinghouse is able to provide this credit guarantee by requiring a cash deposit, usually called the **margin bond** or **performance bond**, from the participants to the contract. Derivatives clearinghouses manage these deposits, occasionally requiring additional deposits, so effectively that they have never failed to pay in the nearly 100 years they have existed. We will say more about this process later and illustrate how it works.

Exchange markets are said to have **transparency**, which means that full information on all transactions is disclosed to exchanges and regulatory bodies. All transactions are centrally reported within the exchanges and their clearinghouses, and specific laws require that these markets be overseen by national regulators. Although this would seem a strong feature of exchange markets, there is a definite cost. Transparency means a loss of privacy: National regulators can see what transactions have been done. Standardization means a loss of flexibility: A participant can do only the transactions that are permitted on the exchange. Regulation means a loss of both privacy and flexibility. It is not that transparency or regulation is good and the other is bad. It is simply a trade-off.

Derivatives exchanges exist in virtually every developed (and some emerging market) countries around the world. Some exchanges specialize in derivatives and others are integrated with securities exchanges.

Although there have been attempts to create somewhat non-standardized derivatives for trading on an exchange, such attempts have not been particularly successful. Standardization is a critical element by which derivatives exchanges are able to provide their services. We will look at this point again when discussing the alternative to standardization: customized OTC derivatives.

2.2. Over-the-Counter Derivatives Markets

The OTC derivatives markets comprise an informal network of market participants that are willing to create and trade virtually any type of derivative that can legally exist. The backbone of these markets is the set of dealers, which are typically banks. Most of these banks are members of a group called the International Swaps and Derivatives Association (ISDA), a worldwide organization of financial institutions that engage in derivative transactions, primarily as dealers. As such, these markets are sometimes called *dealer markets*. Acting as principals, these dealers informally agree to buy and sell various derivatives. It is *informal* because the dealers are not obligated to do so. Their participation is based on a desire to profit, which they do by purchasing at one price and selling at a higher price. Although it might seem that a dealer who can "buy low, sell high" could make money easily, the process in practice is not that simple. Because OTC instruments are not standardized, a dealer cannot expect to buy a derivative at one price and simultaneously sell it to a different party who happens to want to buy the same derivative at the same time and at a higher price.

To manage the risk they assume by buying and selling customized derivatives, OTC derivatives dealers typically hedge their risks by engaging in alternative but similar transactions that pass the risk on to other parties. For example, if a company comes to a dealer to buy a derivative on the euro, the company would effectively be transferring the risk of the euro to the dealer. The dealer would then attempt to lay off (get rid of) that risk by engaging in an alternative but similar transaction that would transfer the risk to another party. This hedge might involve another derivative on the euro or it might simply be a transaction in the euro itself. Of course, that begs the question of why the company could not have laid off the risk itself and avoided the dealer. Indeed, some can and do, but laying off risk is not simple. Unable to find identical offsetting transactions, dealers usually have to find *similar* transactions with which they can lay off the risk. Hedging one derivative with a different kind of derivative on the same underlying is a similar but not identical transaction. It takes specialized knowledge and complex models to be able to do such transactions effectively, and dealers are more capable of doing so than are ordinary companies. Thus, one might think of a dealer as a middleman, a sort of financial wholesaler using its specialized knowledge and resources to facilitate the transfer of risk. In the same manner that one could theoretically purchase a consumer product from a manufacturer, a network of specialized middlemen and retailers is often a more effective method.

Because of the customization of OTC derivatives, there is a tendency to think that the OTC market is less liquid than the exchange market. That is not necessarily true. Many OTC instruments can easily be created and then essentially offset by doing the exact opposite transaction, often with the same party. For example, suppose Corporation A buys an OTC derivative from Dealer B. Before the expiration date, Corporation A wants to terminate the position. It can return to Dealer B and ask to sell a derivative with identical terms. Market conditions will have changed, of course, and the value of the derivative will not be the same, but the transaction can be conducted quite easily with either Corporation A or Dealer B netting a gain at the expense of the other. Alternatively, Corporation A could do this transaction with a different dealer, the result of which would remove exposure to the underlying risk but would leave two transactions open and some risk that one party would default to the other. In contrast to this type of OTC liquidity, some exchange-traded derivatives have very little trading interest and thus relatively low liquidity. Liquidity is always driven by trading interest, which can be strong or weak in both types of markets.

OTC derivative markets operate at a lower degree of regulation and oversight than do exchange-traded derivative markets. In fact, until around 2010, it could largely be said that the OTC market was essentially unregulated. OTC transactions could be executed with only the minimal oversight provided through laws that regulated the parties themselves, not the specific instruments. Following the financial crisis of 2007–2009, new regulations began to blur the distinction between OTC and exchange-listed markets. In both the United States (the Wall Street Reform and Consumer Protection Act of 2010, commonly known as the Dodd–Frank Act) and Europe (the Regulation of the European Parliament and of the Council on OTC Derivatives, Central Counterparties, and Trade Repositories), regulations are changing the characteristics of OTC markets. In general, world policy-makers have advanced an agenda to make global derivatives markets more resilient and robust, pursuing increased transparency and lowered systemic risk.

When the full implementation of these new laws takes place, a number of OTC transactions will have to be cleared through central clearing agencies, information on most OTC transactions will need to be reported to regulators, and entities that operate in the OTC market will be more closely monitored. There are, however, quite a few exemptions that cover a significant percentage of derivative transactions. Clearly, the degree of OTC regulation, although increasing in recent years, is still lighter than that of exchange-listed market regulation. Many transactions in OTC markets will retain a degree of privacy with lower transparency, and most importantly, the OTC markets will remain considerably more flexible than the exchange-listed markets.

EXAMPLE 2   Exchange-Traded versus Over-the-Counter Derivatives

1. Which of the following characteristics is **not** associated with exchange-traded derivatives?
   A. Margin or performance bonds are required.
   B. The exchange guarantees all payments in the event of default.
   C. All terms except the price are customized to the parties' individual needs.
2. Which of the following characteristics is associated with over-the-counter derivatives?
   A. Trading occurs in a central location.
   B. They are more regulated than exchange-listed derivatives.
   C. They are less transparent than exchange-listed derivatives.
3. Market makers earn a profit in both exchange and over-the-counter derivatives markets by:
   A. charging a commission on each trade.
   B. a combination of commissions and markups.
   C. buying at one price, selling at a higher price, and hedging any risk.
4. Which of the following statements *most* accurately describes exchange-traded derivatives relative to over-the-counter derivatives? Exchange-traded derivatives are more likely to have:
   A. greater credit risk.
   B. standardized contract terms.
   C. greater risk management uses.

Solution to 1: C is correct. Exchange-traded contracts are standardized, meaning that the exchange determines the terms of the contract except the price. The exchange guarantees against default and requires margins or performance bonds.

Solution to 2: C is correct. OTC derivatives have a lower degree of transparency than exchange-listed derivatives. Trading does not occur in a central location but, rather, is quite dispersed. Although new national securities laws are tightening the regulation of OTC derivatives, the degree of regulation is less than that of exchange-listed derivatives.

Solution to 3: C is correct. Market makers buy at one price (the bid), sell at a higher price (the ask), and hedge whatever risk they otherwise assume. Market makers do not charge a commission. Hence, A and B are both incorrect.

Solution to 4: B is correct. Standardization of contract terms is a characteristic of exchange-traded derivatives. A is incorrect because credit risk is well-controlled in exchange markets. C is incorrect because the risk management uses are not limited by being traded over the counter.

3. TYPES OF DERIVATIVES: INTRODUCTION, FORWARD CONTRACTS

As previously stated, derivatives fall into two general classifications: forward commitments and contingent claims. The factor that distinguishes forward commitments from contingent claims is that forward commitments *obligate* the parties to engage in a transaction at a future date on terms agreed upon in advance, whereas contingent claims provide one party the *right but not the obligation* to engage in a future transaction on terms agreed upon in advance.

3.1. Forward Commitments

Forward commitments are contracts entered into at one point in time that require both parties to engage in a transaction at a later point in time (the expiration) on terms agreed upon at the start. The parties establish the identity and quantity of the underlying, the manner in which the contract will be executed or settled when it expires, and the fixed price at which the underlying will be exchanged. This fixed price is called the **forward price**.

As a hypothetical example of a forward contract, suppose that today Markus and Johannes enter into an agreement that Markus will sell his BMW to Johannes for a price of €30,000. The transaction will take place on a specified date, say, 180 days from today. At that time, Markus will deliver the vehicle to Johannes's home and Johannes will give Markus a bank-certified check for €30,000. There will be no recourse, so if the vehicle has problems later, Johannes cannot go back to Markus for compensation. It should be clear that both Markus and Johannes must do their due diligence and carefully consider the reliability of each other. The car could have serious quality issues and Johannes could have financial problems and be unable to pay the €30,000. Obviously, the transaction is essentially unregulated. Either party could renege on his obligation, in response to which the other party could go to court, provided a formal contract exists and is carefully written. Note finally that one of the two parties is likely to end up gaining and the other losing, depending on the secondary market price of this type of vehicle at expiration of the contract.

This example is quite simple but illustrates the essential elements of a forward contract. In the financial world, such contracts are very carefully written, with legal provisions that guard against fraud and require extensive credit checks. Now let us take a deeper look at the characteristics of forward contracts.

3.1.1. Forward Contracts

The following is the formal definition of a forward contract:

A forward contract is an over-the-counter derivative contract in which two parties agree that one party, the buyer, will purchase an underlying asset from the other party, the seller, at a later date at a fixed price they agree on when the contract is signed.

In addition to agreeing on the price at which the underlying asset will be sold at a later date, the two parties also agree on several other matters, such as the specific identity of the underlying, the number of units of the underlying that will be delivered, and where the future delivery will occur. These are important points but relatively minor in this discussion, so they can be left out of the definition to keep it uncluttered.

As noted earlier, a forward contract is a commitment. Each party agrees that it will fulfill its responsibility at the designated future date. Failure to do so constitutes a default and the non-defaulting party can institute legal proceedings to enforce performance. It is important to recognize that although either party could default to the other, only one party at a time can default. The party owing the greater amount could default to the other, but the party owing the lesser amount cannot default because its claim on the other party is greater. The amount owed is always based on the net owed by one party to the other.

To gain a better understanding of forward contracts, it is necessary to examine their payoffs. As noted, forward contracts—and indeed all derivatives—take (derive) their payoffs from the performance of the underlying asset. To illustrate the payoff of a forward contract, start with the assumption that we are at time $t = 0$ and that the forward contract expires at a later date, time $t = T$.[4] The spot price of the underlying asset at time 0 is S_0 and at time T is S_T. Of course, when we initiate the contract at time 0, we do not know what S_T will ultimately be. Remember that the two parties, the buyer and the seller, are going long and short, respectively.

At time $t = 0$, the long and the short agree that the short will deliver the asset to the long at time T for a price of $F_0(T)$. The notation $F_0(T)$ denotes that this value is established at time 0 and applies to a contract expiring at time T. $F_0(T)$ is the forward price.

So, let us assume that the buyer enters into the forward contract with the seller for a price of $F_0(T)$, with delivery of one unit of the underlying asset to occur at time T. Now, let us roll forward to time T, when the price of the underlying is S_T. The long is obligated to pay $F_0(T)$, for which he receives an asset worth S_T. If $S_T > F_0(T)$, it is clear that the transaction has worked out well for the long. He paid $F_0(T)$ and receives something of greater value. Thus, the contract

---

[4]Such notations as $t = 0$ and $t = T$ are commonly used in explaining derivatives. To indicate that $t = 0$ simply means that we initiate a contract at an imaginary time designated like a counter starting at zero. To indicate that the contract expires at $t = T$ simply means that at some future time, designated as T, the contract expires. Time T could be a certain number of days from now or a fraction of a year later or T years later. We will be more specific in later readings that involve calculations. For now, just assume that $t = 0$ and $t = T$ are two dates—the initiation and the expiration—of the contract.

effectively pays off $S_T - F_0(T)$ to the long, which is the value of the contract at expiration. The short has the mirror image of the long. He is required to deliver the asset worth S_T and accept a smaller amount, $F_0(T)$. The contract has a payoff for him of $F_0(T) - S_T$, which is negative. Even if the asset's value, S_T, is less than the forward price, $F_0(T)$, the payoffs are still $S_T - F_0(T)$ for the long and $F_0(T) - S_T$ for the short. We can consolidate these results by writing the short's payoff as the negative of the long's, $-[S_T - F_0(T)]$, which serves as a useful reminder that the long and the short are engaged in a zero-sum game, which is a type of competition in which one participant's gains are the other's losses. Although both lose a modest amount in the sense of both having some costs to engage in the transaction, these costs are relatively small and worth ignoring for our purposes at this time. In addition, it is worthwhile to note how derivatives transform the performance of the underlying. The gain from owning the underlying would be $S_T - S_0$, whereas the gain from owning the forward contract would be $S_T - F_0(T)$. Both figures are driven by S_T, the price of the underlying at expiration, but they are not the same.

For an example, a buyer enters a forward contract to buy gold at a price of $F_0(T) = \$1,312.90$ per ounce four months from now. The spot price of gold is $S_0 = \$1,207.40$ per ounce. Four months in the future, the price of the underlying gold is $S_T = \$1,275.90$ per ounce. The buyer's gain from the forward contract, the payoff from the contract, is the value of gold (at maturity) less the forward price: $S_T - F_0(T) = 1,275.90 - 1,312.90 = -\$37.00$ per ounce. Because the value of gold when the contract matures is less than the forward price, $S_T < F_0(T)$, the buyer has incurred a loss. Notably, the forward contract seller has a contract payoff, $+\$37.00$, that is the negative of that of the contract buyer. The gain on owning the underlying, which is $S_T - S_0 = 1,275.90 - 1,207.40 = \$68.40$, differs from the gain ($-\$37.00$) on the forward contract.

The buyer also enters a forward contract to buy oil at a price of $F_0(T) = \$71.86$ per barrel four months from now. The spot price of oil is $S_0 = \$71.11$ per barrel. Four months in the future, the price of the underlying oil is $S_T = \$80.96$ per barrel. The buyer's gain from the forward contract, the payoff from the contract, is the value of oil less the forward price: $S_T - F_0(T) = 80.96 - 71.86 = \$9.10$ per barrel. Unlike the forward contract on gold above, because the value of oil when the contract matures is greater than the forward price, $S_T > F_0(T)$, the buyer of the forward contract realizes a gain.

Exhibit 1 illustrates the payoffs from both buying and selling a forward contract.

EXHIBIT 1   Payoffs from a Forward Contract

A. Payoff from Buying = $S_T - F_0(T)$

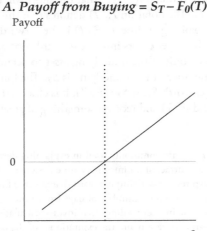

Payoff

S_T

B. Payoff from Selling = −[S_T − $F_0(T)$]

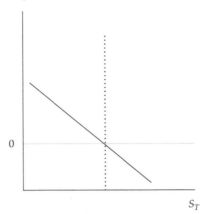

The long hopes the price of the underlying will rise above the forward price, $F_0(T)$, whereas the short hopes the price of the underlying will fall below the forward price. Except in the extremely rare event that the underlying price at T equals the forward price, there will ultimately be a winner and a loser.

An important element of forward contracts is that no money changes hands between parties when the contract is initiated. Unlike in the purchase and sale of an asset, there is no value exchanged at the start. The buyer does not pay the seller some money and obtain something. In fact, forward contracts have zero value at the start. They are neither assets nor liabilities. As you will learn in later readings, their values will deviate from zero later as prices move. Forward contracts will almost always have non-zero values at expiration.

As noted previously, the primary purpose of derivatives is for risk management. Although the uses of forward contracts are covered in depth later in the curriculum, there are a few things to note here about the purposes of forward contracts. It should be apparent that locking in the future buying or selling price of an underlying asset can be extremely attractive for some parties. For example, an airline anticipating the purchase of jet fuel at a later date can enter into a forward contract to buy the fuel at a price agreed upon when the contract is initiated. In so doing, the airline has hedged its cost of fuel. Thus, forward contracts can be structured to create a perfect hedge, providing an assurance that the underlying asset can be bought or sold at a price known when the contract is initiated. Likewise, speculators, who ultimately assume the risk laid off by hedgers, can make bets on the direction of the underlying asset without having to invest the money to purchase the asset itself.

Finally, forward contracts need not specifically settle by delivery of the underlying asset. They can settle by an exchange of cash. These contracts—called **non-deliverable forwards** (NDFs), **cash-settled forwards**, or **contracts for differences**—have the same economic effect as do their delivery-based counterparts. For example, for a physical delivery contract, if the long pays $F_0(T)$ and receives an asset worth S_T, the contract is worth $S_T − F_0(T)$ to the long at expiration. A non-deliverable forward contract would have the short simply pay cash to the long in the amount of $S_T − F_0(T)$. The long would not take possession of the underlying asset, but if he wanted the asset, he could purchase it in the market for its current price of S_T. Because he received a cash settlement in the amount of $S_T - F_0(T)$, in buying the asset the long would have to pay out only $S_T - [S_T - F_0(T)]$, which equals $F_0(T)$. Thus, the long could acquire the asset, effectively paying $F_0(T)$, exactly as the contract promised. Transaction costs do make cash settlement different from physical delivery, but this point is relatively minor and can be disregarded for our purposes here.

As previously mentioned, forward contracts are OTC contracts. There is no formal forward contract exchange. Nonetheless, there are exchange-traded variants of forward contracts, which are called futures contracts or just futures.

4. TYPES OF DERIVATIVES: FUTURES

Futures contracts are specialized versions of forward contracts that have been standardized and that trade on a futures exchange. By standardizing these contracts and creating an organized market with rules, regulations, and a central clearing facility, the futures markets offer an element of liquidity and protection against loss by default.

Formally, a futures contract is defined as follows:

> *A futures contract is a standardized derivative contract created and traded on a futures exchange in which two parties agree that one party, the buyer, will purchase an underlying asset from the other party, the seller, at a later date and at a price agreed on by the two parties when the contract is initiated and in which there is a daily settling of gains and losses and a credit guarantee by the futures exchange through its clearinghouse.*

First, let us review what standardization means. Recall that in forward contracts, the parties customize the contract by specifying the underlying asset, the time to expiration, the delivery and settlement conditions, and the quantity of the underlying, all according to whatever terms they agree on. These contracts are not traded on an exchange. As noted, the regulation of OTC derivatives markets is increasing, but these contracts are not subject to the traditionally high degree of regulation that applies to securities and futures markets. Futures contracts first require the existence of a futures exchange, a legally recognized entity that provides a market for trading these contracts. Futures exchanges are highly regulated at the national level in all countries. These exchanges specify that only certain contracts are authorized for trading. These contracts have specific underlying assets, times to expiration, delivery and settlement conditions, and quantities. The exchange offers a facility in the form of a physical location and/or an electronic system as well as liquidity provided by authorized market makers.

Probably the most important distinctive characteristic of futures contracts is the daily settlement of gains and losses and the associated credit guarantee provided by the exchange through its clearinghouse. When a party buys a futures contract, it commits to purchase the underlying asset at a later date and at a price agreed upon when the contract is initiated. The counterparty (the seller) makes the opposite commitment, an agreement to sell the underlying asset at a later date and at a price agreed upon when the contract is initiated. The agreed-upon price is called the **futures price**. Identical contracts trade on an ongoing basis at different prices, reflecting the passage of time and the arrival of new information to the market. Thus, as the futures price changes, the parties make and lose money. Rising (falling) prices, of course, benefit (hurt) the long and hurt (benefit) the short. At the end of each day, the clearinghouse engages in a practice called **mark to market**, also known as the **daily settlement**. The clearinghouse determines an average of the final futures trades of the day and designates that price as the **settlement price**. All contracts are then said to be *marked to the settlement price*. For example, if the long purchases the contract during the day at a futures price of £120 and the settlement price at the end of the day is £122, the long's account would be marked for a gain of £2. In other words, the long has made a profit of £2 and that amount is credited to his account, with the money coming from the account of the short, who has lost £2. Naturally, if the futures price decreases, the long loses money and is charged with that loss, and the money is transferred to the account of the short.[5]

The account is specifically referred to as a **margin** account. Of course, in equity markets, margin accounts are commonly used, but there are significant differences between futures margin accounts and equity margin accounts. Equity margin accounts involve the extension of credit. An investor deposits part of the cost of the stock and borrows the remainder at a rate of interest. With futures margin accounts, both parties deposit a required minimum sum of money, but the remainder of the price is not borrowed. This required margin is typically less than 10% of the futures price, which is considerably less than in equity margin trading. In the example above, let us assume that the required margin is £10, which is referred to as the **initial margin**. Both the long and the short put that amount into their respective margin accounts. This money is deposited there to support the trade, not as a form of equity, with the remaining amount borrowed. There is no formal loan created as in equity markets. A futures margin is more of a performance bond or good faith deposit, terms that were previously mentioned. It is simply an amount of money put into an account that covers possible future losses.

Associated with each initial margin is another figure called the **maintenance margin**. The maintenance margin is the amount of money that each participant must maintain in the account after the trade is initiated, and it is always significantly lower than the initial margin. Let us assume that the maintenance margin in this example is £6. If the buyer's account is marked to market with a credit of £2, his margin balance moves to £12, while the seller's account is charged £2 and his balance moves to £8. The clearinghouse then compares each participant's balance with the maintenance margin. At this point, both participants more than meet the maintenance margin.

Let us say, however, that the price continues to move in the long's favor and, therefore, against the short. A few days later, assume that the short's balance falls to £4, which is below the maintenance margin requirement of £6. The short will then get a **margin call**, which is a request to deposit additional funds. The amount that the short has to deposit, however, is *not* the £2 that would bring his balance up to the maintenance margin. Instead, the short must deposit enough funds to bring the balance up to the initial margin. So, the short must come up with £6. The purpose of this rule is to get the party's position significantly above the minimum level and provide some breathing room. If the balance were brought up only to the maintenance level, there would likely be another margin call soon. A party can choose not to deposit additional funds, in which case the party would be required to close out the contract as soon as possible and would be responsible for any additional losses until the position is closed.

As with forward contracts, neither party pays any money to the other when the contract is initiated. Value accrues as the futures price changes, but at the end of each day, the

---

[5]The actual amount of money charged and credited depends on the contract size and the number of contracts. A price of £120 might actually refer to a contract that has a standard size of £100,000. Thus, £120 might actually mean 120% of the standard size, or £120,000. In addition, the parties are likely to hold more than one contract. Hence, the gain of £2 referred to in the text might really mean £2,000 (122% minus 120% times the £100,000 standard size) times the number of contracts held by the party.

mark-to-market process settles the gains and losses, effectively resetting the value for each party to zero.

The clearinghouse moves money between the participants, crediting gains to the winners and charging losses to the losers. By doing this on a daily basis, the gains and losses are typically quite small, and the margin balances help ensure that the clearinghouse will collect from the party losing money. As an extra precaution, in fast-moving markets, the clearinghouse can make margin calls during the day, not just at the end of the day. Yet there still remains the possibility that a party could default. A large loss could occur quickly and consume the entire margin balance, with additional money owed.[6] If the losing party cannot pay, the clearing-house provides a guarantee that it will make up the loss, which it does by maintaining an insurance fund. If that fund were depleted, the clearinghouse could levy a tax on the other market participants, though that has never happened.

Some futures contracts contain a provision limiting price changes. These rules, called **price limits**, establish a band relative to the previous day's settlement price, within which all trades must occur. If market participants wish to trade at a price above the upper band, trading stops, which is called **limit up**, until two parties agree on a trade at a price lower than the upper limit. Likewise, if market participants wish to trade at a price below the lower band, which is called **limit down**, no trade can take place until two parties agree to trade at a price above the lower limit. When the market hits these limits and trading stops, it is called **locked limit**. Typically, the exchange rules provide for an expansion of the limits the next day. These price limits, which may be somewhat objectionable to proponents of free markets, are important in helping the clearinghouse manage its credit exposure. Just because two parties wish to trade a futures contract at a price beyond the limits does not mean they should be allowed to do so. The clearinghouse is a third participant in the contract, guaranteeing to each party that it ensures against the other party defaulting. Therefore, the clearinghouse has a vested interest in the price and considerable exposure. Sharply moving prices make it more difficult for the clearinghouse to collect from the parties losing money.

Most participants in futures markets buy and sell contracts, collecting their profits and incurring their losses, with no ultimate intent to make or take delivery of the underlying asset. For example, the long may ultimately sell her position before expiration. When a party re-enters the market at a later date but before expiration and engages in the opposite transaction—a long selling her previously opened contract or a short buying her previously opened contract—the transaction is referred to as an offset. The clearinghouse marks the contract to the current price relative to the previous settlement price and closes out the participant's position.

At any given time, the number of outstanding contracts is called the **open interest**. Each contract counted in the open interest has a long and a corresponding short. The open interest figure changes daily as some parties open up new positions, while other parties offset their old positions. It is theoretically possible that all longs and shorts offset their positions before expiration, leaving no open interest when the contract expires, but in practice there is nearly always some open interest at expiration, at which time there is a final delivery or settlement.

---

[6]For example, let us go back to when the short had a balance of £4, which is £2 below the maintenance margin and £6 below the initial margin. The short will get a margin call, but suppose he elects not to deposit additional funds and requests that his position be terminated. In a fast-moving market, the price might increase more than £4 before his broker can close his position. The remaining balance of £4 would then be depleted, and the short would be responsible for any additional losses.

When discussing forward contracts, we noted that a contract could be written such that the parties engage in physical delivery or cash settlement at expiration. In the futures markets, the exchange specifies whether physical delivery or cash settlement applies. In physical delivery contracts, the short is required to deliver the underlying asset at a designated location and the long is required to pay for it. Delivery replaces the mark-to-market process on the final day. It also ensures an important principle that you will use later: *The futures price converges to the spot price at expiration*. Because the short delivers the actual asset and the long pays the current spot price for it, the futures price at expiration has to be the spot price at that time. Alternatively, a futures contract initiated right at the instant of expiration is effectively a spot transaction and, therefore, the futures price at expiration must equal the spot price. Following this logic, in cash settlement contracts, there is a final mark to market, with the futures price formally set to the spot price, thereby ensuring automatic convergence.

In discussing forward contracts, we described the process by which they pay off as the spot price at expiration minus the forward price, $S_T - F_0(T)$, the former determined at expiration and the latter agreed upon when the contract is initiated. Futures contracts basically pay off the same way, but there is a slight difference. Let us say the contract is initiated on Day 0 and expires on Day T. The intervening days are designated Days 1, 2, ..., T. The initial futures price is designated $f_0(T)$ and the daily settlement prices on Days 1, 2, ..., T are designated $f_1(T), f_2(T), ..., f_T(T)$. There are, of course, futures prices within each trading day, but let us focus only on the settlement prices for now. For simplicity, let us assume that the long buys at the settlement price on Day 0 and holds the position all the way to expiration. Through the mark-to-market process, the cash flows to the account of the long will be

$$f_1(T) - f_0(T) \text{ on Day 1}$$
$$f_2(T) - f_1(T) \text{ on Day 2}$$
$$f_3(T) - f_2(T) \text{ on Day 3}$$
$$...$$
$$f_T(T) - f_{T-1}(T) \text{ on Day } T$$

These add up to

$$f_T(T) - f_0(T) \text{ on Day } T.$$

And because of the convergence of the final futures price to the spot price,

$$f_T(T) - f_0(T) = S_T - f_0(T),$$

which is the same as with forward contracts.[7] Note, however, that the timing of these profits is different from that of forwards. Forward contracts realize the full amount, $S_T - f_0(T)$, at expiration, whereas futures contracts realize this amount in parts on a day-to-day basis. Naturally, the time value of money principle says that these are not equivalent amounts of money. But the differences tend to be small, particularly in low-interest-rate environments, some of these amounts are gains and some are losses, and most futures contracts have maturities of less than a year.

---

[7]Because of this equivalence, we will not specifically illustrate the profit graphs of futures contracts. You can generally treat them the same as those of forwards, which were shown in Exhibit 1.

But the near equivalence of the profits from a futures and a forward contract disguises an important distinction between these types of contracts. In a forward contact, with the entire payoff made at expiration, a loss by one party can be large enough to trigger a default. Hence, forward contracts are subject to default and require careful consideration of the credit quality of the counterparties. Because futures contracts settle gains and collect losses daily, the amounts that could be lost upon default are much smaller and naturally give the clearinghouse much greater flexibility to manage the credit risk it assumes.

Unlike forward markets, futures markets are highly regulated at the national level. National regulators are required to approve new futures exchanges and even new contracts proposed by existing exchanges as well as changes in margin requirements, price limits, and any significant changes in trading procedures. Violations of futures regulations can be subject to governmental prosecution. In addition, futures markets are far more transparent than forward markets. Futures prices, volume, and open interest are widely reported and easily obtained. Futures prices of nearby expiring contracts are often used as proxies for spot prices, particularly in decentralized spot markets, such as gold, which trades in spot markets all over the world.

In spite of the advantages of futures markets over forward markets, forward markets also have advantages over futures markets. Transparency is not always a good thing. Forward markets offer more privacy and fewer regulatory encumbrances. In addition, forward markets offer more flexibility. With the ability to tailor contracts to the specific needs of participants, forward contracts can be written exactly the way the parties want. In contrast, the standardization of futures contracts makes it more difficult for participants to get exactly what they want, even though they may get close substitutes. Yet, futures markets offer a valuable credit guarantee.

Like forward markets, futures markets can be used for hedging or speculation. For example, a jewelry manufacturer can buy gold futures, thereby hedging the price it will have to pay for one of its key inputs. Although it is more difficult to construct a futures strategy that hedges perfectly than to construct a forward strategy that does so, futures offer the benefit of the credit guarantee. It is not possible to argue that futures are better than forwards or vice versa. Market participants always trade off advantages against disadvantages. Some participants prefer futures, and some prefer forwards. Some prefer one over the other for certain risks and the other for other risks. Some might use one for a particular risk at a point in time and a different instrument for the same risk at another point in time. The choice is a matter of taste and constraints.

The third and final type of forward commitment we will cover is swaps. They go a step further in committing the parties to buy and sell something at a later date: They obligate the parties to a sequence of multiple purchases and sales.

5. TYPES OF DERIVATIVES: SWAPS

The concept of a swap is that two parties exchange (swap) a series of cash flows. One set of cash flows is variable or floating and will be determined by the movement of an underlying asset or rate. The other set of cash flows can be variable and determined by a different underlying asset or rate, or it can be fixed. Formally, a swap is defined as follows:

A swap is an over-the-counter derivative contract in which two parties agree to exchange a series of cash flows whereby one party pays a variable series that will be determined by an underlying asset or rate and the other party pays either (1) a variable series determined by a different underlying asset or rate or (2) a fixed series.

As with forward contracts, swap contracts also contain other terms—such as the identity of the underlying, the relevant payment dates, and the payment procedure—that are negotiated between the parties and written into the contract. A swap is a bit more like a forward contract than a futures contract in that it is an OTC contract, so it is privately negotiated and subject to default. Nonetheless, the similarities between futures and forwards apply to futures and swaps and, indeed, combinations of futures contracts expiring at different dates are often compared to swaps.

As with forward contracts, either party can default but only one party can default at a particular time. The money owed is always based on the net owed by one party to the other. Hence, the party owing the lesser amount cannot default to the party owing the greater amount. Only the latter can default, and the amount it owes is the net of what it owes and what is owed to it, which is also true with forwards.

Swaps are relatively young financial instruments, having been created only in the early 1980s. Thus, it may be somewhat surprising to learn that the swap is the most widely used derivative, a likely result of its simplicity and embracement by the corporate world. The most common swap is the **fixed-for-floating interest rate swap**. In fact, this type of swap is so common that it is often called a "plain vanilla swap" or just a "vanilla swap," owing to the notion that vanilla ice cream is considered plain (albeit tasty).

Let us examine a scenario in which the vanilla interest rate swap is frequently used. Suppose a corporation borrows from a bank at a floating rate. It would prefer a fixed rate, which would enable it to better anticipate its cash flow needs in making its interest payments.[8] The corporation can effectively convert its floating-rate loan to a fixed-rate loan by adding a swap, as shown in Exhibit 2.

EXHIBIT 2   Using an Interest Rate Swap to Convert a Floating-Rate Loan to a Fixed-Rate Loan

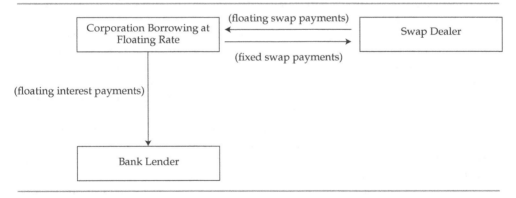

The interest payments on the loan are tied to a specific floating rate. For a dollar-based loan, that rate has historically been US dollar Libor.[9] The payments would be based on the rate from

---

[8]Banks prefer to make floating-rate loans because their own funding is typically short term and at floating rates. Thus, their borrowing rates reset frequently, giving them a strong incentive to pass that risk on to their customers through floating-rate loans.

[9]Libor is being phased out, as the panel of banks will no longer be required to submit quotations after 2021. In anticipation of this, market participants and regulators have been working to develop alternative reference rates.

the Libor market on a specified reset date times the loan balance times a factor reflecting the number of days in the current interest calculation period. The actual payment is made at a later date. Thus, for a loan balance of, say, $10 million with monthly payments, the rate might be based on Libor on the first business day of the month, with interest payable on the first business day of the next month, which is the next reset date, and calculated as $10 million times the rate times 30/360. The 30/360 convention, an implicit assumption of 30 days in a month, is common but only one of many interest calculation conventions used in the financial world. Often, "30" is replaced by the exact number of days since the last interest payment. The use of a 360-day year is a common assumption in the financial world, which originated in the pre-calculator days when an interest rate could be multiplied by a number like 30/360, 60/360, 90/360, etc., more easily than if 365 were used.

Whatever the terms of the loan are, the terms of the swap are typically set to match those of the loan. Thus, a Libor-based loan with monthly payments based on the 30/360 convention would be matched with a swap with monthly payments based on Libor and the 30/360 convention and the same reset and payment dates. Although the loan has an actual balance (the amount owed by borrower to creditor), the swap does not have such a balance owed by one party to the other. Thus, it has no principal, but it does have a balance of sorts, called the **notional principal**, which ordinarily matches the loan balance. A loan with only one principal payment, the final one, will be matched with a swap with a fixed notional principal. An amortizing loan, which has a declining principal balance, will be matched with a swap with a pre-specified declining notional principal that matches the loan balance.

As with futures and forwards, no money changes hands at the start; thus, the value of a swap when initiated must be zero. The fixed rate on the swap is determined by a process that forces the value to zero, a procedure that will be covered later in the curriculum. As market conditions change, the value of a swap will deviate from zero, being positive to one party and negative to the other.

As with forward contracts, swaps are subject to default, but because the notional amount of a swap is not typically exchanged, the credit risk of a swap is much less than that of a loan.[10] The only money passing from one party to the other is the net difference between the fixed and floating interest payments. In fact, the parties do not even pay each other. Only one party pays the other, as determined by the net of the greater amount owed minus the lesser amount. This does not mean that swaps are not subject to a potentially large amount of credit risk. At a given point in time, one party could default, effectively owing the value of all remaining payments, which could substantially exceed the value that the non-defaulting party owes to the defaulting party. Thus, there is indeed credit risk in a swap. This risk must be managed by careful analysis before the transaction and by the potential use of such risk-mitigating measures as collateral.

There are also interest rate swaps in which one party pays on the basis of one interest rate and the other party pays on the basis of a different interest rate. For example, one party might make payments at Libor, whereas the other might make payments on the basis of the U. S. Treasury bill rate. The difference between Libor and the T-bill rate, often called the TED

---

[10]It is possible that the notional principal will be exchanged in a currency swap, whereby each party makes a series of payments to the other in different currencies. Whether the notional principal is exchanged depends on the purpose of the swap. This point will be covered later in the curriculum. At this time, you should see that it would be fruitless to exchange notional principals in an interest rate swap because that would mean each party would give the other the same amount of money when the transaction is initiated and re-exchange the same amount of money when the contract terminates.

spread (T-bills versus Eurodollar), is a measure of the credit risk premium of London banks, which have historically borrowed short term at Libor, versus that of the U.S. government, which borrows short term at the T-bill rate. This transaction is called a basis swap. There are also swaps in which the floating rate is set as an average rate over the period, in accordance with the convention for many loans. Some swaps, called overnight indexed swaps, are tied to a Fed funds–type rate, reflecting the rate at which banks borrow overnight. As we will cover later, there are many other different types of swaps that are used for a variety of purposes. The plain vanilla swap is merely the simplest and most widely used.

Because swaps, forwards, and futures are forward commitments, they can all accomplish the same thing. One could create a series of forwards or futures expiring at a set of dates that would serve the same purpose as a swap. Although swaps are better suited for risks that involve multiple payments, at its most fundamental level, a swap is more or less just a series of forwards and, acknowledging the slight differences discussed above, more or less just a series of futures.

EXAMPLE 3   Forward Contracts, Futures Contracts, and Swaps

1. Which of the following characterizes forward contracts and swaps but not futures?
   A. They are customized.
   B. They are subject to daily price limits.
   C. Their payoffs are received on a daily basis.
2. Which of the following distinguishes forwards from swaps?
   A. Forwards are OTC instruments, whereas swaps are exchange traded.
   B. Forwards are regulated as futures, whereas swaps are regulated as securities.
   C. Swaps have multiple payments, whereas forwards have only a single payment.
3. Which of the following occurs in the daily settlement of futures contracts?
   A. Initial margin deposits are refunded to the two parties.
   B. Gains and losses are reported to other market participants.
   C. Losses are charged to one party and gains credited to the other.

Solution to 1: A is correct. Forwards and swaps are OTC contracts and, therefore, are customized. Futures are exchange traded and, therefore, are standardized. Some futures contracts are subject to daily price limits and their payoffs are received daily, but these characteristics are not true for forwards and swaps.

Solution to 2: C is correct. Forwards and swaps are OTC instruments and both are regulated as such. Neither is regulated as a futures contract or a security. A swap is a series of multiple payments at scheduled dates, whereas a forward has only one payment, made at its expiration date.

Solution to 3: C is correct. Losses and gains are collected and distributed to the respective parties. There is no specific reporting of these gains and losses to anyone else. Initial margin deposits are not refunded and, in fact, additional deposits may be required.

This material completes our introduction to forward commitments. All forward commitments are firm contracts. The parties are required to fulfill the obligations they agreed to. The benefit of this rigidity is that neither party pays anything to the other when the contract is initiated. If one party needs some flexibility, however, it can get it by agreeing to pay the other party some money when the contract is initiated. When the contract expires, the party who paid at the start has some flexibility in deciding whether to buy the underlying asset at the fixed price. Thus, that party did not actually agree to do anything. It had a choice. This is the nature of contingent claims.

6. CONTINGENT CLAIMS: OPTIONS

A **contingent claim** is a derivative in which the outcome or payoff is dependent on the outcome or payoff of an underlying asset. Although this characteristic is also associated with forward commitments, a contingent claim has come to be associated with a *right*, but not an *obligation*, to make a final payment contingent on the performance of the underlying. Given that the holder of the contingent claim has a choice, the term *contingent claim* has become synonymous with the term *option*. The holder has a choice of whether or not to exercise the option. This choice creates a payoff that transforms the underlying payoff in a more pronounced manner than does a forward, futures, or swap. Those instruments provide linear payoffs: As the underlying goes up (down), the derivative gains (loses). The further up (down) the underlying goes, the more the derivative gains (loses). Options are different in that they limit losses in one direction. In addition, options can pay off as the underlying goes down. Hence, they transform the payoffs of the underlying into something quite different.

6.1. Options

We might say that an option, as a contingent claim, grants the right but not the obligation to buy an asset at a later date and at a price agreed on when the option is initiated. But there are so many variations of options that we cannot settle on this statement as a good formal definition. For one thing, options can also grant the right to sell instead of the right to buy. Moreover, they can grant the right to buy or sell earlier than at expiration. So, let us see whether we can combine these points into an all-encompassing definition of an option.

> *An option is a derivative contract in which one party, the buyer, pays a sum of money to the other party, the seller or writer, and receives the right to either buy or sell an underlying asset at a fixed price either on a specific expiration date or at any time prior to the expiration date.*

Unfortunately, even that definition does not cover every unique aspect of options. For example, options can be created in the OTC market and customized to the terms of each party, or they can be created and traded on options exchanges and standardized. As with forward contracts and swaps, customized options are subject to default, are less regulated, and are less transparent than exchange-traded derivatives. Exchange-traded options are protected against default by the clearinghouse of the options exchange and are relatively transparent and regulated at the national level. As noted in the definition above, options can be terminated early or at their expirations. When an option is terminated, either early or at expiration, the holder of the option chooses whether to exercise it. If he exercises it, he either buys or sells the underlying asset, but he does not have both rights. The right to buy is one type of option, referred to as a **call** or **call option**, whereas the right to sell is another type of option, referred to as a **put** or **put option**. With one very unusual and advanced exception that we do not cover, an option is either a call or a put, and that point is made clear in the contract.

An option is also designated as exercisable early (before expiration) or only at expiration. Options that can be exercised early are referred to as **American-style**. Options that can be exercised only at expiration are referred to as **European-style**. *It is extremely important that you do not associate these terms with where these options are traded.* Both types of options trade on all continents.

As with forwards and futures, an option can be exercised by physical delivery or cash settlement, as written in the contract. For a call option with physical delivery, upon exercise the underlying asset is delivered to the call buyer, who pays the call seller the exercise price. For a put option with physical delivery, upon exercise the put buyer delivers the underlying asset to the put seller and receives the strike price. For a cash settlement option, exercise results in the seller paying the buyer the cash equivalent value as if the asset were delivered and paid for.

The fixed price at which the underlying asset can be purchased is called the **exercise price** (also called the "strike price," the "strike," or the "striking price"). This price is somewhat analogous to the forward price because it represents the price at which the underlying will be purchased or sold if the option is exercised. The forward price, however, is set in the pricing of the contract such that the contract value at the start is zero. The strike price of the option is chosen by the participants. The actual price or value of the option is an altogether different concept.

As noted, the buyer pays the writer a sum of money called the **option premium**, or just the "premium." It represents a fair price of the option, and in a well-functioning market, it would be the value of the option. Consistent with everything we know about finance, it is the present value of the cash flows that are expected to be received by the holder of the option during the life of the option. At this point, we will not get into how this price is determined, but you will learn that later. For now, there are some fundamental concepts you need to understand, which form a basis for understanding how options are priced and why anyone would use an option.

Because the option buyer (the long) does not have to exercise the option, beyond the initial payment of the premium, there is no obligation of the long to the short. Thus, only the short can default, which would occur if the long exercises the option and the short fails to do what it is supposed to do. Thus, in contrast to forwards and swaps, in which either party could default to the other, default in options is possible only from the short to the long.

Ruling out the possibility of default for now, let us examine what happens when an option expires. Using the same notation used previously, let S_T be the price of the underlying at the expiration date, T, and X be the exercise price of the option. Remember that a call option allows the holder, or long, to pay X and receive the underlying. It should be obvious that the long would exercise the option at expiration if S_T is greater than X, meaning that the underlying value is greater than what he would pay to obtain the underlying. Otherwise, he would simply let the option expire. Thus, on the expiration date, the option is described as having a payoff of $Max(0, S_T - X)$.

Because the holder of the option would be entitled to exercise it and claim this amount, it also represents the value of the option at expiration. Let us denote that value as c_T. Thus,

$$c_T = Max(0, S_T - X) \qquad \text{(payoff to the call buyer)},$$

which is read as "take the maximum of either zero or $S_T - X$." For example, suppose you buy a call option with an exercise price of 50 and an expiration of three months for a premium of 1.50 when the stock is trading at 45. At expiration, consider the outcomes when the stock's price is 45, 50, or 55. The buyer's payoffs would be:

For $S_T = 45$, payoff = $c_T = Max(0, S_T - X) = Max(0, 45 - 50) = Max(0, -5) = 0$.

For $S_T = 50$, payoff = $c_T = Max(0, S_T - X) = Max(0, 50 - 50) = Max(0, 0) = 0$.

For $S_T = 55$, payoff = $c_T = Max(0, S_T - X) = Max(0, 55 - 50) = Max(0, 5) = 5$.

Thus, if the underlying value exceeds the exercise price ($S_T > X$), then the option value is positive and equal to $S_T - X$. The call option is then said to be **in the money**. If the underlying value is less than the exercise price ($S_T < X$), then $S_T - X$ is negative; zero is greater than a negative number, so the option value would be zero. When the underlying value is less than the exercise price, the call option is said to be **out of the money**. When $S_T = X$, the call option is said to be **at the money**, although at the money is, for all practical purposes, out of the money because the value is still zero.

This payoff amount is also the value of the option at expiration. It represents value because it is what the option is worth at that point. If the holder of the option sells it to someone else an instant before expiration, it should sell for that amount because the new owner would exercise it and capture that amount. To the seller, the value of the option at that point is $-Max(0, S_T - X)$, which is negative to the seller if the option is in the money and zero otherwise.

Using the payoff value and the price paid for the option, we can determine the profit from the strategy, which is denoted with the Greek symbol Π. Let us say the buyer paid c_0 for the option at time 0. Then the profit is

$$\Pi = Max(0, S_T - X) - c_0 \quad \text{(profit to the call buyer)},$$

Continuing with the example with underlying prices at expiration of 45, 50, or 55, the call buyer's profit would be:

For $S_T = 45$, profit = $Max(0, S_T - X) - c_0 = Max(0, 45 - 50) - 1.50 = -1.50$.

For $S_T = 50$, profit = $Max(0, S_T - X) - c_0 = Max(0, 50 - 50) - 1.50 = -1.50$.

For $S_T = 55$, profit = $Max(0, S_T - X) - c_0 = Max(0, 55 - 50) - 1.50 = 3.50$.

To the seller, who received the premium at the start, the payoff is

$$-c_T = -Max(0, S_T - X) \quad \text{(payoff to the call seller)},$$

At expiration, the call seller's payoffs are:

For $S_T = 45$, payoff = $-c_T = -Max(0, S_T - X) = -Max(0, 45 - 50) = 0$.

For $S_T = 50$, payoff = $-c_T = -Max(0, S_T - X) = -Max(0, 50 - 50) = 0$.

For $S_T = 55$, payoff = $-c_T = -Max(0, S_T - X) = -Max(0, 55 - 50) = -5$.

The call seller's profit is

$$\Pi = -Max(0, S_T - X) + c_0 \quad \text{(profit to the call seller)},$$

Finally, at expiration, the call seller's profit for each underlying price at expiration are:

For $S_T = 45$, profit $= -Max(0, S_T - X) + c_0 = -Max(0,45 - 50) + 1.50 = 1.50$.

For $S_T = 50$, profit $= -Max(0, S_T - X) + c_0 = -Max(0,50 - 50) + 1.50 = 1.50$.

For $S_T = 55$, profit $= -Max(0, S_T - X) + c_0 = -Max(0,55 - 50) + 1.50 = -3.50$.

For any given price at expiration, the call seller's payoff or profit is equal to the negative of the call buyer's payoff or profit.

EXAMPLE 4   Call Option Payoffs and Profit at Expiration

Consider a call option selling for $7 in which the exercise price is $100 and the price of the underlying is $98.
1. Determine the value at expiration and the profit for a call buyer under the following outcomes:
   A. The price of the underlying at expiration is $102.
   B. The price of the underlying at expiration is $94.
2. Determine the value at expiration and the profit for a call seller under the following outcomes:
   A. The price of the underlying at expiration is $91.
   B. The price of the underlying at expiration is $101.

Solution to 1:
A. If the price of the underlying at expiration is $102,
    The call buyer's value at expiration $= c_T = Max(0, S_T - X)$
    $= Max(0,102 - 100) = \$2$.
    The call buyer's profit $= \prod = c_T - c_0 = 2 - 7 = -\$5$.
B. If the price of the underlying at expiration is $94,
    The call buyer's value at expiration $= c_T = Max(0, S_T - X)$
    $= Max(0,94 - 100) = \$0$.
    The call buyer's profit $= \prod = c_T - c_0 = 0 - 7 = -\$7$.

Solution to 2:
A. If the price of the underlying at expiration is $91,
    The call seller's value at expiration $= -c_T = -Max(0, S_T - X)$
    $= -Max(0,91 - 100) = \$0$.
    The call seller's profit $= \prod = -c_T + c_0 = 0 + 7 = \$7$
B. If the price of the underlying at expiration is $101,
    The call seller's value at expiration $= -c_T = -Max(0, S_T - X)$
    $= -Max(0,101 - 100) = -\$1$.
    The call seller's profit $= \prod = -c_T + c_0 = -1 + 7 = \$6$.

Exhibit 3 illustrates the payoffs and profits to the call buyer and seller as graphical representations of these equations, with the payoff or value at expiration indicated by the dark line and the profit indicated by the light line. Note in Panel A that the buyer has no upper limit on the profit and has a fixed downside loss limit equal to the premium paid for the option. Such a condition, with limited loss and unlimited gain, is a temptation to many unsuspecting investors, but keep in mind that the graph does not indicate the frequency with which gains and losses will occur. Panel B is the mirror image of Panel A and shows that the seller has unlimited losses and limited gains. One might suspect that selling a call is, therefore, the worst investment strategy possible. Indeed, it is a risky strategy, but at this point these are only simple strategies. Other strategies can be added to mitigate the seller's risk to a substantial degree.

EXHIBIT 3   Payoff and Profit from a Call Option

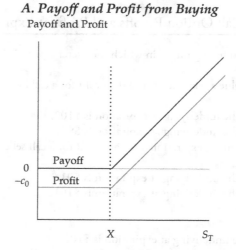

A. Payoff and Profit from Buying

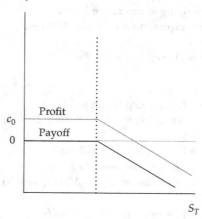

B. Payoff and Profit from Selling

Now let us consider put options. Recall that a put option allows its holder to sell the underlying asset at the exercise price. Thus, the holder should exercise the put at expiration if the underlying asset is worth less than the exercise price ($S_T < X$). In that case, the put is said to be in the money. If the underlying asset is worth the same as the exercise price ($S_T = X$), meaning the put is at the money, or more than the exercise price ($S_T > X$), meaning the put is out of the money, the option holder would not exercise it and it would expire with zero value. Thus, the payoff to the put holder is

$$p_T = Max(0, X - S_T) \qquad \text{(payoff to the put buyer)},$$

If the put buyer paid p_0 for the put at time 0, the profit is

$$\Pi = Max(0, X - S_T) - p_0 \qquad \text{(profit to the put buyer)},$$

And for the seller, the payoff is

$$-p_T = -Max(0, X - S_T) \qquad \text{(payoff to the put seller)},$$

And the profit is

$$\Pi = -Max(0, X - S_T) + p_0 \qquad \text{(profit to the put seller)},$$

To illustrate the payoffs and profit to a put buyer and put seller, assume the put price (p_0) is 1.50, the exercise price (X) is 20.00, and the stock price at expiration (S_T) is either 18.00 or 22.00. The put buyer's payoff is:

For $S_T = 18$, payoff $= p_T = Max(0, X - S_T) = Max(0, 20 - 18) = 2$.
For $S_T = 22$, payoff $= p_T = Max(0, X - S_T) = Max(0, 20 - 22) = 0$.

The put buyer's profit is:

For $S_T = 18$, profit $= Max(0, X - S_T) - p_0 = Max(0, 20 - 18) - 1.50 = 0.50$.
For $S_T = 22$, profit $= Max(0, X - S_T) - p_0 = Max(0, 20 - 22) - 1.50 = -1.50$.

The put seller's payoff is:

For $S_T = 18$, payoff $= -p_T = -Max(0, X - S_T) = -Max(0, 20 - 18) = -2$.
For $S_T = 22$, payoff $= -p_T = -Max(0, X - S_T) = -Max(0, 20 - 22) = 0$.

Finally, the put seller's profit is:

For $S_T = 18$, profit $= -Max(0, X - S_T) + p_0 = -Max(0, 20 - 18) + 1.50 = -0.50$.
For $S_T = 22$, profit $= -Max(0, X - S_T) + p_0 = -Max(0, 20 - 22) + 1.50 = 1.50$.

For a given stock price at expiration, the put seller's payoff or profit are the negative of the put buyer's payoff or profit.

EXAMPLE 5   Put Option Payoffs and Profit at Expiration

Consider a put option selling for $4 in which the exercise price is $60 and the price of the underlying is $62.
1. Determine the value at expiration and the profit for a put buyer under the following outcomes:
   A. The price of the underlying at expiration is $62.
   B. The price of the underlying at expiration is $55.

2. Determine the value at expiration and the profit for a put seller under the following outcomes:
    A. The price of the underlying at expiration is $51.
    B. The price of the underlying at expiration is $68.

Solution to 1:
A. If the price of the underlying at expiration is $62,
    The put buyer's value at expiration $= p_T = Max(0, X - S_T)$
    $= Max(0, 60 - 62) = \$0$.
    The put buyer's profit $= \Pi = p_T - p_0 = 0 - 4 = -\$4$.
B. If the price of the underlying at expiration is $55,
    The put buyer's value at expiration $= p_T = Max(0, X - S_T)$
    $= Max(0, 60 - 55) = \$5$.
    The put buyer's profit $= \Pi = p_T - p_0 = 5 - 4 = \$1$.

Solution to 2:
A. If the price of the underlying at expiration is $51,
    The put seller's value at expiration $= -p_T = -Max(0, X - S_T)$
    $= -Max(0, 60 - 51) = -\$9$.
    The put seller's profit $= \Pi = -p_T + p_0 = -9 + 4 = -\$5$.
B. If the price of the underlying at expiration is $68,
    The put seller's value at expiration $= -p_T = -Max(0, X - S_T)$
    $= -Max(0, 60 - 68) = \$0$.
    The put seller's profit $= \Pi = -p_T + p_0 = 0 + 4 = \$4$.

Exhibit 4 illustrates the payoffs and profits to the buyer and seller of a put.

EXHIBIT 4   Payoff and Profit from a Put Option

A. Payoff and Profit from Buying

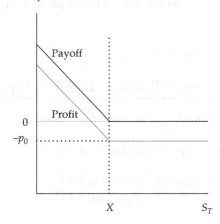

B. Payoff and Profit from Selling
Payoff and Profit

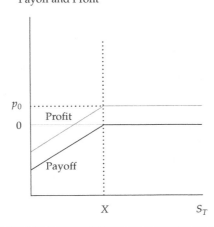

The put buyer has a limited loss, and although the gain is limited by the fact that the underlying value cannot go below zero, the put buyer does gain more the lower the value of the underlying. In this manner, we see how a put option is like insurance. Bad outcomes for the underlying trigger a payoff for both the insurance policy and the put, whereas good outcomes result only in loss of the premium. The put seller, like the insurer, has a limited gain and a loss that is larger the lower the value of the underlying. As with call options, these graphs must be considered carefully because they do not indicate the frequency with which gains and losses will occur. At this point, it should be apparent that buying a call option is consistent with a bullish point of view and buying a put option is consistent with a bearish point of view. Moreover, in contrast to forward commitments, which have payoffs that are linearly related to the payoffs of the underlying (note the straight lines in Exhibit 1), contingent claims have payoffs that are non-linear in relation to the underlying. There is linearity over a range—say, from 0 to X or from X upward or downward—but over the entire range of values for the underlying, the payoffs of contingent claims cannot be depicted with a single straight line.

We have seen only a snapshot of the payoff and profit graphs that can be created with options. Calls can be combined with puts, the underlying asset, and other calls or puts with different expirations and exercise prices to create a diverse set of payoff and profit graphs, some of which are covered later in the curriculum.

Before leaving options, let us again contrast the differences between options and forward commitments. With forward commitments, the parties agree to trade an underlying asset at a later date and at a price agreed upon when the contract is initiated. Neither party pays any cash to the other at the start. With options, the buyer pays cash to the seller at the start and receives the right, but not the obligation, to buy (if a call) or sell (if a put) the underlying asset at expiration at a price agreed upon (the exercise price) when the contract is initiated. In contrast to forwards, futures, and swaps, options do have value at the start: the premium paid by buyer to seller. That premium pays for the *right*, eliminating the *obligation*, to trade the underlying at a later date, as would be the case with a forward commitment.

Although there are numerous variations of options, most have the same essential features described here. There is, however, a distinctive family of contingent claims that emerged in the early 1990s and became widely used and, in some cases, heavily criticized. These instruments are known as credit derivatives.

7. CONTINGENT CLAIMS: CREDIT DERIVATIVES

Credit risk is surely one of the oldest risks known to mankind. Human beings have been lending things to each other for thousands of years, and even the most primitive human beings must have recognized the risk of lending some of their possessions to their comrades. Until the last 20 years or so, however, the management of credit risk was restricted to simply doing the best analysis possible before making a loan, monitoring the financial condition of the borrower during the loan, limiting the exposure to a given party, and requiring collateral. Some modest forms of insurance against credit risk have existed for a number of years, but insurance can be a slow and cumbersome way of protecting against credit loss. Insurance is typically highly regulated, and insurance laws are usually very consumer oriented. Thus, credit insurance as a financial product has met with only modest success.

In the early 1990s, however, the development of the swaps market led to the creation of derivatives that would hedge credit risk. These instruments came to be known as **credit derivatives**, and they avoided many of the regulatory constraints of the traditional insurance industry. Here is a formal definition:

> *A credit derivative is a class of derivative contracts between two parties, a credit protection buyer and a credit protection seller, in which the latter provides protection to the former against a specific credit loss.*

One of the first credit derivatives was a **total return swap**, in which the underlying is typically a bond or loan, in contrast to, say, a stock or stock index. The credit protection buyer offers to pay the credit protection seller the total return on the underlying bond. This total return consists of all interest and principal paid by the borrower plus any changes in the bond's market value. In return, the credit protection seller typically pays the credit protection buyer either a fixed or a floating rate of interest. Thus, if the bond defaults, the credit protection seller must continue to make its promised payments, while receiving a very small return or virtually no return from the credit protection buyer. If the bond incurs a loss, as it surely will if it defaults, the credit protection seller effectively pays the credit protection buyer.

Another type of credit derivative is the **credit spread option**, in which the underlying is the credit (yield) spread on a bond, which is the difference between the bond's yield and the yield on a benchmark default-free bond. As you will learn in the fixed-income material, the credit spread is a reflection of investors' perception of credit risk. Because a credit spread option requires a credit spread as the underlying, this type of derivative works only with a traded bond that has a quoted price. The credit protection buyer selects the strike spread it desires and pays the option premium to the credit protection seller. At expiration, the parties determine whether the option is in the money by comparing the bond's yield spread with the strike chosen, and if it is, the credit protection seller pays the credit protection buyer the established payoff. Thus, this instrument is essentially a call option in which the underlying is the credit spread.

A third type of credit derivative is the **credit-linked note (CLN)**. With this derivative, the credit protection buyer holds a bond or loan that is subject to default risk (the underlying reference security) and issues its own security (the credit-linked note) with the condition that if the bond or loan it holds defaults, the principal payoff on the credit-linked note is reduced accordingly. Thus, the buyer of the credit-linked note effectively insures the credit risk of the underlying reference security.

These three types of credit derivatives have had limited success compared with the fourth type of credit derivative, the **credit default swap (CDS)**. The credit default swap, in particular, has achieved much success by capturing many of the essential features of insurance while avoiding the high degree of consumer regulations that are typically associated with traditional insurance products.

In a CDS, one party—the credit protection buyer, who is seeking credit protection against a third party—makes a series of regularly scheduled payments to the other party, the credit protection seller. The seller makes no payments until a credit event occurs. A declaration of bankruptcy is clearly a credit event, but there are other types of credit events, such as a failure to make a scheduled payment or an involuntary restructuring. The CDS contract specifies what constitutes a credit event, and the industry has a procedure for declaring credit events, though that does not guarantee the parties will not end up in court arguing over whether something was or was not a credit event.

Formally, a credit default swap is defined as follows:

A credit default swap is a derivative contract between two parties, a credit protection buyer and a credit protection seller, in which the buyer makes a series of cash payments to the seller and receives a promise of compensation for credit losses resulting from the default of a third party.

A CDS is conceptually a form of insurance. Sellers of CDSs, oftentimes banks or insurance companies, collect periodic payments and are required to pay out if a loss occurs from the default of a third party. These payouts could take the form of restitution of the defaulted amount or the party holding the defaulting asset could turn it over to the CDS seller and receive a fixed amount. The most common approach is for the payout to be determined by an auction to estimate the market value of the defaulting debt. Thus, CDSs effectively provide coverage against a loss in return for the protection buyer paying a premium to the protection seller, thereby taking the form of insurance against credit loss. Although insurance contracts have certain legal characteristics that are not found in credit default swaps, the two instruments serve similar purposes and operate in virtually the same way: payments made by one party in return for a promise to cover losses incurred by the other.

Exhibit 5 illustrates the typical use of a CDS by a lender. The lender is exposed to the risk of non-payment of principal and interest. The lender lays off this risk by purchasing a CDS from a CDS seller. The lender—now the CDS buyer—promises to make a series of periodic payments to the CDS seller, who then stands ready to compensate the CDS buyer for credit losses.

EXHIBIT 5   Using a Credit Default Swap to Hedge the Credit Risk of a Loan

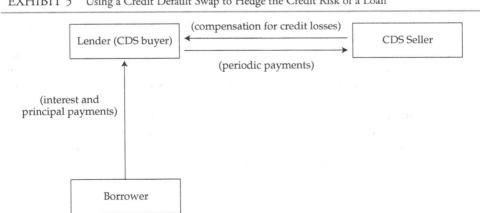

Clearly, the CDS seller is betting on the borrower's not defaulting or—more generally, as insurance companies operate—that the total payouts it is responsible for are less than the total payments collected. Of course, most insurance companies are able to do this by having reliable actuarial statistics, diversifying their risk, and selling some of the risk to other insurance companies. Actuarial statistics are typically quite solid. Average claims for life, health, and casualty insurance are well documented, and insurers can normally set premiums to cover losses and operate at a reasonable profit. Although insurance companies try to manage some of their risks at the micro level (e.g., charging smokers more for life and health insurance), most of their risk management is at the macro level, wherein they attempt to make sure their risks are not concentrated. Thus, they avoid selling too much homeowners insurance to individuals in tornado-prone areas. If they have such an exposure, they can use the reinsurance market to sell some of the risk to other companies that are not overexposed to that risk. Insurance companies attempt to diversify their risks and rely on the principle of uncorrelated risks, which plays such an important role in portfolio management. A well-diversified insurance company, like a well-diversified portfolio, should be able to earn a return commensurate with its assumed risk in the long run.

Credit default swaps should operate the same way. Sellers of CDSs should recognize when their credit risk is too concentrated. When that happens, they become buyers of CDSs from other parties or find other ways to lay off the risk. Unfortunately, during the financial crisis that began in 2007, many sellers of CDSs failed to recognize the high correlations among borrowers whose debt they had guaranteed. One well-known CDS seller, AIG, is a large and highly successful traditional insurance company that got into the business of selling CDSs. Many of these CDSs insured against mortgages. With the growth of the subprime mortgage market, many of these CDS-insured mortgages had a substantial amount of credit risk and were often poorly documented. AIG and many other CDS sellers were thus highly exposed to systemic credit contagion, a situation in which defaults in one area of an economy ripple into another, accompanied by bank weaknesses and failures, rapidly falling equity markets, rising credit risk premiums, and a general loss of confidence in the financial system and the economy. These presumably well-diversified risks guaranteed by CDS sellers, operating as though they were insurance companies, ultimately proved to be poorly diversified. Systemic financial risks can spread more rapidly than fire, health, and casualty risks. Virtually no other risks, except those originating from wars or epidemics, spread in the manner of systemic financial risks.

Thus, to understand and appreciate the importance of the CDS market, it is necessary to recognize how that market can fail. The ability to separate and trade risks is a valuable one. Banks can continue to make loans to their customers, thereby satisfying the customers' needs, while laying off the risk elsewhere. In short, parties not wanting to bear certain risks can sell them to parties wanting to assume certain risks. If all parties do their jobs correctly, the markets and the economy work more efficiently. If, as in the case of certain CDS sellers, not everyone does a good job of managing risk, there can be serious repercussions. In the case of AIG and some other companies, taxpayer bailouts were the ultimate price paid to keep these large institutions afloat so that they could continue to provide their other critical services to consumers. The rules proposed in the new OTC derivatives market regulations—which call for greater regulation and transparency of OTC derivatives and, in particular, CDSs—have important implications for the future of this market and these instruments.

EXAMPLE 6   Options and Credit Derivatives

1. An option provides which of the following?
   A. Either the right to buy or the right to sell an underlying
   B. The right to buy and sell, with the choice made at expiration
   C. The obligation to buy or sell, which can be converted into the right to buy or sell
2. Which of the following is **not** a characteristic of a call option on a stock?
   A. A guarantee that the stock will increase
   B. A specified date on which the right to buy expires
   C. A fixed price at which the call holder can buy the stock
3. A credit derivative is which of the following?
   A. A derivative in which the premium is obtained on credit
   B. A derivative in which the payoff is borrowed by the seller
   C. A derivative in which the seller provides protection to the buyer against credit loss from a third party

Solution to 1: A is correct. An option is strictly the right to buy (a call) or the right to sell (a put). It does not provide both choices or the right to convert an obligation into a right.

Solution to 2: A is correct. A call option on a stock provides no guarantee of any change in the stock price. It has an expiration date, and it provides for a fixed price at which the holder can exercise the option, thereby purchasing the stock.

Solution to 3: C is correct. Credit derivatives provide a guarantee against loss caused by a third party's default. They do not involve borrowing the premium or the payoff.

8. TYPES OF DERIVATIVES: ASSET-BACKED SECURITIES AND HYBRIDS

Although these instruments are covered in more detail in the fixed-income material, we would be remiss if we failed to include them with derivatives. But we will give them only light coverage here.

As discussed earlier, derivatives take (derive) their value from the value of the underlying, as do mutual funds and exchange-traded funds (ETFs). A mutual fund or an ETF holding bonds is virtually identical to the investor holding the bonds directly. Asset-backed securities (ABSs) take this concept a step further by altering the payment streams. ABSs typically divide the payments into slices, called tranches, in which the priority of claims has been changed from equivalent to preferential. For example, in a bond mutual fund or an ETF, all investors in the fund have equal claims, and so the rate of return earned by each investor is exactly the same. If a portfolio of the same bonds were assembled into an ABS, some investors in the ABS would have claims that would supersede those of other investors. The differential nature of these claims becomes relevant when either prepayments or defaults occur.

Prepayments mostly affect only mortgages. When a portfolio of mortgages is assembled into an ABS, the resulting instrument is called a **collateralized mortgage obligation** (CMO). Commonly but not always, the credit risk has been reduced or eliminated, perhaps by a CDS, as discussed earlier. When homeowners pay off their mortgages early due to refinancing at lower rates, the holders of the mortgages suffer losses. They expected to receive a stream of returns that is now terminated. The funds that were previously earning a particular rate will now have to be invested to earn a lower rate. These losses are the mirror images of the gains homeowners make when they proudly proclaim that they refinanced their mortgages and substantially lowered their payments.

CMOs partition the claims against these mortgages into different tranches, which are typically called A, B, and C. Class C tranches bear the first wave of prepayments until that tranche has been completely repaid its full principal investment. At that point, the Class B tranche holders bear the next prepayments until they have been fully repaid. The Class A tranche holders then bear the next wave of prepayments.[11] Thus, the risk faced by the various tranche holders is different from that of a mutual fund or ETF, which would pass the returns directly through such that investors would all receive the same rates of return. Therefore, the expected returns of CMO tranches vary and are commensurate with the prepayment risk they assume. Some CMOs are also characterized by credit risk, perhaps a substantial amount, from subprime mortgages.

When bonds or loans are assembled into ABSs, they are typically called **collateralized bond obligations** (CBOs) or **collateralized loan obligations** (CLOs). These instruments (known collectively as **collateralized debt obligations**, or CDOs) do not traditionally have much prepayment risk but they do have credit risk and oftentimes a great deal of it. The CDO structure allocates this risk to tranches that are called senior, mezzanine, or junior tranches (the last sometimes called equity tranches). When defaults occur, the junior tranches bear the risk first, followed by the mezzanine tranches, and then the senior tranches. The expected returns of the tranches vary according to the perceived credit risk, with the senior tranches having the highest credit quality and the junior the lowest. Thus, the senior tranches have the lowest expected returns and the junior tranches have the highest.

An asset-backed security is formally defined as follows:

> *An asset-backed security is a derivative contract in which a portfolio of debt instruments is assembled and claims are issued on the portfolio in the form of tranches, which have different priorities of claims on the payments made by the debt securities such that prepayments or credit losses are allocated to the most-junior tranches first and the most-senior tranches last.*

ABSs seem to have only an indirect and subtle resemblance to options, but they are indeed options. They promise to make a series of returns that are typically steady. These returns can be lowered if prepayments or defaults occur. Thus, they are contingent on prepayments and defaults. Take a look again at Exhibit 4, Panel B (the profit and payoff of a short put option).

---

[11]The reference to only three tranches is just a general statement. There are many more types of tranches. Our discussion of the three classes is for illustrative purposes only and serves to emphasize that there are high-priority claims, low-priority claims, and other claims somewhere in the middle.

If all goes well, there is a fixed return. If something goes badly, the return can be lowered, and the worse the outcome, the lower the return. Thus, holders of ABSs have effectively written put options.

This completes the discussion of contingent claims. Having now covered forward commitments and contingent claims, the final category of derivative instruments is more or less just a catch-all category in case something was missed.

8.1. Hybrids

The instruments just covered encompass all the fundamental instruments that exist in the derivatives world. Yet, the derivatives world is truly much larger than implied by what has been covered here. We have not covered and will touch only lightly on the many hybrid instruments that combine derivatives, fixed-income securities, currencies, equities, and commodities. For example, options can be combined with bonds to form either callable bonds or convertible bonds. Swaps can be combined with options to form swap payments that have upper and lower limits. Options can be combined with futures to obtain options on futures. Options can be created with swaps as the underlying to form swaptions. Some of these instruments will be covered later. For now, you should just recognize that the possibilities are almost endless.

We will not address these hybrids directly, but some are covered elsewhere in the curriculum. The purpose of discussing them here is for you to realize that derivatives create possibilities not otherwise available in their absence. This point will lead to a better understanding of why derivatives exist, a topic we will get to very shortly.

EXAMPLE 7   Forward Commitments versus Contingent Claims

1. Which of the following is **not** a forward commitment?
   A. An agreement to take out a loan at a future date at a specific rate
   B. An offer of employment that must be accepted or rejected in two weeks
   C. An agreement to lease a piece of machinery for one year with a series of fixed monthly payments
2. Which of the following statements is true about contingent claims?
   A. Either party can default to the other.
   B. The payoffs are linearly related to the performance of the underlying.
   C. The most the long can lose is the amount paid for the contingent claim.

Solution to 1: B is correct. Both A and C are commitments to engage in transactions at future dates. In fact, C is like a swap because the party agrees to make a series of future payments and in return receives temporary use of an asset whose value could vary. B is a contingent claim. The party receiving the employment offer can accept it or reject it if there is a better alternative.

Solution to 2: C is correct. The maximum loss to the long is the premium. The payoffs of contingent claims are not linearly related to the underlying, and only one party, the short, can default.

9. DERIVATIVES UNDERLYINGS

Before discussing the purposes and benefits of derivatives, we need to clarify some points that have been implied so far. We have alluded to certain underlying assets, this section will briefly discuss the underlyings more directly.

9.1. Equities

Equities are one of the most popular categories of underlyings on which derivatives are created. There are two types of equities on which derivatives exist: individual stocks and stock indexes. Derivatives on individual stocks are primarily options. Forwards, futures, and swaps on individual stocks are not widely used. Index derivatives in the form of options, forwards, futures, and swaps are very popular. Index swaps, more often called equity swaps, are quite popular and permit investors to pay the return on one stock index and receive the return on another index or a fixed rate. They can be very useful in asset allocation strategies by allowing an equity manager to increase or reduce exposure to an equity market or sector without trading the individual securities.

In addition, options on stocks are frequently used by companies as compensation and incentives for their executives and employees. These options are granted to provide incentives to work toward driving the stock price up and can result in companies paying lower cash compensation. Some companies also issue warrants, which are options sold to the public that allow the holders to exercise them and buy shares directly from the companies.

9.2. Fixed-Income Instruments and Interest Rates

Options, forwards, futures, and swaps on bonds are widely used. The problem with creating derivatives on bonds, however, is that there are almost always many issues of bonds. A single issuer, whether it is a government or a private borrower, often has more than one bond issue outstanding. For futures contracts, with their standardization requirements, this problem is particularly challenging. What does it mean to say that a futures contract is on a German bund, a US Treasury note, or a UK gilt? The most common solution to this problem is to allow multiple issues to be delivered on a single futures contract. This feature adds some interesting twists to the pricing and trading strategies of these instruments.

Until now, we have referred to the underlying as an *asset*. Yet, one of the largest derivative underlyings is not an asset. It is simply an interest rate. An interest rate is not an asset. One cannot hold an interest rate or place it on a balance sheet as an asset. Although one can hold an instrument that pays an interest rate, the rate itself is not an asset. But there are derivatives in which the rate, not the instrument that pays the rate, is the underlying. In fact, we have already covered one of these derivatives: The plain vanilla interest rate swap in which Libor is the underlying.[12] Instead of a swap, an interest rate derivative could be an option. For example, a call option on 90-day Libor with a strike of 5% would pay off if at expiration Libor exceeds 5%. If Libor is below 5%, the option simply expires unexercised.

Interest rate derivatives are the most widely used derivatives. With that in mind, we will be careful in using the expression *underlying asset* and will use the more generic *underlying*.

---

[12]As you will see later, there are also futures in which the underlying is an interest rate (Eurodollar futures) and forwards in which the underlying is an interest rate (forward rate agreements, or FRAs).

9.3. Currencies

Currency risk is a major factor in global financial markets, and the currency derivatives market is extremely large. Options, forwards, futures, and swaps are widely used. Currency derivatives can be complex, sometimes combining elements of other underlyings. For example, a currency swap involves two parties making a series of interest rate payments to each other in different currencies. Because interest rates and currencies are both subject to change, a currency swap has two sources of risk. Although this instrument may sound extremely complicated, it merely reflects the fact that companies operating across borders are subject to both interest rate risk and currency risk and currency swaps are commonly used to manage those risks.

9.4. Commodities

Commodities are resources, such as food, oil, and metals, that humans use to sustain life and support economic activity. Because of the economic principle of comparative advantage, countries often specialize in the production of certain resources. Thus, the commodities market is extremely large and subject to an almost unimaginable array of risks. One need only observe how the price of oil moves up as tension builds in the Middle East or how the price of orange juice rises on a forecast of cold weather in Florida.

Commodity derivatives are widely used to speculate in and manage the risk associated with commodity price movements. The primary commodity derivatives are futures, but forwards, swaps, and options are also used. The reason that futures are in the lead in the world of commodities is simply history. The first futures markets were futures on commodities. The first futures exchange, the Chicago Board of Trade, was created in 1848, and until the creation of currency futures in 1972, there were no futures on any underlying except commodities.

There has been a tendency to think of the commodities world as somewhat separate from the financial world. Commodity traders and financial traders were quite different groups. Since the creation of financial futures, however, commodity and financial traders have become relatively homogeneous. Moreover, commodities are increasingly viewed as an important asset class that should be included in investment strategies because of their ability to help diversify portfolios.

9.5. Credit

As we previously discussed, credit is another underlying and quite obviously not an asset. Credit default swaps (CDSs) and collateralized debt obligations (CDOs) were discussed extensively in an earlier section. These instruments have clearly established that credit is a distinct underlying that has widespread interest from a trading and risk management perspective. In addition, to the credit of a single entity, credit derivatives are created on multiple entities. CDOs themselves are credit derivatives on portfolios of credit risks. In recent years, indexes of CDOs have been created, and instruments based on the payoffs of these CDO indexes are widely traded.

9.6. Other

This category is included here to capture some of the really unusual underlyings. One in particular is weather. Although weather is hardly an asset, it is certainly a major force in how some entities perform. For example, a ski resort needs snow, farmers need an adequate but not excessive amount of rain, and public utilities experience strains on their capacity during temperature extremes. Derivatives exist in which the payoffs are measured as snowfall, rainfall, and temperature. Although these derivatives have not been widely used—because of some complexities in pricing, among other things—they continue to exist and may still have a future. In addition, there are derivatives on electricity, which is also not an asset. It cannot be held in the traditional sense because it is created and consumed almost instantaneously. Another unusual type of derivative is based on disasters in the form of insurance claims.

Financial institutions will continue to create derivatives on all types of risks and exposures. Most of these derivatives will fail because of little trading interest, but a few will succeed. If that speaks badly of derivatives, it must be remembered that most small businesses fail, most creative ideas fail, and most people who try to become professional entertainers or athletes fail. It is the sign of a healthy and competitive system that only the very best survive.

The Size of the Derivatives Market

In case anyone thinks that the derivatives market is not large enough to justify studying, we should consider how big the market is. Unfortunately, gauging the size of the derivatives market is not a simple task. OTC derivatives contracts are private transactions. No reporting agency gathers data, and market size is not measured in traditional volume-based metrics, such as shares traded in the stock market. Complicating things further is the fact that derivatives underlyings include equities, fixed-income securities, interest rates, currencies, commodities, and a variety of other underlyings. All these underlyings have their own units of measurement. Hence, measuring how "big" the underlying derivatives markets are is like trying to measure how much fruit consumers purchase; the proverbial mixing of apples, oranges, bananas, and all other fruits.

The exchange-listed derivatives market reports its size in terms of volume, meaning the number of contracts traded. Exchange-listed volume, however, is an inconsistent number. For example, US Treasury bond futures contracts trade in units covering $100,000 face value. Eurodollar futures contracts trade in units covering $1,000,000 face value. Crude oil trades in 1,000-barrel (42 gallons each) units. Yet, one traded contract of each gets equal weighting in volume totals.

FIA (a global trade organization for futures, options, and centrally cleared derivatives markets) publishes detailed information about the industry. For 2017, global trading volume was 14.8 billion futures contracts, 10.4 billion options contracts, and a combined total of 25.2 billion contracts. Of nine futures instrument types, the largest three categories were interest rate futures (21.4% of global trading), equity index futures (16.9%), and currency futures (14.6%). Of nine options instrument types, the largest three categories were equity index options (48.4% of global trading), individual equity options (33.5%), and currency options (7.9%). Because options and futures contracts are typically short lived, the number of open-interest contracts is substantially less than the amount of trading volume. For the end of December 2017, open-interest futures contracts were 0.24 billion, open-interest option contracts were 0.60 billion, and the combined total was 0.84 billion contracts.

OTC volume is even more difficult to measure. There is no count of the number of contracts that trade. In fact, *volume* is an almost meaningless concept in OTC markets because any notion of volume requires a standardized size. If a customer goes to a swaps dealer and enters into a swap to hedge a $50 million loan, there is no measure of how much volume that transaction generated. The $50 million swap's notional principal, however, does provide a measure to some extent. Forwards, swaps, and OTC options all have notional principals, so they can be measured in that manner. Another measure of the size of the derivatives market is the market value of these contracts. As noted, forwards and swaps start with zero market value, but their market value changes as market conditions change. Options do not start with zero market value and almost always have a positive market value until expiration, when some options expire out of the money.

The OTC industry has taken both of these concepts—notional principal and market value—as measures of the size of the market. Notional principal is probably a more accurate measure. The amount of a contract's notional principal is unambiguous: It is written into the contract and the two parties cannot disagree over it. Yet, notional principal terribly overstates the amount of money actually at risk. For example, a $50 million notional principal swap will have nowhere near $50 million at risk. The payments on such a swap are merely the net of two opposite series of interest payments on $50 million. The market value of such a swap is the present value of one stream of payments minus the present value of the other. This market value figure will always be well below the notional principal. Thus, market value seems like a better measure except that, unlike notional principal, it is not unambiguous. Market value requires measurement, and two parties can disagree on the market value of the same transaction.

Notional principal and market value estimates for the global OTC derivatives market are collected semi-annually by the Bank for International Settlements of Basel, Switzerland, and published on its website (http://www.bis.org/statistics/derstats.htm). At the end of 2017, notional principal was more than $532 trillion and market value was about $27 trillion. A figure of $600 trillion is an almost unfathomable number and, as noted, is a misleading measure of the amount of money at risk.[13] The market value figure of $11 trillion is a much more realistic measure, but as noted, it is less accurate, relying on estimates provided by banks. Interest rate contracts constituted 81.9% of the total notional amount outstanding. The relative sizes of the other categories were 16.4% for foreign exchange contracts and less than 2% for credit derivatives, equity-linked contracts, and commodity contracts.

The exchange-listed and OTC markets use different measures and each of those measures is subject to severe limitations. About all we can truly say for sure about the derivatives market is, "It is big."

10. THE PURPOSES AND BENEFITS OF DERIVATIVES

Economic historians know that derivatives markets have existed since at least the Middle Ages. It is unclear whether derivatives originated in the Asian rice markets or possibly in medieval trade fairs in Europe. We do know that the origin of modern futures markets is the creation of the Chicago Board of Trade in 1848. To understand why derivatives markets exist, it is useful to take a brief look at why the Chicago Board of Trade was formed.

In the middle of the 19th century, midwestern America was rapidly becoming the center of agricultural production in the United States. At the same time, Chicago was evolving into a

---

[13]To put it in perspective, it would take almost 17 million years for a clock to tick off 532 trillion seconds!

major American city, a hub of transportation and commerce. Grain markets in Chicago were the central location to which midwestern farmers brought their wheat, corn, and soybeans to sell. Unfortunately, most of these products arrived at approximately the same time of the year, September through November. The storage facilities in Chicago were strained beyond capacity. As a result, prices would fall tremendously and some farmers reportedly found it more economical to dump their grains in the Chicago River rather than transport them back to the farm. At other times of the year, prices would rise steeply. A group of businessmen saw this situation as unnecessary volatility and a waste of valuable produce. To deal with this problem, they created the Chicago Board of Trade and a financial instrument called the "to-arrive" contract. A farmer could sell a to-arrive contract at any time during the year. This contract fixed the price of the farmer's grain on the basis of delivery in Chicago at a specified later date. Grain is highly storable, so farmers can hold on to the grain and deliver it at almost any later time. This plan substantially reduced seasonal market volatility and made the markets work much better for all parties.

The traders in Chicago began to trade these contracts, speculating on movements in grain prices. Soon, it became apparent that an important and fascinating market had developed. Widespread hedging and speculative interest resulted in substantial market growth, and about 80 years later, a clearinghouse and a performance guarantee were added, thus completing the evolution of the to-arrive contract into today's modern futures contract.

Many commodities and all financial assets that underlie derivatives contracts are not seasonally produced. Hence, this initial motivation for futures markets is only a minor advantage of derivatives markets today. But there are many reasons why derivative markets serve an important and useful purpose in contemporary finance.

10.1. Risk Allocation, Transfer, and Management

Until the advent of derivatives markets, risk management was quite cumbersome. Setting the actual level of risk to the desired level of risk required engaging in transactions in the underlyings. Such transactions typically had high transaction costs and were disruptive of portfolios. In many cases, it is quite difficult to fine-tune the level of risk to the desired level. From the perspective of a risk taker, it was quite costly to buy risk because a large amount of capital would be required.

Derivatives solve these problems in a very effective way: They allow trading the risk without trading the instrument itself. For example, consider a stockholder who wants to reduce exposure to a stock. In the pre-derivatives era, the only way to do so was to sell the stock. Now, the stockholder can sell futures, forwards, calls, or swaps, or buy put options, all while retaining the stock. For a company founder, these types of strategies can be particularly useful because the founder can retain ownership and probably board membership. Many other excellent examples of the use of derivatives to transfer risk are covered elsewhere in the curriculum. The objective at this point is to establish that derivatives provide an effective method of transferring risk from parties who do not want the risk to parties who do. In this sense, risk allocation is improved within markets and, indeed, the entire global economy.

The overall purpose of derivatives is to obtain more effective risk management within companies and the entire economy. Although some argue that derivatives do not serve this purpose very well (we will discuss this point in Section 11), for now you should understand that derivatives can improve the allocation of risk and facilitate more effective risk management for both companies and economies.

10.2. Information Discovery

One of the advantages of futures markets has been described as *price discovery*. A futures price has been characterized by some experts as a revelation of some information about the future. Thus, a futures price is sometimes thought of as predictive. This statement is not strictly correct because futures prices are not really forecasts of future spot prices. They provide only a little more information than do spot prices, but they do so in a very efficient manner. The markets for some underlyings are highly decentralized and not very efficient. For example, what is gold worth? It trades in markets around the world, but probably the best place to look is at the gold futures contract expiring soonest. What is the value of the S&P 500 Index when the US markets are not open? As it turns out, US futures markets open before the US stock market opens. The S&P 500 futures price is frequently viewed as an indication of where the stock market will open.

Derivative markets can, however, convey information not impounded in spot markets. By virtue of the fact that derivative markets require less capital, information can flow into the derivative markets before it gets into the spot market. The difference may well be only a matter of minutes or possibly seconds, but it can provide the edge to astute traders.

Finally, we should note that futures markets convey another simple piece of information: What price would one accept to avoid uncertainty? If you hold a stock worth $40 and could hedge the next 12 months' uncertainty, what locked-in price should you expect to earn? As it turns out, it should be the price that guarantees the risk-free rate minus whatever dividends would be paid on the stock. Derivatives—specifically, futures, forwards, and swaps—reveal the price that the holder of an asset could take and avoid the risk.

What we have said until now applies to futures, forwards, and swaps. What about options? As you will learn later, given the underlying and the type of option (call or put), an option price reflects two characteristics of the option (exercise price and time to expiration), three characteristics of the underlying (price, volatility, and cash flows it might pay), and one general macroeconomic factor (risk-free rate). Only one of these factors, volatility, is not relatively easy to identify. But with the available models to price the option, we can infer what volatility people are using from the actual market prices at which they execute trades. That volatility, called **implied volatility**, measures the expected risk of the underlying. It reflects the volatility that investors use to determine the market price of the option. Knowing the expected risk of the underlying asset is an extremely useful piece of information. In fact, for options on broad-based market indexes, such as the S&P 500, the implied volatility is a good measure of the general level of uncertainty in the market. Some experts have even called it a measure of fear. Thus, options provide information about what investors think of the uncertainty in the market, if not their fear of it.[14]

In addition, options allow the creation of trading strategies that cannot be done by using the underlying. As the exhibits on options explained, these strategies provide asymmetrical performance: limited movement in one direction and movement in the other direction that changes with movements in the underlying.

10.3. Operational Advantages

We noted earlier that derivatives have lower transaction costs than the underlying. The transaction costs of derivatives can be high relative to the value of the derivatives, but these costs

---

[14]The Chicago Board Options Exchange publishes a measure of the implied volatility of the S&P 500 Index option, which is called the VIX (volatility index). The VIX is widely followed and is cited as a measure of investor uncertainty and sometimes fear.

are typically low relative to the value of the underlying. Thus, an investor who wants to take a position in, say, an equity market index would likely find it less costly to use the futures to get a given degree of exposure than to invest directly in the index to get that same exposure.

Derivative markets also typically have greater liquidity than the underlying spot markets, a result of the smaller amount of capital required to trade derivatives than to get the equivalent exposure directly in the underlying. Futures margin requirements and option premiums are quite low relative to the cost of the underlying.

One other extremely valuable operational advantage of derivative markets is the ease with which one can go short. With derivatives, it is nearly as easy to take a short position as to take a long position, whereas for the underlying asset, it is almost always much more difficult to go short than to go long. In fact, for many commodities, short selling is nearly impossible.

10.4. Market Efficiency

In the study of portfolio management, you learn that an efficient market is one in which no single investor can consistently earn returns in the long run in excess of those commensurate with the risk assumed. Of course, endless debates occur over whether equity markets are efficient. No need to resurrect that issue here, but let us proceed with the assumption that equity markets—and, in fact, most free and competitive financial markets—are reasonably efficient. This assumption does not mean that abnormal returns can never be earned, and indeed prices do get out of line with fundamental values. But competition, the relatively free flow of information, and ease of trading tend to bring prices back in line with fundamental values. Derivatives can make this process work even more rapidly.

When prices deviate from fundamental values, derivative markets offer less costly ways to exploit the mispricing. As noted earlier, less capital is required, transaction costs are lower, and short selling is easier. We also noted that as a result of these features, it is possible, indeed likely, that fundamental value will be reflected in the derivatives markets before it is restored in the underlying market. Although this time difference could be only a matter of minutes, for a trader seeking abnormal returns, a few minutes can be a valuable opportunity.

All these advantages of derivatives markets make the financial markets in general function more effectively. Investors are far more willing to trade if they can more easily manage their risk, trade at lower cost and with less capital, and go short more easily. This increased willingness to trade increases the number of market participants, which makes the market more liquid. A very liquid market may not automatically be an efficient market, but it certainly has a better chance of being one.

Even if one does not accept the concept that financial markets are efficient, it is difficult to say that markets are not more effective and competitive with derivatives. Yet, many blame derivatives for problems in the market. Let us take a look at these arguments.

11. CRITICISMS AND MISUSES OF DERIVATIVES

The history of financial markets is filled with extreme ups and downs, which are often called bubbles and crashes. Bubbles occur when prices rise for a long time and appear to exceed fundamental values. Crashes occur when prices fall rapidly. Although bubbles, if they truly exist, are troublesome, crashes are even more so because nearly everyone loses substantial wealth in a crash. A crash is then typically followed by a government study commissioned to find the causes of the crash. In the last 30 years, almost all such studies have implicated derivatives as having some role in causing the crash. Of course, because derivatives are widely used and involve a high degree of leverage, it is a given that they would be seen in a crash. It is unclear whether derivatives are the real culprit or just the proverbial smoking gun used by someone to do something wrong.

The two principal arguments against derivatives are that they are such speculative devices that they effectively permit legalized gambling and that they destabilize the financial system. Let us look at these points more closely.

11.1. Speculation and Gambling

As noted earlier, derivatives are frequently used to manage risk. In many contexts, this use involves hedging or laying off risk. Naturally, for hedging to work, there must be speculators. Someone must accept the risk. Derivatives markets are unquestionably attractive to speculators. All the benefits of derivatives draw speculators in large numbers, and indeed they should. The more speculators that participate in the market, the cheaper it is for hedgers to lay off risk. These speculators take the form of hedge funds and other professional traders who willingly accept risk that others need to shed. In recent years, the rapid growth of these types of investors has been alarming to some but almost surely has been beneficial for all investors.

Unfortunately, the general image of speculators is not a good one. Speculators are often thought to be short-term traders who attempt to exploit temporary inefficiencies, caring little about long-term fundamental values. The profits from short-term trading are almost always taxed more heavily than the profits from long-term trading, clearly targeting and in some sense punishing speculators. Speculators are thought to engage in price manipulation and to trade at extreme prices.[15] All of this type of trading is viewed more or less as just a form of gambling.

Yet, there are notable differences between gambling and speculation. Gambling typically benefits only a limited number of participants and does not generally help society as a whole. But derivatives trading brings extensive benefits to financial markets, as explained earlier, and thus does benefit society as a whole. In short, the benefits of derivatives are broad, whereas the benefits of gambling are narrow.

Nonetheless, the argument that derivatives are a form of legalized gambling will continue to be made. Speculation and gambling are certainly both forms of financial risk taking, so these arguments are not completely off base. But insurance companies speculate on loss claims, mutual funds that invest in stocks speculate on the performance of companies, and entrepreneurs go up against tremendous odds to speculate on their own ability to create successful businesses. These so-called speculators are rarely criticized for engaging in a form of legalized gambling, and indeed entrepreneurs are praised as the backbone of the economy. Really, all investment is speculative. So, why is speculation viewed as such a bad thing by so many? The answer is unclear.

11.2. Destabilization and Systemic Risk

The arguments against speculation through derivatives often go a step further, claiming that it is not merely speculation or gambling per se but rather that it has destabilizing consequences. Opponents of derivatives claim that the very benefits of derivatives (low cost, low capital requirements, ease of going short) result in an excessive amount of speculative trading that brings

---

[15]Politicians and regulators have been especially critical of energy market speculators. Politicians, in particular, almost always blame rising oil prices on speculators, although credit is conspicuously absent for falling oil prices.

instability to the market. They argue that speculators use large amounts of leverage, thereby subjecting themselves and their creditors to substantial risk if markets do not move in their hoped-for direction. Defaults by speculators can then lead to defaults by their creditors, their creditors' creditors, and so on. These effects can, therefore, be systemic and reflect an epidemic contagion whereby instability can spread throughout markets and an economy, if not the entire world. Given that governments often end up bailing out some banks and insurance companies, society has expressed concern that the risk managed with derivatives must be controlled.

This argument is not without merit. Such effects occurred in the Long-Term Capital Management fiasco of 1998 and again in the financial crisis of 2008, in which derivatives, particularly credit default swaps, were widely used by many of the problem entities. Responses to such events typically take the course of calling for more rules and regulations restricting the use of derivatives, requiring more collateral and credit mitigation measures, backing up banks with more capital, and encouraging, if not requiring, OTC derivatives to be centrally cleared like exchange-traded derivatives.

In response, however, we should note that financial crises—including the South Sea and Mississippi bubbles and the stock market crash of 1929, as well as a handful of economic calamities of the 19th and 20th centuries—have existed since the dawn of capitalism. Some of these events preceded the era of modern derivatives markets, and others were completely unrelated to the use of derivatives. Some organizations, such as Orange County, California, in 1994–1995, have proved that derivatives are not required to take on excessive leverage and nearly bring the entity to ruin. Proponents of derivatives argue that derivatives are but one of many mechanisms through which excessive risk can be taken. Derivatives may seem dangerous, and they can be if misused, but there are many ways to take on leverage that look far less harmful but can be just as risky.

Another criticism of derivatives is simply their complexity. Many derivatives are extremely complex and require a high-level understanding of mathematics. The financial industry employs many mathematicians, physicists, and computer scientists. This single fact has made many distrust derivatives and the people who work on them. It is unclear why this reason has tarnished the reputation of the derivatives industry. Scientists work on complex problems in medicine and engineering without public distrust. One explanation probably lies in the fact that scientists create models of markets by using scientific principles that often fail. To a physicist modeling the movements of celestial bodies, the science is reliable and the physicist is unlikely to misapply the science. The same science applied to financial markets is far less reliable. Financial markets are driven by the actions of people who are not as consistent as the movements of celestial bodies. When financial models fail to work as they should, the scientists are often blamed for either building models that are too complex and unable to accurately capture financial reality or misusing those models, such as using poor estimates of inputs. And derivatives, being so widely used and heavily leveraged, are frequently in the center of it all.

EXAMPLE 8   Purposes and Controversies of Derivative Markets

1. Which of the following is **not** an advantage of derivative markets?
    A. They are less volatile than spot markets.
    B. They facilitate the allocation of risk in the market.
    C. They incur lower transaction costs than spot markets.

2. Which of the following pieces of information is **not** conveyed by at least one type of derivative?
   A. The volatility of the underlying
   B. The most widely used strategy of the underlying
   C. The price at which uncertainty in the underlying can be eliminated
3. Which of the following responds to the criticism that derivatives can be destabilizing to the underlying market?
   A. Market crashes and panics have occurred since long before derivatives existed.
   B. Derivatives are sufficiently regulated that they cannot destabilize the spot market.
   C. The transaction costs of derivatives are high enough to keep their use at a minimum level.

Solution to 1: A is correct. Derivative markets are not by nature more or less volatile than spot markets. They facilitate risk allocation by making it easier and less costly to transfer risk, and their transaction costs are lower than those of spot markets.

Solution to 2: B is correct. Options do convey the volatility of the underlying, and futures, forwards, and swaps convey the price at which uncertainty in the underlying can be eliminated. Derivatives do not convey any information about the use of the underlying in strategies.

Solution to 3: A is correct. Derivatives regulation is not more and is arguably less than spot market regulation, and the transaction costs of derivatives are not a deterrent to their use; in fact, derivatives are widely used. Market crashes and panics have a very long history, much longer than that of derivatives.

An important element of understanding and using derivatives is having a healthy respect for their power. Every day, we use chemicals, electricity, and fire without thinking about their dangers. We consume water and drive automobiles, both of which are statistically quite dangerous. Perhaps these risks are underappreciated, but it is more likely the case that most adults learn how to safely use chemicals, electricity, fire, water, and automobiles. Of course, there are exceptions, many of which are foolish, and foolishness is no stranger to the derivatives industry. The lesson here is that derivatives can make our financial lives better, but like chemicals, electricity, and all the rest, we need to know how to use them safely, which is why they are an important part of the CFA curriculum.

Later in the curriculum, you will learn a great deal about how derivatives are priced. At this point, we introduce the pricing of derivatives. This material not only paves the way for a deeper understanding of derivatives but also complements earlier material by helping you understand how derivatives work.

12. ELEMENTARY PRINCIPLES OF DERIVATIVE PRICING

Pricing and valuation are fundamental elements of the CFA Program. The study of fixed-income and equity securities, as well as their application in portfolio management, is solidly grounded on the principle of valuation. In valuation, the question is simple: What is something worth? Without an answer to that question, one can hardly proceed to use that *something* wisely.

Determining what a derivative is worth is similar to determining what an asset is worth. As you learn in the fixed-income and equity readings, value is the present value of future cash flows, with discounting done at a rate that reflects both the opportunity cost of money and the risk. Derivatives valuation applies that same principle but in a somewhat different way.

Think of a derivative as *attached* to an underlying. We know that the derivative *derives* its value from the value of the underlying. If the underlying's value changes, so should the value of the derivative. The underlying takes its value from the discounted present value of the expected future cash flows it offers, with discounting done at a rate reflecting the investor's risk tolerance. But if the value of the underlying is embedded in the value of the derivative, it would be double counting to discount the derivative's expected future cash flows at a risky discount rate. That effect has already been incorporated into the value of the underlying, which goes into the value of the derivative.

Derivatives usually take their values from the underlying by constructing a hypothetical combination of the derivatives and the underlyings that eliminates risk. This combination is typically called a **hedge portfolio**. With the risk eliminated, it follows that the hedge portfolio should earn the risk-free rate. A derivative's value is the price of the derivative that forces the hedge portfolio to earn the risk-free rate.

This principle of derivative valuation relies completely on the ability of an investor to hold or store the underlying asset. Let us take a look at what that means.

12.1. Storage

As noted previously, the first derivatives were agricultural commodities. Most of these commodities can be stored (i.e., held) for a period of time. Some extreme cases, such as oil and gold, which are storable for millions of years, are excellent examples of fully storable commodities. Grains, such as wheat and corn, can be stored for long but not infinite periods of time. Some commodities, such as bananas, are storable for relatively short periods of time. In the CFA Program, we are more interested in financial assets. Equities and currencies have perpetual storability, whereas bonds are storable until they mature.

Storage incurs costs. Commodity storage costs can be quite expensive. Imagine storing 1,000 kilograms of gold or a million barrels of oil. Financial assets, however, have relatively low storage costs. Some assets pay returns during storage. Stocks pay dividends and bonds pay interest. The net of payments offered minus storage costs plays a role in the valuation of derivatives.

An example earlier in this reading illustrates this point. Suppose an investor holds a dividend-paying stock and wants to eliminate the uncertainty of its selling price over a future period of time. Suppose further that the investor enters into a forward contract that commits him to deliver the stock at a later date, for which he will receive a fixed price. With uncertainty eliminated, the investor should earn the risk-free rate, but in fact, he does not. He earns more because while holding the stock, he collects dividends. Therefore, he should earn the risk-free rate *minus* the dividend yield, a concept known as the cost of carry, which will be covered in great detail in later readings. The cost of carry *plus* the dividends he earns effectively means that he makes the risk-free rate. Now, no one is claiming that this is a good way to earn the risk-free rate. There are many better ways to do that, but this strategy could be executed.

There is one and only one forward price that guarantees that this strategy earns a return of the risk-free rate minus the dividend yield, or the risk-free rate after accounting for the dividends collected. If the forward price at which contracts are created does not equal this price, investors can take advantage of this discrepancy by engaging in arbitrage, which is discussed in the next section.

Forwards, futures, swaps, and options are all priced in this manner. Hence, they rely critically on the ability to store or hold the asset. Some underlyings are not storable. We previously mentioned electricity. It is produced and consumed almost instantaneously. Weather is also not storable. Fresh fish have very limited storability. Although this absence of storability may not be the reason, derivative markets in these types of underlyings have not been particularly successful, whereas those in underlyings that are more easily storable have often been successful.

The opposite of storability is the ability to go short—that is, to borrow the underlying, sell it, and buy it back later. We discussed earlier that short selling of some assets can be difficult. It is not easy to borrow oil or soybeans. There are ways around this constraint, but derivatives valuation is generally much easier when the underlying can be shorted. This point is discussed in more depth later in the curriculum.

12.2. Arbitrage

What we have been describing is the foundation of the principle of **arbitrage**. In well-functioning markets with low transaction costs and a free flow of information, the same asset cannot sell for more than one price. If it did, someone would buy it in the cheaper market and sell it in the more expensive market, earning a riskless profit. The combined actions of all parties doing this would push up the lower price and push down the higher price until they converged. For this reason, arbitrage is often referred to as the **law of one price**. Of course, for arbitrage to be feasible, the ability to purchase and sell short the asset is important.

Obviously, this rule does not apply to all markets. The same consumer good can easily sell for different prices, which is one reason why people spend so much time shopping on the internet. The costs associated with purchasing the good in the cheaper market and selling it in the more expensive market can make the arbitrage not worthwhile. The absence of information on the very fact that different prices exist would also prevent the arbitrage from occurring. Although the internet and various price-comparing websites reduce these frictions and encourage all sellers to offer competitive prices, consumer goods are never likely to be arbitragable.[16]

Financial markets, of course, are a different matter. Information on securities prices around the world is quite accessible and relatively inexpensive. Most financial markets are fairly competitive because dealers, speculators, and brokers attempt to execute trades at the best prices. Arbitrage is considered a dependable rule in the financial markets. Nonetheless, there are people who purport to make a living as arbitrageurs. How could they exist? To figure that out, first consider some examples of arbitrage.

---

[16] If the same consumer good sells for different prices in markets with a relatively free flow of information (e.g., via price-comparing websites), it still may not be possible to truly arbitrage. Buying the good at a lower price and selling it at a higher price but less than the price of the most expensive seller may not be practical, but the most expensive seller may be driven out of business. When everyone knows what everyone else is charging, the same effect of arbitrage can still occur.

The simplest case of an arbitrage might be for the same stock to sell at different prices in two markets. If the stock were selling at $52 in one market and $50 in another, an arbitrageur would buy the stock at $50 in the one market and sell it at $52 in the other. This trade would net an immediate $2 profit at no risk and would not require the commitment of any of the investor's capital. This outcome would be a strong motivation for all arbitrageurs, and their combined actions would force the lower price up and the higher price down until the prices converged.

But what would be the final price? It is entirely possible that $50 is the true fundamental value and $52 is too high. Or $52 could be the true fundamental value and $50 is too low. Or the true fundamental value could lie somewhere between the two. Arbitrage does not tell us the true fundamental value. It is not an *absolute* valuation methodology, such as the discounted cash flow equity valuation model. It is a *relative* valuation methodology. It tells us the correct price of one asset or derivative *relative to* another asset or derivative.

Now, consider another situation, illustrated in Exhibit 6. Observe that we have one stock, AXE Electronics, that today is worth $50 and one period later will be worth either $75 or $40. We will denote these prices as AXE = $50, AXE$^+$ = $75, and AXE$^-$ = $40. Another stock, BYF Technology, is today worth $38 and one period later will be worth $60 or $32. Thus, BYF = $38, BYF$^+$ = $60, and BYF$^-$ = $32. Assume that the risk-free borrowing and lending rate is 4%. Also assume no dividends are paid on either stock during the period covered by this example.

EXHIBIT 6   Arbitrage Opportunity with Stock AXE, Stock BYF, and a Risk-Free Bond

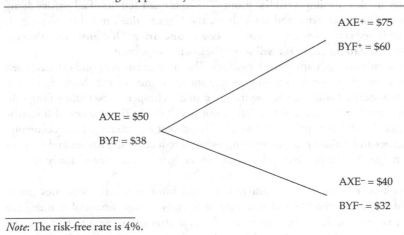

AXE$^+$ = $75

BYF$^+$ = $60

AXE = $50

BYF = $38

AXE$^-$ = $40

BYF$^-$ = $32

Note: The risk-free rate is 4%.

The opportunity exists to make a profit at no risk without committing any of our funds, as demonstrated in Exhibit 7. Suppose we borrow 100 shares of stock AXE, which is selling for $50, and sell them short, thereby receiving $5,000. We take $4,750 and purchase 125 shares of stock BYF (125 × $38 = $4,750). We invest the remaining $250 in risk-free bonds at 4%. This transaction will not require us to use any funds of our own: The short sale will be sufficient to fund the investment in BYF and leave money to invest in risk-free bonds.

EXHIBIT 7   Execution of Arbitrage Transaction with Stock AXE, Stock BYF, and a Risk-Free Bond

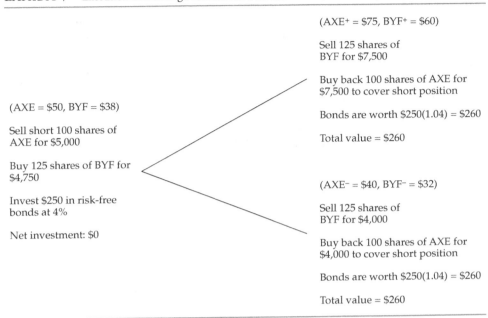

(AXE⁺ = $75, BYF⁺ = $60)

Sell 125 shares of
BYF for $7,500

Buy back 100 shares of AXE for
$7,500 to cover short position

Bonds are worth $250(1.04) = $260

Total value = $260

(AXE = $50, BYF = $38)

Sell short 100 shares of
AXE for $5,000

Buy 125 shares of BYF for
$4,750

Invest $250 in risk-free
bonds at 4%

Net investment: $0

(AXE⁻ = $40, BYF⁻ = $32)

Sell 125 shares of
BYF for $4,000

Buy back 100 shares of AXE for
$4,000 to cover short position

Bonds are worth $250(1.04) = $260

Total value = $260

If the top outcome in Exhibit 7 occurs, we sell the 125 shares of BYF for 125 × $60 = $7,500. This amount is sufficient to buy back the 100 shares of AXE, which is selling for $75. But we will also have the bonds, which are worth $250 × 1.04 = $260. If the bottom outcome occurs, we sell the 125 shares of BYF for 125 × $32 = $4,000—enough money to buy back the 100 shares of AXE, which is selling for $40. Again, we will have the risk-free bonds, worth $260. Regardless of the outcome, we end up with $260.

Recall that we invested no money of our own and end up with a sure $260. It should be apparent that this transaction is extremely attractive, so everyone would do it. The combined actions of multiple investors would drive down the price of AXE and/or drive up the price of BYF until an equilibrium is reached, at which point this transaction would no longer be profitable. As noted earlier, we cannot be sure of the correct fundamental price, but let us assume that BYF's price remains constant. Then AXE would fall to $47.50. Alternatively, if we assume that AXE's price remains constant, then the price of BYF would rise to $40. These values are obtained by noting that the prices for both outcomes occur according to the ratio 1.25 ($75/$60 = 1.25; $40/$32 = 1.25). Thus, their initial prices should be consistent with that ratio. If BYF is $38, AXE should be $38 × 1.25 = $47.50. If AXE is $50, BYF should be $40.00 because $40.00 × 1.25 = $50. Of course, the two prices could settle in between. Arbitrage is only a relative pricing method. It prices the two stocks in relation to each other but does not price either on the basis of its own fundamentals.

Of course, this example is extremely simplified. Clearly, a stock price can change to more than two other prices. Also, if a given stock is at one price, another stock may be at any other price. We have created a simple case here to illustrate a point. But as you will learn later in the curriculum, when derivatives are involved, the simplification here is relatively safe. As we know, the price of a derivative is determined by the price of the underlying. Hence, when the underlying is at one particular price, the derivative's price will be determined by that price. The two assets need not be two stocks; one can be a stock and the other can be a derivative on the stock.

To see that point, consider another type of arbitrage opportunity that involves a forward contract. Recall from the previous example that at the start, AXE sells for $50. Suppose we borrow $50 at 4% interest by issuing a risk-free bond, use the money to buy one share of stock AXE, and simultaneously enter into a forward contract to sell this share at a price of $54 one period later. The stock will then move to either $75 or $40 in the next period. The forward contract requires that we deliver the stock and accept $54 for it. And of course, we will owe $50 × 1.04 = $52 on the loan.

Now consider the two outcomes. Regardless of the outcome, the end result is the same. The forward contract fixes the delivery price of the stock at $54:

AXE goes to $75

Deliver stock to settle forward contract	+ $54
Pay back loan	− $52
Net	+ $2

AXE goes to $40

Deliver stock to settle forward contract	+ $54
Pay back loan	− $52
Net	+ $2

In either case, we made $2, free and clear. In fact, we can even accommodate the possibility of more than two future prices for AXE and we will always make $2.[17] The key point is that we faced no risk and did not have to invest any of our own money, but ended up with $2, which is clearly a good trade. The $2 is an arbitrage profit. But where did it originate?

It turns out that the forward price, $54, was an inappropriate price given current market conditions. In fact, it was just an arbitrary price made up to illustrate the point. To eliminate the opportunity to earn the $2 profit, the forward price should be $52, which is equal, not coincidentally, to the amount owed on the loan. It is also no coincidence that $52 is the price of the asset increased by the rate of interest. We will cover this point later in the curriculum, but for now consider that you have just seen your first derivative pricing model.[18]

Of course, many market participants would do this transaction as long as it generated an arbitrage profit. These forces of arbitrage would either push the forward price down or the stock price up, or both, until an equilibrium is reached that eliminates the opportunity to profit at no risk with no commitment of one's own funds.

To summarize, the forces of arbitrage in financial markets assure us that the same asset cannot sell for different prices, nor can two equivalent combinations of assets that produce the same results sell for different prices. Realistically, some arbitrage opportunities can exist on a temporary basis, but they will be quickly exploited, bringing relative prices back in line with each other. Other apparent arbitrage opportunities will be too small to warrant exploiting.

---

[17]A good study suggestion is to try this example with any future stock price. You should get the same result, a $2 risk-free profit.

[18]This illustration is the quick look at forward pricing alluded to in Section 2.

Not to be naive, however, we must acknowledge that there is a large industry of people who call themselves arbitrageurs. So, how can such an industry exist if there are no opportunities for riskless profit? One explanation is that most of the arbitrage transactions are more complex than the simple examples used here. Many involve estimating information, which can result in differing opinions. Arbitrage involving options, for example, usually requires an estimate of a stock's volatility. Different participants have different opinions about the volatility. It is quite possible that the two counterparties trading with each other believe that each is arbitraging against the other.[19]

But more importantly, the absence of arbitrage opportunities is upheld, ironically, only if participants believe that arbitrage opportunities do exist. If traders believe that no opportunities exist to earn arbitrage profits, then traders will not follow market prices and compare those prices with what they ought to be. Thus, eliminating arbitrage opportunities requires that participants be alert in watching for arbitrage opportunities. In other words, strange as it may sound, disbelief and skepticism concerning the absence of arbitrage opportunities are required for the no-arbitrage rule to be upheld.

Markets in which arbitrage opportunities are either nonexistent or quickly eliminated are relatively efficient markets. Recall that efficient markets are those in which it is not possible to consistently earn returns in excess of those that would be fair compensation for the risk assumed. Although abnormal returns can be earned in a variety of ways, arbitrage profits are definitely examples of abnormal returns. Thus, they are the most egregious violations of the principle of market efficiency.

Throughout the derivatives component of the CFA curriculum, we will use the principle of arbitrage as a dominant theme and assume that arbitrage opportunities cannot exist for any significant length of time nor can any one investor consistently capture them. Thus, prices must conform to models that assume no arbitrage. But we do not want to take the absence of arbitrage opportunities so seriously that we give up and believe that arbitrage opportunities never exist. Otherwise, they will arise and someone else will take them. Consider the rule of arbitrage a law that will be broken from time to time but one that holds far more often than not and one that should be understood and respected.

EXAMPLE 9   Arbitrage

1. Which of the following is a result of arbitrage?
   A. The law of one price
   B. The law of similar prices
   C. The law of limited profitability
2. When an arbitrage opportunity exists, what happens in the market?
   A. The combined actions of all arbitrageurs force the prices to converge.
   B. The combined actions of arbitrageurs result in a locked-limit situation.
   C. The combined actions of all arbitrageurs result in sustained profits to all.

---

[19]In reality, many of the transactions that arbitrageurs do are not really arbitrage. They are quite speculative. For example, many people call themselves arbitrageurs because they buy companies that are potential takeover targets and sell the companies they think will be the buyers. This transaction is not arbitrage by any stretch of the definition. Some transactions are called "risk arbitrage," but this term is an oxymoron. As an investment professional, you should simply be prepared for such misuses of words, which simply reflect the flexibility of language.

3. Which of the following accurately defines arbitrage?
   A. An opportunity to make a profit at no risk
   B. An opportunity to make a profit at no risk and with the investment of no capital
   C. An opportunity to earn a return in excess of the return appropriate for the risk assumed
4. Which of the following ways best describes how arbitrage contributes to market efficiency?
   A. Arbitrage penalizes those who trade too rapidly.
   B. Arbitrage equalizes the risks taken by all market participants.
   C. Arbitrage improves the rate at which prices converge to their relative fair values.

Solution to 1: A is correct. Arbitrage forces equivalent assets to have a single price. There is nothing called the law of similar prices or the law of limited profitability.

Solution to 2: A is correct. Prices converge because of the heavy demand for the cheaper asset and the heavy supply of the more expensive asset. Profits are not sustained, and, in fact, they are eradicated as prices converge. Locked-limit is a condition in the futures market and has nothing to do with arbitrage.

Solution to 3: B is correct. An opportunity to profit at no risk could merely describe the purchase of a risk-free asset. An opportunity to earn a return in excess of the return appropriate for the risk assumed is a concept studied in portfolio management and is often referred to as an abnormal return. It is certainly desirable but is hardly an arbitrage because it requires the assumption of risk and the investment of capital. Arbitrage is risk free and requires no capital because selling the overpriced asset produces the funds to buy the underpriced asset.

Solution to 4: C is correct. Arbitrage imposes no penalties on rapid trading; in fact, it tends to reward those who trade rapidly to take advantage of arbitrage opportunities. Arbitrage has no effect of equalizing risk among market participants. Arbitrage does result in an acceleration of price convergence to fair values relative to instruments with equivalent payoffs.

SUMMARY

This first reading on derivatives introduces you to the basic characteristics of derivatives, including the following points:

- A derivative is a financial instrument that derives its performance from the performance of an underlying asset.
- The underlying asset, called the underlying, trades in the cash or spot markets and its price is called the cash or spot price.
- Derivatives consist of two general classes: forward commitments and contingent claims.
- Derivatives can be created as standardized instruments on derivatives exchanges or as customized instruments in the over-the-counter market.

- Exchange-traded derivatives are standardized, highly regulated, and transparent transactions that are guaranteed against default through the clearinghouse of the derivatives exchange.
- Over-the-counter derivatives are customized, flexible, and more private and less regulated than exchange-traded derivatives, but are subject to a greater risk of default.
- A forward contract is an over-the-counter derivative contract in which two parties agree that one party, the buyer, will purchase an underlying asset from the other party, the seller, at a later date and at a fixed price they agree upon when the contract is signed.
- A futures contract is similar to a forward contract but is a standardized derivative contract created and traded on a futures exchange. In the contract, two parties agree that one party, the buyer, will purchase an underlying asset from the other party, the seller, at a later date and at a price agreed on by the two parties when the contract is initiated. In addition, there is a daily settling of gains and losses and a credit guarantee by the futures exchange through its clearinghouse.
- A swap is an over-the-counter derivative contract in which two parties agree to exchange a series of cash flows whereby one party pays a variable series that will be determined by an underlying asset or rate and the other party pays either a variable series determined by a different underlying asset or rate or a fixed series.
- An option is a derivative contract in which one party, the buyer, pays a sum of money to the other party, the seller or writer, and receives the right to either buy or sell an underlying asset at a fixed price either on a specific expiration date or at any time prior to the expiration date.
- A call is an option that provides the right to buy the underlying.
- A put is an option that provides the right to sell the underlying.
- Credit derivatives are a class of derivative contracts between two parties, the credit protection buyer and the credit protection seller, in which the latter provides protection to the former against a specific credit loss.
- A credit default swap is the most widely used credit derivative. It is a derivative contract between two parties, a credit protection buyer and a credit protection seller, in which the buyer makes a series of payments to the seller and receives a promise of compensation for credit losses resulting from the default of a third party.
- An asset-backed security is a derivative contract in which a portfolio of debt instruments is assembled and claims are issued on the portfolio in the form of tranches, which have different priorities of claims on the payments made by the debt securities such that prepayments or credit losses are allocated to the most-junior tranches first and the most-senior tranches last.
- Derivatives can be combined with other derivatives or underlying assets to form hybrids.
- Derivatives are issued on equities, fixed-income securities, interest rates, currencies, commodities, credit, and a variety of such diverse underlyings as weather, electricity, and disaster claims.
- Derivatives facilitate the transfer of risk, enable the creation of strategies and payoffs not otherwise possible with spot assets, provide information about the spot market, offer lower transaction costs, reduce the amount of capital required, are easier than the underlyings to go short, and improve the efficiency of spot markets.
- Derivatives are sometimes criticized for being a form of legalized gambling and for leading to destabilizing speculation, although these points can generally be refuted.
- Derivatives are typically priced by forming a hedge involving the underlying asset and a derivative such that the combination must pay the risk-free rate and do so for only one derivative price.
- Derivatives pricing relies heavily on the principle of storage, meaning the ability to hold or store the underlying asset. Storage can incur costs but can also generate cash, such as dividends and interest.

- Arbitrage is the condition that two equivalent assets or derivatives or combinations of assets and derivatives sell for different prices, leading to an opportunity to buy at the low price and sell at the high price, thereby earning a risk-free profit without committing any capital.
- The combined actions of arbitrageurs bring about a convergence of prices. Hence, arbitrage leads to the law of one price: Transactions that produce equivalent results must sell for equivalent prices.

PROBLEMS

1. A derivative is *best* described as a financial instrument that derives its performance by:
    A. passing through the returns of the underlying.
    B. replicating the performance of the underlying.
    C. transforming the performance of the underlying.
2. Derivatives are similar to insurance in that both:
    A. have an indefinite life span.
    B. allow for the transfer of risk from one party to another.
    C. allow for the transformation of the underlying risk itself.
3. A beneficial opportunity created by the derivatives market is the ability to:
    A. adjust risk exposures to desired levels.
    B. generate returns proportional to movements in the underlying.
    C. simultaneously take long positions in multiple highly liquid fixed-income securities.
4. Compared with exchange-traded derivatives, over-the-counter derivatives would *most likely* be described as:
    A. standardized.
    B. less transparent.
    C. more transparent.
5. Exchange-traded derivatives are:
    A. largely unregulated.
    B. traded through an informal network.
    C. guaranteed by a clearinghouse against default.
6. The clearing and settlement process of an exchange-traded derivatives market:
    A. provides a credit guarantee.
    B. provides transparency and flexibility.
    C. takes longer than that of most securities exchanges.
7. Which of the following statements *best* portrays the full implementation of post-financial-crisis regulations in the OTC derivatives market?
    A. Transactions are no longer private.
    B. Most transactions need to be reported to regulators.
    C. All transactions must be cleared through central clearing agencies.
8. A characteristic of forward commitments is that they:
    A. provide linear payoffs.
    B. do not depend on the outcome or payoff of an underlying asset.
    C. provide one party the right to engage in future transactions on terms agreed on in advance.

9. In contrast to contingent claims, forward contracts:
   A. have their prices chosen by the participants.
   B. could end in default by either party.
   C. can be exercised by physical or cash delivery.
10. Which of the following statements *best* describes the payoff from a forward contract?
    A. The buyer has more to gain going long than the seller has to lose going short.
    B. The buyer profits if the price of the underlying at expiration exceeds the forward price.
    C. The gains from owning the underlying versus owning the forward contract are equivalent.
11. Which of the following statements regarding the settlement of forward contracts is correct?
    A. Contract settlement by cash has different economic effects from those of a settlement by delivery.
    B. Non-deliverable forwards and contracts for differences have distinct settlement procedures.
    C. At cash settlement, when the long party acquires the asset in the market, it effectively pays the forward price.
12. A futures contract is *best* described as a contract that is:
    A. standardized.
    B. subject to credit risk.
    C. marked to market throughout the trading day.
13. Which of the following statements explains a characteristic of futures price limits? Price limits:
    A. help the clearinghouse manage its credit exposure.
    B. can typically be expanded intra-day by willing traders.
    C. establish a band around the final trade of the previous day.
14. Which of the following statements describes an aspect of margin accounts for futures?
    A. The maintenance margin is always less than the initial margin.
    B. The initial margin required is typically at least 10% of the futures price.
    C. A margin call requires a deposit sufficient to raise the account balance to the maintenance margin.
15. Which of the following factors is shared by forwards and futures contracts?
    A. Timing of profits
    B. Flexible settlement arrangements
    C. Nearly equivalent profits by expiration
16. Which of the following derivatives is classified as a contingent claim?
    A. Futures contracts
    B. Interest rate swaps
    C. Credit default swaps
17. In contrast to contingent claims, forward commitments provide the:
    A. right to buy or sell the underlying asset in the future.
    B. obligation to buy or sell the underlying asset in the future.
    C. promise to provide credit protection in the event of default.
18. Which of the following derivatives provide payoffs that are non-linearly related to the payoffs of the underlying?
    A. Options
    B. Forwards
    C. Interest-rate swaps

19. An interest rate swap is a derivative contract in which:
    A. two parties agree to exchange a series of cash flows.
    B. the credit seller provides protection to the credit buyer.
    C. the buyer has the right to purchase the underlying from the seller.
20. Forward commitments subject to default are:
    A. forwards and futures.
    B. futures and interest rate swaps.
    C. interest rate swaps and forwards.
21. A swap is:
    A. more like a forward than a futures contract.
    B. subject to simultaneous default by both parties.
    C. based on an exchange of two series of fixed cash flows.
22. A plain vanilla interest rate swap is also known as:
    A. a basis swap.
    B. a fixed-for-floating swap.
    C. an overnight indexed swap.
23. The notional principal of a swap is:
    A. not exchanged in the case of an interest rate swap.
    B. a fixed amount whenever it is matched with a loan.
    C. equal to the amount owed by one swap party to the other.
24. Which of the following derivatives is *least likely* to have a value of zero at initiation of the contract?
    A. Futures
    B. Options
    C. Forwards
25. The buyer of an option has a contingent claim in the sense that the option creates:
    A. a right.
    B. an obligation.
    C. a linear payoff with respect to gains and losses of the underlying.
26. Which of the following options grants the holder the right to purchase the underlying prior to expiration?
    A. American-style put option
    B. European-style call option
    C. American-style call option
27. A credit derivative is a derivative contract in which the:
    A. clearinghouse provides a credit guarantee to both the buyer and the seller.
    B. seller provides protection to the buyer against the credit risk of a third party.
    C. the buyer and seller provide a performance bond at initiation of the contract.
28. The junior and senior tranches of an asset-backed security:
    A. have equivalent expected returns.
    B. have claims on separate underlying portfolios.
    C. may be differentially impacted by prepayments or credit losses.
29. In a declining interest rate environment, compared with a CMO's Class A tranche, its Class C tranche will be repaid:
    A. earlier.
    B. at the same pace.
    C. later.

30. For a given CDO, which of the following tranches is *most likely* to have the highest expected return?
    A. Equity
    B. Senior
    C. Mezzanine

31. Which of the following derivatives allows an investor to pay the return on a stock index and receive a fixed rate?
    A. Equity swap
    B. Stock warrant
    C. Index futures contract

32. Which of the following is *most likely* the underlying of a plain vanilla interest rate swap?
    A. 180-day Libor
    B. 10-year US Treasury bond
    C. Bloomberg Barclay's US Aggregate Bond Index

33. Currency swaps are:
    A. rarely used.
    B. commonly used to manage interest rate risk.
    C. executed by two parties making a series of interest rate payments in the same currency.

34. Which of the following statements regarding commodity derivatives is correct?
    A. The primary commodity derivatives are futures.
    B. Commodities are subject to a set of well-defined risk factors.
    C. Commodity traders and financial traders today are distinct groups within the financial world.

35. Compared with the underlying spot market, derivative markets are *more likely* to have:
    A. greater liquidity.
    B. higher transaction costs.
    C. higher capital requirements.

36. Which of the following characteristics is *least likely* to be a benefit associated with using derivatives?
    A. More effective management of risk
    B. Payoffs similar to those associated with the underlying
    C. Greater opportunities to go short compared with the spot market

37. Which of the following statements *best* represents information discovery in the futures market?
    A. The futures price is predictive.
    B. Information flows more slowly into the futures market than into the spot market.
    C. The futures market reveals the price that the holder of the asset can take to avoid uncertainty.

38. The derivative markets tend to:
    A. transfer liquidity from the broader financial markets.
    B. not reflect fundamental value after it is restored in the underlying market.
    C. offer a less costly way to exploit mispricing in comparison to other free and competitive financial markets.

39. Which of the following statements *most likely* contributes to the view that derivatives have some role in causing financial crashes?
    A. Derivatives are the primary means by which leverage and related excessive risk is brought into financial markets.
    B. Growth in the number of investors willing to speculate in derivatives markets leads to excessive speculative trading.
    C. Restrictions on derivatives, such as enhanced collateral requirements and credit mitigation measures, in the years leading up to crashes introduce market rigidity.

40. In contrast to gambling, derivatives speculation:
    A. has a positive public image.
    B. is a form of financial risk taking.
    C. benefits the financial markets and thus society.
41. Derivatives may contribute to financial contagion because of the:
    A. centrally cleared nature of OTC derivatives.
    B. associated significant costs and high capital requirements.
    C. reliance by derivatives speculators on large amounts of leverage.
42. The complex nature of derivatives has led to:
    A. reliable financial models of derivatives markets.
    B. widespread trust in applying scientific principles to derivatives.
    C. financial industry employment of mathematicians and physicists.
43. Which of the following is *most likely* to be a destabilizing consequence of speculation using derivatives?
    A. Increased defaults by speculators and creditors
    B. Market price swings resulting from arbitrage activities
    C. The creation of trading strategies that result in asymmetric performance
44. The law of one price is *best* described as:
    A. the true fundamental value of an asset.
    B. earning a risk-free profit without committing any capital.
    C. two assets that will produce the same cash flows in the future must sell for equivalent prices.
45. Arbitrage opportunities exist when:
    A. two identical assets or derivatives sell for different prices.
    B. combinations of the underlying asset and a derivative earn the risk-free rate.
    C. arbitrageurs simultaneously buy takeover targets and sell takeover acquirers.

For questions 46–49, consider a call option selling for $4 in which the exercise price is $50

46. Determine the value at expiration and the profit for a *buyer* if the price of the underlying at expiration is $55.
    A. $5
    B. $1
    C. −$1
47. Determine the value at expiration and the profit for a *buyer* if the price of the underlying at expiration is $48.
    A. −$4
    B. $0
    C. $2
48. Determine the value at expiration and the profit for a *seller* if the price of the underling at expiration is $49.
    A. $4
    B. $0
    C. −$1
49. Determine the value at expiration and the profit for a *seller* if the price of the underling at expiration is $52.
    A. −$2
    B. $5
    C. $2

For questions 50–52, consider the following scenario

Suppose you believe that the price of a particular underlying, currently selling at $99, is going to increase substantially in the next six months. You decide to purchase a call option expiring in six months on this underlying. The call option has an exercise price of $105 and sells for $7.

50. Determine the profit if the price of the underlying six months from now is $99.
    A. $6
    B. $0
    C. −$7
51. Determine the profit if the price of the underlying six months from now is $112.
    A. $7
    B. $0
    C. −$3
52. Determine the profit if the price of the underlying six months from now is $115.
    A. $0
    B. $3
    C. −$3

For questions 53–55, consider the following scenario

Suppose you believe that the price of a particular underlying, currently selling at $99, is going to decrease substantially in the next six months. You decide to purchase a put option expiring in six months on this underlying. The put option has an exercise price of $95 and sells for $5.

53. Determine the profit for you if the price of the underlying six months from now is $100.
    A. $0
    B. $5
    C. −$5
54. Determine the profit for you if the price of the underlying six months from now is $95.
    A. $0
    B. $5
    C. −$5
55. Determine the profit for you if the price of the underlying six months from now is $85.
    A. $10
    B. $5
    C. $0

CHAPTER 2

BASICS OF DERIVATIVE PRICING AND VALUATION

Don M. Chance, PhD, CFA

LEARNING OUTCOMES

The candidate should be able to:

- explain how the concepts of arbitrage, replication, and risk neutrality are used in pricing derivatives;
- explain the difference between value and price of forward and futures contracts;
- calculate a forward price of an asset with zero, positive, or negative net cost of carry;
- explain how the value and price of a forward contract are determined at expiration, during the life of the contract, and at initiation;
- describe monetary and nonmonetary benefits and costs associated with holding the underlying asset and explain how they affect the value and price of a forward contract;
- define a forward rate agreement and describe its uses;
- explain why forward and futures prices differ;
- explain how swap contracts are similar to but different from a series of forward contracts;
- explain the difference between value and price of swaps;
- explain the exercise value, time value, and moneyness of an option;
- identify the factors that determine the value of an option and explain how each factor affects the value of an option;
- explain put–call parity for European options;
- explain put–call–forward parity for European options;
- explain how the value of an option is determined using a one-period binomial model;
- explain under which circumstances the values of European and American options differ.

1. INTRODUCTION

It is important to understand how prices of derivatives are determined. Whether one is on the buy side or the sell side, a solid understanding of pricing financial products is critical to effective investment decision making. After all, one can hardly determine what to offer or bid for a financial product, or any product for that matter, if one has no idea how its characteristics combine to create value.

Understanding the pricing of financial assets is important. Discounted cash flow methods and models, such as the capital asset pricing model and its variations, are useful for determining the prices of financial assets. The unique characteristics of derivatives, however, pose some complexities not associated with assets, such as equities and fixed-income instruments. Somewhat surprisingly, however, derivatives also have some simplifying characteristics. For example, as we will see in this reading, in well-functioning derivatives markets the need to determine risk premiums is obviated by the ability to construct a risk-free hedge. Correspondingly, the need to determine an investor's risk aversion is irrelevant for derivative pricing, although it is certainly relevant for pricing the underlying.

The purpose of this reading is to establish the foundations of derivative pricing on a basic conceptual level. The following topics are covered:

- How does the pricing of the underlying asset affect the pricing of derivatives?
- How are derivatives priced using the principle of arbitrage?
- How are the prices and values of forward contracts determined?
- How are futures contracts priced differently from forward contracts?
- How are the prices and values of swaps determined?
- How are the prices and values of European options determined?
- How does American option pricing differ from European option pricing?

This reading is organized as follows. Sections 2–4 explore two related topics, the pricing of the underlying assets on which derivatives are created and the principle of arbitrage. Sections 5–7 describe the pricing and valuation of forwards, futures, and swaps. Sections 8–12 introduce the pricing and valuation of options. Section 13 provides a summary.

2. BASIC DERIVATIVE CONCEPTS, PRICING THE UNDERLYING

In this section, we will briefly review the concepts associated with derivatives, the types of derivatives, and the pricing principles of the underlying assets. We will also look at arbitrage, a critical concept that links derivative pricing to the price of the underlying.

2.1. Basic Derivative Concepts

The definition of a derivative is as follows:

> *A derivative is a financial instrument that derives its performance from the performance of an underlying asset.*

A derivative is created as a contract between two parties, the buyer and the seller. Derivatives trade in markets around the world, which include organized exchanges, where highly standardized and regulated versions exist, and over-the-counter markets, where customized and more lightly regulated versions trade. The basic characteristics of derivatives that influence pricing are not particularly related to where the derivatives trade, but are critically dependent on the types of derivatives.

The two principal types of derivatives are forward commitments and contingent claims. A forward commitment is an obligation to engage in a transaction in the spot market at a future date at terms agreed upon today.[1] By entering into a forward commitment, a party locks in the terms of a transaction that he or she will conduct later. The word "commitment" is critical here. A forward contract is a firm obligation.

There are three types of forward commitments: forward contracts, futures contracts, and swap contracts. These contracts can be referred to more simply as forwards, futures, and swaps.

*A **forward contract** is an over-the-counter derivative contract in which two parties agree that one party, the buyer, will purchase an underlying asset from the other party, the seller, at a later date at a fixed price they agree upon when the contract is signed.*

*A **futures contract** is a standardized derivative contract created and traded on a futures exchange in which two parties agree that one party, the buyer, will purchase an underlying asset from the other party, the seller, at a later date at a price agreed upon by the two parties when the contract is initiated and in which there is a daily settling of gains and losses and a credit guarantee by the futures exchange through its clearinghouse.*

*A **swap contract** is an over-the-counter derivative contract in which two parties agree to exchange a series of cash flows whereby one party pays a variable series that will be determined by an underlying asset or rate and the other party pays either 1) a variable series determined by a different underlying asset or rate or 2) a fixed series.*

As these definitions illustrate, forwards and futures are similar. They both establish the terms of a spot transaction that will occur at a later date. Forwards are customized, less transparent, less regulated, and subject to higher counterparty default risk. Futures are standardized, more transparent, more regulated, and generally immune to counterparty default. A swap is equivalent to a series of forward contracts, a point that will be illustrated later.

A contingent claim is a derivative in which the outcome or payoff is determined by the outcome or payoff of an underlying asset, conditional on some event occurring. Contingent claims include options, credit derivatives, and asset-backed securities. Because credit derivatives and asset-backed securities are highly specialized, this reading will focus only on options.

Recall the definition of an option:

*An **option** is a derivative contract in which one party, the buyer, pays a sum of money to the other party, the seller or writer, and receives the right to either buy or sell an underlying asset at a fixed price either on a specific expiration date or at any time prior to the expiration date.*

---

[1] Remember that the term "spot market" refers to the market in which the underlying trades. A transaction in the spot market involves a buyer paying for an asset and receiving it right away or at least within a few days, given the normal time required to settle a financial transaction.

Options can be either customized over-the-counter contracts or standardized and traded on exchanges.

Because derivatives take their prices from the price of the underlying, it is important to first understand how the underlying is priced. We will approach the underlying from a slightly different angle, one that emphasizes the often-subtle costs of holding the underlying, which turn out to play a major role in derivative pricing.

2.2. Pricing the Underlying

The four main types of underlying on which derivatives are based are equities, fixed-income securities/interest rates, currencies, and commodities. Equities, fixed-income securities (but not interest rates), currencies, and commodities are all assets. An interest rate is not an asset, but it can be structured as the underlying of a derivative.[2]

Consider a generic underlying asset. This asset is something of value that you can own. Some assets are financial assets, such as equities, bonds, and currencies, and some are real assets, such as commodities (e.g., gold, oil, and agricultural products) and certain physical objects (e.g., houses, automobiles, and computers).

The price of a financial asset is often determined using a present value of future cash flows approach. The value of the financial asset is the expected future price plus any interim payments such as dividends or coupon interest discounted at a rate appropriate for the risk assumed. Such a definition presumes a period of time over which an investor anticipates holding an asset, known as the holding period. The investor forecasts the price expected to prevail at the end of the holding period as well as any cash flows that are expected to be earned over the holding period. He then takes that predicted future price and expected cash flows and finds their current value by discounting them to the present. Thereby, the investor arrives at a fundamental value for the asset and will compare that value with its current market price. Based on any differential relative to the cost of trading and his confidence in his valuation model, he will make a decision about whether to trade.

2.2.1. The Formation of Expectations

Let us first assume that the underlying does not pay interest or dividends, nor does it have any other cash flows attributable to holding the asset. Exhibit 1 illustrates the basic idea behind the valuation process. Using a probability distribution, the investor forecasts the future over a holding period spanning time 0 to time T. The center of the distribution is the expected price of the asset at time T, which we denote as $E(S_T)$, and represents the investor's prediction of the spot price at T. The investor knows there is risk, so this prediction is imperfect—hence the reason for the probability distribution. Nonetheless, at time 0 the investor makes her best prediction of the spot price at time T, which becomes the foundation for determining what she perceives to be the value of the asset.[3]

---

[2] This is a good example of why it is best not to use the term "underlying *asset*" when speaking of derivatives. Not all derivatives have underlying assets, but all have underlyings, some of which are not assets. Some other examples of non-asset underlyings used in derivatives are weather, insurance claims, and shipping rates. There are also some derivatives in which the underlying is another derivative.

[3] The distribution shown here is symmetrical and relatively similar to a normal distribution, but this characterization is for illustrative purposes only. We are making no assumptions about symmetry or normality at this point.

EXHIBIT 1   The Formation of Expectations for an Asset

$$E(S_T)$$

0   T

2.2.2. The Required Rate of Return on the Underlying Asset

To determine the value of the asset, this prediction must be converted into its price or present value. The specific procedure is to discount this expected future price, but that is the easy part. Determining the rate at which to discount the expected future price is the hard part. We use the symbol k to denote this currently unknown discount rate, which is often referred to as the required rate of return and sometimes the expected rate of return or just the expected return. At a minimum, that rate will include the risk-free rate of interest, which we denote as r. This rate represents the opportunity cost, or so-called time value of money, and reflects the price of giving up your money today in return for receiving more money later.

2.2.3. The Risk Aversion of the Investor

At this point, we must briefly discuss an important characteristic of investors: their degree of risk aversion. We can generally characterize three potential types of investors by how they feel about risk: risk averse, risk neutral, or risk seeking.

Risk-neutral investors are willing to engage in risky investments for which they expect to earn only the risk-free rate. Thus, they do not expect to earn a premium for bearing risk. For risk-averse investors, however, risk is undesirable, so they do not consider the risk-free rate an adequate return to compensate them for the risk. Thus, risk-averse investors require a risk premium, which is an increase in the expected return that is sufficient to justify the acceptance of risk. All things being equal, an investment with a higher risk premium will have a lower price. It is very important to understand, however, that risk premiums are not automatically earned. They are merely expectations. Actual outcomes can differ. Clearly stocks that decline in value did not earn risk premiums, even though someone obviously bought them with the expectation that they would. Nonetheless, risk premiums must exist in the long run or risk-averse investors would not accept the risk.

The third type of investor is one we must mention but do not treat as realistic. Risk seekers are those who prefer risk over certainty and will pay more to invest when there is risk, implying a negative risk premium. We almost always assume that investors prefer certainty over uncertainty, so we generally treat a risk-seeking investor as just a theoretical possibility and not a practical reality.[4]

---

[4] People who gamble in casinos or play lotteries appear to be risk-seekers, given the advantage of the casino or the lottery organizer, but they are merely earning utility from the game itself, not necessarily from the expected financial outcome.

We will assume that investors are risk averse. To justify taking risk, risk-averse investors require a risk premium. We will use the Greek symbol λ (lambda) to denote the risk premium.[5]

2.2.4. The Pricing of Risky Assets

Exhibit 2 illustrates the process by which an investor obtains the current price, S_0, by discounting the expected future price of an asset with no interim cash flows, $E(S_T)$, by r (the risk-free rate) plus λ (the risk premium) over the period from 0 to T.

EXHIBIT 2   Discounting the Expected Future Price to Obtain the Current Price

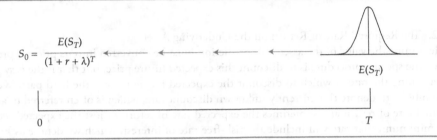

2.2.5. Other Benefits and Costs of Holding an Asset

Many assets generate benefits and some incur costs to their owners. Some of these costs are monetary and others are nonmonetary. The dividends paid by companies and coupon interest paid by borrowers on their bonds represent obvious benefits to the holders of these securities. With currencies representing investments that earn the risk-free rate in a foreign country, they too generate benefits in the form of interest. Barring default, interest payments on bonds and currencies are relatively certain, so we will treat them as such. Dividend payments are not certain, but dividends do tend to be fairly predictable. As such, we will make an assumption common to most derivative models that dividends are certain.[6]

There is substantial evidence that some commodities generate a benefit that is somewhat opaque and difficult to measure. This benefit is called the **convenience yield**. It represents a nonmonetary advantage of holding the asset. For most financial assets, convenience yields are either nonexistent or extremely limited. Financial assets do not possess beauty that might make a person enjoy owning them just to look at them. Convenience yields are primarily associated with commodities and generally exist as a result of difficulty in either shorting the commodity or unusually tight supplies. For example, if a commodity cannot be sold short without great difficulty or cost, the holder of the commodity has an advantage if market conditions suggest that the commodity should be sold. Also, if a commodity is in short supply, the holders of the commodity can sometimes extract a price premium that is believed by some to be higher than what would be justified in well-functioning markets. The spot price

---

[5]Although the risk-free rate is invariant with a country's economy, the risk premium varies with the amount of risk taken. Thus, while the risk-free rate is the same when applied to every investment, the risk premium is not the same for every investment.
[6]Some derivative models incorporate uncertain dividends and interest, but those are beyond the scope of this introductory reading.

of the commodity could even be above the market's expectation of its future price, a condition that would seem to imply a negative expected return. This scenario raises the question of why anyone would want to hold the commodity if its expected return is negative. The convenience yield provides a possible explanation that attributes an implied but non-financial expected return to the advantage of holding a commodity in short supply. The holder of the commodity has the ability to sell it when market conditions suggest that selling is advisable and short selling is difficult.

One cost incurred in owning commodities is the cost of storage. One could hardly own gold, oil, or wheat without incurring some costs in storing these assets. There are also costs incurred in protecting and insuring some commodities against theft or destruction. Depending on the commodity, these costs can be quite significant. For financial assets, however, the storage costs are so low that we can safely ignore them.

Finally, there is the opportunity cost of the money invested. If a person buys an asset, he forgoes interest on his money. The effect on this interest is reflected by compounding the price paid for the asset to a future value at the risk-free rate of interest. Thus, an investor who buys a stock that costs £50 in a market in which the risk-free rate is 4% will effectively have paid £50 × 1.04 = £52 a year later. Of course, the stock could be worth any value at that time, and any gain or loss should be determined in comparison to the effective price paid of £52.

As we described earlier, we determine the current price of an asset by discounting the expected future price by the sum of the risk-free rate (r) plus the risk premium (λ). When we introduce costs and benefits of holding the asset, we have to make an adjustment. With the exception of this opportunity cost of money, we will incorporate the effect of these costs and benefits by determining their value at the end of the holding period. Under the assumption that these costs and benefits are certain, we can then discount them at the risk-free rate to obtain their present value. There is a logic to doing it this way (i.e., finding their future value and discounting back to the present, as opposed to finding their present value directly). By finding their future value, we are effectively saying that the costs and benefits adjust the expected payoff at the end of the holding period. But because they are certain, we can discount their effects at the risk-free rate. So we have effectively just found their present value. The net effect is that the costs reduce the current price and the benefits increase the current price. We use the symbol θ (theta) to denote the present value of the costs and γ (gamma) as the present value of any benefits.

The net of the costs and benefits is often referred to by the term **carry**, or sometimes **cost of carry**. The holding, storing, or "carrying" of an asset is said to incur a net cost that is essentially what it takes to "carry" an asset. Exhibit 3 illustrates the effect in which the carry adjusts the price of an asset in the valuation process.

EXHIBIT 3   Pricing an Asset That Incurs Costs and Generates Benefits

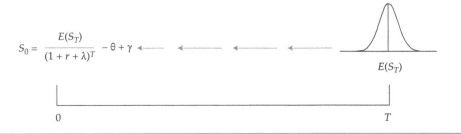

EXAMPLE 1   Pricing the Spot Asset

1. Which of the following factors does **not** affect the spot price of an asset that has no interim costs or benefits?
   A. The time value of money
   B. The risk aversion of investors
   C. The price recently paid by other investors

2. Which of the following does **not** represent a benefit of holding an asset?
   A. The convenience yield
   B. An optimistic expected outlook for the asset
   C. Dividends if the asset is a stock or interest if the asset is a bond

Solution to 1: C is correct. The price recently paid by other investors is past information and does not affect the spot price. The time value of money and the risk aversion of investors determine the discount rate. Only current information is relevant as investors look ahead, not back.

Solution to 2: B is correct. An optimistic forecast for the asset is not a benefit of holding the asset, but it does appear in the valuation of the asset as a high expected price at the horizon date. Convenience yields and dividends and interest are benefits of holding the asset.

To recap, although the various underlyings differ with respect to the specifics of pricing, all of them are based on expectations, risk, and the costs and benefits of holding a specific underlying. Understanding how assets are priced in the spot market is critical to understanding how derivatives are priced. To understand derivative pricing, it is necessary to establish a linkage between the derivative market and the spot market. That linkage occurs through arbitrage.

3. THE PRINCIPLE OF ARBITRAGE

Arbitrage is a type of transaction undertaken when two assets or portfolios produce identical results but sell for different prices. If a trader buys the asset or portfolio at the cheaper price and sells it at the more expensive price, she will generate a net inflow of funds at the start. Because the two assets or portfolios produce identical results, a long position in one and a short position in the other means that at the end of the holding period, the payoffs offset. Hence, no money is gained or lost at the end of the holding period, so there is no risk. The net effect is that the arbitrageur receives money at the start and never has to pay out any money later. Such a situation amounts to free money, like walking down the street, finding money on the ground, and never having to give it up. Exhibit 4 illustrates this process for assets A and B, which have no dividends or other benefits or costs and pay off identically but sell for different prices, with $S_0^A < S_0^B$.

EXHIBIT 4   Executing an Arbitrage

Given: Assets A and B produce the same values at time
T but at time 0, A is selling for less than B.

$S_0^A < S_0^B$: $S_T^A = S_T^B$:
Buy A at S_0^A Sell A for S_T^A
Sell B at S_0^B Buy B for S_T^B
Cash flow = $S_0^B - S_0^A (> 0)$ Cash flow = $S_T^A - S_T^B (= 0)$

0 T

3.1. The (In)Frequency of Arbitrage Opportunities

When arbitrage opportunities exist, traders exploit them very quickly. The combined actions of many traders engaging in the same transaction of buying the low-priced asset or portfolio and selling the high-priced asset or portfolio results in increased demand and an increasing price for the former and decreased demand and a decreasing price for the latter. This market activity will continue until the prices converge. Assets that produce identical results can thus have only one true market price. This rule is called the "law of one price." With virtually all market participants alert for the possibility of earning such profits at no risk, it should not be surprising that arbitrage opportunities are rare.

In practice, prices need not converge precisely, or even all that quickly, because the transaction cost of exploiting an opportunity could exceed the benefit. For example, say you are walking down the sidewalk of the Champs-Élysées in Paris and notice a €1 coin on the sidewalk. You have a bad back, and it would take some effort to bend over. The transaction cost of exploiting this opportunity without any risk could exceed the benefit of the money. Some arbitrage opportunities represent such small discrepancies that they are not worth exploiting because of transaction costs.

Significant arbitrage opportunities, however, will be exploited. A significant opportunity arises from a price differential large enough to overcome the transaction costs. Any such price differential will continue to be exploited until the opportunity disappears. Thus, if you find a €10 note on the Champs-Élysées sidewalk, there is a good chance you will find it worth picking up (even with your bad back), and even if you do not pick it up, it will probably not be there for long. With enough people alert for such opportunities, only a few will arise, and the ones that do will be quickly exploited and disappear. In this manner, arbitrage makes markets work much more efficiently.

3.2. Arbitrage and Derivatives

It may be difficult to conceive of many investments that would produce identical payoffs. Even similar companies such as McDonald's and Burger King, which are in the same line of business, do not perform identically. Their performance may be correlated, but each has its own unique characteristics. For equity securities and with no derivatives involved, about the only such situation that could exist in reality is a stock that trades simultaneously in two different markets, such as Royal Dutch Shell, which trades in Amsterdam and London but is a single company. Clearly there can be only one price. If those two markets operate in different currencies, the currency-adjusted prices should be the same. Bonds issued by the same borrower are also potentially arbitrageable. All bonds of an issuer will be priced off of the term structure of interest rates. Because of this common factor, bonds of different maturities can be arbitraged against each other. But in general, two securities are unlikely to perform identically.

The picture changes, however, if we introduce derivatives. For most derivatives, the pay-offs come (derive) directly from the value of the underlying at the expiration of the derivative. Although no one can predict with certainty the value of the underlying at expiration, as soon as that value is determined, the value of the derivative at expiration becomes certain. So, while the performance of McDonald's stock may have a strong correlation to the performance of Burger King's stock, neither completely determines the other. But derivatives on McDonald's stock and derivatives on Burger King's stock are completely determined by their respective stocks. All of the uncertainty in a derivative comes from the uncertainty in the underlying. As a result, the price of the derivative is tied to the price of the underlying. That being the case, the derivative can be used to hedge the underlying, or vice versa.

Exhibit 5 illustrates this point. When a long position in the underlying is combined with a short position in the derivative to produce a perfect hedge, all of the risk is eliminated and the position should earn the risk-free rate. If not, arbitrageurs begin to trade. If the position generates a return in excess of the risk-free rate, the arbitrageurs see an opportunity because the hedged position of the underlying (long asset and short derivative) earns more than the risk-free rate and a risk-free loan undertaken as a borrower incurs a cost equal to the risk-free rate. Therefore, implementing the hedged position and borrowing at the risk-free rate earns a return in excess of the risk-free rate, incurs a cost of the risk-free rate, and has no risk. As a result, an investor can earn excess return at no risk without committing any capital. Arbitrageurs will execute this transaction in large volumes, continuing to exploit the pricing discrepancy until market forces push prices back in line such that both risk-free transactions earn the risk-free rate.

EXHIBIT 5   Hedging the Underlying with a Derivative (or Vice Versa)

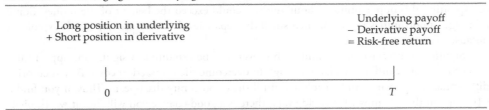

Out of this process, one and only one price can exist for the derivative. Otherwise, there will be an arbitrage opportunity. We typically take the underlying price as given and infer the unique derivative price that prohibits any arbitrage opportunities. Most derivatives pricing models are established on this foundation. We simply assume that no arbitrage opportunities can exist and infer the derivative price that guarantees there are no arbitrage opportunities.

3.3. Arbitrage and Replication

Because a long asset and a short derivative on the asset can be combined to produce a position equivalent to a risk-free bond, it follows that the long asset and a short risk-free asset (meaning to borrow at the risk-free rate) can be combined to produce a long derivative. Alternatively, a short derivative and the short risk-free asset can be combined to produce a short asset position. Exhibit 6 shows this process, referred to as **replication**. Replication is the creation of an asset or portfolio from another asset, portfolio, and/or derivative.

EXHIBIT 6   Arbitrage, Replication, and Derivatives

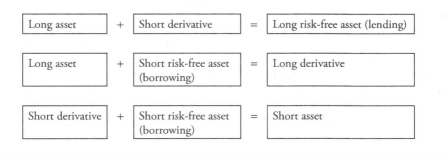

If all assets are correctly priced to prohibit arbitrage, however, the ability to replicate seems useless. Why would one replicate an asset or derivative if there is no cost advantage? Buying a government security to earn the risk-free rate is easier than buying the asset and selling a derivative to produce a risk-free position. At this point, that is certainly a reasonable question. As we progress through this material, however, we will relax the assumption that everything is always correctly priced and we will admit the possibility of occasional arbitrage opportunities. For example, it may be more profitable to hedge a portfolio with a derivative to produce a risk-free rate than to invest in the risk-free asset. In addition, we might find that replication can have lower transaction costs. For example, a derivative on a stock index combined with the risk-free asset [Long derivative (Stock index futures) + Long risk-free asset (Lending) = Long asset (Stock index)] can potentially replicate an index fund at lower transaction costs than buying all the securities in the index. Replication is the essence of arbitrage. The ability to replicate something with something else can be valuable to investors, either through pricing differentials, however temporary, or lower transaction costs.

3.4. Risk Aversion, Risk Neutrality, and Arbitrage-Free Pricing

Most investors are risk averse. They do not accept risk without the expectation of a return commensurate with that risk. Thus, they require risk premiums to justify the risk. One might think that this point implies a method for pricing derivatives based on the application of a risk premium to the expected payoff of the derivative and its risk. As we will describe later, this methodology is not appropriate in the pricing of derivatives.

As previously described, a derivative can be combined with an asset to produce a risk-free position. This fact does not mean that one *should* create such a combination. It merely means that one *can* do so. The derivative price is the price that guarantees the risk-free combination of the derivative and the underlying produces a risk-free return. The derivative price can then be inferred from the characteristics of the underlying, the characteristics of the derivative, and the risk-free rate. The investor's risk aversion is not a factor in determining the derivative price. Because the risk aversion of the investor is not relevant to pricing the derivative, one can just as easily obtain the derivative price by assuming that the investor is risk neutral. That means that the expected payoff of the derivative can be discounted at the risk-free rate rather than the risk-free rate plus a risk premium. Virtually all derivative pricing models ultimately take this form: discounting the expected payoff of the derivative at the risk-free rate.

The entire process of pricing derivatives is not exactly as we have described it at this point. There is an intermediate step, which entails altering the probabilities of the outcomes from the true probabilities to something called risk-neutral probabilities. We will illustrate this process later in this reading. The important point to understand is that while the risk aversion of investors is relevant to pricing assets, it is not relevant to pricing derivatives. As such, derivatives pricing is sometimes called **risk-neutral pricing**. Risk-neutral pricing uses the fact that arbitrage opportunities guarantee that a risk-free portfolio consisting of the underlying and the derivative must earn the risk-free rate. There is only one derivative price that meets that condition. Any mispricing of the derivative will lead to arbitrage transactions that drive the derivative price back to where it should be, the price that eliminates arbitrage opportunities.

The overall process of pricing derivatives by arbitrage and risk neutrality is called **arbitrage-free pricing**. We are effectively determining the price of a derivative by assuming that the market is free of arbitrage opportunities. This notion is also sometimes called the **principle of no arbitrage**. If there are no arbitrage opportunities, combinations of assets and/or derivatives that produce the same results must sell for the same price. The correct derivative price assures us that the market is free of arbitrage opportunities.

3.5. Limits to Arbitrage

As we previously described, there may be reasons to not pick up a coin lying on the ground. Likewise, some small arbitrage profits are never exploited. A bond selling for €1,000 might offer an arbitrage profit by trading a derivative on the bond and a risk-free asset at a total cost of €999, but the profit of €1 might be exceeded by the transaction costs. Such small differentials can easily remain essentially trapped within the bounds of transaction costs. In addition, arbitrage can require capital. Not everyone can borrow virtually unlimited amounts of money at what amounts to a risk-free rate. Moreover, some transactions can require additional capital to maintain positions. The corresponding gains from an offsetting position might not be liquid. Hence, on paper the position is hedged, but in practice, one position has a cash outflow while the other generates gains on paper that are realized only later. Borrowing against those future gains is not always easy.

Moreover, some apparent arbitrage transactions are not completely risk free. As you will learn later, option pricing requires knowledge of the volatility of the underlying asset, which is information that is not easy to obtain and subject to different opinions. Executing an arbitrage can entail risk if one lacks accurate information on the model inputs.

Some arbitrage positions require short-selling assets that can be difficult to short. Some securities are held only by investors who are unwilling to lend the securities and who, by policy, are not arbitrageurs themselves. Some commodities, in particular, can be difficult and costly to sell short. Hence, the arbitrage might exist in only one direction, which keeps the price from becoming seemingly too high or seemingly too low but permitting it to move virtually without limit in the opposite direction.

Arbitrage positions rely on the ultimate realization by other investors of the existence of the mispricing. For some investors, bearing these costs and risks until other investors drive the price back to its appropriate level can be nearly impossible.

The arbitrage principle is the essence of derivative pricing models. Yet, clearly there are limits to the ability of all investors to execute arbitrage transactions. In studying derivative pricing, it is important to accept the no-arbitrage rule as a paradigm, meaning a framework for analysis and understanding. Although no market experts think that arbitrage opportunities never occur, it is a common belief that finding and exploiting them is a challenging and highly competitive process that will not yield frequent success. But it is important that market participants stay alert for and exploit whatever arbitrage opportunities arise. In response, the market functions more efficiently.

EXAMPLE 2   Arbitrage

1. Which of the following *best* describes an arbitrage opportunity? It is an opportunity to:
   A. earn a risk premium in the short run.
   B. buy an asset at less than its fundamental value.
   C. make a profit at no risk with no capital invested.
2. What *most likely* happens when an arbitrage opportunity exists?
   A. Investors trade quickly and prices adjust to eliminate the opportunity.
   B. Risk premiums increase to compensate traders for the additional risk.
   C. Markets cease operations to eliminate the possibility of profit at no risk.
3. Which of the following *best* describes how derivatives are priced?
   A. A hedge portfolio is used that eliminates arbitrage opportunities.
   B. The payoff of the underlying is adjusted downward by the derivative value.
   C. The expected future payoff of the derivative is discounted at the risk-free rate plus a risk premium.
4. An investor who requires no premium to compensate for the assumption of risk is said to be which of the following?
   A. Risk seeking
   B. Risk averse
   C. Risk neutral
5. Which of the following is a limit to arbitrage?
   A. Clearinghouses restrict the transactions that can be arbitraged.
   B. Pricing models do not show whether to buy or sell the derivative.
   C. It may not always be possible to raise sufficient capital to engage in arbitrage.

Solution to 1: C is correct because it is the only answer that is based on the notion of when an arbitrage opportunity exists: when two identical assets or portfolios sell for different prices. A risk premium earned in the short run can easily have occurred through luck. Buying an asset at less than fair value might not even produce a profit.

Solution to 2: A is correct. The combined actions of traders push prices back in line to a level at which no arbitrage opportunities exist. Markets certainly do not shut down, and risk premiums do not adjust and, in fact, have no relevance to arbitrage profits.

Solution to 3: A is correct. A hedge portfolio is formed that eliminates arbitrage opportunities and implies a unique price for the derivative. The other answers are incorrect because the underlying payoff is not adjusted by the derivative value and the discount rate of the derivative does not include a risk premium.

Solution to 4: C is correct. Risk-seeking investors give away a risk premium because they enjoy taking risk. Risk-averse investors expect a risk premium to compensate for the risk. Risk-neutral investors neither give nor receive a risk premium because they have no feelings about risk.

Solution to 5: C is correct. It may not always be possible to raise sufficient capital to engage in arbitrage. Clearinghouses do not restrict arbitrage. Pricing models show what the price of the derivative should be.

Thus, comparison with the market price will indicate if the derivative is overpriced and should be sold or if it is underpriced and should be purchased.

4. PRICING AND VALUATION OF FORWARD CONTRACTS: PRICING VS. VALUATION; EXPIRATION; INITIATION

In equity markets, analysis is undertaken with the objective of determining the value, sometimes called the fundamental value, of a stock. When a stock trades in the market for a price that differs from its fundamental value, investors will often buy or sell the stock based on the perceived mispricing. The fundamental value of a stock is typically determined by analyzing the company's financial statements, projecting its earnings and dividends, determining a discount rate based on the risk, and finding the present value of the future dividends. These steps make up the essence of dividend discount models. Other approaches include comparing the book value of a company to its market value, thereby using book value as a proxy for fundamental value, or by application of a price/earnings ratio to projected next-period earnings, or by discounting free cash flow. Each of these approaches purports to estimate the company's fundamental value, leading to the notion that a company is worth something that may or may not correspond to its price in the market.

In derivative markets, the notion of valuation as a representation of fundamental value is still a valid concept, but the terminology can be somewhat different and can lead to some confusion. Options are not a problem in this regard. They can be analyzed to determine their fundamental value, and the market price can be compared with the fundamental value. Any difference can then presumably be exploited via arbitrage. The combined actions of numerous investors should ultimately lead to the market price converging to its fundamental value, subject to the above limits to arbitrage.

The world of forwards, futures, and swaps, however, uses different terminology with respect to price and value. These contracts do not require the outlay of cash at the start the way an option, stock, or bond does. Forwards, futures, and swaps start off with values of zero. Then as the underlying moves, their values become either positive or negative. The forward, futures, or swap price is a concept that represents the fixed price or rate at which the underlying will be purchased at a later date. It is not an amount to be paid at the start. This fixed price or rate is embedded into the contract while the value will fluctuate as market conditions change. But more importantly, the value and price are not at all comparable with each other.

Consider a simple example. Suppose you own a stock priced at $102. You have a short forward contract to sell the stock at a price of $100 one year from now. The risk-free rate is 4%. Your position is riskless because you know that one year from now, you will sell the stock for $100. Thus, you know you will get $100 one year from now, which has a present value of $100/(1.04) = $96.15. Notice the discounting at the risk-free rate, which is appropriate because the position is riskless. Your overall position is that you own an asset worth $102 and are short a contract worth something, and the two positions combine to have a value of $96.15. Therefore, the forward contract must have a value of $96.15 − $102 = −$5.85. Your forward contract is thus worth −$5.85. To the party on the opposite side, it is worth +$5.85.[7] The price of the forward contract is still $100, which was set when you created the contract at an earlier date. As you can see, the $100 forward price is not comparable to the $5.85 value of the contract.

Although the forward price is fixed, any new forward contract calling for delivery of the same asset at the same time will have a different price. We will cover that point in more detail later. For now, it is important to see that your contract has a price of $100 but a value of −$5.85, which are two entirely different orders of magnitude. This information does not imply that the forward contract is mispriced. The value is the amount of wealth represented by owning the forward contract. The price is one of the terms the parties agreed on when they created the contract.[8] This idea applies in the same manner for futures and swaps.

4.1. Pricing and Valuation of Forward Commitments

In this section, we will go into pricing forward commitments in a little more detail. Let us start by establishing that today, at time 0, we create a forward commitment that expires at time T. The value of the underlying today is S_0. At expiration the underlying value is S_T, which is not known at the initiation of the contract.

4.1.1. Pricing and Valuation of Forward Contracts

Previously, we noted that price and value are entirely different concepts for forward commitments. We gave an example of a forward contract with a price of $100 but a value of −$5.85 to the seller and +$5.85 to the buyer. In the next subsection, we will delve more deeply into understanding these concepts of pricing and valuation for forward contracts.

4.1.1.1. Pricing and Valuation of Forward Contracts at Expiration   Recall that a forward contract specifies that one party agrees to buy the underlying from the other at the expiration date at a price agreed on at the start of the contract. Suppose that you enter into a contract with another party in which you will buy a used car from that party in one year at a price of $10,000. Then $10,000 is the forward price. One year later, when the contract expires, you are committed to paying $10,000 and accepting delivery of the car. Let us say that at that time, you check the used car market and find that an identical car is worth $10,800. How much is your forward contract worth to you at that time? It obligates you to pay $10,000 for a car that you would otherwise have to pay $10,800. Thus, the contract benefits you by $800, so its value is $800. If you were on the opposite side of the transaction, its value would be −$800. If the market price of the car were below $10,000, the contract would have negative value to you and the mirror image positive value to the seller.

---

[7]This concept of the value of the forward contract as it evolves toward expiration is sometimes referred to as its mark-to-market value. The same notion is applicable to swaps. In futures, of course, contracts are automatically marked to market by the clearinghouse, and gains and losses are converted into actual cash flows from one party to the other.

[8]The forward price is more like the exercise price of the option. It is the price the two parties agree will be paid at a future date for the underlying. Of course, the option has the feature that the holder need not ever pay that price, which is the case if the holder chooses not to exercise the option.

This example leads us to our first important derivative pricing result. The forward price, established at the initiation date of contract is $F_0(T)$. Let us denote the value at expiration of the forward contract as $V_T(T)$. This value is formally stated as

$$V_T(T) = S_T - F_0(T) \tag{1}$$

In words,

> *The value of a forward contract at expiration is the spot price of the underlying minus the forward price agreed to in the contract.*

In the financial world, we generally define value as the value to the long position, so the above definition is generally correct but would be adjusted if we look at the transaction from the point of view of the short party. In that case, we would multiply the value to the long party by -1 to calculate the value to the short party. Alternatively, the value to the short party is the forward price minus the spot price at expiration.

If a forward contract could be initiated right at the instant of expiration, the forward price would clearly be the spot price. Such a contract would essentially be a spot transaction.

4.1.1.2. Pricing and Valuation at Initiation Date   In Exhibit 7, we see the nature of the problem of pricing a forward contract. We are situated at time 0, facing an uncertain future. At the horizon date, time T, the underlying price will be S_T. Of course, at time 0 we do not know what S_T will turn out to be. Yet at time 0, we need to establish the forward price, $F_0(T)$, which is the price we agree to pay at time T to purchase the asset.

EXHIBIT 7   The Time Horizon of Forward Contracts

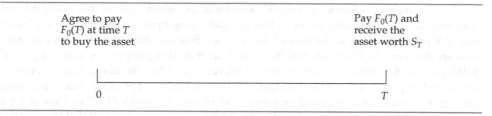

When a forward contract is initiated, neither party pays anything to the other. It is a valueless contract, neither an asset nor a liability. Therefore, its value at initiation is zero:

$$V_0(T) = 0 \tag{2}$$

The forward price that the parties agree to at the initiation date of the contract is a special price that results in the contract having zero value and prohibiting arbitrage. This is our first important result:

> *Because neither the long nor the short pays anything to the other at the initiation date of a forward contract, the value of a forward contract when initiated is zero.*

If this statement were not true and one party paid a sum of money to the other, the party receiving the money could find another party and engage in the opposite transaction, with no money paid to the other on this second contract. The two transactions would completely offset, thereby eliminating the risk. Yet, the first party would have captured some cash from the second and consequently earned an arbitrage profit because his position is completely hedged. He would walk away with money and never have to worry about paying it back. The forward price is the price the two parties agree on that generates a value of zero at the initiation date. Finding that price is actually quite easy.

Consider a very simple asset price at S_0 today that pays no dividends or interest, nor does it yield any nonfinancial benefits or incur any carrying costs. As described earlier, we can peer into the future, but at best we can make only a forecast of the price of this asset at our horizon date of time T. That forecast was previously referred to as the expected spot price at expiration, $E(S_T)$. On the surface, it might seem that pricing a forward contract would somehow involve a discounting of the expected spot price. As we said earlier, however, that is not how derivatives are priced—they are priced using arbitrage.

Suppose we hold the asset and enter into a forward contract to sell the asset at the price $F_0(T)$. It should be easy to see that we have constructed a risk-free position. We know that the asset, currently worth S_0, will be sold later at $F_0(T)$ and that this price should guarantee a risk-free return. Thus, we should find the following relationship,

$$\frac{F_0(T)}{S_0} = (1 + r)^T \qquad (3)$$

We can easily solve for the forward price to obtain

$$F_0(T) = S_0(1 + r)^T \qquad (4)$$

Or, in words,

> *The forward price is the spot price compounded at the risk-free rate over the life of the contract.*

There is a nice logic to this relationship. While the spot price is what someone would have to pay today to buy the asset, a forward contract locks in the purchase price at the horizon date. When that date arrives, the investor will own the asset. Instead of buying the asset today, suppose the investor uses the forward contract to guarantee that she will own the asset at the horizon date. By using the forward contract, the investor will not have committed the money, S_0, that would have forgone interest at the rate r for the period 0 to T. Notice how the risk premium on the asset does not directly appear in the pricing relationship. It does appear implicitly, because it determines the spot price paid to buy the asset. Knowing the spot price, however, eliminates the necessity of determining the risk premium. The derivatives market can simply let the spot market derive the risk premium.

As a simple example, let us say the underlying price, S_0, is £50, the risk-free rate, r, is 3%, and the contract expires in three months, meaning that $T = 3/12 = 0.25$. Then the forward price is £50$(1.03)^{0.25}$ = £50.37. Thus, the two parties would agree that the buyer will pay £50.37 to the seller in three months, and the seller will deliver the underlying to the buyer at expiration.

Now suppose the asset generates cash payments and/or benefits and incurs storage costs. As we discussed, the net cost of carry consists of the benefits, denoted as γ (dividends or interest plus convenience yield), minus the costs, denoted as θ, both of which are in present value form.

To put these concepts in future value form, we simply compound them at the risk-free rate, $(\gamma - \theta)(1 + r)^T$. Because this is their value at the expiration date of the contract, we can add them to $F_0(T)$ in Equation 3, thereby restating that equation as

$$(1 + r)^T = \frac{F_0(T) + (\gamma - \theta)(1 + r)^T}{S_0}$$

The numerator is how much money we end up with at T. Rearranging, we obtain the forward price as

$$F_0(T) = (S_0 - \gamma + \theta)(1 + r)^T$$

or

$$F_0(T) = S_0(1 + r)^T - (\gamma - \theta)(1 + r)^T \tag{5}$$

From Equation 5, we can see that the forward price determined using Equation 4 is reduced by the future value of any benefits and increased by the future value of any costs. In other words,

The forward price of an asset with benefits and/or costs is the spot price compounded at the risk-free rate over the life of the contract minus the future value of those benefits and costs.

Again, the logic is straightforward. To acquire a position in the asset at time T, an investor could buy the asset today and hold it until time T. Alternatively, he could enter into a forward contract, committing him to buying the asset at T at the price $F_0(T)$. He would end up at T holding the asset, but the spot transaction would yield benefits and incur costs, whereas the forward transaction would forgo the benefits but avoid the costs.

Assume the benefits exceed the costs. Then the forward transaction would return less than the spot transaction. The formula adjusts the forward price downward by the expression $-(\gamma - \theta)$ $(1 + r)^T$ to reflect this net loss over the spot transaction. In other words, acquiring the asset in the forward market would be cheaper because it forgoes benefits that exceed the costs. That does not mean the forward strategy is better. It costs less but also produces less. Alternatively, if the costs exceeded the benefits, the forward price would be higher because the forward contract avoids the costs at the expense of the lesser benefits.

Returning to our simple example, suppose the present value of the benefits is $\gamma = £3$ and the present value of the costs is $\theta = £4$. The forward price would be $£50(1.03)^{0.25} - (£3 - £4)$ $(1.03)^{0.25} = £51.38$. The forward price, which was £50.37 without these costs and benefits, is now higher because the carrying costs exceed the benefits.

The value of the contract when initiated is zero provided the forward price conforms to the appropriate pricing formula. To keep the analysis as simple as possible, consider the case in which the asset yields no benefits and incurs no costs. Going long the forward contract or going long the asset produces the same position at T: ownership of the asset. Nonetheless, the strategies are not equivalent. Going long the forward contract enables the investor to avoid having to pay the price of the asset, S_0, so she would collect interest on the money. Thus, the forward strategy would have a value of S_0, reflecting the investment of that much cash invested in risk-free bonds, plus the value of the forward contract. The spot strategy would have a value of S_0, reflecting the investment in the asset. These two strategies must have equal values. Hence, the value of the forward contract must be zero.

Although a forward contract has zero value at the start, it will not have zero value during its life. We now take a look at what happens during the life of the contract.

5. PRICING AND VALUATION OF FORWARD CONTRACTS: BETWEEN INITIATION AND EXPIRATION; FORWARD RATE AGREEMENTS

We previously worked an example in which a forward contract established with a price of $100 later has a value of −$5.85 to the seller and +$5.85 to the buyer. Generally we would say the value is $5.85. We explained that with the spot price at $102, a party that is long the asset and short the forward contract would guarantee the sale of the asset priced at $102 at a price of $100 in one year. The present value of $100 in one year at 4% is $96.15. Thus, the party guarantees that his $102 asset will be effectively sold at a present value of $96.15, for a present value loss of $5.85.

In general, we can say that

The value of a forward contract is the spot price of the underlying asset minus the present value of the forward price.

Again, the logic is simple. A forward contract provides a type of synthetic position in the asset, for which we promise to pay the forward price at expiration. Thus, the value of the forward contract is the spot price of the asset minus the present value of the forward price. Let us write out this relationship using $V_t(T)$ as the value of the forward contract at time t, which is some point in time after the contract is initiated and before it expires:

$$V_t(T) = S_t - F_0(T)(1 + r)^{-(T-t)} \qquad (6)$$

Note that we are working with the spot price at t, but the forward price was fixed when the contract was initiated.[9]

Now, recall the problem we worked in which the underlying had a price of £50 and the contract was initiated with a three-month life at a price of £50.37. Move one month later, so that the remaining time is two months: $T - t = 2/12 = 0.167$. Let the underlying price be £52. The value of the contract would be £52 − £50.37(1.03)$^{-0.167}$ = £1.88.

If the asset has a cost of carry, we must make only a small adjustment:

$$V_t(T) = S_t - (\gamma - \theta)(1 + r)^t - F_0(T)(1 + r)^{-(T-t)} \qquad (7)$$

Note how we adjust the formula by the net of benefits minus costs. The forward contract forgoes the benefits and avoids the costs of holding the asset. Consequently, we adjust the value downward to reflect the forgone benefits and upward to reflect the avoided costs. Remember that the costs (θ) and benefits (γ) are expressed on a present value basis as of time 0. We need their value at time t. We could compound them from 0 to T and then discount them back

---

[9]An alternative approach to valuing a forward contract during its life is to determine the price of a new forward contract that would offset the old one. The discounted difference between the new forward price and the original forward price will lead to the same value.

to t by the period $T - t$, but a shorter route is to simply compound them from 0 to t. In the problem we previously worked, in which we priced the forward contract when the asset has costs and benefits, the benefits (γ) were £3 and the costs (θ) were £4, giving us a forward price of £51.38. We have now moved one month ahead, so $t = 1/12 = 0.0833$ and $T - t = 2/12 = 0.167$. Hence the value of the forward contract would be £52 − (£3 − £4)(1.03)$^{0.0833}$ − £51.38(1.03)$^{-0.167}$ = £1.88. Notice how the answer is the same as in the case of no costs and benefits, as this effect is also embedded in the original forward price and completely offsets.

It is important to note that although we say that Equation 7 holds during the life of the contract at some arbitrary time t, it also holds at the initiation date and at expiration. For the initiation date, we simply change t to 0 in Equation 7. Then we substitute Equation 5 for $F_0(T)$ in Equation 7, obtaining $V_0(T) = 0$, confirming that the value of a forward contract at initiation is zero. At expiration, we let $t = T$ in Equation 7 and obtain the spot price minus the forward price, as presented in Equation 1.[10]

5.1. A Word about Forward Contracts on Interest Rates

Forward contracts in which the underlying is an interest rate are called **forward rate agreements**, or FRAs. These instruments differ slightly from most other forward contracts in that the underlying is not an asset. Changes in interest rates, such as the value of an asset, are unpredictable. Moreover, virtually every company and organization is affected by the uncertainty of interest rates. Hence, FRAs are very useful devices for many companies. FRAs are forward contracts that allow participants to make a known interest payment at a later date and receive in return an unknown interest payment. In that way, a participant whose business will involve borrowing at a future date can hedge against an increase in interest rates by buying an FRA (the long side) and locking in a fixed payment and receiving a random payment that offsets the unknown interest payment it will make on its loan. Note that the FRA seller (the short side) is hedging against a decrease in interest rates. Also, consider that the FRA seller could be a lender wishing to lock in a fixed rate on a loan it will make at a future date.

Even though FRAs do not involve an underlying asset, they can still be combined with an underlying asset to produce a hedged position, thereby leading to fairly straightforward pricing and valuation equations. The math is a little more complex than the math for forwards on assets, but the basic ideas are the same.

FRAs have often historically been based on Libor, the London Interbank Offered Rate, which represents the rate on a Eurodollar time deposit, a loan in dollars from one London bank to another. Other rates such as Euribor (Euro Interbank Offered Rate) and Tibor (Tokyo Interbank Offered Rate) have also been used.[11] As an example, assume we are interested in going long a 30-day FRA with a fixed rate (the FRA rate) in which the underlying is 90-day Libor. A long position means that in 30 days, we will make a known interest payment and receive an interest payment corresponding to the discounted difference between 90-day Libor on that day and the FRA rate. We can either enter into a 30-day FRA on 90-day Libor or create a synthetic FRA. To do the latter, we would go long a 120-day Eurodollar time deposit and short a 30-day Eurodollar time deposit. Exhibit 8 shows the structure of this strategy. We omit

---

[10]You might be wondering whether the cost and benefit terms disappear when $t = T$. With the costs and benefits defined as those incurred over the period t to T, at expiration their value is zero by definition.

[11]Libor is being phased out, as the panel of banks will no longer be required to submit quotations after 2021. In anticipation of this, market participants and regulators have been working to develop alternative reference rates.

some of the details here, such as how much face value we should take on the two Eurodollar transactions as well as the size of the FRA. Those technical issues are covered in more advanced material. At this time, we focus on the fact that going long over the 120-day period and short over the 30-day period leaves an investor with no exposure over the 30-day period and then converts to a position that starts 30 days from now and matures 90 days later. This synthetic position corresponds to a 30-day FRA on 90-day Libor. Exhibit 8 illustrates this point.[12]

EXHIBIT 8   Real FRA and Synthetic FRA (30-Day FRA on 90-Day Libor)

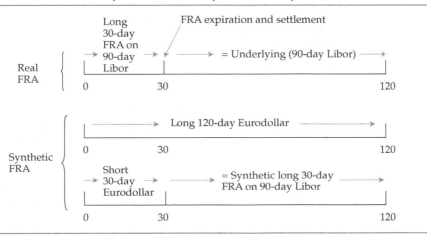

FRAs, and indeed all forward contracts relating to bonds and interest rates, are closely tied to the term structure of interest rates, a concept covered in virtually all treatments of fixed-income securities. Buying a 120-day zero-coupon bond and selling a 30-day zero-coupon bond produces a forward position in a 90-day zero-coupon bond that begins in 30 days. From that forward position, one can infer the forward rate. It would then be seen that the FRA rate *is* the forward rate, even though the derivative itself is not a forward contract on a bond.

EXAMPLE 3   Forward Contract Pricing and Valuation

1. Which of the following *best* describes the difference between the price of a forward contract and its value?
   A. The forward price is fixed at the start, and the value starts at zero and then changes.
   B. The price determines the profit to the buyer, and the value determines the profit to the seller.
   C. The forward contract value is a benchmark against which the price is compared for the purposes of determining whether a trade is advisable.

---

[12]The real FRA we show appears to imply that an investor enters into a Eurodollar transaction in 30 days that matures 90 days later. This is not technically true. The investor does, however, engage in a cash settlement in 30 days that has the same value and economic form as such a transaction. Specifically, settlement at expiration of the FRA is an amount equal to the discounted difference between the underlying 90-day Libor rate on that day and the FRA rate multiplied by a notional principal amount. These details are covered in the Level II and Level III CFA Program curriculum.

2. Which of the following *best* describes the value of the forward contract at expiration? The value is the price of the underlying:
   A. minus the forward price.
   B. divided by the forward price.
   C. minus the compounded forward price.
3. Which of the following factors does *not* affect the forward price?
   A. The costs of holding the underlying
   B. Dividends or interest paid by the underlying
   C. Whether the investor is risk averse, risk seeking, or risk neutral
4. Which of the following *best* describes the forward rate of an FRA?
   A. The spot rate implied by the term structure
   B. The forward rate implied by the term structure
   C. The rate on a zero-coupon bond of maturity equal to that of the forward contract

Solution to 1: A is correct. The forward price is fixed at the start, whereas the value starts at zero and then changes. Both price and value are relevant in determining the profit for both parties. The forward contract value is not a benchmark for comparison with the price.

Solution to 2: A is correct because the holder of the contract gains the difference between the price of the underlying and the forward price. That value can, of course, be negative, which will occur if the holder is forced to buy the underlying at a price higher than the market price.

Solution to 3: C is correct. The costs of holding the underlying, known as carrying costs, and the dividends and interest paid by the underlying are extremely relevant to the forward price. How the investor feels about risk is irrelevant, because the forward price is determined by arbitrage.

Solution to 4: B is correct. FRAs are based on Libor, and they represent forward rates, not spot rates. Spot rates are needed to determine forward rates, but they are not equal to forward rates. The rate on a zero-coupon bond of maturity equal to that of the forward contract describes a spot rate.

As noted, we are not covering the details of derivative pricing but rather are focusing on the intuition. At this point, we have covered the intuition of pricing forward contracts. We now move to futures contracts.

6. PRICING AND VALUATION OF FUTURES CONTRACTS

Futures contracts differ from forward contracts in that they have standard terms, are traded on a futures exchange, and are more heavily regulated, whereas forward contracts are typically private, customized transactions. Perhaps the most important distinction is that they are marked to market on a daily basis, meaning that the accumulated gains and losses from the previous day's trading session are deducted from the accounts of those holding losing positions and transferred to the accounts of those holding winning positions. This daily settling of gains and losses enables the futures exchange to guarantee that a party that earns a profit from a futures transaction will not have to worry about collecting the money. Thus, futures exchanges provide a credit guarantee, which is facilitated through the use of a clearinghouse. The clearinghouse collects and disburses cash flows from the parties on a daily basis, thereby settling obligations quickly before they accumulate to much larger amounts. There is no absolute assurance that a clearinghouse will not fail, but none has ever done so since the first one was created in the 1920s.

The pattern of cash flows in a futures contract is quite similar to that in a forward contract. Suppose you enter into a forward contract two days before expiration in which you agree to buy an asset at €100, the forward price. Two days later, the asset is selling for €103, and the contract expires. You therefore pay €100 and receive an asset worth €103, for a gain of €3. If the contract were cash settled, instead of involving physical delivery, you would receive €3 in cash, which you could use to defer a portion of the cost of the asset. The net effect is that you are buying the asset for €103, paying €100 plus the €3 profit on the forward contract.

Had you chosen a futures contract, the futures price at expiration would still converge to the spot price of €103. But now it would matter what the futures settlement price was on the next to last day. Let us assume that price was €99. That means on the next to last day, your account would be marked to market for a loss of €1, the price of €100 having fallen to €99. That is, you would be charged €1, with the money passed on to the opposite party. But then on the last day, your position would be marked from €99 to €103, a gain of €4. Your net would be €1 lost on the first day and €4 gained on the second for a total of €3. In both situations you gain €3, but with the forward contract, you gain it all at expiration, whereas with the futures contract, you gain it over two days. With this two-day example, the interest on the interim cash flow would be virtually irrelevant, but over longer periods and with sufficiently high interest rates, the difference in the amount of money you end up with could be noticeable.

The value of a futures contract is the accumulated gain or loss on a futures contract since its previous day's settlement. When that value is paid out in the daily settlement, the futures price is effectively reset to the settlement price and the value goes to zero. The different patterns of cash flows for forwards and futures can lead to differences in the pricing of forwards versus futures. But there are some conditions under which the pricing is the same. It turns out that if interest rates were constant, forwards and futures would have the same prices. The differential will vary with the volatility of interest rates. In addition, if futures prices and interest rates are uncorrelated, forwards and futures prices will be the same. If futures prices are positively correlated with interest rates, futures contracts are more desirable to holders of long positions than are forwards. The reason is because rising prices lead to futures profits that are reinvested in periods of rising interest rates, and falling prices leads to losses that occur in periods of falling interest rates. It is far better to receive cash flows in the interim than all at expiration under such conditions. This condition makes futures more attractive than forwards, and therefore their prices will be higher than forward prices. A negative correlation between futures prices and interest rates leads to the opposite interpretation, with forwards being more desirable than futures to the long position. The more desirable contract will tend to have the higher price.

The practical realities, however, are that the derivatives industry makes virtually no distinction between futures and forward prices.[13] Thus, we will make no distinction between futures and forward pricing, except possibly in noting some subtle issues that may arise from time to time.

---

[13]At the time of this writing, many forwards (and swaps) are being processed through clearinghouses, a response to changes brought about by key legislation in several countries that was adopted following the financial crises of 2008. These OTC instruments are thus being effectively marked to market in a similar manner to the futures contracts described here. The full extent of this evolution of OTC trading through clearinghouses is not yet clear.

EXAMPLE 4   Futures Pricing and Valuation

1. Which of the following *best* describes how futures contract payoffs differ from forward contract payoffs?
   A. Forward contract payoffs are larger.
   B. They are equal, ignoring the time value of money.
   C. Futures contract payoffs are larger if the underlying is a commodity.
2. Which of the following conditions will not make futures and forward prices equivalent?
   A. Interest rates are constant.
   B. Futures prices are uncorrelated with interest rates.
   C. The volatility of the forward price is different from the volatility of the futures price.
3. With respect to the value of a futures contract, which of the following statements is *most* accurate? The value is the:
   A. futures price minus the spot price.
   B. present value of the expected payoff at expiration.
   C. accumulated gain since the previous settlement, which resets to zero upon settlement.

Solution to 1: B is correct. Forward payoffs occur all at expiration, whereas futures payoffs occur on a day-to-day basis but would equal forward payoffs ignoring interest. Payoffs could differ, so forward payoffs are not always larger. The type of underlying is not relevant to the point of which payoff is larger.

Solution to 2: C is correct. Constant interest rates or the condition that futures prices are uncorrelated with interest rates will make forward and futures prices equivalent. The volatility of forward and futures prices has no relationship to any difference.

Solution to 3: C is correct. Value accumulates from the previous settlement and goes to zero when distributed.

---

7. PRICING AND VALUATION OF SWAP CONTRACTS

Recall the structure of a forward contract, as depicted in Exhibit 7. The investor is at time 0 and needs to determine the price, $F_0(T)$, that she will agree to pay at time T to purchase the asset. This price is set such that there is no value to the contract at that time. Value can arise later as prices change, but when initiated, the contract has zero value. Neither party pays anything to the other at the start.

Now consider a swap starting at time 0 and ending at time T. We will let this swap be the type that involves a fixed payment exchanged for a floating payment. The contract specifies that the two parties will make a series of n payments at times that we will designate as 1, 2, ..., n, with the last payment occurring at time T. On each of these payment dates, the owner of the swap makes a payment of $FS_0(n, T)$ and receives a payment based on the value of the underlying at the time of each respective payment, $S_1, S_2, ..., S_n$. So from the point of view of the buyer, the sequence of cash flows from the swap is $S_1 - FS_0(n, T)$, $S_2 - FS_0(n, T)$, ..., $S_n - FS_0(n, T)$. The notation $FS_0(n, T)$ denotes the fixed payment established at time 0 for a swap consisting of n payments with the last payment at time T. We denote the time to each payment as t_1, t_2, ..., t_n, where $t_n = T$. This structure is shown in Exhibit 9.

EXHIBIT 9   Structure of Cash Flows in a Swap

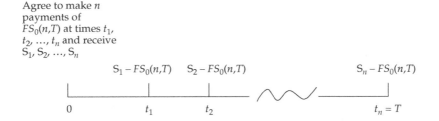

Comparing Exhibit 7 with Exhibit 9 reveals some similarities. A swap is in some sense a series of forward contracts, specifically a set of contracts expiring at various times in which one party agrees to make a fixed payment and receive a variable payment. Now consider Exhibit 10, which breaks down a swap into a series of implicit forward contracts, with the expiration of each forward contract corresponding to a swap payment date.

EXHIBIT 10   A Swap as a Series of Forward Contracts

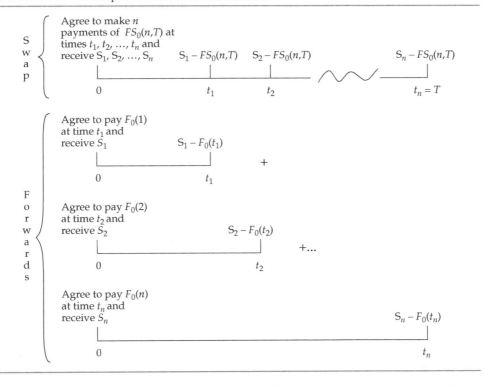

Recall from the material on forward contracts that the forward price is determined by the spot price and the net cost of carry (Equation 5), the latter being partially determined by the length of time of the contract. It should be obvious that a forward contract expiring at time t_1

will not have the same price, $F_0(t_1)$, as a forward contract expiring at time t_2, $F_0(t_2)$, and likewise for all of the implicit remaining forward contracts expiring up through time t_n. The cost of carrying an asset over different time periods will vary by the length of the time periods. In other words, the prices of the implicit forward contracts embedded in a swap will not be equal:

$$F_0(t_1) \neq F_0(t_2) \neq \ldots \neq F_0(t_n)$$

But for a swap, all the fixed payments are equal. So, how can we equate a swap to a series of forward contracts? It turns out that we can, and in doing so, we recall a valuable point about forward pricing.

Recall that the forward price is the price that produces a zero value of the contract at the start. Zero value is essential if there is no exchange of cash flows from one party to the other. And although no exchange of cash flows is customary, it is not mandatory. The parties could agree on any forward price at the start. If the zero-value forward price were $30 and the parties agreed on a price of $28, it should be apparent that the buyer would be getting a great price. The seller, being rational, would require that the buyer compensate him at the start. The seller should be getting $30 at expiration and instead will get $28. So the buyer should compensate the seller to the amount of the present value of $2 at expiration. If the parties agree on a price greater than $30, similar compensation would have to be paid from seller to buyer.

A forward transaction that starts with a zero value is called an at-market forward. A forward transaction that starts with a nonzero value is called an off-market forward. There is generally no prohibition on the use of off-market forward contracts, so two parties can engage in a series of forward contracts at whatever fixed price they so desire. Assume they agree on the price $FS_0(T)$. That is, each forward contract will be created at the fixed price that corresponds to the fixed price of a swap of the same maturity with payments made at the same dates as the series of forward contracts. That means that some of the forward contracts would have positive values and some would have negative values, but their combined values would equal zero.

Now, it sounds like that price would be hard to find, but it is not. We would not, however, go about finding it by taking random guesses. Doing so would take seemingly forever. Along the way, we would notice that some of these implicit forward contracts would have positive values and some would have negative values. If the positives outweighed the negatives, then the overall swap value would be positive, which is too high. Likewise, we might plug in a number that would produce an overall negative value, with the implicit forward contract values tending to be predominantly negative, which is too low.

Not surprisingly, we can find that price easily by appealing to the principle of arbitrage. We said that the principle of arbitrage will guide us *all the way through* derivative pricing. We will omit the details, but here is the general idea.

Suppose we buy an asset that pays the amounts S_1, S_2, ..., S_n at times t_1, t_2, ..., t_n. These are unknown amounts. A simple example would be a floating-rate bond for which the S values represent the coupons that are unknown at the start but ultimately are determined by the evolution of interest rates. Then suppose we finance the purchase of that asset by borrowing money that we promise to repay with equal fixed payments of $FS_0(T)$. That strategy replicates the swap. As you have already learned, replication is the key to pricing.

Valuation of the swap during its life again appeals to replication and the principle of no arbitrage. We will find a way to reproduce the remaining payments on the swap with other transactions. The value of that strategy is the value of the swap.

To obtain the fixed rate on the swap or to value it later during its life, we will need information from the market for the underlying. As we previously noted, there are derivatives on bonds and interest rates, equities, currencies, and commodities. It is not possible to provide a general and simple statement of how to price swaps that covers all of these cases, but that topic is covered in advanced material.

EXAMPLE 5   Swap Pricing and Valuation

1. A swap is equivalent to a series of:
   A. forward contracts, each created at the swap price.
   B. long forward contracts, matched with short futures contracts.
   C. forward contracts, each created at their appropriate forward prices.
2. If the present value of the payments in a forward contract or swap is not zero, which of the following is most likely to be true?
   A. The contract cannot legally be created.
   B. The contract must be replicated by another contract with zero value.
   C. The party whose stream of payments to be received is greater has to pay the other party the present value difference.

Solution to 1: A is correct. Each implicit forward contract is said to be off-market, because it is created at the swap price, not the appropriate forward price, which would be the price created in the forward market.

Solution to 2: C is correct. The party whose stream of payments to be received is greater has to pay the other party the present value difference. Such a contract can legally be created, but the party receiving the greater present value must compensate the other party with a cash payment at the start. Replication is never required.

---

8. PRICING AND VALUATION OF OPTIONS

Unlike a forward, futures, or swap contract, an option is clearly an asset to the holder and a liability to the seller. The buyer of an option pays a sum of money, called the premium, and receives the right to buy (a call) or sell (a put) the underlying. The seller receives the premium and undertakes a potential obligation because the buyer has the right, but not the obligation, to exercise the option. Options are, therefore, contingent claims. Pricing the option is the same as assigning its value. Some confusion from that terminology may still arise, in that an option could trade in the market for an amount that differs from its value.

As mentioned, there are two general types of options. Calls represent the right to buy, and puts represent the right to sell. There are also two important exercise characteristics of options. American options allow exercise at any time up to the expiration, while European options allow exercise only at expiration. It is important to understand that the terms "American" and "European" have no relationship to where the options are traded. Because the right to exercise can be a complex feature of an option, European options are easier to understand, and we will focus on them first.

We will use the same notation used with forwards. We start by assuming that today is time 0, and the option expires at time T. The underlying is an asset currently priced at S_0, and at time T, its price is S_T. Of course, we do not know S_T until we get to the expiration. The option has an exercise or strike price of X. The symbols we use are as follows:

For calls,
> c_0 = value (price) of European call today
> c_T = value (price) of European call at expiration
> C_0 = value (price) of American call today
> C_T = value (price) of American call at expiration

For puts,
> p_0 = value (price) of European put today
> p_T = value (price) of European put at expiration
> P_0 = value (price) of American put today
> P_T = value (price) of American put at expiration

8.1. European Option Pricing

Recall that in studying forward contracts earlier in this reading, the first thing we learned is how a forward contract pays off at expiration. Then we backed up and determined how forward contracts are priced and valued prior to expiration. We follow that same approach for options.

8.1.1. Value of a European Option at Expiration

Recall that a European call option allows the holder to buy the underlying at expiration by paying the exercise price. Therefore, exercise is justified only if the value of the underlying exceeds the exercise price. Otherwise, the holder would simply let the call expire. So if the call is worth exercising ($S_T > X$), the holder pays X and receives an asset worth S_T. Thus, the option is worth $S_T - X$. If the call is not worth exercising ($S_T \geq X$), the option simply expires and is worth nothing at expiration.[14] Thus, the value of the option at expiration is the greater of either zero or the underlying price at expiration minus the exercise price, which is typically written as

$$c_T = \text{Max}(0, S_T - X) \tag{8}$$

This formula is also sometimes referred to as the **exercise value** or **intrinsic value**. In this reading, we will use the term exercise value.

Taking a simple example, if the exercise price is €40 and the underlying price is at expiration €43, the call is worth $c_T = \text{Max}(€0, €43 - €40) = \text{Max}(€0, €3) = €3$. If the underlying price at expiration is €39, the call is worth $c_T = \text{Max}(0, €39 - €40) = \text{Max}(€0, -€1) = €0$.

---

[14]In all the remaining material, we identify conditions at expiration, such as $S_T > X$ and $S_T \leq X$. Here we merged the equality case ($S_T = X$) with the less-than case (<). We could have done it the other way around ($S_T < X$ and $S_T \geq X$), which would have had no effect on our interpretations or any calculations of option value. For convenience, in some situations we will use one specification and in some the other.

For puts, the holder has the right to sell the underlying at X. If the underlying is worth less than X at expiration $(X > S_T)$, the put will be exercised and worth $X - S_T$ because it allowed the holder to avoid the loss in value of the asset of that amount. If the underlying is equal to or worth more than the exercise price at expiration $(S_T \geq X)$, the put will simply expire with no value. So, the put is worth the greater of either zero or the exercise price minus the price of the underlying at expiration.

$$p_T = \text{Max}(0, X - S_T) \tag{9}$$

As discussed above, this formula is referred to as the exercise value or intrinsic value, and as noted, we will use the term exercise value.

Using the same example as with the call, if the underlying is €43 at expiration, the put is worth $p_T = \text{Max}(€0, €40 - €43) = \text{Max}(0, -€3) = €0$. If the underlying is €39 at expiration, the put is worth $p_T = \text{Max}(€0, €40 - €39) = \text{Max}(€0, €1) = €1$.

Thus, the holder of an option looks out into the future and sees these relationships as the payoff possibilities. That does not mean the holder knows what S_T will be, but the holder knows that all of the uncertainty of the option payoff is determined by the behavior of the underlying.

The results of this section can be restated as follows:

The value of a European call at expiration is the exercise value, which is the greater of zero or the value of the underlying minus the exercise price.

The value of a European put at expiration is the exercise value, which is the greater of zero or the exercise price minus the value of the underlying.

To understand option pricing, we have to work our way forward in a gradual manner. The next valuable steps involve using our intuition to identify some characteristics that will influence the value of the option. We might not be able to quantify their effects just yet, but we can rationalize why these factors affect the value of an option.

8.1.2. Effect of the Value of the Underlying

The value of the underlying is obviously a critical element in determining the value of an option. It is the uncertainty of the underlying that provides the motivation for using options. It is easy to rationalize the direction of the effect of the underlying.

A call option can be viewed as a mean of acquiring the underlying, whereas a put option can be viewed as a means of selling the underlying. Thus, a call option is logically worth more if the underlying is worth more, and a put option is logically worth more if the underlying is worth less.

The value of the underlying also forms one of the boundaries for calls. The value of a call option cannot exceed the value of the underlying. After all, a call option is only a means of acquiring the underlying. It can never give the holder more benefit than the underlying. Hence, the value of the underlying forms an upper boundary on what a call is worth. The underlying does not provide an upper or lower boundary for puts. That role is played by the exercise price, as we will see in the next section.

To recap what we learned here,

The value of a European call option is directly related to the value of the underlying.

The value of a European put option is inversely related to the value of the underlying.

8.1.3. Effect of the Exercise Price

The exercise price is a critical factor in determining the value of an option. The exercise price is the hurdle beyond which the underlying must go to justify exercise. For a call, the underlying must rise above the exercise price, and for a put, the underlying must fall below the exercise price, to justify exercise. When the underlying is beyond the exercise price in the appropriate direction (higher for a call, lower for a put), the option is said to be **in the money**. When the underlying is precisely at the exercise price, the option is said to be **at the money**. When the underlying has not reached the exercise price (currently lower for a call, higher for a put), the option is said to be **out of the money**. This characterization of whether the option is in-, at-, or out-of-the-money is referred to as the option's **moneyness**.

For a call option, a lower exercise price has two benefits. One is that there are more values of the underlying at expiration that are above the exercise price, meaning that there are more outcomes in which the call expires in-the-money. The other benefit is that assuming the call expires in-the-money, for any value of the underlying, the option value is greater the lower the exercise price. In other words, at expiration the underlying value S_T will be above the exercise price far more often, the lower is X. And if S_T is indeed higher than X, the payoff of $S_T - X$ is greater, the lower is X.

For puts, the effect is just the opposite. To expire in-the-money, the value of the underlying must fall below the exercise price. The higher the exercise price, the better chance the underlying has of getting below it. Likewise, if the value of the underlying does fall below the exercise price, the higher the exercise price, the greater the payoff. So, if X is higher, S_T will be below it more often, and if S_T is less than X, the payoff of $X - S_T$ is greater, the higher is X for whatever value of S_T occurs.

The exercise price also helps form an upper bound for the value of a European put. If you were holding a European put, the best outcome you could hope for is a zero value of the underlying. For equities, that would mean complete failure and dissolution of the company with shareholders receiving no final payment.[15] In that case, the put would pay $X - S_T$, but with S_T at zero, the put would pay X. If the underlying value goes to zero during the life of the European put, however, the holder cannot collect that payoff until expiration. Nonetheless, the holder would have a risk-free claim on a payoff of X at expiration. Thus, the most the put would be worth is the present value of X, meaning X discounted from expiration to the current day at the risk-free rate.[16] Although the holder cannot collect the payoff by exercising the option, he could sell it for the present value of X.

---

[15]You might think this point means that people who buy puts are hoping the company goes bankrupt, a seemingly morbid motivation. Yet, put buyers are often people who own the stock and buy the put for protection. This motivation is no different from owning a house and buying fire insurance. You do not want the house to burn down. If your sole motivation in buying the insurance were to make a profit on the insurance, you would want the house to burn down. This moral hazard problem illustrates why it is difficult, if not impossible, to buy insurance on a house you do not own. Likewise, executives are prohibited from owning puts on their companies' stock. Individual investors can own puts on stocks they do not own, because they cannot drive the stock price down.

[16] For the put holder to truly have a risk-free claim on X at expiration, given zero value of the underlying today, the underlying value must go to zero and have no possibility of any recovery. If there is any possibility of recovery, the underlying value would not go to zero, as is often observed when a legal filing for bankruptcy is undertaken. Many equities do recover. If there were some chance of recovery but the equity value was zero, demand for the stock would be infinite, which would push the price up.

To recap these results,

The value of a European call option is inversely related to the exercise price.

The value of a European put option is directly related to the exercise price.

8.1.4. Effect of Time to Expiration

Logic suggests that longer-term options should be worth more than shorter-term options. That statement is usually true but not always. A call option unquestionably benefits from additional time. For example, the right to buy an asset for $50 is worth a lot more if that right is available for two years instead of one. The additional time provides further opportunity for the underlying to rise above the exercise price. Although that means there is also additional time for the underlying to fall below the exercise price, it hardly matters to the holder of the call because the loss on the downside is limited to the premium paid.

For a European put option, the additional time still provides more opportunity for the underlying price to fall below the exercise price, but with the additional risk of it rising above the exercise price mitigated by the limited loss of the premium if the put expires out-of-the-money. Thus, it sounds as if puts benefit from longer time, but that is not necessarily true. There is a subtle penalty for this additional time. Put option holders are awaiting the sale of the underlying, for which they will receive the exercise price. The longer they have to wait, the lower the present value of the payoff. For some puts, this negative effect can dwarf the positive effect. This situation occurs with a put the longer the time to expiration, the higher the risk-free rate of interest, and the deeper it is in-the-money. The positive effect of time, however, is somewhat more dominant.

Note that we did not mention this effect for calls. For calls, the holder is waiting to pay out money at expiration. More time lowers the value of this possible outlay. Hence, a longer time period helps call option buyers in this regard.

To recap these results,

The value of a European call option is directly related to the time to expiration.

The value of a European put option can be either directly or inversely related to the time to expiration. The direct effect is more common, but the inverse effect can prevail with a put the longer the time to expiration, the higher the risk-free rate, and the deeper it is in-the-money.

8.1.5. Effect of the Risk-Free Rate of Interest

We have already alluded to the effect of the risk-free rate. For call options, a longer time to expiration means that the present value of the outlay of the exercise price is lower. In other words, with a longer time to expiration, the call option holder continues to earn interest on the money that could be expended later in paying the exercise price upon exercise of the option. If the option is ultimately never exercised, this factor is irrelevant, but it remains at best a benefit and at worst has no effect. For puts, the opposite argument prevails. A longer time to expiration with a higher interest rate lowers the present value of the receipt of the exercise price upon exercise. Thus, the value today of what the put holder might receive at expiration is lower. If the put is ultimately never exercised, the risk-free rate has no effect. Thus, at best, a higher risk-free rate has no effect on the value of a put. At worst, it decreases the value of the put.

These results are summarized as follows:

The value of a European call is directly related to the risk-free interest rate.

The value of a European put is inversely related to the risk-free interest rate.

8.1.6. Effect of Volatility of the Underlying

In studying the pricing of equities, we are conditioned to believe that volatility has a negative effect. After all, investors like return and dislike risk. Volatility is certainly an element of risk. Therefore, volatility is bad for investors, right? Well, partially right.

First, not all volatility is bad for investors. Unsystematic volatility should be irrelevant. Investors can hold diversified portfolios. Systematic volatility is clearly undesirable, but do not think that this means that volatility should be completely avoided where possible. If volatility were universally undesirable, no one would take risks. Clearly risks have to be taken to provide opportunity for reward.

With options, volatility of the underlying is, however, universally desirable. The greater the volatility of the underlying, the more an option is worth. This seemingly counterintuitive result is easy to understand with a little explanation.

First, let us make sure we know what volatility really means. In studying asset returns, we typically represent volatility with the standard deviation of the return, which measures the variation from the average return. The S&P 500 Index has an approximate long-run volatility of around 20%. Under the assumption of a normal distribution, a standard deviation of 20% implies that about 68% of the time, the returns will be within plus or minus one standard deviation of the average. About 95% of the time, they will be within plus or minus two standard deviations of the average. About 99% of the time, they will be within plus or minus three standard deviations of the average. When the distribution is non-normal, different interpretations apply, and in some extreme cases, the standard deviation can be nearly impossible to interpret.

Standard deviation is not the only notion of volatility, however, and it is not even needed at this point. You can proceed fairly safely with a measure as simple as the highest possible value minus the lowest, known as the range. The only requirement we need right now is that the concept of volatility reflects dispersion—how high and how low the underlying can go.

So, regardless of how we measure volatility, the following conditions will hold:

1. A call option will have a higher payoff the higher the underlying is at expiration.
2. A call option will have a zero payoff if it expires with the underlying below the exercise price.

If we could impose greater volatility on the underlying, we should be able to see that in Condition 1, the payoff has a better chance of being greater because the underlying has a greater possibility of large positive returns. In Condition 2, however, the zero payoff is unaffected if we impose greater volatility. Expiring more out-of-the-money is not worse than expiring less out-of-the-money, but expiring more in-the-money is better than expiring less-in-the-money.[17]

---

[17]Think of an option expiring out-of-the-money as like it being dead. (Indeed, the option is dead.) Being "more dead" is not worse than being "less dead."

For puts, we have

1. A put option will have a higher payoff the lower the underlying is at expiration.
2. A put option will have a zero payoff if it expires with the underlying above the exercise price.

If we could impose greater volatility, we would find that it would have a beneficial effect in (1) because a larger positive payoff would have a greater chance of occurring. In (2), the zero payoff is unaffected. The greater of the option expiring more out-of-the-money is irrelevant. Expiring more out-of-the-money is not worse than expiring less out-of-the-money.

Thus, we summarize our results in this section as

The value of a European call is directly related to the volatility of the underlying.

The value of a European put is directly related to the volatility of the underlying.

The combined effects of time and volatility give rise to the concept of the time value of an option. The **time value** of an option is the difference between the market price of the option and its intrinsic value. It represents the market valuation of the potential for higher exercise value relative to the potential for lower exercise value given the volatility of the underlying. Time value of an option is not to be confused with the time value of money, which is the notion of money later being worth less than money today as a result of the combined effects of time and interest. Time value results in an option price being greater with volatility and time but declining as expiration approaches. At expiration, no time value remains and the option is worth only its exercise value. As such, an option price is said to decay over time, a process characterized as **time value decay**, which is covered in more advanced material.

8.1.7. Effect of Payments on the Underlying and the Cost of Carry

We previously discussed how payments on the underlying and carrying costs enter into the determination of forward prices. They also affect option prices. Payments on the underlying refer to dividends on stocks and interest on bonds. In addition, some commodities offer a convenience yield benefit. Carrying costs include the actual physical costs of maintaining and/or storing an asset.

Let us first consider the effect of benefits. Payments of dividends and interest reduce the value of the underlying. Stocks and bonds fall in value as dividends and interest are paid. These benefits to holders of these securities do not flow to holders of options. For call option holders, this reduction is a negative factor. The price of the underlying is hurt by such payments, and call holders do not get to collect these payments. For put holders, the effect is the opposite. When the value of the underlying is reduced, put holders are helped.

Carrying costs have the opposite effect. They raise the effective cost of holding or shorting the asset. Holding call options enables an investor to participate in movements of the underlying without incurring these costs. Holding put options makes it more expensive to participate in movements in the underlying than by short selling because short sellers benefit from carrying costs, which are borne by owners of the asset.

To summarize the results from this section,

A European call option is worth less the more benefits that are paid by the underlying and worth more the more costs that are incurred in holding the underlying.

A European put option is worth more the more benefits that are paid by the underlying and worth less the more costs that are incurred in holding the underlying.

9. LOWER LIMITS FOR PRICES OF EUROPEAN OPTIONS

What we have learned so far forms a framework for understanding how European options are priced. Let us now go a step further and establish a minimum price for these options.

First, we need to look at a call option as similar to the purchase of the underlying with a portion of the purchase price financed by borrowing. If the underlying is a stock, this transaction is usually called a margin transaction. Assume that the underlying is worth S_0. Also assume that you borrow cash in the amount of the present value of X, promising to pay X back T periods later at an interest rate of r. Thus, $X/(1 + r)^T$ is the amount borrowed, and X is the amount to be paid back. Now move forward to time T and observe the price of the underlying, S_T. Upon paying back the loan, the overall strategy will be worth $S_T - X$, which can be positive or negative.

Next, consider an alternative strategy of buying a call option expiring at T with an exercise price of X, the same value as the face value of the loan. We know that the option payoffs will be $S_T - X$ if it expires in-the- money ($S_T > X$) and zero if not ($S_T \leq X$). Exhibit 11 compares these two strategies.[18]

EXHIBIT 11   Call Option vs. Leveraged (Margin) Transaction

	Outcome at T	
	Call Expires Out-of-the-Money ($S_T \leq X$)	Call Expires In-the-Money ($S_T > X$)
Call	0	$S_T - X$
Leveraged transaction		
Asset	S_T	S_T
Loan	$-X$	$-X$
Total	$S_T - X$	$S_T - X$

When the call expires in-the-money, both transactions produce identical payoffs. When the call expires out-of-the-money, the call value is zero, but the leveraged transaction is almost surely a loss. Its value $S_T - X$ is negative or zero at best (if S_T is exactly equal to X).

If two strategies are found to produce equivalent results in some outcomes but one produces a better result in all other outcomes, then one strategy dominates the former. Here we see that the call strategy dominates the leveraged strategy. Any strategy that dominates the other can never have a lower value at any time. Why would anyone pay more for one strategy than for another if the former will never produce a better result than the latter? Thus, the value of the call strategy, c_0, has to be worth at least the value of the leveraged transaction, S_0 (the value of the asset), minus $X/(1 + r)^T$ (the value of the loan). Hence, $c_0 \geq S_0 - X/(1 + r)^T$.

The inequality means that this statement provides the lowest price of the call, but there is one more thing we need to do. It can easily be true that $X/(1 + r)^T > S_0$. In that case, we are

---

[18]Note in Exhibit 11, and in others to come, that the inequality $\leq$ is referred to as out-of-the-money. The case of equality is technically referred to as at-the-money but the verbiage is simplified if we continue to call it out-of-the-money. It is certainly not in-the-money and at-the-money is arguably the same as out-of-the-money. Regardless of one's preference, the equality case can be attached to either of the two outcomes with no effect on our conclusions.

saying that the lowest value is a negative number, but that statement is meaningless. A call can never be worth less than zero, because its holder cannot be forced to exercise it. Thus, we tend to express this relationship as

$$c_0 \geq \text{Max}\left[0, S_0 - X/(1 + r)^T\right] \tag{10}$$

which represents the greater of the value of zero or the underlying price minus the present value of the exercise price. This value becomes the lower limit of the call price.

Now consider an analogous result for puts. Suppose we want to profit from a declining price of the underlying. One way to do this is to sell the underlying short. Suppose we do that and invest cash equal to the present value of X into risk-free bonds that pay X at time T. At time T, given a price of the underlying of S_T, the short sale pays off $-S_T$, a reflection of the payment of S_T to cover the short sale. The bonds pay X. Hence, the total payoff is $X - S_T$.

Now, compare that result with the purchase of a put expiring at T with exercise price of X. If the put expires in-the-money ($S_T < X$), it is worth $X - S_T$. If it expires out-of-the-money ($S_T \geq X$), it is worth zero. Exhibit 12 illustrates the comparison of the put with the short sale and bond strategy. We see that for the in-the-money case, the put and short sale and bond strategies match each other. For the out-of-the-money case, however, the put performs better because the short sale and bond strategy pays $X - S_T$. With $S_T \geq X$, this payment amount is negative. With the put dominating the short sale and bond strategy, the put value cannot be less than the value of the short sale and bond strategy, meaning $p_0 \geq X/(1 + r)^T - S_0$. But as with calls, the right-hand side can be negative, and it hardly helps us to say that a put must sell for more than a negative number. A put can never be worth less than zero, because its owner cannot be forced to exercise it. Thus, the overall result is expressed succinctly as

$$p_0 \geq \text{Max}\left[0, X/(1 + r)^T - S_0\right] \tag{11}$$

EXHIBIT 12   Put vs. Short Sale and Bond Purchase

	Outcome at T	
	Put Expires In-the-Money ($S_T < X$)	Put Expires Out-of-the-Money ($S_T \geq X$)
Put	$X - S_T$	0
Short sale and bond purchase		
Short sale	$-S_T$	$-S_T$
Bond	X	X
Total	$X - S_T$	$X - S_T$

Let us look at some basic examples. Assume the exercise price is €60, the risk-free rate is 4%, and the expiration is nine months, so $T = 9/12 = 0.75$. Consider two cases:

Underlying: $S_0 = $ €70

$$\text{Minimum call price} = \text{Max}[0, €70 - €60/(1.04)^{0.75}] = \text{Max}(0, €11.74) = €11.74$$

$$\text{Minimum put price} = \text{Max}[0, €60/(1.04)^{0.75} - €70] = \text{Max}(0, -€11.74) = €0.00$$

Underlying: $S_0 = €50$

Minimum call price = $Max[0, €50 - €60/(1.04)^{0.75}] = Max(0, -€8.26) = €0.00$

Minimum put price = $Max[0, €60/(1.04)^{0.75} - €50] = Max(0, €8.26) = €8.26$

To recap, in this section we have established lower limits for call and put option values. Formally restating these results in words,

The lowest value of a European call is the greater of zero or the value of the underlying minus the present value of the exercise price.

The lowest value of a European put is the greater of zero or the present value of the exercise price minus the value of the underlying.

EXAMPLE 6   Basic Principles of European Option Pricing

1. Which of the following factors does *not* affect the value of a European option?
   A. The volatility of the underlying
   B. Dividends or interest paid by the underlying
   C. The percentage of the investor's assets invested in the option
2. Which of the following statements imply that a European call on a stock is worth more?
   A. Less time to expiration
   B. A higher stock price relative to the exercise price
   C. Larger dividends paid by the stock during the life of the option
3. Why might a European put be worth less the longer the time to expiration?
   A. The cost of waiting to receive the exercise price is higher.
   B. The risk of the underlying is lower over a longer period of time.
   C. The longer time to expiration means that the put is more likely to expire out-of-the-money.
4. The loss in value of an option as it moves closer to expiration is called what?
   A. Time value decay
   B. Volatility diminution
   C. Time value of money
5. How does the minimum value of a call or put option differ from its exercise value?
   A. The exercise price is adjusted for the time value of money.
   B. The minimum value reflects the volatility of the underlying.
   C. The underlying price is adjusted for the time value of money.

Solution to 1: C is correct. The investor's exposure to the option is not relevant to the price one should pay to buy or ask to sell the option. Volatility and dividends or interest paid by the underlying are highly relevant to the value of the option.

Solution to 2: B is correct. The higher the stock price and the lower the exercise price, the more valuable is the call. Less time to expiration and larger dividends reduce the value of the call.

Solution to 3: A is correct. Although the longer time benefits the holder of the option, it also has a cost in that exercise of a longer-term put comes much later. Therefore, the receipt of the exercise price is delayed. Longer time to expiration does not lower the risk of the underlying. The longer time also does not increase the likelihood of the option expiring out-of-the-money.

Solution to 4: A is correct. An option has time value that decays as the expiration approaches. There is no such concept as volatility diminution. Time value of money relates only to the value of money at one point in time versus another.

Solution to 5: A is correct. The minimum value formula is the greater of zero or the difference between the underlying price and the present value of the exercise price, whereas the exercise value is the maximum of zero and the appropriate difference between the underlying price and the exercise price. Volatility does not affect the minimum price. It does not make sense to adjust the underlying price for the time value of money for the simple reason that it is already adjusted for the time value of money.

10. PUT–CALL PARITY, PUT–CALL–FORWARD PARITY

One of the first concepts that a trader learns in options is the parity relationship between puts and calls. Even though the word "parity" means "equivalence," puts and calls are not equivalent. There is, however, a relationship between the call price and the price of its corresponding put, which we refer to as put–call parity.

Suppose Investor A owns an asset that has a current price of S_0. Assume the asset makes no cash payments and has no carrying costs. The end of the holding period is time T, at which point the asset will be worth S_T. Fearing the possibility that S_T will decline, Investor A buys a put option with an exercise price of X, which can be used to sell the asset for X at time T. This put option has a premium of p_0. Combined with the value of the asset, the investor's current position is worth $S_0 + p_0$, which is the investor's money at risk. This strategy of holding the asset and a put is sometimes called a **protective put**.

At expiration, the value of the asset is S_T. The value of the put will be either zero or $X - S_T$. If the asset increases in value such that $S_T \geq X$, then the overall position is worth S_T. The asset has performed well, and the investor will let the put expire. If the asset value declines to the point at which $S_T < X$, the asset is worth S_T, and the put is worth $X - S_T$, for a total of X. In other words, the investor would exercise the put, selling the asset for X, which exceeds the asset's current value of S_T.

This strategy seems like a reasonable and possibly quite attractive investment. Investor A receives the benefit of unlimited upside potential, with the downside performance truncated at X. Exhibit 13 shows the performance of the protective put. The graph on the left illustrates the underlying asset and the put. The graph on the right shows their combined effects.

EXHIBIT 13   Protective Put (Asset Plus Long Put)

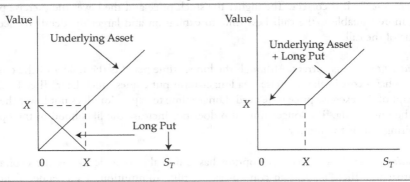

Consider Investor B, an options trader. At time 0, this investor buys a call option on this asset with an exercise price of X that expires at T and a risk-free zero-coupon bond with a face value of X that matures at T. The call costs c_0, and the bond costs the present value of X, which is $X/(1 + r)^T$. Thus, Investor B has invested funds of $c_0 + X/(1 + r)^T$. This strategy is sometimes known as a **fiduciary call**. If the underlying price exceeds the exercise price at expiration, the call will be worth $S_T - X$, and the bond will mature and pay a value of X. These values combine to equal S_T. If the underlying price does not exceed the exercise price at expiration, the call expires worthless and the bond is worth X for a combined value of X.

Exhibit 14 shows the performance of the fiduciary call. The graph on the left shows the call and bond, and the graph on the right shows the combined effects of the two strategies.

EXHIBIT 14   Fiduciary Call (Long Call Plus Risk-Free Bond)

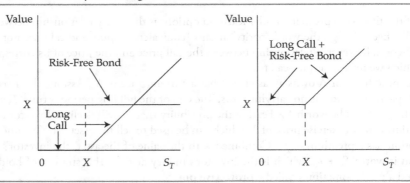

Comparing Exhibit 13 with Exhibit 14 shows that a protective put and a fiduciary call produce the same result. Exhibit 15 shows this result more directly by identifying the payoffs in the various outcomes. Recall that Investor A committed funds of $S_0 + p_0$, while Investor B committed funds of $c_0 + X/(1 + r)^T$. If both investors receive the same payoffs at time T regardless of the asset price at T, the amounts they invest at time 0 have to be the same. Thus, we require

$$S_0 + p_0 = c_0 + X/(1 + r)^T \tag{12}$$

This relationship is known as **put–call parity**.

EXHIBIT 15   Protective Put vs. Fiduciary Call

	Outcome at T	
	Put Expires In-the-Money $(S_T < X)$	Call Expires In-the-Money $(S_T \geq X)$
Protective put		
Asset	S_T	S_T
Long put	$X - S_T$	0
Total	X	S_T
Fiduciary call		
Long call	0	$S_T - X$
Risk-free bond	X	X
Total	X	S_T

For a simple example, assume call and put options with an exercise price of ¥100,000 in which the underlying is at ¥90,000 at time 0. The risk-free rate is 2% and the options expire in two months, so $T = 2/12 = 0.167$. To completely fill in the puzzle, we would need to know the put or call price, from which we could obtain the other. For now, let us write this relationship as

$$p_0 - c_0 = X/(1 + r)^T - S_0$$

The right side would be ¥100,000/(1.02)$^{0.167}$ – ¥90,000 = ¥9,670. Thus, the put price should exceed the call price by ¥9,670. Thus, if the call were priced at ¥5,000, the put price would be ¥14,670. If we knew the put price, we could obtain the call price. Put–call parity does not tell us which price is correct, and it requires knowledge of one price to get the other. Alternatively, it can tell us the difference in the put and call prices.

Put–call parity must hold, at least within transaction costs, or arbitrage opportunities would arise. For example, suppose Investor C observes market prices and finds that the left-hand side of put–call parity, $S_0 + p_0$, is less than the right-hand side, $c_0 + X/(1 + r)^T$. Thus, the put and the stock cost less than the call and the bond. Knowing that there should be equality (parity), Investor C executes an arbitrage transaction, selling the overpriced transactions (the call and the bond) and buying the underpriced transactions (the asset and the put).[19] By selling the higher priced side and buying the lower priced side, Investor C will take in more money than she will pay out, a net inflow of $c_0 + X/(1 + r)^T - (S_0 + p_0)$. At expiration, the long put and long asset will offset the short call and bond, as shown in Exhibit 16.

---

[19]Selling the bond is equivalent to borrowing, meaning to issue a loan.

EXHIBIT 16   Put–Call Parity Arbitrage

| | | Outcome at T | |
Transaction	Cash Flow at Time 0	Put Expires In-the-Money $(S_T < X)$	Call Expires In-the-Money $(S_T \geq X)$
Buy asset	$-S_0$	S_T	S_T
Buy put	$-p_0$	$X - S_T$	0
Sell call	$+c_0$	0	$-(S_T - X)$
Borrow	$+X/(1 + r)^T$	$-X$	$-X$
Total	$-S_0 - p_0 + c_0 + X/(1 + r)^T > 0$	0	0

In simple terms, if $S_T < X$, the short call expires out-of-the-money and the put is exercised to sell the asset for X. This cash, X, is then used to pay off the loan. The net effect is that no money flows in or out at T. If $S_T \geq X$, the put expires out-of-the money, and the short call is exercised, meaning that Investor C must sell the asset for X. This cash, X, is then used to pay off the loan. Again, no money flows in or out. The net effect is a perfect hedge in which no money is paid out or received at T. But there was money taken in at time 0. Taking in money today and never having to pay it out is an arbitrage profit. Arbitrage opportunities like this, however, will be noticed by many investors who will engage in the same transactions. Prices will adjust until parity is restored, whereby $S_0 + p_0 = c_0 + X/(1 + r)^T$.

Put–call parity provides tremendous insights into option pricing. Recall that we proved that going long the asset and long a put is equivalent to going long a call and long a risk-free bond. We can rearrange the put–call parity equation in the following ways:

$$S_0 + p_0 = c_0 + X/(1 + r)^T$$
$$\Rightarrow$$
$$p_0 = c_0 - S_0 + X/(1 + r)^T$$
$$c_0 = p_0 + S_0 - X/(1 + r)^T$$
$$S_0 = c_0 - p_0 + X/(1 + r)^T$$
$$X/(1 + r)^T = S_0 + p_0 - c_0$$

By using the symbols and the signs in these versions of put–call parity, we can see several important interpretations. In the equations below, plus signs mean long and minus signs mean short:

$$p_0 = c_0 - S_0 + X/(1 + r)^T \quad \Rightarrow \quad \text{long put = long call, short asset, long bond}$$
$$c_0 = p_0 + S_0 - X/(1 + r)^T \quad \Rightarrow \quad \text{long call = long put, long asset, short bond}$$
$$S_0 = c_0 - p_0 + X/(1 + r)^T \quad \Rightarrow \quad \text{long asset = long call, short put, long bond}$$
$$X/(1 + r)^T = S_0 + p_0 - c_0 \quad \Rightarrow \quad \text{long bond = long asset, long put, short call}$$

You should be able to convince yourself of any of these points by constructing a table similar to Exhibit 15.[20]

10.1. Put–Call–Forward Parity

Recall that we demonstrated that one could create a risk-free position by going long the asset and selling a forward contract.[21] It follows that one can synthetically create a position in the asset by going long a forward contract and long a risk-free bond. Recall our put–call parity discussion and assume that Investor A creates his protective put in a slightly different manner. Instead of buying the asset, he buys a forward contract and a risk-free bond in which the face value is the forward price. Exhibit 17 shows that this strategy is a synthetic protective put. Because we showed that the fiduciary call is equivalent to the protective put, a fiduciary call has to be equivalent to a protective put with a forward contract. Exhibit 18 demonstrates this point.

EXHIBIT 17   Protective Put with Forward Contract vs. Protective Put with Asset

	Outcome at T	
	Put Expires In-the-Money ($S_T < X$)	Put Expires Out-of-the-Money ($S_T \geq X$)
Protective put with asset		
Asset	S_T	S_T
Long put	$X - S_T$	0
Total	X	S_T
Protective put with forward contract		
Risk-free bond	$F_0(T)$	$F_0(T)$
Forward contract	$S_T - F_0(T)$	$S_T - F_0(T)$
Long put	$X - S_T$	0
Total	X	S_T

---

[20]As a further exercise, you might change the signs of each term in the above and provide the appropriate interpretations.
[21]You might wish to review Exhibit 6.

EXHIBIT 18   Protective Put with Forward Contract vs. Fiduciary Call

	Outcome at T	
	Put Expires In-the-Money $(S_T < X)$	Call Expires In-the-Money $(S_T \geq X)$
Protective Put with Forward Contract		
Risk-free bond	$F_0(T)$	$F_0(T)$
Forward contract	$S_T - F_0(T)$	$S_T - F_0(T)$
Long put	$X - S_T$	0
Total	X	S_T
Fiduciary Call		
Call	0	$S_T - X$
Risk-free bond	X	X
Total	X	S_T

It follows that the cost of the fiduciary call must equal the cost of the synthetic protective put, giving us what is referred to as **put–call–forward parity**,

$$F_0(T)/(1 + r)^T + p_0 = c_0 + X/(1 + r)^T \qquad (13)$$

Returning to our put–call parity example, a forward contract on ¥90,000 expiring in two months with a 2% interest rate would have a price of ¥90,000(1.02)$^{0.167}$ = ¥90,298. Rearranging Equation 13, we have

$$p_0 - c_0 = [X - F_0(T)]/(1 + r)^T$$

The right-hand side is (¥100,000 − ¥90,298)/(1.02)$^{0.167}$ = ¥9,670, which is the same answer we obtained using the underlying asset rather than the forward contract. Naturally these two models give us the same answer. They are both based on the assumption that no arbitrage is possible within the spot, forward, and options markets.

So far we have learned only how to price options in relation to other options, such as a call versus a put or a call or a put versus a forward. We need a way to price options versus their underlying.

EXAMPLE 7   Put–Call Parity

1. Which of the following statements *best* describes put–call parity?
   A. The put price always equals the call price.
   B. The put price equals the call price if the volatility is known.
   C. The put price plus the underlying price equals the call price plus the present value of the exercise price.

2. From put–call parity, which of the following transactions is risk-free?
   A. Long asset, long put, short call
   B. Long call, long put, short asset
   C. Long asset, long call, short bond

Solution to 1: C is correct. The put and underlying make up a protective put, while the call and present value of the exercise price make up a fiduciary call. The put price equals the call price for certain combinations of interest rates, times to expiration, and option moneyness, but these are special cases. Volatility has no effect on put–call parity.

Solution to 2: A is correct. The combination of a long asset, long put, and short call is risk free because its payoffs produce a known cash flow of the value of the exercise price. The other two combinations do not produce risk-free positions. You should work through the payoffs of these three combinations in the form of Exhibit 12.

11. BINOMIAL VALUATION OF OPTIONS

Because the option payoff is determined by the underlying, if we know the outcome of the underlying, we know the payoff of the option. That means that the price of the underlying is the only element of uncertainty. Moreover, the uncertainty is not so much the value of the underlying at expiration as it is whether the underlying is above or below the exercise price. If the underlying is above the exercise price at expiration, the payoff is $S_T - X$ for calls and zero for puts. If the underlying is below the exercise price at expiration, the payoff is zero for calls and $X - S_T$ for puts. In other words, the payoff of the option is straightforward and known, as soon as we know whether the option expires in- or out-of-the-money. Note that for forwards, futures, and swaps, there is no such added complexity. The payoff formula is the same regardless of whether the underlying is above or below the hurdle.

As a result of this characteristic of options, derivation of an option pricing model requires the specification of a model of a random process that describes movements in the underlying. Given the entirely different nature of the payoffs above and below the exercise price, it might seem difficult to derive the option price, even if we could model movements in the underlying. Fortunately, the process is less difficult than it first appears.

At this level of treatment, we will start with a very simple model that allows only two possible movements in the underlying—one going up and one going down from where it is now. This model with two possible outcomes is called the **binomial model**. Start with the underlying at S_0, and let it go up to S_1^+ or down to S_1^-. We cannot arbitrarily set these values at just anything. We will be required to know the values of S_1^+ and S_1^-. That does not mean we know which outcome will occur. It means that we know only what the possibilities are. In doing so, we effectively know the volatility. Assume the probability of the move to S_1^+ is q and the probability of the move to S_1^- is $1 - q$. We specify the returns implied by these moves as up and down factors, u and d, where

$$u = \frac{S_1^+}{S_0}, \quad d = \frac{S_1^-}{S_0} \tag{14}$$

Now, consider a European call option that expires at time 1 and has an exercise price of X. Let the call prices be c_0 today and c_1^+ and c_1^- at expiration. Exhibit 19 illustrates the model.

Our objective is to determine the price of the option today, meaning to determine a formula for c_0. Knowing what we know about arbitrage and the pricing of forward contracts, it would seem we could construct a risk-free portfolio involving this option.

EXHIBIT 19   The Binomial Option Pricing Model

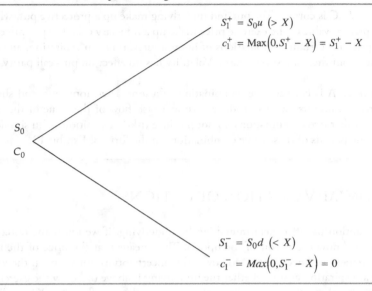

$$S_1^+ = S_0 u \ (> X)$$
$$c_1^+ = \text{Max}\left(0, S_1^+ - X\right) = S_1^+ - X$$

S_0
c_0

$$S_1^- = S_0 d \ (< X)$$
$$c_1^- = Max\left(0, S_1^- - X\right) = 0$$

Because call options and the underlying move together, one possibility is that buying the underlying and selling a call could create a hedge. Indeed it does, but one unit of each is not the appropriate balance. Let us sell one call and hold h units of the underlying. The value h is unknown at the moment, but we will be able to determine its value. The value today of a combination of h units of the underlying and one short call is

$$V_0 = hS_0 - c_0$$

Think of V_0 as the amount of money invested. Depending on which of the two paths is taken by the underlying, the value of this portfolio at time 1 will be

$$V_1^+ = hS_1^+ - c_1^+$$

or

$$V_1^- = hS_1^- - c_1^- \tag{15}$$

If the portfolio were hedged, then V_1^+ would equal V_1^-. We can set V_1^+ and V_1^- equal to each other and solve for the value of h that assures us that the portfolio is hedged:

$$V_1^+ = V_1^-$$
$$\Rightarrow hS_1^+ - c_1^+ = hS_1^- - c_1^-$$
$$\Rightarrow h = \frac{c_1^+ - c_1^-}{S_1^+ - S_1^-} \tag{16}$$

The values on the right-hand side are known, so we can easily calculate h. Thus, we can derive the number of units of the underlying that will perfectly hedge one unit of the short call.

We know that a perfectly hedged investment should earn the risk-free rate, r. Thus, the following statement must be true:

$$V_1^+ \text{ (or } V_1^-) = V_0(1 + r)$$

We can substitute the value of V_1^+ or V_1^- from Equation 15 into the above equation. Then we do a little algebra, which is not important to this discussion, and obtain the formula for the option price,

$$c_0 = \frac{\pi c_1^+ + (1 - \pi) c_1^-}{1 + r}$$

where

$$\pi = \frac{1 + r - d}{u - d} \tag{17}$$

Equation 17 shows that the value of the call today is a weighted average of the next two possible call prices at expiration, where the weights, π and $1 - \pi$, are given by the second formula in Equation 17.

This formula sheds a great deal of light on option pricing. Notice the following:

- The volatility of the underlying, which is reflected in the difference between S_1^+ and S_1^- and affects c_1^+ and c_1^-, is an important factor in determining the value of the option.
- The probabilities of the up and down moves, q and $1 - q$, do not appear in the formula.[22]
- The values π and $1 - \pi$ are similar to probabilities and are often called synthetic or pseudo probabilities. They produce a weighted average of the next two possible call values, a type of expected future value.
- The formula takes the form of an expected future value, the numerator, discounted at the risk-free rate.

On the first point, if volatility increases, the difference between S_1^+ and S_1^- increases, which widens the range between c_1^+ and c_1^-, leading to a higher option value. The upper payoff, c_1^+, will be larger and the lower payoff, c_1^-, will still be zero.[23] On the second point, the actual probabilities of the up and down moves do not matter. This result is because of our ability to construct a hedge and the rule of arbitrage. On the third point, the irrelevance of the actual probabilities is replaced by the relevance of a set of synthetic or pseudo probabilities, π and $1 - \pi$, which are called **risk-neutral probabilities**. On the fourth point, these risk-neutral probabilities are used to find a synthetic expected value, which is then discounted at the risk-free rate. Thus, the option is valued as though investors are risk neutral. As we discussed extensively earlier, that is not the same as assuming that investors are risk neutral.

If the option does not trade at the specified formula, Equation 17, investors can engage in arbitrage transactions. If the option is trading too high relative to the formula, investors can sell the call, buy h shares of the underlying, and earn a return in excess of the risk-free

---

[22]We introduced them earlier to help make this point, but ultimately they serve no purpose.

[23]Although the lower payoff is zero in this example, that will not always be the case.

rate, while funding the transaction by borrowing at the risk-free rate. The combined actions of arbitrageurs will result in downward pressure on the option price until it converges to the model price. If the option price is too low, buying the call, selling short h units of the asset, and investing the proceeds in risk-free bonds will generate risk-free cash that will earn more than the risk-free rate. The combined actions of arbitrageurs doing this will pressure the call price to rise until it reaches the price given by the model.

We will omit the details, but the hedge portfolio can also be constructed with puts.[24] Changing the c's to p's leads to the binomial put option pricing formula,

$$p_0 = \frac{\pi p_1^+ + (1 - \pi) p_1^-}{1 + r} \tag{18}$$

with the risk-neutral probability π determined by the same formula as for calls, as shown in Equation 17.

Let us construct a simple example. Let S_0 be £40 and the risk-free rate be 5%. The up and down factors are $u = 1.20$ and $d = 0.75$. Thus, the next two possible prices of the asset are $S_1^+ = £40(1.20) = £48$ and $S_1^- = £40(0.75) = £30$. Consider a call and a put that have exercise prices of £38. Then the next two possible values of the call and put are

$$c_1^+ = \text{Max}(0, £48 - £38) = £10$$
$$c_1^- = \text{Max}(0, £30 - £38) = £0$$
$$p_1^+ = \text{Max}(0, £38 - £48) = £0$$
$$p_1^- = \text{Max}(0, £38 - £30) = £8$$

Next we compute the risk-neutral probability,

$$\pi = \frac{1 + 0.05 - 0.75}{1.20 - 0.75} = 0.667$$

The values of the call and put are

$$c_0 = \frac{0.667(£10) + (1 - 0.667)£0}{1.05} = £6.35$$

and

$$p_0 = \frac{0.667(£0) + (1 - 0.667)£8}{1.05} = £2.54$$

The binomial model, as we see it here, is extremely simple. In reality, of course, there are more than two possible next-period prices for the underlying. As it turns out, we can extend the number of periods and subdivide an option's life into an increasing number of smaller time periods. In that case, we can obtain a more accurate and realistic model for option pricing, one that is widely used in practice. Given our objective in this reading of understanding the basic ideas behind derivative pricing, the one-period model is sufficient for the time being.

---

[24] A long position in h units of the underlying would be hedged with one long put. The formula for h is the same as the one given here for calls, with call prices in the numerator instead of put prices.

EXAMPLE 8   Binomial Valuation of Options

1. Which of the following terms directly represents the volatility of the underlying in the binomial model?
   A. The standard deviation of the underlying
   B. The difference between the up and down factors
   C. The ratio of the underlying value to the exercise price.
2. Which of the following is *not* a factor in pricing a call option in the binomial model?
   A. The risk-free rate
   B. The exercise price
   C. The probability that the underlying will go up
3. Which of the following *best* describes the binomial option pricing formula?
   A. The expected payoff is discounted at the risk-free rate plus a risk premium.
   B. The spot price is compounded at the risk-free rate minus the volatility premium.
   C. The expected payoff based on risk-neutral probabilities is discounted at the risk-free rate.

Solution to 1: B is correct. The up and down factors express how high and how low the underlying can go. Standard deviation does not appear directly in the binomial model, although it is implicit. The ratio of the underlying value to the exercise price expresses the moneyness of the option.

Solution to 2: C is correct. The actual probabilities of the up and down moves are irrelevant to pricing options. The risk-free and exercise price are, of course, highly relevant.

Solution to 3: C is correct. Risk-neutral probabilities are used, and discounting is at the risk-free rate. There is no risk premium incorporated into option pricing because of the use of arbitrage.

We have now seen how to obtain the price of a European option. Let us now consider what happens if the options are American, meaning they have the right to be exercised early.

12. AMERICAN OPTION PRICING

First, we will use upper case letters for American call and put prices: C_0 and P_0. Second, we know that American options possess every characteristic of European options and one additional trait: They can be exercised at any time prior to expiration. Early exercise cannot be required, so the right to exercise early cannot have negative value. Thus, American options cannot sell for less than European options. Thus, we can state the following:

$$C_0 \geq c_0$$
$$P_0 \geq p_0 \tag{19}$$

Given the price of the underlying at S_0, the early-exercise feature means that we can exercise the option at any time. So, we can claim the value $\text{Max}(0, S_0 - X)$ for calls and $\text{Max}(0, X - S_0)$ for puts. These values establish new minimum prices for American calls and puts,

$$C_0 = \text{Max}(0, S_0 - X)$$
$$P_0 = \text{Max}(0, X - S_0) \tag{20}$$

For call options, we previously learned that a European call has a minimum value given by Equation 10, which is restated here:

$$c_0 \geq \text{Max}\left[0, S_0 - X/(1 + r)^T\right]$$

Comparing $\text{Max}(0, S_0 - X)$ (the minimum for American calls) with $\text{Max}[0, S_0 - X/(1 + r)^T]$ (the minimum for European calls) reveals that the latter is either the same or higher. There are some circumstances in which both minima are zero, some in which the American minimum is zero and the European minimum is positive, and some in which both are positive, in which case $S_0 - X/(1 + r)^T$ is unquestionably more than $S_0 - X$. Given that an American call price cannot be less than a European call price, we have to reestablish the American call minimum as $\text{Max}[0, S_0 - X/(1 + r)^T]$.

For put options, we previously learned that a European put has a minimum value given by Equation 11, which is restated here:

$$p_0 \geq \text{Max}\left[0, X/(1 + r)^T - S_0\right]$$

Comparing $\text{Max}(0, X - S_0)$ (the minimum for American puts) with $\text{Max}[0, X/(1 + r)^T - S_0]$ (the minimum for European puts) reveals that the former is never less. In some circumstances, they are both zero. In some, $X - S_0$ is positive and $X/(1 + r)^T - S_0$ is negative, and in some cases both are positive but $X - S_0$ is unquestionably more than $X/(1 + r)^T - S_0$. Thus, the American put minimum value is the exercise value, which is $\text{Max}(0, X - S_0)$.

So, now we have new minimum prices for American calls and puts:

$$C_0 \geq \text{Max}\left[0, S_0 - X/(1 + r)^T\right]$$
$$P_0 \geq \text{Max}(0, X - S_0) \tag{21}$$

Thus, in the market these options will trade for at least these values.

Let us return to the previous examples for the minimum values. The exercise price is €60, the risk-free rate is 4%, and the expiration is $T = 0.75$. Consider the two cases below:

Underlying: $S_0 = €70$

- The minimum European call price was previously calculated as €11.74. The exercise value of the American call is $\text{Max}(0, €70 - €60) = €10$. The American call has to sell for at least as much as the European call, so the minimum price of the American call is €11.74.
- The minimum European put price was €0.00. This is also the exercise value of the American put [$\text{Max}(0, €60 - €70) = €0.00$], so the minimum price of the American put is still €0.00.

Underlying: $S_0 = €50$

- The minimum European call price was previously calculated as €0.00. The exercise value of the American call is Max(0,€50 − €60) = €0.00, so €0.00 is still the minimum price of the American call.
- The minimum European put price was previously calculated as €8.26. The exercise value of the American put is Max(0,€60 − €50) = €10. So, €10 is the minimum price of the American put.

The call result leads us to a somewhat surprising conclusion. With the exception of what happens at expiration when American and European calls are effectively the same and both worth the exercise value, an American call is always worth more in the market than exercised. That means that an American call will never be exercised early. This result is probably not intuitive.

Consider a deep in-the-money call. One might think that if the holder expected the underlying to not increase any further, exercise might be justified. Yet, we said the call would sell for more in the market than its exercise value. What is the rationale? If the investor thinks the underlying will not go up any further and thus expects no further gains from the option, why would she prefer the underlying? Would the investor be happier holding the underlying, which she believes is not expected to increase? Moreover, she would tie up more funds exercising to acquire the underlying than if she just held on to the option or, better yet, sold it to another investor.

So far, however, we have left out a possible factor that can affect early exercise. Suppose the underlying is a stock and pays dividends. When a stock goes ex-dividend, its price instantaneously falls. Although we will omit the details, an investor holding a call option may find it worthwhile to exercise the call just before the stock goes ex-dividend. The capture of the dividend, thereby avoiding the ex-dividend drop in the price of the underlying, can make early exercise worthwhile. If the underlying is a bond, coupon interest can also motivate early exercise. But if there are significant carrying costs, the motivation for early exercise is weakened. Storage costs lend a preference for owning the option over owning the underlying.

Because the minimum value of an American put exceeds the minimum value of the European put, there is a much stronger motivation for early exercise. Suppose you owned an American put on a stock that is completely bankrupt, with a zero stock price and no possibility of recovery. You can either wait until expiration and capture its exercise value of Max(0, $X − S_T$) = Max(0, $X − 0$) = Max(0, X) = X, or you can capture that value by exercising now. Obviously now is better. As it turns out, however, the underlying does not need to go all the way to zero. There is a critical point at which a put is so deep in-the-money that early exercise is justified. This rationale works differently for a call. A deep in-the-money put has a limit to its ultimate value. It can get no deeper than when the underlying goes to zero. For a call, there is no limit to its moneyness because the underlying has no upper limit to its price.

Although dividends and coupon interest encourage early exercise for calls, they discourage early exercise for puts. The loss from the decline in the price of the underlying that is avoided by exercising a call just before the decline works to the benefit of a put holder. Therefore, if a put holder were considering exercising early, he would be better off waiting until right after the dividend or interest were paid. Carrying costs on the underlying, which discourage exercise for calls, encourage exercise for puts.

At this point, we cannot determine the critical prices at which American options are best exercised early. We require more knowledge and experience with option pricing models, which is covered in more advanced material.

EXAMPLE 9   American Option Pricing

1. With respect to American calls, which of the following statements is *most* accurate?
   A. American calls should be exercised early if the underlying has reached its expected maximum price.
   B. American calls should be exercised early if the underlying has a lower expected return than the risk-free rate.
   C. American calls should be exercised early only if there is a dividend or other cash payment on the underlying.
2. The effect of dividends on a stock on early exercise of a put is to:
   A. make early exercise less likely.
   B. have no effect on early exercise.
   C. make early exercise more likely.

Solution to 1: C is correct. Cash payments on the underlying are the only reason to exercise American calls early. Interest rates, the expected return on the underlying, and any notion of a maximum price is irrelevant. But note that a dividend does not mean that early exercise should automatically be conducted. A dividend is only a necessary condition to justify early exercise for calls.

Solution to 2: A is correct. Dividends drive down the stock price when the dividend is paid. Thus, all else being equal, a stock paying dividends has a built-in force that drives down the stock price. This characteristic discourages early exercise, because stock price declines are beneficial to holders of puts.

SUMMARY

This reading on derivative pricing provides a foundation for understanding how derivatives are valued and traded. Key points include the following:

- The price of the underlying asset is equal to the expected future price discounted at the risk-free rate, plus a risk premium, plus the present value of any benefits, minus the present value of any costs associated with holding the asset.
- An arbitrage opportunity occurs when two identical assets or combinations of assets sell at different prices, leading to the possibility of buying the cheaper asset and selling the more expensive asset to produce a risk-free return without investing any capital.
- In well-functioning markets, arbitrage opportunities are quickly exploited, and the resulting increased buying of underpriced assets and increased selling of overpriced assets returns prices to equivalence.
- Derivatives are priced by creating a risk-free combination of the underlying and a derivative, leading to a unique derivative price that eliminates any possibility of arbitrage.
- Derivative pricing through arbitrage precludes any need for determining risk premiums or the risk aversion of the party trading the option and is referred to as risk-neutral pricing.
- The value of a forward contract at expiration is the value of the asset minus the forward price.

- The value of a forward contract prior to expiration is the value of the asset minus the present value of the forward price.
- The forward price, established when the contract is initiated, is the price agreed to by the two parties that produces a zero value at the start.
- Costs incurred and benefits received by holding the underlying affect the forward price by raising and lowering it, respectively.
- Futures prices can differ from forward prices because of the effect of interest rates on the interim cash flows from the daily settlement.
- Swaps can be priced as an implicit series of off-market forward contracts, whereby each contract is priced the same, resulting in some contracts being positively valued and some negatively valued but with their combined value equaling zero.
- At expiration, a European call or put is worth its exercise value, which for calls is the greater of zero or the underlying price minus the exercise price and for puts is the greater of zero and the exercise price minus the underlying price.
- European calls and puts are affected by the value of the underlying, the exercise price, the risk-free rate, the time to expiration, the volatility of the underlying, and any costs incurred or benefits received while holding the underlying.
- Option values experience time value decay, which is the loss in value due to the passage of time and the approach of expiration, plus the moneyness and the volatility.
- The minimum value of a European call is the maximum of zero and the underlying price minus the present value of the exercise price.
- The minimum value of a European put is the maximum of zero and the present value of the exercise price minus the price of the underlying.
- European put and call prices are related through put–call parity, which specifies that the put price plus the price of the underlying equals the call price plus the present value of the exercise price.
- European put and call prices are related through put–call–forward parity, which shows that the put price plus the value of a risk-free bond with face value equal to the forward price equals the call price plus the value of a risk-free bond with face value equal to the exercise price.
- The values of European options can be obtained using the binomial model, which specifies two possible prices of the asset one period later and enables the construction of a risk-free hedge consisting of the option and the underlying.
- American call prices can differ from European call prices only if there are cash flows on the underlying, such as dividends or interest; these cash flows are the only reason for early exercise of a call.
- American put prices can differ from European put prices, because the right to exercise early always has value for a put, which is because of a lower limit on the value of the underlying.

PROBLEMS

1. For a risk-averse investor, the price of a risky asset, assuming no additional costs and benefits of holding the asset, is:
   A. unrelated to the risk-free rate.
   B. directly related to its level of risk.
   C. inversely related to its level of risk.

2. An arbitrage opportunity is *least likely* to be exploited when:
   A. one position is illiquid.
   B. the price differential between assets is large.
   C. the investor can execute a transaction in large volumes.

3. An arbitrageur will *most likely* execute a trade when:
   A. transaction costs are low.
   B. costs of short-selling are high.
   C. prices are consistent with the law of one price.

4. An arbitrage transaction generates a net inflow of funds:
   A. throughout the holding period.
   B. at the end of the holding period.
   C. at the start of the holding period.

5. Which of the following combinations replicates a long derivative position?
   A. A short derivative and a long asset
   B. A long asset and a short risk-free bond
   C. A short derivative and a short risk-free bond

6. Most derivatives are priced by:
   A. assuming that the market offers arbitrage opportunities.
   B. discounting the expected payoff of the derivative at the risk-free rate.
   C. applying a risk premium to the expected payoff of the derivative and its risk.

7. The price of a forward contract:
   A. is the amount paid at initiation.
   B. is the amount paid at expiration.
   C. fluctuates over the term of the contract.

8. Assume an asset pays no dividends or interest, and also assume that the asset does not yield any non-financial benefits or incur any carrying cost. At initiation, the price of a forward contract on that asset is:
   A. lower than the value of the contract.
   B. equal to the value of the contract.
   C. greater than the value of the contract.

9. With respect to a forward contract, as market conditions change:
   A. only the price fluctuates.
   B. only the value fluctuates.
   C. both the price and the value fluctuate.

10. The value of a forward contract at expiration is:
    A. positive to the long party if the spot price is higher than the forward price.
    B. negative to the short party if the forward price is higher than the spot price.
    C. positive to the short party if the spot price is higher than the forward price.

11. At the initiation of a forward contract on an asset that neither receives benefits nor incurs carrying costs during the term of the contract, the forward price is equal to the:
    A. spot price.
    B. future value of the spot price.
    C. present value of the spot price.

12. Stocks BWQ and ZER are each currently priced at $100 per share. Over the next year, stock BWQ is expected to generate significant benefits whereas stock ZER is not expected to generate any benefits. There are no carrying costs associated with holding either stock over the next year. Compared with ZER, the one-year forward price of BWQ is *most likely*:

    A. lower.

    B. the same.

    C. higher.

13. If the net cost of carry of an asset is positive, then the price of a forward contract on that asset is *most likely*:

    A. lower than if the net cost of carry was zero.

    B. the same as if the net cost of carry was zero.

    C. higher than if the net cost of carry was zero.

14. If the present value of storage costs exceeds the present value of its convenience yield, then the commodity's forward price is *most likely*:

    A. less than the spot price compounded at the risk-free rate.

    B. the same as the spot price compounded at the risk-free rate.

    C. higher than the spot price compounded at the risk-free rate.

15. Which of the following factors *most likely* explains why the spot price of a commodity in short supply can be greater than its forward price?

    A. Opportunity cost

    B. Lack of dividends

    C. Convenience yield

16. When interest rates are constant, futures prices are *most likely*:

    A. less than forward prices.

    B. equal to forward prices.

    C. greater than forward prices.

17. In contrast to a forward contract, a futures contract:

    A. trades over-the-counter.

    B. is initiated at a zero value.

    C. is marked-to-market daily.

18. To the holder of a long position, it is more desirable to own a forward contract than a futures contract when interest rates and futures prices are:

    A. negatively correlated.

    B. uncorrelated.

    C. positively correlated.

19. The value of a swap typically:

    A. is non-zero at initiation.

    B. is obtained through replication.

    C. does not fluctuate over the life of the contract.

20. The price of a swap typically:

    A. is zero at initiation.

    B. fluctuates over the life of the contract.

    C. is obtained through a process of replication.

21. The value of a swap is equal to the present value of the:

    A. fixed payments from the swap.

    B. net cash flow payments from the swap.

    C. underlying at the end of the contract.

22. If no cash is initially exchanged, a swap is comparable to a series of forward contracts when:

    A. the swap payments are variable.

    B. the combined value of all the forward contracts is zero.

    C. all the forward contracts have the same agreed-on price.

23. For a swap in which a series of fixed payments is exchanged for a series of floating payments, the parties to the transaction:
   A. designate the value of the underlying at contract initiation.
   B. value the underlying solely on the basis of its market value at the end of the swap.
   C. value the underlying sequentially at the time of each payment to determine the floating payment.

24. A European call option and a European put option are written on the same underlying, and both options have the same expiration date and exercise price. At expiration, it is possible that both options will have:
   A. negative values.
   B. the same value.
   C. positive values.

25. At expiration, a European put option will be valuable if the exercise price is:
   A. less than the underlying price.
   B. equal to the underlying price.
   C. greater than the underlying price.

26. The value of a European call option at expiration is the greater of zero or the:
   A. value of the underlying.
   B. value of the underlying minus the exercise price.
   C. exercise price minus the value of the underlying.

27. For a European call option with two months until expiration, if the spot price is below the exercise price, the call option will *most likely* have:
   A. zero time value.
   B. positive time value.
   C. positive exercise value.

28. When the price of the underlying is below the exercise price, a put option is:
   A. in-the-money.
   B. at-the-money.
   C. out-of-the-money.

29. If the risk-free rate increases, the value of an in-the-money European put option will *most likely*:
   A. decrease.
   B. remain the same.
   C. increase.

30. The value of a European call option is inversely related to the:
   A. exercise price.
   B. time to expiration.
   C. volatility of the underlying.

31. The table below shows three European call options on the same underlying:

	Time to Expiration	Exercise Price
Option 1	3 months	$100
Option 2	6 months	$100
Option 3	6 months	$105

The option with the highest value is *most likely*:
   A. Option 1.
   B. Option 2.
   C. Option 3.

32. The value of a European put option can be either directly or inversely related to the:
    A. exercise price.
    B. time to expiration.
    C. volatility of the underlying.

33. Prior to expiration, the lowest value of a European put option is the greater of zero or the:
    A. exercise price minus the value of the underlying.
    B. present value of the exercise price minus the value of the underlying.
    C. value of the underlying minus the present value of the exercise price.

34. A European put option on a dividend-paying stock is *most likely* to increase if there is an increase in:
    A. carrying costs.
    B. the risk-free rate.
    C. dividend payments.

35. Based on put–call parity, a trader who combines a long asset, a long put, and a short call will create a synthetic:
    A. long bond.
    B. fiduciary call.
    C. protective put.

36. Which of the following transactions is the equivalent of a synthetic long call position?
    A. Long asset, long put, short call
    B. Long asset, long put, short bond
    C. Short asset, long call, long bond

37. Which of the following is *least likely* to be required by the binomial option pricing model?
    A. Spot price
    B. Two possible prices one period later
    C. Actual probabilities of the up and down moves

38. To determine the price of an option today, the binomial model requires:
    A. selling one put and buying one offsetting call.
    B. buying one unit of the underlying and selling one matching call.
    C. using the risk-free rate to determine the required number of units of the underlying.

39. Assume a call option's strike price is initially equal to the price of its underlying asset. Based on the binomial model, if the volatility of the underlying decreases, the lower of the two potential payoff values of the hedge portfolio:
    A. decreases.
    B. remains the same.
    C. increases.

40. Based on the binomial model, an increase in the actual probability of an upward move in the underlying will result in the option price:
    A. decreasing.
    B. remaining the same.
    C. increasing.

41. If a call option is priced higher than the binomial model predicts, investors can earn a return in excess of the risk-free rate by:
    A. investing at the risk-free rate, selling a call, and selling the underlying.
    B. borrowing at the risk-free rate, buying a call, and buying the underlying.
    C. borrowing at the risk-free rate, selling a call, and buying the underlying.

42. An at-the-money American call option on a stock that pays no dividends has three months remaining until expiration. The market value of the option will *most likely* be:
    A. less than its exercise value.
    B. equal to its exercise value.
    C. greater than its exercise value.

43. At expiration, American call options are worth:
    A. less than European call options.
    B. the same as European call options.
    C. more than European call options.

44. Which of the following circumstances will *most likely* affect the value of an American call option relative to a European call option?
    A. Dividends are declared
    B. Expiration date occurs
    C. The risk-free rate changes

45. Combining a protective put with a forward contract generates equivalent outcomes at expiration to those of a:
    A. fiduciary call.
    B. long call combined with a short asset.
    C. forward contract combined with a risk-free bond.

46. Holding an asset and buying a put on that asset is equivalent to:
    A. initiating a fiduciary call.
    B. buying a risk-free zero-coupon bond and selling a call option.
    C. selling a risk-free zero-coupon bond and buying a call option.

47. If an underlying asset's price is less than a related option's strike price at expiration, a protective put position on that asset versus a fiduciary call position has a value that is:
    A. lower.
    B. the same.
    C. higher.

48. Based on put–call parity, which of the following combinations results in a synthetic long asset position?
    A. A long call, a short put, and a long bond
    B. A short call, a long put, and a short bond
    C. A long call, a short asset, and a long bond

49. For a holder of a European option, put–call–forward parity is based on the assumption that:
    A. no arbitrage is possible within the spot, forward, and option markets.
    B. the value of a European put at expiration is the greater of zero or the underlying value minus the exercise price.
    C. the value of a European call at expiration is the greater of zero or the exercise price minus the value of the underlying.

50. Under put–call–forward parity, which of the following transactions is risk free?
    A. Short call, long put, long forward contract, long risk-free bond
    B. Long call, short put, long forward contract, short risk-free bond
    C. Long call, long put, short forward contract, short risk-free bond

CHAPTER 3

PRICING AND VALUATION OF FORWARD COMMITMENTS

Adam Schwartz, PhD, CFA

LEARNING OUTCOMES

The candidate should be able to:

- describe the carry arbitrage model without underlying cashflows and with underlying cashflows;
- describe how equity forwards and futures are priced, and calculate and interpret their no-arbitrage value;
- describe how interest rate forwards and futures are priced, and calculate and interpret their no-arbitrage value;
- describe how fixed-income forwards and futures are priced, and calculate and interpret their no-arbitrage value;
- describe how interest rate swaps are priced, and calculate and interpret their no-arbitrage value;
- describe how currency swaps are priced, and calculate and interpret their no-arbitrage value;
- describe how equity swaps are priced, and calculate and interpret their no-arbitrage value.

1. INTRODUCTION TO PRICING AND VALUATION OF FORWARD COMMITMENTS

Forward commitments include forwards, futures, and swaps. A forward contract is a promise to buy or sell an asset at a future date at a price agreed to at the contract's initiation. The forward contract has a linear payoff function, with both upside and downside risk.

A swap is essentially a promise to undertake a transaction at a set price or rate at several dates in the future. The technique we use to price and value swaps is to identify and construct a portfolio with cash flows equivalent to those of the swap. Then, we can use tools, such as the law of one price, to determine swap values from simpler financial instruments, such as a pair of bonds with a cash flow pattern similar to those of our swap.

Look out for the big picture: value additivity, arbitrage, and the law of one price are important valuation concepts.

Forwards and swaps are widely used in practice to manage a broad range of market risks. As well, more complex derivative instruments can sometimes be understood in terms of their basic building blocks: forwards and option-based components. Here are just some of the many and varied uses for forwards, futures, and swaps that you might encounter in your investment career:

- Use of equity index futures and swaps by a private wealth manager to hedge equity risk in a low tax basis, concentrated position in his high-net-worth client's portfolio.
- Use of interest rate swaps by a defined benefits plan manager to hedge interest rate risk and to manage the pension plan's duration gap.
- Use of derivatives (total return swaps, equity futures, bond futures, etc.) overlays by a university endowment for tactical asset allocation and portfolio rebalancing.
- Use of interest rate swaps by a corporate borrower to synthetically convert floating-rate debt securities to fixed-rate debt securities (or vice versa).
- Use of VIX futures and inflation swaps by a firm's market strategist to infer expectations about market volatility and inflation rates, respectively.

1.1. Principles of Arbitrage-Free Pricing and Valuation of Forward Commitments

In this section, we examine arbitrage-free pricing and valuation of forward commitments— also known as the no-arbitrage approach to pricing and valuing such instruments. We introduce some guiding principles that heavily influence the activities of arbitrageurs, who are price setters in forward commitment markets.

There is a distinction between the pricing and the valuation of forward commitments. Forward commitment pricing involves determining the appropriate forward commitment price or rate when initiating the forward commitment contract. Forward commitment valuation involves determining the appropriate value of the forward commitment, typically after it has been initiated.

Our approach to pricing and valuation is based on the assumption that prices adjust to prevent arbitrage profits. Hence, the material will be covered from an arbitrageur's perspective. Key to understanding this material is to think like an arbitrageur. Specifically, the arbitrageur seeks to make a profit following two rules:

Rule #1: Do not use your own money; and
Rule #2: Do not take any price risk.

To make a profit, subject to these restrictions, the arbitrageur may need to borrow or lend money and buy or sell assets. The no-arbitrage approach considers the contract's cash flows from contract initiation (Time 0) to contract maturity (Time T). If an initial investment requires an outflow of 100 euros, then we will present it as a −100 euro cash flow. Cash inflows to the arbitrageur have a positive sign, and outflows are negative.

Pricing and valuation tasks based on the no-arbitrage approach imply an inability to create a portfolio that earns a risk-free profit without making a positive net investment of capital. In other words, if cash and forward markets are priced correctly with respect to each other, we cannot create such a portfolio. That is, we cannot create money today with no risk or future liability. This approach is built on the **law of one price**, which states that if two investments have equivalent future cash flows regardless of what will happen in the future, then these two investments should have the same current price. Alternatively, if the law of one price is violated, someone could buy the cheaper asset and sell the more expensive asset, resulting in a gain at no risk and with no commitment of capital. The law of one price can be used with the value additivity principle, which states that the value of a portfolio is simply the sum of the values of each instrument held in the portfolio.

Throughout this discussion of forward commitments, the following key assumptions are made: (1) replicating instruments are identifiable and investable; (2) market frictions are nil; (3) short selling is allowed with full use of proceeds; and (4) borrowing and lending are available at a known risk-free rate.

Our analyses will rely on the **carry arbitrage model**, a no-arbitrage approach in which the underlying instrument is either bought or sold along with establishing a forward position—hence the term "carry." Carry arbitrage models are also known as cost-of-carry arbitrage models or cash-and-carry arbitrage models. Carry arbitrage models account for costs to carry/hold the underlying asset. Carry costs include financing costs plus storage and insurance costs (for physical underlying, like gold). The carry arbitrage model must also adjust for any carry benefits (i.e., negative carry costs), including dividends and interest (such as bond coupons) received. Typically, each type of forward commitment will result in a different model, but common elements will be observed. Carry arbitrage models are a great first approximation to explaining observed forward commitment prices in many markets.

The central theme here is that forward commitments are generally priced so as to preclude arbitrage profits. Section 3 demonstrates how to price and value equity, interest rate, fixed-income, and currency forward contracts. We also explain how these results apply to futures contracts.

1.2. Pricing and Valuing Generic Forward and Futures Contracts

In this section, we examine the pricing of forward and futures contracts based on the no-arbitrage approach. The resulting carry arbitrage models are based on the replication of the forward contract payoff with a position in the underlying that is financed through an external source. Although the margin requirements, mark-to-market features, and centralized clearing in futures markets result in material differences between forward and futures markets in some cases, we focus mainly on cases in which the particular carry arbitrage model can be used in both markets.

1.2.1. Forwards and Futures

Forward and futures contracts are similar in that they are both agreements in which one party is legally obligated to sell and the other party is legally obligated to buy an asset (financial or otherwise) at an agreed price at some specific date in the future. The main difference is that a futures contract is an exchange-traded financial instrument. Contracts trading on an organized exchange, such as the Chicago Mercantile Exchange (CME), incorporate standard features to facilitate trading and ensure both parties fulfill their obligations. For example, a gold futures contract traded on the CME (COMEX) features a standard contract size of 100 ounces, agreed upon deliverable assets (gold bars, perhaps), and a limited choice of maturity dates. To ensure performance of the long and the short parties, the futures exchange requires the posting and daily maintenance of a margin account.

A forward contract is an agreement to buy or sell a specific asset (financial or otherwise) at an agreed price at some specific date in the future. Forward contracts are bilateral non-exchange traded contracts, offering flexibility in terms of size, type of the underlying asset, expiration date, and settlement date. This customization comes at a price of potential credit risk and ability to unwind the position. Since the financial crisis, best practices for OTC contracts suggest daily settlement and margin requirements for forward contracts similar to those required by futures exchanges. Without daily settlement, a forward contract may accumulate (or may lose) value over time. Some of the differences and similarities between forwards and futures are summarized in Exhibit 1.

EXHIBIT 1   Characteristics of Futures and Forward Contracts

Futures	Forwards
Exchange-traded	Negotiated between the contract counterparties
Standardized dates and deliverables	Customized dates and deliverables
Trades guaranteed by a clearinghouse	Trading subject to counterparty risk
Initial value = 0	Initial value = 0 (Typically, but not required)
An initial margin deposit specified by the exchange is required. The margin account is adjusted for gains and losses daily. If daily losses cause the margin balance to drop below a limit set by the futures exchange (i.e., maintenance margin), additional funds must be deposited, or the position will be closed.	Margin requirements may be specified by the counterparties.
Daily settlement marks the contract price equal to the market price and contract value = 0.	Contract may outline a settlement schedule. The forward may accumulate (or lose) value between settlement periods or until maturity (if no early settlements are required).

Forward price (F) or **futures price** (f) refers to the price that is negotiated between the parties to the forward or futures contract, respectively.

Our notation will be as follows, let:
S_t represent spot price (cash price for immediate delivery) of the underlying instrument at any time t,
F_t represent forward price at any time t, and
f_t represent futures price at any time t.

Therefore, S_0, F_0, and f_0 denote, respectively, the spot, forward, and futures price, respectively, established at the initiation date, 0. The initial forward price is established to make the contract value zero for both the long and short parties. The forward (delivery) price does not change during the life of the contract. Time T represents the time at which the contract expires and the future transaction is scheduled to take place. Thus, S_T, F_T, and f_T are the spot, forward, and futures price, respectively, at expiration time T. Between initiation at time 0 and expiration at time T, the spot price of the underlying asset may fluctuate to a new value, S_t. The price of a newly created forward or futures contract at time t with the same underlying and expiration (at time T) may differ from the price agreed to at time 0. So, our forward or futures contract established at time 0 may have a positive or negative value at time t. V_t and v_t will later be used to describe, respectively, the value of a forward and futures contract at any time t.

As we approach expiration, the price of a newly created forward or futures contract will approach the price of a spot transaction. At expiration, a forward or futures contract is equivalent to a spot transaction in the underlying. This property is often called **convergence**, and it implies that at time T, both the forward price and the futures price are equivalent to the spot price—that is,

$$\text{Convergence property: } F_T = f_T = S_T.$$

The convergence property is intuitive. For example, the one-year forward price of gold (that is, the price set today to purchase gold one year from now) might be very different from the spot price of gold. However, the price to buy gold one hour in the future should be very close to the spot price. As the maturity of the forward or futures contract approaches, the forward or futures price will converge to the spot price. If the forward or futures price were higher than the spot at maturity, an arbitrageur would:

1. Sell the forward or futures contract.
2. Borrow funds using a loan to buy the asset.
3. Make delivery at expiration of the contract, repay the loan, and keep the profit.

As market participants exploit this arbitrage opportunity, the forward or futures price will fall due to selling pressure.

If the futures price is below spot price, an arbitrageur would short sell the asset, invest the short-sale proceeds at the risk-free rate, and then enter into a long futures contract. He or she would take delivery of the asset at the futures contract expiration and use it to cover the short. The profit is simply the difference between the short-sale price and the futures price, after adjusting for carrying and financing costs. These actions on the part of arbitrageurs would act to enforce the convergence property.

Prior to expiration, the price of a newly created futures or forward contract will usually differ from the spot price. The forward and futures prices may even differ slightly from each other. For example, when the possibility of counterparty default exists or when the underlying asset price (such as a bond) is correlated with interest rates (which might impact the financing costs for daily settlement), the futures price might vary slightly from the forward price. For most cases, the generalist may assume the price of a futures contract and a forward contract will be same. That is $F_t = f_t$ before expiration.

Exhibit 2 shows the convergence property for a stock index futures/forward contact under continuous compounding and varying dividend yields. To carry a stock index, we must forego the interest rate that could be otherwise earned on our money, but we will collect dividend payments. As shown in Exhibit 2, the convergence path to the spot price at maturity depends on the costs and benefits of carrying the underlying asset. Here the stock index pays a dividend yield, which is a carry benefit. To hold the stock index, we must forego interest that could otherwise be earned on the investment. This financing rate (interest rate, r_c), assumed to be 2% in the following graph, is a cost to carry the index.

EXHIBIT 2   Convergence Property: Convergence of Forward Price to Spot Price (r_c = 2% and Index Level = 100)

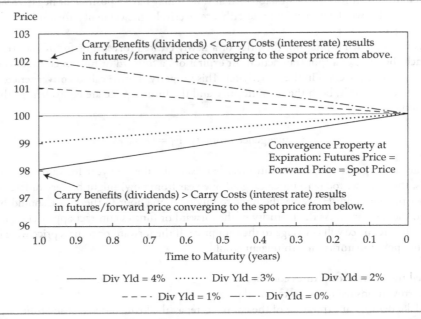

As maturity of the contract approaches (at time = T), the price of a newly created forward or futures contract will approach the spot price so that at expiration $F_T = f_T = S_T$, according to the convergence property. Prior to expiration, the forward/futures prices may be above, below, or nearly equal to the current spot price S_t. For futures contracts, the difference between the spot price and the futures price is the **basis**. As the maturity date nears, the basis converges toward zero. According to the convergence property, the future price approaches the spot price as we move toward expiration. At expiration, the futures price is equal to the price today for delivery today (i.e., spot price). If the convergence property does not hold, arbitrage will force the prices to be equal at contract expiration. The nature of the pricing relationship between the spot and forward/futures prices shown here will be explained shortly using the carry arbitrage model. For example, carry arbitrage will help us understand why assets with carry benefits (dividends) greater than carry costs (costs to finance and store the underlying) will have forward prices that converge to the spot price from below.

As market prices change, the value of existing futures and forward positions will change also. The market value of the forward or futures contract, termed **forward value** or **futures value**, respectively, and sometimes just value, refers to the monetary value of an existing forward or futures contract. When the forward or futures contract is established, the price is negotiated so that the value of the contract on the initiation date is zero. Subsequent to the initiation date, the value can be significantly positive or negative.

For example, an industrial firm requires platinum to manufacture certain components used in automobile manufacturing. The firm enters a long forward contract on 10 March. Under the terms of the contract, the firm agrees to buy 4,500 ounces of platinum on 10 September for $900 per ounce from a metal producer. From the firm's point of view, this is effectively a six-month long forward contract at a price of F_0 = $900. If the price (technically, the September forward price) of platinum increases to $1,100 in May, the firm will be happy to have locked in a purchase price of $900 (long forward contract value is positive). If the price of platinum decreases to $800, the firm must still honor the forward agreement to buy platinum at $900 (long forward contract value is negative). To describe the value of a forward contract, let V_t be the value of the forward contract at any time t.

When the forward contract is established, the forward price is negotiated so that the market value of the forward contract on the initiation date is zero. Most forward contracts are structured this way and are referred to as **at market contracts**. Again, we assume no margin requirements. No money changes hands, meaning that the initial value is zero, so, $V_0 = 0$.

At expiration, the value of a forward contract V_T is realized and, as shown next, is straightforward to compute. Remember, the profit on any completed transaction is the sale price minus the purchase price. The profit or value of the forward contract at expiration is also the sale price minus the purchase price. At initiation, a forward or futures contract allows for either a future purchase price or a future sale price, F_0, to be known at time 0. In a long forward, a buyer can lock in a purchase price, F_0. In a short forward, a seller can lock in a sale price, F_0. Again, a forward contract allows a buyer or a seller to fix an initial price F_0, either the purchase price (long forward) or the sale price (short forward). The party long the forward effectively agrees to buy an asset in the future (at time T) at a price set today (at time 0), F_0.

At expiration, the asset can be sold in the spot market at a price S_T. Therefore, a *long* position in a forward contract has a value at expiration of:

$$V_T = S_T - F_0.$$

A short position effectively locks in a sale price of F_0. It is the negative of the long position. Therefore, the value of a short forward position at expiration is the sale price minus the purchase price of the asset:

$$-V_T = -(S_T - F_0) = F_0 - S_T.$$

For example, in January a fund manager agrees to sell a bond portfolio in May for $F_0 = £10,000,000$. The fund manager locks in the sale price, F_0. If the spot price of the bond portfolio at expiration (S_T) is £9,800,000, then the short forward contract will have an expiration value to the fund manager of:

$$-V_T = £10,000,000 - £9,800,000 = £200,000.$$

The fund manager makes a profit by selling at a higher price than the market price at expiration.

Value may accumulate or diminish with the passage of time in forward contracts, which is why forward contracts require the posting of collateral. Futures contract values, on the other hand, are settled by margining at the end of each trading day when the contract is marked-to-market. The gains and losses in the position over time accumulate in the futures traders' margin accounts. Prior to daily settlement, during the trading hours the market value of a long position in a futures contract is the current futures price less the future price at the last time the contract was marked-to-market times the multiplier, N_f (the multiplier is the standard contract size set by the futures exchange).

For a long futures contract, the value accumulated during the trading day (v_t) is:

$$v_t = \text{Multiplier} \times (\text{Current futures price} - \text{Previous settlement price}) \text{ or}$$
$$v_t = N_f \times (f_t - f_{t-1}).$$

Assume an investor is long one contract ($N_f = 100$ ounces/contract) of June gold, which settled at \$1,300/ounce on the previous trading day. So, the investor is effectively agreeing to purchase 100 ounces of gold in June for \$1,300 per ounce or \$130,000 total. The trader need not pay the entire \$130,000 today but must post a deposit in a margin account to guarantee his/her performance. During the current trading day, the price of June gold increases to \$1,310. Before marking-to-market, the value of the long contract is $100 \times (\$1,310 - \$1,300) = +\$1,000$. After marking-to-market, the gain or loss is reflected in the trader's margin account and the new contract price is set equal to the settlement price. The futures contract value after daily settlement is 0 or $v_t = 0$.

2. CARRY ARBITRAGE

We first consider a generic forward contract, meaning that we do not specify the underlying as anything more than just an asset. As we move through this section, we will continue to address specific additional factors to bring each carry arbitrage model closer to real markets. Thus, we will develop several different carry arbitrage models, each one applicable to a specific forward commitment contract. We start with the simpler of the two base cases, carry of an asset without cash flows to the underlying, then move to the more complex case of forwards on assets with underlying cash flows, such as bonds with coupon payments or stocks that pay dividends.

2.1. Carry Arbitrage Model When There Are No Underlying Cash Flows

Carry arbitrage models receive their name from the literal interpretation of carrying the underlying asset over the life of the forward contract. If an arbitrageur enters a forward contract to sell an underlying instrument for delivery at time T, then to offset this exposure, one strategy is to buy the underlying instrument at time 0 with borrowed funds and carry it to the forward expiration date (time T). The asset can then be sold (or even delivered) under the terms of a forward contract. The risks of this scenario are illustrated in Exhibit 3.

EXHIBIT 3   Cash Flows from Carrying an Underlying Asset and Offsetting Short Forward Position

	Time 0	Time T
Borrowing Funds to Purchase and Carry an Underlying Asset		
Underlying	$-S_0$ (purchase)	$+S_T$ (sale)
Borrowed funds	$+S_0$ (inflow)	$-FV(S_0)$ (repayment)
Net Cash Flow	$+S_0 - S_0 = 0$	$+ST - FV(S_0)$
Short Forward Position		
Short Forward	$V_0 = 0$	$V_T = F_0 - S_T$
Overall Position: Long Asset + Borrowed Funds + Short Forward		
	$+S_0 - S_0 + V_0 = 0$	$+S_T - FV(S_0) + V_T = 0$
		$+S_T - FV(S_0) + (F_0 - S_T) = 0$
		$+F_0 - FV(S_0) = 0$
Net	**0**	$\mathbf{F_0 = FV(S_0)}$

The underlying asset is bought for S_0 with borrowed funds. The asset can be sold at time T for a price, S_T. At time T, the borrowed funds must be repaid at a cost of $FV(S_0)$; note that FV stands for the future value function. Clearly, when S_T is below (above) $FV(S_0)$, our underlying transaction will suffer a loss (earn a profit). A short forward position can be added to our long position in the underlying asset to offset any profit or loss in the underlying. Both positions have no initial (time 0) cash flow. To prevent arbitrage, the overall portfolio (Asset + Borrowed funds + Short forward) should have a value of zero at time T. If the cost to finance the purchase of the asset, $FV(S_0)$, is equal to the initially agreed upon forward price, F_0, then there is no arbitrage profit. So, we should have $F_0 = FV(S_0)$.

For now, we will keep the significant technical issues to a minimum. When possible, we will just use FV and PV to denote future value and present value, respectively. At this point we are not yet concerned about compounding conventions, day count conventions, or even the appropriate risk-free interest rate proxy.

Carry arbitrage models rest on the no-arbitrage assumptions. Therefore, the arbitrageur does not use his or her own money to acquire positions but borrows to purchase the underlying. Borrowing (if the underlying asset is purchased) and lending the proceeds (if the underlying asset is sold) are done at the risk-free interest rate. Furthermore, the arbitrageur offsets all transactions, meaning he/she does not take any price risk. We do not consider other risks, such as liquidity risk and counterparty credit risk, as they would unnecessarily complicate our basic presentation.

If we assume continuous compounding (r_c), then $FV(S_0) = S_0\,exp^{r_cT}$. If we assume annual compounding (r), then $FV(S_0) = S_0(1 + r)^T$. Note that in practice, observed interest rates are derived from market prices. For example, a T-bill price implies the T-bill rate. Significant errors can occur if the quoted interest rate is used with the wrong compounding convention. When possible, we just use basic present value and future value representations to minimize confusion.

To help clarify, we first illustrate the price exposure solely from holding the underlying asset. Exhibit 4 shows the cash flows from carrying the underlying, a non-dividend-paying stock, assuming $S_0 = 100$, r = 5%, and T = 1. For illustration purposes, we allow the stock price at expiration to go down to $S_T^- = 90$ or up to $S_T^+ = 110$. The initial transactions will generate cash flows shown at times 0 and T. In practice, the set of transactions (market purchases, bank transactions) are executed simultaneously at each time period, not sequentially. Here are the two transactions at time 0 that produce a levered equity purchase.

Step 1.   Purchase one unit of the underlying at time 0 (an outflow).
Step 2.   Borrow the purchase price at the risk-free rate (an inflow).

EXHIBIT 4   Cash Flows for Long Financial Position

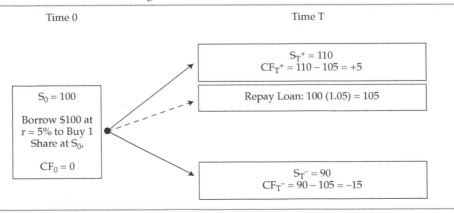

At time T (= 1), the stock price can jump up to $S_T^+ = 110$ or jump down to $S_T^- = 90$. Because the two outcomes are different, the strategy at this point has price risk. After the loan is repaid, the net cash flow will be +5 if the stock jumps up to 110 or −15 if the stock price jumps down to 90. To eliminate price risk, we must add another step to our list of simultaneous transactions. As suggested by Exhibit 3, we sell (go short) a forward contract to set a price today for the future sale of our underlying, and that price ($F_0 = FV(S_0)$) is 105.

Step 3.   Sell a forward at $F_0 = 105$. For a short forward contract, F_0 is the price agreed to at time 0 to sell the asset at Time T.

The resulting portfolio with its offsetting transaction is illustrated in Exhibit 5.

EXHIBIT 5   Cash Flow for Long Financial Position with Short Forward Contract

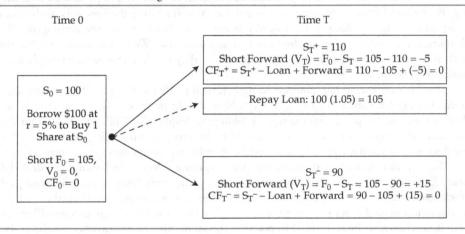

Regardless of the value of the underlying at maturity, we owe 105 on the loan. Notice that at expiration the underlying is worth 90 or 110. Since we agreed to sell the asset at 105, the forward contract value is either 15 or −5, respectively. If the asset is selling for 90 at time T, the forward contract allows us to sell our underlying position for 15 more (105 − 90) than in the spot market. The combination of the proceeds from the sale of the underlying and the value of the short forward at maturity is always 105 (= 90 + 15 or 110 − 5), which is precisely the amount necessary to pay off the loan. So, there is zero net cash flow at expiration under any and all circumstances. Since this transaction has no risk (no uncertainty about value at time T), we require that the no-arbitrage forward price (F_0) is simply the future value of the underlying growing at the risk-free rate, or

$$F_0 = \text{Future value of underlying} = FV(S_0). \tag{1}$$

In our example, $F_0 = FV(S_0) = 105$. In fact, with annual compounding and T = 1, we have simply $F_0 = S_0(1 + r)^T = 100(1 + 0.05)^1$. The future value refers to the amount of money equal to the spot price invested at the compounded risk-free interest rate during the time period. It is not to be confused with or mistaken for the mathematical expectation of the spot price at time T.

Without market frictions, arbitrage may be possible when mispricing occurs. To better understand the arbitrage mechanics, suppose that $F_0 = 106$. Based on the prior information, we observe that the forward price is higher than the price suggested by the carry arbitrage model—recall $F_0 = FV(S_0) = 105$. Because the carry arbitrage model value is lower than the market's forward price, we conclude that the market's forward price is too high and should be sold. An arbitrage opportunity exists, and it will involve selling the forward contract at 106 (Step 1). Step 2 occurs when a second transaction is needed to borrow funds to undertake Step 3, purchase of the underlying instrument so that gains (or losses) in the underlying will offset losses (or gains) on the forward contract. Note, the second step ensures the arbitrageur does not use his or her own money. The third transaction, the purchase of the underlying security, guarantees the arbitrageur does not take any market price risk. Note that all three transactions are done simultaneously. To summarize, the arbitrage transactions for $F_0 > FV(S_0)$ can be represented in the following three steps:

Step 1. Sell the forward contract on the underlying.
Step 2. Borrow the funds to purchase the underlying.
Step 3. Purchase the underlying.

Exhibit 6 shows the resulting cash flows from these transactions. This strategy is known as carry arbitrage because we are carrying—that is, we are long—the underlying instrument. At time T, we earn an arbitrage profit of +1. We do not use any of our own money and make a profit no matter the price of the underlying at maturity (i.e., 110, 90, or anything else). Since the profit of +1 at maturity occurs under every circumstance, it is considered risk-free. Any situation that allows a risk-free profit with no upfront cost will not be available for very long. It represents a clear arbitrage opportunity, one that will be pursued until forward prices fall and eliminate the arbitrage opportunity.

Note that if the forward price, F_0, were 106, the value of the forward contract at time 0 would be the PV of the +1 cash flow at Time T. Thus, at time 0, the value of our short forward is $V_0 = PV[F_0 - FV(S_0)] = (106 - 105)/(1 + 0.05)^1 = 0.9524$.

EXHIBIT 6   Cash Flow with Forward Price Greater Than Carry Arbitrage Model Price

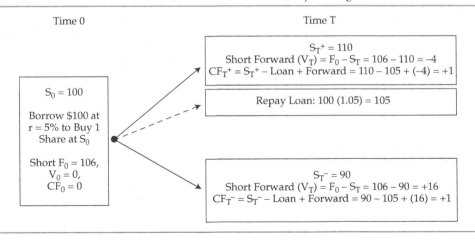

Suppose instead we observe a lower forward price, $F_0 = 104$. Based on the prior information, we conclude that the forward price is too low when compared to the forward price determined by the carry arbitrage model of $F_0 = FV(S_0) = 105$. Since the forward price is too low, Step 1 is to buy the forward contract, and the value at T is $S_T - F_0$. The arbitrageur does not want any price risk, so Step 2 is to sell short the underlying instrument. To accomplish Step 2, we must borrow the asset and sell it. Note that when an arbitrageur needs to sell the underlying, it must be assumed that he/she does not hold it in inventory and thus must sell it short. If the underlying were held in inventory, the investment in it would not be accounted for in the analysis. When the transaction calls for selling a derivative instrument, such as a forward contract, it is always just selling—technically, not short selling.

The long forward contract will allow us to cover our short later. The arbitrageur will then lend the short sale proceeds of 100 at the risk-free rate (Step 3). The deposit of 100 will grow to 105 at time T. Clearly, we will have a profit of +1 when we buy the asset at 104 and deliver it to clear the short. Again, to summarize, the arbitrage transactions when the forward price is too low—that is, $F_0 < FV(S_0)$—involve the following three steps:

Step 1.   Buy the forward contract on the underlying.
Step 2.   Sell the underlying short.
Step 3.   Lend the short sale proceeds.

We must replace the asset at a price of S_T, but we have +105 from the loan and a long forward at 104. Remember, the value of a long forward at time T is $V_T = S_T - F_0$. So, using the prior information, the value of the forward at expiration will be $90 - 104 = -14$ (if $S_T^- = 90$) or $110 - 104 = +6$ (if $S_T^+ = 110$). Thus, the cash flows at maturity will be $CF^- = +105 - 14 - 90 = +1$ or $CF^+ = +105 + 6 - 110 = +1$. Again, we make a profit equal to the mispricing of +1 regardless of the stock value at time T. It is an arbitrage profit, since it was done with no money invested and with no risk.

Note that this set of transactions is the exact opposite of the prior case in Exhibit 6. This strategy is known as **reverse carry arbitrage** because we are doing the opposite of carrying the underlying instrument; that is, we are selling short the underlying instrument.

Therefore, unless $F_0 = FV(S_0)$, there is an arbitrage opportunity. Notice that if $F_0 > FV(S_0)$, then the forward contract is sold and the underlying is purchased. Thus, arbitrageurs drive down the forward price and drive up the underlying price until $F_0 = FV(S_0)$ and a risk-free positive cash flow today (i.e., in PV terms) no longer exists. Further, if $F_0 < FV(S_0)$, then the forward contract is purchased and the underlying is sold short. In this case, the forward price is driven up and the underlying price is driven down. Absent market frictions, arbitrageurs' market activities will drive forward prices to equal the future value of the underlying, bringing the law of one price into effect once again. Most importantly, if the forward contract is priced at its equilibrium price, there will be no arbitrage profit.

EXAMPLE 1   Forward Contract Price

An Australian stock paying no dividends is trading in Australian dollars for A\$63.31, and the annual Australian interest rate is 2.75% with annual compounding.

1.   Based on the current stock price and the no-arbitrage approach, which of the following values is *closest* to the equilibrium three-month forward price?
     A.   A\$63.31
     B.   A\$63.74
     C.   A\$65.05

2. If the interest rate immediately falls 50 bps to 2.25%, the three-month forward price
    will:
    A. decrease.
    B. increase.
    C. be unchanged.

Solution to 1: B is correct. Based on the information given, $S_0 = $ A\$63.31, r = 2.75%
(annual compounding), and T = 0.25. Therefore,

$$F_0 = FV(S_0) = 63.31(1 + 0.0275)^{0.25} = A\$63.7408.$$

Solution to 2: A is correct, because the forward price is directly related to the interest
rate. Specifically,

$$F_0 = FV(S_0) = 63.31(1 + 0.0225)^{0.25} = A\$63.6632.$$

Therefore, we see in this case that a decrease in interest rates resulted in a decrease
in the forward price. This relationship between forward prices and interest rates will
generally hold so long as the underlying is not also influenced by interest rates.

As we see in Example 1, the quoted forward price does not directly reflect expectations of
future underlying prices. The only factors that matter are the current price (S_0), the interest rate
and time to expiration, and, of course, the absence of arbitrage. Other factors will be included
later as we make the carry arbitrage model more realistic, but we will not be including expectations of future underlying prices. So, if we can carry the asset, an opinion that the underlying
will increase in value, perhaps even substantially, has no bearing on the forward price.

We now turn to the task of understanding the value of an existing forward contract.
There are many circumstances in which, once a forward contract has been entered, one wants
to know the contract's fair value. The goal is to calculate the position's value at current market
prices. The need may arise from market-based accounting, for example, in which the accounting statements need to reflect the current fair value of various instruments. Finally, it is simply
important to know whether a position in a forward contract is making money or losing money
(that is, the profit or loss from exiting the contract early).

The forward value prior to maturity is based on arbitrage. A timeline to help illustrate forward valuation is shown in Exhibit 7. Suppose the first transaction involves buying a forward
contract with a price of F_0 at Time 0 with expiration at Time T. Now consider selling a new
forward contract with price F_t at Time t, again with expiration at Time T. Exhibit 7 shows the
potential cash flows. Remember the equivalence at expiration between the forward price, the
futures price, and the underlying price will hold: $F_T = f_T = S_T$. Note that the middle of
the timeline, "Time t" is the valuation date of the forward contract. Note also that we are seeking the forward value; therefore, this set of transactions would result in cash flows only if it is
executed. We need not actually execute the transactions; we just need to see what they would
produce if we did. This point is analogous to the fact that if we are holding a liquid asset, we
need not sell it to determine its value; we can simply observe its market price, which gives us
an estimate of the price at which we could sell the asset.

EXHIBIT 7   Long Forward Interim Value Timeline

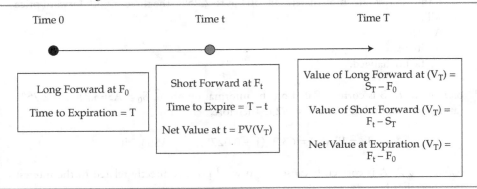

Importantly, there are now three different points in time to consider: Time 0, Time t, and Time T. Note that once the offsetting forward is entered at time t, the net position is not subject to market risk. That is, the S_T terms cancel (in Exhibit 7), so the cash flow at Time T is not influenced by what happens to the spot price. The position is completely hedged. Therefore, the value observed at Time t of the original forward contract initiated at Time 0 and expiring at Time T is simply the present value of the difference in the forward prices, $PV(F_t - F_0)$, at Time t. To be clear, the PV discounts the time T cash flow at the risk-free rate, r, to Time t. Equation 2a shows the long forward value at time t under annual compounding.

Value of Long Forward Contract Prior to Maturity (Time t) =

V_t (long) = Present value of the difference in forward prices:

$$V_t = PV[F_t - F_0] = \frac{[F_t - F_0]}{(1 + r)^{T-t}},$$ (2a)

where F_t is the current forward price and F_0 is the initial forward price.

Alternatively,

$$V_t = S_t - PV[F_0] = S_t - \frac{F_0}{(1 + r)^{T-t}}.$$ (2b)

Equation 2b can be derived from Equation 2a. Assuming annual compounding,

$$F_t = S_t(1 + r)^{(T-t)}, \text{ so } PV[F_t] = PV[S_t(1 + r)^{(T-t)}]$$

$$= S_t(1 + r)^{(T-t)} / (1 + r)^{(T-t)} = S_t.$$

While both are correct, Equation 2a may be useful in cases when market frictions may cause the observed forward price, F_t, to differ slightly from the correct arbitrage-free price. Equation 2b may be more intuitive and has the advantage that the spot price, S_t, may be more readily observed than the forward price, F_t.

As in Equation 2a, the long forward contract value can be viewed as the present value, determined using the given interest rate, of the difference in forward prices—the initial one and the new one that is priced at the point of valuation. If we know the underlying price at Time t, S_t, we can estimate the forward price, $F_t = FV(S_t)$, and we can then solve for the forward value as in Equation 2a.

The interim valuation of a short forward contract is determined in a similar fashion. The short position value is also the present value of differences in forward prices and simply the negative of the long position value. So that,

Value of short forward contract prior to maturity (Time t) $= -V_t$

$$-V_t = PV[F_0 - F_t] = \frac{[F_0 - F_t]}{(1 + r)^{T-t}},$$

or alternatively,

$$= PV[F_0] - S_t = \frac{F_0}{(1 + r)^{T-t}} - S_t$$

EXAMPLE 2   Forward Contract Value

Assume that at Time 0 we entered into a one-year long forward contract with price F_0 = 105. Nine months later, at Time t = 0.75, the observed price of the underlying stock is $S_{0.75}$ = 110 and the interest rate is 5%. The value of the existing forward contract expiring in three months will be *closest* to:

A. −6.34.
B. 6.27.
C. 6.34.

Solution: B is correct. Note that, $S_{0.75}$ = 110, r = 5%, and T − t = 0.25.

Therefore, the three-month forward price at Time t is equal to $F_t = FV(S_t) = 110(1 + 0.05)^{0.25} = 111.3499$.

Based on F_0 = 105, we find that the value of the existing forward entered at Time 0 and valued at Time t using the difference method (Equation 2a) is:

$$V_t = PV[F_t - F_0] = (111.3499 - 105)/(1 + 0.05)^{0.25} = 6.2729.$$

Alternatively, using Equation 2b we have,

$$V_t = S_t - PV[F_0] = 110 - [105/(1 + 0.05)^{0.25}] = 6.2729.$$

Now that we have the basics of forward pricing and forward valuation, we introduce some other realistic carrying costs that influence pricing and valuation.

2.2. Carry Arbitrage Model When Underlying Has Cash Flows

We have seen that forward pricing and valuation are driven by arbitrageurs seeking to exploit mispricing by either carrying or reverse carrying the underlying instrument. Carry arbitrage, when $F_0 > FV(S_0)$, requires paying the interest cost from borrowing to fund purchase of the underlying, whereas reverse carry arbitrage, when $F_0 < FV(S_0)$, results in receiving the interest benefit from lending the proceeds from short-selling the underlying. For many instruments, there are other significant carry costs and benefits. We will now incorporate into forward pricing various costs and benefits related to the underlying instrument. For this reason, we need to introduce some notation.

Let CB denote the **carry benefits**: cash flows the owner might receive for holding the underlying assets (e.g., dividends, foreign currency interest, and bond coupon payments). Let CB_T denote the future value of underlying carry benefits at time T and CB_0 denote the present value at time 0 of underlying carry benefits. Let CC denote the **carry costs**. For financial instruments, carry costs are essentially zero. For commodities, however, carrying costs include such factors as waste, storage, and insurance. Let CC_T denote the future value of underlying carry costs at time T and CC_0 denote the present value of underlying carry costs at time 0. We do not cover commodities in this reading, but you should be aware of these costs. Moreover, you should note that carry costs are similar to financing costs. Holding a financial asset does not generate direct carry costs, but it does result in the opportunity cost of the interest that could be earned on the money tied up in carrying the spot asset. Remember, the financing costs at the risk-free rate are included in the calculation of $F_0 = FV[S_0]$. Other carrying costs that are common to physical assets (such as storage and insurance) are equivalent concepts. For example, to buy and hold gold, money is taken out of the bank (opportunity cost = r, the risk-free rate) to purchase the asset, and money must be paid to store and insure it. The cost to finance the spot asset purchase, the cost to store it, and any benefits that may result from holding the asset will all play a part in determination of the forward price.

The key forward pricing equation can be expressed as:

$$F_0 = \text{Future value of the underlying adjusted for carry cash flows}$$

$$= FV[S_0 + CC_0 - CB_0] \tag{3}$$

Equation 3 relates the forward price of an asset to the spot price by considering the cost of carry. It is sometimes referred to as the **cost of carry model** or future-spot parity. Carry costs and a positive rate of interest increase the burden of carrying the underlying instrument through time; hence, these costs are added in the forward pricing equation. Conversely, carry benefits decrease the burden of carrying the underlying instrument through time; hence, these benefits are subtracted in the forward pricing equation.

Based on Equation 3, $F_0 = FV(S_0 + CC_0 - CB_0)$, if there are no explicit carry costs $(CC_0 = 0)$ as with many financial assets, then we have:

$$F_0 = FV(S_0) - FV(CB_0) = FV(S_0) - FV(\text{Benefits}).$$

For a stock paying a dividend (D), a benefit, prior to maturity of the forward contract, we have the forward contract price (F_0):

$$F_0 = FV(S_0 - PV(D)) = FV(S_0) - FV(D).$$

In words, the initial forward price (F_0) is equal to the future value of carrying the underlying (S_0) minus the future value of any ownership benefits, $(FV(D))$, for a dividend paying stock, prior to expiration. Note the FV computation for the stock price will likely use a different time period than the FV computation for the dividends. This is because the dividend FV is only compounded from the time the dividend is collected until the expiration of the forward contract. So, FV(PV(D)) for a dividend collected at time t and held to expiration at time T would be $FV(PV(D)) = FV(D/(1 + r)^t) = (1 + r)^T \times [(D/(1 + r)^t) = D(1 + r)^{T-t}$. The calculation of F_0 for a dividend paying stock is illustrated in Example 3.

EXAMPLE 3   Forward Contract Price with Underlying Cash Flows

A US stock paying a $10 dividend in two months is trading at $1,000. Assume the US interest rate is 5% with annual compounding.

1. Based on the current stock price and the no-arbitrage approach, which of the following values is *closest* to the equilibrium three-month forward price?
    A. $1,002.23
    B. $1,022.40
    C. $1,025.31

2. If the dividend is instead paid in one month, the three-month forward price will:
    A. decrease.
    B. increase.
    C. be unchanged.

Solution to 1: A is correct. Based on the information given, we know $S_0 = \$1,000$, r = 5% (annual compounding), and T = 0.25. After 2 months, we will receive the benefit of a $10 dividend, which earns interest for 1 month. Therefore,

$$F_0 = FV(S_0) - FV(D) = 1,000(1 + 0.05)^{3/12} - 10(1 + 0.05)^{1/12}$$

$$= \$1,012.2722 - \$10.0407 = \$1,002.2315.$$

Using Equation 3, we could have arrived at the same result. Here $CC_0 = 0$, and CB_0 is the PV of the dividend at time $0 = 10/(1 + 0.05)^{2/12} = \$9.919$. Then,

$$F_0 = FV(S_0 + CC_0 - CB_0) = FV(1,000 + 0 - 9.919)$$

$$= (990.081) \times (1 + 0.05)^{3/12} = \$1,002.23.$$

Solution to 2: A is correct. The benefit of the dividend occurs one month earlier, so we can collect interest for one additional month. The future value of the dividend would be slightly higher. So, the forward price would decrease slightly,

$$F_0 = FV(S_0) - FV(D) = 1,000(1 + 0.05)^{3/12} - 10(1 + 0.05)^{2/12}$$

$$= \$1,012.2722 - \$10.0816 = \$1,002.1906.$$

The value for a long forward position when the underlying has carry benefits or carry costs is found in the same way as described previously except that the new forward price (F_t), as well as the initial one (F_0), are adjusted to account for these benefits and costs. Specifically,

V_t = Present value of the difference in forward prices adjusted for carry benefits and costs

$= PV[F_t - F_0]$.

This equation is Equation 2a. The forward value is equal to the present value of the difference in forward prices. The PV discounts the risk-free cash flow $[F_t - F_0]$ at time T to time t. The benefits and costs are reflected in this valuation equation because they are incorporated into the forward prices, where $F_t = FV(S_t + CC_t - CB_t)$ and $F_0 = FV(S_0 + CC_0 - CB_0)$. Again, the forward value is simply the present value of the difference in forward prices.

EXAMPLE 4   Forward Contract Price with Carry Costs and Benefits

A long one-year forward contract on a productive asset was entered at a forward price of ₡1,000. Now, seven months later, the underlying asset is selling for ₡1,050. The PV of the cost to store, insure, and maintain the asset for the next 5 months is ₡4.00, and the asset will generate income over the next 5 months with a PV of ₡28.00. Assume annual compounding for all costs and benefits and a risk-free rate of 2%.

Based on the current spot price and the no-arbitrage approach, which of the following values is *closest* to the equilibrium five-month forward value?

A. ₡34.22
B. ₡33.50
C. ₡35.94

Solution to 1: A is correct. Based on the information given, we know the following: $F_0 = 1,000$, $S_t = 1,050$, $CC_t = 4$, $CB_t = 28$, $t = 7$ months, $T - t = 5$ months, and $r = 2\%$. The new forward price is $F_t = FV(S_t + CC_t - CB_t)$. So, with annual compounding, we have:

$$F_t = (1,050 + 4 - 28)(1 + 0.02)^{5/12} = ₡1,034.50 \text{ and}$$
$$V_t = PV[F_t - F_0) = [₡1,034.50 - ₡1000]/(1 + 0.02)^{5/12} = ₡34.22.$$

Now let us consider stock indexes, such as the EURO STOXX 50 or the US Russell 3000. With stock indexes, it is difficult to account for the numerous dividend payments paid by underlying stocks that vary in timing and amount. A **dividend index point** is a measure of the quantity of dividends attributable to a particular index. It is a useful measure of the amount of dividends paid, a very useful number for arbitrage trading. To simplify the problem, a continuous dividend yield is often assumed. This means it is assumed that dividends accrue continuously over the period in question rather than on specific discrete dates, which is not an unreasonable assumption for an index with a large number of component stocks.

The focus of the carry arbitrage model with continuous compounding is again the future value of the underlying adjusted for carry costs and benefits and can be expressed as:

$$F_0 = S_0 \exp^{(r_c + CC - CB)T} \tag{4}$$

(Future value of the underlying adjusted for carry).

Note that in this context, r_c, CC, and CB are continuously compounded rates.

The carry arbitrage model can also be used when the underlying asset requires storage costs, needs to be insured, and suffers from spoilage. In these cases, rather than lowering the carrying burden, these costs make it more expensive to carry and hence the forward price is higher. We now apply these results to equity forward and futures contracts.

3. PRICING EQUITY FORWARDS AND FUTURES

We now apply the concepts of arbitrage-free pricing and valuation to the specific types of forward and futures contracts typically used in investment management. We cover, in turn, equity, interest rate, fixed income, and currency forwards and futures. In doing so, we take account of the cash flows generated by the underlying (e.g., dividends, bond coupon payments, foreign currency interest) and the unique features of each of these contracts.

3.1. Equity Forward and Futures Contracts

Although we alluded to equity forward pricing and valuation in the last section, we will now illustrate with concrete examples the application of carry arbitrage models to equity forward and futures contracts. Remember that here we assume that forward contracts and futures contracts are priced in the same way. Additionally, remember that it is vital to treat the compounding convention of interest rates appropriately.

If the underlying is a stock, then the carry benefit is the dividend payments as illustrated in the next two examples.

EXAMPLE 5   Equity Futures Contract Price with Continuously Compounded Interest Rates

---

The continuously compounded dividend yield on the EURO STOXX 50 is 3%, and the current stock index level is 3,500. The continuously compounded annual interest rate is 0.15%. Based on the carry arbitrage model, the three-month futures price will be *closest* to:

A. 3,473.85.
B. 3,475.15.
C. 3,525.03.

Solution: B is correct. Based on the carry arbitrage model (see Equation 4), the futures price is

$$f_0 = S_0 \exp^{(r_c + CC - CB)T}$$

We assume the carry costs (CC) are 0 for a financial asset, such as a stock index. The carry benefit (CB), in this case a 3% continuous dividend yield, is greater than the financing cost r_c (0.15%), so the futures price will be below the spot price. The futures price, the future value of the underlying adjusted for carry (i.e., the dividend payments, over the next 3-months) is:

$$f_0 = 3,500 \exp^{(0.0015 + 0 - 0.03)(3/12)} = 3,475.15.$$

EXAMPLE 6   Equity Forward Pricing and Forward Valuation with Discrete Dividends

Suppose Nestlé common stock is trading for CHF70 and pays a CHF2.20 dividend in one month. Further, assume the Swiss one-month risk-free rate is 1.0%, quoted on an annual compounding basis. Assume that the stock goes ex-dividend the same day the single stock forward contract expires. Thus, the single stock forward contract expires in one month.

The one-month forward price for Nestlé common stock will be *closest* to:

A. CHF66.80.
B. CHF67.86.
C. CHF69.94.

Solution: B is correct. In this case, we have $S_0 = 70$, $r = 1.0\%$, $T = 1/12$, and $FV(CB_0) = 2.20 = CB_T$. Therefore,

$$F_0 = FV(S_0 + CC_0 - CB_0) = FV(S_0) + FV(CC_0) - FV(CB_0)$$
$$= 70(1 + 0.01)^{1/12} + 0 - 2.20 = CHF67.86.$$

As shown in Equation 2a, the value of a forward contract is simply the present value (discounted from time T to time t) of the difference in the initial forward price and the current forward price, that is V_t (long) $= PV[F_t - F_0]$. We will employ this basic principal to value various forward and swap contracts. Here, we find the current value (at time t) of an equity forward contract initially entered at time 0. To reiterate, the value prior to expiration is the present value of the difference in the initial equity forward price and the current equity forward price as illustrated in the next example.

EXAMPLE 7   Equity Forward Valuation

Suppose we bought a one-year forward contract at 102, and there are now three months to expiration. The underlying is currently trading for 110, and interest rates are 5% on an annual compounding basis.

1. If there are no other carry cash flows, the forward value of the existing contract will be *closest* to:
   A. −10.00.
   B. 9.24.
   C. 10.35.

2. If a dividend payment is announced between the forward's valuation and expiration dates, assuming the news announcement does not change the current underlying price, the forward value will *most likely*:
   A. decrease.
   B. increase.
   C. be the same.

   Suppose that instead of buying a forward contract, we buy a one-year *futures* contract at 102 and there are now three months to expiration. Today's futures price is 112.35. There are no other carry cash flows.

3. After marking to market, the futures value of the existing contract will be *closest* to:
   A. −10.35.
   B. 0.00.
   C. 10.35.

Solution to 1: B is correct. For this case, we have $F_0 = 102$, $S_{0.75} = 110$, $r = 5\%$, and $T - t = 0.25$. Note that the new forward price at t is simply $F_t = FV(S_t) = 110(1 + 0.05)^{0.25} = 111.3499$. Therefore, from Equation 2a we have:

$$V_t = PV[F_t - F_0] = (111.3499 - 102)/(1 + 0.05)^{0.25} = 9.2366, \text{ or}$$

alternatively, using Equation 2b,

$$V_t = S_t - PV[F_0] = 110 - 102/(1 + 0.05)^{0.25} = 9.2366.$$

Thus, we see that the current forward value is greater than the difference between the current underlying price of 110 and the initial forward price of 102 due to interest costs resulting in the new forward price being 111.35.

Solution to 2: A is correct. The old forward price is fixed. The discounted difference in the new forward price and the old forward price is the value. If we impose a new dividend, it would lower the new forward price and thus lower the value of the old forward contract.

Solution to 3: B is correct. Futures contracts are marked to market daily, which implies that the market value, resulting in profits and losses, is received or paid at each daily settlement. Hence, the equity futures value is zero each day after settlement has occurred.

We turn now to the widely used interest rate forward and futures contracts.

3.2. Interest Rate Forward and Futures Contracts

Libor, which stands for London Interbank Offered Rate, is a widely used interest rate that serves as the underlying for many derivative instruments. It represents the rate at which London banks can borrow from other London banks. When these loans are in dollars, they are known as Eurodollar time deposits, with the rate referred to as dollar Libor. There are, however, Libor rates for all major non-dollar currencies. Average Libor rates are derived and posted daily at 11:30 a.m. London time. Lenders and participants in the interest rate derivatives market use these posted Libor rates to determine the interest payments on loans and the payoffs of various derivatives. In 2008, financial regulators and many market participants began to suspect that the daily quoted Libor rates, which were compiled by the British Bankers Association (BBA), were being manipulated by certain banks that submitted their rates to the BBA for use in determining average Libor rates. The manipulation of Libor by some participants has resulted in the search for a new market reference rate (MRR), which would serve as a reliable reference for financial transactions. Candidates to replace Libor include SOFR (Secured Overnight Financing Rate), which would be determined by the Federal Reserve Bank of New York, and SONIA (Sterling Overnight Index Average), administered by the Bank of England. Libor is expected to be published until the end of 2021. Which MRR will replace Libor has yet to be decided, so for the examples in this section, we will continue to use Libor.

Currently, there are active forward and futures markets for derivatives based on Libor. We will use the symbol L_m to represent our spot MRR. Our focus will be on forward markets, as represented by forward rate agreements. In order to understand the forward market, however, let us first look at the MRR spot market.

Assume the following notation:

L_m = MRR spot rate (set at time t = 0) for an m-day deposit

NA = notional amount, quantity of funds initially deposited

NTD = number of total days in a year, used for interest calculations (360 in the Libor market)

t_m = accrual period, fraction of year for an m-day deposit—t_m = m/NTD = m/360 (for the Libor market)

TA = terminal amount, quantity of funds repaid when the Libor deposit is withdrawn

For example, suppose we are considering a 90-day Eurodollar deposit (m = 90). Dollar Libor is quoted at 2%; thus, L_{90} = 0.02. If $50,000 is initially deposited, then NA = $50,000. Libor is stated on an actual over 360-day count basis (often denoted ACT/360) with interest paid on an add-on basis. Add-on basis is the convention in the Libor market. The idea is that the interest is added on at the end—in contrast, for example, to the discount basis, in which the current price is discounted based on the amount paid at maturity. Hence, t_m = 90/360 = 0.25. Accordingly, the terminal amount can be expressed as:

$$TA = NA \times [1 + L_m t_m], \text{ and the interest paid is } TA - NA = NA \times [L_m t_m].$$

In this example, TA = $50,000 × [1 + 0.02(90/360)] = $50,250 and the interest is $50,250 − $50,000 = $250.

Now let us turn to the forward market for Libor (i.e., MRR). A **forward rate agreement** (FRA) is an over-the-counter (OTC) forward contract in which the underlying is an interest rate on a deposit. An FRA involves two counterparties: the fixed-rate payer (long), who is also the floating-rate receiver, and the fixed-rate receiver (short), who is also the floating-rate payer. Thus, a fixed-payer (long) FRA will profit when the MRR rises. If the floating rate is above the rate in the forward agreement, the long position can be viewed as having the benefit of borrowing at below market rates. The long will receive a payment. A long FRA would be well suited for a firm planning to borrow in the future and wishing to hedge against rising rates. A fixed-receiver (short) FRA might be a bank or financial institution hoping to lock in a fixed lending rate in the future. The fixed receiver, as the name implies, receives an interest payment based on a fixed rate and makes an interest payment based on a floating rate. If we are the fixed receiver, then it is understood without saying that we also are the floating payer, and vice versa. Because there is no initial exchange of cash flows, to eliminate arbitrage opportunities, the FRA price is the fixed interest rate such that the FRA value is zero on the initiation date.

FRAs are identified in the form of "X × Y," where X and Y are months and the multiplication symbol, ×, is read as "by." To grasp this concept and the notion of exactly what is the underlying in an FRA, consider a 3×9 FRA, which is pronounced "3 by 9." The 3 indicates that the FRA expires in three months. After three months, we determine the FRA payoff based on an underlying rate. The underlying is implied by the difference in the 3 and the 9. That is, the payoff of the FRA is determined by a six-month (180-day) MRR (such as Libor) when the FRA expires in three months. The notation 3×9 is market convention, though it can seem confusing at first. If Libor is the MRR, the rate on the FRA will be determined by the relationship between the spot rate on a nine-month Libor deposit and the spot rate on a three-month Libor deposit when the FRA is initiated. A long FRA will effectively replicate going long a nine-month Libor deposit and short a three-month Libor deposit. Note that although market convention quotes the time periods as months, the calculations use days based on the assumption of 30 days in a month.

The contract established between the two counterparties settles in cash the difference between a fixed interest payment established on the initiation date and a floating interest payment established on the FRA expiration date. The underlying of an FRA is neither a financial asset nor even a financial instrument; it is just an interest payment. It is also important to understand that the parties to an FRA are not necessarily engaged in a Libor deposit in the spot market. The Libor spot market is simply the benchmark from which the payoff of the FRA is determined. Although a party may use an FRA in conjunction with a Libor deposit, it does not have to do so any more than a party that uses a forward or futures on a stock index has to have a position in the stock index.

In Exhibit 8, we illustrate the key time points in an FRA transaction. The FRA is created and priced at Time 0, the initiation date, and expires h days later. The underlying instrument has m days to maturity as of the FRA expiration date. Thus, the FRA payoff is based on the spot m-day MRR observed in h days from FRA initiation. We can only observe spot market reference rates, such as spot Libor. To price the FRA, we require two spot rates: L_h, which takes us to the expiration of the FRA, and L_T, which takes us to the underlying maturity.

The FRA helps hedge single period interest rate risk for an m-day period beginning h days in the future. After the initial FRA rate (FRA_0) is established, we may also wish to determine a value for our FRA at a later date (Time g). As the MRR changes, our interest rate agreement may take on a positive or negative value.

EXHIBIT 8   Important FRA Dates, Expressed in Days from Initiation

Initiation Date	Evaluation Date	FRA Expires	Underlying Matures
			m
0	g	h	h + m = T

Using the notation in Exhibit 8, let FRA_0 denote the fixed forward rate set at Time 0 that expires at Time h wherein the underlying Libor deposit has m days to maturity at expiration of the FRA. Thus, the rate set at initiation of a contract expiring in 30 days in which the underlying is a 90-day MRR, denoted as a 1×4 FRA, will be such a number as 1% or 2.5%. Like all standard forward contracts, no money changes hands when an FRA is initiated, so our objective is to price the FRA, meaning to determine the fixed rate (FRA_0), such that the value of the FRA contract is zero on the initiation date.

When any interest rate derivative expires, there are technically two ways to settle at expiration: "advanced set, settled in arrears" and "advanced set, advanced settled." It is important to note that FRAs are typically settled based on "advanced set, advanced settled," whereas swaps and interest rate options are normally based on "advanced set, settled in arrears." Let us look at both approaches, because they are both used in the interest rate derivatives markets.

In the earlier example of a Libor deposit of $50,000 for 90 days at 2%, the rate was set when the money was deposited, and interest accrued over the life of the deposit. A payment of $50,250 (interest of $250 + principal of $50,000) was made at maturity, 90 days later. Here the term **advanced set** is used because the reference interest rate is set at the time the money is deposited. The advanced set convention is almost always used because most issuers and buyers of financial instruments want to know the rate on the instrument while they have a position in it.

In an FRA, the term "advanced" refers to the fact that the interest rate is set at Time h, the FRA expiration date, which is the time the underlying deposit starts. The term **settled in arrears** is used when the interest payment is made at Time h + m, the maturity of the underlying instrument. Thus, an FRA with advanced set, settled in arrears works the same way as a typical bank deposit as described in the previous example. At Time h, the interest rate is set at L_m, and the interest payment is made at Time T (h + m). Alternatively, when **advanced settled** is used, the settlement is made at Time h. Thus, in an FRA with the advanced set, advanced settled feature, the FRA expires and settles at the same time. Importantly, advanced set, advanced settled is almost always used in FRAs; although we will see advanced set, settled in arrears when we cover interest rate swaps, and it is also used in interest rate options. From this point forward in this discussion, all FRAs will be advanced set, advanced settled, as they are in practice.

The settlement amounts for advanced set, advanced settled are discounted in the following manner:

Settlement amount at h for receive-floating (Long):

$$NA \times \{[L_m - FRA_0]\ t_m\}/[1 + D_m t_m].$$

Again, the FRA is a forward contract on interest rates; long FRA (floating receiver) wins when rates increase. Note the floating rate (Libor perhaps, L_m) is received and thus has a positive sign. Since floating is received, the fixed rate (FRA_0) is paid (outflow). The FRA rate (fixed at t = 0 for the period m, which runs from time h to time T) is an outflow for the long and has a negative sign. For receive fixed (short), the FRA rate is an inflow and the floating rate L_m is an outflow.

Settlement amount at h for receive-fixed (Short):

$$NA \times \{[FRA_0 - L_m]\, t_m\}/[1 + D_m t_m].$$

The divisor, $1 + D_m t_m$, is a discount factor applied to the FRA payoff. It reflects the fact that the rate on which the payoff is determined, L_m, is obtained on day h from the spot market (advanced set), which uses settled in arrears. The discount factor is, therefore, appropriately applied to the FRA payment because the payment is received in advance, not in arrears. That is, the FRA payment is made early (advanced settled), but the interest on the loan is not due until later (settled in arrears). So, the settlement amount at time h is discounted to account for the fact that interest can be earned for m days on the advanced payment. Often it is assumed at time h that $D_m = L_m$, and we will commonly do so here, but it can be different.

Again, it is important to not be confused by the role played by an MRR, such as Libor spot market in an FRA. In the Libor spot market, deposits are made by various parties that are lending to banks. These rates are used as the benchmark for determining the payoffs of FRAs. The two parties to an FRA do not necessarily engage in any Libor spot transactions. Again, Libor spot deposits are settled in arrears, whereas FRA payoffs are settled in advance—hence the discounting.

EXAMPLE 8   Calculating Interest on Libor Spot and FRA Payments

In 30 days, a UK company expects to make a bank deposit of £10,000,000 for a period of 90 days at 90-day Libor set 30 days from today. The company is concerned about a possible decrease in interest rates. Its financial adviser suggests that it negotiate today a 1×4 FRA, an instrument that expires in 30 days and is based on 90-day Libor. The company enters a £10,000,000 notional amount 1×4 receive-fixed FRA that is advanced set, advanced settled (note the company is the short-side of this FRA contract). The appropriate discount rate for the FRA settlement cash flows is 2.40%. After 30 days, 90-day Libor in British pounds is 2.55%.

1. The interest actually paid at maturity on the UK company's bank deposit will be *closest* to:
   A. £60,000.
   B. £63,750.
   C. £67,500.
2. If the FRA was initially priced so that FRA0 = 2.60%, the payment received to settle it will be *closest* to:
   A. −£2,485.08.
   B. £1,242.54.
   C. £1,250.00.

3. If the FRA was initially priced so that FRA0 = 2.50%, the payment received to settle it will be *closest* to:
    A. −£1,242.54.
    B. £1,242.54.
    C. £1,250.00.

Solution to 1: B is correct. This is a simple deposit of £10,000,000 for 90 days at the prevailing 90-day Libor. Since m = 90, we use L_{90} = 2.55%. Therefore, TA = 10,000,000 × [1 + 0.0255(0.25)] = £10,063,750. So, the interest paid at maturity is £63,750.

Solution to 2: B is correct. In this example, m = 90 (number of days in the deposit), t_m = 90/360 (fraction of year until deposit matures observed at the FRA expiration date), and h = 30 (number of days initially in the FRA). The settlement amount of the 1 × 4 FRA at h for receive-fixed (the short) is:

$$NA \times \{[FRA_0 - L_m]t_m\}/[1 + D_m t_m]$$

$$= 10,000,000 \times \{[0.0260 - 0.0255](0.25)\}/[1 + 0.0240(0.25)]$$

$$= £1,242.54.$$

Since the short FRA involves paying floating, the short benefited from a decline in rates. Note D_m does not equal L_m in this example.

Solution to 3: A is correct. The data are similar to those in the previous question, but the initial FRA rate is now 2.50% and not 2.60%. Thus, the settlement amount of the 1 × 4 FRA at time h for receive-fixed (the short) is:

$$NA \times \{[FRA_0 - L_m]t_m\}/[1 + D_m t_m]$$

$$= 10,000,000 \times \{[0.0250 - 0.0255](0.25)\}/[1 + 0.0240(0.25)]$$

$$= -£1,242.54.$$

The short-side in the FRA suffered from a rise in rates because it is paying floating.

At this point, we highlight a few key concepts about FRAs and how to price and value them:

1. An FRA is a forward contract on interest rates. The long side of the FRA, fixed-rate payer (floating-rate receiver), incurs a gain when rates increase and incurs a loss when rates decrease. Conversely, the short side of the FRA, fixed-rate receiver (floating-rate payer), incurs a loss when rates increase and incurs a gain when rates decrease.
2. The FRA price, FRA_0, is the implied forward rate for the period beginning when the FRA expires to the underlying loan maturity. So, we require two spot rates to determine the initial forward rate. Therefore, pricing an FRA is like pricing a forward contract.
3. Although the interest on the underlying loan will not be paid until the end of the loan, the payoff on the FRA will occur at the expiration of the FRA (advanced settled). Therefore, the payoff of an FRA is discounted back to the expiration of the FRA.

As noted in point 2, the FRA price is the implied forward rate for the period beginning when the FRA expires at time h and running m days to the underlying loan maturity at time T. It is similar to any other forward contract. We wish to identify the appropriate FRA_0 rate that makes the value of the FRA equal to zero on the initiation date. The concept used to derive FRA_0 can be understood through a simple example.

Recall that with simple interest, a one-period forward rate is found by solving the expression $[1 + y(1)]\ [1 + F(1)] = [1 + y(2)]^2$, where $y(1)$ denotes the one-period yield to maturity and $y(2)$ the two-period yield to maturity. F denotes the forward rate in the next period. We can observe the spot rates $y(1)$ and $y(2)$. The forward rate is implied from those two rates. Borrowing or lending along the 2-year path must cost the same as borrowing or lending along the path using the 1-year spot and the 1-year forward. The solution for $F(1)$ is simply $F(1) = ([1 + y(2)]^2/[1 + y(1)])$ $- 1$. Assume the one-year spot rate is 3% and the two-year spot rate is 4%. To prevent arbitrage, $F(1) = ([1 + 0.04]^2/[1 + 0.03])] - 1 = 0.0501$. If the forward rate was not 5.01%, an arbitrageur could make a risk-free profit through borrowing along one path and lending along another.

As depicted in Exhibit 9, the rate for an FRA is computed in the same manner. We derive the forward rate (or FRA rate, FRA_0) from two spot rates (such as Libor): the longer rate L_T and the shorter rate L_h. Borrowing or lending at L_T for T days should cost the same as borrowing or lending for h days at L_h and subsequently borrowing or lending for m days at FRA_0.

EXHIBIT 9   FRA Rates from Spot Market Reference Rate (MRR = LIBOR)

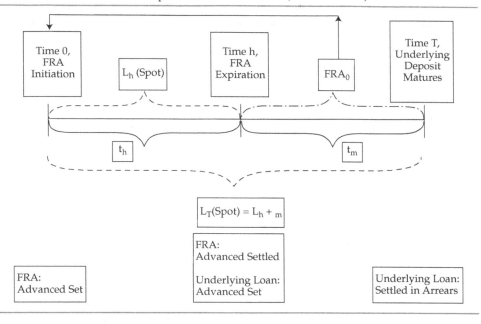

We can solve for the FRA rate by considering that the two paths must be equal to prevent arbitrage or:

$$[1 + L_h t_h][1 + FRA_0 t_m] = [1 + L_T t_T].$$

The solution in annualized form is shown in Equation 5:

$$FRA_0 = \{[1 + L_T t_T]/[1 + L_h t_h] - 1\}/t_m. \qquad (5)$$

The result is the forward rate in the term structure.

So, if 180-day Libor is 2.0% and 90-day Libor is 1.5%, then the price of a 3×6 FRA would be:

$$FRA_0 = \{[1 + L_T t_{180}]/[1 + L_h t_{90}] - 1\}/t_{90}$$

$$= \{[1 + 0.02(180/360)]/[1 + 0.015(90/360)] - 1\}/(90/360)$$

$$= 0.024907 \text{ or } 2.49\%.$$

This result can be compared with the result from a simple approximation technique. Note that for this FRA, 90 is half of 180. Thus, we can use a simple arithmetic average equation—here, $(1/2)1.5\% + (1/2)X = 2.0\%$—and solve for the missing variable X: X = 2.5%. Knowing this approximation will always be biased slightly high, we know we are looking for an answer that is a little less than 2.5%. This is a helpful way to check your final answer.

EXAMPLE 9   FRA Fixed Rate

1. Based on market quotes on Canadian dollar (C$) Libor, the six-month C$ Libor and the nine-month C$ Libor rates are presently at 1.5% and 1.75%, respectively. Assume a 30/360-day count convention. The 6×9 FRA fixed rate (FRA0) will be *closest* to:
   A. 2.00%.
   B. 2.23%.
   C. 2.25%.
   Now consider the following information for problems 2 and 3.
   Assume a 30/360-day count convention and the following spot rates:
   1-Month USD Libor is 2.48%, 3-Month USD Libor is 2.58%, 6-Month USD Libor is 2.62%, and 1-Year USD Libor is 2.72%.
2. Given these four spot rates in the Libor term structure, how many FRA rates can be calculated?
   A. 4 FRA rates
   B. 6 FRA rates
   C. 12 FRA rates
3. The 1×3 FRA fixed rate will be *closest* to:
   A. 2.43%.
   B. 2.53%.
   C. 2.62%.

Solution to 1: B is correct. Based on the information given, we know $L_{180} = 1.50\%$ and $L_{270} = 1.75\%$. The 6×9 FRA rate is thus:

$$FRA_0 = \{[1 + L_T t_T]/[1 + L_h t_h] - 1\}/t_m$$

$$FRA_0 = \{[1 + 0.0175(270/360)]/[1 + 0.015(180/360)] - 1\}/(90/360)$$

$$FRA_0 = [(1.013125/1.0075) - 1]/(0.25) = 0.022333, \text{ or } 2.23\%.$$

Solution to 2: B is correct. Based on the four Libor spot rates given, we can compute six separate FRA rates as follows: 1×3, 1×6, 1×12, 3×6, 3×12, and 6×12 FRA rates.

Solution to 3: C is correct. Based on the information given, we know $L_{30} = 2.48\%$ and $L_{90} = 2.58\%$. The 1×3 FRA rate is thus:

$$FRA_0 = \{[1 + L_T t_T]/[1 + L_h t_h] - 1\}/t_m$$

$$FRA_0 = \{[1 + 0.0258(90/360)]/[1 + 0.0248(30/360)] - 1\}/(60/360)$$

$$FRA_0 = [(1.00645/1.00207) - 1]/(0.1667) = 0.026220, \text{ or } 2.62\%.$$

We can now value an existing FRA (with rate FRA_0) using the same general approach as we did with the forward contracts previously covered. Specifically, we can enter into an offsetting transaction at the new rate that would be set on an FRA that expires at the same time as our original FRA. By taking the opposite position, the new FRA offsets the old one. That is, if we are long the old FRA, we will pay fixed and receive the floating rate L_m at h. We can go short a new FRA and receive fixed (with rate FRA_g) that will obligate us to pay L_m at h.

Consider the following strategy. Let us assume that we initiate an FRA that expires in 90 days and is based on 90-day Libor (so, a 3×6 FRA). The fixed rate at initiation $FRA_0 = 2.49\%$ and $t_m = 90/360$. We are long the FRA, so we will pay the fixed rate of 2.49% and receive floating Libor. Having entered the long FRA, we wish to value our position 30 days later, at Time g, when there are 60 days remaining in the life of the FRA (note that this is now a 2×5 FRA, as one month has passed since FRA initiation). Assume, at this point, the rate on an FRA based on 90-day Libor that expires in 60 days (FRA_g) is 2.59%. Remember, the original FRA has a fixed rate set at 2.49% when it was initiated. Now, 30 days later, a new offsetting FRA can be created at 2.59%. To value the original FRA (at Time g), we short a new FRA that will receive fixed at 2.59% and pay floating Libor at time h. Effectively, we are now receiving fixed at 2.59% and paying fixed at 2.49%. The value of the offset position is 10 bps times (90/360), as follows, times the notional amount, which is then discounted to back to Time g:

$$10 \text{ bps: } FRA_g - FRA_0 = 2.59\% - 2.49\% = 0.10\%$$

$$90/360: t_m = m/NTD, \text{ as } L_m \text{ is the 90-day Libor rate underlying both FRAs}$$

Because the cash flows at T are now known with certainty at g, this offsetting transaction at Time g has eliminated any floating-rate risk at Time T. That is, we had a long FRA at time 0 and added a short FRA at time g. Since the notional amounts and times to maturity of the offsetting transaction are the same, the floating portion of the FRA cash flows (L_m) at time T will exactly cancel, $[L_m - FRA_0] + [FRA_g - L_m] = [FRA_g - FRA_0]$.

Our task, however, is to determine the fair value of the original FRA at Time g. Therefore, we need the present value of this Time T cash flow at Time g. That is, the value of the original FRA is the PV of the difference in the new FRA rate and the old FRA rate times the notional amount. Specifically, we let V_g be the value at Time g of the original FRA that was initiated at Time 0, expires at Time h, and is based on m-day Libor, L_m. Note that discounting will be over the period $T - g$. With D_{T-g} as the discount rate and NA as the notional amount. So,

$$\text{Long FRA value at Time g: } V_g = \text{NA} \times \{[\text{FRA}_g - \text{FRA}_0] \, t_m\}/[1 + D_{(T-g)} t_{(T-g)}]. \tag{6}$$

Thus, the Time g value of the receive-floating FRA initiated at Time 0 (V_g) is just the present value of the difference in FRA rates, one entered at Time g and one entered at Time 0. Traditionally, it is assumed that the discount rate, D_m, is equal to the underlying floating rate, L_m, but that is not necessary. Note that here it is $D_{(T-g)}$.

The value of a receive-fixed or short FRA at time g is the negative of the long value ($-V_g$), so we have: $-V_g = -1 \times (\text{NA} \times \{[\text{FRA}_g - \text{FRA}_0] \, t_m\}/[1 + D_{(T-g)} \, t_{(T-g)}])$.

$$\text{Short FRA value at Time g} = \text{NA} \times \{[\text{FRA}_0 - \text{FRA}_g] \, t_m\}/[1 + D_{(T-g)} \, t_{(T-g)}] \tag{6a}$$

EXAMPLE 10   FRA Valuation

Suppose we entered a receive-floating (long) 6×9 FRA with Canadian dollar notional amount of C$10,000,000 at Time 0. The six-month spot C$ Libor was 0.628%, and the nine-month C$ Libor was 0.712%. Also, assume the 6×9 FRA rate is quoted in the market at 0.877%. After 90 days have passed, the three-month C$ Libor is 1.25% and the six-month C$ Libor is 1.35%, which we will use as the discount rate to determine the value at g.

Assuming the appropriate discount rate is C$ Libor, the value of the original receive-floating 6×9 FRA will be *closest* to:

A. C$14,105.
B. C$14,200.
C. C$14,625.

Solution: A is correct. Initially, we have $L_{180} = 0.628\%$, $L_{270} = 0.712\%$, and $\text{FRA}_0 = 0.877\%$.

After 90 days (g = 90), we have $L_{90} = 1.25\%$ and $L_{180} = 1.35\%$. Interest rates rose during this period; hence, the FRA has gained value because the position is receive-floating. First, we compute the new FRA rate at Time g and then estimate the fair FRA value as the discounted difference in the new and old FRA rates. The new FRA rate at Time g, denoted FRA_g, is the rate on an FRA expiring in 90 days in which the underlying is 90-day C$ Libor (so, a 3×6 FRA). That rate is found using Equation 5. The shorter spot rate is now for h − g (180 − 90 = 90) days, which is the new time until both FRAs expire. The reference spot rate for the underlying maturity is now in T − g (270 − 90 = 180) days.

$$\text{FRA}_g = \{[1 + L_{180} \, t_{(T-g)}]/[1 + L_{90} \, t_{(h-g)}] - 1\}/t_m,$$

T − g = 180 days and h − g = 90 days, so we have:

$$FRA_g = \{[1 + L_{180} (180/360)]/[1 + L_{90} (90/360)] − 1\}/(90/360).$$

Substituting the values given in this problem, we find:

$$FRA_g = \{[1 + 0.0135 (180/360)]/[1 + 0.0125 (90/360)] − 1\}/(90/360) =$$
$$[(1.006750/1.003125) − 1]/0.25 = 0.014455, \text{ or } 1.445\%.$$

Therefore, using Equation 6, we have:

$$V_g = 10,000,000 \times \{[0.01445 − 0.00877] (90/360)\}/[1 + 0.0135 (180/360)]$$

$$= 14,105.$$

We now turn to the specific features of various forward and futures markets. The same general principles will apply, but the specifics will be different.

4. PRICING FIXED-INCOME FORWARD AND FUTURES CONTRACTS

Fixed-income forward and futures contracts have several unique issues that influence the specifics of the carry arbitrage model. First, in some countries the prices of fixed-income securities (termed "bonds" here) are quoted without the interest that has accrued since the last coupon date. The quoted price is sometimes known as the clean price. Naturally when buying a bond, one must pay the full price, which is sometimes called the dirty price, so the accrued interest is included. Nonetheless, it is necessary to understand how the quoted bond price and accrued interest compose the true bond price and the effect this convention has on derivatives pricing. The quotation convention for futures contracts, whether based on clean or dirty prices, usually corresponds to the quotation convention in the respective bond market. In this section, we will largely treat forwards and futures the same, except in certain places where noted.

In general, accrued interest is computed based on the following linear interpolation formula:

$$\text{Accrued interest} = \text{Accrual period} \times \text{Periodic coupon amount, or}$$
$$AI = (NAD/NTD) \times (C/n),$$

where NAD denotes the number of accrued days since the last coupon payment, NTD denotes the number of total days during the coupon payment period, n denotes the number of coupon payments per year (commonly n = 2 for semi-annual), and C is the stated annual coupon amount. For example, after two months (60 days), a 3% semi-annual coupon bond with par of 1,000 would have accrued interest of $AI = (60/180) \times (30/2) = 5$. Note that accrued interest is expressed in currency units (not percent), and the number of total days (NTD) depends on the coupon payment frequency. As in the example, semi-annual indicates coupons are paid twice per year, so with 360 days per year, NTD = 360/2= 180.

Second, fixed-income futures contracts often have more than one bond that can be delivered by the seller. Because bonds trade at different prices based on maturity and stated coupon, a mathematical adjustment to the amount required when settling a futures contract, known as the conversion factor (CF), is used to make all deliverable bonds approximately equal in price. According to the Chicago Mercantile Exchange, "A conversion factor is the approximate decimal price at which \$1 par of a security would trade if it had a six percent yield-to-maturity." So, the CF adjusts each bond to an equivalent 6% coupon bond (i.e., benchmark bond). Other exchanges use different conversion factors, and these are illustrated later in the text and examples.

Third, when multiple bonds can be delivered for a particular futures contract, a cheapest-to-deliver bond typically emerges after adjusting for the conversion factor. The conversion factor adjustment, however, is not precise. Thus, if there are several candidates for delivery, the bond that will be delivered is the one that is least expensive for the seller to purchase in the open market to settle the obligation.

For bond markets in which the quoted price includes the accrued interest and in which futures or forward prices assume accrued interest is in the bond price quote, the futures or forward price simply conforms to the general formula we have previously discussed. Recall that the futures or forward price is simply the future value of the underlying in which finance costs, carry costs, and carry benefits are all incorporated, or

$$F_0 = \text{Future value of underlying adjusted for carry cash flows}$$

$$= FV(S_0 + CC_0 - CB_0).$$

Let Time 0 be the forward contract trade initiation date and Time T be the forward contract expiration date, as shown in Exhibit 10. For the fixed-income bond, let Y denote the time to maturity of the bond at Time T, when the forward contract expires. Therefore, T + Y denotes the underlying instrument's current (Time 0) time to maturity. Let B_0 denote the quoted bond price observed at Time 0 of a fixed-rate bond that matures at Time T + Y and pays a fixed coupon rate.

EXHIBIT 10   Timeline for Bond Futures and Forwards

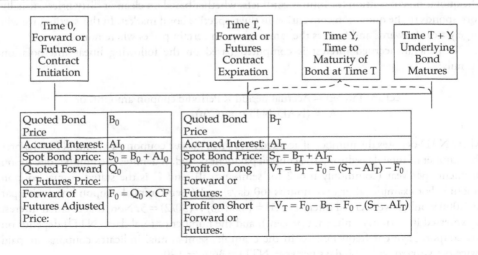

Time 0, Forward or Futures Contract Initiation		Time T, Forward or Futures Contract Expiration		Time Y, Time to Maturity of Bond at Time T	Time T + Y Underlying Bond Matures
Quoted Bond Price	B_0	Quoted Bond Price	B_T		
Accrued Interest:	AI_0	Accrued Interest:	AI_T		
Spot Bond price:	$S_0 = B_0 + AI_0$	Spot Bond Price:	$S_T = B_T + AI_T$		
Quoted Forward or Futures Price:	Q_0	Profit on Long Forward or Futures:	$V_T = B_T - F_0 = (S_T - AI_T) - F_0$		
Forward of Futures Adjusted Price:	$F_0 = Q_0 \times CF$	Profit on Short Forward or Futures:	$-V_T = F_0 - B_T = F_0 - (S_T - AI_T)$		

For bonds quoted without accrued interest, let AI_0 denote the accrued interest at Time 0. The carry benefits are the bond's fixed coupon payments, so $CB_0 = PVCI$, meaning the present value of all coupon interest (CI) paid over the forward contract horizon from Time 0 to Time T. The corresponding future value of these coupons paid over the contract horizon to time T is $CB_T = FVCI$. Finally, there are no carry costs, and thus $CC = 0$. To be consistent with prior notation, we have:

$$S_0 = \text{Quoted bond price} + \text{Accrued interest} = B_0 + AI_0.$$

We could just insert this price (S_0) into the previous equation, letting $CB_0 = PVCI$, and thereby obtain the futures price the straightforward and traditional way. But fixed-income futures contracts often permit delivery of more than one bond and use the conversion factor system to provide this flexibility. In these markets, the futures price, F_0, is defined as the quoted futures price, Q_0, times the conversion factor, CF. Note that in this section, we will use the letter F to denote either the quoted forward price or the futures price times the conversion factor. In fact, the futures contract settles against the quoted bond price *without* accrued interest. Thus, as shown in Exhibit 10, the total profit or loss on a long position in fixed-income futures at expiration (Time T) is the quoted bond price minus the initial futures price or:

$$v_T = B_T - F_0. \text{ Moreover, based on our notation, we can also say,}$$
$$v_T = (S_T - AI_T) - F_0.$$

The fixed-income forward or futures price including the conversion factor, termed the "adjusted price," can be expressed as:

$$\begin{aligned}
F_0 &= Q_0 \times CF \\
&= \text{FV of underlying adjusted for carry cash flows from Times 0 to T} \\
&= FV[S_0 + CC_0 - CB_0] = FV[S_0 + 0 - PVCI] = FV[B_0 + AI_0 - PVCI].
\end{aligned} \tag{7}$$

In other words, the actual futures price is F_0, but in the market the availability of multiple deliverable bonds gives rise to the adjustment factor. Hence, the price you would see quoted is Q_0, where $Q_0 = F_0/CF$.

Recall that the bracketed term $B_0 + AI_0 - PVCI$ in Equation 7 is just the full spot price S_0 minus the present value of the coupons over the life of the forward or futures contract. The fixed-income forward or futures price (F_0) is thus the future value of the quoted bond price plus accrued interest less any coupon payments made during the life of the contract. Again, the quoted bond price plus the accrued interest is the spot price: It is in fact the price you would have to pay to buy the bond. Market conventions in some countries just happen to break this price out into the quoted price plus the accrued interest.

Why Equation 7 must hold is best understood by illustrating what happens when the futures price is not in equilibrium. In fact, in the following scenario, the futures are overpriced relative to the bond, giving rise to an arbitrage opportunity.

Assume we observe a 3-month forward contract, so $T = 0.25$, on a bond that expires at some time in the future, $T + Y$, and this bond is currently quoted (B_0) at 107% of par. There are no coupon payments for this bond over the life of the forward contract, so $PVCI = 0.0$. Other pertinent details of the bond and futures are presented in Exhibit 11.

EXHIBIT 11   Bond and Futures Information for Illustrating Disequilibrium and Arbitrage Opportunity

Bond		
Quoted Bond Price	B_0	107.00
PV of Coupon Interest	PVCI	0
Accrued Interest at Time 0	AI_0	0.07
Accrued Interest at Time T	AI_T	0.20
Futures		
Quoted Futures Price	Q_0	135.00
Conversion Factor	CF	0.80
Adjusted Futures Price	$F_0 (= Q_0 \times CF)$	108.00
Interest Rate		
For Discounting/Compounding	r	0.20%

We observe that the full spot price of the bond is:

$$S_0 = B_0 + AI_0 = 107 + 0.07 = 107.07.$$

The futures price (F_0), which is the future value adjusted for carry cash flows (using Equation 7), is:

$$F_0 = FV[B_0 + AI_0 - PVCI] = (107 + 0.07 - 0)(1.002)^{0.25} = 107.12.$$

Note that the adjusted futures price using the quoted futures price ($Q_0 = 135$) and the conversion factor (CF = 0.80) is $F_0 = 108$. Adding the accrued interest at expiration ($AI_T = 0.20$) to the adjusted futures price gives 108.20. Remember, if you are selling a bond you receive the accrued interest; if you are buying a bond you pay the accrued interest. The adjusted futures price plus accrued interest should equal the future value of the full bond price adjusted for any carry cash flows given by Equation 7. Here, the adjusted futures price (including accrued interest) is 108.20, while the cost to buy and carry the bonds is 107.12. This implies that the futures contract is overpriced by (108.2 − 107.12) = 1.08, thus there is an arbitrage opportunity. In this case, we would simultaneously: 1) sell the overpriced futures contract; 2) borrow funds to purchase the bonds; and 3) buy the underpriced deliverable bonds.

So, to capture the 1.08 with no risk, an arbitrageur might wish to buy this bond and carry it and short the futures contract at 108. At maturity, the arbitrageur simply delivers the bond to cover the futures contract and repays the loan. Arbitrage should allow for the capture of any over (or under) pricing. Selling the futures contract at 108 involves no initial cash flow. The short futures locks in a sale price of 108 + 0.2 = 108.20 for the bond just purchased for 107.07. Since there are no carry benefits, it costs the arbitrageur 107.12, = FV(107.07) = (107.07) $(1+0.002)^{0.25}$, to carry the bond to expiration. The result is a risk-free profit at expiration of 1.08, = 108.00 + 0.2 − 107.12, for which the Time 0 PV is 1.0795, = $1.08(1.002)^{-0.25}$.

The value of the Time 0 cash flows should be zero to prevent an arbitrage opportunity. This example shows the arbitrage profit as a 1.0795 cash flow at Time 0 or 1.08 at time T per bond. If the value had been negative—meaning the full bond price exceeded the adjusted future price plus accrued interest—then the arbitrageur would conduct the reverse carry arbitrage of short selling the bond, lending the proceeds, and buying the futures (termed reverse carry arbitrage because the underlying is not carried but is sold short).

In equilibrium, the adjusted futures price of the bond plus any accrued interest must equal the cost of buying and holding the spot bond until time T. That is, to eliminate an arbitrage opportunity:

$$F_0 + AI_T = FV[B_0 + AI_0 - PVCI], \text{ which implies, } F_0 = FV(S_0) - AI_T - FVCI.$$

In this example, equilibrium is not met. The adjusted futures price, $F_0 = 108$, promises a profit of $(108 - 106.92) = 1.08$ at expiration, since

$$FV(S_0) - AI_T - FVCI = 107.12 - 0.2 - 0 = 106.92.$$

For clarity, substituting for F_0 and S_0 and solving for the quoted futures price (Q_0) results in Equation 8, the conversion factor adjusted futures price (i.e., quoted futures price):

$$Q_0 = [1/CF] \{FV [B_0 + AI_0] - AI_T - FVCI\} \tag{8}$$

In this example we have,

$$Q_0 = [1/CF] \{FV[B_0 + AI_0] - AI_T - FVCI\}$$
$$= (1/0.8) \{(1 + 0.002)^{0.25}(107 + 0.07) - 0.20 - 0.0\} = 133.65.$$

Recall, a futures price of 135 was used as the quoted price, Q_0 (108 was the adjusted futures price). Any quoted futures price higher than the equilibrium futures price of 133.65 (106.92 adjusted) will present arbitrage opportunities; hence, the arbitrage transaction of selling the futures contract resulted in a riskless positive cash flow.

EXAMPLE 11   Estimating the Euro-Bund Futures Price

Euro-bund futures have a contract value of €100,000, and the underlying consists of long-term German debt instruments with 8.5 to 10.5 years to maturity. They are traded on the Eurex. Suppose the underlying 2% coupon (semi-annual payment) German bund is quoted at €108 and has accrued interest of €0.083 (15 days since last coupon paid). The euro-bund futures contract matures in one month (30 days). At contract expiration, the underlying bund will have accrued interest of €0.25; there are no coupon payments due until after the futures contract expires; and the current one-month risk-free rate is 0.1%. The conversion factor is 0.729535.

In this case, we have the following:

$$T = 1/12, CF = 0.729535, B_0 = 108, FVCI = 0, AI_0 = (15/180 \times 2\%/2) = €0.083,$$
$$AI_T = (45/180 \times 2\%/2) = €0.25, \text{ and } r = 0.1\%.$$

The equilibrium euro-bund quoted futures price (Q_0) based on the carry arbitrage model will be *closest* to:

A. €147.57.
B. €147.82.
C. €148.15.

Solution: B is correct. The carry arbitrage model for forwards and futures is simply the future value of the underlying with adjustments for unique carry features. With bond futures, the unique features include the conversion factor, accrued interest, and any coupon payments. Thus, the equilibrium euro-bund futures price can be found using the carry arbitrage model (Equation 8):

$$Q_0 = [1/CF]\{FV[B_0 + AI_0] - AI_T - FVCI\}.$$

Thus, we have:

$$Q_0 = [1/0.729535][(1 + 0.001)^{1/12}(108 + 0.083) - 0.25 - 0] = 147.82.$$

Note that the same result can be found by $Q_0 = F_0/CF$, where:

$$F_0 = FV(S_0) - AI_T - FVCI = (1 + 0.001)^{1/12}(108 + 0.083) - 0.25 - 0 = 107.84.$$

In equilibrium, the quoted euro-bund futures price should be approximately €147.82 based on the carry arbitrage model.

Because of the mark-to-market settlement procedure, the value of a bond future is essentially the price change since the previous day's settlement. That value is captured at the settlement at the end of the day, at which time the value of the bond futures contract, like other futures contracts, resets to zero.

We now turn to the task of estimating the fair value of the bond forward contract at a point in time during its life. Without daily settlement, the value of a forward is not formally realized until expiration. Suppose the first transaction is buying (at Time 0) an at-market bond forward contract priced at F_0 with expiration of Time T. Later (at Time t) consider selling a new bond forward contract priced at F_t, again with expiration of Time T. At the maturity of the forward contracts, we take delivery of the bond under the long forward and use it to make delivery under the short forward. Assuming the same underlying, there is no price risk. The net cash flow at maturity is the difference in the price at which we sold, F_t, and the price we agreed to pay, F_0, or $(F_t - F_0)$. To confirm the price risk on the underlying bond is zero, we could also add the values of the long and the short forward positions at expiration $V_{Long} + V_{Short} = (B_T - F_0) + (F_t - B_T) = F_t - F_0$. Since the position is riskless, the value to the long at time t should be:

$$V_t = \text{Present value of difference in forward prices at time t} = PV[F_t - F_0].$$

As a simple example of bond forward contract valuation, assume that two forward contracts have been entered as follows: long forward at $F_0 = 119.12$ and short forward at

$F_t = 119.92$. Time t is one month before expiration, and both forward contracts expire at Time T. Therefore, time to expiration in one-month is $T - t = 1/12$. Finally, assume the appropriate interest rate for discounting is $r = 0.5\%$.

The forward value observed at Time t for the Time T maturity bond forward contracts is simply the present value of the difference in their forward prices —denoted $PV_{t,T}(F_t - F_0)$. That is, we have:

$$V_t = (119.92 - 119.12)/(1 + 0.005)^{1/12} = 0.7997.$$

EXAMPLE 12   Estimating the Value of a Euro-Bund Forward Position

Suppose that one month ago, we purchased *five* euro-bund forward contracts with two months to expiration and a contract notional value of €100,000 each at a price of 145 (quoted as a percentage of par). The euro-bund forward contract now has one month to expiration. The current annualized one-month risk-free rate is 0.1%. Based on the current forward price of 148, the value of the euro-bund forward position will be *closest* to:

A. €2,190.
B. €14,998.
C. €15,012.

Solution: B is correct. Because we are given both forward prices, the solution is simply the present value of the difference in forward prices at expiration.

$$V_t = PV[F_t - F_0] = (148 - 145)/(1 + 0.001)^{1/12} = 2.99975.$$

This is 2.9997 per €100 par value because this forward price was quoted as a percentage of par. Because five contracts each with €100,000 par were entered, we have $0.029997(€100,000)5 = €14,998.75$. Note that when interest rates are low and the forward contract has a short maturity, then the present value effect is minimal (about €1.25 in this example).

We conclude this section with some observations on the similarities and differences between forward and futures contracts.

4.1. Comparing Forward and Futures Contracts

For every market considered here, the carry arbitrage model provides an approach for both pricing and valuing forward contracts. Recall the two generic expressions:

$$F_0 = FV(S_0 + CC_0 - CB_0) \text{ (Forward pricing)}$$
$$V_t = PV[F_t - F_0] \text{ (Forward valuation)}$$

Carry costs (CC) and financing costs increase the forward price, and carry benefits (CB) decrease the forward price. The arbitrageur is carrying the underlying, and costs increase the burden whereas benefits decrease the burden. The forward value can be expressed as either the present value of the difference in forward prices or as a function of the current underlying price adjusted for carry cash flows and the present value of the initial forward price.

Futures prices are generally found using the same model, but futures values are different because of the daily marking to market. Recall that the futures values are zero at the end of each trading day because profits and losses are taken daily.

In summary, the carry arbitrage model provides a compelling way to price and value forward and futures contracts. Stated concisely, the forward or futures price is simply the future value of the underlying adjusted for any carry cash flows. The forward value is simply the present value of the difference in forward prices at an intermediate time in the contract. The futures value is zero after marking to market. We turn now to pricing and valuing swaps.

5. PRICING AND VALUING SWAP CONTRACTS

Based on the foundational concepts we have studied on using the carry arbitrage model for pricing and valuing forward and futures contracts, we now apply this approach to pricing and valuing swap contracts.

A swap contract is an agreement to exchange (or swap) a series of cash flows at certain periodic dates. For example, an interest rate swap might exchange quarterly cash flows based on a floating rate for those based on a fixed rate. An interest rate swap is like an FRA except that it hedges multiperiod interest-rate risk, whereas an FRA only hedges single-period interest-rate risk. Similarly, in a currency swap the counterparties agree to exchange two series of interest payments, each denominated in a different currency, with the exchange of principal payments at inception and at maturity. Swap contracts can be synthetically created as either a portfolio of underlying instruments (such as bonds) or a portfolio of forward contracts (such as FRAs). Swaps are most easily understood as a portfolio of underlying bonds, so we will follow that approach.

Cash flows from a generic receive-floating and pay-fixed interest rate swap are shown in Exhibit 12. The cash flows are determined by multiplying a specified notional amount by a (fixed or floating) reference rate. In a fixed-for-floating interest rate swap (i.e., pay-fixed, receive-floating, also known as a plain vanilla swap), the fixed-rate payer in the swap would make a series of payments based on a fixed rate of interest applied to the notional amount. The counterparty would receive their fixed payments in return for making payments based on a floating rate applied to the same notional amount. The floating rate used as a reference will be referred to as the market reference rate (MRR). In our examples, we will use Libor as the MRR.

EXHIBIT 12   Generic Swap Cash Flows: Pay-Fixed, Receive-Floating

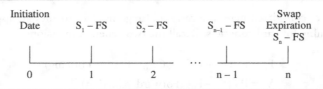

Our generic swap involves a series of n future cash flows at points in time represented simply here as 1, 2, ..., n. Let S_i denote the floating interest rate cash flow based on some underlying, and let FS denote the cash flow based on some fixed interest rate. Notice how the cash flows are netted. If the floating rate S_i increases above the agreed fixed rate FS, so $S_i > FS$, the fixed-rate payer (i.e., floating-rate receiver) will receive positive cash flow. If rates fall, so $S_i < FS$, the fixed-rate receiver (i.e., floating-rate payer) will receive the positive cash flow. We assume that the last cash flow occurs at the swap expiration. Later we will let S_i denote the floating cash flows tied to currency movements or equity movements.

We again will rely on the arbitrage approach for determining the pricing of a swap. This procedure involves finding the fixed rate such that the value of the swap at initiation is zero. Recall that the goal of the arbitrageur is to generate positive cash flows with no risk and no investment of one's own capital. To understand swap valuation, we match the swap cash flows by synthetically creating a replicating portfolio from other instruments. The swap must have the same value as the synthetic portfolio, or arbitrage will result. A pay-fixed, receive-floating swap is equivalent to a short position (i.e., issuer) in a fixed-rate bond and a long position (i.e., investor) in a floating-rate bond. Assuming both bonds were initially priced at par, the initial cash flows are zero and the par payments at maturity offset each other. In other words, the **swap rate** is the rate at which the present value of all the expected floating-rate payments received over the life of the floating-rate bond equal the present value of all the expected fixed-rate payments made over the life of the fixed-rate bond. Thus, the fixed bond payment should be equivalent to the fixed swap payment. Exhibit 13 shows the view of a swap as a pair of bonds. Note that the coupon dates on the bonds match the settlement dates on the swap, and the maturity date matches the expiration date of the swap. As with all derivative instruments, numerous technical details have been simplified here. We will explore some of these details shortly.

EXHIBIT 13   Receive-Floating, Pay-Fixed as a Portfolio of Bonds

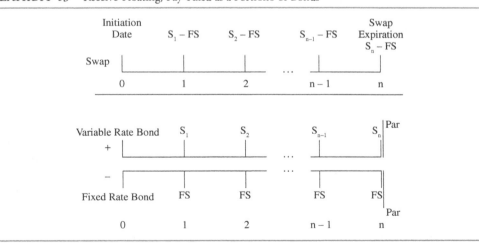

It is worth noting that our replicating portfolio did not need to use a pair of bonds. Swaps can also be viewed as a portfolio of forward or futures contracts. However, in practice futures have standardized characteristics, so there is rarely a set of futures contracts that can perfectly replicate a swap. In addition, because a single forward contract can be viewed as a portfolio of a call and a put (a long call and a short put at the same strike price equal to the swap's fixed rate would replicate the payoffs on a pay-fixed swap), a swap can also be viewed as a portfolio of options. The procedure is fairly straightforward in all cases. Just match the swap cash flows with the cash flows from a portfolio of marketable underlying instruments and rely on the law of one price and the absence of arbitrage to provide a value. Again, bonds are perhaps the best instruments to replicate a swap because they are easy to value.

Market participants often use swaps to transform one series of cash flows into another. For example, suppose that because of the relative ease of issuance, REB, Inc. sells a fixed-rate bond to investors. Based on careful analysis of the interest rate sensitivity of the company's assets, REB's leadership deems a Libor-based variable rate bond to be a more appropriate liability. By entering a receive-fixed, pay-floating interest rate swap, REB can create a synthetic floating-rate bond, as illustrated in Exhibit 15. REB issues fixed-rate bonds and thus must make periodic fixed-rate-based payments to the bond investors, denoted FIX. REB then enters a receive-fixed (FIX) and pay-floating (FLT) interest rate swap. The two fixed-rate payments cancel, leaving on net the floating-rate payments. Thus, we say that REB has created a synthetic floating-rate bond.

EXHIBIT 14   REB's Synthetic Floating-Rate Bond Based on Fixed-Rate Bond Issuance with Receive-Fixed Swap

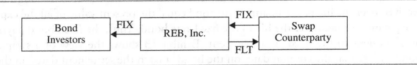

The example in Exhibit 14 is for a swap in which the underlying is an interest rate.

There are also currency swaps and equity swaps. Currency swaps can be used in a similar fashion, but the risks being addressed are both interest rate and currency exposures. Equity swaps can also be used in a similar fashion, but the risk being addressed is equity exposure.

Swaps have several technical nuances that can have a significant influence on pricing and valuation. Differences in payment frequency and day count methods often have a material impact on pricing and valuation. Another issue is identifying the appropriate discount rate to apply to the future cash flows. We turn now to examining three types of swap contracts—interest rate, currency, and equity—with a focus on pricing and valuation.

5.1. Interest Rate Swap Contracts

In this section we will focus on the pricing and valuing of interest rate swap contracts. Our approach will view a swap as a pair of bonds, a long position in one bond and a short position in another bond. At inception of a fixed-for-floating swap, a fixed rate is selected so that the present value of the floating-rate payments is equal to the present value of the fixed-rate payments, meaning the swap value is zero for both parties at inception. The fixed rate (FS) is the swap rate. Determining the swap rate is equivalent to pricing the swap. As the market rates change and time passes over the term of the swap, the value of the swap changes. The swap value (the value of the two constituent bonds) can be positive (an asset) or negative (a liability) to the pay-fixed or receive-fixed swap holders.

Swaps are OTC products with many variations. For example, a plain vanilla Libor-based interest rate swap can involve different frequencies of cash flow settlements and day count conventions. In fact, a swap can have both semi-annual payments and quarterly payments as well as actual day counts and day counts based on 30 days per month. Unless stated otherwise, we will assume for simplicity that the notional amounts are all equal to one (NA = 1). Swap values per 1 notional amount can be simply multiplied by the actual notional amount to arrive at the swap's fair market value.

Interest rate swaps have two legs, typically a floating leg (FLT) and a fixed leg (FIX). The floating leg cash flow—denoted S_i because the rate ($r_{FLT,i}$) may change (or float) during each period i—can be expressed as:

$$S_i = AP_{FLT} \times r_{FLT,i} = (NAD_{FLT}/NTD_{FLT}) \times r_{FLT,i}$$

and the fixed leg cash flow (denoted FS) can be expressed as:

$$FS = AP_{FIX} \times r_{FIX} = (NAD_{FIX}/NTD_{FIX}) \times r_{FIX}.$$

AP denotes the accrual period, $r_{FLT,i}$ denotes the observed floating rate appropriate for Time i, NAD denotes the number of accrued days during the payment period, NTD denotes the total number of days during the year applicable to each cash flow, and r_{FIX} denotes the fixed swap rate. The accrual period accounts for the payment frequency and day count methods. The two most popular day count methods are known as 30/360 and ACT/ACT. As the name suggests, 30/360 treats each month as having 30 days; thus, a year has 360 days. ACT/ACT treats the accrual period as having the actual number of days divided by the actual number of days in the year (365 or 366). Finally, the convention in the swap market is that the floating interest rate is assumed to be advanced set and settled in arrears; thus, $r_{FLT,i}$ is set at the beginning of the period and paid at the end. If we assume constant and equal accrual periods (so, $AP_{FLT} = AP_{FIX}$), the receive-fixed, pay-floating *net* cash flow can be expressed as:

$$FS - S_i = AP \times (r_{FIX} - r_{FLT,i}),$$

and the pay-fixed, receive-floating *net* cash flow can be expressed as:

$$S_i - FS = AP \times (r_{FLT,i} - r_{FIX}).$$

As a simple example, if the fixed rate is 5%, the floating rate is 5.2%, and the accrual period is 30 days based on a 360-day year, the payment of a receive-fixed, pay-floating swap is calculated as:

$$FS - S_i = (30/360) \times (0.05 - 0.052) = -0.000167 \text{ per notional of 1.}$$

Because the floating rate exceeds the fixed rate, the receive-fixed (pay-floating) party would pay this amount (0.000167 per notional of 1) to the pay-fixed (receive-floating) party. In other words, only a single net payment is made by the receive-fixed party to the counterparty. The sign of the net payment is negative as it is an outflow (i.e., negative cash flow) for the receive-fixed (pay-floating) party. Moreover, assuming the notional amount (NA) is £100 million, the net payment made by the receive-fixed party is £16,700 (= −0.000167 × £100,000,000). Finally, if, instead, the fixed rate exceeds the floating rate, the sign of the net payment would be positive as it would be an inflow (i.e., positive cash flow) to the receive-fixed party from the pay-fixed counterparty.

We now turn to swap pricing. Exhibit 15 shows the cash flows for an interest rate swap along with a pair of bonds of equal par value. Suppose (at Step 1) the arbitrageur enters a receive-fixed, pay-floating interest rate swap with some initial value, V_{swap}. Replicating this swap with bonds would entail being long a fixed-rate bond (as the arbitrageur is receiving the fixed-rate coupon) and short a floating-rate bond (as she is paying the floating rate). Therefore, to price this swap, the arbitrageur creates the *opposite* of the replicating portfolio. So, at Step 2 she purchases a floating-rate bond whose value is denoted V_{FLT}. Note that the terms of the variable rate bond are selected to match exactly the floating payments of the swap. Next, a fixed-rate bond is sold short (Step 3)—equivalent to borrowing funds—with terms to match exactly the fixed payments of the swap.

EXHIBIT 15   Cash Flows for Receive-Fixed, Pay-Floating Swap Offset with Bonds

Position	Step	Time 0	Time 1	Time 2	...	Time n
Swap	Receive-fixed, pay-floating swap	V_{swap}	$+FS - S_1$	$+FS - S_2$	...	$+FS - S_n$
Offsetting Portfolio	Buy floating-rate bond	$-V_{FLT}$	$+S_1$	$+S_2$	...	$+S_n + Par$
	Short-sell fixed-rate bond	$+V_{FIX}$	$-FS$	$-FS$	...	$-(FS + Par)$
	Net Cash Flows	$V_{swap} = -V_{FLT}$ $+ V_{FIX} = 0$	0	0	0	0

This portfolio offsets the cash flows from the swap, so the net cash flows from Time 1 to Time n will all be equal to zero. So, in equilibrium we must have $V_{swap} = -V_{FLT} + V_{FIX} = 0$ to prevent an arbitrage opportunity. The value of a receive-fixed, pay-floating swap is:

$$V_{swap} = \text{Value of fixed bond} - \text{Value of floating bond} = V_{FIX} - V_{FLT}. \qquad (9)$$

The value of a receive-fixed, pay-floating interest rate swap is simply the value of buying a fixed-rate bond and issuing (i.e., selling) a floating-rate bond. Remember, the fixed-rate and floating-rate bond values are just the PVs of all the expected interest and par payments. Pricing the swap means to determine the fixed rate (r_{FIX}) such that the value of the swap at initiation is zero. Said differently, to price the swap, the value of the fixed bond must equal the value of the floating bond in Equation 9.

As stated earlier, the value of a fixed bond (V_{FIX}) is the sum of the PV(All coupons) + PV(Par). If C is the coupon amount and par is 1, the value of a fixed-rate bond is, $V_{FIX} =$ sum of PV of all coupons (C) + PV of par value, or:

$$\text{Value fixed bond rate: } V_{FIX} = C\sum_{i=1}^{n} PV_i(1) + PV_n(1). \qquad (10)$$

Notice the coupon amount in Equation 10 is multiplied by a summation term. This term includes the present value discount factors, PV(1), for each cash flow (or coupon payment). These PV factors are derived from the term structure of interest rates at the time of valuation. The summation adds up the PV factor for each coupon as it sequentially occurs. The sum of the PV of all the coupons is added to the PV of par at maturity (Time n).

The present value expression is based on spot rates and is computed using the formula,

$PV_i(1) = \dfrac{1}{1 + Rspot_i\left(\dfrac{NAD_i}{NTD}\right)}$. Spot interest rates ($Rspot_i$) will help us value each individual cash

flow. As an illustration, consider the following term structure of rates for USD cash flows and the computation of their associated PV factors, as shown in Exhibit 16:

EXHIBIT 16   Present Value Factors Using the Term Structure

Days to Maturity	US$ Spot Interest Rates (%)	Present Value (US$1)
90	2.10	0.994777
180	2.25	0.988875
270	2.40	0.982318
360	2.54	0.975229
	Sum:	3.941199

The PV factors are computed for each rate in the term structure as:

$$PV_i(1) = \frac{1}{1 + Rspot_i\left(\dfrac{NAD_i}{NTD}\right)}.$$

Using this formula, we compute the PV factor for a unit cash flow of 1. For example, at 90 days, we have a spot rate of 2.10%, which implies a discount (PV) factor of 0.994777 = $1/ [1 + 0.0210 (90/360)]. Similarly, for 360 days, we have a spot rate of 2.54%, which implies a PV factor of 0.975229 = 1/[1 + 0.0254(360/360)].

The present value factors make it straightforward to value a fixed-rate bond under a given term structure. For example, the value of a fixed 4% bond with quarterly interest payments and Par = 1 under the term structure in Exhibit 16 can be computed using Equation 10. The quarterly coupon payment, C, is 4%/4 on par of 1 or 0.01/quarter.

$$V_{FIX} = C\sum_{i=1}^{n} PV_i(1) + PV_n(1) = 0.01(3.941199) + 0.975229(1) = 1.014641.$$

So, using Equation 10 and the PV factors and their sum from Exhibit 16, we can quickly value the bond at 101.464% of par.

To find the fixed rate needed to price a swap, we first make a slight modification to the notation in Equation 10. Since the coupon C is just the fixed interest rate multiplied by Par (and Par is assumed to be 1), we can substitute $r_{FIX} = C$, so that:

$$V_{FIX} = r_{FIX}\sum_{i=1}^{n} PV_i(1) + PV_n(1).$$

The value of a floating-rate bond, V_{FLT}, at the reset date is 1 (par) because the interest payment is set to match the discount rate. Recall that when the YTM (discount rate) of a bond is equal to the coupon rate, the bond sells at par. Here, we assume par is 1. Because the floating rate and the discount rate are initially the same for our floating bond, at the reset date we have $V_{FLT} = par = 1$.

Setting the value of the fixed bond in Equation 10 equal to 1 (the value of the floating bond at swap initiation, so $V_{FIX} = 1 = V_{FLT}$), we obtain:

$$V_{FIX} = r_{FIX} \sum_{i=1}^{n} PV_i(1) + PV_n(1) = 1.$$

This expression leads to the swap pricing equation, which sets r_{FIX} for the fixed bond:

$$r_{FIX} = \frac{1 - PV_n(1)}{\sum_{i=1}^{n} PV_i(1)} \text{ (Swap Pricing Equation).} \qquad (11)$$

The fixed swap rate, the "price" that swap traders quote among one another, is simply one minus the *final* present value term divided by the sum of present values. The fixed swap leg cash flow (FS) for a unit of notional amount (NA) is simply the fixed swap rate adjusted for the accrual period, or:

$$FS = AP_{FIX} \times r_{FIX} \text{ (Fixed swap cash flow per unit of NA).}$$

We can multiply FS times the notional amount later to find the cash flow for a swap in practice.

EXAMPLE 13   Solving for the Fixed Swap Rate Based on Present Value Factors

Suppose we are pricing a five-year Libor-based interest rate swap with annual resets (30/360 day count). The estimated present value factors, $PV_i(1)$, are given in the following table.

Maturity (years)	Present Value Factors
1	0.990099
2	0.977876
3	0.965136
4	0.951529
5	0.937467

The fixed rate of the swap (r_{FIX}) will be *closest* to:

A. 1.0%.
B. 1.3%.
C. 1.6%.

Solution: B is correct. Note that the sum of present values is:

$$\sum_{i=1}^{5} PV_i(1) = 0.990099 + 0.977876 + 0.965136 + 0.951529 + 0.937467 = 4.822107.$$

Since the final cash flow for a bond consists of the nth coupon plus par, we use the PV factor for the last cash flow, here cash flow 5, twice in Equation 11. We sum it with the other PV factors for the individual coupons in the denominator, and we apply it to Par in the numerator. Therefore, the solution for the fixed swap rate is:

$$r_{FIX} = \frac{1 - 0.937467}{4.822107} = 0.012968, \quad \text{or} \quad 1.2968\%.$$

From pricing a swap in Example 13, we now turn to interest rate swap valuation for a receive fixed (pay floating) swap. As noted previously, the fixed-rate receiver is effectively long a fixed bond and short a floating-rate bond. After initiation, this position will have a positive value when the fixed bond is trading at a premium to par (i.e., interest rates have fallen).

At any time after initiation, the market value of an existing swap can be understood by pricing a new offsetting swap. Assume $r_{FIX,0}$ is the swap rate at initiation. After initiation, the term structure of interest rates will likely imply a different swap rate, $r_{FIX,t}$.

The approach to value a multi-period swap is like the approach to valuing a single period FRA (i.e., multiplying the PV of the difference between the old FRA and the new FRA rates by a notional amount; Equation 6). Valuation is based on arbitrage transactions. Our initial swap position at Time 0 as a floating-rate payer would be offset by a position at Time t as a floating-rate receiver. The floating cash flows from paying and receiving will offset at each date (i), but the fixed payments will be different. We still receive the fixed rate, $r_{FIX,0}$, initially agreed to, but for the purposes of valuation we additionally assume the role as a fixed-rate payer at the new rate, $r_{FIX,t}$. The cash flows per unit of NA at each future date will always be based on the difference between the rate we initially received at Time 0 and the current rate paid at Time t, so $(FS_0 - FS_t) = AP(r_{FIX,0} - r_{FIX,t})$. Thus, the value of a *receive-fixed swap* at some future point in Time (t) is simply the sum of the present values of the difference in fixed swap rates times the stated notional amount (NA), or:

$$V_{SWAP,t} = NA \times (FS_0 - FS_t) \times \sum_{i=1}^{n} PV_i \text{ (Value of receive-fixed swap).} \quad (12)$$

In our valuation equation, n is the number of remaining cash flows from time t. Although this n may be different than the number of cash flows initially used to price the swap at time 0, we use the same notation. It is also important to be clear on which side of the swap this value applies. Notice the cash flow FS_0 in Equation 12 is positive. This is because the swap was initially set up (at Time 0) as a receive-fixed (FS_0), pay-floating swap. To establish a value, the swap is offset with a pay-fixed, receive-floating swap at Time t. Thus, when FS_0 has a positive sign, Equation 12 provides the value to the party initially receiving fixed. The negative of this amount is the value to the fixed-rate payer.

Now, since the *fixed-rate payer is effectively long a floating bond and short a fixed bond*, the position will have positive value when the fixed bond is trading at a discount to par (i.e., interest rates have risen). The fixed-rate payer is also the floating receiver and thus benefits as interest rates rise. At any date, the market value of a swap to the *fixed-rate payer* is based on the present value of the difference between the new offsetting fixed cash flow FS_t to be received and the fixed cash flow FS_0 he or she originally agreed to pay. It will be the negative of the receive-fixed swap value ($V_{SWAP,t}$) given by Equation 12, and we can compute it as follows:

$$-V_{SWAP,t} = -1 \left[NA \times (FS_0 - FS_t) \times \sum_{i=1}^{n} PV_i \right]$$

$$= NA \times (FS_t - FS_0) \times \sum_{i=1}^{n} PV_i \text{ (Value of pay-fixed swap).} \quad (12a)$$

Exhibit 17 provides a summary of the swap legs and the associated replicating and offsetting portfolios for each swap leg. The replicating portfolio (at time 0) provides the same cash flows as our swap. The offsetting portfolio (at time t) will offset the cash flows from our replication of the swap and help us determine a value. Note that the floating cash flows at Time 0 and Time t cancel each other out. For valuation purposes, this allows us to focus on the difference in fixed swap rates. So, the value of a receive-fixed swap at time t is based on the difference between the initial fixed swap rate and the fixed swap rate at time t, or $r_{FIX,0} - r_{FIX,t}$, as shown in the last row of Exhibit 17.

EXHIBIT 17   Swaps and Related Replicating and Offsetting Portfolios

Swap		Receive-Fixed, Pay-Floating			Pay-Fixed, Receive-Floating		
		Portfolio Position		Rates	Portfolio Position		Rates
Replicating Portfolio	Initiation t = 0	Long Fixed-Rate Bond	Short Floating-Rate Bond	$r_{FIX,0}$ $- r_{FLT,0}$	Long Floating-Rate Bond	Short Fixed-Rate Bond	$r_{FLT,0}$ $- r_{FIX,0}$
Offsetting Portfolio	Time = t	Short Fixed-Rate Bond	Long Floating-Rate Bond	$r_{FLT,t}$ $- r_{FIX,t}$	Short Floating-Rate Bond	Long Fixed-Rate Bond	$r_{FIX,t}$ $- r_{FLT,t}$
Rates for Swap Valuation	Time = t			$r_{FIX,0}$ $- r_{FIX,t}$			$r_{FIX,t}$ $- r_{FIX,0}$

The examples illustrated here show swap valuation only on a payment date. If a swap is being valued between payment dates, some adjustments are necessary. We do not pursue this topic here.

EXAMPLE 14   Solving for Receive-Fixed Swap Value Based on Present Value Factors

Suppose two years ago we entered a €100,000,000 seven-year receive-fixed Libor-based interest rate swap with annual resets. The fixed rate in the swap contract entered two years ago was 2.0%. The estimated present value factors, $PV_i(1)$, are repeated from the previous example.

Maturity (years)	Present Value Factors
1	0.990099
2	0.977876
3	0.965136
4	0.951529
5	0.937467
Sum	4.822107

We know from the previous example that the current equilibrium fixed swap rate is close to 1.30% (two years after the swap was originally entered).

1. The value for the swap party receiving the fixed rate will be *closest* to:
   A. −€5,000,000.
   B. €3,375,000.
   C. €4,822,000.
2. The value for the swap party paying the fixed rate will be *closest* to:
   A. −€4,822,000.
   B. −€3,375,000.
   C. €5,000,000.

Solution to 1: B is correct. $r_{FIX,0} = 2.0\%$, and $r_{FIX,t} = 1.3\%$. We assume annual resets (AP = 360/360 = 1), so the cash flow per unit notional is $FS_0 = 2.0\%$ and $FS_t = 1.3\%$. The swap value to the fixed-rate receiver is:

$$V_{SWAP,t} = NA \times (FS_0 - FS_t) \times \sum_{i=1}^{5} PV_i$$
$$= €100,000,000 \times (0.02 - 0.013) \times 4.822107 = €3,375,000.$$

Solution to 2: B is correct. The equivalent pay-fixed swap value is simply the negative of the receive-fixed swap value:

$$-V_{SWAP,t} = NA \times (FS_t - FS_0) \times \sum_{i=1}^{5'} PV_i$$
$$= €100,000,000 \times (0.013 - 0.02) \times 4.822107$$
$$= -€3,375,000.$$

6. PRICING AND VALUING CURRENCY SWAP CONTRACTS

A currency swap is a contract in which two counterparties agree to exchange future interest payments in different currencies. In a currency swap, one party is long a bond (fixed or floating) denominated in one currency and short a bond (fixed or floating) in another currency. The procedure for pricing and valuing currency swaps is like the pricing and valuation of interest rate swaps. Currency swaps come in a wide array of types and structures. We review a few key features:

1. Currency swaps often involve an exchange of notional amounts at both the initiation of the swap and at the expiration of the swap.
2. The payment on each leg of the swap is in a different currency unit, such as euros and Japanese yen, and the payments are not netted.
3. Each leg of the swap can be either fixed or floating.

Pricing a currency swap involves solving for three key variables: two fixed interest rates (each in a different currency) and one notional amount. We must determine the appropriate notional amount in one currency, given the notional amount in the other currency, as well as two fixed-interest rates such that the currency swap value is zero at initiation.

We will focus on fixed-for-fixed currency swaps, so we essentially trade cash flows on a bond in one currency for cash flows on a bond in another currency. Let k be the currency units, such as euros and yen. Letters are used here rather than numbers to avoid confusion with calendar time. The value of a fixed-rate bond in currency k with par of 1 can be expressed generically as the present value of the coupons plus the present value of par, or:

$$V_k = C_k \sum_{i=1}^{n} PV_i(1) + PV_n(Par_k).$$

C_k is the coupon in currency k, and Par_k is the Par value paid at maturity in currency k. The value of a fixed-for-fixed currency swap, V_{CS}, is the difference in the price of two bonds. That is, the value of a currency swap is simply the value of a bond in currency a (V_a) less the value of a bond in currency b (V_b), expressed in terms of currency a, as follows:

$$V_{CS} = V_a - S_0 V_b.$$

Here, S_0 is the spot exchange rate at time 0. To make each party indifferent between the two bonds, the par or principal notional amounts are set to reflect the current spot exchange rate. This will lead to the swap having zero value ($V_{CS} = 0$) at inception (to prevent any arbitrage opportunity), so

$$V_a = S_0 V_b.$$

The swap value may change after initiation as the exchange rate and interest rates on the two currencies fluctuate. Currency swap valuation is best understood by considering an example. Exhibit 18 provides an illustration of an at-market 10-year receive-fixed US$ and pay-fixed € swap. The US$ bond has an annual coupon of US$30 and par of US$1,150. The annual coupon amount of the euro-denominated bond is €9 with par of €1,000. Both bonds are assumed to be trading at par (note, this is $1,150 for the US$ bond, not the usual $1,000) and have a 10-year maturity. We proceed as follows:

- Step 1: We enter the receive-fixed US$ and pay-fixed € swap.
  In Steps 2 and 3, we create a portfolio to offset the swap cash flows.
- Step 2 involves short-selling a US bond (so, paying the fixed US$ coupon on the bond) to offset the US dollar inflows from the swap.
- Step 3 involves purchasing a euro bond (so, receiving the fixed € coupon on the bond), which provides offsetting cash flows for the pay-fixed € portion of the swap.

EXHIBIT 18   Numerical Example of Currency Swap Offset with Bonds

Position	Step	Time 0	Time 1	Time 2	...	Time 10
Swap	1. Receive-fixed US$, pay-fixed euro swap		+$30 − ($1.5/€) x €9 = +$16.5	+$30 − ($1.1/€) x €9 = +$20.1	...	+($30 + $1,150) − ($1.2/€) x (€9 + €1,000) = −$30.8
		0				

EXHIBIT 18   (Continued)

Position	Step	Time 0	Time 1	Time 2	...	Time 10
Offsetting Bond Portfolio	2. Short-sell US$ bond	+$1,150	−$30	−$30	...	−($30 + $1,150)
	3. Buy euro bond	−($1.15/€) x €1,000 = −$1,150	+($1.5/€) x €9 = +$13.5	+($1.1/€) x €9 = +$9.9	...	+($1.2/€) x (€9 + €1,000) = $1,210.8
Offsetting Portfolio Cash Flows		0	−$16.5	−$20.1	...	+$30.8
Overall Net Cash Flows		0	0	0	0	0

The cash flows from the bond portfolio will exactly offset the cash flows from the swap. This illustration assumes a current spot exchange rate (S_0) at which €1 trades for US$1.15, so $S_0 = \$1.15/€1$. Selected future spot exchange rates are $S_1 = \$1.50/€1$, $S_2 = \$1.10/€1$, and $S_{10} = \$1.20/€1$. These future spot exchange rates are used to show the conversion of future euro cash flows into US dollars, but notice that the overall net cash flows are all zero regardless of the future spot exchange rates. In other words, we could have used any numbers for S_1, S_2, and S_{10}. Regardless of exchange rates in the future, the bond portfolio and the swap always have offsetting cash flows. Since the portfolio and swap produce identical (although opposite) cash flows, the law of one price will allow us to determine a value for our swap in terms of a pair of bonds.

Since the net cash flows are 0 at every time t, the portfolio must be worth 0 initially. Exhibit 18 provides the intuition for solving for the notional amount (NA). For a zero cash flow at initiation, the NA (or par value) of the bond denominated in currency a (NA_a) must equal the spot exchange S_0 rate times the notional amount (or par value) of the bond denominated in currency b (NA_b). That is,

$$NA_a = S_0 \times NA_b.$$

The exchange rate is stated as number of units of currency a to buy one unit of currency b. The spot exchange rate in Exhibit 18 is $1.15/€1, so currency a (in the numerator) is US$. At the prevailing exchange rate S_0, it takes $1.15 to buy one euro. $NA_a = \$1,150$ and $S_0 = \$1.15/€1$, so $NA_b = \$1,150/(\$1.15/€1) = €1,000$. Therefore, the swap value at initiation is equal to zero, as it should be:

$$V_{CS} = V_a - S_0 V_b = \$1,150 - (\$1.15/€1) \times €1,000 = 0.$$

At any time during the life (tenor) of the swap shown in Exhibit 18, the opposite cash flows from the offsetting bond transactions result in a zero net cash flow. If the initial swap value is not at market or zero, then there are arbitrage opportunities. If the initial swap value is positive, then a set of arbitrage transactions would be implemented to capture the initial value with no net cash outflow. If the initial swap value is negative, then the opposite set of transactions would be implemented. The goal is to determine the fixed rates of the swap such that the current swap value is zero.

Because the fixed swap rate does not depend on the notional amounts, the fixed swap rates are found in the same manner as the fixed swap rate in an interest rate swap. For emphasis, we repeat the equilibrium fixed swap rate equations for each currency:

$$r_a = \frac{1 - PV_{n,a}(1)}{\sum_{i=1}^{n} PV_{i,a}(1)} \quad \text{and} \quad r_b = \frac{1 - PV_{n,b}(1)}{\sum_{i=1}^{n} PV_{i,b}(1)}. \tag{13}$$

We now have a solution for each of the three swap variables: one notional amount ($NA_a = S_0 \times NA_b$) and two fixed interest rates from Equation 13. Again, the fixed swap rate in each currency is simply one minus the final present value term divided by the sum of present values. We need to be sure that the present value terms are expressed in the appropriate currency. We illustrate currency swap pricing with spot rates by way of an example.

EXAMPLE 15   Currency Swap Pricing with Spot Rates

A US company needs to borrow 100 million Australian dollars (A\$) for one year for its Australian subsidiary. The company decides to issue US\$-denominated bonds in an amount equivalent to A\$100 million. Then, the company enters into a one-year currency swap with quarterly reset (30/360 day count) and the exchange of notional amounts at initiation and at maturity. At the swap's initiation, the US company receives the notional amount in Australian dollars and pays to the counterparty, a swap dealer, the notional amount in US dollars. At the swap's expiration, the US company pays the notional amount in Australian dollars and receives from the counterparty the notional amount in US dollars. Based on interbank rates, we observe the following spot rates today, at Time 0, and compute their PV factors and sums:

Days to Maturity	A\$ Spot Interest Rates (%)	Present Value (A\$1)	US\$ Spot Interest Rates (%)	Present Value (US\$1)
90	2.50	0.993789[a]	0.10	0.999750
180	2.60	0.987167	0.15	0.999251[b]
270	2.70	0.980152	0.20	0.998502
360	2.80	0.972763	0.25	0.997506
	Sum:	3.933870	Sum:	3.995009

[a] A\$0.993789 = 1/[1 + 0.0250(90/360)].
[b] US\$0.999251 = 1/[1 + 0.00150(180/360)].

Assume that the counterparties in the currency swap agree to an A\$/US\$ spot exchange rate of 1.140 (expressed as number of Australian dollars for US\$1).

1. The annual fixed swap rates for Australian dollars and US dollars, respectively, will be *closest* to:
   A. 2.80% and 0.10%.
   B. 2.77% and 0.25%.
   C. 2.65% and 0.175%.

2. The notional amount (in US$ millions) will be *closest* to:
   A. 88.
   B. 100.
   C. 114.
3. The fixed swap quarterly payments in the currency swap will be *closest* to:
   A. A$692,000 and US$55,000.
   B. A$220,000 and US$173,000.
   C. A$720,000 and US$220,000.

Solution to 1: B is correct. Since the PV factors are given, we do not need to compute them from the spot rates. Using Equation 13, the Australian dollar periodic fixed swap rate is:

$$r_{AUD} = \frac{1 - PV_{n,AUD}(1)}{\sum_{i=1}^{4} PV_{i,AUD}(1)} = \frac{1 - 0.972763}{3.933870}$$

$$= 0.00692381 \text{ or } 0.692381\%.$$

The US dollar periodic fixed swap rate is:

$$r_{USD} = \frac{1 - PV_{n,USD}(1)}{\sum_{i=1}^{4} PV_{i,USD}(1)} = \frac{1 - 0.997506}{3.995009}$$

$$= 0.00062422 \text{ or } 0.062422\%.$$

The annualized rate is simply (360/90) times the period results: 2.7695% for Australian dollars and 0.2497% for US dollars.

Solution to 2: A is correct. The US dollar notional amount is calculated as A$100 million divided by the current spot exchange rate, A$1.140/US$1. From $NA_a = S_0 \times NA_b$, we have A$100,000,000 = A$1.14/US$1 × N_b. Solving for N_b we have US$87,719,298 = A$100,000,000/(A$1.14/US$1).

Solution to 3: A is correct. The fixed swap quarterly payments in currency units equal the *periodic* swap rate times the appropriate notional amounts. From the answers to 1 and 2, we have

$$FS_{A\$} = NA_{A\$} \times (AP) \times r_{A\$}$$
$$= A\$100,000,000 \times (90/360) \times (0.027695)$$
$$= A\$692,375$$

and

$$FS_{US\$} = NA_{US\$} \times (AP) \times r_{US\$}$$
$$= US\$87,719,298 \times (90/360) \times (0.002497)$$
$$= US\$54,759.$$

One approach to pricing currency swaps is to view the swap as a pair of fixed-rate bonds. The main advantage of this approach is that all foreign exchange considerations are moved to the initial exchange rate. We do not need to address future foreign currency transactions. Also, note that a fixed-for-floating currency swap (i.e., pay-fixed currency a, receive-floating currency b) is simply a fixed-for-fixed currency swap (i.e., pay-fixed currency a, receive-fixed currency b) paired with a fixed-for-floating interest rate swap (i.e., pay-fixed currency b, receive-floating currency b). Also, we do not technically "price" a floating-rate swap because we do not designate a single coupon rate and because the value of such a swap is par on any reset date. Thus, we have the capacity to price any variation of currency swaps.

We now turn to currency swap valuation. Recall that with currency swaps, there are two main sources of risk: interest rates associated with each currency and their exchange rate. The value of a fixed-for-fixed currency swap at some future point in time, say Time t, is simply the difference in a pair of fixed-rate bonds, one expressed in currency a and one expressed in currency b. To express the bonds in the same currency units, we convert the currency b bond into units of currency a through a spot foreign exchange transaction at a new rate, S_t. The value of a "receive currency a, pay currency b" (fixed-for-fixed) swap at any time t expressed in terms of currency a is the difference in bond values:

$$V_{CS} = V_a - S_t V_b.$$

Substituting the valuation equation for each of the bonds, we have:

$$V_{CS} = \left(FS_a \sum_{i=1}^{n} PV_i(1) + NA_a \ PV_n(1)\right) - S_t\left(FS_b \sum_{i=1}^{n} PV_i(1) + NA_b \ PV_n(1)\right).$$

Note that the fixed swap amount (FS) is the per-period fixed swap rate times the notional amount. Therefore, the currency swap valuation equation can be expressed as:

$$V_{CS} = NA_a\left(r_{Fix,a} \sum_{i=1}^{n} PV_i(1) + PV_n(1)\right) - S_t NA_b\left(r_{Fix,b} \sum_{i=1}^{n} PV_i(1) + PV_n(1)\right). \quad (14)$$

As mentioned, the terms in Equation 14 represent the difference in value of two fixed-rate bonds. The first term in braces is the value of a long position in a bond with face value of 1 unit of currency a, which is then multiplied by the notional amount of the swap in currency a (NA_a). This product represents the value of the cash inflows to the counterparty receiving interest payments in currency a. The second term (after the minus sign) implies outflows and represents the value of a short bond position with face value of 1 unit of currency b, which is multiplied by the product of the swap notional amount in currency b (NA_b) and the current (Time t) exchange rate, S_t (stated in units of currency a per unit of currency b). This gives the value of the payments, in currency a terms, made by the party receiving interest in currency a and paying interest in currency b. V_{CS} is then the value of the swap to the party receiving currency a, while the value of the swap to the party receiving currency b is simply the negative of that amount, $-V_{CS}$.

Equation 14 seems formidable, but it is a straightforward idea. We hold a bond in currency a, and we are short a bond in currency b (which we must express in terms of currency a). It is best understood by an example of a firm that has entered a currency swap and needs to determine the current value.

Example 16 continues the case of the company using a currency swap to effectively convert a bond issued in US dollars into a bond issued in Australian dollars. In studying the problem, take care to identify currency a (implied by how the exchange rate, S_t, is given) and the party receiving interest payments in currency a in the swap.

EXAMPLE 16   Currency Swap Valuation with Spot Rates

This example builds on the previous example addressing currency swap pricing. Recall that a US company needed to borrow 100 million Australian dollars (A$) for one year for its Australian subsidiary. The company decided to borrow in US dollars (US$) an amount equivalent to A$100 million by issuing US-denominated bonds. The company then entered a one-year currency swap with a swap dealer. The swap uses quarterly reset (30/360 day count) and exchange of notional amounts at initiation and at maturity. At the swap's expiration, the US company pays the notional amount in Australian dollars and receives from the dealer the notional amount in US dollars. The fixed rates were found to be 2.7695% for Australian dollars and 0.2497% for US dollars. Initially, the notional amount in US dollars was determined to be US$87,719,298 with a spot exchange rate of A$1.14 for US$1.

Assume 60 days have passed since swap initiation and we now observe the following updated market information:

Days to Maturity	A$ Spot Interest Rates (%)	Present Value (A$1)	US$ Spot Interest Rates (%)	Present Value (US$1)
30	2.00	0.998336	0.50	0.999584
120	1.90	0.993707	0.40	0.998668
210	1.80	0.989609	0.30	0.998253
300	1.70	0.986031	0.20	0.998336
	Sum:	3.967683	*Sum:*	3.994841

The currency spot exchange rate (S_t) is now A$1.13 for US$1.

1. The current value to the swap dealer in A$ of the currency swap entered 60 days ago will be *closest* to:
   A. −A$13,557,000.
   B. A$637,620.
   C. A$2,145,200.
2. The current value to the US firm in US$ of the currency swap entered 60 days ago will be *closest* to:
   A. −$2,673,705.
   B. −$1,898,400.
   C. $334,730.

Solution to 1: C is correct. The US firm issues $87.7 million of bonds and enters a swap with the swap dealer. The initial exchange rate is given as 1.14A$/1US$, so currency a is A$. The swap dealer is receiving quarterly interest payments in currency a (A$). The swap is diagrammed for Example 15 and 16 as shown below:

Swap Cash Flows:

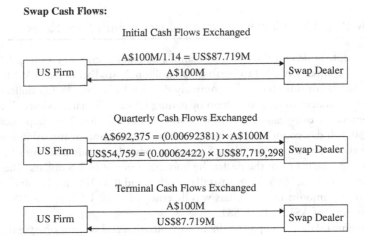

Initial Cash Flows Exchanged

A$100M/1.14 = US$87.719M

US Firm ← A$100M → Swap Dealer

Quarterly Cash Flows Exchanged

A$692,375 = (0.00692381) × A$100M

US Firm → US$54,759 = (0.00062422) × US$87,719,298 ← Swap Dealer

Terminal Cash Flows Exchanged

A$100M

US Firm → US$87.719M → Swap Dealer

After 60 days, the new exchange rate is 1.13A$/1US$ and the term structure of interest rates has changed in both markets. Equation 14 gives the value of the swap at Time t, V_{CS}. This is the value of the swap to the party receiving interest payments in Australian dollars, which is the swap dealer. Thus, using Equation 14, the value to the swap dealer receiving A$ is:

$$V_{CS} = NA_a\left(r_{Fix,a}\sum_{i=1}^{n} PV_i(1) + PV_n(1)\right) - S_t NA_b\left(r_{Fix,b}\sum_{i=1}^{n} PV_i(1) + PV_n(1)\right)$$

V_{CS} = A$100,000,000 × [0.00692381 (3.967683) + 0.986031] − 1.13 (A$/1US$) × (US$87,719,298) × [0.00062422 (3.994841) + 0.998336]

= A$2,145,203.

The first term in Equation 14 represents the PV of the dealer's incoming cash flows in A$, effectively a long position in an A$ bond. Remember, the dealer is receiving quarterly interest payments in A$ and will receive the A$100M terminal payment at swap maturity. To compute the PV of the A$ cash flows, the notional amount is multiplied by a term inside the braces, which represents the periodic interest rate multiplied by the sum of the PV factors for the four payments plus the PV factor for the terminal cash flow (where the PV factors reflect the new term structure). The second term is the PV of the dealer's US$ outflows (effectively a short bond in currency b, here US$). The PV of the quarterly interest payments and terminal payment are calculated using the new term structure and converted into A$ at S_t. Thus, we have the value of the long A$ bond minus the value of short US$ bond (stated in A$ terms). This gives V_{CS}, which is the value of the swap to the party receiving currency a and is the value from the perspective of the swap dealer.

Solution to 2: B is correct. In terms of Solution 1, the current value of the swap to the US firm is $-V_{CS}$. This represents the value to the firm making interest payments in currency a (A$).

$-V_{CS}$ = −A$2,145,203, which when converted to US$ at S_t is:

$-V_{CS}$ = −A$2,145,203 × (1US$/1.13A$) = −US$1,898,410.

Note that the US company initially issues a bond in US$ in their home market and uses the swap to effectively convert to an A$ bond issue. Understanding the swap as two bonds, the US firm is long a US$ bond (US$ is currency b in this example, which the US firm is receiving) and short a bond in A$ (currency a, which the US firm is paying). The swap offsets the US firm's US$ bond issue. The swap allows the US firm to make A$ interest payments to the swap dealer, or to effectively issue a bond in A$ (currency a).

Alternatively, if the exchange rate had been stated as $S_t = 1US\$/1.13A\$$ or equivalently as $S_t = \$0.885/A\$$, then currency a would be US$. In that case, the swap value, V_{CS}, can be understood in terms of the firm receiving US$ since the swap gives the US firm the equivalent of a long position in a US$ bond. The first term in the following equation represents the value of the US$ bond to the US firm in the swap. The second term is the value of the A$ bond position (short for the US firm) expressed in US$ terms.

$$V_{CS} = NA_a\left(r_{Fix,a}\sum_{i=1}^{n}PV_i(1) + PV_n(1)\right) - S_t NA_b\left(r_{Fix,b}\sum_{i=1}^{n}PV_i(1) + PV_n(1)\right)$$

$$V_{CS} = \$87,719,298 \times [0.00062422\,(3.994841) + 0.998336] - (1US\$/A\$1.13) \times$$
$$(A\$100,000,000) \times [0.00692381\,(3.967683) + 0.986031]$$

$$= -US\$1,898,410.$$

The swap value is negative to the US firm due to changes in the term structure and exchange rate. The A$ has strengthened against the US$, so now the US firm must pay periodic interest and principal cash flows in A$ at a rate of 1.13A$/1US$. That is, for each US$ the US firm gets fewer A$ for making payments to the dealer. The new term structure now offers lower interest rates to A$ borrowers, and this also contributes to the negative swap value for the US firm. The firm had agreed to pay higher periodic A$ rates in the swap, but now the present value of those outflows has increased.

7. PRICING AND VALUING EQUITY SWAP CONTRACTS

Drawing on our prior definition of a swap, we define an equity swap in the following manner: An **equity swap** is an OTC derivatives contract in which two parties agree to exchange a series of cash flows whereby one party pays a variable series that will be determined by an equity and the other party pays either (1) a variable series determined by a different equity or rate or (2) a fixed series. An equity swap is used to convert the returns from an equity investment into another series of returns, which, as noted, either can be derived from another equity series or can be a fixed rate. Equity swaps are widely used in equity portfolio investment management to modify returns and risks. Equity swaps allow parties to benefit from returns of an equity or index without owning any shares of the underlying equity. An equity swap may also be used to hedge risk exposure to an equity or index for a certain period.

We examine three types of equity swaps: 1) *receive-equity return, pay-fixed*; 2) *receive-equity return, pay-floating*; and 3) *receive-equity return, pay-another equity return*. Like interest rate swaps and currency swaps, equity swaps have several unique nuances. We highlight just a few. First, the underlying reference instrument for the equity leg of an equity swap can be an individual stock, a published stock index, or a custom portfolio. Second, the equity leg cash flow(s) can be with or without dividends. Third, all the interest rate swap nuances exist with equity swaps that have a fixed or floating interest rate leg.

We focus here on viewing an equity swap as a portfolio of an equity position and a bond. The equity swap cash flows can be expressed as follows:

$$\text{NA(Equity return} - \text{Fixed rate)} \text{ (for receive-equity, pay-fixed),}$$
$$\text{NA(Equity return} - \text{Floating rate)} \text{ (for receive-equity, pay-floating), and}$$
$$\text{NA(Equity return}_a - \text{Equity return}_b) \text{ (for receive-equity, pay-equity),}$$

where a and b denote different equities. Note that an equity-for-equity swap can be viewed simply as a receive-equity a, pay-fixed swap combined with a pay-equity b, receive-fixed swap. The fixed payments cancel out, and we have synthetically created an equity-for-equity swap.

The cash flows for an equity leg (S_i) of an equity swap can be expressed as:

$$S_i = NA_E \, R_E,$$

where R_E denotes the periodic return of the equity either with or without dividends as specified in the swap contract, and NA_E denotes the notional amount. The cash flows for a fixed-interest rate leg (FS) of an equity swap are the same as those of an interest rate swap, or:

$$FS = NA_E \times AP_{FIX} \times r_{FIX},$$

where AP_{FIX} denotes the accrual period for the fixed leg (for which we assume the accrual period is constant) and r_{FIX} here denotes the fixed rate on the equity swap.

EXAMPLE 17   Equity Swap Cash Flows

Suppose we entered a receive-equity index and pay-fixed swap. It is quarterly reset, 30/360 day count, €5,000,000 notional amount, pay-fixed (1.6% annualized, quarterly pay, or 0.4% per quarter).

1. If the equity index return was 4.0% for the quarter (not annualized), the equity swap cash flow will be *closest* to:
   A. −€220,000.
   B. −€180,000.
   C. €180,000.
2. If the equity index return was −6.0% for the quarter (not annualized), the equity swap cash flow will be *closest* to:
   A. −€320,000.
   B. −€180,000.
   C. €180,000.

Solution to 1: C is correct. Note that the equity index return is reported on a quarterly basis. It is not an annualized number. The fixed leg is often reported on an annual basis. Thus, one must carefully interpret the different return conventions. In this case, receive-equity index counterparty cash flows ($S_i - FS = NA_E \times (R_E - r_{FIX})$) are as follows:

€5,000,000 × (0.040 − 0.004) = €180,000 (Receive 4%, pay 0.4% for the quarter).

Solution to 2: A is correct. Similar to 1, we have ($S_i - FS = NA_E \times (R_E - r_{FIX})$):

€5,000,000 × (−0.060 − 0.004) = −€320,000 (Receive −6%, pay 0.4% for the quarter).

When the equity leg of the swap is negative, then the receive-equity counterparty must pay both the equity return as well as the fixed rate (or whatever are the payment terms). Note also that equity swaps may cause liquidity problems. As seen here, if the equity return is negative, then the receive-equity return, pay-floating or pay-fixed swap may result in a large negative cash flow for the receive-equity return party.

For equity swaps, the equity position could be a wide variety of claims, including the return on a stock index with or without dividends and the return on an individual stock with or without dividends. For our objectives here, we ignore the influence of dividends with the understanding that the equity swap leg assumes all dividends are reinvested in the equity position. The arbitrage transactions for an equity swap when dividends are not included are extremely complex and beyond our objectives. The equity leg of the swap is produced by selling the equity position on a reset date and reinvesting the original equity notional amount (NA_E), leaving a remaining balance that is the cash flow required of the equity swap leg (S_i). Technically, we just sell off any equity value in excess of NA_E or purchase additional shares to return the equity value to NA_E, effectively generating S_i. Exhibit 19 shows the cash flows from an equity swap offset with an equity and bond portfolio.

EXHIBIT 19   Cash Flows for Receive-Fixed, Pay-Equity Swap Offset with Equity and Bond Portfolio

Position	Steps	Time 0	Time 1	Time 2	...	Time n
Equity Swap	1. Receive-fixed, pay-equity swap	$-V_{EQ}$	$+FS - S_1$	$+FS - S_2$	...	$+FS - S_n$
Offset Portfolio	2. Buy NA_E of equity	$-NA_E$	$+S_1$	$+S_2$	...	$+S_n + NA_E$
	3. Short sell fixed-rate bond	$+V_{FIX}$, (C = FS)	$-FS$	$-FS$	...	$-(FS + Par)$
	Net cash flows	$-V_{EQ} - NA_E + V_{FIX}$	0	0	0	$NA_E - Par$

Assume a portfolio manager has a large position in a stock that he/she expects to underperform in the future. Perhaps for liquidity or tax reasons, the manager prefers not to sell the stock but considers a receive-fixed, pay equity swap. Exhibit 19 shows the cash flows from such a swap as well as the offsetting portfolio (to eliminate arbitrage), which will assist us in valuing the swap. In Step 1, we enter a receive-fixed, pay equity swap. Steps 2 and 3 provide the offsetting cash flows to those of the swap, which are buy NA_E worth of equity and short sell a fixed-rate bond (with coupon equal to the fixed interest rate leg cash flows), respectively. Notice that from Time 1 to $n - 1$ the sum of these three transactions is always zero. Note also that the final (Time n) cash flow for the long position in the equity includes the periodic return (S_n) plus the sale proceeds of the underlying equity position (NA_E). For the terminal cash flows to equal zero, we must either set the bond par value to equal the initial equity position (NA_E = Par) or finance this difference. In this latter case, the bond par value could be different from the notional amount of equity.

As shown, the swap and pair of offsetting transactions produce 0 net cash flow from period 1 to period $n - 1$. In equilibrium, we require $-V_{EQ} - NA_E + V_{FIX} - PV(Par - NA_E) = 0$. That is, if the portfolio has initial value with no required cash outflow, then arbitrage will be possible. Hence, the equity swap value is:

$$V_{EQ} = V_{FIX} - NA_E - PV(Par - NA_E).$$

Assuming equilibrium ($V_{EQ} = 0$), the fixed swap rate can be expressed as the r_{FIX} rate such that $V_{FIX} = NA_E + PV(Par - NA_E)$. Note that assuming NA_E = Par = 1 and using our fixed bond pricing (Equation 10), we have the pricing equation for an equity swap:

$$r_{FIX} = \frac{1 - PV_n(1)}{\sum_{i=1}^{n} PV_i(1)}.$$

You should recognize that the pricing of an equity swap is identical to Equation 11 for the pricing of a comparable interest rate swap, even though the future cash flows are dramatically different. If the swap required a floating payment, there would be no need to price the swap; the floating side effectively prices itself at par automatically at the start. If the swap involves paying one equity return against another, there would also be no need to price it. You could effectively view this arrangement as *paying equity "a" and receiving the fixed rate* as specified and *receiving equity "b" and paying the same fixed rate*. The fixed rates would cancel.

Finding the value of an equity swap after the swap is initiated, say at Time t (so, $V_{EQ,t}$), is similar to valuing an interest rate swap except that rather than adjusting the floating-rate bond for the last floating rate observed (remember, advanced set), we adjust the value of the notional amount of equity, as shown in Equation 15:

$$V_{EQ,t} = V_{FIX}(C_0) - (S_t/S_{t-1})NA_E - PV(Par - NA_E), \tag{15}$$

where $V_{FIX}(C_0)$ denotes the value at Time t of a fixed-rate bond initiated with coupon C_0 at Time 0, S_t denotes the current equity price, S_{t-1} denotes the equity price observed at the last reset date, and PV() denotes the present value function from the swap maturity date to Time t.

EXAMPLE 18   Equity Swap Pricing

In Examples 13 and 14 related to interest rate swaps, we considered a five-year, annual reset, 30/360 day count, Libor-based swap. The following table provides the present values per €1, PV_i (1).

Maturity (years)	Present Value Factors
1	0.990099
2	0.977876
3	0.965136
4	0.951529
5	0.937467

Assume an annual reset Libor floating-rate bond trading at par. The fixed rate was previously found to be 1.2968% (see Example 13). Given these same data (just shown), the fixed interest rate in the EURO STOXX 50 equity swap is *closest* to:

A. 0.0%.
B. 1.1%.
C. 1.3%.

Solution: C is correct. The fixed rate on an equity swap is the same as that on an interest rate swap, or 1.2968% as in Example 13. That is, the fixed rate on an equity swap is simply the fixed rate on a comparable interest rate swap.

$$\sum_{i=1}^{5} PV_i(1) = 0.990099 + 0.977876 + 0.965136 + 0.951529 + 0.937467$$
$$= 4.822107.$$

Using Equation 11, the solution for the fixed swap rate is:

$$r_{FIX} = \frac{1 - 0.937467}{4.822107} = 0.012968, \text{ } or \text{ } 1.2968\%.$$

EXAMPLE 19   Equity Swap Valuation

Suppose six months ago we entered a receive-fixed, pay-equity five-year annual reset swap in which the fixed leg is based on a 30/360 day count. At the time the swap was entered, the fixed swap rate was 1.5%, the equity was trading at 100, and the notional amount was 10,000,000. Now all spot interest rates have fallen to 1.2% (a flat term structure), and the equity is trading for 105. Assume the Par value of the bond is equal to NA_E.

1. The current fair value of this equity swap is *closest* to:
    A. −€300,000.
    B. −€500,000.
    C. €500,000.

2. The value of the equity swap will be *closest* to zero if the stock price is:
   A. 100.
   B. 102.
   C. 105.

Solution to 1: A is correct. Because we have not yet passed the first reset date, there are five remaining cash flows for this equity swap. The fair value of this swap is found by solving for the fair value of the implied fixed-rate bond. We then adjust for the equity value. The fixed rate of 1.5% results in fixed cash flows of 150,000 at each settlement. Applying the respective present value factors, which are based on the new spot rates of 1.2% (i.e., new term structure is flat), gives us the following:

Date (Years)	Present Value Factors (PV)	Fixed Cash Flow	PV (Fixed Cash Flow)
0.5	0.994036	150,000	149,105
1.5*	0.982318	150,000	147,348
2.5	0.970874	150,000	145,631
3.5	0.959693	150,000	143,954
4.5	0.948767	10,150,000	9,629,981
		Total:	10,216,019

* Answers may differ due to rounding: $PV(1.5) = 1/(1 + 3 \times (0.012/2)) = 0.982318$.

Using Equation 15, we have,

$$V_{EQ,t} = V_{FIX}(C_0) - (S_t/S_{t-1})NA_E - PV(Par - NA_E).$$

Therefore, the fair value of this equity swap is:

$$V_{EQ,t} = 10,216,019 - [(105/100) \times 10,000,000] - 0 = -283,981.$$

Solution to 2: B is correct. The value of the fixed leg of the swap is 102.16% of par, = $(10,216,019/10,000,000) \times 100]$. Therefore, a stock price (S_t) of 102.1602 will result in a value of zero for the swap, as follows:

$$V_{EQ,t} = 10,216,019 - [(102.1602/100) \times 10,000,000] - 0 = 0.$$

SUMMARY

This reading on forward commitment pricing and valuation provides a foundation for understanding how forwards, futures, and swaps are both priced and valued.

Key points include the following:

• The arbitrageur would rather have more money than less and abides by two fundamental rules: Do not use your own money, and do not take any price risk.

- The no-arbitrage approach is used for the pricing and valuation of forward commitments and is built on the key concept of the law of one price, which states that if two investments have the same future cash flows, regardless of what happens in the future, these two investments should have the same current price.
- Throughout this reading, the following key assumptions are made:
  - Replicating and offsetting instruments are identifiable and investable.
  - Market frictions are nil.
  - Short selling is allowed with full use of proceeds.
  - Borrowing and lending are available at a known risk-free rate.
- Carry arbitrage models used for forward commitment pricing and valuation are based on the no-arbitrage approach.
- With forward commitments, there is a distinct difference between pricing and valuation. Pricing involves the determination of the appropriate fixed price or rate, and valuation involves the determination of the contract's current value expressed in currency units.
- Forward commitment pricing results in determining a price or rate such that the forward contract value is equal to zero.
- Using the carry arbitrage model, the forward contract price (F_0) is:

$$F_0 = FV(S_0) = S_0(1 + r)^T \text{ (assuming annual compounding, r)}$$

$$F_0 = FV(S_0) = S_0 \exp^{r_c T} \text{ (assuming continuous compounding, } r_c)$$

- The key forward commitment pricing equations with carry costs (CC) and carry benefits (CB) are:

$$F_0 = FV[S_0 + CC_0 - CB_0] \text{ (with discrete compounding)}$$

$$F_0 = S_0 \exp^{(r_c + CC - CB)T} \text{ (with continuous compounding)}$$

Futures contract pricing in this reading can essentially be treated the same as forward contract pricing.

- The value of a forward commitment is a function of the price of the underlying instrument, financing costs, and other carry costs and benefits.
- The key forward commitment valuation equations are:

$$\text{Long Forward:} \quad V_t = PV[F_t - F_0] = \frac{[F_t - F_0]}{(1 + r)^{T-t}}$$

and

$$\text{Short Forward:} \quad -V_t = PV[F_0 - F_t] = \frac{[F_0 - F_t]}{(1 + r)^{T-t}},$$

With the PV of the difference in forward prices adjusted for carry costs and benefits. Alternatively,

$$\text{Long Forward:} \quad V_t = S_t - PV[F_0] = S_t - \frac{F_0}{(1 + r)^{T-t}}$$

and

$$\text{Short Forward: } - V_t = PV[F_0] - S_t = \frac{F_0}{(1 + r)^{T-t}} - S_t$$

- With equities and fixed-income securities, the forward price is determined such that the initial forward value is zero.
- A forward rate agreement (FRA) is a forward contract on interest rates. The FRA's fixed interest rate is determined such that the initial value of the FRA is zero.
- FRA settlements amounts at Time h are:

$$\text{Pay-fixed (Long): } NA \times \{[L_m - FRA_0] \ t_m\}/[1 + D_m t_m] \text{ and}$$

$$\text{Receive-fixed (Short): } NA \times \{FRA_0 - L_m] \ t_m\}/[1 + D_m t_m].$$

- The FRA's fixed interest rate (annualized) at contract initiation is:

$$FRA_0 = \{[1 + L_T t_T]/[1 + L_h t_h] - 1\}/t_m.$$

- The Time g value of an FRA initiated at Time 0 is:

$$\text{Long FRA: } V_g = NA \times \{[FRA_g - FRA_0] \ t_m\}/[1 + D_{(T-g)} \ t_{(T-g)}] \text{ and}$$

$$\text{Short FRA: } -V_g = NA \times \{[FRA_0 - FRA_g] \ t_m\}/[1 + D_{(T-g)} \ t_{(T-g)}].$$

- The fixed-income forward (or futures) price including conversion factor (i.e., adjusted price) is:

$$F_0 = Q_0 \times CF = FV[S_0 + CC_0 - CB_0] = FV[B_0 + AI_0 - PVCI],$$

and the conversion factor adjusted futures price (i.e., quoted futures price) is:

$$Q_0 = [1/CF] \ \{FV \ [B_0 + AI_0] - AI_T - FVCI\}.$$

- The general approach to pricing and valuing swaps as covered here is using a replicating portfolio or offsetting portfolio of comparable instruments, typically bonds for interest rate and currency swaps and equities plus bonds for equity swaps.
- The swap pricing equation, which sets r_{FIX} for the implied fixed bond in an interest rate swap, is:

$$r_{FIX} = \frac{1 - PV_n(1)}{\sum_{i=1}^{n} PV_i(1)}.$$

- The value of an interest rate swap at a point in Time t after initiation is the sum of the present values of the difference in fixed swap rates times the stated notional amount, or:

$$V_{SWAP,t} = NA \times (FS_0 - FS_t) \times \sum_{i=1}^{n} PV_i \text{ (Value of receive-fixed swap)}$$

and

$$-V_{SWAP,t} = NA \times (FS_t - FS_0) \times \sum_{i=1}^{n} PV_i \text{ (Value of pay-fixed swap)}.$$

- With a basic understanding of pricing and valuing a simple interest rate swap, it is a straight-forward extension to pricing and valuing currency swaps and equity swaps.
- The solution for each of the three variables, one notional amount (NA_a) and two fixed rates (one for each currency, a and b), needed to price a fixed-for-fixed currency swap are:

$$NA_a = S_0 \times NA_b; \quad r_a = \frac{1 - PV_{n,a}(1)}{\sum_{i=1}^{n} PV_{i,a}(1)} \quad \text{and} \quad r_b = \frac{1 - PV_{n,b}(1)}{\sum_{i=1}^{n} PV_{i,b}(1)}.$$

- The currency swap valuation equation, for valuing the swap at time t (after initiation), can be expressed as:

$$V_{CS} = NA_a \left(r_{Fix,a} \sum_{i=1}^{n} PV_i(1) + PV_n(1) \right) - S_t NA_b \left(r_{Fix,b} \sum_{i=1}^{n} PV_i(1) + PV_n(1) \right).$$

- For a receive-fixed, pay equity swap, the fixed rate (r_{FIX}) for the implied fixed bond that makes the swap's value (V_{EQ}) equal to "0" at initiation is:

$$r_{FIX} = \frac{1 - PV_n(1)}{\sum_{i=1}^{n} PV_i(1)}$$

- The value of an equity swap at Time t ($V_{EQ,t}$), after initiation, is:

$$V_{EQ,t} = V_{FIX}(C_0) - (S_t/S_{t-1})NA_E - PV(Par - NA_E)$$

where $V_{FIX}(C_0)$ is the Time t value of a fixed-rate bond initiated with coupon C_0 at Time 0, S_t is the current equity price, S_{t-1} is the equity price at the last reset date, and $PV()$ is the PV function from the swap maturity date to Time t.

PROBLEMS

The following information relates to Questions 1–5

Donald Troubadour is a derivatives trader for Southern Shores Investments. The firm seeks arbitrage opportunities in the forward and futures markets using the carry arbitrage model.

Troubadour identifies an arbitrage opportunity relating to a fixed-income futures contract and its underlying bond. Current data on the futures contract and underlying bond are presented in Exhibit 1. The current annual compounded risk-free rate is 0.30%.

EXHIBIT 1   Current Data for Futures and Underlying Bond

Futures Contract		Underlying Bond	
Quoted futures price	125.00	Quoted bond price	112.00
Conversion factor	0.90	Accrued interest since last coupon payment	0.08
Time remaining to contract expiration	Three months	Accrued interest at futures contract expiration	0.20
Accrued interest over life of futures contract	0.00		

Troubadour next gathers information on a Japanese equity index futures contract, the **Nikkei 225 Futures Contract**:

> Troubadour holds a long position in a Nikkei 225 futures contract that has a remaining maturity of three months. The continuously compounded dividend yield on the Nikkei 225 Stock Index is 1.1%, and the current stock index level is 16,080. The continuously compounded annual interest rate is 0.2996%.

Troubadour next considers an equity forward contract for Texas Steel, Inc. (TSI). Information regarding TSI common shares and a TSI equity forward contract is presented in Exhibit 2.

EXHIBIT 2   Selected Information for TSI

- The price per share of TSI's common shares is $250.
- The forward price per share for a nine-month TSI equity forward contract is $250.562289.
- Assume annual compounding.

Troubadour takes a short position in the TSI equity forward contract. His supervisor asks, "Under which scenario would our position experience a loss?"

Three months after contract initiation, Troubadour gathers information on TSI and the risk-free rate, which is presented in Exhibit 3.

EXHIBIT 3   Selected Data on TSI and the Risk-Free Rate (Three Months Later)

- The price per share of TSI's common shares is $245.
- The risk-free rate is 0.325% (quoted on an annual compounding basis).
- TSI recently announced its regular semiannual dividend of $1.50 per share that will be paid exactly three months before contract expiration.
- The market price of the TSI equity forward contract is equal to the no-arbitrage forward price.

1. Based on Exhibit 1 and assuming annual compounding, the arbitrage profit on the bond futures contract is *closest* to:
    A. 0.4158.
    B. 0.5356.
    C. 0.6195.
2. The current no-arbitrage futures price of the Nikkei 225 futures contract is *closest* to:
    A. 15,951.81.
    B. 16,047.86.
    C. 16,112.21.
3. Based on Exhibit 2, Troubadour should find that an arbitrage opportunity relating to TSI shares is
    A. not available.
    B. available based on carry arbitrage.
    C. available based on reverse carry arbitrage.
4. The *most appropriate* response to Troubadour's supervisor's question regarding the TSI forward contract is:
    A. a decrease in TSI's share price, all else equal.
    B. an increase in the risk-free rate, all else equal
    C. a decrease in the market price of the forward contract, all else equal.

5. Based on Exhibits 2 and 3, and assuming annual compounding, the per share value of Troubadour's short position in the TSI forward contract three months after contract initiation is *closest* to:
   A. $1.6549.
   B. $5.1561.
   C. $6.6549.

The following information relates to Questions 6–14

Sonal Johnson is a risk manager for a bank. She manages the bank's risks using a combination of swaps and forward rate agreements (FRAs).

Johnson prices a three-year Libor-based interest rate swap with annual resets using the present value factors presented in Exhibit 1.

EXHIBIT 1   Present Value Factors

Maturity (years)	Present Value Factors
1	0.990099
2	0.977876
3	0.965136

Johnson also uses the present value factors in Exhibit 1 to value an interest rate swap that the bank entered into one year ago as the pay-fixed (receive-floating) party. Selected data for the swap are presented in Exhibit 2. Johnson notes that the current equilibrium two-year fixed swap rate is 1.12%.

EXHIBIT 2   Selected Data on Fixed for Floating Interest Rate Swap

Swap notional amount	$50,000,000
Original swap term	Three years, with annual resets
Fixed swap rate (since initiation)	3.00%

One of the bank's investments is exposed to movements in the Japanese yen, and Johnson desires to hedge the currency exposure. She prices a one-year fixed-for-fixed currency swap involving yen and US dollars, with a quarterly reset. Johnson uses the interest rate data presented in Exhibit 3 to price the currency swap.

EXHIBIT 3   Selected Japanese and US Interest Rate Data

Days to Maturity	Yen Spot Interest Rates	US Dollar Spot Interest Rates
90	0.05%	0.20%
180	0.10%	0.40%
270	0.15%	0.55%
360	0.25%	0.70%

Johnson next reviews an equity swap with an annual reset that the bank entered into six months ago as the receive-fixed, pay-equity party. Selected data regarding the equity swap, which is linked to an equity index, are presented in Exhibit 4. At the time of initiation, the underlying equity index was trading at 100.00.

EXHIBIT 4   Selected Data on Equity Swap

Swap notional amount	$20,000,000
Original swap term	Five years, with annual resets
Fixed swap rate	2.00%

The equity index is currently trading at 103.00, and relevant US spot rates, along with their associated present value factors, are presented in Exhibit 5.

EXHIBIT 5   Selected US Spot Rates and Present Value Factors

Maturity (years)	Spot Rate	Present Value Factors
0.5	0.40%	0.998004
1.5	1.00%	0.985222
2.5	1.20%	0.970874
3.5	2.00%	0.934579
4.5	2.60%	0.895255

Johnson reviews a 6 × 9 FRA that the bank entered into 90 days ago as the pay-fixed/receive-floating party. Selected data for the FRA are presented in Exhibit 6, and current Libor (i.e., MRR) data are presented in Exhibit 7. Based on her interest rate forecast, Johnson also considers whether the bank should enter into new positions in 1 × 4 and 2 × 5 FRAs.

EXHIBIT 6   6 × 9 FRA Data

FRA term	6 × 9
FRA rate	0.70%
FRA notional amount	US$20,000,000
FRA settlement terms	Advanced set, advanced settle

EXHIBIT 7   Current Libor (Market Reference Rate)

30-day Libor	0.75%
60-day Libor	0.82%
90-day Libor	0.90%
120-day Libor	0.92%
150-day Libor	0.94%
180-day Libor	0.95%
210-day Libor	0.97%
270-day Libor	1.00%

Three months later, the 6 × 9 FRA in Exhibit 6 reaches expiration, at which time the three-month US dollar Libor is 1.10% and the six-month US dollar Libor is 1.20%. Johnson determines that the appropriate discount rate for the FRA settlement cash flows is 1.10%.

6. Based on Exhibit 1, Johnson should price the three-year Libor-based interest rate swap at a fixed rate *closest* to:
   A. 0.34%.
   B. 1.16%.
   C. 1.19%.

7. From the bank's perspective, using data from Exhibit 1, the current value of the swap described in Exhibit 2 is *closest* to:
   A. −$2,951,963.
   B. −$1,849,897.
   C. −$1,943,000.

8. Based on Exhibit 3, Johnson should determine that the annualized equilibrium fixed swap rate for Japanese yen is *closest* to:
   A. 0.0624%.
   B. 0.1375%.
   C. 0.2496%.

9. From the bank's perspective, using data from Exhibits 4 and 5, the fair value of the equity swap is *closest* to:
   A. −$1,139,425.
   B. −$781,322.
   C. −$181,323.

10. Based on Exhibit 5, the current value of the equity swap described in Exhibit 4 would be zero if the equity index was currently trading the *closest* to:
    A. 97.30.
    B. 99.09.
    C. 100.00.

11. From the bank's perspective, based on Exhibits 6 and 7, the value of the 6 × 9 FRA 90 days after inception is *closest* to:
    A. $14,820.
    B. $19,647.
    C. $29,635.

12. Based on Exhibit 7, the no-arbitrage fixed rate on a new 1 × 4 FRA is *closest* to:
    A. 0.65%.
    B. 0.73%.
    C. 0.98%.

13. Based on Exhibit 7, the fixed rate on a new 2 × 5 FRA is *closest* to:
    A. 0.61%.
    B. 1.02%.
    C. 1.71%.

14. Based on Exhibit 6 and the three-month US dollar Libor at expiration, the payment amount that the bank will receive to settle the 6 × 9 FRA is *closest* to:
    A. $19,945.
    B. $24,925.
    C. $39,781.

The following information relates to Questions 15–20

Tim Doyle is a portfolio manager at BestFutures Group, a hedge fund that frequently enters into derivative contracts either to hedge the risk of investments it holds or to speculate outside of those investments. Doyle works alongside Diane Kemper, a junior analyst at the hedge fund. They meet to evaluate new investment ideas and to review several of the firm's existing investments.

Carry Arbitrage Model

Doyle and Kemper discuss the carry arbitrage model and how they can take advantage of mis-pricing in bond markets. Specifically, they would like to execute an arbitrage transaction on a Eurodollar futures contract in which the underlying Eurodollar bond is expected to make an interest payment in two months. Doyle makes the following statements:

Statement 1:   If the Eurodollar futures price is less than the price suggested by the carry arbitrage model, the futures contract should be purchased.

Statement 2:   Based on the cost of carry model, the futures price would be higher if the underlying Eurodollar bond's upcoming interest payment was expected in five months instead of two.

Three-Year Treasury Note Futures Contract

Kemper then presents two investment ideas to Doyle. Kemper's first investment idea is to pur-chase a three-year Treasury note futures contract. The underlying 1.5%, semi-annual three-year Treasury note is quoted at a clean price of 101. It has been 60 days since the three-year Treasury note's last coupon payment, and the next coupon payment is payable in 120 days. Doyle asks Kemper to calculate the full spot price of the underlying three-year Treasury note.

10-Year Treasury Note Futures Contract

Kemper's second investment idea is to purchase a 10-year Treasury note futures contract. The underlying 2%, semi-annual 10-year Treasury note has a dirty price of 104.17. It has been 30 days since the 10-year Treasury note's last coupon payment. The futures contract expires in 90 days. The quoted futures contract price is 129. The current annualized three-month risk-free rate is 1.65%. The conversion factor is 0.7025. Doyle asks Kemper to calculate the equilibrium quoted futures contract price based on the carry arbitrage model.

Japanese Government Bonds

After discussing Kemper's new investment ideas, Doyle and Kemper evaluate one of their existing forward contract positions. Three months ago, BestFutures took a long position in eight 10-year Japanese government bond (JGB) forward contracts, with each contract having a contract notional value of 100 million yen. The contracts had a price of JPY153 (quoted as a percentage of par) when the contracts were purchased. Now, the contracts have six months left to expiration and have a price of JPY155. The annualized six-month interest rate is 0.12%. Doyle asks Kemper to value the JGB forward position.

Interest Rate Swaps

Additionally, Doyle asks Kemper to price a one-year plain vanilla swap. The spot rates and days to maturity at each payment date are presented in Exhibit 1.

EXHIBIT 1   Selected US Spot Rate Data

Days to Maturity	Spot Interest Rates (%)
90	1.90
180	2.00
270	2.10
360	2.20

Finally, Doyle and Kemper review one of BestFutures's pay-fixed interest rate swap positions. Two years ago, the firm entered into a JPY5 billion five-year interest rate swap, paying the fixed rate. The fixed rate when BestFutures entered into the swap two years ago was 0.10%. The current term structure of interest rates for JPY cash flows, which are relevant to the interest rate swap position, is presented in Exhibit 2.

EXHIBIT 2   Selected Japanese Interest Rate Data

Maturity (Years)	Yen Spot Interest Rates (%)	Present Value Factors
1	0.03	0.9997
2	0.06	0.9988
3	0.08	0.9976
Sum		2.9961

Doyle asks Kemper to calculate the value of the pay-fixed interest rate swap.

15. Which of Doyle's statements regarding the Eurodollar futures contract price is correct?
    A. Only Statement 1
    B. Only Statement 2
    C. Both Statement 1 and Statement 2
16. The full spot price of the three-year Treasury note is:
    A. 101.00.
    B. 101.25.
    C. 101.50.
17. The equilibrium 10-year Treasury note quoted futures contract price is *closest* to:
    A. 147.94.
    B. 148.89.
    C. 149.78.
18. The value of the JGB long forward position is *closest* to:
    A. JPY15,980,823.
    B. JPY15,990,409.
    C. JPY16,000,000.

19. Based on Exhibit 1, the fixed rate of the one-year plain vanilla swap is *closest* to:
    A. 0.12%.
    B. 0.55%.
    C. 0.72%.
20. Based on Exhibit 2, the value of the pay-fixed interest rate swap is *closest* to:
    A. −JPY6,491,550.
    B. −JPY2,980,500.
    C. −JPY994,793.

CHAPTER 4

VALUATION OF CONTINGENT CLAIMS

Robert E. Brooks, PhD, CFA, and David Maurice Gentle, MEc, BSc, CFA

LEARNING OUTCOMES

The candidate should be able to:

- describe and interpret the binomial option valuation model and its component terms;
- calculate the no-arbitrage values of European and American options using a two-period binomial model;
- identify an arbitrage opportunity involving options and describe the related arbitrage;
- calculate and interpret the value of an interest rate option using a two-period binomial model;
- describe how the value of a European option can be analyzed as the present value of the option's expected payoff at expiration;
- identify assumptions of the Black–Scholes–Merton option valuation model;
- interpret the components of the Black–Scholes–Merton model as applied to call options in terms of a leveraged position in the underlying;
- describe how the Black–Scholes–Merton model is used to value European options on equities and currencies;
- describe how the Black model is used to value European options on futures;
- describe how the Black model is used to value European interest rate options and European swaptions;
- interpret each of the option Greeks;
- describe how a delta hedge is executed;
- describe the role of gamma risk in options trading;
- define implied volatility and explain how it is used in options trading.

1. INTRODUCTION AND PRINCIPLES OF A NO-ARBITRAGE APPROACH TO VALUATION

A contingent claim is a derivative instrument that provides its owner a right but not an obligation to a payoff determined by an underlying asset, rate, or other derivative. Contingent claims include options, the valuation of which is the objective of this reading. Because many investments contain embedded options, understanding this material is vital for investment management.

Our primary purpose is to understand how the values of options are determined. Option values, as with the values of all financial instruments, are typically obtained using valuation models. Any financial valuation model takes certain inputs and turns them into an output that tells us the fair value or price. Option valuation models, like their counterparts in the forward, futures, and swaps markets, are based on the principle of no arbitrage, meaning that the appropriate price of an option is the one that makes it impossible for any party to earn an arbitrage profit at the expense of any other party. The price that precludes arbitrage profits is the value of the option. Using that concept, we then proceed to introduce option valuation models using two approaches. The first approach is the binomial model, which is based on discrete time, and the second is the Black–Scholes–Merton (BSM) model, which is based on continuous time.

The reading is organized as follows. Section 1 introduces the principles of the no-arbitrage approach to pricing and valuation of options. In Sections 2–7, the binomial option valuation model is explored, and in Sections 8–10, the BSM model is covered. In Sections 11–13, the Black model, being a variation of the BSM model, is applied to futures options, interest rate options, and swaptions. Finally, in Sections 14–19, the Greeks are reviewed along with implied volatility.

1.1. Principles of a No-Arbitrage Approach to Valuation

Our approach is based on the concept of arbitrage. Hence, the material will be covered from an arbitrageur's perspective. Key to understanding this material is to think like an arbitrageur. Specifically, like most people, the arbitrageur would rather have more money than less. The arbitrageur, as will be detailed later, follows two fundamental rules:

Rule #1: Do not use your own money.
Rule #2: Do not take any price risk.

Clearly, if we can generate positive cash flows today and abide by both rules, we have a great business—such is the life of an arbitrageur. If traders could create a portfolio with no future liabilities and positive cash flow today, then it would essentially be a money machine that would be attractive to anyone who prefers more cash to less. In the pursuit of these positive cash flows today, the arbitrageur often needs to borrow to satisfy Rule #1. In effect, the arbitrageur borrows the arbitrage profit to capture it today and, if necessary, may borrow to purchase the underlying. Specifically, the arbitrageur will build portfolios using the underlying instrument to synthetically replicate the cash flows of an option. The underlying instrument is the financial instrument whose later value will be referenced to determine the option value. Examples of underlying instruments include shares, indexes, currencies, and interest rates. As we will see, with options we will often rely on a specific trading strategy that changes over time based on the underlying price behavior.

Based on the concept of comparability, the no-arbitrage valuation approach taken here is built on the concept that if two investments have the same future cash flows regardless of what happens, then these two investments should have the same current price. This principle is known as the **law of one price**. In establishing these foundations of option valuation, the following key assumptions are made: (1) Replicating instruments are identifiable and investable. (2) There are no market frictions, such as transaction costs and taxes. (3) Short selling is allowed with full use of proceeds. (4) The underlying instrument follows a known statistical distribution. (5) Borrowing and lending at a risk-free interest rate is available. When we develop the models in this reading, we will be more specific about what these assumptions mean, in particular what we mean by a known statistical distribution.

In an effort to demonstrate various valuation results based on the absence of arbitrage, we will rely heavily on cash flow tables, which are a representation of the cash flows that occur during the life of an option. For example, if an initial investment requires €100, then from an arbitrageur's perspective, we will present it as a −€100 cash flow. If an option pays off ¥1,000, we will represent it as a +¥1,000 cash flow. That is, cash outflows are treated as negative and inflows as positive.

We first demonstrate how to value options based on a two-period binomial model. The option payoffs can be replicated with a dynamic portfolio of the underlying instrument and financing. A dynamic portfolio is one whose composition changes over time. These changes are important elements of the replicating procedure. Based on the binomial framework, we then turn to exploring interest rate options using a binomial tree. Although more complex, the general approach is shown to be the same.

The multiperiod binomial model is a natural transition to the BSM option valuation model. The BSM model is based on the key assumption that the value of the underlying instrument follows a statistical process called geometric Brownian motion. This characterization is a reasonable way to capture the randomness of financial instrument prices while incorporating a pre-specified expected return and volatility of return. Geometric Brownian motion implies a lognormal distribution of the return, which implies that the continuously compounded return on the underlying is normally distributed.

We also explore the role of carry benefits, meaning the reward or cost of holding the underlying itself instead of holding the derivative on the underlying.

Next we turn to Fischer Black's futures option valuation model (Black model) and note that the model difference, versus the BSM model, is related to the underlying futures contract having no carry costs or benefits. Interest rate options and swaptions are valued based on simple modifications of the Black model.

Finally, we explore the Greeks, otherwise known as delta, gamma, theta, vega, and rho. The Greeks are representations of the sensitivity of the option value to changes in the factors that determine the option value. They provide comparative information essential in managing portfolios containing options. The Greeks are calculated based on an option valuation model, such as the binomial model, BSM model, or the Black model. This information is model dependent, so managers need to carefully select the model best suited for their particular situation. In the last section, we cover implied volatility, which is a measure derived from a market option price and can be interpreted as reflecting what investors believe is the volatility of the underlying.

The models presented here are useful first approximations for explaining observed option prices in many markets. The central theme is that options are generally priced to preclude arbitrage profits, which is not only a reasonable theoretical assumption but is sufficiently accurate in practice.

We turn now to option valuation based on the binomial option valuation model.

2. BINOMIAL OPTION VALUATION MODEL

The binomial model is a valuable tool for financial analysts. It is particularly useful as a heuristic device to understand the unique valuation approach used with options. This model is extensively used to value path-dependent options, which are options whose values depend not only on the value of the underlying at expiration but also how it got there. The path-dependency feature distinguishes this model from the Black–Scholes–Merton option valuation model (BSM model) presented in the next section. The BSM model values only path-independent options, such as European options, which depend on only the values of their respective underlyings at expiration. One particular type of path-dependent option that we are interested in is American options, which are those that can be exercised prior to expiration. In this section, we introduce the general framework for developing the binomial option valuation models for both European and American options.

The binomial option valuation model is based on the no-arbitrage approach to valuation. Hence, understanding the valuation of options improves if one can understand how an arbitrageur approaches financial markets. An arbitrageur engages in financial transactions in pursuit of an initial positive cash flow with no possibility of a negative cash flow in the future. As it appears, it is a great business if you can find it.[1]

To understand option valuation models, it is helpful to think like an arbitrageur. The arbitrageur seeks to exploit any pricing discrepancy between the option price and the underlying spot price. The arbitrageur is assumed to prefer more money compared with less money, assuming everything else is the same. As mentioned earlier, there are two fundamental rules for the arbitrageur.

Rule #1:   Do not use your own money. Specifically, the arbitrageur does not use his or her own money to acquire positions. Also, the arbitrageur does not spend proceeds from short selling transactions on activities unrelated to the transaction at hand.

Rule #2:   Do not take any price risk. The focus here is only on market price risk related to the underlying and the derivatives used. We do not consider other risks, such as liquidity risk and counterparty credit risk.

We will rely heavily on these two rules when developing option valuation models. Remember, these rules are general in nature, and as with many things in finance, there are nuances.

---

[1] There is not a one-to-one correspondence between arbitrage and great investment opportunities. An arbitrage is certainly a great investment opportunity because it produces a risk-free profit with no investment of capital, but all great investment opportunities are not arbitrage. For example, an opportunity to invest €1 today in return for a 99% chance of receiving €1,000,000 tomorrow or a 1% chance of receiving €0 might appear to be a truly great investment opportunity, but it is not arbitrage because it is not risk free and requires the investment of capital.

In Exhibit 1, the two key dates are the option contract initiation date (identified as Time 0) and the option contract expiration date (identified as Time T). Based on the no-arbitrage approach, the option value from the initiation date onward will be estimated with an option valuation model.

EXHIBIT 1   Illustration of Option Contract Initiation and Expiration

Let S_t denote the underlying instrument price observed at Time t, where t is expressed as a fraction of a year. Similarly, S_T denotes the underlying instrument price observed at the option expiration date, T. For example, suppose a call option had 90 days to expiration when purchased (T = 90/365), but now only has 35 days to expiration (t = 55/365). Further, let c_t denote a European-style call price at Time t and with expiration on Date t = T, where both t and T are expressed in years. Similarly, let C_t denote an American-style call price. At the initiation date, the subscripts are omitted, thus $c = c_0$. We follow similar notation with a put, using the letter p, in place of c. Let X denote the exercise price.[2]

For example, suppose on 15 April a 90-day European-style call option contract with a 14 July expiration is initiated with a call price of c = €2.50 and T = 90/365 = 0.246575.

At expiration, the call and put values will be equal to their intrinsic value or exercise value. These **exercise values** can be expressed as

$$c_T = Max(0, S_T - X) \text{ and}$$

$$p_T = Max(0, X - S_T),$$

respectively. If the option values deviate from these expressions, then there will be arbitrage profits available. The option is expiring, there is no uncertainty remaining, and the price must equal the market value obtained from exercising it or letting it expire.

Technically, European options do not have exercise values prior to expiration because they cannot be exercised until expiration. Nonetheless, the notion of the value of the option if it could be exercised, $Max(0, S_t - X)$ for a call and $Max(0, X - S_t)$ for a put, forms a basis for understanding the notion that the value of an option declines with the passage of time. Specifically, option values contain an element known as time value, which is just the market valuation of the potential for higher exercise value relative to the potential for lower exercise value. The time value is always non-negative because of the asymmetry of option payoffs at expiration. For example, for a call, the upside is unlimited, whereas the downside is limited to zero. At expiration, time value is zero.

Although option prices are influenced by a variety of factors, the underlying instrument has a particularly significant influence. At this point, the underlying is assumed to be the only uncertain factor affecting the option price. We now look in detail at the one-period binomial option valuation model. The one-period binomial model is foundational for the material that follows.

---

[2] In financial markets, the exercise price is also commonly called the strike price.

3. ONE-PERIOD BINOMIAL MODEL

Exhibit 2 illustrates the one-period binomial process for an asset priced at S. In the figure on the left, each dot represents a particular outcome at a particular point in time in the binomial lattice. The dots are termed nodes. At the Time 0 node, there are only two possible future paths in the binomial process, an up move and a down move, termed arcs. The figure on the right illustrates the underlying price at each node. At Time 1, there are only two possible outcomes: S^+ denotes the outcome when the underlying goes up, and S^- denotes the outcome when the underlying goes down.

EXHIBIT 2   One-Period Binomial Lattice with Underlying Distribution Illustrated

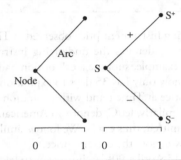

At Time 1, there are only two possible outcomes and two resulting values of the underlying, S^+ (up occurs) and S^- (down occurs). Although the one-period binomial model is clearly unrealistic, it will provide key insights into the more realistic multiperiod binomial as well as the BSM model.

We further define the total returns implied by the underlying movements as

$$u = \frac{S^+}{S} \text{ (up factor) and}$$

$$d = \frac{S^-}{S} \text{ (down factor).}$$

The up factors and down factors are the total returns; that is, one plus the rate of return. The magnitudes of the up and down factors are based on the volatility of the underlying. In general, higher volatility will result in higher up values and lower down values.

We briefly review option valuation within a one-period binomial tree. With this review, we can move quickly to option valuation within a two-period binomial lattice by performing the one-period exercise three times.

We consider the fair value of a two-period call option value measured at Time 1 when an up move occurs, that is c^+. Based on arbitrage forces, we know this option value at expiration is either

$$c^{++} = Max(0, S^{++} - X) = Max(0, u^2S - X), \text{ or}$$

$$c^{+-} = Max(0, S^{+-} - X) = Max(0, udS - X).$$

At this point, we assume that there are no costs or benefits from owning the underlying instrument. Now consider the transactions illustrated in Exhibit 3. These transactions are presented as cash flows. Thus, if we write a call option, we receive money at Time Step 0 and may have to pay out money at Time Step 1. Suppose the first trade is to write or sell one call option within the single-period binomial model. The value of a call option is positively related to the value of the underlying. That is, they both move up or down together. Hence, by writing a call option, the trader will lose money if the underlying goes up and make money if the underlying falls. Therefore, to execute a hedge, the trader will need a position that will make money if the underlying goes up. Thus, the second trade needs to be a long position in the underlying. Specifically, the trader buys a certain number of units, h, of the underlying. The symbol h is used because it represents a hedge ratio.

Note that with these first two trades, neither arbitrage rule is satisfied. The future cash flow could be either $-c^- + hS^-$ or $-c^+ + hS^+$ and can be positive or negative. Thus, the cash flows at the Time Step 1 could result in the arbitrageur having to pay out money if one of these values is less than zero. To resolve both of these issues, we set the Time Step 1 cash flows equal to each other—that is, $-c^+ + hS^+ = -c^- + hS^-$—and solve for the appropriate hedge ratio:

$$h = \frac{c^+ - c^-}{S^+ - S^-} \geq 0 \tag{1}$$

We determine the hedge ratio such that we are indifferent to the underlying going up or down. Thus, we are hedged against moves in the underlying. A simple rule for remembering this formula is that the hedge ratio is the value of the call if the underlying goes up minus the value of the call if the underlying goes down divided by the value of the underlying if it goes up minus the value of the underlying if it goes down. The up and down patterns are the same in the numerator and denominator, but the numerator contains the option and the denominator contains the underlying.

Because call prices are positively related to changes in the underlying price, we know that h is non-negative. As shown in Exhibit 3, we will buy h underlying units as depicted in the second trade, and we will finance the present value of the net cash flows as depicted in the third trade. If we assume r denotes the per period risk-free interest rate, then the present value calculation, denoted as PV, is equal to $1/(1 + r)$. We need to borrow or lend an amount such that the future net cash flows are equal to zero. Therefore, we finance today the present value of $-hS^- + c^-$ which also equals $-hS^+ + c^+$. At this point we do not know if the finance term is positive or negative, thus we may be either borrowing or lending, which will depend on c, h, and S.

EXHIBIT 3   Writing One Call Hedge with h Units of the Underlying and Finance

Strategy	Time Step 0	Time Step 1 Down Occurs	Time Step 1 Up Occurs
1) Write one call option	$+c$	$-c^-$	$-c^+$
2) Buy h underlying units	$-hS$	$+hS^-$	$+hS^+$
3) Borrow or lend	$-PV(-hS^- + c^-)$ $= -PV(-hS^+ + c^+)$	$-hS^- + c^-$	$-hS^+ + c^+$
Net Cash Flow	$+c - hS$ $-PV(-hS^- + c^-)$	0	0

The value of the net portfolio at Time Step 0 should be zero or there is an arbitrage opportunity. If the net portfolio has positive value, then arbitrageurs will engage in this strategy, which will push the call price down and the underlying price up until the net is no longer positive. We assume the size of the borrowing will not influence interest rates. If the net port-folio has negative value, then arbitrageurs will engage in the opposite strategy—buy calls, short sell the underlying, and lend—pushing the call price up and the underlying price down until the net cash flow at Time 0 is no longer positive. Therefore, within the single-period binomial model, we have

$$+c - hS - PV(-hS^- + c^-) = 0$$

or, equivalently,

$$+c - hS - PV(-hS^+ + c^+) = 0.$$

Therefore, the **no-arbitrage approach** leads to the following single-period call option valuation equation:

$$c = hS + PV(-hS^- + c^-) \qquad (2)$$

or, equivalently, $c = hS + PV(-hS^+ + c^+)$. In words, long a call option is equal to owning h shares of stock partially financed, where the financed amount is $PV(-hS^- + c^-)$, or using the per period rate, $(-hS^- + c^-)/(1 + r)$.[3]

We will refer to Equation 2 as the no-arbitrage single-period binomial option valuation model. This equation is foundational to understanding the two-period binomial as well as other option valuation models. The option can be replicated with the underlying and financing, a point illustrated in the following example.

EXAMPLE 1   Long Call Option Replicated with Underlying and Financing

Identify the trading strategy that will generate the payoffs of taking a long position in a call option within a single-period binomial framework.

A.   Buy $h = (c^+ + c^-)/(S^+ + S^-)$ units of the underlying and financing of $-PV(-hS^- + c^-)$
B.   Buy $h = (c^+ - c^-)/(S^+ - S^-)$ units of the underlying and financing of $-PV(-hS^- + c^-)$
C.   Short sell $h = (c^+ - c^-)/(S^+ - S^-)$ units of the underlying and financing of $+PV(-hS^- + c^-)$

Solution: B is correct. The following table shows the terminal payoffs to be identical between a call option and buying the underlying with financing.

---

[3] Or, by the same logic, $PV(-hS^+ + c^+)$, which is $(-hS^+ + c^+)/(1 + r)$.

Strategy	Time Step 0	Time Step 1 Down Occurs	Time Step 1 Up Occurs
Buy 1 call option	$-c$	$+c^-$	$+c^+$
OR A REPLICATING PORTFOLIO			
Buy h underlying units	$-hS$	$+hS^-$	$+hS^+$
Borrow or lend	$-PV(-hS^- + c^-)$ $= -PV(-hS^+ + c^+)$	$-hS^- + c^-$	$-hS^+ + c^+$
Net	$-hS - PV(-hS^- + c^-)$	$+c^-$	$+c^+$

Recall that by design, h is selected such that $-hS^- + c^- = -hS^+ + c^+$ or $h = (c^+ - c^-)/(S^+ - S^-)$. Therefore, a call option can be replicated with the underlying and financing. Specifically, the call option is equivalent to a leveraged position in the underlying.

Thus, the no-arbitrage approach is a replicating strategy: A call option is synthetically replicated with the underlying and financing. Following a similar strategy with puts, the no-arbitrage approach leads to the following no-arbitrage single-period put option valuation equation:

$$p = hS + PV(-hS^- + p^-) \tag{3}$$

or, equivalently, $p = hS + PV(-hS^+ + p^+)$ where

$$h = \frac{p^+ - p^-}{S^+ - S^-} \le 0 \tag{4}$$

Because p^+ is less than p^-, the hedge ratio is negative. Hence, to replicate a long put position, the arbitrageur will short sell the underlying and lend a portion of the proceeds. Note that a long put position would be replicated by trading h units of the underlying. With h negative, this trade is a short sale, and because $-h$ is positive, the value $-hS$ results in a positive cash flow at Time Step 0.

EXAMPLE 2   Long Put Option Replicated with Underlying and Financing

Identify the trading strategy that will generate the payoffs of taking a long position in a put option within a single-period binomial framework.

A. Short sell $-h = -(p^+ - p^-)/(S^+ - S^-)$ units of the underlying and financing of $-PV(-hS^- + p^-)$
B. Buy $-h = (p^+ - p^-)/(S^+ - S^-)$ units of the underlying and financing of $-PV(-hS^- + p^-)$
C. Short sell $h = (p^+ - p^-)/(S^+ - S^-)$ units of the underlying and financing of $+PV(-hS^- + p^-)$

Solution: A is correct. Before illustrating the replicating portfolio, we make a few observations regarding the hedge ratio. Note that by design, h is selected such that $-hS^- + p^- = -hS^+ + p^+$ or $h = (p^+ - p^-)/(S^+ - S^-)$. Unlike calls, the put hedge ratio is not positive (note that $p^+ < p^-$ but $S^+ > S^-$). Remember that taking a position in $-h$ units of the underlying is actually short selling the underlying rather than buying it. The following table shows the terminal payoffs to be identical between a put option and a position in the underlying with financing.

Strategy	Time Step 0	Time Step 1 Down Occurs	Time Step 1 Up Occurs
Buy 1 Put Option	$-p$	$+p^-$	$+p^+$
OR A REPLICATING PORTFOLIO			
Short sell $-h$ Underlying Units	$-hS$	$+hS^-$	$+hS^+$
Borrow or Lend	$-PV(-hS^- + p^-)$ $= -PV(-hS^+ + p^+)$	$-hS^- + p^-$	$-hS^+ + p^+$
Net	$-hS - PV(-hS^- + p^-)$	$+p^-$	$+p^+$

Therefore, a put option can be replicated with the underlying and financing. Specifically, the put option is simply equivalent to a short position in the underlying with financing in the form of lending.

What we have shown to this point is the no-arbitrage approach. Before turning to the expectations approach, we mention, for the sake of completeness, that the transactions for replicating the payoffs for writing options are the reverse for those of buying them. Thus, for writing a call option, the writer will be selling stock short and investing proceeds (i.e. lending), whereas for a put, the writer will be purchasing stock on margin (i.e. borrowing). Once again, we see the powerful result that the same basic conceptual structure is used for puts and calls, whether written or purchased. Only the exercise and expiration conditions vary.

The no-arbitrage results that have been presented can be expressed as the present value of a unique expectation of the option payoffs.[4] Specifically, the **expectations approach** results in an identical value as the no-arbitrage approach, but it is usually easier to compute. The formulas are viewed as follows:

$$c = PV[\pi c^+ + (1 - \pi)c^-] \text{ and} \qquad (5)$$

$$p = PV[\pi p^+ + (1 - \pi)p^-] \qquad (6)$$

where the probability of an up move is

$$\pi = [FV(1) - d]/(u - d)$$

---

[4] It takes a bit of algebra to move from the no-arbitrage expression to the present value of the expected future payoffs, but the important point is that both expressions yield exactly the same result.

Recall the future value is simply the reciprocal of the present value or $FV(1) = 1/PV(1)$. Thus, if $PV(1) = 1/(1 + r)$, then $FV(1) = (1 + r)$. Note that the option values are simply the present value of the expected terminal option payoffs. The expected terminal option payoffs can be expressed as

$$E(c_1) = \pi c^+ + (1 - \pi)c^- \text{ and}$$

$$E(p_1) = \pi p^+ + (1 - \pi)p^-$$

where c_1 and p_1 are the values of the options at Time 1. The present value and future value calculations are based on the risk-free rate, denoted r.[5] Thus, the option values based on the expectations approach can be written and remembered concisely as

$$c = PV_r[E(c_1)] \text{ and}$$

$$p = PV_r[E(p_1)]$$

The expectations approach to option valuation differs in two significant ways from the discounted cash flow approach to securities valuation. First, the expectation is not based on the investor's beliefs regarding the future course of the underlying. That is, the probability, π, is objectively determined and not based on the investor's personal view. This probability has taken several different names, including risk-neutral (RN) probability. Importantly, we did not make any assumption regarding the arbitrageur's risk preferences: The expectations approach is a result of this arbitrage process, not an assumption regarding risk preferences. Hence, they are called risk-neutral probabilities. Although we called them probabilities from the very start, they are not the true probabilities of up and down moves.

Second, the discount rate is *not* risk adjusted. The discount rate is simply based on the estimated risk-free interest rate. The expectations approach here is often viewed as superior to the discounted cash flow approach because both the subjective future expectation as well as the subjective risk-adjusted discount rate have been replaced with more objective measures.

EXAMPLE 3 Single-Period Binomial Call Value

A non-dividend-paying stock is currently trading at €100. A call option has one year to mature, the periodically compounded risk-free interest rate is 5.15%, and the exercise price is €100. Assume a single-period binomial option valuation model, where u = 1.35 and d = 0.74.

1. The optimal hedge ratio will be *closest* to:
   A. 0.57.
   B. 0.60.
   C. 0.65.

---

[5] We will suppress "r" most of the time and simply denote the calculation as PV. The "r" will be used at times to reinforce that the present value calculation is based on the risk-free interest rate.

2. The call option value will be *closest* to:
   A. €13.
   B. €15.
   C. €17.

Solution to 1: A is correct. Given the information provided, we know the following:

$$S^+ = uS = 1.35(100) = 135$$
$$S^- = dS = 0.74(100) = 74$$
$$c^+ = Max(0, uS - X) = Max(0, 135 - 100) = 35$$
$$c^- = Max(0, dS - X) = Max(0, 74 - 100) = 0$$

With this information, we can compute both the hedge ratio as well as the call option value. The hedge ratio is:

$$h = \frac{c^+ - c^-}{S^+ - S^-} = \frac{35 - 0}{135 - 74} = 0.573770$$

Solution to 2: C is correct. The risk-neutral probability of an up move is

$$\pi = [FV(1) - d]/(u - d) = (1.0515 - 0.74)/(1.35 - 0.74) = 0.510656,$$

where $FV(1) = (1 + r) = 1.0515$.

Thus the call value by the expectations approach is

$$c = PV[\pi c^+ + (1 - \pi)c^-] = 0.951022[(0.510656)35 + (1 - 0.510656)0] = €16.998,$$

where $PV(1) = 1/(1 + r) = 1/(1.0515) = 0.951022$.

Note that the call value by the no-arbitrage approach yields the same answer:

$$c = hS + PV(-hS^- + c^-) = 0.573770(100) + 0.951022[-0.573770(74) + 0] = €16.998.$$

The value of a put option can also be found based on put–call parity. Put–call parity can be remembered as simply two versions of portfolio insurance, long stock and long put or lend and long call, where the exercise prices for the put and call are identical. Put–call parity with symbols is

$$S + p = PV(X) + c \tag{7}$$

Put–call parity holds regardless of the particular valuation model being used. Depending on the context, this equation can be rearranged. For example, a call option can be expressed as a position in a stock, financing, and a put, or

$$c = S - PV(X) + p$$

EXAMPLE 4   Single-Period Binomial Put Value

You again observe a €100 price for a non-dividend-paying stock with the same inputs as the previous box. That is, the call option has one year to mature, the periodically compounded risk-free interest rate is 5.15%, the exercise price is €100, u = 1.35, and d = 0.74. The put option value will be *closest* to:

A. €12.00.
B. €12.10.
C. €12.20.

Solution: B is correct. For puts, we know the following:

$$p^+ = Max(0,100 - uS) = Max(0,100 - 135) = 0$$
$$p^- = Max(0,100 - dS) = Max(0,100 - 74) = 26$$

With this information, we can compute the put option value based on risk-neutral probability from the previous example or [recall that PV(1) = 0.951022]

$$p = PV[\pi p^+ + (1 - \pi)p^-] = 0.951022[(0.510656)0 + (1 - 0.510656)26] = €12.10$$

Therefore, in summary, option values can be expressed either in terms of replicating portfolios or as the present value of the expected future cash flows. Both expressions yield the same valuations.

4. BINOMIAL MODEL: TWO-PERIOD (CALL OPTIONS)

The two-period binomial lattice can be viewed as three one-period binomial lattices, as illustrated in Exhibit 4. Clearly, if we understand the one-period model, then the process can be repeated three times. First, we analyze Box 1 and Box 2. Finally, based on the results of Box 1 and Box 2, we analyze Box 3.

EXHIBIT 4   Two-Period Binomial Lattice as Three One-Period Binomial Lattices

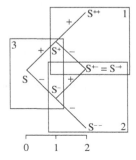

At Time 2, there are only three values of the underlying, S^{++} (an up move occurs twice), S^{--} (a down move occurs twice), and $S^{+-} = S^{-+}$ (either an up move occurs and then a down move or a down move occurs and then an up move). For computational reasons, it is extremely helpful that the lattice recombines—that is, $S^{+-} = S^{-+}$, meaning that if the underlying goes up and then down, it ends up at the same price as if it goes down and then up. A recombining binomial lattice will always have just one more ending node in the final period than the number of time steps. In contrast, a non-recombining lattice of n time steps will have 2^n ending nodes, which poses a tremendous computational challenge even for powerful computers.

For our purposes here, we assume the up and down factors are constant throughout the lattice, ensuring that the lattice recombines—that is $S^{+-} = S^{-+}$. For example, assume $u = 1.25$, $d = 0.8$, and $S_0 = 100$. Note that $S^{+-} = 1.25(0.8)100 = 100$ and $S^{-+} = 0.8(1.25)100 = 100$. So the middle node at Time 2 is 100 and can be reached from either of two paths.

The two-period binomial option valuation model illustrates two important concepts, self-financing and dynamic replication. Self-financing implies that the replicating portfolio will not require any additional funds from the arbitrageur during the life of this dynamically rebalanced portfolio. If additional funds are needed, then they are financed externally. Dynamic replication means that the payoffs from the option can be exactly replicated through a planned trading strategy. Option valuation relies on self-financing, dynamic replication.

Mathematically, the no-arbitrage approach for the two-period binomial model is best understood as working backward through the binomial tree. At Time 2, the payoffs are driven by the option's exercise value.

For calls:

$$c^{++} = \text{Max}(0, S^{++} - X) = \text{Max}(0, u^2S - X),$$

$$c^{+-} = \text{Max}(0, S^{+-} - X) = \text{Max}(0, udS - X), \text{ and}$$

$$c^{--} = \text{Max}(0, S^{--} - X) = \text{Max}(0, d^2S - X)$$

For puts:

$$p^{++} = \text{Max}(0, X - S^{++}) = \text{Max}(0, X - u^2S),$$

$$p^{+-} = \text{Max}(0, X - S^{+-}) = \text{Max}(0, X - udS), \text{ and}$$

$$p^{--} = \text{Max}(0, X - S^{--}) = \text{Max}(0, X - d^2S)$$

At Time 1, the option values are driven by the arbitrage transactions that synthetically replicate the payoffs at Time 2. We can compute the option values at Time 1 based on the option values at Time 2 using the no-arbitrage approach based on Equations 1 and 2. At Time 0, the option values are driven by the arbitrage transactions that synthetically replicate the value of the options at Time 1 (again based on Equations 1 and 2).

We illustrate the no-arbitrage approach for solving the two-period binomial call value. Suppose the annual interest rate is 3%, the underlying stock is $S = 72$, $u = 1.356$, $d = 0.541$, and the exercise price is $X = 75$. The stock does not pay dividends. Exhibit 5 illustrates the results.

EXHIBIT 5   Two-Period Binomial Tree with Call Values and Hedge Ratios

Item	Value
Underlying	132.389
Call	57.389

Item	Value
Underlying	97.632
Call	33.43048
Hedge Ratio	0.72124

Item	Value
Underlying	52.81891
Call	0

Item	Value
Underlying	72
Call	19.47407
Hedge Ratio	0.56971

Item	Value
Underlying	38.952
Call	0
Hedge Ratio	0

Item	Value
Underlying	21.07303
Call	0

We now verify selected values reported in Exhibit 5. At Time Step 2 and assuming up occurs twice, the underlying stock value is $u^2S = (1.356)^272 = 132.389$, and hence, the call value is 57.389 [= Max(0,132.389 − 75)]. The hedge ratio at Time Step 1, assuming up occurs once, is

$$h^+ = \frac{c^{++} - c^{+-}}{S^{++} - S^{+-}} = \frac{57.389 - 0}{132.389 - 52.819} = 0.72124$$

The RN probability of an up move throughout this tree is

$$\pi = [FV(1) - d]/(u - d) = (1.03 - 0.541)/(1.356 - 0.541) = 0.6$$

With this information, we can compute the call price at Time 1 when an up move occurs as

$$c = PV[\pi c^{++} + (1 - \pi)c^{+-}] = (1/1.03)[(0.6)57.389 + (1 - 0.6)0] = 33.43048$$

and at Time Step 0,

$$h = \frac{c^+ - c^-}{S^+ - S^-} = \frac{33.43048 - 0}{97.632 - 38.952} = 0.56971$$

Thus, the call price at the start is

$$c = PV[\pi c^+ + (1 - \pi)c^-] = (1/1.03)[(0.6)33.43048 + (1 - 0.6)0] = 19.47$$

From the no-arbitrage approach, the call payoffs can be replicated by purchasing h shares of the underlying and financing −PV(−hS⁻ + c⁻). Therefore, we purchase 0.56971 shares of stock for 41.019 [= 0.56971(72)] and borrow 21.545 {or in cash flow terms, −21.545 = (1/1.03)[−0.56971(38.952) + 0]}, replicating the call values at Time 0. We then illustrate Time 1 assuming that an up move occurs. The stock position will now be worth 55.622 [= 0.56971(97.632)], and the borrowing must be repaid with interest or 22.191 [= 1.03(21.545)].

Note that the portfolio is worth 33.431 (55.622 − 22.191), the same value as the call except for a small rounding error. Therefore, the portfolio of stock and the financing dynamically replicates the value of the call option.

The final task is to demonstrate that the portfolio is self-financing. Self-financing can be shown by observing that the new portfolio at Time 1, assuming an up move occurs, is equal to the old portfolio that was formed at Time 0 and liquidated at Time 1. Notice that the hedge ratio rose from 0.56971 to 0.72124 as we moved from Time 0 to Time 1, assuming an up move occurs, requiring the purchase of additional shares. These additional shares will be financed with additional borrowing. The total borrowing is 36.98554 {= −PV(−hS^{+-} + c^{+-}) = −(1/1.03)[−0.72124(52.81891) + 0]}. The borrowing at Time 0 that is due at Time 1 is 22.191. The funds borrowed at Time 1 grew to 36.98554. Therefore, the strategy is self-financing.

The two-period binomial model can also be represented as the present value of an expectation of future cash flows. Based on the one-period results, it follows by repeated substitutions that

$$c = PV[\pi^2 c^{++} + 2\pi(1 − \pi)c^{+-} + (1 − \pi)^2 c^{--}] \tag{8}$$

and

$$p = PV[\pi^2 p^{++} + 2\pi(1 − \pi)p^{+-} + (1 − \pi)^2 p^{--}] \tag{9}$$

Therefore, the two-period binomial model is again simply the present value of the expected future cash flows based on the RN probability. Again, the option values are simply the present value of the expected terminal option payoffs. The expected terminal option payoffs can be expressed as

$$E(c_2) = \pi^2 c^{++} + 2\pi(1 − \pi)c^{+-} + (1 − \pi)^2 c^{--}$$

and

$$E(p_2) = \pi^2 p^{++} + 2\pi(1 − \pi)p^{+-} + (1 − \pi)^2 p^{--}$$

Thus, the two-period binomial option values based on the expectations approach can be written and remembered concisely as

$$c = PV_r[E\pi(c_2)] \text{ and}$$

$$p = PV_r[E\pi(p_2)]$$

It is vital to remember that this present value is over two periods, so the discount factor with discrete rates is $PV = [1/(1 + r)^2]$. Recall the subscript "r" just emphasizes the present value calculation and is based on the risk-free interest rate.

EXAMPLE 5   Two-Period Binomial Model Call Valuation

You observe a €50 price for a non-dividend-paying stock. The call option has two years to mature, the periodically compounded risk-free interest rate is 5%, the exercise price is €50, u = 1.356, and d = 0.744. Assume the call option is European-style.

1. The probability of an up move based on the risk-neutral probability is *closest* to:
   A. 30%.
   B. 40%.
   C. 50%.
2. The current call option value is *closest* to:
   A. €9.53.
   B. €9.71.
   C. €9.87.
3. The current put option value is *closest* to:
   A. €5.06.
   B. €5.33.
   C. €5.94.

Solution to 1: C is correct. Based on the RN probability equation, we have:

$$\pi = [FV(1) - d]/(u - d) = [(1 + 0.05) - 0.744]/(1.356 - 0.744) = 0.5 \text{ or } 50\%$$

Solution to 2: B is correct. The current call option value calculations are as follows:

$$c^{++} = Max(0, u^2S - X) = Max[0, 1.356^2(50) - 50] = 41.9368$$
$$c^{-+} = c^{+-} = Max(0, udS - X) = Max[0, 1.356(0.744)(50) - 50] = 0.44320$$
$$c^{--} = Max(0, d^2S - X) = Max[0, 0.744^2(50) - 50] = 0.0$$

With this information, we can compute the call option value:

$$c = PV[E(c_2)] = PV[\pi^2 c^{++} + 2\pi(1 - \pi)c^{+-} + (1 - \pi)^2 c^{--}]$$

$$= [1/(1 + 0.05)]^2[0.5^2 41.9368 + 2(0.5)(1 - 0.5)0.44320 + (1 - 0.5)^2 0.0]$$

$$= 9.71$$

It is vital to remember that the present value is over two periods, hence the single-period PV is squared. Thus, the current call price is €9.71.

Solution to 3: A is correct. The put option value can be computed simply by applying put–call parity or $p = c + PV(X) - S = 9.71 + [1/(1 + 0.05)]^2 50 - 50 = 5.06$. Thus, the current put price is €5.06.

5. BINOMIAL MODEL: TWO-PERIOD (PUT OPTIONS)

We now turn to consider American-style options. It is well-known that non-dividend-paying call options on stock will not be exercised early because the minimum price of the option exceeds its exercise value. To illustrate by example, consider a call on a US$100 stock, with an exercise price of US$10 (that is, very deep in the money). Suppose the call is worth its exercise value of only US$90. To get stock exposure, one could fund and pay US$100 to buy the stock, or fund and pay only US$90 for the call and pay the last US$10 at expiration only if the stock is at or above US$100 at that time. Because the latter choice is preferable, the call must be worth more than the US$90 exercise value. Another way of looking at it is that it would make no sense to exercise this call because you do not believe the stock can go any higher and you would thus simply be obtaining a stock that you believe would go no higher. Moreover, the stock would require that you pay far more money than you have tied up in the call. It is always better to just sell the call in this situation because it will be trading for more than the exercise value.

The same is not true for put options. By early exercise of a put, particularly a deep in-the-money put, the sale proceeds can be invested at the risk-free rate and earn interest worth more than the time value of the put. Thus, we will examine how early exercise influences the value of an American-style put option. As we will see, when early exercise has value, the no-arbitrage approach is the only way to value American-style options.

Suppose the periodically compounded interest rate is 3%, the non-dividend-paying underlying stock is currently trading at 72, the exercise price is 75, $u = 1.356$, $d = 0.541$, and the put option expires in two years. Exhibit 6 shows the results for a European-style put option.

EXHIBIT 6   Two-Period Binomial Model for a European-Style Put Option

Item	Value
Underlying	132.389
Put	0

Item	Value
Underlying	97.632
Put	8.61401
Hedge Ratio	−0.27876

Item	Value
Underlying	72
Put	18.16876
Hedge Ratio	−0.43029

Item	Value
Underlying	52.81891
Put	22.18109

Item	Value
Underlying	38.952
Put	33.86353
Hedge Ratio	−1

Item	Value
Underlying	21.07303
Put	53.92697

The Time 1 down move is of particular interest. The exercise value for this put option is 36.048 [= Max(0,75 − 38.952)]. Therefore, the exercise value is higher than the put value. So, if this same option were American-style, then the option would be worth more exercised than not exercised. Thus, the put option should be exercised. Exhibit 7 illustrates how the analysis changes if this put option were American-style. Clearly, the right to exercise early translates into a higher value.

EXHIBIT 7   Two-Period Binomial Model for an American-Style Put Option

Item	Value
Underlying	132.389
Put	0

Item	Value
Underlying	97.632
Put	8.61401
Hedge Ratio	−0.27876

Item	Value
Underlying	52.81891
Put	22.18109

Item	Value
Underlying	72
Put	~~18.16876~~ 19.01710
Hedge Ratio	~~−0.43029~~ −0.46752

Item	Value
Underlying	38.952
Put	~~33.86353~~ 36.04800
Hedge Ratio	−1

Item	Value
Underlying	21.07303
Put	53.92697

American-style option valuation requires that one work backward through the binomial tree and address whether early exercise is optimal at each step. In Exhibit 7, the early exercise premium at Time 1 when a down move occurs is 2.18447 (36.048 − 33.86353). Also, if we replace 33.86353 with 36.048—in bold below for emphasis—in the Time 0 calculation, we obtain a put value of

$$p = PV[\pi p^+ + (1 - \pi)p^-] = (1/1.03)[(0.6)8.61401 + (1 - 0.6)\textbf{36.048}] = 19.02$$

Thus, the early exercise premium at Time 0 is 0.85 (19.02 − 18.17). From this illustration, we see clearly that in a multiperiod setting, American-style put options cannot be valued simply as the present value of the expected future option payouts, as shown in Equation 9. American-style put options can be valued as the present value of the expected future option payout in a single-period setting. Hence, when early exercise is a consideration, we must address the possibility of early exercise as we work backward through the binomial tree.

EXAMPLE 6   Two-Period Binomial American-Style Put Option Valuation

Suppose you are given the following information: $S_0 = 26$, $X = 25$, $u = 1.466$, $d = 0.656$, $n = 2$ (time steps), $r = 2.05\%$ (per period), and no dividends. The tree is provided in Exhibit 8.

EXHIBIT 8   Two-Period Binomial American-Style Put Option

Item	Value
Underlying	26
Put	4.01174
Hedge Ratio	−0.35345

Item	Value
Underlying	38.116
Put	0
Hedge Ratio	0

Item	Value
Underlying	17.056
Put	7.44360
Hedge Ratio	−0.99970

Item	Value
Underlying	55.87806
Put	0

Item	Value
Underlying	25.00410
Put	0

Item	Value
Underlying	11.18874
Put	13.81126

The early exercise premium of the above American-style put option is *closest* to:

A. 0.27.
B. 0.30.
C. 0.35.

Solution: A is correct. The exercise value at Time 1 with a down move is 7.944 [= Max(0,25 − 17.056)]. Thus, we replace this value in the binomial tree and compute the hedge ratio at Time 0. The resulting put option value at Time 0 is thus 4.28143 (see Exhibit 9).

EXHIBIT 9   Solution

Item	Value
Underlying	26
Put	~~4.01174~~ 4.28143
Hedge Ratio	~~−0.35345~~ −0.37721

Item	Value
Underlying	38.116
Put	0
Hedge Ratio	0

Item	Value
Underlying	17.056
Put	~~7.44360~~ 7.94400
Hedge Ratio	−0.99970

Item	Value
Underlying	55.87806
Put	0

Item	Value
Underlying	25.00410
Put	0

Item	Value
Underlying	11.18874
Put	13.81126

In Exhibit 9, the early exercise premium at Time 1 when a down move occurs is 0.5004 (7.944 − 7.44360). Thus, if we replace 7.44360 with 7.944—in bold below for emphasis—in the Time 0 calculation, we have the put value of

$$p = PV[\pi p^+ + (1 - \pi)p^-] = (1/1.0205)[(0.45)0 + (1 - 0.45)\mathbf{7.944}] = 4.28$$

Thus, the early exercise premium at Time 0 when a down move occurs 0.27 (= 4.28 − 4.01).

6. BINOMIAL MODEL: TWO-PERIOD (ROLE OF DIVIDENDS & COMPREHENSIVE EXAMPLE)

We now briefly introduce the role of dividend payments within the binomial model. Our approach here is known as the escrow method. Because dividends lower the value of the stock, a call option holder is hurt. Although it is possible to adjust the option terms to offset this effect, most option contracts do not provide protection against dividends. Thus, dividends affect the value of an option. We assume dividends are perfectly predictable; hence, we split the underlying instrument into two components: the underlying instrument without the known dividends and the known dividends.[6] For example, the current value of the underlying instrument without dividends can be expressed as

$$\hat{S} = S - \gamma$$

where γ denotes the present value of dividend payments. We use the ^ symbol to denote the underlying instrument without dividends. In this case, we model the uncertainty of the stock based on $\hat{S}$ and not S. At expiration, the underlying instrument value is the same, $\hat{S}_T = S_T$, because we assume any dividends have already been paid. The value of an investment in the stock, however, would be $S_T + \gamma_T$, which assumes the dividend payments are reinvested at the risk-free rate.

To illustrate by example, consider a call on a US$100 stock with exercise price of US$95. The periodically compounded interest rate is 1.0%, the stock will pay a US$3 dividend at Time Step 1, u = 1.224, d = 0.796, and the call option expires in two years. Exhibit 10 shows some results for an American-style call option. The computations in Exhibit 10 involve several technical nuances that are beyond the scope of our objectives. The key objective here is to see how dividend-motivated early exercise influences American options.

The Time 1 up move is particularly interesting. At Time 0, the present value of the US$3 dividend payment is US$2.970297 (= 3/1.01). Therefore, 118.7644 = (100 − 2.970297)1.224 is the stock value without dividends at Time 1, assuming an up move occurs. The exercise value for this call option, including dividends, is 26.7644 [= Max(0,118.7644 + 3 − 95)], whereas

---

[6] The reading focuses on regular, "known" dividends. In the case of large, special dividends, option exchanges may adjust the exercise price.

the value of the call option per the binomial model is 24.9344. In other words, the stock price just before it goes ex-dividend is $118.7644 + 3 = 121.7644$, so the option can be exercised for $121.7644 - 95 = 26.7644$. If not exercised, the stock drops as it goes ex-dividend and the option becomes worth 24.9344 at the ex-dividend price. Thus, by exercising early, the call buyer acquires the stock just before it goes ex-dividend and thus is able to capture the dividend. If the call is not exercised, the call buyer will not receive this dividend. The American-style call option is worth more than the European-style call option because at Time Step 1 when an up move occurs, the call is exercised early, capturing additional value.

EXHIBIT 10   Two-Period Binomial Model for an American-Style Call Option with Dividends

Item	Value
Underlying	145.3676
Call	50.3676

Item	Value
Underlying	118.7644
Call	~~24.9344~~ 26.7644
Hedge Ratio	0.9909

Item	Value
Underlying	94.5364
Call	0

Item	Value
Underlying	100
Call	~~12.3438~~ 13.2497
Hedge Ratio	~~−0.6004~~ 0.6445

Item	Value
Underlying	77.2356
Call	0
Hedge Ratio	0

Item	Value
Underlying	61.4796
Call	0

We now provide a comprehensive binomial option valuation example. In this example, we contrast European-style exercise with American-style exercise.

EXAMPLE 7   Comprehensive Two-Period Binomial Option Valuation Model Exercise

Suppose you observe a non-dividend-paying Australian equity trading for A$7.35. The call and put options have two years to mature, the periodically compounded risk-free interest rate is 4.35%, and the exercise price is A$8.0. Based on an analysis of this equity, the estimates for the up and down moves are u = 1.445 and d = 0.715, respectively.

1. Calculate the European-style call and put option values at Time Step 0 and Time Step 1. Describe and interpret your results.
2. Calculate the European-style call and put option hedge ratios at Time Step 0 and Time Step 1. Based on these hedge ratios, interpret the component terms of the binomial option valuation model.
3. Calculate the American-style call and put option values and hedge ratios at Time Step 0 and Time Step 1. Explain how your results differ from the European-style results.

Solution to 1: The expectations approach requires the following preliminary calculations:

RN probability: $\pi = [FV(1) - d]/(u - d)$

$$= [(1 + 0.0435) - 0.715]/(1.445 - 0.715) = 0.45$$

$$c^{++} = Max(0, u^2S - X)$$

$$= Max[0, 1.445^2(7.35) - 8.0] = 7.347$$

$$c^{+-} = Max(0, udS - X)$$

$$= Max[0, 1.445(0.715)7.35 - 8.0] = 0$$

$$c^{--} = Max(0, d^2S - X)$$

$$= Max[0, 0.715^2(7.35) - 8.0] = 0$$

$$p^{++} = Max(0, X - u^2S)$$

$$= Max[0, 8.0 - 1.445^2(7.35)] = 0$$

$$p^{+-} = Max(0, X - udS)$$

$$= Max[0, 8.0 - 1.445(0.715)7.35] = 0.406$$

$$p^{--} = Max(0, X - d^2S)$$

$$= Max[0, 8.0 - 0.715^2(7.35)] = 4.24$$

Therefore, at Time Step 1, we have (note that $c_2|\,_1^+$ is read as the call value expiring at Time Step 2 observed at Time Step 1, assuming an up move occurs)

$$E(c_2|\,_1^+) = \pi c^{++} + (1 - \pi)c^{+-} = 0.45(7.347) + (1 - 0.45)0 = 3.31$$

$$E(c_2|\,_1^-) = \pi c^{-+} + (1 - \pi)c^{--} = 0.45(0.0) + (1 - 0.45)0.0 = 0.0$$

$$E(p_2|\,_1^+) = \pi p^{++} + (1 - \pi)p^{+-} = 0.45(0.0) + (1 - 0.45)0.406 = 0.2233$$

$$E(p_2|\,_1^-) = \pi p^{-+} + (1 - \pi)p^{--} = 0.45(0.406) + (1 - 0.45)4.24 = 2.51$$

Thus, because $PV_{1,2}(1) = 1/(1 + 0.0435) = 0.958313$, we have the Time Step 1 option values of

$$c^+ = PV_{1,2}\big[E(c_2|\,_1^+)\big] = 0.958313(3.31) = 3.17$$

$$c^- = PV_{1,2}\big[E(c_2|\,_1^-)\big] = 0.958313(0.0) = 0.0$$

$$p^+ = PV_{1,2}\big[E(p_2|\,_1^+)\big] = 0.958313(0.2233) = 0.214$$

$$p^- = PV_{1,2}\big[E(p_2|\,_1^-)\big] = 0.958313(2.51) = 2.41$$

At Time Step 0, we have

$$E(c_2|_0) = \pi^2c^{++} + 2\pi(1 - \pi)c^{+-} + (1 - \pi)^2c^{--}$$

$$= 0.45^2(7.347) + 2(0.45)(1 - 0.45)0 + (1 - 0.45)^2 0 = 1.488$$

$$E(p_2|_0) = \pi^2 p^{++} + 2\pi(1 - \pi)p^{+-} + (1 - \pi)^2 p^{--}$$

$$= 0.45^2(0) + 2(0.45)(1 - 0.45)0.406 + (1 - 0.45)^2 4.24 = 1.484$$

Thus,

$$c = PV_{rf,0,2}[E(c_2|_0)] = 0.91836(1.488) = 1.37 \text{ and}$$

$$p = PV_{rf,0,2}[E(p_2|_0)] = 0.91836(1.484) = 1.36$$

With the two-period binomial model, the call and put values based on the expectations approach are simply the present values of the expected payoffs. The present value of the expected payoffs is based on the risk-free interest rate and the expectations approach is based on the risk-neutral probability. The parameters in this example were selected so that the European-style put and call would have approximately the same value. Notice that the stock price is less than the exercise price by roughly the present value factor or $7.35 = 8.0/1.0435^2$. One intuitive explanation is put–call parity, which can be expressed as $c - p = S - PV(X)$. Thus, if $S = PV(X)$, then $c = p$.

Solution to 2: The computation of the hedge ratios at Time Step 1 and Time Step 0 will require the option values at Time Step 1 and Time Step 2. The terminal values of the options are given in Solution 1.

$$S^{++} = u^2 S = 1.445^2(7.35) = 15.347$$

$$S^{+-} = udS = 1.445(0.715)7.35 = 7.594$$

$$S^{--} = d^2 S = 0.715^2(7.35) = 3.758$$

$$S^+ = uS = 1.445(7.35) = 10.621$$

$$S^- = dS = 0.715(7.35) = 5.255$$

Therefore, the hedge ratios at Time 1 are

$$h_c^+ = \frac{c^{++} - c^{+-}}{S^{++} - S^{+-}} = \frac{7.347 - 0.0}{15.347 - 7.594} = 0.9476$$

$$h_c^- = \frac{c^{-+} - c^{--}}{S^{-+} - S^{--}} = \frac{0.0 - 0.0}{7.594 - 3.758} = 0.0$$

$$h_p^+ = \frac{p^{++} - p^{+-}}{S^{++} - S^{+-}} = \frac{0.0 - 0.406}{15.347 - 7.594} = -0.05237$$

$$h_p^- = \frac{p^{-+} - p^{--}}{S^{-+} - S^{--}} = \frac{0.406 - 4.24}{7.594 - 3.758} = -1.0$$

In the last hedge ratio calculation, both put options are in the money (p^{-+} and p^{--}). In this case, the hedge ratio will be −1, subject to a rounding error. We now turn to interpreting the model's component terms. Based on the no-arbitrage approach, we have for the call price, assuming an up move has occurred, at Time Step 1,

$$c^+ = h_c^+ S^+ + PV_{1,2}(-h_c^+ S^{+-} + c^{+-})$$

$$= 0.9476(10.621) + (1/1.0435)[-0.9476(7.594) + 0.0] = 3.1684$$

Thus, the call option can be interpreted as a leveraged position in the stock. Specifically, long 0.9476 shares for a cost of 10.0645 [= 0.9476(10.621)] partially financed with a 6.8961 {= (1/1.0435)[−0.9476(7.594) + 0.0]} loan. Note that the loan amount can be found simply as the cost of the position in shares less the option value [6.8961 = 0.9476(10.621) − 3.1684]. Similarly, we have

$$c^- = h_c^- S^- + PV_{1,2}\left(-h_c^- S^{--} + c^{--}\right)$$
$$= 0.0(5.255) + (1/1.0435)[-0.0(3.758) + 0.0] = 0.0$$

Specifically, long 0.0 shares for a cost of 0.0 [= 0.0(5.255)] with no financing. For put options, the interpretation is different. Specifically, we have

$$p^+ = PV_{1,2}\left(-h_p^+ S^{++} + p^{++}\right) + h_p^+ S^+$$
$$= (1/1.0435)[-(-0.05237)15.347 + 0.0] + (-0.05237)10.621 = 0.2140$$

Thus, the put option can be interpreted as lending that is partially financed with a short position in shares. Specifically, short 0.05237 shares for a cost of 0.55622 [= (−0.05237)10.621] with financing of 0.77022 {= (1/1.0435)[−(−0.05237)15.347 + 0.0]}. Note that the lending amount can be found simply as the proceeds from the short sale of shares plus the option value [0.77022 = (0.05237)10.621 + 0.2140]. Again, we have

$$p^- = PV_{1,2}\left(-h_p^- S^{-+} + p^{-+}\right) + h_p^- S^-$$
$$= (1/1.0435)[-(-1.0)7.594 + 0.406] + (-1.0)5.255 = 2.4115$$

Here, we short 1.0 shares for a cost of 5.255 [= (−1.0)5.255] with financing of 7.6665 {= (1/1.0435)[−(−1.0)7.594 + 0.406]}. Again, the lending amount can be found simply as the proceeds from the short sale of shares plus the option value [7.6665 = (1.0)5.255 + 2.4115].

Finally, we have at Time Step 0

$$h_c = \frac{c^+ - c^-}{S^+ - S^-} = \frac{3.1684 - 0}{10.621 - 5.255} = 0.5905$$

$$h_p = \frac{p^+ - p^-}{S^+ - S^-} = \frac{0.2140 - 2.4115}{10.621 - 5.255} = -0.4095$$

The interpretations remain the same at Time Step 0:

$$c = h_c S + PV_{0,1}(-h_c S^- + c^-)$$
$$= 0.5905(7.35) + (1/1.0435)[-0.5905(5.255) + 0.0] = 1.37$$

Here, we are long 0.5905 shares for a cost of 4.3402 [=0.5905(7.35)] partially financed with a 2.97 {= (1/1.0435)[−0.5905(5.255) + 0.0] or = 0.5905(7.35) − 1.37} loan.

$$p = PV_{0,1}(-h_p S^+ + p^+) + h_p S$$
$$= (1/1.0435)\{-[-0.4095(10.621)] + 0.214\} + (-0.4095)7.35 = 1.36$$

Here, we short 0.4095 shares for a cost of 3.01 [= (−0.4095)7.35] with financing of 4.37 (= (1/1.0435){−[−0.4095(10.621)] + 0.214} or = (0.4095)7.35 + 1.36).

Solution to 3: We know that American-style call options on non-dividend-paying stock are worth the same as European-style call options because early exercise will not occur. Thus, as previously computed, $c^+ = 3.17$, $c^- = 0.0$, and $c = 1.37$. Recall that the call exercise value (denoted with EV) is simply the maximum of zero or the stock price minus the exercise price. We note that the EVs are less than or equal to the call model values; that is,

$$c_{EV}^+ = Max(0, S^+ - X) = Max(0, 10.621 - 8.0) = 2.621 \ (< 3.1684)$$

$$c_{EV}^- = Max(0, S^- - X) = Max(0, 5.255 - 8.0) = 0.0 \ (= 0.0)$$

$$c_{EV} = Max(0, S - X) = Max(0, 7.35 - 8.0) = 0.0 \ (< 1.37)$$

Therefore, the American-style feature for non-dividend-paying stocks has no effect on either the hedge ratio or the option value. The binomial model for American-style calls on non-dividend-paying stocks can be described and interpreted the same as a similar European-style call. This point is consistent with what we said earlier. If there are no dividends, an American-style call will not be exercised early.

This result is not true for puts. We know that American-style put options on non-dividend-paying stock may be worth more than the analogous European-style put options. The hedge ratios at Time Step 1 will be the same as European-style puts because there is only one period left. Therefore, as previously shown, $p^+ = 0.214$ and $p^- = 2.41$.

The put exercise values are

$$p_{EV}^+ = Max(0, X - S^+) = Max(0, 8.0 - 10.621) = 0 \ (< 0.214)$$

$$p_{EV}^- = Max(0, X - S^-) = Max(0, 8.0 - 5.255) = 2.745 \ (> 2.41)$$

Because the exercise value for the put at Time Step 1, assuming a down move occurred, is greater than the model value, we replace the model value with the exercise value. Hence,

$$p^- = 2.745$$

and the hedge ratio at Time Step 0 will be affected. Specifically, we now have

$$h_p = \frac{p^+ - p^-}{S^+ - S^-} = \frac{0.2140 - 2.745}{10.621 - 5.255} = -0.4717$$

and thus the put model value is

$$p = (1/1.0435)[0.45(0.214) + 0.55(2.745)] = 1.54$$

Clearly, the early exercise feature has a significant impact on both the hedge ratio and the put option value in this case. The hedge ratio goes from −0.4095 to −0.4717. The put value is raised from 1.36 to 1.54.

We see through the simple two-period binomial model that an option can be viewed as a position in the underlying with financing. Furthermore, this valuation model can be expressed as the present value of the expected future cash flows, where the expectation is taken under the RN probability and the discounting is at the risk-free rate.

Up to this point, we have focused on equity options. The binomial model can be applied to any underlying instrument though often requiring some modifications. For example, currency options would require incorporating the foreign interest rate. Futures options would require a binomial lattice of the futures prices. Interest rate options, however, require somewhat different tools that we now examine.

7. INTEREST RATE OPTIONS & MULTIPERIOD MODEL

In this section, we will briefly illustrate how to value interest rate options. There are a wide variety of approaches to valuing interest rate options. We do not delve into how arbitrage-free interest rate trees are generated. The particular approach used here assumes the RN probability of an up move at each node is 50%.

Exhibit 11 presents a binomial lattice of interest rates covering two years along with the corresponding zero-coupon bond values. The rates are expressed in annual compounding. Therefore, at Time 0, the spot rate is $(1.0/0.970446) - 1$ or 3.04540%.[7] Note that at Time 1, the value in the column labeled "Maturity" reflects time to maturity not calendar time. The lattice shows the rates on one-period bonds, so all bonds have a maturity of 1. The column labeled "Value" is the value of a zero-coupon bond with the stated maturity based on the rates provided.

EXHIBIT 11   Two-Year Binomial Interest Rate Lattice by Year

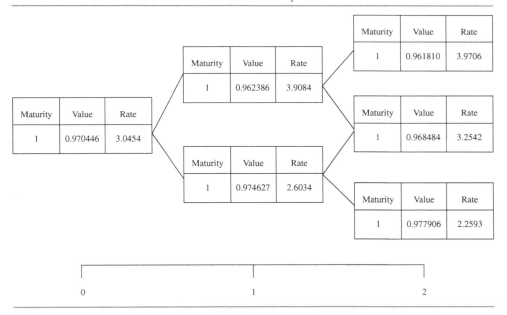

---

[7] The values in the first box from the left are observed at t = 0. The values in the remainder of the lattice are derived by using a technique that is outside the scope of this reading.

The underlying instrument for interest rate options here is the spot rate. A call option on interest rates will be in the money when the current spot rate is above the exercise rate. A put option on interest rates will be in the money when the current spot rate is below the exercise rate. Thus, based on the notation in the previous section, the current spot rate is denoted S. Option valuation follows the expectations approach discussed in the previous section but taken only one period at a time. The procedure is illustrated with an example.

EXAMPLE 8   Option on Interest Rates

This example is based on Exhibit 11. Suppose we seek to value two-year European-style call and put options on the periodically compounded one-year spot interest rate (the underlying). Assume the notional amount of the options is US\$1,000,000 and the call and put exercise rate is 3.25% of par. Assume the RN probability is 50% and these option cash settle at Time 2 based on the observed rates.[8]

Solution: Using the expectations approach introduced in the last section, we have (per US\$1) at Time Step 2

$$c^{++} = \text{Max}(0, S^{++} - X) = \text{Max}[0, 0.039706 - 0.0325] = 0.007206$$

$$c^{+-} = \text{Max}(0, S^{+-} - X) = \text{Max}[0, 0.032542 - 0.0325] = 0.000042$$

$$c^{--} = \text{Max}(0, S^{--} - X) = \text{Max}[0, 0.022593 - 0.0325] = 0.0$$

$$p^{++} = \text{Max}(0, X - S^{++}) = \text{Max}[0, 0.0325 - 0.039706] = 0.0$$

$$p^{+-} = \text{Max}(0, X - S^{+-}) = \text{Max}[0, 0.0325 - 0.032542] = 0.0$$

$$p^{--} = \text{Max}(0, X - S^{--}) = \text{Max}[0, 0.0325 - 0.022593] = 0.009907$$

At Time Step 1, we have

$$c^{+} = PV_{1,2}[\pi c^{++} + (1 - \pi)c^{+-}]$$

$$= 0.962386[0.5(0.007206) + (1 - 0.5)0.000042]$$

$$= 0.003488$$

$$c^{-} = PV_{1,2}[\pi c^{+-} + (1 - \pi)c^{--}]$$

$$= 0.974627[0.5(0.000042) + (1 - 0.5)0.0]$$

$$= 0.00002$$

---

[8] In practice, interest rate options usually have a settlement procedure that results in a deferred payoff. The deferred payoff arises from the fact that the underlying interest rate is based on an instrument that pays interest at the end of its life. For the instrument underlying the interest rate, the interest payment occurs after the interest has accrued. To accommodate this reality in this problem, we would have to introduce an instrument that matures at time three. The purpose of this example is merely to illustrate the procedure for rolling backward through an interest rate tree when the underlying is the interest rate. We simplify this example by omitting this deferred settlement. In Section 12, we discuss in detail the deferred settlement procedure and incorporate it into the pricing model.

$$p^+ = PV_{1,2}[\pi p^{++} + (1 - \pi)p^{+-}]$$

$$= 0.962386[0.5(0.0) + (1 - 0.5)0.0]$$

$$= 0.0$$

$$p^- = PV_{1,2}[\pi p^{+-} + (1 - \pi)p^{--}]$$

$$= 0.974627[0.5(0.0) + (1 - 0.5)0.009907]$$

$$= 0.004828$$

Notice how the present value factors are different for the up and down moves. At Time Step 1 in the + outcome, we discount by a factor of 0.962386, and in the − outcome, we discount by the factor 0.974627. Because this is an option on interest rates, it should not be surprising that we have to allow the interest rate to vary.

Therefore, at Time Step 0, we have

$$c = PV_{rf,0,1}[\pi c^+ + (1 - \pi)c^-]$$

$$= 0.970446[0.5(0.003488) + (1 - 0.5)0.00002]$$

$$= 0.00170216$$

$$p = PV_{rf,0,1}[\pi p^+ + (1 - \pi)p^-]$$

$$= 0.970446[0.5(0.0) + (1 - 0.5)0.004828]$$

$$= 0.00234266$$

Because the notional amount is US$1,000,000, the call value is US$1,702.16 [= US$1,000,000(0.00170216)] and the put value is US$2,342.66 [= US$1,000,000(0.00234266)]. The key insight is to just work a two-period binomial model as three one-period binomial models.

We turn now to briefly generalize the binomial model as it leads naturally to the Black–Scholes–Merton option valuation model.

7.1. Multiperiod Model

The multiperiod binomial model provides a natural bridge to the Black–Scholes–Merton option valuation model presented in the next section. The idea is to take the option's expiration and slice it up into smaller and smaller periods. The two-period model divides the expiration into two periods. The three-period model divides expiration into three periods and so forth. The process continues until you have a large number of time steps. The key feature is that each time step is of equal length. Thus, with a maturity of T, if there are n time steps, then each time step is T/n in length.

For American-style options, we must also test at each node whether the option is worth more exercised or not exercised. As in the two-period case, we work backward through the binomial tree testing the model value against the exercise value and always choosing the higher one.

The binomial model is an important and useful methodology for valuing options. The expectations approach can be applied to European-style options and will lead naturally to the BSM model in the next section. This approach simply values the option as the present value of the expected future payoffs, where the expectation is taken under the risk-neutral probability and the discounting is based on the risk-free rate. The no-arbitrage approach can be applied to either European-style or American-style options because it provides the intuition for the fair value of options.

8. BLACK–SCHOLES–MERTON (BSM) OPTION VALUATION MODEL, INTRODUCTION AND ASSUMPTIONS OF THE BSM MODEL

The BSM model, although very complex in its derivation, is rather simple to use and interpret. The objective here is to illustrate several facets of the BSM model with the objective of highlighting its practical usefulness. After a brief introduction, we examine the assumptions of the BSM model and then delve into the model itself.

8.1. Introductory Material

Louis Bachelier published the first known mathematically rigorous option valuation model in 1900. By the late 1960s, there were several published quantitative option models. Fischer Black, Myron Scholes, and Robert Merton introduced the BSM model in 1973 in two published papers, one by Black and Scholes and the other by Merton. The innovation of the BSM model is essentially the no-arbitrage approach introduced in the previous section but applied with a continuous time process, which is equivalent to a binomial model in which the length of the time step essentially approaches zero. It is also consistent with the basic statistical fact that the binomial process with a "large" number of steps converges to the standard normal distribution. Myron Scholes and Robert Merton won the 1997 Nobel Prize in Economics based, in part, on their work related to the BSM model.[9] Let us now examine the BSM model assumptions.

8.2. Assumptions of the BSM Model

The key assumption for option valuation models is how to model the random nature of the underlying instrument. This characteristic of how an asset evolves randomly is called a stochastic process. Many financial instruments enjoy limited liability; hence, the values of instruments cannot be negative, but they certainly can be zero. In 1900, Bachelier proposed the normal distribution. The key advantages of the normal distribution are that zero is possible, meaning that bankruptcy is allowable, it is symmetric, it is relatively easy to manipulate, and it is additive (which means that sums of normal distributions are normally distributed). The key disadvantage is that negative stock values are theoretically possible, which violates the limited liability principal of stock ownership. Based on research on stock prices in the 1950s and 1960s, a preference emerged for the lognormal distribution, which means that log returns are distributed normally. Black, Scholes, and Merton chose to use the lognormal distribution.

Recall that the no-arbitrage approach requires self-financing and dynamic replication; we need more than just an assumption regarding the terminal distribution of the underlying instrument. We need to model the value of the instrument as it evolves over time, which is what we mean by a stochastic process. The stochastic process chosen by Black, Scholes, and Merton is called geometric Brownian motion (GBM).

---

[9] Fischer Black passed away in 1995 and the Nobel Prize is not awarded posthumously.

Exhibit 12 illustrates GBM, assuming the initial stock price is S = 50. We assume the stock will grow at 3% (μ = 3% annually, geometrically compounded rate). This GBM process also reflects a random component that is determined by a volatility (σ) of 45%. This volatility is the annualized standard deviation of continuously compounded percentage change in the underlying, or in other words, the log return. Note that as a particular sample path drifts upward, we observe more variability on an absolute basis, whereas when the particular sample path drifts downward, we observe less variability on an absolute basis. For example, examine the highest and lowest lines shown in Exhibit 12. The highest line is much more erratic than the lowest line. Recall that a 10% move in a stock with a price of 100 is 10 whereas a 10% move in a stock with a price of 10 is only 1. Thus, GBM can never hit zero nor go below it. This property is appealing because many financial instruments enjoy limited liability and cannot be negative. Finally, note that although the stock movements are rather erratic, there are no large jumps—a common feature with marketable financial instruments.

EXHIBIT 12   Geometric Brownian Motion Simulation (S = 50, μ = 3%, σ = 45%)

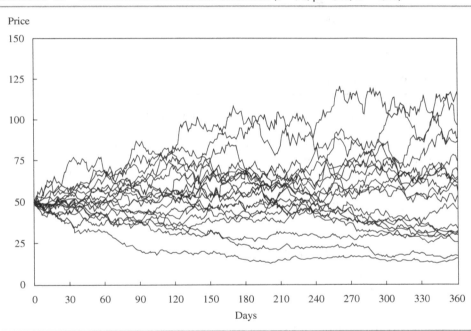

Within the BSM model framework, it is assumed that all investors agree on the distributional characteristics of GBM except the assumed growth rate of the underlying. This growth rate depends on a number of factors, including other instruments and time. The standard BSM model assumes a constant growth rate and constant volatility.

The specific assumptions of the BSM model are as follows:

- The underlying follows a statistical process called geometric Brownian motion, which implies that the continuously compounded return is normally distributed.
- Geometric Brownian motion implies continuous prices, meaning that the price of underlying instrument does not jump from one value to another; rather, it moves smoothly from value to value.

- The underlying instrument is liquid, meaning that it can be easily bought and sold.
- Continuous trading is available, meaning that in the strictest sense one must be able to trade at every instant.
- Short selling of the underlying instrument with full use of the proceeds is permitted.
- There are no market frictions, such as transaction costs, regulatory constraints, or taxes.
- No arbitrage opportunities are available in the marketplace.
- The options are European-style, meaning that early exercise is not allowed.
- The continuously compounded risk-free interest rate is known and constant; borrowing and lending is allowed at the risk-free rate.
- The volatility of the return on the underlying is known and constant.
- If the underlying instrument pays a yield, it is expressed as a continuous known and constant yield at an annualized rate.

Naturally, the foregoing assumptions are not absolutely consistent with real financial markets, but, as in all financial models, the question is whether they produce models that are tractable and useful in practice, which they do.

EXAMPLE 9   BSM Model Assumptions

Which is the *correct* pair of statements? The BSM model assumes:

A. the return on the underlying has a normal distribution. The price of the underlying can jump abruptly to another price.
B. brokerage costs are factored into the BSM model. It is impossible to trade continuously.
C. volatility can be predicted with certainty. Arbitrage is non-existent in the marketplace.

Solution: C is correct. All four of the statements in A and B are incorrect within the BSM model paradigm.

---

9. BSM MODEL: COMPONENTS

We turn now to a careful examination of the BSM model.

The BSM model is a continuous time version of the discrete time binomial model. Given that the BSM model is based on continuous time, it is customary to use a continuously compounded interest rate rather than some discretely compounded alternative. Thus, when an interest rate is used here, denoted simply as r, we mean solely the annualized continuously compounded rate.[10] The volatility, denoted as σ, is also expressed in annualized percentage terms. Initially, we focus on a non-dividend-paying stock. The BSM model, with some adjustments, applies to other underlying instruments, which will be examined later.

---

[10] Note $e^r = 1 + r_d$, where r_d is the annually compounded rate.

The BSM model for stocks can be expressed as

$$c = SN(d_1) - e^{-rT}XN(d_2) \qquad (10)$$

and

$$p = e^{-rT}XN(-d_2) - SN(-d_1) \qquad (11)$$

where

$$d_1 = \frac{\ln(S/X) + (r + \sigma^2/2)T}{\sigma\sqrt{T}}$$

$$d_2 = d_1 - \sigma\sqrt{T}$$

$N(x)$ denotes the standard normal cumulative distribution function, which is the probability of obtaining a value of less than x based on a standard normal distribution. In our context, x will have the value of d_1 or d_2. $N(x)$ reflects the likelihood of observing values less than x from a random sample of observations taken from the standard normal distribution.

Although the BSM model appears very complicated, it has straightforward interpretations that will be explained. $N(x)$ can be estimated by a computer program or a spreadsheet or approximated from a lookup table. The normal distribution is a symmetric distribution with two parameters, the mean and standard deviation. The standard normal distribution is a normal distribution with a mean of 0 and a standard deviation of 1.

Exhibit 13 illustrates the standard normal probability density function (the standard bell curve) and the cumulative distribution function (the accumulated probability and range of 0 to 1). Note that even though GBM is lognormally distributed, the $N(x)$ functions in the BSM model are based on the standard normal distribution. In Exhibit 13, we see that if $x = -1.645$, then $N(x) = N(-1.645) = 0.05$. Thus, if the model value of d is -1.645, the corresponding probability is 5%. Clearly, values of d that are less than 0 imply values of $N(x)$ that are less than 0.5. As a result of the symmetry of the normal distribution, we note that $N(-x) = 1 - N(x)$.

EXHIBIT 13   Standard Normal Distribution

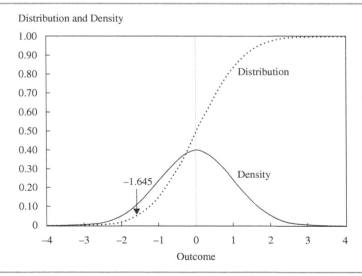

The BSM model can be described as the present value of the expected option payoff at expiration. Specifically, we can express the BSM model for calls as $c = PV_r[E(c_T)]$ and for puts as $p = PV_r[E(p_T)]$, where $E(c_T) = Se^{rT}N(d_1) - XN(d_2)$ and $E(p_T) = XN(-d_2) - Se^{rT}N(-d_1)$. The present value term in this context is simply e^{-rT}. As with most valuation tasks in finance, the value today is simply the present value of the expected future cash flows. It is important to note that the expectation is based on the risk-neutral probability measure defined in Section 3. The expectation is not based on the investor's subjective beliefs, which reflect an aversion to risk. Also, the present value function is based on the risk-free interest rate not on the investor's required return on invested capital, which of course is a function of risk.

Alternatively, the BSM model can be described as having two components: a stock component and a bond component. For call options, the stock component is $SN(d_1)$ and the bond component is $e^{-rT}XN(d_2)$. The BSM model call value is the stock component minus the bond component. For put options, the stock component is $SN(-d_1)$ and the bond component is $e^{-rT}XN(-d_2)$. The BSM model put value is the bond component minus the stock component.

The BSM model can be interpreted as a dynamically managed portfolio of the stock and zero-coupon bonds.[11] The goal is to replicate the option payoffs with stocks and bonds. For both call and put options, we can represent the initial cost of this replicating strategy as

$$\text{Replicating strategy cost} = n_S S + n_B B$$

where the equivalent number of underlying shares is $n_S = N(d_1) > 0$ for calls and $n_S = -N(-d_1) < 0$ for puts. The equivalent number of bonds is $n_B = -N(d_2) < 0$ for calls and $n_B = N(-d_2) > 0$ for puts. The price of the zero-coupon bond is $B = e^{-rT}X$. Note, if n is positive, we are buying the underlying and if n is negative we are selling (short selling) the underlying. The cost of the portfolio will exactly equal either the BSM model call value or the BSM model put value.

For calls, we are simply buying stock with borrowed money because $n_S > 0$ and $n_B < 0$. Again the cost of this portfolio will equal the BSM model call value, and if appropriately rebalanced, then this portfolio will replicate the payoff of the call option. Therefore, a call option can be viewed as a leveraged position in the stock.

Similarly, for put options, we are simply buying bonds with the proceeds from short selling the underlying because $n_S < 0$ and $n_B > 0$. The cost of this portfolio will equal the BSM model put value, and if appropriately rebalanced, then this portfolio will replicate the payoff of the put option. Note that a short position in a put will result in receiving money today and $n_S > 0$ and $n_B < 0$. Therefore, a short put can be viewed as an over-leveraged or over-geared position in the stock because the borrowing exceeds 100% of the cost of the underlying.

Exhibit 14 illustrates the direct comparison between the no-arbitrage approach to the single-period binomial option valuation model and the BSM option valuation model. The parallel between the h term in the binomial model and $N(d_1)$ is easy to see. Recall that the term hedge ratio was used with the binomial model because we were creating a no-arbitrage portfolio. Note for call options, $-N(d_2)$ implies borrowing money or short selling $N(d_2)$ shares of a zero-coupon bond trading at $e^{-rT}X$. For put options, $N(-d_2)$ implies lending money or buying $N(-d_2)$ shares of a zero-coupon bond trading at $e^{-rT}X$.

---

[11] When covering the binomial model, the bond component was generically termed financing. This component is typically handled with bank borrowing or lending. With the BSM model, it is easier to understand as either buying or short selling a risk-free zero-coupon bond.

EXHIBIT 14   BSM and Binomial Option Valuation Model Comparison

Option Valuation	Call Option		Put Option	
Model Terms	Underlying	Financing	Underlying	Financing
Binomial Model	hS	$PV(-hS^- + c^-)$	hS	$PV(-hS^- + p^-)$
BSM Model	$N(d_1)S$	$-N(d_2)e^{-rT}X$	$-N(-d_1)S$	$N(-d_2)e^{-rT}X$

If the value of the underlying, S, increases, then the value of $N(d_1)$ also increases because S has a positive effect on d_1. Thus, the replicating strategy for calls requires continually buying shares in a rising market and selling shares in a falling market.

Within the BSM model theory, the aggregate losses from this "buy high/sell low" strategy, over the life of the option, adds up exactly to the BSM model option premium received for the option at inception.[12] This result must be the case; otherwise there would be arbitrage profits available. Because transaction costs are not, in fact, zero, the frequent rebalancing by buying and selling the underlying adds significant costs for the hedger. Also, markets can often move discontinuously, contrary to the BSM model's assumption that prices move continuously, thus allowing for continuous hedging adjustments. Hence, in reality, hedges are imperfect. For example, if a company announces a merger, then the company's stock price may jump substantially higher, contrary to the BSM model's assumption.

In addition, volatility cannot be known in advance. For these reasons, options are typically more expensive than they would be as predicted by the BSM model theory. In order to continue using the BSM model, the volatility parameter used in the formula is usually higher (by, say, 1% or 2%, but this can vary a lot) than the volatility of the stock actually expected by market participants. We will ignore this point for now, however, as we focus on the mechanics of the model.

EXAMPLE 10   Illustration of BSM Model Component Interpretation

Suppose we are given the following information on call and put options on a stock: S = 100, X = 100, r = 5%, T = 1.0, and σ = 30%. Thus, based on the BSM model, it can be demonstrated that PV(X) = 95.123, d_1 = 0.317, d_2 = 0.017, $N(d_1)$ = 0.624, $N(d_2)$ = 0.507, $N(-d_1)$ = 0.376, $N(-d_2)$ = 0.493, c = 14.23, and p = 9.35.

1. The initial trading strategy required by the no-arbitrage approach to replicate the call option payoffs for a buyer of the option is:
   A. buy 0.317 shares of stock and short sell −0.017 shares of zero-coupon bonds.
   B. buy 0.624 shares of stock and short sell 0.507 shares of zero-coupon bonds.
   C. short sell 0.317 shares of stock and buy 0.017 shares of zero-coupon bonds.

---

[12] The validity of this claim does not rest on the validity of the BSM model assumptions; rather the validity depends only on whether the BSM model accurately predicts the replication cost.

2. Identify the initial trading strategy required by the no-arbitrage approach to replicate the put option payoffs for a buyer of the put.
   A. Buy 0.317 shares of stock and short sell −0.017 shares of zero-coupon bonds.
   B. Buy 0.624 shares of stock and short sell 0.507 shares of zero-coupon bonds.
   C. Short sell 0.376 shares of stock and buy 0.493 shares of zero-coupon bonds.

Solution to 1: B is correct. The no-arbitrage approach to replicating the call option involves purchasing $n_S = N(d_1) = 0.624$ shares of stock partially financed with $n_B = -N(d_2) = -0.507$ shares of zero-coupon bonds priced at $B = Xe^{-rT} = 95.123$ per bond. Note that by definition the cost of this replicating strategy is the BSM call model value or $n_S S + n_B B = 0.624(100) + (-0.507)95.123 = 14.17$. Without rounding errors, the option value is 14.23.

Solution to 2: C is correct. The no-arbitrage approach to replicating the put option is similar. In this case, we trade $n_S = -N(-d_1) = -0.376$ shares of stock—specifically, short sell 0.376 shares—and buy $n_B = N(-d_2) = 0.493$ shares of zero-coupon bonds. Again, the cost of the replicating strategy is $n_S S + n_B B = -0.376(100) + (0.493)95.123 = 9.30$. Without rounding errors, the option value is 9.35. Thus, to replicate a call option based on the BSM model, we buy stock on margin. To replicate a put option, we short the stock and buy zero-coupon bonds.

Note that the $N(d_2)$ term has an additional important interpretation. It is a unique measure of the probability that the call option expires in the money, and correspondingly, $1 - N(d_2) = N(-d_2)$ is the probability that the put option expires in the money. Specifically, the probability based on the RN probability of being in the money, not one's own estimate of the probability of being in the money nor the market's estimate. That is, $N(d_2) = Prob(S_T > X)$ based on the unique RN probability.

10. BSM MODEL: CARRY BENEFITS AND APPLICATIONS

We now turn to incorporating various carry benefits into the BSM model. Carry benefits include dividends for stock options, foreign interest rates for currency options, and coupon payments for bond options. For other underlying instruments, there are carry costs that can easily be treated as negative carry benefits, such as storage and insurance costs for agricultural products. Because the BSM model is established in continuous time, it is common to model these carry benefits as a continuous yield, denoted generically here as γ^c or simply γ.

The BSM model requires a few adjustments to accommodate carry benefits. The carry benefit-adjusted BSM model is

$$c = Se^{-\gamma T}N(d_1) - e^{-rT}XN(d_2) \tag{12}$$

and

$$p = e^{-rT}XN(-d_2) - Se^{-\gamma T}N(-d_1) \tag{13}$$

where

$$d_1 = \frac{\ln(S/X) + (r - \gamma + \sigma^2/2)T}{\sigma\sqrt{T}}$$

Note that d_2 can be expressed again simply as $d_2 = d_1 - \sigma\sqrt{T}$. The value of a put option can also be found based on the carry benefit-adjusted put–call parity:

$$p + Se^{-\gamma T} = c + e^{-rT}X \tag{14}$$

The carry benefit-adjusted BSM model can again be described as the present value of the expected option payoff at expiration. Now, however, $E(c_T) = Se^{(r-\gamma)T}N(d_1) - XN(d_2)$ and $E(p_T) = XN(-d_2) - Se^{(r-\gamma)T}N(-d_1)$. The present value term remains simply e^{-rT}. Carry benefits will have the effect of lowering the expected future value of the underlying

Again, the carry benefit-adjusted BSM model can be described as having two components, a stock component and a bond component. For call options, the stock component is $Se^{-\gamma T}N(d_1)$ and the bond component is again $e^{-rT}XN(d_2)$. For put options, the stock component is $Se^{-\gamma T}N(-d_1)$ and the bond component is again $e^{-rT}XN(-d_2)$. Although both d_1 and d_2 are reduced by carry benefits, the general approach to valuation remains the same. An increase in carry benefits will lower the value of the call option and raise the value of the put option.

Note that $N(d_2)$ term continues to be interpreted as the RN probability of a call option being in the money. The existence of carry benefits has the effect of lowering d_1 and d_2, hence the probability of being in the money with call options declines as the carry benefit rises. This RN probability is an important element to describing how the BSM model is used in various valuation tasks.

For stock options, $\gamma = \delta$, which is the continuously compounded dividend yield. The dividend-yield BSM model can again be interpreted as a dynamically managed portfolio of the stock and zero coupon bonds. Based on the call model above applied to a dividend yielding stock, the equivalent number of units of stock is now $n_S = e^{-\delta T}N(d_1) > 0$ and the equivalent number of units of bonds remains $n_B = -N(d_2) < 0$. Similarly with puts, the equivalent number of units of stock is now $n_S = -e^{-\delta T}N(-d_1) < 0$ and the equivalent number of units of bonds again remains $n_B = N(-d_2) > 0$.

With dividend paying stocks, the arbitrageur is able to receive the benefits of dividend payments when long the stock and has to pay dividends when short the stock. Thus, the burden of carrying the stock is diminished for a long position. The key insight is that dividends influence the dynamically managed portfolio by lowering the number of shares to buy for calls and raising the number of shares to short sell for puts. Higher dividends will lower the value of d_1, thus lowering $N(d_1)$. Also, higher dividends will lower the number of bonds to short sell for calls and raise the number of bonds to buy for puts.

EXAMPLE 11   BSM Model Applied to Equities

Suppose we are given the following information on an underlying stock and options: $S = 60$, $X = 60$, $r = 2\%$, $T = 0.5$, $\delta = 2\%$, and $\sigma = 45\%$. Assume we are examining European-style options.

1. Which answer *best* describes how the BSM model is used to value a call option with the parameters given?
   A. The BSM model call value is the exercise price times N(d1) less the present value of the stock price times N(d2).
   B. The BSM model call value is the stock price times $e^{-\delta T}$N(d1) less the exercise price times e^{-rT}N(d2).
   C. The BSM model call value is the stock price times $e^{-\delta T}$N(–d1) less the present value of the exercise price times e^{-rT}N(–d2).
2. Which answer *best* describes how the BSM model is used to value a put option with the parameters given?
   A. The BSM model put value is the exercise price times N(d1) less the present value of the stock price times N(d2).
   B. The BSM model put value is the exercise price times $e^{-\delta T}$N(–d2) less the stock price times e^{-rT}N(–d2).
   C. The BSM model put value is the exercise price times e^{-rT}N(–d2) less the stock price times $e^{-\delta T}$N(–d1).
3. Suppose now that the stock does not pay a dividend—that is, δ = 0%. Identify the correct statement.
   A. The BSM model option value is the same as the previous problems because options are not dividend adjusted.
   B. The BSM model option values will be different because there is an adjustment term applied to the exercise price, that is $e^{-\delta T}$, which will influence the option values.
   C. The BSM model option value will be different because d1, d2, and the stock component are all adjusted for dividends.

Solution to 1: B is correct. The BSM call model for a dividend-paying stock can be expressed as $Se^{-\delta T}N(d_1) - Xe^{-rT}N(d_2)$.

Solution to 2: C is correct. The BSM put model for a dividend-paying stock can be expressed as $Xe^{-rT}N(-d_2) - Se^{-\delta T}N(-d_1)$.

Solution to 3: C is correct. The BSM model option value will be different because d_1, d_2, and the stock component are all adjusted for dividends.

EXAMPLE 12   How the BSM Model Is Used to Value Stock Options

Suppose that we have some Bank of China shares that are currently trading on the Hong Kong Stock Exchange at HKD4.41. Our view is that the Bank of China's stock price will be steady for the next three months, so we decide to sell some three-month out-of-the-money calls with exercise price at 4.60 in order to enhance our returns by receiving the option premium. Risk-free government securities are paying 1.60% and the stock is yielding HKD 0.24%. The stock volatility is 28%. We use the BSM model to value the calls.

Which statement is correct? The BSM model inputs (underlying, exercise, expiration, risk-free rate, dividend yield, and volatility) are:

A.   4.60, 4.41, 3, 0.0160, 0.0024, and 0.28.
B.   4.41, 4.60, 0.25, 0.0160, 0.0024, and 0.28.
C.   4.41, 4.41, 0.3, 0.0160, 0.0024, and 0.28.

Solution: B is correct. The spot price of the underlying is HKD4.41. The exercise price is HKD4.60. The expiration is 0.25 years (three months). The risk-free rate is 0.016. The dividend yield is 0.0024. The volatility is 0.28.

For foreign exchange options, $\gamma = r^f$, which is the continuously compounded foreign risk-free interest rate. When quoting an exchange rate, we will give the value of the domestic currency per unit of the foreign currency. For example, Japanese yen (¥) per unit of the euro (€) will be expressed as the euro trading for ¥135 or succinctly 135¥/€. This is called the foreign exchange spot rate. Thus, the foreign currency, the euro, is expressed in terms of the Japanese yen, which is in this case the domestic currency. This is logical, for example, when a Japanese firm would want to express its foreign euro holdings in terms of its domestic currency, Japanese yen.

With currency options, the underlying instrument is the foreign exchange spot rate. Again, the carry benefit is the interest rate in the foreign country because the foreign currency could be invested in the foreign country's risk-free instrument. Also, with currency options, the underlying and the exercise price must be quoted in the same currency unit. Lastly, the volatility in the model is the volatility of the log return of the spot exchange rate. Each currency option is for a certain quantity of foreign currency, termed the notional amount, a concept analogous to the number of shares of stock covered in an option contract. The total cost of the option would be obtained by multiplying the formula value by the notional amount in the same way that one would multiply the formula value of an option on a stock by the number of shares the option contract covers.

The BSM model applied to currencies can be described as having two components, a foreign exchange component and a bond component. For call options, the foreign exchange component is $S e^{-r^f T} N(d_1)$ and the bond component is $e^{-rT} X N(d_2)$, where r is the domestic risk-free rate. The BSM call model applied to currencies is simply the foreign exchange component minus the bond component. For put options, the foreign exchange component is $S e^{-r^f T} N(-d_1)$ and the bond component is $e^{-rT} X N(-d_2)$. The BSM put model applied to currencies is simply the bond component minus the foreign exchange component. Remember that the underlying is expressed in terms of the domestic currency.

EXAMPLE 13   BSM Model Applied to Value Options on Currency

A Japanese camera exporter to Europe has contracted to receive fixed euro (€) amounts each quarter for his goods. The spot price of the currency pair is 135¥/€. If the exchange rate falls to, say, 130¥/€, then the yen will have strengthened because it will take fewer yen to buy one euro. The exporter is concerned that the yen will strengthen because in this case, his forthcoming fixed euro will buy fewer yen. Hence, the exporter is considering buying an at-the-money spot euro put option to protect against this fall; this in essence is a call on yen. The Japanese risk-free rate is 0.25% and the European risk-free rate is 1.00%.

1. What are the underlying and exercise prices to use in the BSM model to get the euro put option value?
    A. 1/135; 1/135
    B. 135; 135
    C. 135; 130
2. What are the risk-free rate and the carry rate to use in the BSM model to get the euro put option value?
    A. 0.25%; 1.00%
    B. 0.25%; 0.00%
    C. 1.00%; 0.25%

Solution to 1: B is correct. The underlying is the spot FX price of 135 ¥/€. Because the put is at-the-money spot, the exercise price equals the spot price.

Solution to 2: A is correct. The risk-free rate to use is the Japanese rate because the Japanese yen is the domestic currency unit per the exchange rate quoting convention. The carry rate is the foreign currency's risk-free rate, which is the European rate.

11. BLACK OPTION VALUATION MODEL AND EUROPEAN OPTIONS ON FUTURES

We turn now to examine a modification of the BSM model when the underlying is a forward or futures contract.

In 1976, Fischer Black introduced a modified version of the BSM model approach that is applicable to options on underlying instruments that are costless to carry, such as options on futures contracts—for example, equity index futures—and options on forward contracts. The latter include interest rate-based options, such as caps, floors, and swaptions.

11.1. European Options on Futures

We assume that the futures price also follows geometric Brownian motion. We ignore issues like margin requirements and marking to market. Black proposed the following model for European-style futures options:

$$c = e^{-rT}[F_0(T)N(d_1) - XN(d_2)] \tag{15}$$

and

$$p = e^{-rT}[XN(-d_2) - F_0(T)N(-d_1)] \tag{16}$$

where

$$d_1 = \frac{\ln[F_0(T)/X] + (\sigma^2/2)T}{\sigma\sqrt{T}} \text{ and}$$

$$d_2 = d_1 - \sigma\sqrt{T}$$

Note that $F_0(T)$ denotes the futures price at Time 0 that expires at Time T, and σ denotes the volatility related to the futures price. The other terms are as previously defined. Black's model is simply the BSM model in which the futures contract is assumed to reflect the carry arbitrage model. Futures option put–call parity can be expressed as

$$c = e^{-rT}[F_0(T) - X] + p \tag{17}$$

As we have seen before, put–call parity is a useful tool for describing the valuation relationship between call and put values within various option valuation models.

The Black model can be described in a similar way to the BSM model. The Black model has two components, a futures component and a bond component. For call options, the futures component is $F_0(T)e^{-rT}N(d_1)$ and the bond component is again $e^{-rT}XN(d_2)$. The Black call model is simply the futures component minus the bond component. For put options, the futures component is $F_0(T)e^{-rT}N(-d_1)$ and the bond component is again $e^{-rT}XN(-d_2)$. The Black put model is simply the bond component minus the futures component.

Alternatively, futures option valuation, based on the Black model, is simply computing the present value of the difference between the futures price and the exercise price. The futures price and exercise price are appropriately adjusted by the N(d) functions. For call options, the futures price is adjusted by $N(d_1)$ and the exercise price is adjusted by $-N(d_2)$ to arrive at difference. For put options, the futures price is adjusted by $-N(-d_1)$ and the exercise price is adjusted by $+N(-d_2)$.

EXAMPLE 14   European Options on Futures Index

The S&P 500 Index (a spot index) is presently at 1,860 and the 0.25 expiration futures contract is trading at 1,851.65. Suppose further that the exercise price is 1,860, the continuously compounded risk-free rate is 0.2%, time to expiration is 0.25, volatility is 15%, and the dividend yield is 2.0%. Based on this information, the following results are obtained for options on the futures contract.[13]

Options on Futures	
Calls	Puts
$N(d_1) = 0.491$	$N(-d_1) = 0.509$
$N(d_2) = 0.461$	$N(-d_2) = 0.539$
c = US$51.41	p = US$59.76

---

[13] We ignore the effect of the multiplier. As of this writing, the S&P 500 futures option contract has a multiplier of 250. The prices reported here have not been scaled up by this amount. In practice, the option cost would by 250 times the option value.

1. Identify the statement that *best* describes how the Black model is used to value a European call option on the futures contract just described.
    A. The call value is the present value of the difference between the exercise price times 0.461 and the current futures price times 0.539.
    B. The call value is the present value of the difference between the current futures price times 0.491 and the exercise price times 0.461.
    C. The call value is the present value of the difference between the current spot price times 0.491 and the exercise price times 0.461.
2. Which statement *best* describes how the Black model is used to value a European put options on the futures contract just described?
    A. The put value is the present value of the difference between the exercise price times 0.539 and the current futures price times 0.509.
    B. The put value is the present value of the difference between the current futures price times 0.491 and the exercise price times 0.461.
    C. The put value is the present value of the difference between the current spot price times 0.491 and the exercise price times 0.461.
3. What are the underlying and exercise prices to use in the Black futures option model?
    A. 1,851.65; 1,860
    B. 1,860; 1,860
    C. 1,860; 1,851.65

Solution to 1: B is correct. Recall Black's model for call options can be expressed as $c = e^{-rT}[F_0(T)N(d_1) - XN(d_2)]$.

Solution to 2: A is correct. Recall Black's model for put options can be expressed as $p = e^{-rT}[XN(-d_2) - F_0(T)N(-d_1)]$.

Solution to 3: A is correct. The underlying is the futures price of 1,851.65 and the exercise price was given as 1,860.

12. INTEREST RATE OPTIONS

With interest rate options, the underlying instrument is a reference interest rate, such as three-month Libor. An interest rate call option gains when the reference interest rate rises and an interest rate put option gains when the reference interest rate falls. Interest rate options are the building blocks of many other instruments.

For an interest rate call option on three-month Libor with one year to expiration, the underlying interest rate is a forward rate agreement (FRA) rate that expires in one year. This FRA is observed today and is the underlying rate used in the Black model. The underlying rate of the FRA is a 3-month Libor deposit that is investable in 12 months and matures in 15 months. Thus, in one year, the FRA rate typically converges to the three-month spot Libor.

Interest rates are typically set in advance, but interest payments are made in arrears, which is referred to as advanced set, settled in arrears. For example, with a bank deposit, the interest rate is usually set when the deposit is made, say t_{j-1}, but the interest payment is made when the deposit is withdrawn, say t_j. The deposit, therefore, has $t_m = t_j - t_{j-1}$ time until maturity. Thus, the rate is advanced set, but the payment is settled in arrears. Likewise with a floating rate loan, the rate is usually set and the interest accrues at this known rate, but the payment is made later. Similarly, with some interest rate options, the time to option expiration (t_{j-1}) when the interest rate is set does not correspond to the option settlement (t_j) when the cash payment is made, if any. For example, if an interest rate option payment based on three-month Libor is US$5,000 determined on January 15th, the actual payment of the US$5,000 would occur on April 15.

Interest rates are quoted on an annual basis, but the underlying implied deposit is often less than a year. Thus, the annual rates must be adjusted for the accrual period. Recall that the accrual period for a quarterly reset 30/360 day count FRA is 0.25 (= 90/360). If the day count is on an actual (ACT) number of days divided by 360 (ACT/360), then the accrual period may be something like 0.252778 (= 91/360), assuming 91 days in the period. Typically, the accrual period in FRAs is based on 30/360 whereas the accrual period based on the option is actual number of days in the contract divided by the actual number of days in the year (identified as ACT/ACT or ACT/365).

The model presented here is known as the standard market model and is a variation of Black's futures option valuation model. Again, let t_{j-1} denote the time to option expiration (ACT/365), whereas let t_j denote the time to the maturity date of the underlying FRA. Note that the interest accrual on the underlying begins at the option expiration (Time t_{j-1}). Let FRA(0, t_{j-1}, t_m) denote the fixed rate on a FRA at Time 0 that expires at Time t_{j-1}, where the underlying matures at Time t_j (= $t_{j-1} + t_m$), with all times expressed on an annual basis. We assume the FRA is 30/360 day count. For example, FRA(0,0.25,0.5) = 2% denotes the 2% fixed rate on a forward rate agreement that expires in 0.25 years with settlement amount being paid in 0.75 (= 0.25 + 0.5) years.[14] Let R_X denote the exercise rate expressed on an annual basis. Finally, let σ denote the interest rate volatility. Specifically, σ is the annualized standard deviation of the continuously compounded percentage change in the underlying FRA rate.

Interest rate options give option buyers the right to certain cash payments based on observed interest rates. For example, an interest rate call option gives the call buyer the right to a certain cash payment when the underlying interest rate exceeds the exercise rate. An interest rate put option gives the put buyer the right to a certain cash payment when the underlying interest rate is below the exercise rate.

With the standard market model, the prices of interest rate call and put options can be expressed as

$$c = (AP)\, e^{-r(t_{j-1} + t_m)} \Big[FRA\big(0, t_{j-1}, t_m\big) N(d_1) - R_X N(d_2) \Big] \tag{18}$$

and

$$p = (AP)\, e^{-r(t_{j-1} + t_m)} \Big[R_X N(-d_2) - FRA\big(0, t_{j-1}, t_m\big) N(-d_1) \Big] \tag{19}$$

---

[14] Note that in other contexts the time periods are expressed in months. For example with months, this FRA would be expressed as FRA(0,3,6). Note that the third term in parentheses denotes the maturity of the underlying deposit from the expiration of the FRA.

where

AP denotes the accrual period in years

$$d_1 = \frac{\ln\left[FRA(0, t_{j-1}, t_m)/R_X\right] + (\sigma^2/2)\, t_{j-1}}{\sigma\sqrt{t_{j-1}}}$$

$$d_2 = d_1 - \sigma\sqrt{t_{j-1}}$$

The formulas here give the value of the option for a notional amount of 1. In practice, the notional would be more than one, so the full cost of the option is obtained by multiplying these formula amounts by the notional amount. Of course, this point is just the same as finding the value of an option on a single share of stock and then multiplying that value by the number of shares covered by the option contract.

Immediately, we note that the standard market model requires an adjustment when compared with the Black model for the accrual period. In other words, a value such as FRA(0, t_{j-1}, t_m) or the strike rate, R_X, as appearing in the formula given earlier, is stated on an annual basis, as are interest rates in general. The actual option premium would have to be adjusted for the accrual period. After accounting for this adjustment, this model looks very similar to the Black model, but there are important but subtle differences. First, the discount factor, $e^{-r(t_{j-1} + t_m)}$, does not apply to the option expiration, t_{j-1}. Rather, the discount factor is applied to the maturity date of the FRA or t_j (= $t_{j-1} + t_m$). We express this maturity as ($t_{j-1} + t_m$) rather than t_j to emphasize the settlement in arrears nature of this option. Second, rather than the underlying being a futures price, the underlying is an interest rate, specifically a forward rate based on a forward rate agreement or FRA(0, t_{j-1}, t_m). Third, the exercise price is really a rate and reflects an interest rate, not a price. Fourth, the time to the option expiration, t_{j-1}, is used in the calculation of d_1 and d_2. Finally, both the forward rate and the exercise rate should be expressed in decimal form and not as percent (for example, 0.02 and not 2.0). Alternatively, if expressed as a percent, then the notional amount adjustment could be divided by 100.

As with other option models, the standard market model can be described as simply the present value of the expected option payoff at expiration. Specifically, we can express the standard market model for calls as c = PV[E(c_{tj})] and for puts as p = PV[E(p_{tj})], where E(c_{tj}) = (AP) [FRA(0, t_{j-1}, t_m)N(d_1) − R_XN(d_2)] and E(p_{tj}) = (AP)[R_XN(−d_2) − FRA(0, t_{j-1}, t_m)N(−d_1)]. The present value term in this context is simply $e^{-rt_j} = e^{-r(t_{j-1} + t_m)}$. Again, note we discount from Time t_j, the time when the cash flows are settled on the FRA.

There are several interesting and useful combinations that can be created with interest rate options. We focus on a few that will prove useful for understanding swaptions in the next section. First, if the exercise rate is selected so as to equal the current FRA rate, then long an interest rate call option and short an interest rate put option is equivalent to a receive-floating, pay-fixed FRA.

Second, if the exercise rate is again selected so it is equal to the current FRA rate, then long an interest rate put option and short an interest rate call option is equivalent to a receive-fixed, pay-floating FRA. Note that FRAs are the building blocks of interest rate swaps.

Third, an interest rate cap is a portfolio or strip of interest rate call options in which the expiration of the first underlying corresponds to the expiration of the second option and so forth. The underlying interest rate call options are termed caplets. Thus, a set of floating-rate loan payments can be hedged with a long position in an interest rate cap encompassing a series of interest rate call options.

Fourth, an interest rate floor is a portfolio or strip of interest rate put options in which the expiration of the first underlying corresponds with the expiration of the second option and so forth. The underlying interest rate put options are termed floorlets. Thus, a floating-rate bond investment or any other floating-rate lending situation can be hedged with an interest rate floor encompassing a series of interest rate put options.

Fifth, applying put–call parity as discussed earlier, long an interest rate cap and short an interest rate floor with the exercise prices set at the swap rate is equivalent to a receive-floating, pay-fixed swap. On a settlement date, when the underlying rate is above the strike, both the cap and the swap pay off to the party. When the underlying rate is below the strike on a settlement date, the party must make a payment on the short floor, just as the case with a swap. For the opposite position, long an interest rate floor and short an interest rate cap result in the party making a payment when the underlying rate is above the strike and receiving one when the underlying rate is below the strike, just as is the case for a pay-floating, receive-fixed swap.

Finally, if the exercise rate is set equal to the swap rate, then the value of the cap must be equal to the value of the floor at the start. When an interest rate swap is initiated, its current value is zero and is known as an at-market swap. When an exercise rate is selected such that the cap value equals the floor value, then the initial cost of being long a cap and short the floor is also zero. This occurs when the cap and floor strike are equal to the swap rate.

EXAMPLE 15   European Interest Rate Options

Suppose you are a speculative investor in Singapore. On 15 May, you anticipate that some regulatory changes will be enacted, and you want to profit from this forecast. On 15 June, you intend to borrow 10,000,000 Singapore dollars to fund the purchase of an asset, which you expect to resell at a profit three months after purchase, say on 15 September. The current three-month Sibor (that is, Singapore Libor) is 0.55%. The appropriate FRA rate over the period of 15 June to 15 September is currently 0.68%. You are concerned that rates will rise, so you want to hedge your borrowing risk by purchasing an interest rate call option with an exercise rate of 0.60%.

1. In using the Black model to value this interest rate call option, what would the underlying rate be?
   A. 0.55%
   B. 0.68%
   C. 0.60%
2. The discount factor used in pricing this option would be over what period of time?
   A. 15 May–15 June
   B. 15 June–15 September
   C. 15 May–15 September

Solution to 1: B is correct. In using the Black model, a forward or futures price is used as the underlying. This approach is unlike the BSM model in which a spot price is used as the underlying.

Solution to 2: C is correct. You are pricing the option on 15 May. An option expiring 15 June when the underlying is three-month Sibor will have its payoff determined on 15 June, but the payment will be made on 15 September. Thus, the expected payment must be discounted back from 15 September to 15 May.

Interest rate option values are linked in an important way with interest rate swap values through caps and floors. As we will see in the next section, an interest rate swap serves as the underlying for swaptions. Thus, once again, we see that important links exist between interest rate options, swaps, and swaptions.

13. SWAPTIONS

A swap option or swaption is simply an option on a swap. It gives the holder the right, but not the obligation, to enter a swap at the pre-agreed swap rate—the exercise rate. Interest rate swaps can be either receive fixed, pay floating or receive floating, pay fixed. A payer swaption is an option on a swap to pay fixed, receive floating. A receiver swaption is an option on a swap to receive fixed, pay floating. Note that the terms "call" and "put" are often avoided because of potential confusion over the nature of the underlying. Notice also that the terminology focuses on the fixed swap rate.

A payer swaption buyer hopes the fixed rate goes up before the swaption expires. When exercised, the payer swaption buyer is able to enter into a pay-fixed, receive-floating swap at the predetermined exercise rate, R_X. The buyer can then immediately enter an offsetting at-market receive-fixed, pay-floating swap at the current fixed swap rate. The floating legs of both swaps will offset, leaving the payer swaption buyer with an annuity of the difference between the current fixed swap rate and the swaption exercise rate. Thus, swaption valuation will reflect an annuity.

Swap payments are advanced set, settled in arrears. Let the swap reset dates be expressed as $t_0, t_1, t_2, ..., t_n$. Let R_{FIX} denote the fixed swap rate starting when the swaption expires, denoted as before with T, quoted on an annual basis, and R_X denote the exercise rate starting at Time T, again quoted on an annual basis. As before, we will assume a notional amount of 1.

Because swap rates are quoted on an annual basis, let AP denote the accrual period. Finally, we need some measure of uncertainty. Let σ denote the volatility of the forward swap rate. More precisely, σ denotes annualized, standard deviation of the continuously compounded percentage changes in the forward swap rate.

The swaption model presented here is a modification of the Black model. Let the present value of an annuity matching the forward swap payment be expressed as

$$PVA = \sum_{j=1}^{n} PV_{0,t_j}(1)$$

This term is equivalent to what is sometimes referred to as an annuity discount factor. It applies here because a swaption creates a series of equal payments of the difference in the market swap rate at expiration and the chosen exercise rate. Therefore, the payer swaption valuation model is

$$PAY_{SWN} = (AP)PVA[R_{FIX}N(d_1) - R_X N(d_2)] \qquad (20)$$

and the receiver swaption valuation model

$$REC_{SWN} = (AP)PVA[R_X N(-d_2) - R_{FIX}N(-d_1)] \qquad (21)$$

where

$$d_1 = \frac{\ln(R_{FIX}/R_X) + (\sigma^2/2)T}{\sigma\sqrt{T}}, \text{ and as always,}$$

$$d_2 = d_1 - \sigma\sqrt{T}$$

As noted with interest rate options, the actual premium would need to be scaled by the notional amount. Once again, we can see the similarities to the Black model. We note that the swaption model requires two adjustments, one for the accrual period and one for the present value of an annuity. After accounting for these adjustments, this model looks very similar to the Black model but there are important subtle differences. First, the discount factor is absent. The payoff is not a single payment but a series of payments. Thus, the present value of an annuity used here embeds the option-related discount factor. Second, rather than the underlying being a futures price, the underlying is the fixed rate on a forward interest rate swap. Third, the exercise price is really expressed as an interest rate. Finally, both the forward swap rate and the exercise rate should be expressed in decimal form and not as percent (for example, 0.02 and not 2.0).

As with other option models, the swaption model can be described as simply the present value of the expected option payoff at expiration. Specifically, we can express the payer swaption model value as

$$PAY_{SWN} = PV[E(PAY_{SWN,T})]$$

and the receiver swaption model value as

$$REC_{SWN} = PV[E(REC_{SWN,T})],$$

where

$$E(PAY_{SWN,T}) = e^{rT}PAY_{SWN} \text{ and}$$
$$E(REC_{SWN,T}) = e^{rT}REC_{SWN}.$$

The present value term in this context is simply e^{-rT}. Because the annuity term embedded the discounting over the swaption life, the expected swaption values are the current swaption values grossed up by the current risk-free interest rate.

Alternatively, the swaption model can be described as having two components, a swap component and a bond component. For payer swaptions, the swap component is (AP) $PVA(R_{FIX})N(d_1)$ and the bond component is $(AP)PVA(R_X)N(d_2)$. The payer swaption model value is simply the swap component minus the bond component. For receiver swaptions, the swap component is $(AP)PVA(R_{FIX})N(-d_1)$ and the bond component is (AP) $PVA(R_X)N(-d_2)$. The receiver swaption model value is simply the bond component minus the swap component.

As with nearly all derivative instruments, there are many useful equivalence relationships. Recall that long an interest rate cap and short an interest rate floor with the same exercise rate is equal to a receive-floating, pay-fixed interest rate swap. Also, short an interest rate cap and long an interest rate floor with the same exercise rate is equal to a pay-floating, receive-fixed interest rate swap. There are also equivalence relationships with swaptions. In a similar way, long a receiver swaption and short a payer swaption with the same exercise rate is equivalent to entering a receive-fixed, pay-floating forward swap. Long a payer swaption and short a receiver swaption with the same exercise rate is equivalent to entering a receive-floating, pay-fixed forward swap. Note that if the exercise rate is selected such that the receiver and payer swaptions have the same value, then the exercise rate is equal to the at-market forward swap rate. Thus, there is again a put–call parity relationship important for valuation.

In addition, being long a callable fixed-rate bond can be viewed as being long a straight fixed-rate bond and short a receiver swaption. A receiver swaption gives the buyer the right to receive a fixed rate. Hence, the seller will have to pay the fixed rate when this right is exercised in a lower rate environment. Recall that the bond issuer has the right to call the bonds. If the bond issuer sells a receiver swaption with similar terms, then the bond issuer has essentially converted the callable bond into a straight bond. The bond issuer will now pay the fixed rate on the underlying swap and the floating rate received will be offset by the floating-rate loan created when the bond was refinanced. Specifically, the receiver swaption buyer will benefit when rates fall and the swaption is exercised. Thus, the embedded call feature is similar to a receiver swaption.

EXAMPLE 16   European Swaptions

Suppose you are an Australian company and have ongoing floating-rate debt. You have profited for some time by paying at a floating rate because rates have been falling steadily for the last few years. Now, however, you are concerned that within three months the Australian central bank may tighten its monetary policy and your debt costs will thus increase. Rather than lock in your borrowing via a swap, you prefer to hedge by buying a swaption expiring in three months, whereby you will have the choice, but not the obligation, to enter a five-year swap locking in your borrowing costs. The current three-month forward, five-year swap rate is 2.65%. The current five-year swap rate is 2.55%. The current three-month risk-free rate is 2.25%.

With reference to the Black model to value the swaption, which statement is correct?

A. The underlying is the three-month forward, five-year swap rate.
B. The discount rate to use is 2.55%.
C. The swaption time to expiration, T, is five years.

Solution: A is correct. The current five-year swap rate is not used as a discount rate with swaptions. The swaption time to expiration is 0.25, not the life of the swap.

---

14. OPTION GREEKS AND IMPLIED VOLATILITY: DELTA

With option valuation models, such as the binomial model, BSM model, and Black's model, we are able to estimate a wide array of comparative information, such as how much the option value will change for a small change in a particular parameter.[15] We will explore this derived information as well as implied volatility in this section. These topics are essential for those managing option positions and in general in obtaining a solid understanding of how option prices change. Our discussion will be based on stock options, though the material covered in this section applies to all types of options.

---

[15] Parameters in the BSM model, for example, include the stock price, exercise price, volatility, time to expiration, and the risk-free interest rate.

The measures examined here are known as the Greeks and include, delta, gamma, theta, vega, and rho. With these calculations, we seek to address how much a particular portfolio will change for a given small change in the appropriate parameter. These measures are sometimes referred to as static risk measures in that they capture movements in the option value for a movement in one of the factors that affect the option value, while holding all other factors constant.

Our focus here is on European stock options in which the underlying stock is assumed to pay a dividend yield (denoted δ). Note that for non-dividend-paying stocks, $\delta = 0$.

14.1. Delta

Delta is defined as the change in a given instrument for a given small change in the value of the stock, holding everything else constant. Thus, the delta of long one share of stock is by definition +1.0, and the delta of short one share of stock is by definition −1.0. The concept of the option delta is similarly the change in an option value for a given small change in the value of the underlying stock, holding everything else constant. The option deltas for calls and puts are, respectively,

$$\text{Delta}_c = e^{-\delta T} N(d_1) \tag{22}$$

and

$$\text{Delta}_p = -e^{-\delta T} N(-d_1) \tag{23}$$

Note that the deltas are a simple function of $N(d_1)$. The delta of an option answers the question of how much the option will change for a given change in the stock, holding everything else constant. Therefore, delta is a static risk measure. It does not address how likely this particular change would be. Recall that $N(d_1)$ is a value taken from the cumulative distribution function of a standard normal distribution. As such, the range of values is between 0 and 1. Thus, the range of call delta is 0 and $e^{-\delta T}$ and the range of put delta is $-e^{-\delta T}$ and 0. As the stock price increases, the call option goes deeper in the money and the value of $N(d_1)$ is moving toward 1. As the stock price decreases, the call option goes deeper out of the money and the value of $N(d_1)$ is moving toward zero. When the option gets closer to maturity, the delta will drift either toward 0 if it is out of the money or drift toward 1 if it is in the money. Clearly, as the stock price changes and as time to maturity changes, the deltas are also changing.

Delta hedging an option is the process of establishing a position in the underlying stock of a quantity that is prescribed by the option delta so as to have no exposure to very small moves up or down in the stock price. Hence, to execute a single option delta hedge, we first calculate the option delta and then buy or sell delta units of stock. In practice, rarely does one have only one option position to manage. Thus, in general, delta hedging refers to manipulating the underlying portfolio delta by appropriately changing the positions in the portfolio. A delta neutral portfolio refers to setting the portfolio delta all the way to zero. In theory, the delta neutral portfolio will not change in value for small changes in the stock instrument. Let N_H denote the number of units of the hedging instrument and Delta_H denote the delta of the hedging instrument, which could be the underlying stock, call options, or put options. Delta neutral implies the portfolio delta plus $N_H \text{Delta}_H$ is equal to zero. The optimal number of hedging units, N_H, is

$$N_H = -\frac{\text{Portfolio delta}}{\text{Delta}_H}$$

Note that if N_H is negative, then one must short the hedging instrument, and if N_H is positive, then one must go long the hedging instrument. Clearly, if the portfolio is options and the hedging instrument is stock, then we will buy or sell shares to offset the portfolio position. For example, if the portfolio consists of 100,000 shares of stock at US$10 per share, then the portfolio delta is 100,000. The delta of the hedging instrument, stock, is +1. Thus, the optimal number of hedging units, N_H, is −100,000 (= −100,000/1) or short 100,000 shares. Alternatively, if the portfolio delta is 5,000 and a particular call option with delta of 0.5 is used as the hedging instrument, then to arrive at a delta neutral portfolio, one must sell 10,000 call options (= −5,000/0.5). Alternatively, if a portfolio of options has a delta of −1,500, then one must buy 1,500 shares of stock to be delta neutral [= −(−1,500)/1]. If the hedging instrument is stock, then the delta is +1 per share.

EXAMPLE 17   Delta Hedging

Apple stock is trading at US$125. We write calls (that is, we sell calls) on 1,000 Apple shares and now are exposed to an increase in the price of the Apple stock. That is, if Apple rises, we will lose money because the calls we sold will go up in value, so our liability will increase. Correspondingly, if Apple falls, we will make money. We want to neutralize our exposure to Apple. Say the call delta is 0.50, which means that if Apple goes up by US$0.10, a call on one Apple share will go up US$0.05. We need to trade in such a way as to make money if Apple goes up, to offset our exposure. Hence, we buy 500 Apple shares to hedge. Now, if Apple goes up US$0.10, the sold calls will go up US$50 (our liability goes up), but our long 500 Apple hedge will profit by US$50. Hence, we are delta hedged.

Identify the *incorrect* statement:

A. If we sell Apple puts, we need to buy Apple stock to delta hedge.
B. Call delta is non-negative (≥ 0); put delta is non-positive (≤ 0).
C. Delta hedging is the process of neutralizing exposure to the underlying.

Solution: A is the correct answer because statement A is incorrect. If we sell puts, we need to short sell stock to delta hedge.

One final interpretation of option delta is related to forecasting changes in option prices. Let $\hat{c}$, $\hat{p}$, and $\hat{S}$ denote some new value for the call, put, and stock. Based on an approximation method, the change in the option price can be estimated with a concept known as a delta approximation or

$$\hat{c} - c \cong \text{Delta}_c\left(\hat{S} - S\right) \text{ for calls and}$$

$$\hat{p} - p \cong \text{Delta}_p\left(\hat{S} - S\right) \text{ for puts.}^{[16]}$$

---

[16] The symbol ≅ denotes approximately. The approximation method is known as a Taylor series. Also note that the put delta is non-positive (≤ 0).

We can now illustrate the actual call values as well as the estimated call values based on delta. Exhibit 15 illustrates the call value based on the BSM model and the call value based on the delta approximation,

$$\hat{c} = c + Delta_c(\hat{S} - S).$$

Notice for very small changes in the stock, the delta approximation is fairly accurate. For example, if the stock value rises from 100 to 101, notice that both the call line and the call (delta) estimated line are almost the same value. If, however, the stock value rises from 100 to 150, the call line is now significantly above the call (delta) estimated line. Thus, we see that as the change in the stock increases, the estimation error also increases. The delta approximation is biased low for both a down move and an up move.

EXHIBIT 15   Call Values and Delta Estimated Call Values (S = 100 = X, r = 5%, σ = 30%, δ = 0)

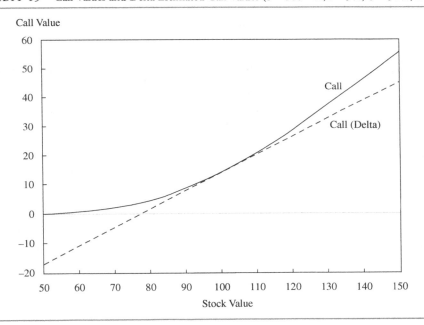

We see that delta hedging is imperfect and gets worse as the underlying moves further away from its original value of 100. Based on the graph, the BSM model assumption of continuous trading is essential to avoid hedging risk. This hedging risk is related to the difference between these two lines and the degree to which the underlying price experiences large changes.

EXAMPLE 18   Delta Hedging

Suppose we know S = 100, X = 100, r = 5%, T = 1.0, σ = 30%, and δ = 5%. We have a short position in put options on 10,000 shares of stock. Based on this information, we note $Delta_c = 0.532$, and $Delta_p = -0.419$. Assume each stock option contract is for one share of stock.

1. The appropriate delta hedge, assuming the hedging instrument is stock, is executed by which of the following transactions? Select the *closest* answer.
   A. Buy 5,320 shares of stock.
   B. Short sell 4,190 shares of stock.
   C. Buy 4,190 shares of stock.
2. The appropriate delta hedge, assuming the hedging instrument is calls, is executed by which of the following transactions? Select the *closest* answer.
   A. Sell 7,876 call options.
   B. Sell 4,190 call options.
   C. Buy 4,190 call options.
3. Identify the correct interpretation of an option delta.
   A. Option delta measures the curvature in the option price with respect to the stock price.
   B. Option delta is the change in an option value for a given small change in the stock's value, holding everything else constant.
   C. Option delta is the probability of the option expiring in the money.

Solution to 1: B is correct. Recall that $N_H = -\dfrac{\text{Portfolio delta}}{\text{Delta}_H}$. The put delta is given as -0.419, thus the short put delta is 0.419. In this case, Portfolio delta = 10,000(0.419) = 4,190 and $\text{Delta}_H = 1.0$. Thus, the number of number of hedging units is $-4,190$ [$= -(4,190/1)$] or short sell 4,190 shares of stock.

Solution to 2: A is correct. Again the Portfolio delta = 4,190 but now $\text{Delta}_H = 0.532$. Thus, the number of hedging units is $-7,875.9$ [$= -(4,190/0.532)$] or sell 7,876 call options.

Solution to 3: B is correct. Delta is defined as the change in a given portfolio for a given small change in the stock's value, holding everything else constant. Option delta is defined as the change in an option value for a given small change in the stock's value, holding everything else constant.

15. GAMMA

Recall that delta is a good approximation of how an option price will change for a small change in the stock. For larger changes in the stock, we need better accuracy. **Gamma** is defined as the change in a given instrument's delta for a given small change in the stock's value, holding everything else constant. Option gamma is similarly defined as the change in a given option delta for a given small change in the stock's value, holding everything else constant. Option gamma is a measure of the curvature in the option price in relationship to the stock price. Thus, the gamma of a long or short position in one share of stock is zero because the delta of a share of stock never changes. A stock always moves one-for-one with itself. Thus, its delta is always $+1$ and, of course, -1 for a short position in the stock. The gamma for a call and put option are the same and can be expressed as

$$\text{Gamma}_c = \text{Gamma}_p = \frac{e^{-\delta T}}{S\sigma\sqrt{T}} n(d_1) \tag{24}$$

where $n(d_1)$ is the standard normal probability density function. The lowercase "n" is distinguished from the cumulative normal distribution—which the density function generates—and that we have used elsewhere in this reading denoted by uppercase "N." The gamma of a call equals the gamma of a similar put based on put–call parity or $c - p = S_0 - e^{-rT}X$. Note that neither S_0 nor $e^{-rT}X$ is a direct function of delta. Hence, the right-hand side of put–call parity has a delta of 1. Thus, the right-hand side delta is not sensitive to changes in the underlying. Therefore, the gamma of a call must equal the gamma of a put.

Gamma is always non-negative. Gamma takes on its largest value near at the money. Options deltas do not change much for small changes in the stock price if the option is either deep in or deep out of the money. Also, as the stock price changes and as time to expiration changes, the gamma is also changing.

Gamma measures the rate of change of delta as the stock changes. Gamma approximates the estimation error in delta for options because the option price with respect to the stock is non-linear and delta is a linear approximation. Thus, gamma is a risk measure; specifically, gamma measures the non-linearity risk or the risk that remains once the portfolio is delta neutral. A gamma neutral portfolio implies the gamma is zero. For example, gamma can be managed to an acceptable level first and then delta is neutralized as a second step. This hedging approach is feasible because options have gamma but a stock does not. Thus, in order to modify gamma, one has to include additional option trades in the portfolio. Once the revised portfolio, including any new option trades, has the desired level of gamma, then the trader can get the portfolio delta to its desired level as step two. To alter the portfolio delta, the trader simply buys or sells stock. Because stock has a positive delta, but zero gamma, the portfolio delta can be brought to its desired level with no impact on the portfolio gamma.

One final interpretation of gamma is related to improving the forecasted changes in option prices. Again, let $\hat{c}$, $\hat{p}$, and $\hat{S}$ denote new values for the call, put, and stock. Again based on an approximation method, the change in the option price can be estimated by a delta-plus-gamma approximation or

$$\hat{c} - c \approx \text{Delta}_c(\hat{S} - S) + \frac{\text{Gamma}_c}{2}(\hat{S} - S)^2 \text{ for calls and}$$

$$\hat{p} - p \approx \text{Delta}_p(\hat{S} - S) + \frac{\text{Gamma}_p}{2}(\hat{S} - S)^2 \text{ for puts.}$$

Exhibit 16 illustrates the call value based on the BSM model; the call value based on the delta approximation,

$$\hat{c} = c + \text{Delta}_c(\hat{S} - S);$$

and the call value based on the delta-plus-gamma approximation,

$$\hat{c} = c + \text{Delta}_c(\hat{S} - S) + \frac{\text{Gamma}_c}{2}(\hat{S} - S)^2.$$

Notice again that for very small changes in the stock, the delta approximation and the delta-plus-gamma approximations are fairly accurate. If the stock value rises from 100 to 150, the call line is again significantly above the delta estimated line but is below the delta-plus-gamma estimated line. Importantly, the call delta-plus-gamma estimated line is significantly closer to the BSM model call values. Thus, we see that even for fairly large changes in the stock, the delta-plus-gamma approximation is accurate. As the change in the stock increases, the estimation error also increases. From Exhibit 16, we see the delta-plus-gamma approximation is biased low for a down move but biased high for an up move. Thus, when estimating how the call price changes when the underlying changes, we see how the delta-plus-gamma approximation is an improvement when compared with using the delta approximation on its own.

EXHIBIT 16   Call Values, Delta Estimated Call Values, and Delta-Plus-Gamma Estimated Call Values (S = 100 = X, r = 5%, σ = 30%, δ = 0)

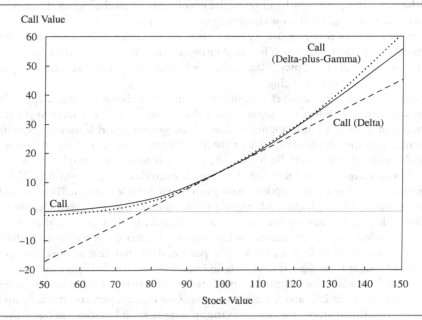

If the BSM model assumptions hold, then we would have no risk in managing option positions. In reality, however, stock prices often jump rather than move continuously and smoothly, which creates "gamma risk." Gamma risk is so-called because gamma measures the risk of stock prices jumping when hedging an option position, and thus leaving us suddenly unhedged.

EXAMPLE 19   Gamma Risk in Option Trading

Suppose we are options traders and have only one option position—a short call option. We also hold some stock such that we are delta hedged. Which one of the following statements is true?

A. We are gamma neutral.
B. Buying a call will increase our overall gamma.
C. Our overall position is a positive gamma, which will make large moves profitable for us, whether up or down.

Solution: B is correct. Buying options (calls or puts) will always increase net gamma. A is incorrect because we are short gamma, not gamma neutral. C is also incorrect because we are short gamma. We can only become gamma neutral from a short gamma position by purchasing options.

16. THETA

Theta is defined as the change in a portfolio for a given small change in calendar time, holding everything else constant. Option theta is similarly defined as the change in an option value for a given small change in calendar time, holding everything else constant. Option theta is the rate at which the option time value declines as the option approaches expiration. To understand theta, it is important to remember the "holding everything else constant" assumption. Specifically, the theta calculation assumes nothing changes except calendar time. Clearly, if calendar time passes, then time to expiration declines. Because stocks do not have an expiration date, the stock theta is zero. Like gamma, theta cannot be adjusted with stock trades.

The gain or loss of an option portfolio in response to the mere passage of calendar time is known as time decay. Particularly with long options positions, often the mere passage of time without any change in other variables, such as the stock, will result is significant losses in value. Therefore, investment managers with significant option positions carefully monitor theta and their exposure to time decay. Time decay is essentially the measure of profit and loss of an option position as time passes, holding everything else constant.

Note that theta is fundamentally different from delta and gamma in the sense that the passage of time does not involve any uncertainty. There is no chance that time will go backward. Time marches on, but it is important to understand how your investment position will change with the mere passage of time.

Typically, theta is negative for options. That is, as calendar time passes, expiration time declines and the option value also declines. Exhibit 17 illustrates the option value with respect to time to expiration. Remember, as calendar time passes, the time to expiration declines. Both the call and the put option are at the money and eventually are worthless if the stock does not change. Notice, however, how the speed of the option value decline increases as time to expiration decreases.

EXHIBIT 17   Option Values and Time to Expiration (S = 100 = X, r = 5%, σ = 30%, δ = 0)

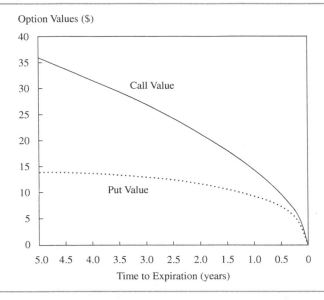

17. VEGA

Vega is defined as the change in a given portfolio for a given small change in volatility, holding everything else constant. Vega measures the sensitivity of a given portfolio to volatility. The vega of an option is positive. An increase in volatility results in an increase in the option value for both calls and puts.

The vega of a call equals the vega of a similar put based on put–call parity or $c - p = S_0 - e^{-rT}X$. Note that neither S_0 nor $e^{-rT}X$ is a direct function of volatility. Therefore, the vega of a call must offset the vega of a put so that the vega of the right-hand side is zero.

Unlike the Greeks we have already discussed, vega is based on an unobservable parameter, future volatility. Although historical volatility can be calculated, there is no objective measure of future volatility. Similar to the concept of expected value, future volatility is subjective. Thus, vega measures the sensitivity of a portfolio to changes in the volatility used in the option valuation model. Option values are generally quite sensitive to volatility. In fact, of the five variables in the BSM, an option's value is most sensitive to volatility changes.

At extremely low volatility, the option values tend toward their lower bounds. The lower bound of a European-style call option is zero or the stock less the present value of the exercise price, whichever is greater. The lower bound of a European-style put option is zero or the present value of the exercise price less the stock, whichever is greater. Exhibit 18 illustrates the option values with respect to volatility. In this case, the call lower bound is 4.88 and the put lower bound is 0. The difference between the call and put can be explained by put–call parity.

EXHIBIT 18   Option Values and Volatility ($S = 100 = X$, $r = 5\%$, $T = 1$, $\delta = 0$)

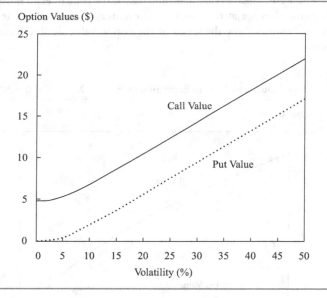

Vega is very important in managing an options portfolio because option values can be very sensitive to volatility changes. Vega is high when options are at or near the money. Volatility is usually only hedged with other options and volatility itself can be quite volatile. Volatility is sometimes considered a separate asset class or a separate risk factor. Because it is rather exotic and potentially dangerous, exposure to volatility needs to be managed, bearing in mind that risk managers, board members, and clients may not understand or appreciate losses if volatility is the source.

18. RHO

Rho is defined as the change in a given portfolio for a given small change in the risk-free interest rate, holding everything else constant. Thus, rho measures the sensitivity of the portfolio to the risk-free interest rate.

The rho of a call is positive. Intuitively, buying an option avoids the financing costs involved with purchasing the stock. In other words, purchasing a call option allows an investor to earn interest on the money that otherwise would have gone to purchasing the stock. The higher the interest rate, the higher the call value.

The rho of a put is negative. Intuitively, the option to sell the stock delays the opportunity to earn interest on the proceeds from the sale. For example, purchasing a put option rather than selling the stock deprives an investor of the potential interest that would have been earned from the proceeds of selling the stock. The higher the interest rate, the lower the put value.

When interest rates are zero, the call and put option values are the same for at-the-money options. Recall that with put–call parity, we have $c - p = S_0 - e^{-rT}X$, and when interest rates are zero, then the present value function has no effect. As interest rates rise, the difference between call and put options increases as illustrated in Exhibit 19. The impact on option prices when interest rates change is relatively small when compared with that for volatility changes and that for changes in the stock. Hence, the influence of interest rates is generally not a major concern.[17]

EXHIBIT 19   Option Values and Interest Rates (S = 100 = X, r = 5%, T = 1, δ = 0)

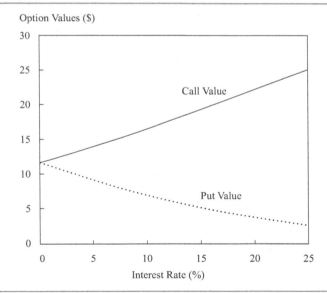

---

[17] An exception to this rule is that with interest rate options, the interest rate is not constant and serves as the underlying. The relationship between the option value and the underlying interest rate is, therefore, captured by the delta, not the rho. Rho is really more generally the relationship between the option value and the rate used to discount cash flows.

19. IMPLIED VOLATILITY

As we have already touched on in Section 17, for most options, the value is particularly sensitive to volatility. Unlike the price of the underlying, however, volatility, is not an observable value in the marketplace. Volatility can be, and often is estimated, based on a sample of historical data. For example, for a three-month option, we might look back over the last three months and calculate the actual historical stock volatility. We can then use this figure as an estimate of volatility over the next three months. The volatility parameter in the BSM model, however, is the *future* volatility. As we know, history is a very frail guide of the future, so the option may appear to be "mispriced" with respect to the actual future volatility experienced. Different investors will have different views of the future volatility. The one with the most accurate forecast will have the most accurate assessment of the option value.

Much like yield to maturity with bonds, volatility can be inferred from option prices. This inferred volatility is called the **implied volatility**. Thus, one important use of the BSM model is to invert the model and estimate implied volatility. The key advantage is that implied volatility provides information regarding the perceived uncertainty going forward and thereby allows us to gain an understanding of the collective opinions of investors on the volatility of the underlying and the demand for options. If the demand for options increases and the no-arbitrage approach is not perfectly reflected in market prices—for example, because of transaction costs—then the preference for buying options will drive option prices up, and hence, the observed implied volatility. This kind of information is of great value to traders in options.

Recall that one assumption of the BSM model is that all investors agree on the value of volatility and that this volatility is non-stochastic. Note that the original BSM model assumes the underlying instrument volatility is constant in our context. That is, when we calculate option values, we have assumed a single volatility number, like 30%. In practice, it is very common to observe different implied volatilities for different exercise prices and observe different implied volatilities for calls and puts with the same terms. Implied volatility also varies across time to expiration as well as across exercise prices. The implied volatility with respect to time to expiration is known as the term structure of volatility, whereas the implied volatility with respect to the exercise price is known as the volatility smile or sometimes skew depending on the particular shape. It is common to construct a three dimensional plot of the implied volatility with respect to both expiration time and exercise prices, a visualization known as the volatility surface. If the BSM model assumptions were true, then one would expect to find the volatility surface flat.

Implied volatility is also not constant through calendar time. As implied volatility increases, market participants are communicating an increased market price of risk. For example, if the implied volatility of a put increases, it is more expensive to buy downside protection with a put. Hence, the market price of hedging is rising. With index options, various volatility indexes have been created, and these indexes measure the collective opinions of investors on the volatility in the market. Investors can now trade futures and options on various volatility indexes in an effort to manage their vega exposure in other options.

Exhibit 20 provides a look at a couple of decades of one such volatility index, the Chicago Board Options Exchange S&P 500 Volatility Index, known as the VIX. The VIX is quoted as a percent and is intended to approximate the implied volatility of the S&P 500 over the next 30 days. VIX is often termed the fear index because it is viewed as a measure of market uncertainty. Thus, an increase in the VIX index is regarded as greater investor uncertainty. From this figure, we see that the implied volatility of the S&P 500 is not constant and goes through periods when the VIX is low and periods when the VIX is high. In the 2008 global financial crisis, the VIX was extremely high, indicating great fear and uncertainty in the equity market. Remember that implied volatility reflects both beliefs regarding future volatility as well as a preference for risk mitigating products like options. Thus, during the crisis, the higher implied volatility reflected both higher expected future volatility as well as increased preference for buying rather than selling options.

EXHIBIT 20   VIX Daily Values, 2 January 1990–18 July 2014

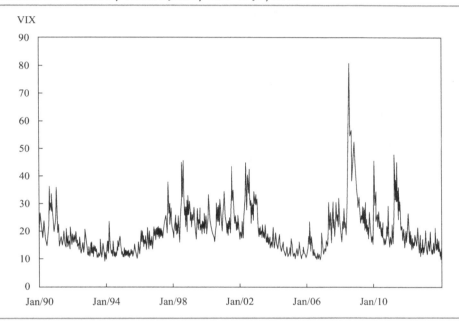

Implied volatility has several uses in option trading. An understanding of implied volatility is essential in managing an options portfolio. This reading explains the valuation of options as a function of the value of the underlying, the exercise price, the expiration date, the risk-free rate, dividends or other benefits paid by the underlying, and the volatility of the underlying. Note that each of these parameters is observable except the volatility of the underlying over the option term looking ahead. This volatility has to be estimated in some manner, such as by calculating historical volatility. But as noted, historical volatility involves looking back in time. There are, however, a vast number of liquid options traded on exchanges around the world so that a wide variety of option prices are observable. Because we know the price and all the parameters except the volatility, we can back out the volatility needed by the option valuation model to get the known price. This volatility is the implied volatility.

Hence, implied volatility can be interpreted as the market's view of how to value options. In the option markets, participants use volatility as the medium in which to quote options. The price is simply calculated by the use of an agreed model with the quoted volatility. For example, rather than quote a particular call option as trading for €14.23, it may be quoted as 30.00, where 30.00 denotes in percentage points the implied volatility based on a €14.23 option price. Note that there is a one-to-one relationship between the implied volatility and the option price, ignoring rounding errors.

The benefit of quoting via implied volatility (or simply volatility), rather than price, is that it allows volatility to be traded in its own right. Volatility is the "guess factor" in option pricing.

All other inputs—value of the underlying, exercise price, expiration, risk-free rate, and dividend yield—are agreed.[18] Volatility is often the same order of magnitude across exercise prices and expiration dates. This means that traders can compare the values of two options, which may have markedly different exercise prices and expiration dates, and therefore, markedly different prices in a common unit of measure, specifically implied volatility.

EXAMPLE 20   Implied Volatility in Option Trading within One Market

Suppose we hold portfolio of options all tied to FTSE 100 futures contracts. Let the current futures price be 6,850. A client calls to request our offer prices on out-of-the-money puts and at-the-money puts, both with the same agreed expiration date. We calculate the prices to be respectively, 190 and 280 futures points. The client wants these prices quoted in implied volatility as well as in futures points because she wants to compare prices by comparing the quoted implied volatilities. The implied volatilities are 16% for the out-of-the-money puts and 15.2% for the at-the-money puts. Why does the client want the quotes in implied volatility?

A. Because she can better compare the two options for value—that is, she can better decide which is cheap and which is expensive.
B. Because she can assess where implied volatility is trading at that time, and thus consider revaluing her options portfolio at the current market implied volatilities for the FTSE 100.
C. Both A and B are valid reasons for quoting options in volatility units.

Solution: C is correct. Implied volatility can be used to assess the relative value of different options, neutralizing the moneyness and time to expiration effects. Also, implied volatility is useful for revaluing existing positions over time.

EXAMPLE 21   Implied Volatility in Option Trading Across Markets

Suppose an options dealer offers to sell a three-month at-the-money call on the FTSE index option at 19% implied volatility and a one-month in-the-money put on Vodaphone (VOD) at 24%. An option trader believes that based on the current outlook, FTSE volatility should be closer to 25% and VOD volatility should be closer to 20%. What actions might the trader take to benefit from her views?

A. Buy the FTSE call and the VOD put.
B. Buy the FTSE call and sell the VOD put.
C. Sell the FTSE call and sell the VOD puts.

---

[18] The risk-free rate and dividend yield may not be entirely agreed, but the impact of variations to these parameters is generally very small compared with the other inputs.

Solution: B is correct. The trader believes that the FTSE call volatility is understated by the dealer and that the VOD put volatility is overstated. Thus, the trader would expect FTSE volatility to rise and VOD volatility to fall. As a result, the FTSE call would be expected to increase in value and the VOD put would be expected to decrease in value. The trader would take the positions as indicated in B.

Regulators, banks, compliance officers, and most option traders use implied volatilities to communicate information related to options portfolios. This is because implied volatilities, together with standard pricing models, give the "market consensus" valuation, in the same way that other assets are valued using market prices.

In summary, as long as all market participants agree on the underlying option model and how other parameters are calculated, then implied volatility can be used as a quoting mechanism. Recall that there are calls and puts, various exercise prices, various maturities, American and European, and exchange-traded and OTC options. Thus, it is difficult to conceptualize all these different prices. For example, if two call options on the same stock had different prices, but one had a longer expiration and lower exercise price and the other had a shorter expiration and higher exercise, which should be the higher priced option? It is impossible to tell on the surface. But if one option implied a higher volatility than the other, we know that after taking into account the effects of time and exercise, one option is more expensive than the other. Thus, by converting the quoted price to implied volatility, it is easier to understand the current market price of various risk exposures.

SUMMARY

This reading on the valuation of contingent claims provides a foundation for understanding how a variety of different options are valued. Key points include the following:

- The arbitrageur would rather have more money than less and abides by two fundamental rules: Do not use your own money and do not take any price risk.
- The no-arbitrage approach is used for option valuation and is built on the key concept of the law of one price, which says that if two investments have the same future cash flows regardless of what happens in the future, then these two investments should have the same current price.
- Throughout this reading, the following key assumptions are made:
  - Replicating instruments are identifiable and investable.
  - Market frictions are nil.
  - Short selling is allowed with full use of proceeds.
  - The underlying instrument price follows a known distribution.
  - Borrowing and lending is available at a known risk-free rate.
- The two-period binomial model can be viewed as three one-period binomial models, one positioned at Time 0 and two positioned at Time 1.
- In general, European-style options can be valued based on the expectations approach in which the option value is determined as the present value of the expected future option

payouts, where the discount rate is the risk-free rate and the expectation is taken based on the risk-neutral probability measure.

- Both American-style options and European-style options can be valued based on the no-arbitrage approach, which provides clear interpretations of the component terms; the option value is determined by working backward through the binomial tree to arrive at the correct current value.
- For American-style options, early exercise influences the option values and hedge ratios as one works backward through the binomial tree.
- Interest rate option valuation requires the specification of an entire term structure of interest rates, so valuation is often estimated via a binomial tree.
- A key assumption of the Black–Scholes–Merton option valuation model is that the return of the underlying instrument follows geometric Brownian motion, implying a lognormal distribution of the price.
- The BSM model can be interpreted as a dynamically managed portfolio of the underlying instrument and zero-coupon bonds.
- BSM model interpretations related to $N(d_1)$ are that it is the basis for the number of units of underlying instrument to replicate an option, that it is the primary determinant of delta, and that it answers the question of how much the option value will change for a small change in the underlying.
- BSM model interpretations related to $N(d_2)$ are that it is the basis for the number of zero-coupon bonds to acquire to replicate an option and that it is the basis for estimating the risk-neutral probability of an option expiring in the money.
- The Black futures option model assumes the underlying is a futures or a forward contract.
- Interest rate options can be valued based on a modified Black futures option model in which the underlying is a forward rate agreement (FRA), there is an accrual period adjustment as well as an underlying notional amount, and that care must be given to day-count conventions.
- An interest rate cap is a portfolio of interest rate call options termed caplets, each with the same exercise rate and with sequential maturities.
- An interest rate floor is a portfolio of interest rate put options termed floorlets, each with the same exercise rate and with sequential maturities.
- A swaption is an option on a swap.
- A payer swaption is an option on a swap to pay fixed and receive floating.
- A receiver swaption is an option on a swap to receive fixed and pay floating.
- Long a callable fixed-rate bond can be viewed as long a straight fixed-rate bond and short a receiver swaption.
- Delta is a static risk measure defined as the change in a given portfolio for a given small change in the value of the underlying instrument, holding everything else constant.
- Delta hedging refers to managing the portfolio delta by entering additional positions into the portfolio.
- A delta neutral portfolio is one in which the portfolio delta is set and maintained at zero.
- A change in the option price can be estimated with a delta approximation.
- Because delta is used to make a linear approximation of the non-linear relationship that exists between the option price and the underlying price, there is an error that can be estimated by gamma.
- Gamma is a static risk measure defined as the change in a given portfolio delta for a given small change in the value of the underlying instrument, holding everything else constant.

- Gamma captures the non-linearity risk or the risk—via exposure to the underlying—that remains once the portfolio is delta neutral.
- A gamma neutral portfolio is one in which the portfolio gamma is maintained at zero.
- The change in the option price can be better estimated by a delta-plus-gamma approximation compared with just a delta approximation.
- Theta is a static risk measure defined as the change in the value of an option given a small change in calendar time, holding everything else constant.
- Vega is a static risk measure defined as the change in a given portfolio for a given small change in volatility, holding everything else constant.
- Rho is a static risk measure defined as the change in a given portfolio for a given small change in the risk-free interest rate, holding everything else constant.
- Although historical volatility can be estimated, there is no objective measure of future volatility.
- Implied volatility is the BSM model volatility that yields the market option price.
- Implied volatility is a measure of future volatility, whereas historical volatility is a measure of past volatility.
- Option prices reflect the beliefs of option market participant about the future volatility of the underlying.
- The volatility smile is a two dimensional plot of the implied volatility with respect to the exercise price.
- The volatility surface is a three dimensional plot of the implied volatility with respect to both expiration time and exercise prices.
- If the BSM model assumptions were true, then one would expect to find the volatility surface flat, but in practice, the volatility surface is not flat.

PROBLEMS

The following information relates to Questions 1–9

Bruno Sousa has been hired recently to work with senior analyst Camila Rocha. Rocha gives him three option valuation tasks.

Alpha Company

Sousa's first task is to illustrate how to value a call option on Alpha Company with a one-period binomial option pricing model. It is a non-dividend-paying stock, and the inputs are as follows.

- The current stock price is 50, and the call option exercise price is 50.
- In one period, the stock price will either rise to 56 or decline to 46.
- The risk-free rate of return is 5% per period.

Based on the model, Rocha asks Sousa to estimate the hedge ratio, the risk-neutral probability of an up move, and the price of the call option. In the illustration, Sousa is also asked to describe related arbitrage positions to use if the call option is overpriced relative to the model.

Beta Company

Next, Sousa uses the two-period binomial model to estimate the value of a European-style call option on Beta Company's common shares. The inputs are as follows.

- The current stock price is 38, and the call option exercise price is 40.
- The up factor (u) is 1.300, and the down factor (d) is 0.800.
- The risk-free rate of return is 3% per period.

Sousa then analyzes a put option on the same stock. All of the inputs, including the exercise price, are the same as for the call option. He estimates that the value of a European-style put option is 4.53. Exhibit 1 summarizes his analysis. Sousa next must determine whether an American-style put option would have the same value.

EXHIBIT 1   Two-Period Binomial European-Style Put Option on Beta Company

Item	Value
Underlying	38
Put	4.5346
Hedge Ratio	−0.4307

Item	Value
Underlying	49.4
Put	0.2517
Hedge Ratio	−0.01943

Item	Value
Underlying	30.4
Put	8.4350
Hedge Ratio	−1

Item	Value
Underlying	64.22
Put	0

Item	Value
Underlying	39.52
Put	0.48

Item	Value
Underlying	24.32
Put	15.68

Time = 0   Time = 1   Time = 2

Sousa makes two statements with regard to the valuation of a European-style option under the expectations approach.

Statement 1:   The calculation involves discounting at the risk-free rate.
Statement 2:   The calculation uses risk-neutral probabilities instead of true probabilities.

Rocha asks Sousa whether it is ever profitable to exercise American options prior to maturity. Sousa answers, "I can think of two possible cases. The first case is the early exercise of an American call option on a dividend-paying stock. The second case is the early exercise of an American put option."

Interest Rate Option

The final option valuation task involves an interest rate option. Sousa must value a two-year, European-style call option on a one-year spot rate. The notional value of the option is 1 million, and the exercise rate is 2.75%. The risk-neutral probability of an up move is 0.50. The current and expected one-year interest rates are shown in Exhibit 2, along with the values of a one-year zero-coupon bond of 1 notional value for each interest rate.

EXHIBIT 2   Two-Year Interest Rate Lattice for an Interest Rate Option

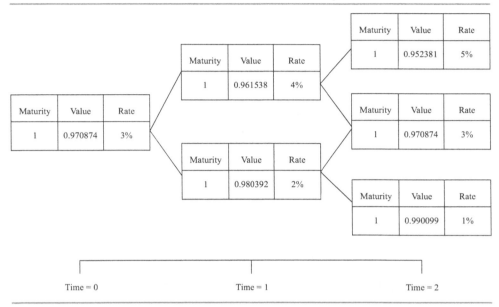

Rocha asks Sousa why the value of a similar in-the-money interest rate call option decreases if the exercise price is higher. Sousa provides two reasons.

Reason 1:   The exercise value of the call option is lower.
Reason 2:   The risk-neutral probabilities are changed.

1. The optimal hedge ratio for the Alpha Company call option using the one-period binomial model is *closest* to:
   A. 0.60.
   B. 0.67.
   C. 1.67.
2. The risk-neutral probability of the up move for the Alpha Company stock is *closest* to:
   A. 0.06.
   B. 0.40.
   C. 0.65.
3. The value of the Alpha Company call option is *closest* to:
   A. 3.71.
   B. 5.71.
   C. 6.19.
4. For the Alpha Company option, the positions to take advantage of the arbitrage opportunity are to write the call and:
   A. short shares of Alpha stock and lend.
   B. buy shares of Alpha stock and borrow.
   C. short shares of Alpha stock and borrow.

5. The value of the European-style call option on Beta Company shares is *closest* to:
   A. 4.83.
   B. 5.12.
   C. 7.61.
6. The value of the American-style put option on Beta Company shares is *closest* to:
   A. 4.53.
   B. 5.15.
   C. 9.32.
7. Which of Sousa's statements about binomial models is correct?
   A. Statement 1 only
   B. Statement 2 only
   C. Both Statement 1 and Statement 2
8. Based on Exhibit 2 and the parameters used by Sousa, the value of the interest rate option is *closest* to:
   A. 5,251.
   B. 6,236.
   C. 6,429.
9. Which of Sousa's reasons for the decrease in the value of the interest rate option is correct?
   A. Reason 1 only
   B. Reason 2 only
   C. Both Reason 1 and Reason 2

The following information relates to Questions 10–17

Trident Advisory Group manages assets for high-net-worth individuals and family trusts.

Alice Lee, chief investment officer, is meeting with a client, Noah Solomon, to discuss risk management strategies for his portfolio. Solomon is concerned about recent volatility and has asked Lee to explain options valuation and the use of options in risk management.

Options on Stock

Lee uses the BSM model to price TCB, which is one of Solomon's holdings. Exhibit 1 provides the current stock price (S), exercise price (X), risk-free interest rate (r), volatility (σ), and time to expiration (T) in years as well as selected outputs from the BSM model. TCB does not pay a dividend.

EXHIBIT 1   BSM Model for European Options on TCB

		BSM Inputs		
S	X	r	Σ	T
$57.03	55	0.22%	32%	0.25

		BSM Outputs			
d_1	$N(d_1)$	d_2	$N(d_2)$	BSM Call Price	BSM Put Price
0.3100	0.6217	0.1500	0.5596	$4.695	$2.634

Options on Futures

The Black model valuation and selected outputs for options on another of Solomon's holdings, the GPX 500 Index (GPX), are shown in Exhibit 2. The spot index level for the GPX is 187.95, and the index is assumed to pay a continuous dividend at a rate of 2.2% (δ) over the life of the options being valued, which expire in 0.36 years. A futures contract on the GPX also expiring in 0.36 years is currently priced at 186.73.

EXHIBIT 2   Black Model for European Options on the GPX Index

Black Model Inputs					
GPX Index	X	r	σ	T	δ Yield
187.95	180	0.39%	24%	0.36	2.2%

Black Model Call Value	Black Model Put Value	Market Call Price	Market Put Price
$14.2089	$7.4890	$14.26	$7.20

Option Greeks					
Delta (call)	Delta (put)	Gamma (call or put)	Theta (call) daily	Rho (call) per %	Vega per % (call or put)
0.6232	−0.3689	0.0139	−0.0327	0.3705	0.4231

After reviewing Exhibit 2, Solomon asks Lee which option Greek letter best describes the changes in an option's value as time to expiration declines.

Solomon observes that the market price of the put option in Exhibit 2 is $7.20. Lee responds that she used the historical volatility of the GPX of 24% as an input to the BSM model, and she explains the implications for the implied volatility for the GPX.

Options on Interest Rates

Solomon forecasts the three-month Libor will exceed 0.85% in six months and is considering using options to reduce the risk of rising rates. He asks Lee to value an interest rate call with a strike price of 0.85%. The current three-month Libor is 0.60%, and an FRA for a three-month Libor loan beginning in six months is currently 0.75%.

Hedging Strategy for the Equity Index

Solomon's portfolio currently holds 10,000 shares of an exchange-traded fund (ETF) that tracks the GPX. He is worried the index will decline. He remarks to Lee, "You have told me how the BSM model can provide useful information for reducing the risk of my GPX position." Lee suggests a delta hedge as a strategy to protect against small moves in the GPX Index.

Lee also indicates that a long position in puts could be used to hedge larger moves in the GPX. She notes that although hedging with either puts or calls can result in a delta-neutral position, they would need to consider the resulting gamma.

10. Based on Exhibit 1 and the BSM valuation approach, the initial portfolio required to replicate the long call option payoff is:
    A. long 0.3100 shares of TCB stock and short 0.5596 shares of a zero-coupon bond.
    B. long 0.6217 shares of TCB stock and short 0.1500 shares of a zero-coupon bond.
    C. long 0.6217 shares of TCB stock and short 0.5596 shares of a zero-coupon bond.

11. To determine the long put option value on TCB stock in Exhibit 1, the correct BSM valuation approach is to compute:
    A. 0.4404 times the present value of the exercise price minus 0.6217 times the price of TCB stock.
    B. 0.4404 times the present value of the exercise price minus 0.3783 times the price of TCB stock.
    C. 0.5596 times the present value of the exercise price minus 0.6217 times the price of TCB stock.

12. What are the correct spot value (S) and the risk-free rate (r) that Lee should use as inputs for the Black model?
    A. 186.73 and 0.39%, respectively
    B. 186.73 and 2.20%, respectively
    C. 187.95 and 2.20%, respectively

13. Which of the following is the correct answer to Solomon's question regarding the option Greek letter?
    A. Vega
    B. Theta
    C. Gamma

14. Based on Solomon's observation about the model price and market price for the put option in Exhibit 2, the implied volatility for the GPX is *most likely*:
    A. less than the historical volatility.
    B. equal to the historical volatility.
    C. greater than the historical volatility.

15. The valuation inputs used by Lee to price a call reflecting Solomon's interest rate views should include an underlying FRA rate of:
    A. 0.60% with six months to expiration.
    B. 0.75% with nine months to expiration.
    C. 0.75% with six months to expiration.

16. The strategy suggested by Lee for hedging small moves in Solomon's ETF position would *most likely* involve:
    A. selling put options.
    B. selling call options.
    C. buying call options.

17. Lee's put-based hedge strategy for Solomon's ETF position would *most likely* result in a portfolio gamma that is:
    A. negative.
    B. neutral.
    C. positive.

CHAPTER 5

CREDIT DEFAULT SWAPS

Brian Rose and Don M. Chance, PhD, CFA

LEARNING OUTCOMES

The candidate should be able to:

- describe credit default swaps (CDS), single-name and index CDS, and the parameters that define a given CDS product;
- describe credit events and settlement protocols with respect to CDS;
- explain the principles underlying and factors that influence the market's pricing of CDS;
- describe the use of CDS to manage credit exposures and to express views regarding changes in the shape and/or level of the credit curve;
- describe the use of CDS to take advantage of valuation disparities among separate markets, such as bonds, loans, equities, and equity-linked instruments.

1. INTRODUCTION

Derivative instruments in which the underlying is a measure of a borrower's credit quality are widely used and well established in a number of countries. We explore basic definitions of such instruments, explain the main concepts, cover elements of valuation and pricing, and discuss applications.

2. BASIC DEFINITIONS AND CONCEPTS

A **credit derivative** is a derivative instrument in which the underlying is a measure of a borrower's credit quality. Four types of credit derivatives are (1) total return swaps, (2) credit spread options, (3) credit-linked notes, and (4) credit default swaps, or CDS. CDS are the most liquid of the four and, as such, are the topic we focus on. In a CDS, one party makes payments to the other and receives in return the promise of compensation if a third party defaults.

In any derivative, the payoff is based on (derived from) the performance of an underlying instrument, rate, or asset that we call the "underlying." For a CDS, the underlying is the credit quality of a borrower. At its most fundamental level, a CDS provides compensation equal to expected recovery when a credit event occurs, but it also changes in value to reflect changes in the market's perception of a borrower's credit quality well in advance of default. The value of a CDS will rise and fall as opinions change about the likelihood and severity of a potential default. The actual event of default might never occur, but a decline in the price of a bond when investors perceive an increase in the likelihood of default is a mark-to-market loss to the bondholder. The most common credit events include bankruptcy, failure to pay, and restructuring. Another type of credit event which may be encountered in sovereign and municipal government bond markets is a moratorium or, more drastically, a repudiation of debt in which the governmental authority declares a moratorium on payments due under the terms of the obligation or challenges the validity of the entire debt obligation. (Other, less common credit events are also defined in the International Swaps and Derivatives Association's Credit Derivatives Definitions, but we will not consider them here.) Credit default swaps are designed to protect creditors against credit events such as these. The industry has expended great effort to provide clear guidance on what credit events are covered by a CDS contract. As with all efforts to write a perfect contract, however, no such device exists and disputes do occasionally arise. We will take a look at these issues later.

In addition to hedging credit risk, investors use CDS to

- leverage their portfolios,
- access maturity exposures not available in the cash market,
- access credit risk while limiting interest rate risk, and
- improve the liquidity of their portfolios given the illiquidity in the corporate bond market.

In addition, the CDS market has increased transparency and insight into the actual cost of credit risk. The higher relative liquidity and relative sophistication of CDS investors allow for more accurate price discovery and facilitate trading during liquidity events when the cash market for bonds becomes illiquid. While many of the applications listed above are beyond the scope of this reading, a basic understanding of this important fixed-income tool is necessary for all investment professionals.

Let's now define a **credit default swap**:

A credit default swap is a derivative contract between two parties, a credit protection buyer and credit protection seller, in which the buyer makes a series of cash payments to the seller and receives a promise of compensation for credit losses resulting from a credit event in an underlying.

In a CDS contract there are two counterparties, the **credit protection buyer** and the **credit protection seller**. The buyer agrees to make a series of periodic payments to the seller over the life of the contract (which are determined and fixed at contract initiation) and receives in return a promise that if default occurs, the protection seller will compensate the protection buyer. If default occurs, the periodic payments made by the protection buyer to the protection seller terminate. Exhibit 1 shows the structure of payment flows.

EXHIBIT 1   Payment Structure of a CDS

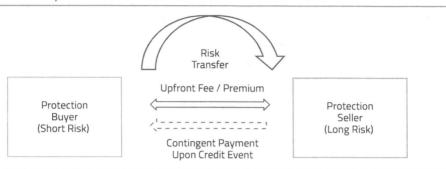

Credit default swaps are somewhat similar to put options. Put options effectively enable the option holder to sell (put) the underlying security to the option seller if the underlying performs poorly relative to the exercise price. Similarly, in the event of a credit event on the underlying security, the buyer of credit protection receives a payment from the credit protection seller equal to the par or notional value of the security less the expected recovery value. If the credit quality of the underlying deteriorates but there is no outright credit event, the credit protection buyer is compensated only if the contract is unwound. How that compensation occurs and how much protection it provides are some points we will discuss.

A CDS does not eliminate credit risk. The definition of a default in the swap contract may not perfectly align with a traditional default event, so the magnitude of the change in value of the contract may differ from the change in value of the underlying. In addition, the credit protection buyer assumes counterparty risk with respect to the credit protection seller. Although there are no guarantees that the credit protection seller will not default, as was seen with several large financial institutions in the financial crisis that started in 2007, most credit protection sellers are relatively high-quality borrowers. If they were not, they could not be active sellers of credit protection.

The majority of CDS are written on debt issued by corporate borrowers, which will be our focus in this reading. But note that CDS can also be written on the debt of sovereign governments and state and local governments. In addition, CDS can be written on portfolios of loans, mortgages, or debt securities.

2.1. Types of CDS

There are three types of CDS: single-name CDS, index CDS, and tranche CDS. Other CDS-related instruments, such as options on CDS (or CDS swaptions) are beyond the scope of this discussion. A CDS on one specific borrower is called a **single-name CDS**. The borrower is called the **reference entity**, and the contract specifies a **reference obligation**, a particular debt instrument issued by the borrower. Only a small subset of issuers, typically with large outstanding liquid debt, have single-name CDS. The designated instrument is usually a senior unsecured obligation, but the reference obligation is not the only instrument covered by the CDS. Any debt obligation issued by the borrower that is ranked equal to or higher than the reference obligation with respect to the priority of claims is covered. The payoff of the CDS is determined by the **cheapest-to-deliver** obligation, which is the debt instrument that can be purchased and delivered at the lowest cost but has the same seniority as the reference obligation.

EXAMPLE 1   Cheapest-to-Deliver Obligation

Assume that a company with several debt issues trading in the market files for bankruptcy (i.e., a credit event takes place). What is the cheapest-to-deliver obligation for a CDS contract where the reference bond is a five-year senior unsecured bond?

A. A subordinated unsecured bond trading at 20% of par
B. A five-year senior unsecured bond trading at 50% of par
C. A two-year senior unsecured bond trading at 45% of par

Solution: C is correct. The cheapest-to-deliver, or lowest-priced, instrument is the two-year senior unsecured bond trading at 45% of par. Although the bond in A trades at a lower dollar price, it is subordinated and, therefore, does not qualify for coverage under the CDS. Note that even though the CDS holder holds the five-year bonds, he will receive payment on the CDS based on the cheapest-to-deliver obligation, not the specific obligation he holds.

A second type of credit default swap, an **index CDS**, involves a portfolio of single-name CDS. This type of instrument allows participants to take positions on the credit risk of a combination of companies, in much the same way that investors can trade index or exchange-traded funds that are combinations of the equities of companies. The two most commonly traded CDS index products are the North American indexes (CDS) and the European, Asian, and Australian indexes (iTraxx). Correlation of defaults is a strong determinant of a portfolio's behavior. For index CDS, this concept takes the form of a factor called **credit correlation**, and it is a key determinant of the value of an index CDS. Analyzing the effects of those correlations is a highly specialized subject, but be aware that much effort is placed on modeling how defaults by certain companies are connected to defaults by other companies. The more correlated the defaults, the more costly it is to purchase protection for a combination of the companies. In contrast, for a diverse combination of companies whose defaults have low correlations, it will be much less expensive to purchase protection.

A third type of CDS is the **tranche CDS**, which covers a combination of borrowers but only up to pre-specified levels of losses—much in the same manner that asset-backed securities are divided into tranches, each covering particular levels of losses. Coverage of tranche CDS is beyond the scope of this reading.

3.   IMPORTANT FEATURES OF CDS MARKETS AND INSTRUMENTS, CREDIT AND SUCCESSION EVENTS, AND SETTLEMENT PROPOSALS

As we will describe in more detail later, the CDS market is large, global, and well organized. The unofficial industry governing body is the International Swaps and Derivatives Association (ISDA), which publishes industry-supported conventions that facilitate the functioning of the market. Parties to CDS contracts generally agree that their contracts will conform to ISDA specifications. These terms are specified in a document called the **ISDA Master Agreement**, which the parties to a CDS sign. In Europe, the standard CDS contract is called the Standard Europe Contract, and in the United States and Canada, it is called the Standard North American Contract. Other standardized contracts exist for Asia, Australia, Latin America, and a few other specific countries.

Each CDS contract specifies a **notional amount**, or "notional" for short, which is the amount of protection being purchased. The notional amount can be thought of as the *size* of the contract. It is important to understand that the total notional amount of CDS can exceed the amount of debt outstanding of the reference entity. As we will discuss later, the credit protection buyer does not have to be an actual creditor holding exposure (i.e., owning a loan, bond, or other debt instrument). It can be simply a party that believes that there will be a change in the credit quality of the reference entity.

As with all derivatives, the CDS contract has an expiration or maturity date, and coverage is provided up to that date. The typical maturity range is 1 to 10 years, with 5 years being the most common and actively traded maturity, but the two parties can negotiate any maturity. Maturity dates are typically the 20th day of March, June, September, or December. The March and September maturity dates are the most liquid, as these are when the index CDS contracts roll.

The buyer of a CDS pays a periodic premium to the seller, referred to as the **CDS spread**, which is a return over a market reference rate required to protect against credit risk. It is sometimes referred to as a credit spread. Conceptually, it is the same as the credit spread on a bond, the compensation for bearing credit risk.

An important advancement in the development of CDS has been in establishing standard annual coupon rates on CDS contracts. (Note that the reference bond will make payments that are referred to collectively as the coupon while a CDS on the reference bond will have its own coupon rate.) Formerly, the coupon rate on the CDS was set at the credit spread. If a CDS required a rate of 4% to compensate the protection seller for the assumption of credit risk, the protection buyer made quarterly payments amounting to 4% annually. Now CDS coupon rates are standardized, with the most common coupons being either 1% or 5%. The 1% rate typically is used for a CDS on an investment-grade company or index, and the 5% rate is used for a CDS on a high-yield company or index. Obviously, either standardized rate might not be the appropriate rate to compensate the seller. Clearly, not all investment-grade companies have equivalent credit risk, and not all high-yield companies have equivalent credit risk. In effect, the standard rate may be too high or too low. This discrepancy is accounted for by an **upfront payment**, commonly called the **upfront premium**. The differential between the credit spread and the standard rate is converted to a present value basis. Thus, a credit spread greater than the standard rate would result in a cash payment from the protection buyer to the protection seller. Similarly, a credit spread less than the standard rate would result in a cash payment from the protection seller to the protection buyer.

Regardless of whether either party makes an upfront payment, the reference entity's credit quality could change during the life of the contract, thereby resulting in changes in the value of the CDS. These changes are reflected in the price of the CDS in the market. Consider a high-yield company with a 5% credit spread and a CDS coupon of 5%. Therefore, there is no upfront payment. The protection buyer simply agrees to make payments equal to 5% of the notional over the life of the CDS. Now suppose that at some later date, the reference entity experiences a decrease in its credit quality. The credit protection buyer is thus paying 5% for risk that now merits a rate higher than 5%. The coverage and cost of protection are the same, but the risk being covered is greater. The value of the CDS to the credit protection buyer has, therefore, increased, and if desired, she could unwind the position to capture the gain. The credit protection seller has experienced a loss in value of the instrument because he is receiving 5% to cover a risk that is higher than it was when the contract was initiated. It should be apparent that absent any other exposure to the reference entity, if the credit quality of the reference entity decreases, the credit protection buyer gains and the credit protection seller loses. The market value of the CDS reflects these gains and losses.

The terminology in CDS markets can be confusing. In equity and fixed-income markets, we think of buyers as being long and sellers as being short. In the CDS market, however, that is not always true. In single-name CDS, the *buyer* of credit protection is *short credit exposure* and the *seller* of credit protection is *long credit exposure*. This is consistent with the fact that in the financial world, "shorts" are said to benefit when things go badly. When credit quality deteriorates, the credit protection buyer benefits, and when it improves, the credit protection seller benefits. To make things even more confusing, though, the opposite is true in CDS index positions: The *buyer* of a CDX is *long* credit exposure and the seller of a CDX is *short* credit exposure. To minimize the confusion, we use the terms *credit protection seller* and *credit protection buyer* throughout our discussion.

3.1. Credit and Succession Events

The **credit event** is what defines default by the reference entity—that is, the event that triggers a payment from the credit protection seller to the credit protection buyer. This event must be unambiguous: Did it occur, or did it not? For the market to function well, the answer to this question must be clear.

As previously mentioned, the most common credit events include bankruptcy, failure to pay, and restructuring. **Bankruptcy** is a declaration provided for by a country's laws that typically involves the establishment of a legal procedure that forces creditors to defer their claims. Bankruptcy essentially creates a temporary fence around the company through which the creditors cannot pass. During the bankruptcy process, the defaulting party works with its creditors and the court to attempt to establish a plan for repaying the debt. If that plan fails, there is likely to be a full liquidation of the company, at which time the court determines the payouts to the various creditors. Until liquidation occurs, the company normally continues to operate. Many companies do not liquidate and are able to emerge from bankruptcy. A bankruptcy filing by the reference entity is universally regarded as a credit event in CDS contracts.

Another credit event recognized in standard CDS contracts is **failure to pay**, which occurs when a borrower does not make a scheduled payment of principal or interest on an outstanding obligation after a grace period, without a formal bankruptcy filing. (Failure to pay credit events are defined in the CDS contract. ISDA contracts define failure to pay events uniformly, but the same is not true for bespoke CDS.) The third type of event, **restructuring**, refers to a number of possible events, including reduction or deferral of principal or interest, change in seniority or priority of an obligation, or change in the currency in which principal or interest is scheduled to be paid. To qualify as a credit event, the restructuring must be either involuntary or coercive. An involuntary credit event is one that is forced on the borrower by the creditors. A coercive credit event is one that is forced on the creditors by the borrower. Debt restructuring is not a credit event in the United States; issuers generally restructure under *bankruptcy*, which *is* a credit event. Restructuring is a credit event in other countries where the use of bankruptcy court to reorganize is less common. The Greek debt crisis is a good example of a restructuring that triggered a credit event.

Determination of whether a credit event occurs is done by a 15-member group within the ISDA called the Determinations Committee (DC). Each region of the world has a Determinations Committee, which consists of 10 CDS dealer (sell-side) banks and 5 non-bank (buy-side) end users. To declare a credit event, there must be a supermajority vote of 12 members.

The Determinations Committees also play a role in determining whether a **succession event** occurred. A succession event arises when there is a change in the corporate structure of the reference entity, such as through a merger, a divestiture, a spinoff, or any similar action in which ultimate responsibility for the debt in question becomes unclear. For example, if a company acquires all of the shares of a target company, it ordinarily assumes the target company's debt as well. Many mergers, however, are more complicated and can involve only partial acquisition of shares. Spinoffs and divestitures can also involve some uncertainty about who is responsible for certain debts. When such a question arises, it becomes critical for CDS holders. The question is ordinarily submitted to a Determinations Committee, and its resolution often involves complex legal interpretations of contract provisions and country laws. If a succession event is declared, the CDS contract is modified to reflect the DC's interpretation of whoever it believes becomes the obligor for the original debt. Ultimately, the CDS contract could be split among multiple entities.

3.2. Settlement Protocols

If the DC declares that a credit event has occurred, the two parties to a CDS have the right, but not the obligation, to settle. **Settlement** typically occurs 30 days after declaration of the credit event by the DC. CDS can be settled by **physical settlement** or by **cash settlement**. The former is less common and involves actual delivery of the debt instrument in exchange for a payment by the credit protection seller of the notional amount of the contract. In cash settlement, the credit protection seller pays cash to the credit protection buyer. Determining the amount of that payment is a critical factor because opinions can differ about how much money has actually been lost. The payment should essentially be the loss that the credit protection buyer has incurred, but determining that amount is not straightforward. Default on a debt does not mean that the creditor will lose the entire amount owed. A portion of the loss could be recovered. The percentage of the loss recovered is called the **recovery rate** (RR). (In most models, the recovery rate applies only to the principal.) The complement is called the **loss given default** (LGD), which is essentially an estimate of the expected credit loss. The **payout amount** is determined as the loss given default multiplied by the notional.

Loss given default = 1 − Recovery rate (%).
Payout amount = LGD × Notional.

Actual recovery can be a very long process, however, and can occur much later than the payoff date of the CDS. To determine an appropriate LGD, the industry conducts an auction in which major banks and dealers submit bids and offers for the cheapest-to-deliver defaulted debt. This process identifies the market's expectation for the recovery rate and the complementary LGD, and the CDS parties agree to accept the outcome of the auction, even though the actual recovery rate can ultimately be quite different, which is an important point if the CDS protection buyer also holds the underlying debt.

EXAMPLE 2 Settlement Preference

A French company files for bankruptcy, triggering various CDS contracts. It has two series of senior bonds outstanding: Bond A trades at 30% of par, and Bond B trades at 40% of par. Investor X owns €10 million of Bond A and owns €10 million of CDS protection. Investor Y owns €10 million of Bond B and owns €10 million of CDS protection.

1. Determine the recovery rate for both CDS contracts.
2. Explain whether Investor X would prefer to cash settle or physically settle her CDS contract or whether she is indifferent.
3. Explain whether Investor Y would prefer to cash settle or physically settle his CDS contract or whether he is indifferent.

Solution to 1: Bond A is the cheapest-to-deliver obligation, trading at 30% of par, so the recovery rate for both CDS contracts is 30%.

Solution to 2: Investor X has no preference between settlement methods. She can cash settle for €7 million [(1 − 30%) × €10 million] and sell her bond for €3 million, for total proceeds of €10 million. Alternatively, she can physically deliver her entire €10 million face amount of bonds to the counterparty in exchange for €10 million in cash.

Solution to 3: Investor Y would prefer a cash settlement because he owns Bond B, which is worth more than the cheapest-to-deliver obligation. He will receive the same €7 million payout on his CDS contract but can sell Bond B for €4 million, for total proceeds of €11 million. If he were to physically settle his contract, he would receive only €10 million, the face amount of his bond.

3.3. CDS Index Products

So far, we have mostly been focusing on single-name CDS. As noted, there are also index CDS products. A company called Markit has been instrumental in producing CDS indexes. Of course, a CDS index is not in itself a traded instrument any more than a stock index is a traded product. As with the major stock indexes, however, the industry has created traded instruments based on the Markit indexes. These instruments are CDS that generate a payoff based on any default that occurs on any entity covered by the index.

The Markit indexes are classified by region and further classified (or divided) by credit quality. The two most commonly traded regions are North America and Europe. North American indexes are identified by the symbol CDX, and European, Asian, and Australian indexes are identified as iTraxx. Within each geographic category are investment-grade and high-yield indexes. The former are identified as CDX IG and iTraxx Main, each comprising 125 entities. The latter are identified as CDX HY, consisting of 100 entities, and iTraxx Crossover, consisting of up to 75 high-yield entities. Investment-grade index CDS are typically quoted in terms of spreads, whereas high-yield index CDS are quoted in terms of prices. Both types of products use standardized coupons. All CDS indexes are equally weighted. Thus, if there are 125 entities, the settlement on one entity is 1/125 of the notional. (Note that some confusion might arise from quoting certain CDS as prices and some as spreads, but keep in mind that the bond market quotes bonds often as prices and sometimes as yields. For example, a Treasury bond can be described as having a price of 120 or a yield of 2.68%. Both terms, combined with the other characteristics of the bond, imply the same concept.)

Markit updates the components of each index every six months by creating new series while retaining the old series. The latest-created series is called the **on-the-run** series, whereas the older series are called **off-the-run** series. When an investor moves from one series to a new one, the move is called a **roll**. When an entity within an index defaults, that entity is removed from the index and settled as a single-name CDS based on its relative proportion in the index. The index then moves forward with a smaller notional.

Index CDS are typically used to take positions on the credit risk of the sectors covered by the indexes as well as to protect bond portfolios that consist of or are similar to the components of the indexes. (An important reminder: When you *buy* a CDS index position, you are *long the credit exposure*, but when you *buy* a single-name CDS position, you have *bought credit protection*. To avoid confusion, we do not talk about buying and selling CDS herein but focus on the desired exposure, using the terms *buy protection* and *sell protection*.)

Standardization is generally undertaken to increase trading volume, which is somewhat limited in the single-name market with so many highly diverse entities. With CDS indexes on standardized portfolios based on the credit risk of well-identified companies, market participants have responded by trading them in large volumes. Indeed, index CDS are typically more liquid than single-name CDS, with average daily trading volume several times that of single-name CDS.

EXAMPLE 3   Hedging and Exposure Using Index CDS

Assume that an investor sells $500 million of protection using the CDX IG index, which has 125 reference entities. Concerned about the creditworthiness of a few of the components, the investor hedges a portion of the credit risk in each. For Company A, he purchases $3 million of single-name CDS protection, and Company A subsequently defaults.

1. What is the investor's net notional exposure to Company A?
2. What proportion of his exposure to Company A has he hedged?
3. What is the remaining notional on his index CDS trade?

Solution to 1: The investor is long $4 million notional credit exposure ($500 million/125) through the index CDS and is short $3 million notional credit exposure through the single-name CDS. His net notional credit exposure is $1 million.

Solution to 2: He has hedged 75% of his exposure ($3 million out of $4 million).

Solution to 3: His index CDS has $496 million remaining notional credit exposure ($500 million original notional minus the $4 million notional related to Company A, which is no longer in the index).

3.4. Market Characteristics

Credit default swaps trade in the over-the-counter market. To better understand this market, we will first review how credit derivatives and specifically CDS were started.

As financial intermediaries, banks draw funds from savings-surplus sectors, primarily consumers, and channel them to savings-deficit sectors, primarily businesses. Corporate lending is a core element of banking. When a bank makes a corporate loan, it assumes two primary risks. One is that the borrower will not repay principal and interest, and the other is that interest rates will change such that the return the bank is earning on its outstanding loans is less than the rate available on comparable instruments in the marketplace. The former is called **credit risk** or **default risk**, and the latter is called **interest rate risk**. There are many ways to manage interest rate risk. Until around the mid-1990s, credit risk was largely managed using traditional methods—such as analysis of the borrower, its industry, and the macroeconomy—as well as control methods, such as credit limits, monitoring, and collateral. In effect, the only defenses against credit risk were to not make a loan, to lend but require collateral (the value of which is also at risk), or to lend and closely monitor the borrower, hoping that any problems could be foreseen and dealt with before a default occurred.

Around 1995, credit derivatives were created to provide a new and potentially more effective method of managing credit risk. They allow credit risk to be transferred from the lender to another party. In so doing, they facilitate the separation of interest rate risk from credit risk. Banks can then provide their most important service—lending—knowing that the credit risk can be transferred to another party if so desired. This ability to easily transfer credit risk allows banks to greatly expand their loan business. Given that lending is such a large and vital component of any economy, credit derivatives facilitate economic growth and have expanded to cover, and indeed are primarily focused on, the short-, intermediate-, and long-term bond markets. In fact, credit derivatives are more effective in the bond market, in which terms and conditions are far more standard, than in the bank loan market. Of the four types of credit derivatives, credit default swaps have clearly established themselves as the most widely used instrument. Indeed, in today's markets CDS are nearly the only credit derivative used to any great extent. CDS transactions are executed in the over-the-counter market by phone, instant message, or the Bloomberg message service. Trade information is reported to the **Depository Trust and Clearinghouse Corporation**, which is a US-headquartered entity providing post-trade clearing, settlement, and information services for many kinds of securities. Regulations require the central clearing of many CDS contracts, meaning that parties will send their contracts through clearinghouses that collect and distribute payments and impose margin requirements, as well as mark positions to market. Central clearing of CDS has risen dramatically since 2010. Currently, slightly more than half of all CDS are centrally cleared, up from just 10% in 2010.

The CDS market today is considerably smaller than it was prior to the 2008 financial crisis. The Bank for International Settlements reported that as of December 2019, the gross notional amount of CDS was about $7.6 trillion with a market value of $199 billion. (For comparison, the notional amounts for interest rate contracts—forward rate agreements, swaps, options—as of December 2019 was about $449 trillion.) As of December 2007, CDS gross notional was $57.9 trillion, nearly 8 times larger.

More than 90% of all CDS market activity is now derived from trading in five major CDS indexes: iTraxx Europe, iTraxx Europe Crossover, iTraxx Europe Senior Financials, CDX IG, and CDS HY.

4. BASICS OF VALUATION AND PRICING

Derivatives are typically priced by solving for the cost of a position that fully offsets the underlying exposure and earns the risk-free rate. In the context of CDS, this "price" is the CDS spread or upfront payment for a particular coupon rate under the contract. Although CDS are referred to as "swaps," they in fact resemble options because of the contingent nature of the payment made by the protection seller to the protection buyer if a credit event occurs as established by the ISDA Determinations Committee as outlined above.

Unlike conventional derivative instruments, the CDS settlement amount under a credit event as declared by the ISDA Determinations Committee is far less clear than for derivatives whose underlying involves actively traded assets, such as equities, interest rates, or currencies. Credit does not "trade" in the traditional sense but, rather, exists implicitly within the bond and loan market. The unique debt structure and composition of each CDS reference entity adds to the complexity of establishing the basis between a CDS contract and a specific outstanding bond or loan.

The details of credit derivative models are beyond the scope of this reading, but it is important for investment industry analysts to have a thorough understanding of the factors that determine CDS pricing.

4.1. Basic Pricing Concepts

In our earlier coverage of credit strategies, we established that the credit valuation adjustment (CVA) may be thought of as the present value of credit risk for a loan, bond, or derivative obligation. In principle, the CVA should, therefore, be a reasonable approximation for the CDS hedge position outlined previously that would leave an investor with a risk-free rate of return. Exhibit 2 summarizes the CVA calculation for a financial exposure.

EXHIBIT 2   Credit Valuation Adjustment

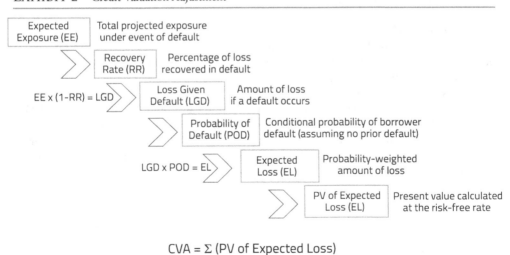

$$\text{CVA} = \Sigma \ (\text{PV of Expected Loss})$$

CVA is a function of expected exposure (EE), recovery rate, loss given default, the **probability of default** (POD) to arrive at an expected loss (EL), and a discount factor to arrive at the present value of expected loss.

Considering each of these CVA components in turn, the expected exposure reflects the notional value of the underlying CDS contract. Recall that the recovery rate is the percentage of loss recovered from a bond in default, whereas the loss given default is a function of the loss severity multiplied by the exposure amount.

The probability of default is a key element of CDS pricing that may be illustrated using a simple example. Consider a one-period CDS swap with no upfront payment where we ignore the time value of money and assume that default is possible only at maturity. The fair price of CDS protection for this period for a given borrower may be estimated as

$$\text{CDS spread} \approx (1 - \text{RR}) \times \text{POD}.$$

For example, if the probability of default is 2% and the recovery rate is 60%, the estimated CDS spread for the period would be 80 bps for the period. Assuming a $100 notional contract value and a period of a year, the CDS contract fair value would be (the present value of) $0.80.

It is important to note that the POD is a conditional probability over time. That is, assuming a two-period case, the probability of default in Period 2 is contingent on "surviving" to (i.e., not defaulting by) the end of Period 1. Note that we simplify the analysis by assuming discrete times of potential default versus the continuous time assumption common in CDS pricing models.

For example, consider a two-year, 5%, $1,000 loan with one interest payment of $50 due in one year and final interest and principal of $1,050 due in two years. Assume further that we estimate a 2% chance of defaulting on the first payment and a 4% chance of defaulting on the second payment. To calculate the POD over the life of the loan, we first determine the **probability of survival** (POS) for Period 1. The POS is 0.98 (100% minus the 2% POD at T_1) multiplied by 0.96 (100% minus the 4% POD at T_2), approximately 94.08%. Thus, the POD over the life of the loan is 100% − 94.08% = 5.92%.

This conditional probability of default is also known as the **hazard rate**, as described in an earlier reading. The hazard rate is the probability that an event will occur *given that it has not already occurred.*

Now consider another possibility, a 10-year bond with an equivalent hazard rate of 2% each year. Suppose we want to know the probability that the borrower will not default during the entire 10-year period. The probability that a default will occur at some point during the 10 years is one minus the probability of no default in 10 years. The probability of no default in 10 years is $0.98 \times 0.98 \ldots 0.98 = 0.98^{10} = 0.817$. Thus, the probability of default is $1 - 0.817 = 0.183$, or 18.3%. This somewhat simplified example illustrates how a low probability of default in any one period can turn into a surprisingly high probability of default over a longer period of time. Note that we have simplified the analysis by assuming a constant hazard rate, which may not be the case in practice.

EXAMPLE 4   Hazard Rate and Probability of Survival

Assume that a company's hazard rate is a constant 8% per year, or 2% per quarter. An investor sells five-year CDS protection on the company with the premiums paid quarterly over the next five years.

1. What is the probability of survival for the first quarter?
2. What is the conditional probability of survival for the second quarter?
3. What is the probability of survival through the second quarter?

Solution to 1: The probability of survival for the first quarter is 98% (100% minus the 2% hazard rate).

Solution to 2: The conditional probability of survival for the second quarter is also 98%, because the hazard rate is constant at 2%. In other words, *conditional on the company having survived the first quarter*, there is a 2% probability of default in the second quarter.

Solution to 3: The probability of survival through the second quarter is 96.04%. The probability of survival through the first quarter is 98%, and the conditional probability of survival through the second quarter is also 98%. The probability of survival through the second quarter is thus 98% × 98% = 96.04%. Alternatively, 1 − 96.04% = 3.96% is the probability of default sometime during the first two quarters.

Understanding the concept of pricing a CDS is facilitated by recognizing that there are essentially two sides, or legs, of a contract. There is the **protection leg**, which is the contingent payment that the credit protection seller may have to make to the credit protection buyer, and the **premium leg**, which is the series of payments the credit protection buyer promises to make to the credit protection seller. Exhibit 3 provides an illustration of the process.

EXHIBIT 3   Determination of CDS Protection vs. Premium Legs

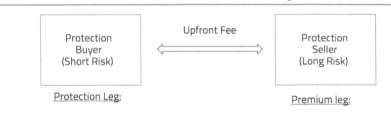

Exhibit 3 shows the upfront payment as the difference in value of the protection and premium legs. The party with a claim on the greater present value must pay the difference at the initiation date of the contract:

Upfront payment = PV (Protection leg) − PV (Premium leg).

If the result is greater (less) than zero, the protection buyer (seller) pays the protection seller (buyer). Actual CDS pricing and valuation models are more mathematically complex but are based on this conceptual framework.

4.2. The Credit Curve and CDS Pricing Conventions

The credit spread of a debt instrument is the rate in excess of a market reference rate (historically, Libor, although Libor is expected to be replaced by the end of 2021) that investors expect to receive to justify holding the instrument. The reference rate may itself contain some credit risk, as it reflects the rate at which commercial banks lend to one another. The credit spread can be expressed roughly as the probability of default multiplied by the loss given default, with LGD in terms of a percentage. The credit spreads for a range of maturities of a company's debt make up its **credit curve**. The credit curve is somewhat analogous to the term structure of interest rates, which is the set of rates on default-free debt over a range of maturities, but the credit curve applies to non-government borrowers and incorporates credit risk into each rate.

The CDS market for a given borrower is integrated with the credit curve of that borrower. In fact, given the evolution and high degree of efficiency of the CDS market, the credit curve is essentially determined by the CDS rates. The curve is affected by a number of factors, a key one of which is the set of aforementioned hazard rates. A constant hazard rate will tend to flatten the credit curve. Upward-sloping credit curves imply a greater likelihood of default in later years, whereas downward-sloping credit curves imply a greater probability of default in the earlier years. Downward-sloping curves are less common and often a result of severe near-term stress in the financial markets. The credit curve would not be completely flat even if the hazard rates are constant, because of discounting. For example, a company issuing 5- and 10-year zero-coupon bonds could have equally likely probabilities of default and hence equal expected payoffs. The present values of the payoffs are not the same, however, and so the discount rates that equate the present value to the expected payoffs will not be the same.

EXAMPLE 5   Change in Credit Curve

A company's 5-year CDS trades at a credit spread of 300 bps, and its 10-year CDS trades at a credit spread of 500 bps.

1. The company's 5-year spread is unchanged, but the 10-year spread widens by 100 bps. Describe the implication of this change in the credit curve.
2. The company's 10-year spread is unchanged, but the 5-year spread widens by 500 bps. Describe the implication of this change in the credit curve.

Solution to 1: This change implies that although the company is not any riskier in the short term, its longer-term creditworthiness is less attractive. Perhaps the company has adequate liquidity for the time being, but after five years it must begin repaying debt or it will be expected to have cash flow difficulties.

Solution to 2: This change implies that the company's near-term credit risk is now much greater. In fact, the probability of default will decrease if the company can survive for the next five years. Perhaps the company has run into liquidity issues that must be resolved soon, and if not resolved, the company will default.

4.3. CDS Pricing Conventions

With corporate bonds, we typically refer to their values in terms of prices or spreads. The spread is a more informative measure than price. A high-yield bond can be offered with a coupon equal to its yield and, therefore, a price of par value. An investment-grade bond with the same maturity can likewise be offered with a coupon equal to its yield, and therefore, its price is at par. These two bonds would have identical prices at the offering date, and their prices might even be close through much of their lives, but they are quite different bonds. Focusing on their prices would, therefore, provide little information. Their spreads are much more informative. With a market reference rate or the risk-free rate as a benchmark, investors can get a sense for the amount of credit risk implied by their prices, maturities, and coupons. The same is true for CDS. Although CDS have their own prices, their spreads are far more informative.

The reference entity will not necessarily have outstanding debt with credit spreads matching the 1% or 5% standardized coupons conventionally used in CDS contracts. Therefore, the present value of the promised payments from the credit protection buyer to the credit protection seller will most likely be different than the present value of the coupons on the reference entity's debt. The present value difference is the upfront premium paid from one party to the other.

Present value of credit spread = Upfront premium + Present value of fixed coupon.

A good rough approximation used in the industry is that the upfront premium is

Upfront premium ≈ (Credit spread − Fixed coupon) × Duration.

The upfront premium must ultimately be converted to a price, which is done by subtracting the percentage premium from 100.

Upfront premium % = 100 − Price of CDS in currency per 100 par.

Note that the duration used here is effective duration, since the cash flows arising from the coupon leg of the CDS are uncertain because they are contingent on the reference entity not defaulting.

EXAMPLE 6   Premiums and Credit Spreads

1. Assume a high-yield company's 10-year credit spread is 600 bps and the duration of the CDS is 8 years. What is the approximate upfront premium required to buy 10-year CDS protection? Assume high-yield companies have 5% coupons on their CDS.
2. Imagine an investor sold five-year protection on an investment-grade company and had to pay a 2% upfront premium to the buyer of protection. Assume the duration of the CDS to be four years. What are the company's credit spreads and the price of the CDS per 100 par?

Solution to 1: To buy 10-year CDS protection, an investor would have to pay a 500 bp coupon plus the present value of the difference between that coupon and the current market spread (600 bps). In this case, the upfront premium would be approximately 100 bps × 8 (duration), or 8% of the notional.

Solution to 2: The value of the upfront premium is equal to the premium (−2%) divided by the duration (4), or −50 bps. The sign of the upfront premium is negative because the seller is paying the premium rather than receiving it. The credit spread is equal to the fixed coupon (100 bps) plus the upfront premium, amortized over the duration of the CDS (−50 bps), or 50 bps. As a reminder, because the company's credit spread is less than the fixed coupon, the protection seller must pay the upfront premium to the protection buyer. The price in currency would be 100 minus the upfront premium, but the latter is negative, so the price is 100 − (−2) = 102.

4.4. Valuation Changes in CDS during Their Lives

As with any traded financial instrument, a CDS has a value that fluctuates during its lifetime. That value is determined in the competitive marketplace. Market participants constantly assess the current credit quality of the reference entity to determine its current value and (implied) credit spread. Clearly, many factors can change over the life of the CDS. By definition, the duration shortens through time. Likewise, the probability of default, the expected loss given default, and the shape of the credit curve will all change as new information is received. The exact valuation procedure of the CDS is precisely the same as it is when the CDS is first issued and simply incorporates the new inputs. The new market value of the CDS reflects gains and losses to the two parties.

Consider the following example of a five-year CDS with a fixed 1% coupon. The credit spread on the reference entity is 2.5%. In promising to pay 1% coupons to receive coverage on a company whose risk justifies 2.5% coupons, the present value of the protection leg exceeds the present value of the payment leg. The difference is the upfront premium, which will be paid by the credit protection buyer to the credit protection seller. During the life of the CDS, assume that the credit quality of the reference entity improves, such that the credit spread is now 2.1%. Now, consider a newly created CDS with the same remaining maturity and 1% coupon. The present value of the payment leg would still be less than the present value of the protection leg, but the difference would be less than it was when the original CDS was created because the risk is now less. Logically, it should be apparent that for the original transaction, the seller has gained and the buyer has lost. The difference between the original upfront premium and the new value is the seller's gain and buyer's loss. A rough approximation of the change in value of the CDS for a given change in spread is as follows:

Profit for the buyer of protection ≈ Change in spread in bps × Duration × Notional.

Alternatively, we might be interested in the CDS percentage price change, which is obtained as

% Change in CDS price = Change in spread in bps × Duration.

The percentage change in the price of a bond is approximately the change in its yield multiplied by its modified duration. For the CDS, the change in yield is analogous to the change in spread, measured in basis points. The duration of the CDS is analogous to the duration of the bond on which the CDS is written.

EXAMPLE 7   Profit and Loss from Change in Credit Spread

An investor buys $10 million of five-year protection, and the CDS contract has a duration of four years. The company's credit spread was originally 500 bps and widens to 800 bps.

1. Does the investor (credit protection buyer) benefit or lose from the change in credit spread?
2. Estimate the CDS price change and estimated profit to the investor.

Solution to 1: The investor owns protection and is therefore short the credit exposure. As the credit spread widens (the credit quality of the underlying deteriorates), the value of the credit protection she owns increases.

Solution to 2: The percentage price change is estimated as the change in spread (300 bps) multiplied by the duration (4), or 12%. The profit to the investor is 12% times the notional ($10 million), or $1.2 million.

4.5. Monetizing Gains and Losses

As with any financial instrument, changes in the price of a CDS give rise to opportunities to unwind the position and either capture a gain or realize a loss. This process is called **monetizing** a gain or loss. Keep in mind that the protection seller is effectively long the reference entity. He has entered into a contract to insure the debt of the reference entity, for which he receives a series of promised payments and possibly an upfront premium. He clearly benefits if the reference entity's credit quality improves because he continues to receive the same compensation but bears less risk. Using the opposite argument, the credit protection buyer benefits from a deterioration of the reference entity's credit quality. Thus, the credit protection seller is more or less long the company's bonds and the credit protection buyer is more or less short the company's bonds. As the company's credit quality changes through time, the market value of the CDS changes, giving rise to gains and losses for the CDS counterparties. The counterparties can realize those gains and losses by entering into new offsetting contracts, effectively selling their CDS positions to other parties.

Going back to the example in the previous section where the credit quality of the reference entity improved—the credit spread on the reference entity declined from 2.5% to 2.1%. The implied upfront premium on a new CDS that matches the terms of the original CDS with adjusted maturity is now the market value of the original CDS. The premium on the new CDS is smaller than that on the original CDS.

Now, suppose that the protection buyer in the original transaction wants to unwind her position. She would then enter into a new CDS as a protection seller and receive the newly calculated upfront premium. As we noted, this value is less than what he paid originally. Likewise, the protection seller in the original transaction could offset his position by entering into a new CDS as a protection buyer. He would pay an upfront premium that is less than what he originally received. The original protection buyer monetizes a loss, and the seller monetizes a gain. The transaction to unwind the CDS does not need to be done with the same original party, although doing so offers some advantages. Central clearing of CDS transactions facilitates the unwind transaction.

At this point, we have identified two ways of realizing a profit or loss on a CDS. One is to effectively exercise the CDS in response to a default. The other is to unwind the position by entering into a new offsetting CDS in the market. A third, less common method occurs if there is no default. A party can simply hold the position until expiration, at which time the credit protection seller has captured all of the premiums and has not been forced to make any payments, and the seller's obligation for any further payments is terminated. The spread of the CDS will go to zero, in much the same manner as a bond converges toward par as it approaches maturity.

The CDS seller clearly gains, having been paid to bear the risk of default that is becoming increasingly unlikely, and the CDS buyer loses. The buyer loses on the CDS because it paid premiums to receive protection in the event of a default, which did not occur. Although the CDS position itself is a loss, the buyer's overall position is not necessarily a loss. If the buyer is a creditor of the reference entity, the premium "loss" is no different than a homeowner's insurance premium payment on his house; he wouldn't consider that payment a loss simply because his house did not burn down.

5. APPLICATIONS OF CDS

Credit default swaps, as demonstrated, facilitate the transfer of credit risk. As simple as that concept seems, there are many different circumstances under which CDS are used. In this section, we consider some applications of this instrument.

Any derivative instrument has two general uses. One is to exploit an expected movement in the underlying. The derivative typically requires less capital and is usually an easier instrument in which to create a short economic exposure as compared with the underlying. The derivatives market can also be more efficient, meaning that it can react to information more rapidly and have more liquidity than the market for the underlying. Thus, information or an expectation of movement in the underlying can often be exploited much more efficiently with the derivative than with the underlying directly.

The other trading opportunity facilitated by derivatives is in valuation differences between the derivative and the underlying. If the derivative is mispriced relative to the underlying, one can take the appropriate position in the derivative and an offsetting position in the underlying. If the valuation assessment is correct and other investors come to the same conclusion, the values of the derivative and underlying will converge, and the investor will earn a return that is essentially free of risk because the risk of the underlying has been hedged away by holding offsetting positions in the derivative and the underlying. Whether this happens as planned depends on both the efficiency of the market and the quality of the valuation model. Differences can also exist between the derivative and other derivatives on the same underlying.

These two general types of uses are also the major applications of CDS. We will refer to them as managing credit exposures, meaning the taking on or shedding of credit risk in light of changing expectations and/or valuation disparities. With valuation disparities, the focus is on differences in the pricing of credit risk in the CDS market relative to that of the underlying bonds.

5.1. Managing Credit Exposures

The most basic application of a CDS is to increase or decrease credit exposure. The most obvious such application is for a lender to buy protection to reduce its credit exposure to a borrower. For the seller of protection, the trade adds credit exposure. A lender's justification for using a CDS seems obvious. The lender may have assumed too much credit risk but does not want to sell the bond or loan because there can be significant transaction costs, because later it may want the bond or loan back, or because the market for the bond or loan is relatively illiquid. If the risk is temporary, it is almost always easier to temporarily reduce risk by using a CDS. Beyond financial institutions, any organization exposed to credit risk is potentially a candidate for using CDS.

The justification for selling credit protection is somewhat less obvious. The seller can be a CDS dealer, whose objective is to profit from making markets in CDS. A dealer typically attempts to manage its exposure by either diversifying its credit risks or hedging the risk by entering into a transaction with yet another party, such as by shorting the debt or equity of the reference entity, often accompanied by investment of the funds in a repurchase agreement, or repo. If the dealer manages the risk effectively, the risk assumed in selling the CDS is essentially offset when the payment for assuming the risk exceeds the cost of removing the risk. Achieving this outcome successfully requires sophisticated credit risk modeling.

Although dealers make up a large percentage of protection sellers, not all sellers are dealers. Consider that any bondholder is a buyer of credit and interest rate risk. If the bondholder wants only credit risk, it can obtain it by selling protection, which would require far less capital and incur potentially lower overall transaction costs than buying the bond. Moreover, the CDS can be more liquid than the bond, so the position can be unwound much more easily.

As noted, it is apparent why a party making a loan might want credit protection. Consider, however, that a party with no exposure to the reference entity might also purchase credit protection. Such a position is called a **naked credit default swap**, and it has resulted in some controversy in regulatory and political circles. In buying protection without owning the underlying, the investor is taking a position that the entity's credit quality will deteriorate, whereas the seller of protection without owning the underlying is taking the position that the entity's credit quality will improve or that the CDS was overpriced.

Some regulators and politicians believe it is inappropriate for a party with no exposure to a borrower to speculate that the borrower's financial condition will deteriorate. This controversy accelerated during the financial crisis of 2008–2009 because many investors bought protection without owning the underlying and benefited from the crisis.

The counterargument, however, is that elsewhere in the financial markets, such bets are made all of the time in the form of long puts, short futures, and short sales of stocks and bonds. These instruments are generally accepted as a means of protecting oneself against poor performance in the financial markets. Credit protection is also a means of protecting oneself against poor performance. In addition, proponents of naked CDS argue that they bring liquidity to the credit market, potentially providing more stability, not less. Nonetheless, naked CDS trading is banned in Europe for sovereign debt, although it is generally permitted otherwise.

CDS trading strategies, with or without naked exposure, can take several forms. An investor can choose to be long or short the credit exposure, as we have previously discussed. Alternatively, the party can be a credit protection seller on one reference entity and a credit protection buyer on a different entity. This is called a **long/short credit trade**. This transaction is a bet that the credit position of one entity will improve relative to that of another. The two entities might be related in some way or might produce substitute goods. For example, one might take a position that because of competition and changes in the luxury car industry, the credit quality of Daimler will improve and that of BMW will weaken, so selling protection on Daimler and buying protection on BMW would be appropriate. Similarly, an investor may undertake a long/short trade based on other factors, such as environmental, social, and governance (ESG) considerations. For instance, an investor may be concerned about a company's poor ESG-related practices and policies relative to another company. In this case, the investor could buy protection using the CDS of a company with weak ESG practices and policies and sell protection using the CDS of a company with strong ESG practices and policies. Example 8 provides a case study of ESG considerations in a long/short ESG trade.

EXAMPLE 8   Long/Short Trade with ESG Considerations

Overview

An analyst is evaluating two US apparel companies: Atelier and Trapp. Atelier is a large company that focuses on high-end apparel brands. It is profitable despite a high cost structure. Trapp is smaller and less profitable than Atelier. Trapp focuses on less expensive brands and strives to keep costs low. Both companies purchase their merchandise from suppliers all over the world. The analyst recognizes that apparel companies must maintain adequate oversight over their suppliers to control the risks of reputational damage and inventory disruptions. Supplier issues are particularly relevant for Atelier and Trapp following a recent fire that occurred at the factory of Global Textiles, a major supplier to both companies. The fire resulted in multiple casualties and unfavorable news headlines.

The analyst notices a significant difference in the way Atelier and Trapp approach ESG considerations. After the fire at its supplier, Atelier signed an "Accord on Fire and Building Safety," which is a legally binding agreement between global apparel manufacturers, retailers, and trade unions in the country where the fire occurred. After signing the accord, Atelier made a concerted effort to fix and enhance machinery in factories of its suppliers. Its objective was to improve workplace safety—notably, to reduce lost employee time due to factory incidents and the rate of factory accidents and fatalities.

Investors view Atelier's corporate governance system favorably because management interests and stakeholder interests are strongly aligned. Atelier's board of directors includes a high percentage of independent directors and is notably diverse. In contrast, Trapp's founder is the majority owner of the company and serves as CEO and chairman of the board of directors. Furthermore, Trapp's board is composed mainly of individuals who have minimal industry expertise. As a consequence, Trapp's board was unprepared to adequately respond to the Global Textiles fire. Given the lack of independence and expertise of Trapp's board, investors consider Trapp's corporate governance system to be poor. Because of its emphasis on low costs and reflecting its less experienced board, Trapp chose not to sign the accord.

Implications for CDS

Single-name CDS on both Atelier and Trapp are actively traded in the market, although Trapp's CDS is less liquid. Before the Global Textiles fire, five-year CDS for Trapp traded at a spread of 250 bps, compared to a spread of 150 bps for the five-year CDS for Atelier. The difference in spreads reflects Trapp's lower trading liquidity, perceived lower creditworthiness (primarily reflecting its smaller size and lower profitability), and hence higher default risk relative to Atelier.

After the Global Textiles fire, spreads on the CDS for all companies in the apparel sector widened considerably. Credit spreads for the five-year CDS on Atelier widened by 60 bps (to 210 bps), and credit spreads for the five-year CDS on Trapp widened by 75 bps (to 325 bps). The analyst believes that over the longer term, the implications of the fire at Global Textiles will be even more adverse for Trapp relative to Atelier. The analyst's view largely reflects Trapp's higher ESG-related risks, especially the perceived weaker safety in its factories and its weaker corporate governance system. In particular, the analyst believes that spreads of Trapp's CDS will remain wider than their pre-fire level of 250 bps, but Atelier's CDS spreads will return to their pre-fire level of 150 bps.

Describe how the analyst can use CDS to exploit the potential opportunity.

Solution

The analyst can try to exploit the potential opportunity by buying protection (shorting the credit) on Trapp using five-year CDS and selling protection (going long the credit) on Atelier using five-year CDS. This trade would reflect both the anticipated continuing adverse spreads for Trapp relative to the pre-fire level and the return of spreads for Atelier to their lower pre-fire levels. For example, assume Atelier's five-year CDS spread returns to 150 bps from 210 bps, but Trapp's five-year CDS spread narrows to just 300 bps from 325 bps. The difference in spreads between the two companies' CDS would have widened from 115 bps (325 bps – 210 bps) right after the factory fire occurred to 150 bps (300 bps – 150 bps). This 35 bp difference in spread would represent profit (excluding trading costs) to the analyst from the long/short trade.

Similar to a long/short trade involving individual entities (companies), an investor might also create a long/short trade using CDS indexes. For example, if the investor anticipates a weakening economy, she could buy protection using a high-yield CDS index and sell protection using an investment-grade CDS index. As high-yield spreads widen relative to investment-grade spreads, the trade would realize a profit. As another example, a trader expecting a strengthening in the Asian economy relative to the European economy could buy protection using a European CDS index and sell protection using an Asian CDS index. As Asia spreads narrow relative to European spreads, the trade would realize a profit.

Another type of long/short trade, called a **curve trade**, involves buying single-name or index protection at one maturity and selling protection on the same reference entity at a different maturity. Consider two CDS maturities, which we will call the short-term and the long-term to keep things simple. We will assume the more common situation of an upward-sloping credit curve, meaning that long-term CDS rates (and credit spreads) are higher than short-term rates. If the curve changes shape, it becomes either steeper or flatter. A steeper (flatter) curve means that long-term credit risk increases (decreases) relative to short-term credit risk. An investor who believes that long-term credit risk will increase relative to short-term credit risk (credit curve steepening) can buy protection by buying a long-term single-name CDS or selling a long-term CDS index and sell protection by selling a short-term single-name CDS or buying a short-term CDS index. In the short run, a curve-steepening trade is bullish. It implies that the short-term outlook for the reference entity is better than the long-term outlook. In the short run, a curve-flattening trade is bearish. It implies that the short-run outlook for the reference entity looks worse than the long-run outlook and reflects the expectation of near-term problems for the reference entity.

EXAMPLE 9   Curve Trading

An investor owns some intermediate-term bonds issued by a company and has become concerned about the risk of a near-term default, although he is not very concerned about a default in the long term. The company's two-year CDS currently trades at 350 bps, and the four-year CDS is at 600 bps.

1. Describe a potential curve trade that the investor could use to hedge the default risk.
2. Explain why an investor may prefer to use a curve trade as a hedge against the company's default risk rather than simply buying protection on the reference entity.

Solution to 1: The investor anticipates a flattening credit curve for the reference company, with spreads rising at the shorter end of the curve. Thus, he would buy credit protection on the two year (buy the two-year single-name CDS) while selling credit protection further out on the curve (sell the four-year single-name CDS).

Solution to 2: The long/short trade reduces the cost of buying near-term credit protection, with the cost of the credit protection offset by the premium received from selling protection further out on the curve. This works only as long as the investor's expectations about the relative risk of near- and longer-term default hold true.

Of course, there can be changes to the credit curve that take the form of simple shifts in the general level of the curve, whereby all spreads go up or down by roughly equal amounts. As with long-duration bonds relative to short-duration bonds, the values of longer-term CDS will move more than those of shorter-term CDS. As an example, a trader who believes that all spreads will go up will want to be a buyer of credit protection but will realize that longer-term CDS will move more than short-term CDS. Thus, she might want to buy protection at the longer part of the curve and hedge by selling protection at the shorter part of the curve. She will balance the sizes of the positions so that the volatility of the position she believes will gain in value will be more than that of the other position. If more risk is desired, she might choose to trade only the more volatile leg.

6. VALUATION DIFFERENCES AND BASIS TRADING

Different investors will have different assessments of the price of credit risk. Such differences of opinion will lead to valuation disparities. Clearly, there can be only one appropriate price at which credit risk can be eliminated, but that price is not easy to determine. The party that has the best estimate of the appropriate price of credit risk can capitalize on its knowledge or ability at the expense of another party. Any such comparative advantage can be captured by trading the CDS against either the reference entity's debt or equity or derivatives on its debt or equity, but such trading is critically dependent on the accuracy of models that isolate the credit risk component of the return. The details of those models are left to CDS specialists, but it is important for candidates to understand the basic ideas.

The yield on the bond issued by the reference entity to a CDS contains a factor that reflects the credit risk. In principle, the amount of yield attributable to credit risk on the bond should be the same as the credit spread on a CDS. It is, after all, the compensation paid to the party assuming the credit risk, regardless of whether that risk is borne by a bondholder or a CDS seller. But there may be a difference in the credit risk compensation in the bond market and CDS market. This differential pricing can arise from mere differences of opinions, differences in models used by participants in the two markets, differences in liquidity in the two markets, and supply and demand conditions in the repo market, which is a primary source of financing for bond purchases. A difference in the credit spreads in these two markets is the foundation of a strategy known as a **basis trade**.

The general idea behind most basis trades is that any such mispricing is likely to be temporary and the spreads should return to equivalence when the market recognizes the disparity. For example, suppose the bond market implies a 5% credit risk premium whereas the CDS market implies a 4% credit risk premium. The trader does not know which is correct but believes these two rates will eventually converge. From the perspective of the CDS, its risk premium is too low relative to the bond credit risk premium. From the perspective of the bond, its risk premium is too high relative to the CDS market, which means its price is too low. So, the CDS market could be pricing in too little credit risk, and/or the bond market could be pricing in too much credit risk. Either market could be correct; it does not matter. The investor would buy the bond at a price that appears to overestimate its credit risk and, at the same time, buy credit protection at what appears to be an unjustifiably low premium, simultaneously hedging interest rate risk exposure with a duration strategy or interest rate derivatives. The risk is balanced because the default potential on the bond is protected by the CDS. If convergence occurs, the trade would capture the 1% differential in the two markets.

To determine the profit potential of such a trade, it is necessary to decompose the bond yield into the risk-free rate plus the funding spread plus the credit spread. The risk-free rate plus the funding spread is essentially the market reference rate. The credit spread is then the excess of the yield over the market reference rate and can be compared with the credit spread in the CDS market. If the spread is higher in the bond market than in the CDS market, it is said to be a negative basis. If the spread is higher in the CDS market than in the bond market, it is said to be a positive basis. Note that in practice, the above decomposition can be complicated by the existence of embedded options, such as with callable and convertible bonds or when the bond is not selling near par. Those factors would need to be accounted for in the calculations.

EXAMPLE 10   Bonds vs. Credit Default Swaps

An investor wants to be long the credit risk of a given company. The company's bond currently yields 6% and matures in five years. A comparable five-year CDS contract has a credit spread of 3.25%. The investor can borrow at Libor, which is currently 2.5%.

1. Calculate the bond's credit spread.
2. Identify a basis trade that would exploit the current situation.

Solution to 1: The bond's credit spread is equal to the yield (6%) minus the market reference rate (2.5%). Therefore, the bond's credit spread is currently 3.5%.

Solution to 2: The bond and CDS markets imply different credit spreads. Credit risk is cheap in the CDS market (3.25%) relative to the bond market (3.5%). The investor should buy protection in the CDS market at 3.25% and go long the bond, with its 3.5% credit spread, netting 25 bps.

Another type of trade using CDS can occur within the instruments issued by a single entity. Credit risk is an element of virtually every unsecured debt instrument or the capital leases issued by a company. Each of these instruments is priced to reflect the appropriate credit risk. Investors can use the CDS market to first determine whether any of these instruments is incorrectly priced relative to the CDS and then buy the cheaper one and sell the more expensive one. Again, there is the assumption that the market will adjust. This type of trading is much more complex, however, because priority of claims means that not all of the instruments pay off equally if default occurs.

EXAMPLE 11   Using CDS to Trade on a Leveraged Buyout

An investor believes that a company will undergo a leveraged buyout (LBO) transaction, whereby it will issue large amounts of debt and use the proceeds to repurchase all of the publicly traded equity, leaving the company owned by management and a few insiders.

1. Why might the CDS spread change?
2. What equity-versus-credit trade might an investor execute in anticipation of such a corporate action?

Solution to 1: Taking on the additional debt will almost surely increase the probability of default, thereby increasing the CDS spread.

Solution to 2: The investor might consider buying the stock and buying credit protection. Both legs will profit if the LBO occurs because the stock price will rise as the company repurchases all outstanding equity and the CDS price will rise as its spread widens to reflect the increased probability of default.

CDS indexes also create an opportunity for a type of arbitrage trade. If the cost of the index is not equivalent to the aggregate cost of the index components, an investor might go long the cheaper instrument and short the more expensive instrument. There is the implicit assumption that convergence will occur. If it does, the investor gains the benefit while basically having neutralized the risk. Transaction costs in this type of arbitrage trade can be quite significant and nullify the profit potential for all but the largest investors.

SUMMARY

- A credit default swap (CDS) is a contract between two parties in which one party purchases protection from another party against losses from the default of a borrower for a defined period of time.
- A CDS is written on the debt of a third party, called the reference entity, whose relevant debt is called the reference obligation, typically a senior unsecured bond.
- A CDS written on a particular reference obligation normally provides coverage for all obligations of the reference entity that have equal or higher seniority.
- The two parties to the CDS are the credit protection buyer, who is said to be short the reference entity's credit, and the credit protection seller, who is said to be long the reference entity's credit.
- The CDS pays off upon occurrence of a credit event, which includes bankruptcy, failure to pay, and, in some countries, involuntary restructuring.
- Settlement of a CDS can occur through a cash payment from the credit protection seller to the credit protection buyer as determined by the cheapest-to-deliver obligation of the reference entity or by physical delivery of the reference obligation from the protection buyer to the protection seller in exchange for the CDS notional.
- A cash settlement payoff is determined by an auction of the reference entity's debt, which gives the market's assessment of the likely recovery rate. The credit protection buyer must accept the outcome of the auction even though the ultimate recovery rate could differ.
- CDS can be constructed on a single entity or as indexes containing multiple entities. Bespoke CDS or baskets of CDS are also common.
- The fixed payments made from CDS buyer to CDS seller are customarily set at a fixed annual rate of 1% for investment-grade debt or 5% for high-yield debt.
- Valuation of a CDS is determined by estimating the present value of the payment leg, which is the series of payments made from the protection buyer to the protection seller, and the present value of the protection leg, which is the payment from the protection seller to the protection buyer in event of default. If the present value of the payment leg is greater than the present value of the protection leg, the protection buyer pays an upfront premium to the seller. If the present value of the protection leg is greater than the present value of the payment leg, the seller pays an upfront premium to the buyer.
- An important determinant of the value of the expected payments is the hazard rate, the probability of default given that default has not already occurred.
- CDS prices are often quoted in terms of credit spreads, the implied number of basis points that the credit protection seller receives from the credit protection buyer to justify providing the protection.
- Credit spreads are often expressed in terms of a credit curve, which expresses the relationship between the credit spreads on bonds of different maturities for the same borrower.

- CDS change in value over their lives as the credit quality of the reference entity changes, which leads to gains and losses for the counterparties, even though default may not have occurred or may never occur. CDS spreads approach zero as the CDS approaches maturity.
- Either party can monetize an accumulated gain or loss by entering into an offsetting position that matches the terms of the original CDS.
- CDS are used to increase or decrease credit exposures or to capitalize on different assessments of the cost of credit among different instruments tied to the reference entity, such as debt, equity, and derivatives of debt and equity.

PROBLEMS

The following information relates to Questions 1–6

UNAB Corporation

On 1 January 20X2, Deem Advisors purchased a $10 million six-year senior unsecured bond issued by UNAB Corporation. Six months later (1 July 20X2), concerned about the portfolio's credit exposure to UNAB, Doris Morrison, the chief investment officer at Deem Advisors, buys $10 million protection on UNAB with a standardized coupon rate of 5%. The reference obligation of the CDS is the UNAB bond owned by Deem Advisors. UNAB adheres to the ISDA CDS protocols.

On 1 January 20X3, Morrison asks Bill Watt, a derivatives analyst, to assess the current credit quality of UNAB bonds and the value of Deem Advisors' CDS on UNAB debt. Watt gathers the following information on UNAB's debt issues currently trading in the market:

Bond 1: A two-year senior unsecured bond trading at 40% of par
Bond 2: A five-year senior unsecured bond trading at 50% of par
Bond 3: A five-year subordinated unsecured bond trading at 20% of par

With respect to the credit quality of UNAB, Watt makes the following statement:

"There is severe near-term stress in the financial markets, and UNAB's credit curve clearly reflects the difficult environment."

On 1 July 20X3, UNAB fails to make a scheduled interest payment on the outstanding subordinated unsecured obligation after a grace period; however, the company does not file for bankruptcy. Morrison asks Watt to determine if UNAB experienced a credit event and, if so, to recommend a settlement preference.

Kand Corporation

Morrison is considering purchasing protection on Kand Corporation debt to hedge the portfolio's position in Kand. She instructs Watt to determine if an upfront payment would be required and, if so, the amount of the premium. Watt presents the information for the CDS in Exhibit 1.

EXHIBIT 1   Summary Data for 10-year CDS on Kand Corporation

Credit spread	700 bps
Duration	7 years
Coupon rate	5%

Morrison purchases 10-year protection on Kand Corporation debt. Two months later the credit spread for Kand Corporation has increased by 200 bps. Morrison asks Watt to close out the firm's CDS position on Kand Corporation by entering into a new, offsetting contract.

Tollunt Corporation

Deem Advisors' chief credit analyst recently reported that Tollunt Corporation's five-year bond is currently yielding 7% and a comparable CDS contract has a credit spread of 4.25%. Since the current market reference rate is 2.5%, Watt has recommended executing a basis trade to take advantage of the pricing of Tollunt's bonds and CDS. The basis trade would consist of purchasing both the bond and the CDS contract.

1. If UNAB experienced a credit event on 1 July, Watt should recommend that Deem Advisors:
   A. prefer a cash settlement.
   B. prefer a physical settlement.
   C. be indifferent between a cash or a physical settlement.
2. According to Watt's statement, the shape of UNAB's credit curve is *most likely*:
   A. flat.
   B. upward-sloping.
   C. downward-sloping.
3. Should Watt conclude that UNAB experienced a credit event?
   A. Yes
   B. No, because UNAB did not file for bankruptcy
   C. No, because the failure to pay occurred on a subordinated unsecured bond
4. Based on Exhibit 1, the upfront premium as a percent of the notional for the CDS protection on Kand Corporation would be *closest* to:
   A. 2.0%.
   B. 9.8%.
   C. 14.0%.
5. If Deem Advisors enters into a new offsetting contract two months after purchasing protection on Kand Corporation, this action will *most likely* result in:
   A. a loss on the CDS position.
   B. a profit on the CDS position.
   C. neither a loss nor a profit on the CDS position.
6. If convergence occurs in the bond and CDS markets for Tollunt Corporation, a basis trade will capture a profit *closest* to:
   A. 0.25%.
   B. 1.75%.
   C. 2.75%.

The following information relates to Questions 7–14

John Smith, a fixed-income portfolio manager at a €10 billion sovereign wealth fund (the Fund), meets with Sofia Chan, a derivatives strategist with Shire Gate Securities (SGS), to discuss investment opportunities for the Fund. Chan notes that SGS adheres to ISDA (International Swaps and Derivatives Association) protocols for credit default swap (CDS) transactions and that any contract must conform to ISDA specifications. Before the Fund can engage in trading CDS products with SGS, the Fund must satisfy compliance requirements.

Smith explains to Chan that fixed-income derivatives strategies are being contemplated for both hedging and trading purposes. Given the size and diversified nature of the Fund, Smith asks Chan to recommend a type of CDS that would allow the Fund to simultaneously fully hedge multiple fixed-income exposures.

Smith and Chan discuss opportunities to add trading profits to the Fund. Smith asks Chan to determine the probability of default associated with a five-year investment-grade bond issued by Orion Industrial. Selected data on the Orion Industrial bond are presented in Exhibit 1.

EXHIBIT 1   Selected Data on Orion Industrial Five-Year Bond

Year	Hazard Rate
1	0.22%
2	0.35%
3	0.50%
4	0.65%
5	0.80%

Chan explains that a single-name CDS can also be used to add profit to the Fund over time. Chan describes a hypothetical trade in which the Fund sells £6 million of five-year CDS protection on Orion, where the CDS contract has a duration of 3.9 years. Chan assumes that the Fund closes the position six months later, after Orion's credit spread narrowed from 150 bps to 100 bps.

Chan discusses the mechanics of a long/short trade. In order to structure a number of potential trades, Chan and Smith exchange their respective views on individual companies and global economies. Chan and Smith agree on the following outlooks.

Outlook 1: The European economy will weaken.
Outlook 2: The US economy will strengthen relative to that of Canada.
Outlook 3: The credit quality of electric car manufacturers will improve relative to that of traditional car manufacturers.

Chan believes US macroeconomic data are improving and that the general economy will strengthen in the short term. Chan suggests that a curve trade could be used by the Fund to capitalize on her short-term view of a steepening of the US credit curve.

Another short-term trading opportunity that Smith and Chan discuss involves the merger and acquisition market. SGS believes that Delta Corporation may make an unsolicited bid at a premium to the market price for all of the publicly traded shares of Zega, Inc. Zega's market capitalization and capital structure are comparable to Delta's; both firms are highly levered. It is anticipated that Delta will issue new equity along with 5- and 10-year senior unsecured debt to fund the acquisition, which will significantly increase its debt ratio.

7. To satisfy the compliance requirements referenced by Chan, the Fund is *most likely* required to:
   A. set a notional amount.
   B. post an upfront payment.
   C. sign an ISDA master agreement.

8. Which type of CDS should Chan recommend to Smith?
   A. CDS index
   B. Tranche CDS
   C. Single-name CDS

9. Based on Exhibit 1, the probability of Orion defaulting on the bond during the first three years is *closest* to:
   A. 1.07%.
   B. 2.50%.
   C. 3.85%.

10. To close the position on the hypothetical Orion trade, the Fund:
    A. sells protection at a higher premium than it paid at the start of the trade.
    B. buys protection at a lower premium than it received at the start of the trade.
    C. buys protection at a higher premium than it received at the start of the trade.

11. The hypothetical Orion trade generated an approximate:
    A. loss of £117,000.
    B. gain of £117,000.
    C. gain of £234,000.

12. Based on the three economic outlook statements, a profitable long/short trade would be to:
    A. sell protection using a Canadian CDX IG and buy protection using a US CDX IG.
    B. buy protection using an iTraxx Crossover and sell protection using an iTraxx Main.
    C. buy protection using an electric car CDS and sell protection using a traditional car CDS.

13. The curve trade that would *best* capitalize on Chan's view of the US credit curve is to:
    A. buy protection using a 20-year CDX and buy protection using a 2-year CDX.
    B. buy protection using a 20-year CDX and sell protection using a 2-year CDX.
    C. sell protection using a 20-year CDX and buy protection using a 2-year CDX.

14. A profitable equity-versus-credit trade involving Delta and Zega is to:
    A. short Zega shares and buy protection on Delta using the 10-year CDS.
    B. go long Zega shares and buy protection on Delta using 5-year CDS.
    C. go long Delta shares and buy protection on Delta using 5-year CDS.

CHAPTER 6

INTRODUCTION TO COMMODITIES AND COMMODITY DERIVATIVES

David Burkart, CFA, and James Alan Finnegan, CAIA, RMA, CFA

LEARNING OUTCOMES

The candidate should be able to:

- compare characteristics of commodity sectors;
- compare the life cycle of commodity sectors from production through trading or consumption;
- contrast the valuation of commodities with the valuation of equities and bonds;
- describe types of participants in commodity futures markets;
- analyze the relationship between spot prices and futures prices in markets in contango and markets in backwardation;
- compare theories of commodity futures returns;
- describe, calculate, and interpret the components of total return for a fully collateralized commodity futures contract;
- contrast roll return in markets in contango and markets in backwardation;
- describe how commodity swaps are used to obtain or modify exposure to commodities;
- describe how the construction of commodity indexes affects index returns.

1. INTRODUCTION

In the upcoming sections, we present the characteristics and valuation of commodities and commodity derivatives. Given that investment in commodities is conducted primarily through futures markets, the concepts and theories behind commodity futures is a primary focus of the reading. In particular, the relationship between spot and futures prices, as well as the underlying components of futures returns, are key analytical considerations.

What do we mean when we talk about investing in commodities? A basic economic definition is that a commodity is a physical good attributable to a natural resource that is tradable and supplied without substantial differentiation by the general public.

Commodities trade in physical (spot) markets and in futures and forward markets. Spot markets involve the physical transfer of goods between buyers and sellers; prices in these markets reflect current (or very near term) supply and demand conditions. Global commodity futures markets constitute financial exchanges of standardized futures contracts in which a price is established in the market today for the sale of some defined quantity and quality of a commodity at a future date of delivery; completion of the contract may permit cash settlement or require physical delivery.

Commodity futures exchanges allow for risk transfer and provide a valuable price discovery mechanism that reflects the collective views of all market participants with regard to the future supply and demand prospects of a commodity. Given the financial (versus physical) nature of their contract execution, commodity exchanges allow important parties beyond traditional suppliers and buyers—speculators, arbitrageurs, private equity, endowments, and other institutional investors—to participate in these price discovery and risk transfer processes. Standardized contracts and organized exchanges also offer liquidity (i.e., trading volumes) to facilitate closing, reducing, expanding, or opening new hedges or exposures as circumstances change on a daily basis.

Forward markets exist alongside futures markets in certain commodities for use by entities that require customization in contract terms. Forwards are largely outside the scope of this reading and are discussed only briefly. Exposure to commodities is also traded in the swap markets for both speculative and hedging purposes. Investment managers may want to establish swap positions to match certain portfolio needs, whereas producers may want to more precisely adjust their commodity risk (e.g., the origin of their cattle or the chemical specifications of their crude oil).

Commodities offer the potential for diversification benefits in a multi-asset class portfolio because of historically low average return correlation with stocks and bonds. In addition, certain academic studies (e.g., Gorton and Rouwenhorst 2006; Erb and Harvey 2006) demonstrate that some commodities have historically had inflation hedging qualities.

Our coverage of the commodities topic is organized as follows: We provide an overview of physical commodity markets, including the major sectors, their life cycles, and their valuation. We then describe futures market participants, commodity futures pricing, and the analysis of commodity returns, including the concepts of contango and backwardation. The subsequent section reviews the use of swap instruments rather than futures to gain exposure to commodities. We then review the various commodity indexes given their importance as benchmarks for the asset class and investment vehicles. Finally, we conclude with a summary of the major points.

2. COMMODITY SECTORS

Commodities are an asset class inherently different from traditional financial assets, such as equities and bonds. These latter assets are securities that are claims on productive capital assets and/or financial assets and thus are expected to generate cash flows for their owners. The intrinsic value of these securities is the present discounted value of their expected future cash flows. Commodities are valued differently. Commodities' value derives from either their use as consumables or as inputs to the production of goods and services. Because a number of commodities need to be processed or have a limited life before spoiling or decaying, an astute analyst will take into account the growth and extraction patterns of the various commodities as well as the logistics associated with transporting these physical goods. Therefore, commodities, while seemingly familiar from everyday life, offer distinct sets of risk exposures for investors.

Fundamental analysis of commodities relies on analyzing supply and demand for each of the products as well as estimating the reaction to the inevitable shocks to their equilibrium or underlying direction. For example, a growing world population demands more crude oil or related products as transportation of goods and people increases. However, technological improvements (e.g., shale drilling or electric vehicles) can disrupt that trend and in the case of armed conflict or adverse weather, for example, may alter it on very short notice! This means that the quantitative analysis of commodities is often imperfect because of high degrees of non-normalcy and shifting correlations. Furthermore, the coefficients to underlying variables are often non-stationary; for example, much corn today is genetically modified to resist heat, rendering drought impact estimates derived from history less predictive. Much of the raw data are held off market by private firms engaged in the commodity industry (such as oil or agricultural companies), which also hinders a purely quantitative approach. Therefore, the framework offered here will be at a high level. We will later provide a breakdown of individual areas for the investor to apply discretionary or quantitative techniques, as circumstances allow. Because the framework can be applied to both supply and demand, we shall set that distinction aside until we focus on individual sectors and commodities. The tools and considerations in fundamental analysis are as follows:

A. Direct announcements: Various government agencies and private companies broadcast production and inventory data that can be used to infer demand, which is often unobservable. Possible public sources include the USDA (US Department of Agriculture), OPEC (Organization of the Petroleum Exporting Countries), the NBS (National Bureau of Statistics of China), and the IEA (International Energy Agency). Setting aside questions of reliability, sometimes estimating current conditions is as straightforward as monitoring official announcements, even with a lag.

B. Component analysis: The more diligent analyst will attempt to break down high-level supply and demand into various components. Applying a stock and flow approach is a logical method. The stock or potential production or demand attempts to set boundaries around what is actually produced or wanted. This can be as general as the amount of arable land in all of Europe or as specific as the current capacity of the Ghawar oil field in Saudi Arabia. The flow considers the utilization of that stock of raw material. Examples include understanding the oil tanker traffic heading to China, estimating the historical yields of US cotton (the amount of fiber per unit of land) in various weather conditions, and estimating the number of piglets per mother hog in Canada.

These examples lend themselves to historical quantitative or conditional analysis. However, care needs to be taken regarding the qualitative aspects of supply and demand; a new policy such as stricter emissions standards can affect both supply (higher standards often strand lower-quality materials) and demand (not all consumers may be properly equipped to utilize a changing standard). Political unrest may not touch an isolated farm but may disrupt consumption.

C. Timing considerations: Stocks and flows from (b) can be further affected by timing issues—such as seasonality and logistics—and, therefore, price reaction. A shock, by definition, is a sudden timing switch; an earthquake that destroys a pipeline does not affect the stock, but it does halt the flow. A more common consideration is seasonality, such as the growing period for crops and people's demand for winter heat generated from natural gas. This last aspect in particular feeds into the shape of the commodity futures curve, as discussed later.

D. Money flow: Short-term and long-term prices can be affected by sentiment and macro monetary conditions, such as inflation. If investor risk tolerance is particularly high or low, then expecting exaggerated price movements would be rational as fundamental conditions are hyped up or beaten down. Alternatively, capital availability from low interest rates can help trigger the building of new mines and affect future supply. Government subsidies of substitute technologies can limit commodity price appreciation (e.g., available funds for electric cars indirectly affect the price of gasoline).

In summary, although the casual investor can perhaps focus solely on public summary statements, the engaged researcher will apply a framework of examining the stock and flow components and their related timing to better understand and weigh the pressures leading to higher or lower prices.

2.1. Commodity Sectors

The world of commodities is relatively broad but can be defined and separated in a reasonable manner. Although there are several ways to segment the asset class by sector, here we use the approach that is the basis for the Bloomberg Commodity Index: energy, grains, industrial (base) metals, livestock, precious metals, and softs (cash crops). This segmentation is more granular than some other indexes but is reasonably consistent with the breakdown in the specialties of most market participants. As noted previously, each sector has a number of individual characteristics that are important in determining the supply and demand for each commodity. A key concept is how easily and cost-effectively the commodity can be produced and stored, as well as such related issues as frequency/timing of consumption, spoilage, insurance, and ease of transportation to consumers. Note that many commodities, such as uranium or water, are traded only in thin, private markets. They are really just individual transactions, as opposed to the markets we are discussing. For the purposes of our coverage, we have to constrain ourselves to primary commodities, recognizing that there are many others that may offer investment opportunities or require hedging. Exhibit 1 reviews each sector and its main characteristics and influences.

EXHIBIT 1   A Description of Commodity Sectors and Factors

	Energy: Fuel transportation, industrial production, and electrical generation. Primary commodities include crude oil, natural gas, coal, and refined products, such as gasoline and heating oil.	
Primary Influences	Stocks: Discovery and depletion of new fields, economic and political costs/certainty of access to those fields, refinery technology and maintenance, power plant type and construction, economic (GDP) size	Flows: Pipeline and tanker reliability, seasonality (summer/winter), adverse weather (cold, hurricanes), automobile/truck sales, geopolitical instability, environmental requirements, economic (GDP) growth

EXHIBIT 1   (Continued)

	Grains: Provide human and animal sustenance but also can be distilled into fuel (e.g., ethanol). Primary commodities include corn, soy, wheat, and rice.	
Primary Influences	Stocks: Arable farmland, storage/port facilities (infrastructure), human and animal population size	Flows: Weather (moisture, temperature), disease, consumer preferences, genetic modification, biofuel substitution, population growth
	Industrial/Base Metals: Materials for durable consumer goods, industry, and construction. Primary commodities include copper, aluminum, nickel, zinc, lead, tin, and iron.	
Primary Influences	Stocks: Mined acreage, smelter capacity, economic (GDP) stage of industrial/consumer development	Flows: Government industrial and environmental policies, economic (GDP) growth, automobile/truck sales, infrastructure investment
	Livestock: Animals raised for human consumption. Primary commodities include hogs, cattle, sheep, and poultry.	
Primary Influences	Stocks: Herd size, processing plant capacity, consumer preferences, feed availability/cost	Flows: Speed of maturation to slaughter weight, economic (GDP) growth/consumer income, disease, adverse weather
	Precious Metals: Certain metals that act as monetary stores of value (as well as industrial uses). Primary commodities include gold, silver, and platinum.	
Primary Influences	Stocks: Mined acreage, smelter capacity, fiat money supply/banking development	Flows: Central bank monetary policy, geopolitics, economic (GDP) growth
	Softs (Cash Crops): Crops sold for income—as opposed to consumed for subsistence—and often originally seen as luxuries. Primary commodities include cotton, cocoa, sugar, and coffee.	
Primary Influences	Stocks: Arable farmland, storage/port facilities (infrastructure), economic (GDP) size	Flows: Weather (moisture, temperature), disease, consumer preferences, biofuel substitution, economic (GDP) growth/ consumer income

As noted in this section, each commodity sector is unique in its fundamental drivers but with the overlapping context of economic and monetary data. With this context in mind, we will now examine the life cycle of the sectors from production to consumption—and their interaction—in more detail.

EXAMPLE 1   Commodity Sector Demand

Industrial activity *most likely* affects the demand for which of the following commodities?

A. Copper
B. Natural gas
C. Softs (e.g., cotton, coffee, sugar and cocoa)

Solution: A is correct. Copper is used for construction, infrastructure development, and the manufacture of durable goods, all of which are economically sensitive. B is incorrect because demand for natural gas is driven primarily by weather conditions (heating or cooling) and only secondarily by industrial activity. C is incorrect because demand for softs is driven primarily by global income.

EXAMPLE 2   Commodity Sector Risks

Which of the following commodity sectors are *least* affected in the short term by weather-related risks?

A. Energy
B. Livestock
C. Precious metals

Solution: C is correct. Weather has very little impact on the availability of precious metals given their ease of storage. Inflation expectations, fund flows, and industrial production are more important factors. A is incorrect because energy demand is strongly influenced by weather (e.g., heating demand in the winter or transportation demand in the summer). B is incorrect because the health of livestock is vulnerable to unfavorable weather conditions increasing the risks of death and disease by extreme cold, wet, and heat.

3. LIFE CYCLE OF COMMODITIES

The life cycle of commodities varies considerably depending on the economic, technical, and structural (i.e., industry, value chain) profile of each commodity, as well as the sector. Conceptually, the commodity production life cycle reflects and amplifies the changes in storage, weather, and political/economic events that shift supply and demand. Recall from the earlier discussion that timing/seasonality is, in effect, an overlay on top of the underlying supply/demand factors. A short life cycle allows for relatively rapid adjustment to outside events, whereas a long life cycle generally limits the ability of supply or demand to react to new conditions. These shifts, in turn, feed into the economics for the valuation and shape of the commodity supply and demand curves, plus their respective price elasticities of demand and supply. Understanding the life cycle builds understanding of, and ideally ability to forecast, what drives market actions and commodity returns.

Among the food commodities, agriculture and livestock have well-defined seasons and growth cycles that are specific to geographic regions. For example, by March of each year, corn planting may be finished in the southern United States but not yet started in Canada. Meanwhile, the corn harvest may be underway in Brazil and Argentina given their reverse seasonal cycle in the Southern Hemisphere. Each geographic location also represents local markets that have different domestic and export demand. These differences affect the nature (level and reliability) of demand and the power of buyers to extend or contract the life cycle.

In comparison, commodities in the energy and metals sectors are extracted all year round. Their life cycle changes are generally at the margin of a continuous process, as opposed to being centered at a discrete time or season. But the products from crude oil and metal ore have seasonal demands depending on weather (e.g., gasoline demand in the summer and heating oil demand in the winter) that affect the life cycle and usage of the underlying commodity. And with all the differences between the varieties even within the same sector, the life cycles depicted have to be representative and selective. The life cycles of several key commodity sectors are as follows.

3.1. Energy

For an example of the differences within a sector, one need look no further than energy. Natural gas can be consumed almost immediately after extraction from the ground. Crude oil, in contrast, has to be transformed into something else; crude is useless in its innate form. The refined products (e.g., gasoline and heating oil), in turn, have a number of potential processing steps depending on the quality of crude oil input and the relative demand for the various products. The steps for the energy complex can be summarized as shown in Exhibit 2.

EXHIBIT 2   Steps for the Energy Complex

Step	Title	Description
1.	Extraction	A drilling location is selected after surveys, and the well is dug. Enough underground pressure for the hydrocarbons to come out naturally may exist, or water or other tools may be required to create such pressure. Water is also used for the fracturing process known as "fracking," which breaks up shale formations to allow for oil or gas to be extracted.
2.	Storage	After extraction, crude oil is commercially stored for a few months on average in the United States, Singapore, and northern Europe and is strategically stored by many countries. In addition, oil may temporarily be stored on tanker ships. Natural gas may be delivered directly to the end consumer. Summer-extracted natural gas is often injected into storage for the winter months.
3.	Consumption Stage	Only natural gas is consumed at this stage because it does not need to be refined. Crude oil requires further processing.
4.	Refining	Crude oil is distilled into its component parts via a process called "cracking." Heat is used to successively boil off the components that are, in turn, cooled down and collected (e.g., gasoline, kerosene), until only the remnants (e.g., asphalt) are left.
5.	Consumption Stage	The distilled products are separated and shipped to their various locations—by ship, pipe, train, or truck—for use by the end consumer.

Sources: Based on information from www.eia.gov/energyexplained/index.php?page=oil_refining#tab1, https://en.wikipedia.org/wiki/Petroleum_refining_processes (accessed 23 April 2019), and authors' research.

Refineries are extraordinarily expensive to build—typically costing several billion US dollars—depending on the processes required to purify and distill the oil. Part of the cost depends on the expected specifications of the crude oil input. Generally speaking, a low-grade, high sulfur source would require more investment than one with an assured lighter, "sweeter" source. Pipelines are also very costly: For example, the Keystone XL pipeline expansion between Canada and the United States was originally estimated to cost $5 billion in 2010, but the estimate was doubled to $10 billion in 2014. Even in countries dealing with violent insurrections (e.g., Libya, Iraq, Nigeria), damage to refineries has been generally modest because of their value to all parties. Pipelines, however, are often destroyed or cut off. Although these costs may appear staggering, they actually pale in comparison with the costs (and risks) of oil exploration, especially in deep offshore locations or geographically remote (or geopolitically risky) regions.

The crude oil market has a number of futures contracts and indexes that follow local grades and origins, but the two most commonly traded set of contracts follow the US-based crude oil (West Texas Intermediate, or WTI, crude oil) and the UK-located Brent crude oil from the North Sea. Likewise, there are futures for natural gas, gasoil, gasoline, and heating oil. Each has different delivery locations and standards, but the WTI and Brent contracts represent a high-quality refinery input that exploration and production companies can use as a hedging device.

EXAMPLE 3   Energy Life Cycle

Which of the following is a primary difference in the production life cycle between crude oil and natural gas?

A. Only crude oil needs to be stored.
B. European companies are the only ones that store crude oil.
C. Natural gas requires very little additional processing after extraction compared with crude oil.

Solution: C is correct. Natural gas can be used after it is extracted from the ground upon delivery, but crude oil must first be processed for later use. A is incorrect because both oil and natural gas are stored before usage. B is incorrect because many countries around the world store crude oil, both commercially and strategically.

3.2. Industrial/Precious Metals

The life cycle of both precious and industrial metals is probably the most flexible because the ore, as well as the finished products, can be stored for months (if not years) given the relative resistance to spoilage of metals (assuming proper storage). Otherwise, the life cycle parallels the energy one outlined previously, as shown in Exhibit 3.

EXHIBIT 3   Copper Purification Process

	Step Name	Description
1.	Extracting and Preparing	Ore (raw earth with ~2% metal content) is removed via a mine or open pit. Ore is then ground into powder and concentrated to roughly 25% purity.
2.	Smelting	The purified ore is heated, and more impurities are removed as slag, increasing the metal content to 60%. Further processes increase the concentration to 99.99%.
3.	Storage/ Logistics	The purified metal is held typically in a bonded warehouse until it is shipped to an end user.

Sources: Based on information from http://resources.schoolscience.co.uk/CDA/14-16/cumining/copch2pg1.html (accessed 23 April 2019), www.madehow.com/Volume-4/Copper.html (accessed 23 April 2019), and authors' research.

Similar to refining crude oil, creating the economies of scale involved in the smelter and ore processing plants is critical. These are huge facilities for which marginal costs (i.e., the cost to convert the last pound or kilogram of processed ore into a useful metal) decline substantially with both the scale of the facility and its utilization (output as a percentage of capacity). As a result, when supply exceeds demand for a given industrial metal, it is difficult for suppliers to either cut back production or halt it entirely. Overproduction often continues until smaller or financially weaker competitors are forced to shut down. Because demand for industrial metals fluctuates with overall economic growth, as was discussed previously, there are substantial incentives for metals producers to invest in new capacity when their utilization (and profit) is high but huge economic and financial penalties for operating these facilities when demand falls off during an economic downturn. Ironically, given the typical economic cycle and the time lag involved after deciding to expand capacity, new supply often arrives just as demand is declining—which exacerbates pricing and profit declines.

With the lack of annual seasonality in the production of metals and ease of storage without spoilage, much of time variability comes from the demand side of the equation (e.g., construction and economic growth).

EXAMPLE 4   Industrial Metals Life Cycle

Because of large economies of scale for processing industrial metals, producers:

A. immediately shut down new capacity when supply exceeds demand.
B. have an incentive to maintain maximum operating production levels when demand declines.
C. find it difficult to cut back production or capacity even when supply exceeds demand or demand slows.

Solution: C is correct. Given the sizable facilities in which metals are produced and their capital requirements, reducing capacity is difficult when demand slows. A is incorrect because of the time lag involved in responding to reduced demand conditions. B is incorrect because producers would face financial losses if they maintained maximum production levels when there is a decline in demand.

3.3. Livestock

Livestock grows year round, but good weather and access to high-quality pasture and feed accelerate weight gain. As a result, there is fluctuation in the availability of animals ready for slaughter. The timing to maturity typically increases with size, with poultry maturing in a matter of weeks, hogs in months, and cattle in a few years. Taking the example of a hog, the life cycle begins with a sow (female hog) giving birth. Normally it takes about six months to raise a piglet to slaughter weight, and during that time it can be fed almost anything to get it up to proper bulk. In mass-scale production, soymeal and cornmeal are the most common foods. In contrast, cattle take longer to raise. For mass-scale breeding, the first one to two years are spent as "feeder cattle," first eating a grass diet in pasture. The next phase covers an additional 6–12 months whereby cattle are in a feed lot being fattened to slaughter weight, generally on a corn-based diet. Note that the various types of feed for these animals are other traded commodities.

The livestock industry in the United States has historically been among the least export-oriented of all the commodities because of the high risk of spoilage once an animal is slaughtered. However, advances in cryogenics (freezing) technologies with regard to chicken, beef, and pork mean that increasingly these products are moving from one part of the world to another in response to differences in production costs and demand. And as emerging and frontier market countries develop middle class consumers capable of purchasing meat protein as a regular part of their diet, there has been increased investment in the livestock and meatpacking industries in such countries as the United States and Brazil. These industries combine low-cost sources of animal feed, large grazing acreage, and strong domestic demand (leading to facilities with substantial economies of scale) as key export points to supply global demand.

Ranchers and slaughterhouses trade hog and cattle futures to hedge against their commitments. Ranchers can hedge both young cattle that are still in pasture (called feeder cattle) and animals being fattened for butchering (called live cattle).

EXAMPLE 5   Livestock Life Cycle

The US livestock sector has been among the least export-oriented commodity sectors because of:

A. low technological innovation in the sector.
B. high risk of spoilage once animals are slaughtered.
C. little or no demand for US livestock from outside the United States.

Solution: B is correct. Livestock incur a high risk of spoilage once they are slaughtered unless the meat is frozen. A is incorrect because advances in cryogenics have improved the ability to export from the United States. C is incorrect because demand for US livestock has expanded internationally, particularly in emerging market countries that are experiencing economic growth.

3.4. Grains

Grains in the Northern Hemisphere follow a similar growth cycle, with an analogous but opposite growth cycle in the Southern Hemisphere. Plants mature according to the following steps: (1) planting (placing the seeds in the ground after preparation/fertilization work); (2) growth (the emerging of the seedling to full height); (3) pod/ear/head formation (the food grain is created by the plant); and (4) harvest (the collection of the grain by the farmer). The timing in North America is shown in Exhibit 4 to illustrate the time it takes to grow each crop.

EXHIBIT 4   Timing for Grain Production in North America

	Corn	Soybeans	Wheat*
Planting	April–May	May–June	Sep.–Oct.
Growth	June–Aug.	July–Aug.	Nov.–March
Pod/Ear/Head Formation	Aug.–Sep.	Sep.	April–May
Harvest	Sep.–Nov.	Sep.–Oct.	June–July

* The hard winter wheat variety, which has a higher protein content, is used here.
Source: Authors' research.

Because demand for grains is year round, they are regularly stored in silos and warehouses globally. Some countries have a central purchasing bureau, and others depend on local or international trading companies to maintain stockpiles. Poor hygienic standards and logistics can result in a substantial loss of value to grains due to mold or insect/animal infestation. Monitoring the purchasing patterns of these government tenders can assist a research analyst in determining grain demand.

Farmers and consumers can trade futures to hedge their exposure to the crop in question, and the contract delivery months reflect the different times of the growing cycle outlined earlier. Ranchers also can use grain futures to hedge against the cost of feeding an animal.

3.5. Softs

Coffee, cocoa, cotton, and sugar are very different soft commodities in this sector, so we will focus on one that is grown and enjoyed broadly—coffee. Coffee is harvested somewhere all year round in the various countries that circle the Equator. After the coffee cherries are picked (still often by hand, to ensure that only ripe ones are taken), the husk and fruit are removed and the remaining bean dried. More than half of coffee uses the dry method in which the harvested cherries are laid out in the sun for two to three weeks. The wet method uses fresh water to soak the cherries, the soft pulp is removed, the bean is fermented for 12–48 hours, and then the bean is dried. The "green" beans are then hulled, sorted, and bagged for their final markets. With most of the consumption in faraway foreign markets, ships are commonly used to transport the beans to their buyer, which may store them in a bonded warehouse. The local buyer roasts the beans and ships them to the retail location (e.g., coffee house or supermarket) for purchase or brewing.

Coffee comes in two main varieties, robusta and arabica, although there are many others. Generally speaking, robusta beans are lower quality with less flavor than the arabica. There are two futures contracts associated with coffee: The robusta variety is traded in London, and the arabica variety is traded in New York. Note that the contracts are for the unroasted or "green" beans. The physical delivery aspect of these contracts allows for sellers to deliver the beans to an authorized bonded warehouse as fulfillment of the contract at expiration. Therefore, farmers and distributors can sell futures contracts to hedge the sales price of production, and coffee roasters can buy futures contracts to hedge coffee bean purchase costs; contract maturities can be selected by each to match their product delivery schedules.

4. VALUATION OF COMMODITIES

The valuation of commodities compared with that of equities and bonds can be summarized by the fact that stocks and bonds represent financial assets and are claims on the economic output of a business, a government, or an individual. Commodities, however, are almost always physical assets. We say "almost always" because some newer classes of commodities, such as electricity or weather, are not physical assets in the sense that you can touch or store them.

Commodities are typically tangible items with an intrinsic (but variable) economic value (e.g., a nugget of gold, a pile of coal, a bushel of corn). They do not generate future cash flows beyond what can be realized through their purchase and sale. In addition, the standard financial instruments that are based on commodities are not financial assets (like a stock or bond) but are derivative contracts with finite lifetimes, such as futures contracts. As with other types of derivatives, commodity derivative contracts can and do have value, but they are contingent on some other factors, such as the price of the underlying commodity. Hence, the valuation of commodities is based not on the estimation of future profitability and cash flows but on a discounted forecast of future possible prices based on such factors as the supply and demand of the physical item or the expected volatility of future prices. On the one hand, this forecast may be quite formal and elaborately estimated by a producer or consumer. One can imagine the detailed inputs available to an oil company based on the labor and capital expenses needed to extract oil, refine it, and transport it to final sale as gasoline in your automobile. On the other hand, this forecast may be instinctively made by a floor trader with little fundamental analysis but instead with professional judgment based on years of experience and perhaps some technical analysis.

As opposed to a stock or bond that receives periodic income, owning a commodity incurs transportation and storage costs. These ongoing expenditures affect the shape of the forward price curve of the commodity derivative contracts with different expiration dates. If storage and transportation costs are substantial, the prices for a commodity futures contract will likely be incrementally higher as one looks farther into the future. However, sometimes the current demand for the commodity can move the spot price higher than the futures price. The spot price reflects the fact that, instead of going long a futures contract, one could buy the commodity today and store it until a future date for use. The expenditure would be the outlay/ investment at today's spot price for the commodity along with (or net of) the future costs one would incur to store and hold it. This time element of commodity storage and supply and demand can generate "roll return" and affect investment returns. These and other factors figure into the assessment of futures pricing, which we will cover later.

Some commodity contracts require actual delivery of the physical commodity at the end of the contract versus settlement in a cash payment (based on the difference between the contract futures price and the spot price prevailing at the time of contract expiration). The force of arbitrage—which reflects the law of one price—may not be entirely enforced by arbitrageurs because some participants do not have the ability to make or take delivery of the physical commodity. In these situations, the relationships that link spot and futures prices are not an equality but are a range that only indicates the limit or boundary of value differences that can occur.

There is an important additional consideration concerning the link between spot and futures prices in commodities. Some of the largest users of commodity futures are businesses seeking to hedge price risk when that price is a critical source of either revenue or cost in their business operations. For example, the airline industry is very dependent on the cost of jet fuel for operating planes. The highly competitive nature of the industry results in tremendous price pressure on airfares, with a need for airlines to fill each flight with as many passengers as possible. The futures and swap markets for jet fuel allow airlines to lower the risk of higher fuel costs by hedging the price of future fuel purchases (particularly against surprise shocks in oil prices).

In addition, the price discovery process of the commodity futures markets provides airlines with insights about future fuel prices that help determine what prices to offer their customers for future flights while still making a profit. In fact, airline ticket sales are—in effect—selling a contract at a price set today for future delivery of a service—namely, a plane flight. In this case, the airlines will typically hedge their price risk and uncertainty about future fuel costs by purchasing ("going long") energy futures contracts.

EXAMPLE 6   Commodities versus Stocks and Bonds

In contrast to financial assets, such as stocks and bonds:

A. commodities are always physical goods.
B. commodities generate periodic cash flows.
C. commodity investment is primarily via derivatives.

Solution: C is correct. The most common way to invest in commodities is via derivatives. A is incorrect because although most commodities are physical goods, certain newer classes, such as electricity or weather, are not tangible. B is incorrect because commodities may incur, rather than generate, periodic cash flow through transportation and storage costs (when the commodities are physically owned).

EXAMPLE 7   Spot Commodity Valuation

What is a key distinction between the valuation of commodities compared with the valuation of stocks and bonds?

A. Valuation of commodities cannot be conducted using technical analysis.
B. Valuation of commodities focuses on supply and demand, whereas valuation of stocks and bonds focuses on discounted cash flows.

C. Valuation of stocks and bonds focuses on future supply and demand, whereas commodity valuation focuses on future profit margins and cash flow.

Solution: B is correct. The valuation of commodities is based on a forecast of future prices based on supply and demand factors, as well as expected price volatility. In contrast, the valuation of stocks and bonds is based on estimating future profitability and/or cash flow. A is incorrect because technical analysis is sometimes applied to valuing commodities. C is incorrect for the reasons stated for choice B.

5. COMMODITIES FUTURES MARKETS: PARTICIPANTS

Public commodity markets are structured as futures markets—that is, as a central exchange where participants trade standardized contracts to make and take delivery at a specified place at a specified future time. As mentioned, futures contracts are derivatives because the value of the contract is derived from another asset. Both futures and forward contracts are binding agreements that establish a price today for delivery of a commodity in the future (or settlement of the contract in cash at expiration). As mentioned at the beginning of the reading, the focus of this reading is on futures, with forwards discussed only briefly.

5.1. Futures Market Participants

The key differences between futures and forward contracts is that futures contracts are standardized agreements traded on public exchanges, such as the Chicago Mercantile Exchange (CME), Intercontinental Exchange (ICE), and the Shanghai Futures Exchange (SHFE), and gains/losses are marked to market every day. Standardization allows a participant to enter into a contract without ever knowing who the counterparty is. In addition, the exchange oversees trading and margin requirements and provides some degree of self-imposed regulatory oversight. In contrast, forward contracts are commonly bilateral agreements between a known party that wants to go long and one that wants to go short. Because of their bilateral nature, forwards are considered to be OTC (over the counter) contracts with less regulatory oversight and much more customization to the specific needs of the hedging (or speculating) party. Often, the counterparty for a forward contract is a financial institution that is providing liquidity or customization in exchange for a fee. Although futures markets require that daily cash movements in the futures price be paid from the losing positions to the winning positions, forward contracts are usually only settled upon expiration or with some custom frequency dictated by the contract.

Early commodity exchanges operated as forward markets, but too often participants would go bankrupt when unrealized losses became realized at the end of the contract. The futures process was introduced to minimize this risk, with the exchange acting as payment guarantor. The first modern organized futures exchange was the Dojima Rice Exchange in Osaka, Japan, which was founded in 1710, although futures contracts were traded in England during the 16th century. The structure of futures markets is important to understand as a way of understanding the goals and roles of the various participants. When we consider any commodity, for every producer of that commodity there is a consumer. Thus, for participants who are long the physical commodity and want to sell it, there are also participants who are short the physical commodity and want to buy it. Therefore, for fairness between the two sets of participants, longs and shorts need to operate on an equal basis. As a coincident observation, the commodity markets are net zero in terms of aggregate futures positions (futures contract longs equal futures contract shorts). In contrast, in markets for stocks and bonds, there is a net long position because the issued stocks' and bonds' market values are equal to the net aggregate positions at the end of each day. Shorting an equity is constrained by the short seller's need to locate shares to short, the requirement to reimburse dividends on borrowed shares, and requirements to post and pay interest on margin that generally exceeds the margin required for long equity positions (as in the United States under Regulation T). In contrast, shorting commodity futures is much simpler, with short investors selling to long investors directly, and thus short investors post the same margin required of long investors.

There are a number of participants in commodity futures markets. First are *hedgers*, who trade in the markets to hedge their exposures related to the commodity. The second are long-term and short-term *traders* and *investors* (including index investors), who speculate on market direction or volatility and provide liquidity and price discovery for the markets in exchange for the expectation of making a profit. Third are the *exchanges* (or clearing houses), which set trading rules and provide the infrastructure of transmitting prices and payments. Fourth are *analysts*, who use the exchange information for non-trading purposes, such as evaluating commodity businesses, creating products that are based on commodity futures (e.g., exchange-traded funds, swaps, and notes), and making public policy decisions. Analysts also include brokers and other financial intermediaries who participate in the markets but do not take a position. Finally, *regulators* of both the exchange and traders exist to monitor and police the markets, investigate malfeasance, and provide a venue for complaints.

5.1.1. Commodity Hedgers

Hedgers tend to be knowledgeable market participants: One would expect that a company that drills for oil knows something about the supply and demand for oil and related forms of energy (at least in the long run). However, hedgers may not be accurate predictors of the future supply and demand for their product. Consider a baker who buys wheat for future delivery and benefits from a surprise drought (has locked in a low price in a supply-constrained market). However, the baker is hurt if the weather is beneficial (has effectively overpaid during a bumper crop). Given that a hedger can make delivery (if short the futures contract) or take delivery (if long the futures contract), he or she is generally motivated by risk mitigation with regard to cash flow, so the risk is more of an opportunity cost than an actual one.

It is important to keep in mind that hedging and speculating are not synonymous with being (respectively) long or short. As Exhibit 5 illustrates with some examples, both long and short positions can be associated with either hedging or speculating.

EXHIBIT 5   Examples of Hedging and Speculating Positions

	Long Position	Short Position
Hedging	Food manufacturer seeking to hedge the price of corn needed for snack chips	Gold mining company seeking to hedge the future price of gold against potential declines
Speculating	Integrated oil company seeking to capitalize on its knowledge of physical oil markets by making bets on future price movements	Commodity trading adviser (CTA) seeking to earn a profit for clients via a macro-commodity investment fund

Note also that hedgers tend to speculate based on their perceived unique insight into market conditions and determine the amount of hedging that is appropriate. From a regulatory standpoint in the United States, the difficulty in clearly distinguishing between hedging and speculating, therefore, has resulted in the separation of commodity producers and consumers from other trading participants regardless of whether commercial participants are actually speculating.

5.1.2. Commodity Traders and Investors

The commodity trading community, like other groups of traders, consists of three primary types: (1) informed investors, (2) liquidity providers, and (3) arbitrageurs. Informed investors largely represent the aforementioned hedgers and speculators, including index and institutional investors. With regard to the hedger, as mentioned previously, a company that drills for oil clearly is familiar with the supply and demand for oil and related forms of energy (at least in the long run). But hedgers may not be accurate predictors of the *future* supply and demand for their product.

Speculators, who believe that they have an information advantage, seek to outperform the hedger by buying or selling futures contracts in conjunction with—or opposite from—the hedger. This trading may be on a micro-second time scale or a multi-month perspective. For example, if a speculator has a superior weather prediction process, he or she has an information advantage and will trade accordingly. Alternatively, a speculator may be willing to act as a liquidity provider, knowing that producers and consumers may not be in the market at the same time. By buying when the producer wants to sell and selling when the consumer is ready to buy, speculators may be able to make a profit. In this sense, speculators are willing to step in, under the right pricing circumstances, to provide insurance to hedgers in return for an expected (albeit not guaranteed) profit.

Finally, arbitrageurs who have the ability to inventory physical commodities can attempt to capitalize on mispricing between the commodity (along with related storage and financing cost) and the futures price. They may own the storage facilities (bonded warehouses, grain silos, feedlots) and work to manage that inventory in conjunction with the futures prices to attempt to make arbitrage-style profits.

5.1.3. Commodity Exchanges

Commodity futures markets are found throughout the world. The CME and ICE are the primary US markets, having consolidated the bulk of the various specialist exchanges. Elsewhere in the Americas, the primary commodity exchange is in Brazil, where B3 trades softs, grains, and livestock. In Europe, the London Metal Exchange (owned by Hong Kong Exchanges and Clearing Limited (HKEX) is the main industrial metals location globally. Energy and shipping are also traded out of London. In Asia, major commodity exchanges include China's Dalian Commodity Exchange and Shanghai Futures Exchange and Japan's Tokyo Commodity Exchange, among others. Finally, Indonesia (palm oil), Singapore (rubber), and Australia (energy, grains, wool) have supplementary commodity futures markets. Given that people all over the world need food, energy, and materials, exchanges have formed globally to meet those needs.

5.1.4. Commodity Market Analysts

Non-market participants use the exchange information to perform research and conduct policy as well as to facilitate market participation. Their activities affect market behavior, albeit in an indirect manner. Research may be commercially based. For example, a manufacturer may want to project and forecast the energy cost of a new process or product as part of an academic study comparing one market structure with another. Commodity prices are a key component in understanding sources of inflation and are used in other indexes that indicate quality of life for consumers and households. Governments that control natural resource extraction (e.g., nationalized oil companies) or tax commodity extraction by private entities are also interested in understanding futures markets to promote or discourage investment and/or raise revenue.

5.1.5. Commodity Regulators

Finally, various regulatory bodies monitor the global commodity markets. In the United States, commodity and futures regulation falls under the Commodity Futures Trading Commission (CFTC), which is a regulatory body separate from the better-known Securities and Exchange Commission. The CFTC delegates much of the direct monitoring to the National Futures Association (NFA)—a self-regulatory body—whose members are the authorized direct participants in the markets with customer responsibilities (e.g., clearing firms, brokers, advisers).

Outside the United States, most other countries have a unified regulatory structure. For example, the China Securities Regulatory Commission regulates both futures and securities (i.e., stocks and bonds). In Europe, most legislation in the area of financial services is initiated at the European Union (EU) level primarily through the European Securities and Markets Authority (ESMA). The Markets in Financial Instruments Directive (MiFID, and subsequently MiFID II), which first came into force in 2007, was a key element of EU financial market integration that focused largely on deregulation (MiFID II took effect in January 2018). Since 2009, existing legislative instruments, particularly for commodity derivative markets, have been revised and new regulations have been introduced with the aim to strengthen oversight and regulation, and they are subject to G–20 commitments. Harmonizing these different regulatory bodies is the International Organization of Securities Commissions (IOSCO), which is the international association of the world's securities and futures markets.

In all regions, the interests of the financial sector strongly influence debates and legislation on financial market regulation, including that of commodities.

EXAMPLE 8   Commodity Market Participants

Commodity traders that often provide insurance to hedgers are *best* described as:

A. arbitrageurs.
B. liquidity providers.
C. informed investors.

Solution: B is correct. Liquidity providers often play the role of providing an insurance service to hedgers who need to unload and transfer price risk by entering into futures contracts. A is incorrect because arbitrageurs typically seek to capitalize and profit on mispricing due to a lack of information in the marketplace. C is incorrect because informed investors predominantly keep commodity futures markets efficient by capitalizing on mispricing attributable to a lack of information in the marketplace.

6. COMMODITY SPOT AND FUTURES PRICING

Commodity prices are typically represented by (1) spot prices in the physical markets and (2) futures prices for later delivery. The **spot price** is simply the current price to deliver a physical commodity to a specific location or purchase it and transport it away from a designated location. Examples of a spot price may be the price quoted at a grain silo, a natural gas pipeline, an oil storage tank, or a sugar refinery.

A **futures price** is a price agreed on to deliver or receive a defined quantity (and often quality) of a commodity at a future date. Although a producer and a consumer can enter into a bilateral contract to exchange a commodity for money in the future, there are (conveniently) many standardized contracts that trade on exchanges for buyers and sellers to use. Recall that a bilateral agreement is a forward contract, compared with a futures contract that is standardized and trades on a futures exchange. One benefit of futures markets is that information regarding contracts (number, price, etc.) is publicly available. In this way, the price discovery process that brings buyers and sellers into agreement is shared broadly and efficiently (in real time) with a global marketplace among the aforementioned market participants. The longest-maturity futures contract outstanding can have maturity extending from about a year (e.g., livestock) to several years (e.g., crude oil).

The difference between spot and futures prices is generally called the **basis**. Depending on the specified commodity and its current circumstances (e.g., supply and demand outlook), the spot price may be higher or lower than the futures price. When the spot price exceeds the futures price, the situation is called **backwardation**, and the opposite case is called **contango**. The origin of the word "contango" is a bit murky, but one theory is that it came from the word "continuation" used in the context of the London Stock Exchange in the mid-1800s. During this period, contango was a fee paid by the buyer to the seller to defer settlement of a trade (hence the near-term price would be less expensive than the longer-term price). The term "backwardation" describes the same arrangement if it were "backward," or reversed (i.e., payment to defer settlement was made by the seller to the buyer).

Backwardation and contango are also used to describe the relationship between two futures contracts of the same commodity. When the near-term (i.e., closer to expiration) futures contract price is higher than the longer-term futures contract price, the futures market for the commodity is in backwardation. In contrast, when the near-term futures contract price is lower than the longer-term futures contract price, the futures market for the commodity is in contango. The price difference (whether in backwardation or contango) is called the calendar spread. Generally speaking and assuming stable spot prices, the producer is willing to take a price in the future that is lower than the current spot price because it provides a level of certainty for the producer's business. The seller of that insurance on the other side of the trade profits because the lower futures price converges to the higher spot price over time. This relationship occurs when future commodity prices are expected to be higher because of a variety of reasons related to economic growth, weather, geopolitical risks, supply disruptions, and so on. As a long owner of a futures contract in contango, value will erode over time as the contract pricing moves closer to the spot price, assuming all else is unchanged. This relationship can be very costly for long holders of contracts if they roll futures positions over time. Although backwardation is "normal" for some contracts, there are other commodities that often trade in contango.

Exhibit 6 is a stylized representation of backwardation in West Texas Intermediate crude oil on CME Group's New York Mercantile Exchange (NYMEX).

EXHIBIT 6   Backwardation

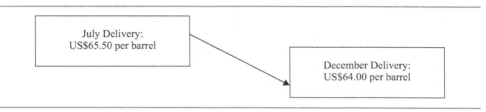

For contracts in a single (common) commodity, such as lean hogs or crude oil, the price differences may be traded as a spread rather than individually.

Exhibit 7 is a stylized representation of contango in lean hogs on the CME.

EXHIBIT 7   Contango

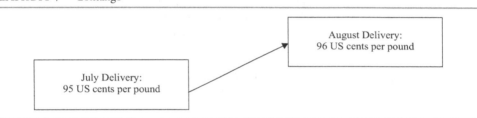

From these examples, the lean hogs July–August calendar spread is −1.0 cent per pound (95 − 96) and the crude oil July–December calendar spread is $1.50 per barrel (65.50 − 64.00).

A positive calendar spread is associated with futures markets that are in backwardation, whereas a negative calendar spread in commodities is associated with futures markets that are in contango. These calendar spreads are traded with their own bid–ask prices, trading range, and order book, similar to the single-month (i.e., nearest to expiration) futures contracts. Note that from this one trade, two contracts (one for each side, or "leg," of the spread) appear on an exchange's trading account and use their respective closing prices to determine profit or loss. Therefore, in the end, all trades and positions are valued at the close-of-day prices.

Commodity futures are settled by either cash or physical delivery. Cash-settled contracts, such as feeder cattle traded on the CME, have no value after the maturity date. Cash settlement is an important innovation in the evolution and development of commodity futures markets. To a certain extent, cash settlement enabled more involvement of two key participants in today's futures markets: speculators and arbitrageurs. It also introduced an entirely new way that hedgers (long or short) could participate in the market to transfer the future price risk of having to sell or buy a commodity without the complications associated with requiring physical delivery. Physical-settled commodity futures contracts require that the title of the actual commodity be transferred by the seller of the futures contract to the buyer at a particular place, on or by a particular date, and of a particular quality specification. For example, under a futures contract with West Texas Intermediate crude oil as the underlying physical commodity, crude oil meeting minimum specifications must be delivered to a particular set of tanks at

Cushing, Oklahoma, in the United States. Meanwhile, a similar futures contract with Brent crude oil as the underlying physical commodity has delivery points in the North Sea off the coast of the United Kingdom and Norway. Supply and demand differences at these two fara-way geographic locations can cause price divergences despite otherwise similar specifications.

Physical delivery also ensures a convergence of the futures and spot markets, which may not necessarily occur in a cash-settled market. Note that this statement does not imply market manipulation in cash-settled markets, because trading costs or other factors may limit complete convergence. The emergence of central exchanges for trading commodity futures facilitated this convergence with standardized contracts. In addition, these exchanges provided centrally established, publicly available pricing, which quickly replaced private pricing that was dependent on both contract terms and the location where transactions occurred.

Physical delivery can become complicated by such factors as quality or variety differences in the commodity. For example, robusta coffee (traded in the United Kingdom) cannot be delivered for arabica coffee (traded in the United States) because it is a different variety of coffee with a different venue for delivery. Likewise, raw (or unprocessed) sugar that is traded in the United States cannot be delivered for white processed sugar that is traded in the United Kingdom. Futures markets can address some of these peculiarities involving quality or differences in supply. When physical delivery is required, some futures contracts require a premium or discount associated with specifications. For example, arabica coffee prices are automatically adjusted based on the country of origin and the location of the warehouse where delivery is made.

In summary, spot prices are highly localized and associated with physical delivery, limiting the degree to which interested participants can seek to hedge or speculate on their future direction. In contrast, futures prices can be global (and if not, at least regional or national) in scope. They also are standardized for trading on exchanges to promote liquidity; act as a reference price point for customized (i.e., forward) contracts; and generate widely available, minimally biased data for market participants and governments to judge supply and demand and to make planning decisions.

In this manner, futures can be used to allocate risk and generate returns for market participants. On the surface, futures trading may seem muddled and chaotic on a micro level but serves as an overall social benefit by sending signals to producers and consumers for hedging and inventory-sizing purposes and to governments for the potential impact of policy decisions.

EXAMPLE 9   Spot and Futures Pricing (1)

The current price of the futures contract nearest to expiration for West Texas Intermediate (WTI) crude oil is $65.00 per barrel, whereas the six-month futures contract for WTI is priced at $60.75 per barrel. Based on this information:

A. the futures market for WTI crude oil is currently in a state of contango.
B. the futures market for WTI crude oil is currently in a state of backwardation.
C. the shipping and delivery cost of WTI crude oil for a futures contract expiring in six months with physical delivery to Cushing, Texas, is $4.25 per barrel.

Solution: B is correct. Commodity futures markets are in a state of backwardation when the spot price is greater than the price of near-term (i.e., nearest to expiration) futures contracts, and correspondingly, the price of near-term futures contracts is greater than longer-term contracts. A is incorrect because the market would be in contango only if the deferred futures price exceeded that of the nearby futures price. C is incorrect because the shipping and delivery costs associated with physical delivery of a commodity are only one component in determining a commodity futures contract price. Geopolitical, seasonal, and other factors also influence the difference in delivery months.

EXAMPLE 10   Spot and Futures Pricing (2)

An important distinction between spot and futures prices for commodities is that:

A. spot prices are universal across regions, but futures prices vary by location.
B. futures prices do not reflect differences in quality or composition for a commodity.
C. spot prices vary across region based on quality/composition and local supply and demand factors.

Solution: C is correct. Spot prices of commodities vary across regions, reflecting logistical constraints and supply and demand imbalances that hinder the movement of materials. A is incorrect because spot prices tend to vary by region while futures are purposely standardized to facilitate trading. B is incorrect because while futures contracts are based on standardized specifications, composition and quality can be assigned premiums or discounts for delivery.

EXAMPLE 11   Spot and Futures Pricing (3)

An arbitrageur has two active positions in the commodity futures markets—one for lean hogs and the other for natural gas. The calendar spread on the lean hogs contract is quoted at −50 cents per pound, and the calendar spread on the natural gas contract is +$1.10 per million BTU (British thermal units). Based on this information, we can say that:

A. only the spreads of these commodities, and not the individual prices, can be traded in commodity markets.
B. the lean hogs futures market is in a state of backwardation and the natural gas futures market is in a state of contango.
C. the lean hogs futures market is in a state of contango and the natural gas futures market is in a state of backwardation.

Solution: C is correct. The spread is the difference between the current spot price for a commodity and the futures contract price. Because futures markets in a state of contango will have futures prices that exceed the spot price, the spread for these markets is negative. Conversely, in a state of backwardation, the spread is positive. A is incorrect because either the individual contract prices or the combined spreads can be traded. B is incorrect because, as mentioned earlier, the negative sign of the spread of lean hogs futures indicates a state of contango, whereas the positive sign of the spread of natural gas futures indicates a state of backwardation.

EXAMPLE 12   Spot and Futures Pricing (4)

A futures price curve for commodities in backwardation:

A. always remains in backwardation in the long term.
B. can fluctuate between contango and backwardation in the long term.
C. reflects structural long-term industry factors, as opposed to dynamic market supply and demand pressures.

Solution: B is correct. During periods of market stress or fundamental structural change in market conditions, some commodity futures price curves can rapidly shift from contango to backwardation or vice versa. A is incorrect because futures price curves can vacillate between contango and backwardation. C is incorrect because the shape of a commodity futures price curve reflects both long-term industry factors as well as market expectations of future supply and demand of the underlying commodity(ies).

---

7. THEORIES OF FUTURES RETURNS

Commodity futures markets have a reputation for volatility, but similar to other asset classes, there are theoretical bases for their long-run behavior. The original purpose of futures markets is for producers and consumers to hedge physical raw materials. In this section, we will discuss the underpinning theories of commodity futures returns, deconstruct the components of futures returns (i.e., at an index level), and close with thoughts on term structure (i.e., contango versus backwardation and implications of rolling futures contracts).

7.1. Theories of Futures Returns

Several theories have been proposed to explain the shape of the futures price curve, which has a dramatic impact on commodity futures returns. This reading covers three of the most important theories: (1) insurance theory, (2) hedging pressure hypothesis, and (3) theory of storage.

7.1.1. Insurance Theory

Keynes (1930), the noted economist and market speculator, proposed one of the earliest known theories on the shape of a commodity futures price curve. Also known as his theory of "normal backwardation," Keynes, in his 1930 tome *A Treatise on Money*, proposed that producers use commodity futures markets for insurance by locking in prices and thus make their revenues more predictable. A commodity producer is long the physical good and thus would be motivated to sell the commodity for future delivery to hedge its sales price. Imagine a farmer who thinks that next year she will grow a certain amount of soybeans on her land. She can sell a portion of her crop today that will be harvested months later to lock in those prices. She can then spend money on fertilizer and seed with more confidence about her budget. She may not be locking in a profit, but she would better understand her financial condition. Keynes's theory assumes that the futures curve is in backwardation "normally" because our farmer would persistently sell forward, pushing down prices in the future. Alternatively, this theory posits that the futures price has to be lower than the current spot price as a form of payment or remuneration to the speculator who takes on the price risk and provides price insurance to the commodity seller. The concept of normal backwardation is illustrated in Exhibit 8, using cotton prices pre- and post-harvest.

EXHIBIT 8   Normal Backwardation

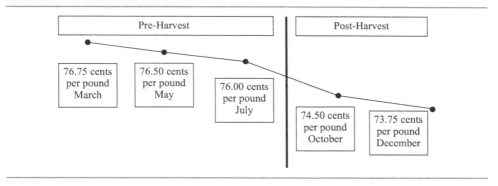

In terms of returns, if the front price is stable (in our example, 76.75 cents), then an investor can buy a further-dated contract (e.g., October) at 74.50 cents and wait for that contract to become the current contract. As the month of October approaches (and assuming no change in front prices), the October contract will reach 76.75 cents at maturity, and the speculator will make a profit of 2.25 cents per pound (note that a contract is 50,000 pounds, so that is a total profit of $1,125 per contract). Even if the contract does not fully converge, this theory holds that there should be positive excess returns (sometimes referred to as the risk premium) via this process to induce buying. As noted earlier, this process acts as a type of insurance for the farmer as well as a return for the investor providing such insurance.

Looking at the evidence, however, markets failed to match Keynes's hypothesis. Kolb (1992) looked at 29 futures contracts and concluded (with some humor) that "normal backwardation is not normal." That is, the presence of backwardation does not necessarily generate positive returns in a statistically significant fashion for the investor (or that contango leads to negative returns, for that matter). This result confirmed other studies, including one by

Fama and French (1987). Therefore, a more sophisticated view developed to explain futures markets in contango (i.e., when the shape of the futures price curve is upward sloping with more distant contract dates), recognizing that certain commodity futures markets often show persistently higher prices in the future as opposed to the backwardation outlined by Keynes. This view is called the hedging pressure hypothesis.

7.1.2. Hedging Pressure Hypothesis

This perspective stemmed from multiple works, most notably outlined by De Roon, Nijman, and Veld (2000), who drew from Cootner (1960). Their research analyzed 20 futures markets from 1986 to 1994 and concluded that hedging pressure plays an important role in explaining futures returns. Hedging pressure occurs when both producers and consumers seek to protect themselves from commodity market price volatility by entering into price hedges to stabilize their projected profits and cash flow. Producers of commodities will tend or want to sell commodities forward and thus sell commodity futures. On the other side, consumers of commodities want to lock in prices of their commodity purchases and buy commodity futures. This theory applies to the aforementioned farmer selling a portion of next year's crop today. It can also apply to a central bank that wants to buy gold during each of the next 12 months as part of its monetary operations or a refinery that may want to lock in the price of its oil purchases and, conversely, the prices of its gasoline and heating oil production.

If the two forces of producers and consumers both seeking price protection are equal in weight, then one can envision a flat commodity curve, such as Exhibit 9 illustrates. In this idealized situation, the natural needs for price insurance by commodity buyers and sellers offset each other. There is no discount on the commodity futures price required to induce speculators to accept the commodity price risk because the hedging needs of both the buyer and seller complement and offset each other.

EXHIBIT 9   Balanced Hedging between Producers and Consumers

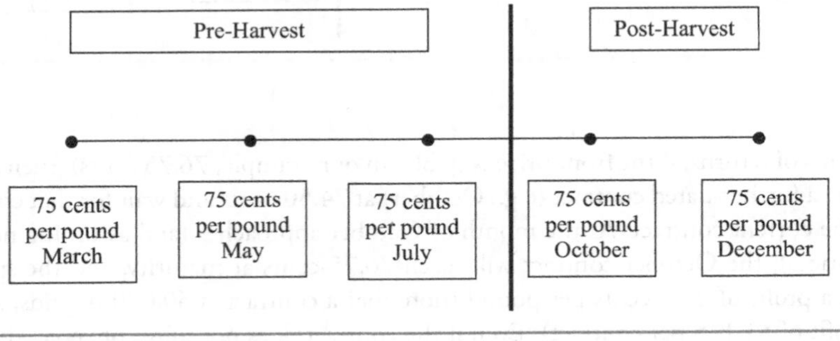

To use a different example, consider the problem of snowfall in the New England region of the United States. On one hand, small municipalities in Vermont, New Hampshire, or Maine may experience high levels of annual snowfall that are a risk to their snow removal budgets. On the other hand, ski resorts in New England have an opposite risk challenge: Low snowfall creates skiing revenue shortfalls (or adds to costs because of the need for man-made snow), whereas high snowfall winters are a potential bonanza for both higher revenue and lower operating costs. This situation is another example of when the hedging needs of two parties can offset each other and create a mutually beneficial outcome.

If commodity producers as a group are more interested in selling forward (seeking price insurance) than commodity consumers (as per the concept of normal backwardation), then the relative imbalance in demand for price protection will lead to the need for speculators to complete the market. But speculators will only do so when futures prices trade at a sufficient discount to compensate for the price risk they will take on. In this case, the shape and structure of the futures price curve can be illustrated as backwardation, as shown in Exhibit 10, which is consistent with Keynes's insurance theory.

EXHIBIT 10   Commodity Producers Exceed Consumers (Backwardation)

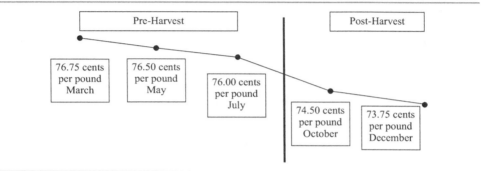

Finally, if the buyers of soybeans (as a group) are especially worried about the availability of the crop in the next harvest but producers of soybeans are less concerned about crop prices, there would be an imbalance in the demand for price insurance away from producers and toward buyers. This situation would lead to a futures price curve that represents a market in contango, as illustrated in Exhibit 11. In this case, the additional demand for price insurance among buyers (versus sellers) of the commodity will lead them to bid up the futures price to induce speculators to take on this price uncertainty risk.

EXHIBIT 11   Commodity Consumers Exceed Producers (Contango)

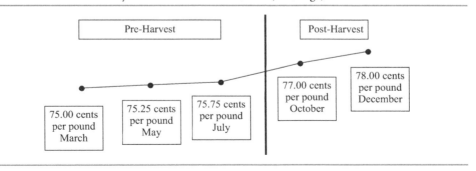

Although this theory is more robust than the Keynes's insurance theory, it is still incomplete. One issue is that producers generally have greater exposure to commodity price risk than consumers do (Hicks 1939). There are companies (as well as countries) that are almost entirely dependent on commodity production and thus are very concentrated in one sector, such as energy (e.g., British Petroleum, ExxonMobil), grains (e.g., Cargill, Louis Dreyfus), and metals (e.g., BHP Billiton, Vale, Rio Tinto, Shenhua).

Commodity consumers, in contrast, are very diffuse and often have other priorities (i.e., few if any individual people hedge their meat consumption or gasoline spending). Companies that purchase and use commodities in their products have a mixed record of price hedging, depending on the importance of the commodities in their cost structure. Clothing companies (e.g., Gap) generally do not hedge cotton because the spending is only a few percentage points of their expense base. Marketing and store experience (seen in rent, occupancy, and depreciation expenses) are much more important. But fast food companies hedge a wide variety of commodity inputs (e.g., livestock, grains, energy) because of the high degree of competition for prepared food at a low price point (e.g., McDonald's, Burger King, Wendy's).

In addition, both producers and consumers speculate on commodity prices, whether it is intended or unintended. Corporate treasury departments that serve as profit centers may adjust their hedges based on their views of the commodity markets. Their primary function may be to hedge, but a profit incentive can lead them to speculate. Individual farmers may not be overly aware of the commodity markets and thus have an inconsistent hedging approach. Trading companies actively trade the futures and physical markets in energy, metals, and grains. The very nature of trading companies is to know what is happening at all times along the value chain of any commodity market and profit from that informational advantage while bringing together buyers and sellers. In their case, profit maximization does not come from the production of commodities but trading around that production. In all of these examples, attempts to hedge may result instead in unintended speculative positions in which a company is not transferring price risk away but instead taking on more risk. The collapse in 1993 of Metallgesellschaft AG, one of Germany's largest industrial conglomerates at the time, from a poorly constructed gasoline, fuel oil, and heating oil hedge is a defining example of flawed commercial hedging.

In summary, despite its intuitive logic, applying the hedging pressure hypothesis remains a challenge because measuring the asymmetry in hedging pressure between buyers and sellers of a commodity is very difficult.

7.1.3. Theory of Storage

This theory, originally postulated by Kaldor (1939), focuses on how the level of commodity inventories helps shape commodity futures price curves. The key issue this theory attempts to address is whether supply or demand of the commodity dominates in terms of its price economics. Recall that commodities are physical assets, not virtual assets like stocks and bonds. Physical assets have to be stored, and storage incurs costs (rent, insurance, inspections, spoilage, etc.). Therefore, a commodity that is regularly stored should have a higher price in the future (contango) to account for those storage costs. In other words, supply dominates demand. In contrast, a commodity that is consumed along a value chain that allows for just-in-time delivery and use (i.e., minimal inventories and storage) can avoid these costs. In this situation, demand dominates supply and current prices are higher than futures prices (i.e., backwardation).

In theoretical terms, available inventory generates a benefit called a convenience yield. Having a physical supply of the commodity available is convenient for consumers of the commodity (e.g., individuals, bread companies, meat processors, refiners) because it acts as a buffer to a potential supply disruption that could otherwise force a shutdown of their operations. Because this type of risk/concern is inversely related to the inventory size and the general availability of the commodity (and confidence in its continued availability), the convenience yield is low when stock is abundant. However, the yield rises as inventories diminish and concerns regarding future availability of the commodity increase.

As a result, the theory of storage states that futures prices can be written this way:

> Futures price = Spot price of the physical commodity + Direct storage costs
> (such as rent and insurance) − Convenience yield.

This equation indicates that price returns and the shape of the curve can move in conjunction with the changes in the available inventory as well as actual and expected supply and demand. For example, when civil war broke out in Libya in 2011, the production of that country's high-quality crude oil was placed in jeopardy, constricting supply. In reaction, the spot price for high-quality crude oil increased. At the same time, the convenience yield increased in the futures contracts closer to expiration because there was a scramble to tap into alternative oil supplies for European refiners. The high quality of Libyan crude oil also restricted which substitute crude oil supplies could be used to replace production from the blocked oil fields and how soon these replacements could be available. The real-world constraints and complications imposed by geography and the logistics of the oil industry resulted in a multi-month delay for replacement supplies. As a result, in the further-out (i.e., longer time to expiration) futures contracts, the reaction was muted as traders assumed that such replacement supplies would be available. Thus the convenience yield remained lower in the deferred months. For this and other reasons, crude oil was pressured to trade in backwardation during 2011.

Unfortunately, while all these theories are reasonable and attractive, they have components that are unobservable or highly volatile and, therefore, not reliably calculable. Commodity producers and consumers regard storage costs as proprietary information. Events (weather, war, technology) can radically adjust convenience yield in a short time with unknown magnitude. Corn suitable for feed may not be suitable for human consumption, so defining inventories is tricky. In the end, we have frameworks and theories, but they are not easily applied and require judgment and analysis by a trader or a valuation system.

EXAMPLE 13   Theories of Commodity Futures Returns (1)

Which of the following *best* describes the insurance theory of futures returns?

A. Speculators will not provide insurance unless the futures price exceeds the spot price.
B. Producers of a commodity will accept a lower future price (versus the spot price) in exchange for the certainty of locking in that price.
C. Commodity futures markets result in a state of contango because of speculators insisting on a risk premium in exchange for accepting price risk.

Solution: B is correct. Under the insurance theory of futures returns, Keynes stated that producers of a commodity would prefer to accept a discount on the potential future spot price in return for the certainty of knowing the future selling price in advance. A is incorrect because the futures price must be below the spot price (normal backwardation) under the insurance theory of futures returns. C is incorrect because the insurance theory of futures returns implies markets are in backwardation, not contango.

EXAMPLE 14   Theories of Commodity Futures Returns (2)

Under the hedging pressure hypothesis, when hedging activity of commodity futures buyers exceeds that of commodity futures sellers, that futures market is *most likely*:

A. flat.
B. in contango.
C. in backwardation.

Solution: B is correct. Under the hedging pressure hypothesis, a market in contango typically results when excess demand for price insurance among commodity futures buyers drives up the futures price to induce speculators to take on price uncertainty risk. A is incorrect because a flat market would likely exist if futures demand activity largely equaled that of supply. C is incorrect because under this scenario, the futures market would be in contango, not backwardation.

EXAMPLE 15   Theories of Commodity Futures Returns (3)

Under the theory of storage, the convenience yield is:

A. not affected by the supply of a commodity.
B. typically low when the supply of a commodity is scarce.
C. typically high when the supply of a commodity is scarce.

Solution: C is correct. Under the theory of storage, the convenience yield of a commodity increases as supply (inventories) diminish and concerns about the future availability increase. A is incorrect because supply levels have a discernible effect on the convenience yield, as mentioned. B is incorrect because the convenience yield would likely be high, as opposed to low, when supply is limited.

EXAMPLE 16   Theories of Commodity Futures Returns (4)

Which of the following represents the formula for a futures price according to the theory of storage?

A. Futures price = Spot price of the physical commodity + Direct storage costs − Convenience yield.
B. Futures price = Spot price of the physical commodity + Direct storage costs + Convenience yield.
C. Futures price = Spot price of the physical commodity − Direct storage costs + Convenience yield.

Solution: A is correct. According to the theory of storage, the futures price reflects the current spot price as well as costs incurred in actually holding the commodity until its delivery. Such costs include direct storage, such as inventory and insurance costs. Finally, because there is a convenience yield (or benefit) to owning a commodity as a form of insurance against potential supply disruptions, this term is subtracted from the current price of the commodity.

8. COMPONENTS OF FUTURES RETURNS

The total return on a commodity investment in futures is different from a total return on the physical assets. So, why do investors tend to use futures to gain their exposure to commodities? Building on the previous section, one can see that physical commodities need to be stored, fed, or perhaps treated against spoilage. Each commodity can be very different in its maintenance requirements; sustaining a hog in Mexico would be very different from storing crude oil in Nigeria.

The total return on commodity futures is traditionally broken into three components:

- the price return (or spot yield),
- the roll return (or roll yield), and
- the collateral return (or collateral yield).

The price return is the change in commodity futures prices, generally the front month contract. Note that this change is different from the change in the price of the physical commodity because lack of standardization of the physical markets makes that a difficult task. Calculating the price return is straightforward, as shown in the following equation:

Price return = (Current price − Previous price)/Previous price.

In addition, as investors move from futures contract to futures contract, they must "roll" that exposure by selling the current contract as it approaches expiration and buying the next contract (assuming a long position). Depending on the shape of the futures curve, there is likely a difference between the two prices. Thus, a portfolio may require buying more far contracts than the near contracts being sold. Investors can observe this scenario if backwardation is driving the shape of the commodity futures price curve.

Example (stylized): Assume an investor has £110 of exposure in wheat futures and the near contract is worth £10 of exposure (so, the investor has £110 exposure divided by £10 per contract, or 11 contracts), but the far (i.e., longer expiration date) contract is worth only £9 of exposure. Therefore, for the investor to roll forward his contracts and maintain a constant level of exposure, he needs to roll the 11 contracts forward and also buy an additional 1 contract to keep the post-roll exposure close to the pre-roll exposure (£110 exposure divided by £9 per contract equals 12.2, or 12 contracts rounded).

In the opposite case, if the futures price curve shape is being driven by contango—with a higher futures price in the far contract—this scenario will require the purchase of fewer commodity contracts than in the near position.

Example: Assume an investor has £108 of exposure in regular unleaded gasoline (or petrol) futures and the near contract is worth £9 of exposure (so, the investor has £108 exposure divided by £9 per contract, or 12 contracts), but the far contract is worth £10 of exposure. Therefore, for the investor to roll forward her contracts and maintain a constant level of exposure, she needs to roll only 11 contracts and sell the extra 1 near contract to keep the post-roll exposure close to the pre-roll exposure (£108 exposure divided by £10 per contract equals 10.8, or 11 contracts rounded).

Note that this roll return is not a return in the sense that it can be independently captured; investors cannot construct a portfolio consisting of only roll returns. Instead, **roll return** is an accounting calculation used to replicate a portion of the total return for a fully collateralized (i.e., with no leverage) commodity index. As defined, the roll return is effectively the accounting difference (in percentage terms) between the near-term commodity futures contract price and the farther-term commodity futures contract price (note that roll return is sometimes defined in monetary terms rather than as a percentage):

Roll return = [(Near-term futures contract closing price − Farther-term futures contract closing price)/Near-term futures contract closing price] × Percentage of the position in the futures contract being rolled.

As an example, consider the roll from the March contract to the April contract for WTI crude oil on 7 February 2019 using the S&P GSCI methodology, which rolls its positions over a five-day period (so 1/5 = 20% per day):

March contract closing price: $52.64/barrel
April contract closing price: $53.00/barrel
($52.64 − $53.00)/$52.64 = −0.68% gross roll return × 20% rollover portion
                                      = −0.13% net roll return (note the negative return in contango).

Note that different indexes use different periods and/or weights in their "rolling methodology." In Section 11, we will further discuss the rolling methodology of various indexes.

In his book *Expected Returns*, Ilmanen (2011) made the argument (challenged by others) that roll return is approximately equal to a risk premium. This concept relates back to Keynes and his theory of "normal backwardation." Keynes proposed that speculators take the other side of the transaction from commodity producers—who sell forward to lock in their cash flows—in an attempt to earn an excess return as compensation for providing price insurance to producers. Ilmanen attempted to demonstrate that positive long-run average returns are associated with positive roll return (i.e., in commodities for which futures prices are in backwardation) and negative long-run average returns are associated with negative roll return. However, because 40% of the commodities examined by Ilmanen (p. 255) had negative roll returns but positive total returns, one cannot directly conclude that backwardation earns a positive total return.

The **collateral return** is the yield (e.g., interest rate) for the bonds or cash used to maintain the investor's futures position(s). The minimum amount of funds is called the initial margin. If an investor has less cash than required by the exchange to maintain the position, the broker who acts as custodian will require more funds (a margin call) or close the position (buying to cover a short position or selling to eliminate a long position). Collateral thus acts as insurance for the exchange that the investor can pay for losses.

For return calculations on indexed investments, the amount of cash would be considered equal to the notional value of the futures. This approach means no leverage. For expected returns, commonly, investors should use a risk-free government bond that most closely matches the term projected. Most commodity indexes use short-term US Treasury bills, but if one is forecasting 10-year returns, then for collateral return purposes, a 10-year constant maturity government bond would have a more appropriate term.

Although indexes will be discussed more fully later in the reading, to illustrate the commodity return elements just discussed, one can use an index—in this case, the aforementioned S&P GSCI, which has one of the longest backtested and live history of the investable commodity indexes. Exhibit 12 shows the disaggregation of its return components.

EXHIBIT 12   Average Annual Return Components of the S&P GSCI, January 1970–March 2019

S&P GSCI Return	Total Return	Spot Return	Roll Return[1]	Collateral Return[1]
Return[2]	6.8%	3.0%	−1.3%	5.0%
Risk[3]	19.8%	19.8%	4.2%	1.1%
Correlation[4]		0.97	−0.11	−0.14

[1] Roll return is defined as the excess return on the S&P GSCI minus the spot of the S&P GSCI. Collateral return is defined as the total return on the S&P GSCI minus the excess return of the S&P GSCI. The excess return measures the returns accrued from investing in uncollateralized nearby commodity futures.

[2] Monthly returns are used.

[3] Risk is defined as annualized standard deviation.

[4] Correlation with the S&P GSCI Total Return.

Source: Author's research based on data from S&P Dow Jones Indices.

As can be seen in the table, over the past 40+ years, the S&P GSCI generated 6.8% in geometrically compounded annualized returns, with about three-quarters derived from interest rates (collateral return). The commodity price spot return component of the index (which has varied over time) contributed to approximately 45% of the total return (3.0% out of 6.8%), whereas the roll return subtracted from the overall return by −1.3% (or 130 bps) on an annualized basis. Investors can see the effect of commodities on inflation via the price return.

The volatility and correlations of the components of index returns are driven by the changes in the spot price return (effectively the same annualized standard deviation of 19.8% as the S&P GSCI with a 97% correlation). The roll return and collateral return do not drive, in general, the monthly returns historically. This link between commodity futures prices and commodity total return indexes helps to define commodities as a separate and investable asset class.

In summary, the total return on a fully collateralized commodity futures contract can be described as the spot price return plus the roll return plus collateral return (risk-free rate return). With an index, a return from rebalancing the index's component weights—a **rebalance return**—would also be added. Using historical data (at the risk of it becoming outdated over time), one can demonstratively use the total return deconstruction to analyze commodities.

EXAMPLE 17   Total Returns for Futures Contracts (1)

A commodity futures market with pricing in backwardation will exhibit which of the following characteristics?

A. The roll return is usually negative.
B. Rolling an expiring futures contract forward will require buying more contracts in order to maintain the same dollar position in the futures markets.
C. Rolling an expiring futures contract forward will require buying fewer contracts in order to maintain the same dollar position in the futures markets.

Solution: B is correct. Commodity futures markets in backwardation exhibit price curves in which longer-dated futures prices are priced lower than near-dated contracts and the nearest-dated contract is priced lower than the current spot price. With a lower futures price on the futures curve, rolling contracts forward in backwardation would require purchasing more contracts to maintain the same dollar position. A is incorrect because the roll return is usually positive, not negative, in markets in backwardation. C is incorrect because an investor would need to purchase more, not fewer, contracts in markets in backwardation to maintain his or her total dollar position.

EXAMPLE 18   Total Returns for Futures Contracts (2)

An investor has realized a 5% price return on a commodity futures contract position and a 2.5% roll return after all her contracts were rolled forward. She had held this position for one year with collateral equal to 100% of the position at a risk-free rate of 2% per year. Her total return on this position (annualized excluding leverage) was:

A. 5.5%.
B. 7.3%.
C. 9.5%.

Solution: C is correct. Total return on a commodity futures position is expressed as

Total return = Price return + Roll return + Collateral return.

In this case, she held the contracts for one year, so the price return of 5% is an annualized figure. In addition, the roll return is also an annual 2.5%. Her collateral return equals 2% per year × 100% initial collateral investment = 2%.

So, her total return (annualized) is

Total return = 5% + 2.5% + 2% = 9.5%.

EXAMPLE 19   Total Returns for Futures Contracts (3)

An investor has a $10,000 position in long futures contracts (for a hypothetical commodity) that he wants to roll forward. The current contracts, which are close to expiration, are valued at $4.00 per contract, whereas the longer-term contract he wants to roll into is valued at $2.50 per contract. What are the transactions—in terms of buying and selling new contracts—he needs to execute in order to maintain his current exposure?

A. Close out (sell) 2,500 near-term contracts and initiate (buy) 4,000 of the longer-term contracts.
B. Close out (buy) 2,500 near-term contracts and initiate (sell) 4,000 of the longer-term contracts.
C. Let the 2,500 near-term contracts expire and use any proceeds to purchase an additional 2,500 of the longer-term contracts.

Solution: A is correct. To roll over the same level of total exposure ($10,000), he will need to do the following:

Sell

$10,000/$4.00 per contract = 2,500 existing contracts.

And replace this position by purchasing

$10,000/$2.50 per contract = 4,000 existing contracts.

---

9. CONTANGO, BACKWARDATION, AND THE ROLL RETURN

To reiterate, contango and backwardation—and the resulting roll return—fundamentally reflect underlying supply and demand expectations and are accounting mechanisms for the commodity term structure. We can gain a sense of these patterns by again examining the history of an index. Recall that from January 1970 to March 2019, the historical roll return of the S&P GSCI subtracted 1.3% from the average annual total return, with a standard deviation of 4.7%. That historical roll return varied over this time period, as depicted in Exhibit 13.

EXHIBIT 13   Historical One-Year S&P GSCI Price and Roll Return (Monthly Returns, January 1970–December 2019)

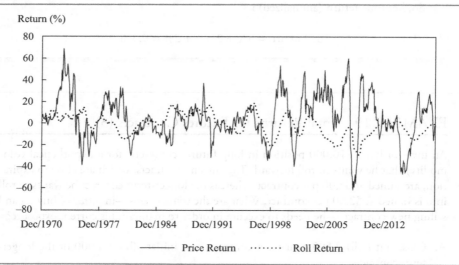

Note: The roll return is rolling monthly.

As the graph shows, periods of either backwardation or contango do not persist indefinitely. A simple review of the Exhibit 13 history demonstrates as much. Furthermore, with a correlation of 3%, roll return is not very indicative of price return, also contrary to popular belief. Positive price returns are associated with negative roll returns as well as positive roll returns. In some cases, certain sectors are indeed associated with contango, as can be seen in Exhibit 14.

EXHIBIT 14   Average Annual Sector Roll Return and Standard Deviation[a]

	S&P GSCI Total	Energy	Industrial Metals	Agriculture	Livestock	Precious Metals	Softs
Mean roll return (annual)[b]	−1.3%	−1.5%	−1.3%	−4.5%	−1.1%	−5.1%	−5.5%
Standard deviation of the mean (annual)[b]	0.4%	0.8%	0.5%	0.4%	0.5%	0.2%	0.6%

EXHIBIT 14   (Continued)

	S&P GSCI Total	Energy	Industrial Metals	Agriculture	Livestock	Precious Metals	Softs
Maximum roll return (annual)[b]	18.9%	31.5%	45.9%	29.2%	35.5%	−0.4%	25.6%
Minimum roll return (annual)[b]	−29.6%	−39.5%	−16.6%	−18.6%	−31.2%	−15.4%	−24.9%

[a] The periods covered vary by sector:
- S&P GSCI total: December 1969–March 2019
- Energy: December 1982–March 2019
- Industrial metals: December 1976–March 2019
- Agriculture: December 1969–March 2019
- Livestock: December 1969–March 2019
- Precious metals: December 1972–March 2019
- Softs: December 1994–March 2019

[b] Calculated using rolling 12-month periods of monthly data.

Sources: Based on data from Bloomberg and Coloma Capital Futures.

Exhibit 14 highlights a few important factors. First, industrial metals, agriculture, livestock, precious metals, and softs have statistically strong negative mean roll returns. Only energy has a statistical possibility of a positive mean roll return, but that opportunity has diminished after 2010. Note from our comparison of the commodity sectors that industrial metals, agriculture, livestock, precious metals, and softs are stored for extended periods in warehouses, silos, and feedlots. In fact, precious metals historically have had negative roll returns because of gold's perpetual storage as an alternative currency. Historically, energy is consumed on a real-time basis apart from various strategic reserves, with the minimal storage buffer thus creating a lower or negative convenience yield. However, since 2010, the emergence of shale oil production in the United States has increased oil's convenience yield to the point that historical scarcity risk is much lower than before. Also, oil supply risk has shifted to China during this period as that country took over the United States' position as the lead oil importer. Finally, OPEC (with the inclusion of Russia and a few other non-OPEC members) regained some pricing power as the cartel achieved some success with supply restriction. Bringing it all together, one can conclude that indexes and long-only strategies that overweight agriculture, livestock, precious metals, and softs should expect to see negative roll returns (or roll yields). Energy commodities (apart from natural gas) have an opportunity for positive roll return, assuming producers successfully withhold supply from the market.

In conclusion, roll return can have an important impact on any single period return but overall has been relatively modest compared with price return. Furthermore, roll return is very sector dependent, which leads to a conclusion that sector diversification or concentration will have a profound impact on an investor's overall roll return based on a diversified portfolio of commodity futures.

EXAMPLE 20   Roll Return

When measuring its contribution to the total return of a commodity futures position, the roll return:

A. typically has a significant contribution to total return over both single and multiple periods.
B. typically has a modest contribution to total return in any single period but can be significant over multiple periods.
C. is always close to zero.

Solution: B is correct. Historically, the roll return has had a relatively modest impact on overall commodity futures return in the short term but can be meaningful over longer time periods. A is incorrect because the roll return is typically modest over shorter periods of time, as noted earlier. C is incorrect because futures contracts generate positive or negative roll returns, depending on the commodity and prevailing market conditions.

10. COMMODITY SWAPS

Instead of futures, some investors can gain market exposure to or hedge risk of commodities via swaps. A **commodity swap** is a legal contract involving the exchange of payments over multiple dates as determined by specified reference prices or indexes relating to commodities. In the world of commodities, a series of futures contracts often forms the basis of the reference prices. For example, an independent oil refiner may want to hedge its oil purchases over an extended period. The refiner may not want to manage a large number of futures contracts but maintain flexibility with regard to its oil supply source. By entering into a swap contract—particularly one that is cash settled instead of physically settled—the refiner can be protected from a price spike and yet maintain flexibility of delivery.

Based on this example, one can see why commercial participants use swaps: The instrument provides both risk management and risk transfer while eliminating the need to set up and manage multiple futures contracts. Swaps also provide a degree of customization not possible with standardized futures contracts. The refiner in the example may negotiate a swap for a specific quality of crude oil (e.g., Heavy Louisiana Sweet instead of West Texas Intermediate, or WTI) as its reference price or a blend of crudes that shifts throughout the year depending on the season. Customization through the use of a swap may also have value by changing the quantity of crude oil hedged over time, such as lowering the exposure during the planned shutdown and maintenance periods at the refinery.

On the other side of the transaction from the refiner (or other hedging or speculating entity) would be a swap dealer, typically a financial intermediary, such as a bank or trading company. The dealer, in turn, may hedge its price risk exposure assumed in the swap through the futures market or, alternatively, negotiate its own swap with another party or arrange an oil purchase contract with a crude oil producer. The dealer may also choose to keep the price risk exposure, seeking to profit from its market information. A diagram demonstrating this swap transaction is shown in Exhibit 15.

EXHIBIT 15   Swap Market Participant Structure

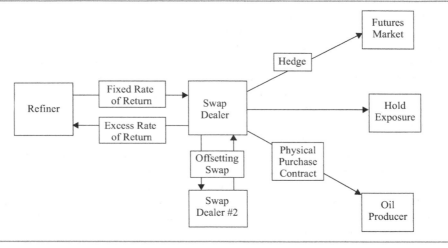

To further understand the diagram in Exhibit 15, assume we had the following scenario:

1. An oil refiner goes long a swap at the end of December that pays the amount exceeding $70 per barrel every month-end through September.
2. The oil refiner would pay a swap counterparty a premium (in this example, $25) for this privilege because it is effectively long a series of call options.

The flow of funds in the swap transaction would be as shown in Exhibit 16.

EXHIBIT 16   Flow of Funds for Swap Transaction Example

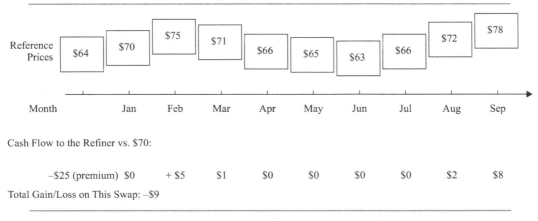

Total gain/loss on this swap to the refiner is −$9 (found by summing the cash flows and ignoring present value calculations or other considerations).

Although this example of a swap lost money and effectively increased the refiner's cost of a barrel of oil by $1 for this time period (given that the net loss on the swap was $9 over nine months), the swap protected the company against the risk of a cash squeeze during those months when an oil price spike could have impaired the liquidity of the company. The swap also defined the cost up front, giving a measure of cash flow predictability. Note that accounting standards and practices for swaps may also have an impact on the attractiveness of swaps. Given that oil prices are subject to many events beyond a company's control, a company looking to protect itself from financing risk may find that a swap can be a valuable tool.

There are many types of swaps available in the marketplace because they are not standardized, exchange-traded contracts like futures. The previous example of the refiner is an example of an "excess return swap." In an excess return swap, the payments to either party are driven primarily by the changes in price of each of the futures contracts that make up the index. The net change in the prices of the underlying futures contracts is defined as the "excess" return, and the excess return is multiplied by the contract's notional amount to determine the payments between buyer and seller.

10.1. Total Return Swap

Another common swap in commodities is a "total return swap." In a total return swap, the change in the level of the index will be equal to the returns generated by the change in price of each of the futures contracts that make up the index plus a return based on interest earned on any cash collateral posted on the purchase of the futures contracts that make up the index. If the level of the index increases, the swap buyer receives payment net of the fee paid to the seller; if the level of the index decreases between two valuation dates, the swap seller receives payment (plus the fee charged to the buyer). This type of swap is generally used by large institutional investors (e.g., pension plans) as opposed to commodity producers or buyers. With a total return swap, the investor seeks exposure to commodity returns, often because of the low return correlation of commodities with other asset classes (e.g., stocks or bonds) or as a reflection of the view that commodities provide a valuable inflation hedge for asset/liability matching (ALM). Therefore, such investors would engage in a total return swap that provides them with long exposure to the future returns from a commodity index that is used as the reference price. Again, accounting treatment with respect to futures often drives these decisions.

As an example of a total return swap, assume an investor who manages a defined benefit retirement plan desires commodity exposure for the reasons noted earlier. Given the size of the portfolio manager's plan assets (assume £2 billion), the manager is seeking approximately 5% exposure of plan assets to commodities. More specifically, the manager has decided that this £100 million exposure (5% of £2 billion) should be to the (hypothetical) China Futures Commodity Index (CFCI) and should remain for five years. Based on this decision, the manager issues a request for proposals (RFP) and, after evaluating the various bidders, contracts with a Swiss bank for a total return swap that will provide the desired exposure.

If on the first day of the swap agreement the CFCI increased by 1%, then the swap dealer would owe the manager £1 million (£100 million × 1%). If on the second day the CFCI declined by 5%, then the manager would owe £5 million to the dealer. Commonly, the dealer will hedge its short index exposure with futures or the physical commodity investments. Because the manager would be seeking the risk–return exposure offered by commodities, the manager would not generally hedge its exposure.

10.2. Basis Swap

Another common commodity swap is a basis swap, in which periodic payments are exchanged based on the values of two related commodity reference prices that are not perfectly correlated. These swaps are often used to adjust for the difference (called the basis) between a highly liquid futures contract in a commodity and an illiquid but related material. For example, a swap may pay the difference between the average daily prices of Brent crude oil (very liquid) and heavy crude oil available for delivery in the Gulf of Mexico (less liquid). This can be a very valuable arrangement for, in this example, refineries on the US Gulf Coast that have heavily invested in processing cheaper heavy crudes that come from such countries as Mexico or Venezuela. Because prices of these crudes do not always move in tandem with more common crudes, such as Brent, they derive a price basis between the two. It should be noted that "basis" has other meanings as well, depending on the commodity in question. For example, in grains, the basis may refer to the difference between the soybean contract and physical soybeans available for delivery at the Mississippi River.

10.3. Variance Swaps and Volatility Swaps

Two final types of relatively common commodity swaps are variance swaps and volatility swaps. Variance swaps of commodities are similar in concept to variance swaps of equities in that there is a variance buyer and a variance seller. Two parties agree to periodically exchange payments based on the proportional difference between an observed/actual variance in the price levels of a commodity (over consecutive time periods), and some fixed amount of variance established at the outset of the contract. If this difference is positive, the variance swap buyer receives a payment; if it is negative, the variance swap seller receives payment. Often the variance differences (observed versus fixed) are capped to limit upside and losses.

Volatility commodity swaps are very similar to variance swaps, with the exception that the direction and amount of payments are determined relative to the observed versus expected volatility for a reference price commodity. In this arrangement, the two sides are not speculating on the level or direction of prices but instead on how volatile prices will be versus expectations. A volatility seller will profit if realized volatility is lower than expectations, whereas the counterparty volatility buyer anticipates higher than expected volatility.

EXAMPLE 21   Commodity Swaps (1)

A portfolio manager enters into a $100 million (notional) total return commodity swap to obtain a long position in commodity exposure. The position is reset monthly against a broad-based commodity index. At the end of the first month, the index is up 3%, and at the end of the second month, the index declines 2%. What are two payments that would occur between the portfolio manager and the swap dealer on the other side of the swap transaction?

A. No payments are exchanged because a net cash flow only occurs when the swap agreement expires.

B. $3 million would be paid by the swap dealer to the portfolio manager (after Month 1), and $2 million would be paid by the portfolio manager to the swap dealer (after Month 2).

C. $3 million would be paid by the portfolio manager to the swap dealer (after Month 1), and $2 million would be paid by the swap dealer to the portfolio manager (after Month 2).

Solution: B is correct. Because the portfolio manager has a long position in the total return commodity swap, he or she will receive payments when the commodity index rises and make payments when the commodity index declines. The payment calculations after the first two months are as follows:

Month 1: $100 million × 3% = $3 million.
Month 2: $100 million × −2% = −$2 million.

A is incorrect because swap payments are made periodically (in this case monthly) and not withheld to the end of the contract. C is incorrect because the payments would be in the opposite direction for each month.

EXAMPLE 22   Commodity Swaps (2)

In a commodity volatility swap, the direction and amount of payments are determined relative to the observed versus reference:

A. direction in the price of a commodity.
B. variance for the price of a commodity.
C. volatility for the price of a commodity.

Solution: C is correct. In a commodity volatility swap, the two sides of the transaction are speculating on expected volatility. A volatility seller will profit if realized volatility is lower than expectations, whereas the volatility buyer benefits from higher than expected volatility. A is incorrect because a volatility swap is based on price volatility, not direction. B is incorrect because a volatility swap is based on price volatility as opposed to price variance (price volatility squared).

---

11. COMMODITY INDEXES

As in other parts of the investment universe, indexes have been created to portray the aggregate movement of commodity prices, investment vehicles, and investing approaches. In fact, one could say that an asset class does not exist without the presence of at least one representative index.

Commodity indexes play three primary roles in commodity sector investments. First, an index can be used as a benchmark to evaluate broader moves in commodity pricing. Second, as a broad indicator, an index can be used for macroeconomic or forecasting purposes by examining statistically significant relationships between movements in the commodity index and other macroeconomic variables. Finally, an index can act as the basis for an investment vehicle or contract providing the information needed to record, monitor, and evaluate price changes that affect contract value.

Although there are a number of commodity indexes, the following are used most frequently for the purposes just mentioned: (1) the S&P GSCI; (2) the Bloomberg Commodity Index (BCOM), formerly known as the Dow Jones–UBS Commodity Index (DJ–UBS); (3) the Deutsche Bank Liquid Commodity Index (DBLCI); (4) the Thomson Reuters/CoreCommodity CRB Index (TR/CC CRB); and (5) the Rogers International Commodities Index (RICI). The following are key characteristics that differentiate each of these indexes:

- The *breadth* of coverage (number of commodities and sectors) included in each index, noting that some commodities have multiple reference contracts (e.g., for crude oil, the common contracts are for West Texas Intermediate in the United States and Brent crude for Europe).
- The relative *weightings* assigned to each component/commodity and the related methodology for how these weights are determined.
- The *rolling methodology* for determining how those contracts that are about to expire are rolled over into future months. This decision has a direct impact on the roll return (or yield) of the overall commodity. Recall that roll return is one of the three key components of overall commodity returns.
- The methodology and frequency for *rebalancing* the weights of the individual commodities, sectors, and contracts in the index to maintain the relative weightings assigned to each investment. As with stocks and bonds within a portfolio, the opportunity to earn positive rebalance returns for commodities depends on the correlation of the underlying components of the index and the propensity of underperforming components to revert back to the mean. For example, a drought may cause cotton prices to increase, but a strong crop the following year will cause prices to collapse. A rebalance sale of the overvalued cotton exposure into an undervalued exposure should "lock in" some of that gain. The rebalance return will likely vary depending on the methodology used by the index.
- The *governance* of indexes is important because it is the process by which all the aforementioned rules are implemented. For example, some indexes are rules-based, whereas others are selection-based. The rules-based indexes follow a quantitative methodology, whereas selection-based indexes are more qualitative in that an index committee picks the commodities. Also, governance oversees the independence of index providers so that, according to best practices of the Index Industry Association, the asset price should be independent from the index provider, which, in turn, should be independent from the product provider (e.g., the exchange-traded fund or swap provider).

For the index to be a viable and useful construct, it should be investable; that is, investors or their agents should be able to replicate the methodology outlined to translate the index concept into a representation of the asset class. For this reason, index providers and investors must be mindful of the venues (physical or electronic) for trading each commodity index, the liquidity and turnover of contracts based on each commodity index, and the term structure of each index (i.e., how far into the future the index extends and which months it covers). The weighting method for components in an index is key to diversification and—combined with rebalancing frequency—influences the opportunity to earn positive rebalance returns.

An index that requires investments in exchanges all over the world is more difficult and expensive for an investor to replicate. An emphasis on illiquid contracts has a negative impact on transaction costs. Contracts without a full yield curve may be a challenge to analyze and trade. In other words, seemingly small execution concerns are magnified when constructing a benchmark that represents an entire asset class, such as commodities. And indexes that choose (perhaps inadvertently) contracts that more commonly trade in backwardation may appear to improve forward-looking performance (because this generates a positive roll return), whereas those that more commonly trade in contango may hurt performance. Exhibit 17 summarizes the various elements of the main indexes discussed.

EXHIBIT 17   Overview of Major Commodity Indexes

	Index				
Element	S&P GSCI	BCOM	DBLCI	TR/CC CRB	RICI
Adoption date	1991	1998	2003	2005 (current version)	1998
Number of commodities	24	23	14	19	38
Weighting method	Production weighted	Production and liquidity weighted	Fixed weight	Fixed weight	Fixed weight
Rolling methodology	Nearby most liquid contract, monthly	Front month to next or second month	Optimized on roll return	Front month to next month	Front month to next month
Rebalancing frequency	Annually	Annually	Annually	Monthly	Monthly
Individual investor funds available?	Yes	Yes	Yes	Yes in some jurisdictions as well as an exchange-traded fund on a related index	Yes

Note: Information is as of 30 April 2019.
Sources: Information from respective sponsor websites, Bloomberg, and authors' research.

Exhibit 17 helps distinguish the key characteristics that differentiate these five commercially important commodity indexes. In terms of coverage (the number of commodities and sectors included in the index), all five of these indexes have broad sector coverage, including energy, grains, livestock, precious metals, industrial metals, and softs. The only exception is the DBLCI, which does not have any livestock exposure. At the other extreme, the RICI includes relatively exotic (and thus illiquid) commodities, such as lumber, oats, and rubber. As a further example of its unique nature, the RICI once included adzuki beans (the red beans found in many Asian cuisines) and palm oil.

11.1. S&P GSCI

The S&P GSCI is the second oldest of the selected commodity indexes. The index is based on 24 commodities and applies liquidity screens to include only those contracts with an established minimum level of trading volume and available historical pricing. It uses a world production value-weighting scheme that gives the largest weight to the most valuable commodity on the basis of physical trade value. It should be no surprise that crude oil has the highest single weight and energy has the highest sector weight (historically as high as 80%) in this index. This approach is most similar to a market-capitalization weighted index of nearly all major bond and stock market indexes. Like some market-capitalization indexes (particularly in emerging or frontier markets), the resulting weights of the S&P GSCI can be highly concentrated. The rolling methodology focuses on owning the front (i.e., near-term) contracts to address the highest liquidity and where supply and demand shocks are most likely to have an impact.

11.2. Bloomberg Commodity Index

The BCOM (formerly the DJ–UBS) is based on 23 commodities. It includes liquidity as both a weighting factor and a screening factor, although the index is selection-based, meaning a committee uses judgment to pick the included commodities. The rules of index construction also place caps on the size of the sectors (33% maximum) and floors on individual commodities (2% minimum). These differences mean that very different index composition and weights can occur. For example, the energy sector currently dominates the S&P GSCI (as high as 80% weight), whereas the BCOM's exposure is much lower (approximately 30%). However, exposure to natural gas as a single component of energy is higher in the BCOM (approximately 9%) than in the S&P GSCI (approximately 3%). Given that natural gas had an annualized roll cost of about 19% (often the highest roll cost of all the commodities), the higher weighting of natural gas in the BCOM implies that the index has to find other sources of return (e.g., price return and rebalance return) to overcome the drag that natural gas inventory storage creates through negative roll return. The rolling methodology focuses on owning the front (i.e., near-term) contracts.

11.3. Deutsche Bank Liquid Commodity Index

The DBLCI uses a fixed-weighting scheme to allocate exposure. The most notable/unique feature of this index is its rolling methodology. Instead of focusing on near-term contracts, it is optimized based on the time value of maximized backwardation/minimized contango for the contracts that fall within the next 12 calendar months. As an example, a June 2014 copper futures contract may be at 1% backwardation versus a May 2014 copper contract. But if the July 2014 copper contract is at a 3% backwardation (1.5% per month, or 3% divided by two months) versus the 1% backwardation per month on the June 2014 contract, then the DBLCI will roll to the July 2014 contract in preference to the June 2014 contract. Therefore, one could argue the DBLCI takes an active decision with regard to roll return positioning as compared with the other indexes.

11.4. Thomson Reuters/CoreCommodity CRB Index

The TR/CC CRB consists of 19 commodities and is a continuation of the first investable commodity index published by the Commodities Research Bureau in 1978 (although an earlier iteration started in 1957). It uses a fixed-weighting scheme to allocate exposure. An index management committee decides the weights based on a number of factors, including diversification, sector representation, liquidity, and economic importance. It also clusters the fixed weights into a number of tiers. As a result, constituents are moved from tier to tier. The rolling methodology focuses on owning the front (i.e., near-term) contracts that mechanically focus on the front month or second front month and do not require a particular calculation.

11.5. Rogers International Commodity Index

The RICI uses a fixed-weighting scheme to allocate exposure among 38 different commodities and was designed by investor Jim Rogers in the late 1990s. An index management committee decides the weights based on a number of factors, including diversification, sector representation, liquidity, and economic importance. Like the TR/CC CRB Index, it also clusters the fixed weights into a number of tiers. As a result, constituents are moved from tier to tier as they gain or lose relative importance as seen by the committee. Energy is the largest weight but is still a highly diversified basket. Some energy constituents are denominated in non-US dollar terms—such as rubber (traded in Japan in Japanese yen) and cocoa (traded in London in British pounds)—which potentially adds a foreign exchange exposure element to the index returns.

11.6. Rebalancing Frequency

Rebalancing frequency plays a role in index returns, especially for those indexes that rebalance more frequently, such as the TR/CC CRB and RICI. Theoretically, from portfolio management theory, rebalancing is more important if a market is frequently mean reverting because there are more peaks to sell and valleys to buy. However, frequent rebalancing can lead to underperformance in a trending market because the outperforming assets are sold but continue up in price, whereas the underperforming assets are purchased but still drift lower.

The relative performance of the monthly rebalanced indexes (TR/CC CRB and RICI) versus the annual rebalance of the other indexes will depend on the length of time of price trends: More frequent mean reversions should favor the former two indexes, but a longer-term trend will more likely favor the annually rebalancing indexes. If an index uses a floating weighting scheme, such as production value (fully or partially), then the higher (lower) futures prices usually coincide with higher (lower) physical prices. Therefore, with this kind of approach, the magnitude of rebalancing weights is generally lower than for a fixed-weight scheme because the post-rebalance weights will generally drift in line with the current portfolio weights. As a result, the S&P GSCI and BCOM indexes typically have lower rebalancing costs and—in a trending market—have an opportunity to outperform their fixed-weight index counterparts, particularly those that have a relatively frequent rebalance period.

11.7. Commodity Index Summary

There is no dominant index based on a particular methodology. Relative performance will occur based on the circumstances of the markets and the time period examined. Evaluating which index is superior for a *long-term* investment generates modest if any value. Per the authors' research, these indexes all have been highly correlated (well above 70%) with each other and have had low (roughly 0%) correlations with traditional asset classes (e.g., US large-cap stocks, US bonds, international stocks). As with equities, for which there are many different index providers, commodity indexes act in parallel even when their returns (and Sharpe ratios) frequently differ dramatically over time.

EXAMPLE 23   Commodity Indexes (1)

All else being equal, compared with an equally weighted commodity index, a production value-weighted index (such as the S&P GSCI) will be:

A. less sensitive to energy sector returns.
B. more sensitive to energy sector returns.
C. equally sensitive to energy sector returns.

Solution: B is correct. The energy sector will make up a sizable portion of a production value-weighted index and thus will be a meaningful driver of returns for such an index. A is incorrect because a production value-weighted index will be more, not less, sensitive to the energy sector. C is incorrect because a production value-weighted index will be more, not equally, sensitive to the energy sector.

EXAMPLE 24   Commodity Indexes (2)

Which of the following statements is *not* correct regarding commodity futures indexes?

A. Commodity sectors in backwardation typically improve index returns.
B. An index that invests in several futures exchanges provides a high degree of diversification.
C. Total returns of the major commodity indexes have low correlation with traditional asset classes, such as equities and bonds.

Solution: B is correct. Commodity futures exchanges throughout the world are highly correlated and thus provide little diversification benefits. A is incorrect because markets in backwardation typically have positive roll yields and thus will likely improve index returns (although the price return may still not be positive and thus the total return may still be negative). C is incorrect because commodity index returns do indeed have historically low correlation with equities and bonds.

SUMMARY

- Commodities are a diverse asset class comprising various sectors: energy, grains, industrial (base) metals, livestock, precious metals, and softs (cash crops). Each of these sectors has a number of characteristics that are important in determining the supply and demand for each commodity, including ease of storage, geopolitics, and weather.
- Fundamental analysis of commodities relies on analyzing supply and demand for each of the products as well as estimating the reaction to the inevitable shocks to their equilibrium or underlying direction.

- The life cycle of commodities varies considerably depending on the economic, technical, and structural (i.e., industry, value chain) profile of each commodity as well as the sector. A short life cycle allows for relatively rapid adjustment to outside events, whereas a long life cycle generally limits the ability of the market to react.
- The valuation of commodities relative to that of equities and bonds can be summarized by noting that equities and bonds represent financial assets whereas commodities are physical assets. The valuation of commodities is not based on the estimation of future profitability and cash flows but rather on a discounted forecast of future possible prices based on such factors as the supply and demand of the physical item.
- The commodity trading environment is similar to other asset classes, with three types of trading participants: (1) informed investors/hedgers, (2) speculators, and (3) arbitrageurs.
- Commodities have two general pricing forms: spot prices in the physical markets and futures prices for later delivery. The spot price is the current price to deliver or purchase a physical commodity at a specific location. A futures price is an exchange-based price agreed on to deliver or receive a defined quantity and often quality of a commodity at a future date.
- The difference between spot and futures prices is generally called the basis. When the spot price is higher than the futures price, it is called backwardation, and when it is lower, it is called contango. Backwardation and contango are also used to describe the relationship between two futures contracts of the same commodity.
- Commodity contracts can be settled by either cash or physical delivery.
- There are three primary theories of futures returns.
  - In insurance theory, commodity producers who are long the physical good are motived to sell the commodity for future delivery to hedge their production price risk exposure.
  - The hedging pressure hypothesis describes when producers along with consumers seek to protect themselves from commodity market price volatility by entering into price hedges to stabilize their projected profits and cash flow.
  - The theory of storage focuses on supply and demand dynamics of commodity inventories, including the concept of "convenience yield."
- The total return of a fully collateralized commodity futures contract can be quantified as the spot price return plus the roll return plus the collateral return (risk-free rate return).
- The roll return is effectively the weighted accounting difference (in percentage terms) between the near-term commodity futures contract price and the farther-term commodity futures contract price.
- A commodity swap is a legal contract between two parties calling for the exchange of payments over multiple dates as determined by several reference prices or indexes.
- The most relevant commodity swaps include excess return swaps, total return swaps, basis swaps, and variance/volatility swaps.
- The five primary commodity indexes based on assets are (1) the S&P GSCI; (2) the Bloomberg Commodity Index, formerly the Dow Jones–UBS Commodity Index; (3) the Deutsche Bank Liquid Commodity Index; (4) the Thomson Reuters/CoreCommodity CRB Index; and (5) the Rogers International Commodities Index.
- The key differentiating characteristics of commodity indexes are
  - the breadth and selection methodology of coverage (number of commodities and sectors) included in each index, noting that some commodities have multiple reference contracts,
  - the relative weightings assigned to each component/commodity and the related methodology for how these weights are determined,
  - the methodology and frequency for rolling the individual futures contracts,

- the methodology and frequency for rebalancing the weights of the individual commodities and sectors, and
- the governance that determines which commodities are selected.

REFERENCES

Cootner, Paul H. 1960. "Returns to Speculators: Telser versus Keynes." *Journal of Political Economy* 68 (4): 396–404. doi:10.1086/258347

De Roon, Frans A., Theo E. Nijman, and Chris Veld. 2000. "Hedging Pressure Effects in Futures Markets." *Journal of Finance* 55 (3): 1437–56. doi:10.1111/0022-1082.00253

Erb, Claude B., and Campbell R. Harvey. 2006. "The Strategic and Tactical Value of Commodity Futures." *Financial Analysts Journal* 62 (2): 69–97. doi:10.2469/faj.v62.n2.4084

Fama, Eugene F., and Kenneth R. French. 1987. "Commodity Futures Prices: Some Evidence on Forecast Power, Premiums and the Theory of Storage." *Journal of Business* 60 (1): 55–73. doi:10.1086/296385

Gorton, Gary, and K. Geert Rouwenhorst. 2006. "Facts and Fantasies about Commodity Futures." *Financial Analysts Journal* 62 (2): 47–68. doi:10.2469/faj.v62.n2.4083

Hicks, John R. 1939. *Value and Capital: An Inquiry into Some Fundamental Principles of Economic Theory.* London: Oxford University Press.

Ilmanen, Antti. 2011. *Expected Returns: An Investor's Guide to Harvesting Market Rewards.* Hoboken, NJ: John Wiley & Sons. doi:10.1002/9781118467190

Kaldor, Nicholas. 1939. "Speculation and Economic Stability." *Review of Economic Studies* 7 (1): 1–27. doi:10.2307/2967593

Keynes, John M. 1930. *The Applied Theory of Money.* vol. 2. A Treatise on Money. London: Macmillan.

Kolb, Robert W. 1992. "Is Normal Backwardation Normal?" *Journal of Futures Markets* 12 (1): 75–91. doi:10.1002/fut.3990120108

PROBLEMS

The following information relates to Questions 1–8

Raffi Musicale is the portfolio manager for a defined benefit pension plan. He meets with Jenny Brown, market strategist with Menlo Bank, to discuss possible investment opportunities. The investment committee for the pension plan has recently approved expanding the plan's permitted asset mix to include alternative asset classes.

Brown proposes the Apex Commodity Fund (Apex Fund) offered by Menlo Bank as a potentially suitable investment for the pension plan. The Apex Fund attempts to produce trading profits by capitalizing on the mispricing between the spot and futures prices of commodities. The fund has access to storage facilities, allowing it to take delivery of commodities when necessary. The Apex Fund's current asset allocation is presented in Exhibit 1.

EXHIBIT 1   Apex Fund's Asset Allocation

Commodity Sector	Allocation (%)
Energy	31.9
Livestock	12.6
Softs	21.7
Precious metals	33.8

Brown explains that the Apex Fund has had historically low correlations with stocks and bonds, resulting in diversification benefits. Musicale asks Brown, "Can you identify a factor that affects the valuation of financial assets like stocks and bonds but does not affect the valuation of commodities?"

Brown shares selected futures contract data for three markets in which the Apex Fund invests. The futures data are presented in Exhibit 2.

EXHIBIT 2   Selected Commodity Futures Data*

Month	Gold Price	Coffee Price	Gasoline Price
July	1,301.2	0.9600	2.2701
September	1,301.2	0.9795	2.2076
December	1,301.2	1.0055	2.0307

* Gold: US$/troy ounce; coffee: US$/pound; gasoline: US$/gallon.

Menlo Bank recently released a report on the coffee market. Brown shares the key conclusion from the report with Musicale: "The coffee market had a global harvest that was greater than expected. Despite the large harvest, coffee futures trading activity is balanced between producers and consumers. This balanced condition is not expected to change over the next year."

Brown shows Musicale the total return of a recent trade executed by the Apex Fund. Brown explains that the Apex Fund took a fully collateralized long futures position in nearby soybean futures contracts at the quoted futures price of 865.0 (US cents/bushel). Three months later, the entire futures position was rolled when the near-term futures price was 877.0 and the farther-term futures price was 883.0. During the three-month period between the time that the initial long position was taken and the rolling of the contract, the collateral earned an annualized rate of 0.60%.

Brown tells Musicale that the pension fund could alternatively gain long exposure to commodities using the swap market. Brown and Musicale analyze the performance of a long position in an S&P GSCI total return swap having monthly resets and a notional amount of $25 million. Selected data on the S&P GSCI are presented in Exhibit 3.

EXHIBIT 3   Selected S&P GSCI Data

Reference Date	Index Level
April (swap initiation)	2,542.35
May	2,582.23
June	2,525.21

1. The Apex Fund is *most likely* to be characterized as:
   A. a hedger.
   B. a speculator.
   C. an arbitrageur.
2. Which factor would *most likely* affect the supply or demand of all four sectors of the Apex Fund?
   A. Weather
   B. Spoilage
   C. Government actions

3. The *most appropriate* response to Musicale's question regarding the valuation factor is:
   A. storage costs.
   B. transportation costs.
   C. expected future cash flows.

4. Which futures market in Exhibit 2 is in backwardation?
   A. Gold
   B. Coffee
   C. Gasoline

5. Based on the key conclusion from the Menlo Bank coffee market report, the shape of the coffee futures curve in Exhibit 2 is *most consistent* with the:
   A. insurance theory.
   B. theory of storage.
   C. hedging pressure hypothesis.

6. Based on Exhibit 2, which commodity's roll returns will *most likely* be positive?
   A. Gold
   B. Coffee
   C. Gasoline

7. The Apex Fund's three-month total return on the soybean futures trade is *closest* to:
   A. 0.85%.
   B. 1.30%.
   C. 2.22%.

8. Based on Exhibit 3, on the June settlement date, the party that is long the S&P GSCI total return swap will:
   A. owe a payment of $552,042.23.
   B. receive a payment of $1,502,621.33.
   C. receive a payment of $1,971,173.60.

The following information relates to Questions 9–15

Jamal Nabli is a portfolio manager at NextWave Commodities (NWC), a commodity-based hedge fund located in the United States. NWC's strategy uses a fixed-weighting scheme to allocate exposure among 12 commodities, and it is benchmarked against the Thomson Reuters/CoreCommodity CRB Index (TR/CC CRB). Nabli manages the energy and livestock sectors with the help of Sota Yamata, a junior analyst.

Nabli and Yamata meet to discuss a variety of factors that affect commodity values in the two sectors they manage. Yamata tells Nabli the following:

Statement 1: Storage costs are negatively related to futures prices.
Statement 2: In contrast to stocks and bonds, most commodity investments are made by using derivatives.
Statement 3: Commodities generate future cash flows beyond what can be realized through their purchase and sale.

Nabli and Yamata then discuss potential new investments in the energy sector. They review Brent crude oil futures data, which are presented in Exhibit 1.

EXHIBIT 1   Selected Data on Brent Crude Oil Futures

Spot Price	Near-Term Futures Price	Longer-Term Futures Price
77.56	73.64	73.59

Yamata presents his research related to the energy sector, which has the following conclusions:

- Consumers have been more concerned about prices than producers have.
- Energy is consumed on a real-time basis and requires minimal storage.

After concluding the discussion of the energy sector, Nabli reviews the performance of NWC's long position in lean hog futures contracts. Nabli notes that the portfolio earned a −12% price return on the lean hog futures position last year and a −24% roll return after the contracts were rolled forward. The position was held with collateral equal to 100% of the position at a risk-free rate of 1.2% per year.

Yamata asks Nabli to clarify how the state of the futures market affects roll returns. Nabli responds as follows:

> **Statement 4:** Roll returns are generally negative when a futures market is in contango.
> **Statement 5:** Roll returns are generally positive when a futures market is in backwardation.

As part of their expansion into new markets, NWC is considering changing its benchmark index. Nabli investigates two indexes as a possible replacement. These indexes both use similar weighting and rebalancing schemes. Index A includes contracts of commodities typically in contango, whereas Index B includes contracts of commodities typically in backwardation. Nabli asks Yamata how the two indexes perform relative to each other in a market that is trending upward.

Because of a substantial decline in drilling activity in the North Sea, Nabli believes the price of Brent crude oil will increase more than that of heavy crude oil. The actual price volatility of Brent crude oil has been lower than its expected volatility, and Nabli expects this trend to continue. Nabli also expects the level of the ICE Brent Index to increase from its current level. Nabli and Yamata discuss how to use swaps to take advantage of Nabli's expectations. The possible positions are (1) a basis swap long on Brent crude oil and short on heavy crude oil, (2) a long volatility swap on Brent crude oil, and (3) a short position in an excess return swap that is based on a fixed level (i.e., the current level) of the ICE Brent Index.

9. Which of Nabli's statements regarding the valuation and storage of commodities is correct?
    A. Statement 1
    B. Statement 2
    C. Statement 3
10. Based on Exhibit 1, Yamata should conclude that the:
    A. calendar spread for Brent crude oil is $3.97.
    B. Brent crude oil futures market is in backwardation.
    C. basis for the near-term Brent crude oil futures contract is $0.05 per barrel.
11. Based on Exhibit 1 and Yamata's research on the energy sector, the shape of the futures price curve for Brent crude oil is most consistent with the:
    A. insurance theory.
    B. theory of storage.
    C. hedging pressure hypothesis.
12. The total return (annualized excluding leverage) on the lean hog futures contract is:
    A. −37.2%.
    B. −36.0%.
    C. −34.8%.

13. Which of Nabli's statements about roll returns is correct?
    A. Only Statement 4
    B. Only Statement 5
    C. Both Statement 4 and Statement 5
14. The *best* response to Nabli's question about the relative performance of the two indexes is that Index B is *most likely* to exhibit returns that are:
    A. lower than those of Index A.
    B. the same as those of Index A.
    C. higher than those of index A.
15. Given Nabli's expectations for crude oil, the *most appropriate* swap position is the:
    A. basis swap.
    B. volatility swap.
    C. excess return swap.

The following information relates to Questions 16–22

Mary McNeil is the corporate treasurer at Farmhouse, which owns and operates several farms and ethanol production plants in the United States. McNeil's primary responsibility is risk management. Katrina Falk, a recently hired junior analyst at Farmhouse, works for McNeil in managing the risk of the firm's commodity price exposures. Farmhouse's risk management policy requires the use of futures to protect revenue from price volatility, regardless of forecasts of future prices, and prohibits risk managers from taking speculative positions.

McNeil meets with Falk to discuss recent developments in two of Farmhouse's commodity markets, grains and livestock. McNeil asks Falk about key characteristics of the two markets that affect revenues and costs. Falk tells McNeil the following:

Statement 1: The life cycle for livestock depends on the product and varies widely by product.

Statement 2: Grains have uniform, well-defined seasons and growth cycles specific to geographic regions.

A material portion of Farmhouse's revenue comes from livestock exports, and a major input cost is the cost of grains imported from outside the United States. Falk and McNeil next discuss three conclusions that Falk reached in an analysis of the grains and livestock markets:

Conclusion 1: Assuming demand for grains remains constant, extreme heat in the regions from which we import our grains will result in a benefit to us in the form of lower grain prices.

Conclusion 2: New tariffs on cattle introduced in our primary export markets will likely result in higher prices for our livestock products in our local market.

Conclusion 3: Major improvements in freezing technology allowing for longer storage will let us better manage the volatility in the prices of our livestock products.

McNeil asks Falk to gather spot and futures price data on live cattle, wheat, and soybeans, which are presented in Exhibit 1. Additionally, she observes that (1) the convenience yield of soybeans exceeds the costs of its direct storage and (2) commodity producers as a group are less interested in hedging in the forward market than commodity consumers are.

EXHIBIT 1   Selected Commodity Price Data*

Market	Live Cattle Price	Wheat Price	Soybeans Price
Spot	109	407	846
Futures	108	407	850

* Live cattle: US cents per pound; wheat and soybeans: US cents per bushel.

A key input cost for Farmhouse in producing ethanol is natural gas. McNeil uses positions in natural gas (NG) futures contracts to manage the risk of natural gas price volatility. Three months ago, she entered into a long position in natural gas futures at a futures price of $2.93 per million British thermal units (MMBtu). The current price of the same contract is $2.99. Exhibit 2 presents additional data about the three-month futures position.

EXHIBIT 2   Selected Information—Natural Gas Futures Three-Month Position*

			Prices	
Commodity	Total Current $ Exposure	Position	Near-Term Futures (Current Price)	Farther-Term Futures
Natural Gas (NG)	5,860,000	Long	2.99	3.03

* NG: $ per MMBtu; 1 contract = 10,000 MMBtu.

The futures position is fully collateralized earning a 3% rate. McNeil decides to roll forward her current exposure in the natural gas position.

Each month, McNeil reports the performance of the energy futures positions, including details on price returns, roll returns, and collateral returns, to the firm's executive committee. A new committee member is concerned about the negative roll returns on some of the positions. In a memo to McNeil, the committee member asks her to explain why she is not avoiding positions with negative roll returns.

16. With respect to its risk management policy, Farmhouse can be *best* described as:
    A. a trader.
    B. a hedger.
    C. an arbitrageur.

17. Which of Falk's statements regarding the characteristics of the grains and livestock markets is correct?
    A. Only Statement 1
    B. Only Statement 2
    C. Both Statement 1 and Statement 2

18. Which of Falk's conclusions regarding commodity markets is correct?
    A. Conclusion 1
    B. Conclusion 2
    C. Conclusion 3

19. Which commodity market in Exhibit 1 is currently in a state of contango?
    A. Wheat
    B. Soybeans
    C. Live cattle

20. Based on Exhibit 1 and McNeil's two observations, the futures price of soybeans is *most* consistent with the:
    A. insurance theory.
    B. theory of storage.
    C. hedging pressure hypothesis.

21. Based on Exhibit 2, the total return from the long position in natural gas futures is *closest* to:
    A. 1.46%.
    B. 3.71%.
    C. 4.14%.

22. The *most appropriate* response to the new committee member's question is that:
    A. roll returns are negatively correlated with price returns.
    B. such roll returns are the result of futures markets in backwardation.
    C. such positions may outperform other positions that have positive roll returns.

CHAPTER 7

CURRENCY MANAGEMENT: AN INTRODUCTION

William A. Barker, PhD, CFA

LEARNING OUTCOMES

The candidate should be able to:

- analyze the effects of currency movements on portfolio risk and return;
- discuss strategic choices in currency management;
- formulate an appropriate currency management program given financial market conditions and portfolio objectives and constraints;
- compare active currency trading strategies based on economic fundamentals, technical analysis, carry-trade, and volatility trading;
- describe how changes in factors underlying active trading strategies affect tactical trading decisions;
- describe how forward contracts and FX (foreign exchange) swaps are used to adjust hedge ratios;
- describe trading strategies used to reduce hedging costs and modify the risk–return characteristics of a foreign-currency portfolio;
- describe the use of cross-hedges, macro-hedges, and minimum-variance-hedge ratios in portfolios exposed to multiple foreign currencies;
- discuss challenges for managing emerging market currency exposures.

1. INTRODUCTION

Globalization has been one of the most persistent themes in recent history, and this theme applies equally to the world of finance. New investment products, deregulation, worldwide financial system integration, and better communication and information networks have opened new global investment opportunities. At the same time, investors have increasingly shed their "home bias" and sought investment alternatives beyond their own borders.

The benefits of this trend for portfolio managers have been clear, both in terms of the broader availability of higher-expected-return investments as well as portfolio diversification opportunities. Nonetheless, investments denominated in foreign currencies also bring a unique set of challenges: measuring and managing foreign exchange risk. Buying foreign-currency denominated assets means bringing currency risk into the portfolio. Exchange rates are volatile and, at least in the short to medium term, can have a marked impact on investment returns and risks—*currency matters*. The key to the superior performance of global portfolios is the effective management of this currency risk.

This reading explores basic concepts and tools of currency management. Section 2 reviews some of the basic concepts of foreign exchange (FX) markets. The material in subsequent sections presumes an understanding of these concepts. Section 3 examines some of the basic mathematics involved in measuring the effects of foreign-currency investments on portfolio return and risk. Sections 4–6 discuss the *strategic* decisions portfolio managers face in setting the target currency exposures of the portfolio. The currency exposures that the portfolio can accept range from a fully hedged position to active management of currency risk. Sections 7–8 discuss some of the *tactical* considerations involving active currency management if the investment policy statement (IPS) extends some latitude for active currency management. A requisite to any active currency management is having a market view; so these sections include various methodologies by which a manager can form directional views on future exchange rate movements and volatility. Sections 9–12 cover a variety of trading tools available to implement both hedging and active currency management strategies. Although the generic types of FX derivatives tools are relatively limited—spot, forward, option, and swap contracts—the number of variations within each and the number of combinations in which they can be used is vast. Section 13 examines some of the issues involved in managing the currency exposures of emerging market currencies—that is, those that are less liquid than the major currencies.

2. REVIEW OF FOREIGN EXCHANGE CONCEPTS

We begin with a review of the basic trading tools of the foreign exchange market: spot, forward, FX swap, and currency option transactions. The concepts introduced in this section will be used extensively in our discussion of currency management techniques in subsequent sections.

Most people think only of spot transactions when they think of the foreign exchange market, but in fact the spot market accounts for less than 40% of the average daily turnover in currencies.[1] Although cross-border *business* may be transacted in the spot market (making and receiving foreign currency payments), the *risk management* of these flows takes place in FX derivatives markets (i.e., using forwards, FX swaps, and currency options). So does the hedging

---

[1] 2013 Triennial Survey, Bank for International Settlements (2013).

of foreign currency assets and liabilities. It is unusual for market participants to engage in any foreign currency transactions without also managing the currency risk they create. Spot transactions typically generate derivative transactions. As a result, understanding these FX derivatives markets, and their relation to the spot market, is critical for understanding the currency risk management issues examined in this reading.

2.1. Spot Markets

In professional FX markets, exchange rate quotes are described in terms of the three-letter currency codes used to identify individual currencies. Exhibit 1 shows a list of some of the more common currency codes.

EXHIBIT 1   Currency Codes

USD	US dollar
EUR	Euro
GBP	British pound
JPY	Japanese yen
MXN	Mexican peso
CHF	Swiss franc
CAD	Canadian dollar
SEK	Swedish krona
AUD	Australian dollar
KRW	Korean won
NZD	New Zealand dollar
BRL	Brazilian real
RUB	Russian ruble
CNY	Chinese yuan
INR	Indian rupee
ZAR	South African rand

An exchange rate is the number of units of one currency (called the *price currency*) that one unit of another currency (called the *base currency*) will buy. For example, in the notation we will use a USD/EUR rate of 1.3650, which means that one euro buys \$1.3650; equivalently, the price of one euro is 1.3650 US dollars. Thus, the euro here is the base currency and the US dollar is the price currency. The exact notation used to represent exchange rates can vary widely between sources, and occasionally the same exchange rate notation will be used by different sources to mean completely different things. The reader should be aware that the notation used here may not be the same as that encountered elsewhere. To avoid confusion, this reading will identify exchange rates using the convention of "P/B," which refers to the price of one unit of the base currency "B" expressed in terms of the price currency "P."

How the professional FX market quotes exchange rates—which is the base currency, and which is the price currency, in any currency pair—is not arbitrary but follows conventions that are broadly agreed on throughout the market. Generally, there is a hierarchy as to which currency will be quoted as the base currency in any given P/B currency pair:

1. Currency pairs involving the EUR will use the EUR as the base currency (for example, GBP/EUR).
2. Currency pairs involving the GBP, other than those involving the EUR, will use the GBP as the base currency (for example, CHF/GBP).
3. Currency pairs involving either the AUD or NZD, other than those involving either the EUR or GBP, will use these currencies as the base currency (for example, USD/AUD and NZD/AUD). The market convention between these two currencies is for a NZD/AUD quote.
4. All other currency quotes involving the USD will use USD as the base currency (for example, MXN/USD).

Readers are encouraged to familiarize themselves with the quoting conventions used in the professional FX market because they are the currency quotes that will be experienced in practice. Exhibit 2 lists some of the most commonly traded currency pairs in global FX markets and their market-standard quoting conventions. These market-standard conventions will be used for the balance of this reading.

EXHIBIT 2   Select Market-Standard Currency Pair Quotes

Quote Convention	Market Name
USD/EUR	Euro-dollar
GBP/EUR	Euro-sterling
USD/GBP	Sterling-dollar
JPY/USD	Dollar-yen
USD/AUD	Aussie-dollar
CHF/USD	Dollar-Swiss
CAD/USD	Dollar-Canada
JPY/EUR	Euro-yen
CHF/EUR	Euro-Swiss
JPY/GBP	Sterling-yen

Another convention used in professional FX markets is that most spot currency quotes are priced out to four decimal places: for example, a typical USD/EUR quote would be 1.3500 and not 1.35. The price point at the fourth decimal place is commonly referred to as a "pip." Professional FX traders also refer to what is called the "big figure" or the "handle," which is the integer to the left side of the decimal place as well as the first two decimal places of the quote. For example, for a USD/EUR quote of 1.3568, 1.35 is the handle and there are 68 pips.

There are exceptions to this four decimal place rule. First, forward quotes—discussed later—will often be quoted out to five and sometimes six decimal places. Second, because of the relative magnitude of some currency values, some currency quotes will only be quoted out to two decimal places. For example, because it takes many Japanese yen to buy one US dollar, the typical spot quote for JPY/USD is priced out to only two decimal places (for example, 86.35 and not 86.3500).[2]

The spot exchange rate is usually for settlement on the second business day after the trade date, referred to as $T + 2$ settlement.[3] In foreign exchange markets—as in other financial markets—market participants confront a two-sided price in the form of a bid price and an offer price (also called an ask price) being quoted by potential counterparties. The **bid price** is the price, defined in terms of the price currency, at which the counterparty providing a two-sided price quote is willing to buy one unit of the **base** currency. Similarly, **offer price** is the price, in terms of the price currency, at which that counterparty is willing to sell one unit of the base currency. For example, given a price request from a client, a dealer might quote a two-sided price on the spot USD/EUR exchange rate of 1.3648/1.3652. This quote means that the dealer is willing to pay USD1.3648 to buy one euro (bid) and that the dealer will sell one euro (offer) for USD1.3652. The market width, usually referred to as dealer's spread or the bid–offer spread, is the difference between the bid and the offer. When transacting on a dealer's bid-offer two-sided price quote, a client is said to either "hit the bid" (selling the base currency) or "pay the offer" (buying the base currency).

An easy check to see whether the bid or offer should be used for a specific transaction is that the party *asking* the dealer for a price should be on the more expensive side of the market. For example, if one wants to buy 1 EUR, 1.3652 is more USD per EUR than 1.3648. Hence, paying the offer involves paying more USD. Similarly, when selling 1 EUR, hitting the bid at 1.3648 means less USD received than 1.3652.

2.2. Forward Markets

Forward contracts are agreements to exchange one currency for another on a future date at an exchange rate agreed on today.[4] In contrast to spot rates, forward contracts are any exchange rate transactions that occur with settlement longer than the usual $T + 2$ settlement for spot delivery.

In professional FX markets, forward exchange rates are typically quoted in terms of "points." The points on a forward rate quote are simply the difference between the forward exchange rate quote and the spot exchange rate quote; that is, the forward premium or discount, with the points scaled so that they can be related to the last decimal place in the spot quote. Forward points are adjustments to the spot price of the base currency, using our standard price/base (P/B) currency notation.

---

[2] Many electronic dealing platforms in the FX market are moving to five decimal place pricing for spot quotes, using what are referred to as "deci-pips." In this case, for example, a USD/EUR spot quote might be shown as 1.37645. Spot quotes for JPY/USD on these systems will be given out to three decimal places.

[3] The exception among the major currencies is CAD/USD, for which standard spot settlement is $T + 1$.

[4] These are sometimes called outright forwards to distinguish them from FX swaps, which are discussed later.

This means that forward rate quotes in professional FX markets are typically shown as the bid–offer on the spot rate and the number of forward points at each maturity.[5] For illustration purposes, assume that the bid–offer for the spot and forward points for the USD/EUR exchange rate are as shown in Exhibit 3.

EXHIBIT 3   Sample Spot and Forward Quotes (Bid–Offer)

Maturity	Spot Rate or Forward Points
Spot (USD/EUR)	1.3549/1.3651
One month	−5.6/−5.1
Three months	−15.9/−15.3
Six months	−37.0/−36.3
Twelve months	−94.3/−91.8

To convert any of these quoted forward points into a forward rate, one would divide the number of points by 10,000 (to scale down to the fourth decimal place, the last decimal place in the USD/EUR spot quote) and then add the result to the spot exchange rate quote.[6] But one must be careful about which side of the market (bid or offer) is being quoted. For example, suppose a market participant was *selling* the EUR forward against the USD. Given the USD/EUR quoting convention, the EUR is the base currency. This means the market participant must use the *bid* rates (i.e., the market participant will "hit the bid") given the USD/EUR quoting convention. Using the data in Exhibit 3, the three-month forward *bid* rate in this case would be based on the bid for both the spot and the forward points, and hence would be:

$$1.3549 + \left(\frac{-15.9}{10,000} \right) = 1.35331$$

This result means that the market participant would be selling EUR three months forward at a price of USD1.35331 per EUR. Note that the quoted points are already scaled to each maturity—they are not annualized—so there is no need to adjust them.

Although there is no cash flow on a forward contract until settlement date, it is often useful to do a mark-to-market valuation on a forward position before then to (1) judge the effectiveness of a hedge based on forward contracts (i.e., by comparing the change in the mark-to-market of the underlying asset with the change in the mark-to-market of the forward), and (2) to measure the profitability of speculative currency positions at points before contract maturity.

As with other financial instruments, the mark-to-market value of forward contracts reflects the profit (or loss) that would be realized from closing out the position at current market prices. To close out a forward position, it must be offset with an equal and opposite forward position using the spot exchange rate and forward points available in the market when the offsetting position is created. When a forward contract is initiated, the forward rate is such

---

[5] Maturity is defined in terms of the time between spot settlement, usually $T + 2$, and the settlement of the forward contract.

[6] Because the JPY/USD exchange rate is only quoted to two decimal places, forward points for the dollar/yen currency pair are divided by 100.

that no cash changes hands (i.e., the mark-to-market value of the contract at initiation is zero). From that moment onward, however, the mark-to-market value of the forward contract will change as the spot exchange rate changes as well as when interest rates change in either of the two currencies.

Consider an example. Suppose that a market participant bought GBP10,000,000 for delivery against the AUD in six months at an "all-in" forward rate of 1.6100 AUD/GBP. (The all-in forward rate is simply the sum of the spot rate and the forward points, appropriately scaled to size.) Three months later, the market participant wants to close out this forward contract. To do that would require selling GBP10,000,000 three months forward using the AUD/GBP spot exchange rate and forward points in effect at that time. Assume the bid–offer for spot and forward points three months prior to the settlement date are as follows:

Spot rate (AUD/GBP)	1.6210/1.6215
Three-month points	130/140

To sell GBP (the base currency in the AUD/GBP quote) means calculating the *bid* side of the market. Hence, the appropriate all-in three-month forward rate to use is

$$1.6210 + 130/10,000 = 1.6340$$

Thus, the market participant originally bought GBP10,000,000 at an AUD/GBP rate of 1.6100 and subsequently sold them at a rate of 1.6340. These GBP amounts will net to zero at settlement date (GBP10 million both bought and sold), but the AUD amounts will not net to zero because the forward rate has changed. The AUD cash flow at settlement date will be equal to

$$(1.6340 - 1.6100) \times 10,000,000 = AUD240,000$$

This amount is a cash *inflow* because the market participant was long the GBP with the original forward position and the GBP subsequently appreciated (the AUD/GBP rate increased).

This cash flow is paid at settlement day, which is still three months away. To calculate the mark-to-market value on the dealer's position, this cash flow must be discounted to the present. The present value of this amount is found by discounting the settlement day cash flow by the three-month discount rate. Because it is an AUD amount, the three-month AUD discount rate is used. If Libor is used and the three-month AUD Libor is 4.80% (annualized), the present value of this future AUD cash flow is then

$$\frac{AUD240,000}{1 + 0.048\left[\dfrac{90}{360}\right]} = AUD237,154$$

This is the mark-to-market value of the original long GBP10 million six-month forward contract when it is closed out three months prior to settlement.

To summarize, the process for marking-to-market a forward position is relatively straightforward:

1. Create an equal and offsetting forward position to the original forward position. (In the example earlier, the market participant is long GBP10 million forward, so the offsetting forward contract would be to sell GBP10 million.)

2. Determine the appropriate all-in forward rate for this new, offsetting forward position. If the base currency of the exchange rate quote is being sold (bought), then use the bid (offer) side of the market.
3. Calculate the cash flow at settlement day. This calculation will be based on the original contract size times the difference between the original forward rate and the rate calculated in Step 2. If the currency the market participant was originally long (short) subsequently appreciated (depreciated), then there will be a cash *inflow*. Otherwise, there will be a cash outflow. (In the earlier example, the market participant was long the GBP and it subsequently appreciated; this appreciation led to a cash inflow at the settlement day.)
4. Calculate the present value of this cash flow at the future settlement date. The currency of the cash flow and the discount rate must match. (In the example earlier, the cash flow at the settlement date is in AUD, so an AUD Libor rate is used to calculate the present value.)

Finally, we note that in the example, the mark-to-market value is given in AUD. It would be possible to translate this AUD amount into any other currency value using the current spot rate for the relevant currency pair. In the example above, this would be done by redenominating the mark-to-market in USD, by selling 240,000 AUD 90-days forward against the USD at the prevailing USD/AUD 90-day forward bid rate. This will produce a USD cash flow in 90 days. This USD amount can then be present-valued at the 90-day US rate to get the USD mark-to-market value of the AUD/GBP forward position. The day-count convention used here is an "actual/360" basis.

2.3. FX Swap Markets

An FX swap transaction consists of offsetting and simultaneous spot and forward transactions, in which the base currency is being bought (sold) spot and sold (bought) forward. These two transactions are often referred to as the "legs" of the swap. The two legs of the swap can either be of equal size (a "matched" swap) or one can be larger than the other (a "mismatched" swap). FX swaps are distinct from currency swaps. Similar to currency swaps, FX swaps involve an exchange of principal amounts in different currencies at swap initiation that is reversed at swap maturity. Unlike currency swaps, FX swaps have no interim interest payments and are nearly always of much shorter term than currency swaps.

FX swaps are important for managing currency risk because they are used to "roll" forward contracts forward as they mature. For example, consider the case of a trader who *bought* GBP1,000,000 one month forward against the CHF in order to set up a currency hedge. One month later, the forward contract will expire. To maintain this long position in the GBP against the CHF, two days prior to contract maturity, given $T + 2$ settlement, the trader must (1) sell GBP1,000,000 against the CHF spot, to settle the maturing forward contract; and (2) buy GBP1,000,000 against the CHF forward. That is, the trader is engaging in an FX swap (a matched swap in this case because the GBP currency amounts are equal).

If a trader wanted to adjust the size of the currency hedge (i.e., the size of the outstanding forward position), the forward leg of the FX swap can be of a different size than the spot transaction when the hedge is rolled. Continuing the previous example, if the trader wanted to increase the size of the long-GBP position by GBP500,000 as the outstanding forward contract expires, the transactions required would be to (1) sell GBP1,000,000 against the CHF spot, to settle the maturing forward contract; and (2) buy GBP1,500,000 against the CHF forward. This would be a mismatched swap.

The pricing of swaps will differ slightly depending on whether they are matched or mismatched swaps. If the amount of the base currency involved for the spot and forward legs of the swap are equal (a matched swap), then these are exactly offsetting transactions; one is a buy, the other a sell, and both are for the same amount. Because of this equality, a common *spot* exchange rate is typically applied to both legs of the swap transaction; it is standard practice to use the mid-market spot exchange rate for a matched swap transaction. However, the *forward* points will still be based on either the bid or offer, depending on whether the market participant is buying or selling the base currency forward. In the earlier example, the trader is *buying* the GBP (the base currency) forward and would hence pay the *offer* side of the market for forward points.

If the FX swap is mismatched, then pricing will need to reflect the difference in trade sizes between the two legs of the transaction. Continuing the example in which the trader increased the size of the long-GBP position by GBP500,000, this mismatched swap is equivalent to (1) a matched swap for a size of GBP1,000,000, and (2) an outright forward contract buying GBP500,000. Pricing for the mismatched swap must reflect this net GBP purchase amount. Because the matched swap would already price the forward points on the offer side of the market, typically this mismatched size adjustment would be reflected in the *spot* rate quoted as the base for the FX swap. Because a net amount of GBP is being *bought*, the spot quote would now be on the *offer* side of the CHF/GBP spot rate quote. (In addition, the trader would still pay the offer side of the market for the forward points.)

We will return to these topics later in the reading when discussing in more depth the use of forward contracts and FX swaps to adjust hedge ratios. (A **hedge ratio** is the ratio of the nominal value of the derivatives contract used as a hedge to the market value of the hedged asset.)

2.4. Currency Options

The final product type within FX markets is currency options. The market for currency options is, in many ways, similar to option markets for other asset classes, such as bonds and equities. As in other markets, the most common options in FX markets are call and put options, which are widely used for both risk management and speculative purposes. However, in addition to these vanilla options, the FX market is also characterized by active trading in exotic options. ("Exotic" options have a variety of features that make them exceptionally flexible risk management tools, compared with vanilla options.)

The risk management uses of both vanilla and exotic currency options will be examined in subsequent sections. Although daily turnover in FX options market is small in *relative* terms compared with the overall daily flow in global spot currency markets, because the overall currency market is so large, the *absolute* size of the FX options market is still very considerable.

3. CURRENCY RISK AND PORTFOLIO RISK AND RETURN

In this section, we examine the effect of currency movements on asset returns and portfolio risk. We then turn to how these effects help determine construction of a foreign asset portfolio.

3.1. Return Decomposition

In this section, we examine how international exposure affects a portfolio's return. A **domestic asset** is an asset that trades in the investor's **domestic currency** (or **home currency**). From a portfolio manager's perspective, the domestic currency is the one in which portfolio valuation and returns are reported. *Domestic* refers to a relation between the currency denomination of the asset and the investor; it is not an inherent property of either the asset or the currency. An example of a domestic asset is a USD-denominated bond portfolio from the perspective of a US-domiciled investor. The return on a domestic asset is not affected by exchange rate movements of the domestic currency.

Foreign assets are assets denominated in currencies other than the investor's home currency. An example of a foreign asset is a USD-denominated bond portfolio from the perspective of a eurozone-domiciled investor (and for whom the euro is the home currency). The return on a foreign asset will be affected by exchange rate movements in the home currency against the **foreign currency**. Continuing with our example, the return to the eurozone-domiciled investor will be affected by the USD return on the USD-denominated bond as well as movements in the exchange rate between the home currency and the foreign currency, the EUR and USD respectively.

The return of the foreign asset measured in foreign-currency terms is known as the **foreign-currency return**. Extending the example, if the value of the USD-denominated bond increased by 10%, measured in USD, that increase is the foreign-currency return to the eurozone-domiciled investor. The **domestic-currency return** on a foreign asset will reflect both the foreign-currency return on that asset as well as percentage movements in the spot exchange rate between the home and foreign currencies. The domestic-currency return is multiplicative with respect to these two factors:

$$R_{DC} = (1 + R_{FC})(1 + R_{FX}) - 1 \tag{1}$$

where R_{DC} is the domestic-currency return (in percent), R_{FC} is the foreign-currency return, and R_{FX} is the percentage change of the foreign currency against the domestic currency.

Returning to the example, the domestic-currency return for the eurozone-domiciled investor on the USD-denominated bond will reflect both the bond's USD-denominated return as well as movements in the exchange rate between the USD and the EUR. Suppose that the foreign-currency return on the USD-denominated bond is 10% and the USD appreciates by 5% against the EUR. In this case, the domestic-currency return to the eurozone investor will be:

$$(1 + 10\%)(1 + 5\%) - 1 = (1.10)(1.05) - 1 = 0.155 = 15.5\%$$

Although the concept is seemingly straightforward, the reader should be aware that Equation 1 hides a subtlety that must be recognized. The term R_{FX} is defined as the percentage change in the foreign currency against the domestic currency. However, this change is *not* always the same thing as the percentage change in the spot rate using market standard P/B quotes (for example, as shown in Exhibit 2). Specifically, it is not always the case that $R_{FX} = \%\Delta S_{P/B}$, where the term on the right side of the equal sign is defined in standard FX market convention (note that %Δ is percentage change).

In other words, R_{FX} is calculated as the change in the directly quoted exchange rate, where the domestic currency is defined as the investor's home currency. Because market quotes are not always in direct terms, analysts will need to convert to direct quotes before calculating percentage changes.

With this nuance in mind, what holds for the domestic-currency return of a single foreign asset also holds for the returns on a multi-currency portfolio of foreign assets, except now the portfolio weights must be considered. More generally, the domestic-currency return on a port-folio of multiple foreign assets will be equal to

$$R_{DC} = \sum_{i=1}^{n} \omega_i (1 + R_{FC,i})(1 + R_{FX,i}) - 1 \tag{2}$$

where $R_{FC,i}$ is the foreign-currency return on the i-th foreign asset, $R_{FX,i}$ is the appreciation of the i-th foreign currency against the domestic currency, and ω_i are the portfolio weights of the foreign-currency assets (defined as the percentage of the aggregate domestic-currency value of the portfolio) and $\sum_{i=1}^{n} \omega_i = 1$. (Note that if short selling is allowed in the portfolio, some of the ω_i can be less than zero.) Again, it is important that the exchange rate notation in this expression (used to calculate $R_{FX,i}$) must be consistently defined with the domestic currency as the price currency.

Assume the following information for a portfolio held by an investor in India. Performance is measured in terms of the Indian rupee (INR) and the weights of the two assets in the portfolio, at the beginning of the period, are 80% for the GBP-denominated asset and 20% for the EUR-denominated asset, respectively. (Note that the portfolio weights are measured in terms of a common currency, the INR, which is the investor's domestic currency in this case.)

	One Year Ago	Today*
INR/GBP spot rate	84.12	85.78
INR/EUR spot rate	65.36	67.81
GBP-denominated asset value, in GBP millions	43.80	50.70
EUR-denominated asset value, in EUR millions	14.08	12.17
GBP-denominated asset value, in INR millions	3,684.46	
EUR-denominated asset value, in INR millions	920.27	
GBP-denominated assets, portfolio weight (INR)	80%	
EUR-denominated assets, portfolio weight (INR)	20%	

* Today's asset values are prior to rebalancing.

The domestic-currency return (R_{DC}) is calculated as follows:

$$R_{DC} = 0.80(1 + R_{FC,GBP})(1 + R_{FX,GBP}) + 0.20(1 + R_{FC,EUR})(1 + R_{FX,EUR}) - 1$$

Note that given the exchange rate quoting convention, the INR is the price currency in the P/B quote for both currency pairs. Adding the data from the table leads to:

$$R_{DC} = 0.80 \left(\frac{50.70}{43.80}\right)\left(\frac{85.78}{84.12}\right) + 0.20 \left(\frac{12.17}{14.08}\right)\left(\frac{67.81}{65.36}\right) - 1$$

This solves to 0.124 or 12.4%.

To get the *expected* future return on a foreign-currency asset portfolio, based on Equation 2, the portfolio manager would need a market opinion for the expected price movement in each of the foreign assets ($R_{A,i}$) and exchange rates ($R_{FX,i}$) in the portfolio. There are typically correlations between all of these variables—correlations between the foreign asset price movements across countries, correlations between movements among various currency pairs, and correlations between exchange rate movements and foreign-currency asset returns. The portfolio manager would need to account for these correlations when forming expectations about future asset price and exchange rate movements.

3.2. Volatility Decomposition

Now we will turn to examining the effect of currency movements on the volatility of domestic-currency returns. Equation 1 can be rearranged as

$$R_{DC} = (1 + R_{FC})(1 + R_{FX}) - 1 = R_{FC} + R_{FX} + R_{FC}R_{FX}$$

When R_{FC} and R_{FX} are small, then the cross-term ($R_{FC}R_{FX}$) is small, and as a result this equation can be approximated as

$$R_{DC} \approx R_{FC} + R_{FX} \tag{3}$$

We return to the example in which the foreign-currency return on the USD-denominated bond was 10% and the USD appreciated by 5% against the EUR. In this example, the domestic-currency return for the Eurozone investor's holding in the USD-denominated bond was approximately equal to 10% + 5% = 15% (which is close to the exact value of 15.5%). We can combine the approximation of Equation 3 with the statistical rule that:

$$\sigma^2(\omega_x X + \omega_y Y) = \omega_x^2 \sigma^2(X) + \omega_y^2 \sigma^2(Y) + 2\omega_x \omega_y \sigma(X)\sigma(Y)\rho(X, Y) \tag{4}$$

where X and Y are random variables, ω are weights attached to X and Y, σ^2 is variance of a random variable, σ is the corresponding standard deviation, and ρ represents the correlation between two random variables. Applying this result to the domestic-currency return approximation of Equation 3 leads to:

$$\sigma^2(R_{DC}) \approx \sigma^2(R_{FC}) + \sigma^2(R_{FX}) + 2\sigma(R_{FC})\sigma(R_{FX})\rho(R_{FC}, R_{FX}) \tag{5}$$

This equation is for the variance of the domestic-currency returns (R_{DC}), but risk is more typically defined in terms of standard deviation because mean and standard deviation are measured in the same units (percent, in this case). Hence, the total risk for domestic-currency returns—that is, $\sigma(R_{DC})$—is the square root of the results calculated in Equation 5.

Note as well that because Equation 5 is based on the addition of all three terms on the right side of the equal sign, exchange rate exposure will generally cause the variance of domestic-currency returns, $\sigma^2(R_{DC})$, to increase to more than that of the foreign-currency returns, $\sigma^2(R_{FC})$, considered on their own. That is, if there was no exchange rate risk, then it would be the case that $\sigma^2(R_{DC}) = \sigma^2(R_{FC})$. Using this as our base-case scenario, adding exchange rate risk exposure to the portfolio usually adds to domestic-currency return variance (the effect is indeterminate if exchange rate movements are negatively correlated with foreign asset returns).

These results on the variance of domestic-currency return can be generalized to a portfolio of foreign-currency assets. If we define the random variables X and Y in Equation 4 in terms of the domestic-currency return (R_{DC}) of two different foreign-currency investments, and the ω_i as portfolio weights that sum to one, then the result is the variance of the domestic-currency returns for the overall foreign asset portfolio:

$$\sigma^2(\omega_1 R_1 + \omega_2 R_2) \approx \omega_1^2 \sigma^2(R_1) + \omega_2^2 \sigma^2(R_2) + 2\omega_1 \omega_2 \sigma(R_1)\sigma(R_2)\rho(R_1, R_2) \tag{6}$$

where R_i is the domestic-currency return of the *i*-th foreign-currency asset. But as shown in Equation 3, the domestic-currency return of a foreign-currency asset (R_{DC}) is itself based on the sum of two random variables: R_{FC} and R_{FX}. This means that we would have to embed the variance expression shown in Equation 5 in *each* of the $\sigma^2(R_i)$ shown in Equation 6 to get the complete solution for the domestic-currency return variance of the overall portfolio. (We would also have to calculate the correlations between *all* of the R_i.) These requirements would lead to a very cumbersome mathematical expression for even a portfolio of only two foreign-currency assets; the expression would be far more complicated for a portfolio with many foreign currencies involved.

Thus, rather than attempt to give the complete mathematical formula for the variance of domestic-currency returns for a multi-currency portfolio, we will instead focus on the key intuition behind this expression. Namely, that the domestic-currency risk exposure of the overall portfolio—that is, $\sigma(R_{DC})$—will depend not only on the variances of *each* of the foreign-currency returns (R_{FC}) and exchange rate movements (R_{FX}) but also on how each of these *interacts* with the others. Generally speaking, negative correlations among these variables will help reduce the overall portfolio's risk through diversification effects.

Note as well that the overall portfolio's risk exposure will depend on the portfolio weights (ω_i) used. If short-selling is allowed in the portfolio, some of these ω_i can be negative as long as the total portfolio weights sum to one. So, for two foreign assets with a strong positive return correlation, short selling one can create considerable diversification benefits for the portfolio. (This approach is equivalent to trading movements in the price spread between these two assets.)

As before with the difference between realized and expected domestic-currency portfolio returns (R_{DC}), there is a difference between realized and expected domestic-currency portfolio risk, $\sigma(R_{DC})$. For Equation 6 to apply to the expected future volatility of the domestic-currency return of a multi-currency foreign asset portfolio, we would need to replace the observed, historical values of the variances and covariances in Equation 6 with their expected future values. This can be challenging, not only because it potentially involves a large number of variables but also because historical price patterns are not always a good guide to future price behavior. Variance and correlation measures are sensitive to the time period used to estimate them and can also vary over time. These variance and correlation measures can either drift randomly with time, or they can be subject to abrupt movements in times of market stress. It should also be clear that these observed, historical volatility and correlation measures need not be the same as the forward-looking *implied* volatility (and correlation) derived from option prices. Although sometimes various survey or consensus forecasts can be used, these too can be sensitive to sample size and composition and are not always available on a timely basis or with a consistent starting point. As with any forecast, they are also not necessarily an accurate guide to future developments; judgment must be used.

Hence, to calculate the expected future risk of the foreign asset portfolio, the portfolio manager would need a market opinion—however derived—on the variance of each of the foreign-currency asset returns (R_{FC}) over the investment horizon as well the variance of future exchange rate movements (R_{FX}) for each currency pair. The portfolio manager would also need a market opinion of how each of these future variables would interact with each other (i.e., their expected correlations). Historical price patterns can serve as a guide, and with computers and large databases, this modeling problem is daunting but not intractable. But the portfolio manager must always be mindful that historical risk patterns may not repeat going forward.

EXAMPLE 1   Portfolio Risk and Return Calculations

The following table shows current and future expected asset prices, measured in their domestic currencies, for both eurozone and Canadian assets (these can be considered "total return" indexes). The table also has the corresponding data for the CAD/EUR spot rate.

	Eurozone		Canada	
	Today	Expected	Today	Expected
Asset price	100.69	101.50	101.00	99.80
CAD/EUR	1.2925	1.3100		

1. What is the expected domestic-currency return for a eurozone investor holding the Canadian asset?
2. What is the expected domestic-currency return for a Canadian investor holding the eurozone asset?
3. From the perspective of the Canadian investor, assume that $\sigma(R_{FC}) = 3\%$ (the expected risk for the foreign-currency asset is 3%) and the $\sigma(R_{FX}) = 2\%$ (the expected risk of exchange rate movements is 2%). Furthermore, the expected correlation between movements in foreign-currency asset returns and movements in the CAD/EUR rate is +0.5. What is the expected risk of the domestic-currency return $[\sigma(R_{DC})]$?

Solution to 1: For the eurozone investor, the $R_{FC} = (99.80/101.00) - 1 = -1.19\%$. Note that, given we are considering the eurozone to be "domestic" for this investor and given the way the R_{FX} expression is defined, we will need to convert the CAD/EUR exchange rate quote so that the EUR is the *price* currency. This leads to $R_{FX} = [(1/1.3100)/(1/1.2925)] - 1 = -1.34\%$. Hence, for the eurozone investor, $R_{DC} = (1 - 1.19\%)(1 - 1.34\%) - 1 = -2.51\%$.

Solution to 2: For the Canadian investor, the $R_{FC} = (101.50/100.69) - 1 = +0.80\%$. Given that in the CAD/EUR quote the CAD is the price currency, for this investor the $R_{FX} = (1.3100/1.2925) - 1 = +1.35\%$. Hence, for the Canadian investor the $R_{DC} = (1 + 0.80\%)(1 + 1.35\%) - 1 = 2.16\%$.

Solution to 3: Because this is a single foreign-currency asset we are considering (not a portfolio of such assets), we can use Equation 5:

$$\sigma^2(R_{DC}) \approx \sigma^2(R_{FC}) + \sigma^2(R_{FX}) + 2\sigma(R_{FC})\sigma(R_{FX})\rho(R_{FC},R_{FX})$$

Inserting the relevant data leads to

$$\sigma^2(R_{DC}) \approx (3\%)^2 + (2\%)^2 + 2(3\%)(2\%)(0.50) = 0.0019$$

> Taking the square root of this leads to $\sigma(R_{DC}) \approx 4.36\%$. (Note that the units in these expressions are all in percent, so in this case 3% is equivalent to 0.03 for calculation purposes.)

4. STRATEGIC DECISIONS IN CURRENCY MANAGEMENT: OVERVIEW

There are a variety of approaches to currency management, ranging from trying to avoid all currency risk in a portfolio to actively seeking foreign exchange risk in order to manage it and enhance portfolio returns.

There is no firm consensus—either among academics or practitioners—about the most effective way to manage currency risk. Some investment managers try to hedge all currency risk, some leave their portfolios unhedged, and others see currency risk as a potential source of incremental return to the portfolio and will actively trade foreign exchange. These widely varying management practices reflect a variety of factors including investment objectives, investment constraints, and beliefs about currency markets.

Concerning beliefs, one camp of thought holds that in the long run currency effects cancel out to zero as exchange rates revert to historical means or their fundamental values. Moreover, an efficient currency market is a zero-sum game (currency "A" cannot appreciate against currency "B" without currency "B" depreciating against currency "A"), so there should not be any long-run gains overall to speculating in currencies, especially after netting out management and transaction costs. Therefore, both currency hedging and actively trading currencies represent a cost to a portfolio with little prospect of consistently positive active returns.

At the other extreme, another camp of thought notes that currency movements can have a dramatic impact on short-run returns and return volatility and holds that there are pricing inefficiencies in currency markets. They note that much of the flow in currency markets is related to international trade or capital flows in which FX trading is being done on a need-to-do basis and these currency trades are just a spinoff of the other transactions. Moreover, some market participants are either not in the market on a purely profit-oriented basis (e.g., central banks, government agencies) or are believed to be "uninformed traders" (primarily retail accounts). Conversely, speculative capital seeking to arbitrage inefficiencies is finite. In short, marketplace diversity is believed to present the potential for "harvesting alpha" through active currency trading.

This ongoing debate does not make foreign-currency risk in portfolios go away; it still needs to managed, or at least, recognized. Ultimately, each portfolio manager or investment oversight committee will have to reach their own decisions about how to manage risk and whether to seek return enhancement through actively trading currency exposures.

Fortunately, there are a well-developed set of financial products and portfolio management techniques that help investors manage currency risk no matter what their individual objectives, views, and constraints. Indeed, the potential combinations of trading tools and strategies are almost infinite, and can shape currency exposures to custom-fit individual circumstance and market opinion. In this section, we explore various points on a spectrum reflecting currency exposure choices (a risk spectrum) and the guidance that portfolio managers use in making strategic decisions about where to locate their portfolios on this continuum. First, however, the implication of investment objectives and constraints as set forth in the investment policy statement must be recognized.

4.1. The Investment Policy Statement

The Investment Policy Statement (IPS) mandates the degree of discretionary currency management that will be allowed in the portfolio, how it will be benchmarked, and the limits on the type of trading polices and tools (e.g., such as leverage) than can be used.

The starting point for organizing the investment plan for any portfolio is the IPS, which is a statement that outlines the broad objectives and constraints of the beneficial owners of the assets. Most IPS specify many of the following points:

- the general objectives of the investment portfolio;
- the risk tolerance of the portfolio and its capacity for bearing risk;
- the time horizon over which the portfolio is to be invested;
- the ongoing income/liquidity needs (if any) of the portfolio; and
- the benchmark against which the portfolio will measure overall investment returns.

The IPS sets the guiding parameters within which more specific portfolio management policies are set, including the target asset mix; whether and to what extent leverage, short positions, and derivatives can be used; and how actively the portfolio will be allowed to trade its various risk exposures.

For most portfolios, currency management can be considered a sub-set of these more specific portfolio management policies within the IPS. The currency risk management policy will usually address such issues as the

- target proportion of currency exposure to be passively hedged;
- latitude for active currency management around this target;
- frequency of hedge rebalancing;
- currency hedge performance benchmark to be used; and
- hedging tools permitted (types of forward and option contracts, etc.).

Currency management should be conducted within these IPS-mandated parameters.

4.2. The Portfolio Optimization Problem

Having described the IPS as the guiding framework for currency management, we now examine the strategic choices that have to be made in deciding the benchmark currency exposures for the portfolio, and the degree of discretion that will be allowed around this benchmark. This process starts with a decision on the optimal foreign-currency asset and FX exposures.

Optimization of a multi-currency portfolio of foreign assets involves selecting portfolio weights that locate the portfolio on the efficient frontier of the trade-off between risk and expected return defined in terms of the investor's domestic currency. As a simplification of this process, consider the portfolio manager examining the expected return and risk of the multi-currency portfolio of foreign assets by using different combinations of portfolio weights (ω_i) that were shown in Equations 2 and 6, respectively, which are repeated here:

$$R_{DC} = \sum_{i=1}^{n} \omega_i (1 + R_{FC,i})(1 + R_{FX,i}) - 1$$

$$\sigma^2(\omega_1 R_1 + \omega_2 R_2) \approx \omega_1^2 \sigma^2(R_1) + \omega_2^2 \sigma^2(R_2) + 2\omega_1 \sigma(R_1) \omega_2 \sigma(R_2) \rho(R_1, R_2)$$

Recall that the R_i in the equation for variance are the R_{DC} for each of the foreign-currency assets. Likewise, recall that the R_{FX} term is defined such that the investor's "domestic" currency is the price currency in the P/B exchange rate quote. In other words, this calculation may require using the algebraic reciprocal of the standard market quote convention. These two equations together show the domestic-currency return and risk for a multi-currency portfolio of foreign assets.

When deciding on an optimal investment position, these equations would be based on the *expected* returns and risks for each of the foreign-currency assets; and hence, including the *expected* returns and risks for each of the foreign-currency exposures. As we have seen earlier, the number of market parameters for which the portfolio manager would need to have a market opinion grows geometrically with the complexity (number of foreign-currency exposures) in the portfolio. That is, to calculate the expected efficient frontier, the portfolio manager must have a market opinion for *each* of the $R_{FC,i}$, $R_{FX,i}$, $\sigma(R_{FC,i})$, $\sigma(R_{FX,i})$, and $\rho(R_{FC,i} R_{FX,i})$, as well as for each of the $\rho(R_{FC,i} R_{FC,j})$ and $\rho(R_{FX,i} R_{FX,j})$. This would be a daunting task for even the most well-informed portfolio manager.

In a perfect world with complete (and costless) information, it would likely be optimal to *jointly* optimize all of the portfolio's exposures—over all currencies and all foreign-currency assets—simultaneously. In the real world, however, this can be a much more difficult task. Confronted with these difficulties, many portfolio managers handle asset allocation with currency risk as a two-step process: (1) portfolio optimization over fully hedged returns; and (2) selection of active currency exposure, if any. Derivative strategies can allow the various risk exposures in a portfolio to be "unbundled" from each other and managed separately. The same applies for currency risks. Because the use of derivatives allows the price risk ($R_{FC,i}$) and exchange rate risk ($R_{FX,j}$) of foreign-currency assets to be unbundled and managed separately, a starting point for the selection process of portfolio weights would be to assume a complete currency hedge. That is, the portfolio manager will choose the exposures to the foreign-currency assets first, and then decide on the appropriate currency exposures afterward (i.e., decide whether to relax the full currency hedge). These decisions are made to simplify the portfolio construction process.

If the currency exposures of foreign assets could be perfectly and costlessly hedged, the hedge would completely neutralize the effect of currency movements on the portfolio's domestic-currency return (R_{DC}).[7] In Equation 2, this would set $R_{FX} = 0$, meaning that the domestic-currency return is then equal to the foreign-currency return ($R_{DC} = R_{FC}$). In Equation 5, this would set $\sigma^2(R_{DC}) = \sigma^2(R_{FC})$, meaning that the domestic-currency return risk is equal to the foreign-currency return risk.

Removing the currency effects leads to a simpler, two-step process for portfolio optimization. First the portfolio manager could pick the set of portfolio weights (ω_i) for the foreign-currency assets that optimize the expected foreign-currency asset risk–return trade-off (assuming there is no currency risk). Then the portfolio manager could choose the desired currency exposures for the portfolio and decide whether and by how far to relax the constraint to a full currency hedge for each currency pair.

---

[7] A "costless" hedge in this sense would not only mean zero transaction costs, but also no "roll yield."

4.3. Choice of Currency Exposures

A natural starting point for the strategic decisions is the "currency-neutral" portfolio resulting from the two-step process described earlier. The question then becomes, How far along the risk spectrum between being fully hedged and actively trading currencies should the portfolio be positioned?

4.3.1. Diversification Considerations

The time horizon of the IPS is important. Many investment practitioners believe that in the long run, adding unhedged foreign-currency exposure to a portfolio does not affect expected long-run portfolio returns; hence in the long run, it would not matter if the portfolio was hedged. (Indeed, portfolio management costs would be reduced without a hedging process.) This belief is based on the view that in the long run, currencies "mean revert" to either some fair value equilibrium level or a historical average; that is, that the *expected* $\%\Delta S = 0$ for a sufficiently long time period. This view typically draws on the expectation that purchasing power parity (PPP) and the other international parity conditions that link movements in exchange rates, interest rates, and inflation rates will eventually hold over the long run.

Supporting this view, some studies argue that in the long-run currencies will in fact mean revert, and hence that currency risk is lower in the long run than in the short run (an early example is Froot 1993). Although much depends on how long run is defined, an investor (IPS) with a very long investment horizon and few immediate liquidity needs—which could potentially require the liquidation of foreign-currency assets at disadvantageous exchange rates—might choose to forgo currency hedging and its associated costs. Logically, this would require a portfolio benchmark index that is also unhedged against currency risk.

Although the international parity conditions may hold in the long run, it can be a *very* long time—possibly decades. Indeed, currencies can continue to drift away from the fair value mean reversion level for much longer than the time period used to judge portfolio performance. Such time periods are also typically longer than the patience of the portfolio manager's oversight committee when portfolio performance is lagging the benchmark. If this very long-run view perspective is not the case, then the IPS will likely impose some form of currency hedging.

Diversification considerations will also depend on the *asset composition* of the foreign-currency asset portfolio. The reason is because the foreign-currency asset returns (R_{FC}) of different asset classes have different correlation patterns with foreign-currency returns (R_{FX}). If there is a negative correlation between these two sets of returns, having at least some currency exposure may help portfolio diversification and moderate the domestic-currency return risk, $\sigma(R_{DC})$. (Refer to Equation 5 in Section 3.)

It is often asserted that the correlation between foreign-currency returns and foreign-currency asset returns tends to be greater for fixed-income portfolios than for equity portfolios. This assertion makes intuitive sense: both bonds and currencies react strongly to movements in interest rates, whereas equities respond more to expected earnings. As a result, the implication is that currency exposures provide little diversification benefit to fixed-income portfolios and that the currency risk should be hedged. In contrast, a better argument can be made for carrying currency exposures in global equity portfolios.

To some degree, various studies have corroborated this relative advantage to currency hedging for fixed income portfolios. But the evidence seems somewhat mixed and depends on which markets are involved. One study found that the hedging advantage for fixed-income portfolios is not always large or consistent (Darnell 2004). Other studies (Campbell 2010;

Martini 2010) found that the optimal hedge ratio for foreign-currency equity portfolios depended critically on the investor's domestic currency. (Recall that the hedge ratio is defined as the ratio of the nominal value of the hedge to the market value of the underlying.) For some currencies, there was no risk-reduction advantage to hedging foreign equities (the optimal hedge ratio was close to 0%), whereas for other currencies, the optimal hedge ratio for foreign equities was close to 100%.

Other studies indicate that the optimal hedge ratio also seems to depend on *market conditions* and longer-term trends in currency pairs. For example, Campbell, Serfaty-de Medeiros, and Viceira (2007) found that there were no diversification benefits from currency exposures in foreign-currency bond portfolios, and hence to minimize the risk to domestic-currency returns these positions should be fully hedged. The authors also found, however, that during the time of their study (their data spanned 1975 to 2005), the US dollar seemed to be an exception in terms of its correlations with foreign-currency asset returns. Their study found that the US dollar tended to appreciate against foreign currencies when global bond prices fell (for example, in times of global financial stress there is a tendency for investors to shift investments into the perceived safety of reserve currencies). This finding would suggest that keeping some exposure to the US dollar in a global bond portfolio would be beneficial. For non-US investors, this would mean under-hedging the currency exposure to the USD (i.e., a hedge ratio less than 100%), whereas for US investors it would mean over-hedging their foreign-currency exposures back into the USD. Note that some currencies—the USD, JPY, and CHF in particular—seem to act as a safe haven and appreciate in times of market stress. Keeping some of these currency exposures in the portfolio—having hedge ratios that are not set at 100%—can help hedge losses on riskier assets, especially for foreign currency equity portfolios (which are more risk exposed than bond portfolios).

Given this diversity of opinions and empirical findings, it is not surprising to see actual hedge ratios vary widely in practice among different investors. Nonetheless, it is still more likely to see currency hedging for fixed-income portfolios rather than equity portfolios, although actual hedge ratios will often vary between individual managers.

4.3.2. Cost Considerations

The costs of currency hedging also guide the strategic positioning of the portfolio. Currency hedges are not a "free good" and they come with a variety of expenses that must be borne by the overall portfolio. Optimal hedging decisions will need to balance the benefits of hedging against these costs.

Hedging costs come mainly in two forms: trading costs and opportunity costs. The most immediate costs of hedging involve trading expenses, and these come in several forms:

- Trading involves dealing on the bid–offer spread offered by banks. Their profit margin is based on these spreads, and the more the client trades and "pays away the spread," the more profit is generated by the dealer. Maintaining a 100% hedge and rebalancing frequently with every minor change in market conditions would be expensive. Although the bid–offer spreads on many FX-related products (especially the spot exchange rate) are quite narrow, "churning" the hedge portfolio would progressively add to hedging costs and detract from the hedge's benefits.
- Some hedges involve currency options; a long position in currency options requires the payment of up-front premiums. If the options expire out of the money (OTM), this cost is unrecoverable.

- Although forward contracts do not require the payment of up-front premiums, they do eventually mature and have to be "rolled" forward with an FX swap transaction to maintain the hedge. Rolling hedges will typically generate cash inflows or outflows. These cash flows will have to be monitored, and as necessary, cash will have to be raised to settle hedging transactions. In other words, even though the currency hedge may *reduce* the volatility of the domestic mark-to-market value of the foreign-currency asset portfolio, it will typically *increase* the volatility in the organization's cash accounts. Managing these cash flow costs can accumulate to become a significant portion of the portfolio's value, and they become more expensive (for cash outflows) the higher interest rates go.

- One of the most important trading costs is the need to maintain an administrative infra-structure for trading. Front-, middle-, and back-office operations will have to be set up, staffed with trained personnel, and provided with specialized technology systems. Settlement of foreign exchange transactions in a variety of currencies means having to maintain cash accounts in these currencies to make and receive these foreign-currency payments. Together all of these various overhead costs can form a significant portion of the overall costs of currency trading.

A second form of costs associated with hedging are the opportunity cost of the hedge. To be 100% hedged is to forgo any possibility of favorable currency rate moves. If skillfully handled, accepting and managing currency risk—or any financial risk—can potentially add value to the portfolio, even net of management fees. (We discuss the methods by which this might be done in Sections 7–8.)

These opportunity costs lead to another motivation for having a strategic hedge ratio of less than 100%: regret minimization. Although it is not possible to accurately predict foreign exchange movements in advance, it is certainly possible to judge after the fact the results of the decision to hedge or not. Missing out on an advantageous currency movement because of a currency hedge can cause *ex post* regret in the portfolio manager or client; so too can having a foreign-currency loss if the foreign-currency asset position was unhedged. Confronted with this *ex ante* dilemma of whether to hedge, many portfolio managers decide simply to "split the difference" and have a 50% hedge ratio (or some other rule-of-thumb number). Both survey evidence and anecdotal evidence show that there is a wide variety of hedge ratios actually used in practice by managers, and that these variations cannot be explained by more "fundamental" factors alone. Instead, many managers appear to incorporate some degree of regret minimization into hedging decisions (for example, see Michenaud and Solnik 2008).

All of these various hedging expenses—both trading and opportunity costs—will need to be managed. Hedging is a form of insurance against risk, and in purchasing any form of insurance the buyer matches their needs and budgets with the policy selected. For example, although it may be possible to buy an insurance policy with full, unlimited coverage, a zero deductible, and no co-pay arrangements, such a policy would likely be prohibitively expensive. Most insurance buyers decide that it is not necessary to insure against every outcome, no matter how minor. Some minor risks can be accepted and "self-insured" through the deductible; some major risks may be considered so unlikely that they are not seen as worth paying the extra premium. (For example, most ordinary people would likely not consider buying insurance against being kidnapped.)

These same principles apply to currency hedging. The portfolio manager (and IPS) would likely not try to hedge every minor, daily change in exchange rates or asset values, but only the larger adverse movements that can materially affect the overall domestic-currency returns (R_{DC}) of the foreign-currency asset portfolio. The portfolio manager will need to balance the benefits and costs of hedging in determining both strategic positioning of the portfolio as well as any latitude for active currency management. However, around whatever strategic positioning decision taken by the IPS in terms of the benchmark level of currency exposure, hedging cost considerations alone will often dictate a *range* of permissible exposures instead of a single point. (This discretionary range is similar to the deductible in an insurance policy.)

5. STRATEGIC DECISIONS IN CURRENCY MANAGEMENT: SPECTRUM OF CURRENCY RISK MANAGEMENT STRATEGIES

The strategic decisions encoded in the IPS with regard to the trade-off between the benefits and costs of hedging, as well as the potential for incremental return to the portfolio from active currency management, are the foundation for determining specific currency management strategies. These strategies are arrayed along a spectrum from very risk-averse passive hedging, to actively seeking out currency risk in order to manage it for profit. We examine each in turn.

5.1. Passive Hedging

In this approach, the goal is to keep the portfolio's currency exposures close, if not equal to, those of a benchmark portfolio used to evaluate performance. Note that the benchmark portfolio often has no foreign exchange exposure, particularly for fixed-income assets; the benchmark index is a "local currency" index based only on the foreign-currency asset return (R_{FC}). However, benchmark indexes that have some foreign exchange risk are also possible.

Passive hedging is a rules-based approach that removes almost all discretion from the portfolio manager, regardless of the manager's market opinion on future movements in exchange rates or other financial prices. In this case, the manager's job is to keep portfolio exposures as close to "neutral" as possible and to minimize tracking errors against the benchmark portfolio's performance. This approach reflects the belief that currency exposures that differ from the benchmark portfolio inject risk (return volatility) into the portfolio without any sufficiently compensatory return. Active currency management—taking positional views on future exchange rate movements—is viewed as being incapable of consistently adding incremental return to the portfolio.

But the hedge ratio has a tendency to "drift" with changes in market conditions, and even passive hedges need periodic rebalancing to realign them with investment objectives. Often the management guidance given to the portfolio manager will specify the rebalancing period—for example, monthly. There may also be allowance for intra-period rebalancing if there have been large exchange rate movements.

5.2. Discretionary Hedging

This approach is similar to passive hedging in that there is a "neutral" benchmark portfolio against which actual portfolio performance will be measured. However, in contrast to a strictly rules-based approach, the portfolio manager now has some limited discretion on how far to allow actual portfolio risk exposures to vary from the neutral position. Usually this discretion is defined in terms of percentage of foreign-currency market value (the portfolio's currency exposures are allowed to vary plus or minus x% from the benchmark). For example, a eurozone-domiciled investor may have a US Treasury bond portfolio with a mandate to keep the hedge ratio within 95% to 105%. Assuming no change in the foreign-currency return (R_{FC}), but allowing exchange rates (R_{FX}) to vary, this means the portfolio can tolerate exchange rate movements between the EUR and USD of up to 5% before the exchange rate exposures in the portfolio are considered excessive. The manager is allowed to manage currency exposures within these limits without being considered in violation of the IPS.

This discretion allows the portfolio manager at least some limited ability to express directional opinions about future currency movements—to accept risk in an attempt to earn reward—in order to add value to the portfolio performance. Of course, the portfolio manager's actual performance will be compared with that of the benchmark portfolio.

5.3. Active Currency Management

Further along the spectrum between extreme risk aversion and purely speculative trading is active currency management. In principle, this approach is really just an extension of discretionary hedging: the portfolio manager is allowed to express directional opinions on exchange rates, but is nonetheless kept within mandated risk limits. The performance of the manager—the choices of risk exposures assumed—is benchmarked against a "neutral" portfolio. But for all forms of active management (i.e., having the discretion to express directional market views), there is no allowance for unlimited speculation; there are risk management systems in place for even the most speculative investment vehicles, such as hedge funds. These controls are designed to prevent traders from taking unusually large currency exposures and risking the solvency of the firm or fund.

In many cases, the difference between discretionary hedging and active currency management is one of emphasis more than degree. The primary duty of the discretionary hedger is to protect the portfolio from currency risk. As a secondary goal, within limited bounds, there is some scope for directional opinion in an attempt to enhance overall portfolio returns. If the manager lacks any firm market conviction, the natural neutral position for the discretionary hedger is to be flat—that is, to have no meaningful currency exposures. In contrast, the active currency manager is supposed to take currency risks and manage them for profit. The primary goal is to add alpha to the portfolio through successful trading. Leaving actual portfolio exposures near zero for extended periods is typically not a viable option.

5.4. Currency Overlay

Active management of currency exposures can extend beyond limited managerial discretion within hedging boundaries. Sometimes accepting and managing currency risk for profit can be considered a portfolio objective. Active currency management is often associated with what are called **currency overlay programs**, although this term is used differently by different sources.

• In the most limited sense of the term, currency overlay simply means that the portfolio manager has outsourced managing currency exposures to a firm specializing in FX management. This could imply something as limited as merely having the external party implement a fully passive approach to currency hedges. If dealing with FX markets and managing currency hedges is beyond the professional competence of the investment manager, whose focus is on managing foreign equities or some other asset class, then hiring such external professional help is an option. Note that typically currency overlay programs involve external managers. However, some large, sophisticated institutional investors may have in-house currency overlay programs managed by a separate group of specialists within the firm.

- A broader view of currency overlay allows the externally hired currency overlay manager to take directional views on future currency movements (again, with the caveat that these be kept within predefined bounds). Sometimes a distinction is made between currency overlay and "foreign exchange as an asset class." In this classification, currency overlay is limited to the currency exposures already in the foreign asset portfolio. For example, if a eurozone-domiciled investor has GBP- and CHF-denominated assets, currency overlay risks are allowed only for these currencies.

- In contrast, the concept of foreign exchange as an asset class does not restrict the currency overlay manager, who is free to take FX exposures in any currency pair where there is value-added to be harvested, regardless of the underlying portfolio. In this sense, the currency overlay manager is very similar to an FX-based hedge fund. To implement this form of active currency management, the currency overlay manager would have a *joint* opinion on a range of currencies, and have market views not only on the expected movements in the spot rates but also the likelihood of these movements (the variance of the expected future spot rate distribution) as well as the expected correlation between future spot rate movements. Basically, the entire portfolio of currencies is actively managed and optimized over all of the expected returns, risks, and correlations among all of the currencies in the portfolio.

We will focus on this latter form of currency overlay in this reading: active currency management conducted by external, FX-specialized sub-advisors to the portfolio.

It is quite possible to have the foreign-currency asset portfolio fully hedged (or allow some discretionary hedging internally) but then also to add an external currency overlay manager to the portfolio. This approach separates the hedging and alpha function mandates of the portfolio. Different organizations have different areas of expertise; it often makes sense to allocate managing the hedge (currency "beta") and managing the active FX exposures (currency "alpha") to those individuals with a comparative advantage in that function.

Adding this form of currency overlay to the portfolio (FX as an asset class) is similar in principle to adding any type of alternative asset class, such as private equity funds or farmland. In each case, the goal is the search for alpha. But to be most effective in adding value to the portfolio, the currency overlay program should add incremental returns (alpha) and/or greater diversification opportunities to improve the portfolio's risk–return profile. To do this, the currency alpha mandate should have minimum correlation with both the major asset classes and the other alpha sources in the portfolio.

Once this FX as an asset class approach is taken, it is not necessary to restrict the portfolio to a single overlay manager any more than it is necessary to restrict the portfolio to a single private equity fund. Different overlay managers follow different strategies (these are described in more detail in Sections 7–8). Within the overall portfolio allocation to "currency as an alternative asset class," it may be beneficial to diversify across a range of active management styles, either by engaging several currency overlay managers with different styles or by applying a fund-of-funds approach, in which the hiring and management of individual currency overlay managers is delegated to a specialized external investment vehicle.

Whether managed internally or externally (via a fund of funds) it will be necessary to monitor, or benchmark, the performance of the currency overlay manager: Do they generate the returns expected from their stated trading strategy? Many major investment banks as well as specialized market-information firms provide a wide range of proprietary indexes that track the performance of the investible universe of currency overlay managers; sometimes they also offer sub-indexes that focus on specific trading strategies (for example, currency positioning based on macroeconomic fundamentals). However, the methodologies used to calculate these various indexes vary between suppliers. In addition, different indexes show different aspects of active currency management. Given these differences between indexes, there is no simple answer for which index is most suitable as a benchmark; much depends on the specifics of the active currency strategy.

EXAMPLE 2   Currency Overlay

Windhoek Capital Management is a South Africa-based investment manager that runs the Conservative Value Fund, which has a mandate to avoid all currency risk in the portfolio. The firm is considering engaging a currency overlay manager to help with managing the foreign exchange exposures of this investment vehicle. Windhoek does not consider itself to have the in-house expertise to manage FX risk.

Brixworth & St. Ives Asset Management is a UK-based investment manager, and runs the Aggressive Growth Fund. This fund is heavily weighted toward emerging market equities, but also has a mandate to seek out inefficiencies in the global foreign exchange market and exploit these for profit. Although Brixworth & St. Ives manages the currency hedges for all of its investment funds in-house, it is also considering engaging a currency overlay manager.

1. Using a currency overlay manager for the Conservative Value Fund is *most likely* to involve:
   A. joining the alpha and hedging mandates.
   B. a more active approach to managing currency risks.
   C. using this manager to passively hedge their foreign exchange exposures.
2. Using a currency overlay manager for the Aggressive Growth Fund is *most likely* to involve:
   A. separating the alpha and hedging mandates.
   B. a less discretionary approach to managing currency hedges.
   C. an IPS that limits active management to emerging market currencies.
3. Brixworth & St. Ives is *more likely* to engage multiple currency overlay managers if:
   A. their returns are correlated with asset returns in the fund.
   B. the currency managers' returns are correlated with each other.
   C. the currency managers' use different active management strategies.

Solution to 1: C is correct. The Conservative Value Fund wants to avoid all currency exposures in the portfolio and Windhoek believes that it lacks the currency management expertise to do this.

Solution to 2: A is correct. Brixworth & St. Ives already does the FX hedging in house, so a currency overlay is more likely to be a pure alpha mandate. This should not change the way that Brixworth & St. Ives manages its hedges, and the fund's mandate to seek out inefficiencies in the global FX market is unlikely to lead to a restriction to actively manage only emerging market currencies.

> *Solution to 3:* C is correct. Different active management strategies may lead to a more diversified source of alpha generation, and hence reduced portfolio risk. Choices A and B are incorrect because a higher correlation with foreign-currency assets in the portfolio or among overlay manager returns is likely to lead to less diversification.

6. STRATEGIC DECISIONS IN CURRENCY MANAGEMENT: FORMULATING A CURRENCY MANAGEMENT PROGRAM

We now try to bring all of these previous considerations together in describing how to formulate an appropriate currency management program given client objectives and constraints, as well as overall financial market conditions. Generally speaking, the *strategic* currency positioning of the portfolio, as encoded in the IPS, should be biased toward a more-fully hedged currency management program the more

- short term the investment objectives of the portfolio;
- risk averse the beneficial owners of the portfolio are (and impervious to *ex post* regret over missed opportunities);
- immediate the income and/or liquidity needs of the portfolio;
- fixed-income assets are held in a foreign-currency portfolio;
- cheaply a hedging program can be implemented;
- volatile (i.e., risky) financial markets are;[8] and
- skeptical the beneficial owners and/or management oversight committee are of the expected benefits of active currency management.

The relaxation of any of these conditions creates latitude to allow a more proactive currency risk posture in the portfolio, either through wider tolerance bands for discretionary hedging, or by introducing foreign currencies as a separate asset class (using currency overlay programs as an alternative asset class in the overall portfolio). In the latter case, the more currency overlay is expected to generate alpha that is uncorrelated with other asset or alpha-generation programs in the portfolio, the more it is likely to be allowed in terms of strategic portfolio positioning.

Investment Policy Statement

Kailua Kona Advisors runs a Hawaii-based hedge fund that focuses on developed market equities located outside of North America. Its investor base consists of local high-net-worth individuals who are all considered to have a long investment horizon, a high tolerance for risk, and no immediate income needs. In its prospectus to investors, Kailua Kona indicates that it actively manages both the fund's equity and foreign-currency exposures, and that the fund uses leverage through the use of loans as well as short-selling.

Exhibit 4 presents the hedge fund's currency management policy included in the IPS for this hedge fund.

---

[8] As we will see, this also increases hedging costs when currency options are used.

EXHIBIT 4   Hedge Fund Currency Management Policy: An Example

Overall Portfolio Benchmark:	MSCI EAFE Index (local currency)
Currency Exposure Ranges:	Foreign-currency exposures, based on the USD market value of the equities actually held by the fund at the beginning of each month, will be hedged back into USD within the following tolerance ranges of plus or minus: • EUR: 20% • GBP: 15% • JPY: 10% • CHF: 10% • AUD: 10% • SEK: 10% Other currency exposures shall be left unhedged.
Rebalancing:	The currency hedges will be rebalanced at least monthly, to reflect changes in the USD-denominated market value of portfolio equity holdings.
Hedging Instruments:	• Forward contracts up to 12 months maturity; • European put and call options can be bought or written, for maturities up to 12 months; and • Exotic options of up to 12 months maturity can be bought or sold.
Reporting:	Management will present quarterly reports to the board detailing net foreign-currency exposures and speculative trading results. Speculative trading results will be benchmarked against a 100% hedged currency exposure.

With this policy, Kailua Kona Advisors is indicating that it is willing to accept foreign-currency exposures within the portfolio but that these exposures must be kept within pre-defined limits. For example, suppose that at the beginning of the month the portfolio held EUR10 million of EUR-denominated assets. Also suppose that this EUR10 million exposure, combined with all the other foreign-currency exposures in the portfolio, matches Kailua Kona Advisors' desired portfolio weights by currency (as a US-based fund, these desired percentage portfolio allocations across all currencies will be based in USD).

The currency-hedging guidelines indicate that the hedge (for example, using a short position in a USD/EUR forward contract) should be between EUR8 million and EUR12 million, giving some discretion to the portfolio manager on the size of the net exposure to the EUR. At the beginning of the next month, the USD values of the foreign assets in the portfolio are measured again, and the process repeats. If there has been either a large move in the foreign-currency value of the EUR-denominated assets and/or a large move in the USD/EUR exchange rate, it is possible that Kailua Kona Advisors' portfolio exposure to EUR-denominated assets will be too far away from the desired percentage allocation.[9] Kailua Kona Advisors will then need to either buy or sell EUR-denominated assets.

---

[9] The overall portfolio percentage allocations by currency will also depend on the price moves of all *other* foreign-currency assets and exchange rates as well, but we will simplify our example by ignoring this nuance.

If movements in the EUR-denominated value of the assets or in the USD/EUR exchange rate are large enough, this asset rebalancing may have to be done before month's end. Either way, once the asset rebalancing is done, it establishes the new EUR-denominated asset value on which the currency hedge will be based (i.e., plus or minus 20% of this new EUR amount).

If the portfolio is not 100% hedged—for example, continuing the Kailua Kona illustration, if the portfolio manager only hedges EUR9 million of the exposure and has a residual exposure of being long EUR1 million—the success or failure of the manager's tactical decision will be compared with a "neutral" benchmark. In this case, the comparison would be against the performance of a 100% fully hedged portfolio—that is, with a EUR10 million hedge.

7. ACTIVE CURRENCY MANAGEMENT: BASED ON ECONOMIC FUNDAMENTALS, TECHNICAL ANALYSIS, AND THE CARRY TRADE

The previous section discussed the *strategic* decisions made by the IPS on locating the currency management practices of the portfolio along a risk spectrum ranging from a very conservative approach to currency risk to very active currency management. In this section, we consider the case in which the IPS has given the portfolio manager (or currency overlay manager) at least some limited discretion for actively managing currency risk within these mandated strategic bounds. This then leads to *tactical* decisions: which FX exposures to accept and manage within these discretionary limits. In other words, tactical decisions involve active currency management.

A market view is a prerequisite to any form of active management. At the heart of the trading decision in FX (and other) markets lies a view on future market prices and conditions. This market opinion guides all decisions with respect to currency risk exposures, including whether currency hedges should be implemented and, if so, how they should be managed.

In what follows, we will explore some of the methods used to form directional views about the FX market. However, a word of caution that cannot be emphasized enough: *There is no simple formula, model, or approach that will allow market participants to precisely forecast exchange rates (or any other financial prices) or to be able to be confident that any trading decision will be profitable.*

7.1. Active Currency Management Based on Economic Fundamentals

This section sets out a broad framework for developing a view about future exchange rate movements based on underlying fundamentals. In contrast to other methods for developing a market view (which are discussed in subsequent sections), at the heart of this approach is the assumption that, in a flexible exchange rate system, exchange rates are determined by logical economic relationships and that these relationships can be modeled.

The simple economic framework is based on the assumption that in the long run, the real exchange rate will converge to its "fair value," but short- to medium-term factors will shape the convergence path to this equilibrium.[10]

---

[10] This model was derived and explained by Rosenberg and Barker (2017).

Recall that the real exchange rate reflects the ratio of the real purchasing power between two countries; that is, the once nominal purchasing power in each country is adjusted by its respective price level as well as the spot exchange rate between the two countries. The long-run equilibrium level for the real exchange rate is determined by purchasing power parity or some other model of an exchange rate's fair value, and serves as the anchor for longer-term movements in exchange rates.

Over shorter time frames, movements in real exchange rates will also reflect movements in the real interest rate differential between countries. Recall that the real interest rate (r) is the nominal interest rate adjusted by the expected inflation rate, or $r = i - \pi^{\varepsilon}$, where i is the nominal interest rate and π^{ε} is the expected inflation rate over the same term as the nominal and real interest rates. Movements in risk premiums will also affect exchange rate movements over shorter-term horizons. The riskier a country's assets are perceived to be by investors, the more likely they are to move their investments out of that country, thereby depressing the exchange rate. Finally, the framework recognizes that there are two currencies involved in an exchange rate quote (the price and base currencies) and hence movements in exchange rates will reflect movements in the *differentials* between these various factors.

As a result, all else equal, the base currency's real exchange rate should appreciate if there is an upward movement in

- its long-run equilibrium real exchange rate;
- either its real or nominal interest rates, which should attract foreign capital;
- expected foreign inflation, which should cause the foreign currency to depreciate; and
- the foreign risk premium, which should make foreign assets less attractive compared with the base currency nation's domestic assets.

The real exchange rate should also increase if it is currently below its long-term equilibrium value. All of this makes intuitive sense.

In summary, the exchange rate forecast is a mix of long-term, medium-term, and short-term factors. The long-run equilibrium real exchange rate is the anchor for exchange rates and the point of long-run convergence for exchange rate movements. Movements in the short- to medium-term factors (nominal interest rates, expected inflation) affect the timing and path of convergence to this long-run equilibrium. A stylized depiction of the price dynamics generated by this interaction between short-, medium-, and longer-term pricing factors is shown in Exhibit 5.

It needs to be stressed that it can be very demanding to model how each of these separate effects—nominal interest rate, expected inflation, and risk premium differentials—change over time and affect exchange rates. It can also be challenging to model movements in the long-term equilibrium real exchange rate. A broad variety of factors, such as fiscal and monetary policy, will affect all of these variables in our simple economic model.[11]

---

[11] A broader discussion of exchange rate economics can be found in Rosenberg and Barker (2017).

EXHIBIT 5   Interaction of Long-Term and Short-Term Factors in Exchange Rates

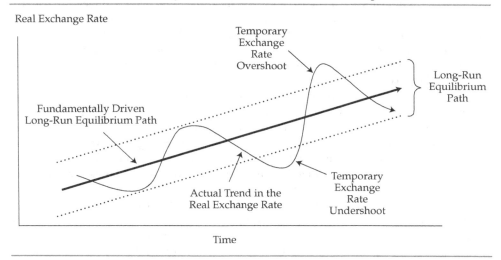

Source: Based on Rosenberg (2002), page 32.

7.2. Active Currency Management Based on Technical Analysis

Another approach to forming a market view is based on technical analysis. This approach is based on quite different assumptions compared with modeling based on economic fundamentals. Whereas classical exchange rate economics tends to view market participants as rational, markets as efficient, and exchange rates as driven by underlying economic factors, technical analysis ignores economic analysis. Instead, technical analysis is based on three broad themes.[12]

First, market technicians believe that in a liquid, freely traded market the historical price data can be helpful in projecting future price movements.[13] The reason is because many traders have already used any useful data external to the market to generate their trading positions, so this information is already reflected in current prices. Therefore, it is not necessary to look outside of the market to form an opinion on future price movements. This means it is not necessary to examine interest rates, inflation rates, or risk premium differentials (the factors in our fundamentally based model) because exchange rates already incorporate these factors.

Second, market technicians believe that historical patterns in the price data have a tendency to repeat, and that this repetition provides profitable trade opportunities. These price patterns repeat because market prices reflect human behavior and human beings have a tendency to react in similar ways to similar situations, even if this repetitive behavior is not always fully rational. For example, when confronted with an upward price trend, many market participants eventually come to believe that it will extrapolate (an attitude of "irrational exuberance" or "this time it is different"). When the trend eventually breaks, a panicked position exit can cause a sharp overshoot of fair value to the downside. Broadly speaking, technical analysis can be seen as the study of market psychology and how market participant emotions—primarily greed and fear—can be read from the price data and used to predict future price moves.

---

[12] Some material in this section is based on Sine and Strong (2012).

[13] In many other asset classes, technical analysis is based on trade volume data as well as price data. But there are no reliable, timely, and high-frequency trade volume data that are publicly available for over-the-counter (OTC) FX markets.

Third, technical analysis does not attempt to determine where market prices *should* trade (fair value, as in fundamental analysis) but where they *will* trade. Because these price patterns reflect trader emotions, they need not reflect—at least immediately—any cool, rational assessment of the underlying economic or fundamental situation. Although market prices may eventually converge to fair value in the long run, the long run can be a very long time indeed. In the meanwhile, there are shorter-term trading opportunities available in trading the technical patterns in the price data.

Combined, these three principles of technical analysis define a discipline dedicated to identifying patterns in the historical price data, especially as it relates to identifying market trends and market turning points. (Technical analysis is less useful in a trendless market.) Technical analysis tries to identify when markets have become **overbought** or **oversold**, meaning that they have trended too far in one direction and are vulnerable to a trend reversal, or correction. Technical analysis also tries to identify what are called **support levels** and **resistance levels**, either within ongoing price trends or at their extremities (i.e., turning points). These support and resistance levels are price points on dealers' order boards where one would except to see clustering of bids and offers, respectively. At these exchange rate levels, the price action is expected to get "sticky" because it will take more order flow to pierce the wall of either bids or offers. But once these price points are breached, the price action can be expected to accelerate as **stops** are triggered. (Stops, in this sense, refer to stop-loss orders, in which traders leave resting bids or offers away from the current market price to be filled if the market reaches those levels. A stop-loss order is triggered when the price action has gone against a trader's position, and it gets the trader out of that position to limit further losses.)

Technical analysis uses visual cues for market patterns as well as more quantitative technical indicators. There is a wide variety of technical indexes based on market prices that are used in this context. Some technical indicators are as simple as using moving averages of past price points. The 200-day moving average of daily exchange rates is often seen as an important indicator of likely support and resistance. Sometimes two moving averages are used to establish when a price trend is building momentum. For example, when the 50-day moving average crosses the 200-day moving average, this is sometimes seen as a price "break out" point.

Other technical indicators are based on more complex mathematical formulae. There is an extremely wide variety of these more mathematical indicators, some of them very esoteric and hard to connect intuitively with the behavior of real world financial market participants.

In summary, many FX active managers routinely use technical analysis—either alone or in conjunction with other approaches—to form a market opinion or to time position entry and exit points. Even though many technical indicators lack the intellectual underpinnings provided by formal economic modeling, they nonetheless remain a prominent feature of FX markets.

7.3. Active Currency Management Based on the Carry Trade

The **carry trade** is a trading strategy of borrowing in low-yield currencies and investing in high-yield currencies. The term "carry" is related to what is known as the cost of carry—that is, of carrying or holding an investment. This investment has either an implicit or explicit cost (borrowing cost) but may also produce income. The net cost of carry is the difference between these two return rates.

If technical analysis is based on ignoring economic fundamentals, then the carry trade is based on exploiting a well-recognized violation of one of the international parity conditions often used to describe these economic fundamentals: uncovered interest rate parity. Recall that uncovered interest rate parity asserts that, *on a longer-term average*, the return on an unhedged foreign-currency asset investment will be the same as a domestic-currency investment. Assuming that the base currency in the P/B quote is the low-yield currency, stated algebraically uncovered interest rate parity asserts that

$$\%\Delta S_{H/L} \approx i_H - i_L$$

where $\%\Delta S_{H/L}$ is the percentage change in the $S_{H/L}$ spot exchange rate (the low-yield currency is the base currency), i_H is the interest rate on the high-yield currency and i_L is the interest rate on the low-yield currency. If uncovered interest rate parity holds, the yield spread *advantage* for the high-yielding currency (the right side of the equation) will, on average, be matched by the *depreciation* of the high-yield currency (the left side of the equation; the low-yield currency is the base currency and hence a positive value for $\%\Delta S_{H/L}$ means a depreciation of the high-yield currency). According to the uncovered interest rate parity theorem, it is this offset between (1) the yield advantage and (2) the currency depreciation that equates, on average, the unhedged currency returns.

But in reality, the historical data show that there are persistent deviations from uncovered interest rate parity in FX markets, at least in the short to medium term. Indeed, high-yield countries often see their currencies *appreciate*, not depreciate, for extended periods of time. The positive returns from a combination of a favorable yield differential plus an appreciating currency can remain in place long enough to present attractive investment opportunities.

This persistent violation of uncovered interest rate parity described by the carry trade is often referred to as the **forward rate bias**. An implication of uncovered interest rate parity is that the forward rate should be an unbiased predictor of future spot rates. The historical data, however, show that the forward rate is not the center of the distribution for future spot rates; in fact, it is a *biased* predictor (for example, see Kritzman 1999). Hence the name "forward rate bias." With the forward rate premium or discount defined as $F_{P/B} - S_{P/B}$ the "bias" in the forward rate bias is that the premium typically overstates the amount of appreciation of the base currency, and the discount overstates the amount of depreciation. Indeed, the forward discount or premium often gets even the *direction* of future spot rate movements wrong.

The carry trade strategy (borrowing in low-yield currencies, investing in high-yield currencies) is equivalent to a strategy based on trading the forward rate bias. Trading the forward rate bias involves buying currencies selling at a forward discount, and selling currencies trading at a forward premium. This makes intuitive sense: It is desirable to buy low and sell high.

To show the equivalence of the carry trade and trading the forward rate bias, recall that covered interest rate parity (which is enforced by arbitrage) is stated as

$$\frac{F_{P/B} - S_{P/B}}{S_{P/B}} = \frac{(i_P - i_B)\left(\frac{t}{360}\right)}{1 + i_B\left(\frac{t}{360}\right)}$$

This equation shows that when the base currency has a lower interest rate than the price currency (i.e., the right side of the equality is positive) the base currency will trade at a forward premium (the left side of the equality is positive). That is, being low-yield currency and trading at a forward premium is synonymous. Similarly, being a high-yield currency means trading at a forward discount. Borrowing in the low-yield currency and investing in the high-yield currency (the carry trade) is hence equivalent to selling currencies that have a forward premium and buying currencies that have a forward discount (trading the forward rate bias). We will return to these concepts in Section 9 when we discuss the roll yield in hedging with forward contracts. Exhibit 6 summarizes several key points about the carry trade.

EXHIBIT 6   The Carry Trade: A Summary

	Buy/Invest	Sell/Borrow
Implementing the carry trade	High-yield currency	Low-yield currency
Trading the forward rate bias	Forward discount currency	Forward premium currency

The gains that one can earn through the carry trade (or equivalently, through trading the forward rate bias) can be seen as the risk premiums earned for carrying an unhedged position—that is, for absorbing currency risk. (In efficient markets, there is no extra reward without extra risk.) Long periods of market stability can make these extra returns enticing to many investors, and the longer the yield differential persists between high-yield and low-yield currencies, the more carry trade positions will have a tendency to build up. But these high-yield currency advantages can be erased quickly, particularly if global financial markets are subject to sudden bouts of stress. This is especially true because the carry trade is a *leveraged* position: borrowing in the low-yielding currency and investing in the high-yielding currency. These occasional large losses mean that the return distribution for the carry trade has a pronounced negative skew.

This negative skew derives from the fact that the **funding currencies** of the carry trade (the low-yield currencies in which borrowing occurs) are typically the safe haven currencies, such as the USD, CHF, and JPY. In contrast, the **investment currencies** (the high-yielding currencies) are typically currencies perceived to be higher risk, such as several emerging market currencies. Any time global financial markets are under stress there is a flight to safety that causes rapid movements in exchange rates, and usually a panicked unwinding of carry trades. As a result, traders running carry trades often get caught in losing positions, with the leverage involved magnifying their losses. Because of the tendency for long periods of relatively small gains in the carry trade to be followed by brief periods of large losses, the carry trade is sometimes characterized as "picking up nickels in front of a steamroller." One guide to the riskiness of the carry trade is the volatility of spot rate movements for the currency pair; all else equal, lower volatility is better for a carry trade position.

We close this section by noting that although the carry trade can be based on borrowing in a single funding currency and investing in a single high-yield currency, it is more common for carry trades to use multiple funding and investment currencies. The number of funding currencies and investment currencies need not be equal: for example, there could be five of one and three of the other. Sometimes the portfolio weighting of exposures between the various funding and investment currencies are simply set equal to each other. But the weights can also be optimized to reflect the trader's market view of the expected movements in each of the exchange rates, as well as their individual risks ($\sigma[\%\Delta S]$) and the expected correlations between movements in the currency pairs. These trades can be dynamically rebalanced, with the relative weights among both funding and investment currencies shifting with market conditions.

8. ACTIVE CURRENCY MANAGEMENT: BASED ON VOLATILITY TRADING

Another type of active trading style is unique to option markets and is known as volatility trading (or simply "vol trading").[14] To explain this trading style, we will start with a quick review of some option basics.

---

[14] In principle, this trading style can be applied to all asset classes with options, not just FX trading. But FX options are the most liquid and widely traded options in the world, so it is in FX where most of volatility trading likely takes place in global financial markets.

The derivatives of the option pricing model show the sensitivity of the option's premium to changes in the factors that determine option value. These derivatives are often referred to as the "Greeks" of option pricing. There is a very large number of first, second, third, and cross-derivatives that can be taken of an option pricing formula, but the two most important Greeks that we will consider here are the following:

- **Delta:** The sensitivity of the option premium to a small change in the price of the underlying[15] of the option, typically a financial asset. This sensitivity is an indication of *price* risk.
- **Vega:** The sensitivity of the option premium to a small change in implied volatility. This sensitivity is an indication of *volatility* risk.

The most important concept to grasp in terms of volatility trading is that the use of options allows the trader, through a variety of trading strategies, to *unbundle* and isolate all of the various risk factors (the Greeks) and trade them separately. Once an initial option position is taken (either long or short), the trader has exposure to *all* of the various Greeks/risk factors. The unwanted risk exposures, however, can then be hedged away, leaving *only* the desired risk exposure to express that specific directional view.

Delta hedging is the act of hedging away the option position's exposure to delta, the price risk of the underlying (the FX spot rate, in this case). Because delta shows the sensitivity of the option price to changes in the spot exchange rate, it thus defines the option's hedge ratio: The size of the offsetting hedge position that will set the *net* delta of the combined position (option plus delta hedge) to zero. Typically, implementing this delta hedge is done using either forward contracts or a spot transaction (spot, by definition, has a delta of one, and no exposure to any other of the Greeks; forward contracts are highly correlated with the spot rate). For example, if a trader was long a call option on USD/EUR with a nominal value of EUR1 million and a delta of +0.5, the delta hedge would involve a short forward position in USD/EUR of EUR0.5 million. That is, the size of the delta hedge is equal to the option's delta times the nominal size of the contract. This hedge size would set the net delta of the overall position (option and forward) to zero.[16] Once the delta hedge has set the net delta of the position to zero, the trader then has exposure *only* to the other Greeks, and can use various trading strategies to position in these (long or short) depending on directional views.

Although one could theoretically trade *any* of the other Greeks, the most important one traded is vega; that is, the trader is expressing a view on the future movements in implied volatility, or in other words, is engaged in volatility trading. Implied volatility is not the same as realized, or observed, historical volatility, although it is heavily influenced by it. By engaging in volatility trading, the trader is expressing a view about the future volatility of exchange rates *but not their direction* (the delta hedge set the net delta of the position to zero).

One simple option strategy that implements a volatility trade is a **straddle**, which is a combination of both an at-the-money (ATM) put and an ATM call. A long straddle buys both of these options. Because their deltas are −0.5 and +0.5, respectively, the net delta of the position is zero; that is, the long straddle is delta neutral. This position is profitable in more volatile markets, when either the put or the call go sufficiently in the money to cover the upfront cost of the two option premiums paid. Similarly, a short straddle is a bet that the spot rate will

---

[15] The underlying asset of a derivative is typically referred to simply as the "underlying."

[16] Strictly speaking, the net delta would be *approximately* equal to zero because forward contracts do not have identical price properties to those of the spot exchange rate. But it is close enough for our purposes here, and we will ignore this small difference.

stay relatively stable. In this case, the payout on any option exercise will be less than the twin premiums the seller has collected; the rest is net profit for the option seller. A similar option structure is a **strangle** position for which a long position is buying out-of-the-money (OTM) puts and calls with the same expiry date and the same degree of being out of the money (we elaborate more on this subject later). Because OTM options are being bought, the cost of the position is cheaper—but conversely, it also does not pay off until the spot rate passes the OTM strike levels. As a result, the risk–reward for a strangle is more moderate than that for a straddle.

The interesting thing to note is that by using delta-neutral trading strategies, volatility is turned into a product that can be actively traded like any other financial product or asset class, such as equities, commodities, fixed-income products, and so on. Volatility is not constant nor are its movements completely random. Instead volatility is determined by a wide variety of underlying factors—both fundamental and technical—that the trader can express an opinion on. Movements in volatility are cyclical, and typically subject to long periods of relative stability punctuated by sharp upward spikes in volatility as markets come under periodic bouts of stress (usually the result of some dramatic event, financial or otherwise). Speculative vol traders—for example, among currency overlay managers—often want to be net-short volatility. The reason is because most options expire out of the money, and the option writer then gets to keep the option premium without delivery of the underlying currency pair. The amount of the option premium can be considered the risk premium, or payment, earned by the option writer for absorbing volatility risk. It is a steady source of income under "normal" market conditions. Ideally, these traders would want to "flip" their position and be long volatility ahead of volatility spikes, but these episodes can be notoriously difficult to time. Most hedgers typically run options positions that are net-long volatility because they are buying protection from unanticipated price volatility. (Being long the option means being exposed to the time decay of the option's time value; that is similar to paying insurance premiums for the protection against exchange rate volatility.)

We can also note that just as there are *currency overlay* programs for actively trading the portfolio's currency exposures (as discussed in Section 5) there can also be *volatility overlay* programs for actively trading the portfolio's exposures to movements in currencies' implied volatility. Just as currency overlay programs manage the portfolio's exposure to currency delta (movements in spot exchange rates), volatility overlay programs manage the portfolio's exposure to currency vega. These volatility overlay programs can be focused on earning speculative profits, but can also be used to hedge the portfolio against risk (we will return to this concept in the discussion of macro hedges in Section 11).

Enumerating all the potential strategies for trading foreign exchange volatility is beyond the scope of this reading. Instead, the reader should be aware that this dimension of trading FX volatility (not price) exists and sees a large amount of active trading. Moreover, the best traders are able to think and trade in both dimensions simultaneously. Movements in volatility are often correlated with directional movements in the price of the underlying. For example, when there is a flight to safety as carry trades unwind, there is typically a spike in volatility (and options prices) at the same time. Although pure vol trading is based on a zero-delta position, this need not always be the case; a trader can express a market opinion on volatility (vega exposure) and still have a directional exposure to the underlying spot exchange rate as well (delta exposure). That is, the overall trading position has net vega and delta exposures that reflect the *joint* market view.

We end this section by explaining how currency options are quoted in professional FX markets. (This information will be used in Sections 9–12 when we discuss other option trading strategies.) Unlike exchanged-traded options, such as those used in equity markets, OTC options for currencies are not described in terms of specific strike levels (i.e., exchange rate levels). Instead, in the interdealer market, options are described in terms of their "delta." Deltas for puts can range from a minimum of −1 to a maximum of 0, with a delta of −0.5 being the point at which the put option is ATM; OTM puts have deltas between 0 and −0.5. For call options, delta ranges from 0 to +1, with 0.5 being the ATM point. In FX markets, these delta values are quoted both in *absolute* terms (i.e., in positive rather than negative values) and as percentages, with standard FX option quotes usually in terms of 25-delta and 10-delta options (i.e., a delta of 0.25 and 0.10, respectively; the 10-delta option is deeper OTM and hence cheaper than the 25-delta option). The FX options market is the most liquid around these standard delta quoting points (ATM, 25-delta, 10-delta), but of course, as a flexible OTC market, options of any delta/strike price can be traded. The 25-delta put option (for example) will still go in the money if the spot price dips below a *specific* exchange rate level; this *implied* strike price is *backed out* of an option pricing model once all the other pricing factors, including the current spot rate and the 25-delta of the option, are put into the option pricing model. (The specific option pricing model used is agreed on by both parties to the trade.)

These standard delta price points are often used to define option trading strategies. For example, a 25-delta strangle would be based on 25-delta put and call options. Similarly, a 10-delta strangle would be based on 10-delta options (and would cost less and have a more moderate payoff structure than a 25-delta strangle). Labeling option structures by their delta is common in FX markets.

EXAMPLE 3   Active Strategies

Annie McYelland works as an analyst at Scotland-based Kilmarnock Advisors, an investment firm that offers several investment vehicles for its clients. McYelland has been put in charge of formulating the firm's market views for some of the foreign currencies that these vehicles have exposures to. Her market views will be used to guide the hedging and discretionary positioning for some of the actively managed portfolios.

McYelland begins by examining yield spreads between various countries and the implied volatility extracted from the option pricing for several currency pairs. She collects the following data:

One-Year Yield Levels	
Switzerland	−0.103%
United States	0.162%
Poland	4.753%
Mexico	4.550%
One-Year Implied Volatility	
PLN/CHF	8.4%
MXN/CHF	15.6%
PLN/USD	20.3%
MXN/USD	16.2%

Note: PLN = Polish zloty; the Swiss yields are negative because of Swiss policy actions.

McYelland is also examining various economic indicators to shape her market views. After studying the economic prospects for both Japan and New Zealand, she expects that the inflation rate for New Zealand is about to accelerate over the next few years, whereas the inflation rate for Japan should remain relatively stable. Turning her attention to the economic situation in India, McYelland believes that the Indian authorities are about to tighten monetary policy, and that this change has not been fully priced into the market. She reconsiders her short-term view for the Indian rupee (i.e., the INR/USD spot rate) after conducting this analysis.

McYelland also examines the exchange rate volatility for several currency pairs to which the investment trusts are exposed. Based on her analysis of the situation, she believes that the exchange rate between Chilean peso and the US dollar (CLP/USD) is about to become much more volatile than usual, although she has no strong views about whether the CLP will appreciate or depreciate.

One of McYelland's colleagues, Catalina Ortega, is a market technician and offers to help McYelland time her various market position entry and exit points based on chart patterns. While examining the JPY/NZD price chart, Ortega notices that the 200-day moving average is at 62.0405 and the current spot rate is 62.0315.

1. Based on the data she collected, all else equal, McYelland's *best* option for implementing a carry trade position would be to fund in:
   A. USD and invest in PLN.
   B. CHF and invest in MXN.
   C. CHF and invest in PLN.

2. Based on McYelland's inflation forecasts, all else equal, she would be *more likely* to expect a(n):
   A. depreciation in the JPY/NZD.
   B. increase in capital flows from Japan to New Zealand.
   C. more accommodative monetary policy by the Reserve Bank of New Zealand.

3. Given her analysis for India, McYelland's short-term market view for the INR/USD spot rate is now *most likely* to be:
   A. biased toward appreciation.
   B. biased toward depreciation.
   C. unchanged because it is only a short-run view.

4. Using CLP/USD options, what would be the *cheapest* way for McYelland to implement her market view for the CLP?
   A. Buy a straddle
   B. Buy a 25-delta strangle
   C. Sell a 40-delta strangle

5. Based on Ortega's analysis, she would *most likely* expect:
   A. support near 62.0400.
   B. resistance near 62.0310.
   C. resistance near 62.0400.

Solution to 1: C is correct. The yield spread between the funding and investment currencies is the widest and the implied volatility (risk) is the lowest. The other choices have a narrower yield spread and higher risk (implied volatility).

Solution to 2: A is correct. All else equal, an increase in New Zealand's inflation rate will decrease its real interest rate and lead to the real interest rate differential favoring Japan over New Zealand. This would likely result in a depreciation of the JPY/NZD rate over time. The shift in the relative real returns should lead to reduced capital flows from Japan to New Zealand (so Choice B is incorrect) and the RBNZ—New Zealand's central bank—is more likely to tighten monetary policy than loosen it as inflation picks up (so Choice C is incorrect).

Solution to 3: B is correct. Tighter monetary policy in India should lead to higher real interest rates (at least in the short run). This increase will cause the INR to appreciate against the USD, but because the USD is the base currency, this will be represented as depreciation in the INR/USD rate. Choice C is incorrect because a tightening of monetary policy that is not fully priced-in to market pricing is likely to move bond yields and hence the exchange rate in the short run (given the simple economic model in Section 7).

Solution to 4: B is correct. Either a long straddle or a long strangle will profit from a marked increase in volatility in the spot rate, but a 25-delta strangle would be cheaper (because it is based on OTM options). Writing a strangle—particularly one that is close to being ATM, which is what a 40-delta structure is—is likely to be exercised in favor of the counterparty if McYelland's market view is correct.

Solution to 5: C is correct. The 200-day moving average has not been crossed yet, and it is higher than the current spot rate. Hence this technical indicator suggests that resistance lies above the current spot rate level, likely in the 62.0400 area. Choice A is incorrect because the currency has not yet appreciated to 62.0400, so it cannot be considered a "support" level. Given that the currency pair has already traded through 62.0310 and is still at least 90 pips away from the 200-day moving average, it is more likely to suspect that resistance still lies above the current spot rate.

9. CURRENCY MANAGEMENT TOOLS: FORWARD CONTRACTS, FX SWAPS, AND CURRENCY OPTIONS

In this section, we focus on how the portfolio manager uses financial derivatives to implement both the *strategic* positioning of the portfolio along the risk spectrum (i.e., the performance benchmark) as well as the *tactical* decisions made in regard to variations around this "neutral" position. The manager's market view—whether based on carry, fundamental, currency volatility, or technical considerations—leads to this active management of risk positioning around the strategic benchmark point. Implementing both strategic and tactical viewpoints requires the use of trading tools, which we discuss in this section.

The balance of this reading will assume that the portfolio's strategic foreign-currency asset exposures and the maximum amount of currency risk desired have already been determined by the portfolio's IPS. We begin at the conservative end of the risk spectrum by describing a passive hedge for a single currency (with a 100% hedge ratio). After discussing the costs and limitations of this approach, we move out further along the risk spectrum by describing strategies in which the basic "building blocks" of financial derivatives can be combined to implement the manager's tactical positioning and construct much more customized risk–return profiles. Not surprisingly, the basic trading tools themselves—forwards, options, FX swaps—are used for both strategic and tactical risk management and by both hedgers and speculators alike (although for different ends). Note that the instruments covered as tools of currency management are not nearly an exhaustive list. For example, exchange-traded funds for currencies are a vehicle that can be useful in managing currency risk.

9.1. Forward Contracts

In this section, we consider the most basic form of hedging: a 100% hedge ratio for a single foreign-currency exposure. Futures or forward contracts on currencies can be used to obtain full currency hedges, although most institutional investors prefer to use forward contracts for the following reasons:

1. Futures contracts are standardized in terms of settlement dates and contract sizes. These may not correspond to the portfolio's investment parameters.
2. Futures contracts may not always be available in the currency pair that the portfolio manager wants to hedge. For example, the most liquid currency futures contracts trade on the Chicago Mercantile Exchange (CME). Although there are CME futures contracts for all major exchange rates (e.g., USD/EUR, USD/GBP) and many cross rates (e.g., CAD/EUR, JPY/CHF), there are not contracts available for all possible currency pairs. Trading these cross rates would need multiple futures contracts, adding to portfolio management costs. In addition, many of the "second tier" emerging market currencies may not have liquid futures contracts available against any currency, let alone the currency pair in which the portfolio manager is interested.
3. Futures contracts require up-front margin (initial margin). They also have intra-period cash flow implications, in that the exchange will require the investor to post additional variation margin when the spot exchange rate moves against the investor's position. These initial and ongoing margin requirements tie up the investor's capital and require careful monitoring through time, adding to the portfolio management expense. Likewise, margin flows can go in the investor's favor, requiring monitoring and reinvestment.

In contrast, forward contracts do not suffer from any of these drawbacks. Major global investment dealers (such as Deutsche Bank, Royal Bank of Scotland, UBS, etc.) will quote prices on forward contracts for practically every possible currency pair, settlement date, and transaction amount. They typically do not require margin to be posted or maintained.

Moreover, the daily trade volume globally for OTC currency forward and swap contracts dwarfs that for exchange-traded currency futures contracts; that is, forward contracts are more liquid than futures for trading in large sizes. Reflecting this liquidity, forward contracts are the predominant hedging instrument in use globally. For the balance of this section, we will focus only on currency forward contracts. However, separate side boxes discuss exchange-traded currency futures contracts and currency-based exchange-traded funds (ETFs).

9.1.1. Hedge Ratios with Forward Contracts

In principle, setting up a full currency hedge is relatively straightforward: match the current market value of the foreign-currency exposure in the portfolio with an equal and offsetting position in a forward contract. In practice, of course, it is not that simple because the market value of the foreign-currency assets will change with market conditions. This means that the actual hedge ratio will typically *drift* away from the desired hedge ratio as market conditions change. A **static hedge** (i.e., unchanging hedge) will avoid transaction costs, but will also tend to accumulate unwanted currency exposures as the value of the foreign-currency assets change. This characteristic will cause a mismatch between the market value of the foreign-currency asset portfolio and the nominal size of the forward contract used for the currency hedge; this is pure currency risk. For this reason, the portfolio manager will typically need to implement a **dynamic hedge** by rebalancing the portfolio periodically. This hedge rebalancing will mean adjusting some combination of the size, number, and maturities of the forward currency contracts.

A simple example will illustrate this rebalancing process. Suppose that an investor domiciled in Switzerland has a EUR-denominated portfolio that, at the start of the period, is worth EUR1,000,000. Assume a monthly hedge-rebalancing cycle. To hedge this portfolio, the investor would sell EUR1,000,000 one month forward against the CHF. Assume that one month later, the EUR-denominated investment portfolio is then actually worth only EUR950,000. To roll the hedge forward for the next month, the investor will engage in a mismatched FX swap. (Recall that a "matched" swap means that both the spot and forward transactions—the near and far "legs" of the swap, respectively—are of equal size.) For the near leg of the swap, EUR1 million will be bought at spot to settle the expiring forward contract. (The euro amounts will then net to zero, but a Swiss franc cash flow will be generated, either a loss or a gain for the investor, depending on how the CHF/EUR rate has changed over the month.) For the far leg of the swap, the investor will sell EUR950,000 forward for one month.

Another way to view this rebalancing process is to consider the case in which the original short forward contract has a three-month maturity. In this case, rebalancing after one month would mean that the manager would have to *buy* 50,000 CHF/EUR two months forward. There is no cash flow at the time this second forward contract is entered, but the *net* amount of euro for delivery at contract settlement two months into the future is now the euro hedge amount desired (i.e., EUR950,000). There will be a net cash flow (denominated in CHF) calculated over these two forward contracts on the settlement date two months hence.

Although rebalancing a dynamic hedge will keep the actual hedge ratio close to the target hedge ratio, it will also lead to increased transaction costs compared with a static hedge. The manager will have to assess the cost–benefit trade-offs of how frequently to dynamically rebalance the hedge. These will depend on a variety of idiosyncratic factors (manager risk aversion, market view, IPS guidelines, etc.), and so there is no single "correct" answer—different managers will likely make different decisions.

However, we can observe that the higher the degree of risk aversion, the more frequently the hedge is likely to be rebalanced back to the "neutral" hedge ratio. Similarly, the greater the tolerance for active trading, and the stronger the commitment to a particular market view, the more likely it is that the actual hedge ratio will be allowed to vary from a "neutral" setting, possibly through entering into new forward contracts. (For example, if the P/B spot rate was seen to be oversold and likely to rebound higher, an actively traded portfolio might buy the base currency through forward contracts to lock in this perceived low price—and thus change the actual hedge ratio accordingly.) The sidebar on executing a hedge illustrates the concepts of rolling hedges, FX swaps and their pricing (bid–offer), and adjusting hedges for market views and changes in market values.

Executing a Hedge

Jiao Yang works at Hong Kong SAR-based Kwun Tong Investment Advisors; its reporting currency is the Hong Kong Dollar (HKD). She has been put in charge of managing the firm's foreign-currency hedges. Forward contracts for two of these hedges are coming due for settlement, and Yang will need to use FX swaps to roll these hedges forward three months.

Hedge #1: Kwun Tong has a short position of JPY800,000,000 coming due on a JPY/HKD forward contract. The market value of the underlying foreign-currency assets has not changed over the life of the contract, and Yang does not have a firm opinion on the expected future movement in the JPY/HKD spot rate.

Hedge #2: Kwun Tong has a short position of EUR8,000,000 coming due on a HKD/EUR forward contract. The market value of the EUR-denominated assets has increased (measured in EUR). Yang expects the HKD/EUR spot rate to decrease.

The following spot exchange rates and three-month forward points are in effect when Yang transacts the FX swaps necessary to roll the hedges forward:

	Spot Rate	Three-Month Forward Points
JPY/HKD	10.80/10.82	−20/−14
HKD/EUR	10.0200/10.0210	125/135

Note: The JPY/HKD forward points will be scaled by 100; the HKD/EUR forward points will be scaled by 10,000

As a result, Yang undertakes the following transactions:

For **Hedge #1**, the foreign-currency value of the underlying assets has not changed, and she does not have a market view that would lead her to want to either over- or under-hedge the foreign-currency exposure. Therefore, to roll these hedges forward, she uses a matched swap. For matched swaps (see Section 2), the convention is to base pricing on the mid-market spot exchange rate. Thus, the spot leg of the swap would be to buy JPY800,000,000 at the mid-market rate of 10.81 JPY/HKD. The forward leg of the swap would require selling JPY800,000,000 forward three months. Selling JPY (the price currency in the JPY/HKD quote) is equivalent to buying HKD (the base currency). Therefore, she uses the offer-side forward points, and the all-in forward rate for the forward leg of the swap is as follows:

$$10.81 + \frac{-14}{100} = 10.67$$

For **Hedge #2**, the foreign-currency value of the underlying assets has increased; Yang recognizes that this implies that she should increase the size of the hedge greater than EUR8,000,000. She also believes that the HKD/EUR spot rate will decrease, and recognizes that this implies a hedge ratio of more than 100% (Kwun Tong Advisors has given her discretion to over- or under-hedge based on her market views). This too means that the size of the hedge should be increased more than EUR8,000,000, because Yang will want a larger short position in the EUR to take advantage of its expected depreciation. Hence, Yang uses a mismatched swap, buying EUR8,000,000 at spot rate against the HKD, to settle the maturing forward contract and then *selling* an amount *more* than EUR8,000,000 forward to increase the hedge size. Because the EUR is the base currency in the HKD/EUR quote, this means using the *bid* side for both the spot rate and the forward points when calculating the all-in forward rate:

$$10.0200 + \frac{125}{10,000} = 10.0325$$

The spot leg of the swap—buying back EUR8,000,000 to settle the outstanding forward transaction—is also based on the bid rate of 10.0200. This is because Yang is selling an amount larger than EUR8,000,000 forward, and the all-in forward rate of the swap is already using the bid side of the market (as it would for a matched swap). Hence, to pick up the net increase in forward EUR sales, the dealer Yang is transacting with would price the swap so that Yang also has to use bid side of the *spot* quote for the spot transaction used to settle the maturing forward contract.

9.1.2. Roll Yield

The roll yield (also called the roll return) on a hedge results from the fact that forward contracts are priced at the spot rate adjusted for the number of forward points at that maturity (see the example shown in Exhibit 3). This forward point adjustment can either benefit or detract from portfolio returns (positive and negative roll yield, respectively) depending on whether the forward points are at a premium or discount, and what side of the market (buying or selling) the portfolio manager is on.

The concept of roll yield is illustrated with the simplified example shown in Exhibit 7.

EXHIBIT 7   The Forward Curve and Roll Yield

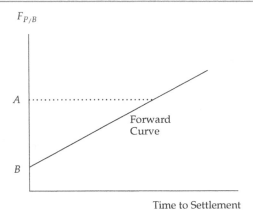

The magnitude of roll yield is given by $|(F_{P/B} - S_{P/B})/S_{P/B}|$ where "$||$" indicates absolute value. The sign depends on whether the investor needs to buy or to sell the base currency forward in order to maintain the hedge. A *positive* roll yield results from buying the base currency at a forward discount or selling it at a forward premium (the intuition here is that it is profitable to "buy low and sell high"). Otherwise, the roll yield is negative (i.e., a positive cost). Examining the case of negative roll yield, assume that to implement the hedge requires buying the base currency in the P/B quote, and that the base currency is trading at a forward premium (as shown in Exhibit 7). By using a long position in a forward contract to implement this hedge, it means paying the forward price of A. All else equal, as time passes the price of the forward contract will "roll down the curve" toward Price B as the forward contract's settlement date approaches. (Note that in reality the curve is not always linear.) At the settlement date of the forward contract, it is necessary to roll the hedging position forward to extend the currency hedge. This rolling forward will involve selling the base currency at the then-current spot exchange rate to settle the forward contract, and then going long another far-dated forward contract (i.e., an FX swap transaction). Note that the portfolio manager originally bought the base currency at Price A and then subsequently sold it at a lower Price B—and that buying high and selling low will be a cost to the portfolio. Or put differently, all else equal, the roll yield would be negative in this case. Note that the "all else equal" caveat refers to the fact that the all-in price of the forward contract consists of the spot rate and forward points, and both are likely to change over the life of the forward contract. It is possible that at the settlement date the spot rate would have moved higher than A, in which case the roll yield would be positive. But the larger the gap between A and B at contract initiation, the less likely this is to occur.

The concept of roll yield is very similar to the concept of forward rate bias (and the carry trade) introduced in Sections 7 and 8. Indeed, a negative roll yield typically indicates that the hedger was trading *against* the forward rate bias by buying a currency at a forward premium (as in Exhibit 7) or selling a currency at a forward discount. This is the exact opposite of trading the forward rate bias, which is to buy at a discount and sell at a premium. Given the equivalence between the forward rate bias and the carry trade, by trading against the forward rate bias the hedger with a negative roll yield is also essentially entering into *negative* carry trade, in effect borrowing at high rates and investing at low rates. On average, this will not be a winning strategy. Given the equivalence between implementing a carry trade, trading the forward rate bias, and earning positive roll yield, we can now complete Exhibit 6 introduced in Section 7 on the carry trade:

EXHIBIT 8   The Carry Trade and Roll Yield

	Buy/Invest	Sell/Borrow	
Implementing the carry trade	High-yield currency	Low-yield currency	Earning a positive roll yield
Trading the forward rate bias	Forward discount currency	Forward premium currency	

Note as well that this concept of roll yield applies to forward and futures contracts used to trade *any* asset class, not just currencies: It applies equally well to forwards and futures on equities, fixed-income securities, commodities, and indeed, any financial product. For example, consider the case of a commodity processor that hedges the costs of its production process by going long corn futures contracts. If the futures curve for corn futures contracts is in contango (upward sloping, as in Exhibit 7), then this hedging position will also face the potential for negative roll yield.

To be fair, it is also possible for the level of, and movement in, forward points to be in the portfolio manager's favor. Extending our previous example, consider the case of a portfolio manager that has to *sell* the base currency to implement the currency hedge. In this case, the manager would be selling the base currency forward at Price A in Exhibit 7 and, all else equal and through entering an FX swap at settlement date, buying the currency back at the lower Price B—essentially, short selling a financial product with a declining price. In this case, the roll yield is positive.

Because the level of and movements in forward points can either enhance or reduce currency-hedged returns, it explains an observed tendency in foreign exchange markets for the amount of currency hedging to generally vary with movements in forward points. As forward points move against the hedger, the amount of hedging activity typically declines as the cost/benefit ratio of the currency hedge deteriorates. The opposite occurs when movements in forward points reduce hedging costs. Essentially the tendency to hedge will vary depending on whether implementing the hedge happens to be trading in the same direction of the forward rate bias strategy or against it. It is easier to sell a currency forward if there is a "cushion" when it is selling at a forward premium. Likewise, it is more attractive to buy a currency when it is trading at a forward discount. This swings the forward rate bias (and carry trade advantage) in favor of the hedge.

Combined with the manager's market view of future spot rate movements, what this concept implies is that, when setting the hedge ratio, the portfolio manager must balance the effect of expected future exchange rate movements on portfolio returns against the expected effect of the roll yield (i.e., the expected cost of the hedge).

A simple example can illustrate this effect. Consider a portfolio manager that needs to sell forward the base currency of a currency pair (P/B) to implement a currency hedge. Clearly, the manager would prefer to sell this currency at as high a price as possible. Assume that given the forward points for this currency pair and the time horizon for the hedge, the expected roll yield (cost of the hedge) is −3%. Suppose the portfolio manager had a market view that the base currency would depreciate by 4%. In this case, the hedge makes sense: It is better to pay 3% for the hedge to avoid an expected 4% loss.

Now, suppose that with a movement in forward points the new forward discount on the base currency is 6% away from the current spot rate. If the manager's market view is unchanged (an expected depreciation of the base currency of 4%), then now the use of the hedge is less clear: Does it make sense to pay 6% for the hedge to avoid an expected 4% loss? A *risk-neutral* manager would not hedge under these circumstances because the net expected value of the hedge is negative. But a *risk-averse* manager might still implement the hedge regardless of the negative net expected value. The reason is because it is possible that the market forecast is wrong and that the *actual* depreciation of the base currency (and realized loss to the portfolio) may be higher than the 6% cost of the hedge. The risk-averse manager must then weigh the *certainty* of a hedge that costs 6% against the *risk* that actual unhedged currency losses might be much higher than that.

Clearly, the cost/benefit analysis has shifted against hedging in this case, but many risk-averse investors would still undertake the hedge anyway. The risk-averse manager would likely only take an unhedged currency position if the difference between the expected cost of the hedge and the expected return on an unhedged position was so great as to make the risk acceptable. Balancing these two considerations would depend on the type of market view the manager held and the degree of conviction in it, as well as the manager's degree of risk aversion. The decision taken will vary among investors, so no definitive answer can be given as to what would be the appropriate hedging choice (different portfolio managers will make different choices given the same opportunity set). But hedging costs will vary with market conditions and the higher the expected cost of the hedge (negative roll yield) the more the cost/benefit calculation moves against using a fully hedged position. Or put another way, if setting up the hedge involves selling the low-yield currency and buying the high-yield currency in the P/B pair (i.e., an implicit carry position), then the more likely the portfolio will be fully hedged or even over-hedged. The opposite is also true: Trading against the forward rate bias is likely to lead to lower hedge ratios, all else equal.

EXAMPLE 4   The Hedging Decision

The reporting currency of Hong Kong SAR-based Kwun Tong Investment Advisors is the Hong Kong dollar (HKD). The investment committee is examining whether it should implement a currency hedge for the firm's exposures to the GBP and the ZAR (the firm has long exposures to both of these foreign currencies). The hedge would use forward contracts. The following data relevant to assessing the expected cost of the hedge and the expected move in the spot exchange rate has been developed by the firm's market strategist.

	Current Spot Rate	Six-Month Forward Rate	Six-Month Forecast Spot Rate
HKD/GBP	12.4610	12.6550	12.3000
HKD/ZAR	0.9510	0.9275	0.9300

1. Recommend whether to hedge the firm's long GBP exposure. Justify your recommendation.
2. Discuss the trade-offs in hedging the firm's long ZAR exposure.

Solution to 1: Kwun Tong is long the GBP against the HKD, and HKD/GBP is selling at a forward premium of +1.6% compared with the current spot rate. All else equal, this is the expected roll yield—which is in the firm's favor, in this case, because to implement the hedge Kwun Tong would be *selling* GBP, the base currency in the quote, at a price *higher* than the current spot rate. Moreover, the firm's market strategist expects the GBP to *depreciate* by 1.3% against the HKD. Both of these considerations argue for hedging this exposure.

Solution to 2: Kwun Tong is long the ZAR against the HKD, and HKD/ZAR is selling at a forward discount of −2.5% compared with the current spot rate. Implementing the hedge would require the firm to *sell* the base currency in the quote, the ZAR, at a price *lower* than the current spot rate. This would imply that, all else equal, the roll yield would go against the firm; that is, the expected cost of the hedge would be 2.5%. But the firm's strategist also forecasts that the ZAR will depreciate against the HKD by 2.2%. This makes the decision to hedge less certain. A risk-neutral investor would not hedge because the expected cost of the hedge is more than the expected depreciation of the ZAR. But this is only a point forecast and comes with a degree of uncertainty—there is a risk that the HKD/ZAR spot rate might depreciate by more than the 2.5% cost of the hedge. In this case, the decision to hedge the currency risk would depend on the trade-offs between (1) the level of risk aversion of the firm; and (2) the conviction the firm held in the currency forecast—that is, the level of certainty that the ZAR would not depreciate by more than 2.5%.

9.2. Currency Options

One of the costs of forward contracts is the opportunity cost. Once fully hedged, the portfolio manager forgoes any upside potential for future currency moves in the portfolio's favor. Currency options remove this opportunity cost because they provide the manager the right, but not the obligation, to buy or sell foreign exchange at a future date at a rate agreed on today. The manager will only exercise the option at the expiry date if it is favorable to do so.[17]

Consider the case of a portfolio manager who is long the base currency in the P/B quote and needs to sell this currency to implement the hedge. One approach is to simply buy an at-the-money put option on the P/B currency pair. Matching a long position in the underlying with a put option is known as a **protective put** strategy. Suppose the current spot rate is 1.3650 and the strike price on the put option bought is 1.3650. If the P/B rate subsequently goes down (P appreciates and B depreciates) by the expiry date, the manager can exercise the option, implement the hedge, and guarantee a selling price of 1.3650. But if the P/B rate increases (P depreciates and B appreciates), the manager can simply let the option expire and collect the currency gains.

Unfortunately, like forward contracts, currency options are not "free goods" and, like any form of insurance, there is always a price to be paid for it. Buying an option means paying an upfront premium. This premium is determined, first, by its **intrinsic value**, which is the difference between the spot exchange rate and the strike price of the option (i.e., whether the option is in the money, at the money, or out of the money, respectively). ATM options are more expensive than OTM options, and frequently these relatively expensive options expire without being exercised.

The second determinant of an option's premium is its **time value**, which in turn is heavily influenced by the volatility in exchange rates. Regardless of exchange rate volatility, however, options are always moving toward expiry. In general, the time value of the option is always declining. This is the time decay of the option's value (theta, one of the "Greeks" of option prices, describes this effect) and is similar in concept to that of negative roll yield on forward contracts described earlier. Time decay always works against the owner of an option.

As with forward contracts, a portfolio manager will have to make judgments about the cost/benefit trade-offs of options-based strategies. Although options do allow the portfolio upside potential from favorable currency movements, options can also be a very expensive form of insurance. The manager will have to balance any market view of potential currency gains against hedging costs and the degree of risk aversion. There is no "right" answer; different managers will make different decisions about the cost/benefit trade-offs when given the same opportunity set.

EXAMPLE 5   Hedging Problems

Brixworth & St. Ives Asset Management is a UK-based firm managing a dynamic hedging program for the currency exposures in its Aggressive Growth Fund. One of the fund's foreign-currency asset holdings is denominated in the Mexican peso (MXN),

---

[17] Almost all options in the FX market are European-style options, which only allow for exercise at the expiry date.

and one month ago Brixworth & St. Ives fully hedged this exposure using a two-month MXN/GBP forward contract. The following table provides the relevant information.

	One Month Ago	Today
Value of assets (in MXN)	10,000,000	9,500,000
MXN/GBP spot rate (bid–offer)	20.0500/20.0580	19.5985/20.0065
One-month forward points (bid–offer)	625/640	650/665
Two-month forward points (bid–offer)	875/900	900/950

The Aggressive Growth Fund also has an unhedged foreign-currency asset exposure denominated in the South African rand (ZAR). The current mid-market spot rate in the ZAR/GBP currency pair is 5.1050.

1. One month ago, Brixworth & St. Ives *most likely* sold:
   A. MXN9,500,000 forward at an all-in forward rate of MXN/GBP 19.6635.
   B. MXN10,000,000 forward at an all-in forward rate of MXN/GBP 20.1375.
   C. MXN10,000,000 forward at an all-in forward rate of MXN/GBP 20.1480.
2. To rebalance the hedge today, the firm would *most likely* need to:
   A. buy MXN500,000 spot.
   B. buy MXN500,000 forward.
   C. sell MXN500,000 forward.
3. Given the data in the table, the roll yield on this hedge at the forward contracts' maturity date is *most likely* to be:
   A. zero.
   B. negative.
   C. positive.
4. Assuming that all ZAR/GBP options considered have the same notional amount and maturity, the *most* expensive hedge that Brixworth & St. Ives could use to hedge its ZAR exposure is a long position in a(n):
   A. ATM call.
   B. 25-delta call.
   C. put with a strike of 5.1050.

Solution to 1: C is correct. Brixworth & St. Ives is long the MXN and hence must sell the MXN forward against the GBP. Selling MXN against the GBP means buying GBP, the base currency in the MXN/GBP quote. Therefore, the offer side of the market must be used. This means the all-in rate used one month ago would have been 20.0580 + 900/10,000, which equals 20.1480. Choice A is incorrect because it uses today's asset value and the bid side of the spot and one-month forward quotes and Choice B is incorrect because it uses the wrong side of the market (the bid side).

Solution to 2: B is correct. The foreign investment went down in value in MXN terms. Therefore Brixworth & St. Ives must reduce the size of the hedge. Previously it had sold MXN10,000,000 forward against the GBP, and this amount must be reduced to

MXN9,500,000 by buying MXN500,000 forward. Choice A is incorrect because hedging is done with forward contracts not spot deals. Choice C is incorrect because selling MXN forward would increase the size of the hedge, not decrease it.

Solution to 3: B is correct. To implement the hedge, Brixworth & St. Ives must sell MXN against the GBP, or equivalently, buy GBP (the base currency in the P/B quote) against the MXN. The base currency is selling forward at a premium, and—all else equal—its price would "roll down the curve" as contract maturity approached. Having to settle the forward contract means then selling the GBP spot at a lower price. Buying high and selling low will define a negative roll yield. Moreover, the GBP has depreciated against the MXN, because the MXN/GBP spot rate declined between one month ago and now, which will also add to the negative roll yield.

Solution to 4: A is correct. The Aggressive Growth Fund is long the ZAR through its foreign-currency assets, and to hedge this exposure it must sell the ZAR against the GBP, or equivalently, buy GBP—the base currency in the P/B quote—against the ZAR. Hedging a required purchase means a long position in a call option (not a put, which is used to hedge a required sale of the base currency in the P/B quote). An ATM call option is more expensive than a 25-delta call option.

10. CURRENCY MANAGEMENT STRATEGIES

In the previous sections, we showed that completely hedging currency risk is possible—but can also be expensive. It can be even more expensive when trying to avoid all downside risk while keeping the full upside potential for favorable currency movements (i.e., a protective put strategy with ATM options). Hedging can be seen as a form of insurance, but it is possible to overpay for insurance. Judgments have to be made to determine at what point the costs outweigh the benefits.

As with any form of insurance, there are always steps that can be taken to reduce hedging costs. For most typical insurance products, these cost-reduction measures include such things as higher deductibles, co-pay arrangements, and lower maximum payouts. The same sorts of measures exist in the FX derivatives market; we will explore these various alterative measures in this section. The key point to keep in mind is that all of these various cost-reduction measures invariably involve some combination of *less downside protection* and/or *less upside potential* for the hedge. In efficient markets, lower insurance premiums mean lower insurance.

These cost-reduction measures also start moving the portfolio away from a passively managed 100% hedge ratio toward discretionary hedging in which the manager is allowed to take directional positions. Once the possibility of accepting some downside risk, and some upside potential, is introduced into the portfolio, the manager is moving away from a rules-based approach to hedging toward a more active style of trading. The portfolio manager can then use the trading tools and strategies described in the following sections to express a market view and/or cut hedging costs.

The variety of trading strategies—involving various combinations of forwards, options, and swaps—that can be deployed to this end is almost infinite. We will not attempt to explore all of them in this reading, but rather to give a sense of the range of trading tools and strategies available for managing currency risk. We begin with Exhibit 9, which gives a high-level description of some of these various trading strategies that will then be explained in more detail in subsequent sections. Note that as this section progresses, we will be describing strategies at different points along the risk spectrum described in Sections 4–6, moving in turn from passive hedge-based approaches to strategies used in more active currency management schemes.

EXHIBIT 9   Select Currency Management Strategies

Forward Contracts	Over-/under-hedging	Profit from market view
Option Contracts	OTM options	Cheaper than ATM
	Risk reversals	Write options to earn premiums
	Put/call spreads	Write options to earn premiums
	Seagull spreads	Write options to earn premiums
Exotic Options	Knock-in/out features	Reduced downside/upside exposure
	Digital options	Extreme payoff strategies

We will make one simplifying assumption for the following sections. Currency management strategies will differ fundamentally depending on whether the base currency of the P/B price quote must be bought or sold to decrease the foreign-currency exposure. To simplify the material and impose consistency on the discussions that follow, we will assume that the portfolio manager must sell the base currency in the P/B quote to reduce currency risk. In addition, unless otherwise noted, the notional amounts and expiration dates on all forward and options contracts are the same.[18]

10.1. Over-/Under-Hedging Using Forward Contracts

When the IPS gives the manager discretion either to over- or under-hedge the portfolio, relative to the "neutral" benchmark, there is the possibility to add incremental value based on the manager's market view. Profits from successful tactical positioning help reduce net hedging costs. For example, if the neutral benchmark hedge ratio is 100% for the base currency being hedged, and the portfolio manager has a market opinion that the base currency is likely to depreciate, then *over*-hedging through a short position in P/B forward contracts might be implemented—that is, the manager might use a hedge ratio higher than 100%. Similarly, if the manager's market opinion is that the base currency is likely to appreciate, the currency exposure might be *under*-hedged.

A variant of this approach would be to adjust the hedge ratio based on exchange rate movements: to increase the hedge ratio if the base currency depreciated, but decrease the hedge ratio if the base currency appreciated. Essentially, this approach is a form of "delta hedging" that tries to mimic the payoff function of a put option on the base currency. That is, this form of dynamic hedging with forward contracts tries to increasingly participate in any upside moves of the base currency, but increasingly hedge any downside moves. Doing so adds

---

[18] Examples of implementing a hedge by *buying* the base currency will be provided in some of the practice examples.

"convexity" to the portfolio, meaning that the hedge's payoff function will be a convex curve when this function is graphed with profit on the vertical axis and the spot rate on the horizontal axis. (Note that this concept of convexity is identical in intent to the concept of convexity describing bonds; as convexity increases, the price of a bond rises more quickly in a declining yield environment and drops more slowly in a rising yield environment. Convexity is a desirable characteristic in both the fixed-income and currency-hedging contexts.)

10.2. Protective Put Using OTM Options

In the previous section, we examined a dynamic hedging strategy using forward contracts that tries to mimic the payoff function of an option and put convexity into the hedge's payoff function. The payoff functions for options are naturally convex to begin with. However, this can be a costly form of convexity (relatively high option premiums), and fully hedging a currency position with a protective put strategy using an ATM option is the most expensive means of all to buy convexity.

One way to reduce the cost of using options is to accept some downside risk by using an OTM option, such as a 25- or 10-delta option. These options will be less costly, but also do not fully protect the portfolio from adverse currency movements. Conversely, it makes sense to insure against larger risks but accept some smaller day-to-day price movements in currencies. As an analogy, it may be possible to buy a home or car insurance policy with a zero deductible—but the premiums would be exorbitant. It may be more rational to have a cheaper insurance policy and accept responsibility for minor events, but insure against extreme damage.

10.3. Risk Reversal (or Collar)

Another set of option strategies involves *selling* options (also known as writing options) to earn income that can be used to offset the cost of buying a put option, which forms the "core" of the hedge. Recall that in this section, we are using the simplifying convention that the manager is long the base currency in the P/B quote; hence puts and not calls would be used for hedging in this case.

One strategy to obtain downside protection at a lower cost than a straight protective put position is to *buy* an OTM put option and *write* an OTM call option. Essentially, the portfolio manager is selling some of the upside potential for movements in the base currency (writing a call) and using the option's premiums to help pay the cost of the long put option being purchased. This approach is similar to creating a collar in fixed-income markets. The portfolio is protected against downside movements, but its upside is limited to the strike price on the OTM call option; the exchange rate risk is confined to a corridor or "collar."

In professional FX markets, having a long position in a call option and a short position in a put option is called a **risk reversal**. For example, buying a 25-delta call and writing a 25-delta put is referred to as a *long* position in a 25-delta risk reversal. The position used to create the collar position we just described (buying a put, writing a call) would be a *short* position in a risk reversal.

The majority of currency hedging for foreign-currency asset portfolios and corporate accounts is based on the use of forward contracts and simple option strategies (protective puts/covered calls and risk reversals/collars). We now begin to transition to more active trading strategies that are designed to express market views for speculative profit.

10.4. Put Spread

A variation of the short risk reversal position is a **put spread**, which is also used to reduce the upfront cost of buying a protective put. The short risk reversal is structured by buying a put option and writing a call option: the premiums received by writing the call help cover the cost of the put. Similarly, the put spread position involves buying a put option and writing another put option to help cover the cost of the long put's premiums. This position is typically structured by buying an OTM put, and writing a deeper-OTM put to gain income from premiums; both options involved have the same maturity.

To continue our previous example, with the current spot rate at 1.3550, the portfolio manager might set up the following put spread: buy a put with a strike of 1.3500 and write a put with a strike of 1.3450. The payoff on the put spread position will then be as follows: there is no hedge protection between 1.3550 and 1.3500; the portfolio is hedged from 1.3500 down to 1.3450; at spot rates below 1.3450, the portfolio becomes unhedged again. The put spread reduces the cost of the hedge, but at the cost of more limited downside protection. The portfolio manager would then use this spread only for cases in which a modest decline in the spot exchange rate was expected, and this position would have to be closely monitored against adverse exchange rate movements.

Note that the put spread structure will not be zero-cost because the deeper-OTM put (1.3450) being written will be cheaper than the less-OTM put (1.3500) being bought. However, there are approaches that will make the put spread (or almost any other option spread position) cheaper or possibly zero-cost: the manager could alter: (a) the strike prices of the options; (b) the notional amounts of the options; or (c) some combination of these two measures.

Altering the strike prices of the put options would mean moving them closer together (and hence more equal in cost). However, this would reduce the downside protection on the hedge. Instead, the portfolio manager could write a larger notional amount for the deeper-OTM option; for example, the ratio for the notionals for the options written versus bought might be 1:2. (In standard FX market notation, this would be a 1 × 2 put spread—the option with exercise price closest to being ATM is given first. However, to avoid confusion it is good practice to specify explicitly in the price quote which is the long and short positions, and what their deltas/strike prices are.) Although this structure may now be (approximately) zero-cost it is not without risks: for spot rates below 1.3450 the portfolio has now seen its exposure to the base currency double-up (because of the 1:2 proportion of notionals) and at a worse spot exchange rate for the portfolio on top of it. Creating a zero-cost structure with a 1 × 2 put spread is equivalent to adding leverage to the options position, because you are selling more options than you are buying. This means that this put spread position will have to be carefully managed. For example, the portfolio manager might choose to close out the short position in the deep-OTM put (by going long/buying an equivalent put option) before the base currency depreciates to the 1.3450 strike level. This may be a costly position exit, however, as the market moves against the manager's original positioning. Because of this, this sort of 1 × 2 structure may be more appropriate for expressing directional opinions rather than as a pure hedging strategy.

10.5. Seagull Spread

An alternative, and somewhat safer approach, would be to combine the original put spread position (1:1 proportion of notionals) with a covered call position. This is simply an extension of the concept behind risk reversals and put spreads. The "core" of the hedge (for a manager long the base currency) is the long position in a put option. This is expensive. To reduce the cost, a short risk reversal position writes a call option while a put spread writes a deep-OTM put option. Of course, the manager can always do both: that is, be long a protective put and then write *both* a call and a deep-OTM put. This option structure is sometimes referred to as a **seagull spread**.

As with the names for other option strategies based on winged creatures, the "seagull" indicates an option structure with at least three individual options, and in which the options at the most distant strikes—the wings—are on the opposite side of the market from the middle strike(s)—the body. For example, if the current spot price is 1.3550, a seagull could be constructed by going *long* an ATM put at 1.3550 (the middle strike is the "body"), *short* an OTM put at 1.3500, and *short* an OTM call at 1.3600 (the latter two options are the "wings"). Because the options in the "wings" are being written (sold) this is called a *short* seagull position. The risk/return profile of this structure gives full downside protection from 1.3550 to 1.3500 (at which point the short put position neutralizes the hedge) and participation in the upside potential in spot rate movements to 1.3600 (the strike level for the short call option).

Note that because *two* options are now being written to gain premiums instead of one, this approach allows the strike price of the long put position to be ATM, increasing the downside protection. The various strikes and/or notional sizes of these options (and hence their premiums) can always be adjusted up or down until a zero-cost structure is obtained. However, note that this particular seagull structure gives away some upside potential (the short call position) as well as takes on some downside risk (if the short put position is triggered, it will disable the hedge coverage coming from the long put position). As always, lower structure costs come with some combination of lower downside protection and/or less upside potential.

There are many variants of these seagull strategies, each of which provides a different risk–reward profile (and net cost). For example, for the portfolio manager wishing to hedge a long position in the base currency in the P/B quote when the current spot rate is 1.3550, another seagull structure would be to write an ATM call at 1.3550 and use the proceeds to buy an OTM put option at 1.3500 and an OTM call option at 1.3600. Note that in this seagull structure, the "body" is now a *short* option position, not a long position as in the previous example, and the "wings" are the long position. Hence, it is a *long* seagull spread. This option structure provides cheap downside protection (the hedge kicks in at the put's 1.3500 strike) while providing the portfolio manager with unlimited participation in any rally in the base currency beyond the 1.3600 strike of the OTM call option. As before, the various option strikes and/or notional sizes on the options bought and written can be adjusted so that a zero-cost structure is obtained.

10.6. Exotic Options

In this section, we move even further away from derivatives and trading strategies used mainly for hedging, and toward the more speculative end of the risk spectrum dominated by active currency management. Exotic options are often used by more sophisticated players in the professional trading market—for example, currency overlay managers—and are less frequently used by institutional investors, investment funds, or corporations for hedging purposes. There are several reasons for this relatively light usage of "exotics" for hedging purposes, some related to the fact that many smaller entities lack familiarity with these products. Another reason involves the difficulty of getting hedge accounting treatment in many jurisdictions, which is more advantageous for financial reporting reasons. Finally, the specialized terms of such instruments make them difficult to value for regulatory and accounting purposes.

In general, the term "exotic" refers to all options that are not "vanilla." In FX, vanilla refers essentially to European-style put and call options. The full range of exotic options is both very broad and constantly evolving; many are extraordinarily complex both to price and even to understand. However, all exotics, no matter how complex, typically share one defining feature in common: They are designed to customize the risk exposures desired by the client and provide them at the lowest possible price.[19] Much like the trading strategies described previously, they usually involve some combination of lower downside protection and/or lower upside potential while providing the client with the specific risk exposures they are prepared to manage, and to do so at what is generally a lower cost than vanilla options.

The two most common type of exotic options encountered in foreign exchange markets are those with **knock-in/knock-out** features and digital options.

An option with a knock-in feature is essentially a vanilla option that is created only when the spot exchange rate touches a pre-specified level (this trigger level, called the "barrier," is not the same as the strike price). Similarly a knock-out option is a vanilla option that ceases to exist when the spot exchange rate touches some pre-specified barrier level. Because these options only exist (i.e., get knocked-in or knocked-out) under certain circumstances, they are more restrictive than vanilla options and hence are cheaper. But again, the knock-in/out features provide less upside potential and/or downside protection.

Digital options are also called binary options, or all-or-nothing options. The expiry value of an in-the-money vanilla option varies based on the amount of difference between the expiry level and strike price. In contrast, digital options pay out a fixed amount if they are determined to be in-the-money. For example, American digital options pay a *fixed* amount if they "touch" their exercise level at any time before expiry (even if by a single pip). This characteristic of "extreme payoff" options makes them almost akin to a lottery ticket. Because of these large payoffs, digital options usually cost more than vanilla options with the same strike price. But digitals also provide highly leveraged exposure to movements in the spot rate. This makes these exotic products more appropriate as trading tools for active currency management, rather than as hedging tools. In practice, digital options are typically used by more sophisticated speculative accounts in the FX market to express directional views on exchange rates.

A full exposition of exotic options is beyond the scope of this reading, but the reader should be aware of their existence and why they exist.

10.7. Section Summary

Clearly, loosening the constraint of a fully hedged portfolio begins to introduce complicated active currency management decisions. The following steps can be helpful to sort things out:

A. First, identify the *base* currency in the P/B quote (currency pair) you are dealing with. Derivatives are typically quoted in terms of either buying or selling the *base* currency when the option is exercised. A move upward in the P/B quote is an appreciation of the base currency.

B. Then, identify whether the base currency must be *bought* or *sold* to establish the hedge. These are the price movements you will be protecting against.

---

[19] Although the price is low for the client compared with vanilla options, exotics are typically nonetheless high profit margin items for investment dealers.

C. If *buying* the base currency is required to implement the hedge, then the core hedge structure will be based on some combination of a long call option and/or a long forward contract. The cost of this core hedge can be reduced by buying an OTM call option or writing options to earn premiums. (But keep in mind, lower hedging costs equate to less downside protection and/or upside potential.)

D. If *selling* the base currency is required to implement the hedge, then the core hedge structure will be based on some combination of a long put option and/or a short forward contract. The cost of this core hedge can be reduced by buying an OTM put option or writing options to earn premiums.

E. The higher the allowed discretion for active management, the lower the risk aversion; and the firmer a particular market view is held, the more the hedge is likely to be structured to allow risk exposures in the portfolio. This approach involves positioning in derivatives that "lean the same way" as the market view. (For example, a market view that the base currency will depreciate would use some combination of short forward contracts, writing call options, buying put options, and using "bearish" exotic strategies.) This directional bias to the trading position would be superimposed on the core hedge position described in steps "c" and "d," creating an active-trading "tilt" in the portfolio.

F. For these active strategies, varying the strike prices and notional amounts of the options involved can move the trading position toward a zero-cost structure. But as with hedges, keep in mind that lower cost implies less downside protection and/or upside potential for the portfolio.

A lot of different hedging tools and strategies have been named and covered in this section. Rather than attempting to absorb all of them by rote memorization (a put spread is "X" and a seagull is "Y"), the reader is encouraged instead to focus on the intuition behind a hedge, and how and why it is constructed. It matters less what name (if any) is given to any specific approach; what is important is understanding how all the moving parts fit together. The reader should focus on a "building blocks" approach in understanding how and why the parts of the currency hedge are assembled in a given manner.

EXAMPLE 6   Alternative Hedging Strategies

Brixworth & St. Ives Asset Management, the UK-based investment firm, has hedged the exposure of its Aggressive Growth Fund to the MXN with a long position in a MXN/GBP forward contract. The fund's foreign-currency asset exposure to the ZAR is hedged by buying an ATM call option on the ZAR/GBP currency pair. The portfolio managers at Brixworth & St. Ives are looking at ways to modify the risk–reward trade-offs and net costs of their currency hedges.

Jasmine Khan, one of the analysts at Brixworth & St. Ives, proposes an option-based hedge structure for the long-ZAR exposure that would replace the hedge based on the ATM call option with either long or short positions in the following three options on ZAR/GBP:

A. ATM put option
B. 25-delta put option
C. 25-delta call option

Khan argues that these three options can be combined into a hedge structure that will have some limited downside risk, but provide complete hedge protection starting at the relevant 25-delta strike level. The structure will also have unlimited upside potential, although this will not start until the ZAR/GBP exchange rate moves to the relevant 25-delta strike level. Finally, this structure can be created at a relatively low cost because it involves option writing.

1. The *best* method for Brixworth & St. Ives to gain some upside potential for the hedge on the Aggressive Growth Fund's MXN exposure using MXN/GBP options is to replace the forward contract with a:
   A. long position in an OTM put.
   B. short position in an ATM call.
   C. long position in a 25-delta risk reversal.
2. While keeping the ATM call option in the ZAR/GBP, the method that would lead to *greatest* cost reduction on the hedge would be to:
   A. buy a 25-delta put.
   B. write a 10-delta call.
   C. write a 25-delta call.
3. Setting up Khan's proposed hedge structure would *most likely* involve being:
   A. long the 25-delta options and short the ATM option.
   B. long the 25-delta call, and short both the ATM and 25-delta put options.
   C. short the 25-delta call, and long both the ATM and 25-delta put options.

Solution to 1: C is correct. The Aggressive Growth Fund has a long foreign-currency exposure to the MXN in its asset portfolio, which is hedged by selling the MXN against the GBP, or equivalently, buying the GBP—the base currency in the P/B quote—against the MXN. This need to protect against an *appreciation* in the GBP is why the hedge is using a *long* position in the forward contract. To set a collar around the MXN/GBP rate, Brixworth & St. Ives would want a long call option position with a strike greater than the current spot rate (this gives upside potential to the hedge) and a short put position with a strike less than the current spot rate (this reduces net cost of the hedge). A long call and a short put defines a long position in a risk reversal.

Choice A is incorrect because, if exercised, buying a put option would increase the fund's exposure to the MXN (sell GBP, buy MXN). Similarly, Choice B is incorrect because, if exercised, the ATM call option would increase the MXN exposure (the GBP is "called" away from the fund at the strike price with MXN delivered). Moreover, although writing the ATM call option would gain some income from premiums, writing options (on their own) is never considered the "best" hedge because the premium income earned is fixed but the potential losses on adverse currency moves are potentially unlimited.

Solution to 2: C is correct. As before, the hedge is implemented in protecting against an *appreciation* of the base currency of the P/B quote, the GBP. The hedge is established with an ATM call option (a long position in the GBP). Writing an OTM call option (i.e., with a strike that is more than the current spot rate of 5.1050) establishes a call spread (although hedge protection is lost if ZAR/GBP expires at or above the strike level). Writing a 25-delta call earns more income from premiums than a deeper-OTM

10-delta call (although the 25-delta call has less hedge protection). Buying an option would increase the cost of the hedge, and a put option on the ZAR/GBP would increase the fund's ZAR exposure if exercised (the GBP is "put" to the counterparty at the strike price and ZAR received).

Solution to 3: A is correct. Once again, the hedge is based on hedging the need to sell ZAR/buy GBP, and GBP is the base currency in the ZAR/GBP quote. This means the hedge needs to protect against an *appreciation* of the GBP (an appreciation of the ZAR/ GBP rate). Based on Khan's description, the hedge provides protection after a certain loss point, which would be a long 25-delta call. Unlimited upside potential after favorable (i.e., down) moves in the ZAR/GBP past a certain level means a long 25-delta put. Getting the low net cost that Khan refers to means that the cost of these two long positions is financed by selling the ATM option. (Together these three positions define a long seagull spread.) Choice B is incorrect because although the first two legs of the position are right, a short position in the put does not provide any unlimited upside potential (from a down-move in ZAR/GBP). Choice C is incorrect because any option-based hedge, given the need to hedge against an up-move in the ZAR/GBP rate, is going to be based on a long call position. C does not contain any of these.

11. HEDGING MULTIPLE FOREIGN CURRENCIES

We now expand our discussion to hedging a portfolio with multiple foreign-currency assets. The hedging tools and strategies are very similar to those discussed for hedging a single foreign-currency asset, except now the currency hedge must consider the *correlation* between the various foreign-currency risk exposures.

For example, consider the case of a US-domiciled investor who has exposures to foreign-currency assets in Australia and New Zealand. These two economies are roughly similar in that they are resource-based and closely tied to the regional economy of the Western Pacific, especially the large emerging markets in Asia. As a result, the movements in their currencies are often closely correlated; the USD/AUD and USD/NZD currency pairs will tend to move together. If the portfolio manager has the discretion to take short positions, the portfolio may (for example) possibly have a net long position in the Australian foreign-currency asset and a net short position in the New Zealand foreign-currency asset. In this case, there may be less need to hedge away the AUD and NZD currency exposures separately because the portfolio's long exposure to the AUD is diversified by the short position on the NZD.

11.1. Cross Hedges and Macro Hedges

A **cross hedge** occurs when a position in one asset (or a derivative based on the asset) is used to hedge the risk exposures of a different asset (or a derivative based on it). Normally, cross hedges are not needed because, as we mentioned earlier, forward contracts and other derivatives are widely available in almost every conceivable currency pair. However, if the portfolio already has "natural" cross hedges in the form of negatively correlated residual currency exposures—as in the long-AUD/short-NZD example in Section 11—this helps moderate portfolio risk ($\sigma[R_{DC}]$) without having to use a direct hedge on the currency exposure.

Sometimes a distinction is made between a "proxy" hedge and a "cross" hedge. When this distinction is made, a *proxy hedge* removes the foreign currency risk by hedging it back to the investor's domestic currency—such as in the example with USD/AUD and USD/NZD discussed in the text. In contrast, a *cross hedge* moves the currency risk from one foreign currency to another foreign currency. For example, a US-domiciled investor may have an exposure to both the Indonesian rupiah (IDR) and the Thai baht (THB), but based on a certain market view, may only want exposure to the THB. In this context, the manager might use currency derivatives as a cross hedge to convert the IDR/USD exposure to a THB/USD exposure. But not all market participants make this sharp of a distinction between proxy hedges and cross hedges, and these terms are often used interchangeably. The most common term found among practitioners in most asset classes is simply a cross hedge, as we are using the term here: hedging an exposure with a closely correlated product (i.e., a proxy hedge when this distinction is made). The cross hedge of moving currency exposures between various *foreign* currencies is more of a special-case application of this concept. In our example, a US investor wanting to shift currency exposures between the IDR and THB would only need to shift the relative size of the IDR/USD and THB/USD forward contracts *already* being used. As mentioned earlier, forwards are available on almost every currency pair, so a cross hedge from foreign currency "A" to foreign currency "B" would be a special case when derivatives on one of the currencies are not available.

EXAMPLE 7   Cross Hedges

Mai Nguyen works at Cape Henlopen Advisors, which runs a US-domiciled fund that invests in foreign-currency assets of Australia and New Zealand. The fund currently has equally weighted exposure to one-year Australian and New Zealand treasury bills (i.e., both of the portfolio weights, $\omega_i = 0.5$). Because the foreign-currency return on these treasury bill assets is risk-free and known in advance, their expected $\sigma(R_{FC})$ is equal to zero.

Nguyen wants to calculate the USD-denominated returns on this portfolio as well as the cross hedging effects of these investments. She collects the following information:

Expected Values	Australia	New Zealand
Foreign-currency asset return R_{FC}	4.0%	6.0%
Foreign-currency return R_{FX}	5.0%	5.0%
Asset risk $\sigma(R_{FC})$	0%	0%
Currency risk $\sigma(R_{FX})$	8.0%	10.0%
Correlation (USD/AUD; USD/NZD)	+0.85	

Using Equation 1, Nguyen calculates that the expected domestic-currency return for the Australian asset is

$$(1.04)(1.05) - 1 = 0.092$$

or 9.2%. Likewise, she determines that the expected domestic-currency return for the New Zealand asset is

$$(1.06)(1.05) - 1 = 0.113$$

or 11.3%. Together, the result is that the expected domestic-currency return (R_{DC}) on the equally weighted foreign-currency asset portfolio is the weighted average of these two individual country returns, or

$$R_{DC} = 0.5(9.2\%) + 0.5(11.3\%) = 10.3\%$$

Nguyen now turns her attention to calculating the portfolio's investment risk $[\sigma(R_{DC})]$. To calculate the expected risk for the domestic-currency return, the currency risk of R_{FX} needs to be multiplied by the *known* return on the treasury bills. The portfolio's investment risk, $\sigma(R_{DC})$, is found by calculating the standard deviation of the right-hand-side of:

$$R_{DC} = (1 + R_{FC})(1 + R_{FX}) - 1$$

Although R_{FX} is a random variable—it is not known in advance—the R_{FC} term is in fact known in advance because the asset return is risk-free. Because of this Nguyen can make use of the statistical rules that, first, $\sigma(kX) = k\sigma(X)$, where X is a random variable and k is a constant; and second, that the correlation between a random variable and a constant is zero. These results greatly simplify the calculations because, in this case, she does not need to consider the correlation between exchange rate movements and foreign-currency asset returns. Instead, Nguyen needs to calculate the risk only on the currency side. Applying these statistical rules to the above formula leads to the following results:

A. The expected risk (i.e., standard deviation) of the domestic-currency return for the Australian asset is equal to $(1.04) \times 8\% = 8.3\%$.
B. The expected risk (i.e., standard deviation) of the domestic-currency return for the New Zealand asset is equal to $(1.06) \times 10\% = 10.6\%$.

Adding all of these numerical values into Equation 4 leads Nguyen to calculate:

$$\sigma^2(R_{DC}) = (0.5)^2(8.3\%)^2 + (0.5)^2(10.6\%)^2 + [(2)0.5(8.3\%)0.5(10.6\%)0.85]$$

$$= 0.8\%$$

The standard deviation of this amount—that is, $\sigma(R_{DC})$—is 9.1%. Note that in the expression, all of the units are in percent, so for example, 8.3% is equivalent to 0.083 for calculation purposes. The careful reader may also note that Nguyen is able to use an exact expression for calculating the variance of the portfolio returns, rather than the approximate expressions shown in Equations 3 and 5. This is because, with risk-free foreign-currency assets, the variance of these foreign-currency returns $\sigma^2(R_{FC})$ is equal to zero.

Nguyen now considers an alternative scenario in which, instead of an equally weighted portfolio (where the $\omega_i = 0.5$), the fund has a long exposure to the New Zealand asset and a short exposure to the Australian asset (i.e., the ω_i are +1 and −1, respectively; this is similar to a highly leveraged carry trade position). Putting these weights into Equations 2 and 4 leads to

$$R_{DC} = -1.0(9.2\%) + 1.0(11.3\%) = 2.1\%$$

$$\sigma^2(R_{DC}) = (1.0)^2(8.3\%)^2 + (1.0)^2(10.6\%)^2 + [-2.0(8.3\%)(10.6\%)0.85]$$

$$= 0.3\%$$

The standard deviation—that is, $\sigma(R_{DC})$—is now 5.6%, less than either of the expected risks for foreign-currency asset returns (results A and B). Nguyen concludes that having long and short positions in positively correlated currencies can lead to much lower portfolio risk, through the benefits of cross hedging. (Nguyen goes on to calculate that if the expected correlation between USD/AUD and USD/NZD increases to 0.95, with all else equal, the expected domestic-currency return risk on the long–short portfolio drops to 3.8%.)

Some types of cross hedges are often referred to as macro hedges. The reason is because the hedge is more focused on the entire portfolio, particularly when individual asset price movements are highly correlated, rather than on individual assets or currency pairs. Another way of viewing a macro hedge is to see the portfolio not just as a collection of financial assets, but as a collection of risk exposures. These various risk exposures are typically defined in categories, such as term risk, credit risk, and liquidity risk. These risks can also be defined in terms of the potential financial scenarios the portfolio is exposed to, such as recession, financial sector stress, or inflation. Often macro hedges are defined in terms of the financial scenario they are designed to protect the portfolio from.

Putting gold in the portfolio sometimes serves this purpose by helping to provide broad portfolio protection against extreme market events. Using a volatility overlay program can also hedge the portfolio against such risks because financial stress is typically associated with a spike in exchange rates' implied volatility. Using a derivative product based on an index, rather than specific assets or currencies, can also define a macro hedge. One macro hedge specific to foreign exchange markets uses derivatives based on fixed-weight baskets of currencies (such derivatives are available in both exchange-traded and OTC form). In a multi-currency portfolio, it may not always be cost efficient to hedge each single currency separately, and in these situations a macro hedge using currency basket derivatives is an alternative approach.

11.2. Minimum-Variance Hedge Ratio

A mathematical approach to determining the optimal cross hedging ratio is known as the **minimum-variance hedge ratio**. Recall that regression analysis based on ordinary least squares (OLS) is used to minimize the variance of $\hat{\varepsilon}$, the residual between actual and fitted values of the regression

$$y_t = \alpha + \beta x_t + \varepsilon_t \text{ where } \hat{\varepsilon}_t = y_t - \left(\hat{\alpha} + \hat{\beta} x_t\right)$$

This same principle can be used to minimize the tracking error between the value of the hedged asset and the hedging instrument. In the regression formula, we substitute the percentage change in the value of the asset to be hedged for y_t, and the percentage change in value of the hedging instrument for x_t (both of these values are measured in terms of the investor's domestic currency). The calculated coefficient in this regression ($\hat{\beta}$) gives the optimal hedging ratio, which means it minimizes the variance of $\hat{\varepsilon}$ and minimizes the tracking error between changes in the value of the hedge and changes in the value of the asset it is hedging. It can be shown that the formula for the minimum-variance hedge ratio—the formula for calculating the $\hat{\beta}$ coefficient in the regression—is mathematically equal to:

$$\frac{\text{covariance } (y, x)}{\text{variance } (x)} = \text{correlation } (y, x) \times \left[\frac{\text{std. dev. } (y)}{\text{std. dev. } (x)}\right]$$

where y and x are defined as before, the change in the domestic-currency value of the asset and the hedge, respectively.

Calculating the minimum-variance hedge ratio typically applies only for "indirect" hedges based on cross hedging or macro hedges; it is not typically applied to a "direct" hedge in which exposure to a spot rate is hedged with a forward contract in that same currency pair. This is because the correlation between movements in the spot rate and its forward contract is likely to be very close to +1. Likewise, the variance in spot price movements and movements in the price of the forward contract are also likely to be approximately equal. Therefore, calculating the minimum-variance hedge ratio by regressing changes in the spot exchange rate against changes in the forward rate will almost always result is a $\hat{\beta}$ regression estimate very close to 1, and hence a minimum-variance hedge ratio close to 100%. So, undertaking the regression analysis is superfluous.

But the minimum-variance hedge ratio can be quite different from 100% when the hedge is *jointly* optimized over *both* exchange rate movements R_{FX} and changes in the foreign-currency value of the asset R_{FC}. A sidebar discusses this case.

There can also be cases when the optimal hedge ratio may not be 100% because of the market characteristics of a specific currency pair. For example, a currency pair may not have a (liquid) forward contract available and hence an alternative cross hedging instrument or a macro hedge must be used instead. We examine when such situations might come up in Section 13.

11.3. Basis Risk

The portfolio manager must be aware that any time a direct currency hedge (i.e., a spot rate hedged against its own forward contract) is replaced with an indirect hedge (cross hedge, macro hedge), **basis risk** is brought into the portfolio. This risk reflects the fact that the price movements in the exposure being hedged and the price movements in the cross hedge instrument are not perfectly correlated, and that the correlation will change with time—and sometimes both dramatically and unexpectedly. For a minimum-variance hedge ratio, this risk is expressed as instability in the $\hat{\beta}$ coefficient estimate as more data become available.

For an example of basis risk, return to the illustration earlier of the foreign-currency asset portfolio that cross hedged a long USD/AUD exposure with a short USD/NZD exposure. It is not only possible, but highly likely, that the correlation between movements in the USD/AUD and the USD/NZD spot rates will vary with time. This varying correlation would reflect movements in the NZD/AUD spot rate. Another example of basis risk would be that the correlation between a multi-currency portfolio's domestic-currency market value and the value of currency basket derivatives being used as a macro hedge will neither be perfect nor constant.

At a minimum, this means that all cross hedges and macro hedges will have to be carefully monitored and, as needed, rebalanced to account for the drift in correlations. It also means that minimum-variance hedge ratios will have to be re-estimated as more data become available. The portfolio manager should beware that sudden, unexpected spikes in basis risk can sometimes turn what was once a minimum-variance hedge or an effective cross hedge into a position that is highly correlated with the underlying assets being hedged—the opposite of a hedge.

Basis risk is also used in the context of forward and futures contracts because the price movements of these derivatives products do not always correspond exactly with those of the underlying currency. This is because the price of the forward contract also reflects the interest rate differential between the two countries in the currency pair as well as the term to contract maturity. But with futures and forwards, the derivatives price converges to the price of the underlying as maturity approaches, which is enforced by arbitrage. This convergence is not the case with cross hedges, which potentially can go disastrously wrong with sudden movements in market risk (price correlations), credit risk, or liquidity risk.

Optimal Minimum-Variance Hedges

For simple foreign-currency asset portfolios, it may be possible to use the single-variable OLS regression technique to do a *joint* optimization of the hedge over both the foreign-currency value of the asset R_{FC} and the foreign-currency risk exposure R_{FX}. This approach will reduce the variance of the all-in domestic-currency return R_{DC}, which is the risk that matters most to the investor, not just reducing the variance of the foreign exchange risk R_{FX}.

Calculating the minimum-variance hedge for the foreign exchange risk R_{FX} proceeds by regressing changes in the spot rate against changes in the value of the hedging instrument (i.e., the forward contract). But as indicated in the text, performing this regression is typically unnecessary; for all intents and purposes, the minimum-variance hedge for a spot exchange rate using a forward contract will be close to 100%.

But when there is only a *single* foreign-currency asset involved, one can perform a joint optimization over both of the foreign-currency risks (i.e., both R_{FC} and R_{FX}) by regressing changes in the domestic-currency return (R_{DC}) against percentage changes in the value of the hedging instrument. Basing the optimal hedge ratio on the OLS estimate for β in this regression will minimize the variance of the domestic-currency return $\sigma^2(R_{DC})$. The result will be a better hedge ratio than just basing the regression on R_{FX} alone because this joint approach will also pick up any *correlations* between R_{FX} and R_{FC}. (Recall from Section 4 that the asset mix in the portfolio, and hence the correlations between R_{FX} and R_{FC}, can affect the optimal hedge ratio.) This single-variable OLS approach, however, will only work if there is a single foreign-currency asset in the portfolio.

Work by Campbell (2010) has shown that the optimal hedge ratio based jointly on movements in R_{FC} and R_{FX} for international *bond* portfolios is almost always close to 100%. However, the optimal hedge ratio for single-country foreign *equity* portfolios varies widely between currencies, and will depend on *both* the investor's domestic currency and the currency of the foreign investment. For example, the optimal hedge ratio for a US equity portfolio will be different for UK and eurozone-based investors; and for eurozone investors, the optimal hedge ratio for a US equity portfolio can be different from that of a Canadian equity portfolio. The study found that the optimal hedge ratio for foreign equity exposures can vary widely from 100% between countries. But as the author cautions, these optimal hedge ratios are calculated on historical data that may not be representative of future price dynamics.

Minimum-Variance Hedge Ratio Example

Annie McYelland is an analyst at Scotland-based Kilmarnock Capital. Her firm is considering an investment in an equity index fund based on the Swiss Stock Market Index (SMI). The SMI is a market-cap weighted average of the twenty largest and most liquid Swiss companies, and captures about 85% of the overall market capitalization of the Swiss equity market.

McYelland is asked to formulate a currency-hedging strategy. Because this investment involves only one currency pair and one investment (the SMI), she decides to calculate the minimum-variance hedge ratio for the entire risk exposure, not just the currency exposure. McYelland collects 10 years of monthly data on the CHF/GBP spot exchange rate and movements in the Swiss Market Index.

McYelland notes that the GBP is the base currency in the CHF/GBP quote and that the formula for domestic-currency returns (R_{DC}) shown in Equation 1 requires that the domestic currency be the price currency. Accordingly, she starts by inverting the CHF/GBP quote to a GBP/CHF quote ($S_{GBP/CHF}$). Then she calculates the monthly percentage changes for this adjusted currency series (%$\Delta S_{GBP/CHF}$) as well as for the SMI (%ΔSMI). This allows her to calculate the monthly returns of an unhedged investment in the SMI with these unhedged returns measured in the "domestic" currency, the GBP:

$$R_{DC} = (1 + R_{FC})(1 + R_{FX}) - 1$$

where R_{FC} = %ΔSMI and R_{FX} = %$\Delta S_{GBP/CHF}$. Because McYelland wants to minimize the variance of these unhedged domestic-currency returns, she calculates the minimum-variance hedge ratio with the following OLS regression:

$$R_{DC} = \alpha + \beta(\%\Delta S_{GBP/CHF}) + \varepsilon$$

The calculated regression coefficients show that $\hat{\alpha} = -0.21$ and $\hat{\beta} = 1.35$. McYelland interprets these results to mean that the estimated $\hat{\beta}$-coefficient is the minimum-variance hedge ratio. This conclusion makes sense because $\hat{\beta}$ represents the sensitivity of the domestic-currency return on the portfolio to percentage changes in the spot rate. In this case, the return on the SMI seems very sensitive to the appreciation of the CHF. Indeed, over the 10 years of data she collected, McYelland notices that the correlation between %ΔSMI and %$\Delta S_{GBP/CHF}$ is equal to +0.6.

On the basis of these calculations, she recommends that the minimum-variance hedge ratio for Kilmarnock Capital's exposure to the SMI be set at approximately 135%. This recommendation means that a *long* CHF1,000,000 exposure to the SMI should be hedged with a *short* position in CHF against the GBP of approximately CHF1,350,000. Because forward contracts in professional FX markets are quoted in terms of CHF/GBP for this currency pair, this would mean a *long* position in the forward contract ($F_{CHF/GBP}$)— that is, *selling* the CHF means *buying* the base currency GBP.

McYelland cautions the Investment Committee at Kilmarnock Capital that this minimum-variance hedge ratio is only approximate and must be closely monitored because it is estimated over historical data that may not be representative of future price dynamics. For example, the +0.6 correlation estimated between %ΔSMI and %$\Delta S_{GBP/CHF}$ is the 10-year *average* correlation; future market conditions may not correspond to this historical average.

12. CURRENCY MANAGEMENT TOOLS AND STRATEGIES: A SUMMARY

This section has covered only some of the most common currency management tools and strategies used in FX markets—there are a great many other derivatives products and strategies that have not been covered. The key points are that there are *many* different hedging and active trading strategies, there are many possible *variations* within each of these strategies, and these strategies can be used in *combination* with each other. There is no need to cover all of what would be a very large number of possible permutations and combinations. Instead, we will close this section with a key thought: Each of these many approaches to either hedging or expressing a directional view on currency movements has its advantages and disadvantages, its risks, and its costs.

As a result, there is no single "correct" approach to initiating and managing currency exposures. Instead, at the strategic level, the IPS of the portfolio sets guidelines for risk exposures, permissible hedging tools, and strategies, which will vary among investors. At the tactical level, at which the portfolio manager has discretion on risk exposures, currency strategy will depend on the manager's management style, market view, and risk tolerance. It will also depend on the manager's perceptions of the relative costs and benefit of any given strategy. Market conditions will affect the cost/benefit calculations behind the hedging decision, as movements in forward points (expected roll yield) or exchange rate volatility (option premiums) affect the expected cost of the hedge; the same hedge structure can be "rich" or "cheap" depending on current market conditions.

Reflecting all of these considerations, different managers will likely make different decisions when confronted with the same opportunity set; and each manager will likely have a good reason for their individual decision. The most important point is that the portfolio manager be aware of all the benefits, costs, and risks of the chosen strategy and be comfortable that any remaining residual currency risks in the hedge are acceptable.

To summarize the key insights of Sections 9–12—and continuing our example of a portfolio manager who is long the base currency in the P/B quote and wants to hedge that price risk—the manager needs to understand the following:

1. Because the portfolio has a *long* exposure to base currency, to neutralize this risk the hedge will attempt to build a *short* exposure out of that currency's derivatives using some combination of forward and/or option contracts.

2. A currency hedge is not a free good, particularly a complete hedge. The hedge cost, real or implied, will consist of some combination of lost upside potential, potentially negative roll yield (forward points at a discount or time decay on long option positions), and upfront payments of option premiums.

3. The cost of any given hedge structure will vary depending on market conditions (i.e., forward points and implied volatility).

4. The cost of the hedge is focused on its "core." For a manager with a long exposure to a currency, the cost of this "core" hedge will be the implicit costs of a short position in a forward contract (no upside potential, possible negative roll yield) or the upfront premium on a long position in a put option. Either of these two forms of insurance can be expensive. However, there are various cost mitigation methods that can be used alone or in combination to reduce these core hedging costs:

   • Writing options to gain upfront premiums.
   • Varying the strike prices of the options written or bought.
   • Varying the notional amounts of the derivative contracts.
   • Using various "exotic" features, such as knock-ins or knock-outs.

5. There is nothing inherently wrong with any of these cost mitigation approaches—but the manager *must* understand that these invariably involve some combination of reduced upside potential and/or reduced downside protection. A reduced cost (or even a zero-cost) hedge structure is perfectly acceptable, but only as long as the portfolio manager fully understands all of the residual risks in the hedge structure and is prepared to accept and manage them.

6. There are often "natural" hedges within the portfolio, in which some residual risk exposures are uncorrelated with each other and offer portfolio diversification effects. Cross hedges and macro hedges bring basis risk into the portfolio, which will have to be monitored and managed.

7. There is no single or "best" way to hedge currency risk. The portfolio manager will have to perform a due diligence examination of potential hedge structures and make a rational decision on a cost/benefit basis.

EXAMPLE 8   Hedging Strategies

Ireland-based Old Galway Capital runs several investment trusts for its clients. Fiona Doyle has just finished rebalancing the dynamic currency hedge for Overseas Investment Trust III, which has an IPS mandate to be fully hedged using forward contracts. Shortly after the rebalancing, Old Galway receives notice that one of its largest investors in the Overseas Investment Trust III has served notice of a large withdrawal from the fund.

Padma Bhattathiri works at Malabar Coast Capital, an India-based investment company. Her mandate is to seek out any alpha opportunities in global FX markets and aggressively manage these for speculative profit. The Reserve Bank of New Zealand (RBNZ) is New Zealand's central bank, and is scheduled to announce its policy rate decision within the week. The consensus forecast among economists is that the RBNZ will leave rates unchanged, but Bhattathiri believes that the RBNZ will surprise the markets with a rate hike.

Jasmine Khan, analyst at UK-based Brixworth & St. Ives Asset Management, has been instructed by the management team to reduce hedging costs for the firm's Aggressive Growth Fund, and that more currency exposure—both downside risk and upside potential—will have to be accepted and managed. Currently, the fund's ZAR-denominated foreign-currency asset exposures are being hedged with a 25-delta risk reversal (on the ZAR/GBP cross rate). The current ZAR/GBP spot rate is 13.1350.

Bao Zhang is a market analyst at South Korea–based Kwangju Capital, an investment firm that offers several actively managed investment trusts for its clients. She notices that the exchange rate for the Philippines Peso (PHP/USD) is increasing (PHP is depreciating) toward its 200-day moving average located in the 42.2500 area (the current spot rate is 42.2475). She mentions this to Akiko Takahashi, a portfolio manager for one of the firm's investment vehicles. Takahashi's view, based on studying economic fundamentals, is that the PHP/USD rate should continue to increase, but after speaking with Zhang she is less sure. After further conversation, Zhang and Takahashi come to the view that the PHP/USD spot rate will either break through the 42.2500 level and gain upward momentum through the 42.2600 level, or stall at the 42.2500 level and then drop down through the 42.2400 level as frustrated long positions exit the market. They decide that either scenario has equal probability over the next month.

Annie McYelland is an analyst at Scotland-based Kilmarnock Capital. The firm is considering a USD10,000,000 investment in an S&P 500 Index fund. McYelland is asked to calculate the minimum-variance hedge ratio. She collects the following statistics based on 10 years of monthly data:

$s(\%\Delta S_{GBP/USD})$	$\sigma(R_{DC})$	$\rho(R_{DC};\%\Delta S_{GBP/USD})$
2.7%	4.4%	0.2

Source: Data are from Bloomberg.

1. Given the sudden liquidity need announced, Doyle's *best* course of action with regard to the currency hedge is to:
   A. do nothing.
   B. reduce the hedge ratio.
   C. over-hedge by using currency options.
2. Given her market view, Bhattathiri would *most likely* choose which of the following long positions?
   A. 5-delta put option on NZD/AUD
   B. 10-delta put option on USD/NZD
   C. Put spread on JPY/NZD using 10-delta and 25-delta options
3. Among the following, replacing the current risk reversal hedge with a long position in which of the following would *best* meet Khan's instructions? (All use the ZAR/GBP.)
   A. 10-delta risk reversal
   B. Put option with a 13.1300 strike
   C. Call option with a 13.1350 strike

4. Which of the following positions would *best* implement Zhang's and Takahashi's market view?
   A. Long a 42.2450 put and long a 42.2550 call
   B. Long a 42.2450 put and short a 42.2400 put
   C. Long a 42.2450 put and short a 42.2550 call
5. Which of the following positions would *best* implement Kilmarnock Capital's minimum-variance hedge?
   A. Long a USD/GBP forward contract with a notional size of USD1.2 million
   B. Long a USD/GBP forward contract with a notional size of USD3.3 million
   C. Short a USD/GBP forward contract with a notional size of USD2.0 million

Solution to 1: A is correct. After rebalancing, the Overseas Investment Trust III is fully hedged; currency risk is at a minimum, which is desirable if liquidity needs have increased. Choices B and C are incorrect because they increase the currency risk exposures.

Solution to 2: A is correct. The surprise rate hike should cause the NZD to appreciate against most currencies. This appreciation would mean a depreciation of the NZD/AUD rate, which a put option can profit from. A 5-delta option is deep-OTM, but the price reaction on the option premiums will be more extreme than a higher-delta option. That is to say, the *percentage* change in the premiums for a 5-delta option for a given percentage change in the spot exchange rate will be higher than the percentage change in premiums for a 25-delta option. In a sense, a very low delta option is like a highly leveraged lottery ticket on the event occurring. With a surprise rate hike, the odds would swing in Bhattathiri's favor. Choice B is incorrect because the price reaction in the USD/NZD spot rate after the surprise rate hike would likely cause the NZD to appreciate; so Bhattathiri would want a call option on the USD/NZD currency pair. Choice C is incorrect because an appreciation of the NZD after the surprise rate hike would best be captured by a call spread on the JPY/NZD rate, which will likely increase (the NZD is the base currency).

Solution to 3: A is correct. Moving to a 10-delta risk reversal will be cheaper (these options are deeper-OTM than 25-delta options) and widen the bands in the corridor being created for the ZAR/GBP rate. Choice B is incorrect because a long put provides no protection against an upside movement in the ZAR/GBP rate, which Brixworth & St. Ives is trying to hedge (recall that the fund is long ZAR in its foreign-currency asset exposure and hence needs to sell ZAR/buy GBP to hedge). Also, if Brixworth & St. Ives exercises the option, they would "put" GBP to the counterparty at the strike price and receive ZAR in return. Although this option position may be considered profitable in its own right, it nonetheless causes the firm to double-up its ZAR exposure. Choice C is incorrect because although an ATM call option on ZAR/GBP will provide complete hedge protection, it will be expensive and clearly more expensive than the current 25-delta risk reversal.

Solution to 4: A is correct. Zhang's and Takahashi's market view is that, over the next month, a move in PHP/USD to either 42.2400 or 42.2600 is equally likely. A strangle would express this view of heightened volatility but without a directional bias, and would require a long put and a long call positions. Choice B is incorrect because it is a put spread; it will profit by a move in PHP/USD between 42.2450 and 42.2400. If it moves below 42.2400 the short put gets exercised by the counterparty and neutralizes the long put. Although less costly than an outright long put position, this structure is not positioned to profit from a move higher in PHP/USD. Choice C is incorrect because it is a short risk reversal position. It provides relatively cheap protection for a down-move in PHP/USD but is not positioned to profit from an up-move in PHP/USD.

Solution to 5: B is correct. The formula for the minimum-variance hedge ratio (h) is:

$$h = \rho(R_{DC};R_{FX}) \times \left[\frac{\sigma(R_{DC})}{\sigma(R_{FX})} \right]$$

After inputting the data from the table, this equation solves to 0.33. This means that for a USD10 million investment in the S&P 500 (long position), Kilmarnock Capital would want to be *short* approximately USD3.3 million in a forward contract. Because the standard market quote for this currency pair is USD/GBP, to be short the USD means one would have to buy the GBP; that is, a *long* position in a USD/GBP forward contract. Choice A is incorrect because it inverts the ratio in the formula. Choice C is incorrect because it shows a short position in the USD/GBP forward, and because it only uses the correlation to set the contract size.

13. CURRENCY MANAGEMENT FOR EMERGING MARKET CURRENCIES

Most of the material in this reading has focused on what might be described as the major currencies, such as the EUR, GBP, or JPY. This focus is not a coincidence: The vast majority of daily flow in global FX markets is accounted for by the top half dozen currencies. Moreover, the vast majority of investable assets globally, as measured by market capitalization, are denominated in the major currencies. Nonetheless, more investors are looking at emerging markets, as well as "frontier markets," for potential investment opportunities. And many developing economies are beginning to emerge as major forces in the global economy. In the following sections, we survey the challenges for currency management and the use of non-deliverable forwards as one tool to address them.

13.1. Special Considerations in Managing Emerging Market Currency Exposures

Managing emerging market currency exposure involves unique challenges. Perhaps the two most important considerations are (1) higher trading costs than the major currencies under "normal" market conditions, and (2) the increased likelihood of extreme market events and severe illiquidity under stressed market conditions.

Many emerging market currencies are thinly traded, causing higher transaction costs (bid–offer spreads). There may also be fewer derivatives products to choose from, especially exchange-traded products. Although many global investment banks will quote spot rates and OTC derivatives for almost any conceivable currency pair, many of these are often seen as "specialty" products and often come with relatively high mark-ups. This mark-up increases trading and hedging costs. (In addition, the underlying foreign-currency asset in emerging markets can be illiquid and lack the full array of derivatives products.)

These higher currency trading costs would especially be the case for "crosses" in these currency pairs. For example, there is no reason why an investor in Chile (which uses the Chilean peso, currency code CLP) could not have an investment in assets denominated in the Thai baht (THB). But the CLP/THB cross is likely to be very thinly traded; there simply are not enough trade or capital flows between these two countries. Typically, any trade between these two currencies would go through a major intermediary currency, usually the USD. Hence, the trade would be broken into two legs: a trade in the CLP/USD pair and another in the THB/USD pair. These trades might go through different traders or trading desks at the same bank; or perhaps one leg of the trade would be done at one bank and the other leg through a different bank. There may also be time zone issues affecting liquidity; one leg of the trade may be relatively liquid at the same time as the other leg of the trade may be more thinly traded. The reason is because liquidity in most emerging market currencies is typically deepest in their domestic time zones. In any event, there are two bid–offer spreads—one for each leg of the trade—to be covered. This is often the case for many of the cross-rate currency pairs among developed market currencies as well. However, the bid–offer spreads are usually tighter for major currency pairs.

The liquidity issue is especially important when trades in these less-liquid currencies get "crowded," for example, through an excessive build-up of carry trades or through a fad-like popularity among investors for investing in a particular region or trading theme. Trades can be much easier to gradually enter into than to quickly exit, particularly under stressed market conditions. For example, after a long period of slow build-up, carry trades into these currencies can occasionally be subject to panicked unwinds as market conditions suddenly turn. This situation typically causes market liquidity to evaporate and leaves traders locked into positions that continue to accumulate losses.

The investment return probability distributions for currency (and other) trades subject to such relatively frequent extreme events have fatter tails than the normal distribution as well as a pronounced negative skew. Risk measurement and control tools (such as value at risk, or VaR) that depend on normal distributions can be misleading under these circumstances and greatly understate the risks the portfolio is actually exposed to. Many investment performance measures are also based on the normal distribution. Historical investment performance measured by such indexes as the Sharpe ratio can look very attractive during times of relative tranquility; but this seeming outperformance can disappear into deep losses faster than most investors can react (investors typically do a poor job of timing crises). As mentioned in the prior section on volatility trading, price volatility in financial markets is very cyclical and implied volatility can be subject to sharp spikes. These volatility spikes can severely affect both option prices and hedging strategies based on options. Even if the initial option protection is in place, it will eventually have to be rolled as options expire—but then at much higher prices for the option buyer.

The occurrence of currency crises can also affect hedging strategies based on forward contracts. Recall that hedging a long exposure to a foreign currency typically involves selling the foreign currency forward. However, when currencies are under severe downward pressure, central banks often react by hiking the policy rate to support the domestic currency. But recall that the higher interest rates go in a country, then, all else equal, the deeper the forward discount for its currency (enforced by the arbitrage conditions of covered interest rate parity). Having to sell the currency forward at increasingly deep discounts will cause losses through negative roll yield and undermine the cost effectiveness of the hedging program.

Extreme price movements in financial markets can also undermine many hedging strategies based on presumed diversification. Crises not only affect the volatility in asset prices but also their correlations, primarily through "contagion" effects. The history of financial markets (circa 2012) has been characterized by a "risk-on, risk-off" environment dominated by swings in investor sentiment between speculative enthusiasm and pronounced flight-to-safety flows. In the process, there is often little differentiation between individual currencies, which tend to get traded together in broader baskets (such as "haven currencies"—USD, JPY, and CHF—and "commodity currencies"—AUD, NZD, and ZAR). Investors who may have believed that they had diversified their portfolio through a broad array of exposures in emerging markets may find instead in crises that they doubled-up their currency exposures. (Likewise, there can be correlated and extreme movements in the underlying assets of these foreign-currency exposures.)

Another potential factor affecting currency management in these "exotic" markets is government involvement in setting the exchange rate through such measures as foreign exchange market intervention, capital controls, and pegged (or at least tightly managed) exchange rates. These measures too can lead to occasional extreme events in markets; for example, when central banks intervene or when currency pegs change or get broken. Short-term stability in these government-influenced markets can lull traders into a false sense of overconfidence and over-positioning. When currency pegs break, the break can happen quickly. Assuming that investment returns will be normally distributed according to parameters estimated on recent historical data, or that correlation factors and liquidity will not change suddenly, can be lethal.

It bears noting that currency crises and government involvement in FX markets is not limited to emerging market currencies, but often occur among the major currencies as well. The central banks of major currencies will, on occasion, intervene in their own currencies or use other polices (such as sharp movements in policy rates) to influence exchange rate levels. These too can lead to extreme events in currency markets.

13.2. Non-Deliverable Forwards

Currencies of many emerging market countries trade with some form of capital controls. Where capital controls exist and delivery in the controlled currency is limited by the local government, it is often possible to use what are known as **non-deliverable forwards** (NDFs). These are similar to regular forward contracts, but they are cash settled (in the non-controlled currency of the currency pair) rather than physically settled (the controlled currency is neither delivered nor received). The non-controlled currency for NDFs is usually the USD or some other major currency. A partial list of some of the most important currencies with NDFs would include the Chinese yuan (CNY), Korean won (KRW), Russian ruble (RUB), Indian rupee (INR), and Brazilian real (BRL). The NDF is essentially a cash-settled "bet" on the movement in the spot rate of these currencies.

For example, a trader could enter into a long position in a three-month NDF for the BRL/USD. Note that the BRL—the currency with capital controls—is the price currency and the base currency, the USD, is the currency that settlement of the NDF will be made in. Assume that the current all-in rate for the NDF is 2.0280 and the trader uses an NDF with a notional size of USD1,000,000. Suppose that three months later the BRL/USD spot rate is 2.0300 and the trader closes out the existing NDF contract with an equal and offsetting spot transaction at this rate. Settlement proceeds by noting that the USD amounts net to zero (USD1,000,000 both bought and sold on settlement date), so the net cash flow generated would normally be in BRL if this was an ordinary forward contract. The net cash flow to the long position in this case would be calculated as

$$(2.0300 - 2.0280) \times 1,000,000 = BRL2,000$$

But with an NDF, there is no delivery in the controlled currency (hence the name *non-deliverable* forward). Settlement must be in USD, so this BRL amount is converted to USD at the then-current spot rate of 2.0300. This leads to a USD cash inflow for the long position in the NDF of

$$BRL2,000 \div 2.0300 \ BRL/USD = USD985.22$$

The credit risk of an NDF is typically lower than for the outright forward because the principal sums in the NDF do not move, unlike with an outright "vanilla" forward contract. For example, in the illustration the cash pay-off to the "bet" was the relatively small amount of USD985.22—there was no delivery of USD1,000,000 against receipt of BRL2,028,000. Conversely, as noted previously, NDFs exist because of some form of government involvement in foreign exchange markets. Sudden changes in government policy can lead to sharp movements in spot and NDF rates, often reversing any investment gains earned during long periods of seeming (but artificial) market calm. The implicit market risk of the NDF embodies an element of "tail risk."

Finally, we note that when capital controls exist, the free cross-border flow of capital that enforces the arbitrage condition underlying covered interest rate parity no longer functions consistently. Therefore, the pricing on NDFs need not be exactly in accord with the covered interest rate parity theorem. Instead, NDF pricing will reflect the individual supply and demand conditions (and risk premia) in the offshore market, which need not be the same as the onshore market of the specific emerging market country. Some of the most active participants in the NDF market are offshore hedge funds and proprietary traders making directional bets on the emerging market currency, rather than corporate or institutional portfolio managers hedging currency exposures. Volatility in the net speculative demand for emerging market exposure can affect the level of forward points. We also note that the type and strictness of capital controls can vary among emerging markets; hence, the need for knowledge of local market regulations is another factor influencing currency risk management in these markets.

SUMMARY

In this reading, we have examined the basic principles of managing foreign exchange risk within the broader investment process. International financial markets create a wide range of opportunities for investors, but they also create the need to recognize, measure, and control exchange rate risk. The management of this risk starts with setting the overall mandate for the portfolio, encoding the investors' investment objectives and constraints into the investment policy statement and providing strategic guidance on how currency risk will be managed in the portfolio. It extends to tactical positioning when portfolio managers translate market views into specific trading strategies within the overall risk management guidelines set by the IPS. We have examined some of these trading strategies, and how a range of portfolio management tools—positions in spot, forward, option, and FX swap contracts—can be used either to hedge away currency risk, or to express a market opinion on future exchange rate movements.

What we have emphasized throughout this reading is that there is no simple or single answer for the "best" currency management strategies. Different investors will have different strategic mandates (IPS), and different portfolio managers will have different market opinions and risk tolerances. There is a near-infinite number of possible currency trading strategies, each with its own benefits, costs, and risks. Currency risk management—both at the strategic and tactical levels—means having to manage the trade-offs between all of these various considerations.

Some of the main points covered in this reading are as follows:

- In professional FX markets, currencies are identified by standard three-letter codes, and quoted in terms of a price and a base currency (P/B).
- The spot exchange rate is typically for $T + 2$ delivery, and forward rates are for delivery for later periods. Both spot and forward rates are quoted in terms of a bid–offer price. Forward rates are quoted in terms of the spot rate plus forward points.
- An FX swap is a simultaneous spot and forward transaction; one leg of the swap is buying the base currency and the other is selling it. FX swaps are used to renew outstanding forward contracts once they mature, to "roll them forward."
- The domestic-currency return on foreign-currency assets can be broken into the foreign-currency asset return and the return on the foreign currency (the percentage appreciation or depreciation of the foreign currency against the domestic currency). These two components of the domestic-currency return are multiplicative.
- When there are several foreign-currency assets, the portfolio domestic-currency return is the weighted average of the individual domestic-currency returns (i.e., using the portfolio weights, which should sum to one).
- The risk of domestic-currency returns (its standard deviation) can be approximated by using a variance formula that recognizes the individual variances and covariances (correlations) among the foreign-currency asset returns and exchange rate movements.
- The calculation of the domestic-currency risk involves a large number of variables that must be estimated: the risks and correlations between all of the foreign-currency asset returns and their exchange rate risks.
- Guidance on where to target the portfolio along the risk spectrum is part of the IPS, which makes this a *strategic* decision based on the investment goals and constraints of the beneficial owners of the portfolio.
- If the IPS allows currency risk in the portfolio, the amount of desired currency exposure will depend on both portfolio diversification considerations and cost considerations.
  - Views on the diversifying effects of foreign-currency exposures depend on the time horizon involved, the type of foreign-currency asset, and market conditions.
  - Cost considerations also affect the hedging decision. Hedging is not free: It has both direct transactional costs as well as opportunity costs (the potential for favorable outcomes is foregone). Cost considerations make a perfect hedge difficult to maintain.
- Currency management strategies can be located along a spectrum stretching from:
  - passive, rules-based, complete hedging of currency exposures;
  - discretionary hedging, which allows the portfolio manager some latitude on managing currency exposures;
  - active currency management, which seeks out currency risk in order to manage it for profit; and to
  - currency overlay programs that aggressively manage currency "alpha."

- There are a variety of methods for forming market views.
  - The use of macroeconomic fundamentals to predict future currency movements is based on estimating the "fair value" for a currency with the expectation that spot rates will eventually converge on this equilibrium value.
  - Technical market indicators assume that, based on market psychology, historical price patterns in the data have a tendency to repeat. Technical indicators can be used to predict support and resistance levels in the market, as well as to confirm market trends and turning points.
  - The carry trade is based on violations of uncovered interest rate parity, and is also based on selling low-yield currencies in order to invest in high-yield currencies. This approach is equivalent to trading the forward rate bias, which means selling currencies trading at a forward premium and buying currencies trading at a forward discount.
  - Volatility trading uses the option market to express views on the distribution of future exchange rates, not their levels.
- Passive hedging will typically use forward contracts (rather than futures contracts) because they are more flexible. However, currency futures contracts are an option for smaller trading sizes and are frequently used in private wealth management.
- Forward contracts have the possibility of negative roll yield (the forward points embedded in the forward price can work for or against the hedge). The portfolio manager will have to balance the advantages and costs of hedging with forward contracts.
- Foreign-currency options can reduce opportunity costs (they allow the upside potential for favorable foreign-currency movements). However, the upfront option premiums must be paid.
- There are a variety of means to reduce the cost of the hedging with either forward or option contracts, but these cost-reduction measures always involve some combination of less downside protection and/or less upside potential.
- Hedging multiple foreign currencies uses the same tools and strategies used in hedging a single foreign-currency exposure; except now the correlation between residual currency exposures in the portfolio should be considered.
- Cross hedges introduce basis risk into the portfolio, which is the risk that the correlation between exposure and its cross hedging instrument may change in unexpected ways. Forward contracts typically have very little basis risk compared with movements in the underlying spot rate.
- The number of trading strategies that can be used, for hedging or speculative purposes, either for a single foreign currency or multiple foreign currencies, is near infinite. The manager must assess the costs, benefits, and risks of each in the context of the investment goals and constraints of the portfolio. There is no single "correct" approach.

REFERENCES

Bank for International Settlements. 2013. "Triennial Central Bank Survey of Foreign Exchange and Derivatives Market Activity."

Campbell, John Y. 2010. "Global Currency Hedging: What Role Should Foreign Currency Play in a Diversified Investment Portfolio?" *CFA Institute Conference Proceedings Quarterly*, vol. 27, no. 4 (December):8–18. doi:10.2469/cp.v27.n4.2

Campbell, John Y., Karine Serfaty-de Medeiros, and Luis. M. Viceira. 2007. "Global Currency Hedging," NBER Working Paper 13088 (May).

Darnell, R. Max. 2004. "Currency Strategies to Enhance Returns." In *Fixed-Income Tools for Enhancing Return and Meeting Client Objectives*. Charlottesville, VA: Association for Investment Management and Research.

Froot, Kenneth A. 1993. "Currency Hedging Over Long Horizons." NBER Working Paper 4355 (April): www.people.hbs.edu/kfroot/oldwebsite/cvpaperlinks/currency_hedging.pdf.

Hnatkovska, Viktoria, and Martin Evans. 2005. "International Capital Flows in a World of Greater Financial Integration." NBER Working Paper 11701 (October).

Kritzman, Mark P. 1999. "The Forward-Rate Bias." In *Currency Risk in Investment Portfolios*. Charlottesville, VA: Association for Investment Management and Research.

Martini, Giulio. 2010. "The Continuum from Passive to Active Currency Management." *CFA Institute Conference Proceedings Quarterly*, vol. 27, no. 1 (March):1–11. doi:10.2469/cp.v27.n1.1

Michenaud, Sébastien, and Bruno Solnik. 2008. "Applying Regret Theory to Investment Choices: Currency Hedging Decisions." *Journal of International Money and Finance*, vol. 27, no. 5:677–694.

Rosenberg, Michael R. 2002. *Deutsche Bank Guide to Exchange-Rate Determination*. London: Irwin Professional Publishing (May).

Rosenberg, Michael R., and William A. Barker. 2017. "Currency Exchange Rates: Understanding Equilibrium Value." CFA Program Curriculum, Level II.

Sine, Barry M. and Robert A. Strong. 2012. "Technical Analysis." CFA Program Curriculum, Level I.

US Department of the Treasury. 2007. "Semiannual Report on International Economic and Exchange Rate Policies, Appendix I." (December).

PROBLEMS

The following information relates to Questions 1–9

Kamala Gupta, a currency management consultant, is hired to evaluate the performance of two portfolios. Portfolio A and Portfolio B are managed in the United States and performance is measured in terms of the US dollar (USD). Portfolio A consists of British pound (GBP) denominated bonds and Portfolio B holds euro (EUR) denominated bonds.

Gupta calculates a 19.5% domestic-currency return for Portfolio A and 0% domestic-currency return for Portfolio B.

1. **Analyze** the movement of the USD against the foreign currency for Portfolio A. **Justify** your choice.

Template for Question 1

Asset	Foreign-Currency Portfolio Return	USD Relative to Foreign-Currency (circle one)
Portfolio A	15%	Appreciated
		Depreciated
Justification		

2. **Analyze** the foreign-currency return for Portfolio B. **Justify** your choice.

Template for Question 2

Asset	Percentage Movement in the Spot Exchange Rate	Foreign-Currency Portfolio Return (circle one)
Portfolio B	EUR appreciated 5% against the USD	Positive
		Negative
Justification		

The fund manager of Portfolio B is evaluating an internally-managed 100% foreign-currency hedged strategy.

3. **Discuss** *two* forms of trading costs associated with this currency management strategy.
   Gupta tells the fund manager of Portfolio B:

   "We need to seriously consider the potential costs associated with favorable currency rate movements, given that a 100% hedge-ratio strategy is being applied to this portfolio."

4. **Explain** Gupta's statement in light of the strategic choices in currency management available to the portfolio manager.
   The investment policy statement (IPS) for Portfolio A provides the manager with discretionary authority to take directional views on future currency movements. The fund manager believes the foreign currency assets of the portfolio could be fully hedged internally. However, the manager also believes existing firm personnel lack the expertise to actively manage foreign-currency movements to generate currency alpha.

5. **Recommend** a solution that will provide the fund manager the opportunity to earn currency alpha through active foreign exchange management.
   Gupta and the fund manager of Portfolio A discuss the differences among several active currency management methods.

6. **Evaluate** each statement independently and select the active currency approach it *best* describes. **Justify** each choice.

Template for Question 6

Gupta's Statements	Active Currency Approach (circle one)	Justification
"Many traders believe that it is not necessary to examine factors like the current account deficit, inflation, and interest rates because current exchange rates already reflect the market view on how these factors will affect future exchange rates."	Carry trade	
	Technical analysis	
	Economic fundamental	

Template for Question 6 (Continued)

Gupta's Statements	Active Currency Approach (circle one)	Justification
"The six-month interest rate in India is 8% compared to 1% in the United States. This presents a yield pick-up opportunity."	Carry trade Technical analysis Economic fundamental	
"The currency overlay manager will estimate the fair value of the currencies with the expectation that observed spot rates will converge to long-run equilibrium values described by parity conditions."	Carry trade Technical analysis Economic fundamental	

The following information is used for Question 7

Gupta interviews a currency overlay manager on behalf of Portfolio A. The foreign currency overlay manager describes volatility-based trading, compares volatility-based trading strategies and explains how the firm uses currency options to establish positions in the foreign exchange market. The overlay manager states:

Statement 1: "Given the current stability in financial markets, several traders at our firm take advantage of the fact that most options expire out-of-the money and therefore are net-short volatility."

Statement 2: "Traders that want to minimize the impact of unanticipated price volatility are net-long volatility."

7. **Compare** Statement 1 and Statement 2 and **identify** which *best* explains the view of a speculative volatility trader and which best explains the view of a hedger of volatility. **Justify** your response.

The following information is used for Questions 8 and 9

The fund manager of Portfolio B believes that setting up a full currency hedge requires a simple matching of the *current* market value of the foreign-currency exposure in the portfolio with an equal and offsetting position in a forward contract.

8. **Explain** how the hedge, as described by the fund manager, will eventually expose the portfolio to currency risk.

9. **Recommend** an alternative hedging strategy that will keep the hedge ratio close to the target hedge ratio. **Identify** the main disadvantage of implementing such a strategy.

The following information relates to Questions 10–15

Guten Investments GmbH, based in Germany and using the EUR as its reporting currency, is an asset management firm providing investment services for local high net worth and institutional investors seeking international exposures. The firm invests in the Swiss, UK, and

US markets, after conducting fundamental research in order to select individual investments. Exhibit 1 presents recent information for exchange rates in these foreign markets.

EXHIBIT 1   Exchange Rate Data

	One Year Ago	Today
Euro-dollar (USD/EUR)*	1.2730	1.2950
Euro-sterling (GBP/EUR)	0.7945	0.8050
Euro-Swiss (CHF/EUR)	1.2175	1.2080

* The amount of USD required to buy one EUR

In prior years, the correlation between movements in the foreign-currency asset returns for the USD-denominated assets and movements in the exchange rate was estimated to be +0.50. After analyzing global financial markets, Konstanze Ostermann, a portfolio manager at Guten Investments, now expects that this correlation will increase to +0.80, although her forecast for foreign-currency asset returns is unchanged.

Ostermann believes that currency markets are efficient and hence that long-run gains cannot be achieved from active currency management, especially after netting out management and transaction costs. She uses this philosophy to guide hedging decisions for her discretionary accounts, unless instructed otherwise by the client.

Ostermann is aware, however, that some investors hold an alternative view on the merits of active currency management. Accordingly, their portfolios have different investment guidelines. For these accounts, Guten Investments employs a currency specialist firm, Umlauf Management, to provide currency overlay programs specific to each client's investment objectives. For most hedging strategies, Umlauf Management develops a market view based on underlying fundamentals in exchange rates. However, when directed by clients, Umlauf Management uses options and a variety of trading strategies to unbundle all of the various risk factors (the "Greeks") and trade them separately.

Ostermann conducts an annual review for three of her clients and gathers the summary information presented in Exhibit 2.

EXHIBIT 2   Select Clients at Guten Investments

Client	Currency Management Objectives
Adele Kastner – A high net worth individual with a low risk tolerance.	Keep the portfolio's currency exposures close, if not equal to, the benchmark so that the domestic-currency return is equal to the foreign-currency return.
Braunt Pensionskasse – A large private-company pension fund with a moderate risk tolerance.	Limited discretion which allows the actual portfolio currency risk exposures to vary plus-or-minus 5% from the neutral position.
Franz Trading GmbH – An exporting company with a high risk tolerance.	Discretion with respect to currency exposure is allowed in order to add alpha to the portfolio.

10. Based on Exhibit 1, the domestic-currency return over the last year (measured in EUR terms) was *higher* than the foreign-currency return for:
    A. USD-denominated assets.
    B. GBP-denominated assets.
    C. CHF-denominated assets.

11. Based on Ostermann's correlation forecast, the expected domestic-currency return (measured in EUR terms) on USD-denominated assets will *most* likely:
    A. increase.
    B. decrease.
    C. remain unchanged.

12. Based on Ostermann's views regarding active currency management, the percentage of currency exposure in her discretionary accounts that is hedged is *most likely:*
    A. 0%.
    B. 50%.
    C. 100%.

13. The active currency management approach that Umlauf Management is *least* likely to employ is based on:
    A. volatility trading.
    B. technical analysis.
    C. economic fundamentals.

14. Based on Exhibit 2, the currency overlay program *most* appropriate for Braunt Pensionskasse would:
    A. be fully passive.
    B. allow limited directional views.
    C. actively manage foreign exchange as an asset class.

15. Based on Exhibit 2, the client *most likely* to benefit from the introduction of an additional overlay manager is:
    A. Adele Kastner.
    B. Braunt Pensionskasse.
    C. Franz Trading GmbH.

The following information relates to Questions 16–19

Li Jiang is an international economist operating a subscription website through which she offers financial advice on currency issues to retail investors. One morning she receives four subscriber e-mails seeking guidance.

Subscriber 1	"As a French national now working in the United States, I hold US dollar-denominated assets currently valued at USD 700,000. The USD/EUR exchange rate has been quite volatile and now appears oversold based on historical price trends. With my American job ending soon, I will return to Europe. I want to protect the value of my USD holdings, measured in EUR terms, before I repatriate these funds back to France. To reduce my currency exposure I am going to use currency futures contracts. Can you explain the factors most relevant to implementing this strategy?"
Subscriber 2	"I have observed that many of the overseas markets for Korean export goods are slowing, while the United States is experiencing a rise in exports. Both trends can combine to possibly affect the value of the won (KRW) relative to the US dollar. As a result, I am considering a speculative currency trade on the KRW/USD exchange rate. I also expect the volatility in this exchange rate to increase."

Subscriber 3   "India has relatively high interest rates compared to the United
                      States and my market view is that this situation is likely to persist.
                      As a retail investor actively trading currencies, I am considering
                      borrowing in USD and converting to the Indian rupee (INR). I
                      then intend to invest these funds in INR-denominated bonds, but
                      without using a currency hedge."

Subscriber 4   "I was wondering if trading in emerging market currencies
                      provides the more opportunities for superior returns through active
                      management than trading in Developed Market currencies."

16. For Subscriber 1, the *most* significant factor to consider would be:
    A. margin requirements.
    B. transaction costs of using futures contracts.
    C. different quoting conventions for future contracts.
17. For Subscriber 2, and assuming all of the choices relate to the KRW/USD exchange rate,
    the *best* way to implement the trading strategy would be to:
    A. write a straddle.
    B. buy a put option.
    C. use a long NDF position.
18. Which of the following market developments would be *most* favorable for Subscriber 3's
    trading plan?
    A. A narrower interest rate differential.
    B. A higher forward premium for INR/USD.
    C. Higher volatility in INR/USD spot rate movements.
19. Jiang's *best* response to Subscriber 4 would be that active trading in trading in emerging
    market currencies:
    A. typically leads to return distributions that are positively skewed.
    B. should not lead to higher returns because FX markets are efficient.
    C. often leads to higher returns through carry trades, but comes with higher risks and
       trading costs.

The following information relates to Questions 20–23

Rika Björk runs the currency overlay program at a large Scandinavian investment fund, which
uses the Swedish krona (SEK) as its reporting currency. She is managing the fund's exposure
to GBP-denominated assets, which are currently hedged with a GBP 100,000,000 forward
contract (on the SEK/GBP cross rate, which is currently at 10.6875 spot). The maturity for
the forward contract is December 1, which is still several months away. However, since the
contract was initiated the value of the fund's assets has declined by GBP 7,000,000. As a result,
Björk wants to rebalance the hedge immediately.

Next Björk turns her attention to the fund's Swiss franc (CHF) exposures. In order to
maintain some profit potential Björk wants to hedge the exposure using a currency option, but
at the same time, she wants to reduce hedging costs. She believes that there is limited upside
for the SEK/CHF cross rate.

Björk then examines the fund's EUR-denominated exposures. Due to recent monetary
tightening by the Riksbank (the Swedish central bank) forward points for the SEK/EUR rate
have swung to a premium. The fund's EUR-denominated exposures are hedged with forward
contracts.

Finally Björk turns her attention to the fund's currency exposures in several emerging markets. The fund has large positions in several Latin American bond markets, but Björk does not feel that there is sufficient liquidity in the related foreign exchange derivatives to easily hedge the fund's Latin American bond markets exposures. However, the exchange rates for these countries, measured against the SEK, are correlated with the MXN/SEK exchange rate. (The MXN is the Mexican peso, which is considered to be among the most liquid Latin American currencies). Björk considers using forward positions in the MXN to cross-hedge the fund's Latin American currency exposures.

20. To rebalance the SEK/GBP hedge, and assuming all instruments are based on SEK/GBP, Björk would buy:
    A. GBP 7,000,000 spot.
    B. GBP 7,000,000 forward to December 1.
    C. SEK 74,812,500 forward to December 1.

21. Given her investment goals and market view, and assuming all options are based on SEK/CHF, the *best* strategy for Björk to manage the fund's CHF exposure would be to buy an:
    A. ATM call option.
    B. ITM call option and write an OTM call option.
    C. OTM put option and write an OTM call option.

22. Given the recent movement in the forward premium for the SEK/EUR rate, Björk can expect that the hedge will experience higher:
    A. basis risk.
    B. roll yield.
    C. premia income.

23. The *most* important risk to Björk's Latin American currency hedge would be changes in:
    A. forward points.
    B. exchange rate volatility.
    C. cross-currency correlations.

The following information relates to Question 24

Kalila Al-Khalili has been hired as a consultant to a Middle Eastern sovereign wealth fund. The fund's oversight committee has asked her to examine the fund's financial characteristics and recommend an appropriate currency management strategy given the fund's Investment Policy Statement. After a thorough study of the fund and its finances, Al-Khalili reaches the following conclusions:

- The fund's mandate is focused on the long-term development of the country, and the royal family (who are very influential on the fund's oversight committee) are prepared to take a long-term perspective on the fund's investments.
- The fund's strategic asset allocation is tilted towards equity rather than fixed-income assets.
- Both its fixed-income and equity portfolios have a sizeable exposure to emerging market assets.
- Currently, about 90% of exchange rate exposures are hedged although the IPS allows a range of hedge ratios.
- Liquidity needs of the fund are minimal, since the government is running a balanced budget and is unlikely to need to dip into the fund in the near term to cover fiscal deficits. Indeed,

the expected lifetime of country's large oil reserves has been greatly extended by recent discoveries, and substantial oil royalties are expected to persist into the future.

24. Based on her investigation, Al-Khalili would *most* likely recommend:
    A. active currency management.
    B. a hedging ratio closer to 100%.
    C. a narrow discretionary band for currency exposures.

The following information relates to Questions 25–27

Mason Darden is an adviser at Colgate & McIntire (C&M), managing large-cap global equity separate accounts. C&M's investment process restricts portfolio positions to companies based in the United States, Japan, and the eurozone. All C&M clients are US-domiciled, with client reporting in US dollars.

Darden manages Ravi Bhatt's account, which had a total (US dollar) return of 7.0% last year. Darden must assess the contribution of foreign currency to the account's total return. Exhibit 1 summarizes the account's geographic portfolio weights, asset returns, and currency returns for last year.

EXHIBIT 1   Performance Data for Bhatt's Portfolio Last Year

Geography	Portfolio Weight	Asset Return	Currency Return
United States	50%	10.0%	NA
Eurozone	25%	5.0%	2.0%
Japan	25%	−3.0%	4.0%
Total	100%		

25. **Calculate** the contribution of foreign currency to the Bhatt account's total return. **Show** your calculations.

    Darden meets with Bhatt and learns that Bhatt will be moving back to his home country of India next month to resume working as a commodity trader. Bhatt is concerned about a possible US recession. His investment policy statement (IPS) allows for flexibility in managing currency risk. Overall returns can be enhanced by capturing opportunities between the US dollar and the Indian rupee (INR) within a range of plus or minus 25% from the neutral position using forward contracts on the currency pair. C&M has a currency overlay team that can appropriately manage currency risk for Bhatt's portfolio.

26. **Determine** the *most appropriate* currency management strategy for Bhatt. **Justify** your response.

Determine the *most appropriate* currency management strategy for Bhatt. (Circle one.)

Passive hedging	Discretionary hedging	Active currency management

Justify your response.

Following analysis of Indian economic fundamentals, C&M's currency team expects continued stability in interest rate and inflation rate differentials between the United States and India. C&M's currency team strongly believes the US dollar will appreciate relative to the Indian rupee.

C&M would like to exploit the perceived alpha opportunity using forward contracts on the USD10,000,000 Bhatt portfolio.

27. **Recommend** the trading strategy C&M should implement. **Justify** your response.

The following information relates to Questions 28–29

Renita Murimi is a currency overlay manager and market technician who serves institutional investors seeking to address currency-specific risks associated with investing in international assets. Her firm also provides volatility overlay programs. She is developing a volatility-based strategy for Emil Konev, a hedge fund manager focused on option trading. Konev seeks to implement an "FX as an asset class" approach distinct to his portfolio to realize speculative gains and believes the long-term strength of the US dollar is peaking.

28. **Describe** how a volatility-based strategy for Konev would *most likely* contrast with Murimi's other institutional investors. **Justify** your response.
29. **Discuss** how Murimi can use her technical skills to devise the strategy.
30. Carnoustie Capital Management, Ltd. (CCM), a UK-based global investment advisory firm, is considering adding an emerging market currency product to its offerings. CCM has for the past three years managed a "model" portfolio of emerging market currencies using the same investment approach as its developed economy currency products. The risk and return measures of the "model" portfolio compare favorably with the one- and three-year emerging market benchmark performance net of CCM's customary advisory fee and estimated trading costs. Mindful of the higher volatility of emerging market currencies, CCM management is particularly pleased with the "model" portfolio's standard deviation, Sharpe ratio, and value at risk (VAR) in comparison to those of its developed economy products.

Recognizing that market conditions have been stable since the "model" portfolio's inception, CCM management is sensitive to the consequences of extreme market events for emerging market risk and return.

Evaluate the application of emerging market and developed market investment return probability distributions for CCM's potential new product.

The following information relates to Questions 31–32

Wilson Manufacturing (Wilson) is an Australian institutional client of Ethan Lee, who manages a variety of portfolios across asset classes. Wilson prefers a neutral benchmark over a rules-based approach, with its investment policy statement (IPS) requiring a currency hedge ratio between 97% and 103% to protect against currency risk. Lee has assessed various currency management strategies for Wilson's US dollar-denominated fixed-income portfolio to optimally locate it along the currency risk spectrum. The portfolio is currently in its flat natural neutral position because of Lee's lack of market conviction.

31. **Identify** the *most likely* approach for Lee to optimally locate Wilson's portfolio on the currency risk spectrum, consistent with the IPS. **Justify** your response with *two* reasons supporting the approach.

Identify the *most likely* approach for Lee to optimally locate Wilson's portfolio on the currency risk spectrum, consistent with IPS. (Circle one.)

Passive Hedging	Discretionary Hedging	Active Currency Management	Currency Overlay

Justify your response with *two* reasons supporting the approach.

1.	2.

Lee and Wilson recently completed the annual portfolio review and determined the IPS is too short-term focused and excessively risk averse. Accordingly, the IPS is revised and foreign currency is introduced as a separate asset class. Lee hires an external foreign exchange sub-adviser to implement a currency overlay program, emphasizing that it is important to structure the program so that the currency overlay is allowed in terms of strategic portfolio positioning.

32. **Discuss** a key attribute of the currency overlay that would *increase* the likelihood it would be allowed in terms of strategic portfolio positioning.

The following information relates to Questions 33–35

Rosario Delgado is an investment manager in Spain. Delgado's client, Max Rivera, seeks assistance with his well-diversified investment portfolio denominated in US dollars.

Rivera's reporting currency is the euro, and he is concerned about his US dollar exposure. His portfolio IPS requires monthly rebalancing, at a minimum. The portfolio's market value is USD2.5 million. Given Rivera's risk aversion, Delgado is considering a monthly hedge using either a one-month forward contract or one-month futures contract.

33. **Determine** which type of hedge instrument combination is *most* appropriate for Rivera's situation. **Justify** your selection.

Determine which type of hedge instrument combination is *most* appropriate for Rivera's situation. (Circle one.)

Static Forward	Static Futures	Dynamic Forward	Dynamic Futures

Justify your selection.

Assume Rivera's portfolio was perfectly hedged. It is now time to rebalance the portfolio and roll the currency hedge forward one month. The relevant data for rebalancing are provided in Exhibit 1.

EXHIBIT 1   Portfolio and Relevant Market Data

	One Month Ago	Today
Portfolio value of assets (USD)	2,500,000	2,650,000
USD/EUR spot rate (bid–offer)	0.8913/0.8914	0.8875/0.8876
One-month forward points (bid–offer)	25/30	20/25

34. **Calculate** the net cash flow (in euros) to maintain the desired hedge. **Show** your calculations.

    With the US dollar currently trading at a forward premium and US interest rates lower than Spanish rates, Delgado recommends trading against the forward rate bias to earn additional return from a positive roll yield.

35. **Identify** *two* strategies Delgado should use to earn a positive roll yield. **Describe** the specific steps needed to execute each strategy.

Identify *two* strategies Delgado should use to earn a positive roll yield.	**Describe** the specific steps needed to execute *each* strategy.
1.	
2.	

CHAPTER **8**

OPTIONS STRATEGIES

Adam Schwartz, PhD, CFA, and Barbara Valbuzzi, CFA

LEARNING OUTCOMES

The candidate should be able to:

- demonstrate how an asset's returns may be replicated by using options;
- discuss the investment objective(s), structure, payoff, risk(s), value at expiration, profit, maximum profit, maximum loss, and breakeven underlying price at expiration of a covered call position;
- discuss the investment objective(s), structure, payoff, risk(s), value at expiration, profit, maximum profit, maximum loss, and breakeven underlying price at expiration of a protective put position;
- compare the delta of covered call and protective put positions with the position of being long an asset and short a forward on the underlying asset;
- compare the effect of buying a call on a short underlying position with the effect of selling a put on a short underlying position;
- discuss the investment objective(s), structure, payoffs, risk(s), value at expiration, profit, maximum profit, maximum loss, and breakeven underlying price at expiration of the following option strategies: bull spread, bear spread, straddle, and collar;
- describe uses of calendar spreads;
- discuss volatility skew and smile;
- identify and evaluate appropriate option strategies consistent with given investment objectives;
- demonstrate the use of options to achieve targeted equity risk exposures.

1. INTRODUCTION

Derivatives are financial instruments through which counterparties agree to exchange economic cash flows based on the movement of underlying securities, indexes, currencies, or other instruments or factors. A derivative's value is thus *derived* from the economic performance of the underlying. Derivatives may be created directly by counterparties or may be facilitated through established, regulated market exchanges. Direct creation between counterparties has the benefit of tailoring to the counterparties' specific needs but also the disadvantage of potentially low liquidity. Exchange-traded derivatives often do not match counterparties' specific needs but do facilitate early termination of the position, and, importantly, mitigate counterparty risk. Derivatives facilitate the exchange of economic risks and benefits where trades in the underlying securities might be less advantageous because of poor liquidity, transaction costs, regulatory impediments, tax or accounting considerations, or other factors.

Options are an important type of contingent-claim derivative that provide their owner with the right but not an obligation to a payoff determined by the future price of the underlying asset. Unlike other types of derivatives (i.e., swaps, forwards, and futures), options have nonlinear payoffs that enable their owners to benefit from movements in the underlying in one direction without being hurt by movements in the opposite direction. The cost of this opportunity, however, is the upfront cash payment required to enter the options position.

Options can be combined with the underlying and with other options in a variety of different ways to modify investment positions, to implement investment strategies, or even to infer market expectations. Therefore, investment managers routinely use option strategies for hedging risk exposures, for seeking to profit from anticipated market moves, and for implementing desired risk exposures in a cost-effective manner.

The main purpose of this reading is to illustrate how options strategies are used in typical investment situations and to show the risk–return trade-offs associated with their use. Importantly, an informed investment professional should have such a basic understanding of options strategies to competently serve his investment clients.

Section 2 of this reading shows how certain combinations of securities (i.e., options, underlying) are equivalent to others. Sections 3–6 discuss two of the most widely used options strategies, covered calls and protective puts. In Sections 7 and 8, we look at popular spread and combination option strategies used by investors. The focus of Section 9 is implied volatility embedded in option prices and related volatility skew and surface. Section 10 discusses option strategy selection. Sections 11 and 12 demonstrate a series of applications showing ways in which an investment manager might solve an investment problem with options. The reading concludes with a summary.

2. POSITION EQUIVALENCIES

It is useful to think of derivatives as building blocks that can be combined to create a specific payoff with the desired risk exposure. A synthetic position can be created for any option or stock strategy. Most of the time, market participants use synthetic positions to transform the payoff profile of their positions when their market views change. We cover a few of these relationships in the following pages. First, a brief recap of put–call parity and put–call–forward parity will help readers to understand such synthetic positions.

As you may remember, put–call parity shows the equivalence (or parity) of a portfolio of a call and a risk-free bond with a portfolio of a put and the underlying, which leads to the relationship between put and call prices. Put–call parity can be expressed in the following formula, where S_0 is the price of the underlying; p_0 and c_0 are the prices (i.e., premiums) of the put and call options, respectively; and $X/(1 + r)^T$ is the present value of the risk-free bond: $S_0 + p_0 = c_0 + X/(1 + r)^T$.

A closely related concept is put–call–forward parity, which identifies the equivalence between buying a fiduciary call, given by the purchase of a call and the risk-free bond, and a synthetic protective put. The latter involves the purchase of a put option and a forward contract on the underlying that expires at the same time as the put option. In the put–call–forward parity formula, S_0 is replaced with a forward contract to buy the underlying, where the forward price is given by $F_0(T) = S_0(1 + r)^T$. Therefore, put–call–forward parity is: $F_0(T)/(1 + r)^T + p_0 = c_0 + X/(1 + r)^T$.

2.1. Synthetic Forward Position

The combination of a long call and a short put with identical strike price and expiration, traded at the same time on the same underlying, is equivalent to a **synthetic long forward position**. In fact, the long call creates the upside and the short put creates the downside on the underlying.

Consider an investor who buys an at-the-money (ATM) call and simultaneously sells a put with the same strike and the same expiration date. Whatever the stock price at expiration, one of the two options will be in the money. If the contract has a physical settlement, the investor will buy the underlying stock by paying the strike price. In fact, on the expiration date, the investor will exercise the call she owns if the stock price is above the strike price. Otherwise, if the underlying price is below the strike price, the put owner will exercise his right to deliver the stock and the investor (who sold the put) must buy it for the strike price. Exhibit 1 shows the values of the two options and the combined position at expiration, compared with the value of the stock purchase at that same time. The stock in this case does not pay dividends.

EXHIBIT 1   Synthetic Long Forward Position at Expiration

Stock price at expiration:	40	50	60
Alternative 1:			
Long 50-strike call payoff	0	0	10
Short 50-strike put payoff	−10	0	0
Total value	−10	0	10
Alternative 2:			
Long stock at 50	−10	0	10
Total value	−10	0	10

We now compare the same option strategy with the payoff of a forward or futures contract in Exhibit 2. The motivation to create a synthetic long forward position could be to exploit an arbitrage opportunity presented by the actual forward price or the need for an alternative to the outright purchase of a long forward position. Frequently, a forward contract is used instead of futures to acquire a stock position because it allows for contract customization.

EXHIBIT 2   Synthetic Long Forward Position vs. Long Forward/Futures

Stock price at expiration:	40	50	60
Alternative 1:			
Long 50-strike call payoff	0	0	10
Short 50-strike put payoff	−10	0	0
Total value	−10	0	10
Alternative 3: Long forward/futures at 50			
Value	−10	0	10

EXAMPLE 1   Synthetic Long Forward Position vs. Long Forward/Futures

A market maker has sold a three-month forward contract on Vodafone that allows the client (counterparty) to buy 10,000 shares at 200.35 pence (100p = £1) at expiration. The current stock price (S_0) is 200p, and the stock does not pay dividends until after the contract matures. The annualized interest rate is 0.70%. The cost (i.e., premium) of puts and calls on Vodafone is identical.

1. Discuss (a) how the market maker can hedge her short forward position upon the sale of the forward contract and (b) the market maker's position upon expiration of the forward contract.
2. Discuss how the market maker can hedge her short forward contract position using a synthetic long forward position, and explain what happens at expiry if the Vodafone share price is above or below 200.35p.

Solution 1:
A. To offset the short forward contract position, the market maker can borrow £20,000 (= 10,000 × S_0/100) and buy 10,000 Vodafone shares at 200p. There is no upfront cost because the stock purchase is 100% financed.
B. At the expiry of the forward contract, the market maker delivers the 10,000 Vodafone shares she owns to the client that is long the forward, and then the market maker repays her loan. The net outflow for the market maker is zero because the following two transactions offset each other:

Amount received for the delivery of shares: 10,000 × 200.35p = £20,035
Repayment of loan: 10,000 × 200p [1 + 0.700% × (90/360)] = £20,035

Solution 2: To hedge her short forward position, the market maker creates a synthetic long forward position. She purchases a call and sells a put, both with a strike price of 200.35p and expiring in three months.

At the expiry of the forward contract, if the stock price is above 200.35p, the market maker exercises her call, pays £20,035 (=10,000 × 200.35p), and receives 10,000 Vodafone shares. She then delivers these shares to the client and receives £20,035.

At the expiry of the forward contract, if the stock price is below 200.35p, the owner of the long put will exercise his option, and the market maker receives the 10,000 Vodafone shares for £20,035. She then delivers these shares to the client and receives £20,035.

Consider now a trader who wants to short a stock over a specified period. He needs to borrow the stock from the market and then sell the borrowed shares. Instead, the trader can create a **synthetic short forward position** by selling a call and buying a put at the same strike price and maturity. When using options to replicate a short stock position, it is important to be aware of early assignment risk that could arise with American-style options. As Exhibit 3 shows, the payoff is the exact opposite of the synthetic long forward position.

The same outcome can be achieved be selling forwards or futures contracts (as seen in Exhibit 3). These instruments are also commonly used to eliminate future price risk. Consider an investor who owns a stock and wants to lock in a future sales price. The investor might enter into a forward or futures contract (as seller) requiring her to deliver the shares at a future date in exchange for a cash amount determined today. Because the initial and final stock prices are known, this investment should pay the risk-free rate. For a dividend-paying stock, the dividends expected to be paid on the stock during the term of the contract will decrease the price of the forward or futures.

EXHIBIT 3   Synthetic Short Forward Position

Stock price at expiration:	40	50	60
Alternative 1:			
Short 50-strike call payoff	0	0	−10
Long 50-strike put payoff	10	0	0
Total value	10	0	−10
Alternative 2:			
Short stock at 50	10	0	−10
Value	10	0	−10
Alternative 3:			
Short forward/futures at 50	10	0	−10
Value	10	0	−10

Synthetic forwards on stocks and equity indexes are often used by market makers that have sold a forward contract to customers—to hedge the risk, the market-maker would implement a synthetic long forward position—or by investment banks wishing to hedge forward exposure arising from structured products.

2.2. Synthetic Put and Call

As already described, market participants can use synthetic positions to transform the payoff and risk profile of their positions. The symmetrical payoffs of long and short stock, forward, and futures positions can be altered by implementing synthetic options positions. For example, the symmetric payoff of a short stock position can become asymmetrical if the investor transforms it into a synthetic long put position by buying a call.

Exhibit 4 shows the payoffs of a synthetic long put position that consists of short stock at 50 and a long call with an exercise price of 50. It can be seen that the payoffs from this synthetic put position at various stock prices at option expiration are identical to those of a long put with a 50-strike price. Of course, all positions are assumed to expire at the same time. Note that the same transformation of payoff and risk profile for a position of short forwards or futures can also be accomplished using long call options.

EXHIBIT 4   Synthetic Long Put

Stock price at expiration:	40	50	60
Alternative 1:			
Short stock at 50	10	0	−10
Long 50-strike call payoff	0	0	+10
Total value	10	0	0
Alternative 2			
Long 50-strike put payoff	10	0	0
Value	10	0	0

EXAMPLE 2   Synthetic Long Put

Three months ago, Wing Tan, a hedge fund manager, entered into a short forward contract that requires him to deliver 50,000 Generali shares, which the fund does not currently own, at €18/share in one month from now. The stock price is currently €16/share. The hedge fund's research analyst, Gisele Rossi, has a non-consensus expectation that the company will report an earnings "beat" next month. The stock does not pay dividends.

1. Under the assumption that Tan maintains the payoff profile of his current short forward position, discuss the conditions for profit or loss at contract expiration.
2. After discussing with Rossi her earnings outlook, Tan remains bearish on Generali. He decides to hedge his risk, however, in case the stock does report a positive

earnings surprise. Discuss how Tan can modify his existing position to produce an asymmetrical, risk-reducing payoff.

Solution 1: If Tan decides to keep the current payoff profile of his position, at the expiry date, given a stock price of S_T, the profit or loss on the short forward will be 50,000 × (€18 − S_T). The position will be profitable only if S_T is below €18; otherwise the manager will incur in a loss.

Solution 2: Tan decides to modify the payoff profile on his short forward position so that, at expiration, it will benefit from any stock price decrease below €16 while avoiding losses if the stock rises above that price. He purchases a call option with a strike price €16 and one month to maturity at a cost (premium) of €0.50. At expiration, the payoffs are as follows:

- On the short forward contract: 50,000 × (€18 − S_T)
- On the long call: 50,000 × {Max[0,(S_T − €16)] − €0.50}
- On the combined position: 50,000 × {(€18 − S_T) + [Max[0,(S_T − €16)] − €0.50]}

If S_T ≤ €16, the call will expire worthless and the profit will amount to 50,000 × (€18 − S_T + 0 − €0.50).

If S_T > €16, the call is exercised and the Generali shares delivered for a maximum profit of 50,000 × (€18 − €16 − €0.50) = €75,000.

In similar fashion, an investor with a long stock position can change his payoff and risk profile into that of a long call by purchasing a put ("protective put" strategy). The long put eliminates the downside risk, whereas the long stock leaves the profit potential unlimited. As shown in Exhibit 5, the strategy has a payoff profile resembling that of a long call. Again, all positions are assumed to expire at the same time. We will have much more to say about the protective put strategy later in this reading. Finally, the payoff profile of a long call can also be achieved by adding a long put to a long forward or futures position, all with the same expiration dates and the same strike and forward (or futures) prices.

EXHIBIT 5   Synthetic Long Call

Stock price at expiration:	40	50	60
Alternative 1:			
Long stock at 50	−10	0	10
Long 50-strike put payoff	10	0	0
Total value	0	0	10
Alternative 2			
Long 50-strike call payoff	0	0	10
Value	0	0	10

3. COVERED CALLS AND PROTECTIVE PUTS

Writing a **covered call** is a very common option strategy used by both individual and institutional investors. In this strategy, a party that already owns shares sells a call option, giving another party the right to buy their shares at the exercise price.[1] The investor owns the shares and has taken on the potential obligation to deliver the shares to the call option buyer and accept the exercise price as the price at which she sells the shares. For her willingness to do this, the investor receives the premium on the option.

When someone simultaneously holds a long position in an asset and a long position in a put option on that asset, the put is often called a **protective put**. The name comes from the fact that the put protects against losses in the value of the underlying asset.

The examples that follow use the convention of identifying an option by the underlying asset, expiration, exercise price, and option type. For example, in Exhibit 6, the PBR October 16 call option sells for 1.42. The underlying asset is Petróleo Brasileiro (PBR) common stock, the expiration is October, the exercise price is 16, the option is a call, and the call premium is 1.42. It is important to note that even though we will refer to this as the October 16 option, it does not expire on 16 October. Rather, 16 reflects the price at which the call owner has the right to buy, otherwise known as the exercise price or strike.

Petróleo Brasileiro (PBR)	October	16	Call
Underlying asset	*Expiration*	*Exercise price*	*Option type*

On some exchanges, certain options may have weekly expirations in addition to a monthly expiration, which means investors need to be careful in specifying the option of interest. For a given underlying asset and exercise price, there may be several weekly and one monthly option expiring in October. The examples that follow all assume a single monthly expiration.

3.1. Investment Objectives of Covered Calls

Consider the option data in Exhibit 6. Suppose there is one month until the September expiration. By convention, option listings show data for a single call or put, but in practice, the most common trading unit for an exchange-traded option is one contract covering 100 shares. Besides call and put premiums for various strike (i.e., exercise) prices and monthly expirations, the option data also shows implied volatilities as well as the "Greeks" (variables so named because most of the common ones are denoted by Greek letters). Implied volatility is the value of the unobservable volatility variable that equates the result of an option pricing model—such as the Black–Scholes–Merton (BSM) model—to the market price of an option, using all other required (and observable) input variables, including the option's strike price, the price of the underlying, the time to option expiration, and the risk-free interest. Before proceeding further, we provide a brief review of the Greeks because they will be an integral part of the discussion of the various option strategies to be presented.

- **Delta** (Δ) is the change in an option's price in response to a change in price of the underlying, all else equal. Delta provides a good approximation of how an option's price will change for

---

[1] When someone creates (writes) a call without owning the underlying asset, it is known as a "naked" call.

a small change in the underlying's price. Delta for long calls is always positive; delta for long puts is always negative. *Delta (Δ) ≈ Change in value of option/Change in value of underlying.*

- **Gamma** (Γ) is the change in an option's delta for a change in price of the underlying, all else equal. Gamma is a measure of the curvature in the option price in relationship to the underlying price. Gamma for long calls and long puts is always positive. *Gamma (Γ) ≈ Change in delta/Change in value of underlying.*

- **Vega** (ν) is the change in an option's price for a change in volatility of the underlying, all else equal. Vega measures the sensitivity of the underlying to volatility. Vega for long calls and long puts is always positive. *Vega (ν) ≈ Change in value of option/Change in volatility of underlying.*

- **Theta** (Θ) is the daily change in an option's price, all else equal. Theta measures the sensitivity of the option's price to the passage of time, known as time decay. Theta for long calls and long puts is generally negative.

Assume the current PBR share price is 15.84 and the risk-free rate is 4%. Now let us consider three different market participants who might logically use covered calls.

EXHIBIT 6   PBR Option Prices, Implied Volatilities, and Greeks

Call Prices			Exercise Price	Put Prices		
SEP	OCT	NOV		SEP	OCT	NOV
1.64	1.95	2.44	15	0.65	0.99	1.46
0.97	1.42	1.90	16	1.14	1.48	1.96
0.51	1.02	1.44	17	1.76	2.09	2.59

Call Implied Volatility				Put Implied Volatility		
SEP	OCT	NOV		SEP	OCT	NOV
64.42%	57.33%	62.50%	15	58.44%	56.48%	62.81%
55.92%	56.11%	60.37%	16	59.40%	56.35%	62.27%
51.07%	55.87%	58.36%	17	59.59%	56.77%	63.40%

Delta: change in option price per change of +1 in stock price, all else equal

Call Deltas				Put Deltas		
SEP	OCT	NOV		SEP	OCT	NOV
0.657	0.647	0.642	15	−0.335	−0.352	−0.359
0.516	0.540	0.560	16	−0.481	−0.460	−0.438
0.351	0.434	0.475	17	−0.620	−0.564	−0.513

Gamma: change in delta per change of +1 in stock price, all else equal

Call Gammas				Put Gammas		
SEP	OCT	NOV		SEP	OCT	NOV
0.125	0.100	0.075	15	0.136	0.102	0.075
0.156	0.109	0.082	16	0.147	0.109	0.080
0.159	0.109	0.086	17	0.140	0.107	0.079

(continued)

EXHIBIT 6   (Continued)

Theta: daily change in option price, all else equal

Call Thetas (daily)				Put Thetas (daily)		
SEP	OCT	NOV		SEP	OCT	NOV
−0.019	−0.012	−0.011	15	−0.015	−0.010	−0.009
−0.018	−0.013	−0.011	16	−0.017	−0.011	−0.010
−0.015	−0.012	−0.011	17	−0.016	−0.011	−0.010

Vega: change in option price per 1% increase in volatility, all else equal

Call Vegas (per %)				Put Vegas (per %)		
SEP	OCT	NOV		SEP	OCT	NOV
0.017	0.024	0.030	15	0.017	0.024	0.030
0.018	0.026	0.031	16	0.018	0.026	0.031
0.017	0.025	0.032	17	0.017	0.025	0.032

3.1.1. Market Participant #1: Yield Enhancement

The most common motivation for writing covered calls is cash generation in anticipation of limited upside moves in the underlying. The call option writer keeps the premium regardless of what happens in the future. Some covered call writers view the premium they receive as an additional source of income in the same way they view cash dividends. For a covered call, a long position in 100 shares of the underlying is required for each short call contract. No additional cash margin is needed if the long position in the underlying is maintained. If the stock price exceeds the strike price at expiry, the underlying shares will be "called away" from the covered call writer and then delivered to satisfy the option holder's right to buy shares at the strike price. It is important to recognize, however, that when someone writes a call option, he is essentially giving up the returns above the strike price to the call holder.

Consider an individual investor who owns PBR and believes the stock price is likely to remain relatively flat over the next few months. With the stock currently trading at just under 16, the investor might think it unlikely that the stock will rise above 17. Exhibit 6 shows that the premium for a call option expiring in September with an exercise price of 17, referred to as the SEP 17 call, is 0.51. She could write that call and receive this premium. Alternatively, she could write a different call, say the NOV 17 call, and receive 1.44. There is a clear trade-off between the size of the option premium and the likelihood of option exercise. The option writer would get more cash from writing the longer-term option (because of a larger time premium), but there is a greater chance that the option would move in the money, resulting in the option being exercised by the buyer and, therefore, the stock being called away from the writer. The view of the covered call writer can be understood in terms of the call option's implied volatility. Essentially, writing the call expresses the view that the volatility of the underlying asset will be lower than the pricing of the option suggests. As shown in Exhibit 6, the implied volatility of the NOV 17 options is 58.36%. By writing the NOV 17 call for 1.44, the covered call investor believes that the volatility of the underlying asset will be less than the option's implied volatility of 58.36%. The call buyer believes the stock will move far enough above the strike price of 17 to provide a payoff greater than the 1.44 cost of the call.

Although it may be acceptable to think of the option premium as income, it is important to remember that the call writer has given up an important benefit of stock ownership: capital gains above the strike price. This dynamic can be seen in Exhibit 7. Consider an investor with a long position in PBR stock (with delta of +1) and a short position in a PBR NOV 17 call. The investor enjoys the benefit of the call premium of 1.44. This cushions the value of the position (Stock – Call, or S – C) as the PBR share price drops. If the PBR stock price drops to 5, the call option will drop to essentially 0. The portfolio will be worth about 6.44, as shown in Exhibit 7. As the stock price increases, however, the short call position begins to limit portfolio gains. If the price of PBR shares rises to 30, the call option delta approaches 1, so the delta of the portfolio (S – C) approaches 0. The portfolio gains from the long PBR stock position will be reduced by losses on the short call position. As the in-the-money option expires, the maximum value of the portfolio will approach 18.44, the exercise price of 17 plus the 1.44 premium, as in Exhibit 7.

EXHIBIT 7   Covered Call Portfolio Value: Long PBR Stock—NOV 17 Call

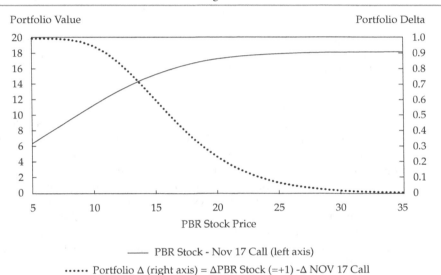

— PBR Stock - Nov 17 Call (left axis)

····· Portfolio Δ (right axis) = ΔPBR Stock (=+1) -Δ NOV 17 Call

3.1.2. Market Participant #2: Reducing a Position at a Favorable Price

Next, consider Sofia Porto, a retail portfolio manager with a portfolio that has become over-weighted in energy companies. She wants to reduce this imbalance. Porto holds 5,000 shares of PBR, an energy company, and she expects the price of this stock to remain relatively stable over the next month. She may decide to sell 1,000 shares for 15.84 each. As an alternative, Porto might decide to write 10 exchange-traded PBR SEP 15 call contracts. This means she is creating 10 option contracts, each of which covers 100 shares. In exchange for this contingent claim, she receives the option premium of 1.64/call × 100 calls/contract × 10 contracts = 1,640. Because the current PBR stock price (15.84) is above the exercise price of 15, the options she writes are in the money. Given her expectation that the stock price will be stable over the next month, it is likely that the option will be exercised. Because Porto wants to reduce the overweighting in energy stocks, this outcome is desirable. If the option is exercised, she has effectively sold the stock at 16.64. She receives 1.64 when she writes the option, and she receives 15 when the option is exercised. Porto could have simply sold the shares at their orig-inal price of 15.84, but in this specific situation, the option strategy resulted in a price improvement of 0.80 ([15 + 1.64] − 15.84) per share, or 5.05% (0.80/15.84), in a month's time.[2] By maintaining the stock position and selling a 15 call, she still risks the possibility of a stock price decline during the coming month resulting in a realized price lower than the current market price of 15.84. For example, if the PBR share price declined to 10 over the next month, Porto would realize only 10 + 1.64 =11.64 on her covered call position.

An American option premium can be viewed as having two parts: exercise value (also called intrinsic value) and time value.[3]

$$\text{Call Premium} = \text{Time Value} + \text{Intrinsic Value} = \text{Time Value} + \text{Max}(0, S - X)$$

In this case, the right to buy at 15 when the stock price is 15.84 has an exercise (or intrinsic) value of 0.84. The option premium is 1.64, which is 0.80 more than the exercise value. This difference of 0.80 is called time value.

$$1.64 = \text{Time Value} + (15.84 - 15)$$

Someone who writes covered calls to improve on the market is capturing the time value, which augments the stock selling price. Remember, though, that giving up part of the return distribution would result in an opportunity loss if the underlying goes up.

3.1.3. Market Participant #3: Target Price Realization

A third popular use of options is really a hybrid of the first two objectives. This strategy involves writing calls with an exercise price near the target price for the stock. Suppose a bank trust department holds PBR in many of its accounts and that its research team believes the stock would be properly priced at 16 per share, which is only slightly higher than its current price. In those accounts for which the investment policy statement permits option activity, the manager might choose to write near-term calls with an exercise price near the target price, 16 in this case. Suppose an account holds 500 shares of PBR. Writing 5 SEP 16 call contracts at 0.97 brings in 485 in cash. If the stock is above 16 in a month, the stock will be called away at the strike price (target price), with the option premium adding an additional 6% positive return to the account.[4] If PBR fails to rise to 16, the manager might write a new OCT expiration call with the same objective in mind.

Although this strategy is popular, the investor should not view it as a source of free money. The stock is currently very close to the target price, and the manager could simply sell it and be satisfied. Although the covered call writing program potentially adds to the return, there is also the chance that the stock could experience bad news or the overall market might pull back, resulting in an opportunity loss relative to the outright sale of the stock. The investor also would have an opportunity loss if the stock rose sharply above the exercise price and it was called away at a lower-than-market price.

The exposure from the short position in the PBR SEP 16 call can be understood in terms of the Greeks in Exhibit 6. Delta measures how the option price changes as the underlying

---

[2] Porto's effective selling price of 16.64 is 0.80 higher than the original price of 15.84: 0.80/15.84 = 5.05%.

[3] In addition to exercise value, some use the term "economic value" for intrinsic value because it is the value of the option if the investor were to exercise it at this very moment and trade out of the stock position.

[4] Relative to a stock price of 16, the option premium of 0.97 is 0.97/16 = 6.06%.

asset price changes, and gamma measures the rate of change in delta.[5] A PBR SEP 16 call has a delta = 0.516 and a gamma of 0.156. A short call will reduce the delta of the portfolio (S − C) from +1 to +0.484 (= +1 [Share] − 0.516 [Short Call]). The lower portfolio delta will reduce the upside opportunity. A share price increase of 1 will result in a portfolio gain of approximately 0.484.[6] The delta of the portfolio is not constant. By selling the PBR 16 call, the portfolio is now "short gamma". Remember, gamma is the rate of change of delta. Although the underlying PBR share has a gamma of 0, the short call will make the gamma of the portfolio −0.156. As the price of PBR shares increases above 16, the delta of the PBR call position will change, at a rate of gamma. Gamma is greatest for a near-the-money option and becomes progressively smaller as the option moves either into or out of the money (as seen in Exhibit 8).

Gamma of an ATM option can increase dramatically as the time to expiration approaches or volatility increases. Traders with large gamma exposure (especially large negative gamma) should be aware of the speed with which the position values can change. The change in portfolio delta and gamma for a PBR SEP 16 covered call as a function of share price can be seen in Exhibit 8. As the price of PBR shares increase, the portfolio delta changes at a rate of gamma. As the share price moves above the exercise price of 16, the portfolio (S − C) delta drops at a rate gamma towards its eventual limit of 0, effectively eliminating any remaining upside in the position.

EXHIBIT 8   Delta vs. Gamma for PBR 16 Covered Call Portfolio

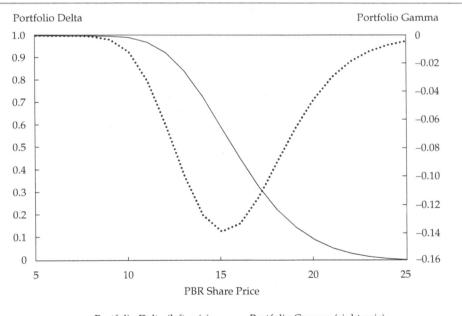

---

[5] Delta is the calculus first derivative of the option price with respect to the underlying asset price. Gamma is the second derivative of the option price with respect to the underlying asset price.

[6] The delta approximates the portfolio price change for very small changes in the underlying price. The delta itself is changing at a rate of gamma. For a change as large as 1%, the actual portfolio value will increase at a rate of less than 0.484 because it is short gamma.

3.1.4. Profit and Loss at Expiration

In the process of learning option strategies, it is always helpful to look at a graphical display of the profit and loss possibilities at the option expiration. Suppose an investor owns PBR, currently trading at 15.84. The investor believes gains may be limited above a price of 17 and decides to write a call against the long share position. The 17 strike calls will have no intrinsic value because the share price is currently 15.84. The investor must now consider the available option maturities (SEP, OCT, and NOV) as shown in Exhibit 6. In deciding which option to write, the investor may consider the option premiums and implied volatilities. Based on the investor's view that volatility will remain low over the next three months, the investor chooses to write the NOV call. At 58.36%, the NOV 17 call has highest implied volatility of the available 17 strike options, so it would be the most overvalued assuming low volatility. The option premium of 1.44 is completely explained by the time value of the NOV option, because the NOV 17 option has no exercise value (Option premium = Time value + Intrinsic value; 1.44 = Time value + Max[0,15.84 − 17]). If the stock is above 17 at expiration, the option holder will exercise the call option and the investor will deliver the shares in exchange for the exercise price of 17. The maximum gain with a covered call is the appreciation to the exercise price plus the option premium.[7]

Some symbols will be helpful in learning these relationships:

S_0 = Stock price when option position opened

S_T = Stock price at option expiration

X = Option exercise price

c_0 = Call premium received or paid

The maximum gain is $(X - S_0) + c_0$. With a starting price of 15.84, a sale price of 17 results in 1.16 of price appreciation. The option writer would keep the option premium of 1.44 for a total gain of 1.16 + 1.44 = 2.60. This is the maximum gain from this strategy because all price appreciation above 17 belongs to the call holder. The call writer keeps the option premium regardless of what the stock does, so if it were to drop, the overall loss is reduced by the option premium received. Exhibit 9 shows the situation. The breakeven price for a covered call is the stock price minus the premium, or $S_0 - c_0$. In other words, the breakeven point occurs when the stock falls by the premium received—in this example, 15.84 − 1.44 = 14.40. The maximum loss would occur if the stock became worthless; it equals the original stock price minus the option premium received, or $S_0 - c_0$.[8] In this single unlikely scenario, the investor would lose 15.84 on the stock position but still keep the premium of 1.44, for a total loss of 14.40.

At option expiration, the *value* of the covered call position is the stock price minus the exercise value of the call. Any appreciation beyond the exercise price belongs to the option buyer, so the covered call writer does not earn any gains beyond that point. Symbolically,

$$\text{Covered Call Expiration Value} = S_T - \text{Max}[(S_T - X),0]. \tag{1}$$

---

[7] If someone writes an in-the-money covered call, there is "depreciation" to the exercise price, so the difference would be subtracted. For instance, if the stock price is 50 and a 45 call sells for 7, the maximum gain is −(50 − 45) + 7 = 2.

[8] Note that with a covered call, the breakeven price and the maximum loss are the same value.

The *profit* at option expiration is the covered call value plus the option premium received minus the original price of the stock:

$$\text{Covered Call Profit at Expiration} = S_T - \text{Max}[(S_T - X),0] + c_0 - S_0. \tag{2}$$

In summary:

$$\text{Maximum gain} = (X - S_0) + c_0$$

$$\text{Maximum loss} = S_0 - c_0$$

$$\text{Breakeven price} = S_0 - c_0$$

$$\text{Expiration value} = S_T - \text{Max}[(S_T - X),0]$$

$$\text{Profit at expiration} = S_T - \text{Max}[(S_T - X),0] + c_0 - S_0$$

EXHIBIT 9   Covered Call P&L Diagram: Stock at 15.84, Write 17 Call at 1.44

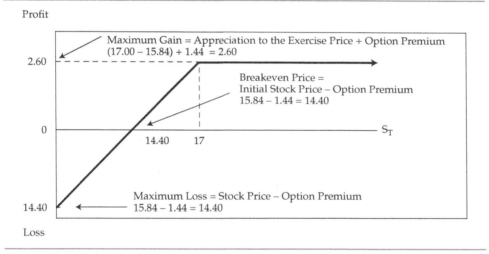

It is important to remember that these profit and loss diagrams depict the situation only at the end of the option's life.[9] Most equity covered call writing occurs with exchange-traded options, so the call writer always has the ability to buy back the option before expiration. If, for instance, the PBR stock price were to decline by 1 shortly after writing the covered call, the call value would most likely also decline. If this investor correctly believed the decline was temporary, he might buy the call back at the new lower option premium, making a profit on that trade, and then write the option again after the share price recovered.

---

[9] It is also important to note that the general shape of the profit and loss diagram for a covered call is the same as that of writing a put. Covered call writing is the most common use of options by individual investors, whereas writing puts is the least common.

EXAMPLE 3   Characteristics of Covered Calls

$$S_0 = \text{Stock price when option position opened} = 25.00$$
$$X = \text{Option exercise price} = 30.00$$
$$S_T = \text{Stock price at option expiration} = 31.33$$
$$c_0 = \text{Call premium received} = 1.55$$

1. Which of the following correctly calculates the maximum gain from writing a covered call?
    A. $(S_T - X) + c_0 = 31.33 - 30.00 + 1.55 = 2.88$
    B. $(S_T - S_0) - c_0 = 31.33 - 25.00 - 1.55 = 4.78$
    C. $(X - S_0) + c_0 = 30.00 - 25.00 + 1.55 = 6.55$
2. Which of the following correctly calculates the breakeven stock price from writing a covered call?
    A. $S_0 - c_0 = 25.00 - 1.55 = 23.45$
    B. $S_T - c_0 = 31.33 - 1.55 = 29.78$
    C. $X + c_0 = 30.00 + 1.55 = 31.55$
3. Which of the following correctly calculates the maximum loss from writing a covered call?
    A. $S_0 - c_0 = 25.00 - 1.55 = 23.45$
    B. $S_T - c_0 = 31.33 - 1.55 = 29.78$
    C. $S_T - X + c_0 = 31.33 - 30.00 + 1.55 = 2.88$

Solution to 1: C is correct. The covered call writer participates in gains up to the exercise price, after which further appreciation is lost to the call buyer. That is, $X - S_0 = 30.00 - 25.00 = 5.00$. The call writer also keeps c_0, the option premium, which is 1.55. So, the total maximum gain is $5.00 + 1.55 = 6.55$.

Solution to 2: A is correct. The call premium of 1.55 offsets a decline in the stock price by the amount of the premium received: $25.00 - 1.55 = 23.45$.

Solution to 3: A is correct. The stock price can fall to zero, causing a loss of the entire investment, but the option writer still keeps the option premium received: $25.00 - 1.55 = 23.45$

4. INVESTMENT OBJECTIVES OF PROTECTIVE PUTS

The protective put is often viewed as a classic example of buying insurance. The investor holds a risky asset and wants protection against a loss in value. He then buys insurance in the form of the put, paying a premium to the seller of the insurance, the put writer. The exercise price of the put is similar to the coverage amount for an insurance policy. The insurance policy deductible is similar to the difference between the current asset price and the strike price of the put. A protective put with a low exercise price is like an insurance policy with a high deductible.

Although less expensive, a low strike put involves greater price exposure before the payoff function goes into the money. For an insurance policy, a higher deductible is less expensive and reflects the increased risk borne by the insured party. For a protective put, a lower exercise price is less costly and has a greater risk of loss in the position.

Like traditional term insurance, this form of insurance provides coverage for a period of time. At the end of the period, the insurance expires and either pays off or not. The buyer of the insurance may or may not choose to renew the insurance by buying another put. A protective put can appear to be a great transaction with no drawbacks, because it provides downside protection with upside potential, but let us take a closer look.

4.1. Loss Protection/Upside Preservation

Suppose a portfolio manager has a client with a 50,000 share position in PBR. Her research suggests there may be a negative shock to the stock price in the next four to six weeks, and he wants to guard against a price decline. Consider the put prices shown in Exhibit 6; the purchase of a protective put presents the manager with some choices. Puts represent a right to sell at the strike price, so higher-strike puts will be more expensive. For this reason, the put buyer may select the 15-strike PBR put. Longer-term American puts are more expensive than their equivalent (same strike price) shorter-maturity puts. The put buyer must be sure the put will not expire before the expected price shock has occurred. The portfolio manager could buy a one-month (SEP) 15-strike put for 0.65. This put insures against the portion of the underlying return distribution that is below 15, but it will not protect against a price shock occurring after the SEP expiration.

Alternatively, the portfolio manager could buy a two-month option, paying 0.99 for an OCT 15 put, or she could buy a three-month option, paying 1.46 for a NOV 15 put. Note that there is not a linear relationship between the put value and its time until expiration. A two-month option does not sell for twice the price of a one-month option, nor does a three-month option sell for three times the price of a one-month option. The portfolio manager can also reduce the cost of insurance by increasing the size of the deductible (i.e., the current stock price minus the put exercise price), perhaps by using a put option with a 14 exercise price. A put option with an exercise price of 14 would have a lower premium but would not protect against losses in the stock until it falls to 14.00 per share. The option price is cheaper, but on a 50,000 share position, the deductible would be 50,000 more than if the exercise price of 15 were selected.[10]

Because of the uncertainty about the timing of the "shock event" she anticipates, the manager might consider the characteristics of the available option maturities. Given our assumptions, three of the BSM model inputs for the available 15 strike options are the same (PBR stock price 15.84, the strike price 15 and the risk-free rate of interest 4%). The difference in the cost of the SEP, OCT, and NOV options will be explained by the differences in time and the term structure of volatility. The BSM model assumes option volatility does not change over time or with strike price. In practice, volatility can vary across time and strike prices. For the 15 puts, the implied volatility is slightly greater for the NOV option, perhaps reflecting other traders' concerns about a shock event before expiration. Because the PBR stock price is 15.84 and the put options are all 15 strike, all three maturities have no intrinsic value.

---

[10] The deductible is $50,000 \times (15.84 - 15.00)$ with a strike price of 15. With a strike price of 14, the deductible would be $50,000 \times (15.84 - 14.00)$, or 50,000 more.

The cost of each PBR 15 strike option is entirely explained by the remaining time value. If the stock price does not fall below 15, the SEP, OCT, and NOV put option values will erode to 0 as they approach their expiration dates. The erosion of the options value with time is approximated by the theta. The daily thetas (Theta/365) for the PBR puts and calls are given in Exhibit 6. Notice, all the theta values in the table are negative. These values approximate the daily losses on the option positions as time passes, all else equal. The NOV 15 put (90 days) has a theta of −0.009 and the SEP 15 put (30 days) has a theta of −0.015. If the NOV 15 option is held for one day, and the price and volatility of the underlying do not change, the put value will decline by approximately 0.009 to approximately 1.45 (= 1.46 − 0.009).

The graph of the BSM theta function for the PBR NOV 15 option as it approaches maturity is shown in Exhibit 10. Notice how the rate of decline changes as maturity approaches. If the PBR price does not drop below 15, the NOV 15 put will expire out-of-the-money and the option price will gradually fall to 0. All else equal, the sum of the daily losses approximated by theta will explain the entire loss of 1.46 in option value over that time. The complex shape of the theta graph in Exhibit 10 results from the nature of the BSM theta formula, which includes terms to reflect the probability that the stock price will fall below the strike price during the remaining time. Note that if the price of PBR remains at 15.84 for the last 10 days to maturity, the BSM put option value will erode to 0 at varying rates averaging about −0.03/day. Assumptions of the BSM model explain the negative peak in theta around three days prior to maturity as the remaining time value rapidly decays to 0. Theta values might help the investor decide which maturity to choose. If he were to buy the cheaper SEP put, the daily erosion of value (−0.015) would be greater than for the more expensive NOV put (−0.009).

EXHIBIT 10   PBR 15 Put Theta over Time

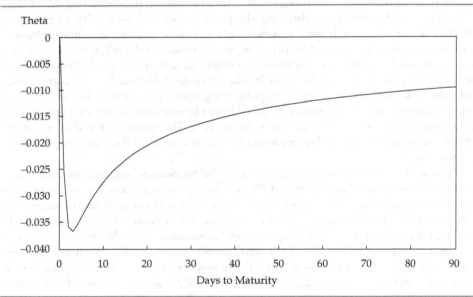

Given the four- to six-week time horizon for the shock event anticipated by the portfolio manager, the OCT put seems appropriate, but there is still the potential to lose the premium without realizing any benefit. With a 0.99 premium for the OCT 15 put and 50,000 shares to protect, the cost to the account would be almost 50,000. One advantage of the NOV option is that although it is more expensive, it has the smallest daily loss of value, as captured by theta. This option also has a greater likelihood of not having expired before the news hits. Also, although the portfolio manager could hold onto the put position until its expiration, she might find it preferable to close out the option prior to maturity and recover some of the premium paid.[11]

4.2. Profit and Loss at Expiration

Exhibit 11 shows the profit and loss diagram for the protective put.[12] The stock can rise to any level, and the position would benefit fully from the appreciation; the maximum gain is unlimited. On the downside, losses are "cut off" once the stock price falls to the exercise price. With a protective put, the maximum loss is the depreciation to the exercise price plus the premium paid, or $S_0 - X + p_0$. At the option expiration, the value of the protective put is the greater of the stock price or the exercise price. The reason is because the stock can rise to any level but has a floor value of the put exercise price. In symbols,

$$\text{Value of Protective Put at Expiration} = S_T + \text{Max}[(X - S_T),0]. \qquad (3)$$

The profit or loss at expiration is the ending value minus the beginning value. The initial value of the protective put is the starting stock price minus the put premium. In symbols,

$$\text{Profit of Protective Put at Expiration} = S_T + \text{Max}[(X - S_T),0] - S_0 - p_0. \qquad (4)$$

EXHIBIT 11 Protective Put P&L Diagram: Stock at 15.84, Buy 15 Put at 1.46

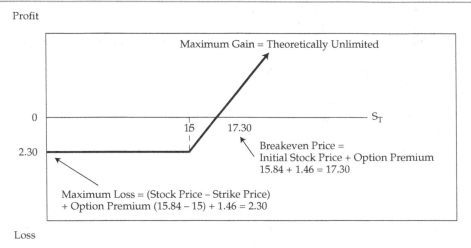

---

[11] A price shock to the underlying asset might increase the market's expectations of future volatility, thereby likely increasing the put premium. By selling the option early, the investor would capture this increase. Also, once the adverse event occurred, there may be no reason to continue to hold the insurance. If the investor no longer needs it, he should cancel it and get part of the purchase price back. In other words, he should sell the put and recapture some of its cost.

[12] Note that the profit and loss diagram for a protective put has a shape similar to a long call position, which is the result of put–call parity. Long the asset and long the put is equivalent to long a call plus long a risk-free bond.

To break even, the underlying asset must rise by enough to offset the price of the put that was purchased. The breakeven point is the initial stock price plus the option premium. In symbols, Breakeven Price $= S_0 + p_0$.

In summary:

$$\text{Maximum gain} = S_T - S_0 - p_0 = \text{Unlimited}$$

$$\text{Maximum loss} = S_0 - X + p_0$$

$$\text{Breakeven price} = S_0 + p_0$$

$$\text{Expiration value} = S_T + \text{Max}[(X - S_T),0]$$

$$\text{Profit at expiration} = S_T + \text{Max}[(X - S_T),0] - S_0 - p_0$$

EXAMPLE 4   Characteristics of Protective Puts

$$S_0 = \text{Stock price when option position opened} = 25.00$$

$$X = \text{Option exercise price} = 20.00$$

$$S_T = \text{Stock price at option expiration} = 31.33$$

$$p_0 = \text{Put premium paid} = 1.15$$

1. Which of the following correctly calculates the gain with the protective put?
   A. $S_T - S_0 - p_0 = 31.33 - 25.00 - 1.15 = 5.18$
   B. $S_T - S_0 + p_0 = 31.33 - 25.00 + 1.15 = 7.48$
   C. $S_T - X - p_0 = 31.33 - 20.00 - 1.15 = 10.18$
2. Which of the following correctly calculates the breakeven stock price with the protective put?
   A. $S_0 - p_0 = 25.00 - 1.15 = 23.85$
   B. $S_0 + p_0 = 25.00 + 1.15 = 26.15$
   C. $S_T + p_0 = 31.33 + 1.15 = 32.48$
3. Which of the following correctly calculates the maximum loss with the protective put?
   A. $S_0 - X + p_0 = 25.00 - 20.00 + 1.15 = 6.15$
   B. $S_T - X - p_0 = 31.33 - 20.00 - 1.15 = 10.18$
   C. $S_0 - p_0 = 25.00 - 1.15 = 23.85$

Solution to 1: A is correct. If the stock price is above the put exercise price at expiration, the put will expire worthless. The profit is the gain on the stock ($S_T - S_0$) minus the cost of the put. Note that the maximum profit with a protective put is theoretically unlimited, because the stock can rise to any level and the entire profit is earned by the stockholder.

Solution to 2: B is correct. Because the option buyer pays the put premium, she does not begin to make money until the stock rises by enough to recover the premium paid.

Solution to 3: A is correct. Once the stock falls to the put exercise price, further losses are eliminated. The investor paid the option premium, so the total loss is the "deductible" plus the cost of the insurance.

5. EQUIVALENCE TO LONG ASSET/SHORT FORWARD POSITION

All investors who consider option strategies should understand that some options are more sensitive to changes in the underlying asset than others. As we have seen, this relationship is measured by delta, an indispensable tool to an options user. Because a long call increases in value and a long put decreases in value as the underlying asset increases in price, call deltas range from 0 to 1 and put deltas range from 0 to −1. (Naturally, the signs are reversed for short positions in these options.) A long position in the underlying asset has a delta of 1.0, whereas a short position has a delta of −1.0. When the share price is close to the strike price, a rough approximation is that a long ATM option will have a delta that is approximately 0.5 (for a call) or −0.5 (for a put). Exhibit 12 shows the delta for the PBR SEP 16 put and call versus share price. As the stock price moves toward 16 (the strike price), the call option delta is approximately 0.52 and the put delta is −0.48. In general, Call Delta − Put Delta = 1 for options on the same underlying with the same BSM model inputs.

EXHIBIT 12   Delta of PBR Options vs. Stock Price

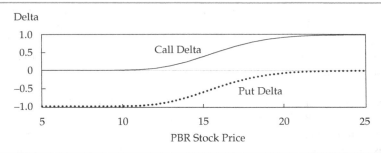

Delta can be applied to a portfolio as well. Suppose on the Tokyo Stock Exchange, Honda Motor Company stock sells for ¥3,500. A portfolio contains 100 shares, and the manager writes one exchange-traded covered call contract with a ¥3,500 strike. The delta of the 100-share position will be $100 \times +1 = +100$. Because the call is at the money, meaning that the stock price and exercise price are equal, it will have a delta of approximately 0.5. The portfolio, however, is short one call contract. From the perspective of the portfolio, the delta of the short call contract is $-0.5 \times 100 = -50$. A short call *loses* money as the underlying price rises. So, this covered call has a **position delta** (which is an overall or portfolio delta) of 50, consisting of +100 points for the stock and −50 points for the short call. Compare this call with a protective put, in which someone buys 100 shares of stock and one contract of an ATM put. Its position delta would also be 50: +100 points for the stock and −50 points for the long put.

Finally, consider a long stock position of 100 shares and a short forward position of 50 shares. Because futures and forwards on non-dividend-paying stocks are essentially proxies for the stock, their deltas are also 1.0 for a long position and −1.0 for a short position. In this example, the short forward position "cancels" half the long stock position, so the position delta is also 50. These examples show three different positions: an ATM covered call, an ATM protective put, and a long stock/short forward position that all have the same delta. For small movements in the price of the underlying asset, these positions will show very similar gains and losses.

5.1. Writing Puts

If someone writes a put option and simultaneously deposits an amount of money equal to the exercise price into a designated account, it is called writing a **cash-secured put**.[13] This strategy is appropriate for someone who is bullish on a stock or who wants to acquire shares at a particular price. The fact that the option exercise price is escrowed provides assurance that the put writer will be able to purchase the stock if the option holder chooses to exercise. Think of the cash in a cash-secured put as being similar to the stock part of a covered call. When an investor sells a covered call, she takes on the obligation to sell a stock, and this obligation is covered by ownership in the shares. When a put option is sold to create a new position, the obligation that accompanies this position is to purchase shares. In order to cover the obligation to purchase shares, the portfolio should have enough cash in the account to make good on this obligation. The short put position is covered or secured by cash in the account.

Now consider two slightly different scenarios using the price data from Exhibit 6. In the first scenario, one investor might be bullish on PBR and is interested in buying the stock at a cheaper price. With the stock at 15.84, she writes the SEP 15 put for 0.65, which is purchased by another investor who is bearish on PBR stock. The option writer will keep the option premium regardless of what the stock price does. If the stock is below 15 at expiration, however, the put would be exercised and the option writer would be obliged to purchase shares from the option holder at the exercise price of 15.

Possible small (and independent) changes to the variables from Exhibit 6 are simulated in Exhibit 13 for the *long* PBR SEP 15 put position. The long put is illustrated here for simplicity— these statistics for the long put position should also help the put writer to understand the risks and returns for her position, because a short position is simply the mirror image of the long position. The initial values are 15.84 for the stock and 0.65 for the put, and the put buyer has acquired a delta of −0.335 and a gamma of 0.136.[14]

As demonstrated in change #1, if the stock price rises by 0.10 from 15.84 to 15.94, the long (short) put will lose (gain) approximately $-0.335 \times 0.10 = -0.0335$ (+0.0335), as the put value drops from 0.65 to approximately 0.617 ($\approx 0.6165 = 0.65 - 0.0335$). Remember, this approximation is good for only a small change in the underlying share price. As the stock price rises, the long put's initial delta, −0.335, will change at a rate of gamma, 0.136, so the delta then becomes −0.321.

---

[13] This strategy is also called a *fiduciary put*. Note that for a European option, the amount deposited would equal the present value of the exercise price. When someone writes a put but does not escrow the exercise price, it is sometimes called a *naked put*. Note that this is a slightly different use of the adjective "naked" than with a naked call. When writing a naked call, the call writer does not have the underlying *asset* to deliver if the call is exercised. When an investor writes a naked put, he has not set aside the *cash* necessary to buy the asset if the put is exercised.

[14] The put writer (short position) will have a delta of $-(-0.335) = +0.335$.

EXHIBIT 13   Long PBR SEP 15 PUT, Greeks and Put Price Changes for Small, Independent Changes in Inputs

	Stock Price (S)	Delta (Δ)	Gamma (Γ)	Option Price (p)
Initial Values	15.84	−0.335	0.136	0.65
Change #1: Stock Price Increases by 0.10, from 15.84 to 15.94				
$\Delta S = +0.10$ $\Delta t = 0$ $\Delta Vol = 0$	**15.94**	Δ changes at rate of Γ, so: $\Delta_1 \approx \Delta_0 + (\Gamma \times \Delta S)$ **−0.321 ≈** **−0.335 + (0.136 × 0.10)**	Γ changes slightly to 0.133	$p_1 \approx p_0 + (\Delta_0 \times \Delta S)$ ***0.617 ≈*** **0.65 + (−0.335 × 0.10)**
Change #2: Time to Expiration Changes by 1 Day, from 30 to 29 Days				
$\Delta S = 0$ $\Delta t = $ **1 day (to 29 Days)** $\Delta Vol = 0$	15.84	−0.335	0.136	$p_1 \approx p_0 + (\Theta \times \Delta t)$ ***0.635 ≈*** **0.65 + (−0.015 × 1)**
Change #3: Implied Volatility Increases by 1 Percentage Point, from 58.44% to 59.44%				
$\Delta S = 0$ $\Delta t = 0$ Δ **Vol = +1%** **(to 59.44%)**	15.84	−0.335	0.136	$p_1 \approx p_0 + (v \times \Delta Vol)$ ***0.667 ≈*** **0.65 + (0.017 × 1)**

The long SEP 15 put position also has a theta of −0.015 and a vega of +0.017.[15] As time decays, the long (short) put option will lose (gain) value at a rate of theta, so the value of long (short) position will decrease (increase) by approximately 0.015/per day. As demonstrated in change #2 (which is separate and independent from change #1), all else equal, the long put value would drop from about 0.65 to 0.635 as the put moves one day closer to expiration (from 30 to 29 days). If the implied volatility of the SEP 15 put were to increase by 1% (from 58.44% to 59.44%), all else equal, the option price would increase by 0.017 to approximately 0.667, as demonstrated in change #3. The increase in volatility would benefit the put holder at the expense of the writer, because the short put position would lose 0.017.

If the stock is above 15 at expiration, the put option will expire unexercised. At the expiration date, the put writer will either keep the premium or have PBR shares put to her at 15. Because the put writer was bullish on PBR and wanted to purchase it at a cheaper price, she may be happy with this result. Netting out the option premium received by the put writer would make her effective purchase price 15.00 − 0.65 = 14.35.

In another scenario, an institutional investor might be interested in purchasing PBR. Suppose the investor wrote the SEP 17 put for 1.76. This strategy will have slightly different values for the Greeks compared with the previous strategy. The delta of the SEP 17 short put position will be +0.62, gamma will be −0.140, and theta will equal +0.016. This position will be more sensitive to changes in the stock price than the SEP 15 put. If the PBR share price increases

---

[15] All else equal, a long put loses time value as it approaches expiration (negative theta). All else equal, a long put increases in value as the volatility is increased (positive vega). In the case of a short put, the signs are reversed.

0.10 from 15.84 to 15.94, the put writer will now profit by approximately +0.62 × 0.10 = 0.062. The higher strike price makes the short SEP 17 put a more bullish position than the SEP 15 put. This dynamic is reflected in the larger delta for the short SEP 17 put at +0.620 (versus +0.335 for the short SEP 15 put).

If the stock is below 17 at expiration, the SEP 17 puts will be exercised and the investor (i.e., put writer) will pay 17 for the shares, resulting in a net price of 17.00 − 1.76 = 15.24. Anytime someone writes an option, the maximum gain is the option premium received, so in this case, the maximum gain is 1.76. The maximum loss when writing a put occurs when the stock falls to zero. The option writer pays the exercise price for worthless stock but still keeps the premium. In this example, the maximum loss would be 17.00 − 1.76 = 15.24. Exhibit 14 shows the corresponding profit and loss diagram.

EXHIBIT 14   Short Put P&L Diagram: Write SEP 17 Put at 1.76

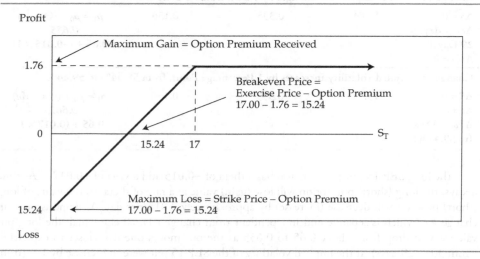

Note the similar shape of the covered call position in Exhibit 9 and the short put in Exhibit 14. Writing a covered call and writing a put are very similar with regard to their risk and reward characteristics.[16]

6. RISK REDUCTION USING COVERED CALLS AND PROTECTIVE PUTS

Covered calls and protective puts may both be viewed as risk-reducing or hedging strategies. In the case of a covered call, some price uncertainty is eliminated for price increases. For a protective put, the price uncertainty is eliminated for price decreases. The risk reduction can be understood by considering hedge statistics.

---

[16] The two strategies are very similar due to put–call parity. Recall that $P = C − S + PV$ of X, implying that $−P \approx −C + S$ (ignoring PV of X), thus showing that a short put payoff profile is similar to that of a covered call.

6.1. Covered Calls

Consider the individual who owns 100 shares of a PBR stock at 15.84. The long position has a delta of +100. Suppose the investor now writes a NOV 17 call contract against this entire position. These options have a delta of 0.475. This covered call position has a position delta of $(100 \times +1.0) - (100 \times 0.475) = +52.5$. A position delta of 52.5 is equivalent (for small changes) to owning 52.5 shares of the underlying asset. An investor can lose more money on a 100-share position than on a 52.5-share position. Even if the stock declines to nearly zero, the loss is reduced only by the amount of the option premium received. Viewed this way, the covered call position is less risky than the underlying asset held alone. The lower position delta will work against the investor if the share price increases. A PBR share price above 17 would result in the shares getting called away, and portfolio gains per share are limited to $2.60 = (X - S_0) + c_0 = (17 - 15.84) + 1.44$.

6.2. Protective Puts

Similar logic applies to the use of protective puts. An investor who buys a put is essentially buying insurance on the stock. An investor owning PBR stock could purchase a NOV 15 put with an option delta of -0.359. The position delta from 100 shares of PBR stock and one NOV 15 put contract would be $+100 + (-0.359 \times 100) = +64.1$ For small changes in price, the protective put portfolio reduces the risk of the 100-share PBR position to the equivalent of a 64.1 share position. This insurance lasts only until NOV. One buys insurance to protect against a risk, and the policyholder should not feel bad if the risk event does not materialize and he does not get to use the insurance. Stated another way, a homeowner should be happy if the fire insurance on his house goes unused. Still, we do not want to buy insurance we do not need, especially if it is expensive. Continually purchasing puts to protect against a possible stock price decline will result in lower volatility in the overall portfolio, but the trade-off between premium cost and risk reduction must be carefully considered. Such continuous purchasing of puts to protect against a possible stock price decline is an expensive strategy that would wipe out most of the long-term gain on an otherwise good investment. The occasional purchase of a protective put to manage a temporary situation, however, can be a sensible risk-reducing activity.

6.3. Buying Calls and Writing Puts on a Short Position

The discussion on protective puts (Stock + Put) and covered calls (Stock − Call) describes risk-reduction strategies for investors with long positions in the underlying asset. How can investors reduce risk when they are short the underlying asset? The short investor is worried the underlying stock will go up and profits if the underlying stock goes down. To offset the risks of a short position, an investor may purchase a call. The new portfolio will be (Call − Stock). The long call will offset portfolio losses when the share price increases.

To generate income from option premiums, the investor may also sell a put. As the stock drops in value, the investor profits from the short stock position, but the portfolio (− Put − Stock) gains will be reduced by the short put. When the share price increases, the short position loses money. The put expires worthless, meaning the investor will keep the put premium. The loss on the short position can still be substantial but is somewhat reduced by the put option premium.

Let us consider these two scenarios using the price data from Exhibit 6. In both cases, the investor is bearish on PBR and shorts the stock at 15.84. In the first case, she purchases the SEP 16 call for 0.97. As the share price increases above 16, the payoff from the call will act to offset losses in the short position. Exhibit 15 illustrates this dynamic. As the share price increases, portfolio losses never exceed 1.13. The profit on the short stock position plus the profit from the in-the-money call equals $(15.84 - S) + [(S - 16) - 0.97] = -1.13$. If the share price decreases, the investor profits from the short but loses the call premium of 0.97. The delta from the short PBR shares is −1. The SEP 16 call delta is 0.516. The overall portfolio delta is still negative at −0.484, making this a bearish strategy. The investor is also long vega from purchasing the call, 0.018, and the position is exposed to time decay, because theta is −0.018 per day. So, she is hoping to profit from increased downside volatility from the short PBR shares while the long call cushions losses from increased upside volatility.

EXHIBIT 15   P&L of Long PBR SEP 16 Call and Short PBR Stock

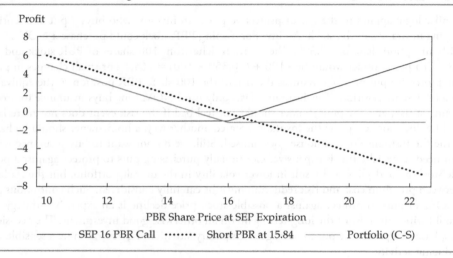

In the second scenario, the investor writes the SEP 15 put for 0.65 and collects the put premium. The upside protection from the long call in the first scenario is not provided by writing a put. The short stock position can have potentially unlimited losses. As shown in Exhibit 16, the potential gain from a falling PBR price now belongs to the put owner. The maximum gain from this strategy is given by the profit on the short stock position plus the profit from the out-of-the-money short put, which equals $(15.84 - S) - [(15 - S) - 0.65] = 1.49$. Losses from the short stock position will be cushioned only by the 0.65 premium collected from writing the put. The delta of the short PBR shares is −1, and the delta of the short put is − (−0.335), so the position delta is $-1 + 0.335 = -0.665$. The investor is bearish and hoping to profit from a downward price move. She is also short vega from writing the put, (−0.017), and benefits from time decay, as theta of the short put is +0.015 (= − [−0.015]). So, she is hoping for reduced volatility to give her an opportunity to collect the put premium without losing from the short on PBR shares.

EXHIBIT 16   P&L of Short PBR SEP 15 Put and Short PBR Stock

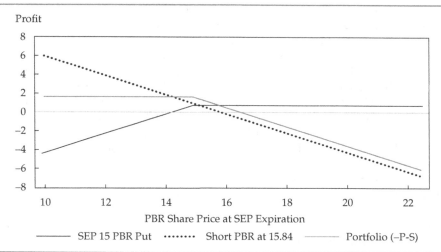

Profit

PBR Share Price at SEP Expiration

——— SEP 15 PBR Put   ········ Short PBR at 15.84   ——— Portfolio (–P–S)

EXAMPLE 5   Risk-Reduction Strategies

Janet Reiter is a US-based investor who holds a limited partnership investment in a French private equity firm. She has received notice from the firm's general partner of an upcoming capital call. Reiter plans to purchase €1,000,000 in three months to meet the capital call due at that time. The current exchange rate is US$1.20/€1, but Reiter is concerned the euro will strengthen against the US dollar. She considers the following instruments to reduce the risk of the planned purchase:

- A three-month USD/EUR call option (to buy euros) with a strike rate $X =$ US$1.25/€1 and costing US$0.02/€1
- A three-month EUR/USD put option (to sell dollars) with a strike rate $X = €0.8080/$US$1 priced at €0.0134/US$1
- A three-month USD/EUR futures contract (to buy euros) with $f_0 =$ US$1.2052/€1

1. Discuss the position required in each instrument to reduce the risk of the planned purchase.
2. Reiter purchases call options for US$20,000, and the exchange rate increases to US$1.29/€1 (EUR currency strengthens) over the next three months. The effective price Reiter pays for her 1,000,000 EUR purchase is closest to:
   A. US$1,270,000.
   B. US$1,290,000.
   C. US$1,310,000.
3. Calculate the price Reiter will pay for the EUR using the three instruments if the exchange rate in three months falls to US$1.10/€1 (EUR currency weakens).

Solution to 1: Reiter could purchase a €1,000,000 call option struck at US$1.25/€1 for US$20,000. If the EUR price were to increase above US$1.25, she would exercise her right to buy EUR for US$1.25. She would also benefit from being able to purchase EUR at a cheaper price should the exchange rate weaken. A call on the euro is like a put on the US dollar. So, a put to sell dollars struck at an exchange rate of $X = €0.8000/US\$1$ can be viewed as a call to buy Euro at an exchange rate of US$1/€0.8000 = US$1.25/€1. Reiter could also buy a put option on USD struck at $X = €0.8080/US\$1$ which would allow her to sell US$1,237,624 (= €1,000,000/[€0.8080/$1]) to receive the €1,000,000 should the dollar weaken below that level. This would cost her €0.0134/US$1 × US$1,237,624 = €16,584 or US$20,525 upfront. If USD appreciated against the EUR, Reiter would still be able to benefit from the lower cost to purchase the EUR. She could instead enter a long position in a three-month futures contract at US$1.2052. Reiter would have the obligation to purchase €1,000,000 at US$1.2052 regardless of the exchange rate in three months. The futures position requires a margin deposit, but no premium is paid.

Solution to 2: A is correct. At an exchange rate of US$1.29/€1, the call with strike of $X = US\$1.25/€1$ will be exercised. Including the call premium (US$0.02/€1), the price effectively paid for the euros is US$1.27/€1 × €1,000,000 = US$1,270,000.

Solution to 3: Both the call and the put options will expire unexercised and Reiter benefits from the lower rate by purchasing €1,000,000 for US$1,100,000. However, she will lose the premiums she paid for the options. For the futures contract, she pays US$1.2052/€1 or US$1,205,200 for €1,000,000 regardless of the more favorable rate.

7. SPREADS AND COMBINATIONS

Option spreads and combinations can be useful option strategies. We first consider money spreads, in which the two options differ only by exercise price. The investor buys an option with a given expiration and exercise price and sells an option with the same expiration but a different exercise price. Of course, the options are on the same underlying asset. The term *spread* is used here because the payoff is based on the difference, or spread, between option exercise prices. For a bull or bear spread, the investor buys one call and writes another call option with a different exercise price, or the investor buys one put and writes another put with a different exercise price.[17] Someone might, for instance, buy a NOV 16 call and simultaneously write a NOV 17 call, or one might buy a SEP 17 put and write a SEP 15 put. An option combination typically uses both puts and calls. The most important option combination is the straddle, on which we focus in this reading. We will investigate spreads first.

7.1. Bull Spreads and Bear Spreads

Spreads are classified in two ways: by market sentiment and by the direction of the initial cash flows. A spread that becomes more valuable when the price of the underlying asset rises is

[17] One important exception to the typical option spread is a *butterfly spread*, which is essentially two simultaneous spreads and can be done using only calls or only puts.

a **bull spread**; a spread that becomes more valuable when the price of the underlying asset declines is a **bear spread**. Because the investor buys one option and sells another, there is typically an initial net cash outflow or inflow. If establishing the spread requires a cash payment by the investor, it is referred to as a debit spread. Debit spreads are effectively long because the long option value exceeds the short option value. If the spread initially results in a cash inflow to the investor, it is referred to as a credit spread. Credit spreads[18] are effectively short because the short option value exceeds the long option value. Any of these strategies can be created with puts or calls. The motivation for a spread is usually to place a directional bet, giving up part of the profit potential in exchange for a lower cost of the position. Some examples will help make this clear.

7.1.1. Bull Spread

Regardless of whether someone constructs a bull spread with puts or with calls, the strategy requires buying one option and writing another with a *higher* exercise price. Because the higher exercise price call is less expensive than the lower strike, a call bull spread involves an initial cash outflow (debit spread). A bull spread created from puts also requires the investor to write the higher-strike option and buy the lower-strike one. Because the higher-strike put is more expensive, a put bull spread involves an initial cash inflow (credit spread).

Let's consider a call bull spread. Suppose, for instance, an investor thought it likely that by the September option expiration, PBR would rise to around 17 from its current level of 15.84. Based on the price data in Exhibit 6, what option strategy would capitalize on this anticipated price movement? If he were to buy the SEP 15 call for 1.64 and the stock rose to 17 at expiration, the call would be worth $S_T - X = 17 - 15 = 2$. If the price of the option was 1.64, the profit is 0.36. The maximum loss is the price paid for the option, or 1.64. If, instead, an investor bought the SEP 16 call for 0.97, at an expiration stock price of 17, the call would be worth 1.00 for a gain of 0.03. A spread could make more sense with the following option values. If he believes the stock will not rise above 17 by September expiration, it may make sense to "sell off" the part of the return distribution above that price. The investor would receive 0.51 for each SEP 17 call sold.

The value of the spread at expiration (V_T) depends on the stock price at expiration S_T. For a bull spread, the investor buys the low strike option (struck at X_L) and sells the high strike option (struck at X_H), so that:

$$V_T = \text{Max}(0, S_T - X_L) - \text{Max}(0, S_T - X_H). \tag{5}$$

Therefore, the value depends on the terminal stock price S_T:

$$V_T = 0 - 0 = 0 \text{ if } S_T \leq X_L$$
$$V_T = S_T - X_L - 0 = S_T - X_L \text{ if } X_L < S_T < X_H$$
$$V_T = S_T - X_L - (S_T - X_H) = X_H - X_L \text{ if } S_T \geq X_H$$

The profit is obtained by subtracting the initial outlay for the spread from the foregoing value of the spread at expiration. To determine the initial outlay, recall that a call option with

---

[18] The use of the term credit spread has a different interpretation than in fixed income investing. For bond investors, the credit spread is a measure of compensation for the bond's default risk.

a lower exercise price will be more expensive than a call option with a higher exercise price. Because we are buying the call with the lower exercise price (for c_L) and selling the call with the higher exercise price (for c_H), the call we buy will cost more than the call we sell ($c_L > c_H$). Hence, the spread will require a net outlay of funds. This net outlay is the initial value of the position, $V_0 = c_L - c_H$, which we call the net premium. The profit is:

$$\Pi = Max(0, S_T - X_L) - Max(0, S_T - X_H) - (c_L - c_H). \tag{6}$$

In this manner, we see that the profit is the profit from the long call, $Max(0, S_T - X_L) - c_L$, plus the profit from the short call, $-Max(0, S_T - X_H) + c_H$. Broken down into ranges, the profit is as follows:

$$\Pi = -c_L + c_H \text{ if } S_T < X_L$$
$$\Pi = S_T - X_L - c_L + c_H \text{ if } X_L < S_T < X_H$$
$$\Pi = X_H - X_L - c_L + c_H \text{ if } S_T \geq X_H$$

If S_T is below X_L, the strategy will lose a limited amount of money. When both options expire out of the money, the investor loses the net premium, $c_L - c_H$. The profit on the upside, if S_T is at least X_H, is also limited to the difference in strike prices minus the net premium.

Consider two alternatives for the call purchase leg of the bull spread: 1) buy the SEP 15 call or 2) buy the SEP 16 call instead. Which is preferred? With Alternative 1, the SEP 15 call costs 1.64. Writing the SEP 17 call brings in 0.51, so the net cost is $1.64 - 0.51 = 1.13$. Traders would refer to this position as a PBR SEP 15/17 bull call spread. The maximum profit would occur at or above the exercise price of 17 because all gains above this level belong to the owner of the PBR SEP 17 call. At an underlying price of 17 or higher, from the trader's perspective, the position is worth 2, which represents the price appreciation from 15 to 17 (i.e., the difference in strikes). The maximum profit is

$$\Pi = X_H - X_L - c_L + c_H = 17 - 15 - 1.64 + 0.51 = 0.87.$$

Another way to look at it is that at a price above 17, the trader exercises the long call, buying the stock at 15, and is forced to sell the stock at 17 to the holder of his short call.

With Alternative 2, the investor buys the SEP 16 call and pays 0.97 for it. Writing the SEP 17 call brings in 0.51, so the net cost would be $0.97 - 0.51 = 0.46$. At an underlying price of 17 or higher, the spread would be worth 1.00, so the maximum profit is

$$\Pi = X_H - X_L - c_L + c_H = 17 - 16 - 0.97 + 0.51 = 0.54.$$

Exhibit 17 compares the profit and loss diagrams for these two alternatives.

To determine the breakeven price with a spread, find the underlying asset price that will cause the exercise value of the two options combined to equal the initial cost of the spread. A spread has two exercise prices. There are also two option premiums. Mathematically, the breakeven price for a call bull spread can be derived from $\Pi = S_T^* - X_L - c_L + c_H = 0$ and is

$$S_T^* = X_L + c_L - c_H,$$

which represents the lower exercise price plus the cost of the spread. In the examples here, Alternative 1 costs 1.13 ($= 1.64 - 0.51$). The breakeven $S_T^* = X_L + c_L - c_H = 15 + 1.64 - 0.51 = 16.13$.

If at option expiration the stock is 16.13, the 15-strike option would be worth 1.13 and the 17-strike call would be worthless. The breakeven price S_T^* is $15.00 + 1.13 = 16.13$, as Exhibit 17 shows.

EXHIBIT 17   Bull Spreads: Current PBR Stock Price = 15.84

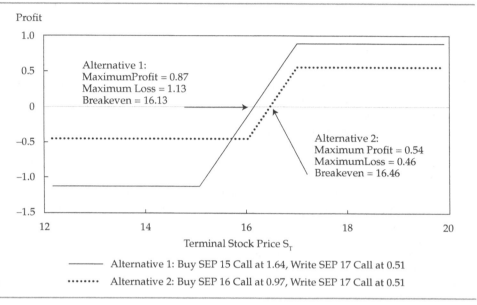

Alternative 1:
MaximumProfit = 0.87
Maximum Loss = 1.13
Breakeven = 16.13

Alternative 2:
Maximum Profit = 0.54
MaximumLoss = 0.46
Breakeven = 16.46

——— Alternative 1: Buy SEP 15 Call at 1.64, Write SEP 17 Call at 0.51
········ Alternative 2: Buy SEP 16 Call at 0.97, Write SEP 17 Call at 0.51

Which of the alternatives is preferable? There is no clear-cut answer. As Exhibit 17 shows, the maximum loss for alternative 1 is $1.64 - 0.51 = 1.13$, compared with a maximum loss of $0.97 - 0.51 = 0.46$ for Alternative 2. However, Alternative 1 is potentially more profitable for a move above 17 and has a lower breakeven price.

With Alternative 1, the breakeven point of 16.13 is less than 2% above the current level of 15.84, whereas with Alternative 2, reaching the breakeven point requires almost a 4% rise in the stock price. There is some additional information in Exhibit 6 the investor may wish to consider. The SEP 15/17 spread involves buying the SEP15 call with implied volatility of 64.42% and selling the SEP 17 call option with implied volatility of 51.07%. The investor may believe the SEP 15 call being purchased is relatively expensive compared with the SEP 17 call being sold. The PBR SEP 16/17 involves buying a SEP 16 call at a cost of 0.97 with an implied volatility of 55.92%. The investor may believe the SEP 16 call represents a better value than the SEP 15 call and so may choose the PBR SEP 16/17 spread.

We can calculate the Greek values for the spread. For example, using Exhibit 6, we see the theta of the PBR SEP 15/17 spread is $-0.004 = -0.019 - (-0.015)$, and the theta of the PBR SEP 16/17 is $-0.003 = -0.018 - (-0.015)$. Therefore, the SEP 16/17 should experience slightly less erosion of value resulting from time decay. The investor may also consider the delta and gamma that each spread would add to her PBR position. The delta of the PBR SEP 15/17 spread is $+0.306 = 0.657 - 0.351$, and the delta of the PBR SEP 16/17 spread is $+0.165 = 0.516 - 0.351$. From the current PBR price of 15.84, the long position in the PBR 15 call will make the SEP 15/17 PBR spread slightly more sensitive to an increase in share price than the SEP 16/17 spread. For the SEP 15/17, we have gamma $= -0.034 = 0.125 - 0.159$ and for the SEP 16/17 gamma $= -0.003 = 0.156 - 0.159$. The more negative gamma value for the SEP

15/17 spread means that the position delta will decrease at a faster rate than the SEP 16/17 spread as the price of PBR shares increase. By carefully selecting the expiration and exercise prices for the options for the spread, an investor can choose the risk–return mix that most closely matches her investment outlook.

7.1.2. Bear Spread

With a bull spread, the investor buys the lower exercise price and writes the higher exercise price. It is the opposite with a bear spread: buy the higher exercise price and sell the lower. Because puts with higher exercise prices are (all else equal) more expensive, a put bear spread will result in an initial cash outflow (be a debit spread). For a call bear spread, the investor buys a higher exercise price call and sells the lower exercise price call. Because the higher exercise price call being purchased is less expensive than the lower strike being sold, a call bear spread will result in an initial cash inflow (credit spread).

If a trader believed PBR stock would be below 15 by the November expiration, one strategy would be to buy the PBR NOV 16 put at 1.96 and write the NOV 15 put at 1.46. This spread has a net cost of 0.50; this amount is the maximum loss, and it occurs at a PBR stock price of 16 or higher. The maximum gain is also 0.50, which occurs at a stock price of 15 or lower. (A useful way to see this result is to realize that reversing the signs of the trades leaves the horizontal axes in a diagram like Exhibit 17 intact, but it flips the profit/loss and cost lines vertically! A debit from buying a spread must be consistent with the seller of the same spread receiving a credit.) Finding the breakeven price uses the same logic as with a bull spread: find the underlying asset price at which the exercise value equals the initial cost. Let p_L represent the lower-strike put premium and p_H the higher-strike put premium. Mathematically, the value of this bear spread position at expiration is:

$$V_T = \text{Max}(0, X_H - S_T) - \text{Max}(0, X_L - S_T). \tag{7}$$

Broken down into ranges, we have the following relations:

$$V_T = X_H - S_T - (X_L - S_T) = X_H - X_L \text{ if } S_T \le X_L$$
$$V_T = X_H - S_T - 0 = X_H - S_T \text{ if } X_L < S_T < X_H$$
$$V_T = 0 - 0 = 0 \text{ if } S_T \ge X_H$$

To obtain the profit, we subtract the initial outlay. Because we are buying the put with the higher exercise price and selling the put with the lower exercise price, the put we are buying is more expensive than the put we are selling. The initial value of the bear spread is $V_0 = p_H - p_L$. The profit is, therefore, $V_T - V_0$, which is:

$$\Pi = \text{Max}(0, X_H - S_T) - \text{Max}(0, X_L - S_T) - (p_H - p_L). \tag{8}$$

We see that the profit is that on the long put, $\text{Max}(0, X_H - S_T) - p_H$, plus the profit from the short put, $-\text{Max}(0, X_L - S_T) + p_L$. Broken down into ranges, the profit is as follows:

$$\Pi = X_H - X_L - p_H + p_L \text{ if } S_T \le X_L$$
$$\Pi = X_H - S_T - p_H + p_L \text{ if } X_L < S_T < X_H$$
$$\Pi = -p_H + p_L \text{ if } S_T \ge X_H$$

The breakeven point, $S_T^* = X_H - p_H + p_L$, sets the profit equal to zero between the strike prices. In this example, $16 - 1.96 + 1.46 = 15.50$. That is, at a stock price of 15.50 on the expiration day, the 16-strike put would be worth 0.50 and the 15-strike put would be worthless. Exhibit 18 shows the profit and loss for a NOV 15/16 bear spread.[19]

EXHIBIT 18   Bear Spread: Current PBR Stock Price = 15.84

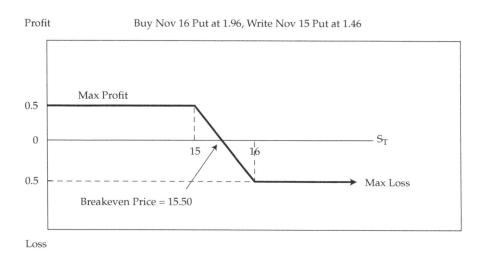

7.1.3. Refining Spreads

It is not necessary that both legs of a spread be established at the same time or maintained for the same period. Options are very versatile, and positions can typically be quickly adjusted as market conditions change. Here are a few examples of different tactical adjustments an option trader might consider.

7.1.3.1. Adding a Short Leg to a Long Position   Consider Carlos Aguila, a trader who in September paid a premium of 1.50 for a NOV 40 call when the underlying stock was selling for 37. A month later, in October, the stock has risen to 48. He observes the following premiums for one-month call options.

---

[19] Bull spreads can also be created with puts, and bear spreads can also be created with calls. In both cases, the result is a credit spread with an initial cash inflow. Recall that American exercise–style options may be exercised at any time prior to expiration. Bull spreads with American puts have an additional risk, which is that the short put could be exercised early when the long put is not yet in the money. If the bull spread uses American calls and the short call is exercised, the long call is deeper in the money, which offsets that risk. A similar point can be applied to bear spreads using calls. Bear spreads with American calls have increased risk, because the short call may be exercised early when the long call may not yet be in the money. Thus, with American options, bull spreads with calls and bear spreads with puts are generally preferred but, of course, not required.

Strike	Premium
40	8.30
45	4.42
50	1.91

This position has become very profitable. The call he bought is now worth 8.30. He paid 1.50, so his profit at this point is 8.30 − 1.50 = 6.80. He thinks the stock is likely to stabilize around its new level and doubts that it will go much higher. Aguila is considering writing a call option with an exercise price of either 45 or 50, thereby converting his long call position into a bull spread. Looking first at the NOV 50 call, he notes that the 1.91 premium would more than cover the initial cost of the NOV 40 call. If he were to write this call, the new profit and loss diagram would look like Exhibit 19. To review, consider the following points:

- At stock prices of 50 or higher, the exercise value of the spread is 10.00. The reason is because both options would be in the money, and a call with an exercise price of 40 would always be worth 10 more at exercise than a call with an exercise price of 50. The initial cost of the call with an exercise price of 40 was 1.50, and there would be a 1.91 cash inflow after writing the call with an exercise price of 50. The profit is 10.00 − 1.50 + 1.91 = 10.41.
- At stock prices of 40 or lower, the exercise value of the spread is zero; both options would be out of the money. The initial cost of the call with an exercise price of 40 was 1.50, and there would be a 1.91 cash inflow after writing the call with an exercise price of 50. The profit is 0 − 1.50 + 1.91 = 0.41.
- Between the two strike prices (40 and 50), the exercise value of the spread rises steadily as the stock price increases. For every unit increase up to the higher strike price, the exercise value of this spread increases by 1.0.

For instance, if the stock price remains unchanged at 48, the exercise value of the spread is 8.00. The reason is because the call with an exercise price of 40 would be worth 8.00 and the call with an exercise price of 50 would be worthless. The initial cost of the 40-strike call was 1.50, and there would be a 1.91 cash inflow when the 50-strike call was written. The profit is 8.00 − 1.50 + 1.91 = 8.41.

Now assume that he has written the NOV 50 call. Aguila needs to be careful how he views this new situation. No matter what happens to the stock price between now and expiration, the position is profitable, relative to his purchase price of the calls with an exercise price of 40. If the stock were to fall by any amount from its current level, however, he would have an opportunity loss. His profit would decrease progressively if the price trended back to 40. Aguila would be correct in saying that the bull spread will make a profit of at least 0.41. But, writing the NOV 50 call only partially hedges against a decline in the value of his new strategy. The position can still lose about 96% of its maximum profit, because only about 4% (0.41/10.41) has been hedged.

EXHIBIT 19   Spread Creation: Buy a Call with Exercise Price of 40 at 1.50; Write a Call Later with Exercise Price of 50 at 1.91

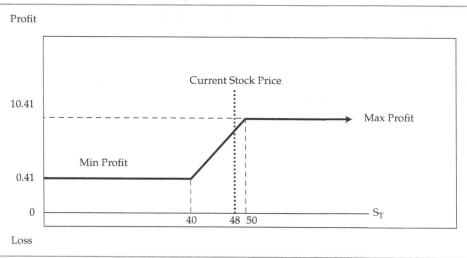

7.1.3.2. Spreads and Delta   A spread strategy may be adapted to a changing market view. Suppose the market has been rising, and Lars Clive, an options trader, expects this trend to continue. Hypothetical company ZKQ currently sells for $44. Suppose Clive buys a NOV 45 call for 5.25. He computes the delta of this call as +0.55 and gamma as +0.028. Initially, Clive will profit at a rate of 0.55 for an increase of $1 in the price of ZKQ stock. For small changes, the delta of his position will increase at a rate of 0.028 for an increase of $1 in the price of ZKQ shares.

Three days later, the stock price has risen to $49, the value of the NOV 45 call has increased to 8.18, and the call delta has increased to +0.68. For the NOV 45 call, the option price increased by 2.93 (= 8.18 − 5.25) instead of by 2.75 (= 5 × 0.55, the stock price change multiplied by the initial delta value). Because delta is changing at a rate gamma, the approximation works best for small changes in share prices. With the stock at $49, a higher-strike NOV 50 call sells for 5.74 and has a delta of +0.55. Now Clive establishes a 45/50 bull call spread by writing the NOV 50 call. Clive is less bullish at the price of 49, and his 45/50 spread portfolio now has a delta of +0.13 = +0.68 − 0.55.

Now suppose another five days pass and the stock price falls to 45. The new option values would be 5.41 for the NOV 45 call and 3.55 for the NOV 50 call. Clive closes out the NOV 50 short call by buying it back. He sold the call for 5.74 and bought it back for 3.55, so he makes 5.74 − 3.55 = 2.19, or 2.19 per contract. He still holds the long position in the NOV 45 call, and his portfolio delta increases to +0.57.

Another four days pass, and ZKQ has risen to 48. The new price for the NOV 50 call is 4.71 with a delta of 0.51. Clive owns the NOV 45 with a price of 7.10 and a delta of 0.66. He then decides to write a NOV 50 call and lower his position delta to 0.15 (= 0.66 − 0.51).

At this point, Clive has had two cash outflows totaling 8.80: the initial 5.25 plus the 3.55 to buy back the NOV 50 call. He has two cash inflows totaling 10.45: the premium income of 5.74 and then 4.71 from the two instances of writing the NOV 50 calls. Exhibit 20 provides a summary of the results of Clive's trades. Because the inflows of 10.45 exceed the outflows of 8.80, he has a resulting profit and loss diagram similar to the plot in Exhibit 19 that we saw in the previous example. Clive's timing was excellent—in each case, he increased his portfolio delta prior to an increase in ZKQ stock and decreased delta before the share price decreased. The important point is that increasing portfolio delta will result in greater profits (losses) when the underlying asset value increases (decreases).

EXHIBIT 20   Spreads and Deltas: A Summary of Results of Clive's Trades

Day	ZKQ Price	Activity	Portfolio Delta	Cash Out	Cash In
1	44	Buy NOV 45 call	0.55	5.25	—
4	49	Sell NOV 50 call	0.13 (= 0.68 − 0.55)	—	5.74
9	45	Buy NOV 50 call	0.57	3.55	—
13	48	Sell NOV 50 call	0.15 (= 0.66 − 0.51)	—	4.71
Total				8.80	10.45
Net Inflow					1.65

Spreads are primarily a directional play on the underlying asset's spot price (and also potentially on its volatility); still, spread traders can attempt to take advantage of changes in price, and it is easy to create a hypothetical example like this one. There obviously is no guarantee that any assumed price trend will continue. In fact, in actual practice, the excellent results shown in Exhibit 20 are exceedingly difficult to achieve. Still, the experienced option user knows to look for opportunistic plays that arise from price swings.

EXAMPLE 6   Spreads

Use the following information to answer questions 1 to 3 on spreads.

$S_0 = 44.50$
OCT 45 call = 2.55, OCT 45 put = 2.92
OCT 50 call = 1.45, OCT 50 put = 6.80

1. What is the maximum gain with an OCT 45/50 bull call spread?
   A. 1.10
   B. 3.05
   C. 3.90
2. What is the maximum loss with an OCT 45/50 bear put spread?
   A. 1.12
   B. 3.88
   C. 4.38
3. What is the breakeven price with an OCT 45/50 bull call spread?
   A. 46.10
   B. 47.50
   C. 48.88

Solution to 1: C is correct. With a bull spread, the maximum gain occurs at the high exercise price. At an underlying price of 50 or higher, the spread is worth the difference in the strike prices, or $50 - 45 = 5$. The cost of establishing the spread is the price paid for the lower-strike option minus the price received for the higher-strike option: $2.55 - 1.45 = 1.10$. The maximum gain is $5.00 - 1.10 = 3.90$.

Solution to 2: B is correct. With a bear spread, an investor buys the higher exercise price and writes the lower exercise price. When this strategy is done with puts, the higher exercise price option costs more than the lower exercise price option. Thus, the investor has a debit spread with an initial cash outlay, which is the most he can lose. The initial cash outlay is the cost of the OCT 50 put minus the premium received from writing the OCT 45 put: $6.80 - 2.92 = 3.88$.

Solution to 3: A is correct. An investor buys the OCT 45 call for 2.55 and sells the OCT 50 call for 1.45, for a net cost of 1.10. She breaks even when the position is worth the price she paid. The long call is worth 1.10 at a stock price of 46.10, and the OCT 50 call will expire out of the money and thus be worthless. The breakeven price is the lower exercise price of 45 plus the 1.10 cost of the spread, or 46.10.

8. STRADDLE

A long **straddle** is an option combination in which one buys *both* puts and calls, with the same exercise price and same expiration date, on the same underlying asset.[20] If someone *writes* both options, it is a short straddle. Because a long call is bullish and a long put is bearish, this strategy may seem illogical. When the Greeks are considered, the trader's position becomes clearer. The classic example is in anticipation of some event in which the outcome is uncertain but likely to significantly affect the price of the underlying asset, regardless of how the event is resolved.

A straddle is an example of a directional play on the underlying volatility, expressing the view that volatility will either increase, for a long straddle, or decrease, for a short straddle, from its current level. A profitable outcome from a long straddle, however, usually requires a significant price movement in the underlying asset. The straddle buyer pays the premium for two options, so to make a profit, the underlying asset must move either above or below the option exercise price by at least the total amount spent on the straddle. As an example, suppose in the next few days there is a verdict expected in a liability lawsuit against an automobile manufacturer. An investor expects the stock to move sharply one way or the other once the verdict is revealed. When the exercise price is chosen close to the current stock price, the straddle is neither a bullish nor a bearish strategy—the delta of the straddle is close to zero. With any other exercise price, there may be a directional bias (non-zero delta) because one of the options will be in the money and one will be out of the money. If the price increases (decreases) significantly, the delta of the call will approach +1 (0), and the put delta will approach 0 (−1), making the delta of the position approximately +1 (−1).

---

[20] If someone buys puts and calls with different exercise prices, the position is called a *strangle*.

Experienced option traders know that it is difficult to make money with a straddle. In the example, other people will also be watching the court proceedings. The market consensus will predict higher volatility once the verdict is announced, and option prices rise when volatility expectations rise. This increased volatility means that both the puts and the calls become expensive well before the verdict is revealed, and the long straddle requires the purchase of both options. To make money, the straddle buyer must be correct in his view that the "true" underlying volatility is higher than the market consensus. Essentially, the bet is that the straddle buyer is right and the other market participants, on average, are wrong by underestimating volatility.

Suppose the underlying stock sells for 50, and an investor selects 30-day options with an exercise price of 50. The call sells for 2.29 and the put for 2.28, for a total investment of 4.57. At prices above 50, the call is in the money. At prices below 50, the put is in the money. For the straddle to be profitable, one of these two options must be profitable enough to pay for the costs of both the put and call. To recover this cost, the underlying asset must either rise or fall by at least 4.57, as shown by the breakeven points in Exhibit 21.

EXHIBIT 21   Long Straddle: Current Stock Price = 50; Buy 50-Strike Call at 2.29, Buy 50-Strike Put at 2.28

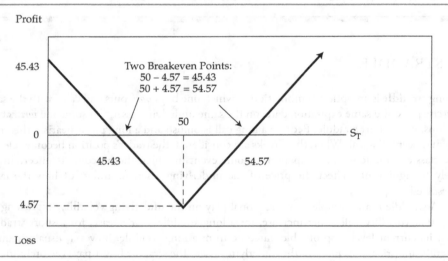

The straddle portfolio and Greeks are shown in Exhibit 22. The long straddle initially has a very low delta (+0.069 for this example) with a high gamma (0.139). The trader does not initially favor an increase or a decrease in the share price but knows the delta may quickly change. Once a direction (increase or decrease in the underlying price) asserts itself, the trader's position will take on a non-zero delta value. The trader's view can be better understood from a vega perspective. The long straddle will be profitable only if the stock price moves enough to recover both premiums. The short straddle writer collects the put and call premiums but will lose if the stock price moves more than 4.57 away from the strike price. The long (short) straddle trade is said to be long (short) volatility. The long straddle is a bet that increased volatility will move the stock price strongly above or below the strike price. The sensitivity of the straddle to changes in volatility is measured by vega. As shown in Exhibit 22, vega for our long straddle is +0.114, meaning the portfolio will profit by approximately 0.114 from increased volatility of 1% in the underlying. A stock price change large enough to cause the price of one option to exceed the cost of the combined premiums is needed to make the straddle trade profitable. A large increase in the underlying price will cause the delta of the call option to approach +1 and the delta of the put to approach 0. A large decrease in the underlying price will cause the delta of the call to drop to 0 and the put delta to approach −1.

EXHIBIT 22   Long and Short Straddle Greeks

	Call	Put	Long Straddle = Call + Put	Short Straddle = −Call + −Put
Cost	2.29	2.28	4.570	−4.570
Delta	0.534	−0.465	0.069	−0.069
Gamma	0.072	0.067	0.139	−0.139
Vega	0.057	0.057	0.114	−0.114
Theta	−0.039	−0.036	−0.075	0.075
Implied Volatility	38%	41%	—	—

Theoretically, the stock can rise to any level, so the maximum profit with the long call is unlimited. If the stock declines, it can fall to no lower than zero. If that happens, the long put would be worth 50. Subtracting the 4.57 cost of the straddle gives a maximum profit of 45.43 from a stock drop. The value of a straddle at expiration is the combined value of the call and the put:

$$V_T = \text{Max}(0, S_T - X) + \text{Max}(0, X - S_T). \tag{9}$$

Broken down into ranges,

$$V_T = X - S_T \text{ if } S_T < X, \text{ and}$$
$$V_T = S_T - X \text{ if } S_T > X.$$

The profit is $V_T - V_0$, or $\Pi = \text{Max}(0, S_T - X) + \text{Max}(0, X - S_T) - c_0 - p_0.$ \hfill (10)

Broken down into ranges,

$$\Pi = X - S_T - c_0 - p_0 \text{ if } S_T < X, \text{ and}$$
$$\Pi = S_T - X - c_0 - p_0 \text{ if } S_T > X.$$

As can be seen in Exhibit 21, the straddle has two breakeven points. The lower breakeven for the straddle is $S_{TL}{}^* = X - c_0 - p_0$, and the upper breakeven is $S_{TH}{}^* = X + c_0 + p_0$.

For the straddle buyer, the worst outcome is if the stock closes exactly at 50, meaning both the put and the call would expire worthless. At any other price, one of the options will have a positive exercise value. Note that at expiration, the straddle is not profitable if the stock price is in the range 45.43 to 54.57. The long straddle shown in Exhibit 21 requires more than a 9% price move in one month to be profitable. A trader who believed such a move was unlikely might be inclined to *write* the straddle, in which case the profit and loss diagram in Exhibit 21 is reversed, with a maximum gain of 4.57 and a theoretically unlimited loss if prices rise. The risk of a long straddle is limited to the amount paid for the two option positions. The straddle can also be understood in terms of theta. As shown in Exhibit 22, theta of the long straddle is

−0.075. All else equal, the long put and call positions will lose their time value as expiration approaches. The long straddle buyer is betting on a large price move in the underlying prior to expiration. If the stock price does not change significantly, the short straddle, which has a positive theta, will benefit from the erosion of time value of the short put and call positions.

8.1. Collars

A **collar** is an option position in which the investor is long shares of stock and then buys a put with an exercise price below the current stock price and writes a call with an exercise price above the current stock price.[21] Collars allow a shareholder to acquire downside protection through a protective put but reduce the cash outlay by writing a covered call. By carefully selecting the options, an investor can often offset most of the put premium paid by the call premium received. Using a collar, the profit and loss on the equity position is limited by the option positions.

For equity investors, the collar typically entails ownership of the underlying asset and the purchase of a put, which is financed with the sale of a call. In a typical investment or corporate finance setting, an interest rate collar may be used to hedge interest rate risk on floating-rate assets or liabilities. For example, a philanthropic foundation funds the grants it makes from income generated by its investment portfolio of floating-rate securities. The foundation's chief investment officer (CIO) wants to hedge interest rate risk (the risk of rates falling on its floating securities) by buying an interest rate floor (a portfolio of interest rate puts) and paying for it by writing a cap (a portfolio of interest rate calls). Should the rates on the portfolio fall, the long floor will provide a lower limit for the income generated by the portfolio. To finance the floor purchase, the foundation sells a cap. The cap will limit the income generated from the floating rate portfolio in the event the floating rate rises. The CIO is still holding a floating-rate securities portfolio but has restricted the returns using the collar. By setting both a minimum and a maximum portfolio return, the CIO may be better able to plan funding requests.

8.1.1. Collars on an Existing Holding

A zero-cost collar involves the purchase of a put and sale of a call with the same premium. In Exhibit 6, for instance, the NOV 15 put costs 1.46 and the NOV 17 call is 1.44, very nearly the same. A collar written in the over-the-counter market can be easily structured to provide a precise offset of the put premium with the call premium.[22]

The value of the collar at expiration is the sum of the value of the underlying asset, the value of the long put (struck at X_1), and the value of the short call (struck at X_2):

$$V_T = S_T + \text{Max}(0, X_1 - S_T) - \text{Max}(0, S_T - X_2), \text{ where } X_2 > X_1. \qquad (11)$$

---

[21] A collar is also called a *fence* or a *hedge wrapper*.

[22] Most collars are structured so that the call and put premiums completely offset each other. If the investor starts with the put at a specific exercise price, he then sells a call that has the same premium. There is one specific call with the same premium, and it has a particular exercise price, which is above the exercise price of the put. An algorithm can be used to search for the exercise price on the call that has the same premium as that of the put, which is then the call that the investor should sell. Most collars are structured and transacted in the over-the-counter market because the exercise price on the call must be a specific one. Exchange-traded options have standardized exercise prices, whereas the exercise prices of over-the-counter options can be set at whatever the investor wants.

The profit is the profit on the underlying share plus the profit on the long put and the short call so that:

$$\Pi = S_T + \text{Max}(0, X_1 - S_T) - \text{Max}(0, S_T - X_2) - S_0 - p_0 + c_0. \tag{12}$$

Broken down into ranges, the total profit on the portfolio is as follows:

$$\Pi = X_1 - S_0 - p_0 + c_0 \text{ if } S_T \leq X_1$$
$$\Pi = S_T - S_0 - p_0 + c_0 \text{ if } X_1 < S_T < X_2$$
$$\Pi = X_2 - S_0 - p_0 + c_0 \text{ if } S_T \geq X_2$$

Consider the risk–return trade-off for a shareholder who previously bought PBR stock at 12 and now buys the NOV 15 put for 1.46 and simultaneously writes the NOV 17 covered call for 1.44. Exhibit 23 shows a profit and loss worksheet for the three positions. Exhibit 24 shows the profit and loss diagram.

EXHIBIT 23   Collar P&L: Stock Purchased at 12, NOV 15 Put Purchased at 1.46, NOV 17 Call Written at 1.44

Stock price at expiration	5	10	15	16	17	20
Profit/loss from long stock	−7.00	−2.00	3.00	4.00	5.00	8.00
Profit/loss from long 15 put	8.54	3.54	−1.46	−1.46	−1.46	−1.46
Profit/loss from short 17 call	1.44	1.44	1.44	1.44	1.44	−1.56
Total	2.98	2.98	2.98	3.98	4.98	4.98

At or below the put exercise price of 15, the collar realizes a profit of $X_1 - S_0 - p_0 + c_0 = 15 - 12 - 1.46 + 1.44 = 2.98$. At or above the call exercise price of 17, the profit is constant at $X_2 - S_0 - p_0 + c_0 = 17 - 12 - 1.46 + 1.44 = 4.98$.

In this example, because the stock price had appreciated before establishing the collar, the position has a minimum gain of at least 2.98 as shown in Exhibit 24. Investors typically establish a collar on a position that is already outstanding.

EXHIBIT 24   Collar P&L Diagram: Stock Purchased at 12, NOV 15 Put Purchased at 1.46, NOV 17 Call Written at 1.44

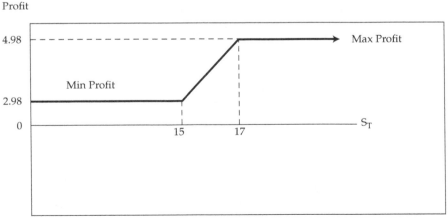

8.1.2. The Risk of a Collar

We have already discussed the risks of covered calls and protective puts. The collar is essentially the simultaneous holding of both of these positions. See Exhibit 25 for the return distribution of a collar. A collar sacrifices the positive part of the return distribution in exchange for the removal of the adverse portion. With the short call option, the option writer sold the right side of the return distribution, which includes the most desirable outcomes. With the long put, the investor is protected against the left side of the distribution and the associated losses. The option premium paid for the put is largely and, often precisely, offset by the option premium received from writing the call. The collar dramatically narrows the distribution of possible investment outcomes, which is risk reducing. In exchange for the risk reduction, the return potential is limited.

The risks of the collar can be understood in terms of the Greeks from Exhibit 6. For example, with a long share the delta of the portfolio = +1. With a collar, the portfolio delta is equal to the delta of the share plus the delta of the long NOV 15 put (−0.359) and short NOV 17 call (−0.475), so the portfolio delta = +1 + (−0.359) + (−0.475) = +0.166. Portfolio gamma, which equals put gamma minus call gamma, will be close to zero, −0.011 (= 0.075 − 0.086). By writing a call and buying a put, the investor reduces the portfolio's delta at a price of 15.84 from +1 to +0.166 and the gamma is very close to zero. If the stock price moves outside the range depicted in Exhibit 25, the delta of the position will approach zero over time. If the share price moves above 17, the NOV 17 call approaches a delta of +1, and the put will approach a delta of 0. The collar is short the call, so above 17 the portfolio delta (long stock with delta = +1 plus a short call with delta = −1) will approach zero. At prices below 15, the NOV 17 call will have a delta approaching 0, but the long put approaches a delta of −1, so the portfolio delta will again approach zero (long stock with delta = +1 plus the long put with delta = −1). The portfolio's sensitivity to changes in the stock price will be limited, as shown in Exhibit 25.

EXHIBIT 25   Collars and Return Distribution: Stock at 15.84, Write NOV 17 Call and Buy NOV 15 Put

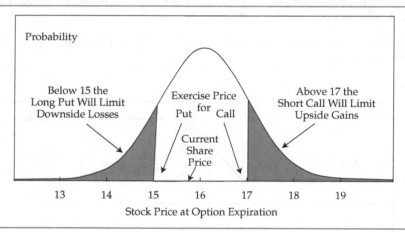

As the chosen put and call exercise prices move successively farther in opposite directions from the current price, the combined collar position begins to replicate the underlying gain/loss pattern of a long position in the underlying security. Conversely, as the chosen strike prices approach and meet each other, the expected returns and volatility become less and less equity-like and eventually converge on those of a risk-free, fixed income return to the time horizon. Thus, a collar position is, economically, intermediate between pure equity and fixed-income exposure.

8.1.3. The Risk of Spreads

Note that the shape of the profit and loss diagram for the bull spread in Exhibit 17 is similar to that of the collar in Exhibit 24. The upside return potential is limited, but so is the maximum loss. As with the risk–return tradeoff with the collar, an option spread takes the tails of the distribution out of play and leaves only price uncertainty between the option exercise prices. Looking at this scenario another way, if someone were to simply buy a long call, the maximum gain would be unlimited and the maximum loss would be the option premium paid. If someone decides to convert this to a spread, doing so limits the maximum gain while simultaneously reducing the total cost.

8.2. Calendar Spread

A strategy in which one sells an option and buys the same type of option but with different expiration dates, on the same underlying asset and with the same strike, is commonly referred to as a **calendar spread**. When the investor buys the more distant call and sells the near-term call, it is a long calendar spread. The investor could also buy a near-term call and sell a longer-dated one, known as a short calendar spread. Calendar spreads can also be done with puts; the investor would still buy a long-maturity put and sell a near-term put with the same strike and underlying to create a long calendar spread. As discussed previously, a portion of the option premium is time value. Time value decays over time and approaches zero as the option expiration date nears. Taking advantage of this time decay is a primary motivation behind a calendar spread. Time decay is more pronounced for a short-term option than for one with a long time until expiration. A calendar spread trade seeks to exploit this characteristic by purchasing a longer-term option and writing a shorter-term option.

Here is an example of how someone might use a calendar spread. Suppose XYZ stock is trading at 45 a share in August. XYZ has a new product to be introduced to the public early the following year. A trader believes this new product introduction will have a positive effect on the share price. Until the excitement associated with this announcement starts to affect the stock price, the trader believes that the stock will languish around the current level. See the option prices, deltas and thetas in Exhibit 26. Based on the bullish outlook for the stock going into January, the trader purchases the XYZ JAN 45 call with a theta (indicator of daily price erosion) of −0.014 for a price of 3.81. Noting that the near-term price forecast is neutral, the trader also decides to sell the XYZ SEP 45 call for 1.55. The theta for the XYZ SEP 45 Call is −0.029. The position costs 2.26 (= 3.81 − 1.55) to create and has an initial theta of +0.015 (= −0.014 − (−0.029)). If the stock price of XYZ remains constant over the next 30 days, the XYZ SEP 45 call will lose time value more rapidly than the JAN 45 call. The delta of calendar spread equals the delta of the JAN 45 call less the delta of the SEP 45 call and will be very low (Delta = +0.041 = 0.572 − 0.531).

Now move forward to the September expiration and assume that XYZ is trading at 45. The September option will now expire with no value, which is a good outcome for the calendar spread trader. The value of the position (now just the XYZ JAN 45 call) is 3.48, a gain of 1.22 over the position cost of 2.26. If the trader still believes that XYZ will stay around 45 into October before starting to move higher, the trader may continue to execute this strategy. An XYZ OCT 45 call might be sold for 1.55 with the hope that it also expires with no value.

EXHIBIT 26   Calendar Spread Call Option Prices, Deltas, and Thetas

150 days until January option expiration. Underlying stock price = 45

Exercise Price	SEP	OCT	JAN
40	5.15	5.47	6.63
45	1.55	2.19	3.81
50	0.22	0.62	1.99
		Delta	
40	0.975	0.902	0.800
45	0.531	0.545	0.572
50	0.121	0.217	0.363
		Theta (daily)	
40	−0.007	−0.011	−0.011
45	−0.029	−0.020	−0.014
50	−0.014	−0.014	−0.013

Just before September option expiration. Underlying stock price = 45

Exercise Price	SEP	OCT	JAN
40	5.00	5.15	6.39
45	0	1.55	3.48
50	0	0.22	1.69

In this example, the calendar spread trader has a directional opinion on the stock but does not believe that the price movement is imminent. Rather, the trader sees an opportunity to capture time value in one or more shorter-lived options that are expected to expire worthless.

A short calendar spread is created by purchasing the near-term option and selling a longer-dated option. Thetas for in-the-money calls may provide motivation for a short calendar spread. Assume a trader purchases the XYZ SEP 40 call with a theta of −0.007 for a price of 5.15. The trader sells the OCT 40 call with a theta of −0.011 for 5.47 to offset the cost of the SEP 40 call. The position nets the trader a cash inflow of 0.32 (= 5.47 − 5.15), and the initial position theta is slightly positive −0.007 − (−0.011) = +0.004.

If the stock price of XYZ remains at 45 (above the strike of 40) at the SEP expiration, the XYZ OCT 40 call will lose time value more rapidly than the SEP 40 call. The trader may close the position at the SEP expiration and make a profit of 0.17 = 0.32 + (5 − 5.15). Note that the profit consists of the 0.32 initial inflow plus the net cost of selling the SEP 40 call (at 5.00) and buying the OCT 40 call (at 5.15). In the event of a larger move, the position values will vary. For a large down move, for example an extreme case in which XYZ loses all of its value (so $S = 0$ at expiration), the long and the short call positions will be approximately worthless and the profit on the spread will be around 0.32 (= 0.32 + [0 − 0])). For a smaller down move to the strike price ($S = 40$ at expiration), the short calendar spread may result in a loss. If the XYZ stock price were to fall to 40 at the SEP expiration, the long position in the SEP 40 call would expire worthless but the OCT 40 call would still have a BSM model value of about 1.00 (not shown in Exhibit 26). This scenario would result in a loss of $0.68 = 0.32 + (0 - 1)$ to close the position. The writer of a calendar spread would typically be looking for a large move away from the strike price in either direction.

In sum, a big move in the underlying market or a decrease in implied volatility will help a short calendar spread, whereas a stable market or an increase in implied volatility will help a long calendar spread. Thus, calendar spreads are sensitive to movement of the underlying but also sensitive to changes in implied volatility.

9. IMPLIED VOLATILITY AND VOLATILITY SKEW

An important factor in the current price of an option is the outlook for the future volatility of the underlying asset's returns, the **implied volatility**. Implied volatility is not observable per se, but it is derived from an option pricing model—such as the Black–Scholes–Merton (BSM) model—and it is value that equates the model price of an option to its market price. Note that all other input variables to the BSM model, including the option's strike price, the price of the underlying, the time to option expiration, and the risk-free interest rate, are observable. Implied volatilities incorporate investors' expectations about the future course of financial asset returns and the level of market uncertainty associated with them.

Implied volatilities for options on a specific asset may differ with strike price (i.e., moneyness), side (i.e., put or call), and time to expiration. In particular, out-of-the-money (OTM) puts typically command higher implied volatilities than ATM or OTM calls. This phenomenon is attributed to investors' reassessments of the probabilities of negative "fat-tailed" market events such as the 2007–2009 global financial crisis.

Implied volatility is often compared with **realized volatility** (i.e., historical volatility), which is the square root of the realized variance of returns and measures the range of past returns for the underlying asset. To calculate the historical volatility for the given option, stock, or equity index, a series of past prices is needed. For example, to calculate the volatility of the S&P 500 Index over the past month (i.e., 21 trading days), it is necessary to first calculate the daily percentage change for each day's index closing price. This is done using the following formula, where P_t is the closing price and P_{t-1} is the prior day's closing price: $(P_t - P_{t-1})/P_{t-1}$. The next step is to apply the standard deviation formula you learned in Level I Quantitative Methods to the daily percentage change data to calculate the standard deviation (i.e., volatility) of the S&P 500 for the selected period, which in this case is the past month.

The standard deviation over the past month is then annualized by multiplying by the square root of the number of periods in a year. Because we assume the average number of trading days in a year and in a month are 252 and 21 (excluding weekends and holidays), respectively, the formula is:

$$\sigma_{Annual}(\%) = \sigma_{Monthly}(\%) \sqrt{\frac{252}{21}}. \tag{13}$$

Note that this example uses one month of daily return data, but the process is equally applicable to any other period.

Obviously, we cannot use the previous formula for realized volatility, which is based on past prices, to obtain implied volatility, which is the expected volatility of future returns of the underlying asset. Instead, the one-month annualized implied volatility can be derived from the current price of an option maturing in one month by using the BSM model. Once the one-month annualized implied volatility is obtained, it can then be converted into an estimate of the volatility expected on the underlying asset over the 21-day life of the option. This expected monthly volatility is given by the one-month annualized implied volatility divided by the square root of the number of 21-day periods in a 252-day trading year, as follows:

$$\sigma_{Monthly}(\%) = \sigma_{Annual}(\%) / \sqrt{\frac{252}{21}} \tag{14}$$

When option prices are compared within or across asset classes or relative to their historical values, they are assessed by their implied volatility. Exhibit 27 shows a comparison of the one-month annualized (ATM) implied volatility at a given point in time for options across three European equity indexes (Euro Stoxx 50, FTSE MIB, and DAX). The DAX shows the lowest implied volatility among the three indexes.

EXHIBIT 27   One-Month Annualized Implied Volatility

Underlying Index	Implied Volatility	Three-Year Low	Three-Year High
Euro Stoxx 50	9.56	9.0	17.9
FTSE MIB	14.22	11.0	21.7
DAX	9.29	7.3	13.9

Using the one-month annualized implied volatility for DAX index options of 9.29%, the volatility expected to materialize in the DAX index over the next month (21 trading days) can be calculated as follows:

$$\sigma_{Monthly}(\%) = 9.29\% / \sqrt{\frac{252}{21}} = 2.68\%$$

So, for example, if an investor buys an ATM one-month (21-day) straddle using puts and calls on the DAX, in order for the strategy to be profitable at expiration, the index must move up or down by at least 2.68%. The investor can compare this price movement needed to reach breakeven with the DAX's realized volatility over similar time horizons in the past. If such a price change is considered reasonable, then the investor can elect to implement the strategy.

The implied volatility of ATM options, calculated from the options' market prices using the BSM model, remains the simplest way to measure the prevailing volatility level. The BSM model assumes that volatility is constant, and notably, before the 1987 stock market crash, there was little volatility skew in equity index markets. Today, however, options prices on several asset classes display persistent volatility skew and, in some circumstances, volatility smile. The implied volatilities of options of a given expiration are thus dependent on their strike prices.

Exhibit 28 plots implied volatility (y-axis) against strike price (x-axis) for options on the same underlying, the FTSE MIB (trading at 19,000), with the same expiration. When the implied volatilities priced into both OTM puts and calls trade at a premium to implied volatilities of ATM options (those with strike price at 19,000), the curve is U-shaped and is called a **volatility smile**, because it resembles the shape of a smile. The more common shape of the implied volatility curve, however, is a **volatility skew**, where the implied volatility increases for OTM puts and decreases for OTM calls, as the strike price moves away from the current price. This shape persists across asset classes and over time because investors have generally less interest in OTM calls whereas OTM put options have found universal demand as portfolio insurance against a market sell-off.

EXHIBIT 28   Implied Volatility Curves for Three-Month Options on FTSE MIB

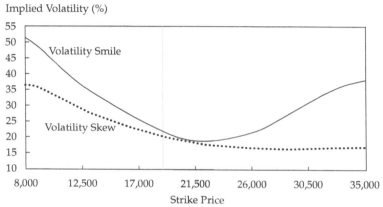

The extent of the skew depends on several factors, including investor sentiment and the relative supply/demand for puts and calls, among others. Several theoretical models try to use these factors to forecast skew variation. However, these models do not lead to unique predictions. In general, we can say that when the implied volatility is significantly higher (relative to historical levels) for puts with strike prices below the underlying asset's price, it means that there is an imbalance in the supply and demand for options. In fact, when investors are looking to hedge the underlying asset, the demand for put options exceeds that for call options. Option traders, who meet this excess demand by selling puts, increase the relative price of these options, thereby raising the implied volatility. A sharp increase in the level of the skew, accompanied with a surge in the absolute level of implied volatility, is an indicator that market sentiment is turning bearish. In contrast, higher implied volatilities (relative to historical levels) for calls with strike prices above the underlying asset's price indicate that investors are bullish and the demand for OTM calls to take on upside exposure is strong.

To better understand how to measure the volatility skew, consider Exhibit 29, which shows the levels of implied volatility at different degrees of moneyness for options expiring in three months on equity indexes where liquid derivatives markets exist. The 90% moneyness option is a put with strike (X) equal to 90% of the current underlying price (S); thus $X/S = 90\%$. The 110% moneyness of the call is calculated similarly. Also shown is the skew, calculated as the difference between the implied volatilities of the 90% put and the 110% call.

EXHIBIT 29   Implied Volatilities and Skew for Three-Month Options

| Index | Implied Volatility by Moneyness | | | 90%–110% |
	ATM	Put: 90%	Call: 110%	Volatility Skew
Nikkei 225	12.9	18.9	12.4	6.5
S&P 500	10.3	17.7	9.4	8.3
Euro Stoxx 50	12.3	17.8	9.3	8.5
DAX	14.5	20.0	11.0	9.0

For most asset classes, the level of option skew varies over time. Exhibit 30 presents the skew on the S&P 500, measured as the difference between the implied volatilities of options with 90% (puts) and 110% (calls) moneyness, and with three months to expiration.

EXHIBIT 30   90% Put–110% Call Implied Volatility Skew for Three-Month Options on S&P 500

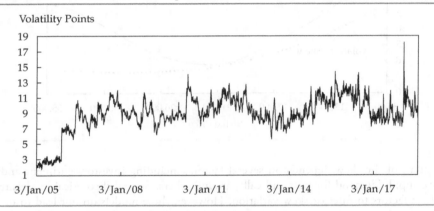

There are trading strategies that attempt to profit from the existence of an implied volatility skew and from changes in its shape over time. A common strategy is to take a long or short position in a **risk reversal**, which is then delta hedged. Using OTM options, a combination of long (short) calls and short (long) puts on the same underlying with the same expiration is a long (short) risk reversal. In particular, when a trader thinks that the put implied volatility is too high relative to the call implied volatility, she creates a long risk reversal, by selling the OTM put and buying the same expiration OTM call. The options position is then delta-hedged by selling the underlying asset. The trader is not aiming to profit from the movement in the overall level in implied volatility. In fact, depending on the strikes of the put and the call, the trade could be vega-neutral. For the trade to be profitable, the trader expects that the call will rise more (or decrease less) in implied volatility terms relative to the put.

Typically, implied volatility is not constant across different maturities, which means that options with the same strike price but with different maturities display different implied volatilities. This determines the **term structure of volatility**, which is often in contango, meaning that the implied volatilities for longer-term options are higher than for near-term ones. When markets are in stress and de-risking sentiment prevails, however, market participants demand short-term options, pushing up their prices and causing the term structure of volatility to invert. Exhibit 31 shows, for options on the S&P 500, a common indicator watched by market participants: the spread between the implied volatilities of 12-month and 3-month ATM options. Values below zero indicate that the term structure is inverted with 3-month options having a higher implied volatility than the 12-month options. In periods when equity markets experience large sell-offs, such as during the 2007–2009 global financial crisis, the term structure of implied volatility typically shows significant inversion. In such periods, the general level of equity volatility and skew also remain high.

EXHIBIT 31   12M–3M Implied Volatility Term Structure of S&P 500 Options

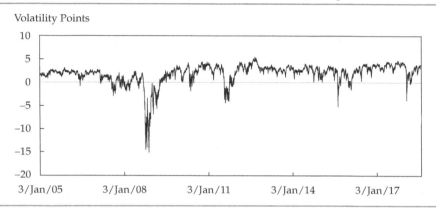

The **implied volatility surface** can be thought of as a three-dimensional plot, for put and call options on the same underlying asset, of days to expiration (*x*-axis), option strike prices (*y*-axis), and implied volatilities (*z*-axis). It simultaneously shows the volatility skew (smile) and the term structure of implied volatility. Considering that implied volatility varies across different option maturities and displays skew, the implied volatility surface is typically not flat as the BSM model may suggest. By observing the implied volatility surface, one can infer changes in market expectations. Several studies have focused on ways to extract information embedded in option market prices. The skew can provide insight into market participants' perceptions about the price movement of the underlying asset over a specified horizon. The general interpretation is that the shape of the volatility skew reflects varying degrees of market participants' fear about future market stress.

10. INVESTMENT OBJECTIVES AND STRATEGY SELECTION

10.1. The Necessity of Setting an Objective

Every trade is based on an outlook on the market. With stocks and most assets, one thinks about the direction of the market: Is it going up or down, or is it stable? When dealing with options, it is not enough to think about the market *direction*; it is also important to think about the Greeks beyond delta: gamma, theta, and vega. Where option valuation is concerned, what matters is not only the direction in which the asset underlying the derivative contract is headed but also the volatility of the underlying and even other investors' perception of that volatility. The investor's investment objective may not be achieved if one of these factors moves in an undesired direction. Gamma could lead to a faster loss or gain, depending on whether the investor is short or long the option, whereas theta could lead to a loss despite the underlying asset moving in the right direction. Vega could rise or fall if market expectations of implied volatility change, leading to a loss or profit for the options position. Furthermore, the option premium paid (if long) or received (if short) must be considered when calculating a position's total profit and loss at maturity. For example, in a simple call option purchase, the underlying asset must go up enough so that the call option reaches breakeven by overcoming the premium paid for the call.

Moreover, with the introduction of volatility-based derivatives, investors increasingly view these investments as a way to protect their portfolios against downside risk and also as a method to improve their portfolios' efficiency. When considering hedging strategies, it is important to differentiate between situations in which the investor's goal is to benefit from rising volatility (long volatility)—for example, in hedging a long stock position—and situations in which the investor wants to benefit from falling volatility (short volatility)—for example, by writing a short straddle position.

Derivatives are used by portfolio managers, traders, and corporations to adjust their risk exposures, to achieve a specific investment objective, or even to infer market expectations in the short term (for example, inferring market expectations for central banks' interest rate decisions). The main advantage of derivatives is that they allow two parties with differing needs and market views to adjust quickly without having to enter into potentially costly and difficult trades in the underlying. Another advantage of using derivatives instead of investing in the physical underlying securities is leverage. The fact that investors can take on a large exposure to the underlying asset by putting up only a fraction of the amount of risk capital is an important feature of derivatives. Liquidity is another key aspect favoring derivatives usage in many markets—for example, the ability to buy or sell credit protection using index credit derivatives (CDS) instead of trading the actual underlying, and likely less liquid, bonds provides a huge liquidity advantage to traders and investors. In sum, given an actual or anticipated portfolio of equities, bonds, rates, currencies, or other assets; a market outlook and a timeframe; and an understanding of the benefits and limitations of derivatives, it is important to set realistic investment objectives, be they for hedging, for taking direction bets, or for capturing arbitrage opportunities.

10.2. Criteria for Identifying Appropriate Option Strategies

Investors use derivatives to achieve a target exposure based on their outlook for the underlying asset. Exhibit 32 shows one way of looking at the interplay of direction and volatility. The strategies identified are most profitable given the expected change in implied volatility and the outlook for the direction of movement of the underlying asset.

EXHIBIT 32   Choosing Options Strategies Based on Direction and Volatility of the Underlying Asset

| | | Outlook on the Trend of Underlying Asset | | |
		Bearish	Trading Range/ Neutral View	Bullish
Expected Move in Implied Volatility	**Decrease**	*Write calls*	*Write straddle*	*Write puts*
	Remain Unchanged	*Write calls and buy puts*	*Calendar spread*	*Buy calls and write puts*
	Increase	*Buy puts*	*Buy straddle*	*Buy calls*

Consider an investor who is bearish about a market. If he expects that implied volatility will increase as the market sells off, then he will buy a put to protect his investments. If instead he believes that volatilities are expected to fall, writing a call would likely be a profitable strategy. Investors need to keep in mind, however, that the two strategies have two different payoffs and risk management implications. As we have seen previously, a position in which the investor writes the call and buys the put is a collar, and it is often associated with holding a long position in the underlying asset. Investors use collars against a long stock position to hedge risk and smooth volatility. In fact, by selling a covered call while purchasing a protective put, the investor establishes a combined position with fixed downside protection while still providing some opportunity for profits.

Now consider an investor who has a bullish view. Buying calls is an option strategy that will allow the investor to benefit if her outlook is correct and implied volatility increases. When implied volatilities are expected to fall, writing a put represents an alternative strategy to take advantage of a bullish market view with declining volatility. If this happens, the position will likely be profitable, because as the stock rises and implied volatility decreases, the short put moves farther out of the money and its price will decrease. The combined position in which the investor is long calls and short puts (i.e., a long risk reversal) is used to implement a bullish view (the investor buys the calls) while lowering the cost (the investor sells the puts) of the long position in the underlying asset that will be established upon exercising the options.

Investors can also decide to sell puts when they want to buy a stock only if the price declines below a determined target price (the strike price of the puts will be the same as this target price). In this case, by selling the put options when implied volatilities are elevated (and the puts are expensive), the investor can realize an effective stock purchase price that is less than the target (strike) price by the size of the premium received.

The purchase of call or put spreads tends to be most appropriate when the investor has a bullish view (call bull spread) or a bearish view (put bear spread) but the underlying market is not clearly trending upward or downward. Furthermore, such spreads are a way to reduce the total cost, given that the spread is normally constructed by buying one option and writing another. Importantly, if the implied volatility curve is skewed, with the implied volatility of OTM puts relatively higher than for nearer-to-the-money options, the cost of a bearish spread is even lower. This is because in the put bear spread, the lower exercise price, more OTM (but relatively more expensive) put is sold and the higher exercise price, nearer-to-the-money (but relatively less expensive) put is purchased.

Now suppose that the market is expected to trade in range. Again, the investor should consider volatility. Suppose he believes the current consensus estimate of volatility implied in option prices is too low and the rate of the change in underlying prices will increase—that is, vega will increase. If the investor is neutral on market direction, the appropriate strategy will be a long straddle, because this strategy takes advantage of an increase in the long call or long put option prices in response to realization of the expected surge in volatility, vega, and gamma. At expiry, the long straddle will be profitable if the price of the call (put) is greater (less) than the upper (lower) breakeven price. In contrast, an investor who expects the market to trade in range and volatility to fall may want to write the straddle instead.

We now consider a strategy that combines a longer-term bullish/bearish outlook on the underlying asset with a near-term neutral outlook. This approach is the calendar spread (or time spread), a strategy using two options of the same type (puts or calls) and same strike price but with different maturity dates. Typically, a long calendar spread—wherein the shorter-maturity option is sold and the longer-maturity option is purchased—is a long volatility trading strategy because the longer-term option has a higher vega than the shorter-term option.

The maximum profit is obtained when the short-term option expires worthless, then implied volatility surges, increasing the price of the remaining long-term option. Although the delta for a calendar spread is approximately zero, gamma is not, so the main risk for the calendar strategy is that the underlying stock price moves too fast and too far from the strike prices. For this reason, the calendar spread is typically implemented in option markets characterized by low implied volatility when the underlying stock is expected to remain in a trading range, but only until the maturity of the short-term option.

11. USES OF OPTIONS IN PORTFOLIO MANAGEMENT

This section uses "mini cases" to illustrate some of the ways in which different market participants use derivative products to solve a problem or to alter a risk exposure. Note that with the wide variety of derivatives available, there are almost always multiple ways in which derivatives might logically be used in a particular situation. These mini cases cover only a few of them.

11.1. Covered Call Writing

Carlos Rivera is a portfolio manager in a small asset management firm focusing on high-net-worth clients. In mid-April, he is preparing for an upcoming meeting with Parker, a client whose daughter is about to marry. Parker and her husband have just decided to pay for their daughter's honeymoon and need to raise $30,000 relatively quickly. The client's portfolio is 70% invested in equities and 30% in fixed income and is by policy slightly aggressive. Currently the Parkers are "asset rich and cash poor," having largely depleted their cash reserves prior to the wedding expenses. The recently revised investment policy statement permits most option activity except the writing of naked calls.

Parker's account contains 5,000 shares of Manzana (MNZA) stock, a stock that she is considering selling in the near future. Rivera's firm has a bearish market outlook for MNZA shares over the next six months. Rivera reviews information on the 44-day exchange-listed options, which expire in May (shown in Exhibit 33). He is considering writing MNZA calls, which will accomplish two objectives. First, the sale of calls will generate the required cash for his client. Secondly, the sale will reduce the delta of Parker's account in line with his firm's bearish short-term outlook for MNZA shares. The current delta of Parker's MNZA position is $5,000(+1)$ or $+5,000$. Exhibit 33 contains call and put price information for May MNZA options with strike prices close to the current market price of MNZA shares ($S_0 = \$169$).

EXHIBIT 33   Manzana Inc. May Options With 44 Days to Expiration, MNZA Stock = $169

Call Premium	Call Delta	Exercise Price	Put Premium	Put Delta	Put or Call Vega
12.55	0.721	160	3.75	−0.289	0.199
9.10	0.620	165	5.30	−0.384	0.224
6.45	0.504	170	7.69	−0.494	0.234
4.03	0.381	175	10.58	−0.604	0.225
2.50	0.271	180	14.10	−0.702	0.199

Discuss the factors that Rivera should consider and the strategy he should recommend to Parker.

Solution:

To generate cash, Rivera will want to write options. The account permits the writing of covered calls. Manzana options trade on an organized exchange with a standard contract size of 100 shares per contract. With 5,000 shares in the account, 50 call contracts would be covered.

If Rivera were to write the MAY 180 calls, doing so would not generate the required cash, $2.50 \times 100 \times 50 = \$12,500$. Writing the MAY 165 calls would generate more than enough income: $9.10 \times 100 \times 50 = \$45,500$. However, the May 165 call is in the money. Although the firm's outlook is bearish for the shares, Rivera feels there is a high likelihood of Parker's MNZA shares being called away at expiration. Writing the May 175 call would generate only $4.03 \times 100 \times 50 = \$20,150$. Although Rivera believes the 175 call would not be exercised, the cash generated would be only about two-thirds of the client's projected need. The May 170 call would generate $6.45 \times 100 \times 50 = \$32,250$, which looks good from a cash-generation perspective. The current price of MNZA shares is 169, so there is a considerable risk that MNZA shares will sell above that level at expiration. If MNZA stock trades above the strike price at the May expiration, then Parker would be exposed to having her shares called at 170. Given the firm's bearish outlook for MNZA shares and, as stated previously, "Parker is considering selling the stock in the near future," this risk might be acceptable. Using the May 170 call option data from Exhibit 33, the delta of Parker's MNZA position would be reduced from +5,000 to $5,000 \times (+1 - 0.504) = +2,480$.[23] The profit graph for the recommended sale of 50 May 170 call contracts against Parker's 5,000 share long position at 169 is shown in Exhibit 34.

EXHIBIT 34   Profit and Loss for MNZA May 170 Covered Call ($S_0 = 169$, $c_0 = 6.45$)

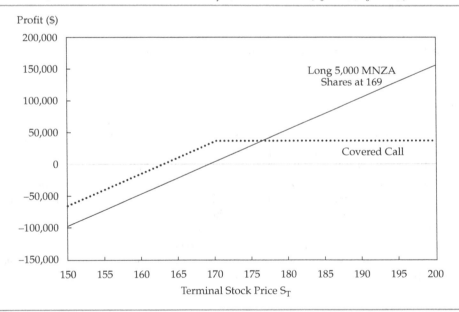

---

[23] Delta for the short calls will approach -1 if the stock price moves strongly above 170 close to maturity. The likelihood of the shares being called away in that scenario would push the position delta to 0 (= +5000 from the shares, −5000 for the short ITM calls).

The $32,250 generated by the call option sales is Parker's to keep. There are two risks, however, that Rivera should point out to Parker using Exhibit 34. The first risk is that his outlook for MNZA shares might be incorrect. The reduced delta may cost his client a potential gain on the long position. If MNZA shares increase above 170, the profits will go to the call owner. Parker's MNZA shares may be called away at 170, limiting her profit to the option premium of $32,500 plus the $5,000 from selling her MNZA shares at a profit of $1 (= $170 − $169) as shown in Exhibit 34.[24] The second risk is that to write the covered call, Parker must continue to hold 5,000 MNZA shares. If the firm's bearish outlook is correct, the shares may drop in value during the next month, resulting in a loss on the long stock position. The loss would be cushioned somewhat by the 6.45 call premium, but a drop of more than 3.8% (below 162.55 = 169 − 6.45; 6.45/169 = 3.8%) results in an overall loss on the position. After Rivera explains the risks to Parker, she elects to write the MNZA 170 calls.

11.2. Put Writing

Oscar Quintera is the chief financial officer for Tres Jotas, a private investment firm in Buenos Aires. He wants to purchase 50,000 MNZA shares for the firm, but at the current price he considers MNZA shares to be a bit expensive. The current share price is $169, and Quintera is willing to buy the stock at a price not higher than $165. Quintera decides to write out-of-the-money puts on MNZA shares.

Discuss the outcome of the transaction, a short position in MNZA May 165 puts, assuming two scenarios:

- Scenario A: MNZA is $163 per share on the option expiration day.
- Scenario B: MNZA is $177 per share on the option expiration day.

Solution:
Quintera can write OTM puts to effectively "get paid" to buy the stock. He sells puts and the firm keeps the cash regardless of what happens in the future. If the stock is above the exercise price at expiration, the put options will not be exercised. Otherwise, the option is exercised, Quintera purchases the stock and, as desired, Tres Jotas becomes an owner of the stock. Exhibit 33 shows the options information for 44-day MAY put options. Because his target price is 165, Quintera writes 500 May MNZA 165 put contracts and receives premium income of $500 \times 100 \times \$5.30 = \$265,000$. The company keeps these funds regardless of future stock price movements. But, the firm is obligated to buy stock at $165 if the put holder chooses to exercise. By writing the puts, Quintera has established a bullish position in MNZA stock. The delta of this MNZA position is $-500 \times 100 \times -0.384 = +19,200$, the equivalent of a long position in 19,200 MNZA shares. The portfolio profit on the short put is shown in Exhibit 35.

---

[24] Note that if the shares are called away at 170, there may also be tax consequences for Parker.

EXHIBIT 35   Short Position Profit for 500 MNZA May 165 Put Contracts

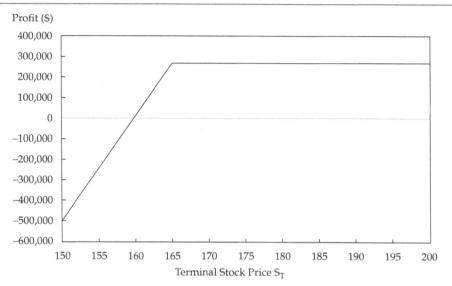

Scenario A:

The stock is $163 per share on the option expiration day. With an exercise price of 165, the put is in the money and will be exercised. Quintera will be assigned to buy 50,000 shares at the exercise price of 165. The cost is 50,000 × $165 = $8,250,000. Quintera is satisfied with the outcome, because the firm keeps the premium income of $265,000, so the net cost of purchase is $8,250,000 − $265,000 = $7,985,000. On 50,000 shares, this means the *effective purchase price* is $7,985,000/50,000 = $159.70, which is below the maximum $165 price Quintera was willing to pay. If the price of MNZA shares drops below 165, the effective purchase price will always be $X − p = 165 − 5.30 = 159.70. This is the breakeven point for the short put position. At prices below the breakeven amount, Quintera would have been better off not writing the put and just buying MNZA shares outright. For example, if the MNZA price fell to $150, Quintera would have been obligated to buy shares at 165, $15 more than the market price. When the $5.30 premium is considered, the $15 difference would amount to a loss of $9.70 per share or $485,000 which can be seen in Exhibit 35.

Scenario B:

The stock price is $177 on the option expiration day. With an exercise price of 165.00, the MNZA puts are out of the money and would not be exercised. Tres Jotas keeps the $265,000 premium received from writing the option. This approach adds to the company's profitability, but Tres Jotas did not acquire the MNZA shares and experienced an opportunity cost relative to an outright purchase of the stock at $169. Any price above 165, will result in earning the premium of $265,000, as can be seen in Exhibit 35.

11.3. Long Straddle

Katrina Hamlet has been following Manzana stock for the past year. She anticipates the announcement of a major new product soon, but she is not sure how the critics will react to it. If the new product is praised, she believes the stock price will increase dramatically. If the product does not impress, she believes the share price will fall substantially. Hamlet has been considering trading around the event with a straddle. The stock is currently priced at $169.00, and she is focused on close-to-the-money (170) calls and puts selling for 6.45 and 7.69, respectively. Her initial strategy is presented as Exhibit 36.

Hamlet expects that the stock will move at least 10% either way once the product announcement is made, making the straddle strategy potentially appropriate. The vega of her position would be $0.234 + 0.234 = +0.468$, meaning a 1% move in the options' volatility would result in a gain of about $0.468 in the value of the straddle. The straddle's delta would be approximately zero, at +0.01 (Call Delta + Put Delta = (0.504 + [−0.494])). This strategy is long volatility. After the market close, Hamlet hears a news story indicating that the product will be unveiled at a trade show in two weeks. The following morning after the market opens, she goes to place her trade and finds that although the stock price remains at $169.00, the option prices have adjusted upward to $10.20 for the call and $10.89 for the put.

Discuss whether the new option premiums have any implications for Hamlet's intended straddle strategy.

EXHIBIT 36   Long Manzana Straddle

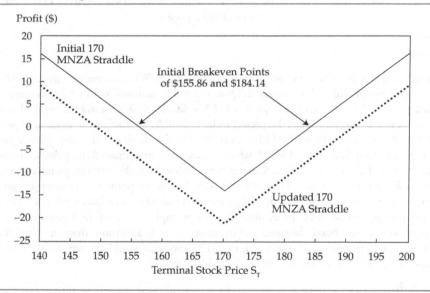

Solution:
Hamlet is betting on a substantial price movement in the underlying MNZA shares to make money with this trade. That price movement, up or down, must be large enough to recover the two premiums paid. In her earlier planning, that total was $6.45 + $7.69 = $14.14. She expects at least a 10% price movement, which on a stock selling for $169.00 would be an increase of $16.90. This price movement would be sufficient to recover the $14.14 cost of the straddle and make her strategy profitable. The breakeven points were $155.86 and $184.14, as shown in Exhibit 36.

The news report about the imminent product unveiling, however, has increased the implied volatility in the options, from about 30% to about 45%, raising their prices and making it more difficult to achieve the new breakeven points. After the news report, Hamlet finds the MAY 170 call now costs $10.20 and the MAY 170 put is trading for $10.89, so the MAY 170 straddle costs $21.09 ($10.20 + $10.89) to implement. Relating back to the vega she calculated the day before, Hamlet computed an initial vega (pre-announcement) of +0.468 for the straddle. Now she sees the approximate 15 percentage point rise in implied volatility (to 45%) in both the put and call. According to her initial vega calculation, she would expect an increase of $15 \times 0.468 = \$7.02$ in her straddle value after the announcement. The announcement increased the price of the straddle by $6.95 (= 21.09 − 14.14), which is very close to the $7.02 increase predicted by the vega calculation. To reach the new breakeven points (170 ± 21.09), she now needs the stock to move by more than 12%, a larger move than 10% from the current level of 169. Given that Hamlet expects only a 10% price movement, she decides against executing this straddle trade.

EXAMPLE 7   Straddle Analytics

Use the following information to answer Questions 1 to 3 on straddles.

XYZ stock price = 100.00
100-strike call premium = 8.00
100-strike put premium = 7.50
Options expire in three months

1. If Yelena Strelnikov, a portfolio manager, buys a straddle on XYZ stock, she is *best* described as expecting a:
   A. higher volatility market.
   B. lower volatility market.
   C. stable volatility market.
2. This strategy will break even at expiration stock prices of:
   A. 92.50 and 108.50.
   B. 92.00 and 108.00.
   C. 84.50 and 115.50.
3. Reaching an upside breakeven point implies an annualized rate of return on XYZ stock *closest* to:
   A. 16%.
   B. 31%.
   C. 62%.

Solution to 1: A is correct. A straddle is directionally neutral in terms of price; it is neither bullish nor bearish. The straddle buyer wants higher volatility and wants it quickly but does not care in which direction the price of the underlying moves. The worst outcome is for the underlying asset to remain stable.

Solution to 2: C is correct. To break even, the stock price must move enough to recover the cost of both the put and the call. These premiums total to $15.50, so the stock must move up at least to $115.50 or down to $84.50.

Solution to 3: C is correct. The price change to a breakeven point is 15.50 points, or 15.5% on a 100 stock. This is for three months. Ignoring compounding, this outcome is equivalent to an annualized rate of 62% on XYZ stock, found by multiplying by 12/3 (15.5% × 4 = 62%).

11.4. Collar

Bernhard Steinbacher has a client with a holding of 100,000 shares in Tundra Corporation, currently trading for €14 per share. The client has owned the shares for many years and thus has a very low tax basis on this stock. Steinbacher wants to safeguard the position's value because the client does not want to sell the shares. He does not find exchange-traded options on the stock. Steinbacher wants to present a way in which the client could protect the investment portfolio from a decline in Tundra's stock price.

Discuss an option strategy that Steinbacher might recommend to his client.

Solution:

In the over-the-counter market, Steinbacher might buy a put and then write an out-of-the money call. This strategy is a collar. The put provides downside protection below the put exercise price, and the call generates income to help offset the cost of the put. The investor decides the strike prices of the put and the call to achieve a specific level of downside protection, while still keeping some benefit from an increase in the stock price. When the strike of the call is set so that the call premium (to be received) exactly offsets the put premium (to be paid), then the position is called a "zero-cost collar." Recalling Exhibit 25 and the underlying return distribution, this strategy effectively sells the right tail of the distribution, which represents potential large gains, in exchange for eliminating the left tail, which represents potential large losses.

11.5. Calendar Spread

Ivanka Dubois is a professional advisor to high-net-worth investors. She expects little price movement in the Euro Stoxx 50 in the next three months but has a bearish long-term outlook. The consensus sentiment favoring a flat market shows no signs of changing over the next few months, and the Euro Stoxx 50 is currently trading at 3500. Exhibit 37 shows prices for two put options with strike price of 3500 that are available on the index. Both options have the same implied volatility.

EXHIBIT 37   3,500 Strike Put Options on Euro Stoxx 50

	Option A	Option B
Current Price	€119	€173
Time to Maturity	3 months	6 months

1. Discuss how Dubois can take advantage of her out-of-consensus view.
2. Analyze four scenarios that Dubois might likely face for the Stoxx 50 index at the expiry of the three-month option (these scenarios are provided at the beginning of the Solution to 2).

Solution to 1: Dubois's view is best implemented with a long position in a calendar spread that combines a longer-term bearish outlook on the underlying asset with a near-term neutral outlook. She is bearish long-term and so would buy a calendar put spread. A long calendar spread is a long volatility trading strategy whereby the maximum profit is obtained when the short-term at the money option expires worthless with the underlying almost unchanged.

Dubois can implement a put calendar spread trade by selling the three-month put option (A) for €119 and buying the six-month same strike put option (B) at the price for €173. Therefore, the cost of establishing this strategy is a net debit of €54 per contract (given by €173 − €119). Remember, Dubois has a bearish long-term outlook. If the put calendar spread is not profitable at the expiry of the three-month put, the short option expires worthless and then she owns the longer-term option free and clear. Thus, Dubois has managed to lower the cost of purchasing a longer-term put option, which could be kept for hedging her portfolio's downside risk.

Solution to 2:   If the put calendar spread position is held until the expiry of the three-month put, then Dubois might likely face one of the four following scenarios for the Euro Stoxx 50. In the first three scenarios, the implied volatility is assumed to remain constant:

- Scenario 1: The index is still trading at 3500 as expected.
- Scenario 2: The index has increased and is trading at 4200.
- Scenario 3: The index has decreased and is trading at 3000.
- Scenario 4: The index has decreased and is trading at 3000, but the implied volatility has significantly increased.

Scenario 1:

The Euro Stoxx 50 is still trading at 3500 as expected. The three-month put option expires worthless, and the original longer-term six-month option, which now has three months remaining to expiration, is worth €119 (because the implied volatility has remained constant). The total cost of the calendar spread was €54, and Dubois can sell the remaining put to a dealer for a profit of €65 (given by €119 − €54). As can be seen in Exhibit 38, which shows the profit and loss diagram for the calendar spread at the time of the expiration of the three-month put, this corresponds to the level of maximum payoff for this strategy.

EXHIBIT 38   P&L for 3,500 Strike Calendar Spread at Expiration of Three-Month Put

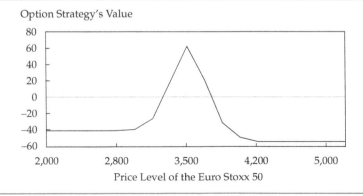

Scenario 2:

The Euro Stoxx 50 has increased and is trading at 4200. The three-month put option expires worthless. Also, the value of the six-month put is near zero, and if Dubois unwinds her (long) put option position she will lose all €54 (given by €173 − €119), the cost of the put calendar spread.

Scenario 3:

The Euro Stoxx 50 index has decreased and is trading at 3000. Dubois must pay €500 (€3,500 − €3,000) to settle the (short) three-month put option at expiration. The (long) put option with three months remaining to expiration is deep in the money and, assuming volatility is still unchanged, it is worth €515 (given by Intrinsic Value of €500 + €15 of Time Value). If Dubois sells this put to a dealer, she will lose €39 (= €515 − €500 − €54) on the put calendar spread.

Scenario 4:

The Euro Stoxx 50 has decreased and is trading at 3000, and the implied volatility has significantly increased. Dubois must pay €500 (€3,500 − €3,000) to settle the (short) three-month put option at expiration. The (long) put option with three months remaining to expiration is deep in the money and, assuming volatility has increased, it is worth €530 (given by Intrinsic Value of €500 + €30 of Time Value). If Dubois sells this put to a dealer, she will realize a loss of €24 (= €530 − €500 − €54) on the put calendar spread. Exhibit 39 adds the profit and loss diagram for the calendar spread at the time of the expiration of the three-month put, assuming that implied volatility of the six-month put has significantly increased.

EXHIBIT 39   P&L for 3,500 Strike Calendar Spread at Expiration of Three-Month Put Assuming an Increase in Implied Volatility

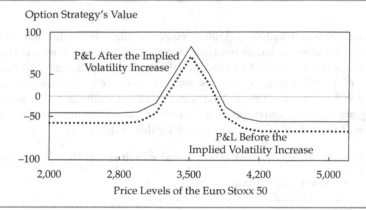

12. HEDGING AN EXPECTED INCREASE IN EQUITY MARKET VOLATILITY

Jack Wu is a fund manager who oversees a stock portfolio valued at US$50 million that is benchmarked to the S&P 500. He expects an imminent significant correction in the US stock market and wants to profit from an anticipated jump in short-term volatility to hedge his portfolio's tail risk.

The VIX Index is currently at 14.87, and the front-month VIX futures trades at 15.60. Wu observes the quotes shown in Exhibit 40 for options on the VIX (these options have same implied volatility). It is important to note that VIX option prices reflect the VIX futures prices. Given that the VIX futures trade at 15.60 while the spot VIX is 14.87, the call is at the money while the put is out of the money by 5.45% (= [14.75 − 15.60]/15.60).

At maturity, the options' payoffs will depend on the settlement price of the relevant VIX futures contracts. The options will expire one month from now, and the contract size is 100.

EXHIBIT 40   Options on VIX Index

	Call Option	Put Option
Option Strike	15.60	14.75
Option Price	2.00	1.55

Discuss the following:

1. A strategy Wu can implement to hedge tail risk in his equity portfolio, by taking advantage of his expected increase in volatility while lowering his hedging cost
2. Profit and loss on the strategy at options expiration
3. Relevant issues and advantages of this strategy

Solution to 1:   Wu decides to purchase the 15.60 call on the VIX and, to partially finance the purchase, he sells an equal number of the 14.75 VIX puts. The total cost of the options strategy is 0.45 (= 2.00 − 1.55) per contract.

Solution to 2:   At maturity, the options' payoffs will depend on the settlement price of the relevant VIX futures. Exhibit 41 shows the profit and loss diagram for the option strategy at the time of the options' expiration. In particular, the horizontal axis shows the values corresponding to the relevant VIX futures contracts.

EXHIBIT 41   Profit and Loss of the VIX Options Strategy

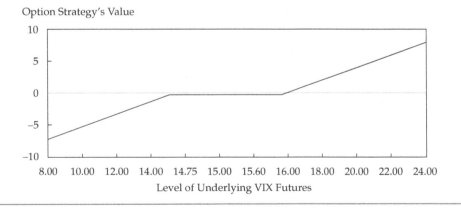

In this case, at the expiry the strategy will be profitable if volatility spikes up (as anticipated) and the VIX futures increase above 16.05. This is calculated as the call strike of 15.60 plus the net cost of the options (15.60 + 0.45). Above this level, the strategy will gain proportionally. In contrast, Wu's option strategy will lose proportionally to its exposure to the short puts if the VIX futures' settlement price is below 14.75 (put strike).

Solution to 3: The hedge ratio that determines the number of calls to buy could be determined based on regression and scenario analysis on the portfolio's profit and loss versus rates of increase in implied volatility during significant stock market sell-offs in the past. Of course, a risk is that past correlations may not be indicative of future correlations. Importantly, the relative advantage of implementing this long volatility hedging strategy by purchasing calls on the VIX over buying VIX futures depends on the difference in leverage available, the difference in payoff profiles (asymmetrical for options and symmetrical for futures), and the shape of the volatility futures term structure, as well as the cost of the options compared with the cost of the index futures.

12.1. Establishing or Modifying Equity Risk Exposure

In this section, we examine some examples in which investors use derivatives for establishing an equity risk exposure, for risk management, or for implementing tactical asset allocation decisions. The choice of derivative that will satisfy the investment goal depends on the outlook for the underlying asset, the investment horizon, and expectations for implied volatility over that horizon.

12.1.1. Long Call

Armando Sanchez is a private wealth advisor working in London. He expects the shares of Markle Co. Ltd. will move from the current price of £60 a share to £70 a share over the next three months, thanks to an increase of positive news flows regarding the company's new fintech services. He also expects that the implied volatilities of options on Markle's stock will stay almost unchanged over the same period. Prices for three-month call options on the stock are shown in Exhibit 42 (note that each call contract represents one share). For his high-net-worth clients whose investment policy statements allow the use of derivatives, Sanchez plans to recommend that they purchase the call option that, based on the budget they intend to spend for implementing the strategy, would maximize profits if the stock price increases to £70 a share or more over the next three months.

EXHIBIT 42   Three-Month Call Options on Markle Co. Ltd.

	Option A	Option B	Option C
Strike	£58.00	£60.00	£70.00
Price	£4.00	£3.00	£0.40
Delta	0.6295	0.5227	0.1184
Gamma	0.0304	0.0322	0.0160

Discuss the option strategy that Sanchez should recommend to his clients.

Solution:
Sanchez has a bullish view because he anticipates a nearly 17% price increase in Markle shares over the next three months, from the current price of £60. He expects that implied volatilities

of the options on Markle shares will stay unchanged, making the purchase of options a profitable strategy if his outlook materializes within the given timeframe.

The best strategy would be a long position in the £60 strike calls (option B). The breakeven price of the position is £63 (£60 + £3), so at option expiry, the overall position would be profitable at any stock price above £63. In contrast, the breakeven price of the 58-strike call (option A) is £62 (£58 + £4) and for the 70-strike call (option C) the breakeven is £70.40 (£70 + £0.40). Therefore, Sanchez would not use option C to implement his strategy because the breakeven price is above his target price of £70/share.

Given the £60 strike call has a lower price (premium) than the £58 strike call, Sanchez's clients can purchase more of these lower-priced options for a given investment size. Moreover, the 60-strike call offers the largest profit potential per unit of premium paid if the stock price increases to £70 (as expected).

$$\text{Call strike £58: } (£70 - £62)/£4 = 2.0$$
$$\text{Call strike £60: } (£70 - £63)/£3 = 2.3$$

Purchasing the £60 strike call (option B) is the most profitable strategy given that Sanchez's expectations are realized. A position in the £60 strike call has a lower delta (= 0.5227) compared with the £58 strike call (delta = 0.6295), so at current prices of the underlying, the change in value of the £60 strike call is lower. If Markle's stock reaches £70 per share during the life of the option, however, the £60 strike call will benefit from having a larger gamma (= 0.0322) compared with the £58 strike call (gamma = 0.0304).

12.1.2. Risk Management: Protective Put Position

Investors use protective puts, collars, and equity swaps against a long stock position to hedge market risk. Here we turn to a practical application of protective puts.

Eliot McLaire manages a Glasgow-based hedge fund that holds 100,000 shares of Relais Corporation, currently trading at €42.00.

Situation A: Before Relais Corporation's quarterly earnings release:

Relais has a quarterly earnings announcement scheduled in one week. Although McLaire expects an earnings increase, he believes the company will miss the consensus earnings estimate, in which case he expects that the maximum drawdown from the current price of €42.00 would be 10%. He would like to protect the fund's position in the company for several days around the earnings announcement while keeping the cost of the protection to a minimum. Exhibit 43 provides information on options prices for Relais Corporation. Note that each put contract represents one share.

EXHIBIT 43   One-Month Put Options on Relais Corporation

	Option A	Option B	Option C
Strike	€40.00	€42.50	€45.00
Price	€1.45	€1.72	€3.46
Delta	−0.4838	−0.5385	−0.7762
Gamma	0.0462	0.0460	0.0346

1. Discuss an options strategy that McLaire can implement to hedge his fund's portfolio against a short-term decline in the share price of Relais Corp.

Solution to 1: McLaire can purchase a protective put with the intent of selling it soon after the earnings announcement. He expects that the maximum drawdown from the current price of €42.00 will be 10%, to €37.80. This expectation narrows the choice of put options based on the following breakeven prices:

Put strike 40.0 (option A): €40.00 − €1.45 = €38.55
Put strike 42.5 (option B): €42.50 − €1.72 = €40.78
Put strike 45.0 (option C): €45.00 − €3.46 = €41.54

The put with strike price of 42.50 (option B) best fits the objective of keeping the cost of adequate protection to a minimum. This is because the 40-strike put (option A) offers limited protection because it is profitable only below €38.55, offering a profit of just €0.75 if the stock falls to €37.80. Furthermore, the 42.50-strike put offers a larger profit per unit of premium paid than the 45.00-strike put if the stock price decreases to €37.80.

Put strike 42.5: (€40.78 − €37.80)/€1.72 = 1.73
Put strike 45.0: (€41.54 − €37.80)/€3.46 = 1.08

The 42.50 strike put has a lower delta (= −0.5385) in absolute value terms than the 45.0 strike put (delta = −0.7762), but it has more gamma. If Relais Corporation's stock falls to €37.80 per share during the life of the option, a position in the 42.50 strike put will benefit from having a larger gamma (= 0.0460) compared with the 45.0 strike put (gamma = 0.0346).

Therefore, McLaire purchases 100,000 of the 42.50-strike puts at €1.72 for a total cost of €172,000.

If Relais Corporation's soon-to-be announced earnings miss the market's expectations, the stock is likely to fall, thereby increasing the long put value and partially offsetting the loss on the stock. If the earnings meet market expectations, then the put may be sold at a price near its purchase price. If the earnings are better than expected and the stock price rises, then the put will decline in value. McLaire would no longer need the "insurance," and he would sell the put position, thereby recovering part of the purchase price.

Situation B: One week later, just after Relais Corporation's earnings release:

McLaire holds the 100,000 puts with the exercise price of €42.50. Seven days have passed since the options' purchase; Relais has just released its earnings, and they turn out to be surprisingly good. Earnings beat the consensus estimate, and immediately after the announcement the stock price rises by 5% to €44.10. Exhibit 44 shows the options' prices on the day of the announcement, after the stock price has increased to €44.10 (the implied volatility remains unchanged).

EXHIBIT 44   23-Day Put Options on Relais

	Option A	Option B	Option C
Strike	€40.00	€42.50	€45.00
Price	€0.15	€0.66	€1.85

EXHIBIT 44   (Continued)

Delta	−0.0923	−0.3000	−0.5916
Gamma	0.0218	0.0460	0.0514
Price Change	−90%	−62%	−47%
Loss on 100,000 Puts from Price Change	€130,000	€106,000	€161,000

2. Discuss how the strategy fared and how McLaire should proceed, assuming earnings beat the consensus estimate and Relais's stock price rises by 5% to €44.10.

Solution to 2:   The 42.50-strike put held by McLaire has 23 days to expiration. The price has declined from €1.72 to €0.66 (−62%), for a total loss of €106,000 (= [€1.72 − €0.66] × 100,000). This is less than the loss McLaire would have incurred if he had purchased the other options. At the same time the value of the 100,000 Relais shares held by the fund has increased by €210,000 (= ($44.10 − $42.00) × 100,000). Now that the earnings announcement has been made, McLaire no longer needs the protection from the put options, so he should sell them and recover €66,000 from the original €172,000 put purchase price.

SUMMARY

This reading on options strategies shows a number of ways in which market participants might use options to enhance returns or to reduce risk to better meet portfolio objectives. The following are the key points.

- Buying a call and writing a put on the same underlying with the same strike price and expiration creates a synthetic long position (i.e., a synthetic long forward position).
- Writing a call and buying a put on the same underlying with the same strike price and expiration creates a synthetic short position (i.e., a synthetic short forward position).
- A synthetic long put position consists of a short stock and long call position in which the call strike price equals the price at which the stock is shorted.
- A synthetic long call position consists of a long stock and long put position in which the put strike price equals the price at which the stock is purchased.
- Delta is the change in an option's price for a change in price of the underlying, all else equal.
- Gamma is the change in an option's delta for a change in price of the underlying, all else equal.
- Vega is the change in an option's price for a change in volatility of the underlying, all else equal.
- Theta is the daily change in an option's price, all else equal.
- A covered call, in which the holder of a stock writes a call giving someone the right to buy the shares, is one of the most common uses of options by individual investors.
- Covered calls can be used to change an investment's risk–reward profile by effectively enhancing yield or reducing/exiting a position when the shares hit a target price.
- A covered call position has a limited maximum return because of the transfer of the right tail of the return distribution to the option buyer.

- The maximum loss of a covered call position is less than the maximum loss of the underlying shares alone, but the covered call carries the potential for an opportunity loss if the underlying shares rise sharply.
- A protective put is the simultaneous holding of a long stock position and a long put on the same asset. The put provides protection or insurance against a price decline.
- The continuous purchase of protective puts maintains the upside potential of the portfolio, while limiting downside volatility. The cost of the puts must be carefully considered, however, because this activity may be expensive. Conversely, the occasional purchase of a protective put to deal with a bearish short-term outlook can be a reasonable risk-reducing strategy.
- The maximum loss with a protective put is limited because the downside risk is transferred to the option writer in exchange for the payment of the option premium.
- With an option spread, an investor buys one option and writes another of the same type. This approach reduces the position cost but caps the maximum payoff.
- A bull spread expresses a bullish view on the underlying and is normally constructed by buying a call option and writing another call option with a higher exercise price (both options have same underlying and same expiry).
- A bear spread expresses a bearish view on the underlying and is normally constructed by buying a put option and writing another put option with a lower exercise price (both options have same underlying and same expiry).
- With either a bull spread or a bear spread, both the maximum gain and the maximum loss are known and limited.
- A long (short) straddle is an option combination in which the investor buys (sells) puts and calls with the same exercise price and expiration date. The long (short) straddle investor expects increased (stable/decreased) volatility and typically requires a large (small/no) price movement in the underlying asset in order to make a profit.
- A collar is an option position in which the investor is long shares of stock and simultaneously writes a call with an exercise price above the current stock price and buys a put with an exercise price below the current stock price. A collar limits the range of investment outcomes by sacrificing upside gain in exchange for providing downside protection.
- A long (short) calendar spread involves buying (selling) a long-dated option and writing (buying) a shorter-dated option of the same type with the same exercise price. A long (short) calendar spread is used when the investment outlook is flat (volatile) in the near term but greater (lesser) return movements are expected in the future.
- Implied volatility is the expected volatility an underlying asset's return and is derived from an option pricing model (i.e., the Black–Scholes–Merton model) as the value that equates the model price of an option to its market price.
- When implied volatilities of OTM options exceed those of ATM options, the implied volatility curve is a volatility smile. The more common shape is a volatility skew, in which implied volatility increases for OTM puts and decreases for OTM calls, as the strike price moves away from the current price.
- The implied volatility surface is a 3-D plot, for put and call options on the same underlying, showing expiration time (x-axis), strike prices (y-axis), and implied volatilities (z-axis). It simultaneously displays volatility skew and the term structure of implied volatility.
- Options, like all derivatives, should always be used in connection with a well-defined investment objective. When using options strategies, it is important to have a view on the expected change in implied volatility and the direction of movement of the underlying asset.

PROBLEMS

The following information relates to Questions 1–10

Aline Nuñes, a junior analyst, works in the derivatives research division of an international securities firm. Nuñes's supervisor, Cátia Pereira, asks her to conduct an analysis of various option trading strategies relating to shares of three companies: IZD, QWY, and XDF. On 1 February, Nuñes gathers selected option premium data on the companies, presented in Exhibit 1.

EXHIBIT 1   Share Price and Option Premiums as of 1 February (share prices and option premiums in €)

Company	Share Price	Call Premium	Option Date/ Strike	Put Premium
		9.45	April/87.50	1.67
IZD	93.93	2.67	April/95.00	4.49
		1.68	April/97.50	5.78
		4.77	April/24.00	0.35
QWY	28.49	3.96	April/25.00	0.50
		0.32	April/31.00	3.00
		0.23	February/80.00	5.52
XDF	74.98	2.54	April/75.00	3.22
		2.47	December/80.00	9.73

Nuñes considers the following option strategies relating to IZD:

Strategy 1: Constructing a synthetic long put position in IZD
Strategy 2: Buying 100 shares of IZD and writing the April €95.00 strike call option on IZD
Strategy 3: Implementing a covered call position in IZD using the April €97.50 strike option

Nuñes next reviews the following option strategies relating to QWY:

Strategy 4: Implementing a protective put position in QWY using the April €25.00 strike option
Strategy 5: Buying 100 shares of QWY, buying the April €24.00 strike put option, and writing the April €31.00 strike call option
Strategy 6: Implementing a bear spread in QWY using the April €25.00 and April €31.00 strike options

Finally, Nuñes considers two option strategies relating to XDF:

Strategy 7: Writing both the April €75.00 strike call option and the April €75.00 strike put option on XDF

Strategy 8: Writing the February €80.00 strike call option and buying the December €80.00 strike call option on XDF

1. Strategy 1 would require Nuñes to buy:
   A. shares of IZD.
   B. a put option on IZD.
   C. a call option on IZD.
2. Based on Exhibit 1, Nuñes should expect Strategy 2 to be *least* profitable if the share price of IZD at option expiration is:
   A. less than €91.26.
   B. between €91.26 and €95.00.
   C. more than €95.00.
3. Based on Exhibit 1, the breakeven share price of Strategy 3 is *closest* to:
   A. €92.25.
   B. €95.61.
   C. €95.82.
4. Based on Exhibit 1, the maximum loss per share that would be incurred by implementing Strategy 4 is:
   A. €2.99.
   B. €3.99.
   C. unlimited.
5. Strategy 5 is *best* described as a:
   A. collar.
   B. straddle.
   C. bear spread.
6. Based on Exhibit 1, Strategy 5 offers:
   A. unlimited upside.
   B. a maximum profit of €2.48 per share.
   C. protection against losses if QWY's share price falls below €28.14.
7. Based on Exhibit 1, the breakeven share price for Strategy 6 is *closest* to:
   A. €22.50.
   B. €28.50.
   C. €33.50.
8. Based on Exhibit 1, the maximum gain per share that could be earned if Strategy 7 is implemented is:
   A. €5.74.
   B. €5.76.
   C. unlimited.
9. Based on Exhibit 1, the *best* explanation for Nuñes to implement Strategy 8 would be that, between the February and December expiration dates, she expects the share price of XDF to:
   A. decrease.
   B. remain unchanged.
   C. increase.
10. Over the past few months, Nuñes and Pereira have followed news reports on a proposed merger between XDF and one of its competitors. A government antitrust committee is

currently reviewing the potential merger. Pereira expects the share price to move sharply upward or downward depending on whether the committee decides to approve or reject the merger next week. Pereira asks Nuñes to recommend an option trade that might allow the firm to benefit from a significant move in the XDF share price regardless of the direction of the move.

The option trade that Nuñes should recommend relating to the government committee's decision is a:

A. collar.

B. bull spread.

C. long straddle.

The following information relates to Questions 11–16

Stanley Kumar Singh, CFA, is the risk manager at SKS Asset Management. He works with individual clients to manage their investment portfolios. One client, Sherman Hopewell, is worried about how short-term market fluctuations over the next three months might impact his equity position in Walnut Corporation. Although Hopewell is concerned about short-term downside price movements, he wants to remain invested in Walnut shares because he remains positive about its long-term performance. Hopewell has asked Singh to recommend an option strategy that will keep him invested in Walnut shares while protecting against a short-term price decline. Singh gathers the information in Exhibit 1 to explore various strategies to address Hopewell's concerns.

Another client, Nigel French, is a trader who does not currently own shares of Walnut Corporation. French has told Singh that he believes that Walnut shares will experience a large move in price after the upcoming quarterly earnings release in two weeks. French also tells Singh, however, that he is unsure which direction the stock will move. French asks Singh to recommend an option strategy that would allow him to profit should the share price move in either direction.

A third client, Wanda Tills, does not currently own Walnut shares and has asked Singh to explain the profit potential of three strategies using options in Walnut: a long straddle, a bull call spread, and a bear put spread. In addition, Tills asks Singh to explain the gamma of a call option. In response, Singh prepares a memo to be shared with Tills that provides a discussion of gamma and presents his analysis on three option strategies:

Strategy 1:   A long straddle position at the $67.50 strike option

Strategy 2:   A bull call spread using the $65 and $70 strike options

Strategy 3:   A bear put spread using the $65 and $70 strike options

EXHIBIT 1   Walnut Corporation Current Stock Price: $67.79
Walnut Corporation European Options

Exercise Price	Market Call Price	Call Delta	Market Put Price	Put Delta
$55.00	$12.83	1.00	$0.24	−0.05
$65.00	$3.65	0.91	$1.34	−0.29
$67.50	$1.99	0.63	$2.26	−0.42
$70.00	$0.91	0.37	$3.70	−0.55
$80.00	$0.03	0.02	$12.95	−0.76

Note: Each option has 106 days remaining until expiration.

11. The option strategy Singh is *most likely* to recommend to Hopewell is a:
    A. collar.
    B. covered call.
    C. protective put.

12. The option strategy that Singh is *most likely* to recommend to French is a:
    A. straddle.
    B. bull spread.
    C. collar.

13. Based on Exhibit 1, Strategy 1 is profitable when the share price at expiration is *closest* to:
    A. $63.00.
    B. $65.24.
    C. $69.49.

14. Based on Exhibit 1, the maximum profit, on a per share basis, from investing in Strategy 2, is *closest* to:
    A. $2.26.
    B. $2.74.
    C. $5.00.

15. Based on Exhibit 1, and assuming the market price of Walnut's shares at expiration is $66, the profit or loss, on a per share basis, from investing in Strategy 3, is *closest* to:
    A. $2.36.
    B. $1.64.
    C. $2.64.

16. Based on the data in Exhibit 1, Singh would advise Tills that the call option with the *largest* gamma would have a strike price *closest* to:
    A. $ 55.00.
    B. $ 67.50.
    C. $ 80.00.

The following information relates to Questions 17–23

Anneke Ngoc is an analyst who works for an international bank, where she advises high-net-worth clients on option strategies. Ngoc prepares for a meeting with a US-based client, Mani Ahlim.

Ngoc notes that Ahlim recently inherited an account containing a large Brazilian real (BRL) cash balance. Ahlim intends to use the inherited funds to purchase a vacation home in the United States with an expected purchase price of US$750,000 in six months. Ahlim is concerned that the Brazilian real will weaken against the US dollar over the next six months. Ngoc considers potential hedge strategies to reduce the risk of a possible adverse currency movement over this time period.

Ahlim holds shares of Pselftarô Ltd. (PSÔL), which has a current share price of $37.41. Ahlim is bullish on PSÔL in the long term. He would like to add to his long position but is concerned about a moderate price decline after the quarterly earnings announcement next month, in April. Ngoc recommends a protective put position with a strike price of $35 using May options and a $40/$50 bull call spread using December options. Ngoc gathers selected PSÔL option prices for May and December, which are presented in Exhibit 1.

EXHIBIT 1   Selected PSÔL Option Prices (all prices in US dollars)

Exercise Price	Expiration Month	Call Price	Put Price
35	May	3.00	1.81
40	December	6.50	10.25
50	December	4.25	20.50

Ahlim also expresses interest in trading options on India's NIFTY 50 (National Stock Exchange Fifty) Index. Ngoc gathers selected one-month option prices and implied volatility data, which are presented in Exhibit 2. India's NIFTY 50 Index is currently trading at a level of 11,610.

EXHIBIT 2   Selected One-Month Option Prices and Implied Volatility Data: NIFTY 50 Index (all prices in Indian rupees)

Exercise Price	Market Call Price	Market Put Price	Implied Call Volatility	Implied Put Volatility
11,200	526.00	61.90	5.87	17.72
11,400	365.45	102.60	10.80	17.01
11,600	240.00	165.80	12.26	16.44
11,800	135.00	213.00	12.14	16.39
12,000	65.80	370.00	11.98	16.56

Ngoc reviews a research report that includes a one-month forecast of the NIFTY 50 Index. The report's conclusions are presented in Exhibit 3.

EXHIBIT 3   Research Report Conclusions: NIFTY 50 Index

One-month forecast:

- We have a neutral view on the direction of the index's move over the next month.
- The rate of the change in underlying prices (vega) is expected to increase.
- The implied volatility of index options is expected to be above the consensus forecast.

Based on these conclusions, Ngoc considers various NIFTY 50 Index option strategies for Ahlim.

17. Which of the following positions would best mitigate Ahlim's concern regarding the purchase of his vacation home in six months?
    A. Sell an at-the-money six-month BRL/USD call option.
    B. Purchase an at-the-money six-month USD/BRL put option.
    C. Take a short position in a six-month BRL/USD futures contract.
18. Based on Exhibit 1, the maximum loss per share of Ngoc's recommended PSÔL protective put position is:
    A. $0.60.
    B. $2.41.
    C. $4.22.

19. Based on Exhibit 1, the breakeven price per share of Ngoc's recommended PSÔL protective put position is:
    A. $35.60.
    B. $36.81.
    C. $39.22.
20. Based on Exhibit 1, the maximum profit per share of Ngoc's recommended PSÔL bull call spread is:
    A. $2.25.
    B. $7.75.
    C. $12.25.
21. Based on Exhibit 1, the breakeven price per share of Ngoc's recommended PSÔL bull call spread is:
    A. $42.25.
    B. $47.75.
    C. $52.25.
22. Based on Exhibit 2, the NIFTY 50 Index implied volatility data *most likely* indicate a:
    A. risk reversal.
    B. volatility skew.
    C. volatility smile.
23. Based on Exhibit 3, which of the following NIFTY 50 Index option strategies should Ngoc recommend to Ahlim?
    A. Buy a straddle.
    B. Buy a call option.
    C. Buy a calendar spread.

CHAPTER 9

SWAPS, FORWARDS, AND FUTURES STRATEGIES

Barbara Valbuzzi, CFA

LEARNING OUTCOMES

The candidate should be able to:

- demonstrate how interest rate swaps, forwards, and futures can be used to modify a portfolio's risk and return;
- demonstrate how currency swaps, forwards, and futures can be used to modify a portfolio's risk and return;
- demonstrate how equity swaps, forwards, and futures can be used to modify a portfolio's risk and return;
- demonstrate the use of volatility derivatives and variance swaps;
- demonstrate the use of derivatives to achieve targeted equity and interest rate risk exposures;
- demonstrate the use of derivatives in asset allocation, rebalancing, and inferring market expectations.

1. MANAGING INTEREST RATE RISK WITH SWAPS

There are many ways in which investment managers and investors can use swaps, forwards, futures, and volatility derivatives. The typical applications of these derivatives involve modifying investment positions for hedging purposes or for taking directional bets, creating or replicating desired payoffs, implementing asset allocation and portfolio rebalancing decisions, and even inferring current market expectations. The following table shows some common uses of these derivatives in portfolio management and the types of derivatives used by investors and portfolio managers.

Common Uses of Swaps, Forwards, and Futures	Typical Derivatives Used
Modifying Portfolio Returns and Risk Exposures (Hedging and Directional Bets)	Interest Rate, Currency, and Equity Swaps and Futures; Fixed-Income Futures; Variance Swaps
Creating Desired Payoffs	Forwards, Futures, Total Return Swaps
Performing Asset Allocation and Portfolio Rebalancing	Equity Index Futures, Government Bond Futures, Index Swaps
Inferring Market Expectations for Interest Rates, Inflation, and Volatility	Fed Funds Futures, Inflation Swaps, VIX Futures

It is important for an informed investment professional to understand how swaps, forwards, futures, and volatility derivatives can be used and their associated risk–return trade-offs. Therefore, the purpose of this reading is to illustrate ways in which these derivatives might be used in typical investment situations. Sections 2–4 of this reading show how swaps, forwards, and futures can be used to modify the risk exposure of an existing position. Sections 5–6 provide a discussion on derivatives on volatility. Sections 7–9 demonstrate a series of applications showing ways in which a portfolio manager might solve an investment problem with these derivatives. The reading concludes with a summary.

1.1. Changing Risk Exposures with Swaps, Futures, and Forwards

Financial managers can use swaps, forwards, and futures markets to quickly and efficiently alter the underlying risk exposure of their asset portfolios or anticipated investment transactions. This section covers a variety of common examples that use swaps, futures, and forwards.

1.1.1. Managing Interest Rate Risk

1.1.1.1. Interest Rate Swaps An interest rate swap is an over-the-counter (OTC) contract between two parties that agree to exchange cash flows on specified payment dates—one based on a *variable* (floating) interest rate and the other based on a *fixed* rate (the "swap rate")—determined at the time the swap is initiated. The swap tenor is when the swap is agreed to expire. Both interest rates are applied to the swap's notional value to determine the size of each payment. Normally, the resulting two payments (one fixed, one floating) are in the same currency but will not be equal, so they are typically netted, with the party owing the greater amount paying the difference to the other party. In this manner, a party that currently has a fixed (floating) risk or other obligation can effectively convert it into a floating (fixed) one.

Interest rate swaps are among the most widely used instruments to manage interest rate risk. In particular, they are designed to manage the risk on cash flows arising from investors' assets and liabilities. Interest rate swaps and futures can also be used to modify the risk and return profile of a portfolio. This is associated with managing a portfolio of bonds that generally involves controlling the portfolio's duration. Although futures are commonly used to make duration changes, swaps can also be used, and we shall see how in this reading. Finally, interest rate swaps are used by financial institutions to hedge the interest rate risk exposure deriving from the issuance of financial instruments sold to clients. Example 1 shows how an interest rate swap is used to convert floating-rate securities into fixed-rate securities. Here the firm initially expects continuing low interest rates, so it issues floating-rate bonds. But after concluding that rates are likely to increase, the firm seeks to convert its interest rate risk to a fixed obligation, even though doing so means making higher payments up front.

EXAMPLE 1   Using an Interest Rate Swap to Convert Floating-Rate Securities into Fixed-Rate Securities

An investment firm has sold £20 million of three-year floating-rate bonds that pay a semiannual coupon equal to the six-month market reference rate plus 50 bps. A few days later, the firm's outlook changes substantially, and it now expects higher rates in the future. The firm enters into an interest rate swap with a tenor of approximately three years and semiannual payments, where the firm pays a fixed par swap rate of 1.25% and receives the six-month reference rate. The swap settlement dates are the same as the coupon payment dates on the floating-rate bonds. At the first swap settlement date, the six-month reference rate is 0.75%.

Analysis: At the first coupon payment and swap settlement date, the six-month reference rate is 0.75% (annualized). This means that on the swap the investment firm will make a net payment of £50,000 as follows:

- Receive based on the reference rate: 0.75% × £20 million × (180/360) = £75,000.
- Pay based on the fixed rate: 1.25% × £20 million × (180/360) = £125,000.
- Net payment *made* by the firm to swap dealer: £125,000 − £75,000 = £50,000.

At the same time, the first semiannual coupon payment on the securities will be (0.75% + 0.50%) × £20 million × (180/360) = £125,000.

The total payment made by the investment firm on the securities and the swap is £175,000 (= £125,000 + £50,000).

Now assume that as we move forward to the second coupon payment and swap settlement date, interest rates have increased and the six-month reference rate is 1.50%.

On the swap, the investment firm will receive a net payment of £25,000 as follows:

- Receive based on the new reference rate: 1.50% × £20 million × (180/360) = £150,000.

- Pay based on the fixed rate: $1.25\% \times £20$ million $\times (180/360) = £125{,}000$.
- Net payment *received* by the firm: $£150{,}000 - £125{,}000 = £25{,}000$.

The coupon payment on the securities will be $(1.50\% + 0.50\%) \times £20$ million $\times (180/360) = £200{,}000$.

The total payment made by the investment firm on the securities and the swap is again $£175{,}000\ (= £200{,}000 - £25{,}000)$.

The investment firm has effectively fixed its all-in borrowing costs. Since this fixed cost is synthesized by a combination of the underlying debt position and the derivative contract, it can be described as a synthetic fixed security.

Why should the investment firm decide to pay a fixed rate of 1.25%, on a semiannual basis, for the remaining life of the securities when the reference rate is only 0.75% today? The reason is that the firm's outlook is now for higher rates in the future, as expressed by market participants in the upward-sloping yield curve. An upward-sloping yield curve reflects that investors require higher risk premium compensation for holding longer-term securities.

The agreed-on fixed rate on the swap is based on the term structure of rates at the time the deal is initiated. If the term structure changes, the new fixed rate agreed on by the counterparties on a swap with the same residual time to maturity as the original one will be different from the original rate. This means that the market value of the swap will become positive or negative. In particular, the investment firm in Example 1 has managed to fix the interest rate on future payments but has given away the opportunity to benefit from possible lower interest rates in the future. If the term structure of interest rates has a parallel shift downward, meaning that all rates across tenors decrease, the value of the swap will become negative from the perspective of the fixed-rate payer, depending on the new swap market fixed rate. The investment firm has managed to achieve the desired fixed profile of future cash flows, but it might incur a loss if the firm wants to unwind the interest rate swap before maturity. Alternatively, if rates rise, as now expected, the swap can be unwound at a profit by the same reasoning in reverse: The value of the swap becomes positive from the fixed-rate payer's view; fixed-rate payment paid is less than floating-rate payment received.

This explanation introduces the concepts of marking to market of the swap and how swaps can be used in fixed-income portfolio management with the objective to hedge the changes in value of a portfolio with fixed cash flows.

When a bond portfolio is fully hedged, its value is immunized with respect to changes in yields. This can be stated as $\Delta P = (N_s)(\Delta S)$, where ΔP is the change in the value of the bond portfolio and ΔS is the change in the value of the swap for a given change in interest rates. The notional principal of the swap (N_s) will be determined as $N_s = \Delta P/\Delta S$. To reduce changes in value of a fixed-rate portfolio, the manager will want to lower the overall duration by exchanging part of this fixed-rate income stream for a floating-rate stream. This can be done by entering an interest rate swap where the portfolio manager will pay the fixed rate and receive the floating rate.

It is important to keep in mind that most of the time, the hedging instrument and the asset or portfolio to be hedged are imperfect substitutes. The result is a market risk, called *basis risk* or *spread risk*—the difference between the market performance of the asset and the derivative instrument used to hedge it. When using an interest rate swap to hedge, it is possible that the changes in the underlying rate of the derivative contract, and thus in the value of the swap, do not perfectly mirror changes in the value of the bond portfolio.

Furthermore, the composition of the bond portfolio could bear additional market risks other than interest rate risk. For instance, suppose a portfolio of corporate bonds is hedged with an interest rate swap. In this case, even if interest rate risk is hedged, the investor is still exposed to credit spread risk.

The main underlying assumptions we will use are that the change in value of the bond portfolio can be approximated by using the concept of modified duration,[1] the yield curve is flat, and it is affected only by parallel shifts. Furthermore, we assume here that the portfolio and the derivative contract used to hedge are perfect substitutes.

A measure for the change in the value of the bond portfolio (ΔP) for a change in interest rates is given by the portfolio's modified duration, $MDUR_P$. The same measure calculated for the interest rate swap, $MDUR_S$, is used to determine the change in the value of the swap, ΔS. The target modified duration for the combined portfolio is $MDUR_T$, and MV_P is the market value of the bond portfolio.

By properly choosing the notional value and the tenor of the swap, the portfolio manager can achieve a combination of the existing portfolio and the interest rate swap that sets the overall portfolio duration to the target duration: $(MV_P)(MDUR_P) + (N_S)(MDUR_S) = (MV_P)(MDUR_T)$.

The equivalence $\Delta P = (N_S)(\Delta S)$ becomes $(MV_P)(MDUR_T - MDUR_P) = (N_S)(MDUR_S)$. To find the swap notional principal, N_S, we need to solve for the following formula:

$$N_S = \left(\frac{MDUR_T - MDUR_P}{MDUR_S} \right)(MV_P) \tag{1}$$

The modified duration of a swap ($MDUR_S$) is the net of the modified durations of the equivalent positions in fixed- and floating-rate bonds. Thus, the position of the pay-fixed party in a pay-fixed, receive-floating swap has the modified duration of a floating-rate bond minus the modified duration of a fixed-rate bond, where the floating- and fixed-rate bonds have cash flows equivalent to the corresponding cash flows of the swap. A pay-fixed, receive-floating swap has a negative (positive) duration from the perspective of a fixed-rate payer (receiver), because the duration of a fixed-rate bond is positive and larger than the duration of a floating-rate bond, which is near zero. Moreover, the negative duration of this position to the fixed-rate payer/floating-rate receiver makes sense in that the position would be expected to benefit from rising interest rates.

---

[1] Although there are various duration measures, we are concerned here with modified duration, which is an approximate measure of how a bond price changes given a small change in the level of interest rates.

EXAMPLE 2   Using an Interest Rate Swap to Achieve a
Target Duration

Consider a portfolio manager with an investment portfolio of €50 million of fixed-rate
German bonds with an average modified duration of 5.5. Because he fears that interest
rates will rise, he wants to reduce the modified duration of the portfolio to 4.5, but
he does not want to sell any of the securities. One way to do this would be to add a
negative-duration position by entering into an interest rate swap where he pays the fixed
rate and receives the floating. A two-year interest rate swap has an estimated modified duration of −2.00 from the perspective of the fixed-rate payer.
    Demonstrate how the manager can use this interest rate swap to achieve the target
modified duration.

Solution: The portfolio manager's goal is for the bonds and the swap to combine to
create a portfolio with a market value of €50 million and a target modified duration of
4.5. This relationship can be expressed as follows:

$$€50,000,000(5.50) + (N_S)(MDUR_S) = €50,000,000(4.50),$$

where

$$N_S = \text{Interest rate swap's notional principal}$$

$$MDUR_S = \text{Interest rate swap's modified duration, set equal to } {-2.00}$$

So, the notional principal of this interest rate swap that the manager should use is
determined using Equation 1, as follows:

$$N_S = [(4.50 - 5.50)/(-2.00)] \times €50,000,000 = €25,000,000.$$

2. MANAGING INTEREST RATE RISK WITH FORWARDS, FUTURES, AND FIXED-INCOME FUTURES

The market in short-term interest rate derivatives is large and liquid, and the instruments
involved are forward rate agreements (FRAs) and interest rate futures. A forward rate agreement is an OTC derivative instrument that is used mainly to hedge a loan expected to be taken
out in the near future or to hedge against changes in the level of interest rates in the future. In
fact, with advanced settled at maturity, an FRA will settle only the discounted difference
between the interest rate agreed on in the contract and the actual rate prevailing at the time of
settlement, applied on the notional amount of the contract. In general, managing short-term
interest rate risk with an interest rate forward contract can also be done with an interest rate
futures contract. Forwards, like swaps, are OTC instruments and are especially useful because
they can be customized, but they do have counterparty risk. In contrast, exchange-traded

interest rate futures contracts are standardized and guaranteed by a clearinghouse, so counter-party risk is virtually zero.[2]

Forward rate agreements and interest rate futures are widely used to hedge the risk associated with interest rates changing from the time a loan or a deposit is anticipated until it is actually implemented. Example 3 demonstrates how interest rate futures are used to lock in an interest rate.

EXAMPLE 3   Using Interest Rate Futures to Lock in an Interest Rate

Amanda Wright, the chief investment officer (CIO) of a US-based philanthropic foundation is expecting a donation of $30 million in two months' time from a member of the foundation's founding family. This significant donation will then be invested for three months and subsequently will be divided into smaller grants to be made to medical and educational institutions supported by the foundation. The current (i.e., spot) three-month reference rate is 2.40% (annualized). The CIO expects interest rates to fall, and she decides to hedge the rate on the deposit with Eurodollar futures.

To provide background information, Eurodollar futures are cash settled on the basis of the market reference rate for an offshore deposit having a principal value of $1 million and a three-month maturity. These contracts are quoted in terms of the "IMM index"[3] that is equal to 100 less the annualized yield on the security. A 1 bp (0.01% or 0.0001) change in the value of the futures contract equates to a $25.00 movement in the contract value. Thus, the basis point value (BPV) of a $1 million face value, 90-day money market instrument is given by

$$BPV = \text{Face value} \times \left(\frac{\text{Days}}{360}\right) \times 0.01\% = \$1,000,000 \times \left(\frac{90}{360}\right) \times 0.01\% = \$25$$

Analysis: Wright buys 30 of the Eurodollar futures contracts at 97.60, locking in a forward rate of 2.40%. After two months, the donation is received and the CIO initiates the deposit at the then-lower spot rate of 2.10%. She unwinds the hedge at a futures price of 97.90, which is 30 bps higher than where the position was initiated.

The foundation will receive $180,000 from the deposit plus the hedge, as follows:

1. Interest obtained on the deposit: 2.10% × $30 million × (90/360) = $157,500.
2. Profit on the hedge is 30 bps (30 × $25 = $750), which for 30 contracts corresponds to $22,500 (= $750 × 30).

---

[2]Regulatory changes in global markets are moving both over-the-counter swaps and forward contracts toward a clearing process as well. The clearing process reduces the risk that one counterparty will default on its obligations (by requiring collateral for trades and by daily marking to market of open positions), and for this reason, the counterparty risk associated with each single trade is virtually zero. However, there is still the risk that a major counterparty will fail to carry out its obligations (e.g., Lehman Brothers), causing operational risks for investors.

[3]The IMM, or International Monetary Market, was established as a division of CME many years ago. The distinction is seldom made today because CME operates as a unified entity, but references to IMM persist today.

> This corresponds to the return on an investment at the initial three-month reference rate of 2.40%, or 2.40% × \$30 million × (90/360) = \$180,000. This calculation demonstrates that by buying the Eurodollar futures, Wright did indeed lock in a forward rate of 2.40%.

Institutional investors and bond traders can decide to use interest rate futures or fixed-income futures (also referred to as "bond futures") contracts, which are longer dated, to hedge interest rate risk exposure. The choice will depend on the maturity of the bond or portfolio to be hedged. Since they are listed, interest rate futures have a limited number of maturities. Furthermore, the nearest months' contracts have higher liquidity than the longer tenors. For these reasons, interest rate futures (e.g., Eurodollar futures) are commonly used to hedge short-term bonds, with up to two to three years remaining to maturity. When using interest rate futures to hedge a short-term bond, an effective and widely adopted technique to construct the hedge is to use a strip of futures contracts. Having measured the responsiveness of the bond to an interest rate change, it is now necessary to measure the sensitivity of each cash flow to changes in the relevant forward rate. Then, one can calculate the number of futures contracts needed to hedge the interest rate exposure for each cash flow. Fixed-income futures contracts remain, however, the preferred instrument to hedge bond positions, given that their liquidity is very high. This is especially true for US Treasury bond futures.

2.1. Fixed-Income Futures

Portfolio managers that want to hedge the duration risk of their bond portfolios usually use fixed-income futures. They are standardized forward contracts listed on an exchange that have as underlying a basket of deliverable bonds with remaining maturities within a predefined range. The most liquid contracts include T-note and T-bond futures listed on the Chicago Board of Trade or the Chicago Mercantile Exchange. Contracts expire in March, June, September, and December, and the underlying assets include Treasury bills, notes, and bonds. In Europe, the most liquid and most heavily traded fixed-income futures are traded on the Eurex, and these are the Euro-Bund (FGBL), Euro-Bobl (FGBM), and Euro-Schatz (FCBS).[4] These futures contracts have German federal government–issued bonds with different maturities as underlying. The Schatz is also known as the short bund futures contract because the maturities of the underlying bonds range from 21 to 27 months. In contrast, maturities of underlying bonds range from 4.5 years to 5.5 years for the Bobl futures contract and are even longer (between 10 years and 30 years) for the Bund futures contract.

Bond futures are used by hedgers to protect an existing bond portfolio against adverse interest rate movements and by arbitrageurs to gain from price differences in equivalent instruments.

A fixed-income futures contract has as its underlying reference assets a basket of deliverable bonds with a range of different coupon levels and maturity dates. Most futures contracts are closed before delivery or rolled into the next contract month. However, in the case of delivery,

---

[4]"Bobl" comes from the German term "Bundesobligation," which corresponds to a federal government bond. "Schatz" is the English word for "Bundesschatzanweisungen," or "Schätze," which is two-year debt issued by the German federal government, whereas "Bunds" represent long-term obligations.

the futures contract seller has the obligation to deliver and the right to choose which security to deliver. For this reason, the duration of a futures contract is usually consistent with the forward behavior of the cheapest underlying deliverable bond. This is called the cheapest-to-deliver (CTD) bond, the eligible bond that the seller will most likely choose to deliver under the futures contract if he decides to deliver (rather than close out the futures position). The price sensitivity of the bond futures will, therefore, reflect the duration of the CTD bond.

Within the underlying basket of bonds, the seller will deliver the CTD bond, the one that presents the greatest profit or smallest loss at delivery. To provide a guide for choosing the CTD bond, the concept of the conversion factor (CF) has been introduced. Given that the short side has the option of delivering any eligible security, a conversion factor invoicing system that allows for a less biased comparison in choosing among deliverable bonds has been established. In fact, the amount the futures contract seller receives at delivery will depend on the conversion factor that, when multiplied by the futures settlement price, will generate a price at which the deliverable bond would trade if its coupon were the notional coupon of the futures contract specification (e.g., 6% coupon and 20 years to maturity). The principal invoice amount at maturity is given in the following equation:[5]

$$\text{Principal invoice amount} = (\text{Futures settlement price}/100) \times CF \times \text{Contract size.} \tag{2}$$

The cheapest-to-deliver bond is determined on the basis of duration, relative bond prices, and yield levels. In particular, a bond with a low (high) coupon rate, a long (short) maturity, and thus a long (short) duration will most likely be the CTD bond if the market yield is above (below) the notional yield of the fixed-income futures contract. The notional yield is usually in line with the prevailing interest rate.

The pricing discrepancy between the price of the cash security and that of the fixed-income futures is the basis. It is determined by the spot cash price less the futures price multiplied by the conversion factor. The possibility of physical delivery of the underlying asset guarantees convergence of futures and spot prices on the delivery date. In fact, the no-arbitrage condition requires the basis to be zero on the delivery date; otherwise, substantial arbitrage profits can be made. However, basis traders look for arbitrage opportunities by capitalizing on relatively small pricing differences. If the basis is negative, a trader would make a profit by "buying the basis"—that is, purchasing the bond and shorting the futures. In contrast, the trader would make a profit by "selling the basis" when the basis is positive; in this case, she would sell the bond and buy the futures. Example 4 demonstrates how to determine the CTD bond for delivery under a Treasury bond futures contract.

EXAMPLE 4   Delivery on a Fixed-Income Futures Contract

A trader has sold 10-year US Treasury bond futures contracts expiring in June and now has the obligation to deliver and the right to choose which security to deliver (the CTD bond). The futures contract reference security is a US Treasury bond with 20 years to

---

[5]If there is accrued interest due on the CTD bond, the futures contract seller will receive the following at delivery: Total invoice amount = Principal invoice amount + Accrued interest.

maturity and a coupon of 6%. The T-bond futures contract size is $100,000. The futures contract settlement price is $143.47. The trader now needs to determine which of the two bonds in the following table is cheapest to deliver.

	Bond A	Bond B
Cash Bond	T 4½ 02/15/36	T 5 05/15/37
Cash Dirty Price	$120.75	$128.50
Bond Purchase Value	$120,750	$128,500
Futures Settlement Price	143.47	143.47
Conversion Factor	0.8388	0.8883
Contract Size	$100,000	$100,000
Principal Invoice Amount	$120,342.64	$127,444.40
Delivery Gain/Loss	−$407.36 = $120,342.64 − $120,750	−$1,055.60 = $127,444.40 − $128,500

Analysis: The trader will try to maximize the difference between the amount received upon delivery, given by the futures contract settlement price (divided by 100) times the conversion factor times $100,000, and the cost of acquiring the bond for delivery, given by its market price plus any accrued interest (i.e., the dirty price). Note that this example assumes no accrued interest.

The conversion factors for both bonds are less than 1 since both bonds have a coupon lower than 6%, the coupon for the futures contract standard. Bond A can be purchased for $120,750 and Bond B for $128,500, both per $100,000 face value. These purchase prices are compared with the amounts received upon delivery. Principal invoice amounts are calculated using Equation 2, as follows:

Principal invoice amount = (Futures settlement price/100) × CF × $100,000.
Bond A: 143.47/100 × 0.8388 × $100,000 = $120,342.64.
Bond B: 143.47/100 × 0.8883 × $100,000 = $127,444.40.

The cheapest to deliver is Bond A, the 4½% T-bond with a maturity date of 02/15/36, since the loss on delivering Bond A ($407.36) is less than the loss on delivering Bond B ($1,055.60).

Continuing with the previous analysis where we hedged a portfolio of fixed-rate securities, we now determine the hedge ratio (HR) expressed as the number of fixed-income futures contracts to be sold or purchased. The relation $\Delta P = (HR)(\Delta F)$ is still valid; note that we saw it previously in the context of swaps as $\Delta P = (N_s)(\Delta S)$, where ΔP is the change in the value of the bond portfolio and ΔF is the change in the value of the fixed-income futures. The "ideal" hedge balances any change in value in the cash securities with an equal and opposite-sign change in the futures' value.

With futures, however, we have to consider the cheapest-to-deliver bond price and the conversion factor. Because the basis of the CTD bond is generally closest to zero, any change in the futures price level (ΔF) will be a reflection of the change in the value of the CTD bond adjusted by its conversion factor. By considering the relative price movement of the bond futures contract to the cheapest-to-deliver bond, we have $\Delta F = \Delta CTD/CF$. By substituting into the equation $\Delta P = (HR)(\Delta F)$, the hedge ratio becomes

$$HR = \frac{\Delta P}{\Delta CTD}(CF) \tag{3}$$

In the case where the bond to hedge is the CTD, then a hedge ratio based on the conversion factor is likely to be quite effective (given that the price of a fixed-income futures contract tends to track closely with that of the cheapest-to-deliver bond).

However, for other securities with different coupons and maturities, the number of bond futures that are used to hedge against price changes of a fixed-rate bond is calculated on the basis of a duration-based hedge ratio. Moreover, the relationship between the bond's price and its yield can also be stated in terms of basis point value and the portfolio's target modified duration, $MDUR_T$, such that the portfolio's target basis point value (BPV_T) is

$$BPV_T = MDUR_T \times 0.01\% \times MV_P \tag{4}$$

In the special case where the objective is to completely hedge the portfolio, $BPV_T = 0$. The effect of the basis point value hedge ratio ($BPVHR$) is then conceptualized as $BPV_P + BPVHR \times BPV_F = 0$. Thus, $BPVHR = -BPV_P/BPV_F$, which uses the basis point value of the portfolio to be hedged (BPV_P) and that of the futures contract (BPV_F), where

$$BPV_P = MDUR_P \times 0.01\% \times MV_P \tag{5}$$

and

$$BPV_F = BPV_{CTD}/CF \tag{6}$$

In Equation 6, the numerator is BPV_{CTD}, the basis point value of the cheapest-to-deliver bond under the futures contract, and the denominator is CF, its conversion factor. The basis point value of the cheapest-to-deliver bond is determined, in a manner analogous to Equations 4 and 5, as

$$BPV_{CTD} = MDUR_{CTD} \times 0.01\% \times MV_{CTD} \tag{7}$$

where $MV_{CTD} = $ (CTD price $/100$) $\times$ Futures contract size.

Finally, for small changes in yield, by substituting into the equation $BPVHR = -BPV_P/BPV_F$, where BPV_F becomes BPV_{CTD}/CF, in the special case of complete hedging, $BPVHR$ in terms of number of futures contracts is

$$BPVHR = \frac{-BPV_P}{BPV_{CTD}} \times \text{Conversion factor} \tag{8}$$

EXAMPLE 5   Hedging Bond Holdings with Fixed-Income Futures

A portfolio manager is holding €50 million (principal) in German bunds (DBRs) and wants to fully hedge the value of the bond investment against a rise in interest rates. The portfolio has a modified duration of 9.50 and a market value of €49,531,000. Moreover, the manager wishes to fully hedge the bond portfolio (so, $BPV_T = 0$) with a short position in Euro-Bund futures with a price of 158.33. The cheapest-to-deliver bond is the DBR 0.25% 02/15/27 that has a price of 98.14, modified duration of 8.623, and conversion factor of 0.619489. The size of the futures contract is €100,000.

Determine the following:

1. The BPV_P of the portfolio to be hedged
2. The BPV_{CTD} of the futures contract hedging instrument
3. The number of Euro-Bund futures contracts to sell to fully hedge the portfolio

Solution to 1: The basis point value of the portfolio (BPV_P), stated in terms of the change in value for a 1 bp (0.01%) change in yield, is calculated using Equation 5, as follows:

$$BPV_P = MDUR_P \times 0.01\% \times MV_P$$

Portfolio Principal	€50,000,000
Portfolio Market Value	€49,531,000
Modified Duration	9.50

$$BPV_P = 9.50 \times 0.0001 \times €49,531,000 = €47,054.45.$$

Thus, the portfolio to be hedged has a BPV_P of €47,054.45 per €50 million notional.

Solution to 2: The basis point value of the CTD bond underlying the futures contract (BPV_{CTD}) is calculated using Equation 7, as follows:

$$BPV_{CTD} = MDUR_{CTD} \times 0.01\% \times MV_{CTD}$$

Futures Hedge	
Euro-Bund Futures Price	158.33
Contract Size	€100,000
Cheapest-to-Deliver Bond	
DBR 0¼ 02/15/27 Gov't.	
Modified Duration	8.623
Bond Price	98.14
Conversion Factor	0.619489

$$BPV_{CTD} = 8.623 \times 0.0001 \times [(98.14/100) \times €100{,}000] = €84.63.$$

So, the BPV of the CTD bond (BPV_{CTD}) is €84.63.

Solution to 3: Using Equation 8 and the Solutions to 1 and 2, we have:

$$BPVHR = \frac{-BPV_P}{BPV_{CTD}} \times CF = \frac{-€47{,}054.45}{€84.63} \times 0.619489 = -344.437 \approx -344$$

Therefore, the number of Euro-Bund futures to *sell* to fully hedge the portfolio is 344 contracts.

In the real world, however, the hedging results are imperfect because (1) the hedge is done with the cheapest-to-deliver bond, and since the CTD bond can change over the holding period, the duration of the futures contract can also change; (2) the relationship between interest rates and bond prices is not linear, owing to convexity; and (3) the term structure of interest rates often changes via non-parallel moves.

Reconsidering Example 2 from before, in which the manager whose portfolio has a modified duration of 5.5 years wants to lower the duration to 4.5 years, the general principle is the same. What needs to be determined is the number of futures contracts that are required to reduce the portfolio's modified duration to the target level. In this more general case, where $MDUR_T$ (and BPV_T) is non-zero, stated in terms of basis point value and $BPVHR$, we have $BPV_P + BPVHR \times BPV_F = BPV_T$.

Solving for $BPVHR$ and substituting for BPV_F, we have the more general version of Equation 8:

$$BPVHR = \left(\frac{BPV_T - BPV_P}{BPV_F} \right)$$

$$= \left(\frac{BPV_T - BPV_P}{BPV_{CTD} / CF} \right)$$

$$= \left(\frac{BPV_T - BPV_P}{BPV_{CTD}} \right) \times CF \qquad (9)$$

EXAMPLE 6   Decreasing Portfolio Duration with Futures

Consider the portfolio manager from Example 5 who now decides to decrease the portfolio's modified duration from 9.50 to 8.50. The yield curve is flat. Additionally, we have already demonstrated that given the portfolio's market value of €49,531,000, the BPV_P is €47,054.50. Finally, assume the CTD bond underlying the Euro-Bund futures is the same as before, DBR 0.25% 02/15/27, with a BPV_{CTD} of €84.63 and a conversion factor of 0.619489.

Determine the following:

1. The BPV_T of the portfolio to be hedged
2. The number of Euro-Bund futures contracts to sell to reduce the portfolio's modified duration to 8.50

Solution to 1: Using Equation 4 with a $MDUR_T$ of 8.50, the portfolio's target basis point value (BPV_T) will be

$$BPV_T = 8.50 \times 0.0001 \times €49,531,000 = €42,101.35.$$

Solution to 2: To achieve the target modified duration of 8.50, the portfolio manager must implement a short position in Euro-Bund futures. Using the same cheapest-to-deliver bond with a BPV_{CTD} of €84.63 and a conversion factor of 0.619489, the number of Euro-Bund futures to sell to decrease the portfolio's duration is calculated using Equation 9:

$$BPVHR = \left(\frac{€42,101.35 - €47,054.50}{€84.63} \right) \times 0.619489$$

$$= -36.26 \approx -36 \text{ futures contracts}$$

Therefore, the number of Euro-Bund futures to *sell* to achieve the target portfolio duration of 8.50 is 36 contracts.

3. MANAGING CURRENCY EXPOSURE

Currency swaps, forwards, and futures can be used to effectively alter currency risk exposures. Currency risk is the risk that the value of a current or future asset (liability) in a foreign currency will decrease (increase) when converted into the domestic currency.

3.1. Currency Swaps

A currency swap is similar to an interest rate swap, but it is different in two ways: (1) The interest rates are associated with different currencies, and (2) the notional principal amounts may or may not be exchanged at the beginning and end of the swap's life.[6]

Currency swaps help the parties in the swap to hedge against the risk of exchange rate fluctuations and to achieve better rate outcomes. In particular, a **cross-currency basis swap** exchanges notional principals because the goal of the transaction is to issue at a more favorable funding rate and swap the amount back to the currency of choice. Firms that need foreign-denominated cash can obtain the funding in their local currency and then swap the local currency for the required foreign currency using a cross-currency basis swap. The swap periodically sets interest rate payments, mostly floating for floating, separately in two different currencies. The net effect is to use a loan in a local currency to take out a loan in a foreign currency while avoiding any foreign exchange risk. In fact, the exchange rate is fixed, as illustrated in Example 7.

---

[6]Although an exchange of notional principals often occurs, the parties may agree not to do this. Some types of hedge transactions are designed to hedge only foreign interest cash flows and not principal payments, so a principal exchange on a currency swap would not be necessary.

EXAMPLE 7   Cross-Currency Basis Swap

Consider a Canadian private equity (PE) firm that is executing a leveraged buyout (LBO) of a small, struggling US-based electronics manufacturer. The goal is to turn around the company by implementing new robotics technology for making servers and infrastructure devices for "bitcoin mining." Exit from the LBO via initial public offering is expected in three years. To execute the LBO and provide working capital for US operations, the PE firm needs USD40 million. The rate on a US dollar loan is the semiannual US dollar reference floating rate plus 100 bps. The PE firm discovers that it can borrow more cheaply in the local Canadian market and decides to fund the LBO in Canadian dollars (CAD) by borrowing CAD50 million for three years at the semiannual Canadian dollar reference floating rate plus 65 bps. Then it contacts a New York–based dealer and requests a quote for a three-year cross-currency basis swap with semiannual interest payments to exchange the CAD50 million into US dollars. The three-year CAD–USD cross-currency basis swap is quoted at −15 bps at a rate of USD/CAD 0.8000 (expressed as US dollars per 1 Canadian dollar). The swap agreement provides that both parties pay the semiannual reference floating rate, but the Canadian dollar rate also includes a "basis." Here the basis is the difference between interest rates in the cross-currency basis swap and those used to determine the forward exchange rates. If covered interest rate parity holds, a forward exchange rate is determined by the spot exchange rate and the interest rate differential between foreign and domestic currencies over the term of the forward rate. However, usually covered interest rate parity does not hold and thus gives rise to the basis.

The basis is quoted on the non-USD leg of the swap. "Paying" the basis would mean borrowing the other currency versus lending US dollars, whereas "receiving" the basis implies lending the other currency versus borrowing US dollars. The three-year CAD–USD cross-currency swap in this case is quoted at −15 bps. This means that the Canadian PE firm, the "lender" of the Canadian dollars in the swap, will receive the Canadian dollar reference rate, assumed to be 1.95%, minus 15 bps every six months in exchange for paying the US dollar reference rate for the US dollars it has "borrowed." Given that the PE firm pays the Canadian dollar floating rate plus 65 bps on its bank loan, the effective spread paid becomes 80 bps (= 65bps + 15 bps). This compares with a spread of 100 bps if instead it borrowed in US dollars.

Analysis: We now examine the cash flows in the cross-currency basis swap, where N is the notional principal of the Canadian dollar leg of the swap and S_0, agreed at the start, is the spot exchange rate for all payments (at inception, on interest payment dates, and at maturity). For the Canadian PE firm, this means that

$$N = CAD50 \text{ million and } S_0 = USD/CAD\ 0.8000.$$

Flows at the inception of the swap.

At inception, the Canadian PE firm delivers Canadian dollars (N) in exchange for US dollars (at a rate of $N \times S_0$).

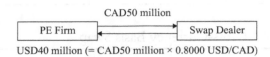

At each payment date, the PE firm makes a floating-rate payment in US dollars and receives a floating-rate payment in Canadian dollars that is passed on to the local Canadian lender. At maturity, the PE firm returns the USD40 million to the dealer and in return receives the CAD50 million, which it uses to pay off its lender.

Periodic payments.
At each swap payment date, the Canadian PE firm receives interest on Canadian dollars (N) in exchange for paying interest on US dollars ($N \times S_0$). Importantly, the "basis" component (of -15 bps) will be included along with the semiannual Canadian dollar reference floating rate.

Suppose that on the first settlement date the semiannual reference floating rate in Canadian dollars is 1.95% and the basis is -15 bps. Therefore, the Canadian dollar rate on the swap is 1.80% ($= 1.95\% - 15$ bps), and we assume the US dollar rate is 2.50% (the semiannual reference floating rate). For the PE firm, the first of a sequence of periodic cash flows resulting from the swap amounts to:

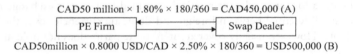

The interest rate payment on the PE firm's loan is CAD50 million $\times$ (1.95% + 0.65%) $\times$ (180/360) = CAD650,000. Considering the CAD450,000 received on the swap (A), the PE firm's net payment is CAD200,000.

At USD/CAD 0.8000, this net payment of CAD200,000 corresponds to a payment of USD160,000, which when added to the USD500,000 paid on the swap (B) totals USD660,000. Importantly, note that had the Canadian PE firm taken out the US loan instead, it would have paid periodically USD700,000 (= USD40 million $\times$ [2.50% + 1.0%] $\times$ [180/360]).

Flows at maturity.
At the maturity of the swap (and after a successful exit from the LBO via a US IPO), the Canadian PE firm swaps back US dollars in exchange for Canadian dollars (USD $\times 1/S_0$).

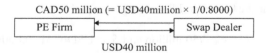

In this specific example, it is worth noting that the exchange rate was assumed not to change.

A common use of currency swaps by investors is in transactions meant to earn extra yield by investing in a foreign bond market and swapping the proceeds into the domestic currency. Given that the investment is hedged against the risk of exchange rate fluctuations, this corresponds to a synthetic domestic yield, but the repackaging allows the investor to earn a higher yield compared with the yield from direct purchase of the domestic asset, because of the level of the basis on the cross-currency swap. For example, during periods when demand for US dollars is strong relative to demand for Japanese yen (JPY), the US–Japan interest rate differential implied by the currency markets may be significantly wider than the actual interest rate differential. During such a period, a US investor might choose among the following two options: (1) Invest in short-term US Treasury bonds, or (2) use a cross-currency swap to lend an equivalent amount of US dollars and buy yen; buy short-term Japanese government debt; each period pay yen and receive US dollars on the swap; and at maturity swap an equivalent amount of yen back into US dollars. When the basis is largely negative, due to relatively weak (strong) demand for yen (US dollars) from swap market participants, the borrowing costs in yen (US dollars) are low (high), making the return from lending US dollars via a cross-currency swap particularly attractive. By choosing Option 2, the investor can earn more than he could from the investment in short-term US Treasury debt.

The rates on the cross-currency basis swaps will depend on the demand for US dollar funding, because when the US dollar reference floating rate is elevated, the counterparty receiving US dollars at initiation of the swap will be willing to receive a lower interest rate on the non-dollar currency periodic payments. Exhibit 1 shows the levels of the basis for one-year cross-currency swaps from May 2016 to April 2018 in the Australian dollar (AUD), the Canadian dollar (CAD), the euro (EUR), and the British pound (GBP) versus USD Libor (quoted as six-month USD Libor versus six-month AUD bank bills, six-month CAD Libor, six-month Euribor, and six-month GBP Libor, respectively). Cross-currency basis spreads vary over time and are driven by credit and liquidity factors, and supply and demand for cross-currency financing. As noted previously, relatively strong demand for US dollar financing against the foreign currency would require the US dollar "borrower" in the swap to accept a lower rate on the periodic foreign currency cash flows it receives—for example, the foreign periodic reference rate less the basis. As shown in Exhibit 1, during the period covered this was the case for US dollar borrowers receiving periodic swap payments in all currencies shown except the Australian dollar.

EXHIBIT 1   Historical Levels for One-Year Cross-Currency Swap Spreads (Basis) vs. Major Currencies (Six-Month Settlement)

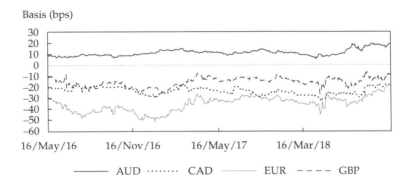

3.2. Currency Forwards and Futures

Currency forwards and futures are actively used to manage currency risk. These two financial instruments are used to hedge against undesired moves in the exchange rate by buying or selling a specified amount of foreign currency, at a defined time in the future and at an agreed-on price at contract initiation. Futures contracts are standardized and best meet dealers' and investors' needs to manage their portfolios' currency risk. Corporations often use customized forward contracts to manage the risk of cash flows in foreign currencies because they can be customized according to their needs.

For example, consider the general partner of a US-based venture capital (VC) firm that is calling down capital commitments for investment in "fintech" startups in Silicon Valley. It will receive in 30 days a payment of CAD50 million from a limited partner residing in Vancouver, British Columbia, and will immediately transfer the funds to its US dollar account. If the Canadian dollar were to depreciate versus the US dollar before the payment date, the US VC firm will receive fewer US dollars in exchange for the CAD50 million. To eliminate the foreign exchange risk associated with receiving this capital commitment, the firm can fix the price of the US dollars now via a forward contract in which it promises to sell CAD50 million for an agreed-on number of US dollars, based on the forward exchange rate, in 30 days.

EXAMPLE 8   Hedging Currency Risk with Futures

Consider the same US-based VC firm that is calling down capital commitments and will receive CAD50 million in 30 days. The general partner now decides to sell futures contracts to lock in the current USD/CAD rate. The hedge ratio is assumed to be equal to 1. The firm hedges its risk by selling Canadian dollar futures contracts with the closest expiry to the future Canadian dollar inflow.

Given a price for the Canadian dollar futures contract of USD/CAD 0.7838 (number of US dollars for 1 Canadian dollar) and a contract size of CAD100,000, determine how many Canadian dollar futures contracts the VC firm must sell to hedge its risk.

Solution: To hedge the risk of the Canadian dollar depreciating against the US dollar, the VC firm must sell 500 futures contracts:

$$\frac{\text{CAD50,000,000}}{\text{CAD100,000}} = 500 \text{ contracts}$$

When the futures contracts expire, the VC firm will receive (pay) any depreciation (appreciation) in the Canadian dollar versus the US dollar compared with the futures contract price of USD0.7838/CAD.[7] If the changes in futures and spot prices are equal during the life of the futures contract, the hedge will be fully effective. A basis risk arises when the differential given by Futures price$_t$ − Spot price$_t$ is either positive or negative. In the absence of arbitrage, between the time when a hedging position is initiated and the time when it is liquidated, this spread may either widen or narrow to zero.

---

[7]Remember that, assuming covered interest rate parity holds, the forward rate $(F_{f/d})$—expressed as units of foreign currency (f) for 1 unit of domestic currency (d)—is calculated from the exchange spot rate $(S_{f/d})$ and the differential between the foreign (i_f) and domestic (i_d) interest rates. The forward rate is calculated on the basis of the following formula: $F_{f/d} = S_{f/d} \times \left[(1 + i_f \times ACT/360)/(1 + i_d \times ACT/360)\right]$.

4. MANAGING EQUITY RISK

Investors can achieve or modify their equity risk exposures using equity swaps and equity forwards and futures. The asset underlying these financial instruments could be an equity index, a single stock, or a basket of stocks.

4.1. Equity Swaps

An equity swap is a derivative contract in which two parties agree to exchange a series of cash flows whereby one party pays a variable series that will be determined by a single stock, a basket of stocks, or an equity index and the other party pays either (1) a variable series determined by a different equity or rate or (2) a fixed series. An equity swap is used to convert the returns from an equity investment into another series of returns, which either can be derived from another equity series or can be a fixed rate. There are three main types of equity swaps:

- receive-equity return, pay-fixed;
- receive-equity return, pay-floating; and
- receive-equity return, pay-another equity return.

Because they are an OTC derivative instrument, each counterparty in the equity swap bears credit risk exposure to the other. For this reason, equity swaps are usually collateralized in order to reduce the credit risk exposure. At the same time, as equity swaps are created in the OTC market, they can be customized as desired by the counterparties.

A total return swap is a slightly modified equity swap; it also includes in the performance any dividends paid by the underlying stocks or index during the period until the swap maturity. The swap has a fixed tenor and may provide for one single payment at the end of the swap's life, although more typically a series of periodic payments would be arranged instead. In another variation, at the time of each periodic payment, the notional amount could be reset or remain unchanged.

Equity swaps provide synthetic exposure to physical stocks. They are preferred by some investors over ownership of shares when access to a specific market is limited, when taxes are levied for owning physical stocks (e.g., stamp duty) but are not levied on swaps, the custodian fees are high, or the cost of monitoring the stock position is elevated (e.g., because of corporate actions). However, it is important to note that equity swaps require putting up collateral, are relatively illiquid contracts, and do not confer voting rights.

Example 9 shows how an equity swap might be used by an institutional investor with a portfolio indexed to the performance of the S&P 500 Index. He believes the stock market will decline over the next six months and would like to temporarily hedge part of the market exposure of his portfolio. He can do this by entering into a six-month equity swap with one payment at termination, exchanging the total return on the S&P 500 for a floating rate. We will consider two scenarios: In the first scenario, in six months the underlying portfolio is up 5%; in the second, it is down 5%.

EXAMPLE 9   Six-Month Equity Swap

An institutional investor holds a $100 million portfolio of US stocks indexed to the S&P 500. He expects the index will fall in the next six months and wants to reduce his market exposure by 30%. He enters into an equity swap with notional principal of $30 million whereby he agrees to pay the return on the index and to receive the floating reference interest rate, assumed to be 2.25%, minus 25 bps—so, 2.00% per annum.

Scenario 1: In the first scenario, the stock market has increased by 5%. Thus, at swap settlement the institutional investor has an obligation to pay 5% × $30 million, or $1.5 million, and would receive 2% × 180/360 × $30 million, or $300,000. The two parties would net the payments and provide for a single payment of $1.2 million, which the institutional investor would pay. Because the portfolio has gained $5 million in this scenario, the profit and loss (P&L) on the combined position (including the original portfolio and the swap) is positive and equal to $3.8 million.

SCENARIO 1 EQUITY PORTFOLIO RISES 5%

US equity portfolio: $100 million × 5% =	+$5,000,000
P&L on the stock portfolio:	+$5,000,000
Swap settlement:	
Pay: $30 million × 5% =	−$1,500,000
Receive: $30 million × 2% × 180/360 =	+$300,000
Net payment on the swap:	−$1,200,000
P&L on the net position (70% of original exposure and 30% hedged): $5,000,000 − $1,200,000 =	+$3,800,000

Scenario 2: In the second scenario, the stock market has decreased by 5%. So, it is slightly more complicated because the equity return that the institutional investor must pay is *negative*, which means he will receive money. He would receive $1.5 million because the S&P 500 had a negative performance in addition to receiving the $300,000. Because the portfolio has lost $5 million in this case, the P&L on the combined position is −$3.2 million. When the swap ends, the institutional investor returns to the same position in which he started, with the equity portfolio fully invested, and it is thereafter subject to full market risk once again.

SCENARIO 2 EQUITY PORTFOLIO DECLINES 5%

US equity portfolio: $100 million × −5% =	−$5,000,000
P&L on the stock portfolio:	−$5,000,000
Swap settlement: *Receive (Pay negative return): $30 million × 5% =*	+$1,500,000
Receive: $30 million × 2% × 180/360 =	+$300,000
Net payment on the swap:	+$1,800,000
P&L on the net position (70% of original exposure and 30% hedged): −$5,000,000 + $1,800,000 =	−$3,200,000

To test the reasonableness of the result, a portfolio comprising 70% equities and 30% money market instruments assumed to earn 2% (1% over the six months) would achieve a return of 3.8% (= 0.7 × 5% + 0.3 × [2%/2]) or $3.8 million on $100 million in the bullish scenario (Scenario 1). In the bearish scenario (Scenario 2), the return would be −3.2% (= 0.7 × −5% + 0.3 × [2%/2]) or −$3.2 million on the initial $100 million portfolio. The total return swap effectively removes the risk associated with 30% of the equity portfolio allocation and converts it into money market equivalent returns.

Consider now a private high-net-worth investor who holds a large, concentrated position in a particular company's stock that pays dividends on a regular basis. She expects that in the next six months the total return from the stock, including the dividends received, will be negative, so she wants to temporarily neutralize her long exposure. At the same time, she does not wish to lose ownership and her voting rights by selling the stock on an exchange.

This investor can enter into a total return swap requiring her to transfer the total performance of the stock (i.e., total return) to the counterparty of the swap, at prespecified dates for an agreed-on fee. Under the terms of the swap, she will pay to the counterparty the share price appreciation plus the dividends received over the life of the contract. If the stock price decreases, she will receive the share price depreciation but net of the dividends. At the same prespecified dates, the investor will receive in exchange from the counterparty an agreed-on floating-rate interest payment based on the swap notional.

Equity swaps that have a single stock as underlying can be cash settled or physically settled. If the swap is cash settled, on the termination date of the contract the equity swap receiver will receive (pay) the equity appreciation (depreciation) in cash. If the swap is physically settled, on the termination date the equity swap receiver will receive the quantity of single stock specified in the contract and pay the notional amount. Let us assume for example that a portfolio manager is the receiver in a six-month equity swap with notional principal of €4.5 million and no interim cash flows that requires physical settlement, at maturity, of 300,000 shares of the Italian insurer Generali. At maturity of the swap, the portfolio manager will receive 300,000 shares of Generali and will pay €4.5 million, which corresponds to a purchase price per share of €15 (= €4.5 million/300,000). He will also pay the interest on the swap based on the agreed-on rate. Now let us also assume that at the swap's maturity the price of Generali is €16. This price implies a gain of €300,000 (= [€16 − €15] × 300,000) for the portfolio manager, assuming he sells the shares received in the swap at €16. If the same swap had cash settlement, instead of physical settlement, at maturity the portfolio manager would have received €300,000—given by €16 (the swap settlement price) less €15 (the agreed price on the swap) and multiplied by 300,000—against the payment of the interest on the swap.

4.2. Equity Forwards and Futures

Equity index futures are an indispensable tool for many investment managers: They are a low-cost instrument to implement tactical allocation decisions, achieve portfolio diversification, and attain international exposure. They are standardized contracts listed on an exchange, and when the underlying is a stock index, only cash settlement is available at contract expiration.

Single stock futures are also available to investors to acquire the desired exposure to a specific stock. This exposure is also achievable with equity forwards, which are OTC contracts that are used when the counterparties need a customized agreement. The underlying of a single stock futures contract is one specified stock, and the investor can receive or pay its performance. At expiration, the contract could require cash settlement or physical settlement using the stock.

In Example 9, rather than using an equity swap, the institutional investor could temporarily remove part of the market risk by selling S&P 500 Index futures. In the practical implementation of a stock index futures trade, we need to remember that the actual futures contract price is the quoted futures price times a designated multiplier. In determining the hedge ratio, the stock index futures price should be quoted on the same order of magnitude as the stock index.

For example, assume that a one-month futures contract on the S&P 500 is quoted at 2,700. Given the multiplier of $250, the actual futures price is equal to $675,000 (= 2,700 × $250). We also assume that the portfolio to be hedged carries average market risk, meaning a beta of 1.0.[8] To hedge 30% of the $100 million portfolio, the portfolio manager would want to sell 44 S&P 500 futures contracts, determined as follows:

$$\frac{\$30 \text{ million}}{2,700(\$250)} = 44.444 \approx 44 \text{ contracts}$$

Suppose the institutional investor sold the 44 futures at 2,700 and at expiration the S&P 500 *rises* by 0.5%. The cash settlement of the contract is at 2,713.5. Because the futures position is short and the index rose, there is a "loss" of 13.5 index points—each point being worth $250—on 44 contracts, for a total cash outflow, paid by the institutional investor, of $148,500:

$$-13.5 \text{ points per contract} \times \$250 \text{ per point} \times 44 \text{ contracts} = -\$148,500 \text{ (a loss)}.$$

If the S&P 500 Index rose by 0.5%, the 30% of the portfolio that has been hedged would also be expected to rise by the same amount, but there is a small difference due to rounding the number of futures contracts used for the hedge:

$$\$30,000,000 \times 0.5\% = \$150,000.$$

If instead the S&P 500 *fell* by 0.5%, the numbers would be the same, but the signs would change. The institutional investor would receive the "gain" because he had a short stock index futures position when the index fell, which would offset the loss on the hedged portion of his stock portfolio. In sum, the equity market risk is hedged away.

In the previous example, the beta of the portfolio was the same as the beta of the equity index futures. This situation usually does not occur, and in most hedging strategies, it is

---

[8]If the portfolio carried above-market risk—say, with a beta of 1.10—the number of contracts needed to hedge would increase by this factor. Similarly, a lower-risk portfolio would require proportionately fewer contracts.

necessary to determine the exact "hedge ratio" in terms of the number of futures contracts. Consider that the investment manager wishes to change the beta of the equity portfolio, β_S, to a target beta of β_T. Because the value of the futures contract begins each day at zero, the dollar beta of the combination of stocks and futures, assuming the target beta is achieved, is $\beta_T S$, where S is the market value of the stock portfolio.[9] The number of futures contracts we shall use is N_f, which can be determined by setting the target dollar beta equal to the dollar beta of the stock portfolio ($\beta_S S$) and the dollar beta of N_f futures ($N_f \beta_f F$), where β_f is the beta of the futures and F is the value per futures contract:

$$\beta_T S = \beta_S S + N_f \beta_f F$$

We then solve for N_f and obtain

$$N_f = \left(\frac{\beta_T - \beta_S}{\beta_f} \right) \left(\frac{S}{F} \right) \tag{10}$$

Note that if the investor wants to increase the portfolio's beta, β_T will exceed β_S and the sign of N_f will be positive, which means that she must buy futures. If she wants to decrease the beta, β_T will be less than β_S, the sign of N_f will be negative, and she must sell futures. This relationship should make sense: Selling futures will offset some of the risk of holding the stock, whereas buying futures will add risk.

In the special case in which the goal is to eliminate market risk, β_T would be set to zero and the formula would reduce to

$$N_f = -\left(\frac{\beta_S}{\beta_f} \right) \left(\frac{S}{F} \right)$$

In this case, the sign of N_f will always be negative, which makes sense, because in order to hedge away all the market risk, futures must be sold.

EXAMPLE 10   Increasing the Beta of a Portfolio with Futures

Paulo Bianchi is the manager of a fund that invests in UK defensive stocks, such as consumer staples producers and utilities. His firm's market outlook for the next quarter has become more positive, so Bianchi decides to increase the beta on the £40 million portfolio he manages from its current level of $\beta_S = 0.85$ to $\beta_T = 1.10$ for the next three months. He will execute this increase in equity market risk exposure using futures on the FTSE 100 Index. The futures contract price is currently £7,300, the contract's multiplier is £10 per index point (so each futures contract is worth £73,000), and its beta, b_f is 1.00.

---

[9]Recall that the market value of the portfolio will still be the same as the market value of the stock, because the value of the futures is zero. The futures value becomes zero whenever it is marked to market, which takes place at the end of each day. In other words, the target beta does not appear to be applied to the value of the futures in the preceding analysis because the value of the futures is zero.

At the end of the three-month period, the UK stock market has increased by 2%. The stock portfolio has increased in value to £40,680,000, calculated as £40,000,000 × [1 + (0.02 × 0.85)]. The FTSE 100 futures contract has risen to £74,460.

1. Determine the appropriate number of FTSE 100 Index futures Bianchi should buy to increase the portfolio's beta to 1.10.
2. Demonstrate how the effective beta of the portfolio of stocks and the FTSE 100 Index futures matched Bianchi's target beta of 1.10.

Solution to 1: Using Equation 10 and the preceding data, the appropriate number of futures contracts to buy to increase the portfolio's beta to 1.10 would be 137.

$$N_f = \left(\frac{\beta_T - \beta_S}{\beta_f}\right)\left(\frac{S}{F}\right) = \left(\frac{1.10 - 0.85}{1.00}\right)\left(\frac{£40,000,000}{£73,000}\right) = 136.99 \text{ (rounded to 137)}$$

Solution to 2: The profit on the futures contracts is 137 × (£74,460 − £73,000) = £200,020. Adding the profit from the futures to the value of the stock portfolio gives a total market value of £40,680,000 + £200,020 = £40,880,020. The rate of return for the combined position is

$$\frac{£40,880,020}{£40,000,000} - 1 = 0.0220, \text{ or } 2.2\%$$

Because the market went up by 2% and the overall gain was 2.2%, the effective beta of the portfolio was

$$\frac{0.0220}{0.020} = 1.10$$

Thus, the effective beta matched the target beta of 1.10.

4.3. Cash Equitization

Cash securitization (also known as "cash equitization" or "cash overlay") is a strategy designed to boost returns by finding ways to "equitize" unintended cash holdings. By purchasing futures contracts, fund managers attempt to replicate the performance of the underlying market in which the cash would have been invested. Given the liquidity of the futures market, doing so would be relatively easy. An alternative solution could be to purchase calls and sell puts on the underlying asset with the same exercise price and expiry date.

In this case, we have a cash holding, implying $\beta_S = 0$, so the number of futures (with beta of β_f) that would need to be purchased in a cash equitization transaction is given by

$$N_f = \left(\frac{\beta_T}{\beta_f}\right)\left(\frac{S}{F}\right) \tag{11}$$

EXAMPLE 11   Cash Equitization

Akari Fujiwara manages a large equity fund denominated in Japanese yen that is indexed to the Nikkei 225 stock index. She determines that the current level of excess cash that has built up in the portfolio amounts to JPY140 million. She decides to purchase futures contracts to replicate the return on her fund's target index. Nikkei 225 index futures currently trade at a price of JPY23,000 per contract, the contract multiplier is JPY1,000 per index point (so each futures contract is worth JPY23 million), and the beta, β_f, is 1.00.

Determine the appropriate number of futures Fujiwara must buy to equitize her portfolio's excess cash position.

Solution: Using Equation 11, which assumes $\beta_S = 0$, the answer is found as follows:

$$N_f = \left(\frac{\beta_T}{\beta_f}\right)\left(\frac{S}{F}\right) = \left(\frac{1.00}{1.00}\right)\left(\frac{\text{JPY}140,000,000}{\text{JPY}23,000,000}\right) = 6.087 \text{ (rounded to 6)}$$

The appropriate number of futures to buy to equitize the portfolio's excess cash position, based on the data provided, would be six contracts.

---

5. VOLATILITY DERIVATIVES: FUTURES AND OPTIONS

With the introduction of volatility futures and variance swaps, many investors now consider volatility an asset class in itself. In particular, long volatility exposure can be an effective hedge against a sell-off in a long equity portfolio, notably during periods of extreme market movements. Empirical studies have identified a negative correlation between volatility and stock index returns that becomes pronounced during stock market downturns. Importantly, variance swaps, which will be discussed in this section, have a valuable convexity feature—as realized volatility increases (decreases), the positive (negative) swap payoffs increase (decrease)—that makes them particularly attractive for hedging long equity portfolios. For example, some investors use strategies that systematically allocate to volatility futures or variance swaps to hedge the "tail" risk of their portfolios. Naturally, the counterparties are selling a kind of insurance; they expect such return tails will not materialize. The effectiveness of such hedges should be compared against more traditional "long volatility" hedging methods, such as implementing a rolling series of out-of-the-money put options or futures. The roll aspect affects portfolio returns, so the term structure should be carefully considered. For example, if futures prices are in backwardation (contango), then overall returns to an investor with a long position in the futures would be enhanced (diminished) owing to positive (negative) roll return. The results are necessarily reversed for the holder of the short futures position. In sum, all these derivatives strategies should be assessed on the basis of their ability to reduce portfolio risk and improve returns. In contrast, a common investment strategy implemented by opportunistic investors involves being systematically short volatility, thereby attempting to capture the risk premium embedded in option prices.

This strategy is most profitable under stable market conditions, but it can lead to large losses if market volatility rises unexpectedly.

5.1. Volatility Futures and Options

The CBOE Volatility Index, known as the VIX or the "fear index," is a measure of investors' expectations of volatility in the S&P 500 over the next 30 days. It is calculated and published by the Chicago Board Options Exchange (CBOE) and is based on the prices of S&P 500 Index options. The CBOE began publishing real-time VIX data in 1993, and in 2004, VIX futures were introduced. Investors cannot invest directly in the VIX but instead must use VIX futures contracts that offer investors a pure play on the level of expected stock market volatility, regardless of the direction of the S&P 500. Volatility futures allow investors to implement their views depending on their expectations about the timing and magnitude of a change in implied volatility. For example, in order for a long VIX futures position to protect an equity portfolio during a downturn, the stock market's implied volatility, as derived from S&P 500 Index options, must increase by more than the consensus expectation of implied volatility prior to the sell-off.

A family of volatility indexes has also been introduced for European equity markets, and they are designed to reflect market expectations of near-term to long-term volatility. The most well known of these is the VSTOXX index, based on real-time option prices on the EURO STOXX 50 index. The family of volatility indexes also includes the VDAX-NEW Index, based on DAX stock index options.

Next, we discuss various shapes of the VIX futures term structure. The CBOE Futures Exchange (CFE) lists nine standard (monthly) VIX index futures contracts and six weekly expirations in VIX futures. Each weekly and monthly contract settles 30 calendar days prior to the subsequent standard S&P 500 Index option's expiration. The weekly futures have lower volumes and open interest than the monthly futures contracts have. Exhibit 2 presents the first six monthly VIX futures contracts at three different fixed points in time for all expires; these are not consecutive days but, rather, are at intervals of about two months apart.

EXHIBIT 2   VIX Futures Contracts

CBOE VIX Futures Expiry	Day 1	Day 60	Day 120
April	16.68	33.46	9.77
May	17.00	19.85	14.05
June	17.00	19.10	14.55
July	17.35	18.50	15.25
August	17.51	18.75	15.60
September	17.80	18.90	16.10

Exhibit 3 shows the shape of the VIX futures term structure corresponding to the data in Exhibit 2. The vertical axis shows the futures prices, and the horizontal scale indicates the month of expiration.

EXHIBIT 3   Shapes of the VIX Futures Term Structure

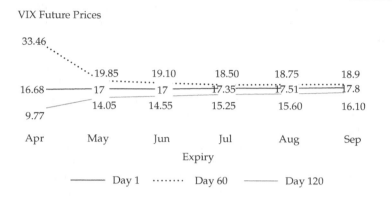

VIX Future Prices

The shape of the VIX futures curve is always changing, reflecting the current volatility environment, investors' expectations regarding the future level of volatility, and the buying and selling activity in VIX futures contracts by market participants. Depending on the mix of these factors, the VIX futures term structure can change from being positively sloped to flat or inverted in just a few months' time.

Day 1 illustrates what happens when volatility is expected to remain stable over the near to long term: The term structure of VIX futures is flat. Day 60 shows the VIX futures in backwardation. This situation typically is a signal that investors expect more volatility in the short term and thus require higher prices for shorter-term contracts than for longer-term ones. In contrast, Day 120 is an example of the VIX futures being in contango. The curve is upward sloped, and it is steep for VIX buyers, with nearly 4.3 volatility points between the April and May expiries. Higher longer-term VIX futures prices are interpreted as an expectation that the VIX will rise because of increasing long-term volatility.

The VIX futures converge to the spot VIX as expiration approaches, so the two must be equal at expiration. When the VIX futures curve is in contango (backwardation) and assuming volatility expectations remain unchanged, the VIX futures price will get "pulled" closer to the VIX spot price, and they will decrease (increase) in price as they approach expiration. Traders calculate the daily roll as the difference between the front-month VIX futures price and the VIX spot price, divided by the number of business days until the VIX futures contract settles. Assuming that the basis declines linearly until settlement, when the term structure is in contango (backwardation), the trader who is long in back-month VIX futures would realize roll-down losses (profits).

Importantly, VIX futures may not reflect the index, especially when the VIX experiences large spikes, because longer-maturity futures contracts are less sensitive to short-term VIX movements. Furthermore, establishing long positions in VIX futures can be very expensive over time. When the short end of the VIX futures curve is much steeper than the long end of the curve, the carrying costs created from the contract roll down are elevated.

This phenomenon is particularly evident for investors who cannot invest directly in futures but must invest in volatility funds that attempt to track the VIX. These funds have attracted interest and substantial money flows because they are easily accessed in the form of exchange-traded products (ETPs) and, in particular, exchange-traded notes (ETNs) that provide exposure to short- and medium-term VIX futures. Some of these products also provide leveraged exposure.

When using these investment products to hedge against a rise in the VIX, the VIX futures term structure should be taken into in consideration because volatility ETPs typically hold a mix of VIX futures that is adjusted daily to keep the average time to expiration of the portfolio constant. The daily rebalancing requires shorter-term futures to be sold and longer-dated futures to be purchased. When the VIX futures are in contango, the cost of rolling over hedges (i.e., negative carry) increases, thereby reducing profits and causing the ETP to underperform relative to the movement in the VIX. In contrast, "inverse" VIX ETPs offer investors the opportunity to profit from decreases in S&P 500 volatility. However, the purchase of these funds implies a directional positioning on volatility, and investors must accept the risk of large losses when volatility increases sharply.

In 2006, VIX options were introduced, providing an asymmetrical exposure to potential increases or decreases in anticipated volatility. VIX options are European style, and their prices depend on the prices of VIX futures with similar expirations because the market makers of VIX options typically hedge the risk of their option positions using VIX futures. To understand the use of VIX calls and puts, it is very important to recognize that the increases in the VIX (and VIX futures) are negatively correlated with the prices of equity assets. In particular, a trader or investor would purchase VIX call options when he expects that volatility will increase owing to a significant sell-off in the equity market. In contrast, VIX put options would be bought to profit from an expectation that volatility will decrease because of stable equity market conditions. Options on the VSTOXX index also exist, but they have lower volumes and open interest than those on the VIX.

6. VOLATILITY DERIVATIVES: VARIANCE SWAPS

Variance swaps are instruments used by investors for taking directional bets on implied versus realized volatility for speculative or hedging purposes. The term "variance swap" refers to the fact that these instruments have a payoff analogous to that of a swap. In a variance swap, the buyer of the contract will pay the difference between the fixed *variance strike* agreed on in the contract and the *realized variance* (annualized) on the underlying over the period specified and applied to a variance notional. In variance swaps, there is no exchange of cash at the contract inception or during the life of the swap. The payoff at expiration of a long variance position will be positive (negative) when realized variance is greater (less) than the swap's variance strike. If the payment amount is positive (negative), the swap seller (buyer) pays the swap buyer (seller). The payoff at settlement is found as follows:

$$\text{Settlement amount}_T = (\text{Variance notional})$$
$$(\text{Realized variance} - \text{Variance strike}) \quad (12)$$

The realized variance is calculated as follows, where $R_i = \ln(P_{i+1}/P_i)$ and N is the number of days observed:

$$\text{Realized variance} = 252 \times \left[\sum_{i=1}^{N-1} R_i^2 / (N-1) \right] \quad (13)$$

Since most market participants are accustomed to thinking in terms of volatility, variance swap traders typically agree on the following two things: (1) a variance swap trade size expressed in **vega notional**, N_{Vega} (not in variance notional), and (2) the strike (X), which represents the expected future variance of the underlying, expressed as volatility (not variance). This approach is intuitive because the vega notional represents the average profit and loss of the variance swap for a 1% change in volatility from the strike. For example, when the vega notional is $50,000, the profit and loss for one volatility point of difference between the realized volatility and the strike will be close to $50,000.

We must bear in mind that this is an approximation because the variance swap payoff is convex and the profit and loss is not linear for changes in the realized volatility. Specifically, to calculate the exact payoff, the variance strike is the strike squared and the **variance notional**, $N_{variance}$, is defined and calculated as

$$\text{Variance notional} = \frac{\text{Vega notional}}{2 \times \text{Strike price}} \tag{14}$$

Thus, given the realized volatility (σ), we have the following equivalence:

$$\text{Settlement amount}_T = N_{Vega}\left(\frac{\sigma^2 - X^2}{2 \times \text{Strike price}}\right) = N_{variance}(\sigma^2 - X^2) \tag{15}$$

The strike on a variance swap is calculated on the basis of the implied volatility skew for a specific expiration, derived from calls and puts quoted in the market. As discussed previously, volatility skew is a plot of the differences in implied volatilities of a basket of options with the same maturity and underlying asset but with different strikes (and thus moneyness). As a rule of thumb, the strike of a variance swap typically corresponds to the implied volatility of the put that has 90% moneyness (calculated as the option's strike divided by the current level of the underlying).

The mark-to-market valuation of a variance swap at time t (VarSwap$_t$) will depend on realized volatility from the swap's initiation to t, RealizedVol(0, t), and implied volatility at t, ImpliedVol(t, T), over the remaining life of the swap ($T - t$). $PV_t(T)$ is the present value at time t of $1 received at maturity T. The value of a variance swap at time t is given by the following formula:[10]

$$\text{Var Swap}_t = \text{Variance notional} \times PV_t(T) \times$$

$$\left\{\frac{t}{T} \times [\text{RealizedVol}(0, t)]^2 + \frac{T-t}{T} \times [\text{Implied Vol}(t, T)]^2 - \text{Strike}^2\right\} \tag{16}$$

Importantly, the sensitivity of a variance swap to changes in implied volatility diminishes over time.

A feature of variance swaps that makes them particularly interesting to investors is that their payoffs are convex in volatility, as seen Exhibit 4. This convexity occurs because being long a variance swap is equivalent to be long a basket of options and short the underlying asset (typically by selling a futures contract). A long position in a variance swap is thus long gamma and has a convex payoff. This characteristic allows volatility sellers to sell variance swaps at a higher price than at-the-money options because the swap's convex payoff profile is attractive to investors who desire a long volatility position as a tail risk hedge.

---

[10]Note that the terms in the braces—RealizedVol, ImpliedVol, and Strike—are all expressed in volatility units. They are squared so that they are expressed in variance units for determining the value of a variance swap.

EXHIBIT 4   The Payoff of a Variance Swap Is Convex in Volatility

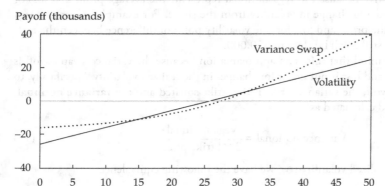

Payoff (thousands)

EXAMPLE 12   Variance Swap Valuation and Settlement

Olivia Santos trades strategies that systematically sell volatility on the S&P 500 Index. She sells $50,000 vega notional of a one-year variance swap on the S&P 500 at a strike of 20% (quoted as annual volatility).

Now six months have passed, and the S&P 500 has experienced a realized volatility of 16% (annualized). On the same day, the fair strike of a new six-month variance swap on the S&P 500 is 19%.

Determine the following:

1. The current value of the variance swap sold by Santos (note that the annual interest rate is 2.5%)
2. The settlement amount at expiration of the swap if the one-year realized volatility is 18%

Solution to 1: Santos sold $50,000 vega notional of a one-year variance swap on the S&P 500 with a strike (in volatility terms) of 20%. The value of the variance swap sold by Santos is found using Equation 16:

$$\text{Var Swap}_t = \text{Variance notional} \times PV_t(T) \times$$

$$\left\{ \frac{t}{T} \times [\text{Realized Vol}(0, t)]^2 + \frac{T-t}{T} \times [\text{Implied Vol}(t, T)]^2 - \text{Strike}^2 \right\}$$

Values for the inputs are as follows:

Volatility strike on existing swap = 20.
Variance strike on existing swap = $20^2 = 400$.
From Equation 14, Variance notional = $\dfrac{\text{Vega notional}}{2 \times \text{Strike}} = \dfrac{\$50,000}{2 \times 20} = 1{,}250.$
Realized Vol$(0, t)^2 = 16^2 = 256$.
Implied Vol$(t, T)^2 = 19^2 = 361$.

$t = 6$ months.

$T = 12$ months.

$PV_t(T) = 1/[1 + (2.5\% \times 6/12)] = 0.987654$ (= Present Value Interest Factor for six months, where the annual rate is 2.5%).

The current value of the swap is

$$\text{VarSwap}_t = 1{,}250 \times (0.987654) \times [(6/12) \times 256 + (6/12) \times 361 - 400]$$
$$= -\$112{,}962.9263.$$

Given that Santos is short the variance swap, the mark-to-market value is positive for her, and it equals $112,963.

Solution to 2: The settlement amount is calculated using Equation 12 as follows:

$$\text{Settlement}_T = \text{Variance notional} \times (\text{Realized variance} - \text{Variance strike})$$
$$= 1{,}250 \times (18^2 - 20^2)$$

$$= -\$95{,}000$$

If the payment amount is positive (negative), the swap seller (buyer) pays the swap buyer (seller). So, in this case, Santos would receive $95,000 from the swap buyer.

7. USING DERIVATIVES TO MANAGE EQUITY EXPOSURE AND TRACKING ERROR

Bernhard Steinbacher has a client with a holding of 100,000 shares in Tundra Corporation, currently trading for €14 per share. The client has owned the shares for many years and thus has a very low tax basis on this stock. Steinbacher wants to safeguard the value of the position since the client does not want to sell the shares. He cannot find exchange-traded options on the stock. Steinbacher wants to present a way in which the client could protect the investment portfolio from a decline in Tundra's stock price.

   Discuss a swap strategy that Steinbacher might recommend to his client.

Solution:

A possible solution is to enter into an equity swap trading the Tundra stock return for the floating reference interest rate. Given Tundra's current share price of €14, the position is worth €1.4 million. Steinbacher can agree to exchange the *total return* on the shares (which includes the price performance and the dividends received) for the reference rate return on this sum of money. Now he needs to determine the time over which the protection is needed and must match the swap tenor to this period. After consulting with his client, Steinbacher decides on six months. The floating reference rate is 0.34%, expressed as an annual rate.

Scenario A:
Over the six months, Tundra pays a €0.10 dividend and the share price rises 1%.

The total return on the stock is $\frac{(14 \times 1.01) - 14 + 0.10}{14} = 1.71\%$. For a six-month period, the reference rate return would be half the annual rate, or 0.17%. Tundra's total return *exceeds* the six-month reference rate return: $(1.71\% - 0.17\%) \times €1.4$ million $= €21,620$, which is a positive amount, so Steinbacher's client would need to *pay* the swap counterparty.

Scenario B:
Over the six months, Tundra pays a €0.10 dividend and the share price falls 1%.

The total return on the stock is $\frac{(14 \times 0.99) - 14 + 0.10}{14} = -0.29\%$. Tundra's total return is less than the six-month reference rate return: $(-0.29\% - 0.17\%) \times €1.4$ million $= -€6,380$, which is a negative amount, so Steinbacher's client would *receive* the negative return and the reference rate return from the swap counterparty (meaning the client will receive a positive cash inflow of €6,380).

7.1. Cash Equitization

Georgia McMillian manages a fund invested in UK stocks that is indexed to the FTSE 100 Index. The fund has £250 million of total assets under management, including £20 million of cash reserves invested at the three-month British pound floating rate of 0.63% (annualized). McMillian does not have an expectation on the direction of UK stocks over the next quarter. However, she is keen to minimize tracking error risk, so she implements a cash equitization strategy attempting to replicate the performance of the FTSE 100 on the cash reserves. Futures on the FTSE 100 settling in three months currently trade at a price of £7,900, the contract's value is £10 per index point (so each futures contract is worth £79,000), and its beta, β_f, is 1.0.

McMillian engages in a synthetic index strategy to gain exposure on a notional amount of £20 million to the FTSE 100 by purchasing equity index futures. The number of futures she must purchase is given by the following:

$$N_f = \left(\frac{\beta_T}{\beta_f}\right)\left(\frac{S}{F}\right) = \left(\frac{1.0}{1.0}\right)\left(\frac{20,000,000}{79,000}\right) = 253.16 \approx 253$$

where the beta of the futures contract, β_f, and the target beta, β_T, are both equal to 1.0.

Scenario: Three months later, the FTSE 100 Index has increased by 5%.

Three months later, the FTSE 100 has increased by 5%, and the original value of £230 million invested in UK stocks has increased to £241.5 million. The price of the FTSE 100 Index futures contract has increased to £8,282.5. Interest on the cash invested at the three-month floating rate amounts to £31,500 (£20,000,000 × 0.63% × 90/360). McMillian bought the futures at £7,900, and the cash settlement of the contract at is £8,282.5. So, there is a "gain" of 382.5 index points, each point being worth £10, on 253 contracts for a total cash inflow of £967,725 (382.5 points per contract × £10 per point × 253 contracts). Adding to the portfolio the profit from the futures and the cash reserves plus the interest earned on the cash gives a total market value for McMillian's portfolio of £262,499,225 (= £241,500,000 + £20,000,000 + £967,725 + £31,500). The rate of return for the combined position is:

$$\frac{£262,499,225}{£250,000,000} - 1 = 0.05, \text{ or } 5\%$$

Importantly, without implementing this strategy, McMillian's return would have been slightly over 4.6%, calculated as (£230 million/£250 million) × 5.0% + (£20 million/£250 million) × 0.63% × (90/360). So, she accomplished her goal of minimizing tracking error by following this strategy.

8. USING DERIVATIVES IN ASSET ALLOCATION

8.1. Changing Allocations between Asset Classes Using Futures

Mario Rossi manages a €500 million portfolio that is allocated 70% to stocks and 30% to bonds. Over the next three-month horizon, he is bearish on eurozone stocks, except for German shares, and is bullish on Italian bonds. So, Rossi wants to reduce the overall allocation to stocks by 10%, to 60%, and achieve the same weight (30%) in Italian stocks (which have a beta of 1.1 with respect to the FTSE MIB Index) and German stocks (which have a beta of 0.9 with respect to the DAX index). He also wants to increase the overall allocation to Italian government bonds (BTPs) by 10%, to 40%. The bond portion of his portfolio has a modified duration of 6.45. In summary, as shown in Exhibit 5, Rossi needs to remove €100 million of exposure to Italian stocks, add €50 million of exposure to German stocks, and add €50 million of exposure to Italian bonds in his portfolio.

EXHIBIT 5   Summary of Rossi's Original and New Asset Allocation

Stock Index	Original (€350 Million, 70%)	New (€300 Million, 60%)	Transaction
FTSE MIB	€250 million (50%)	€150 million (30%)	Sell €100 million
DAX	€100 million (20%)	€150 million (30%)	Buy €50 million
Bonds	Original (€150 Million, 30%)	New (€200 Million, 40%)	Transaction
Italian BTPs	€150 million (30%)	€200 million (40%)	Buy €50 million

Rossi uses stock index futures and bond futures to achieve this objective. Once the notional values to be traded are known, Rossi determines how many futures contracts should be purchased or sold to achieve the desired asset allocation. The FTSE MIB Index futures contract has a price of 23,100 and a multiplier of €5, for a value of €115,500. The DAX index futures contract has a price of 13,000 and a multiplier of €25, for a value of €325,000. Both futures contracts have a beta of 1. The BTP futures contract has a price of 132.50 and a contract size of €100,000. The cheapest-to-deliver bond has a price of €121; a modified duration of 8.19; a BPV_{CTD} (from Equation 7) of €99.10, calculated as 8.19 × 0.0001 × [(121/100) × €100,000)]; and a conversion factor of 0.913292.

1. Determine how many stock index and bond futures contracts Rossi should use to implement the desired asset allocation and whether he should go long or short.
2. At the horizon date (three months later), the value of the Italian stock portfolio has fallen 5% whereas that of the German stock portfolio has increased 1%. The FTSE MIB futures price is 22,000, and the DAX futures price is 13,100. Determine the change in market value of the equity portfolio assuming the futures transactions specified in Part 1 have been carried out (note that you can ignore transaction costs).

3. At the horizon date, the Italian bond yield curve has a parallel shift downward of 25 bps. Determine the change in market value of the bond portfolio assuming the transactions specified in Part 1 have been carried out (note that you can ignore transactions costs).

Solution to 1:
The market value of the Italian stocks is 0.50(€500,000,000) = €250,000,000, and Rossi wants to reduce the exposure to this market by 0.20(€500,000,000) = €100,000,000. The market value of the German stocks is 0.20(€500,000,000) = €100,000,000, and he wants to increase the exposure to this market by 0.10(€500,000,000) = €50,000,000. He decides to sell enough futures contracts on the FTSE MIB to reduce the exposure to Italian stocks by €100 million and to purchase enough futures on the DAX index to increase the exposure to German stocks by €50 million.

The number of stock index futures, N_f, is

$$N_f = \left(\frac{\beta_T - \beta_S}{\beta_f}\right)\left(\frac{S}{F}\right)$$

where β_T is the target beta of zero, β_S is the stock beta of 1.1, β_f is the futures beta of 1.0, S is the market value of the stocks involved in the transaction, and F is the value of the futures contract.

To achieve the desired reduction in exposure to Italian stocks, the market value of the stocks involved in the transaction will be $S = €100,000,000$. The Italian stocks' beta (β_S) is 1.1, and the target beta is $\beta_T = 0$. The FTSE MIB Index futures have a contract value of €115,500 and a beta (β_f) of 1.0:

$$N_f = \left(\frac{\beta_T - \beta_S}{\beta_f}\right)\left(\frac{S}{F}\right) = \left(\frac{0.0 - 1.1}{1.0}\right)\left(\frac{€100,000,000}{€115,500}\right) = -952.38$$

Rossi sells 952 futures contracts (after rounding).

To achieve the desired exposure to German stocks (which have a beta of 0.9), the market value of the stocks involved in the transaction will be $S = €50,000,000$. In this case, $\beta_S = 0.0$ because Rossi is starting with a notional "cash" position from the reduction in Italian stock exposure, and the target beta is now $\beta_T = 0.9$. Given the value of the DAX index futures contract of €325,000 and a beta (β_f) of 1.0, we obtain

$$N_f = \left(\frac{\beta_T - \beta_S}{\beta_f}\right)\left(\frac{S}{F}\right) = \left(\frac{0.9 - 0.0}{1.0}\right)\left(\frac{€50,000,000}{€325,000}\right) = 138.46$$

Rossi buys 138 futures contracts (after rounding).

The market value of the Italian bonds is 0.30(€500,000,000) = €150,000,000, and Rossi wants to increase the exposure to this market by 0.10(€500,000,000) = €50,000,000. He decides to purchase enough Euro-BTP futures so that €50 million exposure in Italian bonds is added to the portfolio. The target basis point value exposure (BPV_T) is determined using Equation 4:

$$BPV_T = MDUR_T \times 0.01\% \times MV_P = 6.45 \times 0.0001 \times €50,000,000 = €32,250$$

The cheapest-to-deliver bond is the BTP 4¾ 09/01/28, which has a conversion factor of 0.913292 and BPV_{CTD} of €99.10. The number of Euro-BTP futures to buy to convert the €50 million in notional cash ($BPV_P = 0$) to the desired exposure in Italian bonds is found using Equation 9:

$$BPVHR = \left(\frac{BPV_T - BPV_P}{BPV_{CTD}} \right) \times CF = [(€32,250 - 0)/€99.10] \times 0.913292 = 297.21$$

Rossi buys 297 Euro-BTP futures contracts (after rounding).

Solution to 2:
The value of the Italian stock portfolio decreases by €7,264,000. This outcome is the net effect of the following:

- The original Italian stock portfolio decreases by €12,500,000 (= €250 million × −5%).
- The short position in 952 FTSE MIB futures gains €5,236,000, calculated as −(22,000 − 23,100) × 952 × €5.
  The value of the German stock portfolio increases by €1,345,000. This outcome is the net effect of the following:

- The original German stock portfolio increases by €1,000,000 (= €100 million × 1%).
- The long position in 138 DAX futures gains €345,000, calculated as (13,100 − 13,000) × 138 × €25.

The total value of the stock position has decreased by €5,919,000 or −1.691% (= −5,919,000/350,000,000).

Had Rossi sold the Italian stocks and then converted the proceeds into German stocks, the equity portfolio would have decreased by €6,000,000 or −1.71% (= −6,000,000/350,000,000). This outcome would have been the net effect of the following:

- A decrease in the new Italian stock portfolio of €7,500,000 (= €150 million × −5%)
- An increase in the new German stock portfolio of €1,500,000 (= €150 million × 1%)

Solution to 3:
The Italian bond yield curve had a parallel shift downward of 25 bps. The value of the Italian bond portfolio increases by €3,224,426. This outcome is the net effect of the following:

- The €150 million portfolio's BPV_P, per Equation 5, is €96,750 (= 6.45 × 0.0001 × €150,000,000). Thus, for a 25 bp decrease in rates, the portfolio value increases by €2,418,750 (= €96,750 × 25).
- The long position in 297 BTP futures has a BPV_{CTD} of €99.10, and the CF is 0.913292. So, using Equation 6, BPV_F is €108.51 (= €99.10/0.913292). Thus, for a 25 bp decrease in rates, the futures position increases in value by €805,676, calculated as follows: BPV_F × Change in yield × Number of futures contracts = €108.51 × 25 × 297.

Had Rossi bought the Italian bonds, the new €200 million bond portfolio would have increased by €3,225,000. The portfolio has a BPV_P of 6.45 × 0.0001 × €200,000,000 = €129,000. Thus, for a 25 bp decrease in rates, the portfolio value increases by €3,225,000 (= €129,000 × 25).

8.2. Rebalancing an Asset Allocation Using Futures

Yolanda Grant manages a portfolio with a target allocation of 40% in stocks and 60% in bonds. Over the last month, the value of the portfolio has increased from €100 million to €106 million, and Grant wants to rebalance it back to the target allocation (40% stocks/60% bonds). As shown in Exhibit 6, the current portfolio has €46 million (43.4%) in European stocks (with beta of 1.2 with respect to the EURO STOXX 50 index) and €60 million (56.6%) in German bunds. The bonds have a modified duration of 9.5.

EXHIBIT 6   Summary of Grant's Current and Rebalanced Allocation

Stocks	Current	Rebalanced	Transaction
European stocks	€46 million (43.4%)	€42.4 million (40%)	Sell €3.6 million
Bonds	**Current**	**Rebalanced**	**Transaction**
German bunds	€60 million (56.6%)	€63.6 million (60%)	Buy €3.6 million

Grant will use stock index futures and bond futures to achieve this objective. Once the notional values to be traded are known, she determines how many futures contracts should be purchased or sold to achieve the desired asset allocation.

The EURO STOXX 50 index futures contract has a price of 3,500 and a multiplier of €10, for a value of €35,000. The Euro-Bund futures contract has a contract size of €100,000. The cheapest-to-deliver bond has a modified duration of 8.623 and a price of 98.14, so (per Equation 7) its BPV_{CTD} is €84.63, calculated as $8.623 \times 0.0001 \times [(98.14/100) \times €100,000)]$. Its conversion factor is 0.619489.

Determine how many stock index and bond futures contracts Grant should use to implement the desired asset allocation and whether she should go long or short.

Solution:
The market value of the European stocks is €46,000,000, and Grant wants to reduce the exposure to this market to 40% or 0.40(€106,000,000) = €42,400,000. She decides to sell enough futures contracts on the EURO STOXX 50 to reduce the allocation to European stocks by 0.034(€106,000,000) = €3,604,000.

To achieve the desired reduction in exposure to European stocks, the market value of the stocks involved in the transaction (S) will be €3,604,000. The European stocks' beta (β_S) is 1.2, and the target beta is $\beta_T = 0$. The EURO STOXX 50 index futures have a contract value (F) of €35,000, with a beta (β_f) of 1.0, so

$$N_f = \left(\frac{\beta_T - \beta_S}{\beta_f} \right) \left(\frac{S}{F} \right) = \left(\frac{0.0 - 1.2}{1.0} \right) \left(\frac{€3,604,000}{€35,000} \right) = -123.57$$

Grant sells 124 futures contracts (after rounding).

The market value of the German bunds is €60,000,000, and Grant wants to increase the exposure to this market to 0.60(€106,000,000) = €63,600,000. She decides to purchase enough Euro-Bund futures so that €3,604,000 (= 0.034 × €106,000,000) of exposure to German bonds is added to the portfolio. The target basis point value (BPV_T) is given by Equation 4, as follows:

$$BPV_T = MDUR_T \times 0.01\% \times MV_P = 9.5 \times 0.0001 \times €3,604,000 = €3,424$$

The cheapest-to-deliver bond has a BPV_{CTD} of €84.63 and a conversion factor of 0.619489. The number of Euro-Bund futures to buy to convert the €3.6 million in notional cash ($BPV_P = 0$) to the desired exposure in German bonds is found using Equation 9:

$$BPVHR = \left(\frac{BPV_T - BPV_P}{BPV_{CTD}}\right) \times CF$$

$$= [(\text{€}3,424 - 0)/\text{€}84.63] \times 0.619489 = 25.06 \approx 25 \text{ contracts}$$

So, Grant should buy 25 Euro-Bund futures contracts.

8.3. Changing Allocations between Asset Classes Using Swaps

Tactical Money Management Inc. (TMM) is interested in changing the asset allocation on a $200 million segment of its portfolio. This money is invested 75% in US stocks and 25% in US bonds. Within the stock allocation, the funds are invested 60% in large cap, 30% in mid-cap, and 10% percent in small cap. Within the bond sector, the funds are invested 80% in US government bonds and 20% in investment-grade corporate bonds.

Given that it is bullish on equities, especially large-cap stocks, over the next year, TMM would like to change the overall allocation to 90% stocks and 10% bonds. Specifically, TMM would like to split the stock allocation into 65% large cap, 25% mid-cap, and 10% small cap. It also wants to change the bond allocation to 75% US government and 25% investment-grade corporate. The current position, the desired new position, and the necessary transactions to get from the current position to the new position are shown in Exhibit 7.

EXHIBIT 7   Summary of TMM's Current and New Asset Allocation

Stock	Current ($150 Million, 75%)	New ($180 Million, 90%)	Transaction
Large cap	$90 million (60%)	$117 million (65%)	Buy $27 million
Mid-cap	$45 million (30%)	$45 million (25%)	None
Small cap	$15 million (10%)	$18 million (10%)	Buy $3 million
Bonds	Current ($50 Million, 25%)	New ($20 Million, 10%)	Transaction
Government	$40 million (80%)	$15 million (75%)	Sell $25 million
Corporate	$10 million (20%)	$5 million (25%)	Sell $5 million

TMM knows these changes would entail a considerable amount of trading in stocks and bonds. So, TMM decides to execute a series of swaps that would enable it to change its position temporarily but more easily and less expensively than by executing the physical transactions. TMM engages Dynamic Dealers Inc. to perform the swaps.

TMM decides to increase the allocation in the large-cap sector by investing in the S&P 500 Index and to increase that in the small-cap sector by investing in the S&P SmallCap 600 Index (SPSC). To reduce the allocation in the overall fixed-income sector, TMM decides to replicate the performance of the Bloomberg Barclays US Treasury Index (BBT) for the government bond sector and the BofA Merrill Lynch US Corporate Index (BAMLC) for the corporate bond sector.

Discuss how TMM can use a combination of equity and fixed-income swaps to synthetically implement its desired asset allocation.

Solution:
To achieve the desired asset allocation, TMM takes the following exposures:

- A long position of $27 million in the S&P 500
- A long position of $3 million in the SPSC
- A short position of $25 million in the BBT
- A short position of $5 million in the BAMLC

The mid-cap exposure of $45 million does not change, so TMM does not need to incorporate a mid-cap index into the swap. TMM uses a combination of equity and fixed-income swaps to achieve its target allocation and structures the swap to have all payments occur on the same dates six months apart. TMM also decides that the swap should mature in one year. If it wishes to extend this period, TMM would need to renegotiate the swap at expiration. Likewise, TMM could decide to unwind the position before one year elapses, which it could do by executing a new swap with opposite payments for the remainder of the life of the original swap.

Every six months and at maturity, each of the equity swaps involves the settlement of the following cash flows:

- *Equity swap 1:* TMM receives the total return of the S&P 500 and makes a floating payment tied to the market reference rate (MRR) minus the agreed-on spread, both on a notional principal of $27 million.
- *Equity swap 2:* TMM receives the total return of the SPSC and makes a floating payment tied to the MRR minus the agreed-on spread, both on a notional principal of $3 million.

The fixed-income swaps will require the following cash flow settlements every six months and at maturity:

- *Fixed-income swap 1:* TMM pays the total return of the BBT and receives floating payments tied to the MRR minus the agreed-on spread, both on notional principal of $25 million.
- *Fixed-income swap 2:* TMM pays the total return of the BAMLC and receives floating payments tied to the MRR minus the agreed-on spread, both on a notional principal of $5 million.

It is important to recognize that this transaction will not perfectly replicate the performance of TMM's equity and fixed-income portfolios, unless they are indexed to the indexes selected as underlying of the swaps. In addition, TMM could encounter a cash flow problem if its fixed-income payments exceed its equity receipts and its portfolio does not generate enough cash to fund its net obligation. The stock and bond portfolio will generate cash only from dividends and interest. Capital gains will not be received in cash unless a portion of the portfolio is sold. But avoiding selling a portion of the portfolio is the very reason why TMM wants to use swaps.

9. USING DERIVATIVES TO INFER MARKET EXPECTATIONS

As mentioned at the beginning of this reading, an important use of derivatives by market participants is for inferring market expectations. These expectations can be for changes in interest rates; for changes in prices for the whole economy (i.e., inflation), individual stocks, or other assets; or even for changes in key factors, such as implied volatility. Exhibit 8 provides a brief list of some of the myriad applications by which information embedded in derivatives prices is used to infer current market expectations. It is important to emphasize that these inferences relate to *current expectations* of future events—they do not foretell what will actually happen—which can change with the arrival of new information.

EXHIBIT 8   Some Typical Applications of Derivatives for Inferring Market Expectations

Use Cases/Applications	Derivative Type
1. Inferring expectations for FOMC moves	Fed funds futures
2. Inferring expectations for inflation rates	CPI (inflation) swaps
3. Inferring expectations for market volatility	VIX futures

The first application in Exhibit 8, using fed funds futures to infer expectations of federal funds rate changes by the Federal Open Market Committee (FOMC), is likely the most common and well-publicized use of derivatives for inferring market expectations, so it is the focus of the following discussion.

9.1. Using Fed Funds Futures to Infer the Expected Average Federal Funds Rate

Market participants are interested in knowing the probabilities of various interest rate level outcomes, deriving from central banks' future decisions, as implied by the pricing of financial instruments. This provides them with an indication about the extent to which markets are "pricing in" future monetary policy changes. Note that such implied probabilities represent the market's view and may diverge from the guidance provided by central banks in their regular communications about the likely future course of monetary policy actions. Furthermore, especially for the longer-term horizon, these inferred probabilities usually do not have strong predictive power. Most information providers and the business media report current implied probability data for selected interest rates and historical analysis charts that show how the implied probabilities of policy rate settings have changed over time.

A commonly followed metric is the probability of a change in the federal funds rate at upcoming FOMC meetings that is implied by the prices of fed funds futures contracts. When the US central bank began its rate hiking cycle in 2015, it declared an intention to maintain a 25 bp "target range" (lower and upper bounds) for the federal funds rate. The Fed regularly communicates its "forward guidance" along with the so-called dot plot, which shows where each FOMC meeting participant believes the federal funds rate should be at the end of the year, for the next few years, and in the longer run.

To derive probabilities of potential upcoming Fed interest rate actions, market participants look at the pricing of fed funds futures, which are tied to the **effective federal funds (FFE) rate**—the rate actually transacted between depository institutions—not the Fed's target federal funds rate. The underlying assumption is that the implied futures market rates are predicting the value of the monthly average effective federal funds rate. As shown in Exhibit 9, where the dots represent forecasts of the federal funds rate by each FOMC member, implied market expectations (dotted line) can diverge significantly from the Fed's forward guidance (solid line, the median of the dots).

EXHIBIT 9   Hypothetical Example of Market's Implied Forecast vs. FOMC Forecast of Federal Funds Rate

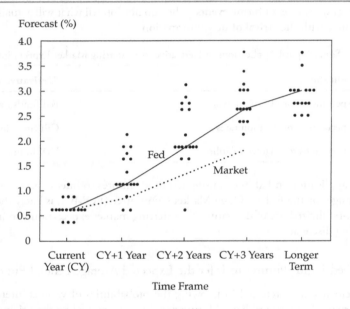

Fed funds futures are traded on the Chicago Board of Trade, and the contract price is quoted as 100 minus the market's expectation for the FFE rate, as follows:

$$\text{Fed funds futures contract price} = 100 - \text{Expected FFE rate.} \qquad (17)$$

At expiration, the contract is cash settled to the simple average (overnight) effective federal funds rate for the delivery month. The overnight rate is calculated and reported daily by the Federal Reserve Bank of New York.

To determine the probability of a change in the federal funds rate, the following formula is used, where the current federal funds rate is the midpoint of the current target range:

$$\frac{\text{Effective federal funds rate implied by futures contract} - \text{Current federal funds rate}}{\text{Federal funds rate assuming a rate hike} - \text{Current federal funds rate}} \qquad (18)$$

9.2. Inferring Market Expectations

Andrew Okyung manages a portfolio of short-term floating-rate corporate debt, and he is interested in understanding current market expectations for any Fed rate actions at the upcoming FOMC meeting. He observes that the current price for the fed funds futures contract expiring after the next FOMC meeting is 97.90. The current federal funds rate target range is set between 1.75% and 2.00%.

Demonstrate how Okyung can use the information provided to determine the following:

1. The expected average FFE rate
2. The probability of a 25 bp interest rate hike at the next FOMC meeting

Solution to 1:
The FFE rate implied by the futures contract price is 2.10% (= 100 − 97.90). Okyung understands that this is the rate that market participants expect to be the average federal funds rate for that month.

Solution to 2:
Okyung knows that given that the FFE rate embedded in the fed funds futures price is 2.10%, there is a high probability that the FOMC will increase rates by 25 bps from its current target range of 1.75%–2.00% to the new target range of 2.00%–2.25%. Given the Fed's declared incremental move size of 25 bps, he calculates the probability of a rate hike as

$$\frac{2.100\% - 1.875\%}{2.125\% - 1.875\%} = 0.90, \text{ or } 90\%$$

where 1.875% is the midpoint of the current target range (1.75%–2.00%) and 2.125% is the midpoint of the new target range (2.00%–2.25%) assuming a rate hike.

Exhibit 10 displays, as a hypothetical example, the trends in implied probabilities (y-axis) derived from fed funds futures prices of an FOMC rate action—either a 25 bp rate hike, a 25 bp rate cut, or no change—at the next FOMC meeting date. Note that the probability of a rate hike or cut is represented as the probability of a move from the current target range at the specified meeting date, and of course, the probabilities of all three actions at a particular meeting date sum to 1.

EXHIBIT 10   Hypothetical Example of Trends of Probabilities for Federal Funds Rate Actions by the FOMC

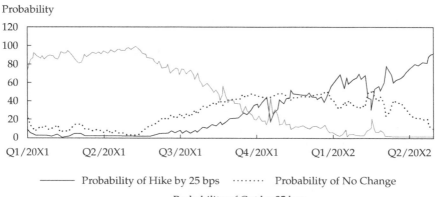

Importantly, typical end-of-month (EOM) activity by large financial and banking institutions often induces "dips" in the FFE rate that create bias issues when using the rate as the basis for probability calculations of potential FOMC rate moves. For example, if such activity increased the price for the relevant fed funds futures contract to 98.05, then the FFE rate would decline to 1.95% (= 100 − 98.05). In this case, using the same equation as before, the probability of an FOMC rate hike decreases from 90% to just 30%:

$$\frac{1.950 - 1.875}{0.25} = 0.30, \text{ or } 30\%$$

To overcome this end-of-month bias, data providers have implemented various methods of "smoothing" the EOM dips. One prominent data provider uses a method that builds a forward rate structure based on where the market believes interest rates will settle in non-FOMC meeting months and then uses these forward rates to make appropriate adjustments. For each FOMC meeting month, it is assumed that an effective rate prevails until the meeting date, and then some rate prevails after the meeting, with the average effective rate over the month being implied by the futures price.

SUMMARY

This reading on swap, forward, and futures strategies shows a number of ways in which market participants might use these derivatives to enhance returns or to reduce risk to better meet portfolio objectives. Following are the key points.

- Interest rate, currency, and equity swaps, forwards, and futures can be used to modify risk and return by altering the characteristics of the cash flows of an investment portfolio.
- An interest rate swap is an OTC contract in which two parties agree to exchange cash flows on specified dates, one based on a floating interest rate and the other based on a fixed rate (swap rate), determined at swap initiation. Both rates are applied to the swap's notional value to determine the size of the payments, which are typically netted. Interest rate swaps enable a party with a fixed (floating) risk or obligation to effectively convert it into a floating (fixed) one.
- Investors can use short-dated interest rate futures and forward rate agreements or longer-dated fixed-income (bond) futures contracts to modify their portfolios' interest rate risk exposure.
- When hedging interest rate risk with bond futures, one must determine the basis point value of the portfolio to be hedged, the target basis point value, and the basis point value of the futures, which itself is determined by the basis point value of the cheapest-to-deliver bond and its conversion factor. The number of bond futures to buy or sell to reach the target basis point value is then determined by the basis point value hedge ratio: $BPVHR = \left(\dfrac{BPV_T - BPV_P}{BPV_{CTD}}\right) \times CF$.
- Cross-currency basis swaps help parties in the swap to hedge against the risk of exchange rate fluctuations and to achieve better rate outcomes. Firms that need foreign-denominated cash can obtain funding in their local currency (likely at a more favorable rate) and then swap the local currency for the required foreign currency using a cross-currency basis swap.
- Equity risk in a portfolio can be managed using equity swaps and total return swaps. There are three main types of equity swap: (1) receive-equity return, pay-fixed; (2) receive-equity

return, pay-floating; and (3) receive-equity return, pay-another equity return. A total return swap is a modified equity swap; it also includes in the performance any dividends paid by the underlying stocks or index during the period until the swap maturity.

- Equity risk in a portfolio can also be managed using equity futures and forwards. Equity futures are standardized, exchange-listed contracts, and when the underlying is a stock index, only cash settlement is available at contract expiration. The number of equity futures contracts to buy or sell is determined by $N_f = \left(\dfrac{\beta_T - \beta_S}{\beta_f} \right) \left(\dfrac{S}{F} \right)$.

- Cash equitization is a strategy designed to boost returns by finding ways to "equitize" unintended cash holdings. It is typically done using stock index futures and interest rate futures.

- Derivatives on volatility include VIX futures and options and variance swaps. Importantly, VIX option prices are determined from VIX futures, and both instruments allow an investor to implement a view depending on her expectations about the timing and magnitude of a change in implied volatility.

- In a variance swap, the buyer of the contract will pay the difference between the fixed variance strike specified in the contract and the realized variance (annualized) on the underlying over the period specified and applied to a variance notional. Thus, variance swaps allow directional bets on implied versus realized volatility.

- Derivatives can be used to infer market participants' current expectations for changes over the short term in inflation (e.g., CPI swaps) and market volatility (e.g., VIX futures). Another common application is using fed funds futures prices to derive the probability of a central bank move in the federal funds rate target at the FOMC's next meeting.

PROBLEMS

1. A US bond portfolio manager wants to hedge a long position in a 10-year Treasury bond against a potential rise in domestic interest rates. He would *most likely:*
   A. sell fixed-income (bond) futures.
   B. enter a receive-fixed 10-year interest rate swap.
   C. sell a strip of 90-day Eurodollar futures contracts.

2. A European bond portfolio manager wants to increase the modified duration of his €30 million portfolio from 3 to 5. She would *most likely* enter a receive-fixed interest rate swap that has principal notional of €20 million and:
   A. a modified duration of 2.
   B. a modified duration of 3.
   C. a modified duration of 4.

3. The CIO of a Canadian private equity company wants to lock in the interest on a three-month "bridge" loan his firm will take out in six months to complete an LBO deal. He sells the relevant interest rate futures contracts at 98.05. In six-months' time, he initiates the loan at 2.70% and unwinds the hedge at 97.30. The effective interest rate on the loan is:
   A. 0.75%.
   B. 1.95%.
   C. 2.70%.

4. A US institutional investor in search of yield decides to buy Italian government bonds for her portfolio but wants to hedge against the risk of exchange rate fluctuations. She enters a cross-currency basis swap, with the same payment dates as the bonds, where at inception she delivers US dollars in exchange for euros for use in purchasing the Italian bonds. The notional principals on the swap are *most likely* exchanged:

   A. at inception only.

   B. at maturity only.

   C. both at inception and at maturity.

5. Continuing from the previous question, assume demand for US dollars is strong relative to demand for euros, so there is a positive basis for "lending" US dollars. By hedging the position in Italian government bonds with the currency basis swap, the US investor will *most likely* increase the periodic net interest payments received from the swap counterparty in:

   A. euros only.

   B. US dollars only.

   C. both euros and US dollars.

6. An equity portfolio manager is invested 100% in US large-cap stocks, but he wants to reduce the current allocation by 20%, to 80%, and allocate 20% to US small caps. He decides not to sell the stocks because of the high transaction costs. Rather, he will use S&P 500 Index futures and Russell 2000 Index futures for achieving the desired exposure in, respectively, US large caps and small caps. To achieve the new allocation, he will for an equivalent of 20% of the portfolio value:

   A. purchase Russell 2000 futures only.

   B. purchase Russell 2000 futures and sell S&P 500 futures.

   C. sell Russell 2000 futures and purchase S&P 500 futures.

7. A volatility trader observes that the VIX term structure is upward sloping. In particular, the VIX is at 13.50, the front-month futures contract trades at 14.10, and the second-month futures contract trades at 15.40. Assuming the shape of the VIX term structure will remain constant over the next three-month period, the trader decides to implement a trade that would profit from the VIX carry roll down. She will *most likely* purchase the:

   A. VIX and sell the VIX second-month futures.

   B. VIX and sell the VIX front-month futures.

   C. VIX front-month futures and sell the VIX second-month futures.

8. The CEO of a corporation owns 100 million shares of his company's stock, which is currently priced at €30 a share. Given the huge exposure of his personal wealth to this one company, he has decided to sell 10% of his position and invest the funds in a floating interest rate instrument. A derivatives dealer suggests that he do so using an equity swap.

   Explain how to structure such a swap.

9. A $30 million investment account of a bank trust fund is allocated one-third to stocks and two-thirds to bonds. The portfolio manager wants to change the overall allocation to 50% stock and 50% bonds and the allocation within the stock fund from 70% domestic stock and 30% foreign stock to 60% domestic and 40% foreign. The bond allocation will remain entirely invested in domestic corporate issues.

   Explain how swaps can be used to implement this adjustment. The market reference rate is assumed to be flat for all swaps, and you do not need to refer to specific stock and bond indexes.

10. Sarah Ko, a private wealth adviser in Singapore, is developing a short-term interest rate forecast for her private wealth clients who have holdings in the US fixed-income markets.

Ko needs to understand current market expectations for possible upcoming central bank (i.e., US Federal Reserve Board) rate actions. The current price for the fed funds futures contract expiring after the next FOMC meeting is 97.175. The current federal funds rate target range is set between 2.50% and 2.75%.

Explain how Ko can use this information to understand potential movements in the current federal funds rate.

The following information relates to Questions 11–17

Global Mega (Global) is a diversified financial services firm. Yasuko Regan, senior trader, and Marcus Whitacre, junior trader, both work on the firm's derivatives desk. Regan and Whitacre assist in structuring and implementing trades for clients in the financial services industry that have limited derivatives expertise. Regan and Whitacre are currently assisting one of Global's clients—Monatize, an asset management firm—with two of its portfolios: Portfolio A and Portfolio B.

Portfolio A is a bond portfolio composed solely of US Treasury bonds. Monatize has asked Global to quote the number of Treasury futures contracts necessary to fully hedge this bond portfolio against a rise in interest rates. Exhibit 1 presents selected data on Portfolio A, the relevant Treasury futures contract, and the cheapest-to-deliver (CTD) bond.

EXHIBIT 1   Selected Data on Portfolio A, the Treasury Futures Contract, and the CTD Bond

Portfolio A		Futures Contract and CTD Bond	
Market value	$143,234,000	Price	145.20
Modified duration	9.10	Modified duration	8.75
Basis point value	$130,342.94	Basis point value	$127.05
		Conversion factor	0.72382
		Contract size	$100,000

After an internal discussion, Monatize elects to not hedge Portfolio A but rather decrease the portfolio's modified duration to 3.10. Regan asks Whitacre to compute the number of Treasury futures contracts to sell in order to achieve this objective. Regan tells Whitacre to assume the yield curve is flat.

Portfolio B is a $100,000,000 equity portfolio indexed to the S&P 500 Index, with excess cash of $4,800,000. Monatize is required to equitize its excess cash to be fully invested, and the firm directs Global to purchase futures contracts to do so. To replicate the return of Portfolio B's target index, Whitacre purchases S&P 500 futures contracts, at a price of 3,300 per contract, that have a multiplier of $250 per index point and a beta of 1.00.

Monatize's CFO and Regan discuss two potential hedging strategies for Portfolio B to protect against a hypothetical extreme sell-off in equities. Regan first suggests that Monatize could enter into a total return equity swap, whereby Monatize agrees to pay the return on the S&P 500 and receive a fixed interest rate at pre-specified dates in exchange for a fee.

Regan next suggests that Monatize could alternatively hedge Portfolio B using variance swaps. Monatize's CFO asks Regan to calculate what the gain would be in five months on a purchase of $1,000,000 vega notional of a one-year variance swap on the S&P 500 at a strike of 15% (quoted as annual volatility), assuming the following:

- Over the next five months, the S&P 500 experiences a realized volatility of 20%;
- At the end of the five-month period, the fair strike of a new seven-month variance swap on the S&P 500 will be 18%; and
- The annual interest rate is 1.50%.

Regan and Whitacre discuss the use of federal funds futures contracts to infer probabilities of future monetary policy changes. Whitacre makes the following three statements about fed funds futures contracts:

Statement 1: Typical end-of-month activity by large financial and banking institutions often induces "dips" in the effective fed funds rate.

Statement 2: Especially for the longer-term horizon, the probabilities inferred from the pricing of fed funds futures usually have strong predictive power.

Statement 3: To derive probabilities of Federal Reserve interest rate actions, market participants look at the pricing of fed funds futures, which are tied to the Federal Reserve's target fed funds rate.

Whitacre then proposes to Regan that Global explore opportunities in bond futures arbitrage. Whitacre makes the following two statements:

Statement 4: If the basis is positive, a trader would make a profit by "selling the basis."

Statement 5: If the basis is negative, a trader would make a profit by selling the bond and buying the futures.

11. Based on Exhibit 1, the number of Treasury futures contracts Whitacre should sell to fully hedge Portfolio A is *closest* to:
    A. 650.
    B. 743.
    C. 1,026.
12. Based on Exhibit 1, the number of Treasury futures contracts Whitacre should sell to achieve Monatize's objective with respect to Portfolio A is *closest* to:
    A. 490.
    B. 518.
    C. 676.
13. The number of S&P 500 futures contracts that Whitacre should buy to equitize Portfolio B's excess cash position is *closest* to:
    A. 6.
    B. 121.
    C. 1,455.
14. The derivative product first suggested by Regan as a potential hedge strategy for Portfolio B:
    A. is a relatively liquid contract.
    B. eliminates counterparty credit risk.
    C. allows Monatize to keep voting rights on its equity portfolio.
15. Based on the CFO's set of assumptions, the gain on the purchase of the variance swap on the S&P 500 in five months would be *closest* to:
    A. $4,317,775.
    B. $4,355,556.
    C. $4,736,334.

16. Which of Whitacre's three statements about fed funds futures is correct?
    A. Statement 1
    B. Statement 2
    C. Statement 3
17. Which of Whitacre's two statements regarding bond futures arbitrage is correct?
    A. Only Statement 4
    B. Only Statement 5
    C. Both Statement 4 and Statement 5

The following information relates to Questions 18–20

Nisqually Uff is the portfolio manager for the Chehalis Fund (the Fund), which holds equities and bonds in its portfolio. Uff focuses on tactical portfolio strategies and uses derivatives to implement his strategies.

Uff has a positive short-term outlook for equities relative to bonds and decides to temporarily increase the beta of the portfolio's equity allocation from 0.9 to 1.2. He will use three-month equity index futures contracts to adjust the beta. Exhibit 1 displays selected data for the Fund's current equity allocation and the relevant futures contract.

EXHIBIT 1   Selected Data for the Fund's Current Equity Allocation and Futures Contract

Current value of the Fund's equity allocation	€168,300,000
Current portfolio beta	0.9
Target portfolio beta	1.2
Index futures contract value	€45,000
Beta of futures contract	1.0

18. Determine the appropriate number of equity index futures contracts that Uff should use to achieve the target portfolio beta. Identify whether the equity index futures contracts should be bought or sold.

One month later, Uff expects interest rates to rise. He decides to reduce the modified duration of the bond allocation of the Fund's portfolio without selling any of its existing bonds. To do so, Uff adds a negative-duration position by entering into an interest rate swap in which he pays the fixed rate and receives the floating rate. Exhibit 2 presents selected data for the Fund's bond allocation and the relevant swap contract.

EXHIBIT 2   Selected Data for the Fund's Bond Allocation and Swap Contract

Current value of the Fund's bond allocation	€90,100,000
Current portfolio average modified duration	7.8000
Target portfolio modified duration	5.0000
Swap modified duration for fixed-rate payer	−2.4848

19. Determine the required notional principal for the interest rate swap in order to achieve the target modified duration for the portfolio.

Six months later, Uff has since closed out both the equity index futures contract position and the interest rate swap position. In response to market movements, he now wants to implement a tactical rebalancing of the Fund's portfolio. Exhibit 3 presents the current and target asset allocations for the Fund's portfolio.

EXHIBIT 3   Current and Target Asset Allocations for the Fund's Portfolio

Asset Class	Current	Target
Equities	€201,384,000 (69.56%)	€188,181,500 (65.0%)
Bonds	€88,126,000 (30.44%)	€101,328,500 (35.0%)
Total	**€289,510,000**	**€289,510,000**

Uff decides to use equity index and bond futures contracts to rebalance the portfolio. Exhibit 4 shows selected data on the Fund's portfolio and the relevant futures contracts.

EXHIBIT 4   Selected Data on Fund's Portfolio and Relevant Futures Contracts

Beta of the Fund's equities relative to index	1.28
Modified duration of the Fund's bonds	4.59
Equity index futures contract value	€35,000
Beta of equity index futures contract	1.00
Basis point value of cheapest-to-deliver (CTD) bond	€91.26
Conversion factor (CF) for CTD bond	0.733194

20. Determine how many equity index and bond futures contracts Uff should use to rebalance the Fund's portfolio to the target allocation. Identify whether the futures contracts should be bought or sold.

The following information relates to Questions 21–22

Canawacta Tioga is the CFO for Wyalusing Corporation, a multinational manufacturing company based in Canada. One year ago, Wyalusing issued fixed-rate coupon bonds in Canada. Tioga now expects Canadian interest rates to fall and remain low for three years. During this three-year period, Tioga wants to use a par interest rate swap to effectively convert the fixed-rate bond coupon payments into floating-rate payments.

21. Explain how to construct the swap that Tioga wants to use with regard to the swap:
    i. tenor
    ii. cash flows
    iii. notional value
    iv. settlement dates

Wyalusing will soon be building a new manufacturing plant in the United States. To fund construction of the plant, the company will borrow in its home currency of CAD because of favorable interest rates. Tioga plans to use a cross-currency basis swap so that Wyalusing will borrow in CAD but make interest payments in USD.

22. Describe how the swap will function, from the perspective of Wyalusing, in terms of the:
    i.   cash flows at inception.
    ii. periodic cash flows.
    iii. cash flows at maturity.

The following information relates to Questions 23–24

Southern Sloth Sanctuary (Sanctuary) is a charitable organization that cares for orphaned and injured sloths from the rain forest in the country of Lushland. The organization is supported by both domestic and international contributions. The Sanctuary's CFO typically invests any funds that are not immediately needed for short-term operational expenses into a domestic index fund that tracks the Lushland 100 stock index, which is denominated in Lushland dollars (LLD).

The Sanctuary just received a large contribution from a local benefactor in the amount of LLD1,000,000. These funds are not needed for short-term operational expenses. The CFO intends to equitize this excess cash position using futures contracts to replicate the return on the Lushland 100 stock index. Exhibit 1 shows selected data for the Lushland 100 Index futures contract.

EXHIBIT 1   Selected Data for Lushland 100 Index Futures Contract

Quoted price of futures contract	1,247
Contract multiplier	LLD 200
Contract beta	1.00

23. Determine the appropriate number of futures contracts that the CFO should buy to equitize the excess cash position.

A Japanese benefactor recently donated a plot of land in Japan to the Sanctuary. Ownership of the land has been transferred to the Sanctuary, which has a binding contract to sell the property for JPY500,000,000. The property sale will be completed in 30 days. The Sanctuary's CFO wants to hedge the risk of JPY depreciation using futures contracts. The CFO assumes a hedge ratio of 1.

24. Describe a strategy to implement the CFO's desired hedge.

CHAPTER 10

INTRODUCTION TO RISK MANAGEMENT

Don M. Chance, PhD, CFA, and Michael E. Edleson, PhD, CFA

LEARNING OUTCOMES

The candidate should be able to:

- define risk management;
- describe features of a risk management framework;
- define risk governance and describe elements of effective risk governance;
- explain how risk tolerance affects risk management;
- describe risk budgeting and its role in risk governance;
- identify financial and non-financial sources of risk and describe how they may interact;
- describe methods for measuring and modifying risk exposures and factors to consider in choosing among the methods.

1. INTRODUCTION

Risk—and risk management—is an inescapable part of economic activity. People generally manage their affairs to be as happy and secure as their environment and resources will allow. But regardless of how carefully these affairs are managed, there is risk because the outcome, whether good or bad, is seldom predictable with complete certainty. There is risk inherent in nearly everything we do, but this reading will focus on economic and financial risk, particularly as it relates to investment management.

All businesses and investors manage risk, whether consciously or not, in the choices they make. At its core, business and investing are about allocating resources and capital to chosen risks. In their decision process, within an environment of uncertainty, these organizations may take steps to avoid some risks, pursue the risks that provide the highest rewards, and measure and mitigate their exposure to these risks as necessary. Risk management processes and tools make difficult business and financial problems easier to address in an uncertain world. Risk is not just a matter of fate; it is something that organizations can actively manage with their decisions, within a risk management framework. Risk is an integral part of the business or investment process. Even in the earliest models of modern portfolio theory, such as mean–variance portfolio optimization and the capital asset pricing model, investment return is linked directly to risk but requires that risk be managed optimally. Proper identification and measurement of risk, and keeping risks aligned with the goals of the enterprise, are key factors in managing businesses and investments. Good risk management results in a higher chance of a preferred outcome—more value for the company or portfolio or more utility for the individual.

Portfolio managers need to be familiar with risk management not only to improve the portfolio's risk–return outcome, but also because of two other ways in which they use risk management at an enterprise level. First, they help to manage their own companies that have their own enterprise risk issues. Second, many portfolio assets are claims on companies that have risks. Portfolio managers need to evaluate the companies' risks and how those companies are addressing them.

This reading takes a broad approach that addresses both the risk management of enterprises in general and portfolio risk management. The principles underlying portfolio risk management are generally applicable to the risk management of financial and non-financial institutions as well.

The concept of risk management is also relevant to individuals. Although many large organizations formally practice risk management, most individuals practice it more informally and some practice it haphazardly, oftentimes responding to risk events after they occur. Although many individuals do take reasonable precautions against unwanted risks, these precautions are often against obvious risks. The more subtle risks are often ignored. Unfortunately, many individuals do not view risk management as a formal, systematic process that would help them achieve not only their financial goals but also the ultimate goal, or maximum utility as economists like to call it, but they should.

Although the primary focus of this reading is on institutions, we will also cover risk management as it applies to individuals. We will show that many common themes underlie risk management—themes that are applicable to both organizations and individuals.

Although often viewed as defensive, risk management is a valuable offensive weapon in the manager's arsenal. In the quest for preferred outcomes, such as higher profit, returns, or share price, management does not usually get to choose the outcomes but does choose the risks it takes in pursuit of those outcomes. The choice of which risks to undertake through the allocation of its scarce resources is the key tool available to management. An organization with a comprehensive risk management culture in place, in which risk is integral to every key strategy and decision, should perform better in the long-term, in good times and bad, as a result of better decision making.

The fact that all businesses and investors engage in risky activities (i.e., activities with uncertain outcomes) raises a number of important questions. The questions that this reading will address include the following:

- What is risk management, and why is it important?
- What risks does an organization (or individual) face in pursuing its objectives?
- How are an organization's goals affected by risk, and how does it make risk management decisions to produce better results?
- How does risk governance guide the risk management process and risk budgeting to integrate an organization's goals with its activities?
- How does an organization measure and evaluate the risks it faces, and what tools does it have to address these risks?

The answers to these questions collectively help to define the process of risk management. This reading is organized along the lines of these questions. Sections 2 and 3 describe the risk management process, and Sections 4–6 discuss risk governance and risk tolerance. Sections 7 and 8 cover the identification of various risks, and Sections 9–11 address the measurement and management of risks.

2. THE RISK MANAGEMENT PROCESS

Risk, broadly speaking, is exposure to uncertainty. Risk is also the concept used to describe all of the uncertain environmental variables that lead to variation in and unpredictability of outcomes. More colloquially, risk is about the chance of a loss or adverse outcome as a result of an action, inaction, or external event.

This last view may make it sound as if risk is something to be avoided. But that is not at all the case. Risk is a key ingredient in the recipe for business or investment success; return without risk is generally a false hope and usually a prescription for falling short of one's goals. Risks taken must be carefully chosen, understood, and well-managed to have a chance at adding value through decisions. Risk and return are the interconnected forces of the financial universe. Many decision makers focus on return, which is not something that is easily controlled, as opposed to risk, or exposure to risk, which may actually be managed or controlled.

Risk exposure is the extent to which the underlying environmental or market risks result in actual risk borne by a business or investor who has assets or liabilities that are sensitive to those risks. It is the state of being exposed or vulnerable to a risk. Risk exposure results from the decisions of an organization or investor to take on risk-sensitive assets and liabilities.

Suppose there is an important announcement in Japan that will result in the yen either appreciating or depreciating by 1%. The range of possible outcomes in real situations is clearly not as simple as the up-or-down 1% case used here, but we will use a simplified example to make an important point. The risk is the uncertain outcome of this event, and the currency risk to a non-Japanese business is the uncertain return or variation in return in domestic currency terms that results from the event. The risk can be described as the range of resulting outcomes and is often thought of in terms of a probability distribution of future returns. Suppose that the underlying amount is ¥1,000,000. The risk exposure of a business may be zero or it could be sizable, depending on whether the business has assets or liabilities tied to this risk—in this case, exposure to that currency. One million yen would, in this example, result in ¥10,000 of risk exposure (1% of ¥1,000,000). Risk management would include, among other things, quantifying and understanding this risk exposure, deciding how and why to have the exposure and how much risk the participant can bear, and possibly mitigating this risk by tailoring the exposure in several ways. The risk management process would inform the decision of whether to operate or invest in this risky currency.

> The word "risk" can be confusing because it is used by different people at different times to mean so many different things. Even when used properly, the term has three related but different meanings, which this example illustrates well. Risk can mean, in turn, the underlying uncertainty, the extent of the risky action taken, or the resulting range of risky outcomes to the organization. In this example, the first meaning is the uncertain +1% or −1% movement of the currency. The second meaning is the ¥1,000,000 worth of risky currency, the position taken by the business. The third meaning is the +¥10,000

or −¥10,000 risky outcome that might accrue to the business for having engaged in this risky activity. A common way of more precisely distinguishing among these three "risks" in usage is: *risk driver* for the underlying risk, *risk position* to describe or quantify the risky action taken, and *risk exposure* for the potential valuation change that may result. In the oversimplified example above, the risk exposure is simply the risk position multiplied by the risk driver. In practice the term "risk" is used interchangeably for all three meanings.

Risk management *is the process by which an organization or individual defines the level of risk to be taken, measures the level of risk being taken, and adjusts the latter toward the former, with the goal of maximizing the company's or portfolio's value or the individual's overall satisfaction, or utility.*

Said differently, risk management comprises all the decisions and actions needed to *best* achieve organizational or personal objectives while bearing a tolerable level of risk. Risk management is *not* about minimizing risk; it is about actively understanding and embracing those risks that best balance the achievement of goals with an acceptable chance of failure, quantifying the exposure, and continually monitoring and modifying it. A company that shied away from all risk would find that it could not operate. In trying to create wealth, all organizations will find themselves "in the risk business." Risk management is not about avoiding risks any more than a practical diet is about avoiding calories. Risk management is not even about predicting risks. "The Doctrine of No Surprises" is a key mantra among many risk managers, but it does not mean they are expected to predict what will happen. Instead, it means that if an unpredictable event, either positive or negative, happens in an uncertain world, the *impact* of that event on the organization or portfolio would not be a surprise and would have been quantified and considered in advance.

For example, a risk manager of a bank would not have been expected to know that a real estate crisis was going to occur and cause significant defaults on the bank's real estate securities. But a good risk manager would help the bank's management decide how much exposure it should have in these securities by quantifying the potential financial impact of such a crisis destroying, say, 60% of the bank's capital. A good risk management process would include a deep discussion at the governance level about the balance between the likely returns and the unlikely—but sizable—losses and whether such losses are tolerable. Management would ensure that the risk analysis and discussion actively affects their investment decisions, that the potential loss is continuously quantified and communicated, and that it will take actions to mitigate or transfer any portion of the risk exposure that cannot be tolerated.[1] The only surprise here should be the market shock itself; the risk manager should have prepared the organization through stress-testing and scenario analysis, continuously reporting in advance on the potential impact of this sizable risk exposure.

A poor risk management process would have ignored the possibility, though small, of such a significant market event and not quantified the potential loss from exposure to a real estate crisis. As such, the bank's management would have had no idea that more than half of the bank's capital could be at risk, not addressed this risk in any governance/risk appetite

---

[1] For example, hedges may be used to limit loss of capital to 20%.

discussion, ignored these risks in its investment decisions, and not taken any action to mitigate this risk. In a good risk management process, most of the work is done before an adverse event happens; in a poor risk management process, perhaps just as much work gets done, but it all comes after the event, which is after the damage has been done.

Good risk management does not prevent losses, but provides a full top-to-bottom framework that rigorously informs the decision-making process—before, during, and after a risk event. Because risks and exposures are dynamic, risk management is a continuous process that is always being reevaluated and revised. If this process is done well, it provides management and staff with the knowledge to navigate as efficiently as possible toward the goals set by the governing body. In turn, this effort increases *ex ante* the value of the business or investment decisions undertaken. Good risk management may allow managers to more quickly or effectively act in the face of a crisis. But *ex post*, even the best risk management may not stop a portfolio from losing money in a market crash nor prevent a business from reduced profits in an economic downturn.

3. THE RISK MANAGEMENT FRAMEWORK

A **risk management framework** flows logically from the definition of risk management that was previously given: It is the infrastructure, process, and analytics needed to support effective risk management in an organization. This process should fully integrate the "risk" and "return" aspects of the enterprise into decisions in support of best achieving its goals within its tolerance for risk. Risk management is not a "one size fits all" solution; it is integral to the enterprise's goals and needs. Thus, it is best achieved through a custom solution. Despite customization, every risk management system or framework should address the following key factors:

- Risk governance
- Risk identification and measurement
- Risk infrastructure
- Defined policies and processes
- Risk monitoring, mitigation, and management
- Communications
- Strategic analysis or integration

Not surprisingly, these factors often overlap in practice. They are defined and discussed here.

Governance is the top-level system of structures, rights, and obligations by which organizations are directed and controlled. Normally performed at the board level, governance is how goals are defined, authority is granted, and top-level decisions are made. The foundation for risk management in the organization is set at the board level as well. **Risk governance** is the top-down process and guidance that directs risk management activities to align with and support the overall enterprise and is addressed in more detail in Sections 4–6. Good governance should include defining an organization's risk tolerance and providing risk oversight. Governance is often driven by regulatory concerns, as well as by the fiduciary role of the governing body. A risk management committee is another facet of governance; it provides top decision makers with a forum for regularly considering risk management issues. To achieve the best results for an organization, risk governance should take an enterprise-wide view. **Enterprise risk management** is an overarching governance approach applied throughout the organization and consistent with its strategy, guiding the risk management framework to focus risk activities on the objectives, health, and value of the *entire* organization.

Risk identification and measurement is the main quantitative core of risk management; but more than that, it must include the qualitative assessment and evaluation of all potential sources of risk and the organization's risk exposures. This ongoing work involves analyzing the environment for relevant risk drivers, which is the common term used for any fundamental underlying factor that results in a risk that is relevant or important to an organization, analyzing the business or portfolio to ascertain risk exposures, tracking changes in those risk exposures, and calculating risk metrics to size these risks under various scenarios and stresses.

Risks are not limited to what is going on in the financial markets. There are many types of risk that can potentially impact a business, portfolio, or individual.

The power of technology has allowed for risk management to be more quantitative and timely. Management can measure and monitor risk, run scenarios, conduct statistical analysis, work with more complex models, and examine more dimensions and risk drivers as well as do it faster. This use of technology needs to be balanced with and supplement—not supplant—experienced business judgment. Technology has made risk infrastructure even more important and beneficial in managing risks.

Risk infrastructure refers to the people and systems required to track risk exposures and perform most of the quantitative risk analysis to allow an assessment of the organization's risk profile. Infrastructure would include risk capture (the important operational process by which a risk exposure gets populated into a risk system), a database and data model, analytic models and systems, a stress or scenario engine, and an ability to generate reports, as well as some amount of skilled and empowered personnel resources dedicated to building and executing the risk framework. With increased reliance on technology, more time and effort must be allotted to test data, models, and results in order to avoid the ironic outcome of the risk of errors coming from within risk systems.

Obviously, the scope of risk infrastructure will be related to the resources, or potential losses, of the organization. Individuals and smaller businesses may rely heavily on an external partner or provider for much of their risk infrastructure and analysis.

Policies and processes are the extension of risk governance into both the day-to-day operation and decision-making processes of the organization. There may be limits, requirements, constraints, and guidelines—some quantitative, some procedural—to ensure risky activities are in line with the organization's predetermined risk tolerance and regulatory requirements. Much of this is just common-sense business practice: updating and protecting data, controlling cash flows, conducting due diligence on investments, handling exceptions and escalations, and making checklists to support important decisions. In a good risk framework, processes would naturally evolve to consider risk at all key decision points, such as investment decisions and asset allocation. Risk management should become an integrated part of the business and not just a policing or regulatory function.

The process of *risk monitoring, mitigation, and management* is the most obvious facet of a risk framework, but also one of the most difficult. Actively monitoring and managing risk requires pulling together risk governance, identification and measurement, infrastructure, and policies and processes and continually reviewing and reevaluating in the face of changing risk exposures and risk drivers. It requires recognizing when risk exposure is not aligned with risk tolerance and then taking action to bring them back into alignment.[2]

Communication of critical risk issues must happen continually and across all levels of the organization. Governance parameters, such as risk tolerances and associated constraints, must

---

[2] Risk mitigation and management is discussed in more detail in Sections 9–11.

be clearly communicated to, and understood by, managers. Risk metrics must be reported in a clear and timely manner. Risk issues must be reviewed and discussed as a standard part of decision making. Changes in exposure must be discussed so that action can be taken as appropriate. There should also be a feedback loop with the governance body so that top-level risk guidance can be validated or updated and communicated back to the rest of the organization.

Strategic analysis and integration help turn risk management into an offensive weapon to improve performance. Good risk management is a key to increasing the value of the overall business or portfolio. A risk management framework should provide the tools to better understand the how and why of performance and help sort out which activities are adding value, and which are not. In investing, rigorous analysis can support better investment decisions and improve strategy and risk-adjusted returns.

EXHIBIT 1   The Risk Management Framework in an Enterprise Context

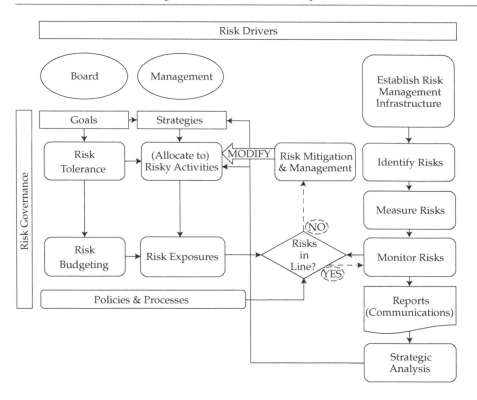

Exhibit 1 illustrates the process of risk management for an enterprise, pulling all the described elements of the risk framework together. Although there are a very high number of risks faced by every organization, most organizations are primarily affected by a small number of key risk drivers, or primary underlying factors that create risk. Along the left side is risk governance, which represents board-level decisions and encompasses and affects the boxes immediately to its right. The governance body, often called a board, defines the goals of the organization and, in turn, decides on its risk tolerance. It may additionally provide guidance on how or where that risk is taken (risk budgeting). The board is also involved in setting high-level policies that will affect most risk management processes. These risk governance activities are a crucial keystone of the risk framework and will be discussed in detail in the next section. When the rest of the risk framework hinges off of these top-down governance elements and is focused on the goals of the entire enterprise (as shown here), the end result is effective enterprise risk management.

The role of management, shown in the middle column, is to plan and execute value-maximizing strategies consistent with their governance guidance. Each management activity in the framework flows not only from management (shown with the arrows) but also from the governance activities on the left. Thus, not only are management's strategies designed to achieve the board's goals, but management also allocates capital to risky activities (its business or investing choices) to execute its strategies consistent with the defined risk tolerance. The risk exposures that result from management's choice of activities should also be aligned with the governing body's risk budget. In addition, management participates actively in setting or implementing policies and establishing procedures that relate to when, how, how much, and by whom each of the other elements of the risk framework are performed.[3]

The rest of the risk management framework comprises a number of important risk activities to help the business achieve all of its strategic and governance goals and mandates. These other elements to implement risk management are shown in the far right column of the illustration. Driven by its need to establish a risk management program to support the enterprise's goals, management would provide the requisite resources for risk management activities by establishing a risk management infrastructure. With risk processes defined and risk infrastructure in place, risks are then identified and measured, which is a regular and continual process of translating risk exposures (produced by the risky activities) into meaningful and generally quantitative risk metrics.

The next major steps—risk monitoring, mitigation, and management—are where much of a firm's day-to-day risk management activity is focused. These activities are split across three boxes in the illustration. Risk levels are continuously monitored, having just been measured.[4] There is a major decision at the monitoring stage: Management must check that all the risks are in line and not outside the limits of the defined risk tolerance or budget.[5] This process involves evaluating the actual risk exposures compared with the organization's risk policies and procedures to ensure that everything is in compliance. If the answer is "no," then risk mitigation and management actions need to be taken to modify risk levels and to bring them back into compliance. There are a variety of methods to accomplish this task, which are addressed in Sections 9–11. Whatever the method, management's allocation of the risk budget to risky activities will be altered by this modification, which includes changing the organization's risk exposures, starting the circle again through the steps on the right, and re-checking to see if risk levels are now consistent with risk policies.

---

[3] In essence, there could be an arrow from policies and processes to every other box to the right, but these rather obvious relationships are intentionally omitted in the diagram to avoid clutter. Likewise, risk exposures inform nearly all the boxes to the right. Risk management is innately quite interrelated.

[4] Continuous usually does not mean real-time; the frequency of monitoring is based on the resources available, the level of systems support, and the need for risk information in the decision process. At large financial firms, this monitoring will generally be daily; for small businesses and individuals it might be quarterly.

[5] This task is generally delegated to a risk manager; but whatever the title, someone must be accountable for this important check.

When risks *are* in line with limits, policies, tolerances, mandates, and so on, then the process moves back to continuous monitoring followed by communicating risk levels.[6] This communication, at a minimum, includes reporting key risk metrics on a regular and timely basis across the organization to assist management in its decision-making process and the board in fulfilling its governance duties. Finally, strategic analysis is supported by the risk measurement, reporting, and other steps of the enterprise risk management process. By analyzing all of the enterprise's strategies and risky activities via the risk measurement lens, management can improve its decision-making process and ascertain where to invest its limited capital and risk budget most fruitfully. This step is generally underappreciated and is an inexpensive and beneficial by-product of having built a risk framework. The last two boxes or steps (reports and strategic analysis) represent important feedback loops to inform and improve both governance and the portfolio of risky activities that make up the business.

There are many feedback loops in properly executed risk management. In practice, most of these steps overlap most of the time and are being performed simultaneously. Good risk management ties together all these steps from the highest governance decisions to lower-level specifics, such as models, reports, and operational checklists.

The risk environment is dynamic, and many of our notions of probabilities and likely risk outcomes change in ways we probably could not predict. The risk management framework should be robust enough to anticipate this dynamism—to expect the unexpected. It should be evolutionary—flexible enough to grow with a company or individual and its new challenges.

The complexity of the risk management framework depends on the complexity of an organization's risk exposures and their resources. But that does not mean that smaller organizations or individuals should skip the risk management process; they may simply be able to do less, or have to work with external partners to assist with large portions of the framework, or be less formal about the process. Ultimately, the key principles just covered are still important even to the smallest organization, even if the specific components do not get assembled as described.

The Risk Management Process for an Individual

Although an individual has neither the resources nor the organizational overhead of a large business, the importance of risk management is not diminished and the risk management framework still applies, albeit most likely in a scaled-down form. Though nearly all of the essential elements of the process illustrated in Exhibit 1 are still useful, the individual can reduce the recipe to six essential ingredients, consistent with the reduced scope of the individual's risk exposures.

The first step for an individual is much like that shown in Exhibit 1 for the most complex organization: the determination of goals or objectives. This step would include most of the elements associated with risk governance, just without all the organizational complexity.

The next functional step involves choosing investments (or other assets) and identifying their risks. Lacking any risk infrastructure, the individual may at this stage already

---

[6] While not obvious in the illustration, communication and reporting should happen whether or not risk levels are in compliance; such communications are even more important when risk levels are out of alignment with tolerances.

require the services of an investment professional or financial adviser. This step and subsequent steps will probably be executed by the adviser, although the individual principal still needs to stay knowledgeable and involved. In the context of the illustration in Exhibit 1, the individual is effectively their own governance body and the adviser serves the role of management.

The next steps for the individual are equivalent to the heart of the risk management process: risk monitoring and risk mitigation and management. The individual would first evaluate their risk exposure (like the diamond or decision step in the illustration), then consider various alternative approaches to modify the risk if necessary, followed by implementing the risk management solution (insuring, hedging, trading, etc.).

The final functional step for an individual's risk management process would be evaluation and review. This step is parallel to the back-end of the risk management illustration, the boxes at the bottom right. This process may occur with much less frequency for an individual—but it is no less important.

Each individual should simplify the risk management process as required so that they do not end up considering it "too esoteric and complicated to worry about" and thus ignoring risk management altogether. The potential costs of avoiding risk management are essentially the same for an individual as for a large corporation or a hedge fund, although perhaps with less money involved.

At its core, business and investing are about allocating resources and capital to chosen risks. Understanding which risks drive better outcomes should be one of the goals of risk management, and it makes good *risk* management inextricably linked with good management generally. When effective risk management is truly integrated at all levels of the decision-making process and the overall management process, the organization has developed an effective *risk culture*. This culture generally produces better results than just considering risk issues as a separate afterthought, and, in turn, it produces *much* better results than ignoring risk issues altogether in the decision-making process. For individuals, the adoption of a risk culture should result in a personal awareness of the many types of risks, their rewards, the costs, the relationships between them, and the methods of aligning the risks borne with the risks and outcomes desired. This awareness should lead to better investment return and/or smaller losses for the risk taken, resulting in higher satisfaction.

There are a number of other benefits from establishing good risk management: (1) Most obvious is less frequent surprises and a better notion of what the damage would be in the event of a surprise; (2) more decision discipline leading to better consideration of trade-offs and better risk-return relationships; (3) better response and risk mitigation stemming from more awareness and active monitoring, which should trim some of the worst losses; (4) better efficiency and fewer operational errors from policies and procedures, transparency, and risk awareness; (5) better relations, with more trust, between the governing body and management, which generally results in more effective delegation; (6) a better image or reputation because analysts and investors perceive a company as prudent and value-focused. Together, all these benefits should lead to higher value for the enterprise.

EXAMPLE 1   Risk Management and Risk Management Framework

1. Which of the following is *not* a goal of risk management?

   A. Measuring risk exposures
   B. Minimizing exposure to risk
   C. Defining the level of risk appetite

2. Which element of a risk management framework sets the overall context for risk management in an organization?

   A. Governance
   B. Risk infrastructure
   C. Policies and processes

3. Which element of risk management makes up the analytical component of the process?

   A. Communication
   B. Risk governance
   C. Risk identification and measurement

4. Which element of risk management involves action when risk exposures are found to be out of line with risk tolerance?

   A. Risk governance
   B. Risk identification and measurement
   C. Risk monitoring, mitigation, and management

Solution to 1: B is correct. The definition of risk management includes both defining the level of risk desired and measuring the level of risk taken. Risk management means taking risks actively and in the best, most value-added way possible and is not about minimizing risks.

Solution to 2: A is correct. Governance is the element of the risk management framework that is the top-level foundation for risk management. Although policies, procedures, and infrastructure are necessary to implement a risk management framework, it is governance that provides the overall context for an organization's risk management.

Solution to 3: C is correct. Risk identification and measurement is the quantitative part of the process. It involves identifying the risks and summarizing their potential quantitative impact. Communication and risk governance are largely qualitative.

Solution to 4: C is correct. Risk monitoring, mitigation, and management require recognizing and taking action when these (risk exposure and risk tolerance) are not in line, as shown in the middle of Exhibit 1. Risk governance involves setting the risk tolerance. Risk identification and measurement involves identifying and measuring the risk exposures.

4. RISK GOVERNANCE – AN ENTERPRISE VIEW

Risk governance is the foundation for risk management. As defined earlier, it is the top-down process and guidance that directs risk management activities to align with and support the goals of the overall enterprise. It typically emanates from a board of directors with fiduciary obligations and risk oversight and who prescribe goals and authorities. Referring back to the definition of risk management, note that risk management is keenly focused on the risk and value of the overall enterprise.

4.1. An Enterprise View of Risk Governance

In addition to the responsibility for risk oversight, there are two other important areas in which the governing body drives the risk framework. First, it determines the organization's goals, direction, and priorities, which combined serve as a key foundation for enterprise risk management. Recall that enterprise risk management is an overarching governance approach applied across the organization that focuses risk activities on the objectives, health, and value of the whole organization. Second, it spells out the risk appetite or tolerance, meaning which risks are acceptable, which risks are to be mitigated and to what extent, and which risks are unacceptable. Risk governance should also provide a sense of the worst losses that could be tolerated in various scenarios, and management should manage risk accordingly. These considerations should flow naturally into decisions about risk budgeting to guide implementation of an optimal program that is consistent with that risk tolerance.

Risk governance is the impact of the governing body of an organization on the risk management framework. It provides context for and clarity on an organization's value drivers and risk appetite, specifies clear authority to management to execute risk management, and ensures risk oversight to continually determine whether risk management is functioning well and consistent with the organization's value maximization. It is the governing body's job to tie the organizational goals and risk framework together; thus, risk governance happens within an enterprise context. Risk governance and risk oversight also entail compliance with regulatory requirements. Risk governance is a difficult and demanding discipline, and if it is going to flourish in an organization, it needs visible commitment from the top.

Providing clear guidance with sufficient leeway to execute strategy is often a difficult balance. Even more challenging is providing for advance discussion and a clear decision and statement of organizational risk appetite. There is usually substantial discussion about this risk appetite *after* a crisis, but too often there is very little discussion during periods of normalcy, when it would be much more beneficial. Because risk is one of the main strategic tools that management can regulate, it is especially important for governing bodies to openly discuss risk, consider scenarios, understand the impact of negative outcomes on the organization, and make it clear where they are not willing to venture. Much like an automobile that comes with a red zone on some dials to establish boundaries for safe operation, risk governance bodies should likewise establish hypothetical red zones to ensure the safe operation of their enterprise.

Enterprise risk management (focusing risk activities on the objectives, health, and value of the *whole* organization) requires that the entire economic balance sheet of the business be considered, not just the assets or one part of the business in isolation. A narrower view of risk management is unlikely to meet the goal of maximizing the value of the entire enterprise.

Pension fund management provides a classic example of the importance of considering enterprise risk management: "Funds" are the assets and "pension" is the liability. But a true enterprise view requires an even broader outlook. A corporate pension fund's manager might try to maximize only the fund's assets, but this would generally do a disservice to the corporation. The assets and liabilities of a pension fund are both sensitive to market variables, so ignoring the liabilities would be ignoring half the risk. With liabilities that are quite bond-like, a pension fund manager using all equities for maximum growth would potentially make the overall fund insolvent in a market collapse with declining interest rates because, in such a situation, the liabilities would increase substantially in value while the assets fell. Risk tolerance for the assets in isolation would be far different from the risk tolerance of the entire enterprise. One should look beyond just the pension liabilities, which are likely to be a small part of the overall enterprise. Broader still, a true enterprise risk view in this case would *also* consider the parent corporation's business risk profile and not just the pension assets and liabilities. In a market collapse, the overall business might be in a recessionary phase, rendering increasing contributions from the corporation to its pension fund quite painful. Factoring the corporate risk profile into the pension fund investment strategy may cause the risk tolerance to be lower in this case.

Risk governance that focuses on the entire enterprise will result in risk management that is much less likely to be at odds with the goals of the organization and more likely to enhance long-run value. Likewise, consideration of a full spectrum of risks, and not just the most obvious quantitative risks, will result in better risk governance.

The enterprise view of risk management is equally applicable and important to an individual, even if the term "enterprise" is not often used in an individual context.[7] The appropriate set of risks for an individual must be viewed not in isolation, but in consideration of the goals and characteristics of the individual in a holistic view. For example, an adviser may be designing an investment portfolio to maximize a client's wealth and optimize the risk–return trade-off at some perceived comfortable level of risk.[8] But the client, whose wealth consists not only of financial assets but also of valuable **human capital**, might prefer that risk allocation decisions be made in view of both forms of capital, optimizing her total wealth. For example, a client with a career in real estate would most likely benefit if her financial portfolio is invested in a way that considers her earnings exposure to real estate related risks. Holdings of real estate securities above a certain level, even if optimal from an isolated portfolio perspective, might make this individual less than optimally diversified from a total wealth perspective. In another example, Investor X, who has substantial inflation-adjusted pension benefits, is different from Investor Y, who has a fixed pension benefit, and different still from Investor Z, who has no pension benefit and retires with solely his own investment portfolio. These three investors will require remarkably different investment solutions, not only to deal with inflation but also to deal with the uncertainty surrounding lifespans. Individuals with different goals and characteristics will need differing investment and risk solutions that are best suited to their individual situations. In fact, because of the extremely variable life cycle of an individual and the discrete nature of many individuals' goals, the enterprise view is even more important to risk management for individuals than it is for institutions.

---

[7] Here, the individual is the governing body, setting individual goals and risk appetite; the financial professional or wealth manager is the "management team" executing much of the rest of the risk framework.

[8] Enterprise risk management is an easier concept for an individual; compared with an organization in which deciding, coordinating, and communicating goals can be a big challenge, the scope of risk management efforts for an individual is smaller and more manageable.

Risk governance extends into management to include ways to ensure that the risk framework of an organization stays consistent with top-level guidance. One useful approach is to provide a regular forum to discuss the risk framework and key risk issues at the management level. In other words, a risk management committee would be a key element of good risk governance. Its activities could parallel the governance body's risk deliberations, but at an operational level as opposed to high-level oversight. In this forum, governance overlaps with many of the other aspects of the organization's risk framework as discussed in Sections 2–3. In fact, if done well, it integrates all of them.

In the same vein, another element of good risk governance is the formal appointment of a responsible executive as chief risk officer (CRO). This officer should be responsible for building and implementing the risk framework for the enterprise and managing the many activities therein. In the same manner that risks are inextricably linked with the core business activities, the CRO is likewise a key participant in the strategic decisions of the enterprise—this position is not solely a policing role. Although the chief executive is responsible for risk as well as all other aspects of an enterprise, it makes no more sense for the CEO to perform the role of the CRO than it would be for the CEO to perform the role of the CFO. Many financial firms now have a CRO in executive management,[9] which had become best practice even in the years prior to the 2008 crisis.

5. RISK TOLERANCE

Perhaps the most important element of good risk governance is the **risk tolerance** discussion and decision within the governing body. Business and investment strategy centers on selecting a portfolio of acceptable risk activities that will maximize value and produce the highest returns possible for the given risk level. At the governance level, the duty is generally not to select these activities—a job that usually falls to management—but to establish the organization's risk appetite. Certain risks or levels of risks may be deemed acceptable, other risks deemed unacceptable, and in the middle are risks that may be pursued in a risk-limited fashion. Said differently, risk tolerance identifies the extent to which the organization is willing to experience losses or opportunity costs and to fail in meeting its objectives.

> The risk tolerance decision *for an individual* is similar, but not identical, to that of a business enterprise. In traditional finance theory, the individual focuses on maximizing unobservable utility, whereas the business maximizes a generally observable value—the market value or equity price of the company. Although individuals are facing life and certain death on an uncertain timetable, most businesses tend to be relatively short-lived organizations, but with an expectation of immortality. The decisions about risk tolerance from those two very different viewpoints can be expected to differ—for example, risk tolerance in organizations often treats its continued existence as a major consideration. In many ways, the individual's risk tolerance decision is the harder one.

The enterprise risk management perspective is the right lens through which to view the risk appetite question. The risk tolerance decision begins with two different analyses that must be integrated—an "inside" view and an "outside" view. First, what shortfalls within an

---

[9] Although this is common for financial firms or other large organizations, many less-complex companies will forgo a formal risk structure. The board still maintains its risk governance responsibilities; and it is up to them to work out with management as to how, and to what extent, to meet these responsibilities.

organization would cause it to fail, or at least fail to achieve some critical goals? Second, what uncertain forces is the organization exposed to? That is, what are its risk drivers? With the answers to these two difficult questions in hand, a board could begin defining dimensions and levels of risk that it finds too uncomfortable to take on. This risk tolerance should be formally chosen and communicated *before* a crisis, and will serve as the high-level guidance for management in its strategic selection of risks. Many organizations will do this *after* a crisis, which is better than not doing it at all but is much like buying insurance after the loss occurs. It is best to take care of it when there seems to be no particularly pressing reason to do so. Similarly, some individuals may not give much thought to their own risk tolerance until after a crisis occurs, when they belatedly decide that the risk was not worth taking.

For example, suppose a Spanish construction equipment manufacturing company's board is determining its risk tolerance. From the inside perspective, it has two main concerns: revenue and liquidity. It determines that it can tolerate a 5%–10% drop in revenue, but that a 20% drop would trigger its debt covenants and put the launch of its new flagship product at risk. Related to this strategy, it needs €40 million of cash flow annually for the next three years for critical capital expenditures and can leave almost none of this cash flow at risk. From the outside perspective, it realizes that there are three main uncertainties or risk drivers over which it has no control: changes in the value of the US dollar, interest rate changes, and market returns on industrial sector equities. Both its business results and its own stock price are strongly correlated with these three risks and could be adversely affected by any of them.

Rather than taking a passive approach as a risk observer, the board in this example uses a top-level analysis to formulate its risk tolerance. In this case, it may decide to limit maximum cash flow variation to €10 million annually and revenue exposure to –10% in a global recession. In addition, it may specify other stated limits, such as the maximum exposure to currency or other risks. This guidance may affect the riskiness of other product strategies that management may pursue. The company may require more expensive financing options to reduce cash flow uncertainty. The governance restrictions may drive risk mitigation programs, such as a hedging strategy, especially for the primary risk drivers that are stated areas of concern.

Governance guidance is important in helping an enterprise target where it should actively pursue risk and where it should mitigate or modify risk. Strategic goals centered on core competencies should be pursued, which leads the company into taking risks that best position the enterprise for success and value creation. Companies sometimes take risks in areas where they have no expertise, which puts their core value creation and their entire organization at peril. A well-functioning risk program would limit or hedge those non-core risks in areas where they have no comparative advantage. Modifying risk is covered in detail in Sections 9–11.

How does a company determine its risk tolerance? There is certainly no formula. Most importantly, a company's goals, its expertise in certain areas, and its strategies will help a board determine which risks the company may pursue and with how much intensity. The ability of a company to respond dynamically to adverse events may allow for a higher risk tolerance. The amount of loss a company can sustain without impairing its status as a going concern should factor into its risk tolerance; some companies are more fragile than others. The competitive landscape matters because both the board's and investors' expectations are usually developed in the context of how a company is positioned in its industry. The government and regulatory landscape is important too, both in their *ex ante* demands on how companies approach risk and in the likely *ex post* reaction in the event of disasters. Quantitative analyses such as scenario analysis, economic models, and sensitivities to macro risk drivers might be used to assess where a board's zone of comfort is bounded. There are other factors that should *not* determine risk tolerance, but in many cases they do. Personal motivations, beliefs, and agendas of board members (the agency problem); company size; whether the market environment seems stable; short-term pressures; and management compensation often affect risk tolerance in ways that might not be in line with the owners' best interests.

Once risk tolerance is determined, the overall risk framework should be geared toward measuring, managing, and communicating compliance with this risk tolerance—getting the risk exposure in line with the enterprise's risk appetite.

This sort of governance exercise not only helps ensure that the organization survives through the worst of times, but also helps ensure a strategic trade-off between risk and return in the decision process, which, in turn, improves potential returns for the given level of risk and value. It is quite easy to find business strategies and investment approaches that produce apparently outsized returns, but they might be at the cost of putting the organization at extreme risk. A somewhat extreme example would be a company selling put options on its own equity, which could produce higher short-term profits but would dramatically increase the chance of the company failing in a steep market decline. Excessive leverage is another risky strategy for boosting short-term profits that may decrease value or lead to failure in the long run. A formal risk governance process with a stated risk tolerance would naturally result in avoidance of many easier, less well-reasoned strategies that entail excessive risk compared with the firm's risk tolerance. Instead, it would lead the strategic discussion into alternative strategies that are more likely to add value while taking reasonable risk within the enterprise's risk tolerance and not simply trade ruin for return. Sincere, good risk governance and risk culture can avoid excessively risky strategies that might put the long-term enterprise value at risk. This approach should produce enhanced value for the enterprise.

6. RISK BUDGETING

Risk budgeting picks up where risk tolerance leaves off. Whereas risk tolerance focuses on the appetite for risk and what is and is not acceptable, risk budgeting has a more specific focus on how that risk is taken. Risk budgeting quantifies and allocates the tolerable risk by specific metrics; it extends and guides implementation of the risk tolerance decision.

Risk budgeting applies to both business management and portfolio management. Its foundation is the perspective that business or portfolio management involves assembling a number of risk activities or securities, which can be collated into an assemblage of various risk characteristics. For example, a traditional view of a portfolio might be that it is allocated 20% to hedge funds, 30% to private equity, and the remaining 50% is split between stocks and bonds. An alternative risk view of the same portfolio might be 70% driven by global equity returns, 20% by domestic equity returns, with the remaining 10% driven by interest rates. The equity component might be allocated 65% to value and 35% to growth. The portfolio might also have 45% illiquid securities and the remainder liquid. Other allocations can be stated in terms of exposures to inflation, long-term interest rates, currencies, and so on. These multiple dimensions for viewing the allocation of a portfolio are not mutually exclusive: they co-exist. If one is evaluating the risk exposure of a portfolio and trying to keep it in line with a stated risk tolerance, one would be far more concerned with the risk characteristics of the investment assets and portfolio rather than their common classifications of stocks, hedge funds, real estate, private equity, and so on. These terms tell us a little about risk but not enough. Equity is traditionally riskier than hedge funds, but some equities are of quite low risk and some hedge funds are of quite high risk. The risk view may be more meaningful and useful in understanding the portfolio risk than the traditional asset allocation view.

Risk budgeting is any means of allocating a portfolio based on some risk characteristics of the investments. In the purest sense, the term "budget" implies that there is a total risk limit for the organization. Although this approach is not formally required,[10] it would certainly be good practice to have a risk budget that is consistent with the organization's risk tolerance. A risk budget provides a means of implementing the risk tolerance at a strategic level, or in other words, a means of bridging from the high-level governance risk decision to the many management decisions, large and small, that result in the actual risk exposures.

A risk budget can be complex and multi-dimensional, or it can be a simple, one-dimensional risk measure. Even the simplest measure can provide significant benefits in developing an effective risk culture. Four well-known single-dimension measures that are often used are standard deviation, beta, value at risk (VaR), and scenario loss, but there are many others. It is common for some hedge funds to budget risk using standard deviation, managing to a fixed-risk fund target, and evaluating individual investments based on their returns and risks as they affect the *ex ante* standard deviation.

More complex forms of risk budgeting use multiple dimensions of risk. One popular approach evaluates risks by their underlying risk classes, such as equity, fixed income, commodity risk, and so on, and then allocates investments by their risk class. Also common are risk factor approaches to risk budgeting, in which exposure to various factors is used to attempt to capture associated risk premiums. An example would be to budget an allocation to give greater emphasis to value stocks based on the belief that they may provide a higher risk-adjusted return than growth stocks. This tactic might be layered over a strategic budget with a certain "beta" as the overall equity risk, supplemented with value and additional factor tilts specified up to some level.

Risk budgeting, although a desirable element of risk governance, cuts across the entire risk management framework, providing a focal point for each of the facets of risk management described in Sections 2 and 3. And although it is true that in practice many organizations operate without a risk budget, it is generally because there has been no specific declaration of their risk tolerance. If a board has a clear understanding of its risk appetite, both the board and management will want some means of implementing a strategic allocation that is consistent with it. Thus, the risk budget becomes a critical overarching construct for the organization's risk framework.

Some individuals may, often through the assistance of a financial planner, engage in some form of risk budgeting, but many do not execute it well or carry it far enough. A classic example of this failure is the tendency of many individuals to invest their financial portfolios in their employers. The risk budget for their total wealth—financial and human capital—is extremely concentrated in one firm and/or one industry. Not surprisingly, such risk budgets typically occur not through formal planning because most formal plans would recognize the problem, but through inaction or inattention.

One major benefit of even the most basic risk budgeting is that it forces risk trade-offs and supports a culture in which risk is considered as a part of all key decisions. Suppose that all the activities a business wants to pursue are in excess of the risk budget. The budgeting of risk should result in an approach, whether explicit or not, of choosing to invest where the return per unit of risk is the highest. Better still, it should also result in a market-benchmarked choice of risk intensity, between possibly doing less of each risky investment or doing more, but with a risk-mitigating hedge. This benefit is extremely important. By choosing between a market

---

[10] One could do risk budgeting even if there were no other risk governance guidance.

hedge or less of a risky investment, one ends up evaluating the investment directly against the market risk–return benchmark. Thus, one is not only comparing risk–return relationships among one's investment choices, but also comparing active versus passive strategies; that is, evaluating investment choices as a whole against the "market return" on a risk-equivalent basis. In other words, one ends up attempting to add active value in each of one's decisions while still staying within the confines of the organization's risk tolerance. The result is even more powerful than merely ensuring that the business is compensated well for the risks they decide to accept. Just having a risk budget in place, forces decision makers to try to add value to the enterprise in every risky decision they make. The risk-budgeting framework makes this consideration innate to the decision process.

EXAMPLE 2   Risk Governance

1. Which of the following approaches is *most* consistent with an enterprise view of risk governance?

   A. Separate strategic planning processes for each part of the enterprise
   B. Considering an organization's risk tolerance when developing its asset allocation
   C. Trying to achieve the highest possible risk-adjusted return on a company's pension fund's assets

2. Which of the following statements about risk tolerance is *most* accurate?

   A. Risk tolerance is best discussed after a crisis, when awareness of risk is heightened.
   B. The risk tolerance discussion is about the actions management will take to minimize losses.
   C. The organization's risk tolerance describes the extent to which the organization is willing to experience losses.

3. Which of the following is *not* consistent with a risk-budgeting approach to portfolio management?

   A. Limiting the beta of the portfolio to 0.75
   B. Allocating investments by their amount of underlying risk sources or factors
   C. Limiting the amount of money available to be spent on hedging strategies by each portfolio manager

4. Who would be the *least* appropriate for controlling the risk management function in a large organization?

   A. Chief risk officer
   B. Chief financial officer
   C. Risk management committee

Solution to 1: B is correct. The enterprise view is characterized by a focus on the organization as a whole—its goals, value, and risk tolerance. It is not about strategies or risks at the individual business line level.

Solution to 2: C is correct. Risk tolerance identifies the extent to which the organization is willing to experience losses or opportunity costs and fail in meeting its objectives. It is best discussed before a crisis and is primarily a risk governance or oversight issue at the board level, not a management or tactical one.

Solution to 3: C is correct. Risk budgeting is any means of allocating a portfolio by some risk characteristics of the investments. This approach could be a strict limit on beta or some other risk measure or an approach that uses risk classes or factors to allocate investments. Risk budgeting does not require nor prohibit hedging, although hedging is available as an implementation tool to support risk budgeting and overall risk governance.

Solution to 4: B is correct. A chief risk officer or a risk management committee is an individual or group that specializes in risk management. A chief financial officer may have considerable knowledge of risk management, may supervise a CRO, and would likely have some involvement in a risk management committee, but a CFO has broader responsibilities and cannot provide the specialization and attention to risk management that is necessary in a large organization.

7. IDENTIFICATION OF RISK – FINANCIAL AND NON-FINANCIAL RISK

Having laid the framework for understanding the concept of risk management and risk governance, we now move into the implementation of the process. One of the first important parts of the process is the identification of risks. In this reading, we identify two general categorizations of risks. The first is the set of risks that originate from the financial markets. Accordingly, we refer to this type of risk as **financial risks**. The second group of risks includes those that emanate from outside the financial markets. As such, we refer to these as **non-financial risks**. Although most risks ultimately have monetary consequences, we reserve the term "financial risks" to refer to the risks that arise from events occurring in the financial markets, such as changes in prices or interest rates.[11] In this reading, we will consider the types of financial and non-financial risks faced by organizations and individuals.

7.1. Financial Risks

The risk management industry has come to classify three types of risks as primarily financial in nature. The three primary types of financial risks are market risk, credit risk, and liquidity risk. **Market risk** is the risk that arises from movements in interest rates, stock prices, exchange

---

[11] We use the term "financial markets" in a very broad sense. A company may also be exposed to commodity price risk, which we would include as a financial risk.

rates, and commodity prices. This categorization is not to say that these four main factors are the underlying drivers of market risks. Market risks typically arise from certain fundamental economic conditions or events in the economy or industry or developments in specific companies. These are the underlying risk drivers, which we will cover later.

Market risks are among the most obvious and visible risks faced by most organizations and many individuals. The financial markets receive considerable attention in the media, and information on financial market activity is abundant. Institutional investors and many corporations devote considerable resources to processing this information with the objective of optimizing performance. Many individuals also devote considerable attention to market risk, and financial publications and television and radio shows are widely followed in the general population. The state of knowledge in risk management is probably greatest in the area of market risk.

The second primary financial risk is credit risk. **Credit risk** is the risk of loss if one party fails to pay an amount owed on an obligation, such as a bond, loan, or derivative, to another party. In a loan, only one party owes money to the other. In some types of derivatives, only one party owes money to the other, and in other types of derivatives, either party can owe the other. This type of risk is also sometimes called default risk and sometimes counterparty risk. As with market risk, the root source of the risk can arise from fundamental conditions in the economy, industry, or weakness in the market for a company's products. Ultimately, default is an asset-specific risk. Bond and derivatives investors must consider credit risk as one of their primary decision tools.[12] Similar to market risk, credit risk is also a highly visible risk with considerable attention paid to defaults, bankruptcies, and the stresses arising from inadequate cash flow in relation to leverage. Credit risk is a particularly significant risk in that although market prices can go down and bounce back up, defaults and bankruptcies have extremely long-term implications for borrowers.

Although market and credit risk are extremely common risks to institutions, they are also assumed by individuals in their personal investments. One other financial risk, however, is much more common to institutions, although it can be faced by individuals, often unknowingly. This third risk is **liquidity risk**, which is the risk of a significant downward valuation adjustment when selling a financial asset. In order to sell an asset, a party may need to reduce the price to a level that is less than the marked value or the seller's assessment of the asset's true value based on the fundamentals of the asset. In certain market conditions, the seller must make a significant price concession. Having to make price concessions is not necessarily unusual and does not imply a poorly functioning market. Indeed, given no shift in demand, a rightward shift of a supply curve in order to sell a larger quantity is entirely consistent with the notion that a seller must lower the price to sell a greater quantity.

All assets have transaction costs in the market, such as the bid–ask spread. The existence of a sell price that is less than a buy price, however, is not a risk but simply a cost. It is the *uncertainty* of that valuation spread that creates this type of risk. Thus, liquidity risk could also be called "transaction cost risk." The liquidity risk of a $10 stock purchased for $10 is not the risk that one would receive the "bid" price of only $9.99 right after one bought it. That $0.01 spread is a known cost when the stock is purchased, so it is not a risk. The risk is that this spread cost might increase dramatically as a result of either changing market conditions or attempting to maintain a position significantly larger than the normal trading volume for the

---

[12] With certain derivatives (swaps and forwards), either party could be forced to pay off to the other, so each party is concerned about whether its counterparty will pay off, meaning that for some products, credit risk is bilateral.

stock. This problem becomes a serious issue for risk management when the liquidation price falls to less than the seller's estimate of the fundamental value of the asset. Although this risk is often associated with illiquid assets,[13] it really stems from a couple of sources. First, market liquidity varies over time and the market for specific assets may become less liquid; second, as the size of a position increases, the cost and uncertainty associated with liquidating it will increase. In some extreme cases, there may be no price above zero at which the seller can sell the asset.

Of course, one might argue that the cost of illiquidity, and liquidity risk, should thus be part of the investor's assessment of fundamental value, and indeed it is for many analysts. If not, liquidity risk can sometimes be confused with a form of valuation denial in which investors believe that they paid an appropriate price and that the market has not converged to its true value. But less liquidity means a thin market and a lack of investor interest, which may be fertile ground for investment opportunities. Although lack of liquidity can offer benefits, such as the opportunity to buy an asset well before everyone else sees that it is an attractive investment, liquidity risk is generally considered to be a negative factor with which risk managers and indeed all investors must contend.

7.2. Non-Financial Risks

Recall that we refer to financial risks as those arising primarily from events occurring in the financial markets. Although most risks have monetary consequences, there are a number of risks that are typically classified as non-financial in nature. These risks arise from a variety of sources, such as from actions within the organization or from external origins, such as the environment as well as from the relationship between the organization and counterparties, regulators, governments, suppliers, and customers.

One important risk of this type is closely related to default risk but deals more with the settling of payments that occur just before a default. This risk is called settlement risk. As an example, suppose Party A enters into a forward contract to purchase ¥200 million of Japanese government bonds from Party B. At expiration if all goes well, Party A would wire the money and Party B would transfer the bonds. Each party fulfills its obligation expecting that the other will do so as well. However, suppose Party A wires the money but Party B does not send the bonds because it has declared bankruptcy. At this point, Party A cannot get the money back, except possibly much later through the potentially slow and cumbersome bankruptcy process.[14] Although the financial consequences are very high, the root source of this risk is the timing of the payment process itself.

Organizations face two types of risks related to the law, and as such, this risk is referred to as legal risk. One risk is simply the risk of being sued over a transaction or for that matter, anything an organization does or fails to do. In financial risk management, however, the major

---

[13] The illiquid nature of an asset is not itself the risk because that is a direct cost borne immediately upon purchase. Still, uncertainty around the valuation of illiquid assets is a pervasive issue, so it is natural to associate liquidity risk with liquidity characteristics. More importantly, though, the term *liquidity risk* also commonly refers to a much broader set of risks for the organization, which are addressed in the next section.

[14] This type of risk often arises because of significant time zone differences. Settlement risk is also called Herstatt risk; Herstatt was the name of a German bank that failed in 1974 after receiving "overnight" payments and then defaulting.

legal concern is that the terms of a contract will not be upheld by the legal system. For example, suppose Bank E enters into a derivatives contract with Party F. Assume that as the underlying changes in price, Party F incurs a loss, whereas there is a corresponding gain to Bank E. But suppose that Party F then identifies a legal issue that it interprets as giving it the right to refuse to pay. If the court upholds Party F's position, Bank E could incur a loss. Litigation always involves uncertainty because even a seemingly weak case can prevail in court.

The following three non-financial risks are related: regulatory risk, accounting risk, and tax risk. They could even be collectively referred to as compliance risk because they all deal with the matter of conforming to policies, laws, rules, and regulations as set forth by governments and authoritative bodies, such as accounting governing boards. Obviously the regulatory, accounting, and tax environment is always subject to change, but the rapid expansion of financial products and strategies in relation to the relatively slow manner in which government and private regulators are able to respond means that laws and regulations are nearly always catching up with the financial world. When these laws and regulations are updated, it can result in significant unexpected costs, back taxes, financial restatements, and penalties.

Another type of non-financial risk is model risk, which is the risk of a valuation error from improperly using a model. This risk arises when an organization uses the wrong model or uses the right model incorrectly. A simple example applicable to both a portfolio manager and a corporate analyst is the assumption of constant dividend growth in the dividend discount model when, in fact, growth is not constant.

Closely related to model risk is tail risk—more events in the tail of the distribution than would be expected by probability models. This risk is a facet of market risk, but it also infects valuations and models when it is ignored or mishandled. Tail risk is known to be especially severe for the normal distribution, which tends to be overused in modeling. As an example, consider the monthly returns on the S&P 500 Index from January 1950 to October 2018. The monthly average return was 0.70%, and the monthly standard deviation was 4.10%. If we rank the monthly returns, we would find that the largest negative return was –21.76%, which occurred in the well-known market crash of October 1987. With a normal distribution, we would find that a return that low would occur only once every 2,199,935 years.[15] The second and third worst monthly returns of –16.94% (October 2008) and –14.58% (August 1998) would occur only once every 6,916 and 654 years respectively. If the normal distribution is a realistic descriptor of returns, results of these magnitudes should *never* have occurred in recorded market history, and yet we have seen three such instances. Interestingly, according to the normal distribution, the largest positive return of 16.30% in October 1974 would occur only once every 888 years. Technically, one could argue that if we go another 2,199,935 years and do not observe a monthly return as low as –21.76%, then the assumption of a normal distribution might seem reasonable, but it seems safe to reject the normal distribution for at least another two million years. Similar comments can apply to the second and third worst returns albeit over shorter periods.

Many quantitative models (e.g., option models) and decision models (e.g., portfolio construction and asset allocation, relying on variances and covariances in analysis and decisions) ignore the existence of fat tails in returns; as a result, market risk is often considered and dealt with in an oversimplified fashion. Tail risk, as the term is used in practice, is important and is discussed separately because financial professionals realize the implicit failure of modeling

---

[15] This calculation and those that follow are based on determining the probability of the given return or less.

market risk. More plainly, ignoring tail risk is a form of model risk. And although tail risk might seem more of a financial risk than a non-financial risk, the mistake occurs internally, arising from poor choices made in modeling.

Most of the internal risks faced by an organization are often grouped together and referred to as operational risk. **Operational risk** is the risk that arises inadequate or failed people, systems, and internal policies, procedures, and processes, as well as from external events that are beyond the control of the organization but that affect its operations. Although the factors that give rise to such risks can arise externally, the risks themselves are largely internal to an organization because it would be expected to have its people, systems and internal policies, procedures, and processes functioning effectively regardless of pressures placed on it by external forces.

Employees themselves are major sources of potential internal risks. Banks are keenly aware of the vulnerability to employee theft, given the ease with which so many employees have access to accounts and systems for making entries. But even perfectly honest employees make mistakes, and some can be quite costly. The employee who credits someone's account $100,000 for a $100 deposit may have made an honest mistake, but it is a mistake that could quickly lead to the rapid disappearance of money. In the past, employees up to senior management have been guilty of perpetrating accounting fraud, not necessarily for their own direct benefit but to make the company look better.

In banks and other companies that trade in the financial markets, there is the risk that a trader or portfolio manager will fail to follow laws, rules, or guidelines and put the company at great financial risk. This individual is commonly described as a "rogue trader." Personified by Nick Leeson of Barings Bank, who in 1995 destroyed the 200-year old company by engaging in a series of highly speculative trades to cover up losses, the rogue trader has become a standard concern of risk managers. Although it was never clear if Leeson's trades were truly unauthorized, his legacy left the fear that institutions bear the risk that one trader can imperil the entire organization by making large and highly speculative trades that put the bank's entire capital base at risk. In essence, a rogue trader is a trader who engages in risky transactions without regard for the organization's limits or conforming to its controls.

Organizations are also threatened by business interruptions, such as those caused by extreme weather and natural disasters. Events such as floods, earthquakes, or hurricanes can cause significant damage and temporarily shut down an organization. Although extreme weather and natural disasters are external forces that are completely out of the control of an organization, it does not excuse the organization from having the appropriate internal procedures for managing problems caused by their external environment. Simple and fairly low-cost actions, such as having generators, backup facilities, or providing employees the option to work remotely, can go a long way toward keeping employees working during extreme weather events and when natural disasters strike. Yet, some organization have not heeded inclement weather forecasts. Failing to react to warnings can result in considerable loss.

In a world that is increasingly digital, cyber risk is a major operational risk that spares no organization and that can have significant consequences. Organizations are expected to understand and manage the risk associated with the disruption of or failure related to their information technology (IT) systems. For example, a hacker breaking into a company's IT system and stealing customer or client data is an external threat. Hacking, however, is not simply a random act of mischief. Companies are aware of the threat of hackers, and hackers can break in to a system only if that system is vulnerable. An organization is responsible for ensuring cyber security and establishing sufficiently robust IT safeguards, such as data encryption, to deter hackers from breaking in and either stealing or causing disruption. Cyber-attacks and data breaches can have serious reputational and compliance consequences. For example, all organizations targeting European citizens must comply with the General Data Protection Regulation (GDPR) and notify regulators and data subjects of any data breaches regarding sensitive personal information within 72 hours. Failure to do so can lead to fines of several million euros, including for organizations based outside the European Union. In addition to the threats posed by hackers and viruses, even secure IT systems themselves are a particular source of risk. Programming errors and bugs can create the possibility of costly mistakes.

Terrorism is another form of operational risks that poses a threat to organizations and individuals. The 1993 attacks on the World Trade Center led many companies to recognize that the New York City financial district was a major terrorist target and that, as such, their operations could be shut down by these acts of violence. When the more destructive attacks of 11 September 2001 occurred, many organizations had already established backup facilities sufficiently far away from that area. Of course, such risk is not confined to major financial centers, and indeed, organizations worldwide have begun to take security measures that address this operational risk.

Some of these operational risks are insurable, at least to a modest extent. We will briefly discuss insurance later, but most companies would much prefer to take proactive steps toward prevention than to incur the inconvenience of losses and then have an outside organization compensate them for their losses.

Solvency risk is the risk that the organization does not survive or succeed because it runs out of cash, even though it might otherwise be solvent.[16] This was probably the most underappreciated component of risk prior to the financial crisis of 2008.[17] The collapse of Lehman Brothers was often associated with an excess of leverage, which was certainly a key factor in its failure. But it was solvency risk that forced the company into bankruptcy. Almost overnight, Lehman's liquidity disappeared because most funding sources would no longer willingly bear Lehman's counterparty risk. Even if it had experienced large market gains on the day it went under, it had already been destroyed by solvency risk. Across the entire financial industry, from hedge funds to pension funds, painful but valuable lessons were learned about the critical importance of funds availability and solvency risk, even if all other risks were well-aligned. Solvency risk is now viewed as one of the key factors in running a successful hedge fund because investors are extremely sensitive to not recovering their investment in the event of a "run on the fund."

Solvency, in the personal or institutional sense, is the availability of funding to continue to operate without liquidating—or at a less extreme level, to be able to make good on liabilities and meet one's cash flow requirements. Solvency risk is the ultimate example of the importance of taking an enterprise view of risk management. For example, a university's investment officer might have a perfectly well-balanced set of risks in the endowment portfolio when viewed in isolation. But as a part of a university, the portfolio may be affected by a deep recession because the university's professional degree revenue, grant money, and donations will fall at the same time as the portfolio's investment value and cash distributions are in decline. Although the

---

[16] Solvency risk is often referred to as liquidity risk by industry professionals, even though the expression *liquidity risk* was used earlier to refer to the risk of valuation shock when selling a security. Although the term "liquidity risk" is used in practice in both contexts, in this reading we will refer to the risk relating to the cash position of an organization as "solvency risk."

[17] Bank runs are perhaps the simplest example of solvency risk. An otherwise solvent bank can easily be ruined by a bank run that wipes out its ability to make good on short-term liabilities.

endowment and university may survive, it might be necessary for the endowment to take many emergency actions that impair its value, simply attributable to the overall solvency risk and the ultimate need of the enterprise to not run out of cash.

Solvency risk is easily mitigated, though never eliminated, by a large number of possible safeguards, none of which is free. Many businesses produce short-term higher returns by essentially ignoring solvency risk, but in doing so, they are not managing risk very well. Since the 2008 crisis, most businesses are keenly aware of the consequences of bad solvency management, and have taken such steps as using less leverage, securing more stable sources of financing, investing in models to provide more transparency on solvency risk, incorporating solvency risk at an enterprise level in risk governance, and holding more cash equivalents and assets with less liquidity risk.

Individuals can also face a number of risks of an operational nature. These include hackers breaking into one's computer and the threat of burglary and robbery. One of the most commonly cited risks for individuals is identity theft. For individuals, however, we consider their primary non-financial risks to be related to their life and health as well as other life-changing events.

Obviously, the health of an individual is an extremely important risk. Poor health can result from poor choices in life, but it can also arise from factors that are outside the control of the individual. These risks can result in direct health care expenses, reduced income because of disability, and reduced lifespan or quality of life. People vary widely in the risk management strategies they undertake to control their health, such as in their choices in diet, exercise, preventive health care, and avoidance of undue health risks. Some individuals address only their financial exposure to health risks, and still others do not take proactive steps to address this risk at all.

Closely related to health risk is mortality risk—the risk of dying relatively young—and longevity risk—the risk of outliving one's financial resources. Not only are these risks a primary determinant of the quality of life, they are also critical factors in investment planning. Although it is probably desirable not to know when one will die, financial planning for one's years in retirement is heavily dependent on one's mortality assumption. Insurance companies, defined benefit pension plans, and vendors of retirement annuities need only know the group average mortality. Mortality tables are reasonably accurate, so these institutions have relatively precise estimates of death rates for groups as a whole. Individuals themselves, however, clearly do not know how long they will live. People who use defined contribution plans must therefore build portfolios and control retirement distributions so that their assets outlive them, which is difficult to do when they do not know when they will die. No one wants to outlive their money, but with an increasingly aging population and good health care, this problem is becoming a greater concern.

There are a number of other major non-financial risks that individuals face, which are generally involved with some sort of life-changing disaster. The largest ones—fire, natural disaster, or massive liability stemming from harming others, such as in a car accident—are generally considered "property and casualty" risks and are insured as such.

8. IDENTIFICATION OF RISK – INTERACTIONS BETWEEN RISKS

In some cases, a risk classified into one category could easily have been classified into another. Indeed, the interactions between risks are numerous. It has been said that market risk begets credit risk, which begets operational risk. That is, given unexpected market moves, one party then owes the other party money. Given the debtor–creditor nature of the relationship, the two parties must have internal operations that process the transactions and pay or collect the money. Thus, whenever there is credit risk, there is settlement risk. If there were no market risk, the other risks in the chain would likely be relatively minor. Legal risk often arises from market or credit risk. Large market moves create losses for one party. There is a long history of parties searching for loopholes in contracts and suing to avoid incurring the loss.

One simple example of an adverse risk interaction is counterparty risk. When trading a derivative contract, it is important to consider the cost of counterparty risk. Suppose Party A buys an out-of-the-money put option with a strike price of ¥1000—a contract theoretically worth ¥100 entitling him to as much as ¥1000 from Counterparty C if an underlying equity index is down. But there is a 2% chance that C could default; and assume that the possibility of default is considered independent of the performance of the equity market. This transaction, with payoffs adjusted for the possibility of default, might price at, say, ¥98 to A. But in reality, the credit risk of C's default is likely dependent on the equity market return. If the probability distribution of default risk overlaps substantially with that of the market being down, which is a likely scenario, then the risks interact, and the cost of risk is higher. In this example, perhaps the probability of C defaulting is 10% or more when the put option is in the money. So, A's expected payoff is lower as a result of facing a credit risk that is compounded by market risk. In fact, it is quite likely that in the extreme event—a deep decline in the equity market when A would presumably receive ¥1000—Party A will in all likelihood get nothing. Thus, the investor bears much more risk than initially thought as a result of the failure to consider the interaction of the two risks. And in doing so, Party A overpaid for the contract. This sort of risk interaction is so common in markets that practitioners have given it a very fitting term—"wrong-way risk." In fact, it was extremely common in the financial crisis of 2008, when holders of many securities based on mortgage credit believed that the risks were well-diversified when in truth, the risks were quite systematic.

Another example of interacting risks was experienced by many banks, funds, and private investment partnerships in 2008, as well as the hedge fund Long-Term Capital Management in 1998. Leverage, which manifested itself in higher market risk, interacted in an extremely toxic manner with liquidity risk and solvency risk and impaired or shuttered many investment firms.[18]

In most adverse financial risk interactions, the whole is much worse than the sum of its parts; the combined risk compounds the individual risks in a non-linear manner. For this example, a 2× levered organization might produce a 2% loss when its unlevered twin or baseline risk bears a 1% loss. If liquidity is a serious issue for the organization, then at a 10% baseline loss, the organization might face some moderate distress from liquidity or funding problems that it ends up losing 25% instead of 20%. It would not be surprising if this organization failed at a 30% baseline loss because of the toxic interplay between levered risk and liquidity problems. This resulting non-linear reaction to risk drivers exists across many risk interactions in many markets, making up-front scenario planning even more valuable to the risk process, a point we will return to later.

---

[18] This example illustrates yet another risk, systemic risk, that is a significant concern to regulators and governments. Stresses and failures in one sector transmit to stresses and failures in other sectors, which can ultimately impact an entire economy. Systemic risk is the ultimate example of interactions among risks.

Earlier, we briefly described a common example of interacting risks for individuals. Suppose an individual works for a publicly traded company and, through an incentive program, receives shares of the company in her company retirement portfolio or for her personal holdings. Company policies may require that employees hold on to these shares for a number of years. When that time has elapsed, however, many individuals fail to recognize the incredibly concentrated risk they are assuming, so they hold on to their shares. An employee's reasoning for not selling the shares is often that the company she works for has been a solid performing company for many years, so she feels no reason to worry. Moreover, the team spirit often imbued in employees generates pride that can make employees believe that there is no better place in which to work and to invest their money. But if something goes wrong in the company or the industry, the employee may lose her job *and* her savings—an incredibly adverse interaction between market risk and human capital risk. The 2003 collapse of Enron remains a powerful historical example, with many loyal and honest employees losing virtually all of their retirement savings by failing to recognize this risk.

In sum, it is important to recognize that risks do not usually arise independently, but generally interact with one another, a problem that is even more critical in stressed market conditions. The resulting combined risk is practically always non-linear in that the total risk faced is worse than the sum of the risks of the separate components. Most risk models and systems do not directly account for risk interactions, which makes the consequences of the risk interaction even worse. Governance bodies, company management, and financial analysts should be keenly aware of the potential risk and damage of risks in combination, and be aware of the dangers of treating risks as separate and unrelated.

EXAMPLE 3   Financial and Non-Financial Sources of Risk

1. Which of the following is *not* a financial risk?

   A. Credit risk
   B. Market risk
   C. Operational risk

2. Which of the following *best* describes an example of interactions among risks?

   A. A stock in Russia declines at the same time as a stock in Japan declines.
   B. Political events cause a decline in economic conditions and an increase in credit spreads.
   C. A market decline makes a derivative counterparty less creditworthy while causing it to owe more money on that derivative contract.

3. Which of the following *best* describes a financial risk?

   A. The risk of an increase in interest rates.
   B. The risk that regulations will make a transaction illegal.
   C. The risk of an individual trading without limits or controls.

4. Which of the following is *not* an example of model risk?

   A. Assuming the tails of a returns distribution are thin when they are, in fact, fat.
   B. Using standard deviation to measure risk when the returns distribution is asymmetric.
   C. Using the one-year risk-free rate to discount the face value of a one-year government bond.

5. Which of the following is the risk that arises when it becomes difficult to sell a security in a highly stressed market?

   A. Liquidity risk
   B. Systemic risk
   C. Wrong-way risk

6. The risks that individuals face based on mortality create which of the following problems?

   A. The risk of loss of income to their families.
   B. Covariance risk associated with their human capital and their investment portfolios.
   C. The interacting effects of solvency risk and the risk of being taken advantage of by an unscrupulous financial adviser.

Solution to 1: C is correct. Operational risk is the only risk listed that is considered non-financial, even though it may have financial consequences. Credit and market risks derive from the possibility of default and market movements, respectively, and along with liquidity risk, are considered financial risks.

Solution to 2: C is correct. Although most risks are likely to be interconnected in some way, in some cases the risks an organization is exposed to will *interact* in such a way that a loss (or gain) in one exposure will lead directly to a loss in a different exposure as well, such as with many counterparty contracts. Conditions in A and B are much more directly linked in that market participants fully expect what follows—for example, in B, an outbreak of war in one region of the world could well cause widespread uncertainty; a flight to quality, such as to government-backed securities; and a widening in spreads for credit-risky securities. In C, in contrast, the reduction in creditworthiness following the market decline may be expected, but owing more money on an already existing contract as a result comes from the interaction of risks.

Solution to 3: A is correct because this risk arises from the financial markets.

Solution to 4: C is correct. The risk-free rate is generally the appropriate rate to use in discounting government bonds. Although government bonds are generally default free, their returns are certainly risky. Assuming a returns distribution has thin tails when it does not and assuming symmetry in an asymmetric distribution are both forms of model risk.

Solution to 5: A is correct. Securities vary highly in how liquid they are. Those with low liquidity are those for which either the number of agents willing to invest or the amount of capital these agents are willing to invest is limited. When markets are stressed, these limited number of investors or small amount of capital dry up, leading to the inability to sell the security at any price the seller feels is reasonable. Systemic risk is the risk of failure of the entire financial system and a much broader risk than liquidity risk. Wrong-way risk is the extent to which one's exposure to a counterparty is positively related to the counterparty's credit risk.

Solution to 6: A is correct. The uncertainty about death creates two risks: mortality risk and longevity risk. The mortality risk (risk of dying relatively young) is manifested by a termination of the income stream generated by the person. In contrast, longevity risk is the risk of outliving one's financial resources.

9. MEASURING AND MODIFYING RISK – DRIVERS AND METRICS

The core element of risk management is the measurement and modification of risk. One cannot modify risk without measuring it. The primary purpose of measuring risk is to determine whether the risk being taken, or being considered, is consistent with the pre-defined risk tolerance. To understand how risk is measured, it is important to understand the basic elements that drive risk.

9.1. Drivers

This section illustrates the origins of risk. Risk is a part of life itself. None of us knows from one day to the next everything that will happen to us in the next 24 hours, let alone over a longer period. We may get a phone call that a relative is extremely sick, or we may be contacted by a head-hunter about an attractive job possibility. We may learn that we are going to be given an award from a prestigious organization, or we may find that our identity has been stolen. All of us can almost surely name something that happened the previous day that was not anticipated. Most of these happenings are minor and often quickly forgotten. Others are serious. Some are good. Some are bad. Some are unpredictable outcomes of known events, such as whether we get an offer following a job interview or whether a medical test reveals that we are healthy or ill. Some events are completely unanticipated, such as getting a phone call from an old friend we have not talked to in many years or having a flat tire on the drive home. Fortunately, the vast majority of risks in life are minor. The ones that are not minor, however, have the potential to be highly unpredictable and financially, and sometimes physically and emotionally, quite costly.

In a conceptual sense, financial risks are no different from the other risks we face in life. All risks arise from the fact that the future is unknown. Financial risks largely emanate from economic risks, and economic risks emanate from the uncertainties of life.

Financial markets generate prices that fluctuate as investors absorb information about the global and domestic state of the economy, the company's industry, and the idiosyncratic characteristics of the company itself. Global and domestic macroeconomies are driven by the companies that operate within them, but much of the tone as well as the ground rules are set by governments and quasi-governmental agencies, such as central banks. Taxes, regulations, laws, and monetary and fiscal policy establish a legal and economic environment and a set of ground rules that greatly affect the degree and quality of economic activity that takes place. Attempts by governments and central banks of different countries to coordinate economic policies can lead to some degrees of success if harmonized, but if not, they can create an environment in which companies engage in practices designed to seek favorable treatment in some countries and avoid unfavorable treatment in others.[19]

All economies, in turn, are composed of industries. Government policies also affect industries, in some cases encouraging economic activity in some industries while discouraging it in others. Some industries are stable, weathering macroeconomic storms quite well, whereas others are highly cyclical.

The uncertainties of global and domestic macroeconomic and central bank policies create risks for economies and industries that we often treat as systematic. Seemingly minor events, such as filling the position of central bank chairperson, are often viewed by investors as major events, signaling possibly a change in policy that can greatly affect the macroeconomy and possibly certain industries.

Moving down to a more fundamental level, investors face the unsystematic or idiosyncratic risks of individual companies. Modern investment analysis prescribes that diversified portfolios bear no unsystematic risk. We are then led to believe that unsystematic risk does not matter in a well-diversified portfolio. But unsystematic risk does matter to the management of a company. It also matters to poorly diversified investors. And it certainly matters to the financial analysts who cover specific companies. And what would appear to be unsystematic risk can oftentimes actually be systematic. For example, poor credit risk management by a major bank can turn into a global financial crisis if that bank is "too big to fail."

In sum, the basic drivers of risk arise from global and domestic macroeconomies, industries, and individual companies. Risk management can control some of this risk, but it cannot control all of it. For example, the risk manager of a company may be able to reduce the likelihood that his company will default, but he cannot control movements in interest rates. For the latter risk, he must accept that interest rate volatility is a given and that he can only position the company to be able to ensure that its risk exposure is aligned with its objective and risk tolerance. In order to do so, he must first be able to measure the risk.

9.2. Metrics

The notion of metrics in the context of risk refers to the quantitative measures of risk exposure. The most basic metric associated with risk is probability. Probability is a measure of the relative frequency with which one would expect an outcome, series of outcomes, or range of outcomes to occur. One can speak about the probability of rolling a six in one roll of a die as 1/6, the chance of rain in the next 24 hours as 20%, or the odds of a central bank taking actions to increase interest rates of 50%. These are all probabilities, differing in concept by the

---

[19] This practice is sometimes called regulatory arbitrage. The policies of certain countries can be more conducive to establishing operations. Examples are the flow of money into countries whose banking laws are less restrictive and more conducive to secrecy and incorporation in or moving a company to a country with lighter regulations or more favorable tax treatment.

fact that the die roll is associated with an objective probability measure, whereas the other two examples are subjective probabilities. It is important to note that probability, in and of itself, is not a sufficient metric of risk. A chance of financial loss of 25% does not tell us everything we need to know. There are other measures of risk that incorporate probability but give us more information.

The standard deviation is a measure of the dispersion in a probability distribution. Although there is a formal mathematical definition of standard deviation, at this point we need only understand the conceptual definition. Standard deviation measures a range over which a certain percentage of the outcomes would be expected to occur. For example, in a normal distribution, about 68% of the time the outcomes will lie within plus or minus one standard deviation of the expected value. Two standard deviations in both directions would cover about 95% of the outcomes, whereas three would encompass 99% of the outcomes. Although standard deviation, or volatility, is widely used in the financial world, it does have significant limitations. In particular, standard deviation may not be an appropriate measure of risk for non-normal distributions. Standard deviation may not exist for return distributions with fat tails.

Moreover, according to modern portfolio theory, the risk captured by an asset's standard deviation overstates the risk of that asset's returns in the context of a diversified portfolio. Investors can easily diversify their holdings, thereby eliminating a portion of the risk in their portfolios by diversifying away the security-specific risk. As a result, most financial valuation theories assert that the ability of investors to eliminate security-specific risk, or non-systematic risk, means that investors should not expect to earn a premium to compensate them for the assumption of this risk. As a consequence, the risk of a security may be better measured by its **beta**, a measure of the sensitivity of a security's returns to the returns on the market portfolio. Beta measures relative risk, meaning how much market risk an asset contributes to a well-diversified portfolio.[20]

Beta describes risk well for a portfolio of equities, but other sources of risk may require other descriptive risk metrics. The risk associated with derivatives is one example of this. Although derivatives are widely used to manage risk, they do so by assuming other risks. Even if the derivative is being used to establish a hedge of an existing exposure to risk, it would still result in the assumption of additional risk because the assumed risk is being used to offset an existing risk. For example, if one purchases a call option denominated in euros to buy Russian rubles, one would be assuming the risk of the ruble/euro exchange rate. Because most derivatives exposures are highly leveraged, it is critical that the risk of derivatives be properly measured. There are several specialized measures of derivatives risk.

The sensitivity of the derivative price to a small change in the value of the underlying asset is called the **delta**. It is perhaps the most important measure of derivatives risk. Yet delta is limited to capturing only small changes in the value of the underlying. Large changes are captured by the concept of **gamma**. Whereas delta is a first-order risk, gamma is considered

---

[20] Earlier, we discussed the fact that unsystematic risk matters to some parties. Here we seem to be saying that it should not matter to anyone. Capital market models almost always assume that investors can diversify quite easily and, as a result, they should not expect to earn a premium for bearing diversifiable risk. This assumption does not mean that everyone's wealth is well-diversified. Investors who do not diversify probably cannot expect to earn a return for bearing diversifiable risk, but it does not mean that these investors should not care about measuring the risk they choose to assume by not diversifying.

a second-order risk because it reflects the risk of changes in delta.[21] Some derivatives, such as options, are also sensitive to changes in the volatility of the underlying. This risk is captured by a concept called **vega**, which is a first-order measure of the change in the derivative price for a change in the volatility of the underlying. Derivatives are also sensitive to changes in interest rates, which are reflected in a measure called **rho**. Most options have relatively low sensitivity to interest rates.[22] These, and other mathematically derived derivatives metrics, are collectively referred to as "the Greeks."

Other asset classes may have their own special metrics to describe risk. One well-known example, **duration**, is a measure of the interest rate sensitivity of a fixed-income instrument. Analogous to delta, it is a first-order risk. The wide variety of financial instrument types and asset classes leads to a proliferation of terminology and risk measures, with most of them having no meaning outside their asset class. As financial organizations and asset risk modeling became more sophisticated and computer power increased, an approach was needed to measure and describe financial risk across the broad spectrum of asset classes. Spurred by the onset of global bank capital regulation, this led to the development of value at risk.

Value at risk or **VaR** is a measure of the size of the tail of the distribution of profits on a portfolio or for an organization. A VaR measure contains three elements: an amount stated in units of currency, a time period, and a probability. For example, assume a London bank determines that its VaR is £3 million at 5% for one day. This statement means that the bank expects to lose a minimum of £3 million in one day 5% of the time. A critical, and often overlooked word, is *minimum*. In this example, the bank expects that its losses will be at least £3 million in one day with 5% probability. In a VaR measure, there is no ultimate maximum that one can state. VaR is thus a minimum extreme loss metric. With a probability of 5% and a measurement period of one day, we can interpret the bank's VaR as expecting a minimum loss of £3 million once every 20 business days. VaR can also be used to measure credit losses, although the construction of the measure is considerably more difficult given the extreme asymmetry of the risk.

VaR is a simple but controversial measure. There are several ways to estimate VaR, each of which has its own advantages and disadvantages. The different measures can lead to highly diverse estimates. Moreover, VaR is subject to the same model risk as derivative pricing models. VaR is based on a particular assumption about the probability distribution of returns or profits. If that assumption is incorrect, the VaR estimate will be incorrect. VaR also requires certain inputs. If those inputs are incorrect, the VaR estimate will be incorrect. Many critics of VaR have argued that naive users of VaR can be lulled into a false sense of security. A presumably tolerable VaR can give the illusion that the risk is under control, when in fact, it is not. Yet, VaR is accepted as a risk measure by most banking regulators and is approved for disclosure purposes in typical accounting standards. As with any risk measure, one should supplement it with other measures.

As emphasized earlier, VaR does not tell the maximum loss. The maximum loss is the entire equity of an organization or the entire value of a portfolio, but the statistics used to estimate VaR can be used to gauge average extreme losses. Conditional VaR or **CVaR** is a common

---

[21] The notion of a first-order risk versus a second-order risk can be seen by considering the following. Suppose A affects B and B, in turn, affects C. A does not affect C directly but does so only indirectly. A is a first-order risk for B and a second-order risk for C.

[22] Options on interest rates, however, have a high sensitivity to interest rates, but only because interest rates are the underlying, and thus, the source of market risk.

tail loss measure, defined as the weighted average of all loss outcomes in the statistical distribution that exceed the VaR loss. Another tail risk metric in the credit risk space that is analogous to CVaR is expected loss given default, which answers the question for a debt security, "If the underlying company or asset defaults, how much do we lose on average?"

VaR focuses on the left tail of the distribution and purports to tell us the expected frequency of extreme negative returns, but it can understate the actual risk. For example, the normal distribution gives us a well-defined measure of extreme negative returns, which are balanced by extreme positive returns. Yet, actual historical return distributions have shown that there are more extreme negative returns than would be expected under the normal distribution. We previously described this concern in the form of tail risk. In response to this concern, statisticians have developed a branch of study that focuses primarily on extreme outcomes, which is called **extreme value theory**, and leads to measures of the statistical characteristics of outcomes that occur in the tails of the distribution. There are mathematical rules that define the statistical properties of such large outcomes, and these rules have been widely used for years in the insurance business. In the past 20 years or so, risk managers have taken to using them to help gauge the likelihood of outcomes that exceed those that would normally be expected.

Two measures in particular that are often used to complement VaR are **scenario analysis** and **stress testing**. These are common sense approaches that ask "If this happens, then how are we affected?" Scenario analysis can be thought of as a package of stress tests, usually with some common underlying theme. A scenario defines a set of conditions or market movements that could occur and would put some pressure on a portfolio. An example might be a sharp increase in interest rates coupled with a significant decline in the value of a currency. The portfolio is then evaluated to determine its expected loss under these scenarios. A different means of posing a scenario analysis is stress testing, which is done by proposing specific asset price moves generally involving extremely large and high pressure scenarios that would occur only rarely but would have the potential for destabilizing the entire organization. The US Federal Reserve and other central banks have begun requiring major banks to stress test their portfolios. Although scenario analysis and stress testing can provide some information, they are, as noted previously for other measures, subject to model risk.

Of course, the measures just mentioned focus primarily on market risk. Credit risk, which is covered in more detail in readings on fixed-income analysis, has long relied heavily on the credit ratings provided by private companies, such as Moody's Analytics, Standard & Poor's, and Fitch Ratings. In effect, a large part of credit analysis for many lenders has been outsourced since the early part of the 20th century. Most lenders, however, do not rely exclusively on these rating companies. They do their own analysis, which focuses on the creditor's liquidity, profitability, and leverage. Liquidity measures, such as the current ratio, may indicate how well a borrower can cover short-term obligations. Solvency ratios, such as cash flow coverage or interest coverage, may reveal whether a borrower generates enough cash or earnings to make its promised interest payments. Profitability measures, such as return on assets, estimate whether a company is sufficiently profitable so that it can easily accommodate debt. Leverage measures, such as the ratio of debt to total assets, reflect whether a company has sufficient equity capital in relation to its debt to absorb losses and negative cash flows without defaulting. Credit analysis also examines the strength and cyclicality of the macroeconomy and the company's industry. Other widely used measures of credit risk include credit VaR, probability of default, expected loss given default, and the probability of a credit rating change.

One of the problems of credit risk measurement is that credit events, such as a ratings downgrade or a default, are relatively rare for a particular organization. Certainly, in the aggregate there are many credit losses, but very few companies that default have a history of defaulting. Without a history to go by, estimating the likelihood of an event that has never actually occurred is extremely difficult. Imagine the challenge of assigning a default probability to Lehman Brothers in 2007. It had been in operation since 1850 and had never defaulted. Yet in 2008, Lehman Brothers, one of the most successful financial companies of all time, filed for bankruptcy. Because of the infrequency of default, risk managers normally attempt to assess default probability by aggregating companies with similar characteristics.[23]

Another useful source of information for risk managers about these rare events is the *ex ante* risk cost that is implied by the market pricing of derivatives. A **credit default swap (CDS)** on an issuing company has an observable price that acts as a signal to a bondholder of the risk cost of a default. Put options, exotic options, insurance contracts, and other financial instruments may contain valuable signals of the cost of rare adverse events, or at least the price of hedging them.

Operational risk is one of the most difficult risks to measure. Consider the operational risk event reported in 2014 in which hackers broke into Home Depot's credit card data base. Assessing the likelihood of such an event and estimating the potential losses would be almost impossible. The threat of litigation alone for years afterward is difficult to quantify. As with credit risk, significant operational risk events are rare but usually quite costly if they do occur. Hence, attempts to quantify the risk usually involve a third party aggregating operational risk events across numerous companies and publishing the statistics.

As mentioned, there are numerous other risks that would likewise be difficult to measure. For example, there is always the possibility of changes in accounting rules, laws, tax rates, and regulatory requirements that can result in significant costs as companies adapt their policies and actions from one regulatory environment to a new one. How would one measure such risks? Moreover, the time period spanned by these risks is extremely long, and in fact, theoretically infinite. Changes in these rules and laws are often motivated by politics. How does one quantify such risks when there are no real numeric measures? Analysis invariably reverts to subjective evaluation of the likelihood of such threats and their potential losses.

As we have described, many risks are measurable, at least on an *ex post* basis. Market-related risks are blessed with large quantities of data, so they are relatively measurable. Credit, operational, and other risks are somewhat rare events. Although it is probably a good thing that such events are indeed rare, their infrequency makes measurement more difficult. Nonetheless, virtually any risk manager will attempt to obtain at least a subjective sense of the expected frequency, likelihood, and cost of these events. With either objective or subjective measurements in mind, risk managers can then proceed to modify these risks accordingly.

10. METHODS OF RISK MODIFICATION – PREVENTION, AVOIDANCE, AND ACCEPTANCE

The notion of risk modification presumes that an analysis has been conducted in the risk governance stage that defines how much risk is acceptable. Coupled with measurements of the actual risk, as discussed in the previous section, the risk manager then proceeds to align the actual risk with the acceptable risk.

---

[23] In some sense, aggregating companies with similar characteristics is what credit ratings do. Companies rated BAA/Baa+ can be quite diverse but all are considered similar with respect to their ability to pay their debts.

It is important to understand, however, that risk modification is not strictly risk reduction. For example, a portfolio with the strategic objective of maintaining a 50/50 split between equity and cash will naturally find that in a market in which cash outperforms equity, the split between equity and cash will tilt toward cash. Thus, the portfolio becomes less risky. Beyond a certain point, the risk of the portfolio is unacceptably low given the return target. Thus, risk modification would take the form of rebalancing by increasing the risk. For the most part, however, risk management focuses more on reducing the risk. Risk reduction is commonly referred to as hedging. A hedge is a transaction put in place to reduce risk. Some hedges are designed to lead to the ultimate in risk reduction—the complete elimination of risk. Others are simply designed to lower the risk to an acceptable level.[24] For some companies, risk management is primarily concerned with keeping the organization solvent. Regardless of the focus, much of what is done to manage risk is the same. In this section, we will examine four broad categories of risk modification: risk prevention and avoidance, risk acceptance, risk transfer, and risk shifting.

10.1. Risk Prevention and Avoidance

One method of managing risk is taking steps to avoid it altogether; however, avoiding risk may not be as simple as it appears. It is difficult to completely avoid risk, but more importantly, it is unclear that every risk should be completely avoided particularly if there are high costs associated with eliminating the risk. Instead we choose a trade-off between cost and benefits. The actual trade-off may be subject to debate because risk assessment and risk management are subject to variation from one person to another.

We could nearly eliminate the risk of being injured or killed in an automobile accident if we choose to never drive or ride in a car. Like any risk-avoidance strategy, however, there would more than likely be a trade-off in terms of the loss of the benefits provided by the activity. We could try to protect our children from all harm, but that may come at the expense of preparing them poorly for adult life. We could invest our entire retirement savings in cash, but would most likely give up protection against inflation and lose out on the opportunity to benefit from long-term economic growth and the performance of investable assets that benefit from that growth.

Insurance companies rely heavily on the techniques of risk prevention and avoidance. An automobile insurance company would prefer that their policyholders never drive their cars. Although it cannot prohibit them from doing so, it can reward them with lower premiums if they drive less and have safe driving records. A life insurance company would prefer that their policyholders do not smoke, and it can reward non-smokers with lower rates.

Nearly every risk we take has an upside, at least as perceived by the person taking the risk. Some counterexamples might seem to belie this point, but not if viewed from the point of view of the risk taker. One could argue that there are no benefits from smoking, but people who smoke may have the opinion that the pleasure they receive exceeds the costs. Casino gambling incurs the risk of significant financial loss and addiction, but it is risk that is acceptable to the consumers who incur it relative to the perceived benefits they receive. The risks of extreme sports, such as skydiving, would seem to be exceeded by the benefits obtained by participants,

---

[24] For example, in the case of the portfolio with a strategic target of 50/50 equity and cash, if equity outperforms cash, the portfolio will tilt toward equity. At some point, a risk-reducing strategy would then be in order. This type of hedge would reduce the risk but not eliminate it.

and yet participants engage in them with apparently much enjoyment. People undertake all types of risky behaviors because they obtain commensurate benefits. These examples are simply cases in which the decision maker chooses to bear a certain degree of risk. They are conceptually the same as an investor who chooses to accept a relatively high degree of risk. Likewise, those who live their lives engaging in very few risky activities are conceptually the same as the investor who keeps only a modest exposure to risky assets.

In organizations, the decision to avoid risk is generally made at the governance level as a part of setting the risk tolerance. Boards will often decide that there are some business or investment activities simply not worth pursuing based on either the goals of the organization or the perceived risk–return trade-off. These are strategic decisions. Boards may exclude some areas or activities to allow management to focus on choosing risks in other areas where they presumably have a better chance of adding value.

We recap this section by noting that risk prevention and avoidance is simply an element of the decision of how much risk to accept, given the trade-off between the risk of loss and the benefit of gain. This could be a direct benefit or an indirect benefit of avoiding or eliminating a risk. Most decisions in life involve a trade-off between benefits and costs, neither of which is necessarily easy to measure. Thus, risk management is an ongoing process of fine-tuning exposure to achieve the level of risk that is desired in relation to the benefits.

If the risk measurement process shows that the risk exceeds the acceptable level, there are three approaches to managing the risk: self-insuring, risk transfer, and risk shifting.

10.2. Risk Acceptance: Self-Insurance and Diversification

In many cases, from both a risk tolerance and a strategic standpoint, it makes sense to keep a risk exposure—but to do so in the most efficient manner possible. Self-insurance is the notion of bearing a risk that is considered undesirable but too costly to eliminate by external means. In some cases, self-insuring means simply to bear the risk. In other cases, it may involve the establishment of a reserve to cover losses. Choosing to not have health insurance can be an optimal choice for some young, healthy adults without responsibility for children. Setting aside some money to cover potential health costs completes the picture of an individual who completely self-insures. Similarly, a young healthy individual who does not buy life insurance but engages in a systematic, well-conceived savings and investment plan is engaging in self-insurance.

One must be careful with this approach, however, because there is a fine line between self-insurance and denial. To the extent that self-insurance results in risks that are completely in line with the enterprise's risk tolerance, it would be an example of good governance. But if there is a risk that is outside the enterprise's risk tolerance, and management decides to bear that risk anyway, saying it is self-insuring, management is basically ignoring that risk, disregarding and violating its risk tolerance, and practicing bad risk governance. For example, an investment management firm, via its risk tolerance decision, may decide that it cannot bear any investment loss exceeding €1 billion and may apply a variety of risk management tools to limit its market and credit risk accordingly. But suppose that the firm makes no move to limit or insure its risks from fraud or a rogue trader on the grounds that it is "self-insuring" this risk, which could result in a loss as high as €3 billion. By leaving itself open to a loss that far exceeds its stated risk tolerance, management is violating the firm's risk governance.

From the perspective of a business organization, self-insurance is obtained by setting aside sufficient capital to cover losses. The banking industry is a classic example of self-insurance.

Although in many countries government insurance may protect depositors, banks self-insure to some extent by maintaining capital and loan loss reserves.

Another form of accepting risk, but doing so in the most efficient manner possible, is diversification. Technically, it is a risk-mitigation technique. But diversification and "the efficient frontier" are so central to modern portfolio analysis that capturing the full benefits of diversification seems the obvious thing for all organizations to pursue—a starting point at which other risk modification could be appended. Although diversification is one form of risk management, it is usually not effective if used in isolation.

In the next two subsections, we discuss how undesired risk can be modified or eliminated by selling the risk to another party. We make two subtle classifications of these methods: risk transfer and risk shifting.

11. METHODS OF RISK MODIFICATION – TRANSFER, SHIFTING, CHOOSING A METHOD FOR MODIFYING

Risk transfer is the process of passing on a risk to another party, often, but not always, in the form of an insurance policy. Insurance is a legal contract in which one party, the insurer, agrees to cover some percentage of a loss incurred by another party, the insured, from a specific event in return for the payment of a premium by the insured. Insurance as a method of risk modification has been in existence for very long time, and in fact, is even mentioned in the Code of Hammurabi almost 4,000 years ago. Insurance has been widely used in the commercial shipping and farming industries going back hundreds of years. Insurance is almost as old as commerce itself.[25]

From the point of view of the insurer, insurance almost always works on the basis of diversification or pooling of risks. An insurer attempts to sell many policies with risks that have low correlations. The insurer assesses the pooled risks and charges a premium that covers the expected aggregate losses and the insurer's operating costs as well as leaves a profit. Insurers need accurate statistics on aggregate risks, but these are often not difficult to obtain. These actuarial data are widely available on accidents, illnesses, property and casualty damage, and death. In principle, a well-diversified insurer does not care if a single insured party has significantly larger-than-average claims as long as there is no reason to believe that the claims are correlated. There will be other parties that have smaller-than-average claims.

Insurers do have to manage their risks carefully. Some risks can be correlated. In the US Gulf Coast region, property insurance, which includes coverage for loss by hurricanes, is typically more expensive than property insurance in other regions. Even with a higher premium, an insurer has to avoid providing too much property coverage in an area where a systemic event, such as a hurricane, can occur in order to diversify its risk exposure.

Although insurers carefully assess their risk and charge premiums that they believe accurately reflect expected losses, they nonetheless remain responsible for potentially large claims. Insurers also manage their risk by avoiding writing too many policies with similar and potentially correlated risks and by selling some of the risk to another insurer, a practice known as

---

[25] It is worth noting that the insurance industry has for a long time referred to itself using the term "risk management." A department of risk management in a large organization is often the group that manages the organization's insurance policies. But since around 1990 or so, the term "risk management" has increasingly come to refer to far more than insurance.

reinsurance. A company that primarily insures property in the US Midwest, which is highly subject to tornado risk, might be willing to accept some Gulf Coast hurricane risk for a reasonable premium. Insurers often write provisions into contracts to exclude coverage of special cases. For example, a war might nullify insurance coverage in an area. Most insurance policies also contain provisions to guard against moral hazards, such as suicide or destroying one's own property. In the last 20 years or so, some insurance companies have issued bonds that permit them to legally avoid paying principal and/or interest if insurance claims exceed a certain amount. These instruments, known as catastrophe bonds, essentially pass some of the insurance risk on to the investors who buy the bonds.

Most insurance policies do not cover *all* of the risk that is insured. It is common for policies to contain a provision known as a deductible. A deductible is a monetary amount of the loss that will be covered by the insured before any claims are paid. Thus, both the insured and the insurer bear some of the risk, although the insurer usually bears the greater amount. Deductibles serve several purposes. Because insurers incur fixed costs for each claim, deductibles reduce the number of small claims. Deductibles also encourage good risk management by the insured parties. Finally, deductibles offer the insured the opportunity to combine risk transfer with self-insurance and thereby achieve a potentially better trade-off of risk and reward.

As noted, the concept of insurance relies on the diversification or pooling of risks. In a few cases, however, the risks are not easy to pool. For example, suppose a volatile but extremely successful actor is signed to star in a movie. The production company knows that it runs the risk that the actor will engage in behavior that damages the ability of the company to finish the movie. The number of volatile and extremely successful actors for whom policies could be written at the same time is somewhat limited. Thus, an insurer would have to bear that risk without the benefit of diversification.

For example, suppose a television network plans to cover the Olympics but is concerned about a possible cancellation or boycott. It might want an insurance policy to cover it against loss. Specialized coverage is possible through such companies as Lloyd's of London. The approximately 350-year old Lloyd's is famous for covering unusual risks. It does so by organizing groups of investors who are willing to bear a risk for a premium. These groups, called syndicates, are subject to the full extent of losses. In many cases, investors in these syndicates have been required to pay substantial amounts of money to cover losses.[26] These examples illustrate how syndicates work. Although there is only one Olympics to insure, there may also be only one actor to insure. Because the two risks are uncorrelated, a company could write policies on both risks and would achieve some diversification. Moreover, there are other unusual risks that can be covered such that the aggregate pool would represent a highly diverse set of risks that have low correlations.

A very slight variation of insurance is a surety bond. With a surety bond, an insurer promises to pay an insured a certain amount of money if a third party fails to fulfill its obligation. For example, if a party engages the services of another party, the first party is covered if the party obligated to provide the service fails to perform to a satisfactory degree. Surety bonds are widely used in commercial activity when one party bears the risk of the potentially high cost of non-performance by another party. A slight variation of a surety bond is a fidelity bond, which is often used to cover against losses that result from employee dishonesty. Bonds of this

---

[26] NBC insured the 1980 Summer Olympics in Moscow through Lloyd's of London to the extent that if a US boycott occurred, Lloyd's would pay NBC for losses that it incurred by prepaying the Soviet Union for broadcasting rights. The United States did boycott the Olympics and NBC collected on its policy.

type work very similarly to insurance and rely on the pooling of uncorrelated risks.[27] Other similar arrangements include indemnity clauses and hold harmless arrangements, such as when two parties sign a contract and one party agrees to hold the other harmless and/or indemnify the other in the event of loss.

The use of insurance by so many as a risk management tool suggests that the cost of risk exceeds the actuarial cost to many individuals and enterprises. *Ex ante* consideration of the cost of a risk in terms of the organization's value or utility ties risk mitigation back to the risk tolerance decision and the most fundamental governance decisions on which value-added strategies to pursue. As an alternative to *ignoring* the cost of risk, the impact on enterprise value should be quite positive.

11.1. Risk Shifting

Whereas risk transfer refers to actions taken that pass the risk on to other parties, **risk shifting** refers to actions that change the distribution of risk outcomes. Risk transfer is often associated with insurance, whereas risk shifting generally involves derivatives as the risk modification vehicle. Although insurance is a form of risk management based on the pooling or diversification of risks, risk shifting diverts some portion of the risk distribution to another market participant who either bears the risk or intermediates that risk by moving it to yet another party. The organization may want to adjust its probability distribution of returns, essentially adjusting the payoff diagram of its risk exposures. An example is a company that is willing to make slightly less profit than it otherwise would if the stock market is up to prevent it from losing too much money if the stock market is down, for example, more than 20% next year. It is adjusting its potential economic outcomes by shifting the probability distribution of its profits conditional on market performance. Risk shifting represents the bulk of hedging and is the most common form of risk modification for financial organizations.

The principal device through which risk shifting is performed is a derivative. We briefly mentioned derivatives earlier in this reading. By definition, a derivative is a financial instrument that derives its price from the price of an underlying asset or rate. Because the price of the underlying and the price of the derivative are so closely related, derivatives can provide essentially the same exposure as the underlying but can do so at lower cost and capital requirements. As such, derivatives permit the efficient shifting of risk across the probability distribution and from one party to another. One can hold the underlying and take an offsetting position in the derivative or vice versa. Whereas insurance can be designed to perform similarly, insurance functions primarily through the pooling of diverse risks. With derivatives, risks are shifted across probability distributions or payoffs and across parties, to leave specific outcomes of the conditional probability distribution with the parties most willing to bear the risk.

There are several types of derivatives, and the manner in which they provide risk shifting varies by type. Derivatives are classified into two categories: forward commitments or contingent claims. Forward commitments are agreements that obligate two parties to undertake a transaction at a future date at a price or rate agreed on when the commitment is made. Forward commitments include such instruments as forward contracts, futures contracts, and swaps. Forward commitments can be used to lock in a future interest rate for a borrower or

---

[27] In the context of surety and fidelity bonds, the word "bond" does not mean a debt obligation issued by one party, the borrower, and bought by another, the lender. In this context, the word refers to assuring one party that it bears no risk for the actions of a specific other party.

lender, the purchase or sale price of an asset, or an exchange rate for a currency. Parties who engage in forward commitments do not pay any money at the initiation of the contract. In lieu of any up-front payment from one party to the other, the two parties agree on the terms of the transaction that will be consummated at the end of the contract. Depending on movements in the price or rate of the underlying, one party will ultimately gain from the transaction while the other will lose or, in the less likely case, both parties could breakeven. For example, a corporate treasurer can use a forward contract to lock in the rate at which a foreign cash flow will be converted into the company's domestic currency. Regardless of movements in the exchange rate during the life of the contract, the foreign cash flow will convert to the domestic currency at a rate that is locked in when the contract is initiated. On the opposite side of the transaction, the party can be a speculator who simply bears the risk, or it can be a dealer who intermediates the risk between the hedger and the speculator. We will discuss dealers in more detail in a few paragraphs.

The other type of derivative is a contingent claim, which is commonly known as an option. An option is a contract between two parties that gives one party the right to buy or sell an underlying asset or to pay or receive a known underlying rate. An option takes the form of either a call option, which provides the right to buy the underlying or to pay a known rate, or a put option, which provides the right to sell the underlying or to receive a known rate.

With a forward commitment, both parties are mutually obligated to each other. Because an option grants the right, but not the obligation, to one party, that party has an advantage over the other. Consequently, that party, the buyer of the option, must pay cash, called the premium, to the seller of the option at the start of the contract. Once the premium is paid, the option buyer has no further obligation. He can either exercise the option or he can let the option expire unexercised. In the latter case, the option buyer incurs a loss equal to the premium. If the option is a call and it is exercised, the buyer pays the fixed price or rate and receives the underlying. If the option is a put and it is exercised, the buyer receives the fixed price or rate and delivers the underlying.[28] If the buyer of the option does exercise it, he may achieve a gain that exceeds the premium paid but the gain could also be less than the premium paid, thereby resulting in a net overall loss. An option buyer could be using the option to speculate on an upward move in the underlying if a call or downward move if a put. Alternatively, the option buyer could be hedging. In the example used earlier for forward commitments, the corporate treasurer anticipating an inflow of cash in a foreign currency could buy a put option to sell that currency, thereby converting it into his domestic cash flow at a known fixed rate. The option gives the treasurer the flexibility to not exercise it if the underlying currency rises in value. This flexibility comes at the cost of having to pay a premium at the start of the transaction, thus shifting the financial outcome across the entire probability distribution of that uncertain currency rate. In contrast, with the forward contract, the treasurer does not have to pay cash at the start but is obligated to convert at the agreed-upon rate.

Derivatives can be created in public forums, such as on derivatives exchanges, or privately between two parties. On derivatives exchanges, there are a large number of individual and institutional traders that make markets in derivatives. For private derivatives transactions, there is an extensive market of large bank and non-bank dealers willing to buy and sell derivatives. In both types of markets, these dealers assume the risk being transferred from parties who

---

[28] Instead of one party delivering the underlying, some options call for settlement in cash of an equivalent amount. Some forward commitments also settle in cash.

originate the transactions. These dealers almost always restructure and transfer some portion, if not all, of the risk by finding other parties that are willing to take on that risk. Ultimately, the risk is assumed by some party willing to accept the risk, producing an economically efficient outcome for all parties.

11.2. How to Choose Which Method for Modifying Risk

Choosing which risk mitigation method to use—risk prevention and avoidance, self-insuring, risk transfer, or risk shifting—is a critical part of the risk management process. Fortunately, the methods are not mutually exclusive, and many organizations use all methods to some extent. No single method provides a clear-cut advantage over the others. As with all decisions, the trade-off is one of costs versus benefits that are weighed in light of the risk tolerance of the organization or individual.

For example, many companies that have extensive foreign operations and are, therefore, highly exposed to exchange rate risk, hedge that risk using derivatives. Some companies prefer forwards, some prefer swaps, some prefer options, and some use multiple instruments. Some companies attempt to hedge currency risk by setting up operations in foreign countries rather than manufacturing domestically and shipping the goods to foreign countries.[29] Some companies manage their currency risk by attempting to balance currency assets and liabilities. Some airlines hedge the risk of oil price changes and others do not. Some airlines that do hedge this risk do so to a far greater degree than others. Additionally, some prefer the certainty of forwards and swaps, whereas others prefer the flexibility of options, even with the up-front cost that options require. Most insurance companies rely on their actuarial knowledge but supplement it with proactive measures, such as selling risk to other parties.

To the extent possible, most organizations should avoid risks that provide few benefits and potentially extreme costs. Reasonable, low-cost precautions against risks with few benefits should always be taken. Thus, risk prevention and risk avoidance are probably the first choice of measures, especially for risks that lie outside the core competencies of the organization and have little reasonable expectation of adding value. Nonetheless, avoidance may not be the best value for its cost. Moreover, avoiding risk may mean avoiding opportunity. Thus, an organization often cannot simply decide not to take a risk, at least not for all undesirable risks.

Organizations that have large amounts of free cash flow may choose to self-insure some risks, but few organizations have so much cash that they can afford to self-insure all risks. Some risks can potentially imperil the entire capital base. Most companies would, however, prefer to self-insure to the extent possible because self-insurance reduces the costs associated with external monitoring and gives the organization the greatest flexibility. Self-insurance and avoidance should generally be clearly addressed at the governance level and be consistent with stated risk tolerance.

Risk transfer, or the use of insurance, is a widely used risk management tactic, but it may not be suitable for many types of risks. Some risks simply are not insurable, at least not in a cost-effective way. Insurance works best when risks can be pooled, and that is not the case for many types of risks, particularly those that can affect a large number of parties at the same

---

[29] Here is another example of the interactions of risks. A decision to manufacture products in a foreign country involves trade-offs between exchange rate risk, political risk, and a variety of other risks germane to that country's economy, not to mention a potentially different degree of operational risk, in the pursuit of higher profits.

time. The use of risk shifting tools, such as derivatives, may not be available for all types of risks, thus limiting their use in risk mitigation. For financial risks that exceed risk appetite, risk shifting is a very common choice.

The various risk management methods are not equal in terms of the risk reduction and the risk profile that remains. For example, contingent claims, such as insurance, provide the flexibility in the form of offering opportunity to profit in one direction and have a loss reduced in the other, but they require payment of cash up front. In contrast, forward commitments lock in an outcome. In other words, they provide little flexibility, but they require no cash payment up front. The risk profile that exists when a contingent claim hedge is put in place differs significantly from the risk profile that exists when a forward commitment hedge is placed. This process requires significant understanding and discussion at all levels of the organization.

To recap, risk takers should identify risks that offer few rewards in light of potential costs and avoid those risks when possible. They should self-insure where it makes sense and diversify to the extent possible. They should consider insurance when risks can be pooled effectively if the cost of the insurance is less than the expected benefit. If derivatives are used, they must consider the trade-off of locking in outcomes with forward commitments versus the flexibility relative to cash cost of contingent claims, which can tailor the desired outcomes or payoffs by shifting the risk. Ultimately, the decision is always one of balancing costs against benefits while producing a risk profile that is consistent with the risk management objectives of the organization.

EXAMPLE 4   Measuring and Modifying Risk

1. From the perspective of an organization, which of the following *best* describes risk drivers?

   A. The probabilities of adverse events
   B. The statistical methods that measure risk
   C. Factors that influence macroeconomies and industries

2. Which of the following concepts directly measures the risk of derivatives?

   A. Probability
   B. Delta and gamma
   C. Beta and standard deviation

3. The *best* definition of value at risk is:

   A. the expected loss if a counterparty defaults.
   B. the maximum loss an organization would expect to incur over a holding period.
   C. the minimum loss expected over a holding period a certain percentage of the time.

4. Which of the following are methods commonly used to supplement VaR to measure the risk of extreme events?

    A. Standard deviation
    B. Loss given default
    C. Scenario analysis and stress testing

5. Which of the following is a true statement about insurable risks?

    A. Insurable risks are less costly.
    B. Insurable risks have smaller loss limits.
    C. Insurable risks are typically diversifiable by the insurer.

Solution to 1: C is correct. Risks (and risk drivers) arise from fundamental factors in macroeconomies and industries.

Solution to 2: B is correct. Delta and gamma are measures of the movement in an option price, given a movement in the underlying. The other answers can reflect some elements of derivatives risk, but they are not direct measures of the risk.

Solution to 3: C is correct. VaR measures a minimum loss expected over a holding period a certain percentage of the time. It is not an expected loss nor does it reflect the maximum possible loss, which is the entire equity of the organization.

Solution to 4: C is correct. Scenario analysis and stress testing both examine the performance of a portfolio subject to extreme events. The other two answers are metrics used in portfolio analysis but are not typically associated with extreme events.

Solution to 5: C is correct. Insurance works by pooling risks. It is not necessarily less costly than derivatives nor does it have lower loss limits.

SUMMARY

Success in business and investing requires the skillful selection and management of risks. A well-developed risk management process ties together an organization's goals, strategic competencies, and tools to create value to help it both thrive and survive. Good risk management results in better decision making and a keener assessment of the many important trade-offs in business and investing, helping managers maximize value.

- Risk and risk management are critical to good business and investing. Risk management is *not* only about avoiding risk.
- Taking risk is an active choice by boards and management, investment managers, and individuals. Risks must be understood and carefully chosen and managed.

- Risk exposure is the extent to which an organization's value may be affected through sensitivity to underlying risks.
- Risk management is a process that defines risk tolerance and measures, monitors, and modifies risks to be in line with that tolerance.
- A risk management framework is the infrastructure, processes, and analytics needed to support effective risk management; it includes risk governance, risk identification and measurement, risk infrastructure, risk policies and processes, risk mitigation and management, communication, and strategic risk analysis and integration.
- Risk governance is the top-level foundation for risk management, including risk oversight and setting risk tolerance for the organization.
- Risk identification and measurement is the quantitative and qualitative assessment of all potential sources of risk and the organization's risk exposures.
- Risk infrastructure comprises the resources and systems required to track and assess the organization's risk profile.
- Risk policies and processes are management's complement to risk governance at the operating level.
- Risk mitigation and management is the active monitoring and adjusting of risk exposures, integrating all the other factors of the risk management framework.
- Communication includes risk reporting and active feedback loops so that the risk process improves decision making.
- Strategic risk analysis and integration involves using these risk tools to rigorously sort out the factors that are and are not adding value as well as incorporating this analysis into the management decision process, with the intent of improving outcomes.
- Employing a risk management committee, along with a chief risk officer (CRO), are hallmarks of a strong risk governance framework.
- Governance and the entire risk process should take an enterprise risk management perspective to ensure that the value of the entire enterprise is maximized.
- Risk tolerance, a key element of good risk governance, delineates which risks are acceptable, which are unacceptable, and how much risk the overall organization can be exposed to.
- Risk budgeting is any means of allocating investments or assets by their risk characteristics.
- Financial risks are those that arise from activity in the financial markets.
- Non-financial risks arise from actions within an organization or from external origins, such as the environment, the community, regulators, politicians, suppliers, and customers.
- Financial risks consist of market risk, credit risk, and liquidity risk.
- Market risk arises from movements in stock prices, interest rates, exchange rates, and commodity prices.
- Credit risk is the risk that a counterparty will not pay an amount owed.
- Liquidity risk is the risk that, as a result of degradation in market conditions or the lack of market participants, one will be unable to sell an asset without lowering the price to less than the fundamental value.
- Non-financial risks consist of a variety of risks, including settlement risk, legal risk, regulatory risk, accounting risk, tax risk, model risk, tail risk, and operational risk.
- Operational risk is the risk that arises either from within the operations of an organization or from external events that are beyond the control of the organization but affect its operations. Operational risk can be caused by employees, the weather and natural disasters, vulnerabilities of IT systems, or terrorism.
- Solvency risk is the risk that the organization does not survive or succeed because it runs out of cash to meet its financial obligations.

- Individuals face many of the same organizational risks outlined here but also face health risk, mortality or longevity risk, and property and casualty risk.
- Risks are not necessarily independent because many risks arise as a result of other risks; risk interactions can be extremely non-linear and harmful.
- Risk drivers are the fundamental global and domestic macroeconomic and industry factors that create risk.
- Common measures of risk include standard deviation or volatility; asset-specific measures, such as beta or duration; derivative measures, such as delta, gamma, vega, and rho; and tail measures such as value at risk, CVaR and expected loss given default.
- Risk can be modified by prevention and avoidance, risk transfer (insurance), or risk shifting (derivatives).
- Risk can be mitigated internally through self-insurance or diversification.
- The primary determinants of which method is best for modifying risk are the benefits weighed against the costs, with consideration for the overall final risk profile and adherence to risk governance objectives.

PROBLEMS

1. Risk management in the case of individuals is *best* described as concerned with:
   A. hedging risk exposures.
   B. maximizing utility while bearing a tolerable level of risk.
   C. maximizing utility while avoiding exposure to undesirable risks.
2. Which of the following may be controlled by an investor?
   A. Risk
   B. Raw returns
   C. Risk-adjusted returns
3. The process of risk management includes:
   A. minimizing risk.
   B. maximizing returns.
   C. defining and measuring risks being taken.
4. Risk governance:
   A. aligns risk management activities with the goals of the overall enterprise.
   B. defines the qualitative assessment and evaluation of potential sources of risk in an organization.
   C. delegates responsibility for risk management to all levels of the organization's hierarchy.
5. The factors a risk management framework should address include all of the following *except*:
   A. communications.
   B. policies and processes.
   C. names of responsible individuals.
6. Which of the following is the correct sequence of events for risk governance and management that focuses on the entire enterprise? Establishing:
   A. risk tolerance, then risk budgeting, and then risk exposures.
   B. risk exposures, then risk tolerance, and then risk budgeting.
   C. risk budgeting, then risk exposures, and then risk tolerance.

7. Which of the following *best* describes activities that are supported by a risk management infrastructure?
   A. Risk tolerance, budgeting, and reporting
   B. Risk tolerance, measurement, and monitoring
   C. Risk identification, measurement, and monitoring

8. Effective risk governance in an enterprise provides guidance on all of the following *except*:
   A. unacceptable risks.
   B. worst losses that may be tolerated.
   C. specific methods to mitigate risk for each subsidiary in the enterprise.

9. A firm's risk management committee would be expected to do all of the following *except*:
   A. approving the governing body's proposed risk policies.
   B. deliberating the governing body's risk policies at the operational level.
   C. providing top decision-makers with a forum for considering risk management issues.

10. Once an enterprise's risk tolerance is determined, the role of risk management is to:
    A. analyze risk drivers.
    B. align risk exposures with risk appetite.
    C. identify the extent to which the enterprise is willing to fail in meeting its objectives.

11. Which factor should *most* affect a company's ability to tolerate risk?
    A. A stable market environment
    B. The beliefs of the individual board members
    C. The ability to dynamically respond to adverse events

12. Risk budgeting includes all of the following *except*:
    A. determining the target return.
    B. quantifying tolerable risk by specific metrics.
    C. allocating a portfolio by some risk characteristics of the investments.

13. A benefit of risk budgeting is that it:
    A. considers risk tradeoffs.
    B. establishes a firm's risk tolerance.
    C. reduces uncertainty facing the firm.

14. Which of the following risks is *best* described as a financial risk?
    A. Credit
    B. Solvency
    C. Operational

15. Liquidity risk is *most* associated with:
    A. the probability of default.
    B. a widening bid–ask spread.
    C. a poorly functioning market.

16. An example of a non-financial risk is:
    A. market risk.
    B. liquidity risk.
    C. settlement risk.

17. If a company has a one-day 5% Value at Risk of $1 million, this means:
    A. 5% of the time the firm is expected to lose at least $1 million in one day.
    B. 95% of the time the firm is expected to lose at least $1 million in one day.
    C. 5% of the time the firm is expected to lose no more than $1 million in one day.

18. An organization choosing to accept a risk exposure may:
    A. buy insurance.
    B. enter into a derivative contract.
    C. establish a reserve fund to cover losses.
19. The choice of risk-modification method is based on:
    A. minimizing risk at the lowest cost.
    B. maximizing returns at the lowest cost.
    C. weighing costs versus benefits in light of the organization's risk tolerance.

CHAPTER 11

MEASURING AND MANAGING MARKET RISK

Don M. Chance, PhD, CFA, and Michelle McCarthy Beck

LEARNING OUTCOMES

The candidate should be able to:

- explain the use of value at risk (VaR) in measuring portfolio risk;
- compare the parametric (variance–covariance), historical simulation, and Monte Carlo simulation methods for estimating VaR;
- estimate and interpret VaR under the parametric, historical simulation, and Monte Carlo simulation methods;
- describe advantages and limitations of VaR;
- describe extensions of VaR;
- describe sensitivity risk measures and scenario risk measures and compare these measures to VaR;
- demonstrate how equity, fixed-income, and options exposure measures may be used in measuring and managing market risk and volatility risk;
- describe the use of sensitivity risk measures and scenario risk measures;
- describe advantages and limitations of sensitivity risk measures and scenario risk measures;
- explain constraints used in managing market risks, including risk budgeting, position limits, scenario limits, and stop-loss limits;
- explain how risk measures may be used in capital allocation decisions;
- describe risk measures used by banks, asset managers, pension funds, and insurers.

1. INTRODUCTION

This reading is an introduction to the process of measuring and managing market risk. Market risk is the risk that arises from movements in stock prices, interest rates, exchange rates, and commodity prices. Market risk is distinguished from credit risk, which is the risk of loss from the failure of a counterparty to make a promised payment, and also from a number of other risks that organizations face, such as breakdowns in their operational procedures. In essence, market risk is the risk arising from changes in the markets to which an organization has exposure.

Risk management is the process of identifying and measuring risk and ensuring that the risks being taken are consistent with the desired risks. The process of managing market risk relies heavily on the use of models. A model is a simplified representation of a real world phenomenon. Financial models attempt to capture the important elements that determine prices and sensitivities in financial markets. In doing so, they provide critical information necessary to manage investment risk. For example, investment risk models help a portfolio manager understand how much the value of the portfolio is likely to change given a change in a certain risk factor. They also provide insight into the gains and losses the portfolio might reasonably be expected to experience and the frequency with which large losses might occur.

Effective risk management, though, is much more than just applying financial models. It requires the application of judgment and experience not only to know how to use the models appropriately but also to appreciate the strengths and limitations of the models and to know when to supplement or substitute one model with another model or approach.

Financial markets operate more or less continuously, and new prices are constantly being generated. As a result, there is a large amount of data on market risk and a lot of collective experience dealing with this risk, making market risk one of the easier financial risks to analyze. Still, market risk is not an easy risk to capture. Although a portfolio's exposures can be identified with some certainty, the potential losses that could arise from those exposures are unknown. The data used to estimate potential losses are generated from past prices and rates, not the ones to come. Risk management models allow the experienced risk manager to blend that historical data with their own forward-looking judgment, providing a framework within which to test that judgment.

We first lay a foundation for understanding value at risk, discuss three primary approaches to estimating value at risk, and cover the primary advantages and limitations as well as extensions of value at risk. We then address the sensitivity measures used for equities, fixed-income securities, and options and also cover historical and hypothetical scenario risk measures. Next, we discuss the use of constraints in risk management, such as risk budgeting, position limits, scenario limits, stop-loss limits, and capital allocation as risk management tools. Lastly, we describe various applications and limitations of risk measures as used by different types of market participants and summarize our discussion.

1.1. Understanding Value at Risk

Value at risk (VaR) was developed in the late 1980s, and over the next decade, it emerged as one of the most important risk measures in global financial markets.

1.1.1. Value at Risk: Formal Definition

Value at risk is the minimum loss that would be expected a certain percentage of the time over a certain period of time given the assumed market conditions. It can be expressed in either currency units or as a percentage of portfolio value. Although this statement is an accurate definition of VaR, it does not provide sufficient clarity to fully comprehend the concept. To better understand what VaR means, let us work with an example. Consider the statement:

> *The 5% VaR of a portfolio is €2.2 million over a one-day period.*

The following three points are important in understanding the concept of VaR:

- VaR can be measured in either currency units (in this example, the euro) or in percentage terms. In this example, if the portfolio value is €400 million, the VaR expressed in percentage terms would be 0.55% (€2.2 million/€400 million = 0.0055).
- VaR is a *minimum* loss. This point cannot be emphasized enough. VaR is often mistakenly assumed to represent *how much one can lose*. If the question is, "how much can one lose?" there is only one answer: *the entire portfolio*. In a €400 million portfolio, assuming no leverage, the most one can lose is €400 million.
- A VaR statement references a time horizon: losses that would be expected to occur over a given period of time. In this example, that period of time is one day. (If VaR is measured on a daily basis, and a typical month has 20–22 business days, then 5% of the days equates to about one day per month.)

These are the explicit elements of a VaR statement: the *frequency* of losses of a given *minimum magnitude* expressed either in *currency* or *percentage* terms. Thus, the VaR statement can be rephrased as follows: A loss of at least €2.2 million would be expected to occur about once every month.

A 5% VaR is often expressed as its complement—a 95% level of confidence. In this reading, we will typically refer to the notion as a 5% VaR, but we should be mindful that it does imply a 95% level of confidence.

Using the example given, it is correct to say any of the following:

- €2.2 million is the minimum loss we would expect 5% of the time.
- 5% of the time, losses would be at least €2.2 million.
- We would expect a loss of no more than €2.2 million 95% of the time.

The last sentence is sometimes mistakenly phrased as "95% of the time we would expect to lose less than €2.2 million," but this statement could be taken to mean that 95% of the time we would incur losses, although those losses would be less than €2.2 million. In fact, a large percentage of the time we will make money.

Exhibit 1 illustrates the concept of VaR using the 5% case. It depicts a probability distribution of returns from a hypothetical portfolio. The distribution chosen is the familiar normal distribution, known sometimes as the bell curve, but that distribution is only one curve that might be used. In fact, there are compelling arguments that the normal distribution is not the right one to use for financial market returns. We discuss these arguments later.

EXHIBIT 1   Illustration of 5% VaR in the Context of a Probability Distribution

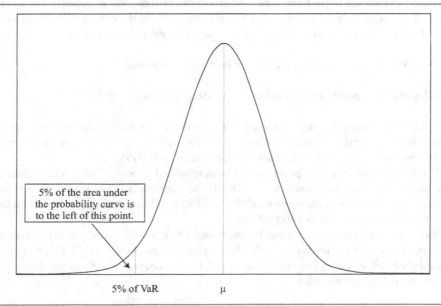

5% of the area under
the probability curve is
to the left of this point.

5% of VaR   μ

Note that the distribution in Exhibit 1 is centered on the value μ. [The symbol μ (Greek: *mu*) is a common symbol used to represent an expected value.] Near the left tail of the distribution is the notation "5% VaR," indicating that 5% of the area under the curve is to the left of the point of the VaR (i.e., the probability of observing a value less than the VaR is 5%).

Thus, it is apparent that VaR is simply a point on the probability distribution of profits or returns from a portfolio. Given the characteristics of the normal distribution, a 5% VaR is equivalent to the point on the distribution that is 1.65 standard deviations below the expected value. Although the concept of VaR can be easily visualized in this manner, actually measuring the VaR is a challenge.

Before we take on that challenge, however, note that there is no formal requirement that VaR be measured at a 5% threshold. It is also common to use a 1% threshold (2.33 standard deviations from the expected value), and some investment managers use a one standard deviation movement (equal to a 16% VaR)—both assuming a normal distribution. There is no definitive rule for what VaR cutoff should be used. A specification with a higher confidence level will produce a higher VaR. It is up to the decision maker to choose an appropriate level.

VaR and Standard Deviations

The 16% VaR relates to a one standard deviation move as follows: In a normal distribution, 50% of the outcomes are to the right of the expected value and 50% are to the left. A one standard deviation interval implies that 68% of the outcomes lie within one standard deviation of the expected value; thus, 34% of the outcomes lie one standard deviation to the left of the expected value and 34% of the outcomes one standard deviation to the right. Adding the 50% of the outcomes that lie to the right of the expected value to the 34% of the outcomes that lie one standard deviation below the expected value means that 84% of all outcomes lie to the right of the point that is one standard deviation to the left of the expected value. Therefore, 16% of all outcomes lie below this point. Thus, a one standard deviation movement is equivalent to a 16% VaR (or an 84% level of confidence).

Just as there is no formal requirement that VaR be measured at a 5% cutoff, there is also no formal requirement that VaR be measured using a daily loss estimate. One could reasonably measure VaR on a weekly, bi-weekly, monthly, quarterly, semiannually, or annual basis. Choosing the VaR threshold and the time horizon are examples of why VaR is not a precise measure but in fact entails considerable judgment.

We should also reiterate that VaR can be expressed as a rate of return or in monetary terms. It is typically easier to process the data necessary to estimate VaR in terms of returns, but VaR is most frequently expressed in terms of profits or losses. This point will become clearer as we work through examples.

EXAMPLE 1   Definition of VaR

1. Given a VaR of $12.5 million at 5% for one month, which of the following statements is correct?
   A. There is a 5% chance of losing $12.5 million over one month.
   B. There is a 95% chance that the expected loss over the next month is less than $12.5 million.
   C. The minimum loss that would be expected to occur over one month 5% of the time is $12.5 million.
2. Which of the following statements is **not** correct?
   A. A 1% VaR implies a downward move of 1%.
   B. A one standard deviation downward move is equivalent to a 16% VaR.
   C. A 5% VaR implies a move of 1.65 standard deviations less than the expected value.

Solution to 1: C is correct because it is the only statement that accurately expresses the VaR. A is incorrect because VaR does not give the likelihood of losing a specific amount. B is incorrect because VaR is not an expected loss; rather, it is a minimum loss.

Solution to 2: A is correct. A 1% VaR (99% confidence) is the point on the distribution 2.33 standard deviations below the expected value. Answers B and C correctly describe a 16% and 5% VaR, respectively.

To this point, we have given only the conceptual definition of VaR. Defining something is one thing; measuring it can be quite challenging. Such is the case for VaR.

2. ESTIMATING VAR

Three methods are typically used to estimate VaR: the parametric (variance–covariance) method, the historical simulation method, and the Monte Carlo simulation method. Each of these will be discussed in turn.

The first step of every VaR calculation, regardless of the VaR method used, is to convert the set of holdings in the portfolio into a set of exposures to **risk factors**, a process called **risk decomposition**. In some instances, this process can be very simple: An equity security can be the risk factor itself. In other instances, the process can be highly complex. For example, a convertible bond issued by a foreign entity has both currency and equity risk factors as well as exposures to multiple points on a yield curve of a given credit quality. Fixed-income instruments and derivatives products often contain distinct risk exposures that require decomposition in order to accurately capture their loss potential.

The second step of VaR estimation requires gathering a data history for each of the risk factors in the VaR model. The three methods use different approaches to specifying these inputs, which will be discussed in the following sections. We will see that the parametric and Monte Carlo methods do not formally require a data history. They require only that the user enter estimates of certain parameters into the computational procedure (expected return, standard deviation, and for some models, skewness and kurtosis). One of the most common sources for estimating parameter inputs for any financial model is historical data, but the user could substitute estimates based on judgment or alternative forecasting models. Indeed, shortly we will override some historical estimates with our own judgment. Nonetheless, the collection of a data history is typically used at least as a starting point in the parametric and Monte Carlo methods, and it is absolutely required for the historical simulation method.

The third step of each method is where the differences between the three VaR methods are most apparent: how each method uses the data to make an estimate of the VaR.

Although most portfolios contain a large number of individual securities and other assets, we will use a two-asset portfolio to illustrate the three VaR methods. Using a limited number of assets permits us to closely observe the essential elements of the VaR estimation procedure without getting mired in the complex mathematics required to accommodate a large number of assets. The objective is to understand the concept of VaR, be aware of how it is estimated, know how it is used, appreciate the benefits of VaR, and be attentive to its limitations. We can achieve these objectives by keeping the portfolio fairly simple.

Our example portfolio has a market value of $150 million and consists of two ETFs—SPDR S&P 500 ETF (SPY), representing the US equity exposure, and SPDR Portfolio Long-Term Corporate Bond ETF (SPLB), representing a corporate bond exposure. We will allocate 80% of the portfolio to SPY and 20% of the portfolio to SPLB. For the sake of simplicity, the two securities will represent the risk factors and the return history of each ETF will serve as the risk factor history used in the VaR model. We have collected a set of two years of daily total return data, reflecting both capital appreciation and dividends on each ETF. The period used for this historical data set is called the **lookback period**. The question of exactly how much data are required to be a representative data set is a complex question that is common to all estimation problems in economics and finance. We will discuss some of the issues on this matter later in this reading.

Exhibit 2 provides statistical summary information based on the two years of daily data in the lookback period, covering the period of 1 July 2015 through 28 June 2019.

EXHIBIT 2   Statistical Estimates from Daily Return Data, 1 July 2015–28 June 2019

	Daily		Annualized	
	Average Return	Standard Deviation	Average Return	Standard Deviation
SPY	0.047%	0.86%	12.51%	13.64%
SPLB	0.031%	0.49%	8.03%	7.73%

Note: The correlation of SPLB and SPY = −0.0607.

SPY produced an annualized average return of about 12.5% with a standard deviation of 13.6%, significantly different from the long-term historical performance of the S&P 500 Index of approximately 10.5% average return and 20% standard deviation. SPLB produced an annualized average return of 8% with a standard deviation of about 7.7%. These numbers compare with an average annual return for long-term corporate bonds of slightly more than 6% and a standard deviation of about 8.5% (historical data are drawn from Malkiel 2007). Although the average return of SPLB in the last four years was higher than that of the overall long-term corporate bond sector, the standard deviations were similar.

The risk and return parameters for each risk factor in Exhibit 2 illustrate how one might collect historical data. It is necessary, however, to critically assess the data and apply judgment to modify the inputs if the lookback period is not representative of the expected performance of the securities (or risk factors) going forward. Exercising our judgment, and believing that we have no information to suggest that future performance will deviate from the long-run historical performance, we adjust our inputs and use returns of 10.5% for SPY and 6% for SPLB, with standard deviations of 20% for SPY and 8.5% for SPLB. These adjustments align the inputs more closely with the long-run historical performance of each sector. In practice, users will want to use estimates they believe are reflective of current expectations, though clearly one user's estimates could differ widely from another's.

Although the returns and standard deviations experienced over the lookback period have been adjusted to more closely align with long-run historical experience, we will use a correlation estimate approximately equal to the observed correlation over our lookback period. We are assuming that the recent historical relationship of equity and fixed-income returns is a reasonable assumption moving forward. To keep the numbers simple, we round the observed correlation of −0.0607 to −0.06.

Exhibit 3 illustrates our input assumptions for the VaR estimations.

EXHIBIT 3   Input Assumptions, 1 July 2015–28 June 2019

	Allocation	Annualized	
		Return	Standard Deviation
SPY	80%	10.5%	20.0%
SPLB	20%	6.0%	8.5%

Note: The correlation of SPLB and SPY = −0.06.

3. THE PARAMETRIC METHOD OF VAR ESTIMATION

The **parametric method** of estimating VaR is sometimes referred to as the analytical method and sometimes the variance–covariance method. The parametric method begins, as does each method, with a risk decomposition of the portfolio holdings. It typically assumes that the return distributions for the risk factors in the portfolio are normal. It then uses the expected return and standard deviation of return for each risk factor to estimate the VaR.

Note that we said that this method *typically* uses the normal distribution. Indeed, that is the common case in practice, but there is no formal requirement that the normal distribution be used. The normal distribution conveniently requires only two parameters—the expected value and standard deviation—to encompass everything there is to know about it. If other distributions are used, additional parameters of the distribution, such as skewness and kurtosis, would be required. We will limit the presentation here to the normal distribution, but be aware that other, more accurately representative distributions could be used but would add complexity to the VaR estimation process.

Recall that in defining VaR, we identified a VaR threshold—a point in the left tail of the distribution, typically either the 5% left tail, the 1% left tail, or a one standard deviation move (16%). If the portfolio is characterized by normally distributed returns and the expected value and standard deviation are known, it is a simple matter to identify any point on the distribution. A normal distribution with expected value μ and standard deviation σ can be converted to a standard normal distribution, which is a special case of the normal distribution in which the expected value is zero and the standard deviation is one. A standard normal distribution is also known as a z-distribution. If we have observed a return R from a normal distribution, we can convert to its equivalent z-distribution value by the transformation:

$$z = \frac{R - \mu}{\sigma}.$$

In a standard normal (z) distribution, a 5% VaR is 1.65 standard deviations below the expected value of zero. A 1% VaR is 2.33 standard deviations below the expected value of zero. A 16% VaR is one standard deviation below the expected value of zero. Thus, in our example, for a 5% VaR, we wish to know the return that is 1.65 standard deviations to the left of the expected return.

To estimate this VaR, we need the expected return and volatility of the portfolio. The expected return is estimated from the following equation:

$$E(R_p) = w_{SPY}E(R_{SPY}) + w_{SPLB}E(R_{SPLB}), \tag{1}$$

where the expected return of the portfolio, $E(R_p)$, is equal to the portfolio weights of SPY (w_{SPY}) and SPLB (w_{SPLB}) multiplied by the expected return of each asset, $E(R_{SPY})$ and $E(R_{SPLB})$.

The volatility of the portfolio, σ_p, is estimated from the following equation:

$$\sigma_p = \sqrt{w_{SPY}^2\sigma_{SPY}^2 + w_{SPLB}^2\sigma_{SPLB}^2 + 2\,w_{SPY}w_{SPLB}\rho_{SPY,SPLB}\sigma_{SPY}\sigma_{SPLB}}, \tag{2}$$

where σ_{SPY} and σ_{SPLB} are the standard deviations (volatilities) of SPY and SPLB, respectively; $\rho_{SPY,SPLB}$ is the correlation between the returns on SPY and SPLB, respectively; and $\rho_{SPY,SPLB}$ $\sigma_{SPY}\sigma_{SPLB}$ is the covariance between SPY and SPLB.

Recall that we estimated these parameters from the historical data, with some modifications to make them more consistent with long-run values. The formal calculations for our portfolio based on these adjusted estimates are as follows:

$$E(R_p) = 0.8(0.105) + 0.2(0.06) = 0.096000$$
$$\sigma_p = \sqrt{(0.8)^2 (0.2)^2 + (0.2)^2 (0.085)^2 + 2(0.8)(0.2)(-0.06)(0.2)(0.085)}$$
$$= 0.159883.$$

Thus, our portfolio, consisting of an 80% position in SPY and a 20% position in SPLB, is estimated to have an expected return of 9.6% and a volatility of approximately 15.99%.

But these inputs are based on annual returns. If we want a one-day VaR, we should adjust the expected returns and volatilities to their daily counterparts. Assuming 250 trading days in a year, the expected return is adjusted by dividing by 250 and the standard deviation is adjusted by dividing by the square root of 250. (Note that the variance is converted by dividing by time, 250 days; thus, the standard deviation must be adjusted by using the square root of time, 250 days.) Thus, the daily expected return and volatility are

$$E(R_p) = \frac{0.096}{250} = 0.000384 \tag{3}$$

and

$$\sigma_p = \frac{0.159883}{\sqrt{250}} = 0.010112. \tag{4}$$

It is important to note that we have assumed that the statistical properties of the return distribution are constant across the year. Earlier, we annualized the daily data in Exhibit 2 in order to see how our estimates compared with long-term estimates. We made some modest adjustments to the annualized data and then, in Equations 3 and 4, returned to using daily data. To estimate an annual VaR, we would need to use annual data, but we would need a longer lookback period in order to have sufficient data points.

It is important to note that we cannot estimate a daily VaR and annualize it to arrive at an annual VaR estimate. First, to assume that a daily distribution of returns can be extrapolated to an annual distribution is a bold assumption. Second, annualizing the daily VaR is not the same as adjusting the expected return and the standard deviation to annual numbers and then calculating the annual VaR. The expected return is annualized by multiplying the daily return by 250, and the standard deviation is annualized by multiplying the daily standard deviation by the square root of 250. Thus, we can annualize the data and estimate an annual VaR, but we cannot estimate a daily VaR and annualize it without assuming a zero expected return.

Having calculated the daily expected return and volatility, the parametric VaR is now easily obtained. With the distribution centered at the expected return of 0.0384% and a one standard deviation move equal to 0.996%, a 5% VaR is obtained by identifying the point on the distribution that lies 1.65 standard deviations to the left of the mean. It is now easy to see why parametric VaR is so named: The expected values, standard deviations, and covariances are the *parameters* of the distributions.

The following step-by-step procedure shows how the VaR is derived:

$$\{[E(Rp) - 1.65\sigma_p](-1)\}(\$150,000,000)$$

Step 1:   Multiply the portfolio standard deviation by 1.65.

$$0.010112 \times 1.65 = 0.016685$$

Step 2:   Subtract the answer obtained in Step 1 from the expected return.

$$0.000384 - 0.016685 = -0.016301$$

Step 3:   Because VaR is expressed as an absolute number (despite representing an expected loss), change the sign of the value obtained in Step 2.

$$\text{Change } -0.016301 \text{ to } 0.016301$$

Step 4:   Multiply the result in Step 3 by the value of the portfolio.

$$\$150,000,000 \times 0.016301 = \$2,445,150$$

Thus, using the parametric method, our estimate of VaR is $2,445,150, meaning that on 5% of trading days the portfolio would be expected to incur a loss of at least $2,445,150. Note that asset managers may stop at Step 3 because at that point the measure is expressed as a percentage of the value of the portfolio, which is the unit this group more commonly uses.

EXAMPLE 2   Parametric VaR

1. The parameters of normal distribution required to estimate parametric VaR are:
   A. expected value and standard deviation.
   B. skewness and kurtosis.
   C. standard deviation and skewness.
2. Assuming a daily expected return of 0.0384% and daily standard deviation of 1.0112% (as in the example in the text), which of the following is *closest* to the 1% VaR for a $150 million portfolio? Express your answer in dollars.
   A. $3.5 million
   B. $2.4 million
   C. $1.4 million
3. Assuming a daily expected return of 0.0384% and daily standard deviation of 1.0112% (as in the example in the text), the daily 5% parametric VaR is $2,445,150. Rounding the VaR to $2.4 million, which of the following values is *closest* to the annual 5% parametric VaR? Express your answer in dollars.
   A. $38 million
   B. $25 million
   C. $600 million

Solution to 1: A is correct. The parameters of a normal distribution are the expected value and standard deviation. Skewness, as mentioned in B and C, and kurtosis, as mentioned in B, are characteristics used to describe a *non*-normal distribution.

Solution to 2: A is correct and is obtained as follows:

Step 1: $2.33 \times 0.010112 = 0.023561$
Step 2: $0.000384 - 0.023561 = -0.023177$
Step 3:   Convert -0.023177 to 0.023177
Step 4: $0.023177 \times \$150$ million $= \$3,476,550$

B is the estimated VaR at a 5% threshold, and C is the estimated VaR using a one standard deviation threshold.

Solution to 3: B is correct. It is found by annualizing the daily return and standard deviation and using these figures in the calculation. The annual return and standard deviation are, respectively, 0.096000 (0.000384×250) and 0.159885 ($0.010112 \times \sqrt{250}$).

Step 1: $0.159885 \times 1.65 = 0.263810$
Step 2: $0.096000 - 0.263810 = -0.167810$
Step 3:   Convert -0.167810 to 0.167810
Step 4: $0.167810 \times \$150$ million $= \$25,171,500$

A incorrectly multiplies the daily VaR by the square root of the number of trading days in a year ($\sqrt{250}$), and C incorrectly multiplies the daily VaR by the approximate number of trading days in a year (250). Neither A nor C make the appropriate adjustment to annualize the standard deviation.

To recap, we see that the parametric VaR method generally makes the assumption that the distribution of returns on the risk factors is normal. Under that assumption, all of the information about a normal distribution is contained in the expected value and standard deviation. Therefore, finding the 5% VaR requires only that we locate the point in the distribution beyond which 5% of the outcomes occur. Although normality is the general assumption of the parametric method, it is not an absolute requirement. Other distributions could be accommodated by incorporating skewness and kurtosis, the third and fourth parameters of the distribution, but that added complexity is not needed to demonstrate the general approach to parametric VaR and is rarely done in practice.

The major advantage of the parametric method is its simplicity and straightforwardness. The assumption of the normal distribution allows us to easily estimate the parameters using historical data, although judgment is required to adjust the parameters when the historical data may be misleading. The parametric method is best used in situations in which one is confident that the normal distribution can be applied as a reasonable approximation of the true distribution and the parameter estimates are reliable or can be turned into reliable estimates by suitable adjustments. It is important to understand that VaR under the parametric method is very sensitive to the parameter estimates, especially the covariances.

One of the major weaknesses of the parametric method is that it can be difficult to use when the investment portfolio contains options. When options are exercised, they pay off linearly with the underlying; however, if never exercised, an option loses 100% of its value. This characteristic leads to a truncated, non-normal distribution that does not lend itself well to the parametric method. But some adjustments can render options more responsive to the parametric method. These adjustments are helpful but not perfect, limiting the usefulness of the parametric method when options are in the portfolio. Additionally, although the expected return and volatility of the underlying fixed income or equity security may be stable over the life of the option, the distribution of the option changes continuously as the value of the underlying, the volatility of the underlying, and the time to expiration all change.

4. THE HISTORICAL SIMULATION METHOD OF VAR ESTIMATION

The **historical simulation method** of VaR uses the *current* portfolio and reprices it using the actual *historical* changes in the key factors experienced during the lookback period. We begin, as with the parametric method, by decomposing the portfolio into risk factors and gathering the historical returns of each risk factor from the chosen lookback period. Unlike the parametric method, however, we do not characterize the distribution using estimates of the mean return, the standard deviation, or the correlations among the risk factors in the portfolio. Instead, we reprice the current portfolio given the returns that occurred on each day of the historical lookback period and sort the results from largest loss to greatest gain. To estimate a one-day VaR at a 5% confidence interval, we choose the point on the resulting distribution beyond which 5% of the outcomes result in larger losses.

Illustrating this point using a full four years of daily observations would be tedious and consume a great deal of space, so we will condense the process quite a bit and then extrapolate the methodology. Exhibit 4 shows the daily returns on the SPY, the SPLB, and our 80% SPY/20% SPLB portfolio over the first five days of our historical data set. Please note that fixed weights are assumed for all days. Neither historical simulation nor Monte Carlo simulation is intended to be a replication of sequences of prices. They are intended to create a sample of one-day returns for a portfolio of given weights.

EXHIBIT 4   First Five Days of Historical Returns on the SPY/SPLB Portfolio Using the 1 July 2015–28 June 2019 Data

Day	SPY Return	SPLB Return	Portfolio Return
1	0.80%	−0.53%	0.53%
2	−0.09%	0.45%	0.02%
3	−0.28%	1.47%	0.07%
4	−0.63%	0.28%	0.56%
5	−1.68%	−0.23%	−1.39%

Notes: The Day 1 portfolio return is obtained by multiplying each holding (SPY, SPLB) by its respective weight in the portfolio (80%/20%) and adding the two results together: 0.80(0.008) + 0.20(−0.0053). Although Exhibit 4 shows only five days of returns, we would, of course, use all of the data at our disposal that is reasonably representative of possible future outcomes.

The historical simulation VaR extracts the portfolio return that lies at the appropriate confidence interval along the distribution. Using Excel's "=percentile(x,y)" function, we calculated the following historical simulation VaRs for our sample portfolio:

- 1% VaR (99% confidence) $2,643,196
- 5% VaR (95% confidence) $1,622,272
- 16% VaR (84% confidence) $880,221

Now, it will be interesting to compare this result with the parametric VaR estimates. Exhibit 5 shows the results side-by-side with the parameters used. The historical simulation method does not directly use these parameters but uses the data itself, and these numbers are the parameters implied by the data itself.

EXHIBIT 5   Comparison of Historical and Parametric VaR Estimates Using 1 July 2015–28 June 2019 Data

	Historical Simulation Method		Parametric Method	
1% VaR	$2,643,196		$3,476,550	
5% VaR	$1,622,272		$2,445,150	
16% VaR	$880,221		$1,459,200	
	Average Return	Standard Deviation	Average Return	Standard Deviation
SPY	12.51%	13.64%	10.50%	20.00%
SPLB	8.03%	7.73%	6.00%	8.50%
Correlation of SPY and SPLB	−0.061		−0.06	

The historical simulation VaRs are much smaller, and the differences stem primarily from the adjustments we made to the historical parameters. We adjusted the volatility and the average return estimates of SPY to more closely reflect the historical norms and slightly raised the volatility of SPLB. Recall, in particular, that our factor history for the S&P 500 exhibited abnormally low volatility relative to the long-run experience.

Additionally, our calculations using the historical simulation method were not constrained by the assumption of a normal distribution as was the case with the parametric method. Exhibit 6 is a histogram of the portfolio returns used in the historical simulation results, overlaid with a normal distribution.

EXHIBIT 6 Histogram of Historical Portfolio Returns (80% SPY and 20% SPLB) Using 1 July 2015–28 June 2019 Data

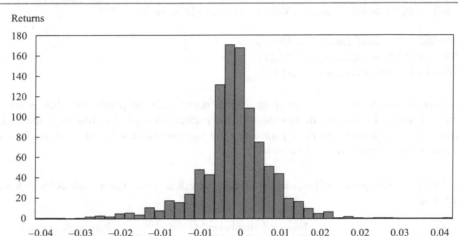

As can be seen, the resulting distribution under the historical simulation method is a departure from a normal distribution. This point again highlights the importance of understanding the underlying assumptions of any VaR model.

There is *no single right way* of estimating VaR. Each method provides an estimate of VaR and is highly sensitive to the input parameters, and similar to many estimation models, they will disagree.

Both the parametric and historical simulation methods in their most basic forms have the limitation that, as with most samples, all observations are weighted equally. The historical simulation method can adjust for this problem, however, by using a weighting methodology that gives more weight to more recent observations and less weight to more distant observations.

The primary advantage of the historical simulation method compared with the parametric method is that the historical simulation method estimates VaR based on what actually happened, so it cannot be dismissed as introducing impossible outcomes. Yet, therein also lies the primary weakness of the historical simulation method: There can be no certainty that a historical event will re-occur or that it would occur in the same manner or with the same likelihood as represented by the historical data. If one uses a relatively short historical data set, such as from January 1987 through December 1988 (a period encompassing the "Black Monday" of 19 October 1987, when stock markets around the world collapsed in a very short time), an occurrence of this magnitude might be projected to occur once every two years, surely an overstatement of its probability. Thus, the historical simulation method is best used when the distribution of returns during the lookback period are expected to be representative of the future.

The historical method is capable of handling the adjustment of one time horizon to another; that is, the information derived from daily data can be extrapolated to estimate an annual VaR, provided the distribution can be assumed to be stationary. In other words, one can convert each daily return to an annual return and then estimate the annual VaR. Although using annual data to estimate an annual VaR is always preferred, that would require a much longer lookback period.

We noted earlier that the parametric method is not well suited for options. Because the historical simulation method captures the returns that actually occurred regardless of the type of financial instrument used, it can accommodate options.

EXAMPLE 3   Historical Simulation VaR

1. Which of the following statements about the historical simulation method of estimating VaR is *most* correct?
   A. A 5% historical simulation VaR is the value that is 5% to the left of the expected value.
   B. A 5% historical simulation VaR is the value that is 1.65 standard deviations to the left of the expected value.
   C. A 5% historical simulation VaR is the fifth percentile, meaning the point on the distribution beyond which 5% of the outcomes result in larger losses.
2. Which of the following is a limitation of the historical simulation method?
   A. The past may not repeat itself.
   B. There is a reliance on the normal distribution.
   C. Estimates of the mean and variance could be biased.

Solution to 1: C is correct. In the historical method, the portfolio returns are arrayed lowest to highest and the observation at the fifth percentile (95% of the outcomes are better than this outcome) is the VaR. A is not correct because it draws a point on the distribution relative to the expected value rather than using the 5% of the outcomes that are in the left-most of the distribution. B confuses the parametric and historical methods. In the parametric method, the 5% VaR lies 1.65 standard deviations below the mean.

Solution to 2: A is correct. The historical simulation method estimates VaR based on the historical distribution of the risk factors. B is not correct; the historical simulation method does not rely on any particular distribution because it simply uses whatever distribution applied in the past. C is not correct because the historical distribution does not formally estimate the mean and variance.

---

5. THE MONTE CARLO SIMULATION METHOD OF VAR ESTIMATION

Monte Carlo simulation is a method of estimating VaR in which the user develops his own assumptions about the statistical characteristics of the distribution and uses those characteristics to generate random outcomes that represent hypothetical returns to a portfolio with the specified characteristics. This method is widely used in the sciences to estimate the statistical distribution of scientific phenomena and has many applications in business and finance. For example, a corporation considering the investment of a large amount of capital in a new project with many uncertain variables could simulate the possible values of these variables and thus gain an understanding of the distribution of the possible returns from this investment. Or, complex options can often be priced by simulating outcomes of the underlying, determining the payoffs of the option, and then averaging the option payoffs and discounting that value back to the present. The reference to the famous Mediterranean casino city allegedly came from an observation made by a scientist that the method is similar to tossing dice at a casino.

Monte Carlo simulation avoids the complexity inherent in the parametric method when the portfolio has a large number of assets. (A large number of assets makes the parameters of the distribution difficult to extract.) There can be many risk factors, and the interactions among these risk factors can be too complex to specify. Moreover, Monte Carlo simulation does not need to be constrained by the assumption of normal distributions. Rather than attempt to determine the expected return and volatility of a combination of multiple statistical processes, one would simply simulate these processes, tabulate the statistical results of the simulations, and thereby gain a measure of the combined effects of these complex component processes on the overall risk.

Monte Carlo simulation requires the generation of random values of the underlying unknowns. In our example, the unknowns are the returns on the two risk factors, represented by the SPY and SPLB ETFs. We can, of course, assume that the statistical properties of the historical returns—their averages, volatilities, and correlation—are appropriate for use in a simulation, or we can modify those values to conform to what we expect to be relevant for the future. For illustrative purposes here, we will simply use the inputs we used in the parametric method.

Recall that we previously assumed for the sake of simplicity that the two securities represent the risk factors. We now decompose the portfolio holdings into these risk factors. First we simulate the returns of these two risk factors, and then we re-price our exposures to the risk factors under the range of simulated returns, recording the results much as we do in the historical simulation method. We then sort the results in order from worst to best. A 5% Monte Carlo VaR would simply be the fifth percentile of the simulated values instead of the historical values.

Yet, it is not quite that simple. We must first decide how many random values to generate. There is no industry standard. The more values we use, the more reliable our answers are but the more time-consuming the procedure becomes. In addition, we cannot just simulate values of two random variables without accounting for the correlation between the two. For example, if you spin two roulette wheels, you can assume they are independent of each other in much the same manner as are two uncorrelated assets. But most assets have at least a small degree of correlation. In our example, we used the historical correlation of about −0.06. Monte Carlo simulation must take that relationship into account.

For simplicity, this reading will not go into detail on either the mathematical techniques that can account for the correlations among risk factor returns or the specific method used to simulate outcomes given average values and volatilities for each risk factor. Both are beyond the scope of this reading.

For this example, we will use 10,000 simulated returns on SPY and SPLB drawn from a normal distribution. Of course, non-normal distributions can be used—and they commonly are in practice—but we want to keep the illustration simple to facilitate comparisons between methods. Each set of simulated returns combines to produce a sample with the expected returns and volatilities as we specified. In addition, the returns will have the pre-specified correlation of −0.06. Each pair of returns is weighted 80/20 as desired. We generate the 10,000 outcomes, sort them from worst to best, and either select the outcome at the 5th percentile for a 5% VaR, the outcome at the 1st percentile for a 1% VaR, or the outcome at the 16th percentile if we want to evaluate the impact of a one standard deviation move. Using the parameters specified in our example, the simulation returns a distribution from which we can draw the following VaR numbers:

$$1\% \text{ VaR} = \$3,541,035$$
$$5\% \text{ VaR} = \$2,517,702$$
$$16\% \text{ VaR} = \$1,524,735$$

Note that these results are fairly close to VaR under the parametric VaR method, where the 5% VaR was $2,445,150. The slight difference arises from the fact that Monte Carlo simulation only *samples* from a population with certain parameters while the parametric method *assumes* those parameters. A sample of a distribution will not produce statistics that match the parameters precisely except in extremely large sample sizes, much larger than the 10,000 used here. Exhibit 7 displays a histogram of the simulated returns overlaid with a bell curve representing a normal distribution. Note how the simulated returns appear more normally distributed than do the historical values, as illustrated in Exhibit 6. This is because we explicitly assumed a normal distribution when running the simulation to generate the values in our example.

EXHIBIT 7   Monte Carlo Simulated Returns 80/20 Portfolio of SPY and SPLB

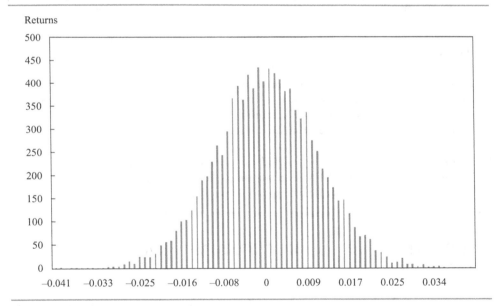

Although we conveniently assumed a normal distribution, one of the advantages of the Monte Carlo method is that it can accommodate virtually *any* distribution. In fact, the flexibility of the Monte Carlo method to handle more complex distributions is its primary attraction. The Monte Carlo and historical simulation methods are much more capable than the parametric method of accurately incorporating the effects of option positions or bond positions with embedded options.

Similar to the historical simulation method, you can scale daily returns to annual returns and extrapolate an estimate of the annual VaR by running a Monte Carlo simulation on these annual returns.

At one time, calculating VaR using the Monte Carlo simulation method was slow, but with the speed of today's computers, it is relatively easy and fast to simulate extremely complex processes for portfolios with thousands of exposures.

EXAMPLE 4 Monte Carlo Simulation VaR

1. When will the Monte Carlo method of estimating VaR produce virtually the same results as the parametric method?
   A. When the Monte Carlo method assumes a non-normal distribution.
   B. When the Monte Carlo method uses the historical return and distribution parameters.
   C. When the parameters and the distribution used in the parametric method are the same as those used in the Monte Carlo method and the Monte Carlo method uses a sufficiently large sample.
2. Which of the following is an advantage of the Monte Carlo method?
   A. The VaR is easy to calculate with a simple formula.
   B. It is flexible enough to accommodate many types of distributions.
   C. The number of necessary simulations is determined by the parameters.

Solution to 1: C is correct. The Monte Carlo method simulates outcomes using whatever distribution is specified by the user. *If* a normal distribution is used *and* a sufficiently large number of simulations are run, the parameters of the Monte Carlo sample will converge with those used in the parametric method and the overall VaR should be very close to that of the parametric method. A is incorrect because the parametric method is not well-adapted to a non-normal distribution. B is incorrect because neither the Monte Carlo method nor the parametric method focuses on historical outcomes.

Solution to 2: B is correct. The method can handle any distribution. A is incorrect because Monte Carlo simulation is not a simple formula. C is incorrect; there is no industry-wide agreement as to the necessary number of simulations.

---

6. ADVANTAGES AND LIMITATIONS OF VAR AND EXTENSIONS OF VAR

The concept of VaR is solidly grounded in modern portfolio analysis. Nonetheless, the implementation of VaR, both in the estimation procedure and in the application of the concept, presents a number of advantages and limitations.

6.1. Advantages of VaR

The use of VaR as a risk measure has the following advantages:

- *Simple concept.* VaR is relatively easy to understand. Although the methodology is fairly technical, the concept itself is not very difficult. So, decision makers without technical backgrounds should be able to grasp the likelihood of possible losses that might endanger the organization. Reporting that a daily 5% VaR is, for example, €2.2 million allows the user to assess the risk in the context of the capital deployed. If a portfolio is expected to incur losses of a minimum of €2.2 million on 5% of the trading days, about once a month, this information is valuable in the context of the size of the portfolio.

- *Easily communicated concept.* VaR captures a considerable amount of information into a single number. If the recipient of the information fully understands the meaning and limitations of VaR, it can be a very significant and practical piece of information.

- *Provides a basis for risk comparison.* VaR can be useful in comparing risks across asset classes, portfolios, and trading units—giving the risk manager a better picture of which constituents are contributing the least and the most to the overall risk. As such, the risk manager can be better informed as he looks for potential hot spots in the organization. This point will be discussed further in a later section.

- *Facilitates capital allocation decisions.* The ability to compare VaR across trading units or portfolio positions provides management with a benchmark that can be used in capital allocation decisions. A proprietary trading firm, for example, can find that its VaR in equity trading is $20 million and its VaR in fixed-income trading is $10 million. If its equity trading portfolio is not expected to take more risk than its fixed-income trading portfolio, then the equity trading activities are taking too much risk or there is too much capital allocated to equity trading. The firm should either make adjustments to realign its VaR or allocate capital in proportion to the relative risks. If a firm is looking to add a position to a portfolio or change the weights of existing portfolio positions, certain extensions of VaR allow the manager to assess the risk of these changes. This topic will be covered in more detail later.

- *Can be used for performance evaluation.* Risk-adjusted performance measurement requires that return or profit be adjusted by the level of risk taken. VaR can serve as the basis for risk adjustment. Without this adjustment, more profitable units could be perceived as more successful; however, when adjusted by VaR, a less profitable unit that poses less risk of loss may be judged more desirable.

- *Reliability can be verified.* VaR is easily capable of being verified, a process known as backtesting. For example, if the daily VaR is $5 million at 5%, we would expect that on 5% of trading days a loss of at least $5 million would be incurred. To determine whether a VaR estimate is reliable, one can determine over a historical period of time whether losses of at least $5 million were incurred on 5% of trading days, subject to reasonable statistical variation.

- *Widely accepted by regulators.* In the United States, the SEC requires that the risk of derivatives positions be disclosed either in the form of a summary table, by sensitivity analysis (a topic we cover later), or by VaR. Thus, VaRs are frequently found in annual reports of financial firms. Global banking regulators also encourage banks to use VaR. These regulations require or encourage the use of VaR, but they do not prescribe how it should be implemented, which estimation method to use, or the maximum acceptable VaR.

6.2. Limitations of VaR

Despite its many advantages, users of VaR must also understand its limitations. The primary limitations of VaR are the following:

- *Subjectivity.* In spite of the apparent scientific objectivity on which it is based, VaR is actually a rather subjective method. As we saw in the descriptions of the three methods of estimating

VaR, there are many decisions to make. At the fundamental level, decisions must be made as to the desired VaR cutoff (5%, 1%, or some other cutoff); over what time horizon the VaR will be measured; and finally, which estimation method will be used. As we have seen here, for each estimation method, there are numerous other discretionary choices to make about inputs, source of data, and so on.

- *Underestimating the frequency of extreme events.* In particular, use of the normal distribution in the parametric method and sometimes in the Monte Carlo method commonly underestimates the likelihood of extreme events that occur in the left tail of the distribution. In other words, there are often more extreme adverse events, called "left-tail events," than would be expected under a normal distribution. As mentioned previously, there is no particular requirement that one use the normal distribution. The historical simulation method uses whatever distribution the data produce. We chose to illustrate the Monte Carlo method with a normal distribution, and it is virtually always used in the parametric method. Nonetheless, the tendency to favor the normal distribution and other simple and symmetrical distributions often leads to an understatement of the frequency of left-tail events.

- *Failure to take into account liquidity.* If some assets in a portfolio are relatively illiquid, VaR could be understated, even under normal market conditions. Additionally, liquidity squeezes are frequently associated with tail events and major market downturns, thereby exacerbating the risk. Although illiquidity in times of stress is a general problem that affects virtually all of a firm's financial decisions, reliance on VaR in non-normal market conditions will lead the user to underestimate the magnitude of potential losses.

- *Sensitivity to correlation risk.* Correlation risk is the risk that during times of extreme market stress, correlations among all assets tend to rise significantly. Thus, markets that provide a reasonable degree of diversification under normal conditions tend to decline together under stressed market conditions, thereby no longer providing diversification.

- *Vulnerability to trending or volatility regimes.* A portfolio might remain under its VaR limit every day but lose an amount approaching this limit each day. Under such circumstances, the portfolio could accumulate substantial losses without technically breaching the VaR constraint. Also, during periods of low volatility, VaR will appear quite low, underestimating the losses that could occur when the environment returns to a normal level of volatility.

- *Misunderstanding the meaning of VaR.* VaR is not a worst-case scenario. Losses can and will exceed VaR.

- *Oversimplification.* Although we noted that VaR is an easily communicated concept, it can also oversimplify the picture. And although VaR does indeed consolidate a considerable amount of information into a single number, that number should be interpreted with caution and an awareness of the other limitations as well as supported by additional risk measures.

- *Disregard of right-tail events.* VaR focuses so heavily on the left tail (the losses) that the right tail (potential gains) are often ignored. By examining both tails of the distribution, the user can get a better appreciation of the overall risk–reward trade-off, which is often missed by concentrating only on VaR.

These limitations are not unique to VaR; they apply equally to any technique or measure used to quantify the expected rewards and risks of investing.

EXAMPLE 5   Advantages and Limitations of VaR

1. Which of the following is **not** an advantage of VaR?
    A. It is a simple concept to communicate.
    B. There is widespread agreement on how to calculate it.
    C. It can be used to compare risk across portfolios or trading units.
2. Which of the following is a limitation of VaR?
    A. It requires the use of the normal distribution.
    B. The maximum VaR is prescribed by federal securities regulators.
    C. It focuses exclusively on potential losses, without considering potential gains.

Solution to 1: B is correct. There is no consensus on how to calculate VaR. A and C are both advantages of VaR, as we noted that VaR is fairly simple to communicate and it can show the contribution of each unit to the overall VaR.

Solution to 2: C is correct. VaR deals exclusively with left-tail or adverse events. A is wrong because although parametric VaR does generally use the normal distribution, the historical simulation method uses whatever distribution occurred in the past and Monte Carlo simulation uses whatever distribution the user chooses. B is incorrect because regulators do not specify maximum VaRs, although they may encourage and require that the measure be used.

6.3. Extensions of VaR

Clearly no single risk model can answer all of the relevant questions a risk manager may have. As a result, VaR has laid a foundation for a number of variations, each of which provides additional information.

As discussed previously, VaR is a minimum loss and is typically expressed as the minimum loss that can be expected to occur 5% of the time. An important and related measure can determine the average loss that would be incurred if the VaR cutoff is exceeded. This measure is sometimes referred to as the **conditional VaR (CVaR)**, although it is not technically a VaR measure. It is the average loss conditional on exceeding the VaR cutoff. So, VaR answers the question, "What is the minimum loss I can expect at a certain confidence?" And CVaR answers the question, "How much can I expect to lose if VaR is exceeded?" CVaR is also sometimes referred to as the **expected tail loss** or **expected shortfall**. CVaR is best derived using the historical simulation and Monte Carlo methods, in which one can observe all of the returns throughout the distribution and calculate the average of the losses beyond the VaR cutoff. The parametric method uses a continuous distribution, so obtaining the average loss beyond the VaR cutoff would require a level of mathematics beyond the scope of this reading.

Using our earlier example, in the historical simulation method, our sample of 500 historical returns was sorted from lowest to highest and the 5% VaR was $1,622,272. With 1,006 returns in the sample, 50 observations (5% of 1,006) lie below the VaR estimate. The average of these losses is \$2,668,389. Thus, when the VaR is exceeded, we would expect an average loss of about \$2.7 million.

For the Monte Carlo method, we generated 10,000 random values and obtained a 5% VaR of \$2,517,705. Given 10,000 random values, 500 observations are in the lowest 5% of the VaR distribution. The CVaR using the Monte Carlo method would be the average of the 500 lowest values, which is \$4,397,756.

Note that once again, the CVaR derived using the historical simulation method is lower than the CVaR derived using the Monte Carlo method. As explained earlier, this result can largely be attributed to the lower volatility of the S&P 500 component in the historical data series.

Beyond assessing tail loss, a risk manager often wants to know how the portfolio VaR will change if a position size is changed relative to the remaining positions. This effect can be captured by a concept called **incremental VaR (IVaR)**. Using our example, suppose the portfolio manager is contemplating increasing the risk by increasing the investment in SPY to 90% of the portfolio. We recalculate the VaR under the proposed allocation, and the incremental VaR is the difference between the "before" and "after" VaR. As an example, using the parametric method, the VaR would be expected to increase from \$2,445,150 to \$2,752,500; thus, the IVaR for the 5% case would be \$307,350. Or, the portfolio manager might wish to add a new asset, thereby reducing the exposure to the existing assets. The risk manager would calculate the VaR under the assumption that the change is made, and then the difference between the new VaR and the old VaR is the IVaR. This measure is useful because it reflects the effect of an anticipated change on the VaR. The risk manager could find that the new VaR will be unacceptably high or that it has possibly even decreased.

A related concept is called **marginal VaR (MVaR)**. It is conceptually similar to incremental VaR in that it reflects the effect of an anticipated change in the portfolio, but it uses formulas derived from calculus to reflect the effect of a very small change in the position. Some people interpret MVaR as a change in the VaR for a \$1 or 1% change in the position, although that is not strictly correct. Nonetheless, this interpretation is a reasonable approximation of the concept behind marginal VaR, which is to reflect the impact of a small change. In a diversified portfolio, marginal VaR may be used to determine the contribution of each asset to the overall VaR; the marginal VaRs for all positions may be proportionately weighted to sum to the total VaR.

Both incremental and marginal VaR address the question of what impact a change in the portfolio holdings might have on the total VaR of the portfolio. Both take into account the potential diversifying effects of various positions or subportfolios, and thus they both can be useful in evaluating the potential effect of a trade before the trade is done.

Another related measure is *ex ante* **tracking error**, also known as **relative VaR**, which is a measure of the degree to which the performance of a given investment portfolio might deviate from its benchmark. It is computed using any of the standard VaR models, described earlier, but the portfolio to which VaR is applied contains the portfolio's holdings *minus* the holdings in the specified benchmark. In other words, the benchmark's holdings, weighted in proportion to the value of the subject portfolio, are entered into the VaR modeling process as short positions. VaR for this measure is typically expressed as a one standard deviation annualized measure. If the portfolio is a perfect match to the benchmark, *ex ante* tracking error will be at or near zero. The more the portfolio differs from the benchmark, the larger the *ex ante* tracking error will be.

EXAMPLE 6   Extensions of VaR

_____

1. Conditional VaR measures the:
   A. VaR over all possible losses.
   B. VaR under normal market conditions.
   C. average loss, given that VaR is exceeded.
2. Which of the following correctly identifies incremental VaR?
   A. The change in VaR from increasing a position in an asset.
   B. The increase in VaR that might occur during extremely volatile markets.
   C. The difference between the asset with the highest VaR and the asset with the second highest VaR.
3. Which of the following statements is correct about marginal VaR?
   A. The marginal VaR is the same as the incremental VaR.
   B. The marginal VaR is the VaR required to meet margin calls.
   C. Marginal VaR estimates the change in VaR for a small change in a given portfolio holding.

Solution to 1: C is correct. Conditional VaR is the average loss conditional on exceeding the VaR. A is not correct because CVaR is not concerned with losses that do not exceed the VaR threshold, and B is incorrect because VaR does not distinguish between normal and non-normal markets.

Solution to 2: A correctly defines incremental VaR. Incremental VaR is the change in VaR from increasing a position in an asset, not a change in VaR from an increase in volatility. B is not correct because incremental volatility reflects the results of intentional changes in exposure, not uncontrollable market volatility. C is not correct because incremental VaR is not the difference in the VaRs of the assets with the greatest and second greatest VaRs.

Solution to 3: C is correct. In A, marginal VaR is a similar concept to incremental VaR in that they both deal with the effect of changes in VaR, but they are not the same concept. B is incorrect because marginal VaR has nothing to do with margin calls.

---

7. OTHER KEY RISK MEASURES – SENSITIVITY RISK MEASURES; SENSITIVITY RISK MEASURES

Just as no single measure of a person's health gives a complete picture of that person's physical condition, no single risk measure gives a full picture of a portfolio's risk profile. As we saw, although VaR has many advantages, it also has many limitations. Therefore, good risk managers will use a comprehensive set of risk tools. In this section, we will look at two additional classes of risk measures: those based on sensitivity analysis and those based on the use of hypothetical or historical scenarios. The former enable us to estimate how our estimated gains and losses change with changes in the underlying risk factors, whereas the latter are based on situations involving considerable market stress from which we estimate how our portfolio will perform.

7.1. Sensitivity Risk Measures

Equity, fixed-income, and options positions can be characterized by a number of exposure measures that reflect the sensitivities of these positions to movements in underlying risk factors. Sensitivity measures examine how performance responds to a single change in an underlying risk factor. Understanding and measuring how portfolio positions respond to the underlying sources of risk are primary objectives in managing risk.

7.1.1. Equity Exposure Measures

The primary equity exposure measure is the beta. In a simple world, a single market factor drives equity returns. The return on a stock is given by the familiar capital asset pricing model (CAPM):

$$E(R_i) = R_F + \beta_i[E(R_M) - R_F],$$

where $E(R_i)$ is the expected return on the asset or portfolio i, R_F is the risk-free rate, $E(R_m)$ is the expected return on the market portfolio, and β_i is the beta, which is the risk measure. The expression $E(R_m) - R_F$ is the equity risk premium, which is the return investors demand for investing in equities rather than risk-free instruments. It should be apparent from this often-used equation that beta measures the sensitivity of the security's expected return to the equity risk premium. The beta is defined as the covariance of the asset return with the market return divided by the variance of the market return. The broad market beta, which is an average of all individual betas, is 1.0. Assets with betas more (less) than 1 are considered more (less) volatile than the market as a whole. The CAPM has a number of extensions, including multifactor models, and risk measures derived from those models can also provide more nuanced information on equity risk exposures.

7.1.2. Fixed-Income Exposure Measures

The primary sensitivity exposure measures for fixed-income investments are duration and convexity. (Note that credit, a major factor driving non-government fixed-income markets, is covered elsewhere.) **Duration** is sometimes described as the weighted-average time to maturity of a bond, in which the bond is treated as partially maturing on each coupon payment date. Duration is a sensitivity measure. Under the assumption that all interest rates that affect a bond change by the same percentage, the duration is a measure of the sensitivity of the bond price to the interest rate change that characterizes all rates. This single rate can be viewed as the bond's yield, y. Given a bond priced at B and yield change of Δy, the rate of return or percentage price change for the bond is approximately given as follows:

$$\frac{\Delta B}{B} \approx -D\frac{\Delta y}{1 + y},$$

where D is the duration. (The $\approx$ sign stands for the phrase "approximately equal" and reflects the fact that the relationship is not exact.) In this expression, it is easy to see that duration does reflect the sensitivity of a bond's price to its yield, although under the restrictive assumption of a single change to all rates. The assumption of a single change to all rates may seem fairly restrictive, but ultimately the assumption is encapsulated by assuming that a single discount rate, the yield, drives the bond price. Duration is considered to be a fairly good sensitivity measure. As previously mentioned, duration is a time measure, the weighted-average maturity of a bond, in which the bond is viewed as maturing progressively as it makes its coupon payments.

The relationship shown here is approximate. The formula is derived under the assumption that the yield change is infinitesimally small, and duration fails to accurately capture bond price movements when yield changes are relatively large. Thus, in the above expression, Δy is for small yield changes. It is not possible, however, to say how small a yield change must be before it is small enough for the expression to hold true. In addition, the expression holds only at any instant in time and only for that instant. Over longer periods, the relationship will be less accurate because of the passage of time and because Δy is likely to be larger. To accommodate longer periods of time and larger yield changes, we can incorporate a second factor called **convexity**, which is denoted C. Convexity describes the sensitivity of a bond's duration to changes in interest rates. Adding convexity to the expression, we obtain the following formula:

$$\frac{\Delta B}{B} \approx -D\frac{\Delta y}{1+y} + \frac{1}{2}C\frac{\Delta y^2}{(1+y)^2}.$$

Convexity can play an important role as a risk measure for large yield changes and long holding periods.

Duration and convexity are essential tools in fixed-income risk management. They allow the risk manager to assess the potential losses to a fixed-income portfolio or position under a given change in interest rates.

7.1.3. Options Risk Measures

Derivatives have their own unique exposure measures. Because forwards, futures, and swaps have payoffs that are linear in relation to their underlying, they can often be evaluated using the same exposure measures as their underlying. Options, however, have non-linear payoffs, which result in them having their own family of exposure measures that incorporate this non-linear behavior.

Although options can be very risky instruments in and of themselves, they are a critical tool for effective risk management and are often used to create an exposure to offset an existing risk in the portfolio. The relative riskiness of an option arises from the high degree of leverage embedded in most options. An additional and very important risk can also arise from the sensitivity of an option to the volatility of the underlying security. We will expand on these points in the next few paragraphs.

The most fundamental risk of an option is its sensitivity to the price of the underlying. This sensitivity is called the option's **delta**. Although delta is derived by using mathematics beyond the scope of this reading, we can provide a simple and reasonably effective definition as follows:

$$\Delta \text{ (delta)} \approx \frac{\text{Change in value of option}}{\text{Change in value of underlying}}$$

Call option deltas range from a value of 0 to a value of 1, whereas put option deltas range from a value of 0 to a value of −1. A value of 0 means that the option value does not change when the value of the underlying changes, a condition that is never absolutely true but can be roughly true for a very deep out-of-the-money option. A call delta of 1 means that the price of the call option changes in unison with the underlying, a condition that is also never absolutely true but is *approximately* true for very deep in-the-money calls. A put delta of −1 means that the price of the put option changes in unison with the underlying but in the opposite direction, a condition that is also never absolutely true but is *approximately* true for very deep in-the-money puts. As expiration approaches, an in-the-money call (put) delta approaches 1 (−1) and an out-of-the-money call (put) delta approaches 0.

Delta can be used to approximate the new price of an option as the underlying changes. For a call option, we can use the following formula:

$$c + \Delta c \approx c + \Delta_c \Delta S.$$

Here, c is the original price of the option and Δc is the change in the price. We approximate the change in the price as the product of the call's delta, Δ_c, and the change in the value of the underlying, ΔS. The same relationship would hold for puts, simply changing the c's to p's.

The delta of an option is somewhat analogous to the duration of a fixed-income security. It is a first-order effect, reflecting the direct change in the value of the option or fixed-income security when the underlying price or yield, respectively, changes. Just as duration captures the effect of only small changes in the yield over a short period of time, delta captures the effect of only small changes in the value of the underlying security over a short period of time. Similar to duration, which has the second-order effect of convexity, we can add a second-order effect for options called **gamma**. Gamma is a measure of how sensitive an option's delta is to a change in the underlying. It is a second-order effect in that it is measuring the sensitivity of the first-order effect, delta. Gamma can be interpreted in several ways. The delta reflects the direct change in the value of the underlying position, whereas gamma reflects the indirect change (i.e., the change in the change). Technically, it reflects the change in the delta, as indicated by the following:

$$\Gamma \text{ (gamma)} \approx \frac{\text{Change in delta}}{\text{Change in value of underlying}}$$

As with convexity, gamma itself is not simple to interpret. For example, a call option might have a delta of 0.6 and a gamma of 0.02. It is not easy to determine whether the gamma is large or small. Using the equation just given, if the value of the underlying increases by 0.10 and the gamma is 0.02, then the delta would increase by 0.002 (0.10×0.02), from 0.6 to 0.602. Gammas get larger as the option approaches at-the-money, and they are large when options approach expiration, unless the option is deeply in or out of the money. Gamma reflects the uncertainty of whether the option will expire in or out of the money. When an option is close to expiration and roughly at the money, a small change in the price of the underlying will determine whether the option expires worthless or in the money. The uncertainty associated with this win-or-lose situation over a very short time frame leads to a large gamma.

Using delta and gamma, the new call price is

$$c + \Delta c \approx c + \Delta_c \Delta S + \frac{1}{2}\Gamma_c (\Delta S)^2,$$

where Γ_c is the gamma of the call. This equation is similar to the corresponding expression that relates yield changes to bond price changes through duration and convexity. Indeed, as we said, gamma is a second-order effect, like convexity.

A third important sensitivity measure for options is **vega**, and it reflects the effect of volatility. Vega is a first-order effect reflecting the relationship between the option price and the volatility of the underlying. Vega is expressed by the following relationship:

$$\text{Vega} \approx \frac{\text{Change in value of option}}{\text{Change in volatility of underlying}}$$

Most options are very sensitive to the volatility of the underlying security. The effect of changing volatility can have a material impact on the value of the option, even when the value of the underlying is not changing.

Using delta, gamma, and vega, the new value of an option given an old value, a change in the value of the underlying, and a change in the volatility can be estimated as follows:

$$c + \Delta c \approx c + \Delta_c \Delta S + \frac{1}{2} \Gamma_c (\Delta S)^2 + \text{vega}(\Delta \sigma),$$

where Δs is the change in volatility.

The expression represents a composite sensitivity relationship for options. It reflects the expected response of an option value to changes in the value and volatility of the underlying, the two primary factors that change in an unpredictable manner and influence the option value. For portfolios that contain options, understanding these relationships and using them to assess the portfolio's response to market movements are essential elements of effective risk management.

These option measures are applicable not only to options but also to portfolios that contain options. For example, the delta of a portfolio consisting of a long position in an S&P 500 ETF and a short position in a call option on the ETF has a delta that is determined by both the ETF and the option. The ETF has a delta of 1; it changes one-for-one with the S&P 500. The option delta, as noted, has a delta between 0 and 1, though technically 0 and −1 because the option position is short. The ETF has no gamma or vega, so the portfolio gamma and vega are determined by the option. The overall deltas, gammas, and vegas are sums of the deltas, gammas, and vegas of the component positions, taking into account the relative amounts of money invested in each position. Risk managers need to know the overall deltas, gammas, vegas, durations, convexities, and betas to get a comprehensive picture of the sensitivity of the entire portfolio to the prices and volatilities of the underlying.

EXAMPLE 7   Sensitivity Risk Measures

1. Which of the following *most* accurately characterizes duration and convexity?
   A. Sensitivity of bond prices to interest rates
   B. First- and second-order effects of yield changes on bond prices
   C. Weighted-average time to maturity based on the coupon payments and principal
2. Which of the following statements about the delta of a call option is **not** correct?
   A. It ranges between 0 and 1.
   B. It precisely captures the change in the call value when the underlying changes.
   C. It approaches 1 for an in-the-money option and 0 for an out-of-the-money option.

3. Which of the following statements about gamma and vega are correct?
   A. Gamma is a second-order effect, and vega is a first-order effect.
   B. Gamma is the effect of volatility, and vega is the effect of changes in volatility.
   C. Gamma is a second-order effect arising from changes in the sensitivity of volatility to the underlying price.

Solution to 1: B is correct. Duration is the first-order effect and convexity the second-order effect of a change in interest rates on the value of a bond. A and C are correct with respect to duration, but not for convexity.

Solution to 2: B is correct. A and C correctly characterize delta, whereas B states that delta is precise, which is incorrect because it gives an approximate relationship.

Solution to 3: A is correct. B is not correct because gamma does not capture the effect of volatility. Vega is the effect of volatility, but it relates to the level and not the change in volatility. C is incorrect because although gamma is a second-order effect on the option value, it is not related to the sensitivity of volatility to the underlying price.

8. SCENARIO RISK MEASURES

A scenario risk measure estimates the portfolio return that would result from a hypothetical change in markets (a hypothetical scenario) or a repeat of a historical event (a historical scenario). As an example, the risk manager might want to understand how her current portfolio would perform if an event, such as the Black Monday of October 1987, were to reoccur. The factor movements that characterized the historical event would be applied to the factor exposures of the current portfolio. Alternatively, the risk manager may develop a hypothetical scenario to describe a market event that has not occurred in the past but which he or she believes has some probability of occurring in the future. The two elements of scenario risk measures that set them apart from sensitivity risk measures are (1) the use of multiple factor movements used in the scenario measures versus the single factor movements typically used in risk sensitivity measures and (2) the typically larger size of the factor movement used in the scenario measures. Scenario risk measures are related to VaR in that they focus on extreme outcomes, but they are not bound by either recent historical events or assumptions about parameters or probability distributions. **Stress tests**, which apply extreme negative stress to a particular portfolio exposure, are closely related to scenario risk measures. Scenario analysis is an open-ended exercise that could look at positive or negative events, although its most common application is to assess the negative outcomes. Stress tests intentionally focus on extreme negative events to assess the impact of such an event on the portfolio.

The two types of scenario risk measures—historical scenarios and hypothetical scenarios— are discussed in the following sections.

8.1. Historical Scenarios

Historical scenarios are scenarios that measure the portfolio return that would result from a repeat of a particular period of financial market history. Historical scenarios used in risk management include such events as the currency crisis of 1997–1998, the market dislocation surrounding the failure of Long-Term Capital Management, the market rout of October 1987, the bursting of the technology bubble in 2001, and the financial crisis of 2008–2009. In order to create a historical scenario, the current set of portfolio holdings is placed into the appropriate valuation models.

Equity positions can often be modeled using their price histories as proxies for their expected behavior, although some practitioners model equities using factor analysis. Valuation models are needed for fixed-income and derivatives products because they have a maturity or an expiration feature that must be accommodated when modeling the portfolio. Historical prices for the fixed-income and derivatives positions currently held in the portfolio may not exist, as in the case of a bond that was issued after the historical period being modeled. Even when historical prices for specific instruments do exist, they may not be relevant to the current characteristics of the instrument. Take the case of a 5-year historical price series for a 10-year bond with 1 year remaining to maturity; the historical price series reflects the price volatility of what used to be a longer bond (e.g., five years ago, the bond had six years remaining to maturity; three years ago, the bond had four years remaining to maturity). The volatility of the bond when it had six years remaining to maturity would be higher than it is today, with only one year remaining to maturity. Using its historical price history would mischaracterize the risk of the current portfolio holding. For this reason, the historical yields, spreads, implied volatilities, prices of the underlying assets in derivatives contracts, and the other input parameters that drive the pricing of these instruments are more important in explaining the risks of these instruments than the price history of the instrument itself.

Some examples may help to show how fixed-income or derivatives valuation models are used in a historical scenario. In the case of a convertible bond, the bond's terms and conditions (e.g., coupon, conversion ratio, maturity) are entered into a convertible bond pricing model. In the case of standard bonds, the terms and conditions of these instruments (e.g., coupon, call features, put features, any amortization or sinking fund features, maturity) are entered into fixed-income pricing models. These modeled fixed-income or derivatives holdings, together with the equity holdings, are then re-priced under the conditions that prevailed during the "scenario period"—a given set of dates in the past. Changes in interest rates, credit spreads, implied volatility levels, and any asset underlying a derivatives product, as well as the historical price changes in the equity portfolio, would all be reflected in the re-priced portfolio. The value of each position is recorded before and after these changes in order to arrive at the gain or loss that would occur under the chosen scenario. Historical scenario events are specifically chosen to represent extreme market dislocations and often exhibit abnormally high correlations among asset classes. It is most common to run the scenario or stress test as if the total price action movement across the period occurs instantaneously, before any rebalancing or management action is possible. The output of the scenario can include

- the total return of the portfolio;
- for long-only asset managers, the total return of the portfolio relative to its benchmark;
- for pensions, insurers, and others whose liabilities are not already incorporated into the portfolio, the total return of the portfolio relative to the change in liabilities under the scenario; and
- any collateral requirements and other cash needs that will be driven by the changes specified in the scenario.

One variation of the historical scenario approach includes running the scenario over multiple days and incorporating actions that the manager might be expected to take during the period. Instead of assuming the shock is a single instant event, this approach assumes it takes place over a number of days and that on each day the portfolio manager can take such actions as selling assets or rebalancing hedges.

Many risk managers are skeptical of this approach because it produces smaller potential loss measures (by design) and does not answer important questions that have been relevant in real crises, such as, "What if the severe price action happens so quickly that the portfolio manager cannot take remedial actions?" Generally, risk managers prefer that a stress testing exercise be tailored to the *initial outcome of a large shock*, to ensure that the event is survivable by a portfolio that uses leverage, and that there will be no unacceptable counterparty exposures or portfolio concentrations before action can be taken to improve the situation. This method also helps to simulate the possibility that liquidity may be unavailable.

Risk managers seeking to measure the impact of a historical scenario need to ensure all relevant risk factors are included. For instance, foreign equities will need to be decomposed into foreign exchange exposure and equity exposure in the analysis. Stress tests typically take the explicit currency approach, which measures the currency exposure of each foreign equity. Alternatively, the risk manager may use an approach that incorporates implicit currency risks, such as companies that may be registered in one country but have earnings flowing in from other countries, and may hedge some of those revenues back to their base currency.

When the historical simulation fully revalues securities under rate and price changes that occurred during the scenario period, the results should be highly accurate. Sometimes, however, scenarios are applied to risk sensitivities rather than the securities themselves. This approach is a simpler form of analysis, but it should not be used for options or option-embedded securities. Although it may be tempting to use delta and gamma or duration and convexity to estimate the impact of a scenario on options or option-embedded securities, these measures are not suited for handling the kinds of extreme movements analyzed in scenario analysis. Although gamma and convexity are second-order adjustments that work with delta and duration to estimate extreme movements, they are inadequate for scenario analysis.

Even in simpler fixed-income cases in which no options are present, care needs to be taken to ensure the analysis does not oversimplify. Duration sensitivities can be used as the inputs to a scenario analysis for straightforward fixed-income instruments, but these sensitivities need to be mapped to the most relevant sectors, credit curves, and yield curve segments before beginning the analysis. If assets are mapped too broadly, the analysis will miss the important differences that could drive the most meaningful outcomes in a given scenario.

It is also important to pay careful attention to how securities or markets that did not yet exist at the time of the scenario are modeled. If, for instance, an analyst is measuring a current portfolio's sensitivity to a recurrence of the 1987 US stock market crash, the analyst needs to determine how to treat stocks in the portfolio that had an initial public offering after 1987. They may need to be mapped to a relevant index or to a similar company or be decomposed into the relevant statistical factors (such as growth, value, volatility, or momentum) by using a factor model before beginning the analysis. Similarly, because credit default swaps did not come into widespread use until 2002, historical scenarios for dates preceding this time would need to be adapted to appropriately reflect the impact of a repeat of that scenario on these new securities.

8.2. Hypothetical Scenarios

Scenarios have a number of benefits. They can reflect the impact of extreme market movements, and they make no specific assumptions regarding normality or correlation. Historical scenarios have the extra benefit of being uncontroversial; no one can claim it is impossible for such events to occur, because they did. One problem with scenario analysis, however, lies in ascribing the probability of a given scenario. Most would agree that it is improbable to assume that the exact historical scenario specified will actually occur in precisely the same way in the future. Another potential problem is that, because it has happened (particularly when it has happened recently), risk managers or portfolio managers are inclined to take precautions that make their portfolios safer for a replay of that historical crisis—and, in the process, make their portfolios more vulnerable to a crisis that has not yet happened.

For that reason, risk managers also use hypothetical scenarios—extreme movements and co-movements in different markets that have not necessarily previously occurred. The scenarios used are somewhat difficult to believe, and it is difficult to assess their probability. Still, they represent the only real method to assess portfolio outcomes under market movements that might be imagined but that have not yet been experienced.

To design an effective hypothetical scenario, it is necessary to identify the portfolio's most significant exposures. Targeting these material exposures and assessing their behavior in various environments is a process called **reverse stress testing**. The risk manager is seeking answers to such questions as the following: What are the top 10 exposures or risk drivers in my portfolio? What would make them risky? What are the top 10 benchmark-relative exposures? Under what scenario would hedges not hedge? Under what scenario would my securities lending activity, ordinarily thought to be riskless, be risky? The ideal use of hypothetical scenarios is, then, not to model every possible future state of every market variable, but rather to target those that are highly significant to the portfolio in order to assess, and potentially address, vulnerabilities.

Reverse stress testing is particularly helpful in estimating potential losses if more than one important exposure is affected in a market crisis, as often happens when participants "crowd" into the same exposures. Sometimes, apparently unrelated markets experience stress at the same time.

The risk manager might also choose to design a hypothetical geopolitical event, estimating its potential effect on markets and the resulting impact on the portfolio. To develop these scenarios, individuals with varying areas of expertise posit an event—such as an earthquake in Country Y, or Country X invades Country Z, or the banking system implodes in Region A. The group conducting the analysis identifies which markets are most likely to be affected as well as any identifiable secondary effects. The next step is to establish a potential range of movement for the affected markets. The final scenario is intended to meet the standard of "rare, but not impossible." The exercise is unlikely to be truly accurate in the face of the real event, but it will often help to identify unexpected portfolio vulnerabilities and outcomes and to think through counterparty credit and operational considerations that could exacerbate or accelerate the scenario.

Hypothetical scenarios are particularly beneficial in being able to stress correlation parameters. The scenario is not constrained to assume that assets will co-move as they have done in the past, which can help identify dangers that other forms of risk analysis may miss. Scenarios can be designed to highlight that correlations often increase in times of stress. This is often achieved by subjecting markets that typically have little or no correlation with one another to the same or similar movements, thereby simulating a temporarily higher correlation. Scenarios can also be devised to pinpoint times when hedging might work poorly—when assets, such as a bond and the credit default swap used to hedge it, that normally have a high correlation might temporarily decouple and move by different percentages or even in different directions. This often occurs when markets experience a "flight to quality"; the swap rate may move down as a result of their relative credit strength, whereas the bond yield might increase given its perceived credit risk.

Once a risk manager has completed a scenario analysis, common questions may be, "What do you do with a scenario analysis? What are the action steps?" If the portfolios are within all other rules and guidelines—their exposures have been kept within desired limits and their VaR or *ex ante* tracking error is within the desired range—scenario analysis provides one final opportunity to assess the potential for negative surprises during a given stress event. The action steps might be to trim back positions that are otherwise within all limits and that appear to present comfortable risk exposures under the current environment but would perform unacceptably during a plausible stress environment. In the case of asset management, where clients have elected to be in a given asset class and the asset manager is constrained by that investment mandate, action steps may include adjusting benchmark-relative risk, disclosing to clients the manager's concerns regarding the risks in the portfolio, or changing counterparty or operational procedures to avoid an unwanted event.

But a caution is in order: A portfolio that has no sensitivity to any stress event is unlikely to earn more than the risk-free rate, or in the case of long-only asset managers, outperform the benchmark index. Stress tests and scenarios analyses are best used in the effort to *understand* a portfolio's risk exposures, not to eliminate them. Effective risk management sets a tolerance range for a stress test or scenario that reflects a higher loss possibility than the investment manager would normally find acceptable. Scenarios should be periodically run again, and action should be taken only if the portfolio exceeds this relatively high tolerance level. It is also important to continually evaluate new threats and new market developments and to periodically refresh the set of scenarios, removing scenarios that are no longer meaningful for the portfolio.

Note also that scenario risk measures and stress tests are best used as the final screen in a series of position constraints that include position size limits, exposure limits, and VaR or *ex ante* tracking error limits. They do not serve well as the initial or primary screen, for reasons that will be discussed shortly.

Parties that use leverage, such as banks and hedge funds, are more likely to use single-factor stress tests rather than multifactor scenario analyses. The focus on a single factor helps in assessing whether a given exposure is likely to impair their capital under a given stress movement; these are pass/fail tests. If capital falls below an acceptable level, it could set off a chain reaction of margin calls, withdrawal of financing, and other actions that threaten the viability of the business.

EXAMPLE 8   Scenario Analysis

1. Which of the following is an example of a reverse stress test?
   A. Identify the top 10 exposures in the portfolio, and then generate a hypothetical stress that could adversely affect all 10 simultaneously.
   B. Find the worst single day's performance that could have occurred for the current portfolio had it been held throughout the past five years.
   C. Find the returns that occurred in all risk factors in the 2008 global financial crisis, reverse the sign on these, and apply them to today's portfolio.
2. Which kind of market participant is *least likely* to use scenario analysis as a pass/fail stress test?
   A. Bank
   B. Long-only asset manager
   C. Hedge fund using leverage

3. What is the *most* accurate approach to scenario analysis for a portfolio that uses options?
    A. Apply the scenario to option delta.
    B. Apply the scenario to option delta + gamma.
    C. Fully reprice the options using the market returns specified under the scenario.

Solution to 1: A is correct. B is not a reverse stress test because reverse stress tests focus more narrowly on trouble spots for a specific portfolio. C would illustrate how the portfolio would have performed in an extremely strong market, quite unlike what occurred in 2008.

Solution to 2: B is correct. Long-only asset managers do not typically use leverage and are thus less likely to become insolvent, making a pass/fail test for solvency less relevant to them. A and C are not correct because parties that use leverage, such as hedge funds and banks, are likely to use stress tests to determine what market movements could impair their capital and lead to insolvency.

Solution to 3: C is correct. Both A and B risk misestimating the actual results of the scenario because both delta and gamma estimate how an option's value might change for a small move in the underlying asset, not the large movements typically used in a scenario analysis.

9. SENSITIVITY AND SCENARIO RISK MEASURES AND VAR

Although both VaR and sensitivity risk measures deal with related concepts, they have their own distinctions. VaR is a measure of losses and the probability of large losses. Sensitivity risk measures capture changes in the value of an asset in response to a change in something else, such as a market index, an interest rate, or an exchange rate; they do not, however, tell us anything about the probability of a given change in value occurring. For example, we could use duration to measure the change in a bond price for an instantaneous 1 bp change in the yield, but duration does not tell us anything about the likelihood of such a change occurring. Similar statements could be made about equities and the various option measures: Betas and deltas do not tell us how likely a change might be in the underlying risk factors, but given a change, they tell us how responsive the asset or derivative would be.

VaR gives us a broader picture of the risk in the sense that it accounts for the probability of losses of certain amounts. In this sense, it incorporates what we know about the probability of movements in the risk factors. Nonetheless, these sensitivity measures are still very useful in that they allow us to take a much more detailed look at the relationships driving the risk. It is one thing to say that a VaR is $2 million for one day at 5%. We know what that means. But it is equally important to understand what is driving the risk. Is it coming from high beta stocks, high duration bonds, or high delta options? If we find our VaR unacceptable, we have to know where to look to modify it. If we simply use VaR by itself, we will blindly rely on a single number without understanding what factors are driving the number.

VaR has much in common with scenario risk measures in that both types of measures estimate potential loss. VaR tends to do so using a model for which input parameters are created based on market returns from a particular time in history. Thus, the VaR estimate is vulnerable if correlation relationships and market volatility during the period in question are not representative of the conditions the portfolio may face in the future. VaR does, however, allow a disciplined method for stressing all factors in the portfolio. Scenario analysis allows either the risk assessment to be fully hypothetical or to be linked to a different and more extreme period of history, helping reduce some of the biases imposed by the VaR model. But there is no guarantee that the scenario chosen will be the "right" one to estimate risk for future markets. Moreover, it is particularly difficult to stress all possible risk factors in a hypothetical scenario in a way that does not embed biases similar to those that occur in VaR modeling.

Each of these measures—sensitivity risk measures, scenario risk measures, and VaR—has distinct limitations and distinct benefits. They are best used in combination because no one measure has the answer, but all provide valuable information that can help risk managers understand the portfolio and avoid unwanted outcomes and surprises.

9.1. Advantages and Limitations of Sensitivity Risk Measures and Scenario Risk Measures

Before portfolios began using risk measures based on modern portfolio theory, the very first risk measure was "position size"—the value invested in a given type of asset. Position size is a very effective risk measure for homogeneous, long-only portfolios, particularly for those familiar with the homogenous asset class in question; an experienced person can assess what the loss potential of such a portfolio is just by knowing its size. But position size is less useful for assessing interest rate risk, even less useful for summarizing the risk of a multi-asset class portfolio, and less useful still at assessing net risk in a portfolio that uses hedging instruments, short positions, and liabilities.

Sensitivity measures address some of the shortcomings of position size measures. Duration, for example, addresses the difference between a 1-year note and a 30-year note; it measures the level of interest rate risk. Option delta and duration (for fixed income) help to display net risk in a portfolio that has hedging or short positions with optionality or interest rate risk.

Sensitivities typically do not often distinguish assets by volatility, though. When measured as the sensitivity to a 1 bp or 1% move, they do not tell the user which portfolio has greater loss potential any more than position size measures do. A high-yield bond portfolio might have the same sensitivity to a 0.01% credit spread movement as an investment-grade portfolio, but they do not have the same risk because the credit spreads of the high-yield portfolio are more likely to move 0.01%, or more, than the credit spreads of the investment-grade bonds. Sensitivity measures do not distinguish by standard deviation/volatility or other higher confidence loss measures. Measuring sensitivity to a one standard deviation movement in an asset's price or yield, however, is one way to overcome this shortcoming of sensitivity.

Granularity: Too Much or Too Little?

Sensitivity measures are aggregated in categories or "buckets." (A bucket is a risk factor description such as "one- to five-year French sovereign debt.") When a number of fixed-income positions are assigned to the same bucket, the effect is an assumption of perfect correlation across the risks encompassed by that bucket. For the "one- to five-year French sovereign debt" risk factor, a short duration position in four-year French sovereign debt will be assumed to fully offset a long duration position in two-year French sovereign debt.

However, this may not be true in the case of a non-parallel interest rate change; these points on the yield curve do not have a correlation coefficient of 1 to one another. The broader the buckets used, the more they can hide this kind of correlation risk; but the narrower the buckets used, the greater the complexity and thus the more difficult to portray portfolios in simple, accessible ways. The width or the narrowness of the risk-factor buckets used to portray sensitivity measures is referred to as granularity.

Scenario analysis and stress testing have well-deserved popularity, and they address many of the shortcomings of VaR described earlier. Sensitivity and scenario risk measures can complement VaR in the following ways:

- They do not need to rely on history. Sensitivity and scenario risk measures can be constructed to test the portfolio's vulnerability to a truly never-before-seen market movement. In this way, they can be free of the volatility and correlation behavior of recent market history, which may simply not be representative of stress conditions. In a scenario analysis, assets that typically have a low correlation with one another can be modeled under an assumption of perfect positive correlation simply by simulating an identical price movement for these assets. Alternatively, they can be modeled under an assumption of perfect negative correlation by simulating identical price movements (i.e., in the opposite direction). A scenario might be designed in which a market that typically exhibits an annual standard deviation of 15% moves by 20% in a single day.
- Scenarios can be designed to overcome any assumption of normal distributions; the shock used could be the equivalent of 1, 10, or 1,000 standard deviations, at the choice of the analyst—or as provided by an actual moment in history.
- Scenarios can be tailored to expose a portfolio's most concentrated positions to even worse movement than its other exposures, allowing liquidity to be taken into account.

But scenario measures are not without their own limitations:

- Historical scenarios are interesting, and illuminating, but are not going to happen in exactly the same way again, making hypothetical scenarios necessary to truly fill the gaps identified with the other risk measures listed.
- Hypothetical scenarios may incorrectly specify how assets will co-move, they may get the magnitude of movements wrong, and they may incorrectly adjust for the effects of liquidity and concentration.
- Hypothetical scenarios can be very difficult to create and maintain. Getting all factors and their relationships accurately represented in the suite of scenarios is a painstaking and possibly never-ending exercise. Accordingly, it is necessary to draw a line of "reasonableness" at which to curtail the scenario analysis, and by the very act of being curtailed, the scenario might miss the real risk.
- It is very difficult to know how to establish the appropriate limits on a scenario analysis or stress test. Because we are proposing hypothetical movements in markets and risk factors, we cannot use history to assign a probability of such a move occurring. What if rates rise instantaneously 0.50%, 1.00%, or 3.00%? How should the short end of the yield curve move versus the long end? How much should credit spreads of different qualities move? It is difficult to choose.

The more extreme the scenario, and the farther from historical experience, the less likely it is to be found believable or actionable by management of a company or a portfolio. This issue tends to lead scenario constructors to underestimate movement in order to appear credible. As an example, prior to the very large drop in real estate values that prevailed in the United States from 2008 to 2010, no similar nationwide price decline had occurred in history. Risk measurement teams at a number of firms did prepare scenarios that estimated the potential outcome if real estate prices declined meaningfully, but their scenarios in many cases were only half as large as the movements that subsequently occurred. Because these large market movements had never before occurred, there was no historical basis for estimating them, and to do so appeared irresponsible. This is an additional risk of scenario analysis: The need to keep the scenario plausible may lead to it being incorrect.

In sum, scenario analyses and stress tests have the opportunity to correct the failings of probabilistic risk measures, such as VaR and *ex ante* tracking error; however, because the version of the future they suggest may be no more accurate than that used in VaR, they may also fail to predict potential loss accurately.

As we can see, each risk measure has elements that are better than the others, and each has important failings. No one measure is the "solution" to risk management. Each is useful and necessary to answer certain questions but not sufficient to answer all possible questions—or to prevent all forms of unexpected loss. Using the measures in combination, to correct each other's failings, is as close to a solution as we come. Designing constraints by using multiple measures is the key practice used by successful risk managers. Viewing a portfolio through these multiple lenses provides a more solid framework for a risk manager or an investor to exercise judgment and can help reduce conceptual bias in portfolio management.

EXAMPLE 9   Limitations of Risk Measures

1. Which of the following is **not** a limitation of VaR?
   A. It does not adjust for bonds of different durations.
   B. It largely relies on recent historical correlations and volatilities.
   C. It can be inaccurate if the size of positions held is large relative to available liquidity.
2. Which of the following statements about sensitivities is true?
   A. When duration is measured as the sensitivity to a 1 bp change in interest rates, it can be biased by choice of the historical period preceding this measure.
   B. Sensitivity measures are the best way to determine how an option can behave under extreme market movements.
   C. Duration effectively assumes that the correlation between a fixed-income exposure and the risk-free rate is 1, whereas beta takes into account the historical correlation between an equity and its comparison index.
3. Which of the following is **not** a limitation of scenario measures?
   A. It is difficult to ascribe probability to a given scenario.
   B. Scenario measures assume a normal distribution, and market returns are not necessarily normal.
   C. They risk being an infinite task; one cannot possibly measure all of the possible future scenarios.

4.   Which measures are based on market returns during a particular historical period?
     A. Hypothetical scenario analysis and duration sensitivity
     B. Historical scenario analysis and VaR
     C. Option delta and vega

Solution to 1: A is correct. Well-executed VaR measures do adjust for bonds of differing duration, and therefore it is not a limitation of VaR. B is incorrect because VaR ordinarily uses some period of recent history as part of the calculation, and this reliance on history is one of its limitations. C is incorrect because VaR can be inaccurate and underestimate risk if portfolio positions are too large relative to the available market liquidity, and this inability to account for the illiquidity of an individual investor's position is an additional limitation of VaR.

Solution to 2: C is correct. Duration assumes that all interest rates that affect a bond change by the same percentage (an effective correlation of 1). A is incorrect because the 1 bp change in rates is applied to current rates, not historical rates. B is incorrect because sensitivity measures are often too small to reveal the most extreme movements for option positions; the larger shocks used in scenario measures are preferable to reveal option characteristics.

Solution to 3: B is correct. Scenario measures do not assume any given distribution, and thus this is not a limitation of scenario analysis. A is incorrect because it is in fact difficult to ascribe probability to many scenarios, and thus this is a limitation of scenario analysis. C is also incorrect because it is in fact impossible to measure all possible future scenarios, and this is a limitation of scenario analysis.

Solution to 4: B is correct. Historical scenarios apply market returns from a particular period to the portfolio, and virtually all VaR methodologies use a historical period to underpin the VaR model (although certain methods may make adjustments if this historical period is seen to be anomalous in some way). A is incorrect because a hypothetical scenario is not based on an actual historical period, and duration sensitivity measures change in value for a given small change in rates, not for a given historical period. C is incorrect because option delta and vega measure how much an option's value will change for a given change in the price of the underlying (delta) or implied volatility (vega), and these are sensitivity measures, not measures based on a particular historical period.

10. USING CONSTRAINTS IN MARKET RISK MANAGEMENT

Designing suitable constraints to be used in market risk management is essential to managing risk effectively. Risk *measurements* in and of themselves cannot be said to be restrictive or unrestrictive: The *limits* placed on the measures drive action. VaR can be measured to a very high confidence level (for example, 99%) or to a low level (for example, 84%). But placing a loose limit on a 99% confidence VaR measure could be less of a constraint than placing a tight limit on an 84% confidence measure. It is not the confidence interval that drives conservatism as much as the limit that is placed on it.

If constraints are too tight, they may limit the pursuit of perceived opportunities and shrink returns or profitability to a sub-optimal level. If constraints are too loose, outsized losses can occur, threatening the viability of the portfolio or business. The concept of "restrictive" or "unrestrictive" relates to the risk appetite of the firm or portfolio and the sizes of losses it can tolerate. Unrestrictive limits are typically set far from current risk levels and permit larger losses than restrictive limits. As an example, for a leveraged portfolio in which insolvency could occur if cumulative daily losses exceed $10 million and the portfolio's current two week, 1% VaR measure is $3 million, an unrestrictive limit might be one set at $10 million. If the portfolio increased positions and went right up to its limit, a misestimation of VaR could result in insolvency; moreover, the fact that losses are expected to exceed the measure at least 1% of the time could mean disaster. But if the limit were set at $4 million, the portfolio might under-allocate the capital it has to invest and fail to make a high enough return on equity to thrive in a competitive environment.

Before applying constraints, particularly those involving such potential loss measures as VaR or a scenario analysis, it is worth considering how far down in the organizational hierarchy to impose them. If applied exclusively to lower level business units, the firm's aggregate risk exposure fails to take advantage of offsetting risks that may occur at higher levels of the organization. As a result, the overall company may never be able to invest according to its risk tolerance because it is "stopped out" by rules lower in the organization. For example, imagine a bank with five trading desks: It might have an overall VaR tolerance of €10 million and might set each trading desk's limit for its standalone VaR at €2 million, which seems reasonable. If there is anything lower than perfect correlation across these desks' positions, however—and particularly if one desk has a short position that to some degree serves as an offset to another desk's long position—the firm will never be able to use its €10 million risk appetite in full. The cure for this problem is over-allocation, with the caveat that a given desk might need to be cut back to its pro rata share in the event that correlations among trading desks are higher than, or the short positions across the different portfolios are not as offsetting as, the over-allocation assumes. Alternatively, some firms might use marginal VaR for each trading desk, allocating each desk a VaR budget such that the total VaR is the sum of each individual desk's marginal VaR. This approach permits each trading desk to "reinvest" the diversification benefits obtained at the aggregate level.

Among the constraints most often used in risk management are risk budgeting, position limits, scenario limits, and stop-loss limits. As is the case in risk measurement, for which multiple measures work better than any one measure alone does, so it is in risk constraints. No one approach on its own works perfectly; they are most effective in combination.

10.1. Risk Budgeting

In **risk budgeting**, the total risk appetite of the firm or portfolio is agreed on at the highest level of the entity and then allocated to sub-activities. Risk budgeting typically rests on a foundation of VaR or *ex ante* tracking error.

A bank might establish a limit on total economic capital or VaR and describe this limit as its risk appetite. Next, it might allocate this risk appetite among the basic risk types (market, credit, and operational) and different business units, geographies, and activities. It allocates to the business unit and/or risk type by specifying a limit, using its chosen measure, for that given activity. For example, it might allow its European business to use 20% of its market risk capital (the portion of its economic capital expected to be used to support market risk taking) and 40% of its credit risk capital, whereas its Asian business might have a different limit. It will set these limits based on the expected long-term profitability of the opportunity set and the demonstrated skill of a business at delivering profitable results, taking into consideration shareholders' expectations regarding the activities the bank is engaged in. As an example of potential shareholder expectations, consider a case in which a firm's shareholder disclosure suggests that the firm's predominant market risk-taking activities are in the Asian markets and that less risk-taking activity is in Europe. Shareholders will be surprised if greater losses are incurred from its European business than its Asian business. Market risk capital limits for the European business should be lower than for the Asian business to be consistent with shareholder disclosures.

A pension fund sponsor might begin with its tolerance for how much of a mismatch it is willing to tolerate overall between the total value of assets and its liabilities—its surplus at risk. Surplus at risk can be the starting point for its asset allocation decision making. Once the broad asset allocation is established, usually expressed via a set of benchmarks, the pension fund sponsor might further establish its tolerance for underperformance in a given asset class and allocate that tolerance to the asset managers selected to manage the assets by assigning each an *ex ante* tracking error budget.

A portfolio manager might have an *ex ante* tracking error budget explicitly provided by the client, or if none is provided by the client, it might instead develop a tracking error budget based on her investment philosophy and market practice. Given this budget, she will seek to optimize the portfolio's exposures relative to the benchmark to ensure that the strategies that generate the most tracking error for the portfolio are those for which she expects the greatest reward.

10.2. Position Limits

Risk budgeting follows a clear logic; but as we have noted, VaR-based measures have a number of drawbacks. One of them is that they perform poorly if portfolios are unusually concentrated, particularly with respect to market liquidity.

Position limits are limits on the market value of any given investment, or the notional principal amount for a derivatives contract. They can be expressed in currency units or as a percentage of some other value, such as net assets. Position limits do not take into account duration, volatility, and correlation, as VaR does, but they are excellent controls on overconcentration. Like risk budgeting, position limits need to be used carefully; if every asset type that a portfolio manager could invest in is constrained, he will have no room to succeed in outperforming the benchmark or generating absolute returns, assuming that is the mandate. Position limits should not be overly prescriptive but should address the event risk and single name risk that VaR handles so poorly, such as

- limits per issuer;
- limits per currency or country;
- limits on categories expected to be minimized in a given strategy, such as high-yield credit or emerging market equities;
- limits on gross size of long–short positions or derivatives activity; and
- limits on asset ownership that correspond to market liquidity measures, such as daily average trading volume.

10.3. Scenario Limits

A scenario limit is a limit on the estimated loss for a given scenario, which if exceeded, would require corrective action in the portfolio.

As discussed in Section 9, scenarios also address shortcomings of VaR, such as the potential for changes in correlation or for extreme movements that might not be predicted using a normal distribution or the historical lookback period used for the VaR measure. Just producing scenario analysis, however, without having any related action steps is not a very valuable exercise.

The action steps that generally follow a scenario analysis are to examine (1) whether the results are within risk tolerance and, in the case of asset managers, (2) whether the results are well incorporated into investor disclosures. To determine whether results are within the established risk tolerance, a tolerance level for each scenario must be developed. It is better to establish a higher tolerance for potential loss under the most extreme scenarios. If the same limit is applied to all scenarios, even extremely unlikely scenarios (e.g., "interest rates rise 1,000,000%"), then the portfolio will simply not be able to take any risk. The risk manager then observes over time whether the portfolio's sensitivity to the scenario is increasing or crosses this high-tolerance bound.

10.4. Stop-Loss Limits

A **stop-loss limit** requires a reduction in the size of a portfolio, or its complete liquidation, when a loss of a particular size occurs in a specified period.

One of the limitations of VaR described in Section 6 was "trending," in which a portfolio remains under its VaR limit each day but cumulatively loses more than expected. This trending can be managed by imposing and monitoring stop-loss limits in addition to the VaR constraints. In one form of a stop-loss limit, the portfolio's positions are unwound if its losses over a pre-specified period exceed a pre-specified level. (Those levels are typically defined to align with the overall risk tolerance.) As an example, a portfolio might have a 10-day, 1% VaR limit of $5 million, but it will be liquidated if its cumulative monthly loss ever exceeds $8 million. The relationship between the stop-loss and the VaR measure can vary depending on management preferences as well as the differing time periods with which the measures are specified.

An alternative approach to a stop-loss limit might instead be to impose a requirement to undertake hedging activity, which may include purchases of protective options, after losses of a given magnitude, with the magnitude of the hedge increasing as losses increase. This approach, called drawdown control or portfolio insurance, is more dynamic and more sophisticated than the simpler stop-loss limit.

10.5. Risk Measures and Capital Allocation

In market risk management, capital allocation is the practice of placing limits on each of a company's activities in order to ensure that the areas in which it expects the greatest reward and has the greatest expertise are given the resources needed to accomplish their goals. Allocating capital wisely ensures that an unproven strategy does not use up all of the firm's risk appetite and, in so doing, deprive the areas most likely to be successful of the capital they need to execute on their strategy.

Economic capital is often used to estimate how much of shareholders' equity could be lost by the portfolio under very unfavorable circumstances. Capital allocation may start with a measurement of economic capital (the amount of capital a firm needs to hold if it is to survive severe losses from the risks in its businesses). The company's actual, physical on-balance-sheet capital must exceed the measure of economic capital, and a minimum level of economic capital must be established to ensure that the company does not take on a risk of loss that will exceed its available capital. The company first establishes its overall risk appetite in economic capital terms, and then it subdivides this appetite among its units. This exercise is similar to risk budgeting, but in the case of corporations, banks, insurers, or hedge funds, it is more likely to be called "capital allocation." Capital allocation is often used in cases in which leverage is used by the portfolio or in which the strategy has meaningful **tail risk**, meaning that losses in extreme events could be far greater than would be expected for a portfolio of assets with a normal distribution. Economic capital is designed to measure how much shareholders' equity could be required to meet tail risk losses. Strategies that have greater-than-expected tail risk include those that sell options, sell insurance, take substantial credit risk, or have unique liquidity or exposure concentration risks. Although risk budgeting more commonly focuses on losses at the one standard deviation level, capital allocation focuses on losses at a very high confidence level in order to capture the magnitude of capital that is placed at risk by the strategy. Capital allocation seeks to understand how much of an investor's scarce resources are, or could be, used by a given portfolio, thereby making it unavailable to other portfolios.

Because a company's capital is a scarce resource and relatively expensive, it should be deployed in activities that have the best chance of earning a superior rate of return. It also should be deployed in a way that investors expect, in activities in which the company has expertise, and in strategies that investors believe the company can successfully execute.

To optimize the use of capital, the "owner" of the capital will typically establish a hurdle rate over a given time horizon; this is often expressed as the expected rate of return per unit of capital allocated. Two potential activities, Portfolio A and Portfolio B, might require different amounts of capital. Portfolio A might require €325,000, and its expected return might be €50,000 per year (15.4%). Portfolio B might have a reasonable expectation of earning €100,000 per year, but it might require €1,000,000 in capital (a 10% return). If the investor has an annualized hurdle rate of 15%, Portfolio A will exceed the hurdle rate and appear a better user of capital than Portfolio B, even though the absolute income for Portfolio B is higher.

Beyond measuring and limiting economic capital, capital allocation is sometimes used as a broad term for allocating costly resources. In some cases, the costly resource is cash; if, for instance, the portfolio has invested in options and futures trading strategies that require heavy use of margin and overcollateralization, its use of economic capital could be low and available cash may be the constraining factor. For other types of investors, such as banks or insurance companies, the capital required by regulatory bodies could be relatively large; as a result, these capital measures may be the most onerous constraint and thus the basis of capital allocation.

When the current measure of economic capital is a smaller number than the portfolio's cash or regulatory capital needs, it may not be the binding constraint. But when it is higher than other measures, it can become the binding constraint, and the one to which hurdle rates should be applied.

EXAMPLE 10   Creating Constraints with Risk Measures

1. Which of the following is **not** an example of risk budgeting?
   A. Giving a foreign exchange trading desk a VaR limit of $10 million
   B. Allowing a portfolio manager to have an *ex ante* tracking error up to 5% in a given portfolio
   C. Reducing the positions in a portfolio after a loss of a 5% of capital has occurred in a single month

2. Which statement is true regarding risk budgeting in cases in which marginal VaR is used?

   A. The total risk budget is never equal to the sum of the individual sub-portfolios' risk budgets.

   B. The total risk budget is always equal to the sum of the individual sub-portfolios' risk budgets.

   C. If the total risk budget is equal to the sum of the individual sub-portfolios' risk budgets, there is a risk that this approach may cause capital to be underutilized.

Solution to 1: C is correct. This is an example of a stop-loss limit, not risk budgeting. The other choices are both examples of risk budgeting.

Solution to 2: B is correct. When using marginal VaR, the total risk budget will be equal to the sum of the individual risk budgets. Choice A is not correct. C is also incorrect; it would be correct if each sub-portfolio's individual VaR measure, not adjusted for its marginal contribution, were used, which could lead to underutilization of capital.

11. APPLICATIONS OF RISK MEASURES

In this section, we examine the practical applications of risk measures. First, we will look at how different types of market participants use risk measures. An understanding of how various market participants use these measures will help as we move to a discussion of their limitations.

11.1. Market Participants and the Different Risk Measures They Use

Three factors tend to greatly influence the types of risk measures used by different market participants:

- The degree to which the market participant is leveraged and the resulting need to assess minimum capitalization/maximum leverage ratios;
- The mix of risk factors to which their business is exposed (e.g., the degree of equity or fixed-income concentration in their portfolios);
- The accounting or regulatory requirements that govern their reporting.

Market participants who use a high degree of leverage typically need to assess their sensitivity to shocks to ensure that they will remain a going concern under very severe, but foreseeable, stresses. This leads them to focus on potential loss measures with a high confidence interval or to focus on rare events that might occur in a short period of time, such as two weeks. Those who use minimal (or no) leverage, such as long-only asset managers, are interested in shock sensitivity as well, but they are likely less concerned with trying to discern the difference between a 99.99% (0.01% VaR) worst case and a 99.95% (0.05% VaR) worst case. Their focus is more likely on avoiding underperformance—for example, failing to keep pace with their market benchmark when markets are doing well. For this reason, they are often more interested in lower confidence intervals—events that are more likely to occur and lead to underperformance for a given strategy. Unleveraged asset managers may also prefer to measure potential underperformance over longer periods of time, such as a quarter or a year, rather than shorter periods.

For portfolios dominated by fixed-income investments, risk managers focus on how sensitive the portfolios are to instantaneous price and yield changes in a variety of categories and typically emphasize duration, credit spread duration, and key rate duration measures. Credit spread duration measures the impact on an instrument's value if credit spreads move while risk-free rates remain unchanged. Key rate duration (sometimes called partial duration) measures the sensitivity of a bond's price to changes in specific maturities on the benchmark yield curve. Risk measurement for fixed-income portfolios is conducted using bond pricing models and by shifting each market rate assumption in the model and aggregating their portfolio's sensitivity to these market rates. Often, these factors are combined into scenarios representing expected central bank policies, inflation expectations, and/or anticipated fiscal policy changes. When portfolios are dominated by equities, risk managers typically categorize the equities by broad country markets, industries, and market capitalization levels. Also, they may additionally regress the returns of their portfolios against fundamental factor histories (such as those for growth, value, momentum, and capitalization size) to understand their exposure to such factors.

Portfolios with full fair value accounting (also called mark-to-market accounting), such as US mutual funds, European UCITS funds, and the held-for-sale portfolios of banks, are very well suited to such risk measures as VaR, economic capital (the amount of capital a firm needs to hold if it is to survive severe losses from the risks in its businesses), duration, and beta—all of which rely on measuring the changes in the fair values of assets. Asset/liability gap models are more meaningful when portfolios are subject to book value accounting in whole or in part.

11.1.1. Banks

Banks need to balance a number of sometimes competing aspects of risk to manage their business and meet the expectations of equity investors/equity analysts, bond investors, credit rating agencies, depositors, and regulatory entities. Some banks apply risk measures differently depending on whether the portfolio being assessed is designated as a "held-to-maturity" portfolio, which requires book value accounting, or a "held-for-sale" or "trading book" portfolio, which requires fair value accounting. Other banks will use fair value measures for all risk assessments regardless of the designation used for accounting purposes. In the following list are some of the factors that banks seek to address through their use of risk tools. In compiling this list, we have assumed that banks may treat measures differently depending on accounting treatment.

- *Liquidity gap:* The extent of any liquidity and asset/liability mismatch. The ability to raise sufficient cash for foreseeable payment needs; a view of the liquidity of assets, as well as the expected repayment date of debt.
- *VaR:* The value at risk for the held-for-sale or trading (fair value) portion of the balance sheet.
- *Leverage:* A leverage ratio is typically computed, sometimes according to a regulatory requirement or to an internally determined measure. Leverage ratios will weight risk assets using a variety of methods and rules and divide this weighted asset figure by equity. The result is that riskier assets will be assigned a greater weighting and less risky assets a lower weighting so that more equity is required to support riskier assets.

- *Sensitivities:* For the held-for-sale portion of their balance sheet, banks measure duration, key rate duration or partial duration, and credit spread duration for interest rate risk positions. Banks will also measure foreign exchange exposure and any equity or commodity exposures. All these exposure measures will include the delta sensitivities of options with any other exposures to the same underlying asset and will also monitor gamma and vega exposures of options. Gamma and vega exposures can be broken out by term to identify how much of these risks come from long-dated versus short-dated options.
- *Economic capital:* This is measured by blending the company's market, credit, and operational risk measures to estimate the total loss the company could suffer at a very high level of confidence (e.g., 99% to 99.99%), usually in one year's time. Economic capital measures are applied to the full balance sheet, including both the held-for-sale and held-for-investment portfolios, and include market, credit, and operational risk capital.
- *Scenario analysis:* Stress tests are applied to the full balance sheet and augment economic capital and liquidity; they are used to identify whether capital is sufficient for targeted, strong negative shocks. Outside of stress testing, significant scenario analysis takes places. Scenario analysis is used to examine how the full balance sheet might be affected by different interest rate, inflation, and credit environments, such as unemployment levels for credit card lenders, home price appreciation/depreciation for mortgage lenders, and business cycle stresses for corporate lenders.

It is common for banks to compute risk measures in distinct business units and geographies and then aggregate these measures to the parent company entity.

11.1.2. Asset Managers

Asset managers are not typically regulated with regard to sufficient capital or liquidity; they are more commonly regulated for fair treatment of investors—that disclosures are full and accurate, that marketing is not misleading, that one client is not favored over the other. In some jurisdictions, certain market risk measures may be used to define risk limits for different fund types.

In asset management portfolios, risk management efforts are focused primarily on volatility, probability of loss, or probability of underperforming a benchmark rather than insolvency. A diversified, unleveraged, long-only fund is unlikely to see asset values decline below zero in the absence of a wholesale withdrawal of assets by the firm's clients. Although service costs and other items make insolvency a technical possibility, in practice, insolvency is a much higher threat for leveraged portfolios. Although derivatives use by asset managers can create effective leverage, these positions are often balanced by an amount of cash in the portfolio equal to the notional exposure created by the derivatives mitigating, if not fully eliminating, the impact of leverage.

Asset managers typically measure and view each portfolio separately with respect to its own constraints and limits. However, there are a few exceptions:

- Long-only asset managers: If the adviser has invested its own capital in any of the funds that it manages, these investments may need to be aggregated for the firm to assess its risk exposures across portfolios.
- Hedge funds: A hedge fund manager needs to aggregate the adviser's side-by-side investment in the various funds it advises.
- Funds of funds: Risk measures for these portfolios typically aggregate the risks of the underlying hedge funds to the master fund level.

An asset manager may choose to aggregate exposures across all funds and strategies to determine if there are unusual concentrations in individual securities or counterparties that would make management actions across all portfolios difficult to carry out (e.g., a single portfolio's holdings in a given security may not pose a liquidity risk, but if the firm were to aggregate all of its holdings in that security, it may find that the portfolio fails to meet the desired liquidity target).

It is important when observing risk measures for asset managers to determine whether the measures represent the backward-looking variability of realized returns in the portfolio as it was then constituted or use the current portfolio and measure its potential loss. Backward-looking returns-based measures (typically including standard deviation, *ex post* tracking error, Sharpe ratio, information ratio, and historical beta) have the value of showing the fund's behavior over time and help assess the skill of the manager. Only an analysis of the current holdings, however, will reveal current risk exposures. Measures that use current holdings typically include VaR, *ex ante* tracking error, duration and forward-looking beta, stress tests, and scenario analyses. All risk and performance measures can be conducted on past portfolio holdings or current portfolio holdings; it is important for the user of any measure to determine which ingredients (which set of portfolio holdings, and for market history, what length and smoothing techniques) have been used in order to use it correctly. Assessing the trends in risk exposures, including whether risk has recently risen or if other important changes have taken place in the strategy, can be accomplished by tracking the risk measures through time.

11.1.2.1. Traditional Asset Managers   Asset managers that use little leverage typically find relative risk measures most meaningful and actionable. The decision to invest in a given asset class is normally the client's, not the adviser's. The adviser seeks to outperform the benchmark representative of the asset class. Exceptions include absolute return funds and asset allocation strategies, but even these can be measured relative to a benchmark. For absolute return strategies, the benchmark is typically cash or a cash-like hurdle rate. When cash is the benchmark, VaR and *ex ante* tracking error will be effectively the same if measured using the same holding period and confidence interval. (Cash has no volatility, so adding a cash benchmark into a relative VaR calculation does not affect the calculation because its zero volatility cancels out its impact; thus, the resulting calculation is the same as the VaR of the portfolio.) Asset allocation funds can use an asset allocation index as the benchmark for a relative risk measure, or they can use a custom combination of market benchmarks.

Although banks, insurers, and other market participants favor measuring VaR in currency terms relevant for the institution (e.g., dollars for a US-based insurer, yen for a Japanese bank) and measure duration and similar statistics as the value change for a 1 bp interest rate change, long-only asset managers generally prefer to express VaR in percentage terms and will divide VaR and duration by the net assets of the portfolio being analyzed. (Note that using returns as the fundamental source of data removes the last step in calculating VaR: multiplying by the size of the portfolio.)

A typical sample of risk measures used by asset managers includes the following:

- *Position limits:* Asset managers use position limits as the most frequent form of risk control for the portfolios they manage, particularly in fund offering documents that need to be understandable to a broad range of investors. Position limits include restrictions on country, currency, sector, and asset class. They may measure them in absolute terms or relative to a benchmark, and they are almost always expressed as a percentage of the portfolio's value.

- *Sensitivities:* Asset managers use the full range of sensitivity measures, including option-adjusted duration, key rate duration, and credit spread duration, and they will typically include the delta exposure of options in these measures. Measures can be expressed in absolute terms as well as relative to a benchmark.
- *Beta sensitivity:* Beta is frequently used for equity-only accounts.
- *Liquidity:* Asset managers often look at the liquidity characteristics of the assets in their portfolios. For equity portfolios, it is common to measure what percentage of daily average trading volume the portfolio holds of each equity security and how many days it would take to liquidate a security if the manager did not want it to be too large a portion of trading volume to avoid taking a price concession.
- *Scenario analysis:* Long-only asset managers typically use stress tests or scenario analyses to verify that the risks in the portfolio are as they have been disclosed to investors and to identify any unusual behavior that could arise in stressed markets.
- *Redemption risk:* Open-end fund managers often assess what percentage of the portfolio could be redeemed at peak times and track this behavior across the funds and asset classes they manage.
- *Ex post versus ex ante tracking error:* Limits on *ex ante* tracking error are often used by traditional asset managers as a key risk metric for the portfolios they manage. It provides an estimate of the degree to which the current portfolio could underperform its benchmark. It is worth noting the distinction between *ex post* tracking error and *ex ante* tracking error: Asset managers use *ex post* tracking error to identify sources of performance and manager skill and *ex ante* tracking error to identify whether today's positions could give rise to unexpected potential performance. *Ex post* tracking error measures the historical deviation between portfolio returns and benchmark returns, and thus both the portfolio holdings and market returns are historical in this measure. *Ex ante* tracking error takes today's benchmark-relative position and exposes it to the variability of past markets to estimate what kind of benchmark-relative performance could arise from the current portfolio. *Ex post* tracking error is a useful tool for assessing manager skill and behavior. The day after a large change in portfolio strategy, *ex ante* tracking will immediately reflect the portfolio's new return profile, whereas *ex post* tracking error will not do so until the new strategy has been in place long enough to dominate the data history. (If *ex post* tracking error is computed using 200 days of history, the day after a large strategy change, only 1 of the 200 data points will reflect the current risk positioning.) Some asset managers focus on maintaining *ex ante* tracking error boundaries for the portfolios they manage to monitor and balance the potential performance impact of the active risks they are taking. **Active share** is a measure of that percentage of the portfolio that differs from the benchmark (i.e., a deviation from the benchmark). It is often monitored to help limit tracking error of the portfolio.
- *VaR:* VaR is less commonly used as a risk measure than *ex ante* tracking error by traditional asset managers, but it is used by some—particularly for portfolios that are characterized as "absolute return" strategies for which a given market benchmark may not serve as the portfolio objective.

11.1.2.2. Hedge Funds   Similar to banks, hedge funds that use leverage need to observe sources and uses of cash through time, including when credit lines could be withdrawn, and need to simulate the interplay between market movements, margin calls, and the redemption rights of investors in order to understand worst-case needs for cash. A sample of the typical range of hedge fund market risk measures includes the following:

- *Sensitivities:* All hedge fund strategies will display some form of sensitivity or exposure, so the full range of sensitivity measures are useful for hedge fund risk management.
- *Gross exposure:* Long–short, market neutral, and arbitrage strategies will typically measure long exposure, short exposure, and gross exposure (the sum of the absolute value of long plus short positions) separately. Gross position risk is an important guide to the importance of correlation risk for the portfolio.
- *Leverage:* Leverage measures are common for hedge funds. It is important to understand how the measure is treating derivatives and what elements appear in the numerator versus the denominator because there are many different ways to execute the measure.
- *VaR:* Hedge funds that use VaR measures tend to focus on high confidence intervals (more than 90%) and short holding periods, and they rarely use a benchmark-relative measure.
- *Scenarios:* Hedge funds commonly use scenario/stress tests that are well tuned to the specific risks of their strategy—in merger arbitrage strategies, for example, the chance that the merger will not take place.
- *Drawdown:* In the case of the following types of hedge fund strategies, standard deviation and historical beta measures can be particularly misleading when seeking to understand what the more extreme risks can be. This is because the strategies listed frequently display decidedly non-normal return distributions, and when this is true, standard deviation is not a good guide to worst-case outcomes. For the following strategies, any historical standard deviation or historical beta measures should be supplemented by a measure of what has been the **maximum drawdown**, often defined as the worst-returning month or quarter for the portfolio or the worst peak-to-trough decline in a portfolio's returns:

  - Strategies that focus on credit risk taking, such as long–short credit, credit arbitrage, or bankruptcy investing
  - Strategies that focus on events, such as merger arbitrage
  - Strategies that make meaningful investments in non-publicly issued assets or other assets that do not reliably have a daily, independent fair value determination
  - Strategies that invest in illiquid asset classes or take large positions relative to market size in any asset class
  - Strategies that sell options or purchase bonds with embedded options
  - Strategies that are highly reliant on correlation relationships, such as equity market neutral

In addition, it is not uncommon for those investing in hedge funds to look at the returns of the hedge fund during a relevant historical period, such as the 2008 financial crisis.

12. PENSION FUNDS AND INSURERS

A defined benefit pension plan is required to make payments to its pensioners in the future that are typically determined as a function of a retiree's final salary. This differs from a defined contribution plan, in which the plan's sponsor may be required to make contributions currently but is not responsible to ensure that they grow to a particular future amount. To meet the required payouts, defined benefit plans have significant market risk management responsibilities. This section describes the practices of defined benefit pension plans only; all mentions in this section of "pension funds" or "pension plans" refer to defined benefit pensions.

The risk management goal for pension funds is to be sufficiently funded to make future payments to pensioners. The requirements for sufficient funding vary from country to country. Different jurisdictions will have regulations concerning such items as how to compute the present value of pension liabilities (including which interest rates are permitted to be used as a discount rate) and what the sponsor of the pension plan is required to contribute when the assets in the pension fund are lower than the present value of the liabilities. In addition, some jurisdictions impose taxes when surplus—the value of the assets less the value of the liabilities—is withdrawn for other use by the plan sponsor. Although these regional differences will shape the practice of pension plan risk management in different countries, it is typically an exercise in ensuring that the plan is not likely to become significantly under- or overfunded. Overfunding occurs when the funding ratio (the assets divided by the present value of the liabilities) is greater than 100%; underfunding occurs when the funding ratio is under 100%. Overfunding may be cured over time by the plan sponsor not needing to make regular contributions to the plan because the number of employees and their salary levels, which drive the pension benefit, are growing. Underfunding, if not cured by growth in the assets in the fund over a suitable time horizon as permitted by regulation, is cured by the plan sponsor contributing to the fund. The pension plan's actions will also vary depending on its age (whether it is a new or established plan) and whether it is currently meaningfully under- or overfunded. Important market risk measures or methods for pension funds often include the following:

- *Interest rate and curve risk:* The first step of risk measurement for pension funds is the analysis of expected payments to pensioners in the future. The expected future cash flows are grouped by maturity. In the case of an international pension fund that must make future payouts in multiple currencies, they may also be grouped by currency. In cases in which the jurisdiction requires a particular fixed-income instrument or curve be used to provide the discount rate for arriving at the present value of the pension liability (such as corporate bonds in the United States, inflation-linked gilts in the United Kingdom, or government bonds in the Netherlands), the liability cash flows will be expressed as a short position at the relevant points on the curve.

- *Surplus at risk:* This measure is an application of VaR. It is computed by entering the assets in the portfolio into a VaR model as long positions and the pension liabilities as short fixed-income positions. It estimates how much the assets might underperform the liabilities, usually over one year, and pension plan sponsors may vary with respect to how high a level of confidence they choose to use (e.g., 84%, 95%, 99%). If the assets in the portfolio were invested precisely in the same fixed-income instruments to which the liabilities have been apportioned and in the same amounts, it would result in zero surplus at risk. In practice, however, it may be impossible to invest in the sizes required in the particular fixed-income instruments specified in the liability analysis, so the pension will invest in other, non-fixed-income investments, such as equities or real assets. The more volatile the investments in the pension fund and the less well correlated these assets are with the liabilities, the higher the surplus at risk. The pension fund may set a threshold level or limit on surplus at risk; when the pension fund's surplus at risk exceeds this limit, pension staff will change the fund's asset allocation to make the assets in the fund better match the liabilities. This liability-focused form of pension investing is commonly referred to as "liability driven investing."

- *Liability hedging exposures versus return generating exposures:* Although matching liabilities is an important goal of pension fund management, it is not the only goal. Pension staff may separate their investment portfolio into investments designed to match the pension liability versus those meant to generate excess returns. The precise instruments linked to the liability cannot always be directly invested in, so a separate portion of the portfolio may be necessary and should perform the function of earning returns that can minimize the chance of having an over- or underfunded status greater than the pension fund's risk tolerance. The return-generating portion of the portfolio also helps to hedge the potential for future changes in the size of the liability that could be caused by longevity risk or by wage growth that exceeds the forecasts currently used to compute the liability.

12.1. Insurers

Insurers in the largest global economies are subject to significant regulation and accounting oversight regarding how they must retain reserves and reflect their liabilities. Regulation may also affect the pricing permitted by product line. It is common for insurers to aggregate risk from underlying business units to arrive at a firm-wide view of risk.

Insurance liabilities vary in their correlation with financial markets. The risk metrics of property and casualty insurance differ significantly from those used for life insurance and annuity products. Property and casualty insurance, including home, auto, corporate liability insurance, and health insurance, are typically not highly correlated with financial asset markets.

Insurers focus on managing a number of forms of insurance risk, for which they may use such tools as reinsurance and geographic dispersion. The market risk management measures in the property and casualty lines of business include the following:

- *Sensitivities and exposures:* Insurers often design an asset allocation for these portfolios and monitor current exposures to remain within the target ranges set forth in the target asset allocation.
- *Economic capital and VaR:* The risk measurement focus for these lines of business is capital at risk and VaR. The premiums earned in these areas are typically set to compensate for the expected payouts (usually defined as a range of possible payouts), so it is only in cases of greater-than-expected payouts that capital is tapped. The risk modeling effort is to estimate what that catastrophic loss amount could be at a given level of probability. Assessment of the risk to economic capital will include the market risks in the portfolio as well as characteristics of the insurance exposures and reinsurance coverage.
- *Scenario analysis:* Insurers use scenario analysis like other market participants that have capital at risk, such as banks and hedge funds. For the property and casualty lines, these scenarios may stress the market risks and the insurance risks in the same scenario.

Insurers do not focus on matching assets with liabilities in their property and casualty lines of business. Investment portfolios are not designed to pay out insurance claims in property and casualty insurance businesses; the premium income is primarily used for that purpose. These investments are designed to achieve a good absolute return within the constraints imposed under regulatory reserve requirements. Riskier assets are discounted relative to safer, fixed-income assets in measuring required reserves.

Life insurance and annuities have stronger ties to the financial markets, even while retaining distinct mortality-based risk profiles. Life liabilities are very long, and the reserves that insurers are required to maintain by insurance regulators are highly dependent on discount rate assumptions. Non-financial inputs include assumptions about mortality and which policyholders will either tap into options in their policy to add coverage at a given level or cancel their policy. Annuities produce returns based on financial assets, with some extra optionality driven by any life insurance elements embedded in the policy. These activities are paired with long-term investment portfolios in a variety of assets that are designed to help the insurer meet future claims.

For life portfolios, market risk measures include the following:

- *Sensitivities:* The exposures of the investment portfolio and the annuity liability are measured and monitored.
- *Asset and liability matching:* The investment portfolio is not designed to be a perfect match to the liabilities, but it is more closely matched to liabilities than is the case in property and casualty insurance.
- *Scenario analysis:* The main focus of risk measurement for the life lines of insurance are measures of potential stress losses based on the differences between the assets in which the insurance company has invested and the liabilities driven by the insurance contracts it has written to its customers. Scenario analyses need to stress both market and non-market sources of cash flow change (in which non-market changes can include changes in longevity).

EXAMPLE 11   Uses of Risk Measures by Market Participants

1. Which type of market participant is *most likely* to consistently express risk measures as a percentage of assets and relative to a benchmark?
   A. Banks
   B. Corporations
   C. Long-only asset managers
2. How does *ex ante* tracking error differ from *ex post* tracking error?
   A. *Ex ante* tracking error takes into account the behavior of options, whereas *ex post* tracking error does not.
   B. *Ex post* tracking error uses a more accurate forecast of future markets than the forecast used for *ex ante* tracking error.
   C. *Ex ante* tracking error uses *current* portfolio holdings exposed to the variability of historical markets, whereas *ex post* tracking error measures the variability of *historical* portfolio holdings in historical markets.

Solution to 1: C is correct. Long-only asset managers most commonly express risk measures in percentage terms and relative to a benchmark, whereas the entities in answers A and B measure risk more commonly in currency units and in absolute terms (not relative to a benchmark). Banks occasionally express risk measures, such as economic capital, as a percentage of assets or other balance sheet measures, but bank risk measures are typically expressed in currency units.

Solution to 2: C is correct. A is incorrect because although *ex post* tracking error accounts for the options that were in the portfolio in the past, *ex ante* tracking error might actually misstate the risk of options if it is computed using the parametric method. B is incorrect because *ex post* tracking error is not aiming to forecast the future; it is only measuring the variability of past results.

SUMMARY

This reading on market risk management models covers various techniques used to manage the risk arising from market fluctuations in prices and rates. The key points are summarized as follows:

- Value at risk (VaR) is the minimum loss in either currency units or as a percentage of portfolio value that would be expected to be incurred a certain percentage of the time over a certain period of time given assumed market conditions.
- VaR requires the decomposition of portfolio performance into risk factors.
- The three methods of estimating VaR are the parametric method, the historical simulation method, and the Monte Carlo simulation method.
- The parametric method of VaR estimation typically provides a VaR estimate from the left tail of a normal distribution, incorporating the expected returns, variances, and covariances of the components of the portfolio.
- The parametric method exploits the simplicity of the normal distribution but provides a poor estimate of VaR when returns are not normally distributed, as might occur when a portfolio contains options.
- The historical simulation method of VaR estimation uses historical return data on the portfolio's current holdings and allocation.
- The historical simulation method has the advantage of incorporating events that actually occurred and does not require the specification of a distribution or the estimation of parameters, but it is only useful to the extent that the future resembles the past.
- The Monte Carlo simulation method of VaR estimation requires the specification of a statistical distribution of returns and the generation of random outcomes from that distribution.
- The Monte Carlo simulation method is extremely flexible but can be complex and time consuming to use.
- There is no single right way to estimate VaR.
- The advantages of VaR include the following: It is a simple concept; it is relatively easy to understand and easily communicated, capturing much information in a single number. It can be useful in comparing risks across asset classes, portfolios, and trading units and, as such, facilitates capital allocation decisions. It can be used for performance evaluation and can be verified by using backtesting. It is widely accepted by regulators.
- The primary limitations of VaR are that it is a subjective measure and highly sensitive to numerous discretionary choices made in the course of computation. It can underestimate the frequency of extreme events. It fails to account for the lack of liquidity and is sensitive to correlation risk. It is vulnerable to trending or volatility regimes and is often misunderstood as a worst-case scenario. It can oversimplify the picture of risk and focuses heavily on the left tail.
- There are numerous variations and extensions of VaR, including conditional VaR (CVaR), incremental VaR (IVaR), and marginal VaR (MVaR), that can provide additional useful information.
- Conditional VaR is the average loss conditional on exceeding the VaR cutoff.
- Incremental VaR measures the change in portfolio VaR as a result of adding or deleting a position from the portfolio or if a position size is changed relative to the remaining positions.
- MVaR measures the change in portfolio VaR given a small change in the portfolio position. In a diversified portfolio, MVaRs can be summed to determine the contribution of each asset to the overall VaR.
- *Ex ante* tracking error measures the degree to which the performance of a given investment portfolio might deviate from its benchmark.

- Sensitivity measures quantify how a security or portfolio will react if a single risk factor changes. Common sensitivity measures are beta for equities; duration and convexity for bonds; and delta, gamma, and vega for options. Sensitivity measures do not indicate which portfolio has greater loss potential.
- Risk managers can use deltas, gammas, vegas, durations, convexities, and betas to get a comprehensive picture of the sensitivity of the entire portfolio.
- Stress tests apply extreme negative stress to a particular portfolio exposure.
- Scenario measures, including stress tests, are risk models that evaluate how a portfolio will perform under certain high-stress market conditions.
- Scenario measures can be based on actual historical scenarios or on hypothetical scenarios.
- Historical scenarios are scenarios that measure the portfolio return that would result from a repeat of a particular period of financial market history.
- Hypothetical scenarios model the impact of extreme movements and co-movements in different markets that have not previously occurred.
- Reverse stress testing is the process of stressing the portfolio's most significant exposures.
- Sensitivity and scenario risk measures can complement VaR. They do not need to rely on history, and scenarios can be designed to overcome an assumption of normal distributions.
- Limitations of scenario measures include the following: Historical scenarios are unlikely to re-occur in exactly the same way. Hypothetical scenarios may incorrectly specify how assets will co-move and thus may get the magnitude of movements wrong. And, it is difficult to establish appropriate limits on a scenario analysis or stress test.
- Constraints are widely used in risk management in the form of risk budgets, position limits, scenario limits, stop-loss limits, and capital allocation.
- Risk budgeting is the allocation of the total risk appetite across sub-portfolios.
- A scenario limit is a limit on the estimated loss for a given scenario, which, if exceeded, would require corrective action in the portfolio.
- A stop-loss limit either requires a reduction in the size of a portfolio or its complete liquidation (when a loss of a particular size occurs in a specified period).
- Position limits are limits on the market value of any given investment.
- Risk measurements and constraints in and of themselves are not restrictive or unrestrictive; it is the limits placed on the measures that drive action.
- The degree of leverage, the mix of risk factors to which the business is exposed, and accounting or regulatory requirements influence the types of risk measures used by different market participants.
- Banks use risk tools to assess the extent of any liquidity and asset/liability mismatch, the probability of losses in their investment portfolios, their overall leverage ratio, interest rate sensitivities, and the risk to economic capital.
- Asset managers' use of risk tools focuses primarily on volatility, probability of loss, or the probability of underperforming a benchmark.
- Pension funds use risk measures to evaluate asset/liability mismatch and surplus at risk.
- Property and casualty insurers use sensitivity and exposure measures to ensure exposures remain within defined asset allocation ranges. They use economic capital and VaR measures to estimate the impairment in the event of a catastrophic loss. They use scenario analysis to stress the market risks and insurance risks simultaneously.
- Life insurers use risk measures to assess the exposures of the investment portfolio and the annuity liability, the extent of any asset/liability mismatch, and the potential stress losses based on the differences between the assets in which they have invested and the liabilities resulting from the insurance contracts they have written.

REFERENCE

Malkiel, Burton. 2007. A *Random Walk Down Wall Street*. New York: W.W. Norton.

PROBLEMS

The following information relates to Questions 1–5

Randy Gorver, chief risk officer at Eastern Regional Bank, and John Abell, assistant risk officer, are currently conducting a risk assessment of several of the bank's independent investment functions. These reviews include the bank's fixed-income investment portfolio and an equity fund managed by the bank's trust department. Gorver and Abell are also assessing Eastern Regional's overall risk exposure.

Eastern Regional Bank Fixed-Income Investment Portfolio

The bank's proprietary fixed-income portfolio is structured as a barbell portfolio: About half of the portfolio is invested in zero-coupon Treasuries with maturities in the 3- to 5-year range (Portfolio P_1), and the remainder is invested in zero-coupon Treasuries with maturities in the 10- to 15-year range (Portfolio P_2). Georges Montes, the portfolio manager, has discretion to allocate between 40% and 60% of the assets to each maturity "bucket." He must remain fully invested at all times. Exhibit 1 shows details of this portfolio.

EXHIBIT 1   US Treasury Barbell Portfolio

	Maturity	
	P_1	P_2
	3–5 Years	10–15 Years
Average duration	3.30	11.07
Average yield to maturity	1.45%	2.23%
Market value	$50.3 million	$58.7 million

Trust Department's Equity Fund

A. **Use of Options:** The trust department of Eastern Regional Bank manages an equity fund called the Index Plus Fund, with $325 million in assets. This fund's objective is to track the S&P 500 Index price return while producing an income return 1.5 times that of the S&P 500. The bank's chief investment officer (CIO) uses put and call options on S&P 500 stock index futures to adjust the risk exposure of certain client accounts that have an investment in this fund. The portfolio of a 60-year-old widow with a below-average risk tolerance has an investment in this fund, and the CIO has asked his assistant, Janet Ferrell, to propose an options strategy to bring the portfolio's delta to 0.90.

B. **Value at Risk**: The Index Plus Fund has a value at risk (VaR) of $6.5 million at 5% for one day. Gorver asks Abell to write a brief summary of the portfolio VaR for the report he is preparing on the fund's risk position.

Combined Bank Risk Exposures

The bank has adopted a new risk policy, which requires forward-looking risk assessments in addition to the measures that look at historical risk characteristics. Management has also become very focused on tail risk since the subprime crisis and is evaluating the bank's capital allocation to certain higher-risk lines of business. Gorver must determine what additional risk metrics to include in his risk reporting to address the new policy. He asks Abell to draft a section of the risk report that will address the risk measures' adequacy for capital allocation decisions.

1. If Montes is expecting a 50 bp increase in yields at all points along the yield curve, which of the following trades is he *most likely* to execute to minimize his risk?
   A. Sell \$35 million of P_2 and reinvest the proceeds in three-year bonds
   B. Sell \$15 million of P_2 and reinvest the proceeds in three-year bonds
   C. Reduce the duration of P_2 to 10 years and reduce the duration of P_1 to 3 years

2. Which of the following options strategies is Ferrell *most likely* to recommend for the client's portfolio?
   A. Long calls
   B. Short calls
   C. Short puts

3. Which of the following statements regarding the VaR of the Index Plus Fund is correct?
   A. The expected maximum loss for the portfolio is \$6.5 million.
   B. Five percent of the time, the portfolio can be expected to experience a loss of at least \$6.5 million.
   C. Ninety-five percent of the time, the portfolio can be expected to experience a one-day loss of no more than \$6.5 million.

4. To comply with the new bank policy on risk assessment, which of the following is the *best* set of risk measures to add to the chief risk officer's risk reporting?
   A. Conditional VaR, stress test, and scenario analysis
   B. Monte Carlo VaR, incremental VaR, and stress test
   C. Parametric VaR, marginal VaR, and scenario analysis

5. Which of the following statements should *not* be included in Abell's report to management regarding the use of risk measures in capital allocation decisions?
   A. VaR measures capture the increased liquidity risk during stress periods.
   B. Stress tests and scenario analysis can be used to evaluate the effect of outlier events on each line of business.
   C. VaR approaches that can accommodate a non-normal distribution are critical to understand relative risk across lines of business.

The following information relates to Questions 6–11

Hiram Life (Hiram), a large multinational insurer located in Canada, has received permission to increase its ownership in an India-based life insurance company, LICIA, from 26% to 49%. Before completing this transaction, Hiram wants to complete a risk assessment of LICIA's investment portfolio. Judith Hamilton, Hiram's chief financial officer, has been asked to brief the management committee on investment risk in its India-based insurance operations.

LICIA's portfolio, which has a market value of CAD260 million, is currently structured as shown in Exhibit 1. Despite its more than 1,000 individual holdings, the portfolio is invested predominantly in India. The Indian government bond market is highly liquid, but the country's mortgage and infrastructure loan markets, as well as the corporate bond market, are relatively illiquid. Individual mortgage and corporate bond positions are large relative to the normal trading volumes in these securities. Given the elevated current and fiscal account deficits, Indian investments are also subject to above-average economic risk.

Hamilton begins with a summary of the India-based portfolio. Exhibit 1 presents the current portfolio composition and the risk and return assumptions used to estimate value at risk (VaR).

EXHIBIT 1   Selected Assumptions for LICIA's Investment Portfolio

	Allocation	Average Daily Return	Daily Standard Deviation
India government securities	50%	0.015%	0.206%
India mortgage/infrastructure loans	25%	0.045%	0.710%
India corporate bonds	15%	0.025%	0.324%
India equity	10%	0.035%	0.996%

Infrastructure is a rapidly growing asset class with limited return history; the first infrastructure loans were issued just 10 years ago.

Hamilton's report to the management committee must outline her assumptions and provide support for the methods she used in her risk assessment. If needed, she will also make recommendations for rebalancing the portfolio to ensure its risk profile is aligned with that of Hiram.

Hamilton develops the assumptions shown in Exhibit 2, which will be used for estimating the portfolio VaR.

EXHIBIT 2   VaR Input Assumptions for Proposed CAD260 Million Portfolio

Method	Average Return Assumption	Standard Deviation Assumption
Monte Carlo simulation	0.026%	0.501%
Parametric approach	0.026%	0.501%
Historical simulation	0.023%	0.490%

Hamilton elects to apply a one-day, 5% VaR limit of CAD2 million in her risk assessment of LICIA's portfolio. This limit is consistent with the risk tolerance the committee has specified for the Hiram portfolio.

The markets' volatility during the last 12 months has been significantly higher than the historical norm, with increased frequency of large daily losses, and Hamilton expects the next 12 months to be equally volatile.

She estimates the one-day 5% portfolio VaR for LICIA's portfolio using three different approaches:

EXHIBIT 3   VaR Results over a One-Day Period for Proposed Portfolio

Method	5% VaR
Monte Carlo simulation	CAD2,095,565
Parametric approach	CAD2,083,610
Historical simulation	CAD1,938,874

The committee is likely to have questions in a number of key areas—the limitations of the VaR report, potential losses in an extreme adverse event, and the reliability of the VaR numbers if the market continues to exhibit higher-than-normal volatility. Hamilton wants to be certain that she has thoroughly evaluated the risks inherent in the LICIA portfolio and compares them with the risks in Hiram's present portfolio.

Hamilton believes the possibility of a ratings downgrade on Indian sovereign debt is high and not yet fully reflected in securities prices. If the rating is lowered, many of the portfolio's holdings will no longer meet Hiram's minimum ratings requirement. A downgrade's effect is unlikely to be limited to the government bond portfolio. All asset classes can be expected to be affected to some degree. Hamilton plans to include a scenario analysis that reflects this possibility to ensure that management has the broadest possible view of the risk exposures in the India portfolio.

6. Given Hamilton's expectations, which of the following models is *most appropriate* to use in estimating portfolio VaR?
   A. Parametric method
   B. Historical simulation method
   C. Monte Carlo simulation method

7. Which risk measure is Hamilton *most likely* to present when addressing the committee's concerns regarding potential losses in extreme stress events?
   A. Relative VaR
   B. Incremental VaR
   C. Conditional VaR

8. The scenario analysis that Hamilton prepares for the committee is *most likely* a:
   A. stress test.
   B. historical scenario.
   C. hypothetical scenario.

9. The scenario analysis that Hamilton prepares for the committee is a valuable tool to supplement VaR *because* it:
   A. incorporates historical data to evaluate the risk in the tail of the VaR distribution.
   B. enables Hamilton to isolate the risk stemming from a single risk factor—the ratings downgrade.
   C. allows the committee to assess the effect of low liquidity in the event of a ratings downgrade.

10. Using the data in Exhibit 2, the portfolio's annual 1% parametric VaR is *closest* to:
    A. CAD17 million.
    B. CAD31 million.
    C. CAD48 million.

11. What additional risk measures would be most appropriate to add to Hamilton's risk assessment?
    A. Delta
    B. Duration
    C. Tracking error

The following information relates to Questions 12–19

Tina Ming is a senior portfolio manager at Flusk Pension Fund (Flusk). Flusk's portfolio is composed of fixed-income instruments structured to match Flusk's liabilities. Ming works with Shrikant McKee, Flusk's risk analyst.

Ming and McKee discuss the latest risk report. McKee calculated value at risk (VaR) for the entire portfolio using the historical method and assuming a lookback period of five years and 250 trading days per year. McKee presents VaR measures in Exhibit 1.

EXHIBIT 1   Flusk Portfolio VaR (in $ millions)

Confidence Interval	Daily VaR	Monthly VaR
95%	1.10	5.37

After reading McKee's report, Ming asks why the number of daily VaR breaches over the last year is zero even though the portfolio has accumulated a substantial loss.

Next, Ming requests that McKee perform the following two risk analyses on Flusk's portfolio:

Analysis 1:   Use scenario analysis to evaluate the impact on risk and return of a repeat of the last financial crisis.

Analysis 2:   Estimate over one year, with a 95% level of confidence, how much Flusk's assets could underperform its liabilities.

Ming recommends purchasing newly issued emerging market corporate bonds that have embedded options. Prior to buying the bonds, Ming wants McKee to estimate the effect of the purchase on Flusk's VaR. McKee suggests running a stress test using a historical period specific to emerging markets that encompassed an extreme change in credit spreads.

At the conclusion of their conversation, Ming asks the following question about risk management tools: "What are the advantages of VaR compared with other risk measures?"

12. Based on Exhibit 1, Flusk's portfolio is expected to experience:
    A. a minimum daily loss of $1.10 million over the next year.
    B. a loss over one month equal to or exceeding $5.37 million 5% of the time.
    C. an average daily loss of $1.10 million 5% of the time during the next 250 trading days.
13. The number of Flusk's VaR breaches *most likely* resulted from:
    A. using a standard normal distribution in the VaR model.
    B. using a 95% confidence interval instead of a 99% confidence interval.
    C. lower market volatility during the last year compared with the lookback period.

14. To perform Analysis 1, McKee should use historical bond:
    A. prices.
    B. yields.
    C. durations.
15. The limitation of the approach requested for Analysis 1 is that it:
    A. omits asset correlations.
    B. precludes incorporating portfolio manager actions.
    C. assumes no deviation from historical market events.
16. The estimate requested in Analysis 2 is *best* described as:
    A. liquidity gap.
    B. surplus at risk.
    C. maximum drawdown.
17. Which measure should McKee use to estimate the effect on Flusk's VaR from Ming's portfolio recommendation?
    A. Relative VaR
    B. Incremental VaR
    C. Conditional VaR
18. When measuring the portfolio impact of the stress test suggested by McKee, which of the following is *most likely* to produce an accurate result?
    A. Marginal VaR
    B. Full revaluation of securities
    C. The use of sensitivity risk measures
19. The risk management tool referenced in Ming's question:
    A. is widely accepted by regulators.
    B. takes into account asset liquidity.
    C. usually incorporates right-tail events.

The following information relates to questions 20–26

Carol Kynnersley is the chief risk officer at Investment Management Advisers (IMA). Kynnersley meets with IMA's portfolio management team and investment advisers to discuss the methods used to measure and manage market risk and how risk metrics are presented in client reports.

The three most popular investment funds offered by IMA are the Equity Opportunities, the Diversified Fixed Income, and the Alpha Core Equity. The Equity Opportunities Fund is composed of two exchange-traded funds: a broadly diversified large-cap equity product and one devoted to energy stocks. Kynnersley makes the following statements regarding the risk management policies established for the Equity Opportunities portfolio:

Statement 1: IMA's preferred approach to model value at risk (VaR) is to estimate expected returns, volatilities, and correlations under the assumption of a normal distribution.

Statement 2: In last year's annual client performance report, IMA stated that a hypothetical $6 million Equity Opportunities Fund account had a daily 5% VaR of approximately 1.5% of portfolio value.

Kynnersley informs the investment advisers that the risk management department recently updated the model for estimating the Equity Opportunities Fund VaR based on the information presented in Exhibit 1.

EXHIBIT 1   Equity Opportunities Fund—VaR Model Input Assumptions

	Large-Cap ETF	Energy ETF	Total Portfolio
Portfolio weight	65.0%	35.0%	100.0%
Expected annual return	12.0%	18.0%	14.1%
Standard deviation	20.0%	40.0%	26.3%

Correlation between ETFs: 0.90
Number of trading days/year: 250

For clients interested in fixed-income products, IMA offers the Diversified Fixed-Income Fund. Kynnersley explains that the portfolio's bonds are all subject to interest rate risk. To demonstrate how fixed-income exposure measures can be used to identify and manage interest rate risk, Kynnersley distributes two exhibits featuring three hypothetical Treasury coupon bonds (Exhibit 2) under three interest rate scenarios (Exhibit 3).

EXHIBIT 2   Fixed-Income Risk Measure

Hypothetical Bond	Duration
Bond 1	1.3
Bond 2	3.7
Bond 3	10.2

EXHIBIT 3   Interest Rate Scenarios

Scenario	Interest Rate Environment
Scenario 1	Rates increase 25 bps
Scenario 2	Rates increase 10 bps
Scenario 3	Rates decrease 20 bps

One of the investment advisers comments that a client recently asked about the performance of the Diversified Fixed-Income Fund relative to its benchmark, a broad fixed-income index. Kynnersley informs the adviser as follows:

Statement 3:   The Diversified Fixed-Income Fund manager monitors the historical deviation between portfolio returns and benchmark returns. The fund prospectus stipulates a target deviation from the benchmark of no more than 5 bps.

Kynnersley concludes the meeting by reviewing the constraints IMA imposes on securities included in the Alpha Core Equity Fund. The compliance department conducts daily oversight using numerous risk screens and, when indicated, notifies portfolio managers to make adjustments. Kynnersley makes the following statement:

Statement 4:   It is important that all clients investing in the fund be made aware of IMA's compliance measures. The Alpha Core Equity Fund restricts the exposure of individual securities to 1.75% of the total portfolio.

20. Based on Statement 1, IMA's VaR estimation approach is *best* described as the:
   A. parametric method.
   B. historical simulation method.
   C. Monte Carlo simulation method.

21. In Statement 2, Kynnersley implies that the portfolio:
   A. is at risk of losing $4,500 each trading day.
   B. value is expected to decline by $90,000 or more once in 20 trading days.
   C. has a 5% chance of falling in value by a maximum of $90,000 on a single trading day.

22. Based *only* on Statement 2, the risk measurement approach:
   A. ignores right-tail events in the return distribution.
   B. is similar to the Sharpe ratio because it is backward looking.
   C. provides a relatively accurate risk estimate in both trending and volatile regimes.

23. Based on Exhibit 1, the daily 5% VaR estimate is *closest* to:
   A. 1.61%.
   B. 2.42%.
   C. 2.69%.

24. Based *only* on Exhibits 2 and 3, it is *most likely* that under:
   A. Scenario 1, Bond 2 outperforms Bond 1.
   B. Scenario 2, Bond 1 underperforms Bond 3.
   C. Scenario 3, Bond 3 is the best performing security.

25. The risk measure referred to in Statement 3 is:
   A. active share.
   B. beta sensitivity
   C. *ex post* tracking error.

26. In Statement 4, Kynnersley describes a constraint associated with a:
   A. risk budget.
   B. position limit.
   C. stop-loss limit.

CHAPTER 12

RISK MANAGEMENT FOR INDIVIDUALS

David M. Blanchett, PhD, CFP, CFA, David M. Cordell, PhD,
CFP, CFA, Michael S. Finke, PhD, and Thomas M. Idzorek, CFA

LEARNING OUTCOMES

The candidate should be able to:

- compare the characteristics of human capital and financial capital as components of an individual's total wealth;
- discuss the relationships among human capital, financial capital, and economic net worth;
- discuss the financial stages of life for an individual;
- describe an economic (holistic) balance sheet;
- discuss risks (earnings, premature death, longevity, property, liability, and health risks) in relation to human and financial capital;
- describe types of insurance relevant to personal financial planning;
- describe the basic elements of a life insurance policy and how insurers price a life insurance policy;
- discuss the use of annuities in personal financial planning;
- discuss the relative advantages and disadvantages of fixed and variable annuities;
- analyze and evaluate an insurance program;
- discuss how asset allocation policy may be influenced by the risk characteristics of human capital;
- recommend and justify appropriate strategies for asset allocation and risk reduction when given an investor profile of key inputs.

1. INTRODUCTION

Risk management for individuals is a key element of life-cycle finance, which recognizes that as investors age, the fundamental nature of their total wealth evolves, as do the risks that they face. **Life-cycle finance** is concerned with helping investors achieve their goals, including an adequate retirement income, by taking a holistic view of the individual's financial situation as he or she moves through life. Individuals are exposed to a range of risks over their lives: They may become disabled, suffer a prolonged illness, die prematurely, or outlive their resources. In addition, from an investment perspective, the assets of individuals could decline in value or provide an inadequate return in relation to financial needs and aspirations. All of these risks have two things in common: They are typically random, and they can result in financial hardship without an appropriate risk management strategy. Risk management for individuals is distinct from risk management for corporations given the distinctive characteristics of households, which include the finite and unknown lifespan of individuals, the frequent preference for stable spending among individuals, and the desire to pass on wealth to heirs (i.e., through bequests). To protect against unexpected financial hardships, risks must be identified, market and non-market solutions considered, and a plan developed and implemented. A well-constructed plan for risk management will involve the selection of financial products and investment strategies that fit an individual's financial goals and mitigate the risk of shortfalls.

In this reading, we provide an overview of the potential risks to an individual or household, an analysis of products and strategies that can protect against some of these risks, and a discussion regarding the selection of an appropriate product or strategy. Following the introduction, Section 2 provides an overview of human and financial capital. Sections 3–5 address the process of risk management, the financial stages of life for an individual, the economic (or holistic) balance sheet, and individual risks and risk exposures. Sections 6–10 discuss the types of products relevant to financial planning, including insurance and annuities. Sections 11–12 contain an insurance program case study and insights on implementing risk management solutions for individuals.

2. HUMAN CAPITAL, FINANCIAL CAPITAL, AND ECONOMIC NET WORTH

To better understand the financial health of an individual—and how to manage the risks faced by that individual—we can use an **economic balance sheet** (or **holistic balance sheet**). We discuss the economic balance sheet in more detail later in the reading, but it is important to note here that an individual's assets are made up of two primary components, **human capital** and **financial capital**, which present unique risk management challenges.

Ibbotson, Milevsky, Chen, and Zhu (2007) define human capital as the net present value of an investor's future expected labor income weighted by the probability of surviving to each future age. Financial capital includes the tangible and intangible assets (outside of human capital) owned by an individual or household. For example, a home, a car, stocks and bonds, a vested[1] retirement portfolio, and money in the bank are all examples of an individual's

---

[1]Vesting refers to ownership of retirement or pension benefits. Once benefits are vested, they belong to the beneficiary. Benefits that are not fully vested can be forfeited or reduced if the individual does not meet future conditions (e.g., if the individual terminates employment before the required number of years of service to the organization).

financial capital (or financial assets). In this section, both human capital and financial capital are explored in greater detail.

2.1. Human Capital

Advances in human capital theory have revolutionized how economists view the household risk management process. Conceptually, future wages or earnings can be thought of as analogous (in a rough sense) to future interest or dividend payments that flow from an individual's work-related skills, knowledge, experience, and other productive attributes that can be converted into wage income—or human capital. Because human capital provides a significant stream of income over decades, its present value is a significant part of most working households' total wealth portfolio. In fact, human capital is often the dominant asset on a household's economic balance sheet. From a risk management perspective, it is critical to understand the approximate total monetary value of an individual's human capital, the investment characteristics of the individual's human capital (i.e., whether the capital is more stock-like or bond-like), and how the approximate value of an individual's human capital relates to the value of the individual's financial capital. Here, we focus on estimating the approximate monetary value of an individual's human capital.

Given that future earnings for many workers are relatively stable over time, earnings can often be compared with the income one might receive from a bond. This analogy is useful because, similar to the way a financial analyst estimates the present value of a bond by discounting future cash flows, we can estimate human capital by discounting the expected future cash flows generated from wages or other income sources. Conceptually, individuals rent out or lease their human capital in the marketplace in exchange for an ongoing income that is a function of the state of the labor market. Some professions will receive a higher rental value (wage rate or salary) than others. Similarly, some professions will see their rental value fluctuate more with changes in the labor market environment.

Estimating the value of human capital is a complex process because the true value cannot be known. One simple approach is to use a discount rate that reflects the risk associated with the future cash flows (i.e., wages). Government employment and teaching are examples of professions that generally lead to relatively stable growth of future cash flows; in these cases, the human capital value would be estimated using a lower discount rate (to reflect the higher degree of certainty). Conversely, investment banking and racecar driving are examples of professions that may experience unstable and less secure future cash flows, so the value of human capital of investment bankers and racecar drivers would be based on a higher discount rate (to reflect the additional risk associated with their professions).

Equation 1 can be used to estimate the value of an individual's human capital today, at Time 0 (HC_0), where w_t is the income from employment in year t, r is the appropriate discount rate, and N is the length of working life in years. Working life typically ends at retirement, although it could also be based on the number of years an individual can potentially work (e.g., a 70-year-old may be retired but still have some remaining human capital that could be traded for income in the labor market):

$$HC_0 = \sum_{t=1}^{N} \frac{w_t}{(1 + r)^t} \tag{1}$$

This simple model in Equation 1 can be expanded using Equation 2, where we define the wage in time period t as a product of the wage in period $t - 1$ and the sum $(1 + g_t)$. That is, the wage in a given period is equal to the previous year's wage increased by g percent (the annual wage growth rate, in nominal terms). We can also modify the discount rate to be the sum of the nominal risk-free rate r_f and a risk adjustment y based on occupational income volatility. Similar to our example earlier contrasting the overall stability of labor income for government workers and teachers to that of investment bankers and racecar drivers, this adjustment recognizes the fact that the income from different professions can vary significantly. The risk adjustment should consider the inherent stability of the income stream as well as the possibility that the income stream will be interrupted by job loss, disability, or death that may be completely unrelated to the type of employment. Additionally, we incorporate mortality, where $p(s_t)$ is the probability of surviving to a given year (or age). Equation 1 uses a simplifying assumption that $p(s_t) = 1$ for each year until retirement (i.e., the individual will survive to retirement with certainty). Using these additional factors, Equation 2 can be restated as:

$$HC_0 = \sum_{t=1}^{N} \frac{p(s_t)\, w_{t-1}(1 + g_t)}{(1 + r_f + y)^t}$$ (2)

EXAMPLE 1   Estimating Human Capital

Identify the key assumptions required to estimate an individual's human capital.

Solution: Human capital can be calculated by using the following formula:

$$HC_0 = \sum_{t=1}^{N} \frac{p(s_t)\, w_{t-1}(1 + g_t)}{(1 + r_f + y)^t}$$

where
$p(s_t)$ = the probability of surviving to year (or age) t
w_t = the income from employment in period t
g_t = the annual wage growth rate
r_f = the nominal risk-free rate
y = risk premium associated with occupational income volatility
N = the length of working life in years

Estimating the Present Value of Human Capital

Using Equation 2, we briefly demonstrate how to estimate the present value of an individual's human capital. John Adam is 60 years old and plans on retiring in 5 years. Adam's annual wage is currently $50,000 and is expected to grow 2% per year. The risk-free rate is 4%. Adam works in a job with a moderate degree of occupational risk; therefore, we assume a risk adjustment based on occupational income volatility of 3%. There is a 99% probability that Adam survives the first year, a 98% probability that he survives the second year, and probabilities of 98%, 97%, and 96% for the following years, respectively. Given this information and using Equation 2, what is the present value of Adam's human capital?

Risk-free rate	= 4%
Income volatility adjustment	= 3%
Total discount rate	= 7%

Year	Wages (2% annual growth)	Present Value of Wages[a]	Probability of Survival	Probability Weighted Wages[b]
1	$51,000	$47,664	99%	$47,187
2	$52,020	$45,436	98%	$44,527
3	$53,060	$43,313	98%	$42,447
4	$54,122	$41,289	97%	$40,050
5	$55,204	$39,360	96%	$37,786
Total value of human capital				**$211,997**

[a]This column illustrates "Wages" discounted by 7% as indicated by the discount rate shown. For example: $47,664 = $51,000/1.07; $45,436 = $52,020/1.07^2; and so on.

[b]The calculation for this column is as follows: $47,187 = $47,664 × 99%. A similar calculation is used for the following years.

How would the estimated value of Adam's human capital change if the wage growth rate were changed to 0%, the risk-free rate decreased to 2%, and the risk adjustment for occupational income volatility also decreased to 2% (using the same base wage and mortality estimates)?

Risk-free rate	= 2%
Income volatility adjustment	= 2%
Total discount rate	= 4%

Year	Wages (No Growth)	Present Value of Wages	Probability of Survival	Probability Weighted Wages
1	$50,000	$48,077	99%	$47,596
2	$50,000	$46,228	98%	$45,303
3	$50,000	$44,450	98%	$43,561
4	$50,000	$42,740	97%	$41,458
5	$50,000	$41,096	96%	$39,453
Total value of human capital				**$217,371**

Reality is typically more complicated than models. Growth rates, nominal risk-free rates, risk adjustments, and mortality are not easily estimated. Additionally, wages do not tend to increase at a constant rate over an individual's lifetime, mortality and disability risk can reduce the value of human capital, and the average growth rate within occupations or even within the overall economy is unknown. In other words, the future payout on human capital, like the future payout on many financial assets, is uncertain. The potential loss of human capital, particularly early in the life cycle, represents an important risk that must be considered. Life and disability insurance, which we discuss later in the reading, are examples of financial instruments that can be used to protect against a random loss in household earnings. As human capital diminishes later in the life cycle, other risks that threaten financial capital and increase spending needs rise in importance. Accordingly, strategies that reduce investment risk and protect against long-term health care expenses and long-life spending needs increase in importance.

Viewing human capital as an asset with its own risk and return characteristics allows us to develop a holistic investment strategy that includes tangible and intangible assets. A total wealth perspective combines human capital with financial capital and incorporates the concept of life-cycle planning (also discussed later) to develop a strategy that maximizes household welfare.

2.2. Financial Capital

Financial capital can be subdivided into various components besides tangible and intangible, such as personal assets and investment assets. Investment assets can be further differentiated into many subtypes with distinctive marketability, tax, and standalone risk characteristics. The relationships between the value of the various components of an individual's financial capital and the value of his or her human capital are important in investment and risk management decision making.

The approach used in financial accounting provides an excellent template for classifying the different financial assets owned by an investor. In financial accounting, the balance sheet includes a summary of all the assets owned by an entity, whether an individual or organization, at a given point in time. Assets are defined broadly as either current or non-current. Current assets are expected to be consumed over the following year; money in a checking account, for example, would be considered a current asset. For an individual, non-current assets—that is, all assets not classified as current assets—include such items as automobiles, real estate, and investments (such as stocks and bonds). Non-current assets differ for a company because they include such items as property, plant, and equipment, as well as intangible assets, such as goodwill.

The financial accounting approach to segmenting assets has important implications when assessing an individual's financial capital because different assets have different roles and each may be exposed to various types of risk. Broadly speaking, an individual's assets can be described as "personal" assets or "investment" assets; personal assets are consumed whereas investment assets are held for their potential to increase in value and fund future consumption. Some assets, such as real estate, can act as both a personal asset (shelter, as an alternative to renting) and an investment asset (to help fund retirement) for an individual.

EXAMPLE 2   Comparing Financial and Human Capital

Describe human capital and financial capital.

Solution: Human capital is commonly defined as the mortality-weighted net present value of an individual's future expected labor income. Financial capital includes the tangible and intangible assets (outside of human capital) owned by an individual or household. For example, a home, a car, stocks, bonds, a vested retirement portfolio, and money in the bank are all examples of an individual's financial capital (or financial assets).

2.2.1. Personal Assets

Personal assets are assets an individual consumes (or uses) in some form in the course of his or her life. Such assets may include automobiles, clothes, furniture, and even a personal residence. In many cases, personal assets are not expected to appreciate in value, and they are often worth more to the individual than their current fair market value.

As mentioned earlier, some assets, like real estate, could be considered a "mixed" asset with both personal and investment characteristics. Another potential example of a mixed asset is collectibles (such as jewelry, wine, stamps, and artwork), which will be discussed separately in a later section. Mixed assets can be especially desirable because they enable individuals to derive satisfaction (i.e., utility) from their current value as well as having the potential to increase in value over time.

Classifying Private Accrued Defined Benefits and Government Retirement Benefits

When separating an individual's total wealth into human capital and financial capital, accrued defined benefits from private pension and government retirement plans—such as the Canada Pension Plan and Old Age Security Pension, the Age Pension in Australia, the mandatory state pension in Germany, and Social Security in the United States—can potentially be classified as either human capital or financial capital. Some practitioners note that accrued defined benefits and government pension benefits are typically a form of deferred labor income, and thus, they prefer to classify these benefits as human capital. Others find it more intuitive to think of accrued defined benefits and social security as a form of human capital that has been converted into a financial asset. In this reading, we classify accrued defined benefits and government pension benefits as components of financial capital.

2.2.2. Investment Assets

Investment assets are the components of an individual's wealth that are often the easiest to identify and typically receive the majority of the attention from financial planners and investment professionals. Investment assets extend beyond relatively tangible investment assets (such as a liquid portfolio) to include less tangible assets (such as an accrued defined benefit pension).

One criterion for subdividing investment assets is marketability, which describes how easy it is to trade an asset. We subdivide marketable assets into publicly traded and non-publicly traded segments, and we define non-marketable assets as those without any ready market (e.g., human capital).

Traditional portfolio construction generally focuses entirely on publicly traded marketable assets, like stocks and bonds, with optimization determining the weights allocated to marketable assets. This approach often ignores the existence of marketable assets that are not publicly traded as well as other non-marketable assets "owned" by the individual (e.g., human capital). In reality, each asset has important risk characteristics that should be considered. In the absence of a generalized framework that can estimate the risk and return of all of the components of an individual's total wealth and their correlations, one must understand the inherent risk and return characteristics of the non-marketable assets and make informed judgments when constructing a holistic portfolio. We will explore this concept more fully later in the reading.

2.2.3. Publicly Traded Marketable Assets

Traditional balance sheets tend to emphasize publicly traded marketable assets because their value and risk characteristics are generally easier to estimate than those of non-publicly traded assets. Publicly traded marketable assets include money market instruments, bonds, and common and preferred equity.

2.2.4. Non-Publicly Traded Marketable Assets

Non-publicly traded marketable assets include real estate, some types of annuities, cash-value life insurance, business assets, and collectibles.

2.2.4.1. Real Estate Real estate—or direct real estate, as it is sometimes called to distinguish it from real estate investment trusts (REITs)—is typically among the largest assets owned by an individual. In many countries, home ownership is common, although the level of home ownership varies materially by country. For example, in Germany, approximately half of households own a home, whereas in China, the number is closer to 90%. To purchase a home, many individuals obtain a mortgage loan. It is common for the home buyer to contribute some percentage of the home's value (e.g., 20%) as a down payment to mitigate some of the risk to the lender. The term of the mortgage loan can vary (e.g., 15 years, 30 years), as can the mortgage's interest rate (which can be either fixed or floating). Mortgage payments are often the largest fixed obligation of homeowners, especially during the early years of a mortgage loan. Mortgages present a unique risk for homeowners because they create a leveraged exposure in a home. For example, a 20% down payment (80% mortgage loan) implies that for any given change in the value of the home, the change in the equity (value less the mortgage loan) of the home will be five times greater than the change in the value of the home. Mortgage loans are either recourse or non-recourse, and the status varies by region. With recourse mortgages, if the borrower defaults on the mortgage, the lender has the right to recover from the borrower any amount due on the loan, whereas non-recourse loans prevent the lender from recovering any further amount from the borrower. Non-recourse loans are thus riskier for lenders because the only available collateral for the loan is the home. As a result, non-recourse loans generally have higher interest rates and/or higher borrower credit standards than recourse loans.

2.2.4.2. Annuities   Annuities are effectively a private defined benefit pension for which an insurance company has guaranteed, or will guarantee, income for life or over some fixed period for the beneficiary (called the annuitant). The estimated balance sheet value of an annuity is comparable to that of a defined benefit pension with a discount for potential insolvency risk, which is difficult to eliminate through diversification or a market hedge. Annuities will be discussed in more detail later in the reading.

2.2.4.3. Cash-Value Life Insurance   A variety of types of life insurance are available, including cash-value life insurance, for which the policy not only provides protection upon a death but also contains some type of cash reserve. This form of insurance usually combines life insurance protection with some type of cash accumulation vehicle. Some insurance policies allow the purchaser to invest in relatively aggressive investments, such as equities, although more conservative investments, such as bonds, are generally more common. Life insurance products will also be discussed at greater length later in the reading.

2.2.4.4. Business Assets   Business assets can represent a significant portion of the total wealth of an individual, especially a self-employed individual. A variety of unique considerations are involved in investing for business owners because their total capital may be very closely tied to the overall performance of the business (i.e., if the business does poorly, it affects not only the value of the business, but also the owner's earnings as well). The value of business assets may best be estimated through recent sales of comparable private businesses within the same industry—often as a multiple of net income or net income with various adjustments (e.g., EBITDA). The value of business assets may vary based on market conditions and will often correlate with other financial assets within a household portfolio. This potential correlation is an important consideration in the risk management process for individuals, particularly small business owners.

2.2.4.5. Collectibles   Collectibles include such items as stamps, paintings, wine, and precious metals (e.g., coins). The value of these assets is often set by auction markets or specialized dealers and involves substantial transaction costs. Collectibles may also provide a flow of utility for the owner. For example, in addition to benefiting from the potential price increase of a painting, the owner is able to display the painting in his or her home and view it daily.

2.2.5. Non-Marketable Assets
The most significant non-marketable financial assets are pensions, whether from a private employer or from a governmental organization. In this section, we consider both types of pensions.

2.2.5.1. Employer Pension Plans (Vested)   There are a variety of retirement plan types across the globe. These accounts can generally be described as either employee-directed savings plans, in which contribution amounts and investments are controlled by the individual (and not guaranteed), or traditional pension plans, which guarantee some level of retirement benefits, typically based on past wages. We include only vested pension benefits as financial assets, because unvested pension benefits are typically contingent on future work and are thus considered to be part of human capital.

The value of a vested traditional defined benefit pension from an employer can be estimated by determining the mortality-weighted net present value of future benefits. The mortality-weighted net present value at Time 0 (now), $mNPV_0$, can be estimated using Equation 3, which is reasonably equivalent to Equation 1. Equation 3 is based on the future expected vested benefit (b_t), the probability of surviving until year t $[p(s_t)]$, and a discount rate (r). The discount rate should vary based on the relative riskiness of the future expected benefit payment—that is, the rate will be higher for riskier future benefit payments—and should reflect whether the benefit is in nominal or real terms:

$$mNPV_0 = \sum_{t=1}^{N} \frac{p(s_t)\, b_t}{(1 + r)^t} \tag{3}$$

Estimating an appropriate discount rate to use in valuing a pension can be quite complex, although it is generally less complex than estimating the discount rate to use in valuing an individual's human capital. There are a number of factors to consider in determining the pension discount rate. As a starting point, one should consider the health of the plan (e.g., its funding status, where the value of the plan's liability is estimated using an appropriate market-based discount rate), the credit quality of the sponsoring company, and any additional credit support. If the company in question has long-term bonds, the yield on the bonds can provide a proxy for an appropriate discount rate. As one example of credit support, the Pension Protection Fund (PPF) was established in the United Kingdom as part of the Pensions Act 2004 to guarantee continued payment of most UK defined benefit pension plans should the employer become insolvent. The existence of PPF insurance helps to decrease the payout risk (and accompanying discount rate) for eligible UK pension plans.

2.2.5.2. Government Pensions   Government pensions are similar to employer pension plans but are generally more secure (in those countries with a high degree of creditworthiness). As with employer pension plans, the vested or accrued benefit amount can be estimated by calculating the mortality-weighted net present value. Given the guaranteed nature of these benefits, government pensions can be considered relatively bond-like. For example, in the United States, retiree government pension benefits (called Social Security retirement benefits) can be thought of as a government bond with benefits indexed to inflation (because Social Security retirement benefits usually increase annually based on inflation). This inflation adjustment is consistent with securities called Treasury Inflation-Protected Securities (TIPS).

Regardless of the domicile, one should consider the financial health of the government entity sponsoring the defined benefit plan as well as the legal framework and any accompanying political risk at the country level.

2.2.6. Account Type

Financial capital is often held in account types that have different tax attributes. Although these account types (and the potential tax benefits surrounding them) vary materially by country, the accounts can generally be described as taxable, tax-deferred, or non-taxable. A taxable account is one for which taxes are due annually on the realized gains, dividends, and/or interest income. A tax-deferred account is one for which taxes on any gains are deferred until some future date, such as when a withdrawal is made from the account. A non-taxable account is one for which taxes are never due, no matter how much the account grows.

2.3. Economic Net Worth

An individual's *net worth* consists of the difference between traditional assets and liabilities that are reasonably simple to measure, such as investment assets, real estate, and mortgages. **Economic net worth**, however, extends net worth to include claims to future assets that can be used for consumption, such as human capital and the present value of pension benefits. When we refer to economic net worth in this reading, we refer to the more holistic accounting of resources that can be used to fund future consumption for the purpose of financial planning over the life cycle.

3. A FRAMEWORK FOR INDIVIDUAL RISK MANAGEMENT

This section contains an overview of the important considerations when developing an effective risk management plan for an individual. First, a risk management strategy for individuals is introduced. Next, the primary financial stages of the life of an individual are discussed. We then incorporate the human capital and financial capital concepts developed in Section 2 into an individual's economic (or holistic) balance sheet, explaining how key components of that balance sheet develop over time. Finally, we identify some of the primary risks to an individual and how they evolve during an individual's lifetime.

3.1. The Risk Management Strategy for Individuals

In general, *risk management* for individuals is the process of identifying threats to the value of household assets and developing an appropriate strategy for dealing with these risks. The risk management strategy provides a framework that allows a household to decide when to avoid, reduce, transfer, or self-insure those risks. There are typically four key steps in the risk management process:

1. Specify the objective.
2. Identify risks.
3. Evaluate risks and select appropriate methods to manage the risks.
4. Monitor outcomes and risk exposures and make appropriate adjustments in methods.

3.1.1. Specify the Objective
The overarching objective of individual risk management is to maximize household welfare through an appropriate balance of risk and safety. Risk represents a possible decrease in future spending caused by unexpected events, such as a market crash, a physical disability, the premature death of a primary earner, or health care expenses. As with investments, this objective is achieved by deciding how much risk a household is willing to bear in order to achieve its long-run spending goals.

3.1.2. Identify Risks
Households face a significant number of risks, including earnings, premature death, longevity, property, liability, and health risks. These risks will be discussed at length in subsequent sections. Each of these risks is associated with a potential loss of financial and/or human capital, and individuals should address each of them to determine how best to address the possibility of loss.

3.1.3. Evaluate Risks and Select Appropriate Methods to Manage the Risks

The existence of a risk exposure does not necessarily require the purchase of an insurance product. The appropriate risk management strategy considers the magnitude of the risk and the range of options available to address that risk. Section 11 will explain the choice among the four techniques of risk avoidance, risk reduction, risk transfer, and risk retention. *Risk avoidance* involves avoiding a risk altogether. For example, one way to avoid the risk to human and financial capital from riding a motorcycle is to simply not own or ride one. *Risk reduction* involves mitigating a risk by reducing its impact on an individual's welfare, either by lowering the likelihood that it will occur or by decreasing the magnitude of loss (for example, by wearing a helmet when riding a motorcycle). *Risk transfer* involves transferring the risk: The use of insurance and annuities to transfer risk to insurers will be discussed later in the reading. *Risk retention* involves retaining a risk and thus maintaining the ability to finance the cost of losses; when funds are set aside to meet potential losses, the individual is said to *self-insure*.

3.1.4. Monitor Outcomes and Risk Exposures and Make Appropriate Adjustments in Methods

Once the appropriate risk management method has been selected, risks must be monitored and updated as the household moves through its life cycle. It is advisable to annually review an insurance/risk management program, including all the ongoing risk exposures and risk management methods. As an individual's goals and personal and financial situation change, these changes will affect risk exposures and optimal risk management strategies. In addition to an annual review, every life change—such as a birth, marriage, inheritance, job change, relocation, divorce, or death—should trigger a review of the risk management plan.

3.2. Financial Stages of Life

Individuals tend to follow a predictable pattern during their lifetimes: They invest in education early in life, embark on a career, start families, accumulate assets, fund growing household expenses, transition into retirement, and ultimately pass on wealth through bequests. In each of these life-cycle stages, the household faces unique goals and risks that require appropriate investment and risk management strategies.

Defining financial stages of life in clear and concise terms does pose a challenge because all individuals are different; however, financial stages are a useful construct when thinking about risk management and the optimal forms of insurance and other products to consider at different ages. Therefore, we divide the financial stages of life for adults into the following seven periods:

- Education phase
- Early career
- Career development
- Peak accumulation
- Pre-retirement
- Early retirement
- Late retirement

3.2.1. Education Phase

The education phase occurs while an individual is investing in knowledge (or human capital) through either formal education or skill development. In theory, the education phase could begin as early as when an individual starts primary school, but this phase typically involves the period when the individual starts developing more specific human capital by attending college or trade school or undertaking an apprenticeship. In some cases, an individual in the education phase may be largely financially dependent on his or her parents or guardians and have little, if any, accumulated financial capital. There is generally little focus on savings or risk management at this point; however, some individuals in this phase may already have families and could benefit from products, such as life insurance, that hedge against the risk of losing human capital.

3.2.2. Early Career

The early career phase normally begins when an individual has completed his or her education and enters the workforce. This stage may begin as early as age 18 (16 in some countries) or as late as the late 20s (or even early 30s), depending on the level of education attained, and generally lasts into the mid-30s. During this period, the individual often marries, perhaps has young children, may purchase a home, and usually begins to save for their children's college expenses. Sometimes, a career-related relocation occurs that could have negative short-term financial implications. Significant family and housing expenses may not allow for much retirement savings. Insurance may be especially valuable during this phase because human capital represents such a large proportion of total wealth and family members are highly dependent on the human capital of one or two individuals to fund expected future consumption.

3.2.3. Career Development

The career development phase normally occurs during the 35–50 age range and is often a time of specific skill development within a given field, upward career mobility, and income growth. This phase often includes accumulation for the children's college educations as well as expenditures for college. Concern intensifies about retirement income planning and financial independence. Higher earners will begin building wealth beyond education and retirement objectives and may make large purchases, such as a vacation home, or travel extensively. Retirement saving tends to increase at a more rapid pace during this phase compared with the early career phase.

3.2.4. Peak Accumulation

In the peak accumulation phase, generally during the ages of 51–60, most people either have reached or are moving toward maximum earnings and have the greatest opportunity for wealth accumulation. This phase may include accumulating funds for other goals and objectives, but it is usually a continuation of retirement income planning, coordination of employee benefits with investment and retirement strategies, and travel. Investors following a life-cycle portfolio strategy will begin to reduce investment risk to emphasize income production for retirement (particularly near the end of this period) and become increasingly concerned about minimizing taxes, given higher levels of wealth and income. There is also potentially more career risk in this phase because if an individual were to lose his or her job, it might be relatively difficult for that individual to find another job with similar pay.

3.2.5. Pre-retirement

The pre-retirement phase consists of the few years preceding the planned retirement age, and it typically represents an individual's maximum career income. Many people in this phase continue to restructure their portfolios to reduce risk and may consider investments that are less volatile. There is further emphasis on tax planning, including the ramifications of retirement plan distribution options.

3.2.6. Early Retirement

The early retirement phase in the cycle is generally defined as the first 10 years of retirement and, for successful investors, often represents a period of comfortable income and sufficient assets to meet expenses. For individuals who are forced to retire because of injury or unemployment, this time may be one of shifting expectations and may involve changing to a lifestyle more commensurate with the individual's savings. This is generally the most active period of retirement and is when an individual is less likely to suffer from cognitive or mobility limitations. The primary objective of the retiree is to use resources to produce activities that provide enjoyment. Some retirees seek a new career, and many will look for a job (part time or full time) that has less stress. It is important to note that upon entering retirement, the need for asset growth does not disappear. For many households, the length of retirement could exceed two decades; given this potential horizon, it is important to continue taking an appropriate level of investment risk in retirees' portfolios.

3.2.7. Late Retirement

The late retirement phase is especially unpredictable because the exact length of retirement is unknown. This uncertainty about longevity for a specific individual is known as longevity risk, which is the risk that an individual outlives his or her financial resources in retirement. Physical activity typically declines during this phase, as does mobility. Although many individuals live comfortably and are in good health until their final days, others experience a long series of physical problems that can deplete financial asset reserves. Cognitive decline can present a risk of financial mistakes, which may be hedged through the participation of a trusted financial adviser or through the use of annuities. Annuities will be discussed in more detail later in the reading.

Two additional concerns may be appropriate to any financial stage. First, depending on the family situation, the need to provide for long-term health care may become apparent. Second, some people may need to devote resources to care for parents or a disabled child for an extended period of time.

EXAMPLE 3   Financial Stages of Life

From a personal financial planning standpoint, what are typical characteristics of someone in the "peak accumulation" phase?

Solution: An individual in the peak accumulation phase of the life cycle would typically have the following characteristics:

- Approximate age of 51–60
- Maximum earnings and opportunity for wealth accumulation
- Increased interest in retirement income planning
- Greater emphasis on stability and less emphasis on growth in the investment portfolio
- Greater concern about tax strategies
- Increased concern about losing employment because it may be more difficult to find new employment

4. THE INDIVIDUAL BALANCE SHEET

A traditional balance sheet includes assets and liabilities that are usually easy to quantify. Our purpose in developing an individual balance sheet is to more comprehensively represent the assets available to fund life-cycle consumption and for wealth preservation and transfer bequests. The primary value of a balance sheet in this context is to illustrate the magnitude of risk exposures for an individual. This perspective is particularly important for individuals who are in life-cycle stages during which human capital is a significant share of overall wealth and for individuals who hold claims on pension assets that grow in value later in the life cycle.

In this section, we attempt to provide a more complete picture of an investor's wealth through the use of an economic balance sheet (or holistic balance sheet), which we initially mentioned in Section 2. Such a balance sheet provides a useful overview of the individual's total wealth portfolio, supplementing traditional balance sheet assets with human capital and pension wealth and expanding liabilities to include consumption and bequest goals. These additional liabilities are important because they often represent leverage created in order to gain access to assets, such as the cost of education to create human capital. They also represent regular payment obligations that may influence the optimal amount of portfolio liquidity and investment risk. Human capital and pension wealth are important because they represent expected income flows that can be drawn on to fund future consumption.

4.1. Traditional Balance Sheet

The simplest balance sheet for an individual investor includes recognizable marketable assets and liabilities. Assets include any type of investment portfolio, retirement portfolio (or plan), real estate, and other tangible and intangible items of value. Liabilities include mortgage debt, credit card debt, auto loans, business debt, and student loans. An example of a simple balance sheet (or statement of net worth) is shown in Exhibit 1, where the assets are netted against the liabilities to determine the net worth of the individual.

EXHIBIT 1   Traditional Balance Sheet as of 31 December 2014

Assets		Liabilities	
Liquid Assets		**Short-Term Liabilities**	
Checking account	€35,000	Credit card debt	€25,000
Certificates of deposit	€100,000	Total short-term liabilities	€25,000
Total liquid assets	€135,000		
Investment Assets		**Long-Term Liabilities**	
Taxable account	€750,000	Car loan*	€25,000
Retirement plan	€600,000	Home mortgage	€500,000
Cash value of life insurance	€25,000	Home equity loan	€90,000
Total investment assets	€1,375,000	Total long-term liabilities	€615,000

(continued)

EXHIBIT 1   (Continued)

Personal Property

House	€2,200,000		
Cars	€160,000		
House contents	€150,000		
Total personal property	€2,510,000		
Total Assets	€4,020,000	Total Liabilities	€640,000
		Net Worth	€3,380,000

Note: A portion of the car loan would likely be short term, but to simplify, we included the entire loan as a long-term liability.

The net value of an asset, or its equity, is calculated by subtracting liabilities associated with that asset from the gross value. For example, an individual may own a home worth £1 million, but if that individual has a £900,000 mortgage, the equity in the home would be only £100,000 (ignoring any additional intangible benefits associated with home ownership).

It should be noted that this traditional balance sheet includes those assets that can be valued easily but ignores other individual assets that are material, such as human capital and pension benefits. For individuals in the earlier life-cycle stages, human capital is larger than other assets on the balance sheet. For those who are eligible to receive a guaranteed retirement income stream, the present value of these assets is significant and can be of great value to older individuals. Although non-marketable and difficult to value precisely, human capital and retirement benefits are extremely important when planning the optimal use of assets and the repayment of liabilities over a life cycle.

4.2. Economic (Holistic) Balance Sheet

The primary goal of an economic (holistic) balance sheet is to arrive at an accurate depiction of an individual's overall financial health by accounting for the present value of all available marketable and non-marketable assets as well as all liabilities. This view allows an individual to map out the optimal level of future consumption and non-consumption goals (such as bequests or other transfers) given the resources that exist today and those that are expected in the future. Although a traditional balance sheet provides information about marketable assets that exist today, it offers limited insight into how these assets should be used to maximize the expected lifetime satisfaction of the individual (a concept economists call "utility"). An economic balance sheet allows an individual to anticipate how available resources can be used to fund consumption over the remaining lifetime.

Exhibit 2 provides a simplified example of an economic balance sheet, which is an expanded version of the traditional balance sheet in Exhibit 1. The traditional assets and liabilities are condensed from the traditional balance sheet in Exhibit 1, with the present value of human capital and pensions added as assets and the present value of lifetime consumption and bequests added as liabilities. For further simplification purposes, we assume that all the assets and liabilities in Exhibit 1 are already calculated at their present value.

EXHIBIT 2   Economic (Holistic) Balance Sheet as of 31 December 2014

Assets		Liabilities	
Financial capital	€4,020,000	Debts	€640,000
Liquid assets		Credit card debt	
Investment assets		Car loan	
Personal property		Home mortgage	
		Home equity loan	
Human capital	€1,400,000	Lifetime consumption needs (present value)	€4,200,000
Pension value	€500,000		
		Bequests	€400,000
Total Assets	€5,920,000	Total Liabilities	€5,240,000
		Economic Net Worth	€680,000

An economic balance sheet that includes the present value of non-marketable assets (e.g., human capital and pensions) and liabilities (e.g., consumption needs and bequests) provides a much more accurate baseline from which to maximize the expected utility of future consumption. Assessing pension and human capital value can also be useful when setting consumption or bequest goals because these assessments provide a more accurate estimation of the future trade-offs an individual will make. Younger households with greater human capital, in addition to spending more to protect the value of this human capital early in the life cycle, will be able to plan for more generous retirement savings goals than households with comparatively lower human capital.

The total economic wealth of an individual changes throughout his or her lifetime, as do the underlying assets that make up that wealth. The total economic wealth of younger individuals is typically dominated by the value of their human capital because younger individuals have not had as much time to save and accumulate financial wealth. As individuals grow older, they are likely to save some of their earnings and will accumulate financial capital. The total value of human capital and the total value of financial capital tend to be inversely related over time as individuals attempt to smooth consumption through borrowing, saving, and eventual spending. When human capital is depleted, an absence of financial capital would result in no wealth to fund an individual's consumption needs. Although some people may live with family or friends at older ages out of necessity, most would prefer to have financial independence in retirement—something that typically requires individuals to save throughout their prime working years.

Although the economic net worth in the hypothetical economic balance sheet was equal to €680,000, it is possible for an individual to have either a surplus or a shortfall. For example, if the individual is not saving enough to adequately fund the lifestyle he or she will want at retirement, that individual may have a shortfall. Alternatively, if the individual is saving more than enough to fund lifestyle needs and has no bequest goals, he or she may have a surplus. In either case, an economic balance sheet provides some perspective about the overall financial situation of an individual based on his or her holistic wealth.

EXAMPLE 4 Traditional vs. Economic Balance Sheet

Contrast a traditional balance sheet with an economic balance sheet.

Solution: A traditional balance sheet includes assets and liabilities that are generally relatively easy to quantify. An economic balance sheet provides a useful overview of one's total wealth portfolio by supplementing traditional balance sheet assets with human capital and pension wealth and including additional liabilities, such as consumption and bequest goals.

4.3. Changes in Economic Net Worth

To provide some context for how the relative value of various household assets changes over a lifetime, we will use the hypothetical example of a British individual at age 25. This 25-year-old is assumed to make £40,000 a year in after-tax income. Over his or her lifetime, real wages are expected to grow at a constant rate of 1% per year, the annual savings rate is 10%, the nominal discount rate is 8%, and the rate of expected inflation is 3%. The value of human capital is estimated using Equation 2. Financial capital at age 25 is assumed to be £10,000, and it is expected to grow at an annual real rate of return of 3% per year. The assumed need from the portfolio is £20,000 for the first year of retirement (age 65) and is increased annually by inflation throughout retirement.

We further assume that at age 30 the individual purchases a home that costs £100,000 in today's currency. The home is purchased with a 10% down payment (which comes from financial capital), with the remainder financed by a 30-year mortgage at a fixed nominal interest rate of 5%. The real growth rate of the value of the home is assumed to be 1%. Total pension benefits of £20,000 per year (in today's currency, at age 25) are assumed to commence at age 65, and the real discount rate for pension retirement benefits is 5%. We assume the benefits are accrued throughout the employment of the individual.

Exhibit 3 shows the values of the assets in the individual's economic balance sheet and how they are expected to change over time. To simplify the concept, we demonstrate graphically how the sample inputs reflect the allocation in the exhibit.

EXHIBIT 3   Life-Cycle Economic Balance Sheet Allocation

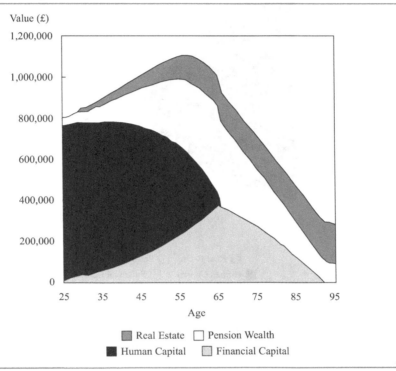

Traditional balance sheet assets, such as investments in marketable securities, real estate, and businesses, vary in importance from one life-cycle stage to the next. In general, tangible assets, such as real estate and personal goods, which provide great value to a young family, dominate a household's portfolio early in the life cycle. As households age, they accumulate financial assets that must be managed efficiently to provide the greatest expected later-life consumption for the amount of risk the household is willing to take. Non-traditional balance sheet assets, such as employer pensions, increase in importance later in the life cycle, providing an important source of stable consumption and affecting the optimal allocation of securities within an investment portfolio. To illustrate, Exhibit 4 provides the relative weights for the various assets included in Exhibit 3.

EXHIBIT 4   Relative Weights of Economic Balance Sheet Allocation

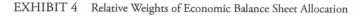

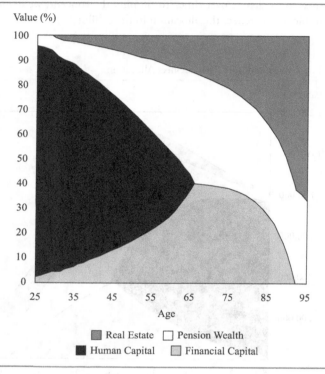

Value (%)

Age

■ Real Estate   □ Pension Wealth
■ Human Capital   ■ Financial Capital

In Exhibit 4, we see that for the typical individual, an investment portfolio represents a significant portion of wealth at age 65 but is still less than 50% of the total economic wealth when home equity, pension wealth, and human capital are also considered. As that individual proceeds through his or her retirement years and funds consumption, the relative share of the investment portfolio declines. In the early retirement stage, total economic wealth is dominated by pension wealth (i.e., the remaining mortality-weighted net present value of benefits) and the value of real estate (i.e., the individual's personal residence). For wealthier individuals, the value of defined benefit pension wealth will likely represent a low percentage of the total wealth portfolio in retirement. To the extent that defined benefit pension wealth has very low credit risk (for example, because of the low default probability of National Insurance in the United Kingdom), a retiree's optimal investment portfolio allocation will be affected. As discussed earlier, one must consider the financial health of both the plan and the sponsor providing the defined benefit pension.

In a related manner, a 65-year-old with £2 million in pension wealth will have a higher level of expected remaining lifetime consumption than a retiree with £1 million in pension wealth and the same traditional balance sheet net worth. Both individuals will need to consider means to safeguard the value of the pension wealth as part of the financial planning process. For example, a pension from a private employer may be subject to company-specific risk. The risk of employer insolvency might be hedged in financial markets by positions in securities and derivatives (if available) that have a negative correlation with the value of the company. As mentioned previously, guarantees of benefit payments may exist, such as the Pension Protection Fund in the United Kingdom that protects many private defined benefit schemes.

The allocation of the different asset types will affect the optimal financial asset allocation decision. A 45-year-old individual in Germany with €1 million in human capital and €500,000 in investment assets should invest differently than a 45-year-old with €3 million in human capital and an identical €500,000 in investment assets. The volatility in the investment portfolio of the individual with lower human capital will have a much greater impact on variation in expected consumption if both individuals have a 40-year planning horizon. Assume that the first 45-year-old with €1.5 million in combined human and financial capital expects to spend approximately €38,000 each year until age 85. The other 45-year-old with €3.5 million in economic net worth expects to spend €88,000 each year. All else being equal, a 40% loss in the first individual's portfolio (0.4 × €500,000 = €200,000) will lead to a 13.2% loss in expected spending per year [(€200,000/40 years)/€38,000] whereas a 40% investment loss to the second individual's portfolio will lead only to a 5.7% decrease in expected consumption [(€200,000/40 years)/€88,000]. For this reason, portfolio recommendations will be less conservative for the investor with high human capital than for the investor with low human capital if both have the same level of risk tolerance.

EXAMPLE 5   Changes in Human and Financial Capital

Describe how the relative values of human capital and financial capital change over an individual's lifetime.

Solution: The total value of human capital and the total value of financial capital tend to be inversely related over time as individuals attempt to smooth consumption through borrowing, saving, and eventual spending. When human capital becomes depleted, without financial capital, an individual will have no wealth to fund his or her lifestyle. Human capital is generally largest for a younger individual, whereas financial capital is generally largest when an individual first retires.

---

5. INDIVIDUAL RISK EXPOSURES

Managing risks to financial and human capital is an essential part of the household financial planning process. In this section, we provide an overview of the risks faced by individuals and discuss how they relate to human and financial capital. In future sections, we introduce financial products that could be used to manage many of these risks.

5.1. Earnings Risk

Earnings risk, within the context of personal risk management, refers to the risks associated with the earning potential of an individual—that is, events that could negatively affect the individual's human and financial capital. As noted previously, health issues can affect earnings, and some health risks are a function of the occupation itself. For example, a construction worker is likely to face higher health-related earnings risk than the average worker. Aside from health issues, unemployment and underemployment represent major factors in earnings risk.

Sometimes, an employee's job performance or a poor "fit" may lead to job loss, but many people find themselves without a job through no fault of their own.

The risk associated with unemployment for reasons other than disability is rather difficult to characterize. In some cases, such as government employees and union members with seniority, the likelihood of unemployment may be very low. Smaller, younger companies may be riskier employers because of dynamic business conditions or cash flow issues. But even large, well-established companies have been known to go out of business or to close unprofitable divisions or locations. In such cases, even an offer to transfer to another location may be undesirable for someone late in his or her working life, for someone with a working spouse and/ or children in school, or for someone who strongly prefers to remain in the same location for a variety of other reasons. Some industries are cyclical and are prone to layoffs, whereas other industries are subject to competitive pressures that may lead to permanent terminations. Self-employed individuals and even some professionals are prone to variability in their earnings. Of course, the cost is the loss or reduction of earnings and may also include the loss of employer contributions to one's retirement fund as well as other benefit programs. A lengthy period of unemployment may itself create more risk because employers are sometimes hesitant to hire people who have been out of work for an extended period of time. If the individual finally finds a job, it may be at a dramatically lower compensation level.

Obviously, the loss of income represents a reduction in both human and financial capital, and this reduction is exacerbated if job opportunities are few, especially in a poor economy or in a region or industry that is particularly affected. For individuals who lose a job as they approach retirement age, it could be very difficult to find another job, even if there are regulations against age discrimination. Aside from the stress on the family budget, unemployment can be psychologically devastating to the individual and his or her family. With earnings risk, as well as health risk (which is discussed in further detail later), an implication in estimating the total value of human capital is that individuals who work in dangerous occupations or in jobs that have a high likelihood of variability or disruption in earnings have either lower future expected earnings or a higher discount rate or both. Financial capital may also be affected by earnings risk because assets will be needed to make up for any loss of income. Furthermore, there may be a need to seek additional training or education to acquire requisite skills, and this retooling can be very expensive.

5.2. Premature Death Risk

The term **premature death risk**, which is sometimes referred to as mortality risk, relates to the death of an individual earlier than anticipated whose future earnings, or human capital, were expected to help pay for financial needs and aspirations of the individual's family. These needs include funding day-to-day living expenses, such as food, housing, and transportation, as well as paying off debts, saving for a child's education, and providing for a comfortable retirement for the surviving spouse. An individual's death may also lead to a reduction in the income of the surviving spouse because some family responsibilities of the deceased individual must now be performed by the surviving spouse (assuming the spouse does not remarry). For a young family, the effect can be especially tragic because the increase in household lifestyle that might have accompanied the career of the deceased may never occur (again, if there is no remarriage).

A risk to consumption needs also occurs if a non-earning member of the family dies. The loss can be estimated as the discounted value of the services provided by the deceased family member plus any out-of-pocket death expenses. If a household's primary caregiver dies, the rest of the family can help with that member's responsibilities, but often additional, paid help is required to replace the primary caregiver's duties. This scenario will mean a dramatic change in lifestyle, compounding the incalculable emotional effect of the death. It could even have a negative impact on the career of the surviving spouse, who may feel drained by the added responsibilities.

Besides the obvious reduction in human capital that the death of an income earner represents, there are also effects on financial capital. Death expenses (including funeral and burial), transition expenses, estate settlement expenses, and the possible need for training or education for the surviving spouse are among the financial costs that may be incurred.

5.3. Longevity Risk

Longevity risk within the context of financial planning relates to the uncertainty surrounding how long retirement will last and specifically the risks associated with living to an advanced age in retirement (e.g., age 100). An extended retirement period may deplete the retiree's resources to the point at which income and financial assets are insufficient to meet post-retirement consumption needs. A common question posed to financial planners is, "How much money do I need to have when I retire?" The answer is dependent on the lifespan of the individual, and longevity is a key variable that can only, at best, be estimated. Other important variables include the nominal rate of return on the portfolio, the rate of inflation, additional sources of income (and whether those sources are adjusted for inflation), and the level of spending. Determining how large a fund an individual will actually have at retirement depends on the amount and timing of contributions, the nominal rate of return, and the amount of time until retirement.

When calculating the sum needed at retirement, financial planners often run a Monte Carlo simulation that is based on an assumed asset allocation to calculate the probability that the funds will last for a specified number of years. Another approach for the time variable is to use a mortality table, adjust for health factors, and add years to be conservative. For example, Friedrich is retiring at age 65, and the mortality tables in his country indicate that a 65-year-old man has an expected lifespan of 20 years. But Friedrich is healthy, exercises regularly, eats well, and has had annual physical examinations, and his parents lived until their late 80s, which was past life expectancy at that time. Friedrich might assume that his retirement will last only 20 years (his life expectancy), but the mortality tables indicate a 50% chance that he will live beyond the forecasted period, which is why it is common to add years to be conservative (e.g., plan for retirement to last 30 years, or until age 95). The decision regarding the additional number of years is obviously subjective. The only way to minimize the likelihood of living beyond the forecasted retirement period would be to use extremely advanced ages (e.g., age 110).

Longevity risk can have a significant impact on the lifestyle of an individual. Even in countries that provide significant pension benefits, income may be inadequate to support the hoped-for lifestyle, and insufficient assets may exacerbate the situation. Making matters worse, many pension programs do not consider inflation. Furthermore, some pension programs, even those sponsored by governmental entities, are unlikely to have sufficient assets to pay future expected liabilities without significant changes to the pension structure. Relying on a pension thus entails its own set of risks.

Longevity risk affects human capital in the sense that an individual who is concerned about "living too long" may choose to work longer than someone else might. Indeed, all else being equal, the person who is concerned about outliving his or her money and who intends to work longer has more human capital, but at the possible expense of a less desirable (i.e., longer) retirement stage.

5.4. Property Risk

Property risk relates to the possibility that a person's property may be damaged, destroyed, stolen, or lost. There are, of course, many different possible events relating to property risk. A house may catch fire, an automobile may be involved in a collision or be damaged in a hailstorm, or a valuable necklace may be lost. In the context of property risk, *direct loss* refers to the monetary value of the loss associated with the property itself. For example, a house fire may cause €50,000 of damage. If the repair process requires that the family live elsewhere while the damage is repaired, the expenses incurred are considered an *indirect loss*. If the family is renting a room to a boarder, the income lost during construction would also be considered an indirect loss. Similarly, if a driver damages his or her automobile by running into a curb, the damage to the automobile is a direct loss and the cost of renting a replacement automobile is an indirect loss.

Because property represents a financial asset, property risk is normally considered to be associated with a potential loss of financial capital. But property used in a business to create income is rightfully considered in a discussion of human capital. That is, this type of business property can be considered a tool that helps drive future earnings, and to the extent that such property is at risk, human capital is also at risk. Business owners should be especially conscious of the fact that in the absence of insurance or other risk management techniques, both financial and human capital is at risk.

5.5. Liability Risk

Liability risk refers to the possibility that an individual or household may be held legally liable for the financial costs associated with property damage or physical injury. In general, one may be *liable* if because of one's action—or inaction when one is legally responsible for taking action—bodily injury, property damage, or other loss is incurred by another person or entity.

For individuals, the most common cause of legal liability involves driving an automobile. An automobile accident may cause bodily injury leading to medical costs, lost income, and even the necessity for long-term care. For the vast majority of people, the potential liability of a major automobile accident exceeds not only their financial capital but also their human capital as well. For example, in some jurisdictions, a liability judgment may result in the confiscation (often termed garnishing) of the wages or other income of the person found liable. Note, though, that the person who is found liable—for example, in an automobile accident—may also have suffered an injury that may affect the individual's financial and/or human capital.

As an example of liability risk, assume that a driver causes an automobile accident in which a passenger in the other car is injured and the other driver's automobile is heavily damaged. In many jurisdictions, the individual who caused the accident is deemed responsible for the repair or replacement of the damaged automobile and the medical expenses and lost income of the victim. As another example, in many countries, a homeowner or even an apartment renter may be deemed legally liable for an accident that causes injury or property damage to a visitor. For example, a guest may accidentally slip on some steps, be seriously injured by the fall, and become incapable of gainful employment. Even if the visitor was careless, laws may specify that the owner or renter of the property is liable.

5.6. Health Risk

Health risk refers to the risks and implications associated with illness or injury. Direct costs associated with illness or injury may include coinsurance, copayments, and deductibles associated with diagnostics, treatments, and procedures. In the context of health insurance, the term *coinsurance* means that the insured must share some of the costs of the specific health care provided. For example, an insurance company may be obligated to pay 80% of the cost of a medical procedure and require that the insured pay the other 20%. *Copayments* refer to the requirement that the insured pay a specified amount of money for a medical service, typically treatment by a physician. For example, a copayment, or "copay," of US$30 may be required for a visit to a primary care physician and US$45 may be required for a visit to a specialist. The remainder of the actual expense is paid by the insurance company. A *deductible* is an amount that the insured is required to spend on health care approved by the insurance company during the plan year before the insurance company pays for anything. For example, there may be a US$500 deductible per person and a US$1,500 total deductible for a family. Insurance companies contend that coinsurance, copayments, and deductibles discourage frivolous use of the health care system, thereby keeping insurance premiums lower.

In some countries, health care costs for individuals can be significant. Obviously, the risk associated with these costs varies considerably both across and within countries and must be considered as a risk to financial capital. Health factors typically have a significant impact on the premiums individuals pay for life, disability, and long-term care insurance.

Health risks manifest themselves in different ways over the life cycle and can have significant implications for human capital as well as for financial capital. For example, if a worker becomes disabled as a result of an accident or health incident, he or she may be unable to work while health expenses are incurred, resulting in a loss to both current assets and future earnings. The impact of a negative health event on human capital can be approximated by using the discounted cash flow framework and estimating the decline in projected cash flows along with an increase in the discount rate arising from increased earnings uncertainty. Illness and injury can also obviously have an adverse impact on life expectancy, potentially resulting in death before planned retirement. Furthermore, health issues involving non-earning members of the family can also be costly. There may be a need for special medical services, housing improvements, specialized vehicles, and other health-related expenses. In the case of the special needs of a child, the financial obligation could continue well beyond the parents' working lives, or even their actual lives.

Although long-term care is a part of the national health care system in some countries, such as Germany and Japan, in others, such as the United States, the cost of long-term care can represent a significant burden on financial capital. In countries where long-term care expenses are incurred by the individual, policies that provide insurance to protect against the cost of long-term care should be considered. Long-term care insurance is designed to cover a portion of the cost of necessities, such as home care, assisted living facilities, and nursing homes.

The risk and cost of long-term care may be considered both a health issue and an issue of insufficient assets at an advanced age—the latter being a component of the aforementioned longevity risk. The risks may also go beyond the immediate family unit. For example, one may have a parent who is not financially capable of paying for long-term care. An added risk is that inflation in long-term care costs (i.e., medical costs) has historically been higher than base inflation.

EXAMPLE 6   Individual Risk Exposures (1)

Describe premature death risk with respect to financial and human capital.

Solution: Within a personal financial planning context, premature death means that an individual dies before fully providing for his or her financial needs (and, if applicable, those of the family). By definition, at that point human capital is eliminated because the deceased individual can no longer generate income. To a lesser degree, there may also be an impact on financial capital. In addition to expenses associated with a funeral and burial, there may be a need for significant transitional funds or even a requirement to settle certain debts or business obligations upon the individual's death. Funds may also be required for education and/or training of the surviving spouse to generate income.

EXAMPLE 7   Individual Risk Exposures (2)

Describe longevity risk within the context of personal financial planning, and explain how it relates to human and financial capital.

Solution: Longevity risk refers to the possibility that an individual may live long enough to deplete his or her resources—to outlive one's money. Longevity risk relates primarily to financial capital—that is, spending one's retirement portfolio. But there is also an aspect of human capital in that one may address longevity risk, in part, by retiring later, thus expanding one's retirement portfolio and reducing the number of years to draw it down while increasing one's human capital.

---

6. LIFE INSURANCE: USES, TYPES, AND ELEMENTS

An individual's balance sheet provides a comprehensive overview of the asset categories held to fund current and future spending. Each of these categories involves some risk of a random loss. Managing these risks involves assessing possible loss exposures and considering market and non-market solutions to both address the possibility of and reduce the magnitude of a loss. We review the range of products that can be used to reduce these risks and present a strategy for analyzing the value of possible treatment options.

What are the consequences of risk? Effective risk management for individuals addresses the trade-offs between expected total wealth and security. Individual life-cycle planning involves assessing expected available resources and planning an optimal earning and spending path over a lifetime. But life does not always unfold as expected. A negative event can threaten the value of assets, and a loss in this value will cause total wealth (and expected future consumption) to fall. For each risk exposure, a solution exists to manage that risk exposure, whether through an altered portfolio allocation, a change in behavior, or the purchase of financial and/or insurance products. Each of these solutions involves a cost that generally results in a lower expected level of consumption over time. Shifting assets from risky to risk-free securities results in the loss of a risk premium. In the case of financial products, purchasing insurance trades a reduction in expected lifetime consumption for an increase in the stability of expected spending after a loss. In this section, we discuss the various types of insurance that individuals may use in financial planning. We then turn our attention to annuities, another financial product available to individuals.

6.1. Life Insurance

Life insurance protects against the loss of human capital for those who depend on an individual's future earnings. In this section, we provide an overview of the key uses of life insurance, the primary types of life insurance, the basic elements of a life insurance policy, how a life insurance policy is priced, and how to determine the appropriate amount of life insurance to purchase, if any.

6.1.1. Uses of Life Insurance

Life insurance provides a hedge against the risk of the premature death of an earner. A family's need for life insurance is related to the risk of the loss of the future earning power of an individual less the expected future spending of that individual. In each case, the risk associated with premature death can be mitigated by transferring the risk to a third party (i.e., by purchasing life insurance). The optimal amount of insurance to purchase is a function of both the expenses of the insurance hedge and the magnitude of the difference in expected lifetime utility with and without that family member.

Life insurance can also be an important estate-planning tool. A life insurance policy can provide immediate liquidity to a beneficiary without the delay involved in the legal process of settling an estate (i.e., distributing assets to beneficiaries) following the death of an individual. This liquidity can be particularly valuable if the estate contains illiquid assets or assets that are difficult to separate and distribute equitably among heirs.

Another possible use of life insurance is as a tax-sheltered savings instrument, notably in the United States. As mentioned previously in this reading, cash-value policies invest a portion of the premium in a tax-advantaged account that represents the difference between the current cost of providing insurance coverage and the premium. The mortality charge is the cost of providing life insurance, which increases with age (as does mortality risk). As mortality risk increases, the accumulated excess premium can be used to pay the increasingly higher costs of providing insurance protection. These excess premiums can be invested in a variety of instruments that can grow over time sheltered from taxation and can eventually be cashed out without paying for older-age life insurance protection.

6.1.2. Types of Life Insurance

There are two main types of life insurance: temporary and permanent. For the purposes of this reading, both types of life insurance are assumed to be non-cancelable: The policy lapses only at the end of the term (for temporary life insurance) or upon death (for permanent life insurance).

Temporary life insurance provides insurance for a certain period of time specified at purchase. This type of coverage is commonly referred to as "term" life insurance. If the individual survives until the end of the period (e.g., 20 years), the policy will terminate unless it can be automatically renewed. Generally, premiums for term life insurance either remain level over the insured period (e.g., 20 years) or increase over the period as mortality risk increases. The cost of term insurance is less than that of permanent insurance, and the cost per year is less for shorter insured periods (e.g., 10 years versus 20 years), again because of increasing mortality risk.

Permanent life insurance provides lifetime coverage, assuming the premiums are paid over the entire period. Policy premiums for permanent life insurance are usually fixed, and there is generally some underlying cash value associated with a permanent insurance policy. There are several types of permanent life insurance that vary by region. Here, we will discuss the two most common types of permanent life insurance: *whole life insurance* and *universal life insurance*.

Whole life insurance remains in force for an insured's entire life (hence the name). Whole life insurance generally requires regular, ongoing fixed premiums, which are typically paid annually, although monthly, quarterly, and semiannual payment options also exist. Failure to pay premiums can result in the lapse of the insurance policy. There is generally a cash value associated with a whole life insurance policy that may be accessed if the insured chooses to do so. The non-cancelability of whole life insurance can make this type of policy appealing to purchase at younger ages, when an individual is typically healthier. Whole life insurance policies can be participating or non-participating. Participating life insurance policies allow potential growth at a higher rate than the guaranteed value, based on the profits of the insurance company. A non-participating policy is one with fixed values: The benefits will not change based on the profits and experience of the insurance company. Universal life insurance is constructed to provide more flexibility than whole life insurance. The policy owner, generally the insured, has the ability to pay higher or lower premium payments and often has more options for investing the cash value. The insurance will stay in force as long as the premiums paid or the cash value is enough to cover the policy expenses of the provider.

Many permanent life insurance policies have a "non-forfeiture clause," whereby the policy owner has the option to receive some portion of the benefits if premium payments are missed (i.e., before the policy lapses). The scenarios permitted by a non-forfeiture clause generally include a cash surrender option (whereby the existing cash value is paid out), a reduced paid-up option (whereby the cash value is used to purchase a single-premium whole life insurance policy), and an extended term option (whereby the cash value is used to purchase a term insurance policy, generally with the same face value as the previous policy).

In addition, a number of potential "riders" can be added to both temporary and permanent life insurance policies. Riders are modifications that add some risk mitigation beyond the basic policy. One example of a common rider is an "accidental death" rider (also referred to as accidental death and dismemberment, or AD&D), which increases the payout if the insured dies or becomes dismembered from an accident. Other common riders include an accelerated death benefit (which may allow insured parties who have been diagnosed as terminally ill to collect all or part of the death benefit while they are still alive), guaranteed insurability (which allows the owner to purchase more insurance in the future at certain predefined intervals), and a waiver of premium (whereby future premiums are waived if the insured becomes disabled). The value of the rider will depend on the level of protection against an unexpected decline in consumption not otherwise provided by a basic policy. An additional way for life insurance policyholders to access the value of the policy is the option to sell the policy to a third party, which is often called a viatical settlement. After purchasing the policy, the third party becomes responsible for paying the premiums and will receive the death benefit when the insured dies.

6.1.3. Basic Elements of a Life Insurance Policy
The basic elements of a life insurance policy include

- the term and type of the policy (e.g., a 20-year temporary insurance policy),
- the amount of benefits (e.g., £100,000),

- limitations under which the death benefit could be withheld (e.g., if death is by suicide within two years of issuance),
- the contestability period (the period during which the insurance company can investigate and deny claims),
- the identity (name, age, gender) of the insured,
- the policy owner,
- the beneficiary or beneficiaries,
- the premium schedule (the amount and frequency of premiums due), and
- modifications to coverage in any riders to the policy.

In addition, for a life insurance policy to be valid, the policy owner generally needs to have an insurable interest in the life of the insured. Thus, the presence of an insurable interest is a basic element of an insurance policy as well.

The insured, the policy owner, the beneficiary (or beneficiaries), and the insurer are the four primary parties involved in any life insurance policy. The insured is the individual whose death triggers the insurance payment. The policy owner is the person who owns the life insurance policy and is responsible for paying premiums. The beneficiary is the individual (or entity) who will receive the proceeds from the life insurance policy when the insured passes away. The actual beneficiary of a jointly owned life insurance policy may be determined by the order of death of the prospective beneficiaries (e.g., a husband and a wife). Lastly, the insurer is the insurance company that writes the policy and is responsible for paying the death benefit. The amount payable to the beneficiary is typically referred to as the "face value" of the life insurance policy.

For most life insurance policies, the policy owner and the insured are the same person. In certain instances, however, a policy owner may choose to obtain insurance to protect against a loss in economic value from the death of another individual. For example, as part of a divorce, one ex-spouse may purchase life insurance on the other ex-spouse. Similarly, a business may purchase life insurance on a key executive under the assumption that the business would be negatively affected by that executive's death.

When the insured is not the policy owner, the policy owner must have an "insurable interest" in the life of the insured. Insurable interest prevents individuals from gambling on the lives of strangers and removes any incentive to hasten the insured person's demise. An insurable interest means that the policy owner must derive some type of benefit from the continued survival of the individual that would be negatively affected should that individual pass away. For example, a spouse has an insurable interest because he or she relies on the income or household services of the other spouse. A business has an insurable interest in key executives who are essential to the ongoing operations of the business.

Life insurance benefits are payable to the beneficiary upon the death of the insured. Usually, some form of documentation or proof of death is required by the life insurance company, such as a death certificate, before benefits are paid to the beneficiary. Death benefits from a life insurance policy can be paid in various forms, such as a lump sum or an annuity, although lump sums are generally more common.

There may be certain situations in which a life insurance company would not be required to pay a benefit. For example, if the insured commits suicide within some predetermined period after purchasing the policy (e.g., two years), or if the insured made material misrepresentations relating to his or her health and/or financial condition during the application process, benefits may not be payable. There is often a maximum contestability period during which the insurer has a legal right to contest the death benefit, after which the insurer cannot deny the claim even if it involves suicide and/or material misstatement.

EXAMPLE 8   Elements of a Life Insurance Policy

Describe the concept of insurable interest for life insurance.

Solution: An insurable interest means that the policy owner must derive some type of benefit from the continued survival of the insured that would be negatively affected should the insured pass away. For example, an individual may rely on a spouse for his or her financial well-being. If the spouse dies, income is no longer generated, leading to financial problems. Another example is a business that may have an insurable interest in a key employee who generates large sales volumes. The purpose of an insurable interest is to prevent individuals from gambling on the lives of others or from having a financial reason to arrange the death of the insured.

---

7. LIFE INSURANCE: PRICING, POLICY COST COMPARISON, AND DETERMINING AMOUNT NEEDED

There are a number of factors that determine how an insurer prices life insurance, and there are many different types of life insurance policies. Although the details of the actuarial calculations are beyond the scope of this reading, it is useful to understand the basic concepts of life insurance pricing.

In general, there are three key considerations in the pricing of life insurance: mortality expectations, a discount rate, and loading.

7.1. Mortality Expectations

One of the most important factors in determining the price for life insurance is the expected mortality of the insured individual (i.e., how long the person is expected to live). Actuaries at insurance companies estimate mortality based on both historical data and future mortality expectations. Generally speaking, life expectancies in most regions of the world have been increasing. Certain attributes, such as age and gender, are obvious factors in evaluating life expectancy. Whether the applicant is a smoker (or has other health risks) is another important factor because smoking is associated with deadly diseases. Exhibit 5 shows an example of the probability of men and women (both smokers and non-smokers) dying at various ages, although these numbers will vary considerably in different countries.

Rather than use a generalized mortality table, life insurance company actuaries typically make adjustments to consider additional factors. The underwriting process serves to categorize applicants according to their perceived riskiness, consistent with the actuaries' specifications. The resulting customized tables consider applicants' health history, particularly conditions that are associated with shorter-than-average life expectancy, such as cancer and heart disease. If an applicant's parents or siblings died at a relatively early age from certain diseases, that applicant may be considered a bigger risk. Excess weight is another health issue leading to shorter life expectancies. Certain activities, such as scuba diving and flying personal aircraft, are deemed to increase mortality risk also. All of these underwriting factors can be collected on a typical life insurance application, and the salesperson who gathers this information can be considered the first level of the underwriting process.

For larger policies, insurance companies may require a physical examination, performed by an insurer-paid nurse or physician, and the examination could include blood pressure, cholesterol and other blood analysis, an electrocardiogram, and other tests. All of these factors can be used to categorize applicants in tables that discriminate among standard risks, preferred (lower) risks, and high risks, and the cost to the insured can vary considerably. Of course, some people have a sufficient number of factors, or serious-enough factors, to make them uninsurable. This underwriting process reduces the likelihood of *adverse selection*. Adverse selection refers to the fact that individuals who know that they have higher-than-average risk are more likely to apply for life insurance. Unless the insurance company performs its underwriting well, mortality experience can be worse than projected.

The Probability of Dying at Certain Ages

Exhibit 5 provides information about the mortality (i.e., the probability of dying) for males and females at different ages.[2] The cost of life insurance is based on the probability that the insured will die during the duration of the policy. The table helps demonstrate why younger (versus older) individuals, females (versus males), and non-smokers (versus smokers) tend to pay less for life insurance—the expected probability of dying in a given year is lower.

EXHIBIT 5   Mortality of Males and Females at Certain Ages

| | Male | | | Female | | |
Age	Composite	Non-Smoker	Smoker	Composite	Non-Smoker	Smoker
35	0.14%	0.09%	0.14%	0.08%	0.07%	0.10%
40	0.21%	0.15%	0.24%	0.12%	0.10%	0.17%
45	0.26%	0.19%	0.35%	0.14%	0.11%	0.23%
50	0.30%	0.23%	0.48%	0.21%	0.15%	0.37%
55	0.42%	0.35%	0.74%	0.32%	0.25%	0.60%
60	0.67%	0.50%	1.21%	0.52%	0.37%	1.00%
65	1.12%	0.84%	2.08%	0.88%	0.59%	1.66%
70	1.81%	1.40%	3.35%	1.48%	0.95%	2.61%
75	3.18%	2.58%	5.34%	2.45%	1.71%	3.93%
80	5.38%	4.65%	7.56%	4.23%	3.33%	6.27%
85	9.71%	8.80%	11.75%	7.77%	6.54%	10.74%
90	17.41%	16.55%	19.04%	13.79%	12.27%	17.34%
95	25.49%	25.16%	26.09%	21.96%	20.82%	24.65%

---

[2]Data are based on the American Academy of Actuaries' 2017 Commissioners Standard Ordinary (CSO) Tables. https://www.soa.org/experience-studies/2015/2017-cso-tables/ accessed 21 November 2018

EXAMPLE 9 Mortality Expectations

If a given male and female are the same age and have equivalent health profiles, evaluate which one should expect to pay more for life insurance.

Solution: A key pricing component of life insurance is expected mortality. From Exhibit 5, one can see that the chance of death for females across the age spectrum is less than it is for males of the same age. Therefore, all else being equal, females should expect to pay less than males for the equivalent life insurance.

7.2. Calculation of the Net Premium and Gross Premium

The *net premium* of a life insurance policy represents the discounted value of the future death benefit. To illustrate a simplified calculation of the net premium, we will consider the example of a one-year, non-renewable term life insurance policy with a death benefit of US$100,000 for Ramon, a 40-year-old non-smoking male. The insurance company insures thousands of people with characteristics like Ramon's. Thus, the life insurance company will experience a predictable distribution of death benefit payments in a given year, although it does not know who among its customers will die during that year.

Premiums are collected at the beginning of the year, and for simplicity, we will assume that death benefit payments occur at the end of the year. As shown in Exhibit 5, and in the absence of other underwriting information, Ramon has a probability of 0.15% of dying within the year. Although the life insurance company will pay a death benefit of either US$100,000 or US$0, we can calculate an expected outflow at the end of the year of US$150, which equals $(0.0015 \times US\$100,000) + (0.9985 \times US\$0)$. Finally, a discount rate, or interest factor, representing an assumption of the insurance company's return on its portfolio, is applied to the expected outflow. Assuming a 5.5% rate, US$150 is discounted by one year to a present value of US$142.18 (US$150/1.055), which is the net premium.

As mentioned previously, life insurance companies typically offer level term policies, under which the insured can pay equal annual premiums for a specified number of years—for example, a five-year level term policy. The calculation still requires discounting expected future death benefit payments back to the present, but we must also consider the fact that the individuals who die within the five-year period will not be paying premiums for the remaining outstanding term.

To determine what the insurance company would actually charge Ramon for the one-year policy, the insurer must consider other factors to calculate the *gross premium*. The gross premium adds a *load* to the net premium, allowing for expenses and a projected profit for the insurance company.

Expenses are incurred by the insurer for both writing a life insurance policy and managing it on an ongoing basis. Expenses associated with writing a life insurance policy include the costs of the underwriting process, which potentially include a sales commission to the agent who sold the policy and the cost of a physical exam. Ongoing expenses include overhead and administrative expenses associated with monitoring the policy, ensuring that premiums are paid on a timely basis, and verifying a potential death claim. Furthermore, most companies provide a low percentage "renewal commission" for the first years of the policy, which encourages the agent to provide needed advice to the policy owner and to try to keep the policy owner from terminating the policy.

Life insurers can be divided into two groups—stock companies and mutual companies. Stock companies are similar to other corporations in that they are owned by shareholders, have a profit motive, and are expected to provide a return to those shareholders. Within the constraints of supply and demand for their product, stock life insurance companies add a projected profit as a part of the load in pricing their policies. In contrast, mutual companies are owned by the policy owners themselves and there is no profit motive. Mutual companies typically charge a gross premium that is somewhat higher than the net premium plus expenses, even though mutual companies do not have profits per se. Then, if mortality experience, expenses, and/or investment returns are better than projected, the amount by which the gross premium exceeds the net premium plus expenses may be paid back to the policy owners as a policy dividend, which is considered a return of premium to the policy owner rather than income.

Premiums for level term policies are higher than those for annually renewable (one-year) policies in the early years. But premiums are lower in the later years of the policies—most notably for longer periods, such as a 20-year level term—because annually renewable term policies often have rapidly increasing premiums. As can be seen in Exhibit 5 earlier in this section, mortality rates begin accelerating rather quickly after age 40. Life insurers sometimes offer low initial rates on annually renewable policies with the expectation that many purchasers of these policies will simply pay the increasing premiums.

Some consumers buy an annually renewable term policy with the intention of taking advantage of the "loss-leader" pricing in the early years and then, when rates rise too much, switching to another company that has a lower premium at the newly attained age. Unfortunately, there is risk in this strategy in that a health issue or accident could make that individual uninsurable, leaving him or her with an annually renewable policy that has an escalating premium.

EXAMPLE 10   Life Insurance Pricing

Discuss the three most relevant elements of life insurance pricing.

Solution: The three most relevant considerations in pricing life insurance are mortality expectations, the discount rate, and loading.

- Mortality expectations: The insurer is concerned about the probability that the insured will die within the term of the policy. Actuaries evaluate mortality expectations based on historical experience, considering such factors as age and gender, the longevity of parents, blood pressure, cholesterol, whether the insured is a smoker, and whether the insured has had any diseases or injuries that are likely to lead to death during the policy term.
- Discount rate: A discount rate, or interest factor, representing an assumption of the insurance company's return on its portfolio, is applied to the expected outflow.
- Loading: After calculating the net premium for a policy, which may be considered the pure price of the insurance, the insurance company adjusts the premium upward to allow for expenses and profit. This adjustment is the load, and the process is called loading.

7.3. Cash Values and Policy Reserves

As noted earlier, although initial premiums are higher, whole life policies offer the advantage of level premiums and an accumulation of cash value within the policy that (1) can be withdrawn by the policy owner when the policy endows (or matures) or when he or she terminates the policy or (2) can be borrowed as a loan while keeping the policy in force. These cash values build up very slowly in the early years, during which the company is making up for its expenses. For example, just the first-year commission on a whole life policy could be equivalent to 100% of the first-year premium; thus, the company is "in the hole" for the first few years and trying to recover the initial expenses. The commissions decline in subsequent early years as the effort required by a sales agent to service the policy is reduced.

Exhibit 6 shows a representation of the build-up of cash value within a whole life policy that endows at a specified age, perhaps age 100. It is important to recognize the interrelationship of the following amounts:

- The premium stays constant.
- The face value stays constant.
- The cash value increases.
- The insurance value decreases.

Essentially, as cash values increase and the insurance value decreases, the ongoing premium is paying for less and less life insurance.

EXHIBIT 6   Build-up of Cash Value in a Whole Life Insurance Policy

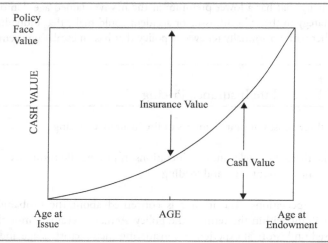

To the extent that the life insurance is intended to replace human capital, it may become unnecessary after the individual's working years are finished. Enough financial capital may have been accrued to make even the immediate death expenses payable from other funds without the need for life insurance. The existence of increasing cash values within a policy adds another dimension to the decision whether to terminate a policy.

Note also that life insurers are typically required by regulators to maintain *policy reserves*, which are a liability on the insurance company's balance sheet. Policy reserves become especially important for whole life policies. With a whole life policy, the insurance company specifies an age at which the policy's face value will be paid as an endowment to the policy owner if the insured person has not died by that time. The insurance company must accumulate reserves during the life of the policy to be able to make that payment. The policy reserve can be defined as follows: Policy reserve = Present value of future benefits – Present value of future net premiums. From the equation, we can infer that as the insured person gets older, the present value of the future death benefit (or the cash value that could be withdrawn) gets larger. At the same time, the present value of the future net premiums gets smaller because fewer premiums remain. Thus, the policy reserves must grow larger over time until, at the time of endowment, the reserves equal the present value of the future benefits. (See Rejda and McNamara 2014, p. 272.)

7.4. Consumer Comparisons of Life Insurance Costs

It may seem easy to compare the cost of two different policies of equal size by simply looking at the first year's premiums. Although this may be the case with term policies, comparing the cost of two whole life insurance policies is much more complex because, for example, one policy may have larger premiums but also faster growth of cash values.

Consumer and/or governmental organizations may provide comparisons of policies from various life insurance companies based on projected data, including assumptions about future dividends and cash values. In many jurisdictions, regulations require that life insurance companies provide consumers with cost data that consider the time value of money and assume a specified number of years. The two most popular indexes for comparison are the *net payment cost index* and the *surrender cost index*, both of which calculate a cost per year per thousand dollars of life insurance coverage under different sets of assumptions. Both methods assume a specific time period, such as 20 years, and a specific compounding discount rate, such as 5%.

The net payment cost index assumes that the insured person will die at the end of a specified period, such as 20 years. Calculation of the net payment cost index includes the following steps:

A. Calculate the future value of an annuity due of an amount equal to the premium, compounded at a 5% discount rate for 20 years. An annuity due—an annuity for which the premium payment is received at the beginning of the period (versus an ordinary annuity, for which the premium payment is received at the end of the period)—is used because premiums are paid at the beginning of the period.

B. Calculate the future value of an ordinary annuity of an amount equal to the projected annual dividend (if any), compounded at 5% for 20 years. An ordinary annuity is used because dividend payments are made at the end of the period.

C. Subtract B from A to get the 20-year insurance cost.

D. Calculate the payments for a 20-year annuity due with a future value equal to C and a discount rate of 5%. This amount is the interest-adjusted cost per year. Again, an annuity due is used because premium payments occur at the beginning of the year.

E. Divide by the number of thousand dollars of face value.

The surrender cost index assumes that the policy will be surrendered at the end of the period and that the policy owner will receive the projected cash value. Calculation of the surrender cost index includes the following steps:

A. Calculate the future value of an annuity due of an amount equal to the premium, compounded at 5% for 20 years. We use an annuity due here for the same reason indicated for the net payment cost index.

B. Calculate the future value of an ordinary annuity of an amount equal to the projected annual dividend (if any), compounded at 5% for 20 years. We use an ordinary annuity here for the same reason indicated for the net payment cost index.

C. Subtract B and the Year 20 projected cash value from A to get the 20-year insurance cost.

D. Calculate the payments for a 20-year annuity due with a future value equal to C and a discount rate of 5%. This amount is the interest-adjusted cost per year.

E. Divide by the number of thousand dollars of face value.

For example, a US$100,000 face value whole life policy has an annual premium of US$2,000, paid at the beginning of the year. Policy dividends of US$500 per year are anticipated, payable at year-end. A cash value of US$22,500 is projected for the end of Year 20.

Net Payment Cost Index Calculation

Future value of premiums (annuity due): US$2,000 annual payment, 20 years, 5%	US$69,439
Future value of dividends (ordinary annuity): US$500 annual payment, 20 years, 5%	−16,533
20-year insurance cost	US$52,906
Annual payments for 20-year insurance cost (annuity due): 20 years, 5%	1,524
Divide by US$ thousands of face value	÷ 100
Net Payment Cost Index, cost per US$ thousand per year	US$15.24

Surrender Cost Index Calculation

Future value of premiums (annuity due): US$2,000 annual payment, 20 years, 5%	US$69,439
Future value of dividends (ordinary annuity): US$500 annual payment, 20 years, 5%	−16,533
20-year cash value (given above)	−22,500
20-year insurance cost	US$30,406
Annual payments for 20-year insurance cost (annuity due): 20 years, 5%	876
Divide by US$ thousands of face value	÷ 100
Surrender Cost Index, cost per US$ thousand per year	US$8.76

The major benefit of these indexes is the ease of comparing policies of the same type. Generally speaking, the lower the index value is, the better the value. However, policies do not always perform as projected. If the insurance company's actual return, expense, and/or mortality experiences are worse than projected, the *ex post* indexes could be larger.

Calculating Life Insurance Needs

Two distinctly different methods are commonly used to calculate the amount of life insurance needed. The *human life value* method is consistent with the concept of human capital. It involves replacing the estimated net contribution to family finances that the insured would generate if that individual did not die during his or her projected earning life. In general, this calculation involves estimating future income that would be generated by the insured, offset by incremental expenses that would be attributable to the insured. The net amounts in each year are then discounted back to the present to calculate the amount of insurance needed. An amount may be added to cover so-called "final expenses," such as funeral and other death expenses.

The *needs analysis* method, as the name implies, is concerned with meeting the financial needs of the family. Needs analysis typically involves estimating living expenses for survivors for an appropriate amount of time, typically until adulthood for surviving children and to projected life expectancy for a surviving spouse. Also included are education costs, final expenses, and any other special expenses. These amounts are discounted back to the present to calculate the total funds needed. Any assets available are subtracted, and the amount remaining is the life insurance needed.

Both the human life value and needs analysis methods are demonstrated in detail in Section 7.5.

7.5. How Much Life Insurance Does One Need?

The optimal amount of life insurance for an individual will vary based on a number of factors. Some individuals with no dependents or bequest goals may not need any insurance, whereas an individual with young children and a non-working spouse may need a significant amount of life insurance. In this section, we outline some of the key considerations to use when determining how much life insurance to purchase.

The primary purpose of life insurance is to replace the present value of future earnings. A 65-year-old individual without children will experience an emotional loss from the premature death of a spouse, as well as some additional short-term expenses, but the economic loss will be modest (or even negative if expected spending needs fall in retirement). Other reasons to consider life insurance include the following:

- *Immediate financial expenses:* These include direct costs associated with death, such as funeral and legal expenses. Although the costs associated vary by region, funerals can be expensive and represent a potentially sizable financial burden on the family. Additional immediate financial expenses could include covering the short-term loss of wages.
- *Legacy goals:* In addition to income replacement, an individual may use life insurance to achieve certain legacy goals. These can include gifts to charities, bequests to family members, and estate planning.

To calculate the amount of insurance needed, one should estimate the amount of money needed to restore the present value of expected earnings that would have occurred if the earner remained alive. Because the purpose of life insurance is to smooth consumption by preventing a drop in spending from an unexpected premature death, the value of life insurance should be equal to the difference in household spending with and without the human capital of the earner. An accurate calculation will adjust household spending needs downward to compensate for the reduction in household size, in addition to estimating the present value of the expected human capital of the insured. The cost of the insurance is obviously an important consideration as well.

Another important consideration when purchasing life insurance is the insurance company's ability to meet its financial obligations. Company financial strength is evaluated by various rating agencies and is important because it provides an indication of the ability of the insurer to meet its obligations and to weather adverse market conditions.

> ## EXAMPLE 11   Appropriateness of Life Insurance
>
> Consider two potential life insurance candidates: (1) a 40-year-old doctor who is married with two young children, substantial student loans, and sizable earnings; and (2) a 35-year-old single person with a moderate amount of financial wealth. Based on the information presented, which person would be a more appropriate candidate for life insurance and why?
>
> *Solution:* The first individual is a much more appropriate candidate for life insurance. Given that the doctor has substantial debt and high earnings, the value of this individual's earnings potential (human capital) is significant. Likewise, with two young children, there is a high dependence on future earnings, representing another reason the earnings potential should be hedged with life insurance. In contrast, the 35-year-old does not have any beneficiaries that would need to be supported. But the younger individual may want to consider purchasing insurance while he or she is still insurable.

8. OTHER TYPES OF INSURANCE

Disability income insurance is designed to mitigate earnings risk as a result of a disability, which refers to the risk that an individual becomes less than fully employed because of a physical injury, disease, or other impairment. Many disabilities for gainfully employed individuals are relatively short rather than lifelong, but the financial disaster associated with the possibility of a lifelong disability can be addressed in a comprehensive risk management plan.

What is meant by disability? The definition of disability used by insurance providers typically specifies one of the following:

- Inability to perform the important duties of one's regular occupation
- Inability to perform the important duties of any occupation for which one is suited by education and experience
- Inability to perform the duties of any occupation

Consider a surgeon who loses the use of his or her dominant hand in an accident. By the first definition, this individual would likely be deemed fully disabled. By the second definition, this individual might be able to work as a general practitioner physician. By the third definition above, as long as the individual was able to be employed (e.g., as a professor at a medical school), he or she might not be considered disabled. For most people, especially professionals with specialized skills, policies that use the first definition are best, even though they are more expensive. In general, a disability income insurance policy will specify that some percentage of the difference between the pre-injury income and the post-injury income would be paid to the insured.

As with all insurance policies, disability income insurance policy standards vary widely in different jurisdictions and even for different companies. For most policies, the premium is fixed and based on the age of the insured at the time of policy issue, and the policies are underwritten for the health and occupation of the insured. Disability income coverage is available

both through individual policies and through many employers. Disability income policies usually include provisions for partial and residual disability. Partial disability means that although
the insured cannot perform all the duties of his or her occupation, the individual can perform enough to remain employed, albeit at a lower income. Partial disability provisions pay a
reduced benefit, providing a financial incentive for the insured to get back to work as soon as
possible. Residual disability refers to the possibility that although the insured can perform all
the duties of his or her occupation, the individual cannot earn as much money as before. Consider the surgeon who can still perform operations but because of a back injury cannot perform
as many surgeries per day as before the injury. The reduction in income would be addressed by
the residual disability benefit, which is smaller than the benefit for full disability.

Typically, insurers will cover compensation only up to specific amounts. Furthermore,
they will insure only up to a specific percentage of compensation, perhaps 60%–80%, for two
reasons. First, if the insured becomes disabled, other expenses decrease, such as certain payroll
taxes, commuting costs, clothing, and food; thus, full replacement is not necessary. Second,
there is a greater chance for fraudulent claims if the disability income payments are close to the
normal compensation.

Other aspects of disability income insurance include the following:

- The *benefit period* specifies how long payments will be made. A specified number of years
  may be stated in the policy, but typically, the benefit period lasts until normal retirement
  age, which varies globally between approximately 55 and 70. The age limit discourages the
  filing of fraudulent claims intended to substitute disability benefits for retirement income.
  Usually, a minimum number of years of benefits, perhaps five, is specified in case the individual should become disabled within that many years of the specified age. For example,
  a 62-year-old who becomes disabled would receive benefits to age 67. This provision encourages individuals to maintain their policies all the way to retirement.
- The *elimination period*, or *waiting period*, specifies the number of days the insured must be
  disabled before payments begin being made. Naturally, the shorter the elimination period,
  the higher the premiums. A typical elimination period for policies in the United States is
  90 days.
- The *rehabilitation clause* provides payments for physical therapy and related services to help
  the disabled person rejoin the workforce as soon as possible.
- The *waiver of premium* clause specifies that premiums need not be paid if the insured
  becomes disabled, and it often includes a reimbursement of premiums during the elimination period.
- The *option to purchase additional insurance rider* allows the insured to increase coverage without further proof of insurability, albeit at the rate appropriate for the insured's current age.
- A *non-cancelable and guaranteed renewable policy* guarantees that the policy will be
  renewed annually as long as premiums are paid and that there will be no changes to
  premiums or promised disability benefits until, usually, age 65. Even if employment
  income declines during the working life, the monthly benefit will remain at the level
  specified in the policy.
- A *non-cancelable* policy cannot be canceled as long as premiums are paid, but the insurer can
  increase premiums for the entire underwriting class that includes the insured. This version
  is less expensive than a non-cancelable and guaranteed renewable policy, but one should be
  aware that insurance companies with significant loss experience are likely to raise rates.
- Inflation adjustments to benefits may be provided by a *cost of living rider*, which will adjust
  benefits with an accepted index or by a specified percentage per year.

Note that, as with virtually all insurance types, any provision in a disability insurance policy that appears advantageous to the insured party will likely increase the premium.

8.1. Property Insurance

Property insurance is used by individuals to manage property risk, which was discussed earlier in the reading. Although property insurance coverage applies to a multitude of situations, for most individuals, the primary areas to cover are the home/residence and the automobile.

8.1.1. Homeowner's Insurance

With regard to a residence, homeowner's insurance is designed to address risks associated with home ownership as well as risks associated with personal property and liability. Renter's insurance is similar to homeowner's insurance but without coverage on the structure. Property insurance protects the insured in case of loss related to his or her property. As we discussed earlier, there are, of course, many different possible events relating to property risk, such as a house fire, an automobile collision, a stolen television, or a lost necklace.

Homeowner's policies may be specified as "all-risks," which means that all risks are included except those specified, or as "named-risks," which means that only those risks specifically listed are covered. All-risks policies are generally more costly. Homeowner's insurance may also be available in either of two versions, based on the way a claim is settled. A policy based on *replacement cost* will reimburse the insured person for the amount required to repair a damaged item or replace a lost, destroyed, or stolen item with a new item of similar quality at current prices. A policy based on *actual cash value* will reimburse the insured person for the replacement cost less depreciation. The replacement cost version is a more expensive policy.

As mentioned earlier in the reading, a *deductible* is the amount of a loss that must be absorbed by the policy owner before the insurance company will make any payment. Deductibles represent a form of active risk retention. If the homeowner's policy has a US$1,000 deductible and there is hail damage of $10,000, the homeowner must pay the first $1,000 and the insurance company would be liable for the remaining $9,000. Deductibles ensure that the homeowner retains some responsibility (and risk) associated with a loss.

As part of their business models, insurance companies price their policies to encourage the use of higher deductibles. For the consumer, this means that a cost–benefit analysis should be performed when determining the optimal deductible level because a larger deductible likely means a lower insurance premium. Imagine that a policy with a $1,000 deductible for a given property has an annual premium of $2,000 and a policy with a $500 deductible has an annual premium of $2,100. The consumer should recognize that selecting the second policy means essentially paying $100 more for a $1,000 insurance policy that has a $500 deductible. An alternative way of looking at it is to ask whether it is worth $100 to insure the second $500 of loss.

Some individuals underinsure their homes to save money, but they do so at their own risk. If a potential loss could exceed the amount of insurance, that individual is retaining risk of that excess amount, either consciously or unconsciously. For individuals who have significant wealth, whose home is a relatively small percentage of their net worth, and who have adequate liquidity, it may make sense to self-insure these types of risks (i.e., maintain only a limited amount of homeowner's insurance or own a policy with a very high deductible).

Mortgage lenders typically require that the homeowner carry enough insurance that if the mortgagor dies, a total loss would trigger payment of an amount at least equal to the outstanding mortgage. Because mortgage balances typically decline over time, insurance contracts covering the outstanding mortgage can be purchased with a decreasing face value and decreasing premiums.

Insurance companies have a different interest from that of mortgage lenders. They want the house to be insured for its full value—less the value of the land because the land will not be destroyed—or at least a high percentage of full value. Premiums are calculated based on this assumption. Although the insurance company is obligated to pay only the face value of the policy in the case of a total loss, it is at a disadvantage if partial losses occur.

Consider a $500,000 (replacement cost) home that, because inflation in home prices has been ignored, is insured for only $250,000. In the absence of other contractual restrictions, if the house sustains $250,000 of damage in a fire, the insurance company would have to pay the entire face value of the policy even though the house sustained only a 50% loss. From the company's standpoint, it should have been receiving the larger premiums for a $500,000 house to pay $250,000 for a 50% loss.

To offset this dilemma, losses are reimbursed at a lower rate if the home is underinsured. It is common for an insurance company to reduce payments if the home is insured for less than 80% of its replacement cost.

Homeowners' liability risks are typically addressed within the insurance policy on the home. That is, there is a provision in the policy for liability coverage for a specified amount in case, for example, a visitor is injured in an accident at the home. This coverage excludes professional liability, such as physicians' malpractice insurance, and business liability, which should be covered with separate policies. The homeowner's policy also excludes liability resulting from intentional acts—for example, throwing a chair through a neighbor's window.

Aside from purchasing homeowner's insurance, one can address homeowner risk through other risk management techniques. The following are some examples:

- Risk of theft of valuable financial documents can be avoided by storing them in a bank's safe deposit box.
- Risk of overall theft can be reduced through the use of high-quality locks, alarms, and surveillance systems.
- Risk of loss or corruption of electronic data can be avoided by storing backups offsite.
- Risk of damage to electronic equipment from a power surge can be reduced by installing surge protectors.
- Risk of loss from fire can be reduced through the use of fire-resistant building materials—and through the easy availability of fire extinguishers.

8.1.2. Automobile Insurance

Automobile property risk can also be addressed through various risk management methods. For example, one might avoid driving in inclement weather conditions. One might require passengers to wear seat belts, reducing their likelihood of injury. One might use common, frequently promoted safe driving techniques or even take alternate routes that are less risky. If buying a new car, one might consider a vehicle with a backup camera and lane-change warning system.

Automobile insurance rates are primarily based on the value of the automobile and the primary operator's age and driving record. Other factors are also included but vary considerably among jurisdictions. Coverages for damage to the automobile are typically divided into two parts. *Collision coverage* is for damage from an accident, and *comprehensive coverage* is for damage from other sources, such as glass breakage, hail, and theft. There may also be coverage available in case one's automobile is damaged by an uninsured or underinsured driver, as well as medical coverage for passengers in the insured's automobile. Insurance companies normally insure automobiles only up to the cost of replacing the automobile with one of the same make and model and in the same condition. If the cost to repair the automobile exceeds its actual cash value, the insurance company typically reimburses only the amount of the actual cash value.

As with homeowner's insurance, automobile owners typically retain some risk through the use of deductibles or by avoiding collision and comprehensive coverage. Again, selecting the amount of the deductible or rejecting property coverage involves a simple cost–benefit analysis. If the individual is able to bear the wealth risk and to afford repairs or a new car if damage occurs, then risk retention will increase expected wealth over time.

Liability associated with automobiles is typically covered under the same policy, with specified limits for bodily injury and property damage. In most countries, some level of third-party coverage is mandatory and additional insurance may be purchased to increase the level of protection. Liability limits often vary for different types of loss—for example, higher limits to cover the costs of physical injury and separate limits to cover the loss of property. If actual liability in an accident exceeds these amounts, the automobile owner is responsible for the remainder.

8.2. Health/Medical Insurance

Any discussion of **health insurance** is highly dependent on the country of residence. In certain countries, health care is governmentally funded and there is no private health insurance. In others, there is a two-tiered system, with governmental coverage for everyone and upgraded coverage for additional payments.

In the United States, one type of insurance approach is called an *indemnity plan*, which allows the insured to go to essentially any medical service provider, but the insured must pay a specified percentage of the "reasonable and customary" fees. Another type of plan is a *preferred provider organization* (PPO), which is a large network of physicians and other medical service providers that charge lower prices to individuals within the plan than to individuals who obtain care on their own. A third type of plan is a *health maintenance organization* (HMO), which allows office visits at no, or very little, cost to encourage individuals to seek help for small medical problems before they become more serious.

Comprehensive major medical insurance covers the vast majority of health care expenses, such as physicians' fees, surgical fees, hospitalization, laboratory fees, x-rays, magnetic resonance imaging (MRIs), and most other expenses that are "reasonable and customary" and part of generally accepted medical care. Aside from the premiums for the actual coverage, major medical insurance includes several other provisions that can substantially influence the total financial outlay. Below are some of the key terms of most health (medical) insurance plans:

- *Deductibles* refer to the amount of health care expenses that the insured person must pay in a year before any expense reimbursement is paid by the insurance company.
- *Coinsurance* specifies the percentage of any expense that the insurance company will pay, often 80%, with the insured person responsible for the remainder.
- *Copayments* are fixed payments that the insured must make for a particular service, such as a doctor's office visit.

- *Maximum out-of-pocket expense* refers to the total amount of expenses incurred within a year beyond which the insurance company pays 100%. It is often expressed in terms of an individual maximum and a family maximum. This concept is often referred to as a stop-loss limit.
- *Maximum yearly benefit* refers to the maximum amount that the insurance company will pay in a year.
- *Maximum lifetime benefit* refers to the maximum amount that the insurance company will pay over an individual's lifetime.
- *Preexisting conditions* refer to health conditions that the insured had when applying for insurance. They may or may not be covered by the insurance company, depending on the policy, laws, and regulations.
- *Preadmission certification* refers to a requirement that the insured receive approval from the insurer before a scheduled (non-emergency) hospital stay or treatment.

Of course, the cost of a plan will be affected by the degree of inclusion and specified value of the preceding provisions. Besides the cost of the plan, health insurance purchasers should be concerned about the breadth and quality of the network of physicians and hospitals available to insured individuals.

8.3. Liability Insurance

To manage liability risk, individuals often obtain **liability insurance**. It is possible that the amount of liability coverage in the homeowner's and automobile insurance policies is less than one thinks is appropriate. In that case, it is reasonable to purchase a *personal umbrella liability insurance* policy. This type of policy has specified limits but pays claims only if the liability limit of the homeowner's or automobile policy is exceeded. For example, consider an individual whose automobile policy specifies a property damage liability limit of US$100,000 and who has an umbrella policy with a liability limit of US$1 million. If that individual is responsible for an automobile accident that causes US$300,000 of damage, the automobile policy would pay the first US$100,000 and the umbrella policy would pay the remaining US$200,000. Umbrella policies are relatively inexpensive.

It is common for people to think of liability insurance coverage in terms of protecting one's own financial assets. Some jurisdictions may specify exempt property—one's home or retirement savings, for example—that cannot be seized in the case that liability for an accident exceeds the amount of insurance coverage. Thus, one might ask oneself, "What is the worst thing that could happen to me in case of an extremely large liability judgment?" But if the goal is to indemnify the injured party—that is, to make the injured party "whole" financially—the amount of insurance purchased should be based on the potential financial catastrophe that could face an injured party.

8.4. Other Types of Insurance

Other types of risks may be present, depending on the individual's situation. For example, when purchasing a home, many individuals purchase *title insurance* (and in some jurisdictions, it is required). The purpose of title insurance is to make sure that ownership of the property is not in doubt. Personal watercraft and trailers may require a separate insurance policy or an endorsement, which is a form of insurance coverage added to an existing policy to cover risks that are not otherwise included in that policy. Again, appropriate levels of risk avoidance, reduction, prevention, and retention will depend on the situation and the size and probability of the potential loss.

One may consider service contracts when purchasing an automobile, home appliance, or other sizable product to avoid repair costs. These types of pseudo-insurance are profit centers for the companies selling them and are often relatively expensive for consumers, partly because of a lack of competition. For example, at the time of purchase of an automobile, one may be offered the opportunity to purchase an extended warranty at the same time from the automobile dealer. There is limited opportunity for price shopping, and the price of the service contract can usually be rolled into the automobile loan. Under these circumstances, the automobile dealer can charge a high rate to the disadvantage of the purchaser. Note that even this type of contract typically involves a deductible.

9. ANNUITIES: TYPES, STRUCTURE, AND CLASSIFICATION

Individuals have a finite but unknown lifespan. The efficient allocation of financial resources across an unknown lifespan is a planning challenge because consumption smoothing requires the allocation of available financial resources across an expected time frame. Humans may plan to spread their resources based on an average lifetime, but this strategy exposes them to the risk of outliving their assets in old age. One efficient strategy is to pool the risk of an unknown lifespan across individuals through the use of an annuity.

Annuities have existed in a variety of forms for thousands of years. The Romans sold a financial instrument called an "annua" that returned a fixed yearly payment, either for life or for a specified period, in return for a lump sum payment. Even today, annuities remain popular risk management tools, especially for older individuals and retirees who want to mitigate the risk associated with outliving their assets (i.e., longevity risk). Annuities are generally purchased from an insurance company; however, government pensions and payouts from employer pension plans are also technically annuities.

Annuities have become increasingly complex over time, and various types exist. With an **immediate annuity**, an amount of money is paid to the insurance company in return for a guarantee of specified future monthly payments over a specified period of time, either a number of years or the life of the insured, who is called the *annuitant*. A **deferred annuity** allows an individual to purchase an income stream to begin at a later date. We further discuss various forms of immediate and deferred annuities in the following sections.

The annuity payment guaranteed by the insurance company is most directly based on the amount of money tendered, the age and gender of the annuitant, and the insurance company's required rate of return (including its cost of funds and its expense and profit factors). Although life insurance helps provide financial protection in case the insured "dies too soon," immediate life annuities provide financial protection in case the insured "lives too long."

In this section, we discuss some of the key aspects of annuities, such as the parties to an annuity contract, the different types of annuities that exist, payout methods, annuity taxation, and the appropriateness of annuities for individuals. We conclude with an overview of how annuities can benefit retirees and provide a framework that explains which retirees may benefit the most from an annuity.

9.1. Parties to an Annuity Contract

There are four primary parties to an annuity contract: the insurer, the annuitant, the contract owner, and the beneficiary. The insurer—generally an insurance company—is the entity that is licensed to sell the annuity. The annuitant is the person who receives the benefits. The contract owner is the individual who purchases the annuity and is typically the annuitant. In some instances, the contract owner and the annuitant may be different: For example, if the annuity is purchased by a company for a retiring employee, then the company is the contract owner and the employee is the annuitant. Lastly, the beneficiary is an individual or entity that will receive any proceeds upon the death of the annuitant. For contracts like a plain vanilla single-premium annuity, there may not be any death benefit; however, with variable annuities and annuities with some kind of minimum guaranteed payment period (e.g., 10 years), often referred to as a "period certain" option, there may be some residual value once the annuitant passes away.

9.2. Classification of Annuities

There are a variety of ways to classify annuities. The two most critical dimensions that help distinguish the primary types of annuities are (1) deferred versus immediate and (2) fixed versus variable. We will expand on these types shortly, but briefly, deferred annuities provide income that begins at a future date after the initial purchase of the annuity. In some cases, the original investment may retain some liquidity prior to initiation of annuity payments if the purchaser retains the right to sell the deferred annuity. In contrast, with immediate payout annuities—or single-premium immediate annuities (SPIAs), as they are often called—the individual permanently exchanges a lump sum for a contract that promises to pay the annuitant an income for life. For both deferred and immediate annuities, the annuity can be invested in what is termed a "fixed" account or a "variable" account.

Many other versions of annuities are available to meet different needs. For example, a *joint life annuity* is based on the expected lifespans of two annuitants, usually husband and wife, and payments are made as long as at least one of the two is alive. All else equal, the monthly payment is lower for this type of annuity because adding a second annuitant extends the payment timespan.

9.2.1. Deferred Variable Annuities

In its most basic form, a deferred variable annuity is similar to a mutual fund, although it is structured as an insurance contract and typically sold by someone licensed to sell insurance products. With most deferred variable annuities, there is a menu of potential investment options from which an individual can choose. Typical investment options might include a predetermined target risk asset allocation consisting of a diversified mix of securities managed by multiple investment managers. Many of the investment managers replicate popular mutual fund strategies for the annuity separate account. Compared with traditional investment programs (e.g., mutual funds), these annuities can be more expensive for investors, and the number of investment fund options within the programs may be limited.

Deferred variable annuity contracts may include a death benefit. A typical death benefit guarantees that the beneficiary named in the contract will receive the entire amount used to purchase the annuity—a feature that has value to the beneficiary only if the individual dies when the value of the contract is less than the initial investment. Like all features of deferred annuities, the death benefit creates a risk for the issuing insurance company. To offset this risk, the insurance company charges a fee. As with mutual funds, individuals maintain control of their money through the right to exit (or sell) the contract, although there can be considerable surrender charges for withdrawing one's money. Also, similar to mutual funds, a deferred variable annuity does not guarantee lifetime income unless the individual (1) adds an additional feature (a contract rider) or (2) annuitizes the contract by converting the value of the deferred variable annuity into an immediate payout annuity. It is worth noting that relatively few deferred variable annuity investors end up "annuitizing."

Adding a guaranteed minimum withdrawal benefit for life rider to a deferred variable annuity can create a guaranteed income stream for life for the investor. The typical guaranteed minimum withdrawal benefit for life promises to pay the individual a fixed percentage (e.g., 4%) of the initial investment value as long as he or she lives. Each payment is subtracted from the current value of the deferred variable annuity contract. If the markets continue to perform well, the initial investment value may not be depleted, and any remaining value will go to the investor's beneficiaries. In a down market, the investment value may be depleted. If this is the case, the insurance company is contractually obligated to continue to pay the investor the guaranteed minimum benefit as long as the investor is alive.

9.2.2. Deferred Fixed Annuities

Deferred fixed annuities provide an annuity payout that begins at some future date. For each dollar invested, the insurance company will tell the investor how much income he or she will receive when annuity payments commence at a specified age in the future. It costs considerably less for a 30-year-old to purchase a dollar of income for life starting at age 65 than it does for a 55-year-old to purchase a dollar of income for life starting at age 65. At any point prior to annuitization (i.e., conversion of the investment into an annuity), the investor can cash out and receive the economic value of the accumulated purchases less any applicable surrender charges, in which case the annuity contract is terminated. Once in retirement, the individual has two options: (1) cash out or (2) begin withdrawing the accumulated funds. In either case, the "economic value" of the accumulated purchases is annuitized, converting the deferred fixed annuity into an immediate fixed. In contrast to deferred variable annuities, which most investors choose not to annuitize, most deferred fixed annuities are eventually annuitized.

9.2.3. Immediate Variable Annuities

With an immediate variable annuity, the individual permanently exchanges a lump sum for an annuity contract that promises to pay the annuitant an income for life. As the name suggests, the amount of the payments varies over time based on the performance of the portfolios that the assets are invested in. A common feature that can be added to an immediate variable annuity for an additional cost is an income floor that protects the annuitant in the event of a down market.

9.2.4. Immediate Fixed Annuities

With immediate fixed annuities, the most common and most utilized type of annuity, an individual trades a sum of money today for a promised income benefit for as long as he or she is alive. The "income yield" for an immediate fixed annuity is the total amount of ongoing annual income received as a percentage of the initial purchase price. For example, if an individual purchases an immediate fixed annuity for $100,000 and in exchange receives a guarantee to be paid $8,000 per year for as long as the individual is alive, the income yield for the annuity would be 8%.

The income yield for immediate fixed annuities, or any type of annuity, varies based on a number of factors. One key factor is the age of the insured individual (or individuals). Exhibit 7 contains the payout rates for two different immediate annuity types: a life-only annuity (which pays benefits only as long as the individual is alive, with no residual benefits) and a life annuity with a 10-year certain payment (whereby benefits are guaranteed to last for at least 10 years). Quotes are included for three different types of annuitants: male, female, and joint (a couple). (The couple consists of a male and a female assumed to be the same age, and the survivor benefit is 100% of the primary benefit; that is, the benefit stays the same as long as either of the couple survives.)

EXHIBIT 7 An Example of Annual Payouts as a Percentage of Initial Premium

	Life Only				Life with 10-Year Period Certain		
Age	Male	Female	Joint	Age	Male	Female	Joint
60	6.28%	5.87%	5.51%	60	6.15%	5.86%	5.42%
65	7.02	6.47	5.96	65	6.75	6.32	5.88
70	8.04	7.31	6.65	70	7.46	7.01	6.59
75	9.53	8.73	7.68	75	8.33	7.93	7.45
80	11.90	10.87	9.35	80	9.30	8.96	8.51
85	15.17	14.27	11.70	85	10.08	9.95	9.45
90	20.10	19.34	14.51	90	10.66	10.49	9.86

Source: www.immediateannuities.com (retrieved December 2014).

There are a number of important takeaways from Exhibit 7. First, the payouts (i.e., income yields) are higher when expected remaining longevity is shorter. For example, a male of 85 will receive a higher income yield than a male of 65 because the older male has a shorter life expectancy. A 65-year-old female will have a smaller payout than a 65-year-old male because females have a longer average life expectancy than males. The income yield is determined by estimating the average longevity of a given annuitant pool. A shorter average payment period will mean higher income for the older annuitants in the pool.

Another takeaway from the table is that the inclusion of a period certain (or return-of-premium feature) will reduce the payout, but to varying degrees. For example, adding the 10-year period certain has a relatively small effect on the income yield for a 60-year-old male (which decreases from 6.28% to 6.15%), but it has a significantly greater impact for the 90-year-old male (whose payout rate decreases from 20.10% to 10.66%). Again, this difference is based on life expectancies. The probability of a 60-year-old male dying in the first 10 years is much smaller than the probability of a 90-year-old male dying over the next 10 years, so the payouts are adjusted accordingly. An individual who is concerned with lifetime income maximization is likely better off not adding any type of rider that includes a residual benefit; however, such a rider may be desirable if an individual has competing goals of generating lifetime income and providing some residual wealth for heirs.

In addition to mortality, another key variable that affects annuity pricing is the expected return the insurance company can earn on premiums. Because insurance companies tend to invest conservatively, the available yield on bonds provides a relatively good proxy, at least from a historical perspective, for how payout rates change over time. When current yields on bonds are lower than historical bond yields and life expectancies are increasing, payouts on annuities will be relatively low by historical standards. Low annuity yields may discourage many individuals from buying annuities if they believe that yields will eventually go back up. In reality, however, lower annuity payout rates simply reflect the increasing cost of hedging longevity risk using available investments.

9.2.5. Advanced Life Deferred Annuities

The final type of annuity that we discuss is a hybrid of a deferred fixed annuity and an immediate fixed annuity. This so-called *advanced life deferred annuity* (ALDA) is often referred to as pure longevity insurance. Although it might sound a bit contradictory, ALDAs are deferred immediate payout annuities. Similar to an immediate fixed annuity, an ALDA involves the permanent exchange of a lump sum for an insurance contract that promises to pay an income. However, in contrast to an immediate payout annuity, for which the payments begin immediately, an ALDA's payments begin later in life—for example, when the individual turns 80 or 85.

Given that a specific monthly benefit may not begin until age 85, a deferred immediate life annuity would clearly cost less to purchase than a regular immediate life annuity. We note three reasons for this lower cost. First, because payments on the deferred annuity begin so far in the future, the insurance company has ample time to earn money on the amount tendered. Second, life expectancy for an 85-year-old is much shorter than for a 65-year-old, so the number of payments made will be fewer. Third, it is quite possible that the annuitant may actually die before any payments are made. For a relatively small premium, longevity insurance can provide additional security and can supplement income in later years.

EXAMPLE 12   Comparing Annuities

Compare fixed immediate annuities and variable immediate annuities.

Solution: Both fixed and variable immediate annuities represent an irrevocable exchange of money for an insurance contract (the annuity contract). With a fixed immediate annuity, payments are "fixed" in either nominal terms or, in some cases, real terms, providing certainty about payment streams. With both fixed and variable immediate annuities, a common feature is a "period certain," whereby the payments continue to a designated beneficiary for a specified period, typically 10 years.

---

10. ANNUITIES: ADVANTAGES AND DISADVANTAGES OF FIXED AND VARIABLE ANNUITIES

In this section, we discuss the relative advantages and disadvantages of both fixed and variable annuities. As a reminder, fixed annuities provide a benefit that is fixed (or known) for life, whereas variable annuities have a benefit that can change over time and that benefit is generally based on the performance of some underlying portfolio or investment. When selecting between fixed and variable annuities, there are a number of important considerations.

10.1. Volatility of Benefit Amount

The most obvious difference between fixed and variable annuities is the type of benefit. Fixed annuities provide a constant income stream that is guaranteed not to change, whereas the income from a variable annuity could change considerably depending on the terms of the annuity payout. Retirees seeking a high level of assurance with respect to benefit payouts are likely better served by a fixed annuity, or a variable annuity that limits the possible change in the benefit over time. Retirees who are risk tolerant may be more interested in a variable annuity. If a retiree is willing to adjust his or her spending over time, that individual may be able to increase the amount spent each year by selecting a variable annuity for which the payment is linked to a risky portfolio of assets.

10.2. Flexibility

The flexibility of an annuity varies materially with the type of annuity and its individual features. For example, an individual who purchases an immediate fixed annuity has effectively traded some amount of wealth for a guarantee of income for life. In most situations, this exchange is irrevocable: The individual who purchased the immediate fixed annuity cannot "undo" the transaction and request the original purchase amount back. The fact that these annuities are irrevocable makes sense from the insurer's perspective because (in theory) if given the option, every individual would request the initial premium back.

Variable annuity payments are typically tied to the performance of an underlying subaccount. This subaccount can often be withdrawn by the annuitant, subject to limitations. Therefore, variable annuities can provide the annuitant with guaranteed income for life as well as the flexibility to access the funds should he or she (or they) need to do so. There may be penalties associated with withdrawing funds from a variable annuity, and in some cases, withdrawals may not be allowed (e.g., in the case of an immediate variable annuity).

10.3. Future Market Expectations

A fixed annuity locks the annuitant into a portfolio of bond-like assets at whatever rate of return exists at the time of purchase. This scenario creates some interest rate risk because the value of these underlying securities will fall if interest rates rise.

If the annuitant assumes that interest rates will vary over time, he or she may be tempted to delay annuitization until interest rates rise. This delay, however, will reduce expected consumption during the delay period because the annuitant receives only market returns on investment assets and no mortality credits. Mortality credits, which will be discussed at greater length shortly, are effectively the difference between the future payout one would receive without pooling one's investments and the future payout one receives when the investment pool includes individuals who have already passed away. Delay of annuitization may also expose the annuitant to the risk that life expectancies will systematically increase during the delay period, which would increase the cost of annuitization (i.e., decrease future potential available payouts). Annuitizing earlier allows the annuitant to hedge the risk of a large increase in future longevity for a population.

Variable annuities allow an annuitant to accept some variation in payments in return for the possibility of higher future payments if the market performs well. Because most retirees will rationally accept some market risk with their investment portfolio, this option allows individuals to increase their retirement income efficiency by benefiting from both a mortality credit and a risk premium. The benefit of accepting market risk varies by type of annuity, and many variable annuity features limit the potential growth in income payments in future time periods. Variable annuities without growth-limiting features, such as minimum income guarantees, are most likely to provide a future income that outpaces inflation on average.

10.4. Fees

The fees associated with variable annuities tend to be higher than those for fixed annuities. These higher fees come from a variety of factors but are primarily attributable to the costs of hedging market risk, administrative expenses, and reduced price competition. Evidence suggests that the price of insurance products is significantly affected by price competition, and immediate fixed annuities are much easier for a consumer to compare (the consumer will simply select the highest annuity payment for the amount he or she will spend). The opaque pricing of variable annuities can reduce price competition if consumers are unable to easily compare the relative efficiency of product characteristics. A thorough price analysis may require weighing the possible added costs of opaque variable annuity features—perhaps using analytical tools to help assess these costs—against the benefits of a potentially higher return.

10.5. Inflation Concerns

Inflation can have a significant negative impact on the real income received from a fixed annuity. For example, if annual inflation averages 3%, after approximately 24 years, the income would be worth approximately half as much as it was worth when the annuity began. In their purest form, fixed annuities are nominal and will not change with inflation; however, it is possible to create a partial inflation hedge by having benefits "step up" some predetermined amount each year (e.g., 3%). Although this adjustment is not a perfect inflation hedge, it does provide a mechanism to ensure that payments increase over time. There are a number of variable annuities (and riders on fixed annuities) that allow the payments to increase or decrease based on changes in inflation. An individual interested in guaranteeing some lifetime level of income that changes with inflation may find these types of policies or riders valuable.

10.6. Payout Methods

The payout methods available from an annuity are similar regardless of whether the annuity is fixed or variable. In certain instances, the annuitant is unable to choose the payout method, especially with some types of government pensions, but there is generally some level of choice when purchasing a private annuity from an insurance company. The primary payout methods were discussed previously but are summarized again here:

- *Life annuity:* Payments are made for the entire life of the annuitant and cease at his or her death.
- *Period-certain annuity:* Payments are made for a specified number of periods without regard to the lifespan or expected lifespan of the annuitant.
- *Life annuity with period certain:* This payment type combines the features associated with a life annuity and a period-certain annuity, so payments are made for the entire life of the annuitant but are guaranteed for a minimum number of years even if the annuitant dies. The most common length of the period certain is 10 years. For example, if the annuitant dies after 6 years, a life annuity with 10 years period certain will make payments to the annuitant's beneficiary for the remaining 4 years and then cease.
- *Life annuity with refund:* This type is similar to a life annuity with period certain, but instead of guaranteeing payments for life or for a certain number of years, a life annuity with refund guarantees that the annuitant (or the beneficiary) will receive payments equal

to the total amount paid into the contract, which is equal to the initial investment amount less fees.

- *Joint life annuity:* With a life annuity on two or more individuals, such as a husband and a wife, payments continue until both members are no longer living. For example, a married couple may purchase an immediate annuity that pays a monthly benefit as long as either one of them is alive. The contract states the benefit that the survivor will receive, which can be as much as 100% of the primary benefit or a smaller amount, such as 50% or 75% of the full benefit. The annuity payments cease when the survivor passes away.

It is important to note that the payout methods are not mutually exclusive. In theory, one could combine each of the different methods into a single annuity. Annuity payments can also be made at different frequencies, such as monthly, quarterly, or annually, although monthly payments are generally the most common. It is also possible to include riders or other methods that specify how the benefit may change over time. For example, it is possible to purchase an annuity for which the payment increases by some fixed percentage (or amount) each year.

10.7. Annuity Benefit Taxation

In some locations, annuities can offer attractive tax benefits, such as tax-deferred growth. For example, in the United States, the growth in an annuity is taxed only when the individual receives income from the annuity. This presents an opportunity for tax-deferred growth, especially for someone who purchases the annuity at a relatively young age or has exhausted other tax-sheltering alternatives. The actual taxation of the benefits varies considerably by type of annuity but is generally based on some average of the difference between the amount paid for the annuity and the benefits received.

The actual method of taxation varies materially by country, and before purchasing an annuity or recommending an annuity for a client, one should become familiar with the applicable tax consequences or consult a local expert on annuity taxation. In general, the potential for tax deferral, combined with a high marginal tax rate on alternative investments, may make annuities attractive for retirees.

10.8. Appropriateness of Annuities

When creating an income stream from a pool of assets, each retiree has a choice. The individual can choose either to receive periodic withdrawals from an investment portfolio (i.e., not annuitize) or to purchase an annuity (i.e., annuitize). This decision is obviously based on a variety of factors and preferences. When discussing the potential benefits of annuitizing, it is important to understand the concept of mortality credits (which we briefly mentioned earlier). Each payment received by the annuitant is a combination of principal, interest, and mortality credits. Mortality credits are the benefits that survivors receive from those individuals in the mortality pool who have already passed away. It is possible to demonstrate this effect visually using a chart (see Exhibit 8).

In Exhibit 8, we show an example of mortality credits for US male individuals, using male mortality rates based on the Society of Actuaries' 2012 Individual Annuity Reserve Table and an interest rate of 3%. We also assume that the individual receives US$70 of annual income for life for an approximate initial cost of US$1,000. Given these assumptions, the annual benefit payment can be decomposed into three parts: interest (based on the remaining assets from the initial investment minus benefits paid), return of premium, and mortality credits.

EXHIBIT 8   Mortality Credits

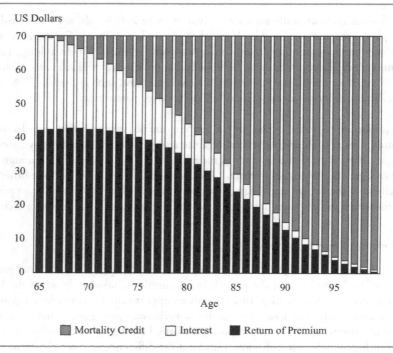

An individual who self-insures longevity risk would receive only (approximately) the interest and return-of-premium portions of Exhibit 8. The additional mortality credits arise because some individuals will pass away early, thereby subsidizing the future benefits of those individuals who are still alive. In this way, an individual can receive more income and additional certainty from purchasing an annuity. However, this certainty comes at a cost because the expected benefits of an annuity are generally not positive. Annuities are a form of insurance, and most forms of insurance, by definition, do not (and should not) have a positive expected value because it would imply that the insurance company lost money on the average policy sold. Moreover, it would likely not be advantageous to purchase an annuity from an insurance company that lost money on the average policy sold because that company would likely eventually go out of business and no longer be able to fund future expected benefit payments.

Therefore, an individual who purchases an annuity is acquiring the benefit of certainty regarding lifetime income in exchange for accepting lower potential wealth at death, as well as lower lifetime income depending on the cost of the annuity. This perspective can be used to create a "retirement income efficient frontier" whereby the decision of how much to annuitize is based on an individual's preference for wealth maximization and aversion to running out of money. This concept is similar to the traditional Markowitz (1952) efficient frontier; but for the retirement income efficient frontier, wealth replaces expected returns on the vertical axis and shortfall risk (which is defined approximately as the risk associated with running out of money over one's lifetime) replaces standard deviation on the horizontal axis. The exact definitions of "wealth" and "shortfall risk" (as well as the terms themselves) have varied across literature but still tend to be relatively consistent. The concept of the retirement income efficient frontier, which is displayed visually in Exhibit 9, is derived from Chen and Milevsky (2003), among others.

EXHIBIT 9   Retirement Income Efficient Frontier

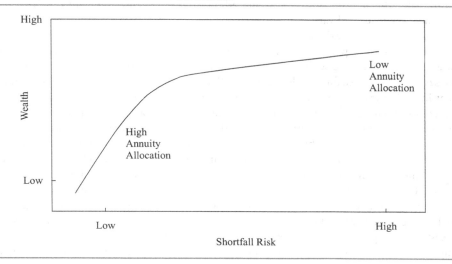

Certain factors can generally be expected to affect a retiree's demand for annuities, either positively or negatively. For example, the following factors would generally suggest increased demand for an annuity:

- Longer-than-average life expectancy
- Greater preference for lifetime income
- Less concern for leaving money to heirs
- More conservative investing preferences (i.e., greater risk aversion)
- Lower guaranteed income from other sources (such as pensions)

The broad international shift away from defined benefit plans and toward defined contribution plans has increased the demand for annuities. Therefore, it is important to have an understanding of annuities and which individuals they are most likely to benefit.

11. RISK MANAGEMENT IMPLEMENTATION: DETERMINING THE OPTIMAL STRATEGY AND CASE ANALYSIS

A variety of factors need to be considered when implementing an optimal risk management strategy for an individual or a household. In this section, we will indicate how human capital affects the asset allocation decision, provide a case study analyzing and critiquing an insurance program, and present appropriate strategies for asset allocation and risk reduction for a given investor.

11.1. Determining the Optimal Risk Management Strategy

As with portfolio selection, the decision to retain risk or to manage risk through insurance or annuities is determined by a household's risk tolerance. At the same level of wealth, a more risk-tolerant household will prefer to retain more risk—either through higher insurance deductibles or by simply buying little or no insurance—than a less risk-tolerant household. Additionally, the amount of overhead and administrative expenses built into the cost of the insurance (the load) will vary by product.

If an individual decides not to insure a risk exposure, he or she may still choose to moderate the impact of a potential loss. The term *loss control* refers to efforts to reduce or eliminate the costs associated with risks. There are three general approaches to loss control. *Risk avoidance* is the purest form of loss control. That is, one can remove the possibility that an event involving loss will occur. For example, one may avoid the risk of loss of a collector car or piece of jewelry by selling the asset. This strategy can be particularly appealing if the asset is no longer providing significant utility, or if the magnitude of the risk exposure rises because of price appreciation. Two other types of loss control are *loss prevention* and *loss reduction*. Loss prevention is the process of taking actions to reduce the probability that a loss event will occur. For example, installing a security system reduces the probability of a break-in that could lead to a loss by theft. Operating an automobile that has a backup camera reduces the probability of causing property damage or personal injury when the automobile is backing up. Installing a swimming pool alarm reduces the probability that a child will drown. Loss reduction is the process of seeking to reduce the size of a loss if a loss event occurs. For example, maintaining a high-quality fire extinguisher in the kitchen may allow a homeowner to contain a fire that would otherwise cause extreme damage. Unlike the loss prevention examples, the fire extinguisher does not reduce the likelihood of the loss event.

As initially discussed in Section 3.1.3, in addition to risk avoidance and risk reduction, individuals can also manage risk through the techniques of *risk transfer* and *risk retention*. Although risk transfer generally involves insurance or annuities, individuals can also use *non-insurance risk transfers* in many situations, and these usually take the form of contracts. For example, an apartment renter may select a long-term lease to lock in the amount of the monthly rent for a longer time during a period of inflation, thus transferring the risk of increased rent to the landlord, who then must absorb the opportunity cost. Incorporation of an individual's business provides a non-insurance risk transfer in many countries. By incorporating, the individual shields his or her personal financial assets from any legal judgment in which the business is found to be at fault.

A systematic risk management approach would be to consider the optimal strategy for each risk exposure. Some guidelines are helpful in deciding when it is appropriate to accept (retain) risk, when it is best to reduce the potential magnitude (or severity) of the risk, and when it makes sense to transfer risk. Small-magnitude risks below a risk retention limit should be retained (i.e., self-insured) and the magnitude/severity reduced to the point where the expected cost is equal to the expected benefit. For example, installing a high-quality fire-rated roof on a house may reduce both the probability of a fire (e.g., from sparks from a house fire next door) and the potential damage from a fire. However, the cost of installing a new, expensive roof may be too high to be justified. In this case, the large-magnitude potential loss from fire can be transferred through property insurance and a deductible can be used to set the optimal amount of risk retention.

A common risk management approach is summarized in Exhibit 10.

EXHIBIT 10   Risk Management Techniques

Loss Characteristics	High Frequency	Low Frequency
High severity	Risk avoidance	Risk transfer
Low severity	Risk reduction	Risk retention

An insurance product can provide indemnification by ensuring that there will be no (or minimal) loss in economic net worth. For example, an insurance claim will provide reimbursement of flood damage to a $20,000 vehicle if the household has a comprehensive insurance policy. If not, the household risks reducing its economic net worth by the size of the loss exposure. Indemnification in life insurance can be more complex. A human life value analysis seeks to replace the loss in human capital. A needs analysis estimates the present value of future consumption that would need to be replaced if the income of a primary earner were lost.

EXAMPLE 13   Risk Management Strategy

Describe *loss control* in risk management.

Solution: Loss control refers to efforts to reduce or eliminate costs associated with risks. A simple method of loss control is to avoid risks (risk avoidance)—for example, by not engaging in high-risk hobbies, such as rock climbing. Another approach to loss control is loss prevention, in which one attempts to reduce the likelihood of a risky event. For example, one may install an alarm system to discourage burglars. Loss reduction refers to approaches that attempt to minimize the size of the loss if a risky event does occur. For example, an airbag in an automobile does not reduce the likelihood of an accident, but it may reduce the seriousness of injuries sustained by those involved in an accident.

11.2. Analyzing an Insurance Program

This section provides a case study of how one might analyze an individual's insurance needs and design an insurance program. In this case, Jacques and Marion Perrier are 40 years old and 38 years old, respectively. They have two children: Henri, age 8, and Émilie, age 6. Jacques is a manager of technical services for a large corporation and earns €100,000 per year. Marion works part-time as a nurse, earning €20,000 after tax per year but plans to return to full-time work in 10 years, when Émilie turns 16. Marion expects that, with adjusted market conditions and after 10 years of inflation, she will earn €60,000 after tax per year as a full-time nurse at that time. Jacques and Marion are in excellent health and maintain a lifestyle that is well within their income.

The family lives in the city in a comfortable condominium that they bought for €250,000 five years ago and that is currently valued at €300,000. They owe €190,000 on a mortgage that still has 25 years to maturity. Although both Jacques and Marion take public transportation to work, they have an automobile, which is 10 years old but in excellent condition with relatively few kilometers of use. Jacques and Marion intend to live in the condominium at least until Jacques's planned retirement at age 60. At that time, they will decide whether to remain in the condominium or move to the small town nearby where Jacques grew up.

Four years ago, when his parents died, Jacques inherited the moderately sized but attractive home where he grew up. It was worth €150,000 at the time and has increased in value to €165,000 (a 10% increase during this period). For two years, the family tried to use the house as a weekend retreat, but they discovered that their children's activities and the desire to go to different places caused them to use the house infrequently. For the past two years, they have rented the house to a middle-aged couple who have no children. There is no debt on the house, and the rent is enough to pay for taxes and other expenses and to generate positive cash flow that Jacques and Marion are using for family vacations.

Both of Jacques's parents died at age 70. Marion's father died at age 80. Her mother, Françoise, is in good health at age 72, and women in her family have generally lived to very old ages. Françoise has a pension but does not have much in assets.

11.2.1. Current Insurance Plan

Life Insurance.   Jacques bought a whole life insurance policy with a death benefit of €200,000 when Henri was born. Jacques is the insured, and his estate is the beneficiary. His employer also provides a €50,000 term life insurance policy that names Marion as the beneficiary. There is no life insurance on Marion.

Health Insurance.   The family is covered by a national health insurance plan.

Disability Insurance.   Jacques's employer provides short-term disability payments for up to six months. As a part-time employee, Marion has no disability benefits.

Long-Term Care Insurance.   Elderly individuals in Jacques and Marion's country are eligible for long-term care at a cost equal to 75% of their pension benefits.

Property Insurance.   The exterior of the condominium is insured through the condominium owners' association. The insured value is increased annually to consider current market and replacement values. Jacques and Marion have a property insurance policy on the contents of their condominium for €20,000. Jacques's parents insured the house for €100,000 15 years ago. They never increased the coverage, and Jacques has maintained the same policy. The automobile has coverage for liability and collision, as well as comprehensive coverage.

Data Summary

- Jacques: age 40; €100,000 annual earnings; €200,000 whole life insurance policy; €50,000 term life insurance policy
- Marion: age 38; €20,000 annual earnings after tax; no life insurance
- Children: Henri, age 8, and Émilie, age 6
- Condominium: €300,000 current value; €190,000 25-year remaining mortgage; exterior of building fully insured; contents insured for €20,000
- Rental home: €165,000 current value; no mortgage; insured for €100,000

11.2.2. Program Review
Life Insurance.   As we discussed earlier, two approaches are commonly used in calculating life insurance needs. The first is the human life value method, which estimates the present value of earnings that must be replaced. As we will demonstrate, the human life value method indicates

that Jacques should purchase approximately €1.11 million of additional life insurance. The second approach is the needs analysis method, which estimates the financial needs of dependents. As we will also demonstrate, the needs analysis method indicates that Jacques should purchase approximately €1.25 million of additional life insurance.

Of course, there is no absolute when calculating life insurance needs because there are so many variables and uncertainties. However, in this case, the two methods generate relatively close numbers. To augment Jacques's current life insurance program, he should purchase at least €1 million in additional term life insurance, but €1.25 million would be more desirable.

Although an annually renewable term policy will be less expensive, a 20-year level term policy should be considered. At the end of 20 years, Jacques will be nearing the end of his working career and the children will be fully grown. Jacques and Marion will have accumulated a high enough level of savings that income replacement will be unnecessary. At that time, the term policy can be allowed to lapse and the €200,000 whole life policy can be retained.

Whole life coverage like Jacques's current policy is relatively expensive, but the pricing and cash build-up at this point in the policy's life indicate that it is probably wise not to replace the policy with term coverage now. Even though life insurance rates have fallen as life expectancies have lengthened and competition has increased, the decline is probably not enough to offset the advantages of the whole life policy at this point. In addition to providing life insurance coverage, the policy's cash-value buildup can be considered a conservative part of the asset allocation of the retirement portfolio.

Marion should be named as the primary beneficiary on the new policy, with Henri and Émilie as secondary beneficiaries, although countries may differ on the exact approach for designating a beneficiary who is a minor. It may be advisable to name a custodian and/or create a trust for Henri and Émilie until they reach adulthood. The old policy should be changed to include these beneficiary designations as well. Making death benefits payable to the estate, as is the case currently on the whole life policy, can make receipt of payments much slower and may subject benefits to greater taxation.

Although Marion's income is modest, her death would cause a financial burden in terms of both lost income and added expenses to replace her family and household responsibilities. Furthermore, her income will increase when she returns to full-time work in 10 years, and financial responsibility for the children will still exist at that time. At Marion's current age and with her excellent health, and because she is female, life insurance rates are very low. However, it is possible that a health issue or accident could cause her rate to increase or even make her uninsurable. Given the complexity of Marion's situation, it is difficult to calculate a recommendation for the amount of life insurance needed.

Life insurance companies typically offer lower rates for larger amounts of coverage in a series of steps. For example, the price per €1,000 of coverage may decrease at €100,000, €250,000, €500,000, and €1,000,000 of coverage. But companies are hesitant to underwrite policies that are large relative to the insured's human life value, or the discounted value of future earnings. A €250,000 policy would take advantage of the price break but would be relatively large for Marion's current income. Still, it is justifiable based on her future employment plan. Purchasing a policy of this size will provide adequate protection for the 10 years until she goes back to work full time, and at that point the children will be more independent, reducing the need for life insurance. As with Jacques, a 20-year level term policy is reasonable.

Life Insurance Needs For Jacques and Marion

As mentioned previously, the *human life value* method is consistent with the concept of human capital and involves replacing the estimated net contributions to family finances that Jacques would generate if he did not die during his projected earning life. Calculating these contributions involves the following steps:

- Start with the actual pre-tax compensation that Jacques would receive from employment: €100,000.
- Adjust for income taxation, and here we assume a 30% rate: €100,000 − €30,000 = €70,000 post-tax compensation.
- Adjust for family expenses attributable to Jacques that will not exist after his death, such as his transportation, travel, clothing, food, entertainment, and insurance premiums. Here, we assume those expenses to be €20,000. So €70,000 − €20,000 = €50,000 income after expenses.
- Add the value of any non-taxable employee benefits that the family will no longer receive, such as employer contributions to retirement plans, which we assume to be €15,000: €50,000 + €15,000 = €65,000.
- Estimate the amount of pre-tax income needed to replace that income on an after-tax basis. Note that the rate of taxation of annual income generated from life insurance proceeds may be different from the rate of taxation of Jacques's employment income, and marginal rates may be lower for lower incomes. Here, we assume a 20% tax rate: €65,000/(1 − t) = €65,000/(1 − 0.20) = €81,250.
- We then apply an annual growth rate, assumed here to be 3%, to consider the effects of inflation and career advancement over the full 20 years until retirement.
- Finally, we discount all the future cash flows back to the present at an appropriate rate, assumed here to be 5%.

Assuming the lost income replacement would be needed by Jacques's family immediately, the human life value calculation can be solved as the present value of an annuity due with growing payments (a so-called "growing annuity due"). Using calculator keystrokes for an annuity due with level payments, the growth of payments can be incorporated by adjusting the discount rate to account for the growth rate of earnings. The adjusted rate i can be calculated as follows, as long as the discount rate is larger than the growth rate:[3] [(1 + Discount rate)/(1 + Growth rate)] − 1, or (1.05/1.03) − 1 = 1.94%. Thus,

- set the calculator for beginning-of-period payments;
- $n = 20$ (the number of years until retirement);
- payment = €81,250; and
- $i = 1.94\%$.

Solving for the present value of an annuity due, the human life value method recommends €1,362,203 of life insurance for Jacques. Because Jacques already has €250,000 of

---

[3]Most individuals' situations would call for a discount rate that is higher than the inflation rate. If that is not the case, or if future cash flows are not projected to grow at a constant rate, the present value can be calculated in the typical manner as the present value of a series of unequal payments.

life insurance, he should purchase an additional €1,112,203, according to this method. This amount would likely be rounded to €1.1 million.

As discussed earlier, the *needs analysis* method is concerned with meeting the financial needs of the family rather than replacing human capital. Needs analysis typically includes the following steps, which are presented in greater detail in Exhibit 11:

- Estimate the amount of cash that will be needed upon the death of the insured person. This amount will include final expenses (funeral and burial) as well as any taxes that may be payable. It is also common to pay off all debt (including mortgages) and to fully fund future education costs. An emergency fund should be created.
- Estimate the capital needed to fund family living expenses. This calculation requires discounting estimated living expenses (i.e., calculating the present value of future cash flow needs) during multiple time frames, typically as follows:
  - Estimate the surviving spouse's living expense needs, assumed here to continue for 52 years, until Marion is 90 years old. Note that when the mortgage and other debts are paid off, living expenses are lower.
  - Estimate the children's living expense needs, assumed here to continue until they are 22 years old. This amount does not include the education fund.
  - Include an additional amount for extra expenses during a transition period after Jacques's death, perhaps covering two years. In general, this period recognizes that there may be some contractual obligations, such as a car lease, that may not terminate upon a person's death.
  - Consider Marion's future income (earnings). Note, however, that Marion may prefer not to go back to work full time as soon as planned because of the extra responsibilities of being a single parent. She may even choose to resign from her part-time job.
- Calculate total needs as the sum of cash needs and capital needs.
- Calculate total capital available, which may include cash/savings, retirement benefits, life insurance, rental property, and other assets.
- Calculate the life insurance need as the difference between the total financial needs and the total capital available.
  Exhibit 11 is a representation of a needs analysis for Jacques.

EXHIBIT 11   Financial Needs: Life Insurance Worksheet

Cash Needs	Euro (€)
Final expenses	10,000
Taxes payable	5,000
Mortgage retirement	190,000
Other debt	10,000
Education fund	200,000
Emergency fund	30,000
Total cash needs	445,000

(continued)

EXHIBIT 11   (Continued)

Capital Needs [present value of annuity due: growth rate = 3%, discount rate = 5%, adjusted rate (as above) = 1.94%]

Marion's living expenses (60,000/year for 52 years)	1,991,941
Children's living expenses:	
Henri (10,000/year for 14 years)	123,934
Émilie (10,000/year for 16 years)	139,071
Transition period needs (10,000/year for 2 years)	19,810
Less Marion's income:	
Until Émilie is 16 (20,000/year for 10 years)	−183,713
Age 48–60 (60,000/year for 12 years)	−398,565[a]
Total capital needs	1,692,478
Total Financial Needs	**2,137,478**
Capital Available	
Cash and savings	30,000
Vested retirement accounts—present value	200,000
Life insurance	250,000
Rental property	165,000
Total capital available	645,000
Life insurance need	**1,492,478**
(Total financial needs less total capital available)	

[a]Calculated in two steps: (1) Compute the amount needed in 10 years, when Marion will begin earning €60,000 per year. Assuming 12 years of earnings from age 48 to age 60, a 3% annual growth in earnings, and a 5% discount rate (1.94% adjusted discount rate), a present value of an annuity due calculation shows that €649,220 will be needed in 10 years. (2) Discount the €649,220 back to the present—10 years at the unadjusted discount rate of 5%—for a total of €398,565. The discount rate is not adjusted during this period because there are no payments to which a growth rate would be applied. We simply discount a future value to the present.

This amount of life insurance under the needs analysis method would likely be rounded to €1.5 million—considerably higher than the €1.11 million calculated earlier using the human life value method. The amount of life insurance selected may depend on which method seems to be more relevant to the family situation. One may view the two values as a reasonable range and use the larger number, the smaller number, or perhaps an average of the two. In many cases, selection of an amount may be further affected by "breakpoints" in the insurance company's premium schedule. The premium rate may decline when insurance coverage reaches, for example, €250,000, €500,000, and €1,000,000.

As a final note, consider that if Jacques dies prematurely, there will be an increased need for life insurance for Marion while Henri and Émilie are still children.

11.2.3. Recommendations

Health Insurance.   Although the Perrier family is covered by national health insurance, they may want to seek private health insurance. In many countries, this type of coverage provides quicker treatment, a wider choice of physicians, and a higher standard of care.

Disability Insurance.   Both Jacques and Marion should consider long-term disability income insurance that guarantees the option to purchase additional coverage without underwriting. This type of policy would allow them to increase coverage as their incomes increase. They should look for "own occupation" coverage that specifies that they would be considered disabled if they could no longer perform the duties of their current positions. They should also select a benefit period that extends at least until their respective retirement ages, possibly age 65. For Jacques, a relatively long, 180-day elimination period would coordinate well with his company's short-term disability plan and would save money. Marion should consider a shorter elimination period, perhaps 90 days, because she has no short-term coverage. Both should choose an option that allows increased coverage based on inflation.

Taxation should be considered in purchasing a disability income policy. In some jurisdictions, premium payments may be deductible for income tax purposes but benefits are taxed. In others, it may make a difference whether the policy is purchased individually or through the employer. In any case, the amount of the benefit selected should be sufficient to replace income, net of any tax advantages and reduction of expenses. Most insurance companies do not like to sell policies with benefits that represent more than 70%–80% of an individual's income (less for high-income individuals) because high percentages create a moral hazard, in that the insured may decide that declaring a disability would give him or her a larger net income without the need to work.

Long-Term Care Insurance.   Although the Perriers' country provides some degree of long-term care assistance, it is possible that the facilities available are not of the standard that would satisfy them. Furthermore, the pricing structure appears to strongly favor individuals with limited income. The Perriers should consider long-term care insurance for themselves, especially if there is a coordination provision with the national plan. At their current ages, rates would be reasonable and would be locked in at the time the policy is purchased. Although stays in long-term care facilities are typically shorter than five years, it would be prudent to purchase a policy that does not have a time limit. Most policies have benefits that are based on a specified amount of money per day. The amount selected should be appropriate for the local cost structure, and the Perriers should pay the extra premium required to receive an automatic inflation adjustment, both before and after any claim.

Long-term care insurance may also be appropriate for Marion's mother, especially because women in her family tend to have long lives. This coverage will be more expensive at her age, but it would alleviate the potential need for care in the home, which would probably be provided by Marion. To avoid the financial and psychological stress of providing home care, a long-term care policy would be useful.

Property Insurance.   Jacques and Marion should check to make sure that the condominium association's insurance coverage is sufficient for the structure. They should also determine whether that policy provides any coverage for contents and, if so, to what extent. It is likely that the condominium association's coverage for contents, if any, is modest, and Jacques and Marion undoubtedly have personal property worth far more than the €20,000 of coverage in their personal policy.

The Perriers should make a thorough valuation of their personal property, even though this is a cumbersome task, and make sure they have or obtain a sufficient amount of coverage. A prudent approach that helps avoid insurance claim problems is to make a written and/or photographic inventory of all contents and improvements within the condominium. Any personal property that has specified limits within their policy should be appraised and scheduled. For example, an expensive necklace should be taken to a jeweler for a formal appraisal, after which the necklace should be added to the insurance policy, which will likely require a higher premium. A copy of the appraisal and inventory should be provided to the insurance company, and another copy should be kept off site in case of a disaster in their condominium.

Property insurance on the house should be reviewed. It appears that the amount of coverage is far less than appropriate. Furthermore, it is not clear whether the transfer of ownership of the property is properly noted on the policy. In the case of a claim, Jacques and Marion may have to deal with legal issues in order to collect. Even if the property ownership issue is clarified, it is likely that the house is insured as the Perrier's residence or secondary residence. However, it is now a rental house, and it requires a different insurance policy. They should also determine whether the rental house's contents are included in the policy. Because they probably are not, it would be worthwhile to explain to the renters that they should obtain their own insurance on the contents (their property). This step is especially important because the Perriers could be considered liable for any loss of the renters' property if, for example, there is a fire caused by faulty wiring.

With regard to auto insurance, the Perriers should make sure that they have substantial liability insurance coverage, especially because it appears that they will have substantial assets to protect. However, they may want to consider whether collision and comprehensive coverage are cost effective for a 10-year-old automobile. Because they seem to drive relatively little, it may make sense to self-insure.

With sufficient liability coverage on the condominium and the auto, the Perriers may qualify for umbrella liability insurance. They should consider this relatively inexpensive coverage to provide additional liability protection relating to the auto and condominium. As a nurse, Marion may want to consider professional liability insurance if it is not provided by her employer. If either Jacques or Marion serves on any type of board of directors of a corporation, public service, or other entity, they should make sure that that entity provides appropriate liability coverage for its directors.

Longevity Insurance.   Marion's mother may be an excellent candidate for longevity insurance. As noted earlier, longevity insurance is typically structured as a life annuity with payments beginning at some future date, such as age 85. Because it is not underwritten, it is generally a poor choice for someone whose life expectancy is shorter than average for his or her age and a good choice for someone whose life expectancy is longer than average, as is the case with Marion's mother. The annuity payments would not start for more than a decade, but they would offer additional income in her later years and help combat inflation, and the cost would be relatively low. Longevity insurance may be viewed as a complement to or even a partial substitute for long-term care insurance. A cost–benefit analysis of the available options should be performed to ensure that the policy selected best matches the goals and financial resources of the household.

12. THE EFFECT OF HUMAN CAPITAL ON ASSET ALLOCATION AND RISK REDUCTION

There are two primary ways to consider how the different subcomponents of an individual's total economic wealth should affect portfolio construction. The first is asset allocation, which includes the overall allocation to risky assets. The second is the underlying asset classes, such as stocks and bonds, selected by the individual. For example, an individual who works in a risky profession that has a high correlation with the stock market might first choose a less aggressive portfolio (e.g., with a lower allocation to stocks than the average person of the same age). Next, the investor would select which individual stocks and bonds (or asset classes) to hold to minimize the overall risk of the portfolio within a total wealth framework.

For many people and for many occupations, human capital is generally considered to be a relatively bond-like asset. For example, dividend growth in the S&P 500 Index exhibited a quarterly volatility of 16.4% from first quarter 1948 to fourth quarter 2013, whereas wage growth volatility was closer to 2.5% over the same period.[4] Among individuals, occupation can have a large impact on the degree of wage growth volatility. For example, Oyer (2008) found that stock market conditions can have a strong impact on the lifetime earnings of MBA students. Asset performance that is strongly correlated with the lifetime earnings of a worker will provide less hedging benefit because the assets magnify, rather than reduce, variability in consumption.

EXAMPLE 14   Human Capital and Asset Allocation (1)

The riskiness of human capital, as well as that of other assets, should affect the allocation of an individual's financial capital. Consider three investors: George, John, and Sam. Each investor owns only two assets—human capital and financial capital—and wants his total wealth (i.e., human capital plus financial capital) to have a 45% stock allocation. If human capital is assumed to be 30% stock-like, what is the optimal allocation for the financial capital of George, John, and Sam?

Person	Human Capital (HC)	Financial Capital (FC)	Total Wealth (TW)
George	$500,000	$150,000	$650,000
John	$800,000	$300,000	$1,100,000
Sam	$150,000	$150,000	$300,000

Solution: The allocation is as follows:

	(A)	(B)	(C)	(D)
	TW × 45%	HC × 30%	(A) – (B)	(C)/FC
Person	Target Equity	HC Equity	FC Equity	FC Equity Allocation %
George	$292,500	$150,000	$142,500	95.00%
John	$495,000	$240,000	$255,000	85.00%
Sam	$135,000	$45,000	$90,000	60.00%

Even within an occupation, each individual has different human capital risks. For example, two people may have the exact same job, but because of random market forces, one could lose his or her job and be unable to find suitable reemployment for an extended period of time.

---

[4]Based on data obtained from the US Bureau of Economic Analysis.

Many financial services workers lost their jobs during the global financial crisis of 2008–2009, and many who became unemployed have been forced to change careers given the lack of available openings. This outcome could have a significant impact on their long-term human capital. Alternatively, a person may have a health shock that seriously reduces their ability to rent his or her human capital for the same wage rate as before. Health shocks that meet the threshold of disability may be partially hedged through the insurance market, and the impact of job loss can be partially hedged through unemployment insurance. Most human capital volatility (other than premature death), however, is difficult to hedge through the insurance market.

If both spouses are employed, this may reduce the overall riskiness of the household's human capital. Each spouse provides his or her own income, each with its own risks, but unless the human capital of the two spouses is highly correlated (e.g., if they are both employed in the same family business), their combined human capital will benefit from diversification. An individual who receives income from numerous sources—such as salaries from different jobs, as well as dividends, interest, and so on—must consider the characteristics of his or her total compensation.

A lower-earning partner may also have a more risky human capital value if the higher-earning partner is tied to a specific geographic location. In the event of a job loss, this household may suffer a more significant decline in human capital value than a household in which both partners are able to move to a location where they can maximize their wage rate. The human capital of a less mobile household will have a lower present value and greater volatility. If human capital is very employer-specific (if the individual would have trouble earning the same wage from a different employer), then it is also less valuable and more risky. A household with a non-working spouse may be in a less vulnerable position than a single-person household if the non-working spouse can exercise the option to rejoin the workforce if the primary earner suffers an unexpected loss in earnings.

Most of the wealth an investor holds outside the investment portfolio (e.g., human capital and defined benefit pensions) tends to be relatively conservative in nature (i.e., more bond-like than stock-like). After an optimal investment policy is determined that establishes a target mix of risky and risk-free assets based on risk tolerance, the total wealth asset allocation should be adjusted as the value of the assets changes over time. For example, younger investors should likely allocate more of their investment portfolio to stocks because the value of human capital (which is bond-like) is highest early in the life cycle. Conversely, older investors should shift more of their wealth toward bonds because their bond-like human capital is gradually depleted as they approach retirement. This investment strategy is consistent with such life-cycle investments as target-date funds (in which the target date is the expected retirement date of the individual), which gradually increase the allocation to bonds as investors get closer to retirement.

The economic (holistic) balance sheet discussed earlier in the reading considers the current value of marketable and non-marketable assets. However, this type of balance sheet does not consider the stochastic nature of each individual asset or how the value of one asset rises and falls with respect to other assets within the portfolio over time. It also does not consider the relative liquidity of each asset category, which can be particularly important when there are limited financial instruments that can be used, for example, to borrow against the value of a pension. The allocation for the financial portfolio should be coordinated with the risk associated with the non-marketable assets in an investor's portfolio, such as human capital. Using this perspective, the financial portfolio can be considered a completion or hedge portfolio, because it is invested in such a way as to optimize the overall risk characteristics of an individual's total wealth.

Human capital is a unique asset class in a number of ways. First, it can require a continued investment in knowledge and skills to maintain or increase its value. Some professions are more risky than others and will provide either greater income variance or income that is more strongly correlated with systematic risks (i.e., will rise and fall with economic cycles). Some forms of human capital are more vulnerable to disability risks or premature death. A precision welder may earn the same income as an accountant, but the welder may be more vulnerable to an injury that would sharply reduce the value of that human capital. Human capital is also more illiquid, and there are limited financial instruments available that can be used to effectively borrow against expected human capital when earnings fall below a desired level of consumption. Some occupations will have an earnings path that is likely to keep pace with inflation, whereas other occupations will not. Employees in some occupations may have invested in human capital that allows them to be very productive in a specific role for their employer. This heavy investment in employer-specific human capital may not easily be rented to another employer for the same wage rate. This places the employee at greater risk of future income volatility. Many who enjoyed steady income growth in the past—for example, mortgage brokers in the United States during the 2000s—were not fully aware of their own human capital risk. Similarly, individuals who work in the real estate industry should likely seek to underweight real estate assets in their portfolios to reduce exposure to real estate from a total wealth perspective. This diversification may be a challenge for those who carry optimistic beliefs about the future growth of their own industry, but history shows that few industries are immune to market shocks.

EXAMPLE 15   Human Capital and Asset Allocation (2)

Describe how investment strategies can be modified to account for human capital risk.

Solution: Investment assets may be strongly or weakly correlated with the human capital value of a worker. The overall volatility of one's economic balance sheet can be reduced by selecting assets that correlate weakly (or even negatively) with human capital. Sector investments may be particularly valuable if they are not a complement to the industry that employs the primary earner. Workers with more volatile assets may also prefer more liquid investments.

EXAMPLE 16   Human Capital and Asset Allocation (3)

Compare investment planning for a young family with investment planning for a newly retired couple.

Solution: A younger household will hold most of its wealth in human capital. For most households, human capital is a bond-like asset that returns a relatively stable income over time. This fact increases the optimal allocation to risky assets within the investment portfolio for younger households. For a newly retired couple, the value of human capital declines relative to the value of the investment portfolio. To balance the total risk of the older household's portfolio, investment portfolio risk should be reduced because investment assets are a larger share of the economic balance sheet (ignoring the impact of charitable bequests and other obligations).

12.1. Asset Allocation and Risk Reduction

An individual or household manages wealth risk mainly to smooth spending over time. A strategy that combines appropriate investments with insurance products, or other risk management tools, can be used to provide the highest level of spending for the level of risk the individual or household is willing to take. Each household will have its own risks and preferences that determine which strategy makes sense.

Investment risk, property risk, and human capital risk can be either idiosyncratic or systematic. Idiosyncratic risks include the risks of a specific occupation, the risk of living a very long life or experiencing a long-term illness, and the risk of premature death or loss of property. Within a total wealth framework, idiosyncratic human capital risks are reduced through investment portfolio strategies and/or through insurance (or annuity) products. Pooling risk allows a household to efficiently reduce idiosyncratic risk. Systematic risks affect all households. For example, a diversified investment portfolio of risky assets will be exposed to the systematic risk that the overall market will fall in value. Earnings can also be affected by systematic risk through a recession or slow economic growth. A cure for cancer might increase overall longevity, placing all households at greater risk of outliving their assets.

The first step in creating strategies for asset allocation and risk reduction is to identify idiosyncratic risk exposures that can be efficiently reduced through diversification or hedging. A young doctor with two children and a lower-earning spouse bears a number of idiosyncratic risks. First, the couple's investment portfolio should be well diversified and not highly correlated with the doctor's income. Second, the household's largest asset, its human capital, could be diminished or lost through disability or premature death. Life insurance and disability insurance provide a hedge that pools idiosyncratic human capital risk. Medical malpractice insurance provides protection against idiosyncratic liability risk. In general, hedging these risks trades a small drop in expected wealth for an increase in the likelihood of smooth spending.

Young households may have additional liquidity constraints that will affect recommended products. A doctor who expects his or her earnings to rise sharply and who has high current expenses may choose to defer retirement saving for a few years. This individual should not, however, avoid paying premiums on insurance used to hedge the value of human capital. Term life insurance can provide ample coverage at a modest price, and the household may consider a longer elimination period on disability insurance to fit the cost into the current budget. The investment portfolio allocation may be of little consequence because the value of the total wealth portfolio consists almost entirely of human capital. Instead, investments may be selected to increase liquidity that can be used to protect current consumption from any short-term income shock.

A 60-year-old couple nearing retirement with grown, independent children and a large investment portfolio will face a different set of risks. Although their combined income may be higher than that of the young doctor, the value of their human capital is far less if they plan to retire in five years. Therefore, for the older couple, risks to the investment portfolio are far more relevant than human capital risks. Life insurance may have value only as a means of covering estate planning and liquidity needs. Disability insurance can likely be dropped. Health and liability remain significant idiosyncratic risk exposures that can be efficiently reduced through health, long-term care, and liability insurance. Home equity can be protected through property insurance; the risk of idiosyncratic regional real estate price variation should also be considered. The couple's risk of outliving their assets can be protected through the purchase of annuities. Market risk can be particularly important because, compared with a younger household, the older couple's investments are a far larger share of total household wealth. An older household may have fewer liquidity constraints and thus more flexibility to retain risks—for example, through higher insurance deductibles and longer elimination periods on long-term care insurance. This older household may also choose to retain the majority of property risk. A rational increase in risk retention can be combined with a reduction in portfolio risk to achieve an efficient balance of total wealth risk. The household will receive a higher expected return (equal to the insurance load) from accepting greater insurable risk while simultaneously reducing the expected return on the investment portfolio by increasing the share of safe assets.

Human capital risks are correlated with market returns and can be at least partially hedged through holistic portfolio construction. Consider a 50-year-old couple, Jennifer and Wade. Jennifer earns US$75,000 a year working as a tenured college professor, and Wade earns US$100,000 selling drilling parts to the oil industry. Jennifer participates in the state public employee pension system, which is currently in good enough financial condition to cover promised benefits for the next 40 years. Wade has US$300,000 saved in a 401(k), half in employer stock. Both are eligible to receive Social Security benefits.

Wade works in a cyclical industry and will see high variability in income but a modest covariance of earnings with the performance of the overall stock market. Although Wade's income today is higher than Jennifer's income, the difference in the present value of their human capital will not be that great. Wade's income is more volatile because it rests largely on the strength of the domestic oil industry. Jennifer may apply a discount rate equivalent to that of current state government bonds because her salary is unlikely to change and her salary risk is comparable to the state's ability to pay general obligation debts. The discount rate on Wade's income may be placed above the historical equity premium because his human capital risk is not easily diversified and is more volatile than the market in general.

To preserve consumption if Wade is laid off for a period of time, the couple should consider holding a significant amount of assets in marketable securities that can be easily liquidated to fund short-term spending needs. These types of assets include money market accounts and short-term government bonds, which can be easily traded in the secondary market. Investment assets held in taxable accounts can be accessed for emergency spending in the event of long-term unemployment. The combination of Jennifer's stable salary and Wade's volatile income allows the couple to take on greater risk than if they lived on Wade's income alone. If Wade and Jennifer have an average level of investment risk tolerance, then they should invest in a mix of stocks and bonds, each within the most tax-efficient account, to create a balanced portfolio appropriate to the couple's risk preferences and the risk of the remainder of the total wealth portfolio.

Wade's more risky human capital is highly correlated with the overall economy, although as previously mentioned, his wages are likely not strongly correlated with the equity market in general. A more efficient investment portfolio will provide a partial hedge against Wade's idiosyncratic human capital risk. The obvious first step would be to sell Wade's investments in employer stock. This may be complicated by restrictions on selling the stock or even Wade's subjective opinion of the potential value of his employer's stock. If Wade is restricted from selling his company stock, an adviser might suggest put options to hedge this risk. To balance the risk to Wade's human capital, the retirement portfolio should overweight sector funds that are either uncorrelated or negatively correlated with the oil industry. Sectors, such as transportation, that perform well when oil prices fall will provide some buffer against fluctuations in the value of Wade's human capital.

The value of Jennifer's pension will likely be a significant share of the couple's total wealth. Discounted at a modest bond rate of comparable duration to the expected pension payments, the value of her pension likely exceeds the US$300,000 that John has saved in his 401(k). If her pension were less secure, which can be estimated based on the percentage of future obligations that can be funded from current assets, then the pension would be discounted at a higher rate. Jennifer's pension can be viewed as a forced savings plan with a promised stable future payout that is comparable to a bond. If the discounted value is estimated to be US$500,000, then this portion of the total portfolio will be characterized as a bond-like asset. Couples with significant pension assets can accept greater risk in the rest of their investment portfolio because poor risky asset performance has less of an impact on future spending when the bulk of consumption will be funded from stable pension income. Wade can take greater risk in his 401(k) because the couple will be able to rely on Jennifer's pension. Note that although it is often difficult to consider, the possibility of divorce should also affect recommendations if pension assets are not allocated to the other spouse. For example, couples may want to hold greater liquidity, and spouses with defined contribution savings or more volatile human capital may choose to take less investment risk.

EXAMPLE 17 Asset Allocation and Risk Reduction

Consider two 35-year-old couples, each of which earns a combined US$150,000 per year. One couple consists of an individual who is employed as a petroleum engineer and a non-working spouse. The other couple consists of two high school teachers. Compare asset allocation and risk reduction strategies for each couple.

Solution: The human capital value of the couple consisting of the petroleum engineer and the non-working spouse is likely lower than the combined human capital value of the high school teachers, although the combined lifetime cumulative wages of the teachers is likely lower than those of the engineer and the spouse. Earnings for the engineer are highly correlated with oil prices, and either rising or falling prices will affect the household's available income in the future. The impact of a disability on employability may be more severe for the engineer than for a teacher. The engineer should thus likely consider a less risky portfolio and should overweight securities that have a low correlation with oil prices. Conversely, the teachers should select a riskier portfolio as a result of their higher human capital and low correlation with individual market sectors.

SUMMARY

The risk management process for individuals is complex given the variety of potential risks that may be experienced over the life cycle and the differences that exist across households. In this reading, key concepts related to risk management and individuals include the following:

- The two primary asset types for most individuals can be described broadly as human capital and financial capital. Human capital is the net present value of the individual's future expected labor income, whereas financial capital consists of assets currently owned by the individual and can include such items as a bank account, individual securities, pooled funds, a retirement account, and a home.

- Economic net worth is an extension of traditional balance sheet net worth that includes claims to future assets that can be used for consumption, such as human capital, as well as the present value of pension benefits.

- There are typically four key steps in the risk management process for individuals: Specify the objective, identify risks, evaluate risks and select appropriate methods to manage the risks, and monitor outcomes and risk exposures and make appropriate adjustments in methods.

- The financial stages of life for adults can be categorized in the following seven periods: education phase, early career, career development, peak accumulation, pre-retirement, early retirement, and late retirement.

- The primary goal of an economic (holistic) balance sheet is to arrive at an accurate depiction of an individual's overall financial health by accounting for the present value of all available marketable and non-marketable assets, as well as all liabilities. An economic (holistic) balance sheet includes traditional assets and liabilities, as well as human capital and pension value, as assets and includes consumption and bequests as liabilities.

- The total economic wealth of an individual changes throughout his or her lifetime, as do the underlying assets that make up that wealth. The total economic wealth of younger individuals is typically dominated by the value of their human capital. As individuals age, earnings will accumulate, increasing financial capital.

- Earnings risk refers to the risks associated with the earnings potential of an individual—that is, events that could negatively affect someone's human and financial capital.

- Premature death risk relates to the death of an individual, such as a family member, whose future earnings (human capital) were expected to help pay for the financial needs and aspirations of the family.

- Longevity risk is the risk of reaching an age at which one's income and financial assets are insufficient to provide adequate support.

- Property risk relates to the possibility that one's property may be damaged, destroyed, stolen, or lost. There are different types of property insurance, depending on the asset, such as automobile insurance and homeowner's insurance.

- Liability risk refers to the possibility that an individual or other entity may be held legally liable for the financial costs of property damage or physical injury.

- Health risk refers to the risks and implications associated with illness or injury. Health risks manifest themselves in different ways over the life cycle and can have significant implications for human capital.

- The primary purpose of life insurance is to help replace the economic value of an individual to a family or a business in the event of that individual's death. The family's need for life insurance is related to the potential loss associated with the future earnings power of that individual.

- The two main types of life insurance are temporary and permanent. Temporary life insurance, or term life insurance, provides insurance for a certain period of time specified at purchase, whereas permanent insurance, or whole life insurance, is used to provide lifetime coverage, assuming the premiums are paid over the entire period.

- Fixed annuities provide a benefit that is fixed (or known) for life, whereas variable annuities have a benefit that can change over time and that is generally based on the performance of some underlying portfolio or investment. When selecting between fixed and variable annuities, there are a number of important considerations, such as the volatility of the benefit, flexibility, future market expectations, fees, and inflation concerns.

- Among the factors that would likely increase demand for an annuity are the following: longer-than-average life expectancy, greater preference for lifetime income, less concern

for leaving money to heirs, more conservative investing preferences, and lower guaranteed income from other sources (such as pensions).
- Techniques for managing a risk include risk avoidance, risk reduction, risk transfer, and risk retention. The most appropriate choice among these techniques often is related to consideration of the frequency and severity of losses associated with the risk.
- The decision to retain risk or buy insurance is determined by a household's risk tolerance. At the same level of wealth, a more risk-tolerant household will prefer to retain more risk, either through higher insurance deductibles or by simply not buying insurance, than will a less risk-tolerant household. Insurance products that have a higher load will encourage a household to retain more risk.
- An individual's total economic wealth affects portfolio construction through asset allocation, which includes the overall allocation to risky assets, as well as the underlying asset classes, such as stocks and bonds, selected by the individual.
- Investment risk, property risk, and human capital risk can be either idiosyncratic or systematic. Examples of idiosyncratic risks include the risks of a specific occupation, the risk of living a very long life or experiencing a long-term illness, and the risk of premature death or loss of property. Systematic risks affect all households.

REFERENCES

Chen, Peng, and Moshe A. Milevsky. 2003. "Merging Asset Allocation and Longevity Insurance: An Optimal Perspective on Payout Annuities." *Journal of Financial Planning*, vol. 16, no. 6 (June): 52–62.

Ibbotson, Roger G., Moshe A. Milevsky, Peng Chen, and Kevin X. Zhu. 2007. *Lifetime Financial Advice: Human Capital, Asset Allocation, and Insurance*. Charlottesville, VA: Research Foundation of CFA Institute.

Markowitz, Harry. 1952. "Portfolio Selection." *Journal of Finance*, vol. 7, no. 1 (March): 77–91.

Oyer, Paul. 2008. "The Making of an Investment Banker: Stock Market Shocks, Career Choice, and Lifetime Income." *Journal of Finance*, vol. 63, no. 6 (December): 2601–2628. doi:10.1111/j.1540-6261.2008.01409.x

Rejda, George E., and Michael J. McNamara. 2014. *Principles of Risk Management and Insurance*, 12th ed. Upper Saddle River, NJ: Prentice Hall.

PROBLEMS

The following information relates to Questions 1–8

Richard Lansky is an insurance and wealth adviser for individuals. Lansky's first meeting of the day is with Gregory Zavris, age 27, a new client who works as a journalist. Gregory's only asset is $5,000 in savings; he has $67,000 in liabilities. During the conversation, Lansky describes the concepts of financial capital and human capital, as well as the components of economic and traditional balance sheets. Gregory asks Lansky:

On which balance sheet are my future earnings reflected?

Gregory does not have medical insurance. He asks Lansky for advice regarding a policy that potentially would allow him to avoid paying for office visits related to minor medical problems.

In the afternoon, Lansky meets with Gregory's parents, Molly and Kirk, ages 53 and 60. Molly is a tenured university professor and provides consulting services to local businesses. Kirk is a senior manager for an investment bank. Lansky determines that Molly's income is more stable than Kirk's.

Kirk and Molly discuss estate planning, and Lansky recommends a whole life insurance policy on Kirk's life, with Molly responsible for paying the premiums. In the event of Kirk's death, Gregory would be entitled to the proceeds from the policy. Lansky explains that one feature of the policy provides for a portion of the benefits to be paid even if a premium payment is late or missed.

Molly tells Lansky that she has recently been reading about annuities and would like to clarify her understanding. Molly makes the following statements.

Statement 1:   Both deferred and immediate annuities provide the same flexibility concerning access to invested funds.

Statement 2:   The income yield for a given amount invested in a life-only immediate annuity is higher for an older person than for a younger person.

At the end of the consultation, Molly asks Lansky for advice regarding her retired aunt, Rose Gabriel, age 69. Molly believes that Gabriel's life annuity and pension benefits will provide enough income to meet her customary lifestyle needs. Gabriel lives in her mortgage-free home; her medical insurance plan covers basic health care expenses. Women in Gabriel's family generally have long life spans but often experience chronic health problems requiring extended nursing at home. Therefore, Molly is concerned that medical expenses might exceed Gabriel's net worth during her final years.

1. Gregory's human capital is:
   A. lower than his financial capital.
   B. equal to his financial capital.
   C. higher than his financial capital.
2. The *most* appropriate response to Gregory's balance sheet question is:
   A. the economic balance sheet only.
   B. the traditional balance sheet only.
   C. both the economic and the traditional balance sheets.
3. Given Gregory's policy preference, which type of medical insurance should Lansky recommend?
   A. Indemnity plan
   B. Preferred provider plan
   C. Health maintenance organization plan
4. In estimating Molly's human capital value, Lansky should apply an income volatility adjustment that is:
   A. less than Kirk's.
   B. the same as Kirk's.
   C. greater than Kirk's.
5. Regarding the whole life insurance policy recommended by Lansky, Kirk would be the:
   A. owner.
   B. insured.
   C. beneficiary.

6. The whole life insurance policy feature described by Lansky is a:
   A. non-forfeiture clause.
   B. waiver-of-premium rider.
   C. guaranteed insurability rider.
7. Which of Molly's statements about annuities is/are correct?
   A. Statement 1 only
   B. Statement 2 only
   C. Both Statement 1 and Statement 2
8. The type of insurance that will *best* address Molly's concern about Gabriel is:
   A. disability insurance.
   B. longevity insurance.
   C. long-term care insurance.

The following information relates to Questions 9–15

Henri Blanc is a financial adviser serving high-net-worth individuals in the United States. Alphonse Perrin, age 55, meets with Blanc for advice about coordinating his employee benefits with his investment and retirement planning strategies.

Perrin has adopted a life-cycle portfolio strategy and plans to retire in 10 years. Recently, he received a promotion and $50,000 salary increase to manage a regional distribution center for a national retail firm. Perrin's spending needs are currently less than his annual income, and he has no debt. His investment assets consist of $2,000,000 in marketable securities (90% equity/10% fixed income) and a vineyard with winery valued at $1,500,000.

Blanc leads Perrin through a discussion of the differences between his financial capital and his human capital, as well as between his traditional balance sheet and his economic balance sheet. Perrin is vested in a defined benefit pension plan based on years of service and prior salary levels. Future benefits will vest annually based on his new salary. Perrin makes the following statements regarding his understanding of pension benefits.

> **Statement 1:** Unvested pension benefits should be classified as human capital.
>
> **Statement 2:** Vested pension benefits should not be classified as financial capital until payments begin.

Perrin asks Blanc to compare his traditional and economic balance sheets. Blanc calculates that the sum of the present values of Perrin's consumption goals and bequests exceeds that of his unvested pension benefits and future earnings.

Perrin tells Blanc that he expects a slower rate of growth in the US economy. Perrin expresses the following concerns to Blanc.

> **Concern 1** Holding all else equal, I wonder what the effect will be on my human capital if the nominal risk-free rate declines?
>
> **Concern 2** My employer projects a slower rate of sales growth in my region; therefore, I am anxious about losing my job.

Perrin is a widower with three adult children who live independently. Perrin's oldest son wishes to inherit the vineyard; the two other children do not want to be involved. Perrin would like to accommodate his children's wishes; however, he wants each child to inherit equal value from his estate. Blanc explains potential uses of life insurance to Perrin and suggests that one of these uses best meets Perrin's immediate needs.

Perrin expresses a preference for a life insurance policy that provides a range of investment options. Perrin selects a policy and asks Blanc to calculate the net payment cost index (per $1,000 of face value, per year), using a life expectancy of 20 years and a discount rate of 5%. Table 1 provides information about Perrin's policy.

TABLE 1   Perrin's Life Insurance Policy

Face value	$500,000
Annual premium (paid at beginning of the year)	$12,000
Policy dividends anticipated per year (paid at end of the year)	$2,000
Cash value projected at the end of 20 years	$47,000

9. Which of Perrin's statements regarding his pension is/are correct?
   A. Statement 1 only
   B. Statement 2 only
   C. Both Statement 1 and Statement 2
10. Blanc's calculations show that Perrin's economic net worth is:
    A. less than his net worth.
    B. equal to his net worth.
    C. greater than his net worth.
11. In response to Perrin's Concern #1, human capital will *most likely*:
    A. decrease.
    B. remain the same.
    C. increase.
12. Perrin's Concern #2 identifies a risk related to:
    A. human capital only.
    B. financial capital only.
    C. both human and financial capital.
13. Which of the following uses of life insurance *best* meets Perrin's immediate needs?
    A. Provides estate liquidity
    B. Acts as a tax-sheltered savings instrument
    C. Replaces lost earning power for dependents
14. The type of life insurance *most appropriate* for Perrin is:
    A. term.
    B. universal.
    C. whole life.
15. The net payment cost index that Blanc should calculate is *closest* to:
    A. $17.48.
    B. $20.00.
    C. $20.19.

The following information relates to Questions 16–23

Adrian and Olivia Barksdale live in Australia with their 16-year-old twins. Adrian, 47, works in a highly cyclical industry as an engineering manager at a bauxite mine. Olivia, 46, is an accountant. The Barksdales are saving for their retirement and college funding for both children. Adrian's annual salary is A$190,000; Olivia's annual salary is A$85,000. The family's living expenses are currently A$95,000 per year.

Both Adrian and Olivia plan to work 18 more years, and they depend on their combined income and savings to fund their goals. The Barksdales' new financial adviser, Duncan Smith, recommends an appropriate disability insurance policy to cover Adrian, given his large salary. Because he has a highly specialized job, Adrian is willing to pay for the most comprehensive policy available.

Smith is also concerned about the Barksdales' existing life insurance coverage. Currently, the Barksdales have a term life policy insuring Adrian with a death benefit of A$100,000. Smith assesses the family's insurance needs in the event Adrian were to die this year. To do so, Smith uses the needs analysis method based on the financial data presented in Exhibit 1 and the following assumptions:

- The discount rate is 6.0%, and the tax rate is 30%.
- Salary and living expenses grow at 3.5% annually.
- Salary and living expenses occur at the beginning of each year.
- The following assumptions apply in the event of Adrian's death:
  - Olivia will continue to work until retirement;
  - Family living expenses will decline by $30,000 per year;
  - Olivia's projected living expense will be $50,000 per year for 44 years; and
  - The children's projected living expenses will be $15,000 per year for 6 years.

EXHIBIT 1   Barksdale Family Financial Needs Worksheet

Cash Needs	AUD (A$)
Final expenses and taxes payable	20,000
Mortgage retirement	400,000
Education fund	300,000
Emergency fund	30,000
Total cash needs	750,000
Capital Available	
Cash and investments	900,000
Adrian: Life insurance	100,000
Total capital available	1,000,000

Next, Smith discusses the advantages and disadvantages of annuities. The Barksdales are interested in purchasing an annuity that offers the following characteristics:

- a payout that begins at retirement,
- the ability to invest in a menu of investment options, and
- a payout that continues as long as either Olivia or Adrian is living.

Olivia's mother, Sarah Brown, is also a client of Smith. She is age 75 and retired, and she needs a known income stream to assist her with current and future expenses. Brown's parents both lived longer than average, and she is concerned about outliving her assets. Smith recommends an annuity.

The Barksdales also worry about longevity risk given their family history and healthy lifestyle. Both spouses want an annuity for their later years (beginning in 40 years) that will ensure the greatest supplemental, level income stream relative to the cost. The Barksdales are willing to forgo the right to cash out the policy.

Smith turns to a discussion about the Barksdales' investment portfolio and how total economic wealth (human capital plus financial capital) might affect asset allocation decisions. The Barksdales' human capital is valued at $2.9 million and estimated to be 35% equity-like. Smith determines that an overall target allocation of 40% equity is appropriate for the Barksdales' total assets on the economic balance sheet.

Smith makes two recommendations regarding the Barksdales' investment portfolio.

Recommendation 1   The portfolio should have lower risk than a portfolio for similar investors in the same lifestyle stage.

Recommendation 2   The portfolio should underweight securities having a high correlation with bauxite demand.

16. Based on Adrian's job and salary, the *most appropriate* disability policy would define disability as the inability to perform duties of:
    A. any occupation.
    B. Adrian's regular occupation.
    C. any occupation for which Adrian is suited by education and experience.

17. Based on the given assumptions and the data in Exhibit 1, the additional amount of life insurance coverage needed is *closest* to:
    A. A$0.
    B. A$331,267.
    C. A$2,078,101.

18. Based on the Barksdales' annuity preferences, which type of annuity should they purchase?
    A. Deferred fixed
    B. Deferred variable
    C. Immediate variable

19. Based on the Barksdales' annuity preferences, which annuity payout method should they choose?
    A. Joint life annuity
    B. Life annuity with refund
    C. Life annuity with period certain

20. Based on Brown's goals and concerns, which type of annuity should Smith recommend for her?
    A. Deferred fixed
    B. Immediate fixed
    C. Immediate variable

21. Which type of annuity *best* satisfies the Barksdales' desire for supplemental income in their later years?
    A. Deferred fixed
    B. Deferred variable
    C. Advanced life deferred

22. Based on Exhibit 1, and meeting the Barksdales' target equity allocation for total economic wealth, the financial capital equity allocation should be *closest* to:
   A. 35.0%.
   B. 54.5%.
   C. 56.1%.
23. Which of Smith's recommendations regarding the Barksdales' investment portfolio is/are correct?
   A. Recommendation 1 only
   B. Recommendation 2 only
   C. Both Recommendation 1 and Recommendation 2

CHAPTER 13

CASE STUDY IN RISK MANAGEMENT: PRIVATE WEALTH

Giuseppe Ballocchi, PhD, CFA

LEARNING OUTCOMES

The candidate should be able to:

- identify and analyze a family's risk exposures during the early career stage;
- recommend and justify methods to manage a family's risk exposures during the early career stage;
- identify and analyze a family's risk exposures during the career development stage;
- recommend and justify methods to manage a family's risk exposures during the career development stage;
- identify and analyze a family's risk exposures during the peak accumulation stage;
- recommend and justify methods to manage a family's risk exposures during the peak accumulation stage;
- identify and analyze a family's risk exposures during the early retirement stage;
- recommend and justify a plan to manage risks to an individual's retirement lifestyle goals.

1. INTRODUCTION AND CASE BACKGROUND

Giving advice on risk management to individuals and families raises a number of challenges. These challenges include the extent to which identified and evaluated risks can be reduced and/or addressed using insurance policies or self-insurance. Families' financial circumstances and risks evolve over time, and financial advisers should review and update the solutions addressing these risks accordingly. Risk management solutions recommended by advisers should consider the family's overall health, wealth, and long-term goals.

This case study explores some of the risk management issues for a married couple living in a hypothetical country in the Eurozone. The case spans several decades and follows the couple through different stages of life from their early career phase, when they are in their late twenties, all the way to retirement. We will show how risk management methods need to change as the family's circumstances evolve. Particularly important prior readings related to this case are the Level III readings "Risk Management for Individuals" and "Overview of Private Wealth Management."

The assumptions used are drawn from what is typical for many countries in Europe. The circumstances and risks that this married couple face are influenced by the environment in which they find themselves. Despite the differences between Europe and other parts of the world, however, their goals, the risks they face, and the assessment of their circumstances, as well as the suggested methods, are by no means unique to the region. The risk analysis methodology and its application would therefore be valid in a much broader context.

For simplicity, we assume that economic conditions and tax rates remain unchanged throughout the four decades that this case study spans. The terms "adviser" and "wealth manager" are used interchangeably throughout this case study. The amounts that appear in exhibits throughout the case study are rounded.

The case is divided into six major sections. Section 1.1 provides background information about the hypothetical country in which the Schmitt family resides. Sections 1–4 provide initial case facts relating to the family's early career stage and risk management analysis, as well as solutions relevant to that stage. In Sections 5 and 6, we revisit the couple in their career development stage when they are 45 years old. In Sections 7–10, we examine their lives at age 55, in peak accumulation phase, and age 64, when they are preparing to retire. The final section provides a summary of the case.

1.1. Background of Eurolandia

This section provides background information about the social security system, healthcare, education and tax rates in the hypothetical country of Eurolandia. The case study assumes that the local social security system and regulatory conditions remain unchanged throughout the period under consideration. Economic conditions are assumed to be stable, with low but stable growth, inflation at 1%, and the risk-free rate (the yield-to-maturity of 30-year government bonds) at 3%. Unless stated otherwise, the amounts of the state pension and social security benefits are expected to increase by 1% annually in real terms.

1.1.1. Government Pension Plan

All Eurolandia residents who are employed are enrolled in the mandatory government pension plan. The plan is expected to provide retirement income for participants who have been enrolled for most of their working lives (35 years at a minimum in most cases) to cover at least basic living expenses upon retirement. This pay-as-you-go scheme fulfills that role at present, but its long-term viability is not necessarily guaranteed. Those who have paid the contributions for most of their working lives can expect to receive about a €13,500 annual pension from the government system. Those who have worked for the government (civil servants) enjoy a higher level of benefits and can expect to receive the higher of €20,000 per year, or 55% of their final salary. The foregoing amounts are what is currently paid to retirees. Unlike the arrangements in many other European countries, in Eurolandia the entitlement to civil servants' pension ends when the retiree dies, and surviving family members are not entitled to further payments.

The foregoing amounts are expected to increase by 2% per year in nominal terms, more than offsetting the 1% inflation rate. Eurolandia's mean annual salary is €35,000.

1.1.2. Health System
Basic health insurance is compulsory for Eurolandia residents, and contributions to the scheme are normally deducted from salary along with the government pension plan contributions. The health insurance offers comprehensive coverage of the vast majority of health care expenses and is considered adequate. It requires those seeking treatment to make small co-payments for a particular service. Supplemental health insurance is available through private companies. It covers optional treatments and offers shorter waiting times as well as access to a selection of privately run facilities that provide a high degree of comfort and that are not covered by the basic health insurance. The government provides basic long-term care.

1.1.3. Unemployment Insurance
Unemployment insurance is compulsory in Eurolandia, and premiums are paid in the form of social security contributions. Unemployment benefits are capped at a low amount, however, far below what a successful professional would earn. Although the modest benefits (€800 per month) run for a limited amount of time, those in long-term unemployment still receive a form of means-tested income support and a range of means-tested benefits, such as housing benefit. Means testing involves assessment of the person's financial resources to determine the need for state benefit support. Those dependent on the social security system would qualify for up to €12,000 per adult per year.

1.1.4. Disability Insurance
As with unemployment insurance, the compulsory social security contributions provide basic disability insurance. This insurance provides benefits in the form of regular income if one is unable to work because of serious illness or disability. As with unemployment insurance, the level of benefits, however, is capped at what is considered to be a low amount of €1,500 per month (€18,000 per year), far below what a successful professional would earn. Government employees, including those working for state schools, qualify for a higher level of coverage after 10 years of service, providing benefits in the form of income replacement of €1,800 per month (€21,600 per year).

1.1.5. Education
Education for children aged six and older is provided and funded by the government. University education up to the first degree level is also funded by the government and is almost free to residents of the European Economic Area (EEA), a free trade zone that, among others, includes European Union countries. Government funding extends to master's-level degrees that are also made accessible through a public subsidy. Government-funded schools and universities enjoy very good reputations.

1.1.6. Social Security Contributions and Tax Rates
To be entitled to the aforementioned social security benefits, employees pay 9% social security contributions on the portion of gross salaries that exceed €15,000 per year. The contributions are deductible from taxable income at source and are capped to a maximum of €10,000 per

family per year. The marginal income tax rates for individuals are listed in Exhibit 1. Unemployment and disability benefits are not subject to income tax.

EXHIBIT 1   Marginal Tax Rates

Yearly Taxable Income (€)	Marginal Tax Rate
0 to 15,000	0%
15,000 to 50,000	30%
Above 50,000	40%

Note: The €15,000 and €50,000 thresholds and the €10,000 cap are annually adjusted for inflation. Mortgage interest is not tax deductible.

The government encourages residents to save for retirement. There are tax incentives for voluntary contributions to government-regulated defined contribution (DC) occupational (employer-sponsored) and private pension savings plans. The government adds 25% to the amount of a member's contribution, meaning that for every €100 a member contributes to the scheme, the amount added becomes €125 thanks to €25 that comes from the government. Members of such schemes can, within certain limits, decide on the asset allocation. There is no tax on investment returns within regulated pension savings plans. Normal retirement age for both men and women is 65 and is expected to remain unchanged. Tax-free lump sum withdrawals from private pension savings plans, amounting to a maximum 25% of the fund, are allowed from age 55. Realized net capital gains on investments held outside regulated pension schemes (including rental property investments) are subject to capital gains taxes of 30% on amounts of gains exceeding €25,000 per person per year. No distinction is made between short-term and long-term holding periods, and the €25,000 level is expected to remain unchanged in the future.

1.2. The Schmitt Family in Their Early Career Stage

The following section provides initial facts as they apply to the Schmitt family. The subsequent sections then explain the risks the Schmitts face as well as the methods for addressing those risks.

1.2.1. Initial Case Facts

Paul and Jessica Schmitt, both 28 years old, recently got married. They are in their early career phase. Both graduated three years ago with master's degrees in, respectively, mathematics and computer science. Upon graduation, Paul found the teaching job to which he aspired, and he has been teaching mathematics at a local school ever since, earning a gross yearly salary of €45,600. After social security and tax deductions, his take-home pay is €33,670. Jessica, a born entrepreneur, joined an IT startup after graduating. Her gross yearly salary is now €24,000, which translates into €20,490 after taxes and social security contributions. Her salary has potential for a significant increase from the current relatively low level. She is also entitled to receive a discretionary bonus if her company becomes profitable. A bonus would potentially constitute a significant portion of her compensation. She could earn a far better fixed salary elsewhere, but she prefers the upside potential that her current position could offer, and she really believes that her company will succeed.

Paul and Jessica have combined savings of €15,000. They have no other financial assets, except for their participation in the government pension plan, to which they have been contributing since they started working three years ago. Their only other notable asset is their old car. The Schmitts have no debt, because their living expenses while they were students were covered by their parents and by government funding. Tuition costs at the state university they attended were negligible. Their monthly expenses are €2,900, including rent of €1,000. Exhibit 2 summarizes the Schmitts' circumstances.

EXHIBIT 2   Summary of the Schmitts' Circumstances

	Jessica	Paul	Combined
Annual gross income (€)	24,000	45,600	69,600
Annual net income (€)	20,490	33,670	54,160
Source of income	Information technology start up	Teaching job at state school	
Annual Living expenses (€)			34,800
Financial assets (€)			15,000
Debt (€)			0
Car (€)			7,000

The Schmitts would like to ensure long-term financial security for the family that they are hoping to start soon. They would also like to buy a house in an area that is very popular with young couples and has seen substantial appreciation of property values. The Schmitts would welcome competent and unbiased financial advice, but they are unsure where to get it. They mention their wish to a relative, Mr. Muller, CFA. He is a retired financial advisor and is happy to help them.

2. IDENTIFICATION AND ANALYSIS OF RISK EXPOSURES: EARLY CAREER STAGE

Muller follows the four key steps in the risk management process for individuals:

1. Specify the objective.
2. Identify risks.
3. Evaluate risks and select appropriate methods to manage the risks.
4. Monitor outcomes and risk exposures and make appropriate adjustments in methods.

2.1. Specify the Schmitts' Financial Objectives

Muller discusses the couple's financial objectives with Paul and Jessica. They describe those objectives as a house purchase in the very near future and hopefully starting a family. They wish to ensure long-term financial security and, looking ahead, a comfortable retirement. Muller acknowledges that most couples of their age usually do not pay much attention to the distant future. Although the Schmitts have almost their entire working career ahead of them, he confirms to them that it is essential to start planning for this long-term objective as early as possible. Moreover, there are likely to be tax advantages to be reaped by optimizing retirement savings, although there may be limited financial resources available to devote to that objective in the Schmitts' current stage of life—the early career stage.

Muller questions the couple about their current circumstances, including employment, and inquires further about the proposed house purchase. The Schmitts are keen to purchase a condominium they like very much at a cost of €270,000. If fully funded by a 25-year repayment mortgage at an initial interest rate of 3.6% per year fixed for 5 years, the monthly mortgage cost would come to approximately €1,360, compared with the €1,000 monthly rent that they are currently paying.

2.2. Identification of Risk Exposures

To better understand the young couple's financial health and to identify and analyze risks the Schmitts face, Muller lists the couple's assets, liabilities, and financial objectives and assesses the characteristics of human capital as components of the Schmitts' total wealth. He observes that they are richly endowed with human capital:

- They are highly trained in fields that are, and are expected to remain, in high demand.
- They are young, in the career development phase, with many working years ahead of them.
- They have been employed for nearly three years, accruing valuable working experience.
- As citizens of an EU country, they are geographically mobile and legally entitled to work in other countries in the region.

Muller describes Paul's human capital, if he continues in his chosen career as a teacher, as very much bond-like. He has the status of a civil servant, a term used to describe someone who works in the state sector. His income is expected to increase with seniority, but has very modest upside potential. Paul benefits from excellent job security, limiting earnings risk from unemployment. Although Paul is entitled to work in many countries, the portability of his human capital as a teacher is limited because the required qualifications to obtain a teaching position vary significantly from country to country. Moreover, the privileges and accrued seniority related to his civil servant status are not easily transferable when moving to another country.

Jessica's human capital, if she remains in the same or a similar role, is very much equity-like. She faces significant uncertainties in her future cash flows from employment, but she can also benefit from substantial rewards if she meets her job objectives and her company does well. Muller and Jessica agree that she faces significant earnings risk, much more so than her husband. This is because she works for a startup that offers no coverage for loss of income resulting from disability or premature death. Only the coverage provided by the country's social insurance system would be available. Unemployment is also much more of a concern for her because, unlike her husband, she does not enjoy the job security of a civil servant. There can also be ambiguity in what triggers her bonus payments and her participation in the company profits. If she becomes a shareholder, following the award of stock options, the resulting asset will have some of the characteristics of a business asset. Jessica's human capital, driven by her globally applicable IT skill set, is portable across countries.

Muller notes that from a financial point of view, the Schmitts' marriage results in human capital diversification, with Paul's human capital being bond-like and Jessica's human capital being equity-like, subject to far more risk and upside than that of her husband.

Exhibits 3 and 4 show the assumptions and the economic balance sheet as summarized by Muller. He repeatedly stresses that any calculations are subject to substantial uncertainty, especially in the early career stage, but such exercise provides a good starting point for the risk analysis that needs to be performed. The asset side at this stage features the rather limited liquid financial assets, the vested state pension benefits (the mortality-weighted net present value [NPV] of the accrued benefit amount), and human capital. Human capital, reflecting the present value (PV) at a wage-risk adjusted discount rate, of the expected stream of income from employment, is calculated using the formula

$$HC_0 = \sum_{t=1}^{t=N} \frac{p(s_t)\, w_{t-1}(1 + g_t)}{(1 + r_f + y)^t} \tag{1}$$

where

HC_0 = human capital
$p(s_t)$ = the probability of surviving to a given year (or age)
w_t = the income from employment in period t
g_t = the annual wage growth rate
r_f = the nominal risk-free rate
y = the risk adjustment based on occupational income volatility
N = the length of working life in years

The human capital values, shown in Exhibit 4, are calculated using the formula in Equation 1 and are based on the assumptions in Exhibit 3.

EXHIBIT 3   Assumptions for the Calculation of Human Capital at Age 28

	Jessica	Paul
Starting salary (net)	€20,490	€33,666
Assumed nominal salary growth rate	6%	3%
Discount rate (nominal risk-free)	3%	3%
Risk adjustment based on occupational income volatility	3%	0%
Remaining length of working life assuming retirement at age 65	37	37

Note: The probability of surviving to a given age is based on mortality tables (not shown here) used in Eurolandia.

The liability side shows financial objectives that can be modeled as liabilities. The €1.87 million present value of lifetime consumption needs is based on an assumed initial €2,900 monthly expenditure (€34,800 per year). Because the Schmitts do not know when they are likely to have children and when they will be incurring higher expenditures, Muller assumes that their expenses will rise by 6% (5% above inflation and assuming they will have a growing family) in each of the next 10 years and increase in line with 1% inflation from then on. Assuming life expectancy of 90 years, the PV of lifetime consumption calculation would cover 62 years in total.

EXHIBIT 4   The Schmitts' Economic Balance Sheet at the Age of 28

Assets (€)		Liabilities (€)	
Savings account	15,000	Debt	0
Accrued entitlement to state retirement benefits (Paul)	21,000		
Accrued DB government retirement plan (Jessica)	11,800		
Paul's human capital	1,174,800	PV of lifetime consumption	1,868,000
Jessica's human capital	694,700		
Total assets	**1,917,300**	**Total liabilities**	**1,868,000**
		Net wealth	**49,300**

Note: Figures are rounded. Because we take a holistic view of assets and liabilities, we include the participation in the country's compulsory retirement program as an asset. The Schmitts' ownership of an old car is disregarded for the purposes of the economic balance sheet.

Miller notes at the outset that both Paul and Jessica are in the early career stage, and they are rich in human capital but have very limited financial assets. They face the financial challenges of starting a family, with the possible purchase of a property. Given their very modest level of financial assets and the fact that their liabilities are very limited, the risk analysis at this stage of life focuses on human capital. The estimation of its present value depends on a range of assumptions and is subject to uncertainty. But liabilities need to be met, especially if the couple has children. For this reason, a careful analysis of any gaps in the current insurance coverage must be conducted. Such analysis will lead to recommendations for risk management in order to preserve and optimize human capital, the most valuable asset that the Schmitts own, and also to meet lifestyle goals. Following systematic examination of their circumstances, Muller identifies the following risks that the Schmitts face and that he will need to evaluate:

- earnings risk resulting from loss of employment
- earnings risk resulting from health and disability
- premature death risk leading to costs imposed on the surviving partner
- car accident and repair costs
- liability risk (e.g., the risk of bodily injury or property damage caused when driving)

In addition to these risks, Muller wants to consider the effect of the proposed house purchase on the Schmitts' financial circumstances.

2.3. Analysis of Identified Risk

Having identified the key risks facing the Schmitts, Mr. Muller, CFA, proceeds to evaluate those risks one by one, considering any existing coverage provided by the employer or the government social security system.

2.3.1. Earnings risk
Earnings risk resulting from loss of employment is particularly relevant for Jessica because of the nature of her employer's business. The likelihood of loss of employment is difficult to

estimate but is higher than the probability of Paul's loss of employment. Because of her limited number of years of service, the amount of any statutory redundancy payments (required by law and related to the number of years of service) due from the employer would be limited. Because they have both been paying social security contributions, they would at least initially be entitled to €800 per month of unemployment benefit, representing just under half of Jessica's net salary and just under a third of Paul's monthly net pay.

Earnings risk resulting from health or disability is highly relevant despite the fact that both Paul and Jessica are young and in good health. If Jessica or Paul were unable to work because of illness or disability, both events more likely than premature death, the benefits from the state social security system would amount to approximately €1,500 per month, replacing most of Jessica's initial €1,708 monthly after-tax income but only just over half of Paul's monthly after-tax income of €2,806. In Jessica's case, one needs to consider that her salary is expected to show healthy growth, as reflected in her human capital estimates, and social security benefits are, over time, set to replace decreasing proportion of her income from employment. Jessica's employment package does not include any disability coverage, while Paul's enhanced coverage resulting from his government employee status would apply only after another seven years of employment.

2.3.2. Premature death risk

In the case of an unlikely scenario of premature death, the risk to the remaining spouse is at this stage of life twofold. First, one-off costs such as the funeral would have to be paid and an emergency fund would have to be established, because the surviving spouse would have no partner to help deal with emergencies. Second, his or her lifestyle would be affected by the fact that the monthly household costs that they currently cover jointly, including rent, would become the remaining spouse's sole responsibility.

2.3.3. Car accident and repair costs

The Schmitts use an old car and have a compulsory third-party insurance policy in place, protecting them in case they need to pay other parties' repair costs or compensation. Given the basic nature of the policy, they are not protected from costs that would arise should they need to have their own car repaired or replaced, exposing them to risk. During their discussions with Muller, however, Paul and Jessica explain that they do not use their car very often.

2.3.4. Liability risk

Muller considers the bulk of liability risk arising from car accidents or from injuries sustained by those who visit one's property. The existing compulsory car policy is basic but does provide liability coverage. Because the Schmitts' property liability (as well as buildings and contents) is insured as part of their rental agreement, he does not consider any other liability risks significant given the local culture.

2.3.5. House purchase

In addition to the aforementioned risks that they already face, the proposed house purchase would increase the couple's vulnerability to unexpected short-term expenditures. The Schmitts already have significant mismatch between financial assets and the sum of liabilities and financial objectives. Human capital is illiquid and represents future cash flows from earnings. The Schmitts' objective of purchasing a property requires a substantial amount of cash for the deposit (down payment), legal/notary's fees, additional transaction costs, and moving expenses. Significant sudden cash needs may arise if, for example, they need to replace their old car. To some extent, such cash needs, except for the house down payment, can be met through borrowing. The interest rates for consumer finance, however, are quite high and typically linked to a floating reference rate, thereby exposing the Schmitts to interest rate risk. Their ability to meet even small, short-term bills and cope with any unexpected expenditures would be limited if they decide to buy a property and use their limited savings to cover the transaction costs.

Muller explains that the house purchase decision itself should be weighed against continuing to rent. Paul and Jessica argue that their monthly spend on rent of €1,000 is not that different from the likely monthly mortgage payment of €1,360, so the house purchase should make little difference to their monthly budget that currently stands at €2,900. Muller points out, however, that the difference that does exist should not be disregarded and that property-related service charges and maintenance costs should be taken into consideration. At an annual 1% of property value (annual cost of €2,700 or €225 per month), the additional cost would dent the Schmitts' ability to build up any savings buffer.

3. RISK MANAGEMENT RECOMMENDATIONS: EARLY CAREER STAGE

Having assessed the risks that the Schmitts face, Muller provides the following recommendations to the young couple:

3.1. Recommendations for Managing Risks

3.1.1. Earnings risk
Earnings risk arising from loss of employment cannot be easily insured. Muller's recommendation is for the Schmitts to build up a savings "buffer" amounting to at least six months' worth of normal expenditures (buffer of €17,400 based on €2,900 monthly spend). That way they could effectively self-insure over time to be able to cope with circumstances during which they would rely on the unemployment benefits provided by the social security system.

Earnings risk resulting from serious illness or disability, exposing the couple to a shortfall in income if they were to rely on state benefits if one was to fall seriously ill or become disabled, can be addressed by taking out disability insurance. Consequently, Muller recommends that each of them take out a disability insurance policy that would replace their current income over and above the disability benefits insurance that the state provides, to maintain their living standards. As their salaries are expected to increase, in Jessica's case substantially from a low starting level, he recommends they go for a policy that guarantees the option to purchase additional coverage without underwriting. The amount of disability income coverage required to replace earnings and supplement the state social security disability benefit is calculated in Exhibit 5. The difference between the amount of recommended coverage for each person reflects the fact that Paul's salary is notably higher than what the disability benefits from the social security system would replace. Muller recommends they buy policies that would provide benefit of €80,000 and €490,000 for Jessica and Paul, respectively. Muller states that the cost of such policy should be in line with fair value and emphasizes the need to carefully compare costs among different providers (*note: the analysis of the cost is beyond the scope of this case study*). He further adds that the policy purchase decision potentially has long term implications, hence the need for in-depth analysis.

EXHIBIT 5   Disability Insurance Coverage Calculation

	Jessica	Paul
Annual salary income (net) to be replaced	€20,490	€33,670
Amount of annual disability coverage provided by the social security system	€18,000	€18,000
Shortfall	€2,490	€15,670
Benefit period (until retirement age)	37 years	37 years
Assumed annual benefit adjustment (nominal)	2%	2%
Discount rate	3%	3%
PV of future earnings replacement required (calculated as PV of annuity due)	€77,700	€489,000

Note: Disability insurance benefits can take the form of a lump sum or a stream of payments over time.

Using calculator keystrokes for an annuity due with level payment, the growth of payments can be incorporated by adjusting the discount rate to account for the growth rate. The adjusted rate can be calculated as follows, as long as the discount rate is larger than the growth rate: (1 + Discount rate)/(1 + Growth rate) – 1, or (1.03/1.02) – 1 = 0.98%. Set the calculator for beginning-of-period payments; $n = 37$, payment = €2,490, and $i = 0.98\%$. Then calculate PV.

3.1.2. Premature death risk

Although the couple has no children or mortgage to pay at present, the financial difficulties faced by the surviving spouse in the event of one person's death should be covered using a life insurance policy. Exhibit 6 illustrates how one could establish the level of life insurance coverage required.

EXHIBIT 6   Calculating the Amount of Life Insurance Coverage

Muller explains that the amount of coverage that the life insurance policy should provide can be calculated using two methods. One is based on the value of human capital (the *human life value* method), which estimates the amount of future earnings that must be replaced. The other is the *needs analysis* method, based on estimating the amount needed to cover survivor's living expenses. He adds that both methods rely on a number of assumptions that may turn out to be inaccurate.

Muller suggests focusing on the needs analysis method at this stage of the Schmitts' careers. He explains that in the absence of debts to be repaid and absence of children whose upbringing would need to be funded, the calculation is relatively simple and involves estimating only two main items:

- Cash needs required upon death of the insured person, including funeral and burial costs, any taxes or debt to be repaid, and establishment of an emergency fund. They agree on a figure of €30,000.
- The surviving spouse's ability to cope with ongoing costs. They currently spend €34,800 per year, of which about half is spent jointly on rent and general expenditures that will remain broadly unchanged in the future. They estimate that the surviving spouse would require at least €25,000 annually for ongoing costs and that those costs would, under such circumstances, grow at 2% in nominal terms. The present value of such annual flow

for the rest of the person's life is then compared with the present value of the survivor's earnings.

	Paul's Life Cover (from Jessica's perspective)	Jessica's Life Cover (from Paul's perspective)
Cash needs		
Funeral and burial costs plus taxes	15,000	15,000
Emergency fund	15,000	15,000
Debts to be repaid	0	0
Total cash needs	**30,000**	**30,000**
Capital needs		
PV of surviving spouse's €25,000 annual living expenses (growing at 2% until death at age 90, discounted at 3%, annuity due)	1,169,000	1,169,000
Less PV of survivor's income until retirement at 65 (annuity due, assuming 3% growth and 3% discount rate for Paul and 6% growth and 3% discount rate plus 3% risk adjustment for Jessica)	758,000	1,246,000
Total capital needs	**411,000**	**−77,000**
Total financial needs	**441,000**	**−47,000**
Capital available:		
Cash, savings, investments	15,000	15,000
PV of vested retirement accounts (attributable to surviving spouse)	11,800	21,000
Existing life insurance coverage	0	0
Total capital available	**27,000**	**36,000**
Additional life insurance needs	414,000	−83,000

Note: Rounding used throughout.

Having analyzed the needs from the surviving partner's point of view, Muller recommends that the couple purchase a life insurance policy on Paul's life. He points out that although life and disability insurance is relevant already, if the Schmitts have children, the level of coverage would need to be reviewed and potentially increased significantly. For now, Paul and Jessica decide on a policy covering Paul's life, providing benefit coverage of €400,000.

3.1.3. Car accident and repair costs

The existing car insurance coverage protects other parties but not the Schmitts. Having considered the cost of taking out more comprehensive coverage and taking into account their sparse use of the car, Muller advises the Schmitts not to spend resources on better coverage but self-insure instead with an adequate savings buffer.

3.1.4. Risks to lifestyle arising from the proposed house purchase

Muller advises the couple against the house purchase at this time. Despite recognizing numerous long-term benefits of home ownership, he argues that delaying the house purchase would lower their risk exposures. Muller also points out that a house cannot be considered fully as an investment asset but rather as a "mixed" asset, with elements of a personal asset (consumer item) as well as an investment asset. In addition, he sees risk to mortgage costs from increasing interest rates (once any fixed-rate period comes to an end). Instead of the house purchase, he suggests the Schmitts draw up a savings plan to build their savings and financial assets, because they risk being left virtually without financial assets if they were to purchase their home in the near future. The Schmitts' total yearly after-tax income of slightly more than €54,000 means that they do have the ability to save, as a simple cash budget in Exhibit 7 shows. The costs of paying the recommended insurance premiums (including the existing car insurance) that Muller estimates could roughly be in the region of €2,500 per year would easily be accommodated by the family budget.

EXHIBIT 7   Summary Annual Budget of the Schmitt Family at Age 28

Combined yearly gross pay	69,600
Less taxes and Social Security contributions	(15,440)
Net pay	54,160
Living costs (including rent)	(34,800)
Net cash available	19,360

Note: Rounded amounts used.

Muller suggests that a comfortable savings buffer, amounting to at least six months of living expenses (i.e., €17,400), should be set aside and be available on demand (e.g., in an easy-access bank account or equivalent). An investment plan should be drawn up once savings in excess of the buffer become available. He recommends that the Schmitts draw up a contingency plan for the critical first year after the home purchase if indeed they go ahead with their intention to buy, in case a sudden liquidity need arises. After the first year, accumulated savings should provide such liquidity buffer. The contingency plan should identify the cheapest way of borrowing, most probably against the house equity.

3.1.5. Other risks

Property insurance will be required if the Schmitts do decide to purchase a home. It is required as a condition for obtaining the mortgage, although Muller suggests that the amount of coverage equals the purchase cost of the property, not just the amount of mortgage debt. This consideration is particularly relevant as the Schmitts would be required to invest almost all of their liquid assets in their new home if the purchase goes ahead.

After a review of the basic health insurance coverage provided by mandatory social security contributions, Muller recommends not to enter into any additional private medical insurance at this time.

3.2. Monitoring Outcomes and Risk Exposures

Muller adds that no risk management strategy is complete without regular monitoring and reviewing of outcomes and risk exposures. He explains that adjustments to the risk management solutions must be made as circumstances change.

4. RISK MANAGEMENT CONSIDERATIONS ASSOCIATED WITH HOME PURCHASE

Contrary to Muller's recommendation, the Schmitts purchase their home in a sought-after area close to Jessica's workplace. The total purchase costs amount to €285,000, including all transaction costs, financed as follows:

1. Personal loan from Jessica's parents amounting to €80,000. The loan is not secured against the property. A secured loan would make obtaining a mortgage from the bank much more challenging, because the bank would not be the sole holder of a lien on the house if Jessica's parents held a secured loan.
2. Personal funds in the amount of €5,000. They reserve the rest of their assets to pay for moving expenses and furniture and to have a minimal liquidity buffer.
3. A 25-year mortgage of €200,000 at 3.6% fixed for five years, resulting in monthly payments of €1,012 consisting of both interest and capital repayment.

A condition of the mortgage is that the property is insured to at least the amount of the mortgage outstanding. The Schmitts take out property insurance with a coverage of €200,000, matching the mortgage amount, but less than what was suggested by Muller.

4.1. Review of Risk Management Arrangements Following the House Purchase

Following the decision to purchase the newly built property, the Schmitts ask Muller to review and update the family's risk management arrangements. They discuss how the risks have changed and how risk management solutions should be modified.

Some risks identified earlier have changed, and new ones have appeared. Earnings risk from unemployment, disability or premature death has not changed, but the level of life coverage needs to be reevaluated because the couple now faces a liability in the form of a mortgage that would, in line with local customs, be expected to be repaid in full if Jessica or Paul died. The same would apply to the loan from Jessica's parents.

EXAMPLE 1 Calculation of Life Insurance Required

Using the needs analysis method (Exhibit 6), recalculate the amount of life insurance coverage the Schmitts require.

Assume that the surviving spouse continues to live in the newly purchased house, and also assume the following:

- The emergency fund would need to be increased to €30,000 because of the near-zero liquid cash resources available following the house purchase.
- The mortgage (€200,000) and loan from Jessica's parents (€80,000) are to be fully repaid, in line with local customs in the country.
- The survivor's annual costs fall to only €19,000 because of the fact that mortgage repayment costs drop out and are only partly offset by maintenance and service charges. Assuming such costs are to be paid for the rest the survivor's life (a further

62 years), and assuming a discount rate of 3% and an annual living cost increase of 2%, the PV of such future costs is about €888,000.

- The PV of the survivor's income from after-tax salary is €758,000 for Jessica and €1,246,000 for Paul, as per Exhibit 6.
- Capital available is now only €12,000 and €21,000, represented by the PV of vested retirement savings accounts for Jessica and Paul, respectively.

Solution:

	Paul's Life Cover (from Jessica's perspective)	Jessica's Life Cover (from Paul's perspective)
Cash needs		
Funeral and burial costs plus taxes	15,000	15,000
Mortgage retirement	200,000	200,000
Other debt (Jessica's parents' loan)	80,000	80,000
Emergency fund	30,000	30,000
Total cash needs	**325,000**	**325,000**
Capital needs		
PV of surviving spouse's living expenses (until death assumed at 90)	888,000	888,000
Less PV of survivor's income until retirement at 65 (annuity due, assuming 3% growth and 3% discount rate for Paul and 6% growth and 3% discount rate plus 3% risk adjustment for Jessica)	758,000	1,246,000
Total capital needs	**130,000**	**−358,000**
Total financial needs	**455,000**	**−33,000**
Capital available:		
Cash, savings, investments	0	0
PV of vested retirement accounts (attributable to surviving spouse)	12,000	21,000
Total capital available (excluding existing insurance coverage)	**12,000**	**21,000**
Insurance coverage required	**443,000**	**−54,000**

Given that the couple already has policy coverage of €400,000 (Paul's life), they should consider raising the amount of coverage of Paul's life.

The Schmitts' advisor explains that they also face property risk and related liability risk. Their existing coverage, arranged to satisfy the mortgage lender, covers the outstanding loan amount of €200,000. Muller recommends that they increase the homeowner's coverage to the full amount of what the property is worth, currently €280,000. The policy, if the cost is reasonable, should also cover the building contents and should provide coverage of legal liability arising from the property.

Muller also points out that the transaction has left the Schmitts with very limited resources. They should aim to build up a cash cushion in the form of instant-access savings. Because they have chosen to borrow at a fixed rate, the Schmitts do not face any near-term risk from rising interest rates.

EXAMPLE 2   Review and Reassessment of Methods

Identify possible upcoming events that should require a reassessment of the family's risk management methods.

Guideline answer: Paul and Jessica are buying their first property, and they hope to start a family. The property purchase and the resulting changes to the risk management solutions have been completed. Preparing for the birth of a child would be the point at which a reassessment of risk management methods becomes highly desirable. This is mainly because a loss of earnings of either Paul or Jessica would seriously impair the Schmitts' ability to pay for the child's upbringing.

---

5. IDENTIFICATION AND ANALYSIS OF RISK EXPOSURES: CAREER DEVELOPMENT STAGE

The Schmitts decide to approach Ms. Stein, CFA, a private wealth management practitioner and a partner in the same firm as Mr. Muller, CFA, who has since passed away. To identify and analyze the Schmitts' risk exposures Stein makes a full inquiry into their financial circumstances. She subsequently discusses their goals and proceeds to identify risks.

5.1. Case Facts: The Schmitts Are 45

In the last 17 years, the Schmitts have made significant progress in their careers and remain in good health. Their incomes and assets have increased, particularly Jessica's salary, which has risen substantially. They have been able to repay most of their mortgage and build up a portfolio of shares of 10 local IT companies whose business they believe they know. The couple is also considering making a speculative investment into residential property (similar in size to their existing property) located in the area where the IT industry is based and where Jessica works. They have repaid the loan from Jessica's parents. They continue to put money aside into an instant-access savings account, building up almost an €80,000 liquidity "buffer." Jessica's employer now offers a defined contribution (DC) company pension scheme into which Jessica and her employer make combined annual contributions of €3,000 (includes the top-up from government). Paul, having spent a number of years working as a teacher in the state education sector, is now entitled to life insurance coverage at three times his salary as part of his employment package. Because he has spent more than 10 years in the teaching role, he is now also entitled to a higher €2,520 monthly benefit in case of disability. This amount is the original €1,800 per month to which tenured state employees were entitled when Paul was 28, subsequently raised annually.

The Schmitts now have two children, Roxane and Peter, who are 12 and 7 years old, respectively. Peter suffers from mental development problems for which there does not appear to be a solution. He needs extra support at school. The Schmitts' living expenses have increased substantially and stand at €65,000 per year. Although Paul and Jessica increased the amount of life insurance coverage after Roxane's birth, they have not updated their insurance arrangements for many years. Exhibit 8 provides a summary of the Schmitts' financial circumstances.

EXHIBIT 8   Summary of the Schmitts' Financial Circumstances at Age 45

	Jessica	Paul	Combined
Yearly gross income (€)	80,000	66,000	**146,000**
Yearly after-tax income (€)	53,650	46,510	**100,160**
Source of income	Department head, IT	Teacher at state school	
Living expenses (€)			**65,000**
Pension provisions	Government pension scheme membership as mandated by law Plus Employer's DC scheme (annual contribution of €3,000 from Jessica and employer)	Government pension scheme as mandated by law. As a civil servant, enjoys better pension conditions No separate private pension fund	
Employer-provided insurance		Life, insurance lump sum coverage 3 × €66,000 = €198,000.	
Private life insurance	€200,000 life policy she took out after the birth of their first child.	Life policy of €440,000	
Disability insurance	Government insurance coverage of €25,200 per year. Private coverage of a lump sum of €112,200 (the original €80,000 policy taken out at age 28, reflecting 2% annual benefit adjustment)	Government insurance coverage of €30,245 per year (includes extra payment reflecting more than 10 years of service) Private coverage of a lump sum of €686,100 (the original €490,000 policy taken out at age 28, reflecting 2% annual benefit adjustment)	

5.2. Financial Objectives in the Career Development Stage

Stein first discusses financial objectives with the 45-year-old Schmitts. They wish to achieve the following goals:

- maximize household welfare and reduce the impact of any unexpected events, such as illness, disability, or premature death;
- plan for future costs of support for Peter; and
- have a comfortable retirement.

To help understand the family's circumstances and identify risks, Stein conducts a valuation of Jessica's and Paul's human capital. The exercise is easier now than was the case in the early career stage. The input parameters are less uncertain, because their salary levels now are more stable and predictable than in the early career stage, and the calculation of present values of expected future earnings is conducted over a shorter time horizon. Exhibit 9 shows the assumptions used, including the reduction in risk adjustment on Jessica's salary. It also shows the resulting economic balance sheet. Although the valuation of human capital varies considerably under different assumptions, the result is that the value of the couple's human capital is substantial, amounting to a combined €1.9 million. Stein notes the financial objectives and notices their dependency on the couple's growing earnings.

EXHIBIT 9   Economic Balance Sheet at the Age of 45

HUMAN CAPITAL ASSUMPTIONS

	Jessica	Paul
Expected salary growth (nominal)	5%	2%
Discount rate (r_f)	3%	3%
Risk adjustment (y)	1%	0%
Length of working life (up to age 65)	20	20
Probability of surviving to age 65	92%	92%

Note: Probability of surviving to a given age is based on mortality tables (not shown here) used in Eurolandia. They are assumed to be the same for men and women.

ECONOMIC BALANCE SHEET

Assets	€	Liabilities	€
Savings account	77,000	Mortgage debt	35,000
Shares of IT companies	130,000		
Accrued DB government retirement plan (Paul)	227,000		
Accrued DB government retirement plan (Jessica)	130,000		
Employer pension value (Jessica)	10,000		
Property (main residence)	320,000		
Paul's human capital	798,000	PV of lifetime consumption needs	2,379,000

Jessica's human capital	1,093,000		
Total assets	**2,805,000**	**Total liabilities**	**2,414,000**
		Net wealth	**391,000**

Note: The present value of lifetime consumption needs is based on the assumption that the family's current level of expenditure (€65,000) from this point increases by 2% a year in nominal terms (1% above inflation) for the rest of their lives. Assumes remaining time period of 45 years and discount rate of 3%. Numbers in the exhibit are rounded.

To better understand the family's regular cash flows, Stein also prepares a summary cash flow budget, shown in Exhibit 10.

EXHIBIT 10   Summary Annual Budget of the Schmitt Family at Age 45

	€
Combined yearly gross pay	146,000
Less taxes and Social Security contributions	45,800
Net pay	**100,200**
Less living costs (including mortgage cost)	65,000
Less (house repair, maintenance, service charges)	3,500
Cash available for insurance and savings	**31,700**
Insurance premiums	3,500
Funds available to save or invest	**28,200**
Currently used primarily to:	
Fund investment portfolio	22,000
Add to savings accounts	3,200
Contribute to Jessica's employer's pension plan	3,000

5.3. Identification and Evaluation of Risks in the Career Development Stage

EXAMPLE 3   Identification of Risks

Identify financial risks the Schmitts face. Discuss each risk in turn.

Guideline answer: The Schmitts face the following main risks:

- Earnings risk resulting from potential loss of employment. The risk of involuntary unemployment remains higher for Jessica than for Paul. Jessica is the higher earner, whereas Paul, a civil servant, could be expected to lose employment only under extreme circumstances. The amount at stake is greater than before because of the salary increases Jessica has enjoyed.

- Earnings risk resulting from disability. The Schmitts remain in good health, so the likelihood of them suffering from disability remains low but is higher than the risk of dying. Their salaries, however, provide their main source of income and funding of their current lifestyles. If one of them were to become disabled, the burden on the rest of the family would not only take the form of lost earnings. It would also limit the range of activities in which the surviving partner could engage, with possible implications for income and costs.
- Premature death risk. This risk remains relevant, because early death could have serious consequences for the family now that children need to be cared for. Not only would costs of bringing up children have to be covered, the surviving spouse would potentially suffer a reduction in income because all family responsibilities would now be performed only by the surviving spouse.
- Risk to the value of their growing but concentrated investment portfolio of shares of IT companies. This is the couple's main investment vehicle but is focused on a volatile sector, whose performance is correlated with Jessica's career prospects.
- Risk to their retirement lifestyle goals. If the couple's contributions to their retirement plans are insufficient or the plans perform poorly, their retirement funding could be insufficient for the standard of living they desire.
- Other risks include property and liability risks.

5.3.1. Assessment of earnings risk

Earnings risk is significant because loss of employment is particularly relevant for Jessica. She is on a relatively high salary and works in a higher-risk sector compared with Paul. If she were to rely on unemployment benefits, at just under €13,500 per year, they would cover a quarter of her net income. In the event Paul were to become unemployed, such benefits would cover less than a third of his net salary.

Earnings risk resulting from disability would seriously affect the couple's ability to maintain their lifestyle and costs associated with providing for the children. In case of disability, Jessica would be entitled to about €25,200 per year, which is less than half of her net salary. Paul is less exposed because his salary is lower and his entitlement to state disability benefit is higher after more than 10 years of service. Relying on state benefits alone would provide €30,245, amounting to almost two-thirds of his net salary. In addition, the Schmitts have existing disability insurance in place, now providing total payout of €112,000 and €686,100 (if treated as a lump sum) in case of Jessica's or Paul's disability, respectively. Stein suggests that the level of coverage is reassessed before recommendation is made.

Premature death risk, now that the couple has children, requires attention. Death of one of the parents would not only have consequences due to one-off costs resulting from the death but would also mean that family expenditures, currently covered jointly, would have to be funded from the survivor's income. Furthermore, the surviving spouse would potentially suffer a reduction in income because family responsibilities would now be performed only by the surviving spouse, most likely preventing him or her from career progression and possibly forcing the person to work part time. Alternatively, such services would have to be provided by others at a cost.

Although the amount of financial assets available to the family has increased substantially in recent years, at an aggregate amount approaching €210,000, they amount to more than the Schmitts' joint yearly gross earnings of €146,000. Stein points out, however, that those amounts are not significant for the couple to be able to cope with unexpected events beyond the short term. The adviser notes the Schmitts would like to avoid the extreme situation where the children would face not only the tragic loss of a parent (or both) but also a deterioration in living standards. Life insurance would provide support for their young children, who are likely to rely on them for financial support for at least the next 10 years and possibly longer in the case of their son Peter.

5.3.2. Analysis of the investment portfolio risks

Risk to the investment portfolio stems from the fact that Jessica and Paul prefer to invest in a relatively small number of companies they believe they know, all of which are IT companies in their home country. Stein points out the correlation between their IT stock holdings and Jessica's human capital, which is also tied to the prospects for the IT sector. If prospects for IT companies suffer, both the value of Jessica's human capital and that of their investment portfolio would decrease at the same time. Their risk-bearing ability is rather limited, which is important because their financial assets are rather modest compared with their spending needs—particularly in the presence of earnings risk related to Jessica's employment, a risk that is difficult to insure against. Moreover, because there is a relatively high concentration of IT employees where the Schmitts live, the value of the real estate that the Schmitts own there is likely to be positively correlated with Jessica's human capital as well.

5.3.3. Analysis of the retirement savings plans

Stein then takes a closer look at the risk to the Schmitts' retirement lifestyle goals. Through their mandatory social security contributions, the couple will be entitled to a government pension. In addition, Jessica's employer now provides a DC company pension, albeit with a limited amount of employer contributions. At the current rate of recently started contributions of €3,000 per year (combining those from Jessica's employer, her own payments, and the tax incentive), and assuming they grow at 3% annually, the estimated fund value would be near €150,000 at the age of 65, according to the fund administrator. At a typical annuity yield of 5%, such a sum would provide annual retirement income of €7,500. Stein estimates that if they remain employed until their retirement, and if there is no impairment in the benefits that are promised, the Schmitts will have a total gross retirement income, including state pensions, amounting to €76,000. This figure is about half of what they are earning now. Although their spending in retirement is likely to be lower than their current consumption, there is a risk that retirement income will be insufficient. Moreover, it is possible, and even likely, that the benefits offered by the state pension may be reduced before they retire, because the state pay-as-you-go system is under a significant strain.

5.3.4. Other risks

Stein also reviews the property and liability risks. The Schmitts have what is considered to be adequate health insurance through the government-mandated plan, which provides even quite advanced and costly treatment. It is a "no frills" arrangement, however, without any additional comfort or luxury environment. Property risk is covered by their existing buildings insurance, which includes liability coverage. The property value insured is the one they took out when buying their property: €200,000, well below the current estimated value of €320,000.

6. RISK MANAGEMENT RECOMMENDATIONS: CAREER DEVELOPMENT STAGE

6.1. Disability Insurance

Exhibit 11 shows Stein's calculation of disability coverage requirement based on the amount of earnings potentially lost in the case of disability.

EXHIBIT 11   Disability Insurance Coverage Calculation at Age 45

	Jessica	Paul
Salary income (net) to be replaced	53,650	46,510
Amount of annual disability coverage currently provided by the social security system	25,200	30,245
Annual shortfall	28,400	16,265
Benefit period (until retirement age)	20 years	20 years
Assumed annual benefit adjustment	2%	2%
Discount rate	3%	3%
PV of future earnings replacement required (annuity due)	519,000	297,000

Note: The purpose is to provide replacement for current income. This table shows the benefit in the form of a lump sum payout.

The current level of coverage is €112,200 for Jessica and €686,100 for Paul. Stein explains that because Paul would now be entitled to a much higher level of disability income from the state system, his level of additional required coverage is now lower. Given Jessica's pay rises in recent years, resulting in higher amounts of income to be replaced in case of disability, Stein recommends that the Schmitts change the level of coverage. Her suggestion is to increase the amount of coverage to €520,000 for Jessica and to reduce it to €300,000 for Paul.

6.2. Life Insurance

Stein explains that the amount of coverage that a life insurance policy should provide can be calculated using either the human capital (the human life value method), which estimates the amount of earnings that must be replaced, or the needs analysis method, based on estimating the amount needed to cover survivors' living expenses. Stein adds that although the methods are distinct in their approach, both rely on a number of assumptions that may turn out to have been inaccurate. For example, it is very difficult to estimate the financial needs of surviving children who are still very young. Exhibit 12 illustrates the two methods.

EXHIBIT 12   Life Insurance Amount Required at Age 45

Human life value method

Stein first works out the amount of lost income replacement, adjusting after-tax income for the amount of annual expenses and the value of the person's employee benefits. Assuming the survivors would need the lost income replacement immediately, she works out the present value of an annuity due.

Human life value method at age 45

	Paul's Life Cover (from Jessica's perspective)	Jessica's Life Cover (from Paul's perspective)
	€	€
Pretax income	66,000	80,000
After-tax income	46,510	53,650
Less adjustment for the deceased person's annual expenses that would not exist	10,000	10,000
Add value of employee benefits (retirement contribution) that family will no longer receive	10,000	4,000
Subtotal (after taxes)	46,510	47,650
Amount of pretax income required to replace after-tax income (30% rate assumed)	66,440	68,070
Annual growth rate (to reflect career advancement)	2%	5%
Discount rate	3%	3%
Present value of annuity due	1,213,000	1,644,000
Less existing life insurance (including €198,000 provided by Paul's employer)	638,000	200,000
Recommended additional life insurance	575,000	1,444,000

Note: Amounts are rounded.

Needs analysis

Stein estimates the cash needs required upon death of the insured person, including funeral and burial costs as well as mortgage debt. She next estimates capital needed to fund the family's living expenses by discounting future cash flow needs to their present value. Stein then considers the amount of the surviving spouse's future income, which she assumes would remain unchanged in real terms because the surviving spouse, being a single parent, would most likely be unable to achieve career progression. Finally, she deducts capital and savings available.

Needs analysis method at age 45

	Paul	Jessica
	€	€
Cash needs		
Cash needs (funeral and burial costs & taxes)	30,000	30,000
Mortgage retirement	35,000	35,000
Total cash needs	**65,000**	**65,000**
Capital needs		
PV of surviving spouse's living costs (assumed to be currently €35,000 for 45 years)	1,281,000	1,281,000
PV of Roxane's living cost (€9,000 for 10 years until graduation at age 22)	86,000	86,000
PV of Peter's living cost (€13,000 for 83 years until age 90)	743,000	743,000
Less PV of survivor's income until retirement at 65	824,000	777,000
Total capital needs	**1,286,000**	**1,333,000**
Total financial needs	**1,351,000**	**1,398,000**
Capital available:		
Cash, savings, investments	207,000	207,000
PV of vested retirement accounts (attributable to surviving spouse)	140,000	227,000
Existing life insurance coverage (including benefit provided by Paul's employer)	638,000	200,000
Total capital available	**985,000**	**634,000**
Additional life insurance needs	366,000	764,000

Note: The annuity-due PV calculations of living costs assume a 2% annual increase and 3% discount rate. A 1% nominal increase in survivor's income is also assumed.

Stein notes that the human life method suggests a significantly higher increase in the recommended life insurance coverage that stems from different approaches used by the two methods. One may view the differing amounts as a range within which to choose the amount of coverage, taking into account the cost of premiums. The amount of life cover selected may depend on which method is more relevant to the family's circumstances. Taking into account the Schmitts' focus on their ability to meet family expenses, Stein recommends that the Schmitts increase their private insurance coverage from the existing €440,000 to €900,000 in the case of Paul and from €200,000 to €1 million in the case of Jessica.

She adds that it is quite important to obtain such coverage while the Schmitts enjoy good health. If they were to develop any medical conditions later in life, obtaining such insurance would be much more problematic, and available coverage would be subject to exclusions and other limitations. She also suggests that the needed coverage can be met by a temporary life insurance, providing coverage until retirement age in about 20 years, when at least one child is expected to be (or is well on its way to being) independent.

6.3. Investment Risk Recommendations

EXAMPLE 4   Investment Risk Recommendations

Recommend and justify changes to the Schmitts' investment portfolio.

Guideline answer: Stein has noted the correlation of the €130,000 of investment hold-ings in IT companies with Jessica's human capital. They should aim to hold an invest-ment portfolio with as low correlation to one's human capital as possible. They should also move away from the concentrated nature of holdings of which they usually hold 10. In order for the Schmitts to achieve better diversification, Stein recommends that, at a minimum, any new investments are no longer made directly into shares of IT companies. Instead, they should be making regular investments into pooled investment vehicles—such as funds that are diversified across a wide range of regions, sectors, and securities—which can be done at low cost. Cost efficiency is paramount because any amount saved from initial charges or annual costs, compounded over many years, may make significant difference to long-term returns. If an active approach to investing is chosen, the additional costs that stem from such an approach should be justified by sufficient active risk-adjusted return.

EXAMPLE 5   Real Estate in Investment Portfolio

The Schmitts earlier mentioned the possibility of making speculative investment in res-idential property (similar in size to their existing property) in the area where IT compa-nies, including Jessica's offices, are based. Identify issues that an adviser should consider before making a recommendation.

Guideline answer: The issue to consider is how the prospects for the local property mar-ket depend on the performance for and employment in the local IT industry. Jessica's own employment prospects depend on this industry, and purchasing a property in the area would increase the Schmitts' exposure to the local IT industry.

Funding of the purchase would also need to be considered because the cost could exceed €300,000 given that the Schmitts' property, similar in size and value to the one they are considering, is worth about €320,000. The Schmitts do not have sufficient resources available. Devoting a large proportion of their investment portfolio to a deposit and funding the rest of the purchase price using a loan would expose them to risks such as interest rate risk. A greater share of their wealth would be tied to the prospects of the local IT industry as they would no longer hold exposure to equities, foregoing benefits from diversification. They should be made aware of the fact that holding an investment property would represent a large, concentrated, illiquid position and that there are costs associated with owning and managing rental property.

6.4. Retirement Planning Recommendation

EXAMPLE 6   Recommendation for Retirement Saving at the Career
              Development Stage

Recommend methods to manage risk to retirement lifestyle goals.

Guideline answer: Analysis of retirement plans identified a significant shortfall in the Schmitts' projected retirement income. To address the risk of having insufficient funds to maintain their lifestyle in retirement, the couple should give serious consideration to increasing the amount dedicated to retirement needs. Their monthly after-tax income of €8,350 exceeds their monthly expenditures by about €2,700, which even after the payment of insurance premiums leaves them with €2,350 (€28,200 per year) to invest. This provides them with an opportunity to boost retirement savings and build up their investment portfolio instead of continuing to build up their liquidity buffer, which is now approaching €80,000 (invested in a low-interest, instant-access bank account). The Schmitts should instead increase contributions into Jessica's pension scheme or open separate private pension plans. Doing so would also allow them to take advantage of the tax benefits of retirement saving because income and capital gains within the regulated plans are tax free, and contributions into the plans are supplemented with the 25% top-up payments from the state. Although the funds from pension plans are normally inaccessible before retirement, the tax advantages, compared with investing outside such plans, can be significant.

6.5. Additional Suggestions

Stein recommends that they update their property insurance coverage to reflect the current market value.

Supplementary private health insurance could be considered to cover dental care, alternative medicine, hospitalization in a private room, and other health costs. The reason in favor of obtaining such coverage now is that it will be cheaper while they are still relatively young and healthy, whereas it would be much more costly to obtain if and when they suffer from preexisting conditions. An important consideration is the lack of portability of such supplementary medical insurance were the Schmitts to move and/or to retire to another country.

Stein concludes her recommendations by adding that a risk management strategy for individuals should not only consist of establishing objectives, identifying risks, evaluating risks, and selecting methods to manage those risks, but also that outcomes and risk exposures should be monitored and methods for addressing them reviewed and adjusted as necessary.

The Schmitts accept their adviser's recommendations. They drop the idea of purchasing a property near the IT business district; they stop adding to their instant-access savings that form their liquidity buffer and instead increase their contributions to Jessica's employer pension plan. The Schmitts continue their contributions to the investment portfolio but start moving away from individual securities, instead investing in diversified equity funds.

7. IDENTIFICATION AND ANALYSIS OF RISK EXPOSURES: PEAK ACCUMULATION STAGE

The Schmitts are now 55 years old and are in their peak accumulation phase. In the last 10 years, they made further progress in their careers. Their incomes continued to increase. Correspondingly, Jessica's employer's contributions into the company pension scheme have increased meaningfully. Jessica herself has also been actively contributing to her employer's occupational pension scheme and into her recently opened private pension, taking advantage of tax incentives. The part of the technology sector in which Jessica's company operates is experiencing volatility arising from a rapidly changing market environment. Paul's employment remains stable. He has been regularly contributing to a private pension plan.

The Schmitts' assets, invested in a number of diversified funds now with a 70% equity (mostly global equity with a small amount in Eurolandia equities) and 30% fixed income mix (split about evenly between domestic government bonds and corporate bonds), have grown substantially thanks to regular investing and investment returns. The value of their property has suffered a decline in real terms as a consequence of the stagnation in Eurolandia's real estate market and of the fact that the area where the property is located has lost its earlier appeal.

Although the Schmitts have already repaid their mortgage, their liabilities have increased. They are still supporting Roxane's living expenses because she just completed her bachelor's degree and is starting post-graduate studies. They are providing the best possible special needs education for Peter, who is now 17 and has made progress but will most likely need assistance for the rest of his life. The Schmitts feel retirement planning has become a crucial issue because they plan to retire in 10 years. They maintain a healthy lifestyle. They meet with Stein to review their risk management arrangements in relation to their lifestyle goals. Together they produce a summary of their financial circumstances, shown in Exhibit 13.

EXHIBIT 13   Summary of the Schmitts' Financial Circumstances at the Age of 55

	Jessica	Paul	Combined
	€	€	€
Yearly gross income	120,000	80,000	200,000
After-tax income	77,888	53,888	131,776
Source of income	Department head, IT	State teaching job	
Living expenses			75,000
Property			340,000
Bank accounts			80,900
Investment portfolio			611,400
Pension provisions	As mandated by law (state pension), plus a company-sponsored pension scheme €113,000 plus €15,000 in private pension savings	As mandated by law. Paul, as a civil servant, plus €47,500 in private pension savings	

| **Disability insurance** | Government insurance coverage of €30,720 per year Private coverage of a lump sum of €633,900 (policy benefit was increased to €520,000 at age 45, adjusted for 2% annual benefit adjustment) | Government insurance cover of €36,870 per year (includes extra payment reflecting more than 10 years of service) Private coverage of a lump sum of €365,700 (policy provided €300,000 at age 45, adjusted for 2% annual benefit adjustment) |
| **Life insurance coverage (up to age 65)** | €1,000,000 private policy *Note*: This amount reflects the recommendation given at age 45. | €900,000 private policy plus 3× salary insurance coverage of €240,000 provided by the employer |

7.1. Review of Objectives, Risks, and Methods of Addressing Them

Stein sets out to establish the Schmitts' financial objectives and review the financial risks they face. She then proceeds to provide recommendations.

7.1.1. Financial objectives
Stein asks the Schmitts to update her on their financial objectives. Paul and Jessica explain that their objectives remain broadly unchanged. They wish to achieve the following:

- Provide financial security for the family in the next 10 years while they remain in full-time employment.
- Have a comfortable retirement, which they anticipate will happen in 10 years when they both reach the age of 65.
- Be in a position (after their retirement) to provide long-term support and assistance for their son Peter for the rest of his life,
- Leave a meaningful inheritance for Roxane.

Stein explains that she will assess the couple's existing insurance arrangements with regard to their financial security while they still are working and earning salaries. She will then focus on assessing risks relating to their three long-term planned goals: the "comfortable retirement," "Peter's long-term assistance," and "inheritance for Roxane" goals.

Stein proceeds to update the Schmitts' financial and economic balance sheets, shown in Exhibit 14.

EXHIBIT 14   Financial and Economic Balance Sheet at Age 55

Human Capital Assumptions

	Jessica	Paul
Expected salary growth (nominal)	2%	2%
Discount rate (r_f)	3%	3%
Risk adjustment (y)	1%	0%
Remaining length of working life (up to age 65)	10	10

Note: Probability of surviving to a given age is based on mortality tables (not shown here) used in Eurolandia.

Economic Balance Sheet (€)

Assets		Liabilities	
Savings account	80,900	Mortgage debt	0
Investment portfolio	611,400		
Accrued DB government retirement plan (Paul)	457,000		
Accrued DB government retirement plan (Jessica)	263,000		
Employer pension value (Jessica)	113,500		
Private pension fund (Jessica)	15,000		
Private pension value (Paul)	47,500		
Property (main residence)	340,000		
Paul's human capital	486,600	PV of lifetime consumption needs	2,235,000
Jessica's human capital	668,100		
Total assets	**3,083,000**	**Total liabilities**	**2,235,000**
		Net wealth	**848,000**

Note: Human capital values are calculated based on an assumption of 2% nominal salary growth rate until retirement in 10 years, discounted at 3%, adjusted for mortality rates and applying a further 1% risk adjustment to Jessica's income.

Lifetime consumption needs are calculated as annuity due based on annual costs of €75,000 over 35 years, with an annual increase of 2%, discounted at 3%.

EXAMPLE 7   Comparison of Economic Balance

Compare the economic balance sheet at age 55, shown in Exhibit 14, with the one produced 10 years ago, shown in Exhibit 9.

Guideline answer: The Schmitts' human capital has decreased in absolute terms over time as they approach retirement, which is now 10 years away. Their human capital has also decreased relative to their financial resources, which have seen a significant increase. The Schmitts have repaid their debts, and their net wealth is now much more substantial than 10 years earlier.

EXAMPLE 8   Liquidity Needs

Discuss the Schmitts' financial position with regard to their ability to meet any unexpected liquidity needs.

Guideline answer: The level of their financial assets provides sufficient liquidity if their circumstances were to change. The Schmitts are now significantly richer in financial assets than they were 10 years earlier. They have a balance of almost €81,000 in their instant-access savings account and more than €600,000 in diversified funds that they should be able to easily exit if such need arose.

7.1.2. Review of Risks and Related Risk Management Methods

Having gathered information about the Schmitts' financial circumstances and goals, Stein identifies the risks and prepares summary information (in Exhibits 15, 16, and 17) to help analyze those risks.

EXHIBIT 15   Earnings Shortfall in Case of Disability at Age 55

	Jessica	Paul
Salary income (net) to be replaced	€77,900	€53,900
Amount of annual disability coverage currently provided by the social security system	€30,720	€36,870
Annual shortfall	€47,180	€17,030

Note: Jessica and Paul's annual earnings shortfalls at the age of 45 were €28,450 and €16,265, respectively. Rounding is used throughout.

EXHIBIT 16   Disability Insurance Coverage Assumptions

Benefit period (until retirement age)	10 years	10 years
Assumed annual benefit adjustment	2%	2%
Discount rate	3%	3%
PV of future earnings replacement required	€452,000	€163,000

EXAMPLE 9   Analysis of Earnings Risk during Peak Accumulation Stage

Using the information provided by the Schmitts to their adviser and the information in Exhibits 13, 15, and 16, analyze the earnings-related risks arising from unemployment and disability that the Schmitts face now that they are in the peak accumulation life stage.

Guideline answer: The Schmitts continue to face earnings risk resulting from unemployment. Jessica continues to work in a sector that shows volatile profitability. A loss of her job at her current age of 55 could make it difficult for her to find alternative employment at significantly above-average salary and level of seniority. Two facts mitigate the seriousness of this concern. First, the Schmitts have a substantial amount of savings and investments to buffer any loss of earnings. Second, Paul's employment appears secure.

The risk to their earnings from disability remains, but the level of coverage should be reassessed because their circumstances have changed and they are closer to retirement.

The amount of annual earnings not protected by the social security system is higher than was the case at age 45 for Jessica because of her salary growth. But the fact that the period over which they would rely on such benefit payments is now only 10 years means that the present value of the disability protection needed is now lower: €452,000 for Jessica and €163,000 for Paul, well below the level of their existing coverage (€633,900 and €365,700).

Stein assesses the level of life insurance coverage needed using the human life and needs analysis methods. Starting with the human life method, the higher level of salaries would be expected to increase the amount of income required to replace the deceased person's earnings. Because the remaining period of earning a salary is now reduced to 10 years until retirement, however, the present value of future earnings would be expected to decline, as Exhibit 17 shows.

EXHIBIT 17   Human Life Method Insurance Coverage Calculation at Age 55

	Paul	Jessica
	€	€
Pretax income	80,000	120,000
After-tax income	53,900	77,900
Less adjustment for the deceased person's annual expenses that will not exist	10,000	10,000
Add value of employee benefits that the family will no longer receive	10,000	4,000
Subtotal (after taxes)	53,900	71,900
Amount of pretax income required to replace after-tax income (30% tax rate)	77,000	102,700
Annual growth rate	2%	2%
Discount rate	3%	3%
Present value of pretax income to be replaced (annuity due, 10 years)	737,000	983,000
Less existing life insurance (including current benefit €240,000 provided by Paul's employer)	1,140,000	1,000,000
Recommended additional life insurance	−403,000	−17,000

Stein should also carry out needs analysis method to help establish the necessary amount of life insurance coverage. The calculation is made simpler by the fact that there are no further debts to repay. The couple's daughter Roxane has graduated and is expected not to require ongoing support once she completes her post-graduate studies in less than two years (Stein excludes the short-term support for Roxane from her calculation in Exhibit 18).

EXHIBIT 18   Needs Analysis Method Insurance Coverage Calculation at Age 55

	Paul's Life Cover (from Jessica's perspective)	Jessica's Life Cover (from Paul's perspective)
Cash needs	€	€
Funeral and burial costs plus taxes	35,000	35,000
Total cash needs	**35,000**	**35,000**
Capital needs		
PV of surviving spouse's living expenses (until age 90)	1,191,800	1,191,800
PV of Peter's living cost (€13,000 per year, growing at 2%, until age 90)	682,000	682,000
Less PV of survivor's income until retirement at 65	685,000	494,000
Total capital needs	**1,188,800**	**1,379,800**
Total financial needs	**1,223,800**	**1,414,800**

Capital available:

Cash, savings, investments	692,300	692,300
PV of vested retirement accounts (attributable to surviving spouse)	392,000	505,000
Existing life insurance coverage (including current benefit €240,000 provided by Paul's employer)	1,140,000	1,000,000
Total capital available	**2,224,300**	**2,197,300**
Additional life insurance needs	−1,000,500	−782,500

Note: The PV of the surviving spouse's expenses is based on annual spend of €40,000 for 35 years, annual growth rate of 2%, and discount rate of 3%. Annuity due is used. The same growth and discount rates are used to calculate the PV of Peter's living cost, and the benefit period is 73 years. The PV of the survivor's income is based on a period of 10 years, 1% growth resulting from limited career progress opportunities in such circumstances, a 3% discount rate, and a 1% additional discount rate risk adjustment for Jessica.

Both the human life value and needs analysis methods suggest that premature death risks are covered by the Schmitts' existing insurance. The amount of existing coverage now substantially exceeds the coverage suggested by the two methods. Stein recommends they reduce the amount of coverage, lowering their monthly premiums. She does point out, however, that one of their objectives is to provide adequate long-term support for Peter and plan for an increase in the cost of doing so when they are no longer able to support him the way they do now (the €13,000 per year would increase substantially then). If Paul or Jessica died before retiring, it would no longer be possible to set funds aside for Peter's future care. Stein suggests the Schmitts consider this factor before adjusting their policy coverage.

Stein notes that the Schmitts have adequate life insurance and satisfactory, although no-frills, health coverage provided by the state. They also have sufficient liquidity to cover incidental expenses—for example, in relation to health care needs not covered by their health insurance. By maintaining a healthy lifestyle, the Schmitts are helping to reduce the health risk. The combination of their existing coverage, government-mandated programs, and the ability to self-insure through their own assets is sufficient. As such, no additional insurance is recommended.

8. ASSESSMENT OF AND RECOMMENDATIONS CONCERNING RISK TO RETIREMENT LIFESTYLE AND BEQUEST GOALS: PEAK ACCUMULATION STAGE

Next, Stein considers the risk to the Schmitts' retirement lifestyle goal. She provides a summary of the retirement assets and then proceeds to establish how much the couple expects to be spending in retirement. Exhibit 19 provides a summary of the retirement plans assuming that the Schmitts retire in 10 years when they are 65. Further assumptions are as follows:

- The Schmitts continue to make social security contributions to the mandatory government pension scheme.
- They also continue making regular payments into their private pensions and Jessica's occupational pension scheme.

- The investment returns of the DC plans remain at 4% per year, slightly lower than the 5% rate seen over the last 10 years, as the assets in the retirement portfolios are gradually moved to lower-risk asset allocation as the retirement date nears.
- The DC plans' final values at age 65 are used to buy an immediate fixed annuity (we assume a 5% annuity "income yield" and no inflation adjustment thereafter).

EXHIBIT 19   The Schmitts' Retirement Assets and Main Risks (not including their investment portfolio)

Assets	Type and Current Value	Expected Growth Rate	Expected Value at Age 65	Expected Annual Gross Pension Benefit (€)	Risks
Paul's mandatory government pension plan	DB pension plan	—	—	€48,950 (55% of the estimated final salary)	Government may reduce retirement benefits due to fiscal pressures
Jessica's mandatory government pension plan	DB pension plan	—	—	€28,191	As above
Jessica's company pension	DC plan, Current value €113,500 Balanced fund	Annual contributions of €14,000, growing at 2% 4% annual investment returns	€350,000	€17,515	Investment risk and interest rate risk that could result in lower annuity income yield
Paul's private pension savings plan	DC plan currently valued at €47,500 Balanced fund	€6,000 annual contributions growing at 2% 3% investment returns	€135,900	€6,795	As above
Jessica's private pension savings plan	DC plan opened recently Valued at €15,000 Uses aggressive, actively managed investment strategy with high risk	€10,000 annual contributions growing at 2%. 8% investment returns	€201,600	€10,080	As above

Note: Jessica has no influence over the terms and conditions of her company pension scheme, which is a mandatory DC plan. Like all beneficiaries, she has the right to vote for the employee representatives on the company's pension fund board. Figures and percentage growth rates are assumed to be net of fees.

Stein estimates that their combined annual retirement income from pension schemes could amount to about €111,500. This figure would be subject to income tax, which she estimates will leave them with after-tax income of €84,000, excluding any income from their investment portfolio (treated separately). To be able to judge whether or not the existing retirement provisions are sufficient, Stein needs to better understand what percentage of salary the Schmitts want to replace in retirement. The couple finds it difficult to be precise about the amounts they will need to spend. They conclude that they should require no more than their current level of annual spending of €75,000 (in real terms). Stein explains that they are in a good position to be able to maintain their current lifestyle even in retirement. She points out, however, the risk from loss of employment, the risk to the state pensions system, and the risk of poor investment returns of the DC plans over the next 10 years. Stein explains each risk in turn:

1. If the Schmitts lose their employment and cannot obtain work with comparable compensation, their pension assets growth and the corresponding estimated values would be at risk because they would no longer be able to fund their regular contributions. Their insurance policies do not provide income replacement in the event of unemployment. Statutory redundancy pay and unemployment benefits would cover a small proportion of their current pay.
2. The other main risk is that the government state pension plan gets overhauled in response to the aging population and fiscal pressures. Such an overhaul could take the form of benefit reduction. A less likely scenario is an increase in the retirement age.
3. Investment risk and inflation risk make up a third risk factor. Investment risk affects the non-government, DC plans that the Schmitts hold. Past returns of the Schmitts' retirement funds over the last decade averaged almost 5% per year, but such returns may not continue into the future. Second, inflation may erode the purchasing power of the income from retirement plans.

If the government pension plans continue to provide benefits at the same level enjoyed by current retirees, they will cover the Schmitts' basic living costs. This income would not provide for any other objectives, such as assistance for or bequeathing assets to their children. The arrangements for those other goals are assessed next.

EXAMPLE 10   Withdrawal of Tax-Free Lump Sum

Regulations in Eurolandia allow members of private pension schemes to withdraw 25% of their retirement assets as a tax-free lump sum from the age of 55, the Schmitts' current age. Taking into account the analysis of their retirement assets, discuss the merits of withdrawing the tax-free lump sum at this stage.

Guideline answer: The potential logic of withdrawing 25% of the DC funds tax free should be assessed in a broad context. The Schmitts have sufficient cash flows from earnings to be able to fund their ongoing expenses and keep adding to their investment portfolio. They are in their peak accumulation stage of their careers and are accumulating assets rather than spending. There appears to be no need for them to access the funds at this stage.

  If they were to withdraw the funds now in order to invest outside their retirement programs, the couple would no longer benefit from the fact that they are accumulating assets without having to pay any capital gains or income taxes within the retirement schemes. Not withdrawing the 25% lump sum now, however, still provides them with the option of withdrawing the tax-free lump sum at a later stage.

8.1. Analysis of Investment Portfolio

Stein turns her attention to the Schmitts' investment portfolio in relation to the couple's two additional goals:

- Provide for their son Peter's care for the rest of his life.
- Leave an inheritance for their daughter Roxane.

She explains to the Schmitts that she needs to understand the time horizon and risk tolerance in relation to the probability of success for each goal. Stein explains that in goals-based investing, their investment portfolio will be treated as a number of sub-portfolios—in this case, only two—each of which is designed to fund an individual goal.

8.1.1. The goal of supporting Peter

Stein first looks into the need to fund support for Peter after the Schmitts' retirement, support that will be required for the rest of Peter's life because he is not expected to ever be in a position to obtain paid employment or to make decisions for himself. Although the state provides a range of benefits to Peter, the Schmitts currently spend €13,000 a year on additional support for their son. They wish to ensure as much as possible that Peter will receive proper assistance, even after they die or otherwise become unable to care directly for him and thus need to hire outside help. This goal is essential for the Schmitts, and they want it to be achieved with the utmost certainty (i.e., with a probability as close to 1 as possible). They are confident that they can fund Peter's long-term care as long as they remain employed for the next 10 years.

Based on average life expectancy in Eurolandia, Peter is expected to outlive his parents by around 40 years, because he was born when they were 38. The Schmitts struggle to establish the period over which they will be able to care for Peter (incurring the €13,000 cost per year and expected to remain unchanged in real terms) without requiring the use of extensive outside help, which currently costs about €30,000 per year. They are also quite worried about possible future inflation despite Eurolandia's low inflation history.

As a base scenario, the Schmitts and their advisor conclude that they should plan for the higher cost resulting from external care to apply in 20 years' time once they reach the age of 75 and Peter is 37. Stein quantifies the amount required to meet that goal, as illustrated in Exhibit 20.

EXHIBIT 20   Net Present Value of Peter's Care

The required funding for the goal of providing for Peter's care for the rest of his life can be modelled as the present value of a deferred-start annuity (even though they would not be buying one now) that begins in 20 years' time. Its duration would equal Peter's life expectancy then (an additional 53 years of life up to the age of 90). The following table shows the PV of such an annuity, with different assumptions, considering a yearly cost of €30,000 in real terms. Because the Schmitts emphasized the need to address inflation risks, the calculations are performed in real terms—that is, the amounts are expressed in euros based on their value at present time when the Schmitts are 55. The discount rate represents the real discount rate.

Real Discount Rate	PV
1.0%	€1,018,000
2.0%	€669,000
3.0%	€451,000

Note: The amounts are rounded to the nearest €1000 for the present value of this annuity due lasting 53 years.

Based on the current level of real interest rates of 2%, the net present value of Peter's care exceeds the current value of the Schmitts' €611,000 investment portfolio. When the Schmitts inquire about the calculations' sensitivity to changes in economic conditions and potential solutions to the shortfall, Stein replies that it would be unrealistic to count on a real discount rate much higher than 2% to reduce the net present value, given the very low real rates experienced for quite some time.

Stein notes, however, that the Schmitts are now in the peak accumulation stage of their careers and can continue to add to the investment portfolio on regular basis: approximately €33,000 per year, with the amount slowly increasing. They would be able to do so while also contributing to their pension plans. Failing to continue contributions to the investment portfolio, however, would pose a serious risk of them being unable to completely fund Peter's long-term support. Second, Stein notes that in her retirement planning assessment, their expenditure assumptions reflect the expectation that the €13,000 annual cost (in real terms) of supporting Peter would continue for the rest of their lives and would not stop when they reach the age of 75, which is what the foregoing deferred-start annuity calculation reflected. In other words, the fact that the Schmitts assume they will be paying €13,000 per year (in real terms) even after they reach 75 means that the additional support needed will be closer to €20,000, rather than €33,000, for as long as they live. She therefore suggests that the PV amount they should plan to use for Peter's care should currently be closer to €500,000.

Before advising them on their portfolio's asset allocation, Stein turns to their other goal.

8.1.2. Leaving inheritance to Roxane

The Schmitts would like to leave inheritance for their children, particularly for Roxane, because they are already making arrangements for Peter's long-term care.[1] The required probability of success for this goal, however, is far lower than what was attributed to Peter's care goal, and the time horizon is much longer because they expect to live for more than 30 years. When Stein asks about the amount they would ideally like Roxane to inherit, the Schmitts state that they hope the amount would be as high as possible, so that she inherits more than just their property—their main residence. Exhibit 21 summarizes the three main known goals.

---

[1]In fact, inheritance law in Eurolandia requires the Schmitts to bequeath a minimum proportion of their wealth to each of the surviving children. They could not, therefore, direct that their entire wealth goes to Peter's care. In this case study, we assume that this legal obligation will be satisfied, so we do not discuss it further.

EXHIBIT 21   The Schmitts' Goals

Goal	NPV	Notes	Time Horizon	Required Probability of Success
Having a comfortable retirement	Not applicable	Goal is already covered by existing pension arrangements, assuming projected earnings growth rates and fund contributions are realized.	10 years	High
Providing for Peter's care	Approximately €500,000	NPV is assumption-dependent	Approximately 20 years	Nearly 100%
Leaving an inheritance for Roxane	As much as possible		>30 years	Around 60%

8.2. Analysis of Asset Allocation

Stein reflects on which asset allocation technique should be used. Using mean–variance optimization is problematic because it is a "single-period" framework," and the Schmitts' stated objectives span multiple periods. She recognizes that asset allocation can be conducted with a goal-based approach, whereby goals are analyzed and modelled and a probability of success specified for each of them. The additional advantage of the goal-based approach is that it enables a far simpler and more intuitive communication with the Schmitts than discussing the risk–return tradeoff in the context of mean–variance optimization.

The idea behind the exercise is to apply goals-based investing techniques by disaggregating the Schmitts' portfolio into two sub-portfolios, each designed to fund a goal with its own time horizon and probability of success.

8.2.1. Peter's care

The Schmitts require that the probability to fulfill this goal be as close as possible to 100%. As such, this sub-portfolio should be worth at least €500,000 in real terms (in today's values) when it becomes necessary to start drawing on it, most probably in around 20 years. Any volatility in the mark-to-market of this portfolio before then, however, is of secondary importance. Stein believes that such portfolio should be invested in inflation-linked government bonds, with long maturities. Yields (including those on inflation-linked bonds) are currently very low, and Stein expects that they may increase over time because of higher inflation expectations (which the inflation-linked bonds would protect them from) or because real rates could rise. Because the time horizon is relatively long, the allocation to inflation-linked bonds can be implemented gradually. The existing portfolio, from which this "sub-fund" will need to be created, is 70% invested in equities and 30% in bonds. By implementing this switch gradually, the Schmitts should be able to minimize capital gains taxes that would otherwise arise from realizing profits on the existing fund holdings. Eurolandia allows residents to pay no tax on the first €25,000 of realized capital gains per year, a level that has remained and is expected to remain unchanged.

> If inflation and, correspondingly, bond coupons on inflation-linked bonds increase in the future, the Schmitts will face a significant tax liability from the income arising from this sub-portfolio. The tax will reduce the inflation protection provided by the portfolio. If this occurs, an adviser can study the possibility of structuring this portfolio as a non-taxable trust but only after considering the costs to create and run the structure, as well as the additional constraints associated with it. Theoretically, the modified duration of this sub-portfolio should match that of the associated goal. Such a match will be challenging, however, because no bonds with such a long modified duration are available.

8.2.2. Leaving an inheritance for Roxane

Given that most of their investment portfolio is allocated to the first sub-portfolio, only €110,000 in investable assets is available to invest in the second sub-portfolio. This sub-portfolio starts off fully allocated to diversified global equity funds to capture the expected returns from equities.

8.3. Recommendations for Risk Management at Peak Accumulation Stage

Having gathered the facts, established the objectives, and analyzed the risks that the Schmitts face, Stein provides a summary of the following recommendations.

8.3.1. Risk to earnings

Stein explains that the risk from unemployment cannot be avoided or insured against using insurance policies but that the Schmitts, thanks to their savings, are self-insuring. Having reviewed their protections against loss of earnings resulting from disability or premature death, she concludes that their existing coverage is more than sufficient. Stein suggests reducing the amount of coverage as well as the premiums they pay where the policies allow for such change.

8.3.2. Recommendations for retirement savings

EXAMPLE 11   Reduction of Risk to Retirement Lifestyle Goals

Recommend and justify methods for reducing risk to retirement lifestyle goals.

Guideline answer: The Schmitts are in a good position to retire comfortably. They should continue contributing to their private pension savings plans up to the legally specified maximum, thereby obtaining the corresponding tax advantage whereby the government adds 25% to their own contributions. Two of their private pension plans are invested in a portfolio that is diversified across asset classes and regions. Over time, the fund holdings are being gradually moved to a lower-risk asset allocation with an increasing proportion of fixed-income government securities.

Jessica's recently opened private pension plan, however, is managed aggressively at the extreme end of what regulated schemes allow. Stein explains that such a high-risk addition to their substantial retirement savings is not necessarily a cause for concern, but she urges the Schmitts to consider moving the fund choice within the scheme to a less risky, more balanced alternative.

8.3.3. Recommendations for the investment portfolio

Stein explains that the first goal, the comfortable retirement, is addressed already through the retirement savings schemes. The other two—funding Peter's support for the rest of his life and leaving an inheritance for Roxane—should be addressed by the following:

- The couple should continue adding to the investment portfolio on regular basis at the existing rate of €33,000 per year or higher. These additional contributions, along with capital gains and reinvested income over time, should result in a healthy growth of the investment portfolio.
- Within the growing portfolio, assets devoted to Peter's care goal, currently amounting to €500,000, should be gradually reallocated from the current 70% equity and 30% fixed income to an increasing proportion of inflation-protected government bonds. Gains on investments should be realized in an orderly fashion to take advantage of the €25,000 of tax-free capital gains per year.

Because the Schmitts continue to save and accumulate assets, it is important to review whether the allocation remains in line with the goals listed in the previous section.

Stein further explains that a detailed Investment Policy Statement will be written for them and further analysis of the actual fund holdings will be carried out. The portfolio allocation will be reviewed periodically, at least once a year. The Investment Policy Statement will be reviewed for any material change in circumstances. She further adds that retirement planning process should also involve an expert, a specialist, on inheritance tax.

9. IDENTIFICATION AND ANALYSIS OF RETIREMENT OBJECTIVES, ASSETS, AND DRAWDOWN PLAN: RETIREMENT STAGE

The Schmitts are about to turn 65, and retirement is imminent. They are in good health, although they occasionally make use of the country's health system. They spend less than in earlier stages of life, and their investment portfolio now amounts to more than €1.5 million. Despite the gradual move from equity funds to fixed-income ones, equities still account for a sizable portion of their holdings: 50% of the total, as result of healthy returns from the asset class. The rest is evenly held in inflation-protected government bonds and corporate bonds. Jessica's income has decreased because she decided to step down from her department management job and is currently employed as a senior IT consultant. The family's living expenses have also come down because Roxane is now independent.

The Schmitts' financial situation and pension assets are summarized in Exhibits 22 and 23.

EXHIBIT 22   Summary of the Schmitts' Financial Circumstances at Age 65

	Jessica	Paul	Combined
Yearly gross income (€)	90,000	89,000	179,000
Source of income	Senior IT consultant	State teaching job	
Living expenses (€)			70,000
Property (€)			420,000
Investment portfolio (€)			1,511,000

EXHIBIT 23   The Schmitts' Retirement Assets

Asset	Current Value at Age 65
Paul's mandatory government pension plan	Annual pension of €48,950 (55% of final salary of €89,000)
Jessica's mandatory government pension plan	Annual pension of €28,190
Jessica's company pension	DC plan. Fund value of €350,000 corresponding to an annual pension of €17,500
Paul's private pension savings plan	€135,000 corresponding to annual pension of €6,750
Jessica's private pension savings plan	€175,000 corresponding to annual pension of €8,750

Note: The annual pension amounts assume that the fund value at retirement is used to purchase a fixed payment annuity at the current 5% annuity yield.

9.1. Key Issues and Objectives

The Schmitts again meet with Stein. They wish to discuss planning for the retirement decision and the management of the investment portfolio. They repeat their objectives, which are as follows:

- Retire shortly with a comfortable level of secure, predictable retirement income for the rest of their lives, and avoid a situation in which they outlive their assets. The Schmitts consider themselves to be healthy and expect to live longer than the average life expectancy. They also state that they wish to make sure to maintain the purchasing power of their retirement income.
- Continue to provide ongoing financial support for Peter, raising the amount devoted to this purpose in 10 years to what they now estimate will need to be €35,000 per year at today's prices.
- Leave a meaningful but as yet unquantified inheritance for Roxane, over and above their residence.
- Help their daughter Roxane with the purchase of her first property in the very near future, up to €150,000.

    The Schmitts would also like to have the option to retire in another country.

9.2. Analysis of Retirement Assets and Drawdown Plan

Stein explains the following:

- Now that the Schmitts are about to retire, there is no further need for life or disability insurance coverage.
- There are no decisions to make with regard to the state pension income that they will soon start drawing, the amounts of which are known with certainty.

    Regarding the employer and private pension schemes they have in place, a plan must be established. She explains that the Schmitts have the following options:

- Purchase annuities that would provide a stream of income for the rest of their lives.
- Withdraw lump sums to use as they wish.
- Leave the funds invested in the retirement schemes.

Up to one-third can be withdrawn from the company pension as a lump sum. The private pension assets offer more flexibility. There is the option of using all or part of them to buy a stream of payments (an annuity) while withdrawing the rest as a lump sum. Stein points out that many considerations must be taken into account.

EXAMPLE 12   Addressing longevity risk

Identify an option that would most likely address the Schmitts' concern about outliving their assets.

A. Purchase annuities.
B. Withdraw lump sums.
C. Leave funds invested in the retirement plans.

Solution: The answer is A. Purchasing annuities would address longevity risk. Annuities involve the purchase of a product that provides a stream of regular income for the rest of the asset owners' lives, regardless of how long they live.

Stein summarizes the key differences between the choice of a lump sum or an annuity:

- With a lump sum withdrawal for the purposes of retirement income, beneficiaries take the longevity risk. The payout is the same regardless of how long they live. This approach normally poses the risk of outliving one's assets. An annuity, instead, is paid for the main beneficiary's entire lifetime, often with residual rights for the spouse (or even children, if below a certain age).
- Ordinary retirement fixed-payment annuities guarantee a nominal amount of regular income. Given the Schmitts' concern about inflation reducing the purchasing power of annuity income, they should consider buying an annuity whose amount is annually adjusted by the inflation index. The drawback is the initial cost, which she estimates would result in them receiving a 4.5% annuity yield instead of 5%.
- The tax treatment of lump sum withdrawals and pension payments varies across jurisdictions. In Eurolandia, lump sums of up to 25% of the total pension plan value can be withdrawn tax free.
- The lump sum payment is final when it occurs. If relevant, any tax arising is also finalized and paid at the same time. With a regular pension, the tax liability cannot be fully estimated in advance because of changes in tax rules and rates. Applicable rules would also change if the Schmitts were to move to another jurisdiction.
- The entitlement to an annuity payment exposes the beneficiary to counterparty risk arising from the provider's inability to honor its obligations.

The relative pretax valuation of a lump sum and the corresponding annuity payment calculation can be performed on the basis of the relevant interest rate curve and life expectancy (including that of any remaining beneficiaries, after the death of the main payee). Stein notes that a number of annuity providers exist on the Eurolandia market and they offer what are considered to be fairly valued annuities. Stein calculates that, on a before-tax basis, the annuity will be more favorable if the Schmitts live past 83 years of age.

With regard to any amounts (of pension fund assets) not used to purchase an annuity, they express preference for a lump sum payment of their pension as opposed to leaving the funds invested in the scheme. This is because of favorable tax treatment of lump sum withdrawals and also because they feel they would have more control of the withdrawn funds, providing them with flexibility. On that note they remind their advisor of their wish to help their daughter Roxane with her planned purchase of a property.

The Schmitts are considering also moving to a sunnier and lower-tax country. In Eurolandia, as in nearly all countries, tax liability depends on tax residence.[2] Some countries offer tax-free status, under certain conditions, to retirees moving there, at least for a certain number of years. One such country is Euromediter, a hypothetical country in the Eurozone.

10. INCOME AND INVESTMENT PORTFOLIO RECOMMENDATIONS: RETIREMENT STAGE

Stein compares the Schmitts' current, pre-retirement income with what they will be receiving from the government pension, the employer's occupational scheme, and the private pension plans. The objective is to provide the Schmitts with regular, inflation-protected income that is sufficient to fund their current level of expenditure of €70,000. This comparison should help determine how much of the pension plan values need to be converted to annuities, as well as what amount can then be withdrawn as lump sum or simply left in the scheme. Stein presents the Schmitts with the proposals shown in Exhibit 24:

EXHIBIT 24   Retirement Income Proposal

	€
State pension Jessica	28,200
State pension Paul	48,950
Total pretax income from state pension	**77,150**
Annuity purchased using 75% of Jessica's company pension plan	11,800
Annuity purchased using 75% of Paul's private pension plan	4,600
Total pretax income from pensions/annuities	**93,600**
Less tax	21,600
After-tax income	**72,000**

Note: Assumes 4.5% annuity yield. Purchased annuities would provide inflation protection.

The recommended arrangement would result in the Schmitts relying on the state pension for a large part of their required retirement income. To bring it up to a sufficient level to maintain their current annual expenditures of €70,000 (in real terms), they would need to convert 75% of Jessica's employer's pension plan and 75% of Paul's private pension plan to an annuity

---

[2] The United States is the most notable exception, because US citizens are liable for US taxes regardless of where they reside.

that provides annual inflation adjustment. The remaining 25% portions of the two pension plans would be withdrawn as a tax-free lump sum (providing a total one-off sum of €121,250).

The remaining pension plan, Jessica's private pension plan, would not be required to provide retirement income. Stein suggests that 25% of the plan can be withdrawn as a tax-free lump sum of €43,750, with the rest kept invested in the plan.

The Schmitts are considering reducing their current living expenses by moving to a Mediterranean country, at the same time benefiting from the available tax break there. Stein provides them with a number of recommendations.

The prospect of retiring to another country has many financial and non-financial implications. It is necessary to consult with experts before making any decisions that are difficult or costly to reverse.

A. A tax expert with up-to-date country knowledge must assess whether the claimed tax advantages really hold.
B. There are estate planning implications, as it must be understood what the applicable laws are (those of the retirement country, those of Eurolandia, or a combination thereof) and the relevant tax regime for estate taxes.
C. The option of moving back to Eurolandia, should the Schmitts wish or need to do so at a later stage, must be examined.
D. If the target retirement country is not in Eurozone and hence does not use the euro (€), currency risk must be assessed and managed.
E. Efficient and inexpensive arrangements must be made for money transfers and currency conversion (if currency conversion is needed).
F. Provision of support for Peter must be assessed.

10.1. Investment Portfolio Analysis and Recommendations

The Schmitts ask Stein for her advice regarding their investment portfolio that stands at €1,511,000. They will also be receiving the tax-free pension lump sum of €165,000 while leaving €131,250 invested in Jessica's private pension plan, bringing the aggregate value of funds available to about €1.8 million.

The Schmitts repeat that, having arranged for regular income stream to cover their retirement expenses, the main objectives for the portfolio are to do the following:

- Provide financial assistance for Peter—a top priority.
- Leave an inheritance for the children, particularly Roxane.
- Provide Roxane with a deposit for her house purchase in the very near future.
- Be able to draw on the investment portfolio to cover unexpected expenses or if a need arises—for example, if their pension income fails to keep up with the rising cost of living, not fully captured by the inflation statistics, or to provide support with their health care if such need arises.

Stein first turns her attention to the Schmitts' top-priority goal: care for Peter, described in Exhibit 25.

EXHIBIT 25

Peter has just turned 27. The Schmitts explain that their current living expenses of €70,000 include about €13,000 in costs related to the support for Peter. That amount is expected to increase to €35,000 in nominal terms in about 10 years because the Schmitts believe that from that age, they will be unable to provide him with the support they currently provide. That amount is expected to remain broadly unchanged (in real terms) for the rest of Peter's life. It would supplement the support he is and will be receiving from the state. Stein calculates the present value of such contribution to support Peter and arrives at an approximate PV figure of €800,000.

Stein then asks the Schmitts about their investment preferences and willingness to bear risk, beyond what they stated as their top priority: Peter's long-term care.

Paul and Jessica explain that they:

- do not want to see their overall investment portfolio fall in value by more than 20% in any given year;
- wish to invest in instruments that can easily be liquidated, because they like to feel that they are in control;
- worry about inflation despite Eurolandia's stability; and
- do not wish to invest in real estate funds.

Stein points out that because their retirement income covers their current needs, the Schmitts have more room to take risk than other couples who require investment income to supplement their pension and fund ordinary living expenses. Their risk tolerance is limited, however, by their requirement that the portfolio as a whole not suffer a loss of more than 20% in a given year even in the case of a market crash. Stein also points out that real estate funds can provide a degree of protection against inflation.

10.2. The Advisor's Recommendations for Investment Portfolio in Retirement

Having considered the Schmitts' financial circumstances, goals, risk tolerances, and preferences, Stein uses her firm's asset allocation tools that are based on the firm's capital markets expectations, assumptions about asset class volatility, and correlation between asset classes. She suggests the following asset allocation to the Schmitts:

- An allocation to international equities and Eurolandia equities of around 35% and 10%, respectively. This allocation would constitute the "risky" part of the portfolio.
- Allocation of 55% to less risky assets, of which they should aim to have 45% in inflation-linked bond funds and 10% in corporate bond funds.

Exhibit 26 summarizes their goals and Stein's investment recommendations.

EXHIBIT 26   Goals and Investment Portfolio as the Schmitts Enter Retirement

Existing Assets	Current Allocation	Goals	Time Horizon	Recommended Asset Allocation
Liquid funds (cash proceeds from pension lump sum)	€165,000	Help Roxane with property purchase deposit	<1 year	Keep funds in cash
Investment portfolio for long-term goals				
Inflation-protected government bond funds	€380,000	Care for Peter (PV of €800,000)	10 years	Inflation-protected government bonds 45% (€739,000) Corporate bond funds 10% (€164,000) Global equities 35% (€575,000), including the actively managed equity funds in Jessica's private pension plan Eurolandia equities 10% (€164,000)
Corporate bond funds	€370,000	Inheritance for Roxane (amount unspecified) and funding for unexpected expenses	Up to 25 years	
Passively managed equity funds	€750,000			
Jessica's private pension plan	€131,250			
Total	Approximately €1.8 million			

Note: In addition to these holdings, the Schmitts keep a cash balance of €85,000 in their bank account and do not expect this to change.

Stein notes that her suggested asset mix requires a further switch into inflation-linked government bond funds. She recommends that the necessary reallocation be implemented with capital gains tax implications in mind. Stein also points out that the portfolio's expected return would be higher if the Schmitts dropped their requirement of limiting the maximum drawdown to 20%, thereby allowing a higher allocation to risky assets.

SUMMARY

This case study follows a family from the early career to the retirement stage. It touches on a small and simplified selection of a wide range of issues and considerations that a family may face. A great range of skills and competencies is required to provide financial advice, ranging from the ability to conduct in-depth risk analysis, all the way to making recommendations on risk mitigation strategies, including the choice of insurance products, to perform asset allocation, tax optimization, retirement planning, and estate planning. All of this must be done with a clear understanding of the applicable legal environment and of the level of access and the cost of accessing financial products. In practice, it is very unlikely that a single financial professional can master all the foregoing competencies. The key to success is to understand at what point the generalist needs to bring in, or refer the client to, a subject matter expert.

In this case study:

- We identify and analyze the Schmitts' risk exposures. We observed that the types of risk exposure change substantially from the early career stage to the early retirement stage.

We conducted the analysis holistically, starting from the economic balance sheet, including human capital.

- We recommend and justify methods to manage the Schmitt family's risk exposures at different stages of their professional life. We use insurance, self-insurance, and adjustments to their investment portfolio.
- We prepare summaries of the Schmitts' risk exposures and the selected methods of managing those risk exposures.
- We recommend and justify modifications to the Schmitts' life and disability insurance at different stages of the income earners' lives.
- Finally, we recommend a justified a plan to manage risk to the Schmitts' retirement lifestyle goals.

PROBLEMS

The following information relates to Questions 1–2

Recently married, Jennifer and Ron Joseph live in the United States. Jennifer, age 26, and Ron, age 28, both earned master's degrees in the high-demand field of computer science. The young couple are in their early career stage and have combined savings of $50,000 with no other financial assets.

Both Jennifer and Ron are in good health and have been working for a few years. Ron works in the private sector as a programmer for a large information technology company, and Jennifer works in the state sector as a public high school teacher. Jennifer benefits from excellent job security with limited earnings risk from unemployment; however, any salary increases over time are expected to be modest. In contrast, Ron faces significant uncertainties in his future employment income, although he could benefit from significant upside in income if he and his employer achieve performance targets.

The Josephs seek financial advice and ask Jeff Berger, a long-time adviser to Ron's parents, to plan a wealth management strategy. Berger explains the concept of an economic balance sheet and the importance of the value of human capital in meeting their financial objectives.

1. **Discuss** key factors that affect the value of the Josephs' human capital.

Berger is concerned about possible financial difficulties for the surviving spouse in the event of the other's premature death. He advises the Josephs to consider mitigating this risk by purchasing life insurance policies.

Berger suggests using the needs analysis method to determine the required insurance amount. He first estimates cash needs for Jennifer and Ron and then estimates that the surviving spouse would live until age 85 and require $35,000 annually for living expenses, and that those expenses would increase 2% annually in nominal terms. He assumes a 2.5% discount rate. Berger also estimates the present value of the surviving spouse's salary income until retirement at age 65 for both Jennifer and Ron. Exhibit 1 presents an abbreviated life insurance worksheet.

EXHIBIT 1   Joseph Family Financial Needs: Life Insurance Worksheet

Cash needs	Ron	Jennifer
Funeral and burial costs plus taxes	$20,000	$20,000
Emergency fund	$15,000	$15,000
Debts to be repaid	$0	$0
Total cash needs	**$35,000**	**$35,000**
Total capital needs	?	?
Total financial needs	?	?
Capital available:		
Cash and investments	$50,000	$50,000
Total capital available	**$50,000**	**$50,000**
Supplemental information:		
PV of surviving spouse's income until retirement at age 65	$748,837 (based on $25,000 starting salary for Jennifer)	$1,304,662 (based on $45,000 starting salary for Ron)

2. **Calculate** the amount of life insurance needs for both Jennifer and Ron individually, based on Berger's assumptions and Exhibit 1.

The following information relates to Questions 3–5

Susan and Robert Hunter, both age 47, live in the United States with their two children, ages 10 and 12. The Hunters both plan to retire at age 67. Susan works as a petroleum engineer at a small oil company, and Robert is a nurse at a local state-owned hospital. The Hunters are saving for retirement and for their children's college education expenses. Susan's annual salary is $135,000 ($90,000 after taxes), and Robert's annual salary is $55,000 ($36,000 after taxes). Their annual household living expenses are $90,000.

The Hunters have $50,000 in their bank account. They also have a stock portfolio consisting of five microcap energy stocks worth around $150,000, which they plan to use to partially fund their retirement needs. The Hunters plan to meet their retirement needs through contributions to pension plans offered by their employers, supplemented by government Social Security income payments starting at age 67. Both contribute 5% of their salaries to their respective defined contribution (DC) plans, but only Susan's company offers a matching contribution up to 10% of her base salary. Susan's DC plan has a current value of $80,000, while Robert's plan has a current value of $40,000. Income and capital gain distributions within the plan are tax free.

The Hunters meet with Helen Chapman seeking financial advice. After reviewing the Hunters' financial objectives, which include funding their retirement and the college education for their two children, Chapman discusses several risks facing the Hunters in their efforts to achieve those objectives.

3. **Evaluate** *each* of the following risks facing the Hunters:
   i.   Premature death risk
   ii. Investment portfolio risk
   iii. Risk to their retirement lifestyle goals
   iv. Earnings risk resulting from potential loss of employment

Chapman reviews the Hunters' existing life insurance policies. Susan Hunter informs Chapman that she currently has a life insurance policy of $200,000 and his wife has a life insurance policy of $300,000. Only Susan has life insurance coverage at work, with coverage at two times her annual salary.

Chapman believes that the Hunters' current coverage is insufficient to provide support for their family in the event of a death. She suggests using the human life value method to estimate the amount of life insurance required. Chapman estimates the present value of the pretax income needed to replace after-tax income to be $1,700,000 for Susan and $394,000 for Robert.

    4. Recommend the additional life insurance the Hunters need. **Justify** your recommendation.

Chapman reviews the Hunters' expected spending needs in retirement and is concerned they will not have saved enough by retirement to support their lifestyle thereafter. Chapman recommends that the Hunters raise their DC plan contributions to 10% of their salaries. The Hunters are reluctant to do so, however, telling Chapman that they would rather save the additional funds to continue building up their bank account balance. The bank account savings are readily accessible compared with the contribution to the DC funds, which will be unavailable until they retire.

    5. Discuss the advantages of the recommendation made by Chapman.

The following information relates to Question 6

James and Wendy Chang, both age 58, plan to retire in nine years. James is a human resource manager for a large US company with a defined contribution (DC) pension plan to which he regularly contributes. Wendy is a freelance computer programmer who works out of a home-based office. She contributes to a private DC plan. Both expect to start receiving Social Security income benefits when they retire at age 67. Their long-term goal is for a comfortable retirement and to provide an inheritance for their two children. The Changs believe they will need to maintain, in real terms, their current level of spending of $100,000 when they retire.

The Changs meet with their financial adviser, Lucie Timan, to discuss the risks to their retirement lifestyle goal. She estimates their Social Security benefit amounts at age 67. In her estimation calculations, Timan assumes a 25% tax rate and a 3% inflation rate. Based on his estimates, the Changs will have total annual pretax retirement income, including Social Security benefits, of $194,500 when they retire at age 67. The Changs tell Timan that they plan to use their DC plans' balances at age 67 to buy an immediate fixed annuity with no inflation adjustment.

    6. Discuss how *each* of the following risk factors could affect the Changs' projected retirement income:
      i. inflation risk
      ii. loss of employment
      iii. poor investment returns

CHAPTER 14

INTEGRATED CASES IN RISK MANAGEMENT: INSTITUTIONAL

Steve Balaban, CFA, Arjan Berkelaar, PhD, CFA, Nasir Hasan, and Hardik Sanjay Shah, CFA

LEARNING OUTCOMES

The candidate should be able to:

- discuss financial risks associated with the portfolio strategy of an institutional investor;
- discuss environmental and social risks associated with the portfolio strategy of an institutional investor;
- analyze and evaluate the financial and non-financial risk exposures in the portfolio strategy of an institutional investor;
- discuss various methods to manage the risks that arise on long-term direct investments of an institutional investor;
- evaluate strengths and weaknesses of an enterprise risk management system and recommend improvements.

1. INTRODUCTION

The focus of this reading is a fictional "case study." The case itself will focus on the portfolio of a sovereign wealth fund (SWF) specifically looking at risk in terms of the SWF's long-term investments. There are three Learning Outcome Statements (LOS) within the case. Prior to the case, we provide two LOS outside the case. These LOS will provide some background information that will be helpful to the candidate in understanding the case.

2. FINANCIAL RISKS FACED BY INSTITUTIONAL INVESTORS

2.1. Long-Term Perspective

Institutional investors (also referred to as *asset owners*) such as pension funds, sovereign wealth funds, endowments, and foundations are distinct from other institutional investors such as banks and insurance companies in terms of the time horizon over which they invest their assets. This long-term perspective allows these institutions to take on certain investment risks that other institutional investors simply cannot bear and to invest in in a broad range of alternative asset classes, including private equity, private real estate, natural resources, infrastructure, and hedge funds. This section will focus on the financial risks associated with the portfolio strategy of long-term institutional investors and in particular will focus on investments in illiquid asset classes. Banks and insurance companies are excluded from the discussion because they are typically much more asset/liability focused and face much tighter regulatory constraints to ensure capital adequacy.

This section will not cover the quantitative aspects of risk management or the mechanics behind various risk metrics, such as standard deviation and conditional value at risk, or risk management techniques, such as Monte Carlo simulation and factor modelling. Those topics are covered in other parts of the CFA Program curriculum. Instead, this reading will cover key risk considerations faced by long-term institutional investors as they invest in a range of traditional and alternative asset classes, including private equity and infrastructure. An important distinguishing feature of long-term institutional investors is their ability to invest in illiquid asset classes. Since the late 1990s, such asset classes have become an ever more important part of the investment portfolios of pension funds, sovereign wealth funds, endowments, and foundations. In this reading, we put particular emphasis on the financial risks that emanate from illiquid investments because these risks tend to be least well quantified but can pose an existential threat to long-term investors if not addressed and managed carefully. The focus is on how market and liquidity risk interact to create potential challenges at the overall portfolio level and affect the institutional investor's ability to meet its long-term objectives.

Section 2.2 briefly discusses the various lenses through which risk management can be viewed. Risk management is a very broad topic, and the goal is to simply provide the reader with a frame of reference. Section 2.3 focuses on the key financial risks that institutional investors face. The focus is on portfolio-level, top-down, long-term financial risk. Risk management for long-term institutional investors should primarily be concerned with events that may jeopardize the organization's ability to meet its long-term objectives. The interaction between market and liquidity risk plays a critical role. In Section 2.4 we discuss the challenges associated with investing in illiquid asset classes from a risk management perspective. We discuss two important aspects of illiquid asset classes: the uncertainty of cash flows and return-smoothing behavior in the return pattern. Section 2.5 describes how institutional investors address and manage liquidity risk at the overall portfolio level.

2.2. Dimensions of Financial Risk Management

The aim of risk management is to avoid an existential threat to the organization. In other words, risk management should focus on what types of events can jeopardize the organization's ability to meet its long-term objectives. Existential threats can arise from both financial risks (e.g., market losses and liquidity risk in the form of the inability to meet cash flows) and non-financial risks (e.g., reputational risks). In this reading, we solely focus on financial risk. Financial risk needs to be viewed through multiple lenses. There is no simple template to financial risk management. It is not simply a matter of calculating, for example, the value at risk of a portfolio. There are several dimensions to sound financial risk management, and we cover them briefly in the following subsections. Our goal is to simply provide a frame of reference for the reader because risk management is a very broad topic.

2.2.1. Top-down vs. bottom-up risk analysis

Risk management requires both a top-down and a bottom-up perspective. From a top-down perspective, the board and chief investment officer (CIO) set overall risk guidelines for the portfolio that serve as guardrails within which the investment team is expected to operate. Risk management involves measuring, monitoring, and reporting portfolio results versus the guidelines. The investment team is tasked with implementing the overall investment strategy either through hiring external asset managers or by directly purchasing and managing securities and assets. The investment team takes a more bottom-up, sub-portfolio approach to managing the risks of each individual portfolio or asset class, while assessing and monitoring their interaction and impact on the risk level of the overall portfolio.

2.2.2. Portfolio-level risk vs. asset-class-specific risk

Although risk management for an institutional investor is ultimately about controlling overall portfolio-level risk, risks also need to be managed and controlled at the asset-class or strategy level so that no particular asset class or strategy will have an undue adverse effect on the overall portfolio. Different asset classes require different risk management techniques. Some risk metrics and methods make sense for publicly traded asset classes, but they may not be meaningful when assessing the risk of, for example, illiquid asset classes or hedge fund investments. For some asset classes, such as public equities, detailed security-level information might be available, whereas for other asset classes, such as hedge funds, only monthly manager returns may be available. In the case of a public equity portfolio, risk analysis might be very granular and rely on sophisticated factor models, whereas risk analysis for hedge fund investments might simply involve calculating the historical volatility of observed returns. Because of differences in data transparency, data frequency, and risk methods used, it is difficult—if not impossible—to aggregate these results at the overall portfolio level. It is not uncommon for institutional investors to have an overall risk management system for portfolio-wide risk metrics in addition to asset-class-specific systems or approaches that provide a more in-depth risk view tailored to a particular asset class.

2.2.3. Return-based vs. holdings-based risk approaches

Financial risk management systems are typically described as being return based (risk estimation relies on the historical return streams of an external manager or a portfolio of securities) or holdings based (risk estimation relies on individual security holdings and the historical returns of those securities in the portfolio). Both approaches have their pros and cons, and they are not mutually exclusive. Return-based systems are relatively easy to implement but may produce risk estimates that are biased because they rely on past returns from a strategy that may be very different today compared with, for example, five years ago. Holdings-based risk systems, in contrast, tend to be more costly and time-consuming to implement. For many institutional investors that invest in hedge funds and illiquid asset classes, holdings-based risk systems for the entire portfolio are typically not feasible because of a lack of transparency on holdings and their related investment strategy (a multi-strategy fund may maintain a long position in a security within one strategy book and a short position in another strategy book), data being available with a one-month to three-month lag, and significant turnover in certain types of hedge fund investments.

2.2.4. Absolute vs. relative risk

Investors are interested in both absolute risk and relative risk. Absolute risk concerns the potential for overall losses and typically relies on overall portfolio-level metrics, such as standard deviation, conditional value at risk, and maximum drawdown. Relative risk concerns underperformance versus policy benchmarks and relies on such metrics as tracking error (the standard deviation of returns relative to a benchmark).

2.2.5. Long-term vs. short-term risk metrics

Modern risk systems used by institutional investors typically focus on calculating volatility, value at risk, and conditional value at risk using sophisticated risk factor techniques. Given the heavy reliance on the current portfolio composition and the granular modeling of each component in the portfolio, these risk systems are most useful in providing an estimate for the potential for near-term losses. Institutional investors are also interested in calculating longer-term risks, such as the probability of losses, the probability of not being able to meet cash flows, and the probability of maintaining purchasing power or meeting a certain return target over longer time periods, such as 5 years, 10 years, 20 years, and so forth.

These long-term risk metrics are typically calculated using Monte Carlo simulation, where asset-class returns are simulated on the basis of a set of forward-looking capital market assumptions (typically expected returns, volatilities, and correlations) and total assets are calculated including cash flows, such as benefit payments and contributions in the case of pension funds and payouts (spending amounts) in case of endowments and foundations. These methods, although typically much less granular than a risk management system, are better able to incorporate future portfolio changes, different rebalancing methods, and cash flows.

2.2.6. Quantitative vs. qualitative risks

At the end of the day, risk management is not simply a quantitative endeavor. Quantitative risk management techniques are backward looking by nature and typically parametric (i.e., they rely on historical data to estimate parameters). Although history can serve as a guide, it does not provide a prediction of the future. Risk management is about assessing the potential for future losses, and quantitative tools need to be complemented with qualitative assessments. However, with qualitative assessments, it is important for risk managers to be aware of their own biases because they are basing these assessments on their own past experience. Thus, it is important for risk managers to recognize and mitigate the backward-looking bias in both quantitative (explicit) and qualitative (implicit) risk analysis.

2.2.7. Pre- and post-investment risk assessment

Finally, although risk management efforts typically focus on measuring the risks of existing investments, a sound risk management philosophy ensures a proper assessment of financial risks prior to making investments. Institutional investors typically put a lot of effort into operational and investment due diligence prior to making investments. In addition to analyzing past investment performance, it is critical when hiring external managers to evaluate the character of the key decision makers, the business ethics of the firm, the investment experience of the team, the quality of operations (such as accounting and trade settlements), and the risk management practices of the external manager. As part of their investment due diligence, institutional investors also look at the quality of the non-executive directors of the fund, the integrity and independence of external auditors, fee structures, master fund and feeder fund structure, custodians, and safekeeping on assets. These considerations are even more important for illiquid investments because it is very difficult to exit from them (investors cannot easily change their mind). After investing, risk management might take on a more quantitative role, but continued due diligence and monitoring are of equal importance. In the case of external managers, this obligation resides with the team responsible for the hiring and firing of the managers. In the case of internal management, an in-house risk management team may be tasked with the ongoing due-diligence and monitoring responsibilities.

The various risk dimensions we have described should provide a sense of the wide-ranging nature of risk management as a discipline. For this reading, we focus exclusively on the key financial risks that long-term institutional investors face. We take a portfolio-level, top-down perspective and are primarily concerned with how illiquid asset classes and the interaction between market and liquidity risk affect an institutional investor's ability to meet its long-term objectives. This risk is unique to long-term institutional investors. The next section will provide a more in-depth description of this risk.

2.3. Risk Considerations for Long-Term Investors

Long-term institutional investors have the ability to invest a significant part of their portfolio in risky and illiquid assets because of their long-term investment horizon and relatively low liquidity needs. The past two decades have seen a steady increase in the allocation to illiquid asset classes, such private equity, private real estate, and infrastructure, by pension funds, sovereign wealth funds, endowments, and foundations. These asset classes create unique risk management challenges and can pose an existential threat if the risks are not addressed and managed carefully. As stated before, the ultimate objective of risk management is to ensure that the organization survives and can meet its long-term objectives.

We start with briefly describing and reviewing the main objectives of long-term institutional investors and their key risk considerations. Exhibit 1 provides an overview by institutional investor type. The ultimate risk consideration for each of these institutional investors is their ability to meet the payouts that they were set up to provide. This risk is largely affected by how the overall investment portfolio performs over time. On the one hand, a very low-risk portfolio that consists primarily of fixed-income investments is unlikely to cause a problem in providing the required payouts in the short run but will almost certainly jeopardize the organization's ability to provide the required payouts in the long run. On the other hand, a very risky and illiquid portfolio is expected to provide high expected returns in the long run but could cause significant pain in the short run during a significant market downturn or financial crisis. Long-term institutional investors aim to strike the right balance between these two extremes in designing their investment policy or strategic asset allocation.

EXHIBIT 1   Objectives and Risk Considerations by Institutional Investor Type

Institutional Investor	Main Objective	Key Risk Consideration
Pension funds	Provide retirement income to plan participants	Inability to meet pension payouts to beneficiaries
Sovereign wealth funds	Varies by type of SWF but most have been set up to provide some future financial support to the government	Inability to provide financial support to the government
Endowments and Foundations	Provide financial support in perpetuity while maintaining intergenerational equity	Inability to provide financial support to the institution or to the mission

This process usually involves a Monte Carlo simulation exercise where asset-class returns are simulated on the basis of a set of forward-looking capital market assumptions and total assets are calculated including cash flows, such as benefit payments and contributions in the case of pension funds and payouts (spending amounts) in the case of endowments and foundations. Monte Carlo simulation allows institutional investors to calculate such metrics as the probability of maintaining purchasing power and the probability of a certain loss or drawdown (e.g., 25%) over a specific time period (e.g., 5 or 10 years) and to determine the appropriate trade-off between two such metrics. What is often ignored in this type of analysis, however, is the important interaction between potential market losses and liquidity. Pension funds, SWFs, endowments, and foundations are unique in that they can often tolerate significantly more market and liquidity risk than other investors. Their long-term investment horizon allows them to survive a significant market correction and even operate in a counter-cyclical way during a market crisis. As institutional investors invest more in such illiquid asset classes as private equity, private real estate, and infrastructure, however, their ability to tolerate market losses may diminish.

Institutional investors need liquidity to meet payouts (retirement payments in the case of pension plans, payouts to the university or foundation in the case of endowments and foundations, etc.), meet capital calls on their illiquid investments, and rebalance their portfolios. During a significant market downturn, these needs can become stretched and impact the institution's ability to meet cash flows, particularly if a large part of the portfolio is invested in illiquid asset classes, such as private equity, real estate, and infrastructure. Exhibit 2 shows the main liquidity needs and the main sources of liquidity for long-term institutional investors. Each of these liquidity needs and sources may be adversely affected during a financial crisis.

EXHIBIT 2   Liquidity Needs and Sources for Institutional Investors

Liquidity Needs	Liquidity Sources
Outflows (e.g., pension payouts to beneficiaries, university payouts, and financial support to the government)	Inflows (e.g., pension contributions, gifts, donations, government savings)
Capital calls for illiquid investments	Distributions from illiquid investments
Portfolio rebalancing	Investment income and proceeds from selling liquid asset classes (cash, fixed income, public equities)

We first start with discussing how liquidity needs may increase during a crisis. First, payouts might increase as the beneficiary requires additional financial support. For example, a university may need additional funds from its endowment to support its operations as other sources of income dry up, or a government might require additional financial support from the sovereign wealth fund to mitigate the crisis situation. Second, there might be an acceleration of capital calls as attractive investment opportunities present themselves during a crisis. Finally, rebalancing flows will be more significant during a crisis because of significant market movements. Good governance and best practice suggest that investors rebalance their portfolios at regular intervals. Sticking to rebalancing practices is particularly important during a financial crisis because failure to rebalance may prevent investors from fully participating in the rebound after the crisis.

Having discussed how the needs for liquidity may increase during a significant market downturn, we next turn to how sources of liquidity might dry up under those circumstances. First, inflows might decrease in a crisis. For example, donors might be struggling financially and donate less to their alma mater, or plan sponsors might be faced with budgetary challenges and, therefore, less inclined to contribute to the pension fund. Second, distributions from illiquid investments might be reduced because there are no attractive exit points due to depressed prices or lower profitability. Finally, investments that are otherwise liquid might become less liquid or simply undesirable to exit from. The main sources of liquidity during a financial crisis are typically cash and fixed-income investments. And most long-term institutional investors hold relatively low allocations to cash and fixed income in their portfolios.

Illiquid asset classes (such as private equity, real estate, and infrastructure) are not available to meet liquidity needs during a crisis. These asset classes cannot be rebalanced or redeemed because they are long term in nature and the assets can be locked up for 5–10 years or even longer. Semi-liquid asset classes, such as hedge fund investments, should not be expected to be liquid and available to meet liquidity needs during a financial crisis because many of these managers might impose redemption gates or have lockups in place or their investments might turn out to be less liquid than anticipated. Finally, although public equity investments are technically liquid, investors may be reluctant to sell part of their public equity portfolio to meet liquidity needs because the market value of these investments may have gone down significantly in a crisis. In addition, investors might not want to redeem from certain active external managers, even if the investments are liquid, because it may impact the future relationship with that manager (particularly for high-demand active managers with limited available capacity).

In conclusion, the main risk that long-term institutional investors face is having insufficient liquidity during a significant market downturn to meet their obligations and rebalance their portfolios. Liquidity needs tend to increase in a crisis while sources of liquidity dry up. This risk increases as institutional investors allocate more to illiquid asset classes. The combination of financial losses and not being able to meet cash flows or rebalance the portfolio because of insufficient liquidity can become a matter of survival. Managing this risk is, therefore, very important for long-term institutional investors. In the next section, we will discuss in more detail the risks associated with illiquid asset classes. In Section 2.5, we will discuss the various ways in which institutional managers manage liquidity risk.

2.4. Risks Associated with Illiquid Asset Classes

Illiquid asset classes, such as private equity, real estate, and infrastructure, offer the potential for returns in excess of those on publicly traded asset classes, such as public equity and fixed income. The higher expected return of these asset classes comes at a cost to investors in the form of illiquidity. Illiquid asset classes are typically subject to a drawdown structure where committed capital is called at an unknown schedule and investors receive profits at an unknown schedule. As a result, investors need to hold suffcient liquid assets to meet capital calls from their private fund managers. The uncertain pattern of cash flows poses both a liquidity and a risk management challenge for investors in illiquid asset classes.

In addition to the importance of adequately managing liquidity needs when investing in illiquid assets, these asset classes tend to be subject to stale pricing, appraisal-based valuations, and a lagged response to movements in public markets. As a result, illiquid asset classes exhibit returns that are smooth, understating the true volatility and correlation with publicly traded asset classes. For example, the standard deviation of observed returns for private equity is often smaller than that of public equity. Although this feature may be appealing for institutional investors, it causes traditional asset allocation models, such as mean–variance optimization, to over-allocate to private asset classes because the Sharpe ratios of observed returns are superior to those of publicly traded asset classes.

Finally, illiquid asset classes cannot be rebalanced easily and costlessly. Although investors could potentially, for example, sell their private equity stakes in the secondary market, this cannot be done instantaneously and investors may have to accept a significantly lower price compared with the true market value.

2.4.1. Cash flow modeling

Illiquid asset classes are subject to a drawdown structure. The investor (typically the limited partner, or LP, in the partnership agreement) commits capital, and this capital gets drawn down over time at the discretion of the general partner, or GP. Investors need to figure out both the commitment strategy (i.e., how much to commit each year) to reach a certain target allocation to illiquid assets and the liquidity needs to meet capital calls when required. Committing too much can pose severe liquidity risk because the percentage allocation to illiquid asset classes may soar due to the so-called denominator effect (total assets under management, or AUM, falls by a larger amount than the repricing of illiquid asset classes). Committing too little may prevent the investor from reaching the target allocation and may result in falling short of return expectations.

In managing liquidity needs and determining the appropriate commitment strategy to illiquid asset classes, investors need to be able to predict future cash flows.

2.4.2. Addressing return smoothing behavior of illiquid asset classes

To calculate the true underlying economic risks of illiquid asset classes as part of their risk management efforts, institutional investors typically use one of two approaches: (1) Use public market proxies in place of private asset classes—for example, use small-cap public equities as a proxy for private equity—or (2) unsmooth observed returns of private asset classes. The objective of the latter is to remove the serial correlation structure of the original return series. The implicit assumption is that the serial correlations in reported returns are entirely due to the smoothing behavior funds engage in when reporting results. A common and simple technique to unsmooth the returns of illiquid asset classes and hedge funds is a method developed by Geltner (1993) to address appraisal-based valuations in real estate. The method proposed by Geltner removes only the first-order serial correlation in observed returns. Okunev and White (2003) extended the method of Geltner (1993) to include higher-order serial correlations. An alternative to the Geltner method is the GLM method proposed by Getmansky, Lo, and Makarov (2004). They assumed that observed returns for illiquid asset classes and hedge funds follow a moving-average process.

To show the effect of these different methods on the annualized volatility of various illiquid asset classes, we use quarterly historical returns for global buyouts, global venture capital, global private real estate, and global private natural resources for the period from Q1 1990 until Q4 2019. Exhibit 3 shows the annualized volatility of the observed returns and the volatility of adjusted returns using the three methods briefly discussed earlier. For the Okunev–White and GLM methods, we use up to four lags. Exhibit 4 shows the beta to global equity returns. For global equity returns, we use quarterly returns for the MSCI World Index from 1990 to 2019.

EXHIBIT 3 Impact of Unsmoothing on Annualized Volatility

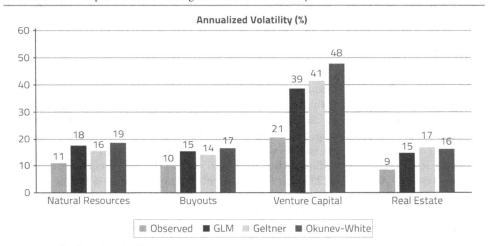

Source: Data is from Cambridge Associates.

EXHIBIT 4 Impact of Unsmoothing on Beta to Public Equities

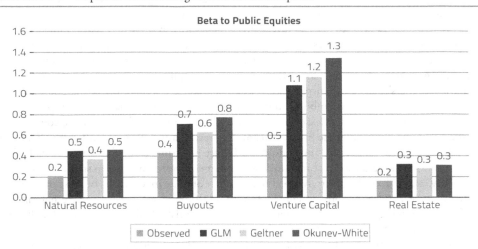

Source: Data is from Cambridge Associates.

As illustrated in Exhibits 3 and 4, after applying unsmoothing techniques, the resulting returns exhibit higher volatility and are typically more correlated with public equity markets.

These unsmoothed return series can then be used along with returns on publicly traded asset classes to determine the covariance matrix to be used in a mean–variance optimization exercise when determining the appropriate allocation to illiquid asset classes and hedge funds. Mean–variance optimization, however, still falls short as an adequate asset allocation tool for institutional investors because it is not able to take into account the illiquid nature of some asset classes. Illiquid asset classes cannot be rebalanced easily without a potential significant price concession. Single-period optimization methods, such as mean–variance optimization, fail when illiquid asset classes are introduced, because such techniques implicitly assume that investors keep portfolio weights constant over time (i.e., portfolio weights are rebalanced perfectly) and they ignore the drawdown structure of illiquid asset classes and the uncertainty of cash flows. Currently, there are not any widely accepted alternatives. Most investors simply constrain the allocations to illiquid asset classes in the mean–variance optimization to achieve reasonable and practical portfolios.

2.4.3. Direct vs. fund investments in illiquid asset classes

In recent years, large pension funds and sovereign wealth funds have increasingly opted to invest directly in illiquid asset classes rather than through the more typical limited partner (LP)–general partner (GP) setup. Some large pension funds and SWFs have built up a large team of merchant banking professionals who are equally capable as a large private equity fund team. The main motivation behind such a move is to save on the high fees that institutional investors typically pay to GPs (2% base fee on committed capital and 20% fee on profits or over a certain hurdle rate). Being able to save on these fees should make the investments more profitable over the long term. Direct investments provide an institutional investor with control over each individual investment. This situation puts the investor in a better position to manage liquidity. In the case of direct investments, there are no unfunded commitments, making it easier to manage capital. The investor also has full discretion over the decision when to exit investments and will not have to be forced to sell in a down market. As a result, direct investments partially alleviate some of the liquidity challenges typically associated with private asset classes and resolve some of the principal–agent issues associated with fund investing.

There are also disadvantages to direct investments in private asset classes. Direct investments in private equity, real estate, or infrastructure require a dedicated and experienced in-house team. In some instances, rather than building out an in-house team for private investments, large pension funds and sovereign wealth funds acquire a general partner. For example, Ontario Teachers' Pension Plan purchased Cadillac Fairview, a large operating company for real estate. Managing and assembling an in-house team adds several challenges compared with the more nimble setup in the case of fund investing. The sourcing of deals may be constrained by the talent and network of the in-house team. As a result, it may be more difficult to diversify the portfolio across geography and industries. Direct investment portfolios may have higher concentration risk because direct investors opt for larger investments due to staffing issues and scalability. This risk could adversely affect the liquidity of these investments because they might be harder to sell and, therefore, potentially less liquid. If the investor relies on external managers for deal sourcing or a partnership agreement, there is a risk of adverse selection. Finally, the governance structure is not set up as well in the case of direct investing compared with fund investments. In contrast to fund managers, employees of a pension fund or sovereign wealth fund may not be able to sit on the board of a private company. Institutional investors may not be able to afford the liability issues associated with direct investing. For fund investments, the investor is a limited partner and has limited liability, whereas with direct investments, the investor may be considered a general partner, with additional liability risks. Finally, institutional investors may find it difficult to adequately compensate internal staff to ensure that they hire and retain talent. This is usually a problem for public pension funds because there is public pressure to keep compensation down.

2.5. Managing Liquidity Risk

In this section, we discuss some of the tools used by institutional investors to manage overall liquidity risk in their portfolios.

   Liquidity management steps:

1. **Establish liquidity risk parameters.**   Institutional investors typically create liquidity guidelines regarding what percentage of assets needs to be liquid and available on a daily or monthly basis. In addition, given the drawdown structure of illiquid asset classes, institutional investors need to keep track of uncalled commitments, not simply invested capital. It is typical for institutional investors to have internal guidelines or bands around the sum of invested capital and uncalled commitments as a percentage of total assets. In addition to such bands, they may have automatic or semiautomatic escalation triggers, such as reducing commitments to illiquid asset classes or even actively seeking to reduce investments through secondary sales once the sum of invested capital plus uncalled commitments reaches a certain level (expressed as a percentage of total assets). These liquidity risk parameters can either be internal or be included in an investment policy statement approved by the board.

2. **Assess the liquidity of the current portfolio and how it evolves over time.**   The second step in managing liquidity risk at the overall portfolio level is to have a clear sense of the liquidity of the portfolio and measure liquidity parameters versus guidelines. Most institutional investors have an internal report that shows what percentage of the portfolio can be liquidated within a day, within a week, within a month, within a quarter, and within a year and what percentage of the portfolio takes more than a year to be liquidated. It is important not only to have a snapshot of that report at a given point in time but also to understand how it evolves over time as the portfolio changes. A good starting point for developing these statistics is to simply look at the legal terms that are in place with external managers. This is particularly relevant for active managers and hedge funds that have redemption notices and lockups included in the investment agreement. In the case of internal management, an even more granular assessment can be made depending on the types of securities being held and using market liquidity measures to gauge how much of these securities can be sold over different time frames during a financial crisis. As discussed in Section 2.3, investors may also want to take into account how redeeming from certain external managers during a crisis may impact the future relationship with that manager (in other words, they may not want to redeem even if the investments are liquid and instead include these investments in a less liquid category).

3. **Develop a cash flow model and project future expected cash flows.**   The third step is to understand and model the various cash flows. As discussed in Section 2.3, institutional investors make payouts (retirement payments, foundation spending, etc.), they receive inflows (gifts and donations for an endowment, pension contributions for a pension plan, etc.), they have to meet capital calls for illiquid asset classes and receive distributions, and they have to rebalance their portfolios. Most institutional investors model each of those

cash flows and project future expected cash flows. Section 2.4 briefly discussed how capital calls and distributions are modeled for illiquid asset classes.

4. **Stress test liquidity needs and cash flow projections.**   The standard cash flow modeling and projections assume business as usual, but it is important to stress test these cash flow projections and liquidity needs. As discussed in Section 2.4, cash flows are affected by market movements. For example, donations might be lower in a crisis and payouts might be higher. Institutional investors stress test their cash flow projections and liquidity needs. It is important to point out that this process is more of an art than a science and there is no universally accepted method for stress testing (as there are universally accepted methods for market risk calculations).

5. **Put in place an emergency plan.**   Finally, institutional investors should put in place an emergency action plan. Such an action plan should include what to liquidate—and in what order—in a crisis to meet cash flows and how to rebalance the portfolio in a crisis. Having such a plan in place can help avoid the risk of panicking in a crisis. Sharing the emergency action plan with the board to get buy-in can also help when a crisis occurs and mitigate the risk of board members pressuring the investment team to make sub-optimal short-term decisions.

Exhibit 5 summarizes the five steps in developing a liquidity management plan.

EXHIBIT 5   Liquidity Management Steps

---

1. Establish liquidity risk parameters.
2. Assess the liquidity of current portfolio, and monitor the evolution over time.
3. Develop a cash flow model and project future cash flows.
4. Stress test liquidity needs and cash flow projections.
5. Develop an emergency action plan.

Long-term institutional investors are able take on certain investment risks that other institutional investors simply cannot bear. Since the late 1990s, they have increasingly invested in a broad range of alternative asset classes, including private equity, private real estate, natural resources, infrastructure, and hedge funds. In this reading, we focus on the financial risks that emanate from illiquid investments because these risks tend to be less well quantified but can pose an existential threat to long-term investors if not addressed and managed carefully. The focus has been on how market and liquidity risk interact to create potential challenges at the overall portfolio level and affect the institutional investor's ability to meet its long-term objectives. We propose several steps institutional investors can take to better manage liquidity at the overall portfolio level.

2.6. Enterprise Risk Management for Institutional Investors

Exhibit 6 provides a high-level view of a risk management framework in an enterprise context:

EXHIBIT 6   Risk Management Framework in an Enterprise Context

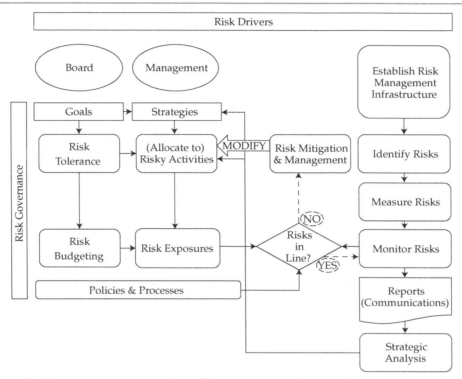

Source: "Risk Management: An Introduction," CFA Program Level I curriculum reading (2021).

We can apply this framework to the setting of an institutional investor in the following manner. The risk management process for an institutional investor starts with the board setting the overall risk tolerance for the organization that is consistent with its objectives and constraints. Risk tolerance should capture the amount of market risk that an institutional investor is willing and able to take in order to maximize expected returns, and it informs the most important investment decision that is made by the board—namely, the strategic asset allocation. Risk tolerance can be expressed in asset-only (for sovereign wealth funds, endowments, and foundations) or asset/liability terms (for pension funds and insurance companies). Typical risk measures used for setting the risk tolerance of institutional investors include volatility, maximum drawdown, and value at risk or conditional value at risk (sometimes referred to as *expected tail loss*, or *ETL*).

In addition to setting the overall risk tolerance (for market losses), the board usually approves additional risk parameters, limits, requirements, and guidelines (some quantitative and others procedural) that are codified in an investment policy statement (IPS). These may include liquidity risk parameters if the institutional investor has a significant allocation to illiquid asset classes, an active risk budget to limit and control the amount of active management pursued by investment staff, restrictions on leverage and the use of derivatives, ethical investment guidelines, and possibly credit risk parameters and constraints in the case of significant fixed-income investments (for example, for an insurance company). These additional guidelines and constraints are put in place to ensure that the investment activities are consistent with the board's risk tolerance and expectations (and with regulatory requirements if applicable).

Management (i.e., the investment team) is tasked with implementing the strategic asset allocation (SAA) and investing the assets either internally or through external managers across the various asset classes included in the SAA. The investment team is also responsible for managing and monitoring the risks associated with the implementation of the SAA and reporting to the board. The objective is not to minimize or eliminate risk but to measure and attribute risk to various risk exposures and factors to ensure that the investments adequately compensate the institution for the risks being taken. Institutional investors typically perform risk factor analysis to better understand the fund's risk exposures, such as exposure to equity risk, interest rate risk, credit risk, inflation risk, currency risk, and liquidity risk. This analysis includes both quantitative modeling and qualitative risk assessments. Quantitative tools may involve sophisticated risk management systems based on returns or holdings, scenario analysis, and stress testing. Other risks are more qualitative in nature, such as potential reputational risk from certain types of investments.

For public equity investments, active risk versus a benchmark needs to be measured and monitored. Institutional investors may have an explicit active risk budget in place. Part of the risk budgeting effort involves ensuring that the active risk budget accurately reflects the areas where most excess return can be expected. In addition, the investment team will want to ensure that most of the active risk in public equities comes from stock picking and not simply from loading on certain equity risk factors, such as growth, momentum, or quality.

For private equity investments, the board may want to understand whether the returns achieved on the investment adequately compensated the fund for giving up liquidity. One way to answer that question is by comparing the returns on the private equity investment with the return of public equities. Currency risk tends to sometimes be overlooked by institutional investors. This risk can have an outsized and unexpected impact on the overall return. Although currency risk can be hedged in some cases, doing so is typically costly or even impossible when investing in emerging and frontier markets. The risk of currency devaluation needs to be acknowledged and assessed prior to making investments. Another risk that gets overlooked is asset allocation drift. The investment portfolio should be rebalanced on a regular basis to bring it back in line with the strategic asset allocation that was approved by the board.

The risk management infrastructure of the institutional investor should be set up to identify and measure the aforementioned risks and monitor how they change over time and whether they are in line with the guidelines set up by the board in the IPS and with additional—more granular—internal guidelines set by the Chief Investment Officer and risk team. The risk team is usually tasked with risk reporting to the various stakeholders, which may include an internal investment committee and the board to ensure adequate risk oversight. The investment team should recognize when risk exposures are not aligned with the overall risk tolerance and guidelines and take action to bring them back into alignment. These actions may involve hedging, rebalancing, and secondary sales or in the case of illiquid investments, reducing commitments.

3. ENVIRONMENTAL AND SOCIAL RISKS FACED BY INSTITUTIONAL INVESTORS

3.1. Universal Ownership, Externalities, and Responsible Investing

In this section, we define universal owners as large institutional investors that effectively own a slice of the whole economy and hence are generally managing their total market exposure, instead of focusing on a subset of issuers. Institutional investors such as sovereign wealth funds and public pension funds usually have large portfolios that are highly diversified and built with a long-term focus. Such portfolios are representative of global capital markets, thereby making such investors "universal owners."

Investing long term in widely diversified holdings inevitably exposes such portfolios to increasing costs related to negative environmental and social externalities. An externality is an impact that an individual's or a corporation's activities have on a third party. If everyone acts in their own self-interest, it could lead to an overall negative outcome for society. Examples of negative environmental externalities include plastic pollution in the ocean, poor air quality due to industrial and vehicular emissions, and water toxicity due to improper effluent management.

Universal owners find it challenging to effectively diversify risks arising from negative environmental and social externalities. Costs that are externalized by one portfolio company can negatively affect the profitability of another portfolio company, thereby adversely affecting the overall portfolio return. For example, a sovereign wealth fund invests in a plastic manufacturer that is saving waste treatment and disposal costs by directly releasing waste pellets and other chemical residues into a nearby river. Water toxicity arising as a result of these actions causes reduced productivity in the agriculture operations downstream, which the asset owner is also invested in. In addition, strengthening regulations related to environmental protection, for example, may lead to monetary fines and penalties, thereby leading to financial risks for a company causing such negative externalities.

According to the UN-backed Principles for Responsible Investment (PRI), environmental costs for universal owners are reflected in portfolio impacts via insurance premiums, taxes, inflated input prices, and the physical costs associated with weather-related disasters (PRI Association 2017). Also, the cost of remediating environmental damage is often significantly higher than the cost of preventing it. Given these facts, it is imperative for large institutional investors to internalize the price of such negative externalities by considering the impact of their investments on society and future generations.

Exhibit 7 provides a non-exhaustive list of environmental and social issues that we have introduced in Level I of the CFA Program curriculum.

EXHIBIT 7   Examples of Environmental and Social Factors

Environmental Issues	Social Issues
Climate change and carbon emissions	Customer satisfaction and product responsibility
Air and water pollution	Data security and privacy
Biodiversity	Gender and diversity
Deforestation	Occupational health and safety
Energy efficiency	Community relations and charitable activities
Waste management	Human rights
Water scarcity	Labor standards

In the next section, we share examples of how some of these environmental and social issues could impact the portfolio strategy for large institutional investors that have a long-term focus toward their investments.

Systemic risks have the potential to destabilize capital markets and lead to serious negative consequences for financial institutions and the broader economy. The unpredictable nature of such megatrends as climate change and their related impacts, both environmental and socioeconomic, pose clear systemic risks to global financial markets. A study carried out by researchers at the Grantham Research Institute on Climate Change and the Environment (2016) at the London School of Economics and Political Science and Vivid Economics projected that climate change could reduce the value of global financial assets by as much as $24 trillion—resulting in permanent damage that would far eclipse that from the 2007–09 financial crisis.

3.2. Material Environmental Issues for an Institutional Investor

For an institutional investor, such as a sovereign wealth fund, such megatrends as climate change and their related risks—both physical and transition risks—have the potential to cause significant harm to a portfolio's value over the medium to long term, particularly for investments in real assets (real estate, infrastructure) and private equity, neither of which are easily divestible. Next, we will discuss the impact of climate-related risks on an institutional investor's portfolio from the perspective of private equity and real asset investments.

3.2.1. Physical climate risks

As we have observed since the beginning of the current century, climate change has profoundly affected the physical world we live in. Annual average temperatures across the globe are continuously rising, and 19 of the 20 warmest years have occurred since 2001 (NASA 2019). Erratic weather patterns, such as heavy precipitation, droughts, and hurricanes, are both more frequent and of higher magnitude. Similarly, wildfires are causing more and more devastation every year. In addition, the chronic issue of sea-level rise is causing coastal flooding. As shown in Exhibit 8, an increase in extreme weather events has occurred.

EXHIBIT 8   Extreme Weather Events on the Rise

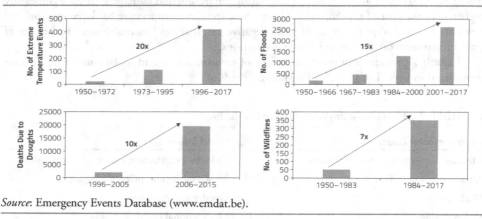

Source: Emergency Events Database (www.emdat.be).

With continued climate change, all these physical climate risks could become more severe in the future and, to a certain extent, become the new normal for the world. Depending on global responses to climate change in the coming decade, the degree of their impact on our economies and investments may be alleviated.

So, what does this mean for the portfolio strategy of large institutional investors with private equity and real asset investments?

3.2.2. Impact on real assets

Should these trends continue, the physical risks that we have discussed could create increased levels of stress on such assets as residential and commercial real estate and infrastructure, such as roads and railways. Rising sea levels that lead to flooding would impact both rents and property valuation for hitherto prime coastal properties. Prolonged exposure to extreme heat would negatively affect the useful life of roads and train tracks, which would lead to accelerated depreciation of such assets and, therefore, more frequent replacement costs for companies and governments (CFA Institute 2020).

Similarly, physical damage caused by frequent, large-scale weather-related events, such as hurricanes or even wildfires—once considered too irregular to insure against—could not only lead to large-scale drawdowns in the portfolio's asset value but also make it difficult or expensive to insure such assets. Most of the flooding-related losses around the world are uninsured, thereby causing additional stress on a country's economy and its people (see Exhibit 9).

EXHIBIT 9   Global Flood Losses and Insurance Levels

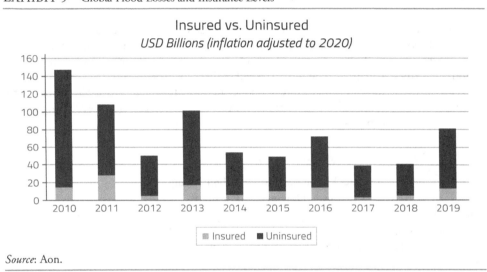

Source: Aon.

Because these physical climate-related risks continue to play out in a much larger and more frequent manner than previously anticipated, they will continue to bring down prices and rental yields of prime real estate, leading to permanent impairments of asset valuations. For a large institutional investor that is looking to preserve capital and provide growth benefits to multiple generations, it is imperative that these risks be factored into the portfolio construction strategies.

3.2.3. Climate transition risks

In line with the 2015 Paris Climate Agreement, countries and companies around the world are already making efforts to dramatically reduce or eliminate their CO_2 emissions in order to limit the global temperature increase in this century to 2 degrees Celsius above preindustrial levels. To keep global warming less than 2°C, scientists project that energy-related CO_2 emissions need to fall 25% by 2030 and reach "net zero" by 2070 (Intergovernmental Panel on Climate Change 2018; IEA 2020).

One of the most ambitious efforts to incentivize decarbonization is the European Union's sustainable finance taxonomy, which helps investors understand whether an economic activity is environmentally sustainable. As of October 2020, looking at the scientific evidence about the current and potential impacts of climate change, it has become clear that the world needs to move toward a low-carbon future if we are to cap global warming at less than 2°C and prevent the negative effects that not doing so would bring to our climate, our ecosystems, and human life. What is currently unclear is the pace at which this decarbonization will happen.

Rapid decarbonization will lead to restrictions on carbon emissions, implementation of some form of carbon pricing, introduction of new technologies, and changes in the consumer behavior. All these effects can create massive disruptions in certain sectors, such as electricity generation (with the increasing cost competitiveness of renewable energy sources as compared with coal) and automobiles (with the impending widespread switch from internal combustion engines to electric vehicles). The International Energy Agency has forecast that in order to reach carbon neutrality by 2050, half of all cars in the world should be electric by 2030 (Lo 2020).

The PRI's Inevitable Policy Response (IPR) project aims to prepare financial markets for climate-related policy risks that are likely to emerge in the short to medium term. The IPR forecast a response by 2025 that will be forceful, abrupt, and disorderly because of the delayed action (see Exhibit 10). The PRI argues that markets have inefficiently priced climate transition risks, but its policy forecast is that a forceful policy response to climate change in the near term is a highly likely outcome, leaving portfolios of institutional investors exposed to significant risks that need to be mitigated.

EXHIBIT 10   IPR Key Policy Forecasts

Coal phase-outs	Sales ban on Internal Combustion Engines (ICE)	Carbon Pricing (Emission Allowances)	Zero carbon power
Early coal phase-out for first mover countries by 2030	Early sales ban for first mover countries by 2035	US\$40–80/tCO$_2$ prices by 2030 for first movers	Significant ramp-up of renewable energy globally
Steady retirement of coal-fired power generation after 2030 in lagging countries	Other countries follow suit as automotive industry reaches tipping point	Global convergence accelerated by Border Carbon Adjustment (BCA) to >=\$100/tCO$_2$ by 2050	Policy support of nuclear capacity increase in a small set of countries, nuclear phased out elsewhere

Carbon Capture and Storage (CCS) & industry decarbonisation	Energy efficiency	Green House Gas (GHG) removal (Land use-based)	Agriculture
Limited CCS support in power,	Increase in coverage and stringency of performance standards	Improved forestry and nature-based solutions	Technical support to improve agricultural yields
Policy incentives primarily for industrial and bioenergy CCS	Utility obligation programs	Stronger enforcement of zero deforestation	Increasing public investment in irrigation and AgTech
Public support for demonstration, and then deployment of hydrogen clusters	Financial and behavioral incentives	Controlled expansion of bioenergy crops	Incremental behavioural incentives away from beef

Source: PRI IPR (www.unpri.org/the-inevitable-policy-response-policy-forecasts/4849.article).

Given the uncertainty around the precise timing and magnitude of the impact of climate change, organizations are increasingly using climate-related scenario analysis to better understand how their businesses might perform under a variety of global warming scenarios—for example, in a world that is 2°C, 3°C, or 4°C warmer. The Task force on Climate-Related Financial Disclosures (TCFD) recommends organizations, including banks, asset managers, and asset owners, use scenario analysis to estimate the implications of such risks and opportunities for their businesses over time and also to inform their strategic thinking. The International Energy Agency and the Intergovernmental Panel on Climate Change both publicly offer a set of climate-related scenarios that are widely used. To learn more about climate-related scenario analysis, refer to the technical supplement issued by the TCFD.

3.2.4. Climate opportunities

Although most of the investor focus in dealing with climate change has been on managing physical and transition risks, exciting investment opportunities are arising in companies focused on climate change mitigation and adaptation. These opportunities exist in secondary markets and, in some cases, investments in real assets and infrastructure projects, such as wind and solar farms and smart grids.

Because the levelized cost of energy for renewable energy generation technologies has considerably decreased since 2010, these have become cost competitive with some conventional generation technologies, such as coal-based power generation, as shown in Exhibit 11.

EXHIBIT 11　2019 Levelized Cost of Energy, Unsubsidized

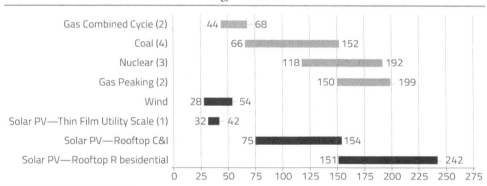

Note: Levelized cost of energy is a measure of the average net present cost of electricity generation for a power plant over its lifetime.

1. Unless otherwise indicated herein, the low end represents a single-axis tracking system and the high end represents a fixed-tilt system.
2. The fuel cost assumption for Lazard's global, unsubsidized analysis for gas-fired generation resources is $3.45/MMBTU.
3. Unless otherwise indicated, the analysis herein does not reflect decommissioning costs, ongoing maintenance-related capital expenditures or the potential economic impacts of federal loan guarantees or other subsidies.
4. High end incorporates 90% carbon capture and compression. Does not include cost of transportation and storage.

Sources: Data is from Lazard (www.lazard.com/perspective/lcoe2019).

This cost competitiveness, coupled with the urgency to decarbonize our economies to avoid the potentially catastrophic physical impacts of climate change, has created secular growth opportunity for such businesses and assets, thereby attracting increasingly large investor attention.

A summary of the business segments where such opportunities may lie follows.

Climate mitigation   This category includes companies that are positioned to benefit, directly or indirectly, from efforts to curb or mitigate the long-term effects of global climate change, to address the environmental challenges presented by global climate change, or to improve the efficiency of resource consumption.

EXHIBIT 12   Climate Mitigation Opportunity Examples

Business Segment	Description
Clean energy	Companies in this segment are involved in the generation of clean energy from such sources as wind, solar, and small hydro. This segment also includes manufacturers of such equipment as windmills and solar panels, as well as related service providers.
Energy efficiency	This segment comprises businesses that provide products and services to improve the efficiency of energy consumption in a variety of processes. Examples include energy efficient transportation and building solution providers and recycling technology.
Batteries and storage	This segment includes companies that help improve battery storage capacity and efficiency. These improvements are critical, for instance, to sustainable growth and wider penetration of some of the previously mentioned technologies, such as clean energy generation and distribution and electric vehicles.
Smart grids	Smart grids are digitally enhanced versions of the conventional electricity grid, with a layer of communication network overlaying the traditional grid. They are a key enabler for energy security and reliability and integration of clean energy resources.
Materials	Such materials as copper and battery-grade lithium are key ingredients in the clean energy value chain because they are required in clean energy power generation, storage solutions, and electric vehicles, resulting in a projected demand rise as the world transitions toward a low-carbon future.

Climate adaptation   This category includes companies that would help better adjust to actual or expected future change in climate with an aim to reduce vulnerability to the harmful effects of climate change, such as food insecurity, sea-level rise, and frequent extreme weather events.

EXHIBIT 13   Climate Adaptation Opportunity Examples

Business Segment	Description
Sustainable agriculture	Companies in this segment are involved in providing products that improve agriculture productivity and reduce the resource consumption in the entire process. Sustainable fish farming and timber production are other activities included here.
Water	This segment consists of businesses that provide products and services to improve the efficiency of water consumption in a variety of processes, including wastewater treatment and reuse.

Many institutional investors are increasing allocations to such sectors as part of their real-asset allocation or as a potential equity alpha opportunity with the expectation that companies in these sectors will outperform the broad equity market over a long period of time as the world transitions to a low carbon future. Evaluating and sufficiently managing both physical and transition climate risks in the portfolio and capturing some of the aforementioned secular growth opportunities could position large institutional investor portfolios to outperform and grow in value in the long term.

3.3. Material Social Issues for an Institutional Investor

Environmental issues, such as climate change and air pollution, are reasonably mature and quite well understood, making them easier to accommodate in discounted cash flow models. Social issues, such as community relation, occupational health and safety, privacy and data security, modern slavery and other human right violations in the supply chain, and inequality, however, are relatively challenging to quantify and integrate into financial models. Most social issues have largely qualitative data reported by companies, such as health and safety policies and initiatives, lists of product quality certifications, and human capital management policies, rather than metrics on which long-term performance can be judged. Nevertheless, these issues have the potential to cause reputational and financial damage to a company and its investors if not managed sufficiently well.

3.3.1. Managing community relations and the social license to operate

For large institutional investors, such as sovereign wealth funds and public pension funds, their investments may have positive social impacts, such as improving essential public infrastructure and services or providing better access to medicine and technology, or negative social impacts, via poor labor standards or forceful relocation and improper rehabilitation of communities by their portfolio companies. Good corporate behavior is usually well received by the community relations, leading to a sustainable and mutually beneficial long-term relationship. In many ways, these aspects are essential to keeping a company's social license to operate.

Let's take a hypothetical example of a sovereign wealth fund (SWF) that has invested in a dam-based hydroelectric power plant in an economically less developed part of its country. Although there will be a positive environmental impact of the project because it will generate electricity from a renewable source, the social impacts of the project could be mixed. On the positive side, rural electrification arising from this project will lead to economic development in the region, thereby improving the standard of living. Dam-based hydroelectric power plants require large-scale land acquisition, often leading to relocation and rehabilitation of indigenous communities. Some locals protest that they have not been sufficiently consulted by the government before issuing consent to establish this project. Moreover, there are allegations of acquisition of land for the project at unfair/poor valuations. In some instances, protesting locals were forcefully removed and relocated by local government authorities, leading to unrest. Eventually, the SWF decides to cease the project implementation owing to this wide variety of instances of pushback from the society.

This example highlights the importance of considering social risks when investing. Despite having the positive intent of supporting development of renewable power generation in a less economically developed part of the country, the SWF faced pushback and reputational damage for not holistically considering the interests of all the stakeholders involved, especially local communities that were the most affected by the project. Some of the best practices in community relation management include extensive stakeholder consultation meetings to better understand their needs and address their concerns, providing alternative employment opportunities to those affected, and ensuring fair land acquisition, rehabilitation, and resettlement practices.

3.3.2. Labor issues in the supply chain

Another increasingly important social topic is the one related to poor labor practices, especially in the supply chain. Driven by globalization, a consumption boom across developed and emerging markets, and the availability of cheap labor in certain parts of the world, a large portion of the manufacturing and assembling activities across such key sectors as technology and garments has been outsourced to developing and frontier markets, such as India, Vietnam, and Malaysia. Although access to cheap, semi-skilled labor has led to better bottom lines for multinational companies, it has also come at the cost of exploitation of workers in such supply chains. Labor rights are being compromised in the form of heavy reliance on temporary workers, excessive or forced overtime, and low wages. Moreover, lax regulations in many countries allow legal prevention of unionization or any form of collective bargaining, thereby making such workers more vulnerable.

Large brands in the apparel industry, such as Nike and Gap, and in the technology space, such as Apple and Samsung, have all been accused of various levels of lapses in their supply chain related to the aforementioned labor management issues. Apart from suffering significant damage to their brands and reputations, which could lead to consumer boycotts, such companies may also face additional costs and/or fines related to product recalls and ad hoc shifting of supply chains.

For SWFs with equity exposure to some of the largest apparel brands and branded tech hardware companies, considering such issues while making investments is of paramount importance because lack of transparency in the supply chain and lapses in labor management may weigh heavily on the resilience of such supply chains amid global-scale disruptions, such as that caused by the COVID-19 pandemic. In addition to the financial risks, reputational risks may also arise because of a view that the SWF implicitly supports such improper and unethical business practices.

3.3.3. The "just" transition

Sustainable development involves meeting the needs of the present generation without compromising the ability of future generations to meet their own needs. Sustainable development includes economic, social, and environmental dimensions, all of which are interrelated. In the transition to environmentally sustainable economies and societies, several challenges may arise—for example, displacement of workers and job losses in certain industries, such as coal mining, fossil fuel extraction/production, and fossil fuel-based power generation. Similarly, increased energy costs due to carbon taxes and higher costs of commodities partly resulting from sustainable production practices may have adverse effects on the incomes of poor households. Therefore, a "just" transition is necessary to ensure that there are limited negative social impacts in our pursuit of positive environmental impacts via avoiding fossil fuels and implementing sustainable agriculture and business practices. Although there is no fixed set of guidelines, the just transition encourages a dialogue between workers, industry, and governments influenced by geographical, political, cultural, and social contexts in order to tackle some of the aforementioned challenges.

CASE STUDY

1. Case Study: Introduction

You are working as a Risk Analyst at a small sovereign wealth fund (SWF) and reporting to the Head of Risk. The SWF is considering making some new investments in direct private equity and direct infrastructure. You have been asked to review risk aspects of these investment opportunities, which will be discussed in an upcoming investment committee meeting. Assuming the investments will be made, you will also have the responsibility to monitor the risk of the investments as well as make recommended improvements to the SWF's risk management system. You are excited about these opportunities and look forward to putting your knowledge and skills learned from the CFA Program to work!

2. Case Study: Background

* Over 20 years ago, the "Republic of Ruritania" discovered an extremely large deposit of crucial rare earth metals that are key elements in the manufacturing of high-speed computers used in science and finance. The entire deposit was sold to various entities allowing Ruritania to secure its financial future. At the same time, the government of Ruritania "dollarized" the economy, moving from the domestic RRR currency to the USD.
* The government of Ruritania (R) decided to form a sovereign wealth fund, R-SWF, in order to grow the capital for future generations. This type of SWF is a "savings fund," intended to share wealth across generations by transforming non-renewable assets into diversified financial assets.
* R-SWF has built up a diversified portfolio of equities, fixed income, and alternative investments.
* In equities and fixed income, the SWF invests in developed markets, emerging markets, and frontier markets through both fund investing and direct investing.
* In alternatives, the SWF invests in private equity (PE), infrastructure, and real estate. Investment methods used include direct investing, making co-investments, and fund investing.
* The case study begins in Section 3 at an investment committee meeting to discuss two potential investments. The next scene, in Section 4, is set three years later, when the performance of the investments are discussed at another investment committee meeting. The final scene, in Section 5, is set five years later and provides additional information on investment performance.

3. R-SWF's Investments: 1.0

Initial Case Facts (1.0)
Today, the investment committee of R-SWF is considering several new investments, including direct private equity and direct infrastructure investments. The investment committee will be discussing risk aspects of the investments, led by the Head of Risk and supported by *you*, a Risk Analyst.

* The investment committee meeting will open with an overview of asset allocation and a few basic discussions on the two proposed investments. However, the focus of the meeting

is on the potential risks of the new investment proposals, not details on the investments themselves. (An in-depth investment committee meeting on the new investments was held last month.)

- The meeting will then move on to a discussion of the potential risks of the two specific direct investments being considered.

    1. Direct infrastructure investment in an airport
    2. Direct PE investment in a beverage manufacturer

- The investment committee meeting will discuss key risks that R-SWF should consider as it decides whether to make new direct investments in PE and infrastructure.
- All investment committee participants (and CFA Program Level III candidates) are provided with a background memo with the following information:

    Memo A: Background on R-SWF's asset allocation and performance
    Memo B: Details on the proposed direct infrastructure investment
    Memo C: Details on the proposed direct private equity investment

---

Investment Committee Meeting MEMO 1.0

To: R-SWF Investment Committee Members
From: R-SWF Chief Investment Officer
Re: Investment Committee Meeting Agenda

Distribution: Head of Risk, Head of PE, Head of Infrastructure, Head of Equities, and
                 Level III Candidates in the CFA Program

An agenda for today's meeting is as follows:

Agenda

- Opening Remarks and Review of Asset Allocation: Chief Investment Officer
- Review of Infrastructure Investment Opportunity: Head of Infrastructure
- Review of Private Equity Investment Opportunity: Head of PE
- Discussion of Risk—Infrastructure Investment: Head of Risk + Everyone
- Discussion of Risk—PE Investment: Head of Risk + Everyone
- Closing Remarks: Chief Investment Officer

    The investment committee meeting will discuss key risks that R-SWF should consider as it determines whether to make new direct investments in PE and infrastructure.

Memo 1A: Asset Allocation and Performance

- Since its inception, over a 25+ year period, R-SWF has built a diversified portfolio of investments. As of last month, the fund had AUM of $50 billion USD, with the fund outperforming its overall benchmark by 150 bps net of fees since inception. Of course, there have been short-term periods of underperformance as the fund pursued its long-term strategy.

- Asset allocation as of last month for the overall fund was as follows:

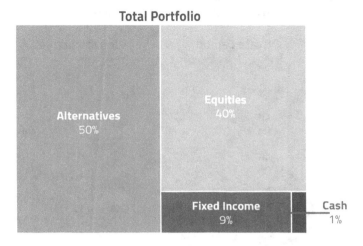

Total Portfolio

- As of last month, R-SWF had approximately 50% of assets invested in alternative investments, consistent with its long-term objectives.
- In today's investment committee meeting, R-SWF is considering two new investments in alternative investments—specifically, in direct private equity and direct infrastructure investments. *(Note: Funding for these two investments will come from a combination of cash, dividends, receivables, and fixed income. The mix will be determined by the Asset/ Liability Committee, or ALCO).*
- Because today's investment committee meeting will focus on alternative investments, we will break the allocation of alternatives down further, as follows:

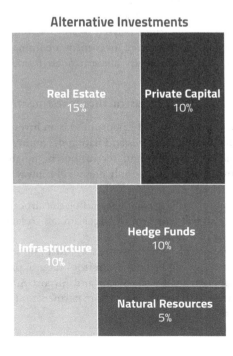

Alternative Investments

- As of last month, R-SWF had approximately 10% of assets invested in private capital and 10% of assets invested in Infrastructure.
- Next, we provide a breakdown of private capital and infrastructure:

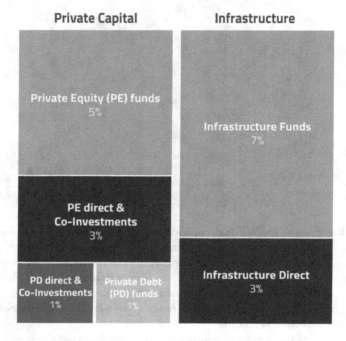

- As of last month, R-SWF had approximately 3% of assets invested in private equity direct and co-investment and 3% of assets invested in direct Infrastructure.
- The investment committee will be discussing risk aspects of the cases, led by the Head of Risk and supported by the Risk Analyst.
- Details on the proposed infrastructure investment are found in Memo 1B.
- Details on the proposed private equity investment are found in Memo 1C.

Memo 1B: Proposed Direct Infrastructure Investment

- The infrastructure direct investment opportunity is an investment in helping modernize an airport in the frontier market island nation of "Sunnyland."
- Sunnyland has beautiful beaches and several hotels, ranging from 3-star to 5-star. However, the Sunnyland Airport has only one small runway that can support airplanes of only up to 10 passengers.
- The Sunnyland government is keen on expanding the airport with a new terminal and new runway. Doing so will allow much larger aircraft to land (up to 150 passengers) and be a major boost to tourism.
- The airport is located about 2 km from the sea, providing scenic views on takeoff and landing. The new runway will be built 1 km from the sea, providing even nicer views.
- R-SWF has been approached by the Sunnyland Airport Authority (SAA) to consider a $100 million investment in a public–private partnership (PPP) on a build–operate–transfer (BOT) basis.

- For R-SWF (with assets of $50 billion), this is a small investment (0.2% of total assets). The investment will be about 2% of total infrastructure assets—$100 million/($100 million + $5,000 million)—which includes investments in funds and direct investments.
- Other facts about this infrastructure investment that are important for the investment committee to understand: *(Note: The focus of the case and investment committee discussion is risks.)*

  - Total project cost of $500 million for new 5 million passenger per annum (pax) terminal
  - $33 million investment to be provided by Airport Operating Group (AOG), which will operate the airport under a management agreement (with fixed fee plus/minus performance incentive)
  - $300 million funding to be provided through non-recourse project finance debt (i.e., approx. 70/30 debt/equity) with 15-year tenor following 3-year grace period
  - 2-year construction period, with fixed price construction contract awarded under tender
  - 25-year concession (including 2-year construction period), with investor consortium entitled to collect all regulated airport charges (e.g., passenger departure charge, landing charges) and commercial revenue (duty free, retail, F&B, car parking), subject to payment of quarterly concession fee of 35% of all revenue to SAA
  - Airport charges (70% of all revenue) are regulated by concession contract—that is, schedule of charges set and then subject to stated formula for future changes (e.g., CPI)
  - Concession agreement includes quality and performance standards to be met for design/construction/development (including timely delivery of new terminal) and operations, respectively
  - Expected IRR for full investment term of 25 years of 15%

Risk Discussion: Infrastructure Investment

The Head of Infrastructure believes the potential return on this project far outweighs the potential risk(s). However, she is happy to discuss potential risks with the investment committee.

Memo 1C: Proposed Direct Private Equity Investment

- The private equity direct investment opportunity is an investment in a local beverage company (Atsui Beverage Company Limited (ABC)) that manufactures and sells carbonated beverages. The investment will be used to modernize the plant.
- ABC is an unlisted beverage company located in the tropical, land-locked nation of "Atsui." Atsui has a developing economy and can be considered a frontier market.
- ABC is the only local manufacturer of carbonated beverages in Atsui. All other beverages are imported.
- ABC's factory is located near a river that allows for transport to the port. Also, the river is known for its unique biodiversity.
- R-SWF's Head of Private Equity has been on several vacations to Atsui and saw an investment opportunity.

- ABC is keen on modernizing its plant, but the founder is worried about giving up control. Thus, the founder is willing to sell only a minority stake of 35% in exchange for $25 million.
- For R-SWF (with assets of $50 billion), this is a small investment (0.05% of total assets). The investment will be about 0.4% of total PE assets—$25 million/ ($25 million + $6,000 million)—which includes investments in funds, co-investments, and direct investments.
- Other facts about this direct PE investment that are important for the investment committee to understand: *(Note: The focus of the case and investment committee discussion is risks.)*
  - R-SWF has been investing in PE for many years in funds. Over the years, R-SWF has developed direct investing capabilities through its co-investments and is now expanding its direct investing program.
  - Because of the increased direct investing capabilities of R-SWF and recent outperformance in returns, R-SWF is looking to increase its private equity allocation to direct investments over the next five years.
  - The government of Atsui has implemented tariffs on all soft drink imports. There is an upcoming election that could change this stance.
  - The cost to modernize the ABC plant is estimated to be $20 million.
  - Over the last 12 months, ABC had a revenue of $50 million. Revenue is expected to increase significantly over the next 10 years—with a modernized plant.
  - Over the last 12 months, ABC had an EBITDA of $7 million. This is an EBITDA margin of 14% and a 10× EBITDA multiple. The Head of PE feels that there is significant room for improvement.
  - With the new technology from the plant modernization, ABC will be able to expand into non-carbonated drinks, such as sports drinks and juices.
  - Once the plant is modernized, productivity will improve significantly, allowing ABC to reduce factory staff headcount by 40%, from 500 employees to 300 employees, which will drive a higher EBITDA margin in the future.
  - With a significant minority, R-SWF will be allowed to have two seats on the board of ABC. So, the board will expand from five members to seven members. R-SWF is planning to have the Head of PE join the board of ABC but hasn't decided on the other board seat.

Risk Discussion: Private Equity Investment

The Head of PE believes the potential return on this project far outweighs the potential risk(s). However, he is happy to discuss potential risks with the Investment Committee.

In-text Question

Please respond to the following question based on **Investment Committee Memo 1.0**.

> As R-SWF's Risk Analyst, do you anticipate liquidity risk will likely be highlighted as a significant financial risk in the upcoming risk discussions for either investment? Explain your thinking.

Guideline Answer:

> No. I do not anticipate the Head of Infrastructure or the Head of PE to highlight liquidity risk as a significant risk for either investment. Although liquidity risk is the main risk that long-term institutional investors face, particularly during a significant market decline, each of these investments represents a small portion of R-SWF's total assets. R-SWF does not have cash flow pressure, unlike many institutional investors that face pressure from the regular payment of liabilities. In addition, R-SWF has been growing over time and is making a concerted effort to expand its direct investment program.
>
> Direct investments typically help mitigate some of the liquidity issues commonly experienced when investing in a fund because direct investment provides a greater amount of control and discretion over when to exit investments. Furthermore, as the direct investment program grows and the proportion of direct investments as part R-SWF's total assets increases, R-SWF's ability to manage capital should improve. I believe there are other financial risks that are more likely to be highlighted as a significant risk for each investment.

Investment Committee Meeting 1.0

Participants

Chief Investment Officer (CIO)
Head of Infrastructure
Head of PE
Head of Risk
Head of Equities
Analysts [no speaking role]

Chief Investment Officer: Good morning, everyone. Welcome to today's investment committee meeting of the sovereign wealth fund of the Republic of Ruritania. After running this money on behalf of our citizens and future generations since its inception, the fund has outperformed our benchmark by 150 basis points, net of fees, and we've grown AUM to $50 billion over 25 years. We are very blessed.

At last month's investment committee meeting, our **Head of Infrastructure** and our **Head of PE** got together to discuss the financials and particulars of two investment opportunities. As they both deserve our attention, today we are joined by our **Head of Risk**, along with our **Head of Equities**, to review them through the lens of risk. Our esteemed junior analysts are in the room with us to observe and provide additional analysis as required.

For now, as we consider our opportunities, I'm mostly here as a facilitator, to pave the way for a robust discussion of investment risk.

Memo A shows us our asset allocation as of mid-June, and we've got 50% in alternatives. We believe in alternatives because our liabilities are negligible and we take a long-term view of things. About 40% of our allocation is in listed equities, with a large portion of that in emerging markets, which we're also big believers in. If we do fund one or both of the two investments on the table, we'll do it with a mix of cash, dividends receivable, and fixed income, but that's not for this committee to decide; the ALCO will go over that at a later date.

In any event, our focus here is private capital, the private equity side. We've got about 3% of our investments in direct private equity and co-investments and about 3% in direct infrastructure.

Again, this meeting is primarily about risk. Let's go to Memo B and ask our **Head of Infrastructure** to talk us through the first investment. It's usually the depth of her infrastructure experience that gives R-SWF the comfort to proceed in the face of risk.

Infrastructure Investment Discussion

Head of Infrastructure: Thank you for the kind words, **CIO**. I'm glad everyone's here so we can apply the full breadth of the investment committee's expertise.

This is an airport BOT project, a PPP in the frontier island nation of Sunnyland, whose primary industry is tourism. The members of our hard-working analyst team who are new to infrastructure have been briefed on the build-operate-transfer models that private developers often adopt under private-public partnerships so they can operate the facilities they have designed and built for a number of years before handing them over to government agencies.

[**Head of Infrastructure** looks around the room to see a few polite nods from the assembled analysts.]

Funds are needed for an airport upgrade: A new terminal and a new, bigger runway will accommodate larger planes. Sunnyland needs to get rid of the passenger bottleneck to allow for an all-important boost in tourism. We're thinking $500 million and two years of construction time should be enough.

Ruritania is prepared to contribute $100 million, and we're insisting on bringing in AOG, a properly experienced airport operator, which will also be investing private equity—about $33 million. The rest of the capital will be no-recourse debt, about $300 million, and an equity injection from the government and other infrastructure investors for the remainder. The debt will be 15-year with a 3-year grace period.

With the BOT arrangements, of course, we take over the airport from the beginning under a 25-year concession agreement for all the cash flows from the terminal. So that's airport charges, like aircraft landing and passenger departure fees, as well as the commercial revenue from duty-free concessions, retail, and so forth, and we remit 35% of what we collect to the Sunnyland Airport Authority on a quarterly basis. If we want to charge more, any increases— say, for CPI adjustments—are worked out according to fixed formulas.

CIO has set the stage for this discussion of risk, and in that spirit, everyone should note the standards and conditions of our agreement with the government. You already know we've got a two-year development program—that's two years to see the revamped airport up and running—so if there are delays or shortfalls in quality, the concession agreement sets out the consequences.

Finally, our expected return for the full 25-year term given our fund's $100 million investment is a 15% IRR.

Chief Investment Officer: Thank you, **Head of Infrastructure**. That's a sufficient return, to be sure, but let's also understand that our involvement can help our friends down in Sunnyland. If we execute this project carefully, it means a boost to the wealth of all Sunnylanders.

You've been there recently, right?

Head of Infrastructure: I have. All indications are that it's an attractive tourist destination. Tourism is key to them now; they lack natural and other resources to diversify the economy. That's what they're depending on to build the economy.

Things are constrained because of the airport. The runway allows only for short, smaller aircraft, so just by increasing runway size and the associated facilities, you're paving a path for the whole nation to grow.

Chief Investment Officer: I ask the assembled team to consider for a minute the responsibilities we have to ourselves, to Ruritania; we all feel partly responsible for its success. When we invest in another sovereign country, such as Sunnyland, we may carry over a similar sense of responsibility, and we take that seriously. While our proposed $100 million investment is just 0.2% of our AUM, this single investment in transportation infrastructure will have an outsized impact on our investees.

With that in mind, let's move to the other proposal on the table. Our **Head of PE** has recently returned from Atsui, the site of the proposed private equity investment outlined in Memo C. Over to you, **Head of PE**.

Private Equity Investment Discussion
Head of PE: Yeah, I just got back. The company is called Atsui Beverage Company or ABC for short, and it was kind of "love at first sight"—or sip. I was on the beach, and a waiter brought me a drink and said it was called the "Mango Special." I thanked him but I was barely listening. You know how it is; my mind was elsewhere. But after the third sip, I was paying less attention to my leisure and more attention to just how good this drink was: refreshing, perfectly sweet, and unlike anything I'd tasted before. You know I'm always thinking about investments, ladies and gents, and I began to think I'd stumbled onto a winner.

I've been back to Atsui three times, and I introduced R-SWF to the team at the ABC plant that makes the Mango Special. I explained how sovereign wealth funds usually partner for the long term, and I built some trust while learning about their business. I know how small this is compared to the rest of our portfolio, but I'm still obsessed with this drink, so I figured out that we can invest $25 million for 35% of the business. They've got $50 million in revenue and $7 million in EBITDA. For those on the team who can't do math quickly like I can, that's a 14% EBITDA margin. And we're looking at a company valuation of roughly 10× EBITDA.

So, wait: Is this a good deal or not?

Well, let's think about it. ABC markets the only locally sourced carbonated beverage in Atsui, *and* tariffs are imposed on foreign competitors. That alone seems pretty great. And they'd use $20 million of our $25 million to modernize the plant. That way, they can turn out product way faster while also gearing up to make non-carbonated drinks like sports drinks and juices. We'd drive efficiency enough to cut headcount from 500 to 300, and that's even better for the EBITDA margin: new equipment, big changes.

I've got the most knowledge on the ground, so I could take a board seat along with someone else from our team. We've gotten pretty comfortable with co-investing, making some money, and developing our skills, and since we're expanding our direct investing effort anyway, this seems like a good fit. It's just $25 million out of our $50 billion pool, so it's a good way to learn, even if some of us think it's risky.

And, you know, sun, mango drinks, and the beach—I bet everyone wants to join the board!

Chief Investment Officer: So, the plant modernization allows for both a meaningful expansion of the product line *and* significant cost savings. But you said that a cut of 200 people underpins those savings?

Head of PE: Yeah.
Chief Investment Officer: OK. Any further questions for **Head of PE**?

Head of Risk: A question from me for **Head of PE**. You mentioned that these guys are the sole beverage manufacturer in Atsui and that there are entry barriers on foreign manufacturers coming in. You've been on the ground, so are local competitors raising their voices about giving ABC some competition?

Head of PE: I've done a lot of local research, and I'm not seeing anyone. When ABC thinks about threats, they think of the big international drink players, who are still scared off by the government's import tariffs.

Chief Investment Officer: A lot of senior officials are keen to grow the local industry. It's a small country, and there's a common emotional investment in ABC's success.

Head of Risk: These do seem like heavy tariffs. **CIO** mentioned they're as high as 100% if you try to buy Coke or Pepsi. The memo says there's an election coming up. Surely there's a risk those entry barriers fall away?

Head of PE: A mango drink is much better than cola, I promise!

Chief Investment Officer: I've done a little outreach myself to people in the know. Combining that with **Head of PE**'s research, I'd say a relaxing of tariffs after the election is a fair assumption.

Head of Equities: I have a question. Will this investment allow for ABC to start exports? Is that part of the expansion plan?

Head of PE: The markets nearby are also tropical, frontier nations. Business relations are decent, and the plant is next to a river that connects to a big port.

Chief Investment Officer: **Head of PE** has explained that the plant workers fish on the freshwater river during their lunch and during breaks, and the river does indeed connect to Atsui's major port. I see good potential for connecting to neighboring buyers.

Head of Risk: But let's remember that this is a frontier market with a developing economy.

Chief Investment Officer: Quite right. Beverages are still somewhat of a luxury item. Nevertheless, there's plenty of growth potential for us and for them.

Head of Equities: Sure, that's encouraging on exports, but **Head of PE** said that ABC sees its competition as the big international drink players, who are still scared off by the government's tariffs. If the election brings in a government keen on foreign investment, that could completely overturn the advantage this particular business has.
     Let's apply a probability to a tariff reduction and to import markets opening up. Pepsi and Coca-Cola have much deeper pockets for waiting out a price war.

Head of PE: I hear you, but maybe I went too far by saying ABC sees them as competitors. Products like the Mango Special and their other drinks don't actually exist in the Coke and

Pepsi product lines, and the Mango Special recipe is so proprietary that if we protect it, it's a real competitive advantage. The other ABC beverages use tropical fruit the multinationals don't have supply chains for, and we believe—I mean, *ABC* believes they have a way of mixing things that no one else can figure out. If that's the case, a path to exports is still there.

With investment, they still have time to get into other juices and diversify. And we're always talking to government officials and to people who could make up the government, and everyone's pretty aligned.

Chief Investment Officer: These risks are tied to the modernization program we're investing in, which means job cuts. In frontier markets, this is very sensitive: Unions may protest, and politicians may make it part of their election agenda, especially given that we're talking about one of the country's more popular companies. We're veering into reputational risk here.

Look, this is a rather small investment, of $25 million, but even a small investment can have an outsized negative impact on us if we don't manage the risk properly.

Thoughts?

Head of PE: We're not just investing and then forgetting things, folks. We're going to be proactive. Before modernization starts, we're going to do some research that shows us what issues are in the minds of all the people of Atsui, not just our workers, and we're going to design new community programs around that. We'll try to make a positive impact first.

We know that cutting employees is sensitive. But by helping many more people than we let go and by giving employees proper training so they have the skills for whatever they're doing next, we're going to be part of a sensible transition.

Head of Equities: That's going to be critical. Community relations is a key component of our social license to operate.

Chief Investment Officer: My dialogue with the **Head of PE** on the ground in Atsui has been ongoing, and he wants us to do right by the community. It's almost an impact investment in and of itself.

Any other questions on the PE investment?

Head of Risk: How comfortable are you with ABC's management? We'll only have a minority stake, and founders are sometimes not the best people to run a business.

So are these people reliable? Do they have the right skill set? The right education? Any worry about potential corruption?

Head of PE: Our due diligence is thorough, and we don't think corruption is an issue. We're new to direct investing, and so we'll be tracking progress extra carefully. And also we're the ones implementing a lot of the modernization, so there'll be more monitoring built in than ever before.

Do we keep management or not? You always have this question in private equity. With all the co-investing we've done, the directors of the funds we partner with find management teams and then keep them and then work *with* them to help them grow.

I see your point that we'd only hold 35% of ABC, but we'll also hold two board seats. I can't predict the future, but we've done a lot of due diligence and we've done a lot of interviews with management, customers, and suppliers. We've interviewed a lot of people who know the management.

We're paying $25 million, and $20 million goes to modernizing the plant. Management will take a little money off the table, and we'll structure it so that they are incentivized in alignment with growth and good oversight. After all, they'll still hold 65%.

We think they'll see that working with us will create success and that willful mismanagement or corruption or taking too much money out of the business works against them in the long run. We're coming to them with our track record through the co-investments we've made, our expertise, and our channels to other markets.

There's always risk, but that's my point of view.

Head of Equities: I support the PE investment. With management having this much skin in the game, their interests are aligned with ours.

Chief Investment Officer: This is a $25 million investment out of our $50 billion fund, and there are impact elements as well that make it more interesting.

Head of PE: Yeah, and to build our direct investment program, we must learn by doing. We've gotten really comfortable with co-investing, and that's great, but to me, it's the people who do this a lot on their own who tend to be really successful.

Yes, there's some risk with management and the government, but a lot of those are risks we're willing to take with one of our first direct investments, where we can get our hands dirty. It's a simple business, right? It's carbonated beverages, and then maybe we go into juices and non-carbonated stuff, right? We can really build the experience of working with management and the other skills that our direct program is going to need.

Hey, maybe our next committee meeting should be in Atsui!

General Discussion on Risk

Chief Investment Officer: I won't argue, but let me ask the committee about a risk that applies to both of these investments. We're an open forum, and so I ask the entire room: What bears more scrutiny?

Head of Risk: The first thing that comes to my mind when we're investing in frontier markets like these is, "How do we deal with the currency risk?" It's hard to hedge these currencies. Meanwhile, they can move wildly against the dollar, turning a really good investment into a really bad investment.

What's your read on this, **Head of PE**?

Head of PE: I'm not stressed about it. When it comes to me and most other visitors to Atsui, we're using US dollars.

Head of Infrastructure: I can speak to the currency risk in Sunnyland. When we're talking about the aviation industry and airports, a lot of revenues for infrastructure investors come in the form of regulated charges. Look at our own concession contract: 70% of the revenues are airport charges. It's typical with these arrangements to outsource the collection of these charges to international organizations like IATA. They collect the revenue from the airline, and almost all of that is paid in dollars, so we're comfortable there.

That leaves the 30% of our revenue coming from commercial sources—retail revenue in the terminal and past the gate and all that duty free and parking. In the big international airports, those transactions take place in the local currency, but we're in a locale that's expressly seeking international tourism. Pricing will be geared to international markets, so we'll have the freedom to price everything in dollars and benchmark the pricing against the affluent traveler.

Head of Risk: I'm glad to hear that.

What about the borrowing side, though? To keep people happy and the logistics simple, I assume any borrowings will come from local banks that use their country's currency.

Head of Infrastructure: It's a good thought, but no. The lenders are big international banks. The in-country banks may participate, but given the size of the loans and how long term these arrangements are—at least in Sunnyland—the local banks just don't have the capacity yet.

Whoever the lenders are, they'll be comfortable knowing the investors are getting their returns mostly in US dollars, which is what the $300 million of debt is denominated in.

Head of Risk: Which brings me to defaults.

Head of Infrastructure: Right, well, this is non-recourse financing, and the concession agreement outlines the terms of default and termination. These are matters that impinge on the direct arrangement between the government and the banks, so while it's something to be aware of, I don't see us getting dragged in.

Head of Risk: Thanks.

Head of Equities: I know the **Head of Risk** was coming to this, but the topic is coming up very often recently.

If you look at the World Economic Forum's "Global Risk Report" since 2017, climate risk and extreme weather feature in the top risks every time. Year over year, the weather gets more erratic. Sea-level rise may be gradual, but it doesn't stop. And while I understand the need to support Sunnyland's economy by expanding the airport, the memo says that the new runway is less than a kilometer from the sea.

Sure, you get a fantastic view when you take off and land, but the sea *is* rising, and the risk of flooding could become real even just during high tide. Running an airport in those conditions would not be possible.

It's a 25-year infrastructure investment. That's long enough for climate risks to materialize and impact operations. We've got to factor this in.

Head of Infrastructure   These points are well taken, but keep in mind that to even get as far as finding interested lenders for the airport, it means we've gone through the due diligence process. The big banks need environmental-impact statements before they jump on board, and even just in our role as equity investors, we had to satisfy ourselves that these kinds of issues were thought through.

Head of Risk: Sure, and naming risks is necessary and commendable, but—

Head of Infrastructure: —But that doesn't mean the risk goes away. Of course.

I'm obviously not an engineer or a contractor, but what I'd say to the committee is that the experts tells us, in the time frame we're looking at, environmental risks are unlikely to materialize, and even so, they're accounted for during the design process. The drainage systems are modified to handle increases in groundwater levels, and the engineers are building in once-in-50-years and once-in-100-years flood scenarios. Those are risks they're confident they can build for.

Chief Investment Officer: None of us are experts here, but my perspective is that we can take comfort from the fact that these kinds of challenges have been around for decades. Consider Kansai International Airport in Japan: People are always saying that it's sinking—and it *has* gone down a tiny bit—but it's been around for over 25 years and it's been fine.

It's important to be aware of it, and I'm glad you brought it up, but indications are that there's nothing really stopping us on this front.

Head of Infrastructure: That's right. We've come to rely on the reports from the technical adviser, and that's a fairly standard approach for us with these sorts of investments.

Head of PE: Agreed.

Head of Risk: What about previous foreign investment in Sunnyland? Did political risk come into play for other investments? What's the general feeling?

Head of PE: **Head of Infrastructure** called me from Sunnyland when I was on the beach in Atsui planning the ABC upgrades, and he asked me to look into it. Investment in Sunnyland has mostly been on the tourism side. There's a mixture of three- and five-star hotels, so major international hotel operators are around. And they're still arriving, but they feel the transportation bottleneck. Those who are there and the ones who are thinking about coming in are happy about the airport project.

Head of Infrastructure: And I haven't heard any horror stories about investors in Sunnyland getting burned because of unfair rule changes. Plus, relations are good. The Sunnyland authorities approached us as a fellow government institution, so we're comfortable on a sort of government-to-government basis.

Chief Investment Officer: One nice thing about an island nation is that it *is* an island. There's less political interference from the neighbors. From what **Head of Infrastructure** was telling me, we can feel positive that our investment in the airport will help the economy and stabilize the local political situation more than the contrary.

Head of Risk: Good to hear. Let's dig a little deeper on the modeling we've done for the airport investment. We expect a 15% IRR over 25 years. That is our base case. Have we done any stress tests to those baseline expectations? What if there are delays and we have to pay a penalty? What if construction costs overrun the budget? What if revenues fall short? Give us an idea of how bad the IRR could get if we don't achieve the base case.

Head of Infrastructure: Sure. I like how you've framed the question, because it covers some key risks.

From our perspective, the biggest risk is traffic—comparing the actual number of visitors and tourists coming in and out of the airport against our projections. We're not experts here, either, but we hired an established traffic consultant who looks at the global tourism numbers and the particulars of our development to make a determination.

The consultant produced a low case and a high case based on different traffic forecasts. The low case is also of interest to the banks, of course, which want confidence that they'll be paid.

Our analysis of the reasonable low case puts IRR down to around 10% or 11%. The high case pushes the return out into the high teens.

There are some sensitivities around CapEx, and we're looking to manage this risk through a fixed-price contract, the language of which says that whatever penalties we'd face for delayed or subpar construction will be passed down to the contractor. We've applied a ±10% sensitivity around that, and it does impinge on the IRR a little bit but not as much as the low-traffic case. If we run into real cost overruns or delays, we're looking at about a 13% IRR.

Head of PE: The airport's key source of revenue is tourist numbers, and we've got an exotic luxury destination on our hands, folks.

Head of Equities: Agreed. And therefore, we need to consider the risk of a prolonged global recession when discretionary vacations and spending take a nosedive. For a small island like Sunnyland, this is a big risk. Some scenario analysis that considers the impact of a downturn that lasts for two or three or even four years seems necessary.

Head of Infrastructure: We've done some work on those scenarios, and it's influenced by a specific responsibility of the government, which they have explicitly accepted, to aggressively promote tourism as soon as, if not before, a recession hits.

Think of the aviation industry, which has been through shocks again and again. With downtimes like the global financial crisis around 2009 and the few instances where travelers were spooked by crashes, the airlines came out with attractive deals and recovery was quick.

Sunnyland's government is used to adjusting and always reduces pricing to attract tourists when they need to. Our sense is that even a prolonged recession isn't a deal killer, because the authorities and the industry will react quickly.

Head of PE: I like your optimism.

Chief Investment Officer   Well, beyond optimism, we're starting from a low base; there's enormous room for growth in Sunnyland.

Head of Risk: If I may, **CIO**, just a follow-up question to the **Head of Equities**' point on the recession: We all experienced the coronavirus pandemic in 2020, and plenty of scientists have warned us that pandemics are going to be more likely—

Head of Equities: —Helped along by climate change!

Head of Risk: Yes, thank you, because of how we're damaging the environment, and again, this investment has a 25-year horizon. What if another pandemic causes rampant restrictions and people are simply not allowed to travel? Has that been factored into our scenario analysis?

Head of Infrastructure: To a limited extent, yes. We pass through 35% of whatever revenue we take on, so our payments to the government are handled that way in the concession agreement. That leaves the crucial aspect of defaults to lenders and what would trigger them.

The built-in debt-service reserve covers us for a period of time, and if travel is on hold for too much longer, then we turn to restructuring or rescheduling the financing.

But let's understand that the COVID-19 pandemic in 2020 was a game-changer, and the language and dynamics of certain contractual agreements were adjusted to avoid straight defaults in these cases. And the concern here is about short-term impact, whereas over 25 years, we expect things to gradually recover, so our concerns are more about keeping the project going and avoiding default during the problem period.

Voting on Infrastructure Investment

Chief Investment Officer: OK, I'm grateful for the expertise we have around this table. I think that's probably good for a committee vote. Let's start with our **Head of Infrastructure**: yes or no?

Head of Infrastructure: Yes.

Chief Investment Officer: How about our **Head of Risk**?

Head of Risk: I have my doubts, but because it is a $100 million investment on AUM of $50 billion, we'll give it a shot. I'll say "yes."

Chief Investment Officer: We have to take a little bit of risk, after all.
     Head of PE, how about you?

Head of PE: Before we ultimately pull the trigger, we should take another look at our other investments and similar memos to see if they're related to tourism and it would mean too much correlation. Besides that, I'm a "yes."

Chief Investment Officer: OK. **Head of Equities**?

Head of Equities: Yes from me as well. Given the size of the investment, I think it's worth taking the risk.

Chief Investment Officer: And I vote "yes."
     As a sovereign wealth fund, beyond our responsibility to manage risks and returns well, we want to give back, and where our participation helps nations develop, we feel a responsibility there as well.

Voting on Private Equity Investment

Chief Investment Officer: All right, very good. Let's move on to our direct private equity investment in ABC. **Head of PE**, what say you?

Head of PE: I'm in. Yes.

Chief Investment Officer: Very good. How about you, **Head of Equities**?

Head of Equities: I'm supportive of this. For one thing, it presents much less risk than the airport in Sunnyland. Yes.

Chief Investment Officer: OK. And our resident infrastructure expert, what say you?

Head of Infrastructure: Well, you might expect me to disagree with **Head of Equities** in terms of the risk—we have a minority position, for one thing. But the investment is small, so I'm fine. Yes.

Chief Investment Officer: OK. And finally, **Head of Risk**?

Head of Risk: **Head of PE** made some very good points. It *is* indeed a simple investment to understand and a chance to gain some experience in direct investment. Even if it doesn't work out financially, there's upside to building our experience and to having a positive impact on the wider community, to name but two areas of non-financial return. Yes from me.

Chief Investment Officer: OK, we have two investments that I'm excited to proceed with. I'd like **Head of Infrastructure** and **Head of PE** to run with those and keep us posted, and now it's time—

Head of PE: —To fight for the open board seat!

Head of Risk: Sounds fun, but actually, let's do this the old-fashioned way by filling the other board seat on the basis of experience?

Head of PE: One free Mango Special to our wise, risk-averse colleague!

Chief Investment Officer: And with that, we'll see everyone for the next investment committee meeting, in a month's time.

—The End—

In-text Questions

Please respond to the following questions based on **Investment Committee Meeting 1.0**.

1. The Head of Infrastructure identified a key risk to the Sunnyland airport investment. Explain what analysis could be shared with you to increase your confidence that the key risk is properly managed prior to making the investment in the Sunnyland airport.
2. Explain how the upcoming election most likely exposes the R-SWF's investment in ABC to financial risk. Discuss whether or not you believe the Head of PE's approach to managing this particular risk is sufficient.

Guideline Answers:

1. During the investment committee meeting, the Head of Infrastructure identified traffic as the key risk to the Sunnyland airport investment. The island might not draw an increased number of tourists simply because the airport can accommodate larger planes and more passengers. Although the Head of Infrastructure alluded to

the fact that he has quantified the financial risk should the level of tourists not meet expectations after the completion of the new airport, I would like to review his scenario analysis to feel comfortable with his assumptions. Scenario analysis would be the best way to manage this financial risk prior to making the investment in Sunnyland.

2. I do not think the Head of PE's approach to managing the financial risk due to the upcoming election is sufficient. My understanding is that the upcoming election will expose ABC to financial risk because the current government has imposed large tariffs on foreign competitors that would like to export their products to Atsui. In the event a different political party, specifically one that opposes such tariffs, wins the upcoming election in Atsui, it could have a significant effect on the profitability of ABC because the company would need to compete for local customers.

Of course, a change in government is not something that ABC can control. Although I believe the steps the Head of PE has taken to manage this particular risk are good, including building rapport with the current government, it is not clear to me that he has conducted a thorough analysis to illustrate the potential financial impact on ABC should the tariffs be reduced or eliminated after the upcoming election. This analysis should be done using scenario analysis. Despite this being a relatively small investment for R-SWF, the financial risk of a change in the tariff policy should be thoroughly modeled and assessed prior to making the investment.

4 R-SWF's Investments: 2.0

Extension of Case Facts (2.0)
After Investment Committee Meeting 1.0, the investment committee of the sovereign wealth fund of Ruritania, R-SWF, added two new significant investments to its portfolio. These investments were direct infrastructure and direct private equity investments—the investments in the airport in Sunnyland and the beverage manufacturer in Atsui, respectively.

- Three years have passed, and the investment committee of R-SWF has decided to conduct an investment review of the two projects.
- Note: The focus of the meeting is on the risks (current and potential) of the new investment proposals, not details on the financial performance of the investments. (An in-depth meeting on the financial performance of the investments was held in the previous month).
- All investment committee participants (and Level III candidates in the CFA Program) are provided with a background memo with the following information:
  - Memo A: Update on R-SWF's asset allocation and performance
  - Memo B: Update on the direct infrastructure investment (airport expansion in Sunnyland) and a list of risks for discussion
  - Memo C: Provides details on the proposed direct private equity investment (investment in ABC) and a list of risks for discussion.

Investment Committee Meeting Memo 2.0

To: R-SWF Investment Committee Members
From: R-SWF Chief Investment Officer
Re: Investment Committee Meeting 2.0 Agenda

Distribution: Head of Risk, Head of PE, Head of Infrastructure, Head of Equities,
    and Junior Staff

Agenda

- Opening Remarks and Asset Allocation CIO—5 minutes
- Infrastructure Update CIO + Head of Infrastructure—5 minutes
- PE Update CIO + Head of PE—5 minutes
- Discussion of Risk—Infrastructure: Head of Infrastructure, Head of Risk, All—
  10 minutes
- Discussion of Risk—PE: Head of PE, Head of Risk, All—10 minutes
- Other Risks: Head of Equities + All—5–10 minutes
- Closing Remarks: CIO—5 minutes

Memo 2A: Asset Allocation and Performance

- Since its inception, R-SWF has built a diversified portfolio of investments. As of last
  month, the fund had AUM of $56 billion USD, with the fund outperforming its
  overall benchmark by 130 bps net of fees since inception. Of course, there have been
  short-term periods of underperformance as the fund pursued its long-term strategy.
- The asset allocation as of last month for the overall fund was as follows:

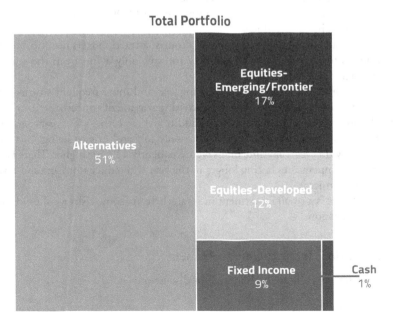

Total Portfolio

- R-SWF had approximately 51% of assets invested in alternative investments, consistent with its long-term objectives.
- Asset allocation was covered extensively in the prior month's investment committee meeting, so today's meeting will not provide any further breakdown.
- The investment committee will be discussing various points of view on risk aspects of the investments—including risk mitigation.
- The discussion will include "other risks" that were perhaps not covered well in the initial discussion. Discussion of environmental and social risks are challenging for long-term direct investing.
- Updates on the airport expansion in Sunnyland infrastructure investment are found in Memo 2B.
- Updates on the PE investment in ABC in Atsui are found in Memo 2C.

Memo 2B: Update on Infrastructure Investment in Sunnyland Airport

Investment Update

- Based on investment committee approval, the $100 million investment in Sunnyland has moved forward in accordance with agreed plans. This amount represents approximately 0.2% of total R-SWF assets.
- The Sunnyland government is happy with the progress of construction, which was completed recently. There was a delay in getting started, but that is Island life. Thankfully, there were no material cost overruns on the project.
- The new terminal is beautifully built and will be a great addition to the island nation as it further develops its tourism capabilities.
- We expect a grand opening of the new terminal in September, in time for the busy fall season. Tourist season is primarily from October through May, with the summer months being very hot (around 40°C) and humid.
- There are rumors that Airport Operating Group (AOG) is looking to renegotiate its contract for a higher fixed fee.
- One of the advantages of Sunnyland as a tourist attraction is its beautiful beaches with easy access to the airport, with the new runway, only 1 km from the sea, providing spectacular views.
- However, climate change has led to rising seas and more frequent storms. Storms are common in island nations; however, the rising seas are of concern.
- In addition, hotter temperatures are of additional concern. A few years ago, the tourist season was September through June, with only July and August being "too hot." However, in May this year, daytime highs were frequently 42°C or higher. There is a risk that the hotter temperatures lasting longer in the year will reduce tourism (and revenues for the airport project).
- Although this is a small investment in total, there are some risks we should focus on in today's discussion.

Risk Discussion: Infrastructure Investment

The following key risks are highlighted for discussion:

- Currency risk
- Expropriation risk by the Sunnyland government

- Risk that revenue from airport is less than expected
- Risk of project delays
- Risk of operating and maintenance costs being higher than projected
- Risk of default of AOG
- Risk that actual future (borrowing) interest rates will be higher than forecast
- Risk of underperformance regarding service quality–not meeting defined standards
- Other risks

Possible Mitigation of the Key Risks

- What should we do to mitigate the key risks?
- What should be our priorities? Action plan?

Memo 2C: Update on PE Investment in Atsui Beverage Company

Investment Update

- Based on investment committee approval, the $25 million investment in ABC has moved forward in accordance with agreed plans. This amount represents approximately 0.05% of total R-SWF assets.
- The modernization of the ABC plant went well, and the product expansion is starting to take shape. However, there several key updates that are unfortunately negative:
  - Atsui and surrounding nations went into a recession last year. Furthermore, a currency devaluation is anticipated. Beverages are considered a luxury item in Atsui.
  - A new government was elected in Atsui last year and took office in January. One of the first orders of business was to reduce tariffs on imported beverages from a 100% tariff to a 20% tariff. This change hurts our cost advantage over foreign brands. It is rumored that tariffs were reduced because Atsui wants to gain favor with foreign governments for potential loans.
  - Because the modern equipment will improve productivity, the original plan was to reduce headcount by 40%. In addition, due to slowing sales, management wanted to reduce staff by a total of 50%. However, labor laws are strict in Atsui. In order to terminate the employment of an Atsui citizen, significant notice (two years) is required. Plus, there is reputational risk for R-SWF for firing factory employees in a frontier market during a recession.
  - In order to make up for lower profits (due to the above reasons), plant management has started to cut corners to save on costs. Unfortunately, one way to do this was to dump waste into the nearby river rather than transport the waste for proper treatment. Although the waste is not toxic, it is starting to spoil the lovely fishing spot near the factory.
  - Another way ABC has tried to cut costs is by reducing employee breaks from one hour to 30 minutes and removing soap from the restrooms, requesting that employees bring their own.
- Although this is a small investment in total, there are some risks we should focus on in today's discussion.

Risk Discussion: Private Equity Investment

The following key risks are highlighted for discussion:

- Currency risk
- Expropriation risk by the Atsui government
- Quality control issues
- Challenges with local management (don't have a majority stake)
- Competitor pressure
- Growing trend of health foods that would result in avoidance of many carbonated beverages
- Elimination of tariffs protecting ABC from foreign-owned manufacturers
- Other risks

Possible Mitigation of the Key Risks

- What should we do to mitigate these risks?
- What should be our priorities? Action plan?

In-text Questions

Please respond to the following questions based on **Investment Committee Memo 2.0**.

4. The investment committee has identified several new risks that were not previously discussed (before Memos 2B and 2C). The CIO asks you to recommend how R-SWF can manage each of the following risks:
   A. Risk of actual future (borrowing) interest rates will be higher than forecast (Memo 2B)
   B. Growing trend of health foods that would result in avoidance of many carbonated beverages (Memo 2C)

Guideline Answers:

4a: R-SWF can manage the risk that actual future (borrowing) interest rates will be higher than forecast by hedging its interest rate exposure for the Sunnyland airport project.

4b: R-SWF can manage the risk of carbonated beverages falling out of favor due to an increasing preference for health foods by working to develop new healthy alternatives to carbonated, presumably sugar-filled drinks. As the production facility expands its ability to produce product, ABC could focus its new product development on healthy alternatives. The company can leverage its experience producing such beverages given the success of its natural mango drink in order to differentiate itself and increase market share.

Investment Committee Meeting 2.0

Participants

Chief Investment Officer (CIO)
Head of Infrastructure
Head of PE
Head of Risk
Head of Equities
Analysts [no speaking role]

Chief Investment Officer: Good morning, everyone, and welcome to today's investment committee meeting of the sovereign wealth fund of the Republic of Ruritania. We're grateful for the opportunity to serve our constituents.

During last month's committee meeting, we reviewed the financial statements of the two projects in question—the airport in Sunnyland and the beverage manufacturer in Atsui. Our **Head of PE** provided the Mango Specials, so thank you for that!

It's been three years—wow, time really flies—since we unanimously approved proceeding with both investments. We'll go through some updates, but today's focus is risks and sensible mitigation measures.

First, though, the bigger picture: In those three years, AUM have grown by $6 billion. We're still outperforming our overall benchmark, but our outperformance has been dulled by difficulties with some assets, primarily real estate, because commercial real estate has underperformed. So that's hurt us a little bit, but as ever, we are long-term investors, and we may reap the benefits of those investments yet.

As we discuss risk mitigation, let's consider environmental and social risks. The greater pressure we've put on ourselves to invest responsibly and sustainably is matched by increased scrutiny from outside observers.

Whether we've decided to make an exit on our own or because of outside pressure, our rather long-term horizon doesn't make it any easier for us to step away from an investment when the time comes. As a contrast, our **Head of Equities** was telling me before the meeting started that he wasn't too happy about how much one of his portfolio companies was polluting, and so he just went ahead and sold the position. It was a liquid investment in a public market, and he was done within the hour. That's a contrast we have to keep in mind.

Allow me to read this comment about ABC from the minutes of the last meeting, as a sort of touchstone for us today: "This is a rather small investment, of $25 million, but even a small investment can have an outsized negative impact on us if we don't manage the risk properly."

But let's begin with Sunnyland airport. **Head of Infrastructure**, why don't you start us off?

Head of Infrastructure: Thanks, **CIO**.

The good news is that the new terminal is pretty much complete and in line with specifications. We received some good reviews, both from locals and the international trade press. The downside is delays: At the outset, we expected a two-year construction program, but we're now well into the third year, unfortunately. There were noticeable cost overruns, and those were borne by the contractor, according to the contract, but there are some delay penalties that have yet to be settled.

The government, the contractor, and ourselves and AOG as investors—we're in discussions about these penalties, and the contractors are pointing to variations they say arose from our side. What they're calling "variations" we see as necessary design thinking for optimizing the commerciality of the retail outlets. The "variations" were pretty minimal, so let's see where our discussions end up. And some further disagreements center around the offices of customs and immigration within the terminal, which the contractor is laying at the foot of the government.

We should also highlight that as we're nearing the startup of terminal operations, the operator, AOG, has started complaining that the costs of training local staff are higher than expected. They haven't said anything formally yet, but I imagine they'll want to renegotiate their fixed-fee contract—nothing too serious.

Meanwhile, the grand opening of the terminal is a month away, in late August. It should be a good, high-profile event, and we should make a good showing. At least four Ruritania representatives, I think.

And then always swirling around our work is the focus of the press on the environmental movement and climate change, so we need to think about the impact on tourism. The main tourist season is September through June, historically, but it's just getting too hot, and so really the prime window for visitors will narrow to October through May.

The debate in the local press is frequently about the impact of so many tourists flying to Sunnyland, and AOG is in dialogue with the airlines about it. We have yet to see how that plays out in terms of impact on the airport operations down the road, but at the grand opening, we'll be able to celebrate the start of the upcoming season in September; bookings are in line with optimistic projections for the first year with the new terminal and runway.

Chief Investment Officer: OK, thank you for that update.

And what can we say about ABC in Atsui?

Head of PE: So, there are positives and negatives. A big positive is that this has been a fantastic learning experience for our direct investment program. But there's been a currency devaluation, and you could argue it's going to get worse because of the recession—the recession that started last year and that you all know so well because we're in the middle of it.

Still, is that good or bad? We do sell to tourists who bring their own currency, and we've got a lot of flexibility to shift our pricing so we can keep prices where they should be relative to our costs, which is positive.

But following the recent election, the new administration is talking about dropping all sorts of import tariffs, including the ones on food and drink. They've basically said, "For sure, we're going to cut them from 100% to 20%."

Obviously, this hurts our cost advantage over foreign brands, and the challenge here is that the new government wants to win favor with foreign governments before asking them for big loans, so the issue is about more than just carbonated drinks.

Chief Investment Officer: There's a rumor that the new president likes Pepsi, so it's almost as if she doesn't want to pay double for a can, but 20% more is OK.

Head of PE: ABC's new modernized equipment is ready to go, but here's the problem: Management is now saying they want to reduce headcount by 50%, instead of just 40%, because of the slowing sales. But labor laws in Atsui are strict, and to let someone go, you usually have to give as much as two years' notice.

Head of Risk:　Two years?

Head of PE:　Yeah, and the other issue is that for us as a sovereign wealth fund, there's reputational risk. Flying in from world cities and firing factory employees in frontier markets mean bad publicity, especially in Atsui and especially during the recession.

　　And here's another thing: In order to make up for lower profits, management has started cutting corners. They're dumping waste in the nearby river rather than paying to transport it to the treatment site. Do you remember how the plant is right next to the river and the employees fish in it during lunch? It's spoiling the fishing spot. This is a problem. And it gets worse: Scientists are saying that the plant site and the river overlap with the range of a rare reptile that is found here and only one other place on earth. So our site has attracted the attention of people with no interest in soda or mangoes.

Head of Risk:　This is a problem.

Head of PE:　Now here's another thing: ABC has tried to cut costs by reducing employee breaks from an hour to 30 minutes and—this is probably a little granular for our meeting, but risks are risks, they have removed soap from the restrooms! Everyone has to bring their own soap now.

　　Now, I know we're a $50 billion sovereign wealth fund—

Chief Investment Officer:　—$56 billion.

Head of PE:　I know we're a $56 billion sovereign wealth fund, and here we are talking about removing soap from a few bathrooms in the tropics where we have a $25 million direct investment, but stuff like this can have a reputational impact.

Head of Risk:　Agreed.

Chief Investment Officer:　Our focus right now is risk, and we should be talking about this. We haven't really faced any of these health and safety or social issues before at the individual investment level, and it's a learning opportunity as we expand our direct investing program. **Head of PE**, when you went to the restroom and found out there was no soap, you had to borrow some from the plant manager. Is that right? Did he give it to you for free, or did he charge you?

Head of PE:　He wanted to charge me, but I didn't need any soap because I had hand sanitizer with me. I got used to carrying hand sanitizer around with me everywhere back in the coronavirus days, so now I just do that when I'm in Atsui.

Chief Investment Officer:　OK, then let's discuss infrastructure.

　　Three years ago when we approved this investment, we talked potential risks, including climate, and we were comfortable with the position that the threat of rising seas was well into the future. We may have to re-evaluate that position.

Head of Risk:　Despite our comfort then, the fact is that storms have become more frequent and the sea level *has* risen measurably—in three short years.

Head of Infrastructure: The lenders have also raised this point, as has our in-country political adviser. I still don't see any impact in the immediate term. If you remember three years ago, much of our comfort came from the environmental-impact assessments, which were required and were factored into the design. What has been constructed can deal with it sufficiently.

The bigger worry is the force of an unanticipated and rare storm that compounds the impact of some already bad flooding. Originally, the engineers planned for a once-in-50-years or once-in-100-years scenario, and it may be that the risk of those events has increased.

There's a discussion to be had with the government about architectural solutions—maybe some proper flood barriers. As for the cost of them, if they'll even work, and whose responsibility that is—those issues are unclear. It's not in anybody's interest for the airport to shut down.

Head of Equities: My experience engaging with large public companies on climate risk tells me that a tiny island like Sunnyland can't have any meaningful impact on a global scale and hence they must focus on adaptation rather than worry too much about mitigation. **Head of Infrastructure** points to one of the more logical solutions: some sort of storm-surge barrier like the Netherlands has relied on for years.

As for who's going to pay for it, let's think beyond our own project for a minute. Rising seas aren't just going to have an impact on the airport; every five-star, beach-facing property will feel it too. The prime hotels feel it, and eventually the whole tourist ecosystem feels it, and with the country so dependent on tourism, my view is that this has to be a government-driven initiative. And a storm-surge barrier that successfully avoids damaging floods will be important enough to private interests, such as real estate and other infrastructure investors, that they'll form part of the funding circle.

Head of Infrastructure: I think that's right. It's a question for the whole economy and for the government. Serious talks are taking place in Sunnyland about a new tax to cover the costs, a sort of climate tax that would go to a host of worsening climate issues.

How the authorities end up structuring that tax will inform whether we can avoid it.

Chief Investment Officer: Understood, but as a sovereign institution, even if we could avoid such a tax to protect our investment value, from a reputational perspective, we should think twice.

Head of PE: **Head of Infrastructure** said that AOG might be asking for a higher fixed fee to operate the new terminal. I'm not sure if this is a question for this point in the meeting, but is there anything we can do to proactively protect ourselves against a higher contract fee in the event AOG gets its renegotiation?

Head of Infrastructure: We all signed a well-structured agreement, and that affords us some decent protection against any meddling in the fee structure, though there are break clauses if anything gets too out of line. Still, there are incentives built into the concession agreement to make sure everyone wins to a greater or lesser extent when traffic goes up.

Equally, we don't want a disgruntled operator. Happy employees, happy travelers, better experience, more traffic.

We haven't been formally approached about this, but let's not dismiss it out of hand just because we have a contract we can hide behind. AOG is a strong global operator. If they did activate a break clause in two or three years' time, that lands us with a responsibility we really don't want, which is finding a new operator. We're still satisfied with their cooperation.

I recommend seeing how talks over the delays play out, and if we find that the government is liable for the delay, we'll request an extension to the concession and then sit down with AOG to positively collaborate on retooling the whole picture.

Chief Investment Officer: OK, we've covered the environmental and reputational risks, the climate risk, and the AOG item as well. Are there any other risks we should examine at this point?

Head of Risk: That covers the important ones. Currency risk and the risk of further delays are less of a concern. With climate change, we can't *solve* it; as **Head of Equities** insists, we have to adapt. It affects the entire nation, so hopefully the government will step in.

And I reinforce the idea of positive negotiations with AOG. We want a happy operator.

Chief Investment Officer: Right. OK, very good.
Head of Risk, it looks like something is still on your mind.

Head of Risk: Thanks for noticing. A little more scrutiny of ABC is warranted. I acknowledge its importance for boosting our direct investment know-how. It's been a great learning experience for **Head of PE** and his team, and it's a very small investment. Even if we lose money, it's not going to move the needle for our fund, but—and this is a substantial "but"—the reputational risk is a big concern.

We don't want to end up in the newspaper firing people during a recession, polluting the river, threatening endangered species, and being rather petty about soap.

Head of Infrastructure: True on all counts.

Head of Risk: Ladies and gentlemen, the writing is on the wall. I propose we exit this investment as soon as possible, if we can. Maybe we can't, and if that's the case, I would remain very concerned.

Head of PE: No, I'm happy you mentioned it, and it's good that it's all coming out in this room. Let me tell you how we see things.

Before we jumped into this as one of our first direct investments, we co-invested and participated in many private equity funds that invest in all kinds of things, including special situations and distressed investments, and we've always gone in with third-party experts or used our own experts. Just because things get a little dicey, it doesn't mean we exit.

When we started, ABC was a conventional, if small, investment. If that's changed and it now is a problem business, we've got a team whose job it is to make lemonade out of lemons, so let's think about passing ABC over to the distressed-asset team before it becomes properly distressed. I'm not saying we keep it or some other team takes it. I'm saying let's at least see if it's a better fit for someone else.

What if we keep going? We've got risks around firing employees, dumping waste in the river, and pettiness around soap. And we're shifting our mindset, and the challenge is less about the return and more about the reputational risk.

So we really need to figure out: Can we change how this business functions to manage that risk? We have a 35% interest, we know that management has skin in the game. But in what game? With management incentivized to improve the bottom line, we're motivating them to cut employees instead of keeping employees happy and avoiding resentment.

So we're asking ourselves a new question: How do we motivate management to keep people inside and outside the plant happy? We have two board seats, and investing more money in modernization seems to make less sense now.

And we've got employees now who don't have much to do, but they're collecting a salary, so why would they leave? And if we can't fire them, it's an issue. Maybe we pay them a percentage—say, half their regular salary—while offering them good training and assistance for eight months to find another job. At the same time, we'd convince management to shift to a less profit-driven focus.

I don't know if any of that will work. Maybe we should have divested earlier, but that's our thinking if we keep holding on.

Head of Equities: And what about the toxic stuff being released into the river?

Head of PE: It's actually not toxic, technically, but we don't even want to be talking about whether it's toxic or not toxic. Ending that practice is an important piece of our talks with management, and so is removing incentives to cut corners.

Can we fundamentally change the way things are going? If we can't, then maybe this is an investment for someone else. Or perhaps we sell our 35% stake back to management?

Chief Investment Officer: Thanks, **Head of PE**. We talked about this being a learning experience. We also talked about it displaying aspects of impact investment. Maybe part of the value is in education. In some less developed areas, they think it's maybe not a big deal to throw things into the river. Can we inform their thinking with the idea that wanting a beautiful river for fishing and enjoyment is a virtue and that it's not really that hard to dispose of waste properly? What can we intelligently say about impact?

Head of Equities: This line of thinking makes sense to me. Our experience in other developing nations as well as developed nations tells us that you'll save some costs in the short term with actions like dumping waste directly into water bodies, but in the long run, regulations catch up to you and the cost of pre-treatment or appropriate handling of waste is much lower than the penalties you get for taking such shortcuts.

If we decide to stay, we have to paint the picture for management that there's a fatal flaw in our approach at the moment. Public perception is one issue, but eventually regulations will be introduced with penalties and obligations to clean up the river.

If we do try to salvage the situation and continue with our investment, there's a path that involves the government. Our pitch should be that if there are legal roadblocks for cutting 50% of the jobs, you might be putting 100% of the jobs at risk because the company won't survive if tariffs are reduced to 20%. The government doesn't want the factory to shut down because of *its* rigid labor laws, so there may well be room for a more, let's say, negotiated conclusion.

It's worth exploring, again, in consultation with the local management.

Chief Investment Officer: Lobbying the government, reframing management's incentives—these are interesting ways to pivot. We should also consider as a committee the extent to which we want to maintain our direct investing/private equity approach or whether there is wisdom in recasting our work as more of an impact program. The committee's analysis has highlighted the difficulties faced by a sovereign wealth fund in cutting staff. It ends up being a headline risk.

The conventional private equity houses can more easily cut jobs for purely financial reasons. However, as a sovereign wealth fund, it is more complicated for us. Imagine the headline: "Government of Ruritania Cuts Jobs in XYZ during a Recession."

Head of Infrastructure: It's not a good look.

Chief Investment Officer: It's not a good look. Right.

Head of Risk: From my point of view, we've covered the main risks for ABC. I like the sequence: We engage with management to change the mindset, and we lobby government on how a two-year notice period and similar restrictions could jeopardize the whole business. We give it another year, and if we're not making progress, we look for an exit option, maybe handing things over to a team that is comfortable with these thorny issues.

Chief Investment Officer: Well summarized. I'm grateful for the focus we are putting on the risks here.

And as for Sunnyland?

Head of Equities: I'd submit to the team that while the world's major governments have *started* taking action on climate change, we're not going to "fix" these problems easily so the planet can just go back to the way it was 30 years ago. The impact will intensify, and we have to adapt.

In my mind, the focus should be on liaising with the government. They will have to drive things because of the scale of the investment required—

Chief Investment Officer: —And because of how long term the investment horizon is.

Team, this is the sort of experienced scrutiny of risk we needed, so thank you very much. This was a highly worthwhile meeting, and let's keep a keen focus on the risks.

—The End—

In-text Questions

Please answer the following question based on **Investment Committee Meeting 2.0.**

1. In the template provided, state the primary environmental risk that has been identified by R-SWF's investment committee for each investment. Recommend how each risk can be managed in the future.

Investment	Primary Environmental Risk	Risk Management Recommendation
Sunnyland Airport		
Atsui Beverage Company		

2. Identify one significant social risk that both investments have in common and that was not originally identified by the investment committee. Discuss whether or not this risk is easily managed once recognized.

Guideline Answers

1. In the template provided, state the primary environmental risk that has been identified by R-SWF's investment committee for each investment. Recommend how each risk can be managed in the future.

Investment	Primary Environmental Risk	Risk Management Recommendation
Sunnyland Airport	Climate change due to rising sea levels	Given the uncertainty around the precise timing and magnitude of the impact of climate change and rising sea levels specifically, R-SWF should use climate-related scenario analysis to better understand how climate change will affect its investment in Sunnyland. In addition, since R-SWF cannot mitigate climate change, it must focus on adaptation strategies. In this case, a strategy to provide protection for the airport against a storm surge or higher sea levels is the most realistic option. An adaptation strategy is consistent with the development mandate of R-SWF's investment in Sunnyland.
Atsui Beverage Company	Waste management due to dumping waste into river	R-SWF must find a way to persuade the board and local management to stop dumping waste in the river in an effort to pursue sustainable development and a "just" transition. Although it might be a cost savings in the short run, in the long run, regulations will catch up. Cleanup of improperly disposed waste is far more costly than appropriately disposing of waste up front. One of the ways to encourage prioritization of protecting the river is to educate the local community about the importance of a healthy river. Community education, the pursuit of sustainable development, and a "just" transition are consistent with the impact investing element of this investment for R-SWF.

2. Reputational risk is very significant in the case of each investment and can have an outsized effect on the performance of the investments. Social issues, such as reputational risk, are generally quite difficult to manage even once identified and understood because they are relatively challenging to quantify and integrate into financial models. Furthermore, best practices include considering the interests of all the stakeholders involved, which is not easy.

In Sunnyland, R-SWF must contribute to any effort to raise funds to implement protection against rising seas. This project will likely be expensive. However, it is not in R-SWF's best interest to appear to be avoiding contributing to the project to accommodate climate change. Doing so could significantly damage R-SWF's reputation in

Sunnyland and beyond given the international attention paid to the construction of the new airport. In theory, reputational risk in this case is relatively simple to manage in that R-SWF simply needs to be a contributor to the project and overall community by supporting efforts to adapt to climate change so as to not destroy Sunnyland's tourism industry. However, execution of such a strategy to mitigate R-SWF's reputational risk in Sunnyland will need to be closely monitored in order to effectively execute it. Managing this type of risk is not easy.

Reputational risk is also very significant in the case of ABC because of two major social issues: (1) occupational health and safety and (2) labor standards. Each of these issues could significantly damage R-SWF's reputation. Removing hand soap from the restrooms is an occupational health and safety issue that could cause reputational damage. Shortening employee breaks and firing people during a recession are social issues related to labor standards.

These types of choices indicate that local management is more concerned about profitability than reputational risk. In order to manage its reputational risk, R-SWF needs to persuade the board to adjust its incentive structure in order to encourage local management to reverse course on these short-sighted, destructive social issues, even if it is expensive. R-SWF does not want to be perceived as an investor that exploits its labor force. Soap should be provided for employees, breaks should be reasonable in length, and rather than firing employees, which can't be effectively executed because of the strict labor laws, ABC should focus on retraining employees for the future of the business. This is a complicated, multifaceted course especially as a minority owner. It isn't easily implemented but can be done. Any changes will need to be monitored to ensure they continue and have the desired outcome—a sustainable and mutually beneficial long-term relationship with the local community.

5 R-SWF's Investments: 3.0

Second Extension of Case Facts (3.0)
You left R-SWF at the end of Year 3 and took a position as a Senior Risk Consultant at Kiken Consulting, a risk consulting firm.

In the summer of Year 5, you are reading the newspaper and notice some commentary on two of the R-SWF investments you had been involved with. You read the following excerpts with nostalgic interest.

Update on Infrastructure Investment
- The infrastructure investment continues to perform poorly because of a combination of the following:
  - lower revenue (fewer tourists) vs. forecast (50% lower than base case)
  - higher costs (mitigating flood damage) vs. forecast (50% higher than base case)
- The medium- and long-term forecast on this investment does not look promising.

Update on PE Investment

- The PE team was able to avoid a diplomatic crisis and reputational risk damage by finding a buyer for the 35% stake. They sold the full position at $27 million.

- The stake was sold to an international beverage company that had been exporting to Atsui. The company's sales had been adversely affected by a weaker Atsui currency. Thus, producing locally is advantageous because it provides a natural foreign exchange hedge.

You set the newspaper down and start thinking about Sunnyland and Atsui when your boss suddenly interrupts you with the following news:

Kiken Consulting has a new client! R-SWF has hired the firm for a risk analysis project. Because you have prior knowledge on R-SWF's approach, your boss has assigned you to the project with a lead role. You are expected to evaluate the strengths and weaknesses of R-SWF's enterprise risk management system and to make recommendations for improvements.

In-text Question

Please respond to the following question.

1. Provide key facts/inputs from the R-SWF case, use them to evaluate the strengths and weaknesses of R-SWF's enterprise risk management processes, and make recommendations for improvements.

Guideline Answer

1. One of the main strengths of R-SWF's risk management process is that R-SWF dedicated an entire internal investment committee meeting to identifying and discussing the potential risks of two relatively small investment opportunities. Ample time was taken to allow senior management of R-SWF to express their concerns and discuss mitigation strategies to reduce potential risks. The investment committee was able to identify various potential risk factors, and senior management voted on both investment opportunities.

    One of the weaknesses of R-SWF's risk management process is that too little effort was made in trying to quantify the various risks and agreeing on specific actions that could be taken if some of those risk materialized. The team, with the help of the Head of Risk, could have done a better job at performing scenario analysis for both investments and presented a base case, an optimistic case, and a pessimistic case. Although the team identified and discussed several risk factors, they should have put together an action plan for risk mitigation and potential hedging tools prior to making the investments. This action plan would be conditional on certain bad outcomes materializing. Finally, since both investments were quite small in the overall scheme and had limited financial and liquidity risk implications for the fund, more consideration could have been given to identifying potential reputational risks and ESG.

REFERENCES

CFA Institute. 2020. "Climate Change Analysis in the Investment Process." CFA Institute (September). www.cfainstitute.org/en/research/industry-research/climate-change-analysis.

Geltner, D. 1993. "Estimating Market Values from Appraised Values without Assuming an Efficient Market." *Journal of Real Estate Research* 8:325–45.

Getmansky, M., A. W. Lo, and I. Makarov. 2004. "An Econometric Model of Serial Correlation and Illiquidity in Hedge Fund Returns." *Journal of Financial Economics* 74:529–609. doi:10.1016/j.jfineco.2004.04.001

Grantham Research Institute on Climate Change and the Environment. "New Study Estimates Global Warming of 2.5 Centigrade Degrees by 2100 Would Put at Risk Trillions of Dollars of World's Financial Assets." Press release (4 April 2016). www.lse.ac.uk/GranthamInstitute/news/us2-5-trillion-of-the-worlds-financial-assets-would-be-at-risk-from-the-impacts-of-climate-change-if-global-mean-surface-temperature-rises-by-2-5c.

IEA. 2020. "World Energy Outlook 2020" (October). www.iea.org/reports/world-energy-outlook-2020.

Intergovernmental Panel on Climate Change. 2018. "Special Report: Global Warming of 1.5 °C" (6 October). www.ipcc.ch/sr15/chapter/spm.

Lo, Joe. 2020. "IEA Outlines How World Can Reach Net Zero Emissions by 2050." *Climate Home News* (13 October). www.climatechangenews.com/2020/10/13/iea-outlines-world-can-reach-net-zero-emissions-2050.

NASA. 2019. "NASA Global Climate Change: Vital Signs of the Planet." https://climate.nasa.gov/vital-signs/global-temperature.

Okunev, J., and D. White. 2003. "Hedge Fund Risk Factors and Value at Risk of Credit Trading Strategies." Working paper, University of New South Wales. doi:10.2139/ssrn.460641

PRI Association. "Macro Risks: Universal Ownership" (12 October 2017). www.unpri.org/sustainable-development-goals/the-sdgs-are-an-unavoidable-consideration-for-universal-owners/306.article.

GLOSSARY

Active share A measure of how similar a portfolio is to its benchmark. A manager who precisely replicates the benchmark will have an active share of zero; a manager with no holdings in common with the benchmark will have an active share of one.

Advanced set An arrangement in which the reference interest rate is set at the time the money is deposited.

Advanced settled An arrangement in which a forward rate agreement (FRA) expires and settles at the same time, at the FRA expiration date.

American-style Type of option contract that can be exercised at any time up to the option's expiration date.

Arbitrage 1) The simultaneous purchase of an undervalued asset or portfolio and sale of an overvalued but equivalent asset or portfolio, in order to obtain a riskless profit on the price differential. Taking advantage of a market inefficiency in a risk-free manner. 2) The condition in a financial market in which equivalent assets or combinations of assets sell for two different prices, creating an opportunity to profit at no risk with no commitment of money. In a well-functioning financial market, few arbitrage opportunities are possible. 3) A risk-free operation that earns an expected positive net profit but requires no net investment of money.

Arbitrage-free pricing The overall process of pricing derivatives by arbitrage and risk neutrality. Also called the *principle of no arbitrage*.

At market contract When a forward contract is established, the forward price is negotiated so that the market value of the forward contract on the initiation date is zero.

At the money An option in which the underlying's price equals the exercise price.

Backwardation A condition in futures markets in which the spot price exceeds the futures price; also, the condition in which the near-term (closer to expiration) futures contract price is higher than the longer-term futures contract price.

Bankruptcy A declaration provided for by a country's laws that typically involves the establishment of a legal procedure that forces creditors to defer their claims.

Base With respect to a foreign exchange quotation of the price of one unit of a currency, the currency referred to in "one unit of a currency."

Basis The difference between the spot price and the futures price. As the maturity date of the futures contract nears, the basis converges toward zero.

Basis risk The risk resulting from using a hedging instrument that is imperfectly matched to the investment being hedged; in general, the risk that the basis will change in an unpredictable way.

Basis trade A trade based on the pricing of credit in the bond market versus the price of the same credit in the CDS market. To execute a basis trade, go long the "underpriced" credit and short the "overpriced" credit. A profit is realized as the implied credit prices converge.

Bear spread An option strategy that becomes more valuable when the price of the underlying asset declines, so requires buying one option and writing another with a *lower* exercise price. A put bear spread involves buying a put with a higher exercise price and selling a put with a lower exercise price. A bear spread can also be executed with calls.

Beta A measure of the sensitivity of a given investment or portfolio to movements in the overall market.

Bid price In a price quotation, the price at which the party making the quotation is willing to buy a specified quantity of an asset or security.

Binomial model   A model for pricing options in which the underlying price can move to only one of two possible new prices.

Bull spread   An option strategy that becomes more valuable when the price of the underlying asset rises, so requires buying one option and writing another with a *higher* exercise price. A call bull spread involves buying a call with a lower exercise price and selling a call with a higher exercise price. A bull spread can also be executed with puts.

Calendar spread   A strategy in which one sells an option and buys the same type of option but with different expiration dates, on the same underlying asset and with the same strike. When the investor buys the more distant (near-term) call and sells the near-term (more distant) call, it is a long (short) calendar spread.

Call   An option that gives the holder the right to buy an underlying asset from another party at a fixed price over a specific period of time.

Call option   An option that gives the holder the right to buy an underlying asset from another party at a fixed price over a specific period of time.

Carry   The net of the costs and benefits of holding, storing, or "carrying" an asset.

Carry arbitrage model   A no-arbitrage approach in which the underlying instrument is either bought or sold along with an opposite position in a forward contract.

Carry benefits   Benefits that arise from owning certain underlyings; for example, dividends, foreign interest, and bond coupon payments.

Carry costs   Costs that arise from owning certain underlyings. They are generally a function of the physical characteristics of the underlying asset and also the interest forgone on the funds tied up in the asset.

Carry trade   A trading strategy that involves buying a security and financing it at a rate that is lower than the yield on that security.

Cash markets   See *spot markets*.

Cash prices   See *spot prices*.

Cash-secured put   An option strategy involving the writing of a put option and simultaneously depositing an amount of money equal to the exercise price into a designated account (this strategy is also called a fiduciary put).

Cash-settled forwards   See *non-deliverable forwards*.

Cash settlement   A procedure used in certain derivative transactions that specifies that the long and short parties settle the derivative's difference in value between them by making a cash payment.

CDS spread   A periodic premium paid by the buyer to the seller that serves as a return over a market reference rate required to protect against credit risk.

Cheapest-to-deliver   The debt instrument that can be purchased and delivered at the lowest cost yet has the same seniority as the reference obligation.

Clearing   The process by which the exchange verifies the execution of a transaction and records the participants' identities.

Collar   An option position in which the investor is long shares of stock and then buys a put with an exercise price below the current stock price and writes a call with an exercise price above the current stock price. Collars allow a shareholder to acquire downside protection through a protective put but reduce the cash outlay by writing a covered call.

Collateralized bond obligations   A structured asset-backed security that is collateralized by a pool of bonds.

Collateralized debt obligation   Generic term used to describe a security backed by a diversified pool of one or more debt obligations.

Collateralized loan obligations   A structured asset-backed security that is collateralized by a pool of loans.

Collateralized mortgage obligation   A security created through the securitization of a pool of mortgage-related products (mortgage pass-through securities or pools of loans).

Collateral return   The component of the total return on a commodity futures position attributable to the yield for the bonds or cash used to maintain the futures position. Also called *collateral yield*.

Commodity swap A type of swap involving the exchange of payments over multiple dates as determined by specified reference prices or indexes relating to commodities.

Conditional VaR (CVaR) The weighted average of all loss outcomes in the statistical (i.e., return) distribution that exceed the VaR loss. Thus, CVaR is a more comprehensive measure of tail loss than VaR is. Sometimes referred to as the *expected tail loss* or *expected shortfall*.

Contango A condition in futures markets in which the spot price is lower than the futures price; also, the condition in which the near-term (closer to expiration) futures contract price is lower than the longer-term futures contract price.

Contingent claims Derivatives in which the payoffs occur if a specific event occurs; generally referred to as options.

Contracts for differences See *non-deliverable forwards*.

Convenience yield A non-monetary advantage of holding an asset.

Convergence The property by which as expiration approaches, the price of a newly created forward or futures contract will approach the price of a spot transaction. At expiration, a forward or futures contract is equivalent to a spot transaction in the underlying.

Convexity A measure of how interest rate sensitivity changes with a change in interest rates.

Cost of carry See *carry*.

Cost of carry model A model that relates the forward price of an asset to the spot price by considering the cost of carry (also referred to as future-spot parity model).

Covered call An option strategy in which a long position in an asset is combined with a short position in a call on that asset.

Credit correlation The correlation of credit (or default) risks of the underlying single-name CDS contained in an index CDS.

Credit curve The credit spreads for a range of maturities of a company's debt.

Credit default swap (CDS) A type of credit derivative in which one party, the credit protection buyer who is seeking credit protection against a third party, makes a series of regularly scheduled payments to the other party, the credit protection seller. The seller makes no payments until a credit event occurs.

Credit derivative A derivative instrument in which the underlying is a measure of the credit quality of a borrower.

Credit derivatives A contract in which one party has the right to claim a payment from another party in the event that a specific credit event occurs over the life of the contract.

Credit event The event that triggers a payment from the credit protection seller to the credit protection buyer.

Credit-linked note (CLN) Fixed-income security in which the holder of the security has the right to withhold payment of the full amount due at maturity if a credit event occurs.

Credit protection buyer One party to a credit default swap; the buyer makes a series of cash payments to the seller and receives a promise of compensation for credit losses resulting from the default.

Credit protection seller One party to a credit default swap; the seller makes a promise to pay compensation for credit losses resulting from the default.

Credit risk The risk that the borrower will not repay principal and interest. Also called *default risk*.

Credit spread option An option on the yield spread on a bond.

Cross-currency basis swap An interest rate swap involving the periodic exchange of floating payments in one currency for another based upon respective market reference rates with an initial and final exchange of notional principal.

Cross hedge A hedge involving a hedging instrument that is imperfectly correlated with the asset being hedged; an example is hedging a bond investment with futures on a non-identical bond.

Currency overlay programs A currency overlay program is a program to manage a portfolio's currency exposures for the case in which those exposures are managed separately from the management of the portfolio itself.

Curve trade Buying a CDS of one maturity and selling a CDS on the same reference entity with a different maturity.

CVaR Conditional VaR, a tail loss measure. The weighted average of all loss outcomes in the statistical distribution that exceed the VaR loss.

Daily settlement See *mark to market* and *marking to market*.

Default risk See *credit risk*.

Deferred annuity An annuity that enables an individual to purchase an income stream that will begin at a later date.

Delta The relationship between the option price and the underlying price, which reflects the sensitivity of the price of the option to changes in the price of the underlying. Delta is a good approximation of how an option price will change for a small change in the stock.

Delta hedging Hedging that involves matching the price response of the position being hedged over a narrow range of prices.

Depository Trust and Clearinghouse Corporation A US-headquartered entity providing post-trade clearing, settlement, and information services.

Derivatives A financial instrument whose value depends on the value of some underlying asset or factor (e.g., a stock price, an interest rate, or exchange rate).

Disability income insurance A type of insurance designed to mitigate earnings risk as a result of a disability in which an individual becomes less than fully employed.

Dividend index point A measure of the quantity of dividends attributable to a particular index.

Domestic asset An asset that trades in the investor's domestic currency (or home currency).

Domestic currency The currency of the investor, i.e., the currency in which he or she typically makes consumption purchases, e.g., the Swiss franc for an investor domiciled in Switzerland.

Domestic-currency return A rate of return stated in domestic currency terms from the perspective of the investor; reflects both the foreign-currency return on an asset as well as percentage movement in the spot exchange rate between the domestic and foreign currencies.

Duration A measure of the approximate sensitivity of a security to a change in interest rates (i.e., a measure of interest rate risk).

Dynamic hedge A hedge requiring adjustment as the price of the hedged asset changes.

Earnings risk The risk associated with the earning potential of an individual.

Economic balance sheet A balance sheet that provides an individual's total wealth portfolio, supplementing traditional balance sheet assets with human capital and pension wealth, and expanding liabilities to include consumption and bequest goals. Also known as *holistic balance sheet*.

Economic net worth The difference between an individual's assets and liabilities; extends traditional financial assets and liabilities to include human capital and future consumption needs.

Effective federal funds (FFE) rate The fed funds rate actually transacted between depository institutions, not the Fed's target federal funds rate.

Enterprise risk management An overall assessment of a company's risk position. A centralized approach to risk management sometimes called firmwide risk management.

Equity swap A swap transaction in which at least one cash flow is tied to the return on an equity portfolio position, often an equity index.

European-style Said of an option contract that can only be exercised on the option's expiration date.

Ex ante tracking error A measure of the degree to which the performance of a given investment portfolio might be expected to deviate from its benchmark; also known as *relative VaR*.

Exercise price The fixed price at which an option holder can buy or sell the underlying. Also called *strike price*, *striking price*, or *strike*.

Exercise value The value obtained if an option is exercised based on current conditions. Also known as *intrinsic value*.

Expectations approach A procedure for obtaining the value of an option derived from discounting at the risk-free rate its expected future payoff based on risk neutral probabilities.

Expected shortfall See *conditional VaR*.

Expected tail loss See *conditional VaR*.

Extreme value theory   A branch of statistics that focuses primarily on extreme outcomes.

Failure to pay   When a borrower does not make a scheduled payment of principal or interest on any outstanding obligations after a grace period.

Fiduciary call   A combination of a European call and a risk-free bond that matures on the option expiration day and has a face value equal to the exercise price of the call.

Financial capital   The tangible and intangible assets (excluding human capital) owned by an individual or household.

Financial risk   The risk that environmental, social, or governance risk factors will result in significant costs or other losses to a company and its shareholders; the risk arising from a company's obligation to meet required payments under its financing agreements.

Fixed-for-floating interest rate swap   An interest rate swap in which one party pays a fixed rate and the other pays a floating rate, with both sets of payments in the same currency. Also called *plain vanilla swap* or *vanilla swap*.

Foreign assets   Assets denominated in currencies other than the investor's home currency.

Foreign currency   Currency that is not the currency in which an investor makes consumption purchases, e.g., the US dollar from the perspective of a Swiss investor.

Foreign-currency return   The return of the foreign asset measured in foreign-currency terms.

Forward commitments   Class of derivatives that provides the ability to lock in a price to transact in the future at a previously agreed-upon price.

Forward contract   An agreement between two parties in which one party, the buyer, agrees to buy from the other party, the seller, an underlying asset at a later date for a price established at the start of the contract.

Forward price   The fixed price or rate at which the transaction, scheduled to occur at the expiration of a forward contract, will take place. This price is agreed to at the initiation date of the forward contract.

Forward rate agreement   An over-the-counter forward contract in which the underlying is an interest rate on a deposit. A forward rate agreement (FRA) calls for one party to make a fixed interest payment and the other to make an interest payment at a rate to be determined at contract expiration.

Forward rate agreements   A forward contract calling for one party to make a fixed interest payment and the other to make an interest payment at a rate to be determined at the contract expiration.

Forward rate bias   An empirically observed divergence from interest rate parity conditions that active investors seek to benefit from by borrowing in a lower-yield currency and investing in a higher-yield currency.

Forward value   The monetary value of an existing forward contract.

Funding currencies   The low-yield currencies in which borrowing occurs in a carry trade.

Futures contract   A variation of a forward contract that has essentially the same basic definition but with some additional features, such as a clearinghouse guarantee against credit losses, a daily settlement of gains and losses, and an organized electronic or floor trading facility.

Futures price   The price at which the parties to a futures contract agree to exchange the underlying (or cash). In commodity markets, the price agreed on to deliver or receive a defined quantity (and often quality) of a commodity at a future date.

Futures value   The monetary value of an existing futures contract.

Gamma   A measure of how sensitive an option's delta is to a change in the underlying. The change in a given instrument's delta for a given small change in the underlying's value, holding everything else constant.

Hazard rate   The probability that an event will occur, given that it has not already occurred.

Health insurance   A type of insurance used to cover health care and medical costs.

Health risk   The risk associated with illness or injury.

Hedge portfolio   A hypothetical combination of the derivative and its underlying that eliminates risk.

Hedge ratio   The relationship of the quantity of an asset being hedged to the quantity of the derivative used for hedging.

Historical simulation method   The application of historical price changes to the current portfolio.

Holistic balance sheet   See *economic balance sheet.*

Home currency   See *domestic currency.*

Human capital   The accumulated knowledge and skill that workers acquire from education, training, or life experience and the corresponding present value of future earnings to be generated by said skilled individual.

Immediate annuity   An annuity that provides a guarantee of specified future monthly payments over a specified period of time.

Implied volatility   The outlook for the future volatility of the underlying asset's price. It is the value (i.e., standard deviation of underlying's returns) that equates the model (e.g., Black–Scholes–Merton model) price of an option to its market price.

Implied volatility surface   A three-dimensional plot, for put and call options on the same underlying asset, of days to expiration (*x*-axis), option strike prices (*y*-axis), and implied volatilities (*z*-axis). It simultaneously shows the volatility skew (or smile) and the term structure of implied volatility.

Incremental VaR (IVaR)   A measure of the incremental effect of an asset on the VaR of a portfolio by measuring the difference between the portfolio's VaR while including a specified asset and the portfolio's VaR with that asset eliminated.

Index CDS   A type of credit default swap that involves a combination of borrowers.

Initial margin   The amount that must be deposited in a clearinghouse account when entering into a futures contract.

Interest rate risk   The risk that interest rates will rise and therefore the market value of current portfolio holdings will fall so that their current yields to maturity then match comparable instruments in the marketplace.

In the money   Options that, if exercised, would result in the value received being worth more than the payment required to exercise.

Intrinsic value   The difference between the spot exchange rate and the strike price of a currency option. See *exercise value.*

Investment currencies   The high-yielding currencies in a carry trade.

ISDA Master Agreement   A standard or "master" agreement published by the International Swaps and Derivatives Association. The master agreement establishes the terms for each party involved in the transaction.

Knock-in/knock-out   Features of a vanilla option that is created (or ceases to exist) when the spot exchange rate touches a pre-specified level.

Law of one price   The condition in a financial market in which two equivalent financial instruments or combinations of financial instruments can sell for only one price. Equivalent to the principle that no arbitrage opportunities are possible.

Liability insurance   A type of insurance used to manage liability risk.

Liability risk   The possibility that an individual or household may be held legally liable for the financial costs associated with property damage or physical injury.

Life-cycle finance   A concept in finance that recognizes as an investor ages, the fundamental nature of wealth and risk evolves.

Life insurance   A type of insurance that protects against the loss of human capital for those who depend on an individual's future earnings.

Limit down   A limit move in the futures market in which the price at which a transaction would be made is at or below the lower limit.

Limit up   A limit move in the futures market in which the price at which a transaction would be made is at or above the upper limit.

Liquidity risk   The risk that a financial instrument cannot be purchased or sold without a significant concession in price due to the size of the market.

Locked limit   A condition in the futures markets in which a transaction cannot take place because the price would be beyond the limits.

Long   The buyer of a derivative contract. Also refers to the position of owning a derivative.

Longevity risk   The risk of outliving one's financial resources.

Long/short credit trade A credit protection seller with respect to one entity combined with a credit protection buyer with respect to another entity.

Lookback period The time period used to gather a historical data set.

Loss given default The amount that will be lost if a default occurs.

Maintenance margin The minimum amount that is required by a futures clearinghouse to maintain a margin account and to protect against default. Participants whose margin balances drop below the required maintenance margin must replenish their accounts.

Margin The amount of money that a trader deposits in a margin account. The term is derived from the stock market practice in which an investor borrows a portion of the money required to purchase a certain amount of stock. In futures markets, there is no borrowing so the margin is more of a down payment or performance bond.

Marginal VaR (MVaR) A measure of the effect of a small change in a position size on portfolio VaR.

Margin bond A cash deposit required by the clearinghouse from the participants to a contract to provide a credit guarantee. Also called a *performance bond*.

Margin call A request for the short to deposit additional funds to bring their balance up to the initial margin.

Market risk The risk that arises from movements in interest rates, stock prices, exchange rates, and commodity prices.

Mark to market The revaluation of a financial asset or liability to its current market value or fair value.

Maximum drawdown The worst cumulative loss ever sustained by an asset or portfolio. More specifically, maximum drawdown is the difference between an asset's or a portfolio's maximum cumulative return and its subsequent lowest cumulative return.

Minimum-variance hedge ratio A mathematical approach to determining the optimal cross hedging ratio.

Monetizing Unwinding a position to either capture a gain or realize a loss.

Moneyness The relationship between the price of the underlying and an option's exercise price.

Monte Carlo simulation A technique that uses the inverse transformation method for converting a randomly generated uniformly distributed number into a simulated value of a random variable of a desired distribution. Each key decision variable in a Monte Carlo simulation requires an assumed statistical distribution; this assumption facilitates incorporating non-normality, fat tails, and tail dependence as well as solving high-dimensionality problems.

Naked credit default swap A position where the owner of the CDS does not have a position in the underlying credit.

No-arbitrage approach A procedure for obtaining the value of an option based on the creation of a portfolio that replicates the payoffs of the option and deriving the option value from the value of the replicating portfolio.

Non-deliverable forwards Forward contracts that are cash settled (in the non-controlled currency of the currency pair) rather than physically settled (the controlled currency is neither delivered nor received).

Non-financial risks Risks that arise from sources other than changes in the external financial markets, such as changes in accounting rules, legal environment, or tax rates.

Notional amount The amount of protection being purchased in a CDS.

Notional principal An imputed principal amount.

Offer price The price at which a counterparty is willing to sell one unit of the base currency.

Off-the-run A series of securities or indexes that were issued/created prior to the most recently issued/created series.

On-the-run The most recently issued/created series of securities or indexes.

Open interest The number of outstanding contracts in a clearinghouse at any given time. The open interest figure changes daily as some parties open up new positions, while other parties offset their old positions.

Operational risk The risk that arises from inadequate or failed people, systems, and internal policies, procedures, and processes, as well as from external events that are beyond the control of the organization but that affect its operations.

Option   A financial instrument that gives one party the right, but not the obligation, to buy or sell an underlying asset from or to another party at a fixed price over a specific period of time. Also referred to as *contingent claim* or *option contract*.

Option premium   The amount of money a buyer pays and seller receives to engage in an option transaction.

Out of the money   Options that, if exercised, would require the payment of more money than the value received and therefore would not be currently exercised.

Overbought   When a market has trended too far in one direction and is vulnerable to a trend reversal, or correction.

Oversold   The opposite of overbought; see *overbought*.

Parametric method   A method of estimating VaR that uses the historical mean, standard deviation, and correlation of security price movements to estimate the portfolio VaR. Generally assumes a normal distribution but can be adapted to non-normal distributions with the addition of skewness and kurtosis. Sometimes called the *variance–covariance method* or the *analytical method*.

Payout amount   The loss given default times the notional.

Performance bond   See *margin bond*.

Permanent life insurance   A type of life insurance that provides lifetime coverage.

Physical settlement   Involves actual delivery of the debt instrument in exchange for a payment by the credit protection seller of the notional amount of the contract.

Position delta   The overall or portfolio delta. For example, the position delta of a covered call, consisting of long 100 shares and short one at-the-money call, is +50 (= +100 for the shares and −50 for the short ATM call).

Premature death risk   The risk of an individual dying earlier than anticipated; sometimes referred to as *mortality risk*.

Premium leg   The series of payments the credit protection buyer promises to make to the credit protection seller.

Price limits   Limits imposed by a futures exchange on the price change that can occur from one day to the next.

Principle of no arbitrage   See *arbitrage-free pricing*.

Probability of default   The probability that a bond issuer will not meet its contractual obligations on schedule.

Probability of survival   The probability that a bond issuer will meet its contractual obligations on schedule.

Property insurance   A type of insurance used by individuals to manage property risk.

Property risk   The possibility that a person's property may be damaged, destroyed, stolen, or lost.

Protection leg   The contingent payment that the credit protection seller may have to make to the credit protection buyer.

Protective put   An option strategy in which a long position in an asset is combined with a long position in a put on that asset.

Put   An option that gives the holder the right to sell an underlying asset to another party at a fixed price over a specific period of time.

Put–call–forward parity   The relationship among puts, calls, and forward contracts.

Put–call parity   An equation expressing the equivalence (parity) of a portfolio of a call and a bond with a portfolio of a put and the underlying, which leads to the relationship between put and call prices.

Put option   An option that gives the holder the right to sell an underlying asset to another party at a fixed price over a specific period of time.

Put spread   A strategy used to reduce the upfront cost of buying a protective put, it involves buying a put option and writing another put option.

Realized volatility   Historical volatility, the square root of the realized variance of returns, which is a measure of the range of past price outcomes for the underlying asset.

Rebalance return   A return from rebalancing the component weights of an index.

Recovery rate   The percentage of the loss recovered.

Reference entity The borrower (debt issuer) covered by a single-name CDS.

Reference obligation A particular debt instrument issued by the borrower that is the designated instrument being covered.

Relative VaR See *ex ante tracking error*.

Replication The creation of an asset or portfolio from another asset, portfolio, and/or derivative.

Resistance levels Price points on dealers' order boards where one would expect to see a clustering of offers.

Restructuring Reorganizing the capital structure of a firm.

Reverse carry arbitrage A strategy involving the short sale of the underlying and an offsetting opposite position in the derivative.

Reverse stress testing A risk management approach in which the user identifies key risk exposures in the portfolio and subjects those exposures to extreme market movements.

Rho The change in a given derivative instrument for a given small change in the risk-free interest rate, holding everything else constant. Rho measures the sensitivity of the option to the risk-free interest rate.

Risk Exposure to uncertainty. The chance of a loss or adverse outcome as a result of an action, inaction, or external event.

Risk budgeting The allocation of an asset owner's total risk appetite among groups or divisions (in the case of a trading organization) or among strategies and managers (in the case of an institutional or individual investor).

Risk decomposition The process of converting a set of holdings in a portfolio into a set of exposures to risk factors.

Risk exposure The state of being exposed or vulnerable to a risk. The extent to which an organization is sensitive to underlying risks.

Risk factors Variables or characteristics with which individual asset returns are correlated. Sometimes referred to simply as *factors*.

Risk governance The top-down process and guidance that directs risk management activities to align with and support the overall enterprise.

Risk management The process of identifying the level of risk an organization wants, measuring the level of risk the organization currently has, taking actions that bring the actual level of risk to the desired level of risk, and monitoring the new actual level of risk so that it continues to be aligned with the desired level of risk.

Risk management framework The infrastructure, process, and analytics needed to support effective risk management in an organization.

Risk-neutral pricing Sometimes said of derivatives pricing, uses the fact that arbitrage opportunities guarantee that a risk-free portfolio consisting of the underlying and the derivative must earn the risk-free rate.

Risk-neutral probabilities Weights that are used to compute a binomial option price. They are the probabilities that would apply if a risk-neutral investor valued an option.

Risk reversal A strategy used to profit from the existence of an implied volatility skew and from changes in its shape over time. A combination of long (short) calls and short (long) puts on the same underlying with the same expiration is a long (short) risk reversal.

Risk shifting Actions to change the distribution of risk outcomes.

Risk tolerance The amount of risk an investor is willing and able to bear to achieve an investment goal.

Risk transfer Actions to pass on a risk to another party, often, but not always, in the form of an insurance policy.

Roll When an investor moves its investment position from an older series to the most current series.

Roll return The component of the return on a commodity futures contract attributable to rolling long futures positions forward through time. Also called *roll yield*.

Scenario analysis Analysis that shows the changes in key financial quantities that result from given (economic) events, such as the loss of customers, the loss of a supply source, or a catastrophic event; a risk management technique involving examination of the performance of a portfolio under specified situations. Closely related to stress testing.

Seagull spread   An extension of the risk reversal foreign exchange option strategy that limits downside risk.

Settled in arrears   An arrangement in which the interest payment is made (i.e., settlement occurs) at the maturity of the underlying instrument.

Settlement   The process that occurs after a trade is completed, the securities are passed to the buyer, and payment is received by the seller.

Settlement price   The official price, designated by the clearinghouse, from which daily gains and losses will be determined and marked to market.

Short   The seller of an asset or derivative contract. Also refers to the position of being short an asset or derivative contract.

Single-name CDS   Credit default swap on one specific borrower.

Solvency risk   The risk that an organization does not survive or succeed because it runs out of cash, even though it might otherwise be solvent.

Spot markets   Markets in which assets are traded for immediate delivery.

Spot price   The current price of an asset or security. For commodities, the current price to deliver a physical commodity to a specific location or purchase and transport it away from a designated location.

Spot prices   The price of an asset for immediately delivery.

Static hedge   A hedge that is not sensitive to changes in the price of the asset hedged.

Stop-loss limit   Constraint used in risk management that requires a reduction in the size of a portfolio, or its complete liquidation, when a loss of a particular size occurs in a specified period.

Stops   Stop-loss orders involve leaving bids or offers away from the current market price to be filled if the market reaches those levels.

Straddle   An option combination in which one buys *both* puts and calls, with the same exercise price and same expiration date, on the same underlying asset. In contrast to this long straddle, if someone *writes* both options, it is a short straddle.

Strangle   A variation on a straddle in which the put and call have different exercise prices; if the put and call are held long, it is a long strangle; if they are held short, it is a short strangle.

Stress testing   A specific type of scenario analysis that estimates losses in rare and extremely unfavorable combinations of events or scenarios.

Stress tests   A risk management technique that assesses the portfolio's response to extreme market movements.

Succession event   A change of corporate structure of the reference entity, such as through a merger, a divestiture, a spinoff, or any similar action, in which ultimate responsibility for the debt in question is unclear.

Support levels   Price points on dealers' order boards where one would expect to see a clustering of bids.

Swap contract   An agreement between two parties to exchange a series of future cash flows.

Swap rate   The "price" that swap traders quote among one another. It is the rate at which the present value of all the expected floating-rate payments received over the life of the floating-rate bond equal the present value of all the expected fixed-rate payments made over the life of the fixed-rate bond.

Synthetic long forward position   The combination of a long call and a short put with identical strike price and expiration, traded at the same time on the same underlying.

Synthetic short forward position   The combination of a short call and a long put at the same strike price and maturity (traded at the same time on the same underlying).

Tail risk   The risk that losses in extreme events could be greater than would be expected for a portfolio of assets with a normal distribution.

Temporary life insurance   A type of life insurance that covers a certain period of time, specified at purchase. Commonly referred to as "term" life insurance.

Term structure of volatility   The plot of implied volatility (y-axis) against option maturity (x-axis) for options with the same strike price on the same underlying. Typically, implied volatility is not constant across different maturities—rather, it is often in contango, meaning that the implied volatilities for longer-term options are higher than for near-term ones.

Theta The change in a derivative instrument for a given small change in calendar time, holding everything else constant. Specifically, the theta calculation assumes nothing changes except calendar time. Theta also reflects the rate at which an option's time value decays.

Time value The difference between the market price of an option and its intrinsic value, determined by the uncertainty of the underlying over the remaining life of the option.

Time value decay Said of an option when, at expiration, no time value remains and the option is worth only its exercise value.

Total return swap A swap in which one party agrees to pay the total return on a security. Often used as a credit derivative, in which the underlying is a bond.

Tranche CDS A type of credit default swap that covers a combination of borrowers but only up to pre-specified levels of losses.

Transparency Said of something (e.g., a market) in which information is fully disclosed to the public and/or regulators.

Underlying An asset that trades in a market in which buyers and sellers meet, decide on a price, and the seller then delivers the asset to the buyer and receives payment. The underlying is the asset or other derivative on which a particular derivative is based. The market for the underlying is also referred to as the *spot market*.

Upfront payment The difference between the credit spread and the standard rate paid by the protection buyer if the standard rate is insufficient to compensate the protection seller. Also called *upfront premium*.

Upfront premium See *upfront payment*.

Value at risk (VaR) The minimum loss that would be expected a certain percentage of the time over a certain period of time given the assumed market conditions.

Variance notional The notional amount of a variance swap; it equals vega notional divided by two times the volatility strike price [i.e., (vega notional)/(2 × volatility strike)].

Vega The change in a given derivative instrument for a given small change in volatility, holding everything else constant. A sensitivity measure for options that reflects the effect of volatility.

Vega notional The trade size for a variance swap, which represents the average profit and loss of the variance swap for a 1% change in volatility from the strike.

Volatility skew The skewed plot (of implied volatility (*y*-axis) against strike price (*x*-axis) for options on the same underlying with the same expiration) that occurs when the implied volatility increases for OTM puts and decreases for OTM calls, as the strike price moves away from the current price.

Volatility smile The U-shaped plot (of implied volatility (*y*-axis) against strike price (*x*-axis) for options on the same underlying with the same expiration) that occurs when the implied volatilities priced into both OTM puts and calls trade at a premium to implied volatilities of ATM options.

ABOUT THE EDITORS
AND AUTHORS

Robert Brooks, PhD, CFA, is the Wallace D. Malone, Jr. endowed chair of Financial Management at The University of Alabama and president of Financial Risk Management, LLC, a financial risk management consulting firm focused on market risks. He has taught for over 30 years, primarily financial risk management classes, and is the author of over 75 articles appearing in the *Journal of Financial and Quantitative Analysis*, *Journal of Derivatives*, *Financial Analysts Journal*, and many others.

Brooks is the co-author of *An Introduction to Derivatives and Risk Management* (Seventh through Tenth Editions) with Don Chance and has authored several books including *Building Financial Risk Management Applications with C++*. He has testified in a subcommittee hearing of the US House of Representatives in Washington, D.C. as well as in a field hearing of the SEC in Birmingham, Alabama. He has consulted with major public utilities, energy companies, auditing firms, corporations, investment bankers, elected municipal officials, and commercial bankers regarding managing financial risks, derivatives valuation, and software development. Further, he has testified in several court cases as well as conducting professional development seminars on various aspects of finance.

Don M. Chance, PhD, CFA, is the James C. Flores chair of MBA Studies and professor of Finance at Louisiana State University. He previously worked in banking and was a member of the finance faculty at Virginia Tech. He is the author or co-author of three books on derivatives and risk management and numerous academic and practitioner articles on a variety of finance topics. He has been a visiting scholar at universities in the United States, Australia, Scotland, Hong Kong, Singapore, and Korea. He has consulted and provided training for numerous companies and organizations, including CFA Institute, which honored him with the C. Stewart Shepard Award in 2015.

David M. Gentle, CFA, is principal of Omega Risk Consulting, which specializes in managing financial risk through the use of hedging and derivatives. Prior to this role, which commenced in 2010, Mr. Gentle was, from 1996, head of Structured Products at Australia's largest fund management firm, AMP Capital Investors, where he managed a range of large options and derivative-based investment products. Previous roles were as a quantitative analyst and researcher at Citibank, NatWest Markets, and Westpac Banking Corporation.

Prior to entering the finance industry, Mr. Gentle was an IT specialist and lecturer at Sydney University. He holds a BSc from the University of NSW, an MEc (Hons) from the University of Sydney, and a Graduate Diploma of Management from Macquarie University. He is a member of CFA Institute and CFA Society Melbourne.

Kenneth Grant is president and founder of General Risk Advisors, LLC. He began his career in the Chicago futures markets and, in the late 1980s, created the risk management group at the Chicago Mercantile Exchange. There, he led a project team responsible for the globalization of the SPAN Margin System—the first portfolio risk management system used on a global, institutional basis. In 1994, he moved to Société Generale as head of Risk Management for the North American Treasury/Capital Markets Group, eventually rising to the role of deputy director. Mr. Grant moved to the hedge fund industry in 1997, joining SAC Capital as its director of Risk Management and later serving as its chief investment strategist. Mr. Grant also spent two years as the head of Global Risk Management at the Tudor Investment Corporation, and 18 months in a similar role for Cheyne Capital. Mr. Grant formed Risk Resources LLC in late 2004 to provide customized, diagnostic risk management services to hedge funds, banks, broker-dealers, and other capital providers. The firm has worked with over 20 companies since its inception representing investment capital in excess of $50 billion. He is the author of *Trading Risk: Enhanced Profitability through Risk Control* (2004), and is principal author of the Managed Funds Association's *Sound Practices for Hedge Fund Managers* (MFA, 2000, 2003, 2005). He served on the MFA's board of directors from 2000 through 2004, was a member of its Executive Committee (2001–2003), and was a founding member of its Hedge Fund Advisory Committee. In 2011, he was awarded a patent for originating processes associated with the reverse engineering of risk management analytics. He is a lecturer in Risk Management in the School of Professional Studies at Columbia University.

John Marsland, CFA, is Chief Operating Officer, Investment at Schroder Investment Management in London and is responsible for global trading and investment operations. Mr. Marsland began his investment career in 1992 at UBS Philips & Drew as a UK economist, and subsequently moved into investment strategy, risk management, and quantitative fund management roles. Mr. Marsland read Economics at Downing College, University of Cambridge, and holds an MSc in Economics from Birkbeck College, University of London. He has been a CFA charterholder since 2000. He has served as a board member and vice-chair of CFA UK and as a member and chair of CFA Institute's Investment Foundations Investment Certificate Advisory Board.

Russell Rhoads, CFA, is director of Education for the CBOE Options Institute. His career before CBOE included positions at a variety of buyside firms including Highland Capital Management, Caldwell & Orkin Investment Counsel, Balyasny Asset Management, and Millennium Management. He is a financial author and editor having contributed to multiple magazines and edited several books for Wiley publishing. He is the author of six market-related books including *Trading VIX Derivatives, Option Spread Trading, Trading Weekly Options,* and *Options Strategies for Advisors and Institutions.* He has also authored material for the CFA program as well as for the CMT designation. He has been widely quoted in the financial press by publications such as the *Wall Street Journal* and *Forbes* and has appeared on several business television networks included Bloomberg TV.

In addition to his duties for the CBOE, Rhoads is an adjunct instructor at Loyola University and the University of Illinois—Chicago. He is a double graduate of the University of Memphis with a BBA and an MS in Finance and received a Master's Certificate in Financial Engineering from Illinois Tech in 2003. He is currently (2017) pursuing a PhD from Oklahoma State University.

Bob Strong, PhD, CFA is University Foundation professor emeritus of Investment Education at the University of Maine. The University of Maine Alumni Association selected him as the 2005 "Distinguished Maine Professor." The Carnegie Foundation named him the 2007 "Maine Professor of the Year." His three textbooks on investments, portfolio management, and derivatives have been used at over 100 universities.

Strong holds a bachelor of science in engineering from the United States Military Academy at West Point, a master of science in business administration from Boston University, and a PhD in finance from Penn State. He has also been a visiting professor of finance at Harvard University where he was deputy director of the Summer Economics Program from 1997 to 1999. Strong served for eight years as the University of Maine's Faculty Athletic Representative to the NCAA. He is past president of the Northeast Business and Economics Association, the Maine CFA Society, and the Bangor Rotary Club. He is an honorary captain in the Maine State Police and is chairman of the board of Bangor Savings Bank.

Barbara Valbuzzi, CFA, is equity strategist at Banca IMI and has over 20 years of experience in trading equity derivatives. Her career developed within the Intesa Sanpaolo group where she held positions as proprietary trader and senior equity derivatives trader. She now applies her trading and relative value experience on the Strategist team that she contributed to set up in 2015, developing trade recommendations and quantitative investment strategies. Early in her career, she served as portfolio manager at UBS Italia.

A graduate in Economics from Bocconi University, she also holds the Chartered Financial Analyst* designation. She is a member of CFA Institute and CFA Society Italy.

Wendy L. Pirie, PhD, CFA, is director of Curriculum Projects in the Education Division at CFA Institute. Prior to joining CFA Institute in 2008, Dr. Pirie taught for over 20 years at a broad range of institutions: large public universities; small, private, religiously affiliated colleges; and a military academy. She primarily taught finance courses but also taught accounting, taxation, business law, marketing, and statistics courses. Dr. Pirie's work has been published in the *Journal of Financial Research*, *Journal of Economics and Finance*, *Educational Innovation in Economics and Business*, and *Managerial Finance*.

Prior to entering academia, she was an auditor with Deloitte & Touche in Toronto, Canada. She is a Chartered Accountant (Ontario) and Certified Public Accountant (Virginia). She completed the ICAEW's Certificate in International Financial Reporting Standards. She holds a PhD in accounting and finance from Queen's University at Kingston, Ontario, and MBAs from the Universities of Toronto and Calgary. She is a member of CFA Institute, New York Society of Security Analysts, and CFA Society Chicago.

INDEX